C000054201

ISBN 978-0-260-71004-8
PIBN 10965627

SESSIONAL PAPERS

VOLUME 5

THIRD SESSION OF THE TENTH PARLIAMENT

OF THE

DOMINION OF CANADA

SESSION 1906-7

VOLUME XLI

☞ See also Numerical List Page 5.

ALPHABETICAL INDEX

TO THE

SESSIONAL PAPERS

TO THE

PARLIAMENT OF CANADA

THIRD SESSION, TENTH PARLIAMENT, 1906-7.

U

V

W

Y

See also Alphabetical Index, page 1.

LIST OF SESSIONAL PAPERS

Arranged in Numerical Order, with their titles at full length; the dates when Ordered and when Presented to the Houses of Parliament; the Name of the Senator or Member who moved for each Sessional Paper, and whether it is ordered to be Printed or Not Printed.

CONTENTS OF VOLUME 1.

(This volume is bound in two parts).

1. Report of the Auditor General, for the fiscal year ended 30th June, 1906. Partial report presented 9th January, 1907, by Hon. W. S. Fielding; also 4th February; 7th February; 21st February; 22nd February, 1st March.......................*Printed for both distribution and sessional papers.*

CONTENTS OF VOLUME 2.

2. Public Accounts of Canada, for the fiscal year ended 30th June, 1906. Presented 27th November, 1906, by Sir Wilfrid Laurier ....*Printed for both distribution and sessional papers.*

3. Estimates of the sums required for the services of Canada for the year ending 31st March, 1908. Presented 29th November, 1906, by Hon. W. S. Fielding.
Printed for both distribution and sessional papers.

3a. Supplementary Estimates for the fiscal period of nine months ending 31st March, 1907. Presented 22nd January, 1907, by Hon. W. S. Fielding......*Printed for both distribution and sessional papers.*

4. Further Supplementary Estimates for the period of nine months ending on the 31st March, 1907. Presented 2nd April, 1907, by Hon. W. S. Fielding....*Printed for both distribution and sessional papers.*

5. Supplementary Estimates for the year ending 31st March, 1908. Presented 19th April, 1907, by Hon. W. S. Fielding.................. ....*Printed for both distribution and sessional papers.*

5a. Further Supplementary Estimates for the year ending 31st March, 1908. Presented 25th April, 1907, by Hon. W. S. Fielding... .. ..*Printed by both distribution and sessional papers.*

6. List of Shareholders in the Chartered Banks of Canada, as on the 31st December, 1906. Presented 25th April, 1907, by Hon. W. S. Fielding........ .... ..*Printed for both distribution and sessional papers.*

CONTENTS OF VOLUME 3.

7. Report of dividends remaining unpaid, unclaimed balances and unpaid drafts and bills of exchange in Chartered Banks of Canada, for five years and upwards, prior to December 31, 1906.
Printed for both distribution and sessional papers.

8. Report of the Superintendent of Insurance for the year ended 31st December, 1906.
Printed for both distribution and sessional papers.

9. Abstract of Statements of Insurance Companies in Canada, for the year ended 31st December, 1906.
Printed for both distribution and sessional papers.

CONTENTS OF VOLUME 4.

10. Report of the Department of Trade and Commerce, for the fiscal year ended 30th June, 1906. Part I.—Canadian Trade. Presented 11th February, 1907, by Hon. W. Paterson.
Printed for both distribution and sessional papers.

10a. Report of the Department of Trade and Commerce, for the year ended 30th June, 1906. Part II.—Trade of Foreign Countries and Treaties and Conventions.
Printed for both distribution and sessional papers.

CONTENTS OF VOLUME 5.

11. Tables of the Trade and Navigation of Canada, for the fiscal year ended 30th June, 1906. Presented 27th November, 1906, by Sir Wilfrid Laurier......*Printed for both distribution and sessional papers.*

12. Inland Revenues of Canada. Excise, &c., for the fiscal year ended 30th June, 1906. Presented 18th December, 1906, by Hon. W. Templeman.........*Printed for both distribution and sessional papers.*

13. Inspection of Weights, Measures Gas and Electric Light, for the fiscal year ended 30th June, 1906. Presented 27th November, 1906, by Hon. W. Templeman.
Printed for both distribution and sessional papers.

CONTENTS OF VOLUME 6.

14. Report on Adulteration of Food, for the fiscal year ended 30th June, 1906. Presented 3rd April, 1907, by Hon. W. Templeman....................*Printed for both distribution and sessional papers.*

15. Report of the Minister of Agriculture, for five months ended 31st March, 1906. Presented 27th November, 1907, by Hon. S. A. Fisher...........*Printed for both distribution and sessional papers.*

16. Report of the Directors and Officers of the Experimental Farms, from 1st December, 1905, to 31st March, 1906. Presented 27th November, 1906, by Hon. S. A. Fisher.
Printed for both distribution and sessional papers.

17. Criminal Statistics for the year ended 30th September, 1906.
Printed for both distribution and sessional papers.

17*a*. Census of the Northwest Provinces, Manitoba, Saskatchewan and Alberta, 1906. Presented 7th February, 1907, by Hon. S. A. Fisher........... *Printed for both distribution and sessional papers.*

17*b*. Return of By-elections for the House of Commons of Canada, held during the year 1906. Presented 15th April, 1907, by Hon. W. S. Fielding........*Printed for both distribution and sessional papers.*

CONTENTS OF VOLUME 7.

18. Report on Canadian Archives, 1906................*Printed for both distribution and sessional papers.*

19. Report of the Minister of Public Works, for the fiscal year ended 30th June, 1906. Presented 21st January, 1907, by Hon. S. A. Fisher............*Printed for both distribution and sessional papers.*

CONTENTS OF VOLUME 8.

19*a*. Reports of the International Waterways Commission, 1906.
Printed for both distribution and sessional papers.

20. Annual Report of the Department of Railways and Canals, for the fiscal year ended 30th June, 1906. Presented 9th January, 1907, by Hon. H. R. Emmerson.
Printed for both distribution and sessional papers.

20*a*. Canal Statistics for the season of navigation, 1905..*Printed for both distribution and sessional papers.*

20*b*. Railway Statistics of Canada for the year ended 30th June, 1906. Presented 21st February, 1907, by Sir Wilfrid Laurier.... .. ..*Printed for both distribution and sessional papers.*

20*c*. First Report of the Board of Railway Commissioners for Canada. February 1st, 1904, to March 31st, 1906. Presented 14th March, 1907, by Hon. H. R. Emmerson.
Printed for both distribution and sessional papers.

CONTENTS OF VOLUME 9.

21. Report of the Department of Marine and Fisheries (Marine), for the year ended 30th June, 190 Presented 11th March, 1907, by Hon. W. S. Fielding.
Printed for both distribution and sessional papers.

21*a*. (No issue for 1906).

21*b*. List of Shipping issued by the Department of Marine and Fisheries, being a list of vessels on the registry books of Canada on the 31st December, 1906.
Printed for both distribution and sessional papers.

CONTENTS OF VOLUME 9—*Concluded.*

CONTENTS OF VOLUME 10.

CONTENTS OF VOLUME 11.

CONTENTS OF VOLUME 12.

CONTENTS OF VOLUME 13.

CONTENTS OF VOLUME 13—*Continued.*

CONTENTS OF VOLUME 13—*Continued.*

CONTENTS OF VOLUME 13—*Continued.*

CONTENTS OF VOLUME 13—*Continued.*

CONTENTS OF VOLUME 13—*Continued.*

CONTENTS OF VOLUME 13—*Continued.*

CONTENTS OF VOLUME 13—*Continued.*

CONTENTS OF VOLUME 13—*Continued.*

91c. Return to an address of the House of Commons, dated 9th January, 1907, for a copy of all orders in council, agreements, valuations, reports, memoranda, letters, telegrams, correspondence and documents of every description, relating to or treating of (*a*) the granting of a closed grazing lease to Brown, Bedingfield, *et al*; (*b*) the enjoyment of and the payment for the privileges granted under said lease. Presented 7th February, 1907.—*Mr. Ames*................................*Not printed.*

91d. Return to an order of the House of Commons, dated 23rd January, 1907, for a copy of all applications for the lease of grazing lands within the provinces of Alberta and Saskatchewan, between the 1st day of February, 1905, and the 1st day of August, 1905. Presented 19th April, 1907.—*Mr. McCarthy (Calgary)*................................*Not printed.*

92. Return to an order of the House of Commons, dated 28th November, 1906, showing: 1. All sums of money paid to the North Atlantic Trading Company, or on their order, to 1st November, 1906, with dates, sums, and names of persons to whom paid. 2. All correspondence between the North Atlantic Trading Company and the government, or any member thereof, or any department, since 1st January, 1906. Presented 9th January, 1907.—*Mr. Wilson (Lennox and Addington)*..*Not printed.*

92a. Return to an order of the House of Commons, dated 17th December, 1906, showing: 1. All claims made on the government by the North Atlantic Trading Company, since the 31st March, 1906. 2. All amounts paid to the said North Atlantic Trading Company by the government of Canada, (*a*) on account of bonuses; (*b*) on account of disbursements, since the 31st March, 1906. 3. A copy of all correspondence had by the government with the said North Atlantic Trading Company since the 31st March, 1906, up to the 1st December, 1906, and of all letters and accounts received from the said company between the above dates. Presented 15th January, 1907.—*Mr. Monk*....*Not printed.*

92b. Report of C. H. Beddoe, accountant of the Department of the Interior, of an audit of the books and accounts of the North Atlantic Trading Company. Presented 1st March, 1907, by Hon. F. Oliver.
Printed for both distribution and sessional papers.

92c. Extract from a Report of the Privy Council, approved by the Governor General on the 19th February, 1907, respecting continental immigration and certain commissions to steamship booking agents. Presented 14th March, 1907, by Hon. F. Oliver................................*Not printed.*

93. Return to an order of the House of Commons, dated 10th December, 1906, showing: All sums paid or credits given by the Record Foundry Company, of Moncton, in respect of purchases from the Intercolonial Railway of scrap iron, copper, babbit metal, lead, sheet lead, and scrap metal of every description, between 1st January, 1904, and 31st March, 1906; said statement to further show date and amount of every such transaction, character, quantity and price per pound, of material purchased and whether and in what instances the same has been offered in public competition or sale by tender. Presented 9th January, 1907.—*Mr. Barker*................................*Not printed.*

94. Return to an order of the House of Commons, dated 14th May, 1906, for a copy of all correspondence, reports, documents and papers relating to any dealings, transactions or negotiations between the government and any company, association, syndicate, or any person or persons on behalf of any company, association or syndicate, who have purchased or acquired, or arranged to purchase or acquire, public lands from the government since 1898; also a statement giving the names, head offices and addresses of the said respective companies, associations and syndicates, together with the amount of land purchased, acquired, or arranged to be purchased or acquired, and the price paid or agreed upon; also a statement giving the names, addresses and occupations of any person or persons, other than companies, associations or syndicates, who have purchased or acquired, or arranged to purchase or acquire, public lands from the government since 1st January, 1898, in areas of more than 160 acres in each instance, and a statement of the area of such lands in each instance; also a copy of all correspondence with such persons, and all documents and papers relating to the sale or disposal of such lands. Presented 10th January, 1907.—*Mr. Borden (Carleton)*.........*Not printed.*

95. Return to an address of the House of Commons, dated 18th December, 1906, for a copy of all orders in council, instructions, reports, letters, telegrams, correspondence and other papers of every kind relating to the negotiations for the Songhees Indian Reserve, and especially all such papers as aforesaid relating to the recent mission of Mr. Pedley, Deputy Superintendent General of Indian Affairs, to the province of British Columbia. Presented 11th January, 1907.—*Mr. Borden (Carleton)*................................*Not printed.*

96. Return to an order of the House of Commons, dated 10th December, 1906, showing the following data: (1) The name of the present homesteader on southeast quarter, section 12, township 30, range 2, west of 5th meridian; (2) date of his entry; (3) by whom it was made; (4) where was it

CONTENTS OF VOLUME 13—*Continued.*

CONTENTS OF VOLUME 13—*Continued.*

CONTENTS OF VOLUME 13—*Continued.*

CONTENTS OF VOLUME 13—*Continued.*

116*d*. Report of E. J. Walsh, C.E., Engineer in charge of the surveys on the Trent Valley Canal, from Lake Simcoe to Georgian Bay, accompanied by plans, profiles and estimates. Presented 15th March, 1907, by Hon. H. R. Emmerson.. ..*Not printed.*

117. Return to an order of the House of Commons, dated 5th December, 1906, for a copy of all letters, telegrams or documents of any description, relating to, (*a*) the appointment of Mr. F. W. Aylmer to the position of resident engineer of the Dominion Public Works at Winnipeg ; and (*b*) his resignation of said position, together with all letters, telegrams, &c., interchanged between Mr Aylmer and any official of the public works department, in this connection. Presented 21st January, 1907.—*Mr. Ames*..*Not printed.*

118. Return to an address of the House of Commons, dated 28th November, 1906, for a copy of all correspondence, tenders, offers of lease or purchase or occupation, of water powers under the control ot the government of Canada, and of any deed of alienation of the same, whether by lease or otherwise, situate within one hundred miles of the city of Montreal. Presented 21st January, 1907.—*Mr. Monk*..*Not printed.*

119. Return to an order of the House of Commons, dated 9th January, 1907, for a copy of all papers and correspondence in connection with registered letters lost between Bethany and Millbrook, and other points in the county of Durham ; more especially concerning a letter posted by one Joseph Hadden, of Bethany, to the Bank of Toronto, at Millbrook. Presented 24th January, 1907.—*Mr. Ward. Not printed.*

120. Return to an order of the House of Commons, dated 3rd December, 1906, for a copy of all thermograph records of temperature on ocean-going vessels taken during the past season ; stating names of vessel, and date of sailing, and port from whence sailing ; also, stating if in cold storage chambers, cool air chambers, ventilated chambers, or unventilated chambers ; also, in case of ventilated chambers, stating the method of ventilation. Presented 24th January, 1907.—*Mr. Smith (Wentworth). Not printed.*

121. Return to an address of the House of Commons, dated 17th December, 1906, for a copy of : 1. All reports made from time to time by the officers of the topographical surveys branch of the department of the interior, in reference to land in townships 10, 11, 12 and 13, ranges 7, 8, 9, 10, 11, 12 and 13, west of the 4th, and townships 7, 8 and 9, ranges 8, 9, 10 and 11, west of the 4th. 2. Orders in council dated the 13th December, 1886, and 21st December, 1897, setting apart certain lands, viz.: those portions of the south half of section 7, the northwest quarter of section 9, and section 21, lying south and east of the river, township 12, range 12 ; that part of section 35 lying south and east of the river, township 11, range 13, and those portions of sections 1 and 2, lying east of the river in township 12, range 13, all west of the 4th meridian, as reserved for watering of stock. 3. Report of inspection referred to in order in council of 21st December, 1903, showing that the land referred to in orders in council dated 13th December, 1886, and 21st December, 1897, were no longer required for the purpose for which they were reserved. 4. All other reports made from time to time to date by officers of the department of the interior regarding the character and fertility of the soil, climate, rainfall, water supply, or topographical features of the area, or any part of the area described in paragraph 1 of this resolution. Presented 28th January, 1907.—*Mr. Ames*............*Not printed.*

122. Orders in Council authorizing the granting of permits to foreigners and foreign corporations to bring fresh fish in American bottoms to any port in British Columbia, to land such fresh fish at such port without payment of duties and tranship the same in bond to any part of the United States of America, &c. Presented 28th January, 1907, by Sir Wilfrid Laurier.................... *Not printed.*

123. Return to an order of the House of Commons, dated 28th November, 1906, for a copy of all correspondence between the government, or any member or official thereof, and any member of the Royal Insurance Commission, or Mr. Shepley, K.C., or Mr. Tilley, barrister, or any other person employed by or on behalf of the government, relating in any way to the work of the commission, to the subjects and methods of conducting the inquiry, to suggestions as to what witnesses be called, what information be sought, and from whom ; together with any reports received or transmitted in reference to the above ; and also, for a copy of all instructions issued by the government, or any member thereof, to the commission, or any counsel employed thereat. Presented 29th January, 1907.—*Mr. Borden (Carleton)*..*Not printed.*

123*a*. Report of the Royal Commission on Life Insurance. Presented 26th February, 1907, by Hon. W. S. Fielding..*Printed for both distribution and sessional papers.*

CONTENTS OF VOLUME 13—*Continued.*

CONTENTS OF VOLUME 13—*Continued.*

CONTENTS OF VOLUME 13—*Continued.*

CONTENTS OF VOLUME 13—*Continued.*

154. Return to an order of the House of Commons, dated 21st January, 1907, for a copy of all reports, papers, surveys, estimates, correspondence and other documents, with reference to the proposed branch line from the Prince Edward Island Railway at or near O'Leary, to a point at or near West Cape. Presented 25th February, 1907.—*Mr. Lefurgey*.................. ....*Not printed.*

155. Return to an order of the House of Commons, dated 3rd December, 1906, for a copy of all correspondence, contracts, appointments of overseers, in respect to Port Bruce Harbour, in the county of Elgin, Ontario, since 1st January, 1905; also a return showing voucher pay-sheets, amount of new material used, from whom purchased, of all day or contract work on said harbour, giving the names of overseers and when appointed, from same date. Presented 26th February, 1907.—*Mr. Marshall. Not printed.*

156. Return to an order of the House of Commons, dated 6th February, 1907, showing: 1. What government dredges operated in the maritime provinces during the years 1900-1, 1901-2, 1902-3, 1903-4, 1904-5, 1905-6. 2. At what ports or places in the maritime provinces dredging was carried on during said years, giving the name of the dredge operating in each place, the number of days each dredge was employed, and the number of cubic yards excavated at each place where dredging was carried on. 3. Where said dredges are at present. Presented 26th February, 1907.—*Mr. Sinclair. Not printed.*

157. Return to an address of the House of Commons, dated 28th November, 1906, for a copy of all orders in council, valuations, letters, telegrams, correspondence, memoranda, conveyances and other documents and papers, from the first day of January, 1900, to the present time, relating to the proposa to acquire lands at Truro, Nova Scotia, for the Intercolonial Railway, and especially all such documents as aforesaid relating to the acquisition of land purchased by the Crown from H. W. Yuill by deed bearing date on or about the 17th October, 1904; also a copy of conveyances bearing date in October, 1904, under which the said Yuill acquired the said property; also all reports touching the question of sites for the construction of a round-house at Truro. Presented 28th February, 1907.—*Mr. Borden (Carleton)*.. ....*Not printed.*

158. Return to an order of the House of Commons, dated 11th February, 1907, showing: 1. What work the Railway Department ordered and performed at public expense to rail and ballast the whole or part of a branch railway from the Intercolonial Railway to the Wallace Quarries, Cumberland County, Nova Scotia, and what length was railed or ballasted. 2. From what point and for what distance the department conveyed ballast for the said work. 3. The length of said branch line. 4. Why the said branch line was not extended to Wallace Village, and what distance farther than constructed it would be necessary to build to give Wallace Village rail connection. 5. If the department hauls cars to said Wallace Quarries at public expense, and why it is done. 6. If shunting charge on the said branch line was cancelled, when it was cancelled, and for what reason. 7. At whose instance or request, or for whose benefit the above-mentioned work was done, and the shunting charge cancelled. 8. How much the department has expended for work on construction of said branch line. 9. Who the owners or operators of the said Wallace Quarries are. 10. What the freight rates collected by the department over the said branch lines are. 11. What similar or any concessions in the matter of construction, reduction of freight rates, or cancellation of shunting charges, to or in relation to any other quarries operated at or near Wallace have been granted by the department. 12. What other quarries operating at or near Wallace, and doing business over the Intercolonial Railway, are charged freight rates or shunting charges, or both, upon or in respect to any branch line used by them. 13. What companies are so operating, and what charges the department makes against them. 14. What owners or operators of the Wallace Quarries above-mentioned are related to the minister of railways, who they are, and how related. Presented 28th February, 1907.—*Mr. McLean (Queen's)*................................ .... *Not printed.*

159. Return to an order of the House of Commons, dated 18th February, 1907, showing: Summary of stock, implements, chattels, grain, hay, roots, and all other kinds of fodder, and their value, on the first day of December, for the years 1905-1906 on the Central Experimental Farm, Ottawa. Presented 28th February, 1907.—*Mr. Jackson (Elgin)*. .. ..*Not printed.*

160. Return to an order of the House of Commons, dated 10th December, 1906, for a copy of the correspondence, telegrams, tenders, and engineer's estimate, in reference to letting the contract for the construction of extension pier at Port Daniel, in county of Bonaventure, on 30th May, 1904. Presented 1st March, 1907.—*Mr. Martin (Queen's)*.............. ....*Not printed.*

CONTENTS OF VOLUME 13—*Continued.*

161. Return to an order of the House of Commons, dated 3rd December, 1906, for a copy of all correspondence, contracts, appointments of overseers, in respect to Port Burwell Harbour, in the county of Elgin, Ontario, since 1st January, 1905; also a return showing pay-sheets, amount of new material used, from whom purchased, of all day or contract work on said harbour, giving names of overseers, and when appointed from the same date. Presented 1st March, 1907.—*Mr. Marshall.* *Not printed.*

162. Copy of Deed, Joseph H. Henderson *et ux* to His Majesty the King, for 34.78 acres of land in the city of Halifax, N.S., for the Intercolonial Railway. Presented 1st March, 1907, by Hon. H. R. Emmerson..*Not printed.*

163. Return to an order of the House of Commons, dated 3rd December, 1906, showing: 1. The present indebtedness to the Dominion Government of the Montreal Turnpike Trust, (*a*) on capital account; (*b*) for arrears of interest. 2. The amount collected at each toll-gate belonging to the said Turnpike Trust during the year ending 31st December, 1905. 3. The names of all parties who have commuted their tolls, and the amount of commutation paid in each case. 4. The amounts expended on each section or road division under the control of said trust, during the said year, ending 31st December, 1905, and the contracts given out during the year, with the name of the contractor, and the date and amount involved in each case. 5. The amount paid out during the said year at each toll-gate and check-gate for salaries of day and night keepers, and other expenditures at each of the toll-gates maintained. 6. The names of all parties holding passes for free use of the road, under the control of said trust, during the said year. 7. The expense of the said trust during the said year, for rent, salaries of the office, giving name and remuneration of each official. 8. The actual indebtedness in detail of the said trust, outside of its bonds, due to the government of Canada. 9. The amount collected during the year 1905 from municipalities, under special agreements made, as their share, pro rata, of the bonded indebtedness of the Turnpike Trust. Presented 1st March, 1907.—*Mr. Monk*..*Not printed.*

164. Return to an order of the House of Commons, dated 16th January, 1907, showing: 1. What amounts were paid into the office of the receiver general during the fiscal year 1905-1906 on account of contractors' deposits for security, and by what contractors these sums were paid. 2. The deposits forfeited to the government during the said fiscal year, names of the contractors and the amounts so forfeited. 3. Cheques received as security from contractors during the said fiscal year, held by the departments which received them, and from whom they were received. 4. The total amount now in the hands of the receiver general and of the several departments, respectively, belonging to this account. Presented 1st March, 1907.—*Mr. Foster*..............................*Not printed.*

165. Return to an address of the House of Commons, dated 10th December 1906, (in so far as the department of customs is concerned), for a copy of all orders in council, correspondence, and all other papers, relating to the Standard Chemical Company (Limited), or Peuchen & Co., in its dealings with the Customs and Inland Revenue Departments, from the date of the incorporation of the said company to the present date. Presented 1st March, 1907.—*Mr. Robitaille*..........*Not printed.*

166. Return (in so far as the department of the interior is concerned) to an address of the Senate dated 7th February, 1907, calling for the orders in council of the 11th of May, 1885, and the 5th of March, 1895, allotting lands in the Northwest Territories under the authority of the Act of 1884, chapter 25, section 7, and all orders in council passed since 1895, relating to grants of lands for this purpose. Also copies of all contracts between the Canadian Northern Railway Company and the government relating to the construction of a line of railway to the Hudson Bay or any portion of the said line of railway. Presented 21st February, 1907.—*Hon. Mr. Ferguson*..............................*Not printed.*

167. Return to an order of the House of Commons, dated 9th January 1907, showing all timber lands in the railway belt in the province of British Columbia, sold or leased by the government, or any department thereof, since the 1st July, 1896, the description and area of such lots, the applications made therefor, the notice of advertisement for sale or tender, the tenders received, the amount of each tender, the tenders accepted, the name and address of the person or company to whom each lot was sold or leased. Presented 4th March, 1907.—*Mr. McCarthy (Calgary)*............*Not printed.*

167a. Return to an order of the House of Commons, dated 11th March, 1907, showing: The timber lands sold or leased by the department of the interior subsequent to the date of those included in Sessional Paper No. 90, brought down to the house on the 9th of April, 1906; the description and area of such lands, the applications made therefor, the notice of advertisement for sale or tender, the tenders received, the amount of each tender, the tenders accepted, the name of the person or com-

CONTENTS OF VOLUME 13—*Continued.*

CONTENTS OF VOLUME 13—*Continued.*

CONTENTS OF VOLUME 13—*Continued.*

who served with or embarked for service with the British forces in South Africa who were not members of the above corps. 3. The names of all British Columbians who were regularly appointed to the medical staff, and were actively engaged in said military operations. 4. The names of nurses, hospital dressers, and orderlies, resident in British Columbia, who were actively engaged in said military operations. Presented 13th March, 1907.—*Mr. Ross (Yale-Cariboo)*..........*Not printed.*

186. Return to an order of the House of Commons, dated 23rd January, 1907, for a copy of all correspondence, with the papers and reports made by superior officers of the Department of Marine and Fisheries, or by Captain Wakeham, or any other person, regarding the dismissal from the service of R. P. Dubé, second mate on board *La Canadienne*; also for a copy of the report made by the said R. P. Dubé to the Department of Marine and Fisheries regarding the fire on the *Aberdeen*, on the 10th November, 1905. Presented 13th March, 1907.—*Mr. Gauvreau*..................*Not printed.*

187. Return to an order of the House of Commons, dated 11th February, 1907, for a copy of the record and all proceedings in the suit in the Exchequer Court of Canada between the King, on the information of the Attorney General of the Dominion of Canada, and H. E. Lyon, plaintiffs, and Malcolm McKenzie and Felix A. Montalbetti, defendants, including all correspondence in connection therewith between the Department of Justice and the Department of the Interior, or any officers thereof, respectively, and between either of the said departments, or any officers thereof, and any other person or persons whatsoever; and including all documents or memorandum in any way relating to the said suit, including instructions to counsel engaged therein on behalf of the plaintiffs; and also all documents on file in the Department of the Interior, relating to the northeast quarter of section 35, in township 7, range 4, west of the 5th meridian. Presented 18th March, 1907.—*Mr. Herron*..................*Not printed.*

187a. Supplementary return to No. 187. Presented 10th April, 1907.....................*Not printed.*

188. Return to an order of the House of Commons, dated 23rd January, 1907, showing: All sales of Dominion lands of 160 acres and upwards, in Manitoba, Saskatchewan and Alberta, which have been made by the government, exclusive of school lands, since the 1st January, 1905, with the price obtained, and dates of sale. Presented 19th March, 1907.—*Mr. Lake*.................*Not printed.*

189. Return to an address of the Senate, dated 6th March, 1907, for copies of all correspondence between the government of Canada or any member thereof with any person whatsoever, and any report from any officer of the government regarding the question of pensions by the state to deserving persons of advanced age; and also a copy of a Bill referred to by the Right Honourable the Minister of Trade and Commerce during a speech made by him in the Senate on the 28th February last, dealing with the sale of annuities by the government of Canada. Presented 19th March, 1907.—*Hon. Mr. Ferguson*..................*Not printed.*

190. A statement in pursuance of section 17 of the Civil Service Insurance Act for the year ending 30th June, 1906. Presented (Senate) 15th March, 1907, by Hon. R. W. Scott..............*Not printed.*

191. Return to an address of the House of Commons, dated 28th March, 1906, for copies of all orders in council, reports, memoranda, correspondence, valuation, documents and papers, of every kind and nature and description, relating to the property situated on the south side of Spring Garden Road, in the city of Halifax, upon which the old drill shed was or is situated; or relating to the leasing, conveying, disposal, or user of the said property, or of any property conveyed to the crown in consideration or in part consideration therefor. Presented 22nd March, 1907.—*Mr. Fowler*..*Not printed.*

192. Return to an order of the House of Commons, dated 11th February, 1907, for a copy of all reports or correspondence between the Railway Commission and the Department of Justice, concerning the trial of one Atkinson, on a charge of manslaughter, in connection with the collision which took place on the Grand Trunk Railway at Richmond, Quebec, in August, 1904. Presented 22nd March, 1907.—*Mr. Worthington*..................*Not printed.*

193. Return to an order of the House of Commons, dated 6th February, 1907, for a copy of all correspondence, telegrams, orders in council, and all other papers and documents in possession of the government, or any member or official thereof, in any way relating to the purchase by the government of what is known as the Warburton property in Charlotteown, for a rifle range, and a right of way for approach to the Hillsboro' bridge. Presented 25th March, 1907.—*Mr. Lefurgey.* *Not printed.*

193a. Supplementary return to No. 193. Presented 15th April, 1907.....................*Not printed.*

CONTENTS OF VOLUME 13—*Continued.*

CONTENTS OF VOLUME 13—*Continued.*

CONTENTS OF VOLUME 13—*Continued.*

CONTENTS OF VOLUME 13—*Concluded.*

TABLES

OF THE

TRADE AND NAVIGATION

OF THE

DOMINION OF CANADA

FOR THE

FISCAL YEAR ENDED JUNE 30

1906

COMPILED FROM OFFICIAL RETURNS

PRINTED BY ORDER OF PARLIAMENT

OTTAWA
PRINTED BY S. E. DAWSON, PRINTER TO THE KING'S MOST
EXCELLENT MAJESTY
1906

[No. 11—1906.]

To His Excellency the Right Honourable Sir Albert Henry George, Earl Grey, Viscount Howick, Baron Grey of Howick, in the County of Northumberland, in the Peerage of the United Kingdom, and a Baronet: Knight Grand Cross of the Most Distinguished Order of Saint Michael and Saint George, &c., &c., Governor General of Canada.

MAY IT PLEASE YOUR EXCELLENCY,—

The undersigned has the honour to present to Your Excellency the Tables of Trade and Navigation of the Dominion of Canada for the Fiscal Year ended June 30, 1906, as prepared from Official Returns and laid before me by the Commissioner of Customs.

All of which is respectfully submitted.

W. PATERSON,
Minister of Customs.

OTTAWA, November 14, 1906.

CUSTOMS DEPARTMENT,
OTTAWA, August 24, 1906.

HON. WILLIAM PATERSON,
Minister of Customs.

I have the honour to hand you the annual statement of the Trade and Navigation of the Dominion of Canada for the fiscal year ended June 30, 1906.

I have the honour to be, sir,
Your obedient servant,

JOHN McDOUGALD,
Commissioner of Customs.

INDEX TO TABLES

INDEX TO TABLES—Concluded.

EXPLANATORY NOTES

In General Statement No. 1 (Pt. ii) of Imports and Goods entered for Consumption, The term 'Entered for Consumption' is the technical term in use at the custom-house, and does not imply that the goods have been actually consumed in Canada, but that they have passed into the possession of the importer and that duty has been paid on that portion liable for duty.

The value of goods imported is governed by Section 58 of the Customs Act, which provides that the value of imported goods subject to ad valorem duty 'shall be the fair market value thereof, when sold for home consumption, in the principal markets of the country whence and at the time when the same were exported directly to Canada.'

In General Statement No. 3 (Pt. ii) of Exports, The term 'The Produce of Canada' includes all imported articles which have been changed in form or enhanced in value by further manufacture in Canada, such as sugar refined in Canada from imported raw sugar, flour ground from imported wheat, and articles constructed or manufactured from imported materials.

'Goods not the produce of Canada' shows the exports of foreign goods which had been previously imported.

Under the Regulations commencing July 1st, 1900, all *Export* entries are delivered at the '*frontier port of exit*,' and the totals thereof are credited to the respective ports where the goods pass outwards from Canada. In view of the more complete returns obtained under this system the additions heretofore made to the export statistics (prior to July 1st, 1900) under the head of 'Short returns' are now omitted.

In this report, the tables of imports and exports at the several ports of entry indicate that merchandise of the value stated was *entered inwards* or *passed outwards* at the ports mentioned, but do not imply that the imports were all for consumption at such ports or that the exports originated there.

The trade by Countries, with the Dominion as a whole, is recorded in the General Statements of Imports and Exports.

The value of 'Goods the Produce of Canada' is their value at the time of exportation at the ports of Canada whence shipped.

The value of 'Goods not the Produce of Canada' is the actual cost of such goods.

The initials N.E.S. mean 'not elsewhere specified.'

" N.O.P. mean 'not otherwise provided for.'

The expression 'Ton' means two thousand pounds, and 'Cwt.' one hundred pounds.

" 'Standard hundred' when applied to deals, means 2,750 feet board measure.

" 'Ton,' applied to square timber, means 40 cubic feet.

In the shipping tables the tonnage is given in net tons.

SPECIAL NOTE.

Under an amendment to the Customs Tariff passed in 1903, provision was made for the collection of a surtax on the goods of any foreign country which treats imports from Canada less favourably than those from other countries.

It is to be particularly noted that the surtax does not apply to the goods of other countries imported from Germany, but only to articles which are the growth, produce or manufacture of Germany. Various classes of goods which are of *other than German origin* therefore appear in these Tables as imports from Germany, entered under the General Tariff and not subject to a surtax.

ERRATA

Part II.—Page 11, Newspapers, &c., total consumption value, for 2,784, read 2,874.

" " 28, Railway cars, tram or horse, General consumption value, for 8,024, read 8,042.

" " 60, Proprietary Medicines, France Import Value, for 36,984 read 36,948,

" " 72, 2nd item, 2nd line, "Embroideries or chiffon," read "Embroidered or Embossed chiffon."

" " 127, Springs, axles, &c., G. B. Total Consumption quantity, for 13,116, read 14,116. Total Consumption quantity for 68,948 read 69,948.

" " 273, Shawls, Total Preferential duty, for 15,508.00, read 15,508.80.

" " 355, Salmon, pickled, for "New Zealand," read "Newfoundland."

" " 363, Other articles of Forest, for "Newfoundland." read "New Zealand."

PART I

TABLES

OF THE

TRADE AND NAVIGATION

No. 1.—Value of total Exports, Imports and Goods entered for Consumption in the Dominion, with the duty collected thereon, for the undermentioned years.

——	Total Exports.	Total Imports.	Entered for Consumption.	Duty.
	$	$	$	$ cts.
Fiscal year ended June 30, 1868	57,567,888	73,459,644	71,985,306	8,819,431 63
do do 1869	60,474,781	70,415,165	67,402,170	8,298,909 71
do do 1870	73,573,490	74,814,339	71,237,603	9,462,940 44
do do 1871	74,173,618	96,092,971	86,947,482	11,843,655 75
do do 1872	82,639,663	111,430,527	107,709,116	13,045,493 50
do do 1873	89,789,922	128,011,281	127,514,594	13,017,730 17
do do 1874	89,351,928	128,213,582	127,404,169	14,421,882 67
do do 1875	77,886,979	123,070,283	119,618,657	15,361,382 12
do do 1876	80,966,435	93,210,346	94,733,218	12,833,114 48
do do 1877	75,875,393	99,327,962	96,300,483	12,548,451 09
do do 1878	79,323,667	93,081,787	91,199,577	12,795,693 17
do do 1879	71,491,255	81,964,427	80,341,608	12,939,540 66
do do 1880	87,911,458	86,489,747	71,782,349	14,138,849 22
do do 1881	98,290,823	105,330,840	91,611,604	18,500,785 97
do do 1882	102,137,203	119,419,500	112,648,927	21,708,837 43
do do 1883	98,085,804	132,254,022	123,137,019	23,172,308 97
do do 1884	91,406,496	116,397,043	108,180,644	20,164,963 37
do do 1885	89,238,361	108,941,486	102,710,019	19,133,558 99
do do 1886	85,251,314	104,424,561	99,602,694	19,448,123 70
do do 1887	89,515,811	112,892,236	105,639,428	22,469,705 83
do do 1888	90,203,000	110,894,630	102,847,100	22,209,641 53
do do 1889	89,189,167	115,224,931	109,673,447	23,784,523 23
do do 1890	96,749,149	121,858,241	112,765,584	24,014,908 07
do do 1891	98,417,296	119,967,638	113,345,124	23,481,069 13
do do 1892	113,963,372	127,406,068	116,978,943	20,550,581 53
do do 1893	118,564,352	129,074,268	121,705,030	21,161,710 93
do do 1894	117,524,949	123,474,940	113,093,983	19,379,822 52
do do 1895	113,638,803	110,781,682	105,252,511	17,887,269 47
do do 1896	121,013,852	118,011,508	110,587,480	20,219,037 32
do do 1897	137,950,253	119,218,609	111,294,021	19,891,996 77
do do 1898	164,152,683	140,323,053	130,698,006	22,157,788 49
do do 1899	158,896,905	162,764,308	154,051,593	25,734,228 75
do do 1900	191,894,723	189,622,513	180,804,316	28,889,110 13
do do 1901	196,487,632	190,415,525	181,237,988	29,106,979 89
do do 1902	211,640,286	212,270,158	202,791,595	32,425,532 31
do do 1903	225,849,724	241,214,961	233,790,516	37,110,354 59
do do 1904	213,521,235	259,211,803	251,464,332	40,954,349 14
do do 1905	203,316,872	266,834,417	261,925,554	42,024,339 92
do do 1906	256,586,630	294,286,015	290,360,807	46,671,101 18

No. 2.—Aggregate Trade of the Dominion by Countries on the basis of Goods entered for Consumption and Exported.

Fiscal Year ended June 30.	Great Britain.	United States.	France.	Germany.	Spain.	Portugal.	Italy.	Holland.
	$	$	$	$	$	$	$	$
1873	107,266,624	89,808,204	2,055,195	1,176,478	502,966	266,188	229,657	229,770
1874	108,083,642	90,524,060	2,569,712	1,022,428	459,027	294,007	236,296	271,043
1875	100,379,969	80,717,803	2,154,065	839,442	390,784	236,790	214,366	260,503
1876	81,457,737	78,003,492	2,394,812	608,355	445,151	199,195	183,199	297,895
1877	81,139,708	77,087,914	1,730,062	404,918	340,757	175,425	242,942	296,860
1878	83,372,719	73,876,437	1,754,394	521,580	325,245	145,941	205,171	266,764
1879	67,288,848	70,904,720	2,247,066	552,999	394,445	161,258	181,933	210,288
1880	80,307,286	62,696,857	1,928,670	532,028	297,245	201,652	623,295	273,837
1881	97,335,378	73,570,337	2,294,043	1,019,198	446,337	165,487	234,723	440,944
1882	95,871,802	96,229,763	2,922,931	1,633,118	570,301	201,656	256,841	613,241
1883	99,197,682	97,701,056	2,934,210	1,942,851	749,897	243,192	322,554	324,800
1884	87,154,242	89,333,366	2,160,804	2,171,346	648,569	240,235	322,499	333,977
1885	83,284,482	86,903,935	2,239,890	2,385,344	481,910	227,096	255,712	361,879
1886	82,143,828	81,436,808	2,509,581	2,408,821	432,540	301,927	215,298	309,559
1887	89,534,079	82,767,265	2,415,001	3,672,985	481,289	204,671	245,560	309,920
1888	79,383,705	91,053,913	2,642,557	3,563,106	427,249	230,397	235,816	332,169
1889	80,422,515	94,059,844	2,562,893	3,836,173	420,794	238,106	186,186	414,302
1890	91,743,935	92,814,783	2,894,154	4,286,136	392,294	291,811	244,545	423,309
1891	91,328,384	94,824,352	2,565,877	4,336,232	555,917	191,148	322,808	404,532
1892	106,254,984	92,125,599	2,770,173	6,526,228	489,652	155,479	490,839	846,167
1893	107,228,906	102,144,986	3,096,164	4,576,224	387,861	135,482	661,403	656,427
1894	107,256,123	88,844,040	3,081,950	7,887,594	445,567	126,469	511,631	625,764
1895	92,988,727	95,932,197	2,920,456	5,421,135	436,580	115,921	415,919	348,164
1896	99,670,030	103,022,434	3,392,482	6,688,990	445,592	88,262	287,676	436,980
1897	106,639,690	111,022,513	3,292,047	7,538,800	436,984	82,337	333,512	480,531
1898	137,499,735	124,410,926	5,000,613	7,421,462	578,462	135,154	495,023	750,486
1899	136,151,978	138,140,687	5,447,017	9,613,025	593,660	92,937	520,684	872,941
1900	152,526,098	178,463,401	5,743,272	10,099,401	647,157	187,801	405,029	767,781
1901	148,347,120	182,867,238	6,979,352	9,162,957	897,893	181,707	642,424	984,840
1902	166,533,983	192,004,734	8,061,042	13,515,747	856,793	234,874	963,641	1,195,856
1903	190,099,222	209,389,119	7,921,647	14,380,336	962,497	293,376	837,555	1,889,869
1904	179,368,950	223,599,447	7,804,453	9,994,827	963,674	210,053	642,891	1,951,398
1905	162,301,480	240,142,642	8,570,437	7,842,068	779,482	227,281	819,610	1,505,474
1906	202,289,527	273,668,593	9,788,078	8,859,871	984,477	218,202	769,610	2,004,640

No. 2.—Aggregate Trade of the Dominion by Countries on the basis of Goods entered for Consumption and Exported—*Concluded.*

Fiscal Year ended June 30.	Belgium.	New-foundland	West Indies.	South America.	China and Japan.	Switzer-land.	Other Countries.	Total.
	$	$	$	$	$	$	$	$
1873	364,456	4,609,552	1,163,425	1,701,633	1,709,856	120,514	1,099,998	217,304,516
1874	534,153	2,657,547	6,086,529	1,686,508	1,263,728	139,674	927,743	216,756,097
1875	337,674	2,806,055	6,139,910	1,064,593	694,472	116,128	1,153,082	197,505,636
1876	374,880	2,675,477	5,291,433	975,762	971,314	56,168	1,764,483	175,699,653
1877	318,724	2,753,748	5,031,667	656,591	455,755	69,066	1,471,734	172,175,876
1878	805,692	2,767,347	4,397,996	669,804	486,244	61,178	1,366,532	170,523,244
1879	219,461	2,280,823	4,753,099	745,830	505,513	94,781	1,291,709	151,832,863
1880	837,897	2,002,261	6,489,257	1,073,421	931,457	94,225	1,314,429	159,693,807
1881	671,267	2,175,773	6,962,516	1,369,731	1,430,734	141,789	1,644,170	189,902,427
1882	645,568	2,468,432	7,018,956	2,314,779	1,635,717	268,093	2,134,932	214,786,130
1883	611,112	2,953,273	7,494,291	2,954,628	1,750,642	336,040	1,706,595	221,222,823
1884	746,528	2,701,120	6,726,486	2,756,371	1,970,541	242,380	2,078,676	199,587,140
1885	551,645	2,022,073	5,698,057	2,802,042	2,528,369	217,666	1,989,280	191,948,380
1886	517,472	2,139,301	5,266,042	2,111,029	2,495,703	203,085	2,363,014	184,854,008
1887	927,580	2,072,946	4,017,593	2,625,066	2,819,584	219,777	2,841,913	195,155,239
1888	505,800	1,945,426	5,870,149	2,487,240	2,261,155	194,938	2,016,480	193,050,100
1889	595,496	1,791,496	6,138,109	2,813,587	2,048,712	166,905	3,167,496	198,862,814
1890	763,146	1,655,400	5,808,189	2,555,849	2,161,816	316,923	3,162,393	209,514,733
1891	728,120	2,218,911	6,360,926	1,782,950	2,202,102	244,319	3,685,842	211,762,420
1892	573,244	2,503,963	7,638,846	1,905,346	3,300,108	193,033	5,168,657	230,942,318
1893	1,268,551	3,247,903	7,390,377	2,099,356	2,766,712	258,464	4,465,666	240,269,382
1894	1,258,692	3,633,154	7,121,172	2,264,677	3,065,768	276,065	4,220,266	230,618,932
1895	693,019	3,065,046	8,681,622	1,610,470	2,906,574	260,040	3,059,444	218,891,314
1896	1,018,789	2,333,721	4,707,243	2,063,145	3,339,429	332,405	3,771,454	231,601,332
1897	1,518,218	2,144,874	4,322,230	2,026,085	3,300,331	223,192	5,882,830	249,244,274
1898	2,204,054	2,632,184	3,829,346	2,505,195	2,829,890	357,003	4,201,156	294,850,689
1899	3,168,136	2,335,323	4,398,902	2,631,635	3,194,849	571,526	5,215,018	312,948,498
1900	4,421,716	2,804,748	4,202,119	2,423,994	2,749,759	529,976	6,726,[illegible]87	372,699,039
1901	6,634,592	2,886,067	4,707,677	2,567,278	3,149,591	603,397	7,113,487	377,725,620
1902	4,156,049	3,498,482	5,472,747	3,440,987	2,555,462	780,183	11,161,301	414,431,881
1903	4,950,732	3,714,157	6,021,294	4,532,008	2,440,999	952,326	11,255,103	459,640,240
1904	4,255,930	3,975,418	8,397,290	5,613,612	3,134,959	1,392,895	13,679,770	464,985,567
1905	3,514,994	4,528,326	10,033,302	6,916,171	3,990,776	1,776,405	12,288,038	465,242,426
1906	4,175,238	4,972,281	9,944,179	9,425,735	3,684,769	2,042,635	14,119,602	546,947,437

No. 3.—Showing the grand aggregate trade from 1868 to 1906 inclusive, on the basis of 'Total Exports and Imports.'

Years.	Total Exports.	Total Imports.	Grand total, Imports and Exports.
	$	$	$
1868	57,567,888	73,459,644	131,027,532
1869	60,474,781	70,415,165	130,889,946
1870	73,573,490	74,814,339	148,387,829
1871	74,173,618	96,092,971	170,266,589
1872	82,639,663	111,430,527	194,070,190
1873	89,789,922	128,011,281	217,801,203
1874	89,351,928	128,213,582	217,565,510
1875	77,886,979	123,070,283	200,957,262
1876	80,966,435	93,210,346	174,176,781
1877	75,875,393	99,327,962	175,203,355
1878	79,323,667	93,081,787	172,405,454
1879	71,491,255	81,964,427	153,455,682
1880	87,911,458	86,489,747	174,401,205
1881	98,290,823	105,330,840	203,621,663
1882	102,137,203	119,419,500	221,556,703
1883	98,085,804	132,254,022	230,339,826
1884	91,406,496	116,397,043	207,803,539
1885	89,238,361	108,941,486	198,179,847
1886	85,251,314	104,424,561	189,675,875
1887	89,515,811	112,892,236	202,408,047
1888	90,203,000	110,894,630	201,097,630
1889	89,189,167	115,224,931	204,414,098
1890	96,749,149	121,858,241	218,607,390
1891	98,417,296	119,967,638	218,384,934
1892	113,963,375	127,406,068	241,369,443
1893	118,564,352	129,074,268	247,638,620
1894	117,524,949	123,474,940	240,999,889
1895	113,638,803	110,781,682	224,420,485
1896	121,013,852	118,011,508	239,025,360
1897	137,950,253	119,218,609	257,168,862
1898	164,152,683	140,323,053	304,475,736
1899	158,896,905	162,764,308	321,661,213
1900	191,894,723	189,622,513	381,517,236
1901	196,487,632	190,415,525	386,903,157
1902	211,640,286	212,270,158	423,910,444
1903	225,849,724	241,214,961	467,064,685
1904	213,521,235	259,211,803	472,733,038
1905	203,316,872	266,834,417	470,151,289
1906	256,586,630	294,286,015	550,872,645

No. 4.—Value of Export, by Countries.

Fiscal year ended June 30.	Great Britain.	United States.	France.	Germany.	Spain.	Portugal.	Italy.	Holland.
	$	$	$	$	$	$	$	$
1873	38,743,848	42,072,526	31,907	76,553	25,080	191,156	177,232	13,142
1874	45,003,882	36,244,311	267,212	65,511	960	193,463	190,211	14,905
1875	40,032,902	29,911,983	212,767	91,019	7,300	170,784	170,408	28,724
1876	40,723,477	31,933,459	553,935	125,768	9,417	127,540	142,787	30,816
1877	41,567,469	25,775,245	319,330	34,324	62,659	129,960	213,692	94,303
1878	45,941,539	25,244,898	369,391	122,254	47,816	104,028	151,861	53,750
1879	36,295,718	27,165,501	714,875	112,090	50,596	135,748	148,472	9,713
1880	45,846,062	33,349,909	812,829	82,237	60,727	165,885	163,787	102,592
1881	53,571,570	36,866,225	662,711	84,932	46,053	108,594	145,997	215,754
1882	45,274,461	47,940,711	825,573	153,114	108,082	149,744	163,755	365,198
1883	47,145,217	41,668,723	617,730	133,697	164,925	179,843	218,113	27,599
1884	43,736,227	38,840,540	390,955	195,575	144,092	172,252	247,151	15,500
1885	41,877,705	39,752,734	303,309	264,075	132,695	166,730	147,550	24,094
1886	41,542,629	36,578,769	534,363	253,298	53,075	245,450	103,601	7,587
1887	44,571,846	37,660,199	341,531	437,536	72,020	146,528	125,681	14,859
1888	40,084,984	42,572,065	397,773	198,543	52,317	155,821	55,090	378
1889	38,105,126	43,522,404	334,210	143,603	13,526	166,021	60,062	1,222
1890	48,353,694	40,522,810	278,552	507,143	69,788	207,777	81,059	1,042
1891	49,280,858	41,138,695	253,734	532,142	67,110	120,611	90,999	14,741
1892	64,906,549	38,988,027	367,539	942,698	93,476	102,370	149,280	567,879
1893	64,080,493	43,923,010	264,047	750,461	44,355	83,001	87,387	282,569
1894	68,538,856	35,809,940	544,986	2,046,052	56,274	79,363	109,188	281,058
1895	61,856,990	41,297,676	335,282	626,976	34,101	58,781	34,325	140,264
1896	66,690,288	44,448,410	581,540	757,531	83,814	41,666	56,759	139,828
1897	77,227,502	49,373,472	690,696	1,045,432	50,452	36,745	108,627	104,422
1898	104,998,818	45,705,336	1,025,262	1,837,448	89,675	87,835	73,765	376,439
1899	99,091,855	45,133,521	1,557,722	2,219,569	59,178	29,641	125,265	372,548
1900	107,736,368	68,619,023	1,374,770	1,715,903	86,456	115,016	260,456	188,199
1901	105,328,956	72,382,230	1,581,331	2,141,552	155,354	85,403	315,063	187,378
1902	117,320,221	71,197,684	1,388,848	2,692,578	161,823	105,495	236,899	320,241
1903	131,202,321	71,783,924	1,341,618	2,097,699	138,553	164,184	295,770	619,329
1904	117,591,376	72,772,932	1,597,928	1,819,223	98,578	109,340	240,963	1,035,327
1905	101,958,771	77,404,071	1,511,298	1,146,654	50,223	128,993	198,973	550,821
1906	133,094,937	97,806,552	2,120,091	1,872,557	55,686	89,598	215,855	824,768

No. 4.—Value of Exports, by Countries—*Concluded.*

Fiscal year ended June 30.	Belgium.	New-foundland.	West Indies.	South America.	China and Japan.	Australia.	Other Countries.	Total.
	$	$	$	$	$	$	$	$
1873	17,754	2,800,555	3,988,493	1,285,434	46,466	41,822	277,954	89,789,922
1874	240,494	1,569,079	3,778,796	1,212,978	39,222	98,733	432,171	89,351,928
1875	59,563	1,901,831	3,945,506	785,797	37,046	181,938	349,411	77,886,979
1876	13,825	1,900,891	3,675,320	688,209	23,075	79,643	938,273	80,966,435
1877	66,912	2,112,106	3,788,858	651,625	37,149	185,610	836,151	75,875,393
1878	49,998	2,094,682	3,414,147	654,357	102,568	370,723	651,655	79,323,667
1879	40,430	1,641,417	3,500,670	741,442	56,551	290,762	587,270	71,491,255
1880	688,811	1,510,300	3,544,103	789,940	37,546	139,901	616,829	87,911,458
1881	258,433	1,523,469	3,147,369	732,111	19,761	146,363	580,881	98,290,823
1882	142,358	1,974,923	2,995,572	941,162	106,675	340,608	655,267	102,137,203
1883	195,705	2,187,338	3,125,031	1,489,957	105,388	375,065	451,473	98,085,804
1884	287,378	1,920,450	3,119,569	1,277,383	60,979	502,181	496,264	91,406,496
1885	72,385	1,670,968	2,535,283	1,461,206	29,918	415,887	383,822	89,238,361
1886	6,565	1,754,980	2,121,570	1,010,034	63,118	259,960	711,315	85,251,314
1887	223,729	1,718,604	2,075,411	1,426,660	69,196	269,471	362,540	89,515,811
1888	17,057	1,523,827	2,601,486	1,510,637	132,448	446,019	454,555	90,203,000
1889	64,756	1,303,335	2,759,455	1,488,999	84,174	661,208	481,051	89,189,167
1890	41,814	1,185,739	2,719,141	1,551,887	61,751	471,028	695,924	96,749,149
1891	72,672	1,467,908	3,122,770	1,063,172	78,791	589,100	523,993	98,417,296
1892	56,212	1,750,714	3,546,559	1,027,525	283,251	436,603	744,693	113,963,375
1893	669,040	2,594,633	3,145,708	1,326,743	341,140	288,352	683,413	118,564,352
1894	708,455	2,818,592	3,443,761	1,392,285	540,849	322,745	832,545	117,524,949
1895	251,402	2,325,196	3,725,426	1,303,474	378,160	417,124	853,626	113,638,803
1896	98,031	1,782,309	2,810,817	1,496,118	668,011	517,258	841,472	121,013,852
1897	354,584	1,692,798	2,643,360	1,405,359	903,922	1,418,289	894,593	137,950,253
1898	973,944	2,167,860	2,749,080	1,060,420	511,919	1,630,714	864,168	164,152,683
1899	849,413	1,808,317	3,043,963	1,456,051	425,350	1,506,138	1,218,374	158,896,905
1900	1,197,798	2,144,070	2,870,343	1,431,107	368,615	1,626,441	2,160,158	191,894,723
1901	2,806,142	2,260,499	2,905,937	1,519,190	699,569	2,311,405	1,807,623	196,487,632
1902	2,444,450	2,381,082	3,298,912	1,781,913	570,586	2,586,554	5,153,000	211,640,286
1903	2,150,550	2,516,576	3,642,176	2,542,056	501,057	2,929,861	3,924,050	225,849,724
1904	1,126,417	2,898,751	3,583,475	2,456,608	568,983	2,622,756	4,898,578	213,521,235
1905	1,739,807	3,473,713	4,401,115	2,880,552	1,520,053	2,194,223	4,157,605	203,316,872
1906	1,565,166	3,213,856	4,575,212	3,623,065	1,467,252	2,082,219	3,979,816	256,586,630

No. 5.—Value of Goods entered for Consumption, by Countries.

Fiscal year ended June 30.	Great Britain.	United States.	France.	Germany.	Spain.	Portugal.	Italy.	Holland.
	$	$	$	$	$	$	$	$
1873	68,522,776	47,735,678	2,023,288	1,099,925	477,886	75,032	52,425	216,628
1874	63,076,437	54,283,072	2,302,500	956,917	458,067	100,544	46,085	256,138
1875	60,347,067	50,805,820	1,941,298	748,423	383,484	66,006	43,958	231,779
1876	40,734,260	46,070,033	1,840,877	482,587	436,034	71,655	40,412	267,079
1877	39,572,239	51,312,669	1,410,732	370,594	278,098	45,465	29,250	202,557
1878 ..	37,431,180	48,631,739	1,385,003	399,326	277 429	41,913	53,310	213,014
1879	30,993,130	43,739,219	1,532,191	440,909	343,849	25,510	33,461	200,575
1880	34,461,224	29,346,948	1,115,841	449,791	236,518	35,767	459,508	171,245
1881	43,583,808	36,704,112	1,631,332	934,266	399,684	56,893	88,726	225,190
1882	50,597,341	48,289,052	2,097,358	1,480,004	462,219	51,912	93,086	248,043
1883 ...	52,052,465	56,032,333	2,316,480	1,809,154	584,972	63,349	104,441	297,201
1884	43,418,015	50,492,826	1,769,849	1,975,771	504,477	67,983	75,348	318,477
1885 ...	41,406,777	47,151,201	1,935,581	2,121,269	349,215	60,366	108,162	337,785
1886	40,601,199	44,858,039	1,975,218	2,155,523	379,465	56,477	106,697	301,972
1887	44,962,233	45,107,066	2,073,470	3,235,449	409,269	58,143	119,889	295,061
1888	39,298,721	48,481,848	2,244,784	3,364,563	374,932	74,576	180,726	331,791
1889	42,317,389	50,537,440	2,228,683	3,692,570	407,268	72,085	126,124	414,080
1890	43,390,241	52,291,973	2,615,602	3,778,993	322,506	84,034	163,486	232,267
1891	42,047,526	53,685,657	2,312,143	3,804,090	488,807	70,537	241,809	389,791
1892	41,348,435	53,137,572	2,402,634	5,583,530	396,176	53,109	341,559	278,288
1893	43,148,413	58,221,976	2,832,117	3,825,763	343,506	52,481	170,564	373,858
1894 ..	38,717,267	53,034,100	2,536,964	5,841,542	389,293	47,106	402,443	344,706
1895	31,131,737	54,634,521	2,585,174	4,794,159	402,479	57,140	381,594	243,900
1896 ..	32,979,742	58,574,024	2,810,942	5,931,459	361,778	4[illegible],[illegible]96	230,917	299,852
1897	29,412,188	61,649,041	2,601,351	6,493 368	386,532	45,592	224,885	376,109
1898	32,500,917	78,705,590	3,975,351	5,584,014	488,787	47,319	421,258	374,047
1899	37,060,123	93,007,166	3,889,295	7,393,456	534,482	63,296	395,599	500,393
1900	44,789,730	109,844,378	4,368,502	8,383,498	560,701	72,785	144,573	579,582
1901	43,018,164	110,485,008	5,398,021	7,021,405	742,539	96,304	327,361	797,462
1902	49,213,762	120,807,050	6,672,194	10,823,169	694,970	129,379	726,742	875,615
1903 ..	58,896,901	137,605,195	6,580,029	12,282,637	823,944	129,192	541,785	12 70,540
1904	61,777,574	150,820,515	6,206,525	8,175,604	865,096	106,713	401,928	916,071
1905	60,342,709	162,738,571	7,059,139	6,695,414	729,259	98,288	620,637	954,653
906	69,194,588	175,862,071	7,667,987	6,987,314	928,791	128,604	553,755	1,179,892

No 5.—Value of Goods entered for Consumption, by Countries—*Concluded.*

Fiscal year ended June 30.	Belgium.	New-foundland	West Indies.	South America.	China and Japan.	Switzer-land.	Other Countries.	Total.
	$	$	$	$	$	$	$	$
1873	346,702	1,808,997	2,174,932	416,199	1,663,390	120,514	780,222	127,514,594
1874	293,659	1,088,468	2,307,733	473,530	1,224,506	139,674	396,839	127,404,169
1875	278,311	904,224	2,194,404	278,796	657,426	116,128	621,733	119,618,657
1876	361,055	774,586	1,616,113	287,553	948,239	56,168	746,567	94,733,218
1877 .. .	251,812	641,642	1,242,809	4,971	418,606	69,066	449,973	96,300,483
1878	255,694	672,665	1,033,849	15,447	383,676	61,178	344,154	91,199,577
1879	179,031	639,406	1,252,429	4,388	448,962	94,781	413,767	80,341,608
1880	149,086	581,961	2,945,154	283,481	893,911	94,225	557,689	71,782,349
1881	412,834	652,304	3,815,147	637,620	1,410,973	141,789	916,926	91,611,604
1882	503,210	493,509	4,023,384	1,373,617	1,529,042	268,093	1,139,057	112,648,927
1883	415,407	765,935	4,369,260	1,464,671	1,645,254	336,040	880,057	123,137,019
1884	459,150	780,670	3.606,917	1.478,988	1,909,562	242,380	1,080,231	108,180,644
1885	479,260	351,105	3,162,774	1,340,836	2,493,451	217,666	1,189,571	102,710,019
1886	510,907	384,321	3,144,472	1,100,995	2,432,585	203,085	1,391,739	99,602,694
1887	703,851	354,342	1,942,182	1,198,406	2,750,388	219,777	2,209,902	105,639,428
1888	488,743	421,599	3,268,663	876,603	2,128,707	193,838	1,117,006	102,847,100
1889	530,740	488,161	3,378,654	1,324,588	1,964,538	166,890	2,025,237	109,673,447
1890	721,332	469,711	3,089,048	1,003,962	2,100,065	316,523	1,995,841	112,765,584
1891	655,448	751,003	3,238,156	719,778	2,123,311	244,319	2,572,749	113,345,124
1892	517,032	753,249	4,092,287	877,821	3,016,857	192,365	3,988,029	116,978,943
1893	599,511	653,270	4,244,669	772,613	2,425,572	258,464	3,782,253	121,705,030
1894	550,237	814,562	3,677,411	872,392	2,524,919	274,825	3,066,216	113,093,983
1895	441,617	739,850	4,794,020	469,172	2,528,414	259,400	1,789,334	105,252,511
1896	920,758	551,412	1,896,426	567,027	2,671,418	332,120	2,413,009	110,587,480
1897	1,163,632	452.076	1,678,870	620,250	2,396,409	222,173	3,571,545	111,294,021
1898	1,230,110	464,324	1,080,266	1,425,653	2,317,971	349,678	1,732,721	130,698,006
1899	2,318,723	527,006	1.354,939	1,175,584	2,769,499	568,768	2,493,264	154,051,598
1900	3,223,918	660,678	1,331,776	992,887	2,381,144	529,176	2,940,988	180,804,316
1901	3,828,450	625,568	1,801,740	1,048,088	2,450,022	602,658	2,995,198	181,237,988
1902	1,711,599	1,117,400	2,173,835	1,659,074	1,984,876	765,010	3,436,920	202,791,595
1903	2,800,182	1,197,581	2,379,275	1,989,952	1,939,942	944.727	4,408,634	233,790,516
1904	3,129,513	1,076,667	4,813,815	3,157,004	2,565,976	1,389,000	6,062,331	251,464,332
1905 . ..	1,775,187	1,054,613	5,638.187	4,035,619	2,470,723	1,766,991	5,945,564	261,925,554
1906	2.610,072	1,758,425	6,591.083	5,869,075	2,217,517	2,012,405	6,799,228	290 360.807

No. 6.—Duty Collected.

Fiscal Y'r ended June 30.	Great Britain.	United States.	France.	Germany.	Spain.	Portugal.	Italy.	Holland.
	$ cts.	$ cts.	$ cts.	$ cts.	$ cts.	$ cts.	$ cts.	$ cts.
1873....	7,398,460 17	2,966,119 34	627,831 95	334,415 51	102,711 21	21,245 21	9,320 80	294,569 02
1874....	7,867,481 41	3,695,564 03	744,059 10	272,234 68	112,918 73	27,674 63	13,626 76	361,153 47
1875....	8,881,997 81	3,860,877 10	604,092 47	173,427 65	113,599 78	28,421 97	8,502 45	394,017 97
1876....	6,075,759 82	4,117,223 40	723,368 24	134,282 11	157,287 53	29,302 21	24,629 25	459,887 63
1877....	6,377,596 23	4,426,394 79	480,340 56	75,762 93	79,515 38	20,322 20	15,783 10	316,156 00
1878....	6,445,985 38	4,794,599 63	400,600 04	79,673 10	87,755 88	13,452 55	19,652 43	308,153 30
1879....	5,561,933 02	5,529,150 64	501,747 90	104,211 80	120,385 81	7,970 14	19,474 58	329,634 07
1880....	6,737,997 05	4,521,311 08	427,937 89	103,156 82	106,720 56	14,935 79	30,031 12	301,570 50
1881....	8,772,949 97	5,657,292 75	597,948 79	215,108 04	167,412 55	25,307 99	40,956 25	372,335 63
1882....	10,011,811 00	7,082,722 29	742,774 93	338,691 39	210,766 86	29,105 63	34,283 98	420,607 91
1883....	9,897,785 16	8,158,023 35	824,963 17	388,556 85	231,866 95	34,135 50	44,340 03	535,741 81
1884....	8,001,370 74	7,420,461 79	645,152 71	554,181 88	192,946 21	34,228 80	32,186 80	493,807 39
1885....	7,617,249 45	6,636,405 83	650,515 29	572,947 91	154,680 24	29,345 65	33,380 25	521,318 20
1886....	7,817,357 45	6,790,080 76	735,666 52	588,168 44	150,268 47	30,510 74	35,667 84	602,570 19
1887....	9,318,920 08	7,299,591 68	699,840 07	1,190,267 30	176,449 17	33,329 81	31,404 53	623,894 26
1888....	8,972,739 84	7,131,006 23	796,242 70	1,214,748 15	171,790 38	36,621 03	42,004 78	704,034 45
1889....	9,450,242 70	7,413,354 83	854,805 00	1,266,638 56	185,969 33	36,895 32	32,456 70	756,785 89
1890....	9,576,965 75	8,220,299 55	957,312 22	1,165,158 67	170,028 06	36,528 91	37,938 11	806,261 40
1891....	9,114,271 75	7,799,318 12	932,032 53	1,320,583 23	217,612 94	30,680 47	44,888 99	741,462 43
1892....	9,074,200 71	7,814,666 93	931,044 99	783,740 50	186,168 39	27,446 98	35,846 83	697,184 17
1893....	9,498,747 08	7,636,075 81	1,058,095 75	857,264 35	180,132 25	27,1[illegible]1 69	30,816 89	815,200 70
1894....	8,245,845 87	6,960,950 68	1,019,568 12	978,224 53	207,724 63	22,894 36	49,073 63	879,107 85
1895....	7,006,676 58	6,897,395 04	985,945 87	892,547 04	184,788 45	24,361 92	46,697 12	755,251 48
1896....	7,358,514 15	7,767,992 63	1,020,804 74	1,329,186 36	162,118 81	22,269 68	39,386 07	792,609 63
1897....	6,205,366 80	8,147,075 10	969,539 64	1,489,755 60	150,587 43	23,191 61	33,474 05	920,096 46
1898....	6,649,428 60	9,941,624 48	1,183,890 30	1,364,159 04	176,764 64	20,606 24	46,466 82	908,046 37
1899....	7,328,191 92	11,713,858 94	1,300,876 33	1,903,223 16	181,346 14	25,559 36	52,842 44	1,061,622 69
1900....	8,074,541 07	13,491,872 86	1,428,019 46	2,189,798 17	183,147 69	28,548 59	26,842 73	1,171,550 06
1901....	7,845,406 49	13,311,749 58	1,794,455 55	1,811,974 55	191,527 27	37,138 80	45,171 84	1,350,098 08
1902....	8,424,693 04	15,155,136 39	2,163,016 40	2,741,263 29	205,803 43	42,700 86	88,174 27	1,306,967 57
1903....	9,841,627 33	17,069,881 19	2,098,633 61	3,255,121 88	212,104 39	45,912 40	87,457 75	1,527,113 35
1904....	10,838,017 31	19,554,585 54	2,113,667 94	2,172,571 04	228,532 66	41,226 25	88,831 12	1,726,681 98
1905....	11,171,010 04	20,580,301 56	2,224,967 73	1,826,789 33	216,933 42	39,295 27	123,388 07	1,570,378 88
1906....	12,944,249 35	22,187,102 94	2,520,034 97	1,852,538 47	289,363 62	44,716 82	118,725 17	1,620,711 72

No. 6.—Duty Collected—*Concluded.*

Fiscal Year ended June 30.	Belgium.	Newfoundland.	West Indies.	South America.	China and Japan.	Switzerland.	Other Countries.	Additional duties, post entries, overcollections, &c.	Total.
	$ cts.	$ cts.	$ cts.	$ cts.	$ cts.	$ cts.	$ cts.	$ cts.	$ cts.
1873	94,504 87	97,147 31	831,930 86	182,660 79	157 95	15,994 95	40,660 23	....	13,017,730 17
1874	51,171 82	54,929 33	935,653 11	194,325 88	26,185 10	21,950 85	42,953 77	....	14,421,882 67
1875	42,489 19	12,584 62	926,463 33	124,963 29	83,469 42	20,917 93	85,557 14	....	15,361,382 12
1876	61,407 14	4,890 45	603,819 86	120,843 58	132,042 28	10,274 57	178,096 41	....	12,833,114 48
1877	50,106 26	9,735 83	435,718 43	1,834 11	68,261 35	12,387 96	178,535 96	....	12,548,451 09
1878	45,144 82	4,921 23	341,240 28	6,874 10	113,447 24	9,855 02	124,338 17	....	12,795,693 17
1879	45,107 35	3,230 76	454,872 58	2,591 84	127,283 34	16,597 54	115,349 29	....	12,939,540 66
1880	41,886 44	3,168 48	1,305,495 00	161,936 81	207,920 61	18,764 19	156,016 88	....	14,138,849 22
1881	90,250 84	3,251 22	1,584,622 00	280,009 74	348,466 71	33,740 02	311,133 47	....	18,500,785 97
1882	119,492 16	1,781 73	1,615,945 44	504,255 74	178,499 40	65,780 72	352,318 25	....	21,708,837 43
1883	106,234 50	7,365 17	1,770,682 99	692,562 12	157,516 29	83,492 95	239,042 13	....	23,172,308 97
1884	103,953 96	4,158 34	1,397,926 55	688,702 68	273,708 37	56,966 92	265,210 23	....	20,164,963 37
1885	121,660 61	2,268 61	1,327,363 99	655,708 66	450,153 25	51,863 04	308,698 01	....	19,133,558 99
1886	132,116 62	2,467 99	1,384,327 91	503,735 53	148,098 67	49,052 66	478,033 91	....	19,448,123 70
1887	166,445 16	1,624 70	968,496 12	848,562 83	222,799 93	59,393 20	828,686 99	....	22,469,705 83
1888	117,228 81	3,211 68	1,831,368 64	641,854 29	162,844 61	43,778 82	340,166 62	....	22,209,641 53
1889	122,116 44	1,087 36	1,727,816 27	849,431 97	185,782 89	38,653 78	845,532 61	7,952 63	23,784,523 23
1890	150,349 40	3,386 14	1,223,589 61	559,312 13	216,956 50	79,331 47	804,400 21	7,089 94	24,014,908 07
1891	126,180 23	3,452 92	1,337,754 14	260,102 71	265,198 43	63,161 46	1,215,178 05	9,190 73	23,481,069 13
1892	104,003 88	4,191 49	272,167 34	75,439 20	273,256 10	49,388 45	201,112 48	20,723 09	20,550,581 53
1893	112,081 99	1,494 56	314,148 32	78,592 25	313,798 23	70,418 15	160,133 95	7,538 96	21,161,710 93
1894	119,020 54	1,623 12	292,464 66	73,489 61	273,712 97	73,695 14	172,318 29	10,108 32	19,379,822 32
1895	93,303 46	1,053 95	380,955 12	68,786 81	230,890 41	72,742 85	231,349 72	14,523 65	17,887,269 47
1896	192,457 64	1,197 81	478,829 02	106,494 83	265,572 02	93,87. 62	521,413 34	64,312 97	20,219,037 32
1897	250,770 38	1,274 89	454,418 06	109,914 69	267,575 35	64,153 55	757,363 19	47,439 87	19,891,996 77
1898	287,411 60	1,690 86	304,971 01	209,761 63	291,747 74	91,525 82	328,978 26	*350,715 08	22,157,788 49
1899	663,898 07	1,669 28	374,161 69	97,167 56	349,381 86	156,108 44	414,930 52	109,390 35	25,734,228 75
1900	916,374 13	2,740 46	363,563 81	120,148 16	279,351 97	143,983 86	414,866 20	53,760 91	28,889,110 13
1901	1,081,162 82	1,190 88	471,923 66	205,344 97	341,473 58	159,147 86	416,207 47	43,006 49	29,106,979 89
1902	387,008 06	7,023 17	550,252 39	199,921 52	370,966 45	199,638 08	509,973 06	72,994 33	32,425,532 31
1903	602,178 47	1,914 12	684,985 96	303,880 29	355,971 92	255250 99	680,547 56	87,773 38	37.110,354 59
1904	444.514 69	2,780 11	1,202,659 24	731,277 80	444-747 26	376,616 39	873,447 83	114,191 98	40,954,349 14
1905	321,094 73	2,435 99	1,184,429 72	591,697 60	489,814 72	469,943 37	982,112 49	229,747 00	42,024,339 92
1906	511,584 66	1,092 68	1,531,148 25	712,435 40	486,583 62	546,901 63	1,070,251 05	233,660 83	46,671,101 18

* Includes $309,999.04 collected at Fort-Cudahy and Dawson, for which no statistical returns have been received.

No. 7.—Percentage of Duty on Total Value of Goods imported and entered for Consumption, Dutiable and Free; and percentage of expenses of collection of Customs Revenue in the Dominion of Canada, during each year from 1868 to 1906, inclusive.

Year.	Percentage of Duty on Total Value of Goods Imported, Dutiable and Free.	Percentage of Duty on Total Value of Goods entered for Consumption, Dutiable and Free.	Percentage Expense of Collection of Customs Revenue.
	p. c.	p. c.	p. c.
1868	12·00	12·25	05·99
1869	11·78	12·31	07·09
1870	12·65	13·28	05·41
1871	12·32	13·62	04·21
1872	11·70	12·11	04·04
1873	10·17	10·20	04·35
1874	11·25	11·32	04·55
1875	12·48	12·83	04·44
1876	13·76	13·44	05·61
1877	12·63	13·03	05·75
1878	13·74	14·03	05·58
1879	15·78	16·10	05·56
1880	16·34	19·70	05·04
1881	17·56	20·19	03·87
1882	18·18	19·27	03·33
1883	17·52	18·82	03·26
1884	17·32	18·64	03·96
1885	17·55	18·61	04·14
1886	18·60	19·50	04·10
1887	19·87	21·24	03·64
1888	20·03	21·57	03·81
1889	20·60	21·65	03·62
1890	19·63	21·21	03·63
1891	19·52	20·06	03·83
1892	16·13	17·56	04·39
1893	16·39	17·38	04·26
1894	15·69	17·13	04·75
1895	16 14	16·99	05·13
1896	17·13	18·28	04·43
1897	16.68	17.87	04·75
1898	15·79	16·95	04·37
1899	15·81	16·70	04·02
1900	15·23	15·98	03·71
1901	15·28	16·06	03·86
1902	15·28	15·99	03·62
1903	15·38	15·87	03·31
1904	15·80	16·28	03·31
1905	15·75	16·04	03·49
1906	15·52	15·73	03·31

No. 8.—COMPARATIVE STATEMENT of the Values of the Imports and Exports into and percentage excess of Imports over Exports,

Fiscal Year.	Importations.				Exports.			
	Merchandise.		Coin and Bullion.	Totals.	Merchandise.		Coin and Buillion.	Totals.
	Dutiable.	Free.			Home Produce.	Foreign produce.		
	$	$	$	$	$	$	$	$
1868	45,250,395	23,314,102	4,895,147	73,459,644	48,504,899	4,196,821	4,866,168	57,567,888
1869	44,081,563	22,086,373	4,247.229	70,415,165	52,400,772	3,855,801	4,218,208	60,474,781
1870	48,665,547	21,813,263	4,335,529	74,814,339	59,043,590	6,527,622	8,002,278	73,573,490
1871	70,295,223	23,064,654	2,733,094	96,092,971	57,630,024	9,853,244	6,690,350	74,173,618
1872	72,157,423	36,519,355	2,753,749	111,430,527	65,831,083	12,798,182	4,010,398	82,639,663
1873	74,217,954	50,787,862	3,005,465	128,011,281	76,538,025	9,405,910	3,845,987	89,789,922
1874	77,070,460	46,919,840	4,223,282	128,213,582	76,741,997	10,614,096	1,995,835	89,351,928
1875	81,504,477	39,355,717	2,210,089	123,070,283	69,709,823	7,137,319	1,039,837	77,886,979
1876	58,794,777	32,195,458	2,220,111	93,210,346	72,491,437	7,234,961	1,240,037	80,966,435
1877	63,986,376	33,167,497	2,174,089	99,327,962	68,030,546	7,111,108	733,739	75,875,393
1878	61,700,190	30,577,871	803,726	93,081,787	67,989,800	11,164,878	168,989	79,323,667
1879	57,052,042	23,273,296	1,639,089	81,964,427	62,431,025	8,355,644	704,586	71,491,255
1880	68,895,483	15,712,457	1,881,807	86,489,747	72,899,697	13,240,006	1,771,755	87,911,458
1881	85,516,908	18.690,657	1,123,275	105,330,840	83,944,701	13,375,117	971'005	98,290,823
1882	93,339,930	24,575,827	1,503,743	119,419,500	94,137,657	7,628,453	371,093	102,137,203
1883	100,827,816	30.150,683	1,275,523	132,254,022	87,702,431	9,751,773	631,600	98,085,804
1884	88,349,492	25,839,885	2,207,666	116,397,043	79,833,098	9,389,106	2,184,292	91,406,496
1885	79,614,108	26,373,134	2,951,244	108,941,486	79,131,735	8,079,646	2,026,980	89,238,361
1886	75,536,758	25,277,246	3,610,557	104,424,561	77,756,704	7,438,079	56,531	85,251,314
1887	85,479,400	26,880,618	532,218	112,892,236	80,960,909	8,549,333	5,569	89,515,811
1888	77,784,037	30,935,121	2,175,472	110,894,630	81,382,072	8,803,394	17,534	90,203,000
1889	80,059,966	34,589,714	575,251	115,224,931	80,272,456	6,938,455	1,978,256	89,189,167
1890	86,258,633	34,516,597	1,083,011	121,858,241	85,257,586	9,051,781	2,439,782	96,749,149
1891	81,286,372	36,870,096	1,811,170	119,967,638	88,671,738	8,798,631	946,927	98,417,296
1892	81,190,844	44,396,694	1,818,530	127,406,068	99,032,466	13,121,791	1,809,118	113,963,375
1893	77,378,091	45,161,977	6,534,200	129,074,268	105,488,798	8,941,856	4,133,698	118,564,352
1894	73,341,506	46,110,362	4,023,072	123,474,940	103,851,764	11,833,805	1,839,380	117,524,949
1895	64,064,587	42,140,475	4,576,620	110,781,682	102,828,441	6,485,043	4,325,319	113,638,803
1896	74,259,940	38,525.249	5,226,319	118,011,508	109,707,805	6,606,738	4,699,309	121,013,852
1897	74,108,590	40,433,825	4,676,194	119,218,609	123,632,540	10,825,163	3,492,550	137,950,253
1898	84,141,104	51,791,105	4,390,844	140,323,053	144,548,662	14,980,883	4,623,138	164,152,683
1899	98,349,633	59,709,541	4,705,134	162,764,308	137,360,792	17,520,088	4,016,025	158,896,905
1900	112,943,896	68,381,179	8,297,438	189,622,513	168,972 301	14,265,254	8,657,168	191,894,723
1901	115,574,658	71,303,573	3,537.294	190,415,525	177,431,386	17,077,757	1,978,489	196,487,632
1902	127,955,254	78,003,499	6,311,405	212,270,158	196,019,763	13,951,101	1,669,422	211,640,286
1903	143,839,632	88,398,532	8,976,797	241,214,961	214,401,674	10,828,087	619,963	225,849,724
1904	156,108,453	95,229,037	7,874,313	259,211,803	198,414,439	12,641,239	2,465,557	213,521,235
1905	157,164,975	99,361,007	10,308,435	266,834,417	190,854,946	10,617,115	1,844,811	203,316,872
1906	176.790,332	110,417,080	7,078,603	294,286,015	235,483,956	11,173,846	9,928,828	256,586,630

from the Dominion of Canada in each Fiscal Year from 1868 to 1906; showing also or of Exports over Imports in each year.

Excess Value of Merchandise Imported over.		Excess of total Exports over total Imports, including Coin and Bullion.	Percentage Excess of total Imp'rts over total Exports, including Coin and Bullion.	Percentage Excess of total Exp'rts over total Imports, including Coin and Bullion.	Percentage, Increase or Decrease.			
					Gross Imports compared with preceding year.		Gross Exports compared with preceding year.	
Canadian Merchandise Exported.	Canadian and Foreign Merchandise Exported.				Increase.	Decrease.	Increase	D'crease
$	$	$	p. c.	p. c.	p. c.	p. c.	p. c.	p. c.
20,059,598	15,862,777		27·6					
13,767,164	9,911,363		16·4			04·1	05·05	
11,435,220	4,907,598		01·7		06·2		21·6	
35,729,853	25,876,609		29·5		28·4		0·8	
42,845,695	30,047,513		34·8		15·0		11·4	
48,467,791	39,061,881		32·5		14·9		08·6	
47,248,303	36,634,207		43·5		00·16			00·5
51,150,371	44,013,052		58·0			0·4		12·8
18,498,798	11,263,837		15·1			24·2	03·9	
29,123,327	22,012,219		30·9		06·5			06·3
24,288,261	13,123,383		17·3			06·3	04·5	
17,894,313	9,438,669		14·6			11·9		09·6
11,708,243		1,421,711		01·6	05·5		22·9	
20,262,864	6,887,747		07·1		21·8		11·8	
23,778,100	16,149,647		14·5		13·3		03·9	
43,276,068	33,524,295		28·8		10·7			03·9
34,356,279	24,967,173		21·4			11·9		06·8
26,855,507	18,775,861		18·0			06·4		02·3
23,057,300	15,619,221		18·3			04·1		04·3
31,399,109	22,849,776		20·7		08·1		05·0	
27,337,086	18,533,692		18·6			01·8	00·7	
34,377,224	27,438,769		22·6		03·9			01·1
35,517,644	26,465,863		20·6		05·4		07·8	
29,484,730	20,686,099		17·9			01·5	01·7	
26,555,072	13,432,281		10·5		06·2		16·0	
17,051,270	8,109,414		08·1		01·3		4·0	
15,600,104	3,766,299		04·8			04·3		00·8
3,376,621		2,857,121		02·21		09·95		03·3
3,077,384		3,002,344		02·54	06·14		6·49	
		18,731,644		15·71	01·02		14·00	
		23,829,630		16·98	17·70		18 99	
20,698,382	3,178,294		02·4		16·00			03·2
12,352,774		2,272,210		01·2	14·16		20·77	
9,446,845		6,072,107		03·2	00·42		02·39	
9,938,990			00·3		11·47		07·71	
17,836,490	7,008,403		06·4		13·63		06·29	
52,923,051	40,281,812		21·4		7·46			05·4
65,671,036	55,053,921		31·2		02·94			4·77
51,723,456	40,549,610		14·69		10·29		26·2	

No. 9.—COMPARATIVE STATEMENT showing the Tonnage of all vessels entered inwards and outwards in the Dominion of Canada, during each Fiscal Year ended June 30, from 1868 to 1906, inclusive.

SHIPPING.

Fiscal Year ended June 30.	Tonnage of Vessels built.	Tonnage of Vessels registered.	Tonnage of Vessels entered Inwards and Outwards (Sea-going and Inland Navigation) exclusive of Coasting.	Tonnage of Vessels employed in the Coasting Trade entered Inwards and Outwards.	Tonnage and value of Vessels sold to other Countries.	
					Tonnage.	Value.
	Tons.	Tons.	Tons.	Tons.	Tons.	$
1868	87,230	113,692	12,982,825	....	....	....
1869	96,439	125,408	10,461,044	....	....	....
1870	93,166	1252	11,415,870	....	....	....
1871	6,001	121,724	13,126,028	....	....	....
1872	4,065	127,371	12,808,160	....	....	....
1873	0,870	2,326	11,748,997	....	....	....
1874	174,404	3,616	11,399,857	....	....	....
1875	188,098	4,002	9,537,155	....	....	....
1876	165,041	144,422	9,911,199	10,300,939	64,134	9,870
1877	7,297	6,260	11,091,244	8,862	46,329	6,44
1878	106,976	100,089	12,054,890	11,047,661	35,039	8,145
1879	3,051	94,882	11,646,812	12,066,683	19,318	529,824
1880	68,756	64,982	13,577,845	14,053,013	6,208	464,327
1881	79,364	0,210	13,802,432	15,116,766	1,608	348,018
1882	68.240	06	13,379,882	14,791,064	161	402,311
1883	73.576	78,229	13,770,735	15,683,566	23,896	6,038

1884	70,287	80,822	14,359,026	15,473,707	1,768	416,756
1885	57,486	65,962	14,084,712	15,944,422	13,177	246,277
1886	37,531	4,672	13,969,232	16,368,274	14,343	25,363
1887	6,298	67,662	14,090,998	17,513,677	1,363	143,772
1888	22,698	3,298	1,308	18,789,279	14,479	9,969
1889	23,835	31,998	16,054,221	19,834,577	1,673	266,817
1890	39,434	5,353	18,446,100	22,797,115	22,844	442,781
1891	55,477	52,506	18,803,648	24,694,580	1,543	280,474
1892	44,321	61,457	18,692,455	24,783,844	36,399	506,747
1893	38,521	45,796	18,539,534	24,579,123	3,317	363,916
1894	23,497	9,878	20,353,081	26,560,968	21,960	243,429
1895	18,728	26,125	19,100,963	25,473,434	16,567	172,563
1896	0,153	14,144	21,870,473	27,431,753	12,203	99,392
1897	12,058	22,959	23,373,933	27,267,975	9,158	164
1898	22,426	27,716	24,746,116	29,653,950	17,210	191,069
1899	22,085	28,257	25,420,110	30,212,496	7,562	126,466
1900	28,544	40,443	26,914,095	33,631,730	13,354	5,618
1901	20,156	35,156	26,029,808	34,444,796	4,490	66,468
1902	28,288	4,336	30,025,404	40,700,907	11,360	25,865
1903	30,856	41,405	33,655,043	44,990,358	1,172	0,602
1904	28,397	33,192	31,202,205	45,505,122	7,208	87,115
1905	21,865	27,583	32,277,820	44,377,261	3,696	100,363
1906	18,724	37,639	34,732,172	46,324,062	9,487	71,825

No. 10.—COMPARATIVE STATEMENT (by Provinces) of the Values of Exports, of Total at each Port in the Dominion of Canada during the Fiscal

PROVINCE OF

Number.	PORTS.	Fiscal Year ended June 30, 1904.				Fiscal
		Exports.	Imports.	Entered for Consumption.	Duty.	Exports.
		$	$	$	$ cts.	$
1	Amherstburg	97,291	229,063	213,404	30,333 97	133,394
2	Belleville	2,788	503,106	501,454	89,017 98	2,185
3	Berlin	....	1,798,860	1,797,072	190,256 67	....
4	Bowmanville	....	212,340	212,340	11,221 66	....
5	Brantford	....	2,108,119	2,105,212	262,237 11	....
6	Bridgeburg	4,234,218	2,734,617	2,506,729	519,857 84	4,481,786
7	Brockville	43,231	1,247,896	1,096,666	156,929 91	44,081
8	Chatham	150,919	1,110,778	1,108,532	163,006 25	12,568
9	Cobourg	2,254	403,920	404,080	26,248 91	8,604
10	Collingwood	12,520	298,384	299,705	32,200 90	13,221
11	Cornwall	148,138	715,170	714,855	29,818 14	410,644
12	Deseronto	235,858	201,278	201,278	22,172 36	237,636
13	Fort William	2,519,555	2,048,161	2,013,082	384,911 19	2,823,895
14	Galt	....	1,025,032	1,025,032	89,150 33	....
15	Gananoque	22,049	447,086	447,086	33,346 89	6,652
16	Goderich	....	531,056	531,459	61,839 49	....
17	Guelph	....	1,531,141	1,530,742	139,874 89	....
18	Hamilton	586	9,328,014	9,210,865	1,234,993 48	1,159
19	Ingersoll	....	225,254	225,254	32,847 19	....
20	Kenora	1,566	319,551	323,205	33,164 67	4,155
21	Kingston	205 534	1,609.621	1,610,673	177,610 38	180,020
22	Lindsay	....	305,053	305,053	28,490 11	....
23	London	....	5,200,343	5,206,295	831,864 80	....
24	Midland	261,339	598,892	600,012	37,532 65	419,879
25	Morrisburg	4,894	65,627	65,627	5,358 43	8,411
26	Napanee	....	148,230	148,241	14,713 60	....
27	Niagara Falls	18,071,625	1,460,169	1,462,977	253,174 68	16,781,777
28	Oshawa	....	348,712	348,712	37,458 17	....
29	Ottawa	64,235	4,688,297	4,689,690	775,993 24	75,940
30	Owen Sound	9,193	517,456	516,739	61,008 93	842
31	Paris	....	607,745	607,745	41,172 85	....
32	Parry Sound	1,388,097	180,635	180,635	34,469 98	1,341,042
33	Peterboro'	....	1,529,371	1,531,277	222,881 15	....
34	Picton	2,439	156,828	156,871	22,400 68	1,326
35	Port Arthur	972,064	2,291,045	2,311,896	197,663 65	1,355,957
36	Port Hope	16,420	184,713	184,713	18,322 01	4,508
37	Prescott	4,233,014	1,243,136	1,216,825	87,396 31	8,002,467
38	St. Catherines	11,870	1,753,951	1,747,309	208,019 32	6,101
39	St. Thomas	19,681	1,373,240	1,397,880	285,653 98	38,089
40	Sarnia	2,002,004	1,493,059	1,289,413	188,170 89	2,379,661
41	Sault St. Marie	3,855,121	1,110,028	1,020,229	150,236 61	4,521,357
42	Simcoe	30	254,117	254,556	35,077 96	84
43	Stratford	12,968	1,348,839	1,346,499	161,733 71	....
44	Toronto	3,150	47,671,288	47,259,131	8,177,506 72	10,948
45	Trenton	45,066	131,440	131,202	19,888 68	22,132
46	Wallaceburg	20,203	122,195	122,195	10,360 09	50,537
47	Whitby	3,100	149,069	149,069	12,357 59	3,127
48	Windsor	3,268,585	3,797,715	3,780,899	593,404 71	3,233,935
49	Woodstock	....	812,954	812,954	95,493 97	....
	Total	41,941,605	108,172,594	106,923,369	16,328,785 68	46,618,115

Imports, of Imports entered for Consumption and of the Amount of Duty collected Years ended, respectively on June 30, 1904, 1905, 1906.

ONTARIO.

Year ended June 30, 1905.			Fiscal Year ended June 30, 1906.				Number.
Imports.	Entered for Con-sumption.	Duty.	Exports.	Imports.	Entered for Con-sumption.	Duty.	
$	$	$ cts.	$	$	$	$ cts.	
433,415	332,300	44,876 54	176,231	336,143	244,695	31,890 09	1
543,502	537,006	89,028 14	3,926	686,059	691,460	115,549 55	2
1,871,873	1,868,663	182,626 61	....	2,168,894	2,169,617	193,506 07	3
170,698	170,698	9,787 03	....	222,536	222,536	13,374 30	4
1,787,565	1,769,931	225,662 86	....	2,236,046	2,232,813	290,453 62	5
2,047,155	1,695,050	358,970 97	4,948,202	1,956,866	2,089,774	479,299 58	6
897,786	906,563	114,954 24	51,754	866,375	754,265	93,955 42	7
1,129,901	1,072,725	179,442 70	17,939	1,147,021	1,092,863	194,047 33	8
353,405	353,405	26,011 86	3,772	282,845	283,410	30,505 44	9
412,987	412,118	39,257 30	106,048	1,258,404	811,899	70,470 81	10
850,304	849,804	37,338 26	359,869	976,557	975,957	28,889 91	11
139,988	139,988	19,160 11	196,100	153,512	153,645	22,077 87	12
2,879,274	2,482,150	412,266 10	11,371,361	2,103,727	2,134,278	406,548 16	13
1,230.640	1,230,640	102,204 13	....	1,208,608	1,208,508	109,581 69	14
371,517	371,517	25,996 52	7,172	383,966	383,966	34,401 40	15
547,352	546,612	61,810 39	1,859	551,299	551,126	64,433 77	16
1,647,190	1,638,374	137,601 72	....	1,732,128	1,731,354	153,170 74	17
9,589,241	9,391,454	1,270,311 06	25	11,070,806	10,974,455	1,564,034 04	18
276,006	227,863	32,609 38	....	333,513	239,579	35,840 09	19
255,393	258,311	36,238 03	4,615	361,028	363,890	55,308 01	20
1,488,368	1,489,565	174,123 28	219,522	1,535,744	1,540,450	177,355 91	21
270,010	270,010	27,052 39	....	292,657	293,423	25,465 50	22
5,191,223	5,118,607	806,889 34	....	5,435,135	5,369,300	855,493 51	23
532,626	520,350	17,057 89	468,502	613,544	621,486	27,444 50	24
46,331	46,331	3,051 25	14,492	46,763	46,840	2,904 12	25
162,836	162,836	9,954 79	....	145,073	145,073	14.225 74	26
2,576,077	2,577,405	536,345 12	16,433,198	2,004,874	1,973,620	379,007 23	27
365,046	365,046	40,684 66	....	413,212	413,212	50,325 69	28
4,762,116	4,624,416	747,507 42	91,976	5,547,048	5,414,984	954,897 26	29
400,114	387,097	49,404 72	28,891	480,281	476,100	58,221 57	30
646,124	645,184	39,535 85	....	661,804	661,904	48,992 85	31
180,144	180,144	44,019 29	1,335,378	196.335	196,335	43,415 91	32
2,352,739	2,171,524	335,597 29	....	3,101,674	2,451,316	369,638 79	33
145,784	144,833	18,104 31	3,487	164,174	162,998	27,413 05	34
2,660,807	2,697,575	141,459 75	4,157,342	1,640,700	1,535,712	195,372 12	35
193,840	193,840	16,116 69	242	220,673	221,146	16,147 66	36
2,559,743	2,503,081	97,251 80	7,994,962	1,257,346	1,237,150	102,294 87	37
1,927,791	1,822,378	201,163 18	4,329	2,027,133	2,019,901	241,770 28	38
1,138,771	1,124,083	184,068 25	48,622	1,107,464	1,139,175	231,440 63	39
2,879,679	3,080,230	426,122 02	3,478,699	2,498,691	2,359,189	290,735 06	40
2,544,254	2,436,051	321,140 58	4,457,478	3,150,330	3,147,235	309,171 03	41
312,835	312,835	28,988 57	....	379,387	380,180	41,249 98	42
1,316,087	1,316,338	160,735 55	5,087	1,416,230	1.412,860	149,105 79	43
50,838,296	50,271,583	9,586,707 17	17,959	58,116,363	57,459,516	9,731,165 16	44
125,110	124,038	19,173 09	1,593	116,135	116,713	24,775 32	45
184,302	184,302	18,567 31	37,223	133,237	133,237	13,569 89	46
116,728	116,728	7,095 24	1,499	110,957	110,957	9,070 99	47
4,521,526	4,505,236	881,283 13	3,676,892	5,174,716	5,084,161	721,070 71	48
651,881	651,656	75,692 73	....	630,254	630,254	67,563 29	49
118,526,380	116,398,474	18,421,046 61	59,725,246	128,654,267	126,064,517	19,166,642 30	

No. 10.—Comparative Statement of the Value of

PROVINCE OF

Number.	Ports.	Fiscal Year ended June 30, 1904.				Fiscal
		Exports.	Imports.	Entered for Consumption.	Duty.	Exports.
		$	$	$	$ cts.	$
1	Abercorn	2,306,541	62,943	62,943	3,791 70	2,036,876
2	Coaticook	10,509,868	166,615	166,615	10,317 49	9,133,026
3	Cookshire	426,850	70,680	70,756	10,540 83	385,958
4	Gaspé	214,133	9,643	9,747	2,976 15	302,946
5	Hemmingford	2,959,229	224,911	224,911	9,138 46	3,304,502
6	Mansonville	47,838	7,731	7,731	548 79	19,329
7	Montreal	67,844,729	80,561,275	74,517,129	12,437,927 95	59,411,278
8	Paspebiac	280,444	38,244	45,281	5,443 35	268,784
9	Percé	24,104	10,650	10,650	1,153 38	32,886
10	Quebec	5,095,034	8,117,739	8,080,569	1,297,220 83	3,717,471
11	Rimouski	243,298	47,534	48,403	9,395 73	270,526
12	St. Armand	5,335,095	41,124	39,669	2,331 42	4,367,312
13	St. Hyacinthe	....	392,998	394,524	37,814 14	....
14	St. Johns	4,774,061	1,961,077	1,961,772	96,318 91	6,294,197
15	Sherbrooke	....	1,162,974	1,162,490	192,767 09	....
16	Sorel	41,705	183,740	183,219	27,519 51	....
17	Stanstead	2,234,173	434,481	431,906	19,822 90	2,387,200
18	Three Rivers	479,095	452,152	454,446	105,219 14	504,758
19	Valleyfield	....	1,100,338	1,100,491	38,423 77	....
	Grand total	102,816,197	95,046,849	88,973,252	14,308,671 54	92,437,049

Exports and Imports at each Port, &c.—*Continued.*

QUEBEC.

Year ended June 30, 1905.			Fiscal Year ended June 30, 1906.				Number.
Imports.	Entered for Consumption.	Duty.	Exports.	Imports.	Entered for Consumption.	Duty.	
$	$	$ cts.	$	$	$	$ cts.	
80,499	80,499	3,502 07	3,006,441	78,654	78,654	3,898 97	1
152,775	152,825	11,261 37	11,121,095	193,644	193,644	11,744 67	2
81,501	81,944	8,531 62	479,925	99,608	100,678	11,052 22	3
11,108	11,108	2,317 24	314,238	11,829	11,871	3,740 22	4
427,153	427,153	6,547 05	3,349,684	575,911	575,911	16,748 02	5
11,655	11,655	675 34	17,943	9,862	9,862	811 55	6
78,451,031	76,332,640	11,591,656 70	81,589,542	82,256,937	80,821,740	13,275,623 17	7
54,848	54,753	8,148 94	325,680	57,652	56,528	8,740 56	8
8,361	8,361	784 39	58,666	7,318	7,338	740 68	9
8,824,728	8,860,273	1,526,131 93	4,163,567	9,157,346	9,136,774	1,502,320 73	10
48,534	46,513	16,294 35	186,198	33,215	35,225	17,997 65	11
54,553	53,654	3,850 96	4,632,212	56,241	56,241	4,390 96	12
401,119	401,118	38,106 82	....	322,057	324,571	42,370 94	13
2,489,078	2,486,999	146,361 27	8,569,252	2,120,922	2,121,302	177,895 90	14
1,222,014	1,223,585	176,666 42	....	1,254,320	1,228,120	182,373 52	15
160,453	160,979	21,054 39	....	228,751	229,928	20,020 42	16
550,814	549,324	18,674 92	3,239,476	916,882	916,882	31,368 05	17
328,148	328,544	81,903 40	219,820	957,900	956,606	126,609 24	18
671,389	670,188	29,235 27	....	1,533,182	1,530,337	35,621 35	19
94,029,761	91,942,115	13,691,704 45	121,273,739	99,872,231	97,392,212	15,474,068 82	

No. 10.—Comparative Statement of the Value

PROVINCE OF

Number.	Ports.	Fiscal Year ended June 30, 1903.				
		Exports.	Imports.	Entered for Consumption.	Duty.	Exports.
		$	$	$	$	$
1	Amherst	349,103	417,424	417,576	72,698 99	328,681
2	Annapolis	223,659	79,113	79,303	6,512 37	273,999
3	Antigonish	12,938	29,521	29,521	7,780 57	15,749
4	Arichat	46,488	14,492	15,317	1,024 03	1,170
5	Baddeck	35,268	6,395	6,425	1,082 27	18,627
6	Barrington	4,895	3,634	3,635	569 22	3,062
7	Canso	133,401	18,819	18,899	1,787 27	174,778
8	Digby	125,722	36,594	36,609	3,461 80	115,426
9	Glace Bay	....	....	....	....	....
10	Halifax	9,203,245	8,370,346	8,466,060	1,668,990 82	8,444,149
11	Kentville	54,659	191,310	191,336	20,386 51	62,681
12	Liverpool	133,076	28,422	28,826	2,497 05	165,340
13	Lockeport	54,467	3,858	4,641	489 84	39,089
14	Lunenburg	557,234	336,158	339,638	19,845 60	543,775
15	Middleton	....	23,445	23,445	4,753 71	....
16	New Glasgow	....	379,071	379,410	53,793 27	....
17	North Sydney	559,471	458,278	460,694	77,356 62	570,736
18	Parrsboro'	688,164	35,704	35,990	1,674 42	700,901
19	Pictou	171,827	212,816	212,847	12,334 77	12,456
20	Port Hawkesbury	244,800	13,631	13,745	1,338 82	170,986
21	Port Hood	19,246	27,427	27,444	5,863 82	61,530
22	Shelburne	309,104	11,539	11,539	1,227 67	54,516
23	Sydney	2,346,963	1,237,479	1,222,056	174,672 17	1,403,478
24	Truro	....	348,524	355,313	95,864 12	....
25	Weymouth	176,338	24,354	24,802	2,358 23	217,016
26	Windsor	283,091	173,478	173,692	8,592 25	415,733
27	Yarmouth	1,363,680	685,817	690,091	59,524 07	1,495,894
	Total	17,096,839	13,167,649	13,268,854	2,306,480 28	15,289,772

PROVINCE OF

Number.	Ports.	Exports.	Imports.	Entered for Consumption.	Duty.	Exports.
1	Bathurst	....	32,674	32,701	5,098 17	133,145
2	Campbellton	202,875	77,868	77,603	13,686 37	361,890
3	Chatham	960,333	116,431	116,019	10,320 09	658,377
4	Dalhousie	256,997	13,900	15,434	5,295 13	253,357
5	Fredericton	27,441	400,209	400,444	37,494 53	47,592
6	McAdam Junction	1,496,866	148,787	148,787	5,532 29	1,228,927
7	Moncton	481,240	508,805	509,257	53,754 48	392,373
8	Newcastle	569,407	27,435	27,698	8,337 91	562,116
9	Sackville	114,489	59,525	59,539	7,518 82	106,006
10	Saint John	13,318,058	6,663,679	6,495,639	1,174,220 73	13,548,041
11	Saint Stephen	364,695	724,003	745,964	46,602 30	556,101
12	Woodstock	139,453	183,215	185,426	23,752 34	82,778
	Total	17,931,854	8,956,531	8,814,511	1,391,613 16	17,930,703

of Exports and Imports at each Port, &c.—*Continued.*

NOVA SCOTIA.

Fiscal Year ended June 30, 1904.			Fiscal Year ended June 30, 1905.				Number.
Imports.	Entered for Consumption.	Duty.	Exports.	Imports.	Entered for Consumption.	Duty.	
$	$	$	$	$	$	$ c.	
550,983	551,016	82,414 46	332,339	594,080	594,496	89,949 65	1
93,366	95,178	6,102 02	193,488	69,778	71,050	6,064 32	2
28,413	28,413	5,695 57	9,505	23,989	23,989	6,571 13	3
3,100	4,565	244 67	2,360	5,150	6,817	575 20	4
3,424	3,474	711 55	12,750	4,531	4,531	955 81	5
6,318	6,276	540 69	....	7,969	7,939	647 62	6
64,991	49,135	4,960 76	127,764	63,973	79,806	12,746 96	7
36,240	36,240	3,490 17	146,285	34,173	34,298	3,582 79	8
....	....	....	....	476,111	476,111	92,329 06	9
8,187,740	7,728,027	1,360,546 94	10,192,631	8,709,717	8,867,759	1,586,925 83	10
127,417	127,468	15,581 04	79,674	128,937	128,934	12,638 62	11
14,364	14,922	1,393 63	116,255	24,155	24,540	2,418 13	12
6,862	7,084	345 45	41,367	7,711	8,104	323 46	13
231,032	262,901	28,619 48	738,744	326,007	346,016	43,432 37	14
51,538	51,538	11,153 16	....	33,261	33,261	6,540 57	15
328,577	329,155	44,742 03	3,450	266,507	267,238	41,066 05	16
433,946	431,197	33,131 54	734,621	392,652	397,325	40,686 17	17
24,522	24,661	1,137 10	778,241	4,795	4,894	856 98	18
205,126	205,515	10,655 85	61,063	198,999	199,633	8,947 39	19
9,173	9,171	818 77	177,850	15,299	15,285	2,916 98	20
10,454	10,415	1,885 99	8,990	8,271	8,277	1,541 39	21
7,283	7,592	783 87	34,603	11,928	11,328	1,610 78	22
1,380,774	1,315,843	170,773 03	1,546,157	1,488,866	1,493,318	146,345 11	23
300,969	303,901	69,650 28	....	289,608	294,347	66,699 15	24
23,318	23,566	2,152 54	260,724	18,477	18,668	1,916 76	25
150,697	150,876	6,042 53	478,610	218,487	218,861	8,033 89	26
606,632	607,391	52,658 77	1,544,800	680,625	675,539	59,634 35	27
12,887,259	12,385,520	1,916,231 89	17,622,271	14,104,056	14,312,364	2,245,956 52	

NEW BRUNSWICK.

Imports.	Entered for Consumption.	Duty.	Exports.	Imports.	Entered for Consumption.	Duty.	Number.
32,862	32,870	4,325 44	....	34,371	34,416	4,672 38	1
49,488	51,370	16,744 85	451,680	52,564	56,594	22,719 18	2
150,210	149,772	13,003 44	827,636	165,894	155,616	11,206 04	3
17,384	18,663	5,229 89	207,580	9,092	9,862	2,276 02	4
467,295	467,295	40,015 03	9,024	460,474	460,675	49,241 38	5
281,456	281,456	56,447 46	1,721,418	120,539	120,539	6,450 68	6
494,222	493,241	46,983 91	629,548	557,315	559,419	60,088 97	7
33,292	33,317	8,706 44	462,603	21,381	21,426	5,249 81	8
66,666	66,703	7,048 91	122,310	52,008	52,022	5,178 40	9
5,582,477	5,560,764	1,091,568 12	18,532,039	6,327,760	6,352,339	1,212,614 42	10
791,322	791,324	34,882 03	473,442	800,967	801,035	40,597 60	11
148,138	153,258	28,916 24	111,673	256,299	261,466	37,721 24	12
8,114,812	8,100,033	1,353,871 76	23,548,953	8,848,664	8,886,409	1,458,016 12	

No. 10.—COMPARATIVE STATEMENT (by Provinces) of the

PROVINCE OF

Number.	PORTS.	Fiscal Year ended June 30, 1904.				Fiscal
		Exports.	Imports.	Entered for Consumption.	Duty.	Exports.
		$	$	$	$ c.	$
1	Grand Forks	32,063	410,917	416,325	60,059 15	766,891
2	Kaslo	1,853	49,426	49,630	7,782 05	2,646
3	Nanaimo	3,580,562	338,355	357,742	82,526 32	2,859,598
4	Nelson	1,398,663	704,036	709,710	143,817 25	1,115,189
5	New Westminster	3,017,716	966,129	970,585	184,830 53	2,711,422
6	Rossland	3,087,418	596,232	600,843	74,134 52	1,829,344
7	Vancouver	4,346,635	6,015,540	5,780,114	1,423,428 25	5,331,402
8	Victoria	1,071,418	2,998,453	2,931,578	747,833 82	2,061,390
	Total	16,536,328	12,079,088	11,816,527	2,724,411 89	16,677,882

PROVINCE OF

Number.	PORTS.	Exports.	Imports.	Entered for Consumption.	Duty.	Exports.
1	Brandon	5,080	992,533	991,236	125,295 72	10,475
2	Emerson	....	....	....	....	2,145,241
3	Winnipeg	1,044,556	13,242,027	13,243,842	2,599,961 52	419,344
	Total	1,049,636	14,234,560	14,235,078	2,725,257 24	2,575,060

PRINCE EDWARD

Number.	PORTS.	Exports.	Imports.	Entered for Consumption.	Duty.	Exports.
1	Charlottetown	695,299	558,672	563,079	139,193 96	644,032
2	Summerside	31,115	101,659	101,748	12,186 12	10,480
	Total	726,414	660,331	664,827	151,380 08	654,512

NORTHWEST TERRITORIES

Number.	PORTS.	Exports.	Imports.	Entered for Consumption.	Duty.	Exports.
1	Calgary	....	1,554,326	1,571,407	212,928 04	....
2	Edmonton	....	....	....	....	....
3	Lethbridge	114,459	1,217,089	1,218,314	144,648 19	211,654
4	North Portal	....	....	....	....	542,251
5	Regina	3,060,649	2,120,348	2,110,728	241,562 10	....
6	Dawson	302,908	1,508,168	1,372,407	339,793 40	839,317
7	White Horse	11,944,346	487,075	487,863	77,378 34	9,540,557
8	Fullerton and Erick	....	....	....	....	....
	Total	15,422,362	6,887,006	6,760,719	1,016,310 07	11,133,779

Value of Exports and Imports, at each Port, &c.—*Concluded.*

BRITISH COLUMBIA.

Year ended June 30, 1905.			Fiscal Year ended June 30, 1906.				
Imports.	Entered for Consumption.	Duty.	Exports.	Imports.	Entered for Consumption.	Duty.	Number.
$	$	$ c.	$	$	$	$ c.	
818,886	822,232	100,760 86	3,563,214	802,268	807,354	112,883 61	1
91,193	91,193	9,128 39	441,947	73,578	73,578	4,545 77	2
381,818	381,361	78,911 82	3,687,390	772,881	775,285	82,581 21	3
899,257	904,003	175,122 09	1,214,655	1,082,421	1,084,246	221,586 04	4
896,240	896,175	162,399 96	5,152,115	928,206	913,884	187,249 65	5
362,710	363,674	56,098 21	507,624	470,353	471,424	56,340 76	6
6,147,861	6,106,952	1,505,706 92	7,283,155	8,254,412	8,193,647	1,862,278 64	7
2,967,054	2,926,478	724,685 12	967,478	3,334,460	3,265,002	809,339 98	8
12,565,019	12,492,068	2,812,813 37	22,817,578	15,718,579	15,584,420	3,336,805 66	

MANITOBA.

Imports.	Entered for Consumption.	Duty.	Exports.	Imports.	Entered for Consumption.	Duty.	Number.
883,644	889,036	140,200 39	13,301	1,104,946	1,111,152	192,555 68	1
495.810	494,850	23,296 60	1,603,047	416,288	415,708	37,251 97	2
12,932,139	12,898,493	2,704,232 69	318,815	17,556,273	17,590,366	3,620,072 03	3
14,311,593	14,282,379	2,867,729 68	1,935,163	19,077,507	19,117,226	3,849,879 68	

ISLAND.

Imports.	Entered for Consumption.	Duty.	Exports.	Imports.	Entered for Consumption.	Duty.	Number.
505,642	502,308	110,997 16	755,008	453,890	457,516	87,560 44	1
88,138	88,063	10,841 84	36,853	81,366	81,301	11,090 81	2
593,780	590,371	121,839 00	791,861	535,256	538,817	98,651 25	

AND YUKON.

Imports.	Entered for Consumption.	Duty.	Exports.	Imports.	Entered for Consumption.	Duty.	Number.
1,005,199	1,014,233	194,942 14	....	1,375,097	1,386,497	281,926 87	1
291,690	296,961	57,934 87	....	462,195	469,833	104,316 04	2
1,021,745	1,023,502	124,358 55	329,217	971,879	971,971	134,213 07	3
1,238,788	1,238,788	58,328 33	540,370	2,537,148	2,537,148	89,137 03	4
649,819	644,423	106,606 96	....	799,117	798,388	144,086 01	5
1,274,708	1,192,362	240,554 66	405,512	951,947	922,579	224,506 78	6
309,125	309,586	53,091 49	7,596,720	359,673	360,027	59,214 88	7
620	620	462 19	....	....	....	....	8
5,791,694	5,720,475	836,279 19	8,871,819	7,457,056	7,446,443	1,037,400 68	

No. 10.—COMPARATIVE STATEMENT (by Provinces) showing the Value of Exports, of collected by the Dominion of Canada, during the Fiscal

Number.	Provinces.	Fiscal Year ended June 30, 1904. Total Exports.	Total Imports.	Entered for Consumption.	Duty.	Fiscal Total Exports.
		$	$	$	$ cts.	$
1	Ontario	41,941,605	108,172,594	106,923,369	16,328,785 68	46,618,115
2	Quebec	102,816,197	95,046,849	88,973,252	14,308,671 54	92,437,049
3	Nova Scotia	17,096,839	13,167,649	13,268,854	2,306,480 28	15,289,772
4	New-Brunswick	17,931,854	8,956,531	8,814,511	1,391,613 16	17,930,703
5	Manitoba	1,049,636	14,234,560	14,235,078	2,725,257 24	2,575,060
6	British Columbia	16,536,328	12,079,088	11,816,527	2,724,411 89	16,677,882
7	Prince Edward Island	726,414	660,331	664,827	151,380 08	654,512
8	Northwest Territories	3,175,108	4,891,763	4,900,449	599,138 33	753,905
9	Yukon District	12,247,254	1,995,243	1,860,270	417,171 74	10,379,874
10	Northeast Territories	.....	.....	.....	.....	.....
	Total	213,521,235	259,204,608	251,457,137	40,952,909 94	203,316,872
	British prepaid postal parcels; duty received through P. O. Department	.....	7,195	7,195	1,439 20	.....
	Grand total	213,521,235	259,211,803	251,464,332	40,954,349 14	203,316,872

Total Imports and of Imports entered for Consumption, and the Amount of Duty
Years ending respectively on June 30, 1904, 1905 and 1906.

Year ended June 30 1905.			Fiscal Year ended June 30, 1906.				
Total Imports.	Entered for Consumption.	Duty.	Total Exports.	Total Imports.	Total Entered for Consumption.	Duty.	Number.
$	$	$ cts.	$	$	$	$ cts.	
118,526,380	116,398,474	18,421,046 61	59,725,246	128,654,267	126,064,517	19,166,642 30	1
94,029,761	91,942,115	13,691,704 45	121,273,739	99,872,231	98,392,212	15,474,068 82	2
12,887,259	12,385,520	1,916,231 89	17,622,271	14,104,056	14,312,364	2,245,956 52	3
8,114,812	8,100,033	1,353,871 76	23,548,953	8,848,664	8,886,409	1,458,016 12	4
14,311,593	14,282,379	2,867,729 68	1,935,163	19,077,507	19,117,226	3,849,879 68	5
12,565,019	12,492,068	2,812,813 37	22,817,578	15,718,579	15,584,420	3,336,805 66	6
593,780	590,371	121,839 00	791,861	535,256	538,817	98,651 25	7
4,207,241	4,217,907	542,170 85	869,587	6,145,436	6,163,837	753,679 02	8
1,583,833	1,501,948	293,646 15	8,002,232	1,311,620	1,282,606	283,721 66	9
620	620	462 19	....	....	....	....	10
266,820,298	261,911,435	42,021,515 95	256,586,630	294,267,616	290,342,408	46,667,421 03	
14,119	14,119	2,823 97	....	18,399	18,399	3,680 15	
266,834,417	261,925,554	42,024,339 92	256,586,630	294,286,015	290,360,807	46,671,101 18	

No. 11.—STATEMENT showing the Value of Goods Entered for Consumption at the undermentioned Ports during the Fiscal Year ended June 30, 1906.

Dutiable Goods.	Brantford	Calgary.	Dawson.	Halifax.	Hamilton.	London.	Montreal.	Ottawa.	Quebec.
	$	$	$	$	$	$	$	$	$
Ale, beer and porter	214	3,313	21,959	23,766	1,759	792	74,145	6,761	1,696
Animals, living	135	2,197	14,188	605	1,623	1,937	9,090	2,521	311
Antiseptic surgical dressing		41	6	1,681	1,029	1,130	38,458	621	397
Bagatelle tables									
Bags containing cement	724	418		599	4,974	3,707	20,130	985	6,956
Baking powder			1,342				85,969		449
Balls, cues and racks for bagatelle tables		49	67	76			1,096	610	85
Baskets	115	148	62	1,368	600	2,543	18,148	848	1,596
Belting, all kinds, except rubber and leather	244	483		987	1,977	18	37,151	40	189
Belts, surgical trusses and suspensory bandages	21	37	183	392	744	269	3,872	1,705	421
Belts, all kinds, N.E.S.	31	65	16	1,166	1,818	1,377	39,378	2,039	2,379
Bells	5	176	22	472	1,539	1,355	13,578	[illegible]	868
Billiard tables		1,280		26	250		3,776	133	20
Blacking, shoe and shoemakers' ink	37	647	103	2,252	3,120	1,452	27,350	1,644	1,091
Blinds, of wood, metal or other material, except textile or paper							3,510	648	
Blue, laundry, all kinds	306		11	900	287	1,346	11,343	1,006	1,684
Boats		201		803	4,531	379	10,575	3,328	3,532
Bolsters and pillows	41			387	607	151	1,231	127	249
Bone, manufactures of									
Books, periodicals and other printed matter	16,122	15,700	5,502	52,819	45,017	65,073	525,526	53,565	30,840
Boot, shoe and stay laces	5	29	12	757	748	437	71,236	121	2,325
Boots, shoes and slippers, except rubber and leather		207	1,575		12,721	3,697	40,742	2,394	
Braces and suspenders and parts of	126	28	18	2,396	468	443	21,682	1,820	1,688
Brass and manufactures of	5,949	6,362	2,420	11,632	37,257	10,739	268,573	16,455	18,550
Breadstuffs, viz.—									
Bread, biscuits, rice, macaroni, sago and tapioca	69	6,804	2,266	16,213	0,272	17,911	357,505	4,472	7,661
Grain, flour and meal	855	14,744	20,714	10,786	5,543	7,662	287	3,885	19,645
British gum, dextrine, sizing cream, &c	1,864			37	2,319	240	21,243	1,164	1,347
Bricks, tiles and manufactures of clay, N.E.S.	1,625	5,664	15	7,407	1,626	19,341	57,848	7,924	4,959
Brooms and brushes	140	372	335	2,132	1,015	4,004	98,242	2,328	1,833
Buttons	294	164	109	2,510	13,071	3,063	109,198	3,528	5,993
Candles			1,148	469	1,323	821	14,639	460	1,660
Canvas for sails				2,027			628		107
Cane, reed or rattan, split, and manufactures of				49	183	186	7,852	1,552	970
Carriages of all kinds, railway cars, trucks and parts of	5,482	23,899	27,423	5,323	15,589	36,089	199,741	35,979	10,756
Carpets, N.E.S.		234					49		

Article									
[illegible]					200		182	2	
[illegible]		158		449	131	242	1,461		
[illegible] of			3	92	973	395	17,015	126	271
[illegible]	3,070	1,763	85	58,670	24,897	19,766	152,687	6,797	56,020
[illegible]	7		6	507	1,206	369	7,044	582	569
Charcoal		7	23	14,776	2,990	1,034	3,005	38	
[illegible]ry		26		516	1,194	62	4,[illegible]2	333	220
Church [illegible]		74		226	15		9,860	560	7,376
[illegible]							347		20
[illegible], springs and movements	617	675	[illegible]2	4,489	11,203	4 022	102,000	3,301	4,811
[illegible]	3	74	7	144	820	125	[illegible]	129	27
[illegible] waterproof, for manufacturers							[illegible]3		
Coal, [illegible]	57,535		2,132	1,139	326,371	246,025	[illegible]	174 171	42,172
[illegible]			94	32	118	163	1,[illegible]8	297	19
[illegible]			3	22,713		48	2[illegible]8		
Cocoa desiccated		43	51			2,172	191		
Cocoa [illegible], shells nibs, and other [illegible]		676	262	20,774	1,589	16,830	289,009	[illegible]00	10,049
Coffee, all kinds, N.E.S. (see Free Goods)	26	89	4,234	4,622	5,687	1,695	28,173	8,405	375
[illegible]	697	517	381	4,106	4,019	1,867	[illegible]50	[illegible]7	2,272
[illegible] and [illegible]et	120	314	34	3,169	7,127	4,448	1,945	4,[illegible]8	9,319
[illegible] and [illegible] of	336	4,515	479	5,545	10,672	2,876	[illegible]8	1,73	1,460
Cordage of all [illegible]	1,005	[illegible]8	1,314	12,724	3,104	202	[illegible]60	2,954	11,974
[illegible] of cork wood	232	4,021	1,136	11,227	2,008	36	[illegible]9	161	7,038
[illegible], &c.	51	92	254	1,809	3,932	489	[illegible]47	[illegible]41	2,549
[illegible] and [illegible]trical	200	76		260	454	634	[illegible]0	[illegible]	325
[illegible] of	35,828	[illegible]89	12,203	121,941	276,011	209,752	3,[illegible]6	1 [illegible]00	253,272
[illegible], bulk				605	127	302	6,399	102	2,114
[illegible]				269		69	3[illegible]8	281	
Curtains, made up	2,519	831	85	10,432	12,798	19,123	120,001	[illegible]8	11,423
Cyclometers and [illegible]								59	
Dressing, [illegible] and [illegible]er									
Drugs, dyes, chemicals, medicines	7,003	4,347	1,165	68,902	75,367	39,594	90 440	72,[illegible]44	31,829
[illegible] and china	3,398	2,224	149	36,201	50,964	62,459	[illegible]7	[illegible]50	50,658
Eggs			19,260	15		52	1,[illegible]8	95	
Elastic	52	61		2,189	750	2,740	6,[illegible]50	1,73	7,314
Electric light [illegible] and pints	476			169	[illegible]6	21	[illegible]8	[illegible]75	190
Electric [illegible], &c.	3,279	7,066	1,[illegible]2	1[illegible]8	,[illegible]76	48,194	[illegible]181	[illegible]2	51,872
[illegible], N.E.S.	15	91		591	1,664	2,629	22 [illegible]5	2,746	1,032
Emery [illegible] and manufactures of [illegible]	6,[illegible]94	3	22	125	1,024	637	11,828	[illegible]6	513
Express [illegible]	12,[illegible]5	14,600	1,878	[illegible]9	7,[illegible]8	24,982	[illegible]6	1,[illegible]8	20,645
Fancy goods	6,909	4,059	1,366	[illegible]3	79,278	78,262	4[illegible]21	4,[illegible]3	68,730
Feathers, bed, &c.			7				13,015	[illegible]2	7,878
Feath[illegible]				5		308			
Fertilizers				12	65	100	545	1,986	2,563
Fibreware, N.E.S.				220	6,406	267	13,997	694	519
[illegible]		33	10		6,598	1,477	4,594	874	72
Fish (see Free Goods)	4,605	3,626	5,328	12,[illegible]76	26,094	17,998	[illegible]3	,1[illegible]5	9,757
Flax, [illegible], jute and manufactures of	6,051	3,917	703	[illegible]6	54,905	64,372	1,235,614	47,228	63,456
Foundry facings	926		31	115	1,651	628	10[illegible]72	472	143
Fruits and nuts (see Free Goods)	59,218	110,551	37,076	1 [illegible]8	176,100	190,549	[illegible]21	[illegible]39	52,897

IMPORTS for Consumption by Ports—*Continued.*

Dutiable Goods.	Sault Ste. Marie.	St. John, N.B.	St. Johns, Que.	Sydney.	Toronto.	Vancouver.	Victoria.	Windsor, Ont.	Winnipeg.
	$	$	$	$	$	$	$	$	$
A[illegible], beer and porter	12	24,930	59	11,175	28,702	38,771	29,172	57	94,458
[illegible]s, living	4,502	1,497	286	385	20,055	104,749	72,174	3,296	120,140
Antiseptic surgical dressing		1,173			12,297	3,198	11	42	6,316
Bagatelle b[illegible]s					148	17			49
Baking [illegible]der					56	46,314	1,126	170	23
Balls, cues and [illegible]cks for bagatelle tables		39		13	4,526	102	28		5
B[illegible], cement	300	63	5,030	288	6,476			2,188	33,761
Basl[illegible]es	63	[illegible]0	178	21	17,855	2,896	823	130	4,[illegible]24
Belting, all [illegible]s, e[illegible]t rubber and leather	846	3,627	74		4[illegible]07	1,185	6,755	5,163	2,167
Bel[illegible]s, [illegible]al tru[illegible]es and suspensory bandages	10	270	2		11,226	883	614	127	3,320
Belts, all kinds, N.E.S.		4,961		151	21,[illegible]69	2,833	97		6,955
Bells	92	1,138		34	8,332	487	34	98	4,457
B[illegible]d [illegible]s				130	23,122	708	40	318	[illegible]7
Blacking, shoe and [illegible]emakers' ink	31	2,022		243	15,466	2,129	721	129	9,579
Blinds, of [illegible], metal or [illegible]her material, except textile or paper		67	29		149		68		30
B[illegible], l[illegible]dy, all kinds		359			3,512	[illegible]3	186	139	3,298
B[illegible]s	1,520	861	378	64	21,421	3,545	2,434	1,467	4,496
Bol[illegible]es and pill [illegible]s		25			3,[illegible]49	20	86	45	2,915
Bone, [illegible] of									
Books, [illegible]s and other printed matter	2,734	45,676	5,405	4,614	[illegible],04	42,221	24,677	34,[illegible]98	[illegible]8
Boot, shoe and stay [illegible]s	18	725		51	49,270	67	60	1	3,060
B[illegible], [illegible]s and [illegible]s, except rubber and leather		1,751			12,573	7,706	4,332		8,619
[illegible]s and [illegible]e[illegible]s and parts of	6	1,459	1	134	16,012	[illegible]7	1,254	12	8,[illegible]05
Brass and [illegible]s of	2,915	16,[illegible]84	1,340	2,615	183,906	29,624	13,714	12,167	107,[illegible]82
Breadstuffs, viz.:—									
[illegible], [illegible]s, rice, macaroni, sago and tapioca	103	13,942	1,[illegible]06	3,669	75,630	186,838	89,058	2,308	44,620
G[illegible]n, flour and [illegible]al	1,[illegible]39	6,680	333	47	156,226	[illegible],199	100,307	186,970	76,824
Bricks, t[illegible]s and [illegible]s of clay, N.E.S.	288	4,831	5,[illegible]85	19[illegible]	32,791	21,679	5,850	10,945	108,185
British gum, [illegible]ine, sizing cream, &c.	110	414	254		15,[illegible]86	89		39	75
Brooms and brushes	547	7,379	84	108	101,395	9,456	2,035	564	27,769
Buttons	30	4,353	181	186	97,076	3,214	2,680	610	9,751
[illegible]s		1,066	13		7,354	10[illegible]39	7,282	66	3,226
Canvas [illegible]r sails		582				88	3,916		
Cane, [illegible]ed or [illegible]an, split and manufactures of		81	6,536		[illegible]1	80	17	4,712	
[illegible]s of all kinds, railway cars, trucks and parts of	5,216	12,995	10,907	696	120,084	34,353	19,309	77,[illegible]90	605,022
[illegible], N.E.S.									
[illegible]t [illegible]s					5[illegible]5				9
[illegible]h [illegible]s		3,383		99	224,883	2,293		317	3,130

Celluloid, manufactures of	98	2,854	2	9	20,021	1,565	50	54	2,485
Cement	2,908	35,123	17,918	16,514	27,413	35,288	611	18,150	116,027
Chalk, prepared	13	468			9,693	376	41	532	1,311
Charcoal		23			4,170	179		617	681
Chicory		26			1,714	1,171	990		1,542
Church vestments		4	98	26	3,095	97	15	50	995
[illegible]	37				15	32	178		
[illegible]ks, clock cases, springs and movements	210	7,709	1,024	11	138,006	10,944	2,385	375	34,447
Clothes [illegible]rs	433	980	18	55	9,454	431	230	179	1,704
Cloths, not [illegible]ed or [illegible]de [illegible]f, for manufacturers									
Coal, bituminous, and [illegible]st	493,551	2,230	6,336		[illegible]	20,469	8,101	745,449	9,865
[illegible]a carpeting, [illegible]ts and matting		167			1,327	401	150		125
" [illegible]uts	8	9,848		6	18,144	792	203	18	596
" desiccated					3,576	1,258	359		724
" paste, chocolate paste, shell, nibs and [illegible]er preparations		3,308	1,378	34	[illegible]	22,169	16,434	658	47,254
Coffee, all kinds, N.E.S. (see Free Goods)	77	6,487	1	11	38,226	7,355	3,704	1,703	18,721
[illegible]llars		4,166		271	55,442	3,467	1,650	50	17,448
[illegible]s, dress and toilet	7	9,085	48	102	80,859	3,649	827	27	15,076
[illegible]r and manufactures of	434	21,501	57	256	16,590	3,470	3,255	5,182	12,381
Cordage of all kinds	2,567	18,868	93	17	[illegible]	12,299	5,830	1,743	10,732
[illegible]ks and other manufactures of cork wood	108	2,114	8	150	36,977	1,913	942	15,812	439
Corsets, clasps, &c		1,023			42,393	2,295	1,766	320	16,792
[illegible]es and [illegible]y, theatrical		427	15	50	7,606	346	955	150	2,055
[illegible]n, manufactures of	3,568	166,709	10,292	14,993	3,108,958	128,114	84,197	32,034	623,497
Crape, black		429		13	[illegible]	15		12	664
Cuffs		176			176	15	127	361	280
Curtains, [illegible]de up	83	17,559		418	309,222	14,074	6,122	10	61,405
Cyclometers and pedometers		49			971	65			242
Dressing, harness and [illegible]									
Drugs, [illegible], [illegible], medicines	5,671	42,709	52,502	1,351	489,476	137,754	222,232	71,692	118,136
Earthenware and china	1,154	136,103	1,479	1,274	549,517	[illegible]	[illegible]	6,863	142,000
Eggs	1,031				324	[illegible]	3,084	82	6,412
Elastic		1,070	1	263	1,[illegible]87	1,199	1,133	46	6,659
Electric light carbons and points	428	1,096	46	481	25,227	1,706	688	721	2,367
Electric apparatus, motors, &c	46,457	22,896	64,268	3,951	310,507	31,592	12,753	22,395	85,315
Embroideries, N.E.S.		276			42,050	2912	361		3,833
Emery wheels and manufactures of emery	454	440	105	306	9,274	2,630	386	564	1,376
Express parcels	16,096	24,446	4,297	3,799	130,160	22,266	13,996	80,698	66,372
Fancy goods	264	104,415	5,270	3,611	1,[illegible]066	36,032	27,048	4,254	178,921
Feathers, bed. &c					5,219	81	187		370
Featherbone					130				
Fertilizers	24	8,366	1,771		1,692	5,075	23	676	140
Fibreware, N.E.S	257	167	327		6,799	1,922	194	144	972
Fireworks		208			4,[illegible]60	1,616	1,190	61	7,[illegible]01
Fish (see Free Goods)	1,325	10,793	1,879	397	[illegible]520	92,937	22,357	2,397	53,062
Flax, hemp, jute and manufactures of	873	61,079	7,856	17,961	878,917	87,228	55,918	8,661	221,200
Foundry facings	237	128			3,421			681	
Fruits and nuts (see Free Goods)	16,242	178,541	6,661	22,282	926,878	290,489	105,022	27,228	772,802
Furniture, [illegible]d, iron or [illegible]ther material	1,856	11,803	375	435	206,548	42,071	14,482	18,160	127,647
Furs and manufactures of furs (see Free Goods)	33	14,996	87	997	324,883	4,031	6,342	16,553	26,840

IMPORTS for Consumption by Ports—*Continued.*

Dutiable Goods.	Brantford.	Calgary.	Dawson.	Halifax.	Hamilton.	London.	Montreal.	Ottawa.	Quebec.
	$	$	$	$	$	$	$	$	$
Furniture, wood, iron or other material	1,989	3,813	2,187	8,885	[illegible]	9,266	[illegible]	15,233	9,224
Furs and manufactures of furs (see Free Goods)	259	706	344	5,979	[illegible]	58,181	651,500	15,634	205,973
Fuses			45	5,074			17,378	46	325
Glass and manufactures of	3,003	12,526	1,002	58,609	56,599	[illegible]	832,082	36,716	78,605
Gloves and mitts	1,247	2,198	1,259	13,064	12,383	[illegible]	621,812	11,703	[illegible]
Gold, silver and manufactures of	244	1,032	2,005	11,899	8,250	9,902	249,240	8,969	10,494
Grease, axle		1,235	67	[illegible]	5,847	1,147	6,603	1,768	
Gunpowder and other explosives	43	1,909	1,099	7,126	18,834	[illegible]	81,386	10,391	6,116
Gutta percha, India rubber and manufactures of	3,421	3,382	56,346	[illegible]	39,768	16,233	165,921	13,046	13,386
Hair and manufactures of	123	70	47	407	819	150	12,360	338	993
Hats, caps and bonnets	4,888	9,986	5,275	42,794	51,085	124,963	604,773	38,516	106,269
Hay			38,991						
Honey			395	416			269		
Hops	182	4,232	803	13,961	4,832	11,853	58,448	2,533	19,914
Ink	543	483	140	3,812	4,284	5,644	47,002	7,589	2,413
Iron and steel and manufactures of (see Free Goods)	850,012	350,770	97,205	423,528	2,327,614	638,501	10,326,081	[illegible]	854,630
Ivory							317	120	
Jellies, jams and preserves	222	5,118	233	7,944	2,285	1,250	24,001	3,926	2,613
Jewellery	413	861	2,843	6,287	51,190	23,217	[illegible]	10,645	11,049
Knitted goods							93		222
Lead and manufactures of			24	9,225	15,854	9,203	[illegible]	1,765	3,040
Leather and manufactures of	12,777	28,560	14,816	[illegible]	90,001	52,895	[illegible]	72,785	[illegible]
Lime	20			3	433	60	2,467	2,553	
Juice and other fruit juices	29	16	114	1,337	148	59	7,424	376	155
Lithographic presses							14,274	40	
" stones, not engraved	94			53	51	189	632		
Machine card clothing		1,411			102		7,566	4,540	923
Magic lanterns and slides therefor	112	39		111	46	102	1 462	997	122
Malt	137		2,219	97			995	61	
" extract					1,620		1,399		35
Marble and manufactures of	423	962		3,728	7,864	1,458	50,044	5,108	1,901
Mattresses	34		5		407		185	376	432
Mats and rugs	2,151	6,953	171	5,223	6,320	10,782	8,518	15,585	2,170
Metals and manufactures of	14,139	8,230	2,755	14,571	109,079	26,328	331,248	32,452	14,210
Milk, condensed			1,093	55		14	2,434	1	31
Mineral substances, N.O.P.	1,606	268	104	6,826	16,413	9,717	98,634	5,946	371
" and aerated waters	35	4,702	133	2,102	1,291	124	105,634	2,188	10,343
Mosaic flooring		213			49	125	1,817	1,809	641

[illegible]e	157	44	3	1,135	506	507	3,549	650	559
[illegible]al [illegible]ts		2,142	457	5,962	4 031	2[illegible]14	[illegible]92	22,172	5,834
[illegible]rd and mustard cake	907	1,011	76	3,030	3[illegible]2	7,550	31,712	4,534	1,549
Oils, all [illegible]ds, N.E.S	18,799	3,056	21,528	203,979	67,[illegible]64	[illegible]179	789,302	22,618	[illegible]9
Oiled cloths, of all kinds, [illegible]k [illegible] and linoleum	7,071	6,794	117	20,209	[illegible]96	[illegible]30	[illegible]9	22,618	41,849
Optical, philosophical, [illegible]c and [illegible]al [illegible]s	363	2,137	1,706	4,431	8,547	2[illegible]027	104 978	7,274	1,550
Packages	2,144	8,950	17,437	50,482	16,522	13,871	[illegible]40	21,835	71,130
Paints and colours	4,[illegible]3	586	89	53,884	22,678	10,264	8[illegible]027	23,301	[illegible]00
Paper and [illegible]es of	7[illegible]94	13,711	9,401	47,698	151,960	0,[illegible]82	[illegible]9	70,673	41,073
Pencils, lead	704	32	60	2,897	7,736	2,981	49,798	3,952	3[illegible]70
[illegible], penholders and [illegible]rs	412	246	461	3,744	3,229	1,612	82,642	2,274	1,174
Perfumery, [illegible] [illegible]c	289	873	55	2,780	5,264	2[illegible]13	50,116	1,618	2,804
Photographic dry [illegible]s		73	20	60	396	77	16,673	26	
Picture and photograph frames	707	432		1,445	1,549	1,206	23,997	2,566	[illegible]47
[illegible]es	649	1,476	1,640	16,849	7,357	15,579	37,015	5,910	9[illegible]3
Plants and trees	281	3,780	21	584	4,386	1,743	8,720	2,506	732
Plaster of Paris		2,740		52			34	71	38
Blates, engraved on wood or metal						106		11,443	179
Pocketbooks, [illegible]s	648	993	143	1,424	4,906	2[illegible]62	59,830	5,514	6,693
Polish or composition, knife or other	508	65	55	3,179	3,086	[illegible]05	18,760	1,018	3,941
Pomades							406	162	
Post office parcels	4,430	18,784	4,296	17,704	19,507	11,904	45,557	20,618	9 652
Precious [illegible]s, N.E.S			400		6,683	1 [illegible]2	40,574	717	4[illegible]8
Printing presses and [illegible]chines and parts of	1,909	1,952	200	5,110	5,663	6[illegible]93	87,790	16,060	7,480
Provisions, viz.—									
Butter, [illegible]e and lard		9,221	18,202	47,236	20,626	5[illegible] 2[illegible]61	86,306	15,322	13,908
[illegible]ts, all k[illegible]ds	162	74,049	90,230	97,752	30,344	2[illegible]40	248,516	190,024	[illegible]50
Regalia and badges	30	434		367	166	168	2,719	97	125
Ribbons, N.E.S	3,698	2,253	27	13,646	20,826	[illegible]67	368,239	19,098	20,731
Rove, imported for the [illegible]e of [illegible]e for r[illegible]t [illegible]									
Railway and travelling rugs		671		1,217	1,340	3,818	14,477	919	2,186
Sails					507	17	527		
Salt (see Free Goods)	282	1,505	196	321	1,430	502	1 669	315	23
Sand, glass, [illegible]ry [illegible]d flint paper	557	26		1,175	4,845	2,127	[illegible]09	2,142	3,616
Sauces, [illegible]ps and soy	337	1,482	740	5,573	3,626	2[illegible]01	4[illegible]3	2,845	1,199
Sausage casings, cleaned	857	1,912	678	2,297	13,071	[illegible]02	[illegible]99	3,163	86
[illegible]s, N.E.S	920	1,430	20	7,896	13,229	12,572	65,671	16,090	46,524
Ships and vessels [illegible]d repairs on				1,200	8,500		2,000	43,000	
Signs of any material and [illegible]ers for signs	23	248	26	665	1,908	1,211	23,464	1,517	1,097
Silk and [illegible]s of	8,539	3,819	3,177	32,766	49,168	66,789	1,268,988	55,999	,[illegible]6
S[illegible]e	2,373		20	1,529	7,352	[illegible]2	,[illegible]8	3,366	557
Soaps	1,919	5,086	1,327	17,959	19,753	8[illegible]7	177,093	9,850	7,260
Spices	178	946	126	18,764	66,474	23,179	61,528	4,804	5,116
Spirits	3,729	25,672	14,526	141,199	22,192	15,051	749,302	59,451	158,606
" wine, not sparkling	753	2,305	2,630	14,294	3,529	2,281	191 907	11,864	32,538
" " sparkling		5,042	3,340	4,176	1,794	1,577	[illegible]0	2,176	1,931
Sponges	52			404	1,733	68	16,721	953	605
Starch	57	289	69	1,000	1,676	3,074	13,157	1,428	767
Stearic acid							618		
Stockinettes for manufacture of rubber boots							5,[illegible]2		

IMPORTS for Consumption by Ports—*Continued.*

Dutiable Goods.	Sault Ste. Marie.	St. John, N.B.	St. Johns, Que.	Sydney.	Toronto.	Vancouver.	Victoria, B.C.	Windsor, Ont.	Winnipeg.
	$	$	$	$	$	$	$	$	$
Fuses	25	89	.....	32	124	4,984	3,193	.....	59
Glass and manufactures of	4,577	80,927	1,242	1,634	674,967	105,241	26,237	52,409	289,393
Gloves and mitts	129	26,504	4,243	1,659	245,929	[illegible]	19,421	2,224	104,134
Gold, silver and manufactures of	112	8,064	51	97	170,274	12,948	7,897	546	[illegible]
Grease, axle	52	414	.....	1,007	26,766	2,565	907	1,578	6,667
Gunpowder and other explosives	1,353	8,986	853	.....	34,391	58,825	14,824	119	211,672
Gutta percha, India rubber and manufactures of	9,711	15,421	1,199	2,909	189,354	35,566	12,019	4,147	54,749
Hair and manufactures of	.....	2,694	15	70	8,640	270	289	15	3,300
Hats, caps and bonnets	1,367	[illegible]	519	5,962	795,662	51,902	27,510	1,103	125,745
Hay	4,657	.....	.....	.....	.....	302	25	.....	28
Honey	117	4	.....	.....	8	3,927	1,144	.....	418
Hops	1,089	8,887	.....	.....	39,813	347	219	1,719	10,313
Ink	18	5,487	136	448	53,229	4,210	2,216	310	8,784
Iron and steel and manufactures of (see Free Goods)	633,639	509,669	251,406	314,347	5,266,510	1,197,348	363,125	966,222	3,959,605
Ivory	.....	.....	.....	.....	53	65	194	.....	.....
Jellies, jams and preserves	.....	4,033	12	1,416	13,492	22,596	7,328	343	27,892
Jewellery	183	7,847	352	397	384,835	9,446	6,516	435	51,574
Knitted goods	.....	.....	63	.....	.....	.....	.....	.....	.....
Lead and manufactures of	546	22,587	.....	685	68,022	5,035	6,609	23,717	10,668
Leather and manufactures of	2,834	30,644	2,576	2,379	755,583	99,750	24,625	1,817	178,691
Lime	3,800	.....	743	.....	997	375	.....	147	13,167
" juice and other fruit juices	.....	1,689	.....	274	5,646	2,181	1,271	67	1,072
Lithographic presses	.....	.....	.....	.....	47,328	.....	.....	.....	42
" stones, not engraved	.....	.....	.....	.....	5,555	119	3	.....	170
Machine card clothing	.....	458	.....	.....	4,786	.....	.....	.....	.....
Magic lanterns and slides therefor	119	73	35	32	2,925	286	180	.....	121
Malt	.....	.....	.....	158	[illegible]	24,549	2,907	.....	15,300
" extract	.....	.....	.....	.....	6,120	.....	.....	.....	249
Marble and manufactures of	313	709	1,834	533	41,707	2,780	1,101	1,005	25,850
Matches	.....	39	40	.....	1,173	526	244	.....	342
Mats and rugs	199	10,097	149	66	[illegible]	20,768	6,427	9,305	35,163
Metals and manufactures of	1,186	25,492	5,478	3,229	448,604	41,445	14,202	20,848	133,583
Milk, condensed	.....	.....	.....	10	.....	1,831	1,222	.....	515
Mineral waters, N.O.P.	2,697	6,171	4,880	1,199	43,776	6,647	3,857	2,941	18,832
" and aerated waters	57	1,877	.....	23	11,103	4,031	6,102	.....	23,633
Mosaic flooring	.....	10	.....	.....	3,481	1,254	396	.....	281
Mucilage	15	669	1	92	7,609	590	306	1,953	[illegible]
Musical instruments	498	7,257	535	1,226	262,838	8,528	4,831	471	37,971

Mustard and mustard cake		3,491			24	4,586	2,484	390	14,850
Oils, all kinds, N.E.S.	3,408	117,341	6,493	1,313	449,299	73,087	40,447	37,819	286,837
Gd lhs, of all kinds, rk matting nd linoleum	734	21,138	60	3,093	247,788	33,920	11,239	4,727	109,199
ical, philosophical, hic nd ital instruments	229	4,283	167	69	151,661	6,749	1,687	657	22,702
Packages	707	70,403	1,792	8,228	77,199	54,657	44,076	3,255	97,676
Paints nd colours	736	19,035	2,661	897	218,672	9,153	30,845	24,048	57,258
Paper nd es of	2,837	58,217	2,343	2,783	1,163,935	77,055	42,922	36,523	230,158
ils, lead	251	5,228	4	9	65,689	3,887	358	180	19,334
Pens, ds nd rulers	9	2,321		25	61,872	1,796	556	258	11,751
Perfumery, nn- lic		2,045	62	115	30,431	6,637	573	2,295	8,672
Photographic dy pls		45			34,938	1,418	766		2,554
le nd photograph frames	499	1,548	47	102	44,001	2,043	878	4,871	6,104
Pls	32	16,289		2,145	47,480	19,678	4,803	2,470	19,470
Plants nd trees	61	291	320	251	14,165	22,823	3,547	2,007	4,927
Plr of ls	325				89	3,805	934	70	21,630
Plates, engraved on wd or metal			27		1,729	80	604		12
Pocket books, purses	69	2,012	55	107	80,930	6,422	3,911	353	18,490
Polish or composition, knife or other	135	2,598	43	169	15,013	2,484	622	1,763	2,781
Pomades					2,292	61		2,996	
Post ffie ds	5,186	14,843	949	23	105,888	19,320	21,931	3,988	46,65
Precious es, N.E.S.					32,069	1,300	575		1,187
Printing presses nd machines and parts of	742	2,678	15	245	167,699	4,364	4,446	619	49,313
Provisions, viz.:—									
Butter, he nd lard	10,906	49,673		4,811	96,731	82,527	35,284	4,513	125,831
Meats, all ids	33,404	81,383	52	6,222	127,794	223,959	100,592	8,581	255,486
Regalia nd ls	211	86		60	2,591	59	315	63	1,240
Ribbons, N.E.S	323	36,498	168	2,256	433,087	19,257	7,376	286	89,447
Rove, imported for the mufacture of twine for rlet bds									
Railway nd travelling rugs		1,733	25	80	8,849	1,119	997		7,378
Sails					150			52	210
Salt (se Free ds)	323	383			5,285	1,115	729	850	13,782
Sand, glass, ny nd flint pr	23	1,248	93	55	31,964	1,583	86	687	3,599
Sauces, catsups nd sy	2	3,497		85	15,839	30,059	12,923	164	13,362
Sausage casings, cleaned	11	3,673		215	13,757	2,072	1,295	257	2,872
Seeds, N.E.S.	122	5,594	1,074		104,230	8,183	14,833	16,072	4,668
Ships and vessels nd ips on	2,215	8,800		35	33,000	1,120	23,710	4,360	
Signs of any mal nd les for signs	140	615	275	72	16,696	2,808	66	1,056	5,381
Silk nd manufactures of	568	68,758	45,736	2,04	2,068,237	72,731	46,932	12,739	209,638
Ste		3,310	241	400	49,963	964	50	1,425	5,714
Soaps	240	12,617	24	743	130,618	34,098	13,004	3,421	31,282
Sps		12,382	1,420	103	67,249	10,192	4,629	504	19,860
Spirits	835	182,389	5,197	27 08	176,617	91,364	128,499	2,966	150,737
" wine, not sparkling	124	7,603	443	90	37,201	30,038	20,546	716	20,336
" " sparkling		970	3		29,500	6,807	33,419	211	16,233
Sponges		202	46		27,586	615	471	40	2,714
Starch	49	4,330		198	4,519	1,426	1,176	600	1,262
Stearic acid					214			11	48
Stockinettes for manufacture of rubber boots, &c.			11,681		9,037				
Stone and manufactures of	709	4,522	447		60,263	2,310	674	5,035	23,198
Straw	61	1,917			26,961	7,970	2,288	3,645	2,748

IMPORTS for Consumption by Ports—*Continued.*

Dutiable Goods.	Brantford	Calgary.	Dawson.	Halifax.	Hamilton.	London.	Montreal.	Ottawa.	Quebec.
	$	$	$	$	$	$	$	$	$
Stone and [illegible] of	339	225	13	1,556	17,314	6,288	126,644	12,894	1,859
Straw	23		1	238	759	874	13,734	474	196
[illegible] and syrups	1,108	1,082	5,298	2,401,734	9,248	[illegible]	5,915,237	8,424	142,592
" [illegible]				107,813	3,164	2,725	617		21,058
" [illegible] and [illegible]	1,293	800	2,695	9,124	8,939	8,864	100,889	2,478	6,984
" glucose, [illegible], [illegible] sugar and syrup	1,596	13	2,023	11	33	8,997	2,091		1
Tallow		1,301		145			1,429	1,544	
Tape lines		297	49	472	1,047	370	9,949	262	608
Tea (see Free [illegible])			193	102	71		11,243	9	358
Teeth, artificial									
Tin and [illegible] of	1,010	612	318	4,097	6,871	3,873	40,872	4,353	1,649
Tobacco and [illegible] of	55	6,184	40,888	24,284	3,567	1,289	233,110	9,657	3,497
" pipes	26	6	134	5,262	5,066	434	229,027	7,470	15,823
Trawls and trawling spoons	97	96		1,222	1,236	486	7,374	2,738	1,800
Turpentine, spirits of	2,360			19,092	16,570	17,626	263,757	9,691	350
[illegible], valises, hat boxes, &c	100	813	48	1,737	1,022	1,600	29,432	3,543	4,590
Twines and manufactures of	229	90		163	1,094	2,411	3,474	802	174
Umbrellas, [illegible] and [illegible]	144	202	6	762	1,459	1,207	8,733	2,390	1,795
Unenumerated articles	957	256	390	3,255	3,020	753	24,659	2,504	2,422
Varnish, lacquers, japans, &c	1,536	106	5	3,611	7,339	2,814	42,776	2,941	4,525
Vegetables	3,692	12,718	35,460	26,109	[illegible]	5,097	206,605	16,558	6,653
Vinegar	83	575	122	405	1,120	307	5,741	401	674
Watches, [illegible] cases, movements, glasses, &c	377	243	3,126	2,838	20,801	10,283	591,758	1,044	466
Wax and [illegible] of		122	36	882	26 818	423	39,756	739	4,337
[illegible]		161		55	88	230	69,666	2,121	10,212
[illegible], thongs and lashes		1,157	129	93	29	198	1,866	15	373
[illegible] and osiers							23		
[illegible] [illegible] and cornice poles					90	632	1,091	1,400	165
Wood and manufactures of	11,493	12,612	6,780	20,064	51,131	32,295	197,797	30,017	21,666
Window shades and rollers			95	188	64	183	2,030	751	
Wool and manufactures of	36,137	23,328	19,793	256,339	739,174	[illegible]	6,991,301	298,501	439,333
Zinc and manufactures of	295			127	58	299	2,553	316	156
Damaged goods				4,776			7,075	739	4,264
Total dutiable goods	1,353,769	1,004,679	733,750	5,340,931	6,633,423	3,336,896	50,490,066	3,331,969	3,945,896

IMPORTS for Consumption by Ports.—*Continued.*

Dutiable Goods	Sault Ste. Marie.	St. John, N.B.	St. Johns, Que.	Sydney.	Toronto.	Vancouver.	Victoria.	Windsor, Ont.	Winnipeg.
	$	$	$	$	$	$	$	$	$
Sugars and syrups		160,932	6,026	107	59,870	1,430,560	5,329	1,911	13,212
" molasses		141,347			6,750		1,992		12,512
" candy and confectionery	141	11,460	70	786	74,439	18,545	7,898	620	30,642
Sugar glucose, saccharine, maple sugar and syrup		51		14	25,087	900	336	320	3
Tallow		8				19	173		1,785
Tape lines	33	329		23	6,567	897	248		6,346
Tea (see Free Goods)		2,394			977	1,596	584	641	1,088
Teeth, artificial									
Tin and manufactures of	87	5,987	4,670	36	36,308	20,070	1,917	8,210	14,357
Tobacco and manufactures of	198	4,[illegible]15	4,137	161	169,926	148,659	38,775	2,851	54,552
" pipes		13,487	1	18	8,[illegible]13	13,428	3,793	27	6,[illegible]68
Trawls and trawling spoons	257	2,103		209	21,810	4,209	1,036		1,416
Trunks, valises, hat boxes, &c	87	2,868	33	155	31,813	3,229	1,707	744	5,132
Turpentine, spirits of		0,[illegible]802		216	181,535	1,873	1,910	18,013	38,179
Twines and manufactures of	15	1,756	386	36	13,658	739	285	101	4,650
Umbrellas, parasols and sunshades	12	765	1,431	75	11,562	5,263	1,937	154	6,416
Unenumerated articles	33	4,842	298		31,472	4,908	2,237	1,900	9,693
[illegible], japans, &c	31	2,132	749	196	51,916	1,597	1,884	254	3,001
Vegetables	8,241	22,356	26	5,691	159,234	63,445	19,859	6,101	76,928
Vinegar		219		13	7,647	5,423	3,668		1,071
Watches, watch cases, movements, glasses, &c	97	933	950	109	257,860	3,093	2,808	70	28,045
Wax and manufactures of	3	663	1,544	13	13,411	1,013	305	936	2,327
Webbing		155	507		46,140	447	716	348	728
Whips, thongs and lashes		5			1,888	513	68		973
Willow and osiers									
Window cornices and cornice poles		371			5,483	520	192	73	425
Wood and manufactures of	13,897	20,808	8,877	1,762	6[illegible]23	54,455	36,010	33,200	347,155
Window shades and rollers	93	593		13	38,005	548	62	334	858
Wool and fabrics of	4,249	3 4,[illegible]74	4,282	16,955	5,240,016	249,140	160,411	43,044	1,015,839
Zinc and manufactures of		405			4,167	797	323	22	908
Damaged goods							33		1,941
Total dutiable goods	1,380,619	3,548,245	614,445	550,782	36,218,342	6,518,608	2,569,673	2,841,688	13,388,075

IMPORTS for Consumption by Ports—*Continued.*

Free Goods.	Brantford	Calgary.	Dawson.	Halifax.	Hamilton.	London.	Montreal.	Ottawa.	Quebec.
PRODUCE OF THE MINE.	$	$	$	$	$	$	$	$	$
Clay	2,206	....	9	728	12,592	1,247	48,166	8,587	1,190
Coal, anthracite	135,740	70	....	121,173	487,227	339,340	1,329,320	587,546	207,241
Minerals	340	....	....	15	20	1,179	28,354	....	....
Ores	192	....	....	....	8,580	....	2,375	20	....
Precious stones, not polished	380	106	25,977	89,239	164,776	2,837	592,526	7,384	53
Salt	....	....	....	40,747	739	....	116,861	25	44,722
Whiting	....	....	....	1,421	343	31	30,406	1,535	914
Other articles	9,277	47	....	6,318	13,248	4,599	56,880	9,976	3,492
Total	148,135	223	25,986	259,641	687,525	349,233	2,204,888	615,073	257,612
FISHERIES.									
Fish of all kinds	....	....	....	1,019,932	....	....	11,863	....	105
" oil	....	....	....	12,041	....	28	29,397	....	20
Other articles	....	....	....	16,085	....	49	904	142	39
Total	....	....	....	1,048,058	....	77	42,164	142	164
FOREST.									
Corkwood	....	....	....	2,309	384	....	25,003	....	....
" bark	....	....	....	....	....	....	94	....	....
Ivory nuts	....	....	....	....	....	....	1,992	....	....
Logs, round, and unmanufactured timber	....	....	....	32,729	....	3,336	1,833	....	1,589
Lumber and timber, planks, &c., sawn, not shaped	66,806	4,078	5,526	31,525	122,516	127,042	756,902	52,792	96,630
Other articles	777	....	....	1,001	10,929	83,216	24,608	15,044	307
Total	67,583	4,078	5,526	67,564	133,829	213,594	810,432	67,836	98,526
ANIMALS AND THEIR PRODUCTS.									
Animals for improvement of stock	25,491	10,710	25	1,045	19,931	25,969	209,588	1,739	37,846
Bristles	....	....	....	4	29,326	8,306	7,804	32	143
Fur skins, not dressed	....	202	9,462	6,229	29,836	5,245	1,935,538	51,932	344,097
Grease	512	3,367	....	2,975	25,642	9,767	9,817	543	4,151
Hides and skins, undressed	4,116	....	....	24,078	157,035	47,305	1,360,711	86	535,325

Silk, raw					349		283,047		
Wool	6,621			2,590	32,751		116,839	178,924	611
Other articles	172	27	12	8,228	4,626	4,939	112,204	3,358	3,229
Total	36,912	14,306	9,499	45,149	299,496	101,531	4,035,548	236,614	925,402
AGRICULTURAL PRODUCTS.									
Broom corn	568			613	18,812	9,226	4,732	3,429	5,152
Fibres, Mexican and vegetable	969			1,615	5,189	2,054	4,037	230	
Fruits, green	31,642	44	1,099	67,033	58,175	32,736	264,416	79,916	36,604
Hemp, undressed	161,631			137,566			390,648		
Indian corn	62,120		11	108,191	46,294	26,277	2,629,931	15,997	81,984
Seeds	3	12		449	9,092	1,987	1,460,113	489	129
Tobacco leaf for excise purposes	25,523	3,793		1,997	180,706	264,741	1,531,879		53,064
Other articles	109,465	402		372,217	5,058	5,355	72,503	6,545	1,815
Total	391,921	4,251	1,110	689,681	323,326	342,376	6,358,259	106,606	178,748
MANUFACTURED AND PARTIALLY MANUFACTURED ARTICLES.									
Bells for churches		110		235	941	49	26,135	821	23,946
Bolting cloth	172				302		546	52	216
Cotton wool and waste	11,125		190	160,719	657,534	29,590	2,147,778	57,906	816,215
Drugs and chemicals	24,569	8,184	205	113,996	128,214	244,609	1,130,480	81,268	37,406
Duck for belting and hose			2,480				40,772		
Fish hooks, nets, seines, &c.				78,232	6,472	217	12,202	3,223	12,268
Gutta percha, crude, rubber, &c.	1,042			151	32,308	83	992,464		7,797
Junk and oakum	4	100		6,684	1,011	106	11,558	1,903	3,012
Metals—									
Brass	2,725			5,053	78,586	66,943	433,920	9,524	1,873
Copper	4,686			9,007	132,179	65,435	2,148,687	8,338	30,171
Iron and steel	31,537	85,746	17,959	82,729	187,929	130,691	1,227,224	82,898	148,393
Tin	488	312		96,342	443,343	101,790	903,484	2,318	22,948
Zinc	11,186	33		13,360	2,463	16,269	190,220		10,675
Other	134	2,700		16,851	30,168	1,263	182,638	125	626
Newspapers and magazines	48	12	8	781	89	501	87,996	217	317
Oil-cake meal and cotton-seed cake and meal				905	1,113	3,890	2,159	42	
Oil, cocoanut and palm		3,243		6	434	3,313	25,319	8	
Pitch and tar, pine	5	31	4	2,829	117	343	3,598		270
Plaits, straw, Tuscan and grass	237			884	827	8,668	29,999	750	151
Rags	1,935		120	165	438	313	124,673	1,641	3,394
Resin or rosin	6,021	4,374		3,716	15,691	2,421	76,994	14,659	14,407
Veneers of ivory									
Other articles	92,126	68,525	713	381,155	731,428	190,955	1,957,941	175,428	163,250
Total	188,040	173,370	21,679	973,800	2,451,587	867,449	11,756,787	441,121	1,297,325

IMPORTS for Consumption by Ports—*Continued.*

Free Goods.	Sault Ste. Marie.	St. John, N.B.	St. Johns, Que.	Sydney.	Toronto.	Vancouver.	Victoria.	Windsor.	Winnipeg.
PRODUCE OF THE MINE.	$	$	$	$	$	$	$	$	$
Clay	8,916	2,190	18,569	46,488	18,818	1,324	163	1,016	1,438
Coal, anthracite	65,059	229,014	699,845	4,745	2,130,151			117,661	35,243
Minerals			3,870		6,903	839	198	88	9
Ores	693,915		1,605	461,225		475		26	
Precious stones, not polished	2,351	1,253			23,532	39,647	30,160		52,331
Salt		47,150		1,186	11	25,898	10,618		27
Whiting		687	18		3,024	12	507	392	2,607
Other articles	743	5,129	8,695	41,057	466,381	433	3,678	11,980	2,287
Total	770,984	285,423	732,602	554,701	2,648,820	68,628	45,324	131,163	93,942
FISHERIES.									
Fish of all kinds		2,060		2,090	214				
Fish oil		2,720			12,256				
Other articles					664	59	54		62
Total		4,780		2,090	13,134	59	54		62
FOREST.									
Corkwood		70			46,546				
Corkwood bark									
Ivory nuts									
Logs, round, and manufactured timber	5,586		514		50	1,871	6,894	6,796	42,468
Lumber and timber, planks, &c., sawn, not shaped	17,998	64,406	93,801	9,974	516,360	32,852	7,580	116,259	332,905
Other articles	8,046		400		47,868	346	200	106,959	90,495
Total	31,630	64,476	94,715	9,974	610,824	35,069	14,683	230,014	465,868
ANIMALS AND THEIR PRODUCE.									
Aminals for improvement of stock	70	36,336	1,042		59,386	7,761	983	19,860	66,648
Bristles		30,024			32,497		3	16,791	5
Fur skins, not dressed	513	1,985	34		774,280	901	22,023		47,544
Grease	2,120	8.274			54,647	2,620	6,393		8,841
Hides and skins, undressed		113,222	18,851		2,692,074		13	4,075	184

Silk, raw			169,072			190			
Wool			8,759		416,644	63			
Other articles	73	7,165	14		300,586	12,686	1,300	1,010	4,594
Total	2,776	197,006	197,772		4,330,114	24,221	30,715	41,736	127,816
AGRICULTURAL PRODUCTS.									
Broom corn		20,721			45,123	3,584	232	148	3,346
Fibres, Mexican and vegetable	78	9,679			23,517	19	1,066	1,634	318
Fruits, green	4,065	74,953	906	9,366	326,003	35,726	9,480	26,571	65,751
Hemp, undressed					141,061				
Indian corn	3,557	110,398	30,622		168,198	12,809	18,134	806,782	679
Seeds		133	274		35,564	2,559	2,761	6,444	99
Tobacco leaf for excise purposes	1,036	8,658	33,602	108	299,116	18,656	15,404	5,435	75,249
Other articles	38	1,009	32	96	178,577	4,200	3,004	634	3,720
Total	8,774	225,551	65,436	9,570	1,217,159	77,553	50,081	847,648	[illegible]
MANUFACTURED AND PARTIALLY MANUFACTURED ARTICLES.									
Bells for [illegible]	120	823			519	10	6	41	1,422
Bolting cloth		10			6,995			7	1,110
Cotton wool and waste	2,022	403,941	9,363	4,162	87,117	8,424	2,283	1,671	12,925
Drugs, dyes and chemicals	5,051	235,619	56,211	5,512	1,413,160	27,119	176,424	94,043	59,005
Duck for belting and hose					62,984	36			
Fish hooks, nets, seines, &c.	7,152	28,321	51	165	90,850	169,714	26,538	2,953	49,576
Gutta percha, crude, [illegible], &c.		12	268,189		646,129	96			64
Junk and oakum	160	3,903			4,155	1,090	2,259	200	3,404
Metals—									
Brass	692	9,948	1,317	2,916	133,280	7,408	1,161	13,383	4,846
Copper	2,457	54,192	2,076	831	250,232	3,134	2,095	17,984	4,657
Iron and steel	125,744	85,752	29,518	74,255	549,982	72,506	58,569	368,074	95,221
Tin	10,986	73,263	6,169	2,827	592,376	478,088	80,786	2,811	78,499
Zinc		11,941		167	96,380	9,727	924	517	3,338
Other	148	14,053	750	24	199,774	6,465	3,992	229	4,723
Newspapers and magazines		219			139,852	12,040	6,486	22,073	1,229
Oil-cake meal and cotton-seed cake and meal	26	2,698	495		3	168	4,170	31	112
Oil, cocoanut and palm		203			95,354	884	2,118	1,462	17,054
Pitch and tar, pine	54	1,027			1,302	483	701	28	1,522
Plaits, straw, Tuscan and grass	120	6,891	4,495	135	101,266	253	486	87	1,019
Rags	32,093	3,930	18		27,651	984	92	808	634
Resin or rosin	1,694	5,282			110,406	3,770	3,659	7,211	15,814
Veneers of ivory									
Other [illegible]	667,495	236,318	8,548	255,562	1,901,559	120,266	42,255	72,530	960,588
Total	856,014	1,178,346	387,200	346,556	6,511,326	922,665	415,004	606,143	1,316,762

IMPORTS for Consumption by Ports—*Continued.*

FREE GOODS.	Brantford	Calgary.	Dawson.	Halifax.	Hamilton.	London.	Montreal.	Ottawa.	Quebec.
MISCELLANEOUS ARTICLES.	$	$	$	$	$	$	$	$	$
Articles for the Dominion Government	19	433	389	120,422	2,377	2,036	316,611	414,933	487,012
" army and navy				2,885					2,287
Coffee, green (see Dutiable)				9,121	64,965	29,301	178,251	22,676	
Models of inventions	501				1,426	10	8,609	25	267
Settlers' effects	31,726	165,875	1,661	21,909	99,354	57,601	326,667	85,715	[illegible]
Tea (see Dutiable)	7,422	18,938		225,875	148,934	72,597	765,070	55,458	51,392
Coin and bullion			119,977	15,698	107,766	3,848	2,536,723	1,062	329
Other articles	6,785	344	3,002	47,025	20,447	12,751	991,665	35,754	18,803
Total	46,453	185,590	125,029	442,935	443,269	158,144	5,123,596	615,623	2,433,101
Total Free	879,044	381,818	188,829	3,526,828	4,341,032	2,032,404	30,331,674	2,083,015	5,190,878
" Dutiable	1,353,769	1,004,679	733,750	5,340,931	6,633,423	3,336,896	50,490,066	3,331,969	3,945,896
Grand total	2,232,813	1.386,497	922,579	8,867,759	10,974,455	5,369,300	80,821,740	5,414,984	[illegible]

IMPORTS for Consumption by Ports—*Continued.*

FREE GOODS.	Sault Ste. Marie.	St. John, N.B.	St. Johns, Que.	Sydney.	Toronto.	Vancouver.	Victoria.	Windsor, Ont.	Winnipeg.
MISCELLANEOUS ARTICLES.	$	$	$	$	$	$	$	$	$
Articles for the Dominion Government	7,818	29,328	377	45	100,020	4,847	14,475	98	12,521
" army and navy	....	....	....	....	....	....	1,435	....	....
Coffee, green (see Duitable)	....	1,955	....	....	149,052	96,537	17,757	1,750	[illegible]
Models of inventions	40	125	....	50	1,416	542	....	334	189
Settlers' effects	37,776	29,803	28,065	8,944	314,745	129,437	55,710	129,395	[illegible]
Tea (see Dutiable)	474	773,925	....	81	781,219	256,964	25,293	2,181	273,466
Coin and bullion	12	222	....	....	4,257,332	7,952	1,497	4,792	364
Other articles	50,318	13,154	690	10,266	306,013	50,565	23,301	247,219	29,429
Total	96,438	848,512	29,132	19,386	5,909,797	546,844	139,468	385,769	2,048,679
Total Free	1,766,616	2,804,094	1,506,857	942,536	21,241,174	1,675,039	695,329	2,242,473	4,202,291
" Dutiable	1,380,619	3,548,245	614,445	550,782	36,218,342	6,518,608	2,569,673	2,841,688	13,388,075
Grand total	3,147,235	6,352,339	2,121,302	1,493,318	57,459,516	8,193,647	3,265,002	5,084,161	17,590,366

No. 12.—EXPORTS of Canadian Produce from the undermentioned Ports—Fiscal Year, 1906.

—	Abercorn.	Bridgeburg.	Coaticook.	Fort William.	Halifax.	Hemmingford.	Montreal.	Nanaimo.	New Westminster.	Niagara Falls.
THE MINE.	$	$	$	$	$	$	$	$	$	$
Arsenic										
Asbestos	20	198,703	19,144		10,030	31,727	214,863		180	
Barytes, ground and unground										
Coal	984				126,958			2,098,648	471	
Chromite (chromic iron)										
Felspar		7,072								
Gold-bearing quartz, dust, nuggets, &c.		7,239			2,100		114,343	178,871	2,540,719	4,636
Gypsum or plaster, crude					9,437					
Metals, viz.—										
Copper, fine, contained in ore, matte, regulus, &c.					1,534	348	382,404	795,380	811,410	
Copper, black or coarse	453	348				905	71,574			
Lead, metallic, contained in ore, &c.							937		68,590	
Lead, pig										2,344
Nickel, fine, contained in ore, matte or speiss							324,288			73
Platinum, contained in concentrates, &c.										
Silver, metallic, contained in ore, concentrates, &c.		40,020			100	4,500	583,456	109,556	250,001	1,251,542
Mica	921	4,995	376		1,965	57,334	20,403			248
Mineral pigment, iron oxides, ochres, &c.						3,304	1,297			
Mineral water	34	1,010			793	111	1,200			16
Oil, mineral, coal and kerosene (crude)										
" " (refined)							128			
Ores, viz.—										
Iron	198	3,049				868	125			46
Antimony					6,157					
Other		14,430			4,460	18,605	28,152		2,808	9,090
Plumbago, crude ore and concentrates, &c.	11						58			2,031
Pyrites		12,662	10							380
Salt					15		800			1,022
Sand and gravel	40	16,498								8,910
Stone, ornamental, granite, marble, &c., unwrought							2,240	620		
" building, freestone, limestone, &c., "										240
" for manufacture of grindstones, rough						1,619				
Other articles	2,215	41,107	211		234	1,986	5,241	337	407	3,666
Total	4,876	347,133	19,741		163,783	121,307	1,751,509	3,183,412	3,674,586	1,284,244

THE FISHERIES.										
Codfish, including haddock, ling and pollock, fresh.					1,150					
" dry salted	10		3		2,470,765	38,854	2,409			
" wet salted					2,743					
" pickled										
Tongues and sounds					2,449					
Mackerel, fresh			1		12,473	34				
" canned					36		207			
" pickled					144,531					
Halibut, fresh	18,462		5		426	4				
" pickled	3,164									
Herring, fresh or frozen		27	65		2,021	82		4,792	208	
" pickled			4		264,054	340	13	10,867	1,630	
" [illegible]d					8	895				
" smoked			8		9,736	14,027	50		298	
Sea fish, [illegible]r, fresh			123		2,360	49,127				
" pickled			122		18,612					
" preserved	25		321		1,779	1,438	337		175	
Oysters, fresh			23		70	6	202			
Lobsters, fresh		3,075			89,508	4,968				8
" canned			498		1,731,959	60,101	63,094			
Bait, fish										
Clams or other			1		272			407		
Salmon, fresh			12,738		18,287	15,945	17,657		50,899	7
" [illegible]			12		47	2				
" canned					5,735	3,603	418,175	712	409,438	
" pickled			64		22,683	4,213	211	10,180	70,903	
Salmon or lake trout			47			78				5
Fish, all other, fresh	6,620	326,926	3,228		2,349	14,958	47		1,096	79,588
" pickled			644		2,521	39			1,241	
Fish oil, cod					29,887		49			
" se[illegible]l					4,536					
" whale					82		40,775			
" [illegible]r					125					
Furs or skins, the produce of fish or [illegible] animals.					13,146	46,940	36,340			
[illegible]		862			3,768	16	405	7	31	12
Total	28,281	330,890	17,907		4,858,118	255,670	579,971	26,965	535,919	79,620
THE FOREST.										
Ashes, pot and pearl			4,666			5,642	23,417			718
All other	1,277	6,191	1,957			335				36,671
Bark for tanning	6,304		1,428				1,187			
Firewood	1,980	2,964	937						188	1,625
Knees and futtocks						7,385				
Logs, cedar, capable of being made into shingle bolts		614							10,359	41
" elm			100			270	2,160			

No. 12.—EXPORTS of Canadian Produce from the undermentioned Ports—Fiscal Year, 1906.

—	Prescott.	Quebec.	Rossland.	St. Armand.	St. Johns, Que.	St. John, N.B.	Sault Ste. Marie	Sydney.	Vancouver.	Winnipeg.
THE MINE.	$	$	$	$	$	$	$	$	$	$
Arsenic	3,116				25					
Asbestos	400	43,857		115,614	8,706	77,519			1,486	
Barytes, ground and unground										
Coal				4,844		9,852		1,365,062	283	48
Chromite (chromic iron)	2,920									
Felspar										
Gold-bearing quartz, dust, nuggets, &c.	708,663		341,620	3,773	120,719				71,913	
Gypsum or plaster, crude						7,408				
Metals, viz.—										
Copper, fine, contained in ore, matte, regulus, &c.	2,342,149		83,886		6,159	83,219	2,167		92,311	
Copper, black, &c.				230						
Lead, metallic, contained in ore, &c.					7				54,703	
Lead, pig		1,637							114,961	
Nickel, fine, contained in ore, matte or speiss	1,564,250					278,325				
Platinum, contained in concentrates, &c.										
Silver, metallic, contained in ore, concentrates, &c.	396,786		20,655	3,646	977,133	20,040			276,178	
Mica	36,983			1	140,877	12,478				
Mineral pigment, iron oxides, ochres, &c.										
Mineral water	31			15	22	23				
Oil, mineral, coal and kerosene, crude										
" " refined						1,685			3	99
Ores, viz.—										
Iron	986						338,200			
Other	63,216			366	79,015	8,128			114	
Plumbago, crude ore and concentrates, &c.										
Salt						2,973	676			
Sand and gravel				122			275			95
Stone, ornamental, granite, marble, &c., unwrought				335	50					
" building, freestone, limestone, &c. "				192					880	
" for manufacture of grindstones, rough				270	233					
Other articles	5,942		40	1,140	2,754	953	6,792		2,411	6
Total	5,125,442	45,494	446,201	130,548	1,335,700	502,603	348,110	1,365,062	615,243	248
THE FISHERIES.										
Codfish, including haddock, ling and pollock, fresh					33	398				

" dry salted		102,925		53,577		57,931			8,909	
" not salted						393				
" tongues and sounds						4,822				
Mackerel, fresh					2,383	7,270				
" pickled				10	1,237	9,771				18
Halibut, fresh	2,030				40	60			20	
Herring, fresh or frozen				7	30	19,372			320	
" pickled		15,960		3		9,244			19,571	
" canned						389			22	
" smoked				4	1	18,714			92	
Sea fish, other, fresh				728	32,571	1,614				
" pickled						4,200			3,173	
" preserved					16	4,025			2,893	
Oysters, fresh		147		98	716	180				
Lobsters, fresh				3		9,629	2,770			
" canned		13,730		774	5,932	206,593	2,028		2	
Bait fish		39								
Clams or other					73	73,495			509	
Salmon, fresh	9,958	4,757		82	8,171	46,845			241,505	
" smoked					44				108	
" canned	7,190				10	10,090			3,688,655	
" pickled	51,438			30		32			[illegible]	
" or lake trout				40	142		3,973			
Fish, all other, fresh	80,708		25	1,525	29,299	8,795	57,391		1,247	13,287
" pickled	6,518	523		1,719	253	1,920	2,747		7,453	
Fish oil, cod		1,380		29	1	2,706				
" other						494			5,155	
Furs or skins, the produce of fish or marine animal	171,710	289			6	75				
Other articles					158	882			8	1,698
Total	329,552	139,750	25	58,629	81,116	499,939	68,909		4,086,474	15,003
THE FOREST.										
Ashes, pot and pearl				455	377	1,876				
All other	1,339			16,941	297					
Bark for tanning				96	48		4,710			
Firewood				7,040	6,288	6,182				60
Knees and futtocks									190	
Logs, cedar, capable of being made into shingle bolts									9,762	
" elm				1,140		3,820				
" hemlock							1,363			
" pine							15,697			
" spruce					13,881		765			
" all other				140	1,952	926	48,605		97,556	
Lumber, viz.—										
Battens										
Basswood	3,385			2,127	13,052	788				
Butternut										
Deals, pine	9,159	61,536		7,299	28,234	18,113				

No. 12.—EXPORTS of Canadian Produce from the undermentioned Ports—Fiscal Year, 1906—*Continued.*

—	Abercorn.	Bridgeburg.	Coaticook.	Fort William.	Halifax.	Hemmingford.	Montreal.	Nanaimo.	New Westminster.	Niagara Falls.
THE FOREST—*Con.*	$	$	$	$	$	$	$	$	$	$
Logs, oak							80			
" pine		765					3,550			504
" spruce	8,891		890		104					
" all other	6,045	2,866	6,581		105	121	20,041	93,196	22,651	1,601
Lumber, viz.—										
Battens					5,533					
Basswood	1,795		3,771		1,965	240	6,257			3,741
Butternut										
Deals, pine		4,818	20,303		5,654	22,671	2,035,143			
Spruce and other			1421		[illegible]	20,669	407,560			
Deal ends			7,384		22,227		181,974			
Laths	1,181	66,978	1,681		79,802	61,874	1,731	3,214		16,424
Palings										
Pickets			1,325				23,807			
Planks and boards	196,222	326,833	371,308		238,607	594,207	706,040	337,862	57,163	628,165
Joists										
Scantling	300		5,926		79,435	5,619				
Shingles	38,141	12,737	20,801		3,888	85,434	11,437	13,940	129,758	7,187
Shooks, box										1,195
" other		595	65,942		26,233	21,088	42,519			2,873
Staves and headings	194	16,065	1,529		3,327	178	25,982	1,395		27,806
All other lumber, N.E.S.	8,281	3,516	43,364		6,722	15,594	42,399			1,487
Match blocks			28,698		450					
Masts and spars					2,214					
Piling	24								2,009	
Poles, hop, hoop, telegraph and other	428	17,768	140		78	17,614	2,405	2,580	8,178	15,770
Posts, cedar, tamarack and other	114	337	460			1,078	101			317
Shingle bolts of pine or cedar									16,063	
Sleepers and railroad ties	1,518		2,923		2,932	64,105	8,320			
Stave bolts		143								35
Timber, square, viz.—										
Ash							1,434			
Birch			10,265		21,162	75	99,791			
Elm						460	7,352			100
Maple							400			275
Oak										
Pine, red							2,300			
" white	30					3,404	8,460			240

All other	595	1,793	875	....	296	786	1,631	....	....	403
Wood, blocks and other, for pulp	17,532	8,497	383,404	....	....	14,327	109,994	....	....	21,343
Other articles of the forest	624	1,255	10	....	671	1	25	....	....	1,229
Total	291,476	474,735	998,089	....	1,170,548	943,180	3,777,497	452,187	246,369	769,850
ANIMALS AND THEIR PRODUCE.										
Animals, horses, one year old or less	....	450	....	....	100	....	....	....	....	....
" " over one year old	4,790	123,626	6,880	....	11,455	7,900	41,315	....	11,480	[illegible]
" cattle, one year old or less	55	1,001	195	....	....	3,812	3,500	....	....	1,237
" " over one year old	607,413	542,949	819,563	....	59,420	150	7,249,168	....	90	[illegible]
" swine	....	2,267	49	....	221	....	2,700	....	693	1,264
" sheep, one year old or less	73,134	259,862	32,177	....	951	52,482	....	....	....	308
" " over one year old	57,996	160,747	41,925	....	4,245	353	110,771	....	2,725	8,183
Poultry	16	22,156	65	....	705	6	134	....	78	6,069
All other	25	4,526	185	....	50	171	1,050	....	435	6,362
Bones	312	3,905	....	....	15	562	1,900	....	....	11,253
Butter	13	3,503	89,614	....	150,834	4,724	[illegible]	42	5,055	841
Cheese	24,495	4,839	3,113,999	....	112,651	23,612	18,868,335	....	....	518,907
Eggs	40	940	39,112	....	26,017	2	385,872	....	14	304
Furs, dressed	....	....	....	....	....	4,203	439	....	....	....
" undressed	2,473	17,552	31,552	....	60,744	413,770	476,330	....	6,749	53,375
Glue and grease scraps	3,104	3,952	138	....	....	51,111	7,283	....	540	65,001
Glue stock	4	632	....	....	11	592	....	....	....	....
Hair	4,240	22,809	1,694	....	....	2,173	8,606	....	....	32,529
Hides and skins, other than fur	385,390	568,863	21,440	....	14,231	175,260	26,039	....	12,819	176,597
Horns and hoofs	716	....	119	....	539	4,145	804	....	42	642
Honey	48	407	23	....	69	....	2,325	....	....	138
Lard	....	....	5,600	....	59	....	6,163	....	....	....
Meats, viz.—										
Bacon	37,390	137	2,201,001	....	1,599	2	3,937,217	....	....	4,384,540
Beef	6,500	158	5,087	....	2,534	....	9,494	....	....	128,295
Hams	....	450	58,674	....	3,097	84	275,689	....	21	29,143
Mutton	....	242	....	....	682	....	....	....	....	248
Pork	....	....	6,770	....	11,497	....	9,941	....	....	9497
Poultry, dressed or undressed	13,282	532	32,429	....	19,529	75	317	....	....	352
Game " "	4	15	6	....	92	13	....	....	....	507
Tongues	....	....	18	....	5	....	612	....	....	[illegible]
Canned	....	1	25,857	....	26,985	....	1,270,934	....	....	14,944
All other, N.E.S	2,500	9,931	59,618	....	2,517	....	48,202	....	....	17,421
Milk and cream, condensed	....	38	....	....	6,529	3,150	38,561	....	....	39,918
Oil, lard	....	....	....	....	....	....	....	....	....	....
" neatsfoot and other animal, N.E.S	....	....	....	....	....	....	....	....	....	....
Sheep pelts	123	13	....	....	....	35	....	....	5,745	23,190
Tails	39	75	....	....	15	....	12	....	....	1,428
Tallow	23	....	....	....	490	....	10,129	....	....	....
Wool	32,460	2	396	....	25	9,735	33,531	....	25,248	7,933

No. 12.—EXPORTS of Canadian Produce from the undermentioned Ports—Fiscal Year, 1906—*Continued.*

—	Prescott.	Quebec.	Rossland.	St. Armand.	St. Johns, Que.	St. John, N.B.	Sault Ste. Marie.	Sydney.	Vancouver.	Winnipeg.
THE FOREST—*Con.*	$ cts.	$	$	$	$	$	$	$	$	$
Lumber—*Con.*										
Spruce and other		856 775		4,057	23,694	1,[illegible]976				
Deal ends		11,358			1,930	6,855				
Laths	52,070	4,771		3,151	109,976	405,713	139,192		7,052	
Palings										
Pickets	8,499				18,379	5,239	48,879		2,508	
Planks and boards	1,589,880	48,399		256,079	3,301,296	632,566	2,827,417	1,567	454,065	
Joists					3,641					
Scantling		18,023		65	4,938	302,362				
Shingles	70,524	4,621		88,682	92,226	102,821	6,374		275	
Shooks, box									831	
" other		92,977		2,837	285	99,538			500	
Staves, other and headings	112	223		3,463	472	10,069			3,475	
All other lumber, N.E.S.	425	2,316	20	8,179	93,793	60,037		128	100	
Match blocks					145	633				
Masts and spars						233			410	
Piling						13,203				
Poles, hop, hoop, telegraph and other	2,885		209		4,222	2,934				
Posts, cedar, tamarack and other				154	992		1,631			
Shingle bolts, of pine or cedar										
Sleepers and railroad ties	9,133	4,351		577	52,979		6,343			
Timber, square, viz.:—										
Ash		9,419								
Birch		66,131				53,212				
Elm	17	243,650			90					
Oak		182,260								
Pine, red		3,324					2,986			
" white		954,410			749					
All other	636	17,790		90	17	9,160				
Wood, blocks and other, for pulp	36,183	199,586		33,488	1,052,775	4,023	75,958			
Other articles of the forest	4,726				1	918		191	15	
Total	1,788,973	2,781,920	229	436,060	4,826,729	3,724,697	3,179,920	1,886	576,739	60
ANIMALS AND THEIR PRODUCE.										
Animals, horses, one year old or less										
" " over one year old	12,169	1,000	395	13,784	6,692	19,132	1,215	1,215	1,345	6,050

" cattle, one year old or less	2,266				325	920				15
" " over one year	846	44,425		724,662	1,550	1,291,074			3,750	140
" swine	6				500				20	114
" sheep, one year old or less	4,742			1,630	35,042			20		
" " over one year old	20,374			24,977	135	16,474		87		
Poultry	351		19	746	52	4			20	
All other	69			526	1,032		90		180	5,615
Bones				9,186	3,159				25	
Butter	7	466		54	21,212	99,350	19	2,640	12,833	40
Cheese		123,935		197,414	6,662	1,409,334			9,643	24
Eggs	22			4	13	31,382	16	60	50	
Furs, dressed					42,511	1,639				
" undressed	36,441	21,547		5,739	266,101	71,926	2,253		8,957	269,218
Grease and grease scraps		1,331		7,842		60				
Glue stock				605	82	330				
Hair				3,473	7,826	1,033				
Hides and skins, other than fur	86,308	1,180	429	153,527	79,502	64,646	182,581		86,260	243
Horns and hoofs		50		2,515	1,927	25			1,500	
Honey				192	51	5	8		78	26
Lard								8	370	
Meats, viz.—										
Bacon				743,797	49	321,324			192	
Beef		5,695		2,825		8,533		90		
Hams				40,406	94	11,469			142	
Mutton				7	3,213			15		
Pork		2,243		15,316	132	2,355		20		
Poultry, dressed or undressed	785			18,332	8,530	6,331		30		
Game	2			559	1,770	270				
Tongues				802						
Canned						25,426			837	
All other, N.E.S.				11,727	3,972	13,462	2		2,609	
Milk and cream, condensed						26,620	44		5,146	
Oil—Neatsfoot and other animal, N.E.S.										
Sheep pelts	14,848				21				231	
Tails	10					97				
Tallow				1,477		5,357			4,710	
Wool	350			226,689		3,574				
Other articles	38	20		459	2,064	627	45	32	19	35
Total	179,634	201,892	843	2,209,272	494,219	3,432,779	186,273	4,217	138,917	281,520
AGRICULTURAL PRODUCTS.										
Balsam		1,452		146	1,070					
Cider				390					18	
Flax				32,706						680
Fruit, viz.—										
Apples, dried		3		44 231		6				
" green or ripe	34	4,701		221,276	5,275	68,472	498		2,263	
Berries, of all kinds	655			606	9	23,858	11,806		200	14

No. 12.—EXPORTS of Canadian Produce from the undermentioned Ports—Fiscal Year, 1906—*Continued.*

—	Abercorn.	Bridgeburg.	Coaticook.	Fort William.	Halifax.	Hemmingford.	Montreal.	Nanaimo.	New Westminster	Niagara Falls.
ANIMALS AND THEIR PRODUCE—*Con.*	$	$	$	$	$	$	$	$	$	$
Other articles	13	2,406	4,822		209	1,797	28,522		14,019	55,095
Total	1,256,598	1,758,986	6,599,008		518,122	758,919	39,486,925	42	85,753	5,772,287
AGRICULTURAL PRODUCTS.										
Balsam	555		4,871			2,081	288			
Cider			2,365		5,018		1,449			
Flax		16,672		70,362						92,463
Fruit, viz.: Apples, dried		2	2,909		1,149	1,400	7,675			11,620
" " green or ripe	9,790	64,651	384,672		882,058	10,196	2,118,645		31	255,814
" Berries, of all kinds		589	18,407		360	908				1,206
" Canned or preserved	44	973	28,348		9,816	869	139,057			18,500
" All other, N.E.S.	36	3,809	1,140		3,768	156	5,008		7	92,822
Grain and products of, viz.:—										
Barley		513	58,305		98		94,091			69,130
Beans		8,681	51		3,281	100	16,890			10,368
Buckwheat			2,337				41,571			8,921
Indian corn					613		5			
Oats	4,147	2,818	28,800	62,373	63,425	7	41,080			148,590
Peas	2,497	17,051	134,305		3,534		115,547			263,109
" split		93	3,352		54,239		960			66,054
Rye										
Wheat	6,773	2,459	1,244,042	11,223,923	112,808		10,428,160			94,130
Other grain					10					2,080
Bran	64,854	9,116	12,389		14,369		145,439			01,061
Flour of wheat	41,493	16,589	560,294		303,955	8,753	2,566,290		1,634	1,158,199
Indian meal					2,348		1,055			500
Oatmeal	59,701	5,461	81,140		126		91,925			4,821
Meal, all other	1,755	1,547	1,489		1,641		6,622			488
Hay	120,681	7,202	81,241		37,215	67,256	94,059			50,721
Hemp					555					
Hops							4,017			
Malt					87		2,122			2
Maple sugar	62	4,241	468		42	2,425	1,322		1,997	6
" syrup	64	197	56		92	180	1,087			43
Nuts							8			90

Seeds—										
Clover	27,447	258,595	18,888			6	28,914			562,428
Grass		11,577			21		38			10,515
All other	32	9,088	92		27	19	9			4,192
Straw	1,156		1,682		483	1,892	98			50
Tobacco, leaf	380	359	1			2,476	7		265	221
Trees, shrubs and plants	37	1,815	19		451	275	59		26	2,811
Vegetables canned or preserved	8,160		487		1,919		5,154			4,673
Potatoes	407	506	1,111		419,508	8,301	1,726		9	236
Turnips	3,829	33,347	971		1,575	434				33,508
All other vegetables		283	658		6,712	803	1,692			229
Cereal foods, prepared	410,973	521	3,444		2,469	27	426,637			3,635
Other articles	195	6,169	674		5,200	948	2,300		62	6,554
Total	765,068	484,984	2,678,808	11,356,658	1,937,972	109,512	17,244,406		4,031	3,989,190
MANUFACTURES.										
Agricultural implements	22,371	14,148	1,736		2,222		167,041			1,823,158
Aluminum in pigs, bars, &c.			11,200			44,087	354,959			
" in any other form					8					
Books, pamphlets, maps, &c.	8,277	7,086	3,189	30	22,619	4,682	59,565		1,460	52,660
Biscuits and bread		4,276			19,227	7	3,554		41	3,406
Bricks	2	93			146		1,594			
Buttons		4,618								763
Candles		9,616								
Cartridges	39				30	16,089	6,002			3,068
Charcoal		3,000					3,011			41
Cement		3	19		1,774	18	207	829	18	570
Cinders										1,023
Clay manufactures of										
Clothing and wearing apparel	356	5,935	1,165		5,574	340	10,311		295	4,785
Coke							910	10,500		
Cordage, rope and twine	461	10,883	14		91,243	10,596	1,107			33,150
Cotton fabrics		290	9,428		35,842	27,738	8,164			89,458
Cottons, other	1,367	111	102		192	2	2,102			7,923
Cotton waste	18,797		943			5,627	724			124
Drugs, chemicals and medicines, N.E.S.	8,215	36,004	61,477		176,496	4,619	214,954	500	1,455	13,757
Dyestuffs		2					1,681			664
Electrical apparatus	55	695			595	619	1,814			10,503
Electrotypes		1,028	11		29	203	106		16	587
Extract of hemlock bark					23,920		550			
Explosives and fulminates of all kinds					40,212					924
Felt, manufactures of	569				150	33				58
Fertilizers	9,904	12,948	20		468	1,044				9,699
Fur, manufactures of		217	50		6,228	371	2,570		20	795
Glass and glassware, N.E.S.		508	9		965	66	4,566		5	711
Grindstones, manufactured			360		1,590					
Gypsum or plaster, ground					132		500			
Hats and caps		100	3		628	66	991			513

No. 12.—Exports of Canadian Produce from the undermentioned Ports—Fiscal Year, 1906.

—	Prescott.	Quebec.	Rossland.	St. Armand.	St. Johns, Que.	St. John, N.B.	Sault Ste. Marie	Sydney.	Vancouver.	Winnipeg.
AGRICULTURAL PRODUCTS—*Con.*	$	$	$	$	$	$	$	$	$	$
Fruits—*Con.*										
Canned or preserved		675		9,633	6	[illegible]	25		641	
All other, N.E.S.	277		8	17,569	1,233	5,806	128		635	
Grain and products of, viz.—										
Barley				2		247,048				
Beans		1,046		771		2,839			372	
Buckwheat					950	3,307				
Indian corn				14	16	23,557				
Oats				894		249,691		1,588	1,577	
Peas				31,510	5,243	38,059	1,345		627	
Peas, split				5,895		[illegible]			675	
Rye										
Wheat	16,890	25,564		20,820	793,972	5,435,596			105	125
Other grain		108		30						
Bran	109	1,590		28,610		[illegible]		95		210
Flour of wheat	75,237	35,913		90,586	21,712	991,356			85,743	820
Bran Meal		110		840	8	[illegible]				
Oatmeal		1,186		29,213		[illegible]				
Meal all other				1,300		[illegible]				
Hay	2,227	1,640		336,237	172,872	[illegible]	50	787	110	
Hops						2,413			6,841	
Malt										
Maple sugar	1	82		99	97	112	6,434		593	
" syrup	22			98	70	182	90		1,322	
Nuts										
Seeds—										
Clover				80,475	4,150	20,666	320			
Grass				1,045			214			113
All other				62	91	5,293				
Straw	128			5,172	4,295	1,769				
Tobacco, leaf				4,104	1,020	10,225				
Trees, shrubs and plants	20			1	33	56	285		152	
Tomatoes canned or preserved				1,690		7,015				
Potatoes	1,047			632	1,555	26,154		501	5,345	
Turnips				943		205	75	6		
All other vegetables	80			2,628	5,827	887	138	26	4,919	48
Cereal foods, prepared				9,452	2,035	163,516		653	6,099	

Other articles	3			1,659	856	33,249	61		3,480	
Total	96,730	74,070	8	990,269	1,022,395	7,753,634	21,469	3,656	121,707	2,010
MANUFACTURES.										
Agricultural implements	4,440			244,832	64	99,474	275		98,878	245
Aluminum in pigs, bars, &c		27,249		130		131,499				
" in any other form				920		49,063				
Books, pamphlets, maps, &c	377	1,624	107	11,106	6,006	22,043	1,349		8,506	415
Biscuits and bread	1	1,084		334	20	4,219			590	
Bricks				95	3		227	178		
Buttons										
Candles										
Cartridges				2	132	3,147			6,501	
Charcoal							47,618		15	
Cement					1	39		1,702	2,979	
Clay, manufactures of										
Clothing and wearing apparel	440	44		1,160	1,203	6,303	679	25	7,443	703
Coke										
Cordage, rope and twine				17,652		93	15,481		110	
Cotton fabrics				35,399	1	12,145			814,513	
Cottons, other		63		769	1,435	4,574			458	
Cotton waste	11			408	16,082	4,138		119		
Drugs, chemicals and medicines, N.E.S	27,503	683	3	14,947	5,412	173,931	7,653	14,663	14,093	125
Dyestuffs					347					
Electrical apparatus	40	220	12	28	152	388	52	468	4,847	5
Electrotypes				88	229	454			8	25
Extract of hemlock bark						41,028				
Explosives and fulminates of all kinds	116,418	784	11	225			29			
Felt, manufactures of					73					
Fertilizers				15,609	36,287	1,123			18,583	
Fur, manufactures of		325		94	2,981	3,390				75
Glass and glassware, N.E.S.	93	153		30	448	360			206	
Grindstones, manufactured						50				
Gypsum or plaster, ground						964				
Hats and caps	2		4	12	77	4	2		17	
Household effects, N.E.S	14,907	3,575	4,574	69,205	56,884	33,614	34,794	120	45,125	4,615
Ice										
Indian rubber, manufactures of	1,983			1,517	2,317	5,446	1,264		87,772	
" scrap and other	4,364		100	39,964	8,963	5,651			505	
Iron and steel and manufactures of, viz.:—										
Stoves				52	122	172			204	
Castings, N.E.S.	48			247	199	954	44	43	6,816	
Pig iron										
Machinery, N.E.S.	12,230	647	105	10,641	19,824	20,334	1,505	28,917	53,296	45
Sewing machines	55		356	620	326	191	275		549	30
Typewriters		55			893	38,110			472	
Scrap iron or steel	700			638	5,477	165				
Hardware, N.E.S.	418	14,934		1,185	2,390	9,372		4,822	2,436	280

No. 12.—EXPORTS of Canadian Produce from the undermentioned Ports—Fiscal Year, 1906—*Continued.*

—	Abercorn.	Bridge-burg.	Coaticook.	Fort William.	Halifax.	Hemming-ford.	Montreal.	Nanaimo.	New Westminster	Niagara Falls.
MANUFACTURES—*Con.*	$	$	$	$	$	$	$	$	$	$
Household effects, N.E.S.	68,735	139,937	35,086	300	43,756	31,749	68,100	1,220	51,841	139,438
Ice		12,535								1,372
India rubber, manufactures of	100	4,775	18,547		2,428	2,554	83,714		25	49,610
" scrap and other	19,976	82,963	14	6,998	3,376	2,767	700		798	9,785
Iron and steel and manufactures of, viz.:										
Stoves	28	91	40		5,520	27	1,467			100
Castings, N.E.S.	8	32,007	157		1,910	5	4,856		352	847
Pig iron		9,075					8,006			
Machinery, N.E.S.	1,368	25,721	2,785		12,408	98,510	31,391		2,217	80,933
Sewing machines	865	1,145	1,611		391	5,279	1,085		260	1,795
Typewriters	386	252	50		1,778	33,320	65,942		90	1,046
Scrap iron or steel	32	100,543				200	8,265	832	11,529	4,604
Hdware, N.E.S.	897	8,888	5,676		7,614	33,943	53,120		401	28,043
Steel and manufactures of	2,406	32,808	1,237	5	10,417	4,992	49,992	1,748	7,897	44,553
Jeweller's sweepings	2,928	1,924	1,450			3,130	24,432		11,467	12,165
Junk	4,261	58,756	1,735		29,220	64,455	79,695			71,323
Lamps and lanterns		125	15		380		2,569			1,331
Leather—										
Sole	37,237		177,931		321,642	2,845	710,463			24,177
Upper			62,158		8,273		120,883			555
Leather, N.E.S	2,600	1,257	29,644		1,468	2,213	164,291			19,290
Boots and shoes	255	710	393		42,454	1,118	16,702		13	1,956
Harness and saddlery	65	418	151		469	206	60		220	165
Other manufactures of	626	365	1,049		748	1,436	1,673		35	2,893
Lime		6,765	22		70		13,140			35,710
Liquors—										
Ale and beer		429	8		180		565			359
Gin	17	1,465	92		287		45			
Whiskey		13,560	9		1,931	67	13,345			110,129
Wines		47	34		2,122	6	662			79
Other spirits, N.E.S.		2,342			28		32,271			
Metals, N.O.P.	445	3,318	52		6,345	8,444	11,914			4,101
Molasses										
Musical instruments, viz.:—										
Organs	1,319	10,088	79,693		190		49,474		15	21,546
Pianos	644	5,080	1,329		4,100		5,195	306	725	15,966
Other		278	3,041		215	48	589		10	3,713
Oakum					57					

Oil cake		8,650	37,530		16		138,321			6,758
Oil, N.E.S		750			1,936		2,255		1,705	20,807
Paper, wall		26	145		7,958	7,124	2,551			944
" N.E.S	28,160	562	57,614		23,460	396,812	766,677			1,290
Photographs	33	318	31		245	13	243		91	369
Plumbago, manufactures of		4								914
Rags	31,579	32,322	2,413		870	2,069	52,517			13,093
Sails					160					
Ships sold to other countries					300					
Soap		14	31		20,316	4	709			185
Starch			295		58		2,077			
Stone, ornamental, viz.:—										
Granite, marble, &c					1,043		675			
Building, viz.:—Freestone, limestone, &c					119					
Sugar of all kinds, N.E.S					934		609		6,270	
Sugar-house syrup										
Tar		4,016			3,030		1,728			
Tin, manufactures of	587		946		1,070	466	3,713			1,800
Tobacco, viz.:—										
Cigars		12			685		1,685			
Cigarettes					98		106			
Snuff										
Stems and cuttings		2,775	208			624	9,767			16,505
All other, N.E.S		500	592		7,517	79	10,145			2,686
Tow										8,680
Vehicles, viz.:—										
Carriages	150	657	90		6,040	1,425	13,868		40	464
" parts of		11			1,822		423			1,526
Carts	265	107	10		25	295	960			16,133
Wagons	115		672				80			710
Automobiles	2,000	900							275	42,952
Bicycles	48	234	93		97		303			41,094
" parts of							163			23,722
Vehicles, all other	455	2,723	1,809		40	452	4,646			1,498
Vinegar		134			69					
Wood, viz.:—										
Barrels, empty			109		882		1,857			75
Household furniture	148	82	3,824		12,772	248	122,028			41,568
Doors, sashes and blinds	8	657	14,307		90	980	91,242			1,060
Boxes and match splints			26,634		72,817	880	2,188			
Mouldings, trimmings and other furnishings			7		354		3,900			93
Pails, tubs, churns, &c		32			38		3,146			1,654
Spool wood and spools			46							25
Wood pulp	40,936	22,475	64,308		51,193	122,637	123,314			131,312
Other manufactures of	7,756	3,172	22,479		58,385	674	61,869		43	71,826
Woollens	4,597	8,593	135		13,782	465	7,973		12	1,017
Other articles	2,567	82,130	9,284		83,452	27,132	196,183	4,202	8,367	95,663
Total	335,015	841,024	757,346	7,333	1,311,340	978,894	4,099,510	20,131	108,108	3,395,447

No. 12.—EXPORTS of Canadian Produce from the undermentioned Ports Fiscal Year 1906.

	Prescott.	Quebec.	Rossland.	St. Armand.	St. Johns, Que.	St. John, N.B.	Sault Ste. Marie	Sydney.	Vancouver.	Winnipeg.
MANUFACTURES—*Con.*	$	$	$	$	$	$	$	$	$	$
Iron and steel and manufactures of										
Steel and manufactures of	892	150	270	1,864	11,230	23,628	2,814	5,188	19,584	2,584
Jeweller's sweepings	350			27,113	460	10,725			1,250	
Junk	2,957			15,376	12,863	43,921	1,438		958	
Lamps and lanterns				4	99	75,365				
Leather										
Sole		13,238		38,130		168,024			2,479	
Upper		2,459		1,528	26	75,334				
Leather, N.E.S.	62	1,245		12,094	4,556	105,022		55	4,388	
Boots and shoes	41	1,256		500	1,525	4,558	840		18,289	
Harness and saddlery	138		48	60	93	1,235		26	130	108
Other manufactures of	585	5,037		514	103	10,058			25	
Lime						140			1,564	
Liquors—										
Ale and beer	9			2	93	78			5	
Gin				3	10					
Whiskey	3,382			187	473	5,899	2,655		8,903	24
Wines				9	189	66			304	
Other spirits, N.E.S.	30			13	5	51,290			6	
Metals, N.O.P.	82	197		1,320	1,159	2,145		2,050	2,223	
Molasses										
Musical instruments, viz.:—										
[illegible]s	45		100	1,989		35,048			3,935	
Pianos	100		1,200	1,735	850	1,160			6,575	
Other					29	120			440	
Oil cake		1,397		13,558		72,191				
Oil, N.E.S.				268	548	11,181		5,904		251
Paper, wall			21	1	13,211	2,630			27	
" N.E.S.	53,985	79,321		30,404	4,769	379,545	3,922		32,593	12
[illegible]s		23		69	301	541	9		48	19
Plumbago, manufactures of	1,457									
Rags	1,225			15,186	2,757	19,953				
Ships sold to other countries									260	
Soap		550		27	15	19,753			10,102	
Starch				2		2,508				
Stone, ornamental, viz.:—										
Granite, marble, &c.					30					
Building, viz.—Freestone, limestone, &c.										

Sugar of all kinds, N.E.S.				4					12,043	
Sugar-house syrup									15,679	
Tar						2,013		85,708		32
Tin, manufactures of				7,533	2,108	1,711			1,536	
Tobacco, viz.:—										
Cigars									267	
Cigarettes									8	
Snuff										
Stems and cuttings	93			83		474				
Tobacco, all other		10,784		972	253	8,128	16		58	6
Carriages	15				375	3,825	80		925	
" parts of				1,797		243		42	80	
Carts				231	860					
Wagons	25			200	275	105		25	291	45
Automobiles									2,700	
Bicycles		21			60	295			10,775	20
" parts of						7			8,487	
Vehicles, all other	270			548	790	11,097	105	800	1,847	93
Barrels, empty	67				27	251				
Toys				2,129						
Household furniture	13,863	10		6,694	1,746	55,072	70	125	656	
Doors, sashes and blinds				1,092		35,804			255	
Matches and match splints				145	3	6,354				
Mouldings, trimmings and other furnishings						304				
Pails, tubs, churns, &c		2,600		1,368		545				
Spool wood and spools		12,435		74	64	738				
Wood pulp	75,524	558,603		1,786	298,907	357,752	503,957		6,685	
Other manufactures of wood	1,181	2,108		12,766	5,857	62,236	3,890	20	25,065	
Woollens	876	11,347		86	1,189	3,758			740	
Other articles	1,909	19,676	25	9,198	40,829	61,588	5,819	594	44,564	7,370
Total	443,193	773,897	6,936	676,571	577,085	2,406,911	636,862	151,594	1,421,661	17,127
MISCELLANEOUS ARTICLES.										
Coffee						60				
Rice										
" meal						5,515				
Paintings in oil, &c				800	3,055	7,405				
Other miscellaneous articles		53		500		1,601			95	
Total		53		1,300	3,055	14,581			95	
Grand total	7,963,524	4,017,076	454,242	4,502,649	8,340,299	18,335,144	4,441,543	1,526,415	6,960,836	315,968

No. 12.—EXPORTS of Canadian Produce from the undermentioned Ports—Fiscal Year, 1906—*Continued.*

Exports.	Abercorn.	Bridgeburg.	Coaticooke.	Fort William.	Halifax.	Hemmingford.	Montreal.	Nanaimo.	New Westminster.	Niagara Falls.
MISCELLANEOUS ARTICLES.	$	$	$	$	$	$	$	$	$	$
Coffee					276		44			
Dried fruits, N.E.S.							64			
Rice										
" meal							24,415			
Paintings	80	80	75		1,850	500	2,711			
Other miscellaneous articles		5,903			15,147	52	4,340		51	2,459
Total	80	5,983	75		17,273	552	31,574		51	2,459
Grand total	2,681,394	4,243,735	11,070,975	11,363,991	9,977,156	3,168,034	66,971,392	3,682,737	4,654,817	15,293,097

No. 13.—STATEMENT of Customs and other Revenue collected throughout the Dominion by Chief Ports and Outports during the Fiscal Year ended June 30, 1906.

ONTARIO.

Chief Port.	Outports.	Customs Duties.	Other Revenues.	Total Revenues.	Remarks.
		$ cts.	$ cts.	$ cts.	
Amherstburg	....	10,782 15			
	Essex Centre	6,276 99			
	Kingsville	2,434 95			
	Leamington	11,863 48	5 25		
	West Dock	532 52			
		31,890 09	5 25	31,895 34	
Belleville	....	109,973 70	40 00		
	Campbellford	5,575 85			
		115,549 55	40 00	115,589 55	
Berlin	....	193.506 07	60 00	193,566 07	
Bowmanville	....	13,363 16			
	Newcastle	11 14			
		13,374 30	....	13,374 30	
Brantford	....	290,453 62	40 00	290,493 62	
Bridgeburg	....	479,299 58	1,769 65	481,069 23	
Brockville	....	93,955 42	20 00	93,975 42	
Chatham	....	109,031 56	44 74		
	Glencoe	3,668 72			
	Ridgetown	8,883 09			
	Rondeau	66,411 56	100 00		
	Tilbury	1,666 16			
	Blenheim	4,381 13			
	Dresden	3 49			
	Romney	1 62			
		194,047 33	144 74	194,192 07	
Cobourg	....	26,212 18			
	Brighton	2,776 08			
	Colbourne	1,517 18			
	Grafton	....			
		30,505 44	....	30,505 44	
Collingwood	....	24,737 43			
	Meaford	45,733 38			
		70,470 81	....	70,470 81	

No. 13.—STATEMENT of Customs Revenue Collected, &c.—Ontario—*Continued.*

Chief Port.	Outports.	Customs Duties.	Other Revenues.	Total Revenues.	Remarks.
		$ cts.	$ cts.	$ cts.	
Cornwall	....	28,681 90	20 00		
	Aultsville	208 01			
		28,889 91	20 00	28,909 91	
Deseronto	....	22,077 87	24 11	22,101 98	
Fort William	....	406,548 16	30 00	406,578 16	
Galt	....	77,430 15			
	Preston	29,254 18			
	Ayr	2,897 36			
		109,581 69	....	109,581 69	
Gananoque	....	33,653 98			
	Rockport	615 84			
	Riverview	11 31			
	Pool's Resort	120 27			
		34,401 40	....	34,401 40	
Goderich	....	13,680 54			
	Clinton	17,780 99			
	Kincardine	6,079 92			
	Seaforth	12,220 19			
	Southampton	6,008 09			
	Wingham	8,664 04			
	Lucknow	....			
		64,433 77	....	64,433 77	
Guelph	....	144,449 55			
	Walkerton	8,705 98			
	Mount Forest	10 71			
	Harriston	2 68			
	Durham	1 47			
	Palmerston	35			
		153,170 74	....	153,170 74	
Hamilton	....	1,469,407 88	1,352 09		
	Burlington	6,086 54			
	Dundas	55,403 45			
	Dunnville	30,856 00			
	Oakville	2,280 17			
		1,564,034 04	1,352 09	1,565,386 13	
Hope	....	16,147 66	....	16,147 66	
Ingersoll	....	35,840 09	....	35,840 09	
Kenora	....	55,308 01	25 00	55,333 01	

No. 13.—STATEMENT of Customs Revenue Collected, &c.—Ontario—*Continued.*

Chief Port.	Outports.	Customs Duties.	Other Revenues.	Total Revenue.	Remarks.
		$ cts.	$ cts.	$ cts.	
Kingston	....	177,336 07	226 54		
	Bath	19 84	....		
		177,355 91	226 54	177,582 45	
Lindsay	....	25,465 50	....	25,465 50	
London	....	843,032 24	167 67		
	Strathroy	12,461 27			
		855,493 51	167 67	855,661 18	
Midland	....	23,673 70			
	Penetanguishene	3,770 80			
		27,444 50	....	27,444 50	
Morrisburg	....	2,119 71	8 00		
	Iroquois	784 41			
		2,904 12	8 00	2,912 12	
Napanee	....	14,225 74	....	14,225 74	
Niagara Falls	....	368,882 25	1,981 66		
	Chippawa	8,286 52			
	Niagara	1,799 80			
	Queenston	38 66			
		379,007 23	1,981 66	380,988 89	
Oshawa	....	50,325 69	....	50,325 69	
Ottawa	....	764,004 81	410 04		
	Alexandria	3,797 82			
	Almonte	8,082 65			
	Arnprior	4,141 53	20 00		
	Carleton Place	5,044 92			
	Pembroke	19,150 57			
	Perth	17,236 01			
	Renfrew	4,727 76			
	North Bay	66,284 95	20 00		
	Smith's Falls	27,967 04			
	Sturgeon Falls	34,459 20	20 00		
	Grenville				
		954,897 26	470 04	955,367 30	
Owen Sound	....	58,165 92	404 93		
	Chesley	55 65			
		58,221 57	404 93	58,626 50	

No. 13.—STATEMENT of Customs Revenue Collected, &c.—Ontario—*Continued.*

Chief Port.	Outports.	Customs Duties.	Other Revenues.	Total Revenues.	Remarks.
		$ cts.	$ cts.	$ cts.	
Paris	....	41,140 99	1 00		
	St. George	7,851 86			
		48,992 85	1 00	48,993 85	
Parry Sound	....	40,993 99			
	Byng Inlet	2,155 06			
	French River	266 86			
		43,415 91	.....	43,415 91	
Peterboro	....	369,638 79	20 00	369,658 79	
Picton	....	24,381 01			
	Wellington	3,032 04			
		27,413 05	....	27,413 05	
Port Arthur	....	175,198 27	420 00		
	Fort Francis	10,725 49	20 00		
	Lee Blain	93 40			
	Rainy River	9,354 96	296 78		
		195,372 12	736 78	196,108 90	
Prescott	....	87,697 03	314 30		
	Cardinal	14,597 84			
		102,294 87	314 30	102,609 17	
St. Catharines	....	171,861 15	137 88		
	Port Colborne	11,541 00	6 25		
	Port Dalhousie	9,504 61			
	Thorold	19,040 27			
	Welland	29,823 25	18 00		
		241,770 28	162 13	241,932 41	
St. Thomas	....	152,615 98	62 35		
	Aylmer	12,117 97			
	Port Burwell	1,400 52			
	Port Stanley	65,306 16	0 10		
		231,440 63	62 45	231,503 08	
Sarnia	....	125,733 06	42 00		
	Courtright	2,386 74			
	Petrolia	19,636 27			
	Point Edward	142,947 97	50 00		
	Stag Island	31 02			
		290,735 06	92 00	290,827 06	

No. 13.—STATEMENT of Customs Revenue Collected, &c.—Ontario—*Continued.*

Chief Port.	Outports.	Customs Duties.	Other Revenues.	Total Revenues.	Remarks.
		$ cts.	$ cts.	$ cts.	
Sault Ste. Marie.	....	192,474 80	786 30		
	Algoma Mills	62,391 78			
	Bruce Mines	6,141 19			
	Little Current	2,569 17			
	Michipicoten River	4,095 09			
	St. Joseph's Island	15 85			
	Sudbury	37,763 72			
	Gore Bay	21 73			
	Thessalon	1,011 31			
	Manitowaning	13 00			
	Cockburn Island	200 32			
	Cutler	2,473 07			
		309,171 03	786 30	309,957 33	
Simcoe	....	23,519 38			
	Tilsonburg	13,484 31			
	Port Dover	2,736 11			
	Port Rowan	1,510 18			
		41,249 98	....	41,249 98	
Stratford	....	80,812 21	20 00		
	Mitchel	8,607 16			
	St. Mary's	18,137 41			
	Listowel	37,988 81			
	Mount Forest	79 81			
	Wiarton	3,480 39	25 00		
		149,105 79	45 00	149,150 79	
Toronto	....	9,399,152 21	10,658 33		
	Aurora and New Market	14,392 11			
	Barrie	20,644 95	0 85		
	Brampton	16,743 65	1 00		
	Georgetown	21,227 26			
	Orangeville	13,156 63			
	Orillia	52,448 02			
	Port Credit	22,000 98			
	Streetsville	4,300 70			
	Toronto Junction	167,098 65			
		9,731,165 16	10,660 18	9,741,825 34	
Trenton	....	24,775 32	....	24,775 32	
Wallaceburg	....	11,914 42			
	Lambton	569 24			
	Sombra	928 57			
	Walpole Island	157 66			
		13,569 89		13,569 89	
Whitby	....	9,070 99		9,070 99	

No. 13.—STATEMENT of Customs Revenue Collected, &c.—Ontario—*Continued.*

Chief Port.	Outports.	Customs Duties.	Other Revenues.	Total Revenues.	Remarks.
		$ cts.	$ cts.	$ cts.	
Windsor........	....	486,712 88	4,073 47		
	Walkerville..........	233,333 48			
	Belle River..........	1,024 35			
		721,070 71	4,073 47	725,144 18	
Woodstock...........	....	64,624 20			
	Norwich............	2,939 09			
		67,563 29		67,563 29	
	Ontario totals.......	19,166,642 30	23,743 29	19,190,385 59	

QUEBEC.

Chief Port.	Outports.	Customs Duties.	Other Revenues.	Total Revenues.	Remarks.
Abercorn	....	3,898 97	202 00	4,100 97	
Coaticook..........	....	11,574 18			
	Island Pond........	12 90			
	Stanhope...........	157 59			
		11,744 67		11,744 67	
Cookshire..........	....	3,911 15			
	Comin's Mills.......	1,323 06	106 24		
	Lake Megantic......	5,729 27	20 00		
	Hereford..........	88 74			
		11,052 22	126 24	11,178 46	
Gaspé	....	3,740 22		3,740 22	
Hemmingford.........	....	500 88	104 92		
	Athelstan...........	15,616 67			
	Franklin Centre....	395 65	10 00		
	Roxham............	35 80			
	Vicars Station......	195 02			
	Corbin				
	Huntingdon	4 00			
		16,748 02	114 92	16,862 94	
Mansonville.........	....	264 07			
	Mansonville Station.	547 48	58 00		
		811 55	58 00	869 55	
Montreal	....	13,226,219 72	89,174 75		
	Dundee............	1,285 03			
	Joliette............	20,301 57	20 00		
	St. Jerome..........	20,337 50	40 00		
	St. Regis...........	120 22			
	Trout River........	120 25	737 00		
	Côteau Landing....	9 95			
	Marieville..........	7,228 93	20 00		
		13,275,623 17	89,991 75	13,365,614 92	

No. 13.—STATEMENT of Customs Revenue Collected, &c.—Quebec—*Continued.*

Chief Port.	Outports.	Customs Duties.	Other Revenues.	Total Revenues.	Remarks.
		$ cts.	$ cts.	$ cts.	
Paspebiac	....	8,538 70	20 00		
	New Richmond	132 73			
	Nouvelle	69 13			
		8,740 56	20 00	8,760 56	
Percé	....	740 68		740 68	
Quebec	....	1,451,584 22	928 69		
	Beauce	2,788 57	40 00		
	Chicoutimi	7,240 71			
	Magdalen Island	484 30	20 00		
	Victoriaville	16,747 13	20 00		
	River du Loup	22,841 31	52 73		
	St. Thomas	42 57			
	Bradore Bay	180 77			
	English Bay (Anticosti Island	411 15			
		1,502,320 73	1,061 42	1,503,382 15	
Rimouski	....	17,980 73	40 00		
	Matane	16 92			
		17,997 65	40 00	18,037 65	
St. Armand	....	4,170 85	111 00		
	Philipsburg	220 11			
		4,390 96	111 00	4,501 96	
St. Hyacinthe	....	41,266 61	40 00		
	Drummondville	1,104 33			
		42,370 94	40 00	42,410 94	
St. Johns	....	130,787 70	71 20		
	Clarenceville	377 38	190 79		
	Frelighsburg	300 44			
	Granby	45,309 73			
	Lacolle	699 29			
	Rouse's Point	65 19			
	Noyan Junction	356 17			
		177,895 90	261 99	178,157 89	
Sherbrooke	....	163,992 43	53 33		
	Richmond	11,386 33			
	Windsor Mills	4,150 30			
	Thetford Mines	2,844 46			
		182,373 52	53 33	182,426 85	
Sorel	....	20,020 42	65 00	20,085 42	

No. 13.—STATEMENT of Customs Revenue Collected, &c.—Quebec—*Continued.*

Chief Port.	Outports.	Customs Duties.	Other Revenues.	Total Revenues.	Remarks.
		$ cts.	$ cts.	$ cts.	
Stanstead	....	8,448 86	76 35		
	Georgeville	711 96			
	Magog	4,112 17			
	Stanstead Junction	18,095 06	450 99		
		31,368 05	527 34	31,895 39	
Three Rivers	....	72,852 64	80 00		
	Grand Mère and Shawinigan Falls	52,508 29			
	Nicolet	1,248 31	20 00		
		126,609 24	100 00	126,709 24	
Valleyfield	....	35,621 35	40 00	35,661 35	
	Quebec totals	15,474,068 82	92,812 99	15,566,881 81	

NEW BRUNSWICK.

Chief Port.	Outports.	Customs Duties.	Other Revenues.	Total Revenues.	Remarks.
Bathurst	....	4,317 97			
	Caraquet	164 75			
	Shippegan	146 63			
	Tracadie	43 93			
		4,672 38	....	4,672 38	
Campbellton	....	22,719 18	23 00	22,742 18	
Chatham	....	10,521 41	20 00		
	Buctouche	185 79			
	Richibucto	498 84			
		11,206 04	20 00	11,226 04	
Dalhousie	....	2,276 02	....	2,276 02	
Fredericton	....	49,241 38	....	49,241 38	
McAdam Junction	....	6,450 68	37 75	6,488 43	
Moncton	....	56,961 42	47 77		
	Cocagne	5 97			
	Alma	13 49			
	Dorchester	802 23			
	Harvey	498 08			
	Hillsboro'	939 45			
	Shediac	868 33			
		60,088 97	47 77	60,136 74	
Newcastle	....	5,249 81	....	5,249 81	

No. 13.—STATEMENT of Customs Revenue Collected, &c.—New Brunswick—*Continued.*

Chief Port.	Outports.	Customs Duties.	Other Revenue.	Total Revenue.	Remarks.
		$ cts.	$ cts.	$ cts.	
Sackville	....	4,725 32			
	Bay Verte	453 08			
	Rockport	....			
		5,178 40	....	5,178 40	
St. John	....	1,200,804 23	7,620 33		
	St. George	1,573 08	400 00		
	Sussex	9,264 30			
	Lepreaux	.. ..			
	Musquash	3 58			
	St. Martins	208 96			
	Back Bay	102 05			
	Beaver Harbour	658 22			
		1,212,614 42	8,020 33	1,220,634 75	
St. Stephen	....	24,870 56	775 00		
	Campobello	939 88	111 70		
	Milltown	5,587 09	50 00		
	North Head	619 72	222 00		
	St. Andrews	4,084 14			
	Upper Mills	3,375 30			
	Lords Cove	889 08			
	Grand Harbour	231 83			
		40,597 60	1,158 70	41,756 30	
Woodstock	....	14,332 09	400 00		
	Aroostook Junction	4,361 28	343 00		
	Centerville	814 93			
	Edmundston	1,843 22			
	Debec	1,931 17			
	Grand Falls	687 45	225 00		
	St. Leonards	513 32	25 00		
	Middle St. Francis	13,237 78	20 00		
	Green River	....			
		37,721 24	1,013 00	38,734 24	
	N. Brunswick totals	1,458,016 12	10,320 55	1,468,336 67	

NOVA SCOTIA.

Chief Port.	Outports.	Customs Duties.	Other Revenue.	Total Revenue.	Remarks.
Amherst	....	82,599 28	20 00		
	Northport	4 45			
	Oxford	1,827 13			
	Pugwash	569 33			
	River Hebert	723 13			
	Spring Hill	4,023 98			
	Tidnish	5 97			
	Wallace	196 38			
		89,949 65	20 00	89,969 65	

No. 13.—STATEMENT of Customs Revenue Collected, &c.—Nova Scotia—*Continued.*

Chief Port.	Outports.	Customs Duties.	Other Revenues.	Total Revenues.	Remarks.
		$ cts.	$ cts.	$ cts.	
Annapolis Royal	....	3,226 33	20 00		
	Bridgetown	1,971 96			
	Clementsport	283 53			
	Thorne's Cove	582 50			
	Port Wade	....			
		6,064 32	20 00	6,084 32	
Antigonish	....	6,523 12			
	Bayfield	12 15			
	Harbour au Bouche	35 86			
		6,571 13	....	6,571 13	
Arichat	....	227 82			
	St. Peter	315 98			
	West Arichat	25 45			
	Descouse	1 89			
	L'Ardoise	3 01			
	River Bourgeoise	1 05			
		575 20	....	575 20	
Baddeck	....	926 60			
	Aspey Bay	13 24			
	St. Anne's	11 67			
	New Campbellton	4 30			
	Ingonish	....			
	Neil's Harbour	....			
	Little Narrows	....			
		955 81	....	955 81	
Barrington	....	188 96			
	Clarks Harbour	389 08			
	Fort La Tour	69 58			
		647 62	....	647 62	
Canso	....	9,848 51			
	Guysboro'	206 29			
	Sherbrooke	88 37			
	Isaac's Harbour	343 57			
	Liscombe	1 41			
	Queensport	50 97			
	Port Mulgrave	2,207 84	25 00		
		12,746 96	25 00	12,771 96	
Digby	....	1,500 99	25 00		
	Bear River	1,335 50			
	Freeport	420 24			
	Sandy Cove	44 81			
	Westport	281 25			
		3,582 79	25 00	3,607 79	

No. 13.—STATEMENT of Customs Revenue Collected, &c.—Nova Scotia—*Continued.*

Chief Port.	Outports.	Customs Duties.	Other Revenue.	Total Revenue.	Remarks.
		$ cts.	$ cts.	$ cts.	
Glace Bay	....	92,329 06	....	92,329 06	
Halifax	....	1,586,827 55	2,482 66		
	Sheet Harbour	98 28			
	Port Dufferin	....			
	Ingram Docks	....			
		1,586,925 83	2,482 66	1,589,408 49	
Kentville	....	* 8,955 37			
	Berwick	530 69			
	Canning	186 17			
	Kingsport	510 13			
	Port Williams	596 86			
	Wolfville	1,614 71			
	Harbourville	....			
	Aylsford Station	244 69			
		12,638 62	....	12,638 62	
Liverpool	....	2,400 25			
	Port Medway	17 88			
		2,418 13	....	2,418 13	
Lockeport	....	323 46	20 00	343 46	
Lunenburg	....	11,135 83	140 00		
	Chester	394 90			
	Bridgewater	30,368 23	420 00		
	Mahone Bay	655 21	20 00		
	La Have	878 20			
		43,432 37	580 00	44,012 37	
Middleton	....	6,345 22			
	Port George	105 16			
	Margaretsville	90 19			
		6,540 57	....	6,540 57	
New Glasgow	....	41,025 97	40 00		
	Merigomish	40 08			
		41,066 05	40 00	41,106 05	
North Sydney	....	40,562 58	76 46		
	Grand Narrows	31 40			
	Little Bras d'Or	....			
	Millsville	....			
	Sydney Mines	92 19			
		40,686 17	76 46	40,762 63	

No. 13.—STATEMENT of Customs Revenue Collected, &c.—Nova Scotia—*Continued.*

Chief Port.	Outports.	Customs Duties.	Other Revenues.	Total Revenues.	Remarks.
		$ cts.	$ cts.	$ cts.	
Parrsboro'	....	748 36			
	Advocate Harbour	19 36			
	Apple River	59 46			
	Port Greville	23 20			
	Five Islands	6 60			
		856 98	....	856 98	
Picton	....	8,687 78			
	Tatamagouche	140 57			
	River John	119 04			
		8,947 39	....	8,947 39	
Port Hawkesbury	....	2,700 88			
	Port Hastings	16 24			
	Whycocomagh	20 81			
	West Bay	28 86			
	Marble Mountain	91 15			
	Orangedale	59 04			
		2,916 98	....	2,916 98	
Port Hood	....	184 55			
	Cheticamp	212 09			
	Margaree	45 26			
	Mabou	352 15			
	Inverness	747 34			
		1,541 39	....	1,541 39	
Shelburne	....	1,460 10	20 00		
	Jordan Bay	1 02			
	North East Harbour	149 66			
		1,610 78	20 00	1,630 78	
Sydney	....	145,129 37	112 20		
	Port Morien	391 12			
	Louisburg	819 05			
	Gabarouse Bay	3 20			
	Main à Dieu	2 37			
		146,345 11	112 20	146,457 31	
Truro	....	64,743 53			
	Economy	5 68			
	Londonderry	1,948 39			
	Little Bass River	1 55			
		66,699 15	....	66,699 15	
Weymouth	....	862 74			
	Belliveau's Cove	82 73			
	Meteghan	538 37			
	Barton	188 02			
	Church Point	244 90			
		1,916 76	....	1,916 76	

No. 13.—STATEMENT of Customs Revenue Collected, &c.—Nova Scotia—*Concluded.*

Chief Port.	Outports.	Customs Duties.	Other Revenues	Total Revenues.	Remarks.
		$ cts.	$ cts.	$ cts.	
Windsor	....	7,663 62	2 05		
	Cheverie	5 02			
	Hantsport	304 74			
	Maitland	48 39			
	Walton	12 12			
		8,033 89	2 05	8,035 94	
Yarmouth	....	58,907 08	500 00		
	Pubnico	74 89			
	Salmon River	173 36			
	Tusket Wedge	9 48	20 00		
	Tusket	469 54			
		59,634 35	520 00	60,154 35	
	Nova Scotia totals.	2,245,956 52	3,943 37	2,249,899 89	

MANITOBA.

Chief Port.	Outports.	Customs Duties.	Other Revenues	Total Revenues.	Remarks.
Brandon	....	151,624 13	60 00		
	Bannerman	....			
	Carberry	2,305 58			
	Deloraine	2,699 68			
	Killarney	6,266 66	200 00		
	Virden	21,983 50	20 00		
	Rapid City	101 89			
	Melita	7,514 24			
		192,555 68	280 00	192,835 68	
Emerson	....	37,251 97	2,218 50	39,470 47	
Winnipeg	....	3,507,889 66	5,219 68		
	Crystal City	4,130 85			
	Gretna	19,098 45			
	Morden	5,142 64	92 00		
	Neepawa	8,406 06			
	Portage la Prairie	54,532 70	40 00		
	Mowbray	1,084 58	5 00		
	Selkirk	2,575 18			
	Stonewall	93 42			
	Manitou	65 35			
	Birtle	317 45			
	Yorkton	2,514 08			
	Gladstone	161 36			
	Minnedosa	394 88			
	Sprague	320 65			
	Pilot Mound	54 99			
	York Factory	395 70			
	Battleford	442 85			
	Moose Factory	12,451 18			
		3,620,072 03	5,356 68	3,625,428 71	
	Manitoba totals	3,849,879 68	7,855 18	3,857,734 86	

No. 13.—STATEMENT of Customs Revenue Collected, &c.—*Continued.*

BRITISH COLUMBIA.

Chief Port.	Outports.	Customs Duties.	Other Revenues.	Total Revenues.	Remarks.
		$ cts.	$ cts.	$ cts.	
Grand Forks	....	42,091 62	418 85		
	Cascade City	1,129 15			
	Midway	23,585 70	268 75		
	Osoyoos	948 97			
	Sidley	1,297 20			
	Greenwood	24,013 00	20 00		
	Fairview	39 17			
	Carson	967 88			
	Keremeos	239 17			
	Phœnix	18,571 75			
		112,883 61	707 60	113,591 21	
Kaslo	....	3,485 96			
	Rykerts	1,059 81			
		4,545 77	....	4,545 77	
Nanaimo	....	63,183 24	1,240 22		
	Comox	4,092 67	20 00		
	Chemainus	6,060 30	20 00		
	Ladysmith	7,576 66	20 00		
	Courtney	121 27			
	Cumberland	202 07			
	Crofton	1,205 50			
	New Alberni	66 64			
	Alberni	72 86			
		82,581 21	1,300 22	83,881 43	
Nelson	....	110,087 96	40 00		
	Cranbrook	33,494 49	40 00		
	Fernie	65,854 39	21 29		
	Fort Steele	17 59			
	Flathead	15 00			
	Waneta	4,308 41			
	Erie	7 20			
	Gateway	7,801 00			
	Eastport	....			
	Kingsgate	....			
		221,586 04	101 29	221,687 33	
New Westminster	....	82,271 56	179 70		
	Alder Grove	217 85			
	Ashcroft	14,624 36	20 00		
	Douglas	3,595 99	28 00		
	Golden	5,048 19	20 00		
	Huntingdon	22,750 75			
	Kamloops	7,896 94			
	Revelstoke	22,329 64	20 00		
	Upper Sumas	146 44			
	Vernon	23,625 20	20 00		
	Ladner	1,402 61			
	Agassiz	50 28			
	Chilliwack	204 64			
	Yale	41 73			
	Steveston	3,043 47			
		187,249 65	287 70	187,537 35	

No. 13.—STATEMENT of Customs Revenue Collected, &c.—British Columbia—*Con.*

Chief Port.	Outports.	Customs Duties.	Other Revenue.	Total Revenue.	Remarks.
		$ cts.	$ cts.	$ cts.	
Rossland	....	46,281 89	20 00		
	Paterson	472 10			
	Trail	9,586 77			
		56,340 76	20 00	56,360 76	
Vancouver	....	1,862,278 64	10,636 15	1,872,914 79	
Victoria	....	805,740 94	6,340 96		
	Stickeen	718 33			
	Sidney	....			
	Duncan's	766 23			
	Port Essington	51 99			
	Metlakatla	46 49			
	Esquimalt	....			
	Massett	51 24			
	Salt Spring Island	142 12			
	Bella Coola	3 11			
	San Juan	....			
	Port Simpson	865 40			
	Fort Simpson	954 13			
		809,339 98	6,340 96	815,680 94	
	B. Columbia totals	3,336,805 66	19,393 92	3,356,199 58	

PRINCE EDWARD ISLAND.

Chief Port.	Outports.	Customs Duties.	Other Revenue.	Total Revenue.	Remarks.
Charlottetown	....	84,094 69	76 20		
	Cardigan	232 49			
	Crapaud	140 52			
	Georgetown	146 95			
	Grand River	1 20			
	Montague Bridge	1,253 39			
	Murray Harbour	125 96			
	Rustico	8 98			
	Souris	967 16			
	St. Peters	513 83			
	Vernon River	61 84			
	New London	13 52			
		87,560 44	76 20	87,636 64	
Summerside	....	8,919 99	45 00		
	Alberton	193 43			
	Malpeque	8 79			
	Port Hill	59 57			
	Tignish	1,909 03			
		11,090 81	45 00	11,135 81	
	P. E. totals	98,651 25	121 20	98,772 45	

No. 13.—STATEMENT of Customs Revenue Collected, &c.—*Continued.*

ALBERTA.

Chief Port.	Outports.	Customs Duties.	Other Revenues.	Total Revenues.	Remarks.
		$ cts.	$ cts.	$ cts.	
Calgary		269,153 57	72 00		
	Canmore	21 24			
	Banff	246 18			
	Medicine Hat	12,505 88	30 50		
		281,926 87	102 50	282,029 37	
Edmonton		104,312 94	40 00		
	Wostok	3 10			
		104,316 04	40 00	104,356 04	
Lethbridge		35,058 37	85 90		
	Cardston	2,322 17			
	Coutts	24,996 90			
	Macleod	20,132 62			
	Maple Creek	12,513 53			
	Pend d'Oreille	10,927 00			
	Pincher Creek	316 98			
	Wild Horse	46 95			
	Wood Mountain	10,070 05	1,272 55		
	Twin Lakes	6,729 20			
	Willow Creek	11,099 30			
		134,213 07	1,358 45	135,571 52	
	Alberta, totals	520,455 98	1,500 95	521,956 93	

SASKATCHEWAN.

Chief Port.	Outports.	Customs Duties.	Other Revenues.	Total Revenues.	Remarks.
North Portal		89,137 03	552 00	89,689 03	
Regina		83,103 15	60 00		
	Broadview	94 99			
	Grenfell	199 22			
	Indian Head	388 05			
	Moosejaw	24,094 05			
	Moosomin	307 95			
	Prince Albert	19,761 56	20 00		
	Qu'Appelle	256 90			
	Saskatoon	15,215 08			
	South Qu'Appelle	187 13			
	Wapella	95 34			
	Whitewood	131 33			
	Wolseley	251 26			
		144,086 01	80 00	144,166 01	
	Saskatchewan, totals	233,223 04	632 00	233,855 04	

No. 13.—STATEMENT of Customs Revenue Collected, &c.—*Concluded.*

YUKON TERRITORY.

Chief Port.	Outports.	Customs Duties.	Other Revenues.	Total Revenues.	Remarks.
		$ cts.	$ cts.	$ cts.	
Dawson	....	221,408 82	1,829 55		
	Forty Mile	2,945 94	250 00		
	Fort McPherson	152 02			
		224,506 78	2,079 55	226,586 33	
White Horse	....	34,754 86	1 00		
	Atlin	434 48			
	Carcross	20,848 61			
	Dalton Trail	53 11			
	White Pass	3,123 82	34 95		
		59,214 88	35 95	59,250 83	
	Yukon Ter. totals	283,721 66	2,115 50	285,837 16	
British Post Office Parcels	....	3,680 17	....	3,680 17	

RECAPITULATION.

Provinces.	Customs Duties.	Other Revenues.	Total Revenues.
	$ cts.	$ cts.	$ cts.
Ontario	19,166,642 30	23,743 29	19,190,385 59
Quebec	15,474,068 82	92,812 99	15,566,881 81
New Brunswick	1,458,016 12	10,320 55	1,468,336 67
Nova Scotia	2,245,956 52	3,943 37	2,249,899 89
Manitoba	3,849,879 68	7,855 18	3,857,734 86
British Columbia	3,336,805 66	19,393 92	3,356,199 58
Prince Edward Island	98,651 25	121 20	98,772 45
Alberta	520,455 98	1,500 95	521,956 93
Saskatchewan	233,223 04	632 00	233,855 04
Yukon Territory	283,721 66	2,115 50	285,837 16
British Post Office Parcels	3,680 17	....	3,680 17
Dominion totals	46,671,101 20	162,438 95	46,833,540 15

No. 14.—SUMMARY STATEMENT of Foreign Merchandise Imported into Canada; the Surtax Tariffs; the Duty Collected by Articles under each Tariff, Consumption and Amount of Duty Collected

	Articles and General Tariff Rates.		Total Imports.		General Tariff.		
			Quantity.	Value.	Quantity.	Value.	Duty.
	DUTIABLE GOODS.			$		$	$ cts.
1	Ale, beer and porter in bottles, 24c. per gall.	Galls.	533,900	361,569	540,021	361,305	129,605 04
2	" " casks, 16c. "	"	226,877	50,511	204,365	42,024	32,698 40
	Total, ale, &c.		760,777	412,080	744,386	403,329	162,303 44
3	Ginger ale, 20 p.c.	$	....	16,171	....	1,360	272 00
	Animals, living, viz.—						
4	Hogs, 1½c. per lb	Lbs.	6,585,642	386,995	124,795	7,233	1,871 93
5	Horned cattle, 20 p.c.	No.	14,297	186,338	14,277	182,963	36,592 60
6	Horses, 20 p.c.	"	17,149	1,078,888	16,340	744,588	148,917 60
7	Sheep, 20 p.c.	"	70,123	201,912	69,985	199,962	39,992 40
8	All other, N.E.S., 20 p.c.	$	....	55,717	....	52,658	10,531 60
	Total, animals		....	1,909,850	225,397	1,187,404	237,906 13
9	Antiseptic surgical dressings such as absorbent cotton, cotton wool, lint, lamb's wool, tow, jute, gauzes and oakum, prepared for use as surgical dressings plain or medicated, 20 p.c.	$	....	68,169	....	57,638	11,527 60
10	Bagatelle tables or boards, 35 p.c.	No.	616	214	615	197	68 95
11	Bags which contained cement, 25 p.c.	$	....	172,475	....	160,072	40,018 00
12	Baking powders, 6c. per lb	Lbs.	378,734	106,636	491,168	138,577	29,470 08
13	Balls, cues and racks and cue tips for bagatelle boards and billiard tables, 35 p.c.	$	....	8,082	....	6,727	2,354 45
14	Baskets of all kinds, N.E.S., 30 p.c.	"	....	58,873	....	34,945	10,483 50
15	Belting of all kinds, except rubber and leather, 20 p.c.	"	....	78,223	....	32,351	6,470 20
16	Belts, surgical, and trusses, electric belts, pessaries and suspensory bandages of all kinds, 20 p.c.	"	....	25,392	....	21,342	4,268 40
17	Belts of all kinds, N.O.P., 35 p.c.	"	....	89,299	....	45,642	15,974 70
18	Bells and gongs, N.E.S., 30 p.c.	"	....	38,714	....	37,042	11,112 60
19	Billiard tables, 35 p.c.	No.	482	32,916	462	28,886	10,110 10
20	Blacking, shoe and shoemakers' ink; shoe, harness and leather dressing, N.O.P., 25 p.c.	$	....	86,830	....	80,534	20,133 50
21	Blinds of wood, metal or other material, not textile or paper, 30 p.c.	"	....	5,502	....	5,502	1,650 60
22	Blueing—Laundry blueing of all kinds, 25 p.c.	"	....	26,542	....	3,243	810 75
23	Boats—open, pleasure sail boats, skiffs and canoes, 25 p.c.	No.	512	91,256	505	90,195	22,548 75
24	Bolsters and pillows, 30 p.c.	$	....	9,969	....	9,101	2,730 30
25	Books, printed; periodicals and pamphlets, N.E.S., 10 p.c.	"	....	1,046,511	....	829,194	82,919 40
26	Books—Novels or works of fiction, or literature of a similar character, unbound or paper bound, or in sheets, including freight rates for railways and telegraph rates, bound in book or pamphlet form, not including Christmas annuals or publications commonly known as juvenile and toy books, 20 p.c.	"	....	99,323	....	80,396	16,079 20

Quantity and Value entered for Consumption under the General, Preferential and
and the Total Quantity and Value of each Article entered for
thereon during the Fiscal Year 1906.

Entered for Home Consumption.									
Preferential Tariff.			Surtax Tariff.			Total.			
Quantity.	Value.	Duty.	Quantity.	Value.	Duty.	Quantity.	Value.	Duty Collected.	
	$	$ cts.		$	$ cts.		$	$ cts.	
			3,928	2,584	1,256 99	543,949	363,889	130,862 03	1
			20,123	7,562	4,292 95	224,488	49,586	36,991 35	2
			24,051	10,146	5,549 94	768,437	413,475	167,853 38	
	13,414	1,788 55					14,774	2,060 55	3
						124,795	7,233	1,871 93	4
						14,277	182,963	36,592 60	5
						16,340	744,588	148,917 60	6
						69,985	199,962	39,992 40	7
	37	4 94		378	100 79		53,073	10,637 33	8
	37	4 94		378	100 79		1,187,819	238,011 86	
	11,523	1,536 58					69,161	13,064 18	9
1	17	3 96				616	214	72 91	10
	9,150	1,525 05		1,050	349 94		170,272	41,892 99	11
12	8	0 48				491,180	138,585	29,470 56	12
	1,355	316 15					8,082	2,670 60	13
	3,588	717 60		19,346	7,738 40		57,879	18,939 50	14
	43,902	5,853 73		290	77 33		76,543	12,401 26	15
	3,841	512 17		209	55 73		25,392	4,836 30	16
	39,565	9,232 20		2,361	1,101 90		87,568	26,308 80	17
	779	155 80		904	361 60		38,725	11,630 00	18
20	4,030	940 36				482	32,916	11,050 46	19
	5,879	979 92					86,413	21,113 42	20
							5,502	1,650 60	21
	23,583	3,930 59					26,826	4,741 34	22
6	600	100 01				511	90,795	22,648 76	23
	810	162 00					9,911	2,892 30	24
	212,055	14,137 84		4,501	600 09		1,045,750	97,657 33	25
	18,474	2,463 43		765	204 03		99,635	18,746 66	26

No. 14.—Summary Statement of Foreign Merchandise

	Articles and General Tariff Rates.		Total Imports.		General Tariff.		
			Quantity.	Value.	Quantity.	Value.	Duty.
	DUTIABLE GOODS.			$		$	$ cts.
	Books—*Con.*						
1	Bank notes, bonds, bills of exchange, cheques, promissory notes, drafts, and all similar work unsigned and cards or other commercial blank forms printed or lithographed, or printed from steel or copper or other plates, and other printed matter, N.E.S., 35 p.c.	$	....	125,035	....	110,414	38,644 90
2	Posters, advertising bills and folders, 15c. per lb	Lbs.	107,787	23,809	106,567	23,569	15,985 05
3	Labels for cigar boxes, fruits, vegetables, meat, fish, confectionery and other goods: also shipping, price or other tags, tickets or labels; and railroad or other tickets whether lithographed or printed or partly printed, N.E.S., 35 p.c	$	....	170,926	....	139,519	48,831 65
4	Maps and charts, N.E.S., 20 p.c	"	....	20,902	....	16,012	3,202 40
5	Newspapers, or supplemental editions or parts thereof partly printed and intended to be completed and published in Canada, 25 p.c	"	....	2,874	....	2,874	718 50
6	Advertising pamphlets, pictorial show cards, illustrated advertising periodicals, illustrated price books, catalognes and price lists, advertising calendars and almanacs; patent medicine or other advertising circulars, fly sheets or pamphlets, 15c. per lb	Lbs.	671,625	161,016	601,138	145,965	90,170 70
7	Chromos, chromotypes, oleographs, or like work produced by any process other than hand painting or drawing, and having any advertisement or advertising matter printed, lithographed, or stamped thereon, or attached thereto, or other similar artistic work, lithographed, printed or stamped on paper or cardboard for business or advertisement purposes, N.O.P., 15c. per lb	"	3,982	900	3,962	898	594 30
8	Printed music, bound or in sheets, 10 p.c.	$	....	110,266	....	88,733	8,873 30
9	Photographs, chromos, chromotypes, artotypes, oleographs, paintings, drawings, pictures, engravings or prints, or proofs therefrom, and similar works of art, N.O.P.; blue prints and building plans, 20 p.c	"	....	606,475	....	336,913	67,382 60
	Total, books	...	......	2,368,037	....	1,774,487	373,402 00
10	Boot, shoe and stay laces of any material, 30 p.c	$	....	135,517	....	46,861	14,058 30
11	Boots and shoes and slippers of all kinds, except rubber and leather, 25 p.c.	"	....	93,594	....	49,452	12,363 00
12	Braces or suspenders, and metal parts of, 35 p.c	"	......	84,992	......	63,547	22,241 45
	Brass and manufactures of—						
13	Nails, tacks, rivets and burrs or washers, 30 p.c	"	....	9,345	....	6,873	2,061 90
14	Pumps, 30 p.c.	"	......	24,020	....	23,166	6,949 80
15	Wire, plain, 10 p.c	Lbs.	176,853	27,287	149,364	21,618	2,161 80

SESSIONAL PAPER No. 11

Imported into Canada, &c.—*Continued.*

Entered for Home Consumption.									
Preferential Tariff.			Surtax Tariff.			Total.			
Quantity.	Value.	Duty.	Quantity.	Value.	Duty.	Quantity.	Value.	Duty Collected.	
	$	$ cts.		$	$ cts.		$	$ cts.	
....	10,258	2,393 64	....	2,944	1,373 87	....	123,616	42,412 41	1
1,220	240	122 00	....	....	....	107,787	23,809	16,107 05	2
....	9,274	2,164 11	....	22,779	10,630 29	....	171,572	61,626 05	3
....	4,852	647 01	....	38	10 13	....	20,902	3,859 54	4
....	....	....	....	....	....	....	2,874	718 50	5
46,101	11,129	4,610 10	8,697	2,412	1,739 40	655,936	159,506	96,520 20	6
20	2	2 00	....	....	....	3,982	900	596 30	7
....	18,669	1,244 70	....	2,864	381 91	....	110,266	10,499 91	8
....	96,246	12,833 22	....	118,596	31,625 47	....	551,755	111,841 29	9
....	381,199	40,618 05	....	154,899	46,565 19	....	2,310,585	460,585 24	
....	73,718	14,743 60	....	12,330	4,932 00	....	132,909	33,733 90	10
....	40,037	6,673 06	....	10,851	3,616 99	....	100,340	22,653 05	11
....	21,182	4,942 71	....	53	24 73	....	84,782	27,208 89	12
....	867	173 40	....	1,605	642 00	....	9,345	2,877 30	13
....	323	64 60	....	39	15 60	....	23,528	7,030 00	14
23,952	3,992	266 19	3,393	1,646	219 48	176,709	27,256	2,647 47	15

No. 14.—SUMMARY STATEMENT of Foreign Merchandise

	Articles and General Tariff Rates.		Total Imports.		General Tariff.		
			Quantity.	Value.	Quantity.	Value.	Duty.
	DUTIABLE GOODS—*Con.*			$		$	$ cts.
	Brass and manufactures of—*Con.*						
1	Wire cloth, &c., N.E.S., 25 p.c.	$	....	44,825	....	12,096	3,024 00
2	Manufactures of, N.O.P. 30 p.c.	"	....	780,840	....	694,033	208,209 90
	Total, brass		....	886,317	....	757,786	222,407 40
	Breadstuffs, &c., viz.—						
3	Arrowroot, 20 p.c.	Lbs.	28,597	1,261	6,747	237	47 40
4	Biscuits of all kinds not sweetened, 25 p.c.	"	274,568	18,530	232,626	13,849	3,462 25
5	Biscuits of all kinds sweetened, 27½ p.c.	"	256,085	35,665	73,325	6,382	1,755 31
6	Macaroni and vermicelli, 25 p.c.	"	2,785,335	106,581	2,793,579	107,068	26,767 00
7	Rice, cleaned, 1¼c. per lb.	"	16,828,664	348,917	9,287,975	203,233	116,099 61
8	Rice, uncleaned, unhulled or paddy, ½c. per lb.	"	13,092,156	296,349	6,454,084	148,552	32,270 41
9	Rice and sago flour and sago, 25 p.c.	"	840,606	15,308	242,842	4,591	1,147 75
10	Tapioca, 25 p.c.	"	2,103,392	54,707	361,672	10,832	2,708 00
	Total, breadstuffs		36,204,403	877,318	19,452,850	494,744	184,257 73
	Grain and products of, viz.—						
11	Barley, 30 p.c.	Bush.	1,923,995	900,588	2,785	1,632	489 60
12	Beans, 15c. per bush	"	27,497	45,941	27,095	45,141	4,064 25
13	Buckwheat, 10c. per bush	"	99	120	99	120	9 90
14	Indian corn for purposes of distillation, 7½c. per bush	"	1,898,183	1,037,026	1,349,776	721,653	101,233 29
15	Oats, 10c. per bush	"	2,616,145	1,196,300	44,000	20,351	4,400 00
16	Pease, N.E.S., 10c. per bush	"	5,065	9,098	5,055	9,080	505 50
17	Rye, 10c. per bush	"	170,361	107,729	24,072	15,068	2,407 20
18	Wheat, 12c. per bush	"	676,696	579,639	64,927	49,741	7,791 24
	Total, grain		7,318,041	3,876,441	1,517,809	862,786	120,900 98
19	Bran, mill feed, &c., 20 p.c.	$	....	72,328	....	67,584	13,516 80
20	Buckwheat meal or flour, ¼c. per lb.	Lbs.	104,902	2,890	104,002	2,866	260 01
21	Indian or corn meal, 25c. per brl.	Brls.	27,054	71,275	26,706	69,830	6,676 50
22	Oatmeal, 20 p.c.	Lbs.	8,749	299	29,091	743	148 60
23	Rolled oats, $\frac{8}{10}$c. per lb.	"	456,927	9,190	430,090	8,482	2,580 55
24	Rye flour, 50c. per brl	Brls.	1,837	6,313	1,820	6,235	910 00
25	Wheat flour, 60c. per brl.	"	43,963	174,079	41,811	161,765	25,086 60
26	Hominy, cracked, evaporated or dried corn, 20 p.c.	$	....	4,919	....	4,922	984 40
27	Cereal foods, prepared, 20 p.c	$	....	153,299	....	152,600	30,520 00
28	All other breadstuffs, N.E.S., 20 p.c.	$	....	76,672	....	62,461	12,492 20
29	Grain, flour and meal, &c., of all kinds, when damaged by water *in transitu*, 20 p.c.	$	....	657	....	657	131 40
	Total, grain products		....	571,951	....	538,145	93,307 06
	Bricks and titles: See Earthenware.						
30	Fire brick and stove linings, N.E.S., 20 p.c.	$	....	51,892	....	47,310	9,462 00
31	Bath brick, 20 p.	"	....	1,503	....	248	49 60
32	Building brick, 20 p.c.	M	21,934	194,897	21,141	185,265	37,053 00
33	Paving brick, 20 p.c.	$	4,104	46,008	4,079	45,548	9,109 60
34	Drain tiles, not glazed, 20 p.c.	$	....	4,727	....	4,328	865 60
35	Drain pipes, sewer pipes, chimney linings or vents, chimney tops, and inverted blocks, glazed or unglazed, 35 p.c.	"	....	131,353	....	112,115	39,240 25
36	Manufactures of clay, N.O.P., 20 p.c.	$	....	30,067	....	28,381	5,676 20
	Total, bricks, &c.		....	460,447	....	423,195	101,456 25

Imported into Canada, &c.—*Continued.*

Entered for Home Consumption.									
Preferential Tariff.			Surtax Tariff.			Total.			
Quantity.	Value.	Duty.	Quantity.	Value.	Duty.	Quantity.	Value.	Duty Collected.	
	$	$ cts.		$	$ cts.		$	$ cts.	
....	32,154	5,358 97	....	575	191 67	....	44,825	8,574 64	1
....	70,078	14,015 60	....	15,661	6,264 40	....	779,772	228,489 90	2
....	107,414	19,878 76	....	19,526	7,333 15	....	884,726	249,619 31	
24,501	1,118	149 10	....	....	....	31,248	1,355	196 50	3
39,135	4,371	728 59	....	....	....	271,761	18,220	4,190 84	4
181,920	29,169	5,348 22	....	....	....	255,245	35,551	7,103 53	5
....	....	....	....	....	....	2,793,579	107,068	26,767 00	6
6,242,175	132,570	52,018 36	84,000	3,450	1,400 00	15,614,150	339,253	169,517 97	7
12,605,889	165,048	42,019 66	....	....	....	19,059,973	313,600	74,290 07	8
699,725	11,891	1,981 87	....	....	....	942,567	16,482	3,129 62	9
1,717,395	43,486	7,247 73	....	....	....	2,079,067	54,318	9,955 73	10
21,510,740	387,653	109,493 53	84,000	3,450	1,400 00	41,047,590	885,847	295,151 26	
240	263	52 60	....	....	....	3,025	1,895	542 20	11
9	21	90	2	8	40	27,106	45,170	4,065 53	12
....	....	....	....	....	....	99	120	9 90	13
....	....	....	....	....	....	1,349,776	721,653	101,233 29	14
2,298	1,705	153 23	....	....	....	46,298	22,056	4,553 23	15
....	....	....	....	....	....	5,055	9,080	505 50	16
....	....	....	....	....	....	24,072	15,068	2,407 20	17
....	....	....	....	....	....	64,927	49,741	7,791 24	18
2,547	1,989	206 73	2	8	40	1,520,358	864,783	121,108 11	
....	4,809	641 23	....	....	....	....	72,393	14,158 03	19
....	....	....	....	....	....	104,002	2,866	260 01	20
7	21	1 16	....	....	....	26,713	69,851	6,677 66	21
3,883	142	18 93	....	....	....	32,974	885	167 53	22
....	....	....	....	....	....	430,090	8,482	2,580 55	23
....	....	....	....	....	....	1,820	6,235	910 00	24
101	355	40 40	....	....	....	41,912	162,120	25,127 00	25
....	....	....	....	....	....	....	4,922	984 40	26
....	3,049	406 60	....	....	....	....	155,649	30,926 60	27
....	13,281	1,770 95	....	56	14 97	....	75,798	14,278 12	28
....	....	....	....	....	....	....	657	131 40	29
....	21,657	2,879 27	....	56	14 97	....	559,858	96,201 30	
....	4,582	610 99	....	....	....	....	51,892	10,072 99	30
....	1,218	162 37	....	....	....	....	1,466	211 97	31
740	9,491	1,265 47	53	141	37 60	21,934	194,897	38,356 07	32
25	460	61 34	....	....	....	4,104	46,008	9,170 94	33
....	399	53 19	....	....	....	....	4,727	918 79	34
....	19,238	4,488 85	....	....	....	....	131,353	43,729 10	35
....	1,135	151 35	....	551	146 93	....	30,067	5,974 48	36
....	36,523	6,793 56	....	692	184 53	....	460,410	108,434 34	

No. 14.—SUMMARY STATEMENT of Foreign Merchandise

	Articles and General Tariff Rates.	Total Imports.		General Tariff.		
		Quantity.	Value.	Quantity.	Value.	Duty.
	DUTIABLE GOODS—*Con.*		$		$	$ cts.
1	British gum, dextrine, sizing cream and enamel sizing, 10 p.c. .... Lbs.	1,793,839	61,603	1,441,187	49,799	4,979 90
2	Brooms and whisks, 20 p.c. .... $	....	3,432	....	3,231	646 20
3	Brushes, 25 p.c. .... "	....	282,605	....	231,157	57,789 25
4	Buttons, pantaloon, wholly of metal, 25 p.c. Gross.	459,247	32,476	326,932	25,300	6,325 00
5	Buttons, shoe, N.E.S., 25 p.c. .... "	5,549	379	5,539	377	94 25
6	Buttons, all kinds, N.O.P., 35 p.c. .... $	....	250,653	....	188,358	65,925 30
	Total, buttons	....	283,508	....	214,035	72,344 55
	Candles—					
7	Paraffine wax, 25 p.c. .... Lbs.	149,308	15,843	145,076	15,450	3,862 50
8	All other, N.E.S., 25 p.c. .... "	564,763	65,840	376,594	47,836	11,959 00
	Total, candles	714,071	81,683	521,670	63,286	15,821 50
9	Cane, reed or rattan, split or otherwise manufactured, N.O.P., 15 p.c. .... $	....	54,815	....	43,457	6,518 55
10	Canvas, to be used for boats' and ships' sails, 5 p.c. .... $	....	7,835	....	180	9 00
	Carriages and vehicles—					
11	Buggies, carriages, pleasure carts and similar vehicles, N.E.S., 35 p.c. .... No.	1,475	107,087	1,355	94,588	33,105 80
12	Cutters, 35 p.c. .... "	15	448	15	448	156 80
13	Farm wagons, 25 p.c. .... "	4,452	186,281	4,451	186,184	46,546 00
14	Freight wagons, drays and similar vehicles, 25 p.c. .... "	905	56,371	904	54,278	13,569 50
15	Finished parts of buggies, carriages and similar vehicles, N.E.S., including parts of cutters, children's carriages, and sleds N.O.P., 35 p.c. .... $	....	96,568	....	95,004	33,251 40
16	Railway cars, passengers, 30 p.c. .... No.	52	368,434	52	368,434	110,530 20
17	" tram or horse, 30 p.c. .... "	24	25,394	18	8,042	2,412 60
18	" box and flat cars, 30 p.c. .... "	473	297,899	473	297,899	89,369 70
19	" cars, parts of, 30 p.c. .... $	....	335,687	....	234,502	70,350 60
20	" or road scrapers, 30 p.c. .... "	....	81,173	....	81,160	24,348 00
21	Sleighs, 25 p.c. .... "	894	17,990	892	17,880	4,470 00
22	Wheelbarrows, and trucks and hand-carts, 30 p.c. .... No.	17,495	103,818	17,440	103,662	31,098 60
23	Bicycles and tricycles, 30 p.c. .... "	2,371	40,404	2,225	33,429	10,028 70
24	" " parts of, 30 p.c. $	....	76,756	....	68,035	20,410 50
25	Children's carriages and sleds, 35 p.c. .... "	....	58,739	....	58,443	20,455 05
	Total, carriages, &c.	....	1,853,049	....	1,701,988	510,103 45
26	Carpets, N.E.S., (see woollens), 35 p.c. .... Yds.	1,681	879	100	49	17 15
27	Carpet sweepers, 30 p.c. .... No.	7,230	15,928	7,230	15,928	4,778 40
28	Cash registers, 30 p.c. .... "	1,631	237,834	1,631	237,834	71,350 20
29	Celluloid, manufactures of, N.E.S., 20 p.c. $	....	46,575	....	36,859	7,371 80
30	Cement, Hydraulic or Waterlime, 12½c. per 100 lbs. .... Cwt.	10,794	4,034	10,794	4,034	1,349 25
31	Cement, Portland, 12½c. per 100 lbs. .... "	2,861,416	971,127	2,120,974	737,567	265,121 86
32	" N.E.S and manf. of N.O.P., 20 p.c. $	....	27,861	....	20,790	4,158 00
	Total, cement	2,872,210	1,003,022	2,131,768	762,391	270,629 11

Imported into Canada &c.—*Continued.*

Entered for Home Consumption.									
Preferential Tariff.			Surtax Tariff.			Total.			
Quantity.	Value.	Duty.	Quantity.	Value.	Duty.	Quantity.	Value.	Duty Collected.	
	$	$ cts.		$	$ cts.		$	$ cts.	
180,623	6,188	412 55	113,648	3,625	483 34	1,735,458	59,612	5,875 79	1
......	86	11 50	......	115	30 60	......	3,432	688 30	2
......	26,117	4,352 95	......	25,461	8,486 92	......	282,735	70,629 12	3
50,603	2,772	462 04	81,712	4,404	1,467 98	459,247	32,476	8,255 02	4
10	2	33	......	......	......	5,549	379	94 58	5
......	31,506	7,351 72	......	30,532	14,248 34	......	250,396	87,525 36	6
......	34,280	7,814 09	......	34,936	15,716 32	......	283,251	95,874 96	
3,432	319	53 18	300	35	11 67	148,808	15,804	3,927 35	7
149,190	13,761	2,293 59	2,728	547	182 35	528,512	62,144	14,434 94	8
152,622	14,080	2,346 77	3,028	582	194 02	677,320	77,948	18,362 29	
......	2,711	271 10	......	8,647	1,729 40	......	54,815	8,519 05	9
......	7,655	255 16	......	......	......	......	7,835	264 16	10
1	104	24 27	......	......	......	1,356	94,692	33,130 07	11
......	......	......	......	......	......	15	448	156 80	12
1	97	16 17	......	......	......	4,452	186,281	46,562 17	13
1	2,093	348 84	......	......	......	905	56,371	13,918 34	14
......	338	78 91	......	......	......	......	95,342	33,330 31	15
......	......	......	......	......	......	52	368,434	110,530 20	16
6	17,352	3,470 40	......	......	......	24	25,394	5,883 00	17
......	......	......	......	......	......	473	297,899	89,369 70	18
......	30,391	6,078 20	......	70,594	28,237 60	......	335,487	104,666 40	19
......	......	......	......	......	......	......	81,160	24,348 00	20
......	......	......	......	......	......	892	17,880	4,470 00	21
2	22	4 40	1	5	2 00	17,443	103,689	31,105 00	22
166	5,327	1,065 40	......	......	......	2,391	38,756	11,094 10	23
......	8,849	1,769 80	......	21	8 40	......	76,905	22,188 70	24
......	276	64 41	......	......	......	......	58,719	20,519 46	25
......	64,849	12,920 80	......	70,620	28,248 00	......	1,837,457	551,272 25	
1,556	790	184 34	25	40	18 69	1,681	879	220 18	26
......	......	......	......	......	......	7,230	15,928	4,778 40	27
......	......	......	......	......	......	1,631	237,834	71,350 20	28
......	5,818	775 78	......	3,898	1,039 57	......	46,575	9,187 15	29
......	......	......	......	......	......	10,794	4,034	1,349 25	30
696,571	215,544	58,047 40	31,037	10,728	5,172 80	2,848,582	963,839	328,342 06	31
......	4,187	558 33	......	2,881	768 30	......	27,858	5,484 63	32
696,571	219,731	58,605 73	31,037	13,609	5,941 10	2,859,376	995,731	335,175 94	

No. 14.—SUMMARY STATEMENT of Foreign Merchandise

	Articles and General Tariff Rates.		Total Imports.		General Tariff.		
			Quantity.	Value.	Quantity.	Value.	Duty.
	DUTIABLE GOODS—*Con.*			$		$	$ cts.
1	Chalk, prepared, 20 p.c.	$	....	23,821	....	20,425	4,085 00
2	Charcoal, 20 p.c.	"	....	34,591	....	19,778	3,955 60
3	Chicory, raw or green, 3c. per lb.	Lbs.	2,997	117	....	....	....
4	" kiln-dried, roasted or ground, 4c. per lb.	"	248,884	12,493	71,305	5,200	2,852 20
	Total, chicory		251,881	12,610	71,305	5,200	2,852 20
5	Church vestments of any material, 20 p.c.	$	....	23,501	....	22,005	4,401 00
6	Cider, clarified or refined, 10c. per gall.	Galls.	739	578	765	529	76 50
7	" not clarified or refined, 5c. per gall.	"	2,072	397	1,598	361	79 90
	Total, cider		2,811	975	2,363	890	156 40
8	Clocks, clock keys and clock movements, 25 p.c	$	....	342,894	....	291,878	72,969 50
9	Clothes wringers, and parts thereof, for domestic use, 35 p.c.	No.	7,578	19,538	7,576	19,528	6,834 80
10	Cloths, not rubbered or made waterproof, whether of wool, cotton, unions, silk or ramie, sixty inches or over in width and weighing not more than seven ounces to the square yard imported exclusively for the manufacture of mackintosh clothing, 15 p.c.	Yds.	113,713	21,609	....	....	....
11	Coal, bituminous, 53c. per ton	Tons.	4,764,805	8,795,763	4,476,050	8,316,627	2,372,306 50
12	" dust, N.E.S., 20p.c. not over 13c. per ton	"	751,214	494,100	746,526	487,461	83,732 92
	Total, coal		5,516,019	9,289,863	5,222,576	8,804,088	2,456,039 42
13	Cocoa carpeting, mats, rugs and matting, 25 p.c.	$	....	4,847	....	775	193 75
14	Cocoa nuts, imported from place of growth by vessel direct to a Canadian port, 50c. per 100	No.	2,464,751	54,108	43,384	938	216 92
15	Cocoa nuts, N.E.S., $1 per 100	"	127,043	3,913	127,043	3,913	1,270 43
	Total, cocoanuts		2,591,794	58,021	170,427	4,851	1,487 35
16	Cocoa nut, desiccated, sweetened or not, 5c. per lb.	Lbs.	116,738	8,475	8,433	789	421 65
17	Cocoa paste, chocolate paste, cocoa and cocoa butter, N.O.P., 4c. per lb.	"	1,333,972	246,259	818,394	147,060	32,735 76
18	Cocoa shells and nibs, chocolate and other preparations of cocoa, N.E.S., 20 p.c.	"	1,372,190	325,786	732,297	192,769	38,553 80
	Total, cocoa		2,706,162	572,045	1,550,691	339,829	71,289 56

Imported into Canada, &c.—*Continued.*

ENTERED FOR HOME CONSUMPTION.

Preferential Tariff.			Surtax Tariff.			Total.			
Quantity.	Value.	Duty.	Quantity.	Value.	Duty.	Quantity.	Value.	Duty Collected.	
	$	$ cts.		$	$ cts.		$	$ cts.	
....	1,618	215 77	....	1,810	482 70	....	23,853	4,783 47	1
....	14,813	1,975 07	....	....	....	....	34,591	5,930 67	2
861	38	17 22	....	....	....	861	38	17 22	3
168,675	7,066	4,498 10	....	....	....	239,980	12,266	7,350 30	4
169,536	7,104	4,515 32	....	....	....	240,841	12,304	7,367 52	
....	1,496	199 54	....	....	....	....	23,501	4,600 54	5
90	119	6 00	....	....	....	855	648	82 50	6
....	....	....	....	....	....	1,598	361	79 90	7
90	119	6 00	....	....	....	2,453	1,009	162 40	
....	4,560	760 04	....	46,649	15,549 72	....	343,087	89,279 26	8
2	10	2 34	....	....	....	7,578	19,538	6,837 14	9
121,236	23,153	2,315 30	....	....	....	121,236	23,153	2,315 30	10
19,500	43,722	6,890 03	....	....	....	4,495,550	8,360,349	2,379,196 53	11
725	1,719	62 88	....	....	....	747,251	489,180	83,795 80	12
20,225	45,441	6,952 91	....	....	....	5,242,801	8,849,529	2,462,992 33	
....	4,080	680 02	....	....	....	....	4,855	873 77	13
2,394,461	52,788	7,981 49	....	....	....	2,437,845	53,726	8,198 41	14
....	....	....	....	....	....	127,043	3,913	1,270 43	15
2,394,461	52,788	7,981 49	....	....	....	2,564,888	57,639	9,468 84	
108,555	7,729	3,618 50	....	....	....	116,988	8,518	4,040 15	16
466,710	93,206	12,445 86	31,716	4,237	1,691 51	1,316,820	244,503	46,873 13	17
646,765	137,678	18,357 13	546	146	38 92	1,379,608	330,593	56,949 85	18
1,113,475	230,884	30,802 99	32,262	4,383	1,730 43	2,696,428	575,096	103,822 98	

No. 14.—SUMMARY STATEMENT of Foreign Merchandise

	Articles and General Tariff Rates.		Total Imports.		General Tariff.		
			Quantity.	Value.	Quantity.	Value.	Duty.
	DUTIABLE GOODS—*Con.*			$		$	$ cts.
1	Coffee, green, N.E.S., 10 p.c.	Lbs.	488,034	56,260	496,303	57,237	5,723 70
2	" extract of, N.E.S., or substitutes therefor of all kinds, 3c. per lb.	"	71,107	10,320	40,639	2,984	1,219 17
3	" roasted or ground, when not imported direct from the country of growth and production, 2c. per lb. and 10 p.c.	"	196,848	38,414	205,969	40,846	8,203 98
4	" roasted or ground, and imitations of and substitutes for, N.O.P., 2c. per lb	"	300,346	33,206	313,747	34,066	6,274 94
5	" condensed with milk, 30 p.c.	"	162	38	147	35	10 50
	Total, coffee		1,056,497	138,238	1,056,805	135,168	21,432 29
6	Collars of cotton or linen, xylonite, xyolite or celluloid, 35 p.c.	Doz.	199,631	184,698	133,888	125,656	43,979 60
7	Combs for dress and toilet, of all kinds, 35 p.c.	$	....	238,750	....	129,362	45,276 70
	Copper and manufactures of—						
8	Nails, tacks, rivets and burrs or washers, 30 p.c.	$	....	3,460	....	2,945	883 50
9	Wire, plain, tinned or plated, 15 p.c.	Lbs.	216,794	40,134	213,281	39,395	5,909 25
10	Wire cloth, &c., 25 p.c.	$	....	3,303	....	643	160 75
11	All other manufactures of, N.O.P., 30 p.c.	"	....	96,090	....	87,398	26,219 40
	Total, copper		....	142,987	....	130,381	33,172 90
12	Cordage, cotton, of all kinds, 25 p.c.	Lbs.	159,360	21,279	65,019	9,172	2,293 00
13	" and twines of all kinds, N.E.S., (see Twines) 25 p.c.	"	2,110,550	240,296	698,567	85,206	21,301 50
	Total, cordage		2,269,910	261,575	763,586	94,378	23,594 50
14	Corks, and other manufactures of cork-wood, or cork-bark, N.O.P., 20 p.c.	$	....	194,404	....	184,620	36,924 00
15	Corsets, 35 p.c.	"	....	113,233	....	111,703	39,096 05
16	Corset clasps, busks, blanks and steels, and corset wires, tipped or untipped, 35 p.c.	"	....	3,031	....	2,841	994 35
17	Costumes and scenery, theatrical, according to material	"	....	21,591	....	20,738	4,198 35
	Cotton, manufactures of—						
18	Duck, gray or white, N.E.S., 22½ p.c.	Yds.	311,873	81,220	220,242	56,863	12,794 45
19	Embroideries, white, 25 p.c.	$	....	536,604	....	505,030	126,257 50
20	Gray, unbleached cotton fabrics, 25 p.c.	Yds.	628,023	45,670	549,382	40,020	10,005 00
21	White or bleached cotton fabrics, 25 p.c.	"	15,483,996	1,274,640	2,870,295	257,029	64,257 25
22	Fabrics, printed, dyed or coloured, N.O.P., 35 p.c.	"	36,259,318	3,608,467	6,172,415	598,359	209,425 65
23	Jeans, coutilles and sateens, imported by corset and dress stay-makers for use in their own factories, 20 p.c.	"	1,076,307	106,080	1,062,391	104,393	20,878 60
24	Handkerchiefs, 35 p.c.	$	....	335,733	....	54,769	19,169 15
25	Batts, batting and sheet wadding, 25 p.c.	Lbs.	129,358	16,135	124,946	15,235	3,808 75
26	Knitting yarn, hosiery yarn or other cotton yarn, 25 p.c.	"	191,473	45,644	123,038	29,355	7,338 75
27	Cotton warps, 25 p.c.	$	....	2,241	....	1,238	309 50
28	Seamless bags, 20 p.c.	"	....	19,364	....	8,557	1,711 40

Imported into Canada, &c.—*Continued.*

ENTERED FOR CONSUMPTION.

Preferential Tariff.			Surtax Tariff.			Total.			
Quantity.	Value.	Duty.	Quantity.	Value.	Duty.	Quantity.	Value.	Duty Collected.	
	$	$ cts.		$	$ cts.		$	$ cts.	
						496,303	57,237	5,723 70	1
30,341	7,242	606 84				70,980	10,226	1,826 01	2
1,515	268	38 08				207,484	41,114	8,242 06	3
124	14	1 66				313,871	34,080	6,276 60	4
15	3	0 60				162	38	11 10	5
31,995	7,527	647 18				1,088,800	142,695	22,079 47	
45,658	41,106	9,591 68	19,962	17,790	8,302 14	199,508	184,552	61,873 42	6
	81,483	19,013 06		27,671	12,913 18		238,516	77,202 94	7
	515	103 00					3,460	986 50	8
3,217	686	68 60	19	14	2 80	216,517	40,095	5,980 65	9
	2,660	443 34					3,303	604 09	10
	8,146	1,629 20		6	2 40		95,550	27,851 00	11
	12,007	2,244 14		20	5 20		142,408	35,422 24	
94,341	12,107	2,421 40				159,360	21,279	4,714 40	12
1,438,858	155,743	31,148 60	19	3	1 00	2,137,444	240,952	52,451 10	13
1,533,199	167,850	33,570 00	19	3	1 00	2,296,804	262,231	57,165 50	
	3,705	493 98		189	50 40		188,514	37,468 38	14
	1,119	261 15		103	48 08		112,925	39,405 28	15
	190	44 33					3,031	1,038 68	16
	97	20 21		36	9 60		20,871	4,228 16	17
93,377	24,402	3,660 35				313,619	81,265	16,454 86	18
	21,058	3,509 66		5,166	1,722 00		531,254	131,489 16	19
78,507	5,636	939 29	32	3	1 00	627,921	45,659	10,945 29	20
12,595,828	1,013,911	168,987 25	70,626	5,715	1,904 97	15,536,749	1,276,655	235,149 47	21
29,676,367	2,950,950	688,559 11	272,180	51,352	23,964·33	36,120,962	3,600,661	921,949 09	22
13,916	1,687	224 95				1,076,307	106,080	21,103 55	23
	282,069	65,816 86		554	258 53		337,392	85,244 54	24
3,728	683	113 84	684	217	72 31	129,358	16,135	3,994 90	25
68,435	16,289	2,714 91				191,473	45,644	10,053 66	26
	1,003	167 17					2,241	476 67	27
	10,805	1,440 69					19,362	3,152 09	28

No. 14.—SUMMARY STATEMENT of Foreign Merchandise

	Articles and General Tariff Rates.		Total Imports.		General Tariff.		
			Quantity.	Value.	Quantity.	Value.	Duty.
	DUTIABLE GOODS—*Con.*			$		$	$ cts.
	Cotton, manufactures of—*Con.*						
1	Sheets and bed quilts and damask of cotton, N.O.P., 30 p.c.	$	...	202,866	...	25,509	7,652 70
2	Shirts of cotton, 35 p.c.	Doz.	39,990	173,242	28,113	116,076	40,626 60
3	Sowing thread on spools, 25 p.c.	$	...	355,694	...	198,448	49,612 00
4	Sewing cotton thread in hanks, 3 and 6 cord, 15 p.	Lbs.	641,002	384,044	545	222	33 30
5	Crochet cotton thread, on spools or tubes or in balls, 25 p.c.	$	...	20,959	...	9,469	2,367 25
6	All other cotton thread, N.E.S., 25 p.c.	Lbs.	2,647	524	917	313	78 25
7	Clothing, N.E.S , 35 p.c.	$	...	672,763	...	414,096	144,933 60
8	Blouses and shirt waists, 35 .c.	"	...	87,949	...	81,221	28,427 35
9	Cotton bags made up by the use of the needle, not otherwise provided for, 35 p.c.	"	...	63,389	...	56,443	19,755 05
10	Lampwicks, 25 p.c.	"	...	10,894	...	5,698	1,424 50
11	Shawls, 30 p.c.	"	...	1,881	...	85	25 50
12	Socks and stockings, 35 p.c.	Doz. prs.	247,094	314,368	33,357	30,102	10,535 70
13	Tape not dyed or coloured, 25 p.c.	$	...	62,322	...	12,438	3,109 50
14	" dyed or , 35 p.c.	"	...	32,530	...	11,610	4,063 50
15	Towels, 30 p.ccoloured.	"	...	98,383	...	2,086	625 80
16	Undershirts and drawers, 35 p.c.	"	...	100,024	...	85,559	29,945 65
17	Uncoloured cotton fabrics, bleached, viz.:—Scrims and window scrims, cambric cloths, muslin apron checks, brilliants, cords, piques, diapers, lenos, mosquito nettings; Swiss jaconet and cambric muslins, and plain, striped or checked lawns, 25 p.c.	Yds.	2,184,317	186,555	265,259	25,962	6,490 50
18	Velvet, velveteens and plush fabrics, N.E.S., 30 p.c.	"	1,842,146	469,779	355,901	105,709	31,712 70
19	Other articles made by the seamstress from cotton fabrics, N.O.P., 35 p.c.	$	...	191,653	...	131,676	46,086 60
	Total, cottons		...	9,501,617	...	2,983,570	903,462 05
20	Crapes, black, 20 p.c.	$	...	13,303	...	2,934	586 80
21	Cuffs of cotton, linen, xylonite, xyolite or celluloid, 35 p.c.	Prs.	45,565	5,151	38,430	4,225	1,478 75
22	Curtains and shams when made up, trimmed or untrimmed, 35 p.c.	$	...	633,991	...	231,734	81,106 90
23	Cyclometers and pedometers, 25 p.c.	"	...	1,683	...	1,156	289 00
	Drugs, dyes, chemicals and medicines—						
	Acids—						
24	Acetic and pyroligneous, N.E.S., not exceeding proof strength, 15c. per gall.	Galls.	61	42	61	42	? 15
25	Acetic and pyroligneous, in excess of the strength of proof, 15c. per gall., and 2c. additional for each degree above proof.	"	7,948	6,211	608	561	908 87
26	Acid, acetic and pyroligneous, crude, of any strength, not exceeding 30 p.c., 25 p.c.	"	49,945	2,864	49,890	2,860	715 00
27	Acid phosphate, N.O.P., 25 p.c.	Lbs.	332,523	19,492	332,363	19,458	4,864 50
28	Acids, mixed, N.E.S., 20 p.c.	"	297,644	7,875	297,340	7,808	1,561 60
29	Muriatic and nitric, 20 p.c.	"	109,875	3,932	107,737	3,540	708 00
30	Sulphuric, 25 p.c.	"	823,210	8,584	821,968	8,540	2,135 00
31	Other, N.E.S., 20 p.c.	"	504,526	46,904	329,508	15,235	3,047 00
32	Aniline dyes, in packages of less than 1 lb. weight, 20 p.c.	"	1,998	722	1,748	132	26 40

Imported into Canada, &c.—*Continued.*

Entered for Home Consumption.									
Preferential Tariff.			Surtax Tariff.			Total.			
Quantity.	Value.	Duty.	Quantity.	Value.	Duty.	Quantity.	Value.	Duty Collected.	
	$	$ cts.		$	$ cts.		$	$ cts.	
....	176,420	35,284 00	....	978	391 20	....	202,907	43,327 90	1
11,550	55,959	13,057 58	330	1,167	544 59	39,993	173,202	54,228 77	2
....	157,071	26,178 62	....	1,497	498 97	....	357,016	76,289 59	3
640,651	383,887	28,388 70	....	....	....	641,196	384,109	38,422 00	4
....	11,455	1,909 19	....	35	11 66	....	20,959	4,288 10	5
1,730	211	35 16	....	....	....	2,647	524	113 41	6
....	232,894	54,343 34	....	26,329	12,286 80	....	673,319	211,563 74	7
....	4,801	1,121 29	....	1,695	790 99	....	87,717	30,339 63	8
....	7,080	1,652 02	....	....	....	....	63,523	21,407 07	9
....	5,143	857 38	....	35	11 67	....	10,876	2,293 55	10
....	1,713	342 60	....	83	33 20	....	1,881	401 30	11
74,778	104,633	24,414 77	138,854	179,760	83,888 07	246,989	314,495	118,838 54	12
....	46,805	7,800 95	....	3,078	1,025 96	....	62,321	11,936 41	13
....	18,186	4,243 41	....	2,734	1,275 81	....	32,530	9,582 72	14
....	94,721	18,944 20	....	760	304 00	....	97,567	19,874 00	15
....	13,223	3,085 52	....	1,242	579 64	....	100,024	33,610 81	16
1,938,584	160,868	26,812 32	7	1	0 33	2,203,850	186,831	33,303 15	17
1,330,969	315,218	63,043 60	156,348	49,292	19,716 80	1,843,218	470,219	114,473 10	18
....	53,605	12,507 31	....	4,154	1,938 58	....	189,435	60,532 49	19
....	6,172,386	1,270,156 04	....	335,847	151,221 41	....	9,491,803	2,324,839 50	
....	9,986	1,331 52	....	383	102 11	....	13,303	2,020 43	20
6,484	851	198 60	651	75	35 00	45,565	5,151	1,712 35	21
....	401,347	93,648 36	....	1,110	518 01	....	634,191	175,273 27	22
....	254	42 33	....	....	....	....	1,410	331 33	23
....	....	....	....	....	....	61	42	9 15	24
7,942	6,201	7,239 79	4	9	10 77	8,554	6,771	8,159 43	25
55	4	0 66	....	....	....	49,945	2,864	715 66	26
160	34	5 67	....	....	....	332,523	19,492	4,870 17	27
304	67	8 93	....	....	....	297,644	7,875	1,570 53	28
2,403	288	38 40	10	56	14 93	110,150	3,884	761 33	29
617	18	3 01	....	....	....	822,585	8,558	2,138 01	30
130,270	25,213	3,361 80	41,185	5,881	1,568 34	500,963	46,329	7,977 14	31
....	....	....	250	590	157 33	1,998	722	183 73	32

No. 14.—SUMMARY STATEMENT of Foreign Merchandise

No.	Articles and General Tariff Rates.		Total Imports.		General Tariff.		
			Quantity.	Value.	Quantity.	Value.	Duty.
	DUTIABLE GOODS—*Con.*			$		$	$ cts.
	Drugs, dyes, &c.—*Con.*						
1	Gelatine and isinglass, 25 p.c	Lbs.	216,768	63,037	146,022	39,489	9,872 25
2	Glue, powdered or sheet, 25 p.c	"	2,811,950	219,005	1,478,535	124,827	31,206 75
3	Glue, liquid, 25 p.c.	$	....	14,659	....	14,144	3,536 00
4	Glycerine, N.E.S., 20 p.c.	Lbs.	1,335,159	115,998	66,361	7,461	1,492 20
5	Glycerine, imported by manufacturers of explosives for use in the manufacture thereof in their own factories, 10 p.c.	"	2,385,224	227,948	346,229	32,285	3,228 50
6	Gums—Camphor, 20 p.c	"	32,770	22,698	24,826	16,435	3,287 00
7	" Opium (crude) $1 per lb	"	75,652	285,317	4,770	9,922	4,770 00
8	" Other, N.E.S., 20 p.c	"	12,542	2,329	12,542	2,329	465 80
9	Liquorice, in paste, rolls and sticks, 20 p.c.	"	2,556,324	192,218	2,196,188	170,357	34,071 40
10	Magnesia, 20 p.c.	"	266,554	8,727	206,333	4,828	965 60
11	Milk food, and other similar preparations, 30 p.c	$	....	90,140	....	50,930	15,279 00
12	Morphine, 20 p.c	Oz.	5,441	6,431	329	671	134 20
13	Opium, powdered, $1.35 per lb.	Lbs.	11,548	36,026	83	240	112 05
14	Proprietary medicines, in liquid form, containing alcohol, 50 p.c	$	....	73,170	....	72,484	36,242 00
15	Proprietary medicines, not otherwise provided for, 25 p.c.	"	....	444,541	....	324,477	81,119 25
16	Potash or potassa, bicarbonate of, 20 p.c.	Lbs.	7,152	730	6,268	506	101 20
17	Salts, glauber, 20 p.c	"	233,923	1,032	67,618	377	75 40
18	Soda, bicarbonate of, 20 p.c	"	5,088,929	46,619	576,615	6,053	1,210 60
19	Sodium, hyposulphite, 20 p.c	$	....	11,278	....	9,018	1,803 60
20	Sulphuric ether, chloroform and solutions of peroxides of hydrogen, 25 p.c.	Lbs.	183,411	32,408	142,526	17,162	4,290 50
21	Thorium, nitrate, 20 p.c	"	....	29	....	....	....
22	Vaseline and all similar preparations of petroleum, for tiolet, medicinal or other purposes, 25 p.c	$	....	14,308	....	14,244	3,561 00
23	Yeast cakes, 6c per lb.	Lbs.	3,681	366	3,616	359	216 96
24	Yeast, compressed, in packages weighing less than 50 lbs., 6c per lb.	"	870	178	870	178	52 20
25	Yeast, compressed, in bulk or mass of not less than 50 lbs., 3c per lb.	"	226,329	48,072	226,329	48,072	6,789 87
26	All other drugs, dyes and chemicals, &c., not otherwise provided for, 20 p.c.	$	....	610,708	....	368,879	73,775 80
	Total, drugs, &c.		....	2,664,598	... .	1,393,903	331,634 65
	Earthen and chinaware:—(See Bricks and Tiles).						
27	Baths, tubs and washstands of earthenware, stone, cement or clay, or of other material, N.O.P., 30 p.c.	$	....	68,153	....	52,062	15,618 60
28	Brown or coloured earthen and stoneware, and Rockingham ware, 30 p.c.	"	....	8,366	....	5,017	1,505 10
29	Decorated, printed or sponged, and all earthenware, N.E.S., 30 p.c.	"	....	191,083	....	54,691	16,407 30
30	Demijohns, churns or crocks, 30 p.c.	"	....	10,272	....	9,211	2,763 30
31	White granite or ironstone ware, C.C. or cream coloured ware, 30 p.c.	"	.. ..	46,284	....	8,737	2,621 10
32	Tableware of china, porcelain or other clay, 30 p.c	"	....	944,555	....	153,394	46,018 20
33	China and porcelain ware, N.E.S., 30 p.c.	"	... .	210,405	....	103,442	31,032 60
34	Earthenware tiles, 35 p.c	"	....	77,824	....	49,351	17,272 85
35	Manufactures of earthenware, N.E.S., 30 p.c.	"	....	117,875	....	98,115	29,434 50
	Total, earthenware		....	1,674,817	.. ....	534,020	162,673 55

Imported into Canada, &c.—*Continued.*

ENTERED FOR HOME CONSUMPTION.

Preferential Tariff.			Surtax Tariff.			Total.			
Quantity.	Value.	Duty.	Quantity.	Value.	Duty.	Quantity.	Value.	Duty Collected.	
	$	$ cts.		$	$ cts.		$	$ cts.	
42,832	15,323	2,553 85	32,977	8,186	2,728 65	221,831	62,998	15,154 75	1
616,125	47,707	7,951 31	657,921	42,984	14,328 01	2,752,581	215,518	53,486 07	2
	488	81 38		52	17 34		14,684	3,634 72	3
1,262,930	105,532	14,071 02				1,329,291	112,993	15,563 22	4
2,065,104	200,729	13,382 01				2,411,333	233,014	16,610 51	5
11,417	7,582	1,010 94				36,243	24,017	4,297 94	6
63,757	252,009	42,504 67	5	12	6 67	68,532	261,943	47,281 34	7
						12,542	2,329	465 80	8
53,027	4,236	564 90				2,249,215	174.593	34,636 30	9
30,139	2,496	332 79	30,082	1,403	374 14	266,554	8,727	1,672 53	10
	39,414	7,882 80					90,344	23,161 80	11
5,112	5,760	768 02				5,441	6,431	902 22	12
118	313	106 20				201	553	218 25	13
				3,192	2,127 98		75,676	38,369 98	14
	122,836	20,473 55		4,621	1,540 80		451,934	103,133 20	15
884	224	29 88				7,152	730	131 08	16
163,090	623	83 07	3,215	32	8 54	233,923	1,032	167 01	17
4,509,311	40,326	5,376 86				5,085,926	46,379	6,587 46	18
	2,060	274 67		200	53 33		11,278	2,131 60	19
10,887	7,446	1,241 01	44,374	7,240	2,413 38	197,787	31,848	7,944 89	20
				29	7 74		29	7 74	21
	2	0 34		62	20 67		14,308	3,582 01	22
						3,616	359	216 96	23
						870	178	52 20	24
						226,329	48,072	6.789 87	25
	179,826	23,977 81		63,504	16,934 58		612,209	114,688 19	26
	1,066,757	153,325 34		138,053	42,312 80		2,598,713	527,272 79	
	15,747	3,149 40		19	7 60		67,828	18,775 60	27
	3,346	669 20					8,363	2,174 30	28
	122,668	24,533 60		14,193	5,677 20		191,552	46,618 10	29
	1,205	241 00		92	36 80		10,508	3,041 10	30
	39,223	7,844 60					47,960	10,465 70	31
	705,415	105,812 25		97,255	38,902 00		956,064	190,732 45	32
	34,715	6,943 00		75,856	30,342 40		214,013	68,318 00	33
	28,877	6,737 96		19	8 87		78,247	24,019 68	34
	16,788	3,357 60		2,921	1,168 40		117,824	33,960 50	35
	967,984	159,288 61		190,355	76,143 27		1,692,359	398,105 43	

No. 14.—SUMMARY STATEMENT of Foreign Merchandise

	Articles and General Tariff Rates.		Total Imports. Quantity.	Total Imports. Value.	General Tariff. Quantity.	General Tariff. Value.	General Tariff. Duty.
	DUTIABLE GOODS—*Con.*			$		$	$ cts.
1	Eggs, 3c. per doz	Doz.	485,229	94,232	462,669	88,937	13,880 07
2	Elastic round or flat, including garter elastic, 35 p.c.	$	....	118,362	....	26,944	9,430 40
3	Electric light carbons and carbon points, of all kinds, N.E.S., 35 p.c.	M.	5,661	48,064	4,914	37,908	13,267 80
4	Electric carbons over 6 inches in circumference, 15 p.c	No.	120	71	120	71	10 65
	Total, electric carbons		....	48,135	....	37,979	13,278 45
5	Electric apparatus, N.E.S., insulators of all kinds, &c., electric and galvanic batteries; telegraph and telephone instruments, 25 p.c.	$	....	2,461,726	....	2,382,118	595,529 50
6	Electric motors, generators, dynamos and sockets, 25 p.c	"	....	1,003,853	....	994,219	248,554 75
	Total, electric apparatus		....	3,465,579	....	3,376,337	844,084 25
7	Embroideries, not otherwise provided for, 35 p.c.	$	....	86,288	....	63,154	22,103 90
8	Emery wheels and manufactures of emery, 25 p.c.	"	.. ..	42,086	.. . .	41,626	10,406 50
9	Express parcels of small value	"	... .	1,065,380	....	1,061,815	277,330 71
	Fancy goods, viz.—						
10	Alabaster, spar, amber, terra cotta, or composition ornaments, 35 p.c.	$	....	3,884	....	3,190	1,116 50
11	Bead ornaments and statuettes, N.E.S., 35 p.c.	"	....	76,233	....	60,779	21,272 65
12	Boxes, fancy, ornamental cases and writing desks, &c., &c., 35 p.c.	"	....	138,631	....	71,983	25,194 05
13	Braids, bracelets, cords, fringes, tassels, &c., 35 p.c.	"	....	454,879	....	217,973	76,290 55
14	Casket gimps and fringes embroidered or embossed chiffon imported by manufacturers of burial caskets or robes for use in such manufacture, 10 p.c.	"	....	9,892	....	9,615	961 50
15	Cases for jewellery, watches, silver ware, plated ware and cutlery, 35 p.c.	"	....	20,007	....	13,709	4,798 15
16	Fancy manufactures of bone, shell, horn and ivory, N.E.S., 35 p.c.	"	....	601	....	332	116 20
17	Fans, 35 p.c.	"	....	12,078	....	10,320	3,612 00
18	Flowers, artificial, 25 p.c	"	....	264,749	....	165,505	41,376 25
19	Feathers, fancy, undressed, 20 p.c.	"	....	5,061	....	4,519	903 80
20	" " N.E.S., 30 p.c.	"	....	272,190	.. . .	114,619	34,385 70
21	" ostrich and vulture, dressed, 30 p.c.	"	....	22,605	....	3,384	1,015 20
22	Ivory or bone dice, draughts, chessmen, &c., 20 p.c.	"	....	791	... .	726	145 20
23	Laces, lace collars and similar goods, lace nets and nettings of cotton, linen, silk or other material, 35 p.c.	"	....	1,704,692	. . ....	561,465	196,512 75
24	Millinery not elsewhere provided for, according to material	"	....	296	....	227	77 45
25	Toys and dolls of all kinds, 35 p.c.	"	....	362,440	....	145,693	50,992 55
26	All other, N.E.S., 35 p.c.	"	....	18,145	....	13,229	4,630 15
	Total, fancy goods		.. . .	3,367,174	....	1,397,268	463,400 65

Imported into Canada, &c.—*Continued.*

Entered for Home Consumption.									
Preferential Tariff.			Surtax Tariff.			Total.			
Quantity.	Value.	Duty.	Quantity.	Value.	Duty.	Quantity.	Value.	Duty Collected.	
	$	$ cts.		$	$ cts.		$	$ cts.	
....	....	....	....	....	....	462,669	88,937	13,880 07	1
....	91,314	21,306 85	....	104	48 53	....	118,362	30,785 78	2
....	....	....	756	10,238	4,777 72	5,670	48,146	18,045 52	3
....	....	....	....	....	....	120	71	10 65	4
....	....	....	....	10,238	4,777 72	....	48,217	18,056 17	
....	66,213	11,035 63	....	9,083	3,027 69	....	2,457,414	609,592 82	5
....	7,732	1,288 67	....	166	55 33	....	1,002,117	249,898 75	6
....	73,945	12,324 30	....	9,249	3,083 02	....	3,459,531	859,491 57	
....	12,053	2,812 48	....	9,775	4,561 66	....	84,982	29,478 04	7
....	271	45 17	....	183	61 01	....	42,080	10,512 68	8
....	3,420	795 67	....	145	49 19	....	1,065,380	278,175 57	9
....	227	52 97	....	467	217 95	....	3,884	1,387 42	10
....	521	121 62	....	15,537	7,250 61	....	76,837	28,644 88	11
....	27,829	6,493 80	....	38,647	18,035 49	....	138,459	49,723 34	12
....	71,834	16,762 24	....	164,947	76,975 38	....	454,754	170,028 17	13
....	28	1 87	....	249	33 20	....	9,892	996 57	14
....	2,346	547 42	....	4,022	1,876 93	....	20,077	7,222 50	15
....	39	9 10	....	155	72 33	....	526	197 63	16
....	40	9 34	....	1,710	797 98	....	12,070	4,419 32	17
....	62,176	10,362 95	....	37,127	12,375 62	....	264,808	64,114 82	18
....	454	60 53	....	88	23 47	....	5,061	987 80	19
....	127,339	25,467 80	....	30,248	12,099 20	....	272,206	71,952 70	20
....	18,941	3,788 20	....	280	112 00	....	22,605	4,915 40	21
....	37	4 93	....	28	7 47	....	791	157 60	22
....	745,823	174,027 54	....	395,609	184,618 45	....	1,702,897	555,158 74	23
....	69	15 57	....	....	....	....	296	93 02	24
....	26,842	6,263 71	....	190,049	88,690 22	....	362,584	145,946 48	25
....	2,794	652 02	....	2,122	990 35	....	18,145	6,272 52	26
....	1,087,339	244,641 61	....	881,285	404,176 65	....	3,365,892	1,112,218 91	

No. 14.—SUMMARY STATEMENT of Foreign Merchandise

No.	Articles and General Tariff Rates.		Total Imports. Quantity.	Total Imports. Value.	General Tariff. Quantity.	General Tariff. Value.	General Tariff. Duty.
	DUTIABLE GOODS—*Con.*			$		$	$ cts.
1	Feathers, bed and other, undressed, N.O.P., 20 p.c.	$	....	26,978	....	27,501	5,500 20
2	Feathers, bed and other, dressed, N.O.P., 30 p.c.	"	....	206	....	122	36 60
3	Feathers, all other, N.E.S., 30 p.c.	"	... .	141	....	27	8 10
4	Featherbone in coils, 20 p.c.	"	....	455	....	443	88 60
5	Fertilizers, compounded or manufactured, 10 p.c.	"	....	167,513	....	157,519	15,751 90
6	Fibre, Kartavert, indurated fibre, vulcanized fibre and like material and manufactures of, N.E.S., 25 p.c.	"	....	44,570	....	44,261	11,065 25
7	Fireworks, firecrackers and torpedoes, all kinds, 25 p.c.	"	....	29,439	... .	29,497	7,374 25
	Fish—						
8	Cod, haddock, ling and pollock, fresh, imported otherwise than in barrels, &c., 50c. per 100 lbs.	Lbs.	1,490,576	53,686	1,490,260	53,674	7,451 39
9	Cod, haddock, ling and pollock, dry salted, 50c. per 100 lbs.	"	615,931	29,564	278,325	12,298	1,391 68
10	Cod, haddock, ling and pollock, wet salted, 50c. per 100 lbs.	"	1,432	101	1,432	101	7 17
11	Cod, haddock, ling and pollock, smoked, 1c. per lb.	"	42,456	2,524	42,586	2,532	425 86
12	Cod, haddock, ling and pollock, pickled, in barrels, 1c. per lb.	"	3,350	96	3,350	96	33 50
13	Halibut, fresh, not in barrels, 50c. per 100 lbs.	"	1,174,598	53,444	1,174,345	53,422	5,871 83
14	Halibut, pickled, in barrels, 1c. per lb.	"	129	12	129	12	1 29
15	Herrings, fresh, not in barrels, 50c. per 100 lbs.	"	13,965	508	12,365	449	61 83
16	Herrings, pickled or salted, ½c. per lb.	"	515,397	23,662	346,306	17,555	1,731 54
17	" smoked, 1c. per lb.	"	4,085	356	4,067	355	40 67
18	Mackerel, fresh, 1c. per lb.	"	15,031	1,626	14,931	1,614	149 31
19	" pickled, 1c. per lb.	"	199,552	8,764	3,566	300	35 66
20	Sea fish, other, fresh, not in barrels, 50c. per 100 lbs.	"	27,806	1,578	27,806	1,578	139 04
21	Sea fish, other, pickled, in barrels, 1c. per lb.	"	204,432	3,384	832	46	8 32
22	Sea fish, other, preserved, N.E.S., 25 p.c.	"	14,716	1,413	4,726	565	141 25
23	Oysters, fresh in shell, 25 p.c.	Brls.	3,507	21,606	3,497	21,528	5,382 00
24	" shelled, in bulk, 10c. per gall.	Galls.	219,504	278,555	219,504	278,555	21,950 40
25	" canned, in cans not over 1 pint, 3c. per can	Cans.	15,866	1,775	15,770	1,768	473 10
26	Oysters, canned, in cans over one pint and not over one quart, 5c. per can	"	17,853	8,958	16,089	7,990	804 45
27	Oysters, canned, in cans exceeding one quart, 5c. additional for each quart or fraction of	"	.. . .	....	38	77	7 60
28	Oysters, prepared and preserved, N.E.S., 25 p.c.	Lbs.	484,356	37,955	482,003	40,783	10,195 75
29	Lobsters, fresh (not alive), 25 p.c.	Brls.	22	231	22	231	57 75
30	" canned, N.E.S., 25 p.c.	Lbs.	519	88	300	44	11 00
31	Bait fish, fresh, not in barrels, 50c. per 100 lbs.	"	16,000	560	....	....	....
32	Salmon, fresh, not in barrels, ½c. per lb.	"	665,278	15,813	665,278	15,813	3,326 40
33	" smoked, 1c. per lb.	"	8,652	981	7,532	905	75 32
34	" canned, prepared or preserved, N.E.S., 25 p.c.	"	1,972	103	1,180	131	32 75

SESSIONAL PAPER No. 11

Imported into Canada, &c.—*Continued.*

Entered for Home Consumption.									
Preferental Tariff.			Surtax Tariff.			Total.			
Quantity.	Value.	Duty.	Quantity.	Value.	Duty.	Quantity.	Value.	Duty Collected.	
	$	$ cts.		$	$ cts.		$	$ cts.	
....	48	6 41	....	302	80 54	....	27,851	5,587 15	1
....	84	16 80	....	....	....	....	206	53 40	2
....	48	9 60	....	66	26 40	....	141	44 10	3
....	12	1 60	....	....	....	....	455	90 20	4
....	7,795	519 71	....	2,194	292 53	....	167,508	16,564 14	5
....	296	49 35	....	13	4 33	....	44,570	1,118 93	6
....	....	....	....	....	....	....	29,497	7,374 25	7
316	12	1 05	....	....	....	1,490,576	53,686	7,452 44	8
....	....	....	....	....	....	278,325	12,298	1,391 68	9
....	....	....	....	....	....	1,432	101	7 17	10
....	....	....	....	....	....	42,586	2,532	425 86	11
....	....	....	....	....	....	3,350	96	33 50	12
....	....	....	....	....	....	1,174,345	53,422	5,871 83	13
....	....	....	....	....	....	129	12	1 29	14
....	....	....	....	....	....	12,365	449	61 83	15
163,287	5,885	544 31	6,054	244	40 35	515,647	23,684	2,316 20	16
18	1	0 12	....	....	....	4,085	356	40 79	17
....	....	....	....	....	....	14,931	1,614	149 31	18
....	....	....	....	....	....	3,566	300	35 66	19
....	....	....	....	....	....	27,806	1,578	139 04	20
....	....	....	....	....	....	832	46	8 32	21
9,735	814	135 72	....	....	....	14,461	1,379	276 97	22
....	....	....	....	....	....	3,497	21,528	5,382 00	23
....	....	....	....	....	....	219,504	278,555	21,950 40	24
....	....	....	....	....	....	15,770	1,768	473 10	25
....	....	....	....	....	....	16,089	7,990	804 45	26
....	....	....	....	....	....	38	77	7 60	27
....	....	....	....	....	....	482,003	40,783	10,195 75	28
....	....	....	....	....	....	22	231	57 75	29
....	....	....	....	....	....	300	44	11 00	30
....	....	....	....	....	....	....	....	....	31
....	....	....	....	....	....	665,278	15,813	3,326 40	32
....	....	....	....	....	....	7,532	905	75 32	33
72	13	2 17	....	....	....	1,252	144	34 92	34

No. 14.—SUMMARY STATEMENT of Foreign Merchandise

	Articles and General Tariff Rates.		Total Imports.		General Tariff.		
			Quantity.	Value.	Quantity.	Value.	Duty.
	DUTIABLE GOODS—Con.			$		$	$ cts.
	Fish—Con.						
1	Salmon, pickled or salted, 1c. per lb	Lbs.	1,437	77	1,437	77	14 37
2	Fish smoked, and boneless fish, N.E.S., 1c. per lb	"	42,042	2,367	41,994	2,363	419 94
3	Anchovies and sardines, packed in oil or otherwise, in tin boxes measuring not more than 5 inches long, 4 inches wide and 3½ inches deep, 5c. per box	Boxes.	147	33	160	32	8 00
4	Anchovies and sardines, in half boxes, measuring not more than 5 inches long, 4 inches wide and 1⅝ inches deep, 2½c. per box	½-boxes.	89,322	11,635	69,291	9,755	1,732 29
5	Anchovies and sardines, in quarter boxes, measuring not more than 4¾ inches long, 3½ inches wide and 1¼ inches deep, 2c. per box	¼-boxes.	1,844,857	133,133	1,780,976	120,147	35,619 52
6	Anchovies and sardines, imported in any other form, 30 p.c	$	....	5,203	....	2,627	788 10
7	Fish preserved in oil, except anchovies and sardines, 30 p.c	$	....	24,188	....	9,374	2,812 20
8	Fish, all other, not in barrels or half-barrels, fresh, 50c. per 100 lbs	Lbs.	410,482	24,062	404,482	23,843	2,022 50
9	Fish, all other, not in barrels or half-barrels, pickled, 50c. per 100 lbs	"	12,546	841	12,434	833	62 17
10	Fish, fresh or dried, N.E.S., imported in barrels or half-barrels, 1c. per lb	"	243,670	10,229	29,670	2,412	296 70
11	Fish, all other, pickled or salted, in barrels, 1c. per lb	"	21,518	707	7,918	367	79 18
12	Fish, prepared or preserved, N.E.S., 25 p.c	Lbs.	670,553	57,379	357,319	31,096	7,774 00
	Fish Oil—						
13	Cod, N.E.S., 20 p.c	Galls.	2,086	1,050	1,808	925	185 00
14	Cod-liver, 20 p.c	"	28,642	14,538	25,446	13,120	2,624 00
15	Whale and spermaceti, N.E.S., 20 p.c	"	3,809	2,361	3,707	2,296	459 20
16	Other, N.E.S., 20 p.c	"	36,781	10,512	36,781	10,512	2,102 40
17	Packages containing oysters or other fish not otherwise provided for, 25 p.c	$	....	12,229	....	11,092	2,773 00
18	Other articles, the produce of the fisheries, not specially provided for, 20 p.c.	"	....	14,097	....	14,065	2,813 00
	Total, fish		....	871,984	....	767,358	122,392 43
	Flax, hemp and jute—manufactures of, viz.—						
19	Bags or sacks of hemp, linen or jute, 20 p.c	"	....	119,253	....	35,464	7,092 80
20	Carpeting, rugs, matting, and mats of hemp or jute, 25 p.c	"	....	92,994	....	30,107	7,526 75
21	Carpet linings and stair pads, 25 p.c	"	....	5,048	....	4,661	1,165 25
22	Sail twine of flax or hemp to be used for boats' and ships' sails, 5 p.c	Lbs.	13,762	2,763	567	117	5 85
23	Damask of linen, stair linen, diaper, napkins, doylies, table and tray cloths, quilts, and like articles of linen, N.O.P. 30 p.c	$	....	729,468	....	98,763	29,628 90
24	Handkerchiefs, 35 p.c	"	....	219,626	....	25,168	8,808 80
25	Horse clothing, shaped or otherwise manufactured, 30 p.c	"	....	2,336	....	1,127	338 10
26	Towels, 30 p.c	"	....	179,627	....	7,681	2,304 30
27	Sheets and sheetings, 30 p.c	Yds.	9,516	2,059	3,154	460	138 00
28	Linens, brown or bleached, 25 p.c	"	672,850	73,316	8,780	1,707	426 75

Imported into Canada, &c.—*Continued.*

ENTERED FOR HOME CONSUMPTION.

Preferential Tariff.			Surtax Tariff.			Total.			
Quantity.	Value.	Duty.	Quantity.	Value.	Duty.	Quantity.	Value.	Duty Collected.	
	$	$ cts.		$	$ cts.		$	$ cts.	
....	....	....	....	....	....	1,437	77	14 37	1
....	....	....	....	....	....	41,994	2,363	419 94	2
12	4	0 40	....	....	....	172	36	8 40	3
236	60	3 93	....	....	....	69,527	9,815	1,736 22	4
42,602	1,980	568 01	....	....	....	1,823,578	122,127	36,187 53	5
....	2,352	470 40	....	27	10 80	....	5,006	1,269 30	6
....	12,990	2,598 00	....	61	24 40	....	22,425	5,434 60	7
6,000	219	20 00	....	....	....	410,482	24,062	2,042 50	8
112	8	0 37	....	....	....	12,546	841	62 54	9
....	....	....	....	....	....	29,670	2,412	296 70	10
....	....	....	....	....	....	7,918	367	79 18	11
276,162	22,275	3,712 71	....	....	....	633,481	53,371	11,486 31	12
....	....	....	....	....	....	1,808	925	185 00	13
22	29	3 87	200	86	22 94	25,668	13,235	2,650 81	14
102	65	8 67	....	....	....	3,809	2,361	467 87	15
....	....	....	....	....	....	36,781	10,512	2,102 40	16
....	25	4 16	....	....	....	....	11,117	2,777 16	17
....	32	4 27	....	....	....	....	14,097	2,817 27	18
....	46,764	8,078 16	....	418	98 49	....	814,540	130,569 08	
....	81,720	10,896 13	....	70	18 67	....	117,254	18,007 60	19
....	61,611	10,268 89	....	395	131 67	....	92,113	17,927 31	20
....	646	107 67	....	....	....	....	5,307	1,272 92	21
13,195	2,646	88 21	....	....	....	13,762	2,763	94 06	22
....	604,167	120,833 40	....	18,538	7,415 20	....	721,468	157,877 50	23
....	190,814	44,524 31	....	210	97 99	....	216,192	53,431 10	24
....	1,049	209 80	....	....	....	....	2,176	547 90	25
....	166,327	33,265 40	....	5,807	2,322 80	....	179,815	37,892 50	26
6,362	1,599	319 80	....	....	....	9,516	2,059	457 80	27
649,214	71,347	11,891 67	718	76	25 33	658,712	73,130	12,343 75	28

No. 14.—SUMMARY STATEMENT of Foreign Merchandise

	Articles and General Tariff Rates.		Total Imports.		General Tariff.		
			Quantity.	Value.	Quantity.	Value.	Duty.
	DUTIABLE GOODS—*Con.*			$		$	$ cts.
	Flax, hemp and jute—*Con.*						
1	Linen duck, canvas, huckabacks, or other manufactures of flax, N.E.S., 25 p.c.	$	....	689,033	....	39,684	9,921 00
2	Linen clothing, N.E.S., 35 p.c.	"	....	14,628	....	5,560	1,946 00
3	" blouses and shirt waists, 35 p.c.	"	....	931	....	521	182 35
4	" thread, 25 p.c.	Lbs.	259,899	167,783	7,789	3,864	966 00
5	Shirts of linen, 35 p.c.	Doz.	529	4,967	284	2,367	828 45
6	Yarn, singles, flax, hemp and jute, N.E.S., 25 p.c.	Lbs.	18,746	2,723	7,196	638	159 50
7	Tapestry, jute, 25 p.c.	$	....	100	....	47	11 75
8	Jute cloth, not otherwise finished than bleached or calendered, 10 p.c.	Yds.	13,609,142	556,845	366,348	14,051	1,405 10
9	Other articles made by the seamstress from linen fabrics, N.O.P., 35 p.c.	$	....	15,016	....	7,248	2,536 80
10	Other manufactures of hemp or jute, N.E.S., or of flax, hemp and jute combined, 25 p.c.	$	....	213,571	....	21,305	5,326 25
	Total, flax, hemp and jute		....	3,092,087	....	300,540	80,718 70
11	Foundry facings of all kinds, 25 p.c.	$	....	21,148	....	14,481	3,620 25
	Fruits, including nuts, viz.—						
12	Dried—Apples, 25 p.c.	Lbs.	34,409	2,868	32,109	2,610	652 50
13	Currants, 1 c. per lb.	"	9,797,568	325,193	10,188,156	341,846	101,881 56
14	Dates, 25 p.c.	"	2,228,770	45,473	2,114,451	42,546	10,636 50
15	Figs, 25 p.c.	"	2,884,796	104,013	2,873,910	103,974	25,993 50
16	Prunes, 1c. per lb.	"	6,808,116	252,777	6,992,257	259,178	68,378 97
17	Raisins, 1c. per lb.	"	16,546,307	674,932	16,853,388	683,679	168,533 88
18	All other, N.E.S., 25 p.c.	"	2,378,942	164,649	2,395,138	165,201	41,300 25
19	Almonds, shelled, 5c. per lb.	"	888,184	155,915	848,783	147,880	29,209 00
20	" not shelled, 3c. per lb.	"	929,642	71,623	868,801	66,944	17,975 95
21	Brazil nuts, not shelled, 3c. per lb.	"	228,515	18,113	217,906	17,250	6,471 50
22	Pecans, not shelled and shelled peanuts, N.E.S., 3c. per lb.	"	628,469	37,323	623,014	38,409	17,888 23
23	Walnuts, not shelled, 3c. per lb.	"	985,965	99,373	1,083,303	98,324	22,977 26
24	All other nuts, N.O.P., 2c. per lb.	"	6,036,912	276,327	5,872,560	278,364	117,451 20
25	" shelled, 5c. per lb.	"	857,048	134,342	952,660	139,777	21,604 49
26	Green—Apples, 40c. per brl.	Brl.	20,240	90,644	20,072	89,558	8,028 80
27	Blackberries, gooseberries, raspberries and strawberries, N.E.S., 2c. per lb.	Lbs.	1,485,586	138,937	1,484,833	138,824	29,696 66
28	Cherries, 2c. per lb.	"	121,613	18,024	120,986	17,937	2,419 72
29	Cranberries, 25 p.c.	Bush.	15,100	39,184	15,091	39,160	9,790 00
30	Currants, 2c. per lb.	Lbs.	610	37	610	37	12 20
31	Grapes, 2c. per lb.	"	2,028,254	142,951	2,002,008	140,616	40,040 16
32	Oranges, lemons and limes, in boxes of capacity not exceeding 2½ cubic feet, 2 c. per box	Boxes.	616,341	1,430,260	611,379	1,398,717	152,844 75
33	Oranges, lemons and limes in ½ boxes of capacity not exceeding 1¼ cubic feet, 13c. per box	½ "	25,302	33,540	25,445	30,087	3,307 84
34	Oranges, lemons and limes, in cases or other packages, N.E.S., 10c per cubic foot holding capacity	cu. ft.	224,539	140,971	225,738	141,727	22,573 80
35	Oranges, lemons and limes, in bulk, $1.50 per 1,000	No.	4,528	102	4,528	102	6 79
36	Oranges, lemons and limes in barrels, not exceeding the capacity of flour barrels, 55c. per brl.	Brls.	21,183	60,012	4,070	13,276	2,238 50
37	Peaches, N.O.P., 1c. per lb.	Lbs.	3,582,669	90,835	3,531,224	89,994	35,312 24
38	Plums, 25 p.c.	Bush.	46,659	62,559	56,647	62,522	15,630 50
39	Quinces, 25 p.c.	"	170	399	170	399	99 75

Imported into Canada, &c.—*Continued.*

ENTERED FOR HOME CONSUMPTION.

Preferential Tariff.			Surtax Tariff.			Total.			
Quantity.	Value.	Duty.	Quantity	Value.	Duty.	Quantity.	Value.	Duty Collected.	
	$	$ cts.		$	$ cts.		$	$ cts.	
	642,578	107,098 19		7,680	2,560 05		689,942	119,579 24	1
	9,347	2,181 19		26	12 13		14,933	4,139 32	2
	410	95 67					931	278 02	3
252,050	163,923	27,321 10	20	21	7 00	259,859	167,808	28,294 10	4
255	2,759	643 81				539	5,126	1,472 26	5
11,550	2,085	347 51				18,746	2,723	507 01	6
	53	8 84					160	20 59	7
13,242,794	542,794	36,186 43				13,609,142	556,845	37,591 53	8
	5,963	1,391 56		1,838	857 73		15,049	4,786 09	9
	192,901	32,150 51		482	160 67		214,688	37,637 43	10
	2,744,739	439,830 09		35,143	13,609 24		3,080,422	534,158 03	
	6,667	1,111 18					21,148	4,731 43	11
						32,109	2,610	652 50	12
643	24	4 29				10,188,799	341,870	101,885 85	13
						2,114,451	42,546	10,636 50	14
108	6	1 00				2,874,018	103,980	25,994 50	15
						6,992.257	259,178	68,378 97	16
						16,853.388	683,679	168,533 88	17
542	47	7 84				2,395,680	165,248	41,308 09	18
1,852	408	61 73				850,635	148.288	29,270 73	19
						868,801	66,944	17,975 95	20
						217,906	17,250	6,471 50	21
						623,014	38,409	17,888 23	22
						1.083,303	98,324	22,977 26	23
675	84	9 00				5,873,235	278,448	117,460 20	24
14,530	1,164	484 33				967,190	140,941	22,088 82	25
						20,072	89,558	8,028 80	26
						1,484,833	138,824	29,696 66	27
						120,986	17,937	2,419 72	28
						15,091	39,160	9,790 00	29
						610	37	12 20	30
						2,002,008	140,616	40,040 16	31
3,254	4,404	542 42				614,633	1,403,121	153,387 17	32
47	34	4 08				25,492	30,121	3,311 92	33
220	166	14 65				225,958	141,893	22,588 45	34
						4,528	102	6 79	35
17,113	46,736	6,274 88				21,183	60,012	8,513 38	36
						3,531,224	89,994	35,312 24	37
						56,647	62,522	15,630 50	38
						170	399	99 75	39

No. 14.—SUMMARY STATEMENT of Foreign Merchandise

	Articles and General Tariff Rates.		Total Imports.		General Tariff.		
			Quantity.	Value.	Quantity.	Value.	Duty.
	DUTIABLE GOODS—*Con.*			$		$	$ cts.
	Fruits—*Con.*						
1	All other, N.E.S., 20 p.c.	$	....	69.729	....	69,465	13,893 00
2	Fruits in air-tight cans or other packages, 2½c. per lb.	Lbs.	2,217,160	116,923	1,038,843	66,423	23,374 20
3	Fruits preserved in brandy or preserved in other spirits, $2 per gall.	Galls.	1,520	498	179	558	358 00
	Total, fruits and nuts		....	4,798,526	....	4,685,384	1,010,581 70
4	Furniture, house, office, cabinet or store furniture of wood, iron or other material, in parts or finished, 30 p.c.	$	....	753,589	....	706,503	211,950 90
	Furs and manufactures of, viz.—						
5	Fur skins wholly or partially dressed, N.E.S., 15 p.c.	"	....	1,142,895	....	557,885	83,682 75
6	Caps, hats, muffs, tippets, capes, coats, cloaks, and other manufactures of fur, N.O.P., 30 p.c.	"	....	287,723	....	137,084	41,125 20
	Total, fur and manufactures of		....	1,430,618	....	694,969	124,807 95
7	Fuses, N.O.P., 20 p.c.	$	....	63,862	....	19,660	3,932 00
	Glass and manufactures of—						
8	Bulbs for electric lights, 10 p.c.	Doz.	215,960	40,609	211,530	40,128	4,012 80
9	Glass carboys or demijohns, empty or filled, bottles, decanters, flasks and phials, 30 p.c.	$	....	242,706	....	204,182	61,254 60
10	Glass jars and glass balls, and cut, pressed or moulded, crystal or glass table ware, decorated or not, 30 p.c.	"	....	330,469	....	308,267	92,480 10
11	Lamp chimneys, glass shades or globes, and blown glass table ware, 30 p.c.	"	....	136,034	....	110,821	33,246 30
12	Ornamental, figured and enamelled coloured glass and memorial or other ornamental window glass, N. O. P., 30 p.c.	"	....	61,756	....	14,266	4,279 80
13	Painted or vitrified, chipped, figured, enamelled and obscured white glass, 30 p.c.	Sq. ft.	168,118	9,308	64,233	5,181	1,554 30
14	Common and colourless window glass, 15 p.c.	"	38,623,833	950,901	24,031,720	618,797	92,819 55
15	Plain, coloured, opaque, stained or tinted or muffled glass in sheets, 20 p.c.	"	821,686	66,048	528,188	41,447	8,289 40
16	Plate glass, not bevelled in sheets or panes, not exceeding 7 square feet each, N.O.P., 10 p.c.	"	742,446	131,619	523,319	97,168	9,716 80
17	Plate glass, not bevelled in sheets or panes, exceeding 7 square feet each, and not exceeding twenty-five square feet each, N.O.P., 25 p.c.	"	764,850	129,965	462,028	71,893	17,973 25
18	" " N.E.S., 35 p.c.	"	917,498	189,137	415,615	81,176	28,411 60
19	" " bevelled, N.O.P., 35 p.c.	"	26,131	5,670	15,820	3,705	1,296 75
20	" " rough rolled, 30 p.c.	"	334,047	26,371	66,242	7,998	2,399 40
21	German looking glass (thin plate), unsilvered or for silvering, 20 p.c.	$	....	2,560	....	2,231	446 20
22	Silvered glass, bevelled or not, framed or not framed, 35 p.c.	"	....	80,029	....	35,831	12,540 85

Imported into Canada, &c.—*Continued.*

Entered for Home Consumption.									
Preferential Tariff.			Surtax Tariff.			Total.			
Quantity.	Value.	Duty.	Quantity.	Value.	Duty.	Quantity.	Value.	Duty Collected.	
	$	$ cts.		$	$ cts.		$	$ cts.	
....	2	0 27	....	....	....	....	69,467	13,893 27	1
1,037,183	44,732	15,557 80	385	48	11 55	2,076,411	111,203	38,943 55	2
....	....	....	....	....	....	179	558	358 00	3
....	97,807	22,962 29	....	48	11 55	....	4,783,239	1,033,555 54	
....	32,546	6,509 20	....	4,701	1,880 40	....	743,750	220,340 50	4
....	228,461	22,846 10	....	323,898	64,779 60	....	1,110,244	171,308 45	5
....	145,847	29,169 40	....	3,724	1,489 60	....	286,655	71,784 20	6
....	374,308	52,015 50	....	327,622	66,269 20	....	1,396,899	243,092 65	
....	42,932	5,724 35	....	310	82 66	....	62,902	9,739 01	7
230	16	1 06	4,200	465	62 00	215,960	40,609	4,075 86	8
....	31,001	6,200 20	....	107,553	43,021 20	....	342,736	110,476 00	9
....	11,457	2,291 40	....	10,741	4,296 40	....	330,465	99,067 90	10
....	452	90 40	....	21,264	8,505 60	....	132,537	41,842 30	11
....	47,440	9,488 00	....	....	....	....	61,706	13,767 80	12
103,885	4,127	825 40	....	....	....	168,118	9,308	2,379 70	13
14,502,853	329,256	24,693 93	....	....	....	38,534,573	948,053	117,513 48	14
291,421	24,435	3,258 10	2,177	166	44 27	821,786	66,048	11,591 77	15
219,127	34,451	2,296 87	....	....	....	742,446	131,619	12,013 67	16
302,822	58,072	9,678 75	....	....	....	764,850	129,965	27,652 00	17
500,329	107,538	25,092 51	....	....	....	915,944	188,714	53,504 11	18
10,311	1,965	458 48	....	....	....	26,131	5,670	1,755 23	19
267,805	18,373	3,674 60	....	....	....	334,047	26,371	6,074 00	20
....	....	....	....	329	87 74	....	2,560	533 94	21
....	28,526	6,656 10	....	15,667	7,311 38	....	80,024	26,508 33	22

No. 14.—SUMMARY STATEMENT of Foreign Merchandise

	Articles and General Tariff Rates.		Total Imports.		General Tariff.		
			Quantity.	Value.	Quantity.	Value.	Duty.
	DUTIABLE GOODS—*Con.*			$		$	$ cts.
	Glass, manufactures of—*Con.*						
1	Stained glass windows, 30 p.c.	$	....	610	....	154	46 20
2	All other glass and manufactures of glass, not otherwise provided for, including bent plate or other sheet glass, 20 p.c.	"	....	167,606	....	138,585	27,717 00
	Total, glass and manufactures of		....	2,671,398	....	1,781,830	398,484 90
3	Gloves and mitts of all kinds, 35 p.c.	"	....	1,167,094	....	626,876	219,406 60
	Gold and silver, manufactures of—						
4	Gold, silver and aluminium leaf, Dutch or schlag metal leaf, 25 p.c.	"	....	45,841	....	13,290	3,322 50
5	Manufactures of gold, N.E.S., 30 p.c.	"	....	14,741	....	14,193	4,257 90
6	Electro-plated ware and gilt ware of all kinds, N.E.S., 30 p.c.	"	....	337,849	....	224,797	67,439 10
7	Sterling or other silverware, 30 p.c.	"	....	180,947	....	74,736	22,420 80
	Total, gold and silver and manufactures of		....	579,378	....	327,016	97,440 30
8	Grease, axle, 20 p.c.	Lbs.	1,632,717	64,660	1,607,949	63,322	12,664 40
	Gunpowder and other explosives, &c.:—						
9	Gun, rifle, sporting and cannister powder, 3c. per lb.	"	86,962	25,711	64,754	20,029	1,942 62
10	Blasting and mining powder, 2c. per lb.	"	949,035	89,240	274,835	12,268	5,496 70
11	Giant powder, nitro, nitro-glycerine and other explosives, 3c. per lb.	"	543,145	94,492	107,527	14,109	3,225 81
12	Gun, rifle and pistol cartridges or other ammunitions, N.O.P., 30 p.c.	$	....	392,510	....	168,225	50,467 50
13	Gun wads, percussion caps, primers and cartridge cases, 30 p.c.	"	....	29,270	....	15,369	4,610 70
14	Gun or pistol covers or cases, game bags, loading tools and cartridge belts of any material, 30 p.c.	"	....	16,049	....	15,142	4,542 60
	Total, gunpowder and explosives		....	647,272	....	245,142	70,285 93
	Gutta percha and India-rubber, manufactures of:—						
15	Boots and shoes, 25 p.c.	$	....	179,631	....	142,948	35,737 00
16	Belting, 25 p.c.	"	....	40,437	....	40,241	10,060 25
17	Clothing, and clothing made waterproof with India-rubber, 35 p.c.	"	....	50,370	....	17,079	5,977 65
18	Hose, including cotton or linen, lined with rubber, 35 p.c.	"	....	52,989	....	50,173	17,560 55
19	Packing, mats and matting, 35 p.c.	"	....	73,488	....	70,614	24,714 90
20	All other, not otherwise provided for, 25 p.c.	"	....	414,828	....	334,470	83,617 50
	Total gutta, percha and manufactures of		....	811,743	....	655.525	177,667 85
	Hair and manufactures of, not otherwise provided for—						
21	Braids, chains or cords, 35 p.c.	$	....	1,117	....	1,117	390 95
22	Curled or dyed, 20 p.c.	Lbs.	5,236	6,292	3,894	5,537	1,107 40
23	Hair cloth of all kinds, 30 p.c.	$	....	11,955	....	2,794	838 20
24	Other manufactures of, N.E.S., 35 p.c.	"	....	12,303	....	10,850	3,797 50
	Total, hair and manufactures of		....	31,667	....	20,298	6,134 05

SESSIONAL PAPER No. 11

Imported into Canada, &c.—*Continued.*

Entered for Home Consumption.									
Preferential Tariff.			Surtax Tariff.			Total.			
Quantity.	Value.	Duty.	Quantity.	Value.	Duty.	Quantity.	Value.	Duty Collected.	
	$	$ cts.		$	$ cts.		$	$ cts.	
....	101	20 20	....	355	142 00	....	610	208 40	1
....	18,504	2,467 48	....	10,053	2,680 87	....	167,142	32,865 35	2
....	715,714	97,193 48	....	166,593	66,151 46	....	2,664,137	561,829 84	
....	326,411	76,163 60	....	212,349	99,096 07	....	1,165,636	394,666 27	3
....	1,531	255 20	....	31,027	10,342 34	....	45,848	13,920 04	4
....	536	107 20	....	12	4 80	....	14,741	4,369 90	5
....	101,244	20,248 80	....	12,118	4,847 20	....	338,159	92,535 10	6
....	78,296	15,659 20	....	2,947	1,178 80	....	155,979	39,258 80	7
....	181,607	36,270 40	....	46,104	16,373 14	....	554,727	150,083 84	
21,344	1,138	151 73	474	55	14 66	1,629,767	64,515	12,830 79	8
21,733	5,619	434 66	....	....	....	86,487	25,648	2,377 28	9
674,200	76,972	8,989 37	....	....	....	949,035	89,240	14,486 07	10
64,350	24,440	1,287 00	....	....	....	171,877	38,549	4,512 81	11
....	229,888	45,977 60	....	....	....	....	398,113	96,445 10	12
....	12,968	2,593 60	....	239	95 60	....	28,576	7,299 90	13
....	906	181 20	....	....	....	....	16,048	4,723 80	14
....	350,793	59,463 43	....	239	95 60	....	596,174	129,844 96	
....	253	42 17	....	20	6 67	....	142,221	35,785 84	15
....	19	3 17	....	....	....	....	40,260	10,063 42	16
....	33,445	7,804 09	....	....	....	....	50,524	13,781 74	17
....	935	218 18	....	154	71 87	....	51,262	17,850 60	18
....	1,364	318 27	....	237	110 60	....	72,215	25,143 77	19
....	56,317	9,386 46	....	23,626	7,875 33	....	414,413	100,879 29	20
....	92,333	17,772 34	....	24,037	8,064 47	....	771,895	203,504 66	
....	....	....	....	....	....	....	1,117	390 95	21
336	551	73 52	1,006	204	54 40	5,236	6,292	1,235 32	22
....	9,119	1,823 80	....	28	11 20	....	11,941	2,673 20	23
....	777	181 33	....	676	315 46	....	12,303	4,294 29	24
....	10,447	2,078 65	....	908	381 06	....	31,653	3,593 7[illegible]	

No. 14.—SUMMARY STATEMENT of Foreign Merchandise

	Articles and General Tariff Rates.		Total Imports.		General Tariff.		
			Quantity.	Value.	Quantity.	Value.	Duty.
	DUTIABLE GOODS—*Con.*			$		$	$ cts.
	Hats, caps and bonnets, N.E.S :—						
1	Beaver, silk or felt, 30 p.c.	$	....	1,301,864	....	615,616	184,684 80
2	Straw, grass, chip or other material, N.E.S., 30 p.c.	"	....	935,086	....	600,526	180,157 80
3	Hat, cap and bonnet shapes, 30 p.c.	"	....	43,529	....	20,225	6,067 50
	Total, hats, caps, &c.		....	2,280,479	....	1,236,367	370,910 10
4	Hay, $2 per ton	Tons.	7,025	99,317	7,014	99,215	14,028 00
5	Honey, in the comb or otherwise, and imitations thereof, 3c. per lb	Lbs.	83,634	7,556	59,266	6,810	1,777 98
6	Hops, 6c. per lb.	"	983,776	184,897	706,342	140,406	42,380 52
7	Ink, writing, 20 p.c	$	....	54,959	....	40,726	8,145 20
8	" printing, 20 p.c	"	....	100,291	....	89,916	17,983 20
	Total, inks		....	155,250	....	130,642	26,128 40
	Iron and manufactures of, steel and manufactures of, or both combined :—						
	Agricultural implements, N.E S., viz. :						
9	Cultivators and weeders, 20 p.c	No.	3,829	26,394	3,827	26,282	5,256 40
10	Drills, grain seed, 20 p.c.	"	2,835	117,233	2,835	117,233	23,446 60
11	Farm road or field rollers, 25 p.c.	"	10	206	10	204	51 00
12	Forks, pronged, 25 p.c.	"	8,565	5,249	8,285	5,105	1,276 25
13	Harrows, 20 p.c.	"	4,387	66,232	4,383	66,166	13,233 20
14	Harvesters, self-binding, 20 p.c	"	932	96,756	927	95,846	19,169 20
15	Hay loaders, 25 p.c.	"	582	26,435	582	26,435	6,608 75
16	Hay tedders, 25 p.c	"	815	34,076	815	34,076	8,519 00
17	Hoes, 25 p.c	"	4,902	873	4,365	743	185 75
18	Horse rakes, 20 p.c.	"	872	20,639	929	21,587	4,317 40
19	Knives, hay or straw, 25 p.c.	"	1,265	60	1,265	60	15 00
20	Lawn mowers, 35 p.c	"	2,697	13,404	2,692	13,296	4,653 60
21	Manure spreaders, 20 p.c	"	1,133	108,054	1,133	108,054	21,610 80
22	Mowing machines, 20 p.c	"	766	24,692	766	24,692	4,938 40
23	Ploughs, 20 p.c.	"	17,034	477,747	17,031	477,647	95,529 40
24	Post hole diggers, 25 p.c	"	1,485	1,326	1,485	1,326	331 50
25	Potato diggers, 25 p.c	"	226	7,484	212	6,604	1,651 00
26	Rakes, N.E.S., 25 p.c.	"	9,620	1,822	9,608	1,819	454 75
27	Reapers, 20 p.c	"	284	13,872	284	13,872	2,774 40
28	Scythes, 25 p.c	Doz.	2,000	10,043	1,464	7,623	1,905 75
29	Sickles or reaping hooks, 25 p.c.	"	41	185	5	15	3 75
30	Spades and shovels and spade and shovel blanks, and iron or steel cut to shape for the same, 35 p.c.	"	19,643	47,037	4,254	22,897	8,013 95
31	Parts of agricultural implements paying 20 p.c., 20 p.c	$	....	472,843	....	472,373	94,474 60
32	All other agricultural implements, N.E.S., 25 p.c	"	....	42,461	....	37,959	9,489 75
33	Anvils and vises, 30 p.c.	"	....	50,792	....	31,301	9,390 30
34	Cart or wagon skeins or boxes, 30 p.c.	Lbs.	167,454	9,404	150,690	9,040	2,712 00
35	Springs, axles, axle bars, N.E.S., and axle blanks and parts thereof, of iron or steel, for railway or tramway or other vehicles, 35 p.c	Cwt.	69,948	143,874	56,042	110,939	38,828 65
36	Bar iron or steel rolled whether in coils, bundles, rods or bars, comprising rounds, ovals, squares and flats, and rolled shapes, N.O.P., $7 per ton.	"	986,461	1,542,046	665,117	1,047,214	232,790 95
37	Butts and hinges, N.E.S., 30 p.c.	$	....	92,706	....	91,634	27,490 20

Imported into Canada, &c.—*Continued.*

Entered for Home Consumption.									
Preferential Tariff.			Surtax Tariff.			Total.			
Quantity.	Value.	Duty.	Quantity.	Value.	Duty.	Quantity.	Value.	Duty Collected.	
	$	$ cts.		$	$ cts.		$	$ cts.	
	684,642	136,928 40		280	112 00		1,300,538	321,725 20	1
	330,946	66,189 20		1,893	757 20		933,365	247,104 20	2
	23,261	4,652 20		43	17 20		43,529	10,736 90	3
	1,038,849	207,769 80		2,216	886 40		2,277,432	579,566 30	
						7,014	99,215	14,028 00	4
25,288	679	505 76				84,554	7,489	2,283 74	5
251,366	38,406	10,054 64	62,557	16,630	5,004 56	1,020,265	195,442	57,439 72	6
	14,279	1,904 05		137	36 54		55,142	10,085 79	7
	10,228	1,363 82		210	55 99		100,354	19,403 01	8
	24,507	3,267 87		347	92 53		155,496	29,488 80	
1	15	2 00				3,828	26,297	5,258 40	9
						2,835	117,233	23,446 60	10
						10	204	51 00	11
280	144	24 02				8,565	5,249	1,300 27	12
3	36	4 80				4,386	66,202	13,238 00	13
						927	95,846	19,169 20	14
						582	26,435	6,608 75	15
						815	34,076	8,519 00	16
537	130	21 66				4,902	873	207 41	17
						929	21,587	4,317 40	18
						1,265	60	15 00	19
5	108	25 20				2,697	13,404	4.678 80	20
						1,133	108,054	21,610 80	21
						766	24,692	4,938 40	22
2	56	7 47				17,033	477,703	95,536 87	23
						1,485	1,326	331 50	24
14	880	146 67				226	7,484	1,797 67	25
12	3	0 50				9,620	1,822	455 25	26
						284	13,872	2,774 40	27
536	2,420	403 35				2,000	10,043	2,309 10	28
36	170	28 34				41	185	32 09	29
10,859	23,865	5,568 64				15,113	46,762	13,582 59	30
	398	53 08					472,771	94,527 68	31
	3,693	615 50		732	243 96		42,384	10,349 21	32
	19,185	3,837 00		306	122 40		50,792	13,349 70	33
16,764	364	72 80				167,454	9,404	2,784 80	34
13,906	32,935	7,684 96				68,948	143,874	46,513 61	35
322,302	494,495	75,204 56	10	20	4 66	987,429	1,541,729	308,000 17	36
	1,022	204 40					92,656	27,694 60	37

No. 14.—SUMMARY STATEMENT of Foreign Merchandise

	Articles and General Tariff Rates.		Total Imports.		General Tariff.		
			Quantity.	Value.	Quantity.	Value.	Duty.
	DUTIABLE GOODS—*Con.*			$		$	$ cts.
	Iron and steel—*Con.*						
1	Castings, iron or steel, in the rough, N.E.S., 25 p.c	$	....	387,693	....	369,076	92,269 00
2	Canada plates: Russia iron; terne plate, and rolled sheets of iron or steel coated with zinc, spelter or other metal, of all widths or thickness, N.O.P., 5 p.c	Cwt.	303,735	699,744	45,675	128,386	6,419 30
3	Cast iron pipe of every description, $8 per ton	"	343,404	447,450	44,664	92,755	17,865 60
4	Cast scrap iron, $2.50 per ton	Tons.	4,866	60,086	2,482	33,765	6,205 00
5	Chains, coil chain, chain links and chain shackles, of iron or steel, $\frac{5}{16}$th of an inch in diam. and over, 5 p.c	Cwt.	40,676	142,062	27,354	97,947	4,897 35
6	Chain, malleable sprocket or link belting, for binders, 20 p.c.	$	....	43,992	....	43,988	8,797 60
7	Chains, N.E.S., 30 p.c.	"	....	99,146	....	79,737	23,921 10
8	Tacks, shoe, 35 p.c.	Lbs.	20,886	2,442	20,746	2,437	852 95
9	Cut tacks, brads, sprigs, or shoe nails, double pointed, and other tacks of iron or steel, N.O.P., 35 p.c.	"	76,730	4,858	73,960	4,782	1,673 70
10	Engines, locomotives for railways, N.E.S., 35 p.c	No.	85	338,179	85	338,179	118,362 65
11	Fire engines, 35 p.c.	"	6	7,150	5	4,150	1,452 50
12	Fire extinguishing machines, 35 p.c	$	....	53,298	....	53,289	18,651 15
13	Gasoline engines, 25 p.c	No.	2,068	405,323	2,066	404,104	101,026 00
14	Steam engines and boilers, 25 p.c.	"	1,702	597,810	1,647	475,112	118,778 00
15	Fittings, iron or steel, for iron or steel pipe, 30 p.c.	Lbs.	6,698,195	387,015	6,549,883	381,443	114,432 90
16	Ferro-silicon, spiegeleisen and ferro-manganese, 5 p.c	Tons.	15,023	462,739	5,540	156,506	7,825 30
17	Forgings of iron or steel, of whatever shape or size, or in whatever stage of manufacture, N.E.S., and steel shafting, turned, compressed or polished; and hammered iron or steel bars or shapes, N.O.P., 30 p.c.	Lbs.	4,112,301	171,276	3,955,775	165,309	49,592 70
18	Hardware, viz.: Builders' cabinet-makers', upholsterers', harnessmakers', saddlers' and carriage hardware, including curry combs and horse boots, N.E.S., 30 p.c	$	....	751,859	....	671,449	201,434 70
19	Horse, mule, and ox shoes, 30 p.c	"	....	14,360	....	14,125	4,237 50
20	Iron or steel ingots, cogged ingots, blooms, slabs, billets, puddled bars, and loops or other forms, N.O.P., less finished than iron or steel bars, but more advanced than pig iron, except castings, $2 per ton	Cwt.	650,943	663,794	534,078	522,735	53,407 80
21	Iron or steel bridges or parts thereof; iron or steel structural work, columns, shapes or sections, drilled, punched, or in any further stage of manufacture than as rolled or cast, N.E.S., 35 p.c.	"	185,678	508,346	184,851	506,949	177,432 15
22	Iron in pigs, $2.50 per ton	Tons.	98,544	1,395,005	61,092	947,967	152,730 00
23	Locks of all kinds, 30 p.c.	$	....	283,455	....	274,962	82,488 60
	Machines, machinery, &c.:—						
24	Automobiles, 25 p.c.	No.	460	672,128	405	547,565	191,149 05
25	Fanning mills, 25 p.c	"	267	3,144	267	3,144	786 00
26	Grain crushers, 25 p.c.	"	1	71	1	71	17 75
27	Wind mills, 25 p.c	"	909	41,934	909	41,934	10,483 50

SESSIONAL PAPER No. 11

Imported into Canada, &c.—*Continued.*

ENTERED FOR HOME CONSUMPTION.

Preferential Tariff.			Surtax Tariff.			Total.			
Quantity.	Value.	Duty.	Quantity.	Value.	Duty.	Quantity.	Value.	Duty.	
	$	$ cts.		$	$ cts.		$	$ cts.	
....	16,716	2,786 02	....	....	....	....	385,792	95,055 02	1
258,060	571,358	19,045 48	....	....	....	303,735	699,744	25,464 78	2
298,740	354,695	79,664 10	....	....	....	343,404	447,450	97,529 70	3
2,384	26,321	3,973 35	....	....	....	4,866	60,086	10,178 35	4
13,263	43,692	1,456 58	....	....	....	40,617	141,639	6,353 93	5
....	....	....	....	....	....	....	43,988	8,797 60	6
....	15,557	3,111 40	....	3,894	1,557 60	....	99,188	28,590 10	7
140	5	1 17	....	....	....	20,886	2,442	854 12	8
634	39	9 11	2,536	37	17 26	77,130	4,858	1,700 07	9
....	....	....	....	....	....	85	338,179	118,362 65	10
....	....	....	....	....	....	5	4,150	1,452 50	11
....	9	2 10	....	....	....	....	53,298	18,653 25	12
2	1,219	203 19	....	....	....	2,068	405,323	101,229 19	13
51	121,187	20,197 86	....	....	....	1,698	596,299	138,975 86	14
146,709	5,391	1,078 20	....	....	....	6,696,592	386,834	115,511 10	15
9,117	295,546	9,851 52	366	10,687	712 47	15,023	462,739	18,389 29	16
108,237	4,427	885 40	34,099	590	236 00	4,098,111	170,326	50,714 10	17
....	79,410	15,882 00	....	1,251	500 40	....	752,110	217,817 10	18
....	....	....	....	212	84 80	....	14,337	4,322 30	19
75,743	100,533	5,049 65	41,122	40,526	5,482 80	650,943	663,794	63,940 25	20
827	1,397	325 99	....	....	....	185,678	508,346	177,758 14	21
35,703	453,011	59,505 16	2	69	6 67	96,797	1,401,047	212,241 83	22
....	6,349	1,269 80	....	1,995	798 00	....	283,306	84,556 40	23
42	73,883	17,239 36	1	24,423	11,397 42	448	645,871	219,785 83	24
....	....	....	....	....	....	267	3,144	786 00	25
....	....	....	....	....	....	1	71	17 75	26
....	....	....	....	....	....	909	41,934	10,483 50	27

No. 14.—SUMMARY STATEMENT of Foreign Merchandise

	Articles and General Tariff Rates.		Total Imports.		General Tariff.		
			Quantity.	Value.	Quantity.	Value.	Duty.
	DUTIABLE GOODS—*Con.*			$		$	$ cts.
	Iron and steel—*Con.*						
	Machines, machinery, &c.—*Con.*						
1	Ore crushers and rock crushers, stamp mills, Cornish and belted rolls, rock drills, air compressors, cranes, derricks, and percussion coal cutters, 25 p.c.	$	....	206,669	....	151,113	37,778 25
	Portable machines:—						
2	Fodder or feed cutters, 25 p.c.	No.	27	704	26	558	139 50
3	Horse powers, 25 p.c.	"	11	556	11	556	139 00
4	Portable engines, 25 p.c.	"	626	712,895	638	717,785	179,446 25
5	Portable saw mills and planing mills, 25 p.c.	"	73	31,382	73	31,382	7,845 50
6	Threshers and separators, 25 p.c.	"	648	358,485	652	359,986	89,996 50
7	All other portable machines, 25 p.c.	"	922	101,628	888	101,453	25,363 25
8	Parts of above articles, 25 p.c.	$	....	142,124	....	142,124	35,531 00
9	Sewing machines, and parts of, 30 p.c.	No.	14,311	286,235	13,456	269,334	80,800 20
10	Slot machines, 25 p.c.	"	2,389	41,628	2,388	41,603	10,400 75
11	Machines, type-writing, 25 p.c.	"	4,972	285,006	4,926	282,897	70,724 25
12	All other machinery composed wholly or in part of iron, or steel, N.O.P., 25 p.c.	$	....	5,335,669	....	4,944,513	1,236,128 25
13	Malleable iron castings and iron or steel castings, N.E.S., 25 p.c.	Cwt.	4,957	16,819	4,957	16,819	4,204 75
14	Nails and spikes, composition and sheathing nails, 15 p.c.	Lbs.	11,159	1,347	6,559	559	83 85
15	Nails and spikes, wrought and pressed, trunk, clout, coopers, cigar box, Hungarian, horse shoe and other nails, N.E.S., 30 p.	"	208,987	14,123	123,991	10,816	3,244 80
16	Nails and spikes, cut, and railway spikes $\frac{1}{2}$c. per lb.	"	2,080,075	38,313	2,108,010	38,559	10,540 05
17	Nails, wire, of all kinds, N.O.P., $\frac{3}{8}$c. per lb.	"	532,975	18,389	529,603	18,299	3,177 51
18	Mould boards, or shaves or plough plates, land sides and other plates for agricultural implements, cut to shape from rolled plates of steel but not moulded, punched, polished or otherwise manufactured, 5 p.c.	Cwt.	67,845	189,327	67,835	189,304	9,465 20
19	Pumps, N.E.S., 25 p.c.	$	....	261,645	....	246,653	61,663 25
20	Iron or steel railway bars or rails of any form, punched or not punched, N.E.S. for railways, which term for the purposes of this item shall include all kinds of railways, street railways and tramways, even although the same are used for private purposes only, and even although they are not used or intended to be used in connection with the business of common carrying of goods or passengers, 30 p.c.	Tons.	49,062	1,197,170	20,634	549,432	144,438 00
21	Railway fish-plates and tie plates, $8 per ton	"	4,337	171,186	3,512	144,243	28,096 00
22	Rolled iron or steel angles, tees, beams, channels, joists, girders, zees, stars or rolled shapes, or trough, bridge, building or structural rolled sections, or shapes, not punched, drilled or further manufactured than rolled, N.E.S., and flat eye bar blanks not punched or drilled, 10 p.c.	Cwt.	1,066,653	1,431,999	616,419	920,942	92,094 20

Imported into Canada, &c.—*Continued.*

ENTERED FOR HOME CONSUMPTION.

Preferential Tariff.			Surtax Tariff.			Total.			
Quantity.	Value.	Duty.	Quantity.	Value.	Duty.	Quantity.	Value.	Duty Collected.	
	$	$ cts.		$	$ cts.		$	$ cts.	
....	52,511	8,751 89	....	2,969	989 67	....	206,593	47,519 81	1
1	146	24 34	....	....	....	27	704	163 84	2
....	....	....	....	....	....	11	556	139 00	3
....	....	....	....	....	....	638	717,785	179,446 25	4
....	....	....	....	....	....	73	31,382	7,845 50	5
....	....	....	....	....	....	652	359,986	89,996 50	6
37	680	113 33	....	....	....	925	102,133	25,476 58	7
....	....	....	....	....	....	....	142,124	35,531 00	8
642	13,954	2,790 80	40	901	360 40	14,138	284,189	83,951 40	9
....	....	....	....	....	....	2,388	41,603	10,400 75	10
7	426	71 00	....	....	....	4,933	283,323	70,795 25	11
....	265,191	44,199 14	....	122,010	40,669 96	....	5,331,714	1,320,997 35	12
....	....	....	....	....	....	4,957	16,819	4,204 75	13
4,600	760	76 00	....	....	....	11,159	1,319	159 85	14
83,368	3,248	649 60	288	51	20 40	207,647	14,115	3,914 80	15
30,065	719	100 22	....	....	....	2,138,075	39,278	10,640 27	16
672	19	2 69	....	....	....	530,275	18,318	3,180 20	17
10	23	0 77	....	....	....	67,845	189,327	9,465 97	18
....	8,180	1,363 32	....	6,387	2,128 96	....	261,220	65,155 53	19
28,623	650,953	133,574 06	621	14,163	5,796 00	49,878	1,214,548	283,808 06	20
875	28,024	4,666 67	....	....	....	4,387	172,267	32,762 67	21
112,238	162,359	10,824 00	337,996	348,698	46,492 96	1,066,653	1,431,999	149,411 16	22

No. 14.—SUMMARY STATEMENT of Foreign Merchandise

	Articles and General Tariff Rates.		Total Imports.		General Tariff.		
			Quantity.	Value.	Quantity.	Value.	Duty.
	DUTIABLE GOODS—*Con.*			$		$	$ cts.
	Iron and steel—*Con.*						
1	Rolled iron or steel hoop, band, scroll or strip, 8 inches or less in width, No. 18 gauge and thicker, N.E.S., $7 per ton	Cwt.	63,296	109,530	46,713	83,897	16,349 55
2	Rolled iron or steel hoop, band, scroll or strip, thinner than No. 18 gauge, N.E.S., 5 p.c.	"	56,963	131,566	38,393	92,235	4,611 75
3	Rolled iron or steel angles, tees, beams, channels, girders and other rolled shapes or sections, weighing less than 35 lbs., per lineal yard, not punched, drilled or further manufactured than rolled, N.O.P., $7 per ton	"	376,692	540,013	214,572	319,239	75,100 20
4	Rolled iron or steel plates or sheets, sheared or unsheared, and skelp iron or steel, sheared or rolled in grooves, N.E.S., $7 per ton	"	256,248	394,302	175,948	274,578	61,581 81
5	Rolled iron or steel plates, not less than 30 inches in width and not less than ¼ inch in thickness, N.O.P., 10 p.c.	"	589,151	904,252	493,886	771,109	77,110 90
6	Rolled iron or steel sheets, No. 17 gauge and thinner, N.O.P., 5 per cent	"	342,848	719,173	148,675	327,397	16,369 85
7	Rolls of chilled iron or steel, 30 p.c.	"	10,496	34,172	10,152	32,882	9,864 60
8	Sad or smoothing, hatters' and tailors' irons, plated wholly or in part or not, 25 p.c.	$	....	16,747	....	16,138	4,034 50
9	Safes, doors for safes and vaults, 30 p.c.	"	....	114,131	....	113,972	34,191 60
10	Screws, iron and steel, commonly called 'Wood Screws,' N.E.S., 35 p.c.	Gross.	208,830	29,483	204,904	28,443	9,955 05
11	Scales, balances, weighing beams and strength testing machines, 30 p.c.	$	....	134,477	....	130,499	39,149 70
12	Sheets flat of galvanized iron or steel, 5 p.c.	Cwt.	369,580	1,101,128	155,508	484,318	24,215 90
13	Sheets iron or steel corrugated, galvanized, 25 p.c.	"	3,296	9,520	1,845	5,848	1,462 00
14	Sheets iron or steel corrugated, not galvanized, 30 p.c.	"	887	2,191	555	1,411	423 30
15	Skates, of all kinds and parts thereof, 35 p.c.	Pairs.	90,107	51,555	10,004	12,935	4,527 25
16	Skelp iron or steel, sheared or rolled in grooves, imported by manufacturers of wrought iron or steel pipe for use only in the manufacture of wrought iron or steel pipe in their own factories, 5 p.c.	Cwt.	680,729	888,257	673,346	872,729	43,636 45
17	Stoves of all kinds and parts thereof, N.E.S., 25 p.c.	$	....	473,422	....	468,141	117,035 25
18	Swedish rolled iron and Swedish rolled steel nail rods under half an inch in diameter for the manufacture of horse-shoe nails, 15 p.c.	Cwt.	20,459	42,429	20,459	42,429	6,364 35
19	Switches, frogs, crossings and intersections for railways, 30 p.c.	"	13,746	55,120	13,522	52,650	15,795 00
	Tubing—						
20	Boiler tubes of wrought iron or steel, including flues and corrugated tubes for marine boilers, 5 p.c.	$	....	472,854	....	391,718	19,585 90
21	Tubes of rolled steel, seamless, not joined or welded, not more than 1½ inches in diameter, 10 p.c.	"	....	4,199	....	4,154	415 40
22	Tubes, seamless steel, for bicycles, 10 p.c.	"	....	10,214	....	9,730	973 00

SESSIONAL PAPER No. 11

Imported into Canad, &c.—*Continued.*

ENTERED FOR HOME CONSUMPTION.

Preferential Tariff.			Surtax Tariff.			Total.			
Quantity.	Value.	Duty.	Quantity.	Value.	Duty.	Quantity.	Value.	Duty Collected.	
	$	$ cts.		$	$ cts.		$	$ cts.	
15,868	24,919	3,702 81	715	714	333 67	63,296	109,530	20,386 03	1
16,344	35,300	1,176 77	2,221	4,015	267 65	56,958	131,550	6,056 17	2
158,494	217,069	36,982 21	3,626	3,705	1,692 14	376,692	510,013	113,774 55	3
80,117	119,433	18,694 29	170	263	79 34	256,235	394,274	80,355 44	4
95,027	132,927	8,861 93	238	216	28 80	589,151	904,252	86,001 63	5
194,175	391,783	13,059 64	....	....	....	342,850	719,180	29,429 49	6
344	1,290	258 00	....	....	....	10,496	34,172	10,122 60	7
....	515	85 85	....	65	21 67	....	16,718	4,142 02	8
....	159	31 80	....	....	....	....	114,131	34,223 40	9
3,919	1,038	242 20	....	....	....	208,823	29,481	10,197 25	10
....	3,112	622 40	....	790	316 00	....	134,401	40,068 10	11
214,072	616,810	20,560 69	....	....	....	369,580	1,101,128	44,776 59	12
1,451	3,672	612 00	....	....	....	3,296	9,520	2,074 00	13
332	780	156 00	....	....	....	887	2,191	579 30	14
181	160	37 33	76,641	36,533	17,048 71	86,826	49,628	21,613 29	15
7,383	15,528	517 61	....	....	....	680,729	888,257	44,154 06	16
....	1,932	322 02	....	2,908	969 32	....	472,981	118,326 59	17
....	....	....	....	....	....	20,459	42,429	6,364 35	13
224	2,470	494 00	....	....	....	13,746	55,120	16,289 00	19
....	78,930	2,631 15	....	2,120	141 33	....	472,768	22,358 38	20
....	45	3 00	....	....	....	....	4,199	418 40	21
....	484	32 27	....	....	....	....	10,214	1,005 27	2

No. 14.—SUMMARY STATEMENT of Foreign Merchandise

	Articles and General Tariff Rates.		Total Imports.		General Tariff.		
			Quantity.	Value.	Quantity.	Value.	Duty.
	DUTIABLE GOODS—*Con.*			$		$	$ cts.
	Iron and steel—*Con.*						
	Tubing—*Con.*						
1	Tubing, wrought iron or steel, plain or galvanized, threaded and coupled or not, over 2 inches in diameter, N.E.S., 15 p.c.	$	......	558,129	....	550,085	82,512 90
2	Tubing, wrought iron or steel, plain or galvanized, threaded and coupled or not, two inches or less in diameter, N.E.S., 35 p.c.	"	....	110,550	....	89,693	31,392 55
3	Other iron or steel tubes or pipes, N.O.P. 30 p.c.	"	....	59,036	....	54,908	16,472 40
4	Ware—Galvanized sheet iron or of galvanized sheet steel, manufactures, N.O.P., 25 p.c.	"	....	27,821	....	26,188	6,547 00
5	Ware—Agate, granite or enamelled iron or steel hollow ware, 35 p.c.	"	....	76,004	....	46,875	16,406 25
6	Ware—Enamelled iron or steel ware, N.E.S.; iron or steel hollow ware, plain black, tinned or coated; and nickel and aluminium kitchen or household hollow ware, N.E.S., 30 p.c.	"	....	167,746	....	154,416	46,324 80
7	Wire bale ties, 30 p.c. ...Bundles of 250	ties.	3,743	4,932	3,743	4,932	1,479 60
8	Wire cloth or wove wire and netting of iron or steel, 30 p.c.	Lbs.	1,132.220	67,813	255,045	20,456	6,136 80
9	Wire screens, doors and windows, 30 p.c.	$	....	5,950	....	3,765	1,129 50
10	Wire fencing, woven, buckthorn strip, and wire fencing of iron or steel, N.E.S., 15 p.c.	Lbs.	1,758,022	73,068	1,692,040	70,070	10,510 50
11	Wire, single or several, covered with cotton, linen, silk, rubber or other material, &c., N.E.S., 30 p.c.	"	2,227,552	356,571	2,002,034	323,941	97,182 30
12	Wire of all kinds, N.O.P., 20 p.c.	"	10,694,693	245,578	6,697,525	162,099	32,419 80
13	Wire rope, stranded or twisted wire, clothes lines, picture or other twisted wire and wire cables, N.E.S., 25 p.c.	"	3,074,975	219,227	708,877	59,211	14,802 75
14	Iron or steel nuts, washers, rivets and bolts with or without threads, and nut, bolt and hinge blanks, and T and strap hinges of all kinds, N.E.S., ¾c. p. lb. and 25 p.c.	"	2,998,947	118,209	2,783,167	112,537	49,008 56
15	Iron or steel scrap, wrought, being waste or refuse, including punchings, cuttings and clippings or iron or steel plates or sheets, having been in actual use; crop ends of tin plate bars, blooms and rails, the same not having been in actual use, $1 per ton.	Cwt.	422,136	325,371	197,030	157,355	9,851 51
16	Pen knives, jack knives, and pocket knives of all kinds, 30 p.c.	$	....	142,643	....	3,923	1,176 90
17	Table cutlery, all kinds, N.O.P., 30 p.c.	"	....	259,964	....	31,448	9,434 40
18	All other cutlery, N.E.S., 30 p.c.	"	. ...	336,002	....	123,772	37,131 60
19	Guns, rifles, including air guns and air rifles (not being toys), muskets, cannons, pistols, revolvers, or other firearms, 30 p.c.	"	....	435,487	....	407,467	122,240 10
20	Bayonets, swords, fencing foils and masks, 30 p.c.	"	....	2,487	....	1,598	479 40
21	Needles, of any material or kind, N.O.P., 30 p.c.	"	....	81,464	....	35,858	10,757 40
22	Steel—chrome steel, 15 p.c.	Cwt.	5,275	24,614	5,275	24,614	3,692 10

Imported into Canada, &c.—*Continued.*

Entered for Home Consumption.									
Preferential Tariff.			Surtax Tariff.			Total.			
Quantity.	Value.	Duty.	Quantity.	Value.	Duty.	Quantity.	Value.	Duty Collected.	
	$	$ cts.		$	$ cts.		$	$ cts.	
....	4,373	437 30	....	....	....	....	554,459	82,950 20	1
....	19,982	4,662 55	....	....	....	....	109,675	36,055 10	2
....	4,128	825 60	....	....	....	....	59,036	17,298 00	3
....	1,195	199 22	....	438	146 00	....	27,821	6,892 22	4
....	6,423	1,498 78	....	22,637	10,563 93	....	75,935	28,468 96	5
....	6,795	1,359 00	....	6,622	2,648 80	....	167,833	50,332 60	6
....	....	....	....	....	....	3,743	4,932	1,479 60	7
876,885	47,331	9,466 20	290	26	10 40	1,132,220	67,813	15,613 40	8
....	2,185	437 00	....	....	....	....	5,950	1,566 50	9
65,892	2,998	299 80	....	....	....	1,757,932	73,068	10,810 30	10
215,930	30,621	6,124 20	5,578	1,279	511 60	2,223,542	355,841	103,818 10	11
1,541,929	35,335	4,711 39	2,450,239	48,009	12,802 39	10,689,693	245,443	49,933 58	12
2,266,008	148,741	24,790 39	30,443	1,722	573 99	3,005,328	209,674	40,167 13	13
222,166	5,747	2,068 75	714	73	31 46	3,006,047	118,357	51,108 77	14
224,939	167,914	7,497 81	....	....	....	421,969	325,269	17,349 32	15
....	101,042	20,208 40	....	37,585	15,034 00	....	142,550	36,419 30	16
....	218,517	43,703 40	....	10,438	4,175 20	....	260,403	57,313 00	17
....	92,184	18,436 80	....	119,786	47,914 40	....	335,742	103,482 80	18
....	26,372	5,274 40	....	835	334 00	....	434,674	127,848 50	19
....	187	37 40	....	702	280 80	....	2,487	797 60	20
....	41,563	8,312 60	....	3,994	1,597 60	....	81,415	20,667 60	21
....	....	....	....	....	....	5,275	24,614	3,692 10	22

No. 14.—Summary Statement of Foreign Merchandise

No.	Articles and General Tariff Rates.		Total Imports. Quantity.	Total Imports. Value.	General Tariff. Quantity.	General Tariff. Value.	General Tariff. Duty.
	DUTIABLE GOODS—*Con.*			$		$	$ cts.
	Iron and steel—*Con.*						
1	Steel plate, Universal mill or rolled edge bridge plates imported by manufacturers of bridges, 10 p.c.	Cwt.	243,768	347,360	242,410	345,594	34,559 40
2	Steel in bars, bands, hoops, scroll or strips, sheets or plates, of any size, thickness or width when of greater value than 2½c. per lb., N.O.P., 5 p.c.	"	173,404	857,031	130,896	571,395	28,569 75
	Tools and implements:						
3	Adzes, cleavers, hatchets, wedges, sledges, hammers, crowbars, cant dogs and track tools; picks, mattocks and eyes or poles for the same, 30 p.c.	$	....	87,782	....	81,393	24,417 90
4	Axes, 25 p.c.	Doz.	6,055	35,116	6,051	35,123	8,780 75
5	Saws, 30 p.c.	$	....	206,528	....	203,774	61,132 20
6	Files and rasps, N.E.S., 30 p.c.	"	....	88,211	....	76,332	22,899 60
7	Tools, hand or machine, of all kinds, N.O.P., 30 p.c.	"	....	1,020,391	....	910,131	273,039 30
8	Knife blades, or blanks, and forks of iron or steel, in the rough, not handled, filed, ground or otherwise manufactured, 10 p.c.	"	....	70	....	....	....
9	Manufactures, articles or wares not specially enumerated or provided for, composed wholly or in part of iron or steel, and whether partly or wholly manufactured, 30 p.c.	$	....	3,024,046	....	2,748,082	824,424 60
	Total, iron and steel		....	38,545,539	....	30,386,326	6,805,278 39
10	Ivory, manufactures of, N.O.P., 20 p.c.	$	....	1,230	....	1,162	232 40
11	Jellies, jams and preserves, N.E.S., 3¼ c. per lb.	Lbs.	1,822,193	137,655	85,340	9,097	2,773 79
12	Jewellery, N.O.P., 30 p.c.	$	....	887,919	....	741,244	222,373 20
13	Knitted goods of every description, N.E.S., 35 p.c.	"	....	1,939	....	537	187 95
	Lead and manufactures of:						
14	Old, scrap, pig and block, 15 p.c.	Cwt.	82,729	271,105	1,570	5,153	772 95
15	Bars and in sheets, 25 p.c.	"	16,108	57,190	1,786	7,883	1,970 75
16	Pipe, 35 p.c.	Lbs.	84,649	5,421	61,779	4,011	1,403 85
17	Shot and bullets, 35 p.c.	"	73,925	2,942	6,806	466	163 10
18	Manufactures of, N.O.P., 30 p.c.	$	....	75,417	....	67,177	20,153 10
	Total, lead		....	412,075	....	84,690	24,463 75
	Leather and manufactures of:						
19	Sole leather, all kinds, 15 p.c.	Lbs.	467,312	118,592	243,073	64,042	9,606 30
20	Leather, belting leather of all kinds, 15 p.c.	"	307,391	107,618	7,812	2,723	408 45
21	Upper leather, not dressed, waxed or glazed, 15 p.c.	"	896	371	896	371	55 65
22	Calf, kid, or goat, lamb and sheep skins, tanned, 15 p.c.	"	5,731	2,141	3,308	1,390	208 50
23	Calf, kid, or goat, lamb and sheep skins, dressed, waxed or glazed, 17½ p.c.	"	420,869	383,484	334,269	300,621	52,609 42
24	Glove leathers, tanned or dressed, coloured or uncoloured, imported by glove manufacturers for use in their own factories in the manufacture of gloves, 10 p.c.	"	679,419	383,565	665,021	368,684	36,868 40

Imported into Canada, &c.—*Continued.*

Entered for Home Consumption.									
Preferential Tariff.			Surtax Tariff.			Total.			
Quantity.	Value.	Duty.	Quantity.	Value.	Duty.	Quantity.	Value.	Duty Collected.	
	$	$ cts.		$	$ cts.		$	$ cts.	
1,358	1,766	117 73	....	....	....	243,768	347,360	34,677 13	1
41,685	278,796	9,293 38	659	6,163	410 85	173,240	856,354	38,273 98	2
....	3,060	612 00	....	2,572	1,028 80	....	87,025	26,058 70	3
....	....	....	....	....	....	6,051	35,123	8,780 75	4
....	1,130	226 00	....	1,624	649 60	....	206,528	62,007 80	5
....	8,828	1,765 60	....	3,051	1,220 40	....	88,211	25,885 60	6
....	57,969	11,593 80	....	51,561	20,624 40	....	1,019,661	305,257 50	7
....	70	4 67	....	....	....	....	70	4 67	8
....	221,104	44,220 80	....	48,715	19,486 00	....	3,017,901	888,131 40	9
....	7,122,569	879,919 16	....	999,082	278,566 04	....	38,507,977	7,963,763 59	
....	68	9 06	....	....	....	....	1,230	241 46	10
1,751,246	129,361	37,944 07	460	72	19 93	1,837,046	138,530	40,737 79	11
....	78,084	15,616 80	....	69,551	27,820 40	....	888,879	265,810 40	12
....	1,355	316 19	....	47	21 93	....	1,939	526 07	13
81,159	265,952	26,595 20	....	....	....	82,729	271,105	27,368 15	14
14,320	49,302	8,217 15	....	....	....	16,106	57,185	10,187 90	15
25,965	1,406	328 06	....	....	....	87,744	5,417	1,731 91	16
66,044	2,405	561 16	....	....	....	72,850	2,871	724 26	17
....	7,668	1,533 60	....	774	309 60	....	75,619	21,996 30	18
....	326,733	37,235 47	....	774	309 60	....	412,197	62,008 52	
224,239	54,550	5,455 00	....	....	....	467,312	118,592	15,061 30	19
317,845	108,588	10,858 80	....	....	....	325,657	111,311	11,267 25	20
....	....	....	....	....	....	896	371	55 65	21
823	673	67 30	1,600	78	15 60	5,731	2,141	291 40	22
70,480	65,607	7,654 34	1.470	1,330	310 33	406,219	367,558	60,574 09	23
3,084	2,927	195 20	11,314	11,954	1,593 85	679,419	383,565	38,657 45	24

No. 14.—SUMMARY STATEMENT of Foreign Merchandise

	Articles and General Tariff Rates.		Total Imports.		General Tariff.		
			Quantity.	Value.	Quantity.	Value.	Duty.
	DUTIABLE GOODS—*Con.*			$		$	$ cts.
	Leather and manufactures of—*Con.*						
1	Harness leather, 17½ p.c.	Lbs.	26,732	12,053	2,491	1,180	206 52
2	Tanners' scrap leather, 15 p.c.	"	143,975	5,265	143,855	5,074	761 10
3	Upper leather, including dongola, cordovan, kangaroo, alligator and chamois skins, or other upper leather, N.E.S., dressed, waxed or glazed, 17½ p.c.	"	221,132	184,828	150,674	129,079	22,589 37
4	Japanned, patent or enamelled leather and Morocco leather, 25 p.c.	"	79,632	90,113	70,560	81,193	20,298 25
5	Skins for Morocco leather, tanned, but not further manufactured, 15 p.c.	"	7,562	2,559	570	234	35 10
6	All other leather and skins, N.O.P., 15 p.c.	"	230,427	77,018	82,266	25,263	3,789 45
7	All other leather and skins dressed, waxed or glazed, &c., N.E.S., 17½ p.c.	"	40,379	21,349	33,081	15,980	2,796 62
	Total, leather		....	1,388,956	....	995,834	150,233 13
	Manufactures of, viz.:						
8	Boots and shoes, 25 p.c.	$	....	1,284,654	....	1,219,911	304,977 75
9	Harness and saddlery, N.E.S., 30 p.c.	"	....	91,092	....	66,581	19,974 30
10	Leather belting, 20 p.c.	"	....	54,819	....	30,979	6,195 80
11	All other manufactures of leather and raw hide, N.O.P., 25 p.c.	"	....	212,048	....	181,019	45,254 75
	Total, leather manufactures		....	1,642,613	....	1,498,490	376,402 60
12	Lime, 20 p.c.	Brls.	134,334	93,630	134,334	93,630	18,726 00
13	Lime juice, and fruit juices, fortified with or containing not more than twenty-five per cent of proof spirits, 60c. per gall.	Galls.	360	687	313	625	187 80
14	Lime juice, and fruit juices, containing more than twenty-five per cent of proof spirits, $2 per gall.	"	52	100	76	293	152 00
15	Lime juice and other fruit syrups and fruit juices, N.O.P., 20 p.c.	"	19,433	22,222	9,140	12,428	2,485 60
	Total, lime juice		19,845	23,009	9,529	13,346	2,825 40
16	Lithographic presses and type-making accessories therefor, 10 p.c.	$	....	64,810	....	53,253	5,325 30
17	Lithographic stones, not engraved, 20 p.c.	"	....	6,772	....	1,309	261 80
18	Machine card clothing, 25 p.c.	"	....	35,746	....	6,812	1,703 00
19	Magic lanterns and slides therefor, 25 p.c.	"	....	11,728	....	7,916	1,979 00
20	Malt, 15c. per bush.	Bush.	94,152	68,240	93,136	65,870	13,970 40
21	Malt, extract of (non-alcoholic), for medicinal and baking purposes, 25 p.c.	$	....	10,787	....	9,690	2,422 50
	Marble and manufactures of:						
22	Marble, sawn only, 20 p.c.	"	....	108,718	....	108,329	21,665 80
23	Rough, not hammered or chiselled, 15 p.c.	"	....	6,827	....	6,827	1,024 05
24	Manufactures of, N.O.P., 35 p.c.	"	....	74,499	....	71,437	25,002 95
	Total, marble		....	190,044	....	186,593	47,692 80
25	Mattresses, including hair, spring and other, 30 p.c.	"	....	7,051	....	6,337	1,901 10
26	Mats and rugs, including door and carriage, N.E.S., 35 p.c.	"	....	364,752	....	89,233	31,231 55

Imported into Canada, &c.—*Continued.*

Entered for Home Consumption.									
Preferential Tariff.			Surtax Tariff.			Total.			
Quantity.	Value.	Duty.	Quantity.	Value.	Duty.	Quantity.	Value.	Duty Collected.	
	$	$ cts.		$	$ cts.		$	$ cts.	
24,241	10,873	1,268 54	...	...	...	26,732	12,053	1,475 06	1
120	191	19 10	...	...	...	143,975	5,265	780 20	2
62,247	44,185	5,155 04	1,478	1,901	443 56	214,399	175,165	28,187 97	3
5,437	4,157	692 84	3,635	4,763	1,587 66	79,632	90,113	22,578 75	4
6,992	2,325	232 50	...	...	...	7,562	2,559	267 60	5
150,929	52,650	5,265 00	...	...	...	233,195	77,913	9,054 45	6
7,298	5,369	626 44	...	...	...	40,379	21,349	3,423 06	7
...	352,095	37,490 10	...	20,026	3,951 00	...	1,367,955	191,674 23	
...	63,052	10,508 85	...	41	13 67	...	1,283,004	315,500 27	8
...	22,197	4,439 40	...	...	...	...	88,778	24,413 70	9
...	21,294	2,839 26	...	...	...	...	52,273	9,035 06	10
...	25,345	4,224 43	...	5,055	1,684 99	...	211,419	51,164 17	11
...	131,888	22,011 94	...	5,096	1,698 66	...	1,635,474	400,113 20	
...	...	...	...	...	...	134,334	93,630	18,726 00	12
...	...	...	...	...	...	313	625	187 80	13
...	...	...	...	...	...	76	293	152 00	14
10,943	11,019	1,469 39	3	4	1 07	20,086	23,451	3,956 06	15
10,943	11,019	1,469 39	3	4	1 07	20,475	24,369	4,295 86	
...	8,431	562 07	...	...	...	...	61,684	5,887 37	16
...	...	...	...	5,463	1,456 79	...	6,772	1,718 59	17
...	27,263	4,543 89	...	1,232	410 66	...	35,307	6,657 55	18
...	1,237	206 23	...	2,617	872 33	...	11,770	3,057 56	19
1,016	2,370	101 60	...	...	...	94,152	68,240	14,072 00	20
...	1,013	168 84	...	...	...	...	10,703	2,591 34	21
...	389	51 89	...	...	...	...	108,718	21,717 69	22
...	...	...	...	...	...	...	6,827	1,024 05	23
...	2,599	606 48	...	8	3 74	...	74,044	25,613 17	24
...	2,988	658 37	...	8	3 74	...	189,589	48,354 91	
...	471	94 20	...	...	...	...	6,808	1,995 30	25
...	263,834	61,562 39	...	10,730	5,007 34	...	363,797	97,801 28	26

No. 14.—Summary Statement of Foreign Merchandise

	Articles and General Tariff Rates.		Total Imports.		General Tariff.		
			Quantity.	Value.	Quantity.	Value.	Duty.
	DUTIABLE GOODS—*Con.*			$		$	$ cts.
	Metal, N. E. S. and manufactures of—						
1	Aluminium, manufactures of, N.O.P., 25 p.c.	$	....	23,565	....	21,605	5,401 25
2	Babbit metal, 10 p.c.	"	....	59,667	....	41,003	4,100 30
3	Britannia metal, manufactures of, not plated, 25 p.c.	"	....	29,358	....	22,259	5,564 75
4	Bronze statuettes and ornaments, 35 p.c.	"	....	5,325	....	4,791	1,676 85
5	Buckles of iron, steel, brass or copper, of all kinds, N.O.P. (not being jewellery), 30 p.c.	"	....	38,604	....	29,770	8,931 00
6	Cages—Bird, parrot, squirrel and rat, of wire, and metal parts thereof, 35 p.c.	"	....	5,260	....	5,260	1,841 00
7	Composition metal for the manufacture of jewellery and filled gold watch cases, 10 p.c.	"	....	6,303	....	6,303	630 30
8	Frames, clasps and fasteners for purses and chatelaine bags or reticules, not more than seven inches in width, imported by the manufacturers of purses and chatelaine bags or reticules for use in their factories, 20 p.c.	"	....	17,385	....	16,684	3,336 80
9	Furniture springs, 30 p.c.	"	....	11,677	....	11,635	3,490 50
10	Phosphor tin and phosphor bronze, in blocks, bars, plates, sheets and wire, 10 p.c.	"	....	12,738	....	11,803	1,180 30
11	Garden or lawn sprinklers, 30 p.c.	"	....	1,050	....	1,050	315 00
12	Gas, coal or other oil and electric light fixtures or parts thereof of metal, including lava or other tips, burners, collars, galleries, shades and shade-holders, 30 p.c.	"	....	343,018	....	329,878	98,963 40
13	Gas mantles and incandescent gas burners. 30 p.c.	"	....	39,891	....	39,413	11,823 90
14	Gas meters, 35 p.c.	No.	2,466	40,776	1,812	34,055	11,919 25
15	German, Nevada and nickel silver, manufactures of, not plated, 25 p.c.	$	....	30,250	....	24,162	6,040 50
16	Lamp springs, 10 p.c.	"	....	2,727	....	2,727	272 70
17	Lamps, side lights, head lights, and lanterns, 30 p.c.	"	....	366,545	....	349,568	104,870 40
18	Nickel-plated ware, N.E.S., 30 p.c.	"	....	157,247	....	140,275	42,082 50
19	Nickel anodes, 10 p.c.	"	....	15,976	....	15,808	1,580 80
20	Patterns of brass, iron, steel or other metal, 30 p.c.	"	....	4,436	....	4,436	1,330 80
21	Pins, N.O.P., 30 p.c.	"	....	106,849	....	35,068	10,520 40
22	Screws, brass or other metal, except iron or steel, N.O.P., 35 p.c.	"	....	6,303	....	6,094	2,132 90
23	Stereotypes, electrotypes and celluloids for almanacs, calendars, illustrated pamphlets, newspaper advertisements or engravings, and all other like work for commercial, trade or other purposes, N.E.S.; and matrices or copper shells for the same, 1½ c. per sq. inch.	Sq. in.	418,449	15,717	394,337	14,915	5,915 17
24	Stereotypes, electrotypes, and celluloids of newspaper columns, and bases for the same, composed wholly or partly of metal or celluloid, ¼ c. per sq. inch.	"	516,639	4,175	516,639	4,175	1,291 61
25	Stereotypes—matrices or copper shells for the same, 1½ c. per sq. inch	"	706	50	706	50	10 59
26	Type for printing, including chases, quoins and slugs of all kinds, 20 p.c.	$	....	115,082	....	71,946	14,389 20
27	Type metal, 10 p.c.	"	....	8,675	....	6,534	653 40

Imported into Canada, &c.—*Continued.*

Entered for Home Consumption.									
Preferential Tariff.			Surtax Tariff.			Total.			
Quantity.	Value.	Duty.	Quantity.	Value.	Duty.	Quantity.	Value.	Duty Collected.	
	$	$ cts.		$	$ cts.		$	$ cts.	
....	416	69 35	....	1,618	539 34	....	23,639	6,009 94	1
....	18,659	1,243 94	....	....	....	....	59,662	5,344 24	2
....	5,467	911 19	....	1,632	544 02	....	29,358	7,019 96	3
....	52	12 14	....	482	224 93	....	5,325	1,913 92	4
....	3,628	725 60	....	5,147	2,058 80	....	38,545	11,715 40	5
....	....	....	....	....	....	....	5,260	1,841 00	6
....	....	....	....	....	....	....	6,303	630 30	
....	....	....	....	701	186 93	....	17,385	3,523 73	8
....	125	25 00	....	....	....	....	11,760	3,515 50	9
....	727	48 48	....	208	27 73	....	12,738	1,256 51	10
....	....	....	....	....	....	....	1,050	315 00	11
....	11,347	2,269 40	....	3,377	1,350 80	....	344,602	102,583 60	12
....	409	81 80	....	348	139 20	....	40,170	12,044 90	13
654	6,721	1,568 21	....	....	....	2,466	40,776	13,487 46	14
....	5,992	998 68	....	96	32 00	....	30,250	7,071 18	15
....	....	....	....	....	....	....	2,727	272 70	16
....	9,166	1,833 20	....	7,306	2,922 40	....	366,040	109,626 00	17
....	12,034	2,406 80	....	4,797	1,918 80	....	157,106	46,408 10	18
....	....	....	....	168	22 40	....	15,976	1,603 20	19
....	....	....	....	....	....	....	4,436	1,330 80	20
....	63,587	12,717 40	....	8,237	3,294 80	....	106,892	26,532 60	21
....	209	48 77	....	....	....	....	6,303	2,181 67	22
23,354	739	233 54	372	30	7 44	418,063	15,684	6,156 15	23
....	....	....	....	....	....	516,639	4,175	1,291 61	24
....	....	....	....	....	....	706	50	10 59	25
....	43,517	5,802 26	....	214	57 07	....	115,677	20,248 53	26
....	2,141	142 74	....	....	....	....	8,675	796 14	27

No. 14.—SUMMARY STATEMENT of Foreign Merchandise

	Articles and General Tariff Rates.		Total Imports.		General Tariff.		
			Quantity.	Value.	Quantity.	Value.	Duty.
	DUTIABLE GOODS—*Con.*			$		$	$ cts.
	Metal, N.E.S. and manufactures of—*Con.*						
1	Pewter, platina and metal composition, N.E.S., 30 p.c.	$	....	2,716	....	2,181	654 30
2	Wire of all kinds, N.O.P., 20 p.c.	Lbs.	65,696	13,051	51,131	11,722	2,344 40
3	Wire, twisted, &c., except iron or steel, N.E.S., 25 p.c.	$	....	279	....	125	31 25
	Total, metal and manufactures of		....	1,484,695	....	1,265,295	353,295 52
4	Milk, condensed, 3¼ c. per lb.	Lbs.	188,249	9,822	74,878	5,369	2,433 43
	Mineral substances, not otherwise provided for—						
5	Asbestus, in any form other than crude, and all manufactures of, 25 p.c.	$	....	138,000	....	123,973	30,993 25
6	Blacklead, 25 p.c.	"	....	34,004	....	26,135	6,533 75
7	Mineral and bituminous substances, not otherwise provided for, 20 p.c.	"	....	77,431	....	56,824	11,364 80
8	Plumbago, not ground or otherwise manufactured, 10 p.c.	"	....	2,791	....	2,791	279 10
9	Plumbago, ground and manufactures of, N.E.S., 25 p.c.	"	....	19,074	....	16,009	4,002 25
	Total, mineral substances		....	271,300	....	225,732	53,173 15
10	Mineral and ærated waters, N.E.S., 20 p.c.	"	....	178,083	....	137,072	27,414 40
11	Mosiac flooring of any material, 30 p.c.	"	....	12,489	....	12,295	3,688 50
12	Mucilage, 25 p.c.	"	....	23,914	....	22,866	5,716 50
	Musical instruments, viz.:—						
13	Brass band instruments, 25 p.c.	"	....	38,534	....	24,473	6,118 25
14	Cabinet organs, 30 p.c.	No.	284	18,429	278	18,065	5,419 50
15	Pipe organs, 30 p.c.	"	1	750	1	750	225 00
16	Parts of organs, 25 p.c.	$	....	22,542	....	22,014	5,503 50
17	Pianofortes, 30 p.c.	No.	816	174,328	793	170,764	51,229 20
18	Pianos, parts of, 25 p.c.	$	....	151,757	....	146,356	36,589 00
19	Other musical instruments, N.E.S., 30 p.c.	"	....	127,048	....	57,521	17,256 30
	Total, musical instruments		....	533,388	....	439,943	122,340 75
20	Mustard, ground, 25 p.c.	Lbs.	628,569	106,777	265,338	15,988	3,997 00
21	" French, liquid, 35 p.c.	$	....	8,082	....	7,590	2,656 50
	Total, mustard		....	114,859	....	23,578	6,653 50
	Oils, mineral—						
22	Coal and kerosene, distilled, purified or refined, naphtha and petroleum, N.E.S., 2½c. per gallon	Galls.	9,225,561	808,597	9,248,472	810,547	231,212 57
23	Products of petroleum, N.E.S., 2½c. per gall	"	1,730,898	181,929	1,630,646	176,341	40,766 31
24	Crude petroleum, gas oils other than benzine and gasoline, 1½c. per gall	"	21,383	1,405	19,680	1,282	295 21
25	Illuminating oils, composed wholly or in part of the products of petroleum, coal, shale or lignite, costing more than thirty cents per gallon, 20 p.c.	"	3,769	1,597	3,357	1,387	277 40

Imported into Canada, &c.—*Continued.*

Entered for Home Consumption.									
Preferential Tariff.			Surtax Tariff.			Total.			
Quantity.	Value.	Duty.	Quantity.	Value.	Duty.	Quantity.	Value.	Duty Collected.	
	$	$ cts.		$	$ cts.		$	$ cts.	
...	172	34 40	...	363	145 20	...	2,716	833 90	1
4,307	736	98 16	8,628	320	85 35	64,066	12,778	2,527 91	2
...	154	25 67	...	...	...	...	279	56 92	3
...	185,998	31,296 73	...	35,044	13,557 21	...	1,486,337	398,149 46	
37,627	2,618	815 29	...	...	...	112,505	7,987	3,248 72	4
...	7,697	1,282 93	...	6,304	2,101 33	...	137,974	34,377 51	5
...	7,772	1,295 40	...	...	...	...	33,907	7,829 15	6
...	12,539	1,671 90	...	8,331	2,221 62	...	77,694	15,258 32	7
...	...	...	...	...	...	...	2,791	279 10	8
...	3.049	508 16	...	...	...	...	19,058	4,510 41	9
...	31,057	4,758 39	...	14,635	4,322 95	...	271,424	62,254 49	
...	9,557	1,274 34	...	30,256	8,068 29	...	176,885	36,757 03	10
...	389	77 80	...	...	...	...	12,684	3,766 30	11
...	1,062	177 04	...	...	...	...	23,928	5,893 54	12
...	11,517	1,919 56	...	1,978	659 34	...	37,968	8,697 15	13
1	37	7 40	5	327	130 80	284	18,429	5,557 70	14
...	...	...	...	...	...	1	750	225 00	15
...	528	88 00	...	...	...	...	22,542	5,591 50	16
16	1,921	384 20	5	1,343	537 20	814	174,028	52,150 60	17
...	...	...	...	5,401	1,800 33	...	151,757	38,389 33	18
...	2,643	528 60	...	69,586	27,834 40	...	129,750	45,619 30	19
...	16,646	2,927 76	...	78,635	30,962 07	...	535,224	156,230 58	
373,233	93,986	15,664 51	...	...	...	638,571	109,974	19,661 51	20
...	...	...	...	...	...	...	7,590	2,656 50	21
...	93,986	15,664 51	...	...	...	...	117,564	22,318 01	
6,728	1,679	112 16	...	...	...	9,255,200	812,226	231,324 73	22
2,663	728	44 39	...	...	...	1,633,309	177,069	40,810 70	23
...	...	...	...	...	...	19,680	1,282	295 21	24
179	103	13 73	...	...	...	3,536	1,490	291 13	25

No. 14.—SUMMARY STATEMENT of Foreign Merchandise

	Articles and General Tariff Rates.		Total Imports.		General Tariff.		
			Quantity.	Value.	Quantity.	Value.	Duty.
	DUTIABLE GOODS—*Con.*			$		$	$ cts.
	Oil, animal—						
1	Lard oil, 25 p.c	Galls.	12,829	6,420	12,600	6,337	1,584 25
2	Neatsfoot, 25 p.c	"	23,313	17,737	23,282	17,714	4,428 50
3	Other animal oil, N.E.S., 20 p.c	"	5,620	2,632	5,432	2,591	518 20
	Vegetable—						
4	Castor, 20 p.c	"	91,024	42,762	4,148	2,904	580 80
5	Cotton seed, 20 p.c	"	1,122,177	320,575	1,075,935	311,877	62,375 40
6	Flaxseed or linseed, raw or boiled, 25 p.c	"	1,184,715	444,437	142,282	57,467	14,366 75
7	Olive, N.E.S., 20 p.c	"	67,849	75,869	60,553	61,741	12,348 20
8	Sesame seed, 25 p.c	"	652	443	652	443	110 75
9	Vegetable oil, not otherwise specified, 20 p.c	"	94,865	52,120	82,706	45,436	9,087 20
10	Lubricating oils composed wholly or in part of petroleum and costing less than 25c. per gall., 2½c. per gall	"	1,916,142	250,018	1,907,029	248,938	47,676 19
11	All other lubricating oils, N.E.S., 20 p.c	"	385,667	144,504	321,039	120,899	24,179 80
12	Essential, 10 p.c	Lbs.	162,199	129,880	148,493	119,774	11,977 40
13	All other oils not elsewhere specified, 20 p.c	Galls.	58,043	24,898	46,256	19,537	3,907 40
	Total, oils		....	2,505,823	....	2,005,215	465,692 33
14	Oiled silk and cloth, and tape or other textile, india-rubbered, flocked or coated, N.O.P., 30 p.c	$	....	177,300	....	157,926	47,377 80
15	Oil cloth, enamelled carriage, floor, shelf and table oil cloth, cork matting or carpets and linoleum, 30 p.c	Sq. yds.	2,486,494	735,806	158,482	29,338	8,801 40
16	Optical, philosophical, photographic and mathematical instruments, N.E.S., 25 p.c	$	....	293,130	....	239,356	59,839 00
17	Spectacles and eye-glasses, 30 p.c	"	....	15,279	....	14,935	4,480 50
18	Spectaclas and eye-glasses—frames and metal parts of, 20 p.c	"	....	46,957	....	46,901	9,380 20
19	Packages, 20 p.c	"	....	945,737	....	859,408	171,881 60
	Paints and colours—						
20	Brocade and bronze powders and gold liquid paint, 25 p.c	"	....	42,414	....	11,599	2,899 75
21	Colours, dry, N.E.S., 20 p.c	Lbs.	2,414,480	139,709	1,838,607	108,361	21,672 20
22	Lead, white, dry, 30 p.c	"	8,248,057	336,142	1,500,247	69,129	4,119 70
23	Lead, white, ground in oil, 35 p.c	"	270,920	12,533	21,304	1,112	389 20
24	Red lead and orange mineral, 5 p.c	"	1,893,914	68,769	361,358	18,136	906 80
25	Ochres, ochrey earths and raw siennas, 20 p.c	"	1,762,682	23,790	1,487,453	18,398	3,679 60
26	Zinc white, 5 p.c	"	4,904,304	198,063	3,572,376	151,396	7,569 80
27	Oxides, fire proofs, umbers and burnt siennas, N.E.S., 25 p.c	"	2,560,789	33,604	1,687,507	17,518	4,379 50
28	Paints and colours and rough stuff and fillers, anti-corrosive and anti-fouling paints commonly used for ships' hulls, and ground and liquid paints, N.E.S., 25 p.c	"	4,719,065	276,741	3,984,656	219,073	54,768 25
29	Paris green, dry, 10 p.c	"	156,748	34,658	1,525	121	12 10
30	Paints and colours ground in spirits, and all spirit varnishes and lacquers, $1.12½c. per gall	Galls.	849	2,765	813	2,640	914 70
31	Putty, 20 p.c	Lbs.	246,980	3,862	238,958	3,761	752 20
	Total, paints		....	1,173,050	....	621,244	102,063 80

Imported into Canada, &c.—*Continued.*

ENTERED FOR HOME CONSUMPTION.

Preferential Tariff.			Surtax Tariff.			Total.			
Quantity.	Value.	Duty.	Quantity.	Value.	Duty.	Quantity.	Value.	Duty collected.	
	$	$ cts.		$	$ cts.		$	$ cts.	
...	...	...	...	...	...	12,600	6,337	1,584 25	1
31	23	3 83	...	...	...	23,313	17,737	4,432 33	2
12	21	2 80	...	...	...	5,444	2,612	521 00	3
87,361	40,000	5,333 42	...	...	...	91,509	42,904	5,914 22	4
24,729	7,939	1,058 54	...	...	...	1,100,664	319,816	63,433 94	5
1,027,730	381,470	63,578 44	...	...	...	1,170,012	438,937	77,945 19	6
8,506	13,132	1,751 27	...	...	...	69,059	74,873	14,099 47	7
...	...	...	...	...	...	652	443	110 75	8
8,109	5,400	720 06	3,230	893	238 14	94,045	51,729	10,045 40	9
...	...	...	...	...	...	1,907,029	248,938	47,676 19	10
17,936	6,780	904 09	169	86	22 93	339,144	127,765	25,106 82	11
4,386	4,514	300 93	8,794	5,358	714 45	161,673	129,646	12,992 78	12
7,333	3,145	419 35	3,598	2,028	540 80	57,187	24,710	4,867 55	13
...	464,934	74,243 01	...	8,365	1,516 32	...	2,478,514	541,451 66	
...	19,241	3,848 20	...	275	110 00	...	177,442	51,336 00	14
2,323,172	707,899	141,579 80	783	409	163 60	2,482,437	737,646	150,544 80	15
...	33,298	5,549 99	...	18,649	6,216 36	...	291,303	71,605 35	16
...	50	10 00	...	300	120 00	...	15,285	4,610 50	17
...	...	...	...	56	14 94	...	46,957	9,395 14	18
...	69,105	9,215 25	...	3,684	982 47	...	932,197	182,079 32	19
...	1,342	223 68	...	29,488	9,829 34	...	42,429	12,952 77	20
303,512	21,728	2,897 13	261,636	8,459	2,255 76	2,403,755	138,548	26,825 09	21
4,980,986	214,060	37,829 51	1,766,824	52,953	4,634 87	8,248,057	336,142	46,584 08	22
249,616	11,421	2,638 78	...	...	...	270,920	12,533	3,027 98	23
818,580	34,185	1,139 46	713,976	16,448	1,096 53	1,893,914	68,769	3,142 79	24
244,963	4,707	627 64	30,266	685	182 65	1,762,682	23,790	4,489 89	25
729,309	20,611	687 06	602,629	26,056	1,737 03	4,904,314	198,063	9,993 89	26
809,718	15,243	2,540 50	61,623	846	282 00	2,558,848	33,607	7,202 00	27
723,735	53,148	8,858 35	24,520	3,482	1,160 70	4,732,911	275,703	64,787 30	28
155,223	34,537	2,302 47	...	...	...	156,748	34,658	2,314 57	29
36	125	27 03	...	...	...	849	2,765	941 73	30
8,022	101	13 49	...	...	...	246,980	3,862	765 69	31
...	411,208	59,785 10	...	138,417	21,178 88	...	1,170,869	183,027 78	

No. 14.—SUMMARY STATEMENT of Foreign Merchandise

	Articles and General Tariff Rates.		Total Imports.		General Tariff.		
			Quantity.	Value.	Quantity.	Value.	Duty.
	DUTIABLE GOODS—*Con.*			$		$	$ cts.
	Paper and manufactures of, N.E.S.—						
1	Albumenized and other papers and films chemically prepared for photographers' use, 30 p.c.	$	....	124,794	....	110,872	33,261 60
2	Bags or sacks, printed or not, 25 p.c.	"	....	33,622	....	31,055	7,763 75
3	Cards for playing, 6c. per pack	Packs	587,748	67,179	349,764	38,248	20,985 84
4	Card board, paste board, in sheets or cut to size, N.E.S., 35 p.c.	$	....	79.526	....	68,441	23,954 35
5	Envelopes, 35 p.c.	Thousand	70,297	64,786	59,190	48,878	17,107 30
6	Paper, felt or straw board, 25 p.c.	$	....	238,923	....	237,415	59,353 75
7	Hangings or wall paper, including borders, 35 p.c.	Rolls of 8 yds.	2,309,680	217,207	2,203,654	186,291	65,201 85
8	Leather board, leatheroid and mfrs. of, 25 p.c.	$	....	36,028	....	35,926	8,981 50
9	Mill board, not straw board, 10 p.c.	"	....	44,780	....	43,141	4,314 10
10	Union collar cloth paper, in rolls or sheets, not glossed or finished, 15 p.c.	"	....	1,108	....	1,108	166 20
11	Union collar cloth paper, in rolls or sheets, glossed or finished, 20 p.c.	"	....	400	....	263	52 60
12	Pads not printed, papier maché ware, N.O.P., and mfrs. of paper, N.E.S., 35 p.c.	"	....	743,934	....	567,435	198,602 25
13	Printing paper of not greater value than 2¼c. per lb., O.C., 15 p.c.	Lbs.	244,638	5,594	244,638	5,594	839 10
14	Printing paper, N.E.S., 25 p.c.	"	8,526,357	515,796	5,996,301	363,923	90,980 75
15	Ruled, border and coated papers and papeteries and boxed papers, 35 p.c.	$	....	212.695	....	165,851	58,047 85
16	Straw board, in sheets or rolls, 25 p.c.	Lbs.	424,264	8,631	424,264	8,631	2,157 75
17	Window blinds of paper of all kinds, 35 p.c.	$	....	376	....	67	23 45
18	Wrapping, 25 p.c.	Lbs.	1,812,485	61,644	1,557,548	49,210	12,302 50
19	All kinds, N.E.S., 25 p.c.	$	....	691,961	....	523,627	130,906 75
	Total, paper		....	3,148,984	....	2,485,976	735,003 24
20	Pencils, lead, in wood or otherwise, 25 p.c.	$	....	175,747	....	126.188	31,547 00
21	Pens, penholders and rulers, of all kinds, 25 p.c.	"	....	180,203	....	139,517	34,879 25
	Perfumery, non-alcoholic, viz.—						
22	Hair oil, tooth and other powders and washes, pomatums, pastes, and all other perfumed preparations, N.O.P., used for the hair, mouth or skin, 30 p.c.	"	....	122,454	....	108,038	32,411 40
23	Photographic dryplates, 30 p.c.	$	....	57,242	....	45,264	13,579 20
24	Picture and photograph frames of any material, 30 p.c.	"	....	101,105	....	81,777	24,533 10
25	Pickles, in bottles, jars or similar vessels, 35 p.c.	Galls.	230,244	204,145	55,003	51,095	17,883 25
26	Pickles, in bulk, 35 p.c.	"	104,574	30,621	102,242	29,251	10,237 85
	Total, pickles		334,818	234,766	157,245	80,346	28,121 10
	Plants and trees, viz.—						
27	Apple trees, 3c. each	No.	203,518	15,105	202,590	14,894	6,077 70
28	Cherry trees, 3c. each	"	48,849	8,004	48,838	7,998	1,465 14
29	Currant bushes, 20 p.c.	"	57,869	1,208	57,869	1,208	241 60
30	Fruit, shade, lawn and ornamental trees, shrubs and plants, N.E.S., 20 p.c.	$	....	61.853	....	60,441	12,088 20
31	Gooseberry bushes, 20 p.c.	No.	59,556	1,537	55,056	1,394	278 80

Imported into Canada, &c.—*Continued.*

Entered for Home Consumption.									
Preferential Tariff.			Surtax Tariff.			Total.			
Quantity.	Value.	Duty.	Quantity.	Value.	Duty.	Quantity.	Value.	Duty collected.	
	$	$ cts		$	$ cts.		$	$ cts.	
....	13,357	2,671 40	....	531	212 40	....	124,760	36,145 40	1
....	984	164 02	....	1,587	529 01	....	33,626	8,456 78	2
237,783	28,953	9,511 32	1,944	144	155 52	589,491	67,345	30,652 68	3
....	9,001	2,100 29	....	2,061	961 82	....	79,503	27,016 46	4
9,753	14,094	3,288 94	880	1,183	552 08	69,823	64,155	20,948 32	5
....	1,604	267 33	....	....	....	....	239,019	59,621 08	6
90,067	22,276	5,197 78	84,092	9,236	4,310 14	2,377,813	217,803	74,709 77	7
....	102	17 00	....	....	....	....	36,028	8,998 50	8
....	1,619	107 99	....	20	2 67	....	44,780	4,424 76	9
....	....	....	....	....	....	....	1,108	166 20	10
....	12	1 61	....	125	33 33	....	400	87 54	11
....	126,828	29,594 00	....	47,368	22,105 13	....	741,631	250,301 38	12
....	....	....	....	....	....	244,638	5,594	839 10	13
2,439,504	145,480	24,246 72	82,052	6,152	2,050 64	8,517,857	515,555	117,278 11	14
....	42,845	9,997 38	....	4,449	2,076 20	....	213,145	70,121 43	15
....	....	....	....	....	....	424,264	8,631	2,157 75	16
....	309	72 10	....	....	....	....	376	95 55	17
241,984	11,508	1,918 07	30,027	1,515	505 01	1,829,559	62,233	14,725 58	18
....	157,866	26,311 53	....	10,973	3,657 67	....	692,466	160,875 95	19
....	576,838	115,467 48	....	85,344	37,151 62	....	3,148,158	887,622 34	
....	4,357	726 28	....	45,339	15,112 98	....	175,834	47,386 26	20
....	38,337	6,389 97	....	2,349	782 99	....	180,203	42,052 21	21
....	14,110	2,822 00	....	650	260 00	....	122,798	35,493 40	22
....	11,865	2,373 00	....	480	191 00	....	57,609	16,143 20	23
....	8,064	1,612 80	....	9,492	3,796 80	....	99,333	29,942 70	24
175,034	151,378	35,322 60	40	49	22 87	230,077	202,522	53,228 72	25
1,086	726	169 42	....	....	....	103,328	29,977	10,407 27	26
176,120	152,104	35,492 02	40	49	22 87	333,405	232,499	63,635 99	
928	211	18 56	....	....	....	203,518	15,105	6,096 26	27
11	6	0 22	....	....	....	48,849	8,004	1,465 36	28
....	....	....	....	....	....	57,869	1,208	241 60	29
....	1,397	186 28	....	15	4 00	....	61,853	12,278 48	30
4,500	143	19 07	....	....	....	59,556	1,537	297 87	31

No 14.—SUMMARY STATEMENT of Foreign Merchandise

	Articles and General Tariff Rates.		Total Imports.		General Tariff.		
			Quantity.	Value.	Quantity.	Value.	Duty.
	DUTIABLE GOODS—*Con.*			$		$	$ cts.
	Plants and trees—*Con.*						
1	Grape vines, 20 p.c.	No.	58,145	781	58,145	781	156 20
2	Peach trees, 3c. each	"	210,070	11,926	210,070	11,926	6,302 10
3	Pear trees, 3c. each	"	11,962	1,082	11,962	1,082	358 86
4	Plum trees, 3c. each	"	45,769	4,665	45,769	4,665	1,373 07
5	Raspberry bushes, 20 p.c.	"	180,841	1,056	176,393	989	197 80
6	Rose bushes, 20 p.c.	"	43,319	4,353	35,218	3,648	729 60
7	Quince trees, 3c. each	"	643	101	643	101	19 29
	Total, plants and trees		....	111,671	....	109,127	29,288 36
8	Plaster of Paris, or gypsum, ground, not calcined, 15 p.c.	Brls.	6,562	1,799	6,562	1,799	269 85
9	Plaster of Paris, or gypsum, calcined or manufactured, 12½c. per 100 lbs	Cwt.	128,667	43,766	128,630	43,729	16,078 78
	Total, plaster of Paris		....	45,565	....	45,528	16,348 63
10	Plates, engraved on wood, steel or on other metal and transfers taken from the same, including engravers' plates, of steel polished, engraved or for engraving thereon, 20 p.c.	$	....	14,887	....	14,811	2,962 20
11	Pocket-books, purses, reticules and musical instrument cases, 30 p.c.	"	....	203,061	....	143,724	43,117 20
12	Polish or composition, knife and other, N.O.P., 25 p.c.	"	....	68,459	....	61,898	15,474 50
13	Pomades, French or flower odours, &c., imported in tins of not less than ten pounds each, 15 p.c.	Lbs.	4,434	5,856	4,434	5,856	878 40
14	" " all other, 30 p.c.	"	62	65	53	62	18 60
	Total, pomades		4,496	5,921	4,487	5,918	897 00
15	Post office parcels and packages	$	....	607,752	....	475,361	115,806 36
16	Precious stones, N.E.S., polished, but not set, pierced or otherwise manufactured, and imitations thereof, 10 p.c.	"	....	85,877	....	63,750	6,375 00
17	Printing presses, printing machines, folding machines book-binders', bookbinding, ruling, embossing and paper cutting machines, N.E.S., 10 p.c.	"	....	387,429	....	330,639	33,063 90
	Provisions, not otherwise specified—						
18	Butter, 4c. per lb	Lbs.	292,212	64,519	105,547	26,160	4,221 88
19	Cheese, 3c. per lb	"	509,416	83,324	354,996	61,961	10,649 88
20	Lard, 2c. per lb.	"	7,661,895	653,044	7,529,199	644,920	150,583 98
21	Lard, compound and similar substances, cottolene and animal stearine of all kinds, N.E.S., 2c. per lb	"	416,111	35,795	225,186	16,129	4,503 72
	Total, provisions		8,879,634	836,682	8,214,928	749,170	169,959 46
	Meats, viz.—						
22	Bacon and hams, shoulders and sides, 2c. per lb.	Lbs.	7,140,369	783,546	7,079,845	775,876	141,596 90
23	Beef, salted, in barrels, 2c. per lb	"	3,478,865	160,949	2,374,515	111.862	47,490 30
24	Canned meats and canned poultry and game, 25 p. c.	"	817,916	99,085	717,734	87,263	21,815 75

Imported into Canada, &c.—*Continued.*

Entered for Home Consumption.									
Preferential Tariff.			Surtax Tariff.			Total.			
Quantity.	Value.	Duty.	Quantity.	Value.	Duty.	Quantity.	Value.	Duty Collected.	
	$	$ cts.		$	$ cts.		$	$ cts.	
....	....	....	....	....	....	58,145	781	156 20	1
....	....	....	....	....	....	210,070	11,926	6,302 10	2
....	....	....	....	....	....	11,962	1,082	358 86	3
....	....	....	....	....	....	45,769	4,665	1,373 07	4
4,448	67	8 94	....	....	....	180,841	1,056	206 74	5
8,061	697	92 97	40	8	2 13	43,319	4,353	824 70	6
....	....	....	....	....	....	643	101	19 29	7
....	2,521	326 04	....	23	6 13	....	111,671	29,620 53	
....	....	....	....	....	....	6,562	1,799	269 85	8
35	13	2 91	....	....	....	128,665	43,742	16,081 69	9
....	13	2 91	....	....	....	....	45,541	16,351 54	
....	....	....	....	76	20 27	....	14,887	2,982 47	10
....	36,227	7,245 40	....	23,010	9,204 00	....	202,961	59,566 60	11
....	4,252	708 71	....	1,524	507 99	....	67,674	16,691 20	12
....	....	....	....	....	....	4,434	5,856	878 40	13
9	3	0 60	....	....	....	62	65	19 20	14
9	3	0 60	....	....	....	4,496	5,921	897 60	
....	130,218	30,601 76	....	2,173	796 57	....	607,752	147,204 69	15
....	15,517	1,034 50	....	6,610	881 29	....	85,877	8,290 79	16
....	42,706	2,847 06	....	14,066	1,875 45	....	387,411	37,786 41	17
37,904	8,784	1,010 75	....	....	....	143,451	34,944	5,232 63	18
13,585	3,328	271 71	50	20	2 00	368,631	65,309	10,923 59	19
424	47	5 66	....	....	....	7,529,623	644,967	150,589 64	20
203,427	16,949	2,712 39	224	28	5 97	428,837	33,106	7,222 08	21
255,340	29,108	4,000 51	274	48	7 97	8,470,542	778,326	173,967 94	
3,297	566	43 98	....	....	....	7,083,142	776,442	141,640 88	22
....	....	....	....	....	....	2,374,515	111,862	47,490 30	23
33,975	5,073	845 62	1,299	250	83 34	753,008	92,586	22,744 71	24

No. 14.—SUMMARY STATEMENT of Foreign Merchandise

No.	Articles and General Tariff Rates.		Total Imports.		General Tariff.		
			Quantity.	Value.	Quantity.	Value.	Duty.
	DUTIABLE GOODS—*Con.*			$		$	$ cts.
	Provisions, meats—*Con.*						
1	Extracts of meats and fluid beef not medicated, and soups, 25 p. c	$	....	85,223	....	80,336	20,084 00
2	Mutton and lamb, fresh, 35 p. c	Lbs.	376,318	19,558	403,242	21,362	7,476 70
3	Pork, barrelled, in brine, 2c. per lb	"	11,215,320	821,653	10,726,109	785,905	214,522 18
4	Poultry and game, N.O.P., 20 p. c	$	....	39,593	....	39,568	7,913 60
5	Dried or smoked meats, and meats preserved in any other way than salted or pickled, N.E.S., 2c. per lb.	Lbs.	1,430,095	162,385	1,433,166	161,744	28,663 32
6	Other meats, fresh, 3c. per lb	"	269,628	29,605	246,094	28,044	7,382 82
7	Other meats, salted, N.E.S, 2c. per lb	"	588,559	50,953	578,316	50,333	11,566 32
	Total, meats		....	2,252,550	....	2,142,293	508,511 89
8	Regalia and badges, 35 p. c	$	....	11,422	....	9,421	3,297 35
9	Ribbons, 35 p. c	"	....	1,157,886	....	1,078,269	377,394 15
10	Railway or travelling rugs and lap dusters of all kinds, 30 p. c	"	....	51,502	....	13,885	4,165 50
11	Sails for boats and ships, 25 p. c	"	....	2,696	....	2,074	518 50
12	Salt, coarse, N.E.S , 5c. per 100 lbs	Lbs.	14,900,108	33,627	14,900,108	33,627	7,450 06
13	Salt, fine, in bulk, 5c. per 100 lbs	"	2,797,950	7,983	2,797,950	7,983	1,398 98
14	Salt, N.E.S., in bags, barrels or other packages, 7½c. per 100 lbs	"	3,674,427	18,221	3,668,006	18,195	2,751 17
	Total, salt		21,372,485	59,831	21,366,064	59,805	11,600 21
15	Sand paper, glass, flint and emery paper and emery cloth, 25 p. c	$	....	106,330	....	104,569	26,142 25
16	Sauces and catsups, in bottles, 35 p. c	Galls.	88,344	116,928	37,519	37,064	12,972 40
17	Sauces and catsups, in bulk, 35 p. c	"	28,712	7,264	26,976	7,125	2,493 75
18	Soy, 35 p. c	"	29,164	6,869	29,179	6,872	2,405 20
	Total, sauces		146,220	131,061	93,674	51,061	17,871 35
19	Sausage casings, N.E.S., 20 p. c	$	....	82,897	....	61,364	12,272 80
	Seeds, viz.—						
20	Garden, field and other seeds for agricultural or other purposes, N.O.P., when in bulk or in large parcels, 10 p.c.	"	....	374,974	....	364,010	36,401 00
21	Garden, field and other seeds for agricultural or other purposes, N.O.P., when in small papers or parcels, 25 p.c.	"	....	6,821	....	4,540	1,135 00
22	Bulbous roots, N.O.P., 20 p. c	"	......	14,388	....	14,107	2,821 40
	Total, seeds		....	396,183	....	382,657	40,357 40
23	Ships, foreign built British, on applying for Canadian coasting license, 25 p. c	$	....	178,450	....	178,450	44,612 50
24	Ships and vessels, repairs, according to materials	"	....	415	....	415	103 75
	Total, ships		....	178,865	....	178,865	44,716 25

SESSIONAL PAPER No. 11

Imported into Canada, &c.—*Continued.*

Entered for Home Consumption.									
Preferential Tariff.			Surtax Tariff.			Total.			
Quantity.	Value.	Duty.	Quantity.	Value.	Duty.	Quantity.	Value.	Duty Collected.	
	$	$ cts.		$	$ cts.		$	$ cts.	
	6,441	1,073 54		296	98 69		87,073	21,256 23	1
						403,242	21,362	7,476 70	2
						10,726,109	785,905	214,522 18	3
	223	29 74					39,791	7,943 34	4
751	94	10 02				1,433,917	161,838	28,673 34	5
						246,094	28,044	7,382 82	6
24	5	0 32				578,340	50,338	11,566 64	7
	12,402	2,003 22		546	182 03		2,155,241	510,697 14	
	1,962	457 85		39	18 20		11,422	3,773 40	8
	11,225	2,619 31		60,838	28,391 11		1,150,332	408,404 57	9
	36,415	7,283 00		1,278	511 20		51,578	11,959 70	10
	622	103 67					2,696	622 17	11
						14,900,108	33,627	7,450 06	12
						2,797,950	7,983	1,398 98	13
						3,668,006	18,195	2,751 17	14
						21,366,064	59,805	11,600 21	
	1,704	284 04		57	19 01		106,330	26,445 30	15
49,031	72,551	16,928 98				86,550	109,615	29,901 38	16
2,424	1,048	244 59				29,400	8,173	2,738 34	17
						29,179	6,872	2,405 20	18
51,455	73,599	17,173 57				145,129	124,660	35,044 92	
	22,055	2,940 68					83,419	15,213 48	19
	5,579	371 98		3,920	522 65		373,509	37,295 63	20
	2,281	380 23					6,821	1,515 23	21
	281	37 47					14,388	2,858 87	22
	8,141	789 68		3,920	522 65		394,718	41,669 73	
							178,450	44,612 50	23
							415	103 75	24
							178,865	44,716 25	

No. 14.—Summary Statement of Foreign Merchandise

No.	Articles and General Tariff Rates.		Total Imports. Quantity.	Total Imports. Value.	General Tariff. Quantity.	General Tariff. Value.	General Tariff. Duty.
	Dutiable Goods—*Con.*			$		$	$ cts.
1	Signs of any material, framed or not, and letters of any material for signs or similar use, 30 p. c.	$	....	66,233	....	59,999	17,999 70
	Silk and manufactures of—						
	Fabrics, N.E.S., 30 p. c.	$	....	2,879,716	....	2,458,121	737,436 30
3	Silk cloth, including satin, imported by manufacturers of burial caskets or burial robes, for use in such manufacture, 10 p. c.	"	....	17,983	....	13,863	1,386 30
4	Silk, when imported by manufacturers of men's neckties, for use exclusively in the manufacture of such neckties in their own factories, 10 p. c.	"	....	493,858	....	320,250	32,025 00
5	Handkerchiefs, 35 p. c.	"	....	121,596	....	100,726	35,254 10
6	Blouses and shirt waists, 35 p. c.	"	....	55,749	....	24,996	8,748 60
7	Clothing, 35 p. c	"	....	254,535	....	89,744	31,410 40
8	Silk in the gum or spun, not more advanced than singles, tram and thrown organzine, not coloured, 15 p. c.	Lbs.	17,955	33,038	2,390	2,752	412 80
9	Sewing and embroidery silk and silk twist, 25 p. c.	$	....	40,187	....	16,463	4,115 75
10	Shawls, 30 p. c.	"	....	8,592	....	5,560	1,668 00
11	Shirts, 35 p. c.	Doz.	213	2,483	49	447	156 45
12	Silk and all manufactures of, not otherwise provided for, or of which silk is the component part of chief value, N.E.S., 35 p. c.	$	....	114,521	....	72,967	25,538 45
13	Socks and stockings, 35 p. c.	Doz. pairs.	1,454	8,755	51	642	224 70
14	Undershirts and drawers, 35 p. c	$	....	6,549	....	644	225 40
15	Velvets, velveteens, plush fabrics, N.E.S., 30 p. c.	Yds.	448,738	282,270	124,143	89,121	26,736 30
	Total, silks.		....	4,319,832	....	3,196,296	905,338 55
	Slate and manufactures of—						
16	Roofing slate, 25 p.c., not over 75c. per square.	Squares.	15,373	60,054	15,373	60,054	11,351 00
17	School writing slates, 25 p.c	$	....	20,524	....	19,600	4,900 00
18	Slate pencils, 25 p.c.	"	....	3,550	....	1,600	400 00
19	Slate, and manufactures of, N.E.S., 30 p.c.	"	....	29,023	....	29,023	8,706 90
	Total, slate and manufactures of.		....	113,151	....	110,277	25,357 90
	Soap—						
20	Common, or laundry, 1c. per lb.	Lbs.	1,738,544	96,151	1,651,623	91,407	16,516 23
21	Castile, mottled or white, 2c. per lb.	"	1,496,144	74,485	1,543,513	75,045	16,610 69
22	Common soft and liquid, 35 p.c.	"	137,755	4,605	79,842	2,831	990 85
23	Harness, 25 p.c	"	16,952	2,242	14,367	1,893	473 25
24	Toilet, 35 p.c	$	....	183,303	....	141,413	49,494 55
25	Soap, N.E.S., including pumice, silver and mineral soaps, sapolio and like articles, 35 p.c.	Lbs.	638,784	54,590	579,588	48,867	17,103 45
26	Pearline and other soap powders, 30 p.c.	"	2,358,048	96,065	2,330,013	94,507	28,352 10
	Total, soap		....	511,441	....	455,963	129,541 12

Imported into Canada, &c.—*Continued.*

ENTERED FOR HOME CONSUMPTION.									
Preferential Tariff.			Surtax Tariff.			Total.			
Quantity.	Value.	Duty.	Quantity.	Value.	Duty.	Quantity.	Value.	Duty Collected.	
	$	$ cts.		$	$ cts.		$	$ cts.	
....	5,293	1,058 60	....	945	378 00	....	66,237	19,436 30	1
....	363,991	72,798 20	....	60,442	24,176 80	....	2,882,554	834,411 30	2
....	43	2 87	....	4,077	543 60	....	17,983	1,932 77	3
....	66,110	4,407 33	....	114,578	15,277 06	....	500,938	51,709 39	4
....	29,117	6,794 13	....	90	42 00	....	129,933	42,090 23	5
....	27,881	6,505 74	....	1,995	930 97	....	54,872	16,185 31	6
....	148,468	34,643 35	....	9,998	4,665 69	....	248,210	70,719 44	7
15,565	30,286	3,028 60	....	....	....	17,955	33,038	3,441 40	8
....	23,206	3,867 93	....	243	81 00	....	39,912	8,064 68	9
....	1,405	281 00	....	1,737	694 80	....	8,702	2,643 80	10
164	2,036	475 10	....	....	....	213	2,483	631 55	11
....	32,815	7,657 27	....	8,394	3.917 25	....	114,176	37,112 97	12
704	4,796	1,119 13	699	3,317	1,547 94	1,454	8,755	2,891 77	13
....	5,905	1,377 93	....	....	....	....	6,549	1,603 33	14
243,370	142,910	28,582 00	85,155	51,216	20,486 40	452,668	283,247	75,804 70	15
....	878,969	171,540 58	....	256,087	72,363 51	....	4,331,352	1,149,242 64	
....	....	....	....	....	....	15,373	60,054	11,351 00	16
....	7	1 17	....	928	309 35	....	20,535	5,210 52	17
....	....	....	....	1,729	576 36	....	3,329	976 36	18
....	....	....	....	....	....	....	29,023	8,706 90	19
....	7	1 17	....	2,657	885 71	....	112,941	26,244 78	
37,075	1,633	247 20	....	....	....	1,688,698	93,040	16,763 43	20
122	6	1 62	....	....	....	1,543,635	75,051	16,612 31	21
57,201	1,688	393 93	712	86	40 13	137,755	4,605	1,424 91	22
2,585	349	58 18	....	....	....	16,952	2,242	531 43	23
....	37,514	8,753 59	....	1,628	759 76	....	180,555	59,007 90	24
3,909	319	74 44	....	....	....	583,497	49,180	17,177 89	25
922	70	14 00	....	....	....	2,330,935	94,577	28,366 10	26
....	41,579	9,542 96	....	1,714	799 89	....	499,256	139,883 97	

No. 14.—Summary Statement of Foreign Merchandise

No.	Articles and General Tariff Rates.		Total Imports.		General Tariff.		
			Quantity.	Value.	Quantity.	Value.	Duty.
	DUTIABLE GOODS—*Con.*			$		$	$ cts.
	Spices—						
1	Ginger and spices of all kinds, N.E.S., unground, 12½ p.c.	Lbs.	3,037,454	248,824	885,933	73,155	9.145 03
2	Ginger and spices of all kinds, N.E.S., ground, 25 p.c.	"	302,118	26,486	252,990	18,735	4,683 75
3	Ginger, preserved, 30 p.c.	"	143,397	8,817	129,429	7,782	2,334 60
4	Nutmegs and mace, 25 p.c.	"	153,696	24,046	38,622	5,377	1,344 25
	Total, spices		3,636,665	308,173	1,306,974	105,049	17,507 63
	Spirits and wines, viz.—						
5	Amyl alcohol or fusel oil, or any substance known as potato spirit or potato oil, $2.40 per gall.	Galls.	3	8	3	8	7 20
6	Ethyl alcohol, or the substance known as alcohol, hydrated oxide of ethyl, or spirits of wine, $2.40 per gall.	"	308,865	58,985	115,661	23,155	277,586 40
7	Methyl alcohol, wood alcohol, wood naphtha, pyroxylic spirits, wood spirits or methylated spirits, $2.40 per gall.	"	20	31	18	28	43 20
8	Absinthe, $2.40 per gall.	"	3,003	4,548	3,082	4,470	7,396 80
9	Arrack or palm spirit, $2.40 per gall.	"	522	830	604	811	1,449 60
10	Brandy, including artificial brandy and imitations of brandy, $2.40 per gall.	"	355,211	539,662	341,754	553,102	820,209 60
11	Cordials and liqueurs of all kinds, N.E.S.; mescal, pulque, rum shrub, schiedam and other schnapps; tafia, angostura and similar alcoholic bitters or beverages, $2.40 per gall.	"	38,347	91,358	35,367	82,274	84,880 80
12	Gin of all kinds, N.E.S., $2.40 per gall.	"	671,963	377,528	727,497	370,027	1,745,992 80
13	Rum, $2.40 per gall.	"	113,667	61,498	133,246	61,104	319.790 40
14	Whiskey, $2.40 per gall.	"	646,543	1,024,593	586,160	929,834	1,406,784 00
15	All spirituous or alcoholic liquors, N.O.P., $2.40 per gall.	"	18,080	12,281	17,335	11,596	41,604 00
16	Spirits and strong waters of any kind, mixed with any ingredient or ingredients, as being or known or designated as anodynes, elixirs, essences, extracts, lotions, tinctures or medicines, or medicinal wines (so called), or ethereal and spirituous fruit essences, N.E.S., $2.40 per gall. and 30 p.c.	"	2,421	15,095	2,282	14,264	9,756 00
17	Medicinal or medicated wines containing not more than 40 p.c. of proof spirit, $1.50 per gall.	"	3,253	9,598	3,119	8,597	4.678 50
18	Alcoholic perfumes and perfumed spirits, bay rum, cologne and lavender waters, hair, tooth and skin washes, and other toilet preparations containing spirits or any kind, in bottles or flasks containing not more than 4 ounces each, 50 p.c.	"	3,931	54,103	3,638	51,769	25,884 50
19	Alcoholic perfumes and perfumed spirits, bay rum, cologne and lavender waters, hair, tooth and skin washes, and other toilet preparations containing spirits of any kind, in bottles, flasks or other packages containing more than 4 ounces each, $2.40 per gall. and 40 p.c.	"	3,478	53,396	3,387	52,800	29,248 80
20	Vermouth containing not more than 36 p.c. of proof spirits, 90 p.c. per gall.	"	19,365	23,353	17,709	20,247	15,928 10

Imported into Canada, &c.—*Continued.*

Entered for Home Consumption.									
Preferential Tariff.			Surtax Tariff.			Total.			
Quantity.	Value.	Duty.	Quantity.	Value.	Duty.	Quantity.	Value.	Duty Collected.	
	$	$ cts.		$	$ cts.		$	$ cts.	
2,150,318	174,297	14,525 08				3,036,251	247,452	23,670 11	1
52,620	7,733	1,289 14				305,610	26,468	5,972 89	2
5,885	995	199 00				135,314	8,777	2,533 60	3
112,808	18,631	3,105 24				151,430	24,008	4,449 49	4
2,321,631	201,656	19,118 46				3,628,605	306,705	36,626 09	
						3	8	7 20	5
			115	105	368 00	115,776	23,260	277,954 40	6
			2	3	6 40	20	31	49 60	7
						3,082	4,470	7,396 80	8
						604	811	1,449 60	9
						341,754	553,102	820,209 60	10
			162	300	518 40	35,529	82,574	85,399 20	11
			55	38	176 00	727,552	370,065	1,746,163 80	12
						133,246	61,104	319,790 40	13
			226	523	723 20	586,386	930,357	1,407,507 20	14
			21	20	67 20	17,356	11,616	41,671 20	15
			63	85	235 60	2,345	14,349	9,991 60	16
						3,119	8,597	4,678 50	17
			358	3,270	2,179 96	3,996	55,039	28,064 46	18
			94	664	654 91	3,481	53,464	29,903 71	19
						17,709	20,247	15,938 10	20

No. 14.—SUMMARY STATEMENT of Foreign Merchandise

	Articles and General Tariff Rates.		Total Imports.		General Tariff.		
			Quantity.	Value.	Quantity.	Value.	Duty.
	DUTIABLE GOODS—Con.			$		$	$ cts.
1	Spirits and wines—Con.						
2	Vermouth containing more than 36 p.c of proof spirits, $2.40 per gall........	Galls.	186	226	80	97	192 00
3	Nitrous ether, sweet spirits of nitre and aromatic spirits of ammonia, $2.40 per gall. and 30 p.c	"	683	1,820	566	1,581	1,832 70
4	Wines, ginger, containing not more than 26 p.c. of proof spirits, 90c. per gall ..	"	2,129	1,706	2,025	1,601	1,822 50
	Wines, ginger, containing more than 26 p.c. of proof spirits, $2.40 per gall....	"	132	129	132	129	316 80
	Total, spirits..		2,191,802	2,330,748	1,993,665	2,187,494	4,795,414 70
	Wines of all kinds, except sparkling wines, including orange, lemon, strawberry, raspberry, elder and currant wines—						
5	Containing 26 p.c. or less of spirits, 25c. per gall. and 30 p.c..............	"	336,509	205,571	320,510	192,473	86,225 00
6	Containing over 26 p.c. and not over 27 p.c., 28c. per gall. and 30 p.c ...	"	7,610	4,105	9,614	4,916	4,166 72
7	Containing over 27 p.c. and not over 28 p.c., 31c. per gall. and 30 p.c ...	"	12,623	7,557	12,473	7,226	6,034 43
8	Containing over 28 p.c. and not over 29 p.c., 34c. per gall. and 30 p.c....	"	24,015	12,568	23,405	11,718	11,473 10
9	Containing over 29 p.c. and not over 30 p.c., 37c. per gall. and 30 p.c....	"	25,811	15,647	25,922	15,964	14,380 34
10	Containing over 30 p.c. and not over 31 p.c., 40c. per gall. and 30 p.c....	"	22,807	18,005	23,700	18,414	15,004 20
11	Containing over 31 p.c. and not over 32 p.c., 43c. per gall. and 30 p.c ...	"	33,471	27,331	33,181	28,272	22,749 45
12	Containing over 32 p.c. and not over 33 p.c., 46c. per gall. and 30 p.c....	"	31,492	32,551	30,026	31,872	23,373 56
13	Containing over 33 p.c. and not over 34 p.c., 49c. per gall. and 30 p.c....	"	30,249	35,442	29,403	34,709	24,820 18
14	Containing over 34 p.c. and not over 35 p.c., 52c. per gall. and 30 p.c....	"	18,747	27,054	17,665	26,380	17,099 80
15	Containing over 35 p.c. and not over 36 p.c., 55c. per gall. and 30 p.c..	"	11,636	19,952	10,786	19,052	11,647 90
16	Containing over 36 p.c. and not over 37 p.c., 58c. per gall. and 30 p.c....	"	3,508	6,510	3,302	6,030	3,724 16
17	Containing over 37 p.c. and not over 38 p.c., 61c. per gall. and 30 p.c....	"	900	3,017	584	1,567	826 34
18	Containing over 38 p.c. and not over 39 p.c., 64c. per gall. and 30 p.c....	"	283	644	283	389	297 82
19	Containing over 39 p.c. and not over 40 p.c., 67c. per gall. and 30 p.c....	"	746	199	746	199	559 52
	Total, wines, non-sparkling......		560,407	416,153	541,600	399,181	242,382 52
	Champagne and all other sparkling wines—						
20	In bottles containing each not more than a quart but more than a pint, old wine measure, $3.30 per doz. and 30 p.c	Doz.	8,243	109,183	8,043	107,885	27,337 20
21	In bottles containing not more than a pint but more than half a pint, old wine measure, $1.65 per doz. and 30 per cent......	"	28,160	196,681	26,976	177,696	44,848 80
22	In bottles containing one-half pint each or less, 82c. per doz. and 30 p.c.		1,671	4,871	1,299	3,139	1,068 48

SESSIONAL PAPER No. 11

Imported into Canada, &c.—*Continued.*

ENTERED FOR HOME CONSUMPTION.

Preferential Tariff.			Surtax Tariff.			Total.			
Quantity.	Value.	Duty.	Quantity.	Value.	Duty.	Quantity.	Value.	Duty Collected.	
	$	$ cts.		$	$ cts.		$	$ cts.	
						80	97	192 00	1
			150	269	587 60	716	1,850	2,420 30	2
						2,025	1,601	1,822 50	3
						132	129	316 80	4
			1,246	5,277	5,517 27	1,994,911	2,192,771	4,800,931 97	
			6,369	10,523	6,332 17	326,879	202,996	92,557 17	5
						9,614	4,916	4,166 72	6
						12,473	7,226	6,034 43	7
						23,405	11,718	11,473 10	8
						25,922	15,964	14,380 34	9
						23,700	18,414	15,004 20	10
						33,181	28,272	22,749 45	11
						30,026	31,872	23,373 56	12
						29,403	34,709	24,820 18	13
						17,665	26,380	17,099 80	14
						10,786	19,052	11,647 90	15
			58	58	68 05	3,360	6,088	3,792 21	16
						584	1,567	826 34	17
						283	389	297 82	18
						746	199	559 52	19
			6,427	10,581	6,400 22	548,027	409,762	248,782 74	
			176	1,392	1,331 20	8,219	109,277	28,668 40	20
			220	917	850 80	27,196	178,613	45,699 60	21
						1,299	3,139	1,068 48	22

No. 14.—SUMMARY STATEMENT of Foreign Merchandise

	Articles and General Tariff Rates.	Total Imports.		General Tariff.		
		Quantity.	Value.	Quantity.	Value.	Duty.
	DUTIABLE GOODS—*Con.*		$		$	$ cts.
	Syirits and wines—*Con.*					
	Champagne—*Con.*					
1	In bottles containing more than one quart each, $3.30 per doz., $1.65 per gall. and 30 p.c. ... Doz. & Galls.	Doz. Galls. 11 27	476	Galls. Doz. 5 9	167	31 35
	Total, wines, sparkling	....	311,211	....	288,887	73,285 83
2	Sponges, 20 p.c. ... $	....	51,521	....	40,052	8,010 40
3	Starch, including farina, corn starch, &c., 1½c. per lb. ... Lbs.	1,024,708	40,575	757,801	26,017	11,366 89
4	Stearic acid, 20 p.c. ... "	179,051	17,050	119,371	10,272	2,054 40
5	Stockinettes for the manufacture of rubber boots and shoes, imported by manufacturers of rubber boots and shoes for use exclusively in the manufacture thereof in their own factories, 15 p.c. ... $	....	72,634	....	58,522	8,778 30
	Stone and manufactures of—					
6	Flagstones, granite, rough freestone, sandstone and all building stone, not hammered or chiselled, 15 p.c. ... Tons.	14,724	66,994	14,528	65,543	9,831 45
7	Granite and freestones, dressed; all other building stone dressed, except marble, 20 p.c. ... "	11,381	65,134	11,346	64,762	12,952 40
8	Granite, sawn only, 20 p.c. ... "	9,495	32,316	9,491	32,077	6,415 40
9	" manufactures of, N.O.P., 35 p.c. $	....	94,717	....	8,045	2,815 75
10	Grindstones, not mounted and not less than 36 inches in diameter, 15 p.c. ... "	....	48,683	....	44,455	6,668 25
11	Grindstones, N.E.S., 25 p.c. ... "	....	10,944	....	10,830	2,707 50
12	Paving blocks, 20 p.c. ... "	....	24,817	....	19,141	3,828 20
13	Manufactures of stone, N.O.P., 30 p.c. ... "	....	26,585	....	24,764	7,429 20
	Total, stone and manufactures of	....	370,190	....	269,617	52,648 15
14	Straw, 20 p.c. ... Tons.	127	941	127	941	188 20
15	" carpeting, rugs, mats and matting, 25 p.c. ... $	....	46,311	....	46,800	11,700 00
16	" manufactures of, not otherwise provided for, 20 p.c. ... "	....	20,655	....	8,253	1,650 60
	Total, straw and manufactures of	....	67,907	....	55,994	13,538 80
	Sugars, syrups and molasses—					
17	Sugar, above No. 16 D.S. in colour, and all refined sugars of whatever kinds, grades or standards, by degrees ... Lbs.	27,086,137	808,652	1,856,411	62,367	23,220 34
18	Sugar, N.E.S., not above No. 16 D.S. in colour, sugar drainings, or pumpings drained in transit, melado or concentrated melado, tank bottoms and sugar concrete, by degrees ... "	390,846,220	8,121,935	76,063,180	1,851,466	539,370 50
19	Syrups and molasses of all kinds, N.O.P., the product of the sugar cane and beet, N.E.S., and all imitations thereof or substitutes thereof, ⅜c. per lb. ... "	3,597,982	56,797	3,032,391	47,424	22,742 94
	Total, sugars and syrups	421,530,339	8,987 384	80,951,982	1,961,257	585,333 78

Imported into Canada, &c.—*Continued.*

Entered for Home Consumption.									
Preferential Tariff.			Surtax Tariff.			Total.			
Quantity.	Value.	Duty.	Quantity.	Value.	Duty.	Quantity.	Value.	Duty Collected.	
	$	$ cts.		$	$ cts.		$	$ cts.	
						Doz. Galls.			
						5 9	167	31 35	1
				2,309	2,182 00		291,196	75,467 83	
	13,744	1,832 48		262	69 85		54,058	9,912 73	2
248,050	13,898	2,480 50	24,254	771	485 09	1,030,105	40,686	14,332 48	3
59,680	6,778	903 74				179,051	17,050	2,958 14	4
	14,112	1,411 20					72,634	10,189 50	5
196	1,451	145 10				14,724	66,994	9,976 55	6
35	372	49 61				11,381	65,134	13,002 01	7
4	239	31 87				9,495	32,316	6,447 27	8
	86,672	20,221 13					94,717	23,039 88	9
	3,182	318 20		1,046	209 20		48,683	7,195 65	10
	114	19 00					10,944	2,726 50	11
	5,676	756 80					24,817	4,585 00	12
	666	133 20		1,155	462 00		26,585	8,024 40	13
	98,372	21,677 91		2,201	671 20		370,190	74,997 26	
						127	941	188 20	14
	159	26 51		128	42 66		47,087	11,769 17	15
	68	9 07		12,334	3,289 11		20,655	4,948 78	16
	227	35 58		12,462	3,331 77		68,683	16,906 15	
26,676,056	839,387	223,010 56	446	18	7 41	28,532,913	901,772	246,238 31	17
344,366,430	7,483,926	1,637,461 77				420,429,610	9,335,392	2,176,832 27	18
126,797	3,483	633 94				3,159,188	50,907	23,376 88	19
371,169,283	8,326,796	1,861,106 27	446	18	7 41	452,121,711	10,288,071	2,446,447 46	

No. 14.—Summary Statement of Foreign Merchandise

	Articles and General Tariff Rates.		Total Imports.		General Tariff.		
			Quantity.	Value.	Quantity.	Value.	Duty.
	DUTIABLE GOODS—*Con.*			$		$	$ cts.
	Sugars, syrups and molasses—*Con.*						
	Molasses produced in the process of the manufacture of cane sugar from the juice of the cane without any admixture with any other ingredient, when imported in the original package in which it was placed at the point of production and not afterwards subjected to any process of treating or mixing—						
1	Testing by polariscope, 40 degrees or over, $1\frac{3}{4}$c. per gall.	Galls.	1,170,958	253,919	1,335,594	309,734	23,372 71
2	Testing by polariscope, 39 degrees or over, $2\frac{3}{4}$c. per gall	"	729	226	2,008	430	55 22
3	Testing by polariscope, 37 degrees or over, $4\frac{3}{4}$c. per gall.	"	243	70	243	70	11 54
	Total, molasses.		1,171,930	254,215	1,337,845	310,234	23,439 47
4	Sugar candy, brown or white, and confectionery, including sweetened gums, candied peel and pop corn, $\frac{1}{2}$c. per lb. and 35 p.c.	Lbs.	2,296,822	304,565	955,477	147,485	56,397 18
5	Glucose or grape sugar, glucose syrup and corn syrup or any syrups containing any admixture thereof, $\frac{3}{4}$c. per lb.	"	2,235,762	41,070	2,226,242	40,639	16,696 83
6	Saccharine or any product containing over one-half per cent thereof, 20 p.c.	"	2,117	1,931	1,967	1,886	377 20
7	Sugar, maple, and maple syrup, 20 p.c.	"	93,719	8,566	27,943	2,999	599 80
8	Tallow, 20 p.c.	"	83,950	5,230	78,009	4,635	927 00
9	Tape lines of any material, 25 p.c.	$	....	28,517	....	16,384	4,096 00
10	Tea of Ceylon, black, 10 p.c.	Lbs.	31,708	4,965	30,398	4,654	465 40
11	" " green, 10 p.c.	"	4,307	439	4,307	439	43 90
12	" India, black, 10 p.c.	"	25,569	3,068	10,676	1,684	168 40
13	" China, black, 10 p.c.	"	30,080	6,468	29,358	6,322	632 20
14	" " green, 10 p.c.	"	6,795	1,410	4,292	1,160	116 00
15	" Japan, green, 10 p.c.	"	40,962	6,265	77,041	9,937	993 70
16	" other countries, black, 10 p.c.	"	5,057	1,556	5,132	1,515	151 50
17	" " green, 10 p.c.	"	23,740	4,317	9,577	1,235	123 50
	Total, teas		168,218	28,488	170,781	26,946	2,694 60
18	Tinware, plain, japanned, or lithographed, and all manufactures of tin, N.E.S., 25 p.c.	$	....	228,971	....	195,026	48,756 50
	Tobacco and manufactures of—						
19	Cigarettes, $3 per lb. and 25 p.c.	Lbs.	28,370	63,313	24,093	56,606	86,430 50
20	Cigars, $3 per lb. and 25 p.c.	"	116,204	402,638	116,505	403,954	450,503 50
21	Tobacco, cut, 55c. per lb.	"	329,116	189,258	321,383	183,860	176,760 65
22	Snuff, 50c. per lb.	"	42,393	18,658	42,714	18,148	21,357 00
23	All other manufactures of tobacco, N.E.S., 50c. per lb	"	162,638	68,258	117,206	51,777	58,603 00
24	Foreign raw leaf tobacco samples, unstemmed, 40c. per lb.	"	22,746	11,877	20	12	8 00
	Total, tobacco and manufactures of.		701,467	754,002	621,921	714,357	793,662 65

SESSIONAL PAPER No. 11

Imported into Canada, &c.—*Continued.*

Entered for Home Consumption.									
Preferential Tariff.			Surtax Tariff.			Total.			
Quantity.	Value.	Duty.	Quantity.	Value.	Duty.	Quantity.	Value.	Duty Collected.	
	$	$ cts.		$	$ cts.		$	$ cts.	
2,401	441	28 03	....	....	....	1,337,995	310,175	23,400 74	1
....	....	....	....	....	....	2,008	430	55 22	2
....	....	....	....	....	....	243	70	11 54	3
2,401	441	28 03	....	....	....	1,340,246	310,675	23,467 50	
1,342,472	156,471	40,985 23	....	....	....	2,297,949	303,956	97,382 41	4
9,520	431	47 60	....	....	....	2,235,762	41,070	16,744 43	5
150	45	6 00	....	....	....	2,117	1,931	383 20	6
24,954	1,793	239 07	....	....	....	51,997	4,792	838 87	7
5,941	595	79 35	....	....	....	83,950	5,230	1,006 35	8
....	11,273	1,878 99	....	789	262 99	....	28,446	6,237 98	9
1,370	327	21 80	....	....	....	31,768	4,981	487 20	10
....	....	....	....	....	....	4,307	439	43 90	11
....	....	....	....	....	....	10,676	1,684	168 40	12
....	....	....	....	....	....	29,358	6,322	632 20	13
....	....	....	....	....	....	4,292	1,160	116 00	14
....	....	....	....	....	....	77,041	9,937	993 70	15
....	....	....	....	....	....	5,132	1,515	151 50	16
....	....	....	....	....	....	9,577	1,235	123 50	17
1,370	327	21 80	....	....	....	172,151	27,273	2,716 40	
....	25,889	4,315 19	....	7,523	2,507 66	....	228,438	55,579 35	18
....	....	....	26	57	123 00	24,119	56,663	86,553 50	19
....	....	....	593	894	2,670 01	117,098	401,848	453,173 51	20
....	....	....	....	....	....	321,383	183,860	176,760 65	21
....	....	....	88	21	58 67	42,802	18,169	21,415 67	22
....	....	....	....	....	....	117,206	51,777	58,603 00	23
....	....	....	....	....	....	20	12	8 00	24
....	....	....	707	972	2,851 68	622,628	715,329	796,514 33	

No. 14.—SUMMARY STATEMENT of Foreign Merchandise

	Articles and General Tariff Rates.		Total Imports.		General Tariff.		
			Quantity.	Value.	Quantity.	Value.	Duty.
	DUTIABLE GOODS—*Con.*			$		$	$ cts.
1	Tobacco pipes of all kinds, pipe mounts, cigar and cigarette holders and cases for same, smokers' sets and cases therefor and tobacco pouches, 35 p.c.	$	....	443,023	....	312,777	109,471 95
2	Trawls, trawling spoons, fly books, sinkers, swivels, and sportsman's fishing bait, and fish hooks, N.E.S., 30 p.c.	"	....	49,518	....	24,074	7,222 20
3	Trunks, valises, hat-boxes, carpet bags, satchels, tool bags or baskets, portmanteaus, flyhooks and parts thereof, N.O.P., 30 p.c.	$	....	102,623	....	82,562	24,768 60
4	Turpentine, spirits of, 5 p.c.	Galls.	898,100	603,059	895,463	601,731	30,086 55
5	Twine, manufactures of, viz.: hammocks and lawn tennis nets, sportsman's fish nets and other articles, N.O.P., 30 p.	$	....	33,197	....	31,979	9,593 70
6	Umbrellas, parasols and sunshades, of all kinds and materials, 35 p.c.	"	....	53,122	....	10,962	3,836 70
7	Unenumerated articles, 20 p.c.	"	....	125,002	....	101,428	20,285 60
8	Varnish, lacquers, japans, japan dryers, liquid dryers and oil finish, N.E.S., 20c. per gall. and 20 p.c.	Galls.	88,906	168,987	65,183	111,701	35,376 80
	Vegetables, viz.—						
9	Melons, 25 p.c.	No.	507,523	35,139	505,689	35,087	8,771 75
10	Potatoes, 15c. per bush.	Bush.	241,605	131,891	222,239	123,115	33,335 86
11	" sweet and yams, 10c. per bush.	"	29,935	25,412	29,811	25,277	2,981 10
12	Tomatoes, fresh, 20c. per bush and 10 p.c.	"	51,486	116,934	51,454	116,586	21,949 40
13	Tomatoes and other vegetables, including corn and baked beans in cans or other pkgs., N.E.S., 1½c. per lb.	Lbs.	2,504,360	129,505	2,672,957	131,671	40,094 36
14	Fresh or dry salted, N.O.P., 25 p.c.	$	....	363,532	....	348,142	87,035 50
	Total, vegetables		....	802,413	....	779,878	194,167 97
15	Vinegar, of any strength not exceeding strength of proof, 15c. per gall.	Galls.	93,683	23,079	29,565	4,066	4,434 75
16	Vinegar, above strength of proof, 2c. additional for each degree	"	9,017	5,880	4,665	2,206	873 17
	Total, vinegar		102,700	28,959	34,230	6,272	5,307 92
17	Watches, 25 p.c.	$	....	82,423	....	77,731	19,432 75
18	Watch cases, 30 p.c.	"	....	74,088	....	73,446	22,033 80
19	Watch actions and movements, 10 p.c.	"	....	767,837	....	764,383	76,438 30
20	Watch glasses and watch keys, 25 p.c.	"	....	11,806	....	6,312	1,578 00
	Total, watches, cases, movements, glasses, &c.		....	936,154	....	921,872	119,482 85
21	Wax, bees, 10 p.c.	Lbs.	31,947	11,174	31,589	11,087	1,108 70
22	Wax, paraffine, 25 p.c.	"	112,612	9,721	104,196	9,186	2,296 50
23	Wax and manufactures of, N.E.S., 20 p.c.	$	....	83,609	....	69,671	13,934 20
	Total, wax and manufactures of		....	104,504	....	89,944	17,339 40

Imported into Canada, &c.—*Continued.*

Entered for Home Consumption.									
Preferential Tariff.			Surtax Tariff.			Total.			
Quantity.	Value.	Duty.	Quantity.	Value.	Duty.	Quantity.	Value.	Duty Collected.	
	$	$ cts.		$	$ cts.		$	$ cts.	
....	97,099	22,656 75	....	30,421	14,196 52	....	440,297	146,325 22	1
....	25,003	5,000 60	....	31	12 40	....	49,108	12,235 20	2
....	16,864	3,372 80	....	2,863	1,145 20	....	102,289	29,286 60	3
1,594	785	26 19	1,043	528	35 20	898,100	603,044	30,147 94	4
....	1,548	309 60	....	....	....	....	33,527	9,903 30	5
....	41,817	9,757 55	....	395	184 33	....	53,174	13,778 58	6
....	21,922	2,923 13	....	1,702	453 88	....	125,052	23,662 61	7
23,331	56,605	10,658 29	38	39	20 53	88,552	168,345	46,055 62	8
....	....	....	....	....	....	105,689	35,087	8,771 75	9
1,400	528	140 00	....	....	....	223,639	123,643	33,475 86	10
65	37	4 33	....	....	....	29,876	25,314	2,985 43	11
....	....	....	....	....	....	51,454	116,586	21,949 40	12
19,498	1,350	194 99	821	144	16 41	2,693,276	133,165	40,305 76	13
....	1,707	284 56	....	2,850	950 00	....	352,699	88,270 06	14
....	3,622	623 88	....	2,994	966 41	....	786,494	195,758 26	
53,624	18,863	5,362 40	10,491	724	2,098 20	93,680	23,653	11,895 35	15
4,802	3,517	3,898 68	....	....	....	9,467	5,723	4,771 85	16
58,426	22,380	9,261 08	10,491	724	2,098 20	103,147	29,376	16,667 20	
....	1,105	184 23	....	3,389	1,129 63	....	82,225	20,746 61	17
....	123	24 60	....	451	180 40	....	74,020	22,238 80	18
....	503	33 54	....	2,451	326 80	....	767,337	76,798 64	19
....	576	96 00	....	4,918	1,639 33	....	11,806	3,313 33	20
....	2,307	338 37	....	11,209	3,276 16	....	935,388	123,097 38	
358	87	5 80	....	....	....	31,947	11,174	1,114 50	21
8,038	469	78 17	378	66	22 00	112,612	9,721	2,396 67	22
....	10,853	1,447 08	....	638	170 11	....	81,162	15,551 39	23
....	11,409	1,531 05	....	704	192 11	....	102,057	19,062 56	

No. 14.—SUMMARY STATEMENT of Foreign Merchandise

	Articles and General Tariff Rates.		Total Imports.		General Tariff.		
			Quantity.	Value.	Quantity.	Value.	Duty.
	DUTIABLE GOODS—*Con.*			$		$	$ cts.
1	Webbing, elastic and non-elastic, 20 p.c.	$	....	203,586	....	139,002	27,800 40
2	Whips of all kinds, including thongs and lashes, 35 p.c.	"	....	8,343	....	4,863	1,702 05
3	Window cornices and cornice poles of all kinds, 30 p.c.	$	....	12,496	....	11,602	3,480 60
4	Window shade or blind rollers, 35 p.c.	"	....	34,616	....	34,345	12,020 75
5	Window shades in the peace or cut and hemmed or mounted on rollers, N.E.S., 35 p.c.	Sq. yds.	88,458	12,095	37,030	4,725	1,653 75
	Total, window cornices, rollers, shades, &c.		....	59,207	....	50,672	17,155 10
	Wood and manufactures of—						
6	Barrels containing petroleum or its products, or any mixture of which petroleum forms a part, when such contents are chargeable with a specific duty, 20c. each	No.	36,765	37,294	36,191	36,719	7,238 20
7	Fishing rods, 30 p.c.	$	....	12,194	....	10,209	3,062 70
8	Handles of all kinds, hickory, 25 p.c.	"	....	38,948	....	39,092	9,773 00
9	" " ash, 25 p.c.	"	....	18,564	....	18,546	4,636 50
10	Caskets and coffins and metal parts thereof, 25 p.c.	"	....	23,869	....	23,869	5,967 25
11	Lasts of wood, 25 p.c.	"	....	29,056	....	29,056	7,264 00
12	Mouldings, plain, gilded or otherwise further manufactured, 25 p.c.	"	....	70,852	....	70,487	17,621 75
13	Rakes, hay, 25 p.c.	No.	27,916	3,313	27,916	3,313	828 25
14	Show cases and metal parts thereof, 35 p.c.	"	2,287	29,572	2,052	28,495	9,973 25
15	Woodenware, churns, washboards, pounders and rolling-pins, 20 p.c.	$	....	10,201	....	10,214	2,042 80
16	Woodenware, pails and tubs, 25 p.c.	"	....	27,096	....	27,143	6,785 75
17	Manufactures of wood, N.O.P., 25 p.c.	"	....	909,048	....	868,705	217,176 25
18	Sawed boards, planks, deals, planed or dressed on one or both sides, when the edges thereof are jointed or tongued and grooved, 25 p.c.	M. ft.	7,610	126,527	7,610	126,513	31,628 25
19	Lumber and timber manufactured, N.E.S., 20 p.c.	"	1,735	25,997	1,735	25,988	5,197 60
20	Umbrella, parasol and sunshade sticks or handles, N.E.S., 20 p.c.	$	....	14,186	....	11,127	2,225 40
21	Veneers of wood, not over $\frac{3}{32}$ of an inch in thickness, 7½ p.c.	"	....	181,598	....	181,560	13,617 48
22	Walking sticks and canes of all kinds, N.E.S., 30 p.c.	"	....	19,463	....	12,926	3,877 80
23	Wood pulp, 25 p.c.	"	....	51,579	....	50,670	12,667 50
24	Willow or osier wares, and all manufactures of like material not otherwise provided for, 25 p.c.	"	....	8,616	....	8,593	2,148 25
	Total, wood and manufactures of		....	1,637,973	....	1,583,225	363,731 98

SESSIONAL PAPER No. 11

Imported into Canada, &c.—*Continued.*

Entered for Home Consumption.									
Preferential Tariff.			Surtax Tariff.			Total.			
Quantity.	Value.	Duty.	Quantity.	Value.	Duty.	Quantity.	Value.	Duty Collected.	
	$	$ cts.		$	$ cts.		$	$ cts.	
	61,740	8,232 08		2,844	758 39		203,586	36,790 87	1
	3,476	811 16		4	1 87		8,343	2,515 08	2
	894	178 80					12,496	3,659 40	3
	271	63 24					34,616	12,083 99	4
51,428	7,370	1,719 66				88,458	12,095	3,373 41	5
	8,535	1,961 70					59,207	19,116 80	
205	205	27 34				36,396	36,924	7,265 54	6
	1,985	397 00					12,194	3,459 70	7
	118	19 67					39,210	9,792 67	8
	18	3 00					18,564	4,639 50	9
							23,869	5,967 25	10
							29,056	7,264 00	11
	368	61 32		15	5 00		70,870	17,688 07	12
						27,916	3,313	828 25	13
238	1,052	245 53	17	42	19 60	2,307	29,589	10,238 38	14
	36	4 80					10,250	2,047 60	15
	21	3 50					27,164	6,789 25	16
	25,655	4,276 20		11,341	3,780 32		905,701	225,232 77	17
						7,610	126,513	31,628 25	18
	9	1 20				1,735	25,997	5,198 80	19
	1,728	230 42		1,331	354 93		14,186	2,810 75	20
	38	1 90					181,598	13,619 38	21
	6,387	1,277 40		150	60 00		19,463	5,215 20	22
	878	146 33		31	10 33		51,579	12,824 16	23
				23	7 67		8,616	2,155 92	24
	38,498	6,695 61		12,933	4,237 85		1,634,656	374,665 44	

No. 14.—SUMMARY STATEMENT of Foreign Merchandise

	Articles and General Tariff Rates.		Total Imports.		General Tariff.		
			Quantity.	Value.	Quantity.	Value.	Duty.
	DUTIABLE GOODS—*Con.*			$		$	$ cts.
	Wool, manufactures of :—						
1	Blankets, 35 p.c.	Lbs.	374,578	108,769	40,492	10,729	3,755 15
2	Cassimeres, cloths and doeskins, 35 p.c.	Yds.	3,075,228	2,003,161	138,347	85,202	29,820 70
3	Coatings and overcoatings, 35 p.c.	"	1,838,061	1,166,954	33,019	20,747	7,261 45
4	Tweeds, 35 p.c.	"	3,962,590	2,092,559	110,756	48,877	17,106 95
5	Felt cloth, N.E.S., 35 p.c.	"	29,556	32,588	15,796	20,495	7,173 25
6	Flannels, 35 p.c.	"	746,067	132,348	106,284	22,585	7,904 75
7	Knitted goods, including knitted underwear, N.E.S., 35 p.c.	$	....	407,059	....	71,749	25,112 15
8	Bed comforters and counterpanes, 35 p.c.	No.	7,691	16,027	1,772	2,741	959 35
9	Shawls, 30 p.c.	$	....	109,982	....	4,678	1,403 40
10	Shirts of wool, 35 p.c.	Doz.	4,146	31,065	585	4,086	1,430 10
11	Socks and stockings of wool, worsted, the hair of the alpaca, goat, &c., 35 p.c.	Doz. pairs.	626,751	1,120,696	16,971	23,255	8,139 25
12	Undershirts and drawers, 35 p.c.	$	....	222,972	....	59,933	20,976 55
13	Yarns costing 30c. p. lb. and over imported on the cop, tube or in the hank by manufacturers of woollen goods for use in their products, 20 p.c.	Lbs.	1,554,524	753,468	27,969	17,569	3,513 80
14	Yarns, N.E.S., 30 p.c.	"	285,419	160,102	10,081	3,557	1,067 10
15	All fabrics and manufactures composed wholly or in part of wool, worsted, &c., N.E.S., 35 p.c.	$	....	5,956,693	.....	1,658,803	580,581 07
16	Women's and children's dress goods, coat linings, Italian cloths, alpacas, orleans, cashmeres, henriettas, serges, buntings, nun's cloth, bengalines, whip cords, twills plains or jasquards of similar fabrics, composed wholly or in part of wool, worsted, the hair of the camel, alpaca, goat or like animal, not exceeding in weight six ounces to the square yard, imported in the gray or unfinished state for the purpose of being dyed or finished in Canada, 25 p.c.	Sq. yds.	499,222	92,610	109,029	24,913	6,228 25
17	Clothing, women's and children's outside garments, 35 p.c.	$	....	488,524	....	108,462	37,961 70
18	Clothing, ready-made, and wearing apparel, N.E.S., composed wholly or in part of wool, worsted, &c., N.E.S., 35 p.c.	"	....	788,804	.....	297,609	104,163 15
19	Carpets, Brussels, 35 p.c.	Yds.	651,228	460,784	5,210	4,182	1,463 70
20	" Tapestry, 35 p.c.	"	1,581,249	564,175	11,254	4,145	1,450 75
21	" Wool, N.E.S., 35 p.c.	"	746,302	542,353	21,952	19,712	6,899 20
22	Felt, pressed, of all kinds, not filled or covered by or with any woven fabric, 20 p.c.	Lbs.	811,667	190,174	620,289	124,904	24,980 80
23	Shoddy, 20 p.c.	"	444,458	40,703	18,790	789	157 80
	Total, wool and manufactures of		....	17,482,570	....	2,639,722	899,510 37
24	Zinc, manufactures of, N.O.P., 25 p.c.	$	....	12,917	....	11,919	2,979 75
25	Damaged goods, under sections 49 to 53 of Rev. Stat., Cap. 32	$	....	18,828	....	13,899	3,137 07
26	Prepaid postal packages, duty received by Customs from Post Office Department	"	....	18,399	....	18,399	3,680 15
27	Special duty on articles shipped to Canada at lower than usual home trade price	"	....	....	....	....	74,409 28
28	Additional duties, post entries over collections, &c.	$	....	....	....	....	159,251 55
	Total, dutiable goods		....	176,790,332	....	112,938,969	33,301,541 57

Imported into Canada, &c.—*Continued.*

Entered for Home Consumption.									
Preferential Tariff.			Surtax Tariff.			Total.			
Quantity.	Value.	Duty.	Quantity.	Value.	Duty.	Quantity.	Value.	Duty Collected.	
	$	$ cts.		$	$ cts.		$	$ cts.	
339,236	98,669	23,023 12	4,082	2,092	976 28	383,810	111,490	27,754 55	1
2,828,325	1,853,932	556,179 60	60,295	38,075	17,768 31	3,026,967	1,977,209	603,768 61	2
1,758,644	1,116,122	334,836 60	30,240	28,060	13,094 65	1,821,903	1,164,929	355,192 70	3
3,708,900	2,008,409	602,522 70	35,038	16,440	7,671 97	3,854,694	2,073,726	627,301 62	4
12,376	10,973	3,291 90	1,384	1,120	522 66	29,556	32,588	10,987 81	5
562,193	93,429	21,800 75	68,604	15,660	7,308 03	737,081	131,674	37,013 53	6
....	258,100	60,224 68	....	74,178	34,616 64	....	404,027	119,953 47	7
5,919	13,286	3,100 13	....	....	....	7,691	16,027	4,059 48	8
....	77,544	15,508 80	....	26,896	10,758 40	....	109,118	27,670 60	9
3,221	25,566	5,965 58	340	1,413	659 40	4,146	31,065	8,055 08	10
560,490	1,012,426	236,234 91	49,260	83,600	39,013 43	626,721	1,119,281	283,387 59	11
....	155,989	36,397 67	....	6,253	2,918 08	....	222,175	60,292 30	12
1,548,680	745,008	99,335 03	19	9	2 40	1,576,668	762,586	102,851 23	13
170,974	102,892	20,578 40	86,735	45,096	18,038 40	267,790	151,545	39,683 90	14
....	4,107,222	1,232,166 60	....	199,623	93,156 94	....	5,965,648	1,905,904 61	15
361,776	63,369	10,561 51	....	....	....	470,805	88,282	16,789 76	16
....	141,231	42,369 30	....	240,818	112,381 60	....	490,511	192,712 60	17
....	377,999	113,399 70	....	113,908	53,157 31	....	789,516	270,720 16	18
649,602	460,335	107,412 28	6,769	3,505	1,635 67	661,581	468,022	110,511 65	19
1,567,191	560,093	130,689 16	356	361	168 46	1,578,801	564,599	132,308 37	20
725,011	515,439	120,269 73	10,301	6,443	3,006 72	757,264	541,594	130,175 65	21
48,325	18,955	2,527 50	159,743	51,659	13,775 72	828,357	195,518	41,284 02	22
425,668	39,914	5,321 89	....	....	....	444,458	40,703	5,479 69	23
....	13,856,902	3,783,717 54	....	955,209	430,631 07	....	17,451,833	5,113,858 98	
....	901	150 18	....	97	32 33	....	12,917	3,162 26	24
....	4,327	782 16	....	602	141 39	....	18,828	4,060 62	25
....	....	....	....	....	....	....	18.399	3,680 15	26
....	....	....	....	....	....	....	....	74,409 28	27
....	....	....	....	....	....	....	....	159,251 55	28
....	54,164,102	11,158,853 14	....	5,943,038	2,210,706 47	....	173,046,109	46,671,101 18	

No. 14.—SUMMARY STATEMENT OF IMPORTS—*Continued.*

ARTICLES.		Imported.		Entered for Home Consumption.	
		Quantity.	Value.	Quantity.	Value.
FREE GOODS.			$		$
PRODUCE OF THE MINE.					
Burrstones in blocks, rough or unmanufactured, not bound up or prepared for binding into mill stones....	No.	1,746	2,661	1,746	2,661
Chalk stone, China or Cornwall stone, Cliff stone, and felspar, ground or unground....	$	....	9,053	....	9,053
Clays, viz.:—					
China clay....	Cwt.	176,084	65,909	176,084	65,909
Fire clay....	$	....	131,130	....	131,130
Pipe clay....	"	....	1,333	....	1,333
Clays, all other, N.E.S....	"	....	22,132	....	22,132
Total, clays....		....	220,504	....	220,504
Coal, anthracite, and anthracite coal dust....	Tons.	2,200,863	10,304,303	2,200,863	10,304,303
Emery, in bulk, crushed or ground....	$	....	21,781	....	21,781
Flint, flints and ground flint stones....	Cwt.	31,108	19,335	31,108	19,335
Fossils....	$	....	15	....	15
Fuller's earth in bulk only, not prepared for toilet or other purposes....	"	....	4,644	....	4,644
Gannister....	Cwt.	12,803	3,119	12,803	3,119
Gravels and sand....	Tons.	116,500	173,727	116,500	173,727
Gypsum, crude (sulphate of lime)....	"	6,332	22,008	6,332	22,008
Pumice and pumice stone, ground or unground....	$	....	9,053	....	9,053
Minerals, viz.—					
Alumina, or oxide of aluminum....	Cwt.	76,074	194,083	76,074	194,083
Cryolite or kryolite....	"	4,054	22,793	4,054	22,793
Litharge....	"	10,165	39,836	10,165	39,836
Total, minerals....		90,293	256,712	90,293	256,712
Mineral waters, natural, not in bottle....	Galls.	8,285	1,754	8,285	1,754
Mineralogical specimens....	$	....	726	....	726
Ores of metals, all kinds, including cobalt ore....	Cwt.	17,678,691	2,270,036	17,678,691	2,270,036
Phosphate rock (fertilizer)....	$	....	20,497	....	20,497
Precious stones, in the rough....	"	....	305,913	....	305,913
Diamonds, unset, diamond dust or bort, and black diamonds for borers....	"	....	1,209,755	....	1,209,755
Salt, imported from the United Kingdom, or any British possession; or imported for the use of the sea or gulf fisheries....	Cwt.	2,030,800	352,214	2,030,800	352,214
Silex or crystallized quartz....	"	7,465	8,347	7,465	8,347
Tufa, calcareous....	"	600	30	600	30
Whiting or whitening, gilders' whiting or Paris white..	"	160,030	44,876	160,030	44,876
Total, mine....		....	15,261,063	....	15,261,063
THE FISHERIES.					
Ambergris....	$	....	141	....	141
Fish offal or refuse and fish skins....	"	....	203	....	203
Fur skins, undressed, the produce of marine animals...	"	....	16,020	....	16,020
Pearl, mother of, unmanufactured....	"	....	3,909	....	3,909
Tortoise and other shells....	"	....	2,989	....	2,989
Turtles....	"	....	793	....	793
Whalebone, unmanufactured....	Lbs.	7	59	7	59
Seed and breeding oysters, imported for the purpose of being planted in Canadian waters....	$	....	525	....	525

No. 14.—SUMMARY STATEMENT OF IMPORTS—*Continued.*

ARTICLES.		Imported.		Entered for Home Consumption.	
		Quantity.	Value.	Quantity.	Value.
FREE GOODS—THE FISHERIES—*Con.*			$		$
Special from Newfoundland.					
Fish —					
Cod, haddock, ling and pollock, fresh	Lbs.	2,610	109	2,610	109
" " " dry, salted or smoked	Cwt.	180,781	812,344	180,781	812,344
" " " pickled	"	2,465	11,464	2,465	11,464
Halibut fresh	Lbs.	8,750	544	8,750	544
Herring "	"	2,075,600	36,162	2,075,600	36,162
" pickled	"	11,146,710	183,171	11,146,710	183,171
" smoked	"	1,640	54	1,640	54
Lobsters fresh in cans	"	30	13	30	13
" preserved in cans	"	244,255	58,760	244,255	58,760
Salmon fresh	"	121,441	10,974	121,441	10,974
" smoked	"	200	31	200	31
" canned	"	528	85	528	85
" pickled	"	640,874	33,993	640,874	33,993
Fish, all other fresh	$	....	2,828	....	2,828
" pickled	Lbs.	54,784	1,721	54,784	1,721
Total, fish from Newfoundland		....	1,152,253	....	1,152,253
Fish oil, viz.—					
Cod	Galls.	102,500	33,959	102,500	63,959
Seal	"	42,341	13,431	42,341	13,431
Other	"	37,839	10,196	37,839	10,196
Total, fish oil		182,680	57,586	182,680	57,586
Other articles, produce of the fisheries, N.E.S.	$	....	85	....	85
Total, fisheries		....	1,234,563	....	1,234,563
THE FOREST.					
Cork-wood	$	....	75,252	....	75,252
Barks, viz.:—Cork-wood	"	....	94	....	94
Hemlock	Cords.	36	171	36	171
Oak and tanners'	"	....	283	....	283
(D) Shovel handles wholly of wood	$	....	35,675	....	35,675
Felloes of hickory wood, rough sawn to shape only, or rough sawn and bent to shape, not planed, smoothed or otherwise manufactured	"	....	26,744	....	26,744
Handle, heading, stave and shingle bolts	"	....	43,356	....	43,356
Hickory billets	"	....	9,833	....	9,833
Hickory sawn to shape for spokes of wheels	"	....	6,681	....	6,681
Hickory spokes, rough turned, not tenoned, mitred, throated, faced, sized, cut to length, round tenoned or polished	"	....	108,100	....	108,100
Hubs for wheels, posts, last blocks, wagon, oar, gun, heading and all like blocks or sticks, rough hewn or sawed only	"	....	14,359	....	14,359
Ivory nuts (vegetable)	"	....	27,009	....	27,009
Fence posts and railroad ties	"	....	508,696	....	508,696
Logs, and round unmanufactured timber	"	....	889,571	....	889,571
Lumber and timber, planks and boards, when not otherwise manufactured than rough sawn or split or creosoted, vulcanized, or treated by any other preserving process, viz.—					
Boxwood	Feet.	5,560	430	5,560	430
Cherry, chestnut, gumwood hickory and whitewood	"	9,660,829	420,524	9,660,829	420,524

No. 14.—SUMMARY STATEMENT OF IMPORTS—*Continued.*

ARTICLES.		Imported.		Entered for Home Consumption.	
		Quantity.	Value.	Quantity.	Value.
FREE GOODS—THE FOREST—*Con.*			$		$
Lumber and timber—*Con.*					
Mahogany	Feet.	1,752,416	197,476	1,752,416	197,476
Oak	"	32,852,223	1,239,259	32,852,223	1,239,259
Pitch pine	"	22,576,299	565,474	22,576,299	565,474
Red wood	"	72,840	2,658	72,840	2,658
Rose wood	"	55,089	4,774	55,089	4,774
Sandal-wood	"	517	56	517	56
Spanish cedar	"	39,387	7,388	39,387	7,388
Sycamore	"	24,951	556	24,951	556
Walnut	"	1,003,318	43,246	1,003,318	43,246
White ash	"	1,715,091	72,034	1,715,091	72,034
African teak, black heart ebony, lignum vitæ, red cedar and satin-wood	$	....	29,835	....	29,835
Timber hewn or sawed, squared or sided, or creosoted	"	....	189,418	....	189,418
Sawed or split boards, planks, deals and other lumber, when not further manufactured than dressed on one side only or creosoted, vulcanized or treated by any preserving process	M ft.	52,401	1,124,638	52,401	1,124,638
Pine and spruce clapboards	"	323	2,860	323	2,860
Laths	M.	468	1,434	468	1,434
Shingles	"	10,301	21,311	10,301	21,311
Staves, not listed or jointed, of wood of all kinds	"	6,622	198,835	6,622	198,835
Total, lumber		....	4,122,206	....	4,122,206
Sawdust of the following woods:—Amaranth, cocoboral, boxwood, cherry, chestnut, walnut, gumwood, mahogany, pitch pine, rosewood, sandal-wood, sycamore, Spanish cedar, oak, hickory, whitewood, African teak, black heart ebony, lignum vitæ, red cedar, redwood, satin-wood, white ash, persimmon and dogwood	$	....	3,623	....	3,623
Wood for fuel	Cords.	38,991	96,021	38,991	96,021
Total, forest		....	5,967,674	....	5,967,674
ANIMALS AND THEIR PRODUCE.					
Animals for improvement of stock, viz.—					
Horses	No.	1,466	820,679	1,482	824,379
Cattle	"	542	57,509	542	57,509
Sheep	"	334	8,688	334	8,688
Swine	"	88	2,364	88	2,364
Dogs	"	343	11,073	343	11,073
Goats	"	22	96	22	96
Fowls, domestic, pure bred	"	3,715	8,703	3,715	8,703
Total, animals for improvement of stock		6,510	909,112	6,526	912,812
Animals brought into Canada, temporarily, and for a period not exceeding three months, for the purpose of exhibition or competition for prizes offered by any agricultural or other association, viz.:—					
Horses	No.	1,476	378,492	....	....
Cattle	"	25	6,125	....	....
Sheep	"	39	260	....	....
All other, N.E.S.	"	....	3,810	....	....
Total, animals for exhibition purposes		1,540	388,687	....	....

No. 14.—SUMMARY STATEMENT OF IMPORTS—*Continued.*

ARTICLES.		Imported.		Entered for Home Consumption.	
		Quantity.	Value.	Quantity.	Value.
FREE GOODS—ANIMALS AND THEIR PRODUCE—*Con.*			$		$
Bees	$	....	596	....	596
Bones, crude, not manufactured, burned, calcined, ground or steamed	Cwt.	33,425	25,528	33,425	25,528
Bone dust, bone black or charred bone and bone ash	"	36,209	52,364	36,209	52,364
Bristles	Lbs.	133,696	112,788	133,696	112,788
Cat-gut or worm gut not manufactured, for whip and other cord	$	....	589	....	589
Egg yolk	"	....	6,240	....	6,240
Fur skins of all kinds, not dressed in any manner, N.E.S	"	....	3,307,225	....	3,307,225
Grease, degras and oleostearine	Lbs.	1,779,780	76,810	1,779,780	76,810
Grease, rough, the refuse of animal fat, for the manufacture of soap and oils only	"	6,496,671	303,907	6,496,671	303,907
Total, grease		8,276,451	380,717	8,276,451	380,717
Guano and other animal manures	Cwt.	4,125	11,640	4,125	11,640
Hair, cleaned or uncleaned, but not curled, dyed or otherwise manufactured	Lbs.	418,934	59,834	418,934	59,834
Horse hair, not further manufactured than simply cleaned and dipped or dyed, for use in the manufacture of horse hair cloth	"	55,423	51,771	55,423	51,771
Hatters' furs, not on the skin	$	....	58,524	....	58,524
Hides and skins raw, whether dry salted or pickled, and tails undressed	"	....	6,552,319	....	6,552,319
Hoofs, horn strips, horn and horn tips, in the rough, not polished or otherwise manufactured than cleaned	"	....	18,993	....	18,993
Ivory, unmanufactured	Lbs.	1,298	6,833	1,298	6,833
Leeches	$	....	247	....	247
Musk in pods or in grains	Oz.	256	2,265	256	2,265
Pelts, raw	$	....	239,955	....	239,955
Pigeons, homing and messenger, pheasants and quails	"	....	3,073	....	3,073
Quills in their natural state or unplumed	"	....	2,461	....	2,461
Rennet, raw and prepared	"	....	65,294	....	65,294
Silk, raw or as reeled from the cocoon, not being doubled, twisted or advanced in manufacture in any way	Lbs.	120,207	451,707	120,207	451,707
Silk in the gum or spun, imported by manufacturers of silk underwear for such manufactures in their own factories	"	448	1,273	448	1,273
Silk cocoons and silk waste	$	....	3,080	....	3,080
Sausage skins or casings, not cleaned	"	....	425	....	425
Wool not further prepared than washed, N.E.S	Lbs.	6,311,837	1,489,268	6,311,837	1,489,268
Totals, animals and their produce		....	14,202,808	....	13,817,821
AGRICULTURAL PRODUCTS.					
Bamboo-reels, not further manufactured than cut into suitable lengths for walking sticks or canes, or for sticks for umbrellas, parasols or sunshades, and bamboos unmanufactured	$	....	6,066	....	6,066
Broom corn	"	....	196,084	....	196,084
Cane and rattans not manufactured	"	....	11,294	....	11,294
Cocoa beans, not roasted, crushed or ground	Lbs.	1,756,791	214,379	1,756,791	214,379
Esparto, or Spanish grass, and other grasses and pulp of, including fancy grasses dried but not coloured or otherwise manufactured	Cwt.	75	501	75	501

No. 14.—SUMMARY STATEMENT OF IMPORTS—*Continued.*

ARTICLES.		Imported.		Entered for Home Consumption.	
		Quantity.	Value.	Quantity.	Value.
FREE GOODS—AGRICULTURAL PRODUCTS—*Con.*			$		$
Fibre, Mexican, Istle or Tampico	"	2,853	31,825	2,853	31,825
" flax and flax tow	"	951	5,978	951	5,978
" vegetable, N.E.S	"	5,420	28,337	5,420	28,337
Total, fibre		9,224	66,140	9,224	66,140
Florist stock, viz.:—					
Palms, bulbs, corms, tubers, rhizomes, arucaria, spiræa and lilies of the valley	$	....	108,712	....	108,712
Fruits, green, viz.:—					
Bananas	Bunches.	1,200,534	1,171,387	1,200,534	1,171,387
Pineapples	No.	2,241,217	193,267	2,241,217	193,267
Guavas, mangoes, plantains, pomegranates and shaddocks	$	....	23,755	....	23,755
Berries, viz.: Wild blueberries, wild strawberries and wild raspberries	"	....	1,642	....	1,642
Total, fruits, green		....	1,390,051	....	1,390,051
Foot grease, the refuse of the cotton seed after the oil has been pressed out, but not when treated with alkalies	Cwt.	1,635	6,877	1,635	6,877
Hemp, undressed	"	123,857	914,382	123,857	914,382
Indian corn, N.E.S	Bush.	10,132,496	5,545,767	9,966,421	5,458,295
Jute butts and jute	Cwt.	6,038	25,654	6,038	25,654
Locust beans and locust bean meal	Lbs.	17,669	738	17,669	738
Manilla grass	Cwt.	96,244	806,651	96,244	806,651
Osiers or willows, unmanufactured	$	....	1,323	....	1,323
Palm leaf, unmanufactured	"	....	253	....	253
Seedling stock for grafting, viz.: Plum, pear, peach and other fruit trees	"	....	5,723	....	5,723
Seeds, viz.:—					
Annato	Lbs.	5,444	435	5,444	435
Beet and mangold	"	560,943	39,503	560,943	39,503
Carrot	"	31,971	5,167	31,971	5,167
Flax	"	76,949,206	1,647,194	76,949,206	1,647,194
Turnip	"	244,150	18,637	244,150	18,637
Mustard	"	128,935	6,143	128,935	6,143
Beans (seed) from Britain	"	7,785	460	7,785	460
Pease " "	"	107,739	4,263	107,739	4,263
Rape seed, sowing	"	244,402	7,249	244,402	7,249
Mushroom spawn	$	....	980	....	980
Total, seeds		78,280,575	1,730,031	78,280,575	1,730,031
Tobacco, unmanufactured, for excise purposes, under conditions of the Inland Revenue Act	Lbs.	14,603,355	2,669,225	14,519,658	2,710,093
Trees, N.E.S	$	....	3,146	....	3,146
Total, agricultural products		....	13,702,997	....	13,656,393
MANUFACTURED AND PARTIALLY MANUFACTURED ARTICLES.					
Admiralty charts	$	....	1,191	....	1,191
Album insides, made of paper	"	....	37	....	37
Artificial limbs	"	....	21,225	....	21,225
Artificial teeth	"	....	105,194	....	105,194
Ash, pot and pearl, in packages of not less than 25 lbs.	Lbs.	287,611	12,420	287,611	12,420
Asphaltum, or asphalt	Cwt.	158,273	172,641	158,273	172,641

No. 14.—SUMMARY STATEMENT OF IMPORTS—*Continued.*

ARTICLES.		Imported.		Entered for Home Consumption.	
		Quantity.	Value.	Quantity.	Value.
FREE GOODS—MANUFACTURED ARTICLES, ETC.—*Con.*			$		$
Astrachan or Russian hair skins and China goat plates or rugs, wholly or partially dressed but not dyed	$		62,553		62,553
Bells, imported for the use of churches	"		70,404		70,404
Binder twine of hemp, jute, manilla or sisal, and of manilla and sisal mixed	Lbs.	14,762,545	1,650,741	14,762,545	1,650,741
Binder twine, articles for the manufacture of	$		67,578		67,578
Blanc fixe and satin white	Lbs.	404,026	4,728	404,026	4,728
Blanketing and lapping and discs or mills for engraving copper rollers, imported by cotton manufacturers, calico printers and wall paper manufacturers for use in their own factories only	$		10,894		10,894
Blast furnace slag	"		19,005		19,005
Bolting cloth, not made up	"		17,593		17,593
Bone pitch, crude only	"		718		718
Books, viz.: Bibles, prayer books, psalm and hymn books and religious tracts, &c	"		238,655		238,655
Books, printed by or for any government or by any association for the promotion of science or letters and official annual reports of religious or benevolent associations and issued in the course of the proceedings of said associations, to their members, and not for the purpose of sale or trade	"		2,895		2,895
Books, embossed, for the blind and books for the instruction of the deaf and dumb and blind	"		340		340
Books, not printed or reprinted in Canada, which are included and used as text books in the curriculum of any university, incorporated college or normal school in Canada; books specially imported for the *bona fide* use of incorporated mechanics' institutes, public libraries, libraries of universities, colleges and schools, or for the library of any incorporated medical, law, literary, scientific or art association or society, and being the property of the organized authorities of such library, and not in any case the property of individuals	"		262,173		262,173
Books, bound or unbound, which have been printed and manufactured more than twelve years	"		20,774		20,774
Books, viz.: Books on the application of science to industries of all kinds, including books on agriculture, horticulture, forestry, fish and fishing, mining, metallurgy, architecture, electric and other engineering, carpentry, ship-building, mechanism, dyeing, bleaching, tanning, weaving and other mechanic arts, and similar industrial books; also books printed in any language other than the English and French languages, or in any two languages not being English and French, or in any three or more languages	"		112,428		112,428
Manuscripts and insurance maps	"		4,115		4,115
Total, books and maps			641,380		641,380
Bookbinder's cloth	$		44,443		44,443
Brick, fire, for use in process of manufacture	M.	24,975	539,962	24,975	539,962
Buckram, for the manufacture of hat and bonnet shapes	Yds.	77,514	11,783	77,514	11,783
Bullion or gold fringe	$		3,982		3,982
Buttons, shoe, papier maché	Gross.	88,233	2,498	88,233	2,498
Canvas or fabric, not frictionized, for the manufacture of bicycle tires, imported by the manufacturers of bicycles for use exclusively in the manufacture of bicycle tires, in their own factories	$		17,125		17,125

No. 14.—SUMMARY STATEMENT OF IMPORTS—*Continued.*

ARTICLES.		Imported.		Entered for Home Consumption.	
		Quantity.	Value.	Quantity.	Value.
FREE GOODS—MANUFACTURED ARTICLES, ETC.—*Con.*			$		$
Caplins, unfinished leghorn hats	$	....	2,099	....	2,099
Carbons over 6 inches in circumference, for use in Canadian manufactures	No.	353,840	70,540	353,840	70,540
Cat-gut or gut cord for musical instruments	$	....	7,090	....	7,090
Celluloid, xylonite or xyolite, in sheets and in lumps, blocks or balls in the rough	"	....	65,492	....	65,492
Chronometers and compasses for ships	"	....	12,339	....	12,339
Citron, lemon and orange rinds, in brine	"	....	1,893	....	1,893
Coal tar and coal pitch	Galls.	2,794,687	154,628	2,794,687	154,628
Coke	Tons.	480,222	1,311,375	480,222	1,311,375
Colours, metalic, viz.: Oxides of cobalt, tin and copper, N.E.S	Lbs.	214,020	66,927	214,020	66,927
Communion plate, imported for the use of churches	$	....	22,589	....	22,589
Coir and coir yarn	Lbs.	308,652	13,923	308,652	13,923
Cotton waste, not dyed, &c.	"	9,548,458	613,100	9,548,458	613,100
Cotton wool or raw cotton	"	68,001,047	7,626,625	68,001,047	7,626,625
Crucibles, clay or plumbago	$	....	32,950	....	32,950
Curling stones	No.	2,466	11,895	2,466	11,895
Diamond drills for prospecting for minerals, not to include motive power	"	26	40,620	26	40,620
Drugs, dyes, chemicals and medicines—					
Acid, boracic	Lbs.	200,141	10,552	200,141	10,552
Acid, hydro-fluo-silicic	"	256,184	7,063	256,184	7,063
Acid, oxalic	"	158,262	8,476	158,262	8,476
Acid, tannic and blood albumen	$	....	10,733	....	10,733
Alazarine and artificial alazarine	Lbs.	30,172	5,921	30,172	5,921
Alum, in bulk only, ground or unground, and alum cake	"	4,768,779	51,914	4,768,779	51,914
Alumina, sulphate of	"	3,750,872	28,147	3,750,872	28,147
Ammonia, nitrate of	"	66,283	4,353	66,283	4,353
Ammonia, sulphate of	"	368,118	11,508	368,118	11,508
Aniline dyes and coal tar dyes, in bulk or packages of not less than 1 lb.	"	1,427,213	368,972	1,427,213	368,972
Aniline salts and arseniate of aniline	"	185,886	15,499	185,886	15,499
Aniline oil, crude	"	15,097	1,358	15,097	1,358
Annatto, liquid or solid	"	89,401	12,507	89,401	12,507
Antimony, or regulus of, not ground, pulverized or otherwise manufactured	"	316,278	42,517	316,278	42,517
Antimony salts	"	87,640	13,780	87,640	13,780
Argols or argal	"	168,213	7,315	168,213	7,315
Arsenic	"	446,975	19,169	446,975	19,169
Beans, viz.:—Nux vomica, crude only	"	163	4	163	4
Tonquin, crude only	"	4,082	2,369	4,082	2,369
Vanilla, crude only	"	16,064	29,689	16,064	29,689
Borax, ground or unground, in bulk of not less than 25 lbs	"	2,493,496	78,277	2,493,496	78,277
Brimstone, crude, or in roll or flour, and sulphur crude in roll or flour	"	43,047,672	436,156	43,047,672	436,156
Bromine	"	633	212	633	212
Burgundy pitch	"	4,920	113	4,920	113
Camwood and sumac or extract thereof	"	782,253	17,077	782,253	17,077
Chloralum or chloride of aluminium	"	50	21	50	21
Chloride of lime in packages of not less than 25 lbs.	"	5,831,183	59,315	5,831,183	59,315
Cochineal	"	7,801	2,304	7,801	2,304
Copper, precipitate of, crude	"	4,988	618	4,988	618
Cream of tartar in crystals	"	1,370,221	213,254	1,370,221	213,254
Cyanide of potassium	"	112,861	20,439	112,861	20,439
Dragon's blood	"	395	257	395	257
Dyes, patent prepared	"	38,951	5,232	38,951	5,232
Dyeing or tanning articles in a crude state used in dyeing or tanning, N.E.S	"	864,217	21,897	864,217	21,897

No. 14.—SUMMARY STATEMENT OF IMPORTS—*Continued.*

ARTICLES.		Imported.		Entered for Home Consumption.	
		Quantity.	Value.	Quantity.	Value.
FREE GOODS—MANUFACTURED ARTICLES, ETC.—*Con.*			$		$
Drugs, dyes, &c.—*Con.*					
Extract of logwood, fustic, oak, and of oak bark and quebracho	Lbs.	17,281,285	413,805	17,281,285	413,805
Ferment cultures to be used in butter making	$	....	36	....	36
Flowers, leaves and roots—					
Roots, medicinal, viz.:—Alkanet, crude, crushed or ground, aconite, calumba, foliæ digitalis, gentian, ginseng, jalap, ipecacuanha, iris, orris root, liquorice, sarsaparilla, squills, taraxacum, rhubarb and valerian, unground	"	....	18,531	....	18,531
Gums, viz.—					
Amber, Arabic, Australian, copal, damar, elemy, kaurie, mastic, sandarac, Senegal, shellac; and white shellac in gum or flake, for manufacturing purposes; and gum tragacanth, gum gedda and gum barberry	Lbs.	1,915,928	353,707	1,915,928	353,707
Chicle or Sappato gum, crude	"	4,214,259	1,049,087	4,214,259	1,049,087
Hemp bleaching compound when imported by manufacturers of rope to be used in their own factories for the manufacture or rope, O.C., Feb. 13, 1902	$	....	12,940	....	12,940
Indigo	Lbs.	54,407	9,092	54,407	9,092
Indigo auxiliary or zinc dust	"	129,669	5,693	129,669	5,693
Indigo, paste and extract of	"	47,981	9,032	47,981	9,032
Iodine, crude	"	14,195	14,335	14,195	14,335
Iron liquor, solutions of acetate or nitrate of iron for dyeing and calico printing	$	....	3,534	....	3,534
Kainite, or German potash salts for fertilizers	Lbs.	674,397	3,411	674,397	3,411
Lac, crude, seed, button, stick and shell	"	233	80	233	80
Lead, nitrate and acetate of not ground	"	452,052	24,373	452,052	24,373
Litmus and all lichens, prepared and not prepared	"	20	5	20	5
Logwood and fustic, ground, and ground oak bark	"	314,577	5,032	314,577	5,032
Madder and munjeet, or Indian madder, ground or prepared and all extracts of	$	....	691	....	691
Manganese, oxide of	Lbs.	244,620	5,508	244,620	5,508
Moss, Iceland, and other mosses	"	636,849	37,304	636,849	37,304
Nut galls and extracts thereof	"	10,870	2,158	10,870	2,158
Ottar or attar of roses, and oil of roses	Oz.	2,155	7,395	2,155	7,395
Persis, or extract of archill and cudbear	Lbs.	4,024	378	4,024	378
Phosphorus	"	1,615	671	1,615	671
Potash, caustic	"	229,797	11,027	229,797	11,027
Potash, chlorate of, not further prepared than ground, and free from admixture with any other substance	"	408,954	28,765	408,954	28,765
Potash, German mineral	"	48,908	950	48,908	950
Potash, muriate and bichromate of, crude	"	2,173,922	66,766	2,173,922	66,766
Potash, red and yellow prussiate of	"	45,094	4,337	45,094	4,337
Quicksilver	"	150,364	69,505	150,364	69,505
Quinine, salts of	Oz.	91,709	17,958	91,709	17,958
Red liquor, a crude acetate of aluminium prepared from pyroligneous acid for dyeing and calico printing	$	....	409	....	409
Safety bate, and tannin preserver when imported by tanners for use exclusively in their own tanneries in tanning leather O.C., March 1, 1899	"	....	457	....	457
Saffron and safflower and extract of, and saffron cake	Lbs.	561	922	561	922
Sal ammoniac	"	462,705	16,070	462,705	16,070
Saltpetre	"	2,516,772	109,005	2,516,772	109,005
Seeds, aromatic, crude, not edible—					
Anise, anise-star, caraway, coriander, cardamon, cumin, fenugreek and fennel	"	122,843	9,010	122,843	9,010
Soda, ash	"	19,287,697	149,949	19,287,697	149,949
Soda, bichromate	"	259,029	9,749	259,029	9,749
Soda, bisulphite of	"	627,285	6,297	627,285	6,297
Soda, caustic	"	9,540,616	181,114	9,540,616	181,114

No. 14.—Summary Statement of Imports—*Continued.*

ARTICLES.		Imported.		Entered for Home Consumption.	
		Quantity.	Value.	Quantity.	Value.
FREE GOODS—MANUFACTURED ARTICLES, ETC.—*Con.*			$		$
Soda, chlorate of	Lbs.	36,512	2,470	36,512	2,470
Soda, nitrate of	"	23,082,434	516,867	23,082,434	516,867
Soda, nitrite of	"	5,689	342	5,689	342
Soda, sal	"	9,922,237	78,692	9,922,237	78,692
Soda, silicate of, in crystal or in solution	"	2,889,605	26,364	2,889,605	26,364
Soda, sulphate of, crude, known as salt cake	"	517,272	2,674	517,272	2,674
Sodium, sulphide of, arseniate, binarseniate, chloride and stannate of soda	"	869,064	10,538	869,064	10,538
Sulphate of iron (copperas)	"	362,915	2,493	362,915	2,493
Sulphate of copper (blue vitriol)	"	1,862,067	95,049	1,862,067	95,049
Tartar emetic and gray tartar	"	30,354	4,864	30,354	4,864
Tartaric acid crystals	"	147,373	30,488	147,373	30,488
Terra japonica, gambier or cutch	"	981,089	44,848	981,089	44,848
Tin crystals	$	....	2,634	....	2,634
Turmeric	Lbs.	44,285	2,521	44,285	2,521
Ultramarine blue, dry or in pulp	"	378,696	22,185	378,696	22,185
Verdigris, or sub-acetate of copper, dry	"	862	142	862	142
Zinc, salts of	"	120,165	4,586	120,165	4,586
Drugs, crude, such as barks, flowers, roots, beans, berries, balsams, bulbs, fruits, insects, grains, gums and gum resins, herbs, leaves, nuts, fruit and stem seeds —which are not edible and which are in a crude state and not advanced in value by refining or grinding or any other process of manufacture and not otherwise provided for	$	....	67,300	....	67,300
Total, drugs, &c.		....	5,081,163	....	5,081,163
Duck for belting and hose, imported by manufacturers of such articles for use in the manufacture thereof in their own factories	$	....	118,337	....	118,337
Fashion plates, tailors', milliners' and mantle-makers'	"	....	4,153	....	4,153
Felt, adhesive, for sheathing vessels	"	....	407	....	407
Fertilizers uncompounded or unmanufactured, N.E.S.	"	....	6,876	....	6,876
Fillets of cotton and rubber, not exceeding 7 inches wide, imported by and for the use of manufacturers of card clothing	"	....	86	....	86
Fisheries, for the use of, viz.—					
Fish hooks for deep sea or lake fishing, not smaller in size than No. 2·0, not including hooks commonly used for sportsman's purposes	"	....	17,282	....	17,282
Bank, cod, pollock and mackerel fish lines; and mackerel, herring, salmon, seal, seine, mullet, net and trawl twine in hanks or coil, barked or not,—in variety of sizes and threads—including gilling thread in balls, and head ropes, barked marline, and net morsels of cotton, hemp or flax, and deep sea fishing nets or seines, when used exclusively for the fisheries, and not including lines or nets commonly used for sportsman's purposes	"	....	677,133	....	677,133
Total, fish hooks, seines, &c.		....	694,415	....	694,415
Glass cut to size for manufacture of dry plates for photographic purposes when imported by the manufacturers of such dry plates for use exclusively in the manufacture thereof in their own factories	$	....	8,876	....	8,876
Glove fasteners, metal, eyelet hooks and eyelets, and shoe lace wire fasteners	"	....	151,573	....	151,573
Globes, geographical, topographical and astronomical	"	....	3,879	....	3,879
Gold beaters' moulds and gold beaters' skins	"	....	1,434	....	1,434

No. 14.—SUMMARY STATEMENT OF IMPORTS—*Continued.*

ARTICLES.		Imported.		Entered for Home Consumption.	
		Quantity.	Value.	Quantity.	Value.
FREE GOODS—MANUFACTURED ARTICLES, ETC.—*Con.*			$		$
Gold and silver sweepings	$		974		974
Gutta percha	Lbs.	825	971	825	971
Hatters' bands (not cords,) bindings, tips and sides, hat sweats and linings, both tips and sides, imported by hat and cap manufacturers, for use in the manufacture of these articles only in their own factories	$		174,254		175,249
Hatters' plush of silk or cotton	"		2,970		2,970
Hemp paper, made on four cylinder machines and calendered to between ·006 and ·008 inch thickness, for the manufacture of shot shells; Primers for shot shells and cartridges, and felt board sized and hydraulic pressed and covered with paper or uncovered, for the manufacture of gunwads, imported by manufacturers of shot shells, cartridges and gunwads, to be used for these purposes only in their own factories	"		23,984		23,984
Ingot moulds	"		153,556		153,556
Iron sand or globules or iron shot and dry putty for polishing glass or granite	Lbs.	442,703	4,670	442,703	4,670
Ivories, piano key	$		111,079		111,079
Junk, old, and oakum	Cwt.	16,408	50,812	16,408	50,812
Jute cloth as taken from the loom, not coloured, cropped, mangled, pressed, calendered, nor finished, in any way	Yds.	18,696,841	843,850	18,696,841	843,850
Jute, flax or hemp yarn, plain, dyed or coloured, jute canvas, not pressed or calendered, imported by manufacturers of carpets, rugs and mats, jute webbing or jute cloth, hammocks, twines and floor oil cloth, for use in the manufacture of any of these articles only, in their own factories	Lbs.	3,313,277	290,892	3,313,277	290,892
Kelp, sea grass and sea weed, N.E.S	Cwt.	415	821	415	821
Lampblack and ivory black	Lbs.	616,824	31,006	616,824	31,006
Lime juice, crude only	Gall.	28,615	5,910	28,615	5,910
Lastings, mohair cloth, or other manufactures of cloth, imported by manufacturers of buttons for use in their own factories, and woven or made in patterns of such size, shape or form, or cut in such manner as to be fit for covering buttons exclusively	$		5,326		5,326
Manilla hoods	"		74		74
Medals of gold, silver or copper, and other metallic articles, actually bestowed as trophies or prizes and received and accepted as honorary distinctions, and cups or other prizes won in *bona fide* competitions	"		2,166		2,166
Mexican saddle trees and stirrups of wood	"		9,438		9,438
Metals, viz.:					
Aluminium in ingots, blocks or bars, strips, sheets or plates	Lbs.	720,723	168,405	720,723	168,405
Anchors	Cwt.	4,795	18,043	4,795	18,043
Bismuth, metallic, in its natural state	Lbs.	529	949	529	949
Brass cups, being rough blanks, for the manufacture of paper shells or cartridges when imported by manufacturers of brass and paper shells and cartridges, for use in their own factories	$		65,119		65,119
Brass, old and scrap or in blocks	Cwt.	20,649	258,787	20,649	258,787
Brass in bolts, bars and rods in coils or otherwise, in lengths not less than 6 feet, unmanufactured	"	10,589	183,861	10,589	183,861
Brass in strips, sheets or plates, not polished, planished, or coated	"	10,912	200,265	10,912	200,265
Brass, tubing, not bent or otherwise manufactured, in lengths not less than 6 feet	Lbs.	853,373	192,247	853,373	192,247
Total, brass			900,279		900,279

No. 14.—Summary Statement of Imports—*Continued.*

ARTICLES.		Imported.		Entered for Home Consumption.	
		Quantity.	Value.	Quantity.	Value.
FREE GOODS—MANUFACTURED ARTICLES, ETC.—*Con.*			$		$
Metals, &c.—*Con.*					
Britannia metal, in pigs, blocks or bars	Cwt.	307	11,104	307	11,104
Copper, old and scrap or in blocks	"	4,452	63,765	4,452	63,765
Copper in pigs or ingots	"	21,825	378,089	21,825	378,089
Copper in bolts, bars and rods in coils or otherwise in lengths not less than 6 feet, unmanufactured	"	112,276	1,922,071	112,276	1,922,071
Copper, in strips, sheets or plates, not planished or coated, &c	"	25,472	519,808	25,472	519,808
Copper tubing in lengths, not less than 6 feet, and not polished, bent or otherwise manufactured	Lbs.	262,761	69,319	262,761	69,319
Copper rollers, for use in calico printing imported by calico printers for use in their own factories	$	....	6,697	....	6,697
Total, copper		....	2,959,749	....	2,959,749
Cream separators and steel bowls for	$	....	625,510	....	625,510
Cream separators, articles for the construction or manufacture of—when imported by manufacturers of cream separators to be used in their own factories for the manufacture of cream separators, O.C., Feb. 12, 1902	"	....	95,578	....	95,578
Iron or steel, rolled round wire rods, in the coil, not over ⅜-inch in diameter, imported by wire manufacturers for use in making wire in the coil in their factories	Cwt.	376,220	478,991	376,220	478,991
Iron or steel masts, or parts of	"	18	367	18	367
Rolled iron tubes not welded, or joined under 1½-inch in diameter, angle iron 9 and 10 gauge, not over 1¼ inch wide, iron tubing lacquered or brass covered, not over 1½-inch diameter, all of which are to be cut to lengths for the manufacture of bedsteads, and to be used for no other purpose, and brass trimmings for bedsteads, imported for the manufacture of iron or brass bedsteads	$	....	212,340	....	212,340
Scrap iron and scrap steel, old and fit only to be re-manufactured, being part of or recovered from any vessel wrecked in waters subject to the jurisdiction of Canada	Cwt.	2,500	1,220	2,500	1,220
Iron or steel beams, sheets, plates, angles, knees and cable chains for wooden, iron, steel or composite ships or vessels	"	210,753	315,664	210,753	315,664
Locomotive and car wheel tires of steel in the rough	"	80,365	161,914	80,365	161,914
Manufactured articles of iron or steel or brass which at the time of their importation are of a class or kind not manufactured in Canada, imported for use in the construction or equipment of ships or vessels	$	....	85,227	....	85,227
Lead, tea	Lbs.	1,905,087	79,886	1,905,087	79,886

No. 14.—SUMMARY STATEMENT OF IMPORTS—*Continued.*

ARTICLES.		Imported.		Entered for Home Consumption.	
		Quantity.	Value.	Quantity.	Value.
FREE GOODS—MANUFACTURED ARTICLES, ETC.—*Con.*			$		$
Metals—Machinery, viz.:					
Mining, smelting and reducing, coal cutting machines except percussion coal cutters, coal heading machines, coal augers and rotary coal drills, core drills, miners' safety lamps, coal washing machinery, coke-making machinery, ore drying machinery, ore roasting machinery, electric or magnetic machines for separating or concentrating iron ores, blast furnace water jackets, converters for metallurgical processes in iron or copper-briquette making machines, ball and rock emery grinding machines, copper plates, plated or not, machinery for extraction of precious metals by the chlorination or cyanide process, monitors, giants and elevators for hydraulic mining, amalgam safes, automatic ore samplers, automatic feeders, jigs classifiers, separators, retorts, buddles, vanners, mercury pumps, pyrometers, bullion furnaces, amalgam cleaners, gold mining slime tables, blast furnace blowing engines, wrought iron tubing, butt or lap-welded, threaded or coupled or not, not less than 2½ inches diameter, imported for use exclusively in mining, smelting, reducing or refining	$	....	868,104	....	879,216
And appliances of all kinds not made in Canada, for use exclusively in alluvial gold mining, until June 30, 1906	"	....	69,932	....	69,932
Of a class or kind not made in Canada for the manufacture of linen	"	....	4,757	....	4,757
Of a class or kind not made in Canada for the manufacture of brass goods such as are mentioned in tariff item 492, viz.: Brass in bolts, blocks, bars, rods, strips, sheets and plates and brass tubing	"	....	4,983	....	4,983
Well digging and apparatus of a class or kind not made in Canada, for drilling for water and oil, not to include motive power	"	....	101,883	....	101,883
Charcoal making	"	....	39,836	....	39,836
And tools not manufactured in Canada, necessary for any factory to be established in Canada for the manufacture of rifles for the Government of Canada	"	....	14,057	....	14,057
All materials or parts in the rough and unfinished, and screws, nuts, bands and springs, to be used in rifles to be manufactured at any such factory for the Government of Canada	"	....	70,253	....	70,253
Machinery of every kind and structural iron and steel, when imported for use in the construction and equipment of factories for the manufacture of sugar from beet root to June 30, 1906	"	... .	7,043	... .	7,043
Platinum wire and platinum in bars, strips, sheets or plates; platinum retorts, pans, condensers, tubing and pipe, imported by manufacturers of sulphuric acid for use in their works	"	....	54,494	.... ..	54,494
Ribs of brass, iron or steel, runners, rings, caps, notches, ferrules, mounts and sticks or canes in the rough, or not further manufactured than cut into lengths suitable for umbrella, parasol or sunshade or walking sticks, imported by manufacturers of umbrellas, parasols and sunshades for use in their factories in the manufacture of umbrellas, parasols, sunshades or walking sticks	"	....	143,781	....	143,781
Sewing machine attachments	"	....	48,141	....	48,141

No. 14.—Summary Statement of Imports—*Continued.*

ARTICLES.		Imported.		Entered for Home Consumption.	
		Quantity.	Value.	Quantity.	Value.
FREE GOODS—MANUFACTURED ARTICLES, ETC.—*Con.*			$		$
Metals—					
Silver, German silver, and nickel silver, in ingots, blocks, bars, strips, sheets or plates, unmanufactured	Lbs.	207,253	54,045	207,253	54,045
Silver tubing, when imported by manufacturers of silverware to be used in their own factories in the manufacture of silverware, O.C., Feb. 12, 1902	$	....	722	....	722
Steel for saws and straw cutters, cut to shape but not further manufactured	Cwt.	11,811	131,399	11,811	131,399
Steel strip and flat steel wire imported by manufacturers of buckthorn and plain strip fencing, for use in their own factories in the manufacture thereof	"	80	277	80	277
Steel wire, Bessemer soft drawn spring, of Nos. 10, 12 and 13 gauge, respectively, and homo steel spring wire of Nos. 11 and 12 gauge, respectively, imported by manufacturers of wire mattresses, to be used in their own factories in the manufacture of such articles	"	3,675	9,186	3,675	9,186
Crucible sheet steel, 11 to 16 gauge, 2½ to 18 inches wide imported by manufacturers of mower and reaper knives for manufacture of such knives in their own factories	"	10,337	42,702	10,337	42,702
Steel of No. 20 gauge and thinner, but not thinner than No. 30 gauge, for the manufacture of corset steels, clock springs and shoe shanks, imported by the manufacturers of such articles for exclusive use in the manufacture thereof in their own factories	"	60	278	60	278
Flat steel wire, of No. 16 gauge or thinner, imported by the manufacturers of crinoline or corset wire and dress stays, for use in the manufacture of such articles in their own factories	"	3,885	22,451	3,885	22,451
Steel valued at 2½ cents per pound and upwards, imported by the manufacturers of skates, for use exclusively in the manufacture thereof in their own factories	"	3,592	16,007	3,592	16,007
Steel, under ½ inch in diameter, or under ½ inch square, imported by the manufacturers of cutlery, or of knobs, or of locks, for use exclusively in the manufacture of such articles in their own factories	"	3,095	7,701	3,095	7,701
Steel for the manufacture of cutlery when imported by manufacturers of cutlery to be used in their own factories in the manufacture of such articles, C.C., Feb. 13, 1902	"	271	637	271	637
Steel of No. 12 gauge and thinner, but not thinner than No. 30 gauge, for the manufacture of buckle clasps, bed fasts, furniture casters and ice creepers, imported by the manufacturers of such articles, for use exclusively in the manufacture thereof in their own factories	"	2,099	5,379	2,099	5,379
Steel of No. 24 and 17 gauge, in sheets sixty-three inches long, and from 18 inches to 32 inches wide, imported by the manufacturers of tubular bow sockets for use in the manufacture of such articles in their own factories	"	1,174	2,349	1,174	2,349
Steel for the manufacture of bicycle chain, imported by the manufacturers of bicycle chain for use in the manufacture thereof in their own factories	"	178	680	178	680

No. 14.—SUMMARY STATEMENT OF IMPORTS—*Continued.*

ARTICLES.	Imported,		Entered for Home Consumption.	
	Quantity.	Value.	Quantity.	Value.
FREE GOODS—MANUFACTURED ARTICLES, ETC.—*Con.*		$		$
Metals—*Con.*				
Steel for the manufacture of files, augers, auger bits, hammers, axes, hatchets, scythes, reaping hooks, hoes, hand-rakes, hay or straw knives, wind mills and agricultural or harvesting forks imported by the manufacturers of such or any of such articles for use exclusively in the manufacture thereof in their own factories .... "	99,399	198,970	99,399	198,970
Steel springs for the manufacture of surgical trusses imported by the manufacturers for use exclusively in the manufacture thereof in their own factories... Lbs.	980	443	980	443
Flat spring steel, steel billets and steel axle bars, imported by manufacturers of carriage springs and carriage axles for use exclusively in the manufacture of springs and axles for carriages or vehicles other than railway or tramway, in their own factories.... Cwt.	93,125	127,105	93,125	127,105
Spiral spring steel for spiral springs for railways, imported by the manufacturers of railway springs for use exclusively in the manufacture of railway spiral springs in their own factories .... "	73,117	123,460	73,117	123,460
Stereotypes, electrotypes and celluloids of newspaper columns in any language other than French and English, and of books, and bases and matrices and copper shells for the same, whether composed wholly or in part of metal or celluloid........ Sq. in.	600,505	15,824	600,505	15,824
Spelter, zinc, in blocks and pigs........ Cwt.	50,137	290,686	50,137	290,686
Tagging metal, plain, japanned or coated, in coils, not over 1½ in. wide, imported by manufacturers of shoe and corset laces for use in their factories........ "	39	649	39	649
Tin in blocks, pigs and bars........ "	33,417	1,171,569	33,417	1,171,569
Tin plates and sheets........ "	605,182	1,869,000	605,182	1,869,000
Tin-foil........ Lbs.	561,623	65,307	561,623	65,307
Total, tin........	....	3,105,876	....	3,105,876
Barbed fencing wire of iron and steel........ Cwt.	446,212	929,660	446,212	929,660
Wire, crucible cast steel........ Lbs.	2,427,406	115,541	2,427,406	115,541
Wire of brass, zinc, iron or steel, screwed or twisted, or flattened and corrugated, for use in connection with nailing machines for the manufacture of boots and shoes........ "	89,142	30,800	89,142	30,800
Galvanized iron or steel wire Nos. 9, 12, and 13 gauge Cwt.	545,339	1,076,589	545,339	1,076,589
Wire rigging for ships and vessels........ "	4,259	19,055	4,299	19,270
Yellow metal, in bars, bolts and for sheathing........ "	2,078	29,995	2,078	29,995
Zinc in blocks, pigs, sheets and plates........ "	24,462	158,438	24,462	158,438
Zinc, seamless drawn tubing........ Lbs.	71	12	71	12
Molasses, the produce of any British country entitled to the benefits of the British preferential tariff, when produced from sugar cane and imported direct by vessel from the country of production in the original package in which it was placed at the point of production and not afterwards subjected to any process of treating or mixing; but not for distillation........ Galls.	4,143,307	779,532	4,144,190	779,736
Syrup or molasses of cane or beet testing under 35 degrees by the polariscope, for use in the manufacture of compressed food for live stock, when imported by the manufacturers of such food, to be used for such manufacture only in their own factories, O.C., Aug. 19, 1899. Lbs.	533,646	5,881	533,646	5,881

No. 14.—SUMMARY STATEMENT OF IMPORTS—*Continued.*

ARTICLES.		Imported. Quantity.	Imported. Value.	Entered for Home Consumption. Quantity.	Entered for Home Consumption. Value.
FREE GOODS—MANUFACTURED ARTICLES, ETC.—*Continued.*			$		$
Newspapers, and quarterly, monthly and semi-monthly magazines, and weekly literary papers, unbound....	$	....	314,363	....	314,363
Noils, being the short wool which falls from the combs in worsted factories; and worsted tops, N.E.S.......	"	....	291,127	....	291,127
Oil cake and oil cake meal, cotton seed cake and meal, palm nut cake and meal	Cwt.	20,611	26,784	20,611	26,784
Oils, viz.: Carbolic or heavy oil	Galls.	87,197	10,422	87,197	10,422
Cotton seed imported by manufacturers of liquid annatto, O.C., January 15, 1898........	"	7,789	2,574	7,789	2,574
Cocoanut and palm in their natural state	"	259,329	155,183	259,329	155,183
Cotton seed for canning fish, O.C., June 4, 1902 ...	"	6,071	1,972	6,071	1,972
Palm bleached, for use as material in Canadian manufactures........	"	160	101	160	101
Olive, for manufacturing soap or tobacco or for canning fish	"	26,475	13,219	26,475	13,219
Petroleum, crude, fuel and gas oils (8233 specific gravity)........	"	19,805,656	667,172	19,805,656	667,172
Rosin oil........	"	....	34,781	....	34,781
Total, oils........		....	885,424	....	885,424
Paper tubes and cones, when imported by manufacturers of cotton yarns or fabrics, to be used in winding yarns thereon, O.C., March 9, 1904........	$	....	5,530	....	5,530
Paper, photographic, plain basic, baryta coated, for albumenizing or sensitizing, when imported by manufacturers of sensitized paper	"	....	22,404	....	22,404
Philosophical and scientific apparatus, utensils, instruments and preparations, including boxes and bottles containing the same, of a class or kind not manufactured in Canada, when specially imported in good faith for use and by order of any society or institution incorporated or established solely for religious, philosophical, educational, scientific or literary purposes, or for the encouragement of the fine arts, or for the use or by order of any college, academy, school or seminary of learning in Canada, and not for sale........	"	....	66,658	....	66,658
Photographs, not exceeding three, sent by friends and not for purpose of sale........	"	....	199	....	199
Piano and organ parts: Key pins, damper springs, jack springs, regulating spoons, bridle wires, damper wires, back check wires, dowel wires, German centre pins, rail hooks, brass brackets, plates, damper rod nuts, damper sockets and screws, shell, brass sapstan screws, brass flange plates and screws, hammer wires, fly felt, butt felt, damper felt, hammer rail cloth, back check felt, catch felt, thin damper felt, whip cloth, bushing cloth, hammer felt, back hammer felt, bridle leather and buckskin, when imported by manufacturers of piano keys, actions, hammers, base dampers and organ keys, to be used exclusively for the manufacture of such articles in their own factories, O.C., June 6, 1901.....	"	....	68,403	....	68,403
Pictorial illustrations of insects, &c., when imported for the use of colleges and schools, scientific and literary societies........	"	....	23	....	23
Pitch and tar (pine) in packages of not less than 15 galls.	Galls.	137,856	14,032	137,856	14,032
Plaits, plain, chip, Manilla, cotton, mohair, straw, Tuscan and grass........	$	....	160,656	....	160,656

No. 14.—Summary Statement of Imports—*Continued.*

Articles.		Imported.		Entered for Home Consumption.	
		Quantity.	Value.	Quantity.	Value.
Free Goods—Manufactured Articles, etc.—*Con.*			$		$
Printing presses (rotary) of a class or kind not made in Canada	No.	97	398,187	97	398,187
Prunella	$	....	1,333	....	1,333
Rags of cotton, linen, jute, hemp and woollen; paper waste clippings, and waste of any kind except mineral	Cwt.	1,697,801	361,722	1,697,801	361,722
Resin or rosin in packages of not less than 100 lbs	"	188,752	349,115	188,752	349,115
Rubber, crude caoutchouc or India rubber unmanufactured	Lbs.	2,490,756	2,394,828	2,490,756	2,394,828
Rubber, recovered, and rubber substitute and hard rubber in sheets	"	3,069,188	357,380	3,069,188	357,380
Rubber powdered and rubber waste	"	330,272	22,543	330,272	22,543
Rubber thread, elastic	"	1,255	2,171	1,255	2,171
Total, rubber		....	2,776,922	....	2,776,922
Soap, whale oil	Lbs.	25,911	688	25,911	688
Spurs and stilts used in the manufacture of earthenware	$	....	880	....	880
Square or round reeds and rawhide centres, textile leather or rubber heads, thumbs and tips, and steel, iron or nickel caps for whip ends, imported by whip manufacturers for use in the manufacture of whips in their own factories	"	....	24,062	....	24,062
Surgical and dental instruments and surgical needles	"	....	198,058	....	197,841
Teasels	"	....	727	....	727
Turpentine, raw or crude	Lbs.	53,474	3,688	53,474	3,688
Vaccine points, articles for the manufacture, viz.: Glass caps, shells, containers and capillary tubes; rubber bulbs, boxes or corks; only when imported by manufacturers of vaccine points, O.C., July 13, 1901	$	....	10	....	10
Varnish, black and bright, for ships' use	Galls.	948	568	948	568
Yarn, Botany yarn, single, in numbers 30 and finer, on mule cops, dry-spun on what is known as the French and Belgian system, not doubled or twisted, in white only, when imported by manufacturers of cashmere socks and stockings, to be used exclusively for the manufacture of such articles in their own factories, O.C., June 6, 1901	Lbs.	150,121	91,810	150,121	91,810
Yarn, cotton, No. 40 and finer	"	1,168,323	382,017	1,168,323	382,017
Yarn, cotton, polished or glazed, when imported by manufacturers of shoe laces for the manufacture of such goods in their own factories, O.C., March 1, 1899	"	24,312	6,136	24,312	6,136
Yarn, of jute, flax or hemp, for the manufacture of towels, when imported by the manufacturers of jute, linen or union towels, to be used in their own factories in the manufacture of such articles, O.C., April 14, 1902	"	96,253	14,428	96,253	14,428
Yarn, mohair	"	1,590	1,400	1,590	1,400
Yarn, spun from the hair of the Alpaca or of the Angora goat, imported by manufacturers of braid for use exclusively in their factories for the manufacture of such braids only	"	192	449	192	449
Yarn, wool or worsted, genapped, dyed or finished, imported by manufacturers of braids, cords, tassels and fringes	"	53,116	25,042	53,116	25,042
Total, yarns		1,493,907	521,282	1,493,907	521,282
Total, manufactures		....	42,653,796	....	42,666,105

No. 14.—SUMMARY STATEMENT OF IMPORTS—*Continued.*

ARTICLES.		Imported.		Entered for Home Consumption.	
		Quantity.	Value.	Quantity.	Value.
MISCELLANEOUS ARTICLES.			$		$
Anatomical preparations and skeletons or parts thereof.	$	....	2,124	... .	2,124
Apparel, wearing, and other personal and household effects, not merchandise, of British subjects dying abroad but domiciled in Canada; books, pictures, family plate or furniture, personal effects and heir-looms left by bequest..	"	....	4,154	... .	4,154
Articles the growth, produce or manufacture of Canada, returned after having been exported	"	... .	784,454	....	784,454
Articles for the use of the Governor General	"	....	12,425	....	12,877
Articles for the personal or official use of Consuls General who are natives or citizens of the country they represent and who are not engaged in any other business or profession	"	....	2,760	... .. .	3,307
Articles imported by or for the use of the Dominion Government, of any of the departments thereof, or by and for the Senate and House of Commons, &c.	"	....	1,831,472	.. ....	1,832,808
Articles for the use of the Army and Navy, viz.: Arms, military or naval clothing, musical instruments for bands, military stores and munitions of war; also articles consigned direct to officers and men on board vessels of His Majesty's navy, for their own personal use	"	....	7,805	....	7,944
Articles ex-warehoused for ships' stores	"	....	....	....	398,052
Articles ex-warehoused for Excise purposes to be manufactured in bond, not elsewhere specified	$	....	....	....	3,007
Articles for the Anglo-American Telegraph Co.	"	....	43	....	43
Bacteriological products or serums for subcutaneous injections	"	....	45,300	....	45,300
Barrels or packages of Canadian manufacture which have been exported filled with Canadian products, when returned, or exported empty and returned filled with foreign products	"	....	29,232	....	29,232
Bird skins and skins of animals not native to Canada, for taxidermic purposes, not further manufactured than prepared for preservation	"	....	660	....	660
Botanical specimens	"	....	21	....	21
Cabinets of coins, collections of medals and of other antiquities, including collections of postage stamps...	"	. ...	20,701	... .	20,701
Casts as models for the use of schools of design	"	....	43	... .	43
Clothing and books, donations of, for charitable purposes	"	....	10,054	....	10,054
Coffee, green, imported direct from the country of growth and production or purchased in bond in the United Kingdom	Lbs.	6,904,567	693,139	6,904,567	693,139
Entomological specimens	$	....	246	... .	246
Ice	"	....	5,049	....	5,049
Models of inventions and of other improvements in the arts, but no article shall be deemed a model which can be fitted for use	"	....	17,401	....	17,401
Paintings in oil or water colours by artists of well known merit, or copies of the old masters by such artists	"	....	827,725	....	827,725
Paintings in oil or water colours, the production of Canadian artists	"	....	713	....	713
Passover bread, O.C.	"	....	15,044	....	15,044
Settlers' effects	"	... .	9,254,511	....	9,254,511
Specimens, models and wall diagrams for illustration of natural history for universities and public museums..	"	.. ..	1,334	....	1,334
Tea of India, black, imported direct or purchased in bond in United Kingdom	Lbs.	8,380,392	1,133,365	8,380,392	1,133,365
Tea of India, green, imported direct or purchased in bond in United Kingdom	"	498,320	62,463	498,320	62,463

SESSIONAL PAPER No. 11

No. 14.—SUMMARY STATEMENT OF IMPORTS—*Continued.*

ARTICLES.		Imported.		Entered for Home Consumption.	
		Quantity.	Value.	Quantity.	Value.
FREE GOODS—MISCELLANEOUS ARTICLES—*Con.*			$		$
Tea of Ceylon, black, imported direct or purchased in bond in United Kingdom	Lbs.	10,041,518	1,491,785	10,041,518	1,491,785
Tea of Ceylon, green, imported direct or purchased in bond in United Kingdom	"	1,480,323	201,311	1,480,323	201,311
Tea of China, black, imported direct or purchased in bond in United Kingdom	"	745,834	106,605	745,834	106,605
Tea of China, green, imported direct or purchased in bond in United Kingdom	"	481,068	70,926	481,068	70,926
Tea of Japan, green, imported direct or purchased in bond in United Kingdom	"	3,833,021	572,053	3,833,021	572,053
Total, teas		25,460,476	3,638,508	25,460,476	3,638,508
Vaccine and ivory vaccine points	$	....	5,018	....	5,018
Coins, gold and silver, except U. S. silver coin	"	....	6,271,006	....	6,271,006
Gold bullion, in bars, blocks, ingots, drops, sheets or plates, unmanufactured	"	....	349,521	....	349,521
Silver bullion, in bars, blocks, ingots, drops, sheets or plates, unmanufactured	"	....	458,076	....	458,076
Total, coin and bullion		....	7,078,603	....	7,078,603
Menageries	$	....	51,036	....	....
Paintings for exhibition	"	....	114,200	....	....
Other articles	"	....	19,007	....	19,007
Total, miscellaneous		....	24,472,782	....	24,711,079
Total, free goods		....	117,495,683	....	117,314,698

No. 15.—STATEMENT showing the Value and Duty of Goods entered for Consumption in Canada during the Fiscal Years 1905 and 1906 respectively; also the Value and Duty Collected on Goods entered for Consumption in Canada from the 'British Empire,' and from 'Other Countries,' during the Fiscal Year 1906.

ARTICLES.	Entered for Consumption.				Entered for Consumption during Fiscal Year 1906.			
	Fiscal Year 1905.		Fiscal Year 1906.		From British Empire.		From other Countries.	
	Value.	Duty.	Value.	Duty.	Value.	Duty.	Value.	Duty.
DUTIABLE GOODS.	$	$ cts.	$	$ cts.	$	$ cts.	$	$ cts.
Ale, beer and porter	323,708	133,104 97	34475	167,853 38	161,485	45,067 60	251,990	2,285 78
" ginger	9,782	1,355 46	14,774	960 55	14,401	1,985 95	373	74 60
Animals, living	1,041,111	208,494 59	1,187,819	238,011 86	412	85 94	1, 71,807	237,925 92
Antiseptic surgical dressing	58,578	11,193 18	69,161	13,064 18	11,548	1,541 58	57,613	11,522 60
Bagatelle tables	201	66 50	214	72 91	17	3 96	197	68 95
Bags [illegible] [illegible]in cement	....	....	170,272	41,892 99	9,150	1,525 05	1,622	40,367 94
Baking powder	122,745	24,466 38	138,585	29,470 56	8	0 48	138,577	29,470 08
Balls, [illegible]es and racks for bagatelle tables	3,978	1,313 01	8,082	2,670 60	1,361	318 25	6,721	2,352 35
Baskets	53,860	17,624 40	57,879	18,939 50	4,698	1,081 80	53,181	17,857 70
Belting, all kinds, except r[illegible]ber and [illegible]r	66,321	10,718 66	76,543	12,401 26	44,559	5,985 13	31,984	6,416 13
Belts, surgical, trusses and suspensory bandages	30,447	5,700 41	25,392	4,836 30	4,030	549 97	21,362	4,286 33
Belts, all kinds, N.E.S	66,031	20,667 82	87,568	26,308 80	1,458	9,923 32	46,110	16,385 48
Bells	39,551	11,846 80	38,725	11,630 00	1,174	277 90	37,551	11,352 10
Billiard tables	34,809	11,858 49	32,916	11,050 46	4,310	1,038 36	28,606	0,012 10
Blacking, shoe and shoemakers' ink, and harness and leather dressing	86,979	21,502 10	86,413	21,113 42	6,586	1,156 67	79,827	19,956 75
Blinds of wood, metal or [illegible]ther material, except textile or paper	1,043	312 90	5,502	1,650 60	....	....	5,502	1,650 60
B[illegible]g, laundry, all kinds	24,899	4,462 89	26,826	4,741 34	23,583	3,930 59	3,243	810 75
Boats	39,114	9,676 93	90,795	2,048 76	1,048	212 01	89,747	22,436 75
Bolsters and pillows	12,538	3,700 30	9,911	2,892 30	846	172 80	9,065	2,719 50
Books, periodicals and other printed matter	1,973,808	379,808 09	2,310,585	460,585 24	429,343	51,612 87	1,881,242	408,972 37
Boot, shoe and stay [illegible]ades	127,309	31,817 90	132,909	33,733 90	82,443	17,511 60	50,466	16,222 30
Boots, sh[illegible]es and [illegible]rs ex[illegible]pt [illegible]ber and [illegible]r.	41,374	26,133 77	100,340	22,653 05	46,603	8,335 89	53,737	4,317 16
Braces, suspenders and parts of	73,144	23,402 37	84,782	27,203 89	23,476	5,746 77	61,306	2,462 12
Brass and manufactures of	722,559	42,891 07	884,726	29,619 31	110,591	20,850 86	774,135	228,768 45
Breadstuffs, viz.—								
Arrowroot, [illegible]s, rice and macaroni	763,949	281,596 58	885,847	295,151 26	1,044	152,466 33	44,803	142,684 93
Grain, flour and meal	1,619,750	268,580 72	1,424,641	217,309 41	26,637	3,715 02	1,398,004	213,594 39

Bricks, tiles and manufactures of clay, N.E.S.	369,561	86,516 46	460,410	108,434 34	38,322	7 254 31	422,088	101,180 03
British gum, dextrine, sizing cream, &c	71,602	7,322 06	59,612	5,875 79	7,927	593 18	51,685	5,282 61
Brooms and brushes	296,412	74,231 26	286,167	71,317 42	32,736	6,088 66	253,431	65,228 76
Buttons	326,349	112,845 48	283,251	95,874 96	47,775	13,019 77	235,476	82,855 19
Candles	86,399	20,540 80	77,948	18,362 29	14,650	2 489 68	63,298	15,872 61
Canvas for sails	5,097	170 17	7,835	264 16	7,835	264 16		
Cane, reed or rattan split, and manufactured	40,150	6,189 65	54,815	8,519 05	3,224	355 05	51,591	8,164 00
Carriages, of all kinds, railway cars, trucks and parts of	1,201,744	367,957 69	1,837,457	551,272 25	67,148	13,630 05	1,770,309	537,642 20
Carpets, N.E.S.	1,907	485 82	879	220 18	791	184 81	88	35 37
Carpet sweepers	14,712	4,413 60	15,928	4,778 40			15,928	4,778 40
Cash registers	244,299	73,292 70	237,834	71,350 20			237,834	71,350 20
Celluloid, manufactures of	54,166	10,762 15	46,575	9,187 15	7,630	1,183 44	38,945	8,003 71
Cement	1,263,828	390,616 17	995,731	335,175 94	222,629	59 686 84	773,102	275,489 10
Chalk, prepared	20,896	4,180 56	23,853	4,783 47	1,733	241 63	22,120	4,541 84
Chicory	10,848	7 766 95	12,304	7,367 52	10,382	6,011 24	1,922	1,356 28
Church vestments	18,395	3,622 19	23,501	4,600 54	1,600	220 34	21,901	4,380 20
Charcoal	46,862	8,667 73	34,591	5,930 67	14,813	1,975 07	19,778	3,955 60
Cider	763	106 85	1,009	162 40	126	12 00	883	150 40
Clocks, clock cases, springs and movements	307,484	80,318 89	343,087	89,279 26	10,663	2,649 37	332,424	86,629 89
Clothes wringers	20,137	7,048 42	19,538	6,837 14	10	2 34	19,528	6,834 80
Cloths, not rubbered or made waterproof for manufactures	50,461	5,055 50	23,153	2,315 30	23,153	2,315 30		
Coal, [illegible] and dust	8,346,352	2,275,614 35	8,849,529	2,462,992 33	45,918	7,041 42	8,803,611	2,455,950 91
Cocoa, carpeting mats and matting	11,289	2,550 94	4,855	873 77	4,404	761 02	451	112 75
" nuts	55,422	10,762 28	57,639	9,468 84	53,708	8,195 06	3,931	1,273 78
" desiccated	4,323	1,813 58	8,518	4,040 15	7,973	3,806 20	545	233 95
" paste, chocolate paste, shells, nibs and other preparations	540,145	98,444 61	575,096	103,822 98	233,657	31,417 65	341,439	72,405 33
Coffee, N.E.S	134,764	21,806 75	142,695	22,079 47	7 712	670 68	134,983	21,408 79
Collars	175,644	57,953 71	184,552	61,873 42	46,017	11,563 35	138,535	50,310 07
Combs, dress and toilet	196,804	64,958 93	238,516	77,202 94	86,210	20,680 34	152,306	56,522 60
Copper and manufactures of	108,926	27,837 08	142,408	35,422 24	13,460	2,680 64	128,948	32,741 60
Cordage of all kinds	232,171	51,263 17	262,231	57,165 50	168,699	33,782 50	93,532	23,383 00
Corks and other manufactures of cork bark	126,984	25,329 33	188,514	37,468 38	19,643	3,681 58	168,871	33,786 80
Corsets, clasps, &c	100,167	34,655 39	115,956	40,443 96	1,605	412 70	114,351	40,031 26
Costumes and scenery, theatrical	15,440	3,130 83	20,871	4,228 16	97	20 21	20,774	4,207 95
Cotton, manufactures of	8,284,340	2,016,588 81	9,491,803	2,324,839 50	6,456,498	1,362,926 98	3,035,305	961,912 52
Crapes	16,430	2,553 77	13,303	2,020 43	10,484	1,456 12	2,819	564 31
Cuffs	4,998	1,639 76	5,151	1,712 35	861	202 10	4,290	1,510 25
Curtains	567,950	157,329 87	634,191	175,273 27	435,253	105,601 79	198,938	69,671 48
Cyclometers and pedometers	582	149 41	1,410	331 33	267	45 58	1,143	285 75
Drugs, dyes, chemicals, medicines	2,265,970	460,459 86	2,598,713	527,272 79	1,127,915	169,308 07	1,470,798	357,964 72
Earthenware and chinaware	1,636,214	384,094 67	1,692,359	398,105 43	988,318	165,553 06	704,041	232,552 37
Eggs	67,559	9,197 01	88,937	13,880 97	891	461 46	88,046	13,.18 61
Elastic	112,903	29,413 66	118,362	30,785 78	91,469	21,361 10	26,893	9,424 68
Electric light carbons and carbon points	67,110	17,846 71	48,217	18,056 17			48,217	18,056 17
Electric apparatus, motors, &c	2,758,357	693,451 13	3,459,531	859,491 57	80,812	14,045 55	3,378,719	845,446 02
Embroideries, N.E.S	68,645	23,650 68	84,982	29,478 04	24,519	7,522 08	60,463	21,955 96
Emery wheels and manufactures of emery	33,250	8,278 83	42,080	10,512 68	271	45 17	41,809	10,467 51

No. 15.—STATEMENT showing the Value and Duty of Goods entered for Consumption in Canada, &c.—*Continued.*

ARTICLES.	Entered for Consumption.				Entered for Consumption during Fiscal Year, 1906.			
	Fiscal Year 1905.		Fiscal Year 1906.		From British Empire.		From other Countries.	
	Value.	Duty.	Value.	Duty.	Value.	Duty.	Value.	Duty.
DUTIABLE GOODS—*Continued.*	$	$ cts.	$	$ cts.	$	$ cts.	$	$ cts.
Express parcels	995,785	264,146 24	1,065,380	278,175 57	3,950	903 41	[illegible]30	277,272 16
Fancy goods	3,068,788	1, 17[illegible]10 51	3,365,892	1,112,218 91	1,483,667	[illegible]5,383 87	1,882,225	716,835 04
Feathers, bed, &c.	39,933	8,508 14	2[illegible]98	5,684 65	305	76 91	27,893	5,607 74
Featherbone	8,946	1,789 20	455	90 20	12	1 60	443	88 60
Fertilizers	128,237	12,581 37	167,508	16,564 14	7,848	525 01	159,660	16,039 13
Fibreware	25,308	6,312 42	44,570	11,118 93	322	55 85	44,248	11,063 08
Flasks	23,346	5,833 59	29,497	7,374 25	1,663	[illegible]5 75	27,834	6,958 50
Fish	752,558	9[illegible]90 38	814,540	130,569 08	87,173	19,232 50	727,367	111,336 58
Flax, hemp, jute and manufactures of	2,502,406	465,200 08	3, 8[illegible]22	3[illegible]58 03	2,801,757	5[illegible]90 50	278,665	78,367 53
Foundry facings	14,957	3,494 99	1,[illegible]48	4,731 43	6,667	1,111 18	14,481	3,620 25
Fruits and nuts	3,903,087	913,306 81	4,783,239	1,033,555 54	341,728	78,097 61	4,441,511	955,457 93
Furniture, wood, iron or other material	693,994	205,230 60	743,750	220,340 50	42,699	9,600 40	[illegible]051	210,740 10
Fuses, N.O.P.	53,313	7,904 07	62,902	9,739 01	42,932	5,724 35	19,970	4,014 66
Furs and manufactures of furs	1,305,200	218,745 30	1,396,899	243,092 65	534,554	79,429 75	862,345	163,662 90
Glass and manufactures	1,946,614	448,929 71	2,664,137	[illegible]629 84	757,774	107,678 60	1,906,363	454,151 24
Gloves and mitts	980,883	332,664 20	1,165,636	[illegible]066 27	436,100	118,569 62	729,536	276,096 65
Gold, silver and manufactures of	502,305	142,328 49	[illegible]27	150,683 84	190,154	38,873 64	364,573	111,210 20
Grease, axle	31,259	6,255 09	64,515	12,830 79	1,174	[illegible]8 93	63,341	12,671 86
Gunpowder and other explosives	411,704	90,614 42	9[illegible]74	129,844 96	353,889	[illegible]086 32	242,285	69,658 64
Gutta percha, India rubber and manufactures of	816,787	213,606 52	771,895	203,504 66	99,242	19,834 24	672,653	183,670 42
Hair and manufactures of	28,967	7,910 72	31,653	8,593 76	13,689	3,077 63	17,964	5,516 13
Hats, caps and bonnets, N.E.S.	2,221,661	[illegible]0 50	2,277,432	579,566 30	1,078,816	219,879 40	1,198,616	359,686 90
Hay	145,618	17,330 00	99,215	4,[illegible]28 0	....	....	99,215	4,[illegible]28 00
Honey	8,418	2,410 02	7,489	2,283 74	845	61 61	6,644	[illegible]2 13
Hops	216,055	43,376 92	195,442	7,[illegible]39 72	45,754	13,190 64	149,688	44,249 08
Ink	158,724	30,035 41	155,496	29,488 80	24,902	3,350 73	[illegible]94	26,138 07
Iron and steel and manufactures of	31,557,739	6, [illegible]757 67	38,507,977	7,963,763 59	7,656,920	978,372 19	30, [illegible]057	6,985 3[illegible]1 40
Ivory	1,616	311 28	[illegible]230	241 46	112	17 86	1,118	23 60
Jellies, jams and preserves	103,352	30,778 67	138,530	40,737 79	130,528	38,503 46	8,002	2,234 33
Jewellery	827,413	248,998 60	888,879	265,810 40	93,142	20,404 30	[illegible]37	245,406 10
Knitted goods	2,287	[illegible]1 17	1,939	526 07	1,446	353 52	493	172 55

Lead and manufactures of	261,555	45,519 41	412,197	62,008 52	7[illegible]10	39,647 42	74,987	22,361 10
Leather and manufactures of	2,642,437	530,470 03	3,003,429	591,787 43	499,321	62,806 33	2, [illegible]008	528,981 10
Lime	71,588	4,317 60	93,630	18,726 00			93,630	18,726 00
Lime juice and other fruit juices	17,826	3,086 42	24,369	4,295 86	11,550	1,575 59	12,819	2,720 27
Lithographic presses	19,735	1,973 50	1,684	5,887 37	8,431	562 07	53,253	5,325 30
" stones not [illegible]	13,683	3,563 39	6,772	1,718 59	36	9 60	6,736	1,708 99
Machine, card clothing	27,824	5,548 57	35,307	6,657 55	28,087	4,769 97	7,220	1,887 58
Magic lanterns and slides for	7,972	2,110 38	11,770	3,057 56	1,533	282 15	10,237	2,775 41
Malt	83,132	16,408 70	68,240	14,072 00	2,370	101 60	65,870	13,970 40
" extracts of	10,072	2,416 94	10,703	2,591 34	1,013	168 84	9,690	2,422 50
Marble and manufactures of	145,466	36,561 09	189,589	48,354 91	6,595	1,309 70	182,994	47,045 21
Mattresses	5,550	1,622 30	6,808	1,995 30	556	119 70	6,252	1,875 60
Mats and rugs	290,479	78,907 48	363,797	97,801 28	303,204	75,585 14	60,593	22,216 14
Metals and [illegible]tes of	1,283,903	347,737 39	1,486,337	398,149 46	[illegible]994	34,572 05	1,289,343	363,577 41
Milk, condensed	7,469	3,174 11	7,987	3,248 72	2,992	894 66	4,995	2,354 06
Mineral substances, N.O.B	221,839	51,273 12	271,424	62,254 49	33,096	5,240 71	8[illegible]328	57,013 78
" and aerated waters	161,160	3,[illegible]95 32	176,885	36,757 03	20,012	3,948 94	156,873	32,808 09
Mosaic flooring	7,580	2,256 70	12,684	3,766 30	389	77 80	12,295	3,688 50
Mucilage	18,503	4,579 45	23,928	5,893 54	[illegible]	179 79	22,855	5,713 75
Musical instruments	453,491	133,673 36	535,224	6[illegible]30 58	24,964	5,570 41	510,260	150,660 17
Mustard and mustard cake	114,200	22,339 72	117,564	22,318 01	94,179	15,721 66	23,385	6,596 35
Oils, all kinds, N.E.S.	2,445,509	528,967 53	2,478,514	541,451 66	489,329	78,968 70	1,989,185	462,482 96
Oiled cloths of all kinds, cork matting and linoleum	771,443	171,431 90	915,088	201,880 80	730,817	146,549 80	184,271	55,331 00
Optical, philosophsical, photographic and mathematical instruments	307,267	74,845 25	353,545	85,610 99	38,175	6,883 34	315,370	8,727 65
Packages	787,463	[illegible]594 37	932,197	182,079 32	311,873	57,769 12	[illegible]324	124,310 20
Paints and colours	1,277,420	150,923 74	1, [illegible]869	183,027 78	431,751	62,481 [illegible]	739,118	120,546 65
Paper and manufactures of	2,950,752	838,121 48	3,148,158	887,622 34	617,386	128,540 83	2,530,772	759,081 51
Pencils, lead	172,629	45,843 21	1[illegible]884	47,386 26	30,441	7,541 28	145,443	39,844 98
Pens, penholders and rulers	160,259	37,650 51	180,203	42,052 21	38,951	6,551 97	1[illegible]52	35,500 24
Perfumery, non [illegible]	100,641	29,092 10	122,798	35,493 40	[illegible]613	3,601 20	[illegible]185	31,892 20
Photographic dry plates	54,273	15,321 90	57,609	[illegible]143 20	11,871	2,374 80	[illegible]238	13,768 40
Picture and photograph frames	88,649	26,976 70	99,333	29,942 70	11,539	2,715 80	87,794	27,226 90
Pickles	222,892	61,212 75	232,499	63,635 99	153,503	35,981 67	78,996	2[illegible]54 32
Plants and trees	79,273	21,423 15	111,671	29,620 53	3,870	595 76	7[illegible]801	[illegible]024 77
Plaster of Paris	40,324	10,306 99	45,541	[illegible]351 54	51	8 61	[illegible]490	16,342 93
Plates engraved on wood or metal	12,015	2,371 67	14,887	2,982 47			14,887	2,982 47
Pocket books, purses, tobacco pouches, &c	208,867	63,478 40	202,961	5[illegible]66 60	40,796	8,832 90	162,165	0,[illegible]33 70
Polish or composition, knife or other	58,677	14,567 89	67,674	16,691 20	5,291	972 63	62,383	15,718 57
Pomades	6,063	936 30	5,121	897 60	6	1 50	5,915	896 10
Post office parcels	596,081	4[illegible]094 34	607,752	7[illegible]204 69	4[illegible]015	34,798 08	4[illegible]737	112,406 61
Precious stones, N.E.S.	82,215	7,460 97	85,877	8,290 79	18,533	1,341 87	67,344	6,948 92
Printing presses, machines and parts	340,674	33,393 00	387,411	3786 41	51,590	3,886 38	335,821	33,900 03
Provisions—Butter, [illegible]e and lard	255,935	5158 64	778,326	173,967 94	30,419	4,242 07	7[illegible]907	169,725 87
" [illegible]ats of all kinds	1,223,081	288,237 12	2,155,241	510,697 14	9,514	15,607 09	2,095,727	495, [illegible]90 05
Regalia and badges	10,198	3,440 68	11,422	3,773 40	2,082	504 40	9,340	3,269 00
Ribbons, N.E.S.	1,095,072	389,568 42	1,150,332	408,404 57	456,777	161,465 41	693,555	246,939 16
Railway and travelling rugs	52,504	12,339 80	51,578	11,959 70	41,264	8,820 60	10,314	3,139 10
Sails	2,103	517 84	2,696	622 17	762	138 67	1,934	483 50
Salt	58,056	,[illegible]04 14	59,805	11,600 21			59,805	11,600 21

No. 15.—STATEMENT showing the Value and Duty of Goods entered for Consumption in Canada, &c.—*Concluded.*

ARTICLES.	Entered for Consumption.				Entered for Consumption during Fiscal Year, 1906.			
	Fiscal Year 1905.		Fiscal Year 1906.		From British Empire.		From other Countries.	
	Value.	Duty.	Value.	Duty.	Value.	Duty.	Value.	Duty.
DUTIABLE GOODS—*Continued.*	$	$ cts.	$	$ cts.	$	$ cts.	$	$ cts.
Sand, glass, emery and flint paper	85,046	21,065 70	106,330	26,445 30	2,232	416 04	104,098	26,029 26
Sauces, catsups and soy	116,039	33,363 86	124,660	35,044 92	75,426	17,813 02	49,234	17,231 90
Sausage casings	71,584	3,[illegible]29 55	83,419	15,213 48	23,132	3,156 08	60,287	12,057 40
Seeds, N.E.S.	477,407	50,528 65	394,718	41,669 73	16,791	1,790 71	377,927	39,879 02
Ships, vessels and repairs on	200,008	[illegible] 00	178,865	44,716 25	....	....	178,865	44,716 25
Signs of any material and letters for signs	49,556	14,472 60	66,237	9,436 30	6,298	1,369 20	59,939	8,[illegible]67 10
Silk and manufactures of	4,379,401	1,[illegible] 55	4,331,352	1,149,212 64	1,927,613	486,564 91	2,403,739	662,677 73
Slate	93,228	21,698 35	112,941	26,244 78	844	251 27	112,097	25,993 51
Soap	[illegible]	124,171 83	499,256	139,883 97	45,091	1,057 24	454,165	[illegible] 73
Spices	274,933	35,852 40	306,705	36,626 69	217,687	21,650 94	89,018	4,[illegible]75 15
Spirits	[illegible]	5,422,601 75	2,192,771	4,800,931 97	1,117,851	[illegible] 60	1,074,920	2,853,869 37
" wine not sparkling	376,679	[illegible] 12	409,762	248,782 74	32,809	22,304 46	376,953	226,478 28
" wine sparkling	232,361	[illegible] 64	291,196	75,467 83	15,031	2,964 26	276,165	72,503 57
Sponges	41,431	7,609 96	54,058	9,912 73	[illegible]	2,293 21	38,042	7,619 52
Starch	41,070	14,303 67	40,686	4,[illegible]32 48	15,534	3,793 44	25,152	1,[illegible]39 04
Stearic acid	4,981	996 20	17,050	2,958 14	6,778	903 74	10,272	2,054 40
Stockinettes for manufacture of rubber boots	66,804	9,363 85	72,634	1,089 50	14,112	1,411 20	58,522	8,778 30
Stone and manufactures of	302,724	60,053 69	370,190	4,997 26	102,550	22,601 71	267,640	52,395 55
Straw and manufactures of	72,662	17,735 73	68,683	6,[illegible]06 15	506	103 32	68,177	6,[illegible]02 83
Sugar and syrups	8,612,179	[illegible] 43	10,288,071	2,446,447 46	8,399,626	1,885,531 24	1,888,445	560,916 22
Molasses	341,051	24,260 63	310,675	23,467 50	1,038	56 55	309,637	23,410 95
Candy and confectionery	262,632	84,979 38	303,956	9,[illegible]82 41	[illegible]	43,194 76	142,090	5,[illegible]87 65
Glucose, saccharine, maple sugar and syrup	12,987	3,843 35	47,793	1,966 50	2,269	292 67	45,524	17,673 83
Tallow	5,053	817 61	5,230	1,006 35	1,557	271 75	3,673	734 60
Tape lines	23,867	5,324 66	28,446	6,237 98	11,384	1,909 17	17,062	4,328 81
Tea (see free)	16,375	1,637 50	27,273	2,716 40	1,788	167 90	25,485	2,548 50
Teeth, artificial	[illegible]	3,492 94	....	....	....	....	....	....
Tin and manufactures of	156,335	37,304 33	228,438	55,579 35	29,515	5,372 86	198,923	50,206 49
Tobacco and manufactures of	[illegible]	[illegible] 80	715,329	796,514 33	128,274	129,591 35	587,055	[illegible] 98
" pipes	[illegible]	[illegible] 50	440,297	146,325 22	252,186	77,440 97	188,111	68,884 25
Trawls and trawling spoons	8,537	4,[illegible]74 40	49,108	12,235 20	25,278	5,083 10	23,830	7,152 10

Turpentine, spirits of	[illegible]	22,995 45	603,044	30,147 94	5,314	261 44	597,730	[illegible] 50
Trunks, valises, hat boxes, &c	[illegible]	25,188 60	[illegible]	9,286 60	[illegible]	3,696 50	84,404	25,590 10
Twines and [illegible]es of	24,900	7,351 10	[illegible]	9,903 30	1,942	427 80	31,585	[illegible] 50
Umbrellas, parasols and [illegible]es	54,003	13,946 26	53,174	13,778 58	42,098	[illegible] 90	11,076	3,922 68
Unenumerated	95,937	17,646 35	[illegible]	23,662 61	29,158	4,379 41	[illegible]	19,283 20
[illegible]h, lacquers, japans, &c	148,082	42,244 86	[illegible]	46,055 62	58,191	11,118 89	110,154	34,936 73
Vegetables	[illegible]	273,127 58	[illegible]	[illegible] 26	[illegible]	16,689 29	720,835	179,068 97
Vinegar	31,584	17,608 63	[illegible]	16,667 20	[illegible]	9,490 98	6,670	7,176 22
Watches, [illegible]h cases, [illegible]ments, glasses, &c	[illegible]	[illegible] 47	935,388	[illegible] 38	26,637	5,796 65	908,751	[illegible] 73
Wax and [illegible]tures of	[illegible]	18,840 48	[illegible]	19,062 56	27,684	4,784 82	74,373	14,277 74
[illegible]g	[illegible]	32,476 81	[illegible]	[illegible] 87	64,226	8,763 28	139,360	28,027 59
Whips, th[illegible]gs and lashes	9,567	2,850 78	8,343	2,515 08	3,923	967 61	[illegible]	1,547 47
[illegible]w, cornices, poles, shades, rollers, &c	4,639	[illegible] 22	59,207	[illegible] 80	8,739	2,032 45	[illegible]	17,084 35
W[illegible]d and manufactures of ([illegible]ding willow and osier)	1,660,553	379,924 14	1,634,656	374,665 44	43,458	8,026 88	[illegible]	366,638 56
Wool and manufactures of	15,572,911	4,446,920 29	[illegible]	5,[illegible] 98	14,740,024	4,115,304 48	2,711,809	[illegible] 50
Zinc and manufactures of	11,912	2,981 65	12,917	3,162 26	962	165 43	11,955	[illegible] 83
Damaged goods	[illegible]	6,247 26	18,828	4,060 62	5,729	1,074 01	[illegible]	2,986 61
Prepaid postal packages, duty received by Customs from Post Office Department	14,119	2,823 97	18,399	3,680 15	18,399	3,680 15	....	....
Additional duties	....	133,361 52	....	159,251 55	....	....	....	159,251 55
Special duty on articles shipped to Canada at lower than usual home trade price	....	96,385 48	....	74,409 28	....	....	....	74,409 28
Total	150,928,787	42,024,339 92	173,046,109	46,671,101 18	61,335,023	15,032,703 11	111,711,086	31,638,398 07

No. 15.—FREE IMPORTS.

ARTICLES.	Entered for Consumption.		Entered for Consumption during Fiscal Year 1906.	
	Fiscal Year 1905.	Fiscal Year 1906.	From British Empire.	From Other Countries.
	Value.	Value.	Value.	Value.
FREE GOODS.	$	$	$	$
PRODUCE OF THE MINE.				
Clay	176,805	220,504	64,091	156,413
Coal, anthracite	12,093,371	10,304,303	162,953	10,141,350
Minerals	203,249	256,712	46,004	210,708
Ores	1,775,158	2,270,036	461,267	1,808,769
Precious stones, not polished	166,274	305,913	220,691	85,222
Salt	340,954	352,214	313,604	38,610
Whiting	51,215	44,876	37,164	7,712
Other articles	1,421,179	1,506,505	404,389	1,102,116
Total	16,228,205	15,261,063	1,710,163	13,550,900
FISHERIES.				
Fish of all kinds	630,660	1,152,253	1,152,253	....
Fish oil	101,434	57,586	57,586	....
Other articles	19,308	24,724	16,636	8,088
Total	751,402	1,234,563	1,226,475	8,088
FOREST.				
Corkwood	79,095	75,252	5,421	69,831
" bark	223	94	....	94
Ivory nuts	21,411	27,009	....	27,009
Logs and round unmanufactured timber	479,791	889,571	1,521	888,050
Lumber and timber, planks, boards, &c.	4,623,766	4,122,206	47,317	4,074,889
Other articles	764,135	853,542	2,082	851,460
Total	5,968,421	5,967,674	56,341	5,911,333
ANIMALS.				
Animals for improvement of stock	767,288	912,812	384,011	528,801
Bristles	98,921	112,788	51,374	61,414
Fur skins, not dressed	2,795,820	3,307,225	319,163	2,988,062
Grease	280,345	380,717	7,012	373,705
Hides and skins, undressed	5,147,073	6,552,319	2,330,075	4,222,244
Silk, raw	444,370	451,707	....	451,707
Wool	1,553,431	1,489,268	910,523	578,745
Other articles	433,479	610,985	270,927	340,058
Total	11,520,727	13,817,821	4,273,085	9,544,736
AGRICULTURAL PRODUCTS.				
Broom corn	175,412	196,084	....	196,084
Fibre, Mexican and vegetable	47,465	66,140	8,614	57,526
Fruit, green	1,143,116	1,390,051	57,144	1,332,907
Hemp, undressed	787,101	914,382	534,252	380,130
Indian corn	5,521,035	5,458,295	1,215	5,457,080
Seeds	299,567	1,730,031	31,750	1,698,281
Tobacco (for excise)	2,377,212	2,710,093	1,947	2,708,146
Other articles	926,496	1,191,317	315,083	876,234
Total	11,277,404	13,656,393	950,005	12,706,388

No. 15.—Free Imports—*Concluded.*

ARTICLES.	Entered for Consumption.		Entered for Consumption during Fiscal Year 1906.	
	Fiscal Year 1905.	Fiscal Year 1906.	From British Empire.	From Other Countries.
	Value.	Value.	Value.	Value.
FREE GOODS.	$	$	$	$
MANUFACTURED AND PARTIALLY MANUFACTURED ARTICLES.				
Bells for churches	40,700	70,404	7,208	63,196
Binder twine	1,294,553	1,650,741	21,818	1,628,923
Books, maps, &c	602,369	641,380	200,137	441,243
Coke	807,842	1,311,375	31,311	1,280,064
Cotton wool and waste	6,039,251	8,239,725	73,976	8,165,749
Drugs, dyes and chemicals	4,111,335	5,081,163	967,710	4,113,453
Duck for belting and hose	89,067	118,337	168	118,169
Fish hooks, nets, seines, &c.	754,143	694,415	315,532	378,883
Gutta percha, crude rubber, &c	2,728,291	2,777,896	3,402	2,774,494
Junk and oakum	50,399	50,812	28,882	21,930
Jute cloth	847,894	843,850	816,814	27,036
Metals—				
Brass	617,790	900,279	125,026	775,253
Copper	1,933,503	2,959,749	31,340	2,928,409
Iron and steel	10,411,559	6,065,039	752,439	5,312,600
Tin	2,633,358	3,105,876	1,708,266	1,397,610
Zinc	141,514	158,450	56,385	102,065
Other	745,482	881,340	182,126	699,214
Newspapers and magazines	225,154	314,363	53,036	261,327
Oil cake and meal and cotton seed cake and meal	46,991	26,784	218	26,566
Oil, cocoanut and palm	144,441	155,183	107,204	47,979
Pitch and tar (pine)	23,098	14,032	1,745	12,287
Plaits, straw, tuscan and grass	168,855	160,656	35,791	124,865
Rags	324,747	361,722	94,251	267,471
Resin or rosin	259,839	349,115	2,616	346,499
Yarns	451,746	521.282	433,588	87,694
Other articles	4,507,431	5,212,137	1,757,368	3,454,769
Total	40,001,352	42,666,105	7,808,357	34,857,748
MISCELLANEOUS.				
Articles for Dominion Government	1,692,365	1,832,808	795,238	1,037,570
" Army and Navy	13,165	7,944	6,255	1,689
Coffee (see dutiable)	591,542	693,139	146,706	546,433
Models of inventions	23,245	17,401	211	17,190
Settlers effects	7,084,659	9,254,511	1,971,469	7,283,042
Tea (see dutiable)	3,654,565	3,638,508	2,933,140	705,368
Coin and bullion	10,308,435	7,078,603	14,593	7,064,010
Other articles	1,881,280	2,188,165	576,966	1,611,199
Total	25,249,256	24,711,079	6,444,578	18,266,501
Total free	110,996,767	117,314,698	22,469,004	94,845,694
Total dutiable	150,928,787	173,046,109	61,335,023	111,711,086
Grand total	261,925,554	290,360,807	83,804,027	206,556,780

No. 16.—General Statement by Countries, showing the Quantity, Value and Duty Collected on Articles Imported and Entered for Consumption in Canada under the provisions of the *French Treaty*, during the Fiscal Year ended June 30, 1906.

Note.—The undermentioned articles are included in General Statement No. 1, part 2, and Summary Statement No. 14, part 1.

Articles.	Countries whence Imported.	Imported.		Entered for Consumption.		Duty.
		Quantity.	Value.	Quantity.	Value.	
		Lbs.	$	Lbs.	$	$ cts.
Prunes	Great Britain	....	....	5,600	119	37 33
	Austria	297,273	9,026	297,273	9,026	1,981 83
	France	166,608	5,662	160,208	5,543	1,068 05
	Total	463,881	14,688	463,081	14,688	3,087 21
Nuts, almonds, shelled	Great Britain	22,908	4,907	16,424	3,193	547 46
	France	137,927	22,863	131,763	21,988	4,392 10
	Spain	615,564	107,512	619,351	107,546	20,644 91
	United States	25,993	5,732	26,263	5,784	875 43
	Total	802,392	141,014	793,801	138,511	26,459 90
" not shelled	Great Britain	19,309	1,395	16,990	1,232	339 80
	France	336,719	24,547	252,881	18,177	5,057 62
	Spain	441,378	33,700	463,753	35,471	9,275 06
	United States	58,507	5,891	75,184	7,135	1,503 68
	Total	855,913	65,533	808,808	62,015	16,176 16
" Brazil nuts, not shelled	France	....	....	520	36	10 40
	United States	6,048	429	6,048	429	120 96
	Total	6,048	429	6,568	465	131 36
" pecans, not shelled and shelled peanuts, N.E.S.	France	37,998	1,640	38,366	1,677	767 32
	Spain	31,213	1,298	31,213	1,298	624 26
	United States	10,640	589	10,640	589	212 80
	Total	79,851	3,527	80,219	3,564	1,604 38
" walnuts, not shelled	Great Britain	28,209	2,037	28,209	2,037	564 18
	France	672,444	71,404	761,354	69,795	15,227 08
	Spain	65,718	4,732	81,185	6,160	1,623 70
	United States	88,104	9,422	81,435	8,529	1,628 70
	Total	854,475	87,595	952,183	86,521	19,043 66
" all other, N.O.P.	France	12,059	1,369	12,827	1,383	256 54
	United States	36,595	2,617	31,989	2,416	639 78
	Total	48,654	3,986	44,816	3,799	896 32
" all other, N.O.P., shelled	Great Britain	1,108	58	6,608	617	132 16
	France	647,341	103,229	782,915	111,112	15,658 30
	Spain	50,201	3,404	45,637	3,229	912 74
	United States	31,186	3,821	32,457	3,910	649 14
	Total	729,836	110,512	867,617	118,868	17,352 34

No. 16.—General Statement by Countries, showing the Quantity, Value and Duty Collected on Articles Imported and Entered for Consumption in Canada under the provisions of the *French Treaty, &c.—Concluded.*

Articles.	Countries whence Imported.	Imported.		Entered for Consumption.		Duty.
		Quantity.	Value.	Quantity.	Value.	
		Lbs.	$	Lbs.	$	$ cts.
Soap, castile	Great Britain	13,889	665	15,689	748	156 89
	France	1,338,601	63,774	1,381,822	64,151	13,818 22
	United States	28,446	1,369	28,446	1,369	284 46
	Total	1,380,936	65,808	1,425,957	66,268	14,259 57
Wines, non-sparkling, containing 26 p.c. or less of alcohol		Galls.		Galls.		
	Great Britain	2,201	2,713	2,180	3,084	545 00
	France	147,914	115,350	146,954	116,696	36,738 50
	Fr. Poss. Africa	....	....	131	75	32 75
	Germany	....	....	2	8	0 50
	Italy	....	....	36	31	9 00
	Portugal	....	....	288	173	72 00
	St. Pierre	167	291	276	466	69 00
	Spain	138,608	52,190	136,998	51,273	34,249 50
	United States	675	460	374	342	93 50
	Total	289,565	171,004	287,239	172,148	71,809 75
Wines, champagne and all other sparkling—						
Wines in bottles containing each not more than a quart, but more than a pint, old wine measure		Doz.		Doz.		
	Great Britain	521	9,554	523	9,280	1,725 90
	France	7,069	93,075	7,248	95,153	23,918 40
	Spain	....	....	5	22	16 50
	United States	85	1,219	60	779	198 00
	Total	7,675	103,848	7,836	105,234	25,858 80
Wines in bottles containing not more than a pint, but more than ½ a pint, old wine measure	Great Britain	595	5,398	582	5,227	960 30
	France	25,877	179,792	25,418	166,568	41,939 70
	Germany	....	....	20	102	33 00
	Spain	....	....	20	36	33 00
	United States	770	5,127	740	4,635	1,221 00
	Total	27,242	190,317	26,780	176,568	44,187 00
Wines in bottles containing ½ pint each or less	Great Britain	14	49	18	53	14 76
	France	1,595	4,571	1,227	2,903	1,006 14
	Spain	....	....	20	48	16 40
	United States	20	93	32	124	26 24
	Total	1,629	4,713	1,297	3,128	1,063 54
Wines in bottles containing more than one quart each		Doz. Galls.		Doz. Galls.		
	Great Britain	6 12	225	2 3	66	11 55
	France	5 15	251	3 6	101	19 80
	Total	11 27	476	5 9	167	31 35

No. 16.—SUMMARY STATEMENT showing the Quantity and Value of Goods imported and entered for consumption, the rates of duty and the amount collected under the operation of the *French Treaty* during the year ending June 30, 1906.

Articles.		Rates of Duty.	Imported.		Entered for Consumption.		Duty.
			Quantity.	Value.	Quantity.	Value.	
				$		$	$ cts.
Prunes............	Lbs.	$\frac{2}{3}$ c. per lb	463,881	14,688	463,681	14,688	3,087 21
Nuts, almonds, shelled ...	"	$3\frac{1}{3}$c. "	802,392	141,014	793,801	138,511	26,459 90
" not shelled.	"	2 c. "	855,913	65,533	808,808	62,015	16,176 16
Brazil nuts, not shelled ...	"	2 c. "	6,048	429	6,568	465	131 36
Pecans, not shelled and shelled peanuts.........	"	2 c. "	79,851	3,527	80,219	3,564	1,604 38
Walnuts, not shelled	"	2 c. "	854,475	87,595	952,183	86,521	19,043 66
All other nuts, N.O.P....	"	2 c. "	48,654	3,986	44,816	3,799	896 32
" shelled....	"	2 c. "	729,836	110,512	867,617	118,868	17,352 34
Soap, castile	"	1 c. " ...	1,380,936	65,808	1,425,957	66,268	14,259 57
Wines, non-sparkling, containing 26 p.c. or less of alcohol...............	Galls.	25c. per gall	289,565	171,004	287,239	172,148	71,809 75
Champagne, and all other sparkling—							
In bottles containing each not more than a quart but more than a pint old wine measure.	Doz.	$3.30 per doz....	7,675	103,848	7,836	105,234	25,858 80
In bottles containing not more than a pint but more than $\frac{1}{2}$ pint, old wine measure	"	$1.65 "	27,242	190,317	26,780	176,568	44,187 00
In bottles containing $\frac{1}{2}$ pint each or less......	"	82c. "	1,629	4,713	1,297	3,128	1,063 54
In bottles containing more than 1 quart each	"	$3.30 " & $1.65 per gall.	Galls. 11 Doz. 27	476	Galls. 5 Doz. 9	167	31 35
Total..................		....	....	963,450	....	951,944	241,961 34

ABSTRACT BY COUNTRIES.

Showing the Value of Goods imported into Canada under the provisions of the *French Treaty,* during the fiscal year ended June 30, 1906.

—	Imported.	Entered for Consumption.	Duty.
	$	$	$ cts.
Great Britain	27,001	25,656	5,035 33
Austria	9,026	9,026	1,981 83
France	687,527	675,283	159,878 17
Fr. Poss. Africa	....	75	32 75
Germany	....	110	33 50
Italy	....	31	9 00
Portugal	....	173	72 00
St. Pierre	291	466	69 00
Spain	202,836	205,083	67,396 07
United States	36,769	36,041	7,453 69
Total	963,450	951,944	241,961 34

No. 17.—STATEMENT of Goods Imported from British and Foreign West Indies (including Guiana) during the Fiscal Year ended June 30, 1906.

DUTIABLE GOODS.	From British West Indies and British Guiana.		From Foreign West Indies and Foreign Guiana.		Total From West Indies and Guiana.	
	Quantity.	Value.	Quantity.	Value.	Quantity.	Value.
		$		$		$
Ale and beer .... Galls.	43	20			43	20
Animals,—Horses .... No.	1	50			1	50
" all other, N.O.P. ..... $		42				42
Breadstuffs—Arrowroot ..... Lbs.	10,193	353			10,193	353
" rice, cleaned ..... "	189,600	4,392			189,600	4,392
Baskets .... $		5				5
Brass manufactures .... "		15				15
Cocoa nuts .... No.	2,464,081	54,090			2,464,081	54,090
Coffee, roasted or ground, not direct .... Lbs.	207	42			207	42
Damaged goods .... $		3,814				3,814
Flax, &c.—Linen duck .... "		4				4
Fruits, green, viz.—						
Oranges, lemons, &c .... Boxes.	3,828	5,204			3,828	5,204
" " ...... ½ "	48	35			48	35
" " Cubic feet holding capacity.	223	196			223	196
" " .... Brls.	18,289	49,381			18,289	49,381
Fruits in air-tight cans .... Lbs.	47,271	3,764			47,271	3,764
Glass manufactures .... $		1				1
Grass, straw or chip manufactures .... "		70				70
Honey .... Lbs.	17,579	459			17,579	459
Iron, scrap, wrought, &c ...... Cwt.	495	186			495	186
Jellies, jams and preserves, N.E.S. .... Lbs.	7,596	454			7,596	454
Lead, old and scrap .... Cwt.	435	840			435	840
Lime juice, N.O.P .... Galls.	1,410	820			1,410	820
Mats and rugs, N.E.S .... $		30				30
Packages .... "		6,788		6		6,794
Spices .... Lbs.	81,430	4,358			81,430	4,358
Spirits .... Galls.	59,344	23,347			59,344	23,347
Sponges .... $		2,569		1,940		4,509
Sugar and syrups .... Lbs.	317,157,885	6,254,132			317,157,885	6,254,132
Molasses .... Galls.			1,037,900	220,337	1,037,900	220,337
Tobacco, &c.—Cigarettes ...... Lbs.			168	168	168	168
" Cigars .... "	326	1,097	101,440	374,267	101,766	375,364
" Tobacco, cut ... "			374	69	374	69
" " pipes, &c. $				11		11
Unenumerated articles .... "		579				579
Vegetables—						
Potatoes, sweet and yams .... Bush.	50	23			50	23
Tomatoes, fresh. .... "	11	33			11	33
Fresh, dry or salted, N.O.P. . $		398				398
Wood manufactures .... "		6				6
Total, dutiable goods		6,417,597		596,798		7,014,395

No. 17.—STATEMENT of Goods Imported from British and Foreign West Indies, &c.—*Concluded.*

Free Goods.		From British West Indies and British Guiana.		From Foreign West Indies and Foreign Guiana.		Total from West Indies and Guiana.	
		Quantity.	Value.	Quantity.	Value.	Quantity.	Value.
			$		$		$
Apparel, wearing	$		100				100
Articles, returned	"		1,363		370		1,733
" for Consuls General	"				289		289
Asphaltum	Cwt.	850	850			850	850
Beans, viz.: Tonquin, crude	Lbs	240	124			240	124
Canadian packages returned	$		22				22
Cocoa beans	Lbs.	467,852	48,553			467,852	48,553
Coffee, green	"	192,184	16,808	3,525	442	195,709	17,250
Coin, gold and silver	$		3,521				3,521
Extract of logwoood, &c	Lbs.	21,190	2,437			21,190	2,437
Palms, bulbs, &c	$		61				61
Fruits, green—							
Bananas	Bunches.	55,092	46,350			55,092	46,350
Pine apples	No.	35,223	2,899			35,223	2,899
Guavas, mangoes, &c	$		6,100				6,100
Fur skins, N.E.S	"		2				2
Grease, rough	Lbs.	400	8			400	8
Hides and skins, raw	$		170,180				170,180
Junk, old, and oakum	Cwt.	41	187			41	187
Lamp-black and ivory black	Lbs.	4,650	653			4,650	653
Lime juice, crude	Galls.	26,587	4,889			26,587	4,889
Lumber and timber—							
African teak, &c	$		19		20		39
Metals—							
Anchors	Cwt.	9	5			9	5
Brass, old and scrap	"	115	906			115	906
Copper "	"	82	607			82	607
Yellow metal	"	33	300			33	300
Molasses	Galls.	4,143,307	779,532			4,143,307	779,532
Rubber	Lbs.	1,900	57			1,900	57
Salt	Cwt.	104,705	14,187	2,427	330	107,132	14,517
Settlers' effects	$		2,685		20		2,705
Shells	"		54				54
Tobacco, unmanufactured	Lbs.			186,387	58,812	186,387	58,812
Turtles	$		28				28
Wool, not further prepared than washed	Lbs.	4,220	276			4,220	276
Total, free goods			1,103,763		60,283		1,164,046
Total, dutiable and free			7,521,360		657,081		8,178,441
Imported through foreign countries			1,813,552		255,652		2,069,204
Imported direct			5,707,808		401,429		6,109,237

No. 17.—STATEMENT of Goods Exported to British and Foreign West Indies (including Guiana) during the Fiscal Year ended June 30, 1906.

ARTICLES.	To British West Indies and British Guiana.		To Foreign West Indies and Foreign Guiana.		Total to West Indies and Guiana.	
	Quantity.	Value.	Quantity.	Value.	Quantity.	Value.
THE MINE.		$		$		$
Coal......Tons.	1,620	6,750			1,620	6,750
Gypsum or plaster, crude...... "	11	96			11	96
Mineral water......Galls.	333	71			333	71
Other articles...... $		520				520
Total, mine......		7,437				7,437
THE FISHERIES.						
Codfish, dry salted...... Cwt.	189,328	1,068,729	5,030	23,476	194,358	1,092,205
" wet salted...... "	199	393			199	393
" pickled salted...... "	5	20			5	20
Tongues and sounds...... Brls.	14	21			14	21
Mackerel, fresh......Lbs.	100	4			100	4
" pickled......Brls.	6,953	67,348	50	591	7,003	67,939
Herrings, pickled...... "	53,073	235,290	445	2,206	53,518	237,496
" canned......Lbs.	220	10			220	10
" smoked...... "	856,859	22,952	25,066	613	881,925	23,565
Sea fish, other, pickled......Brls.	3,658	21,569	77	462	3,735	22,031
" " preserved......Lbs.	14,447	763	1,075	52	15,522	815
Lobsters, canned...... "	24,921	5,290			24,921	5,290
Salmon, smoked...... "	104	12	53	8	157	20
" canned...... "	17,156	1,568			17,156	1,568
" pickled......Brls.	1,115	12,981	34	411	1,149	13,392
Fish, all other, pickled...... "	49	207			49	207
Fish oil, cod......Galls.	1,004	318			1,004	318
" other...... "	80	25			80	25
Other articles......		7				7
Total, fisheries......		1,437,507		27,819		1,465,326
THE FOREST.						
Lumber—						
Laths...... M.	627	1,344			627	1,344
Planks and boards......M. ft.	9,309	144,732	11	131	9,310	144,863
Scantling...... "	490	3,707			490	3,707
Shingles...... M.	21,437	30,814			21,437	30,814
Shooks, other...... $		12,153				12,153
Staves, other and headings...... "		178				178
All lumber, N.E.S...... "		1,724				1,724
Masts and spars...... No.	261	1,844			261	1,844
Total, forest......		196,496		131		196,627
ANIMALS.						
Horses, over one year old...... No.	34	4,110			34	4,110
Cattle, one year old or less...... "	14	1,400			14	1,400
" over one year old...... "	8	455			8	455
Swine...... "	4	80			4	80
Sheep, one year old or less...... "	96	559			96	559
" over one year old...... "	563	3,303			563	3,303
Poultry...... $		177				177
Butter...... Lbs.	373,576	98,739	21,420	4,590	394,996	103,329
Cheese...... "	191,178	29,369	15,520	2,069	206,698	31,438

No. 17.—STATEMENT of Goods Exported to British and Foreign West Indies—*Con.*

ARTICLES.		To British West Indies and British Guiana.		To Foreign West Indies and Foreign Guiana.		Total to West Indies and Guiana.	
		Quantity.	Value.	Quantity.	Value.	Quantity.	Value.
ANIMALS—*Con.*			$		$		$
Eggs	Doz.	169	36			169	36
Glue stock	$		6				6
Hides and skins	"		45				45
Lard	Lbs.	133	10			133	10
Meats—							
Bacon	"	1,810	295			1,810	295
Beef	"	36,379	2,090			36,379	2,090
Ham	"	1,271	187			1,271	187
Mutton	"	17,856	525			17,856	525
Pork	"	143,990	4,555			143,990	4,555
Poultry, dressed	$		125				125
Game	"		2				2
Canned	Lbs.	2,929	301			2,929	301
All other	"	7,796	574			7,796	574
Milk and cream (condensed)	"	76,394	4,838			76,394	4,838
Tallow	"	45	4			45	4
Total, animals			151,785		6,659		158,444
AGRICULTURAL PRODUCTS.							
Fruit,—Apples, green or ripe	Brls.	152	470			152	470
" canned or preserved	$		281				281
" all other, N.E.S	"		170				170
Grain—							
Barley	Bush.	58	55			58	55
Beans	"	480	867	741	1,039	1,221	1,906
Indian corn	"	4	3			4	3
Oats	"	230,629	90,261	1,191	525	231,820	90,786
Pease, whole	"	30,049	29,686	56	70	30,105	29,756
" split	"	85,604	103,424	122	158	85,726	103,582
Other grain	"	1,063	1,306			1,063	1,306
Bran	Cwt.	11,544	10,028			11,544	10,028
Flour, of wheat	Brls.	90,195	357,194	4,261	16,392	94,456	373,586
Indian meal	"	267	1,281			267	1,281
Oatmeal	"	275	1,070			275	1,070
Hay	Tons.	1,115	11,802	9	90	1,124	11,892
Malt	Bush.	72	87			72	87
Maple syrup	Galls.	6	3			6	3
Nuts	Lbs.	35,463	764			35,463	764
Seeds, all other	$		180				180
Straw	Tons.	17	152			17	152
Vegetables, canned or preserved	$		263				263
Potatoes	Bush.	141,323	82,563	5	4	141,328	82,567
Turnips	"	199	69			199	69
All other vegetables	$		1,007				1,007
Cereal foods	"		122				122
Total, agriculture			693.108		18,278		711,386
MANUFACTURES.							
Agricultural implements	$		330				330
Books	"		8,419				8,419
Biscuits and bread	Cwt.	2,200	20,574	7	101	2,207	20,675
Bricks	M.	2	10			2	10
Cement	$		27				27
Clothing and wearing apparel	"		1,137				1,137
Cordage, ropes and twine	"		35,975				35,975

No. 17.—Statement of Goods Exported to British and Foreign West Indies—*Con.*

Articles.		To British West Indies and British Guiana.		To Foreign West Indies and Foreign Guiana.		Total to West Indies and Guiana.	
		Quantity.	Value.	Quantity.	Value.	Quantity.	Value.
MANUFACTURES—*Con.*			$		$		$
Cotton fabrics	Yds.	21,692	2,852	16,332	1,576	38,024	4,428
Drugs, chemicals, &c	$		132,870		75		132,945
Electrical apparatus	"		86				86
Electrotypes	"		2				2
Explosives and fulminates	Lbs.	24	3			24	3
Glass and glassware, N.E.S	$		162				162
Household effects, N.E.S	"		1,790				1,790
India rubber, mfrs. of	"		432				432
Iron and steel—							
Stoves	No.	10	153			10	153
Castings, N.E.S	$		30				30
Machinery, N.E.S	"		3,843				3,843
Type-writers	No.	1	50			1	50
Scrap	Cwt.	60	75			60	75
Hardware, N.E.S	$		1,532		263		1,795
Manufactures of	"		3,091				3,091
Leather—							
Sole	Lbs.	25,993	5,876			25,993	5,876
Upper	"	100	20			100	20
N.E.S	"	3,034	639			3,034	639
Boots and shoes	$		15,519				15,519
Harness and saddlery	"		120				120
Other mfrs. of	"		603				603
Liquors—							
Ale and beer	Galls.	432	143			432	143
Whisky	"	2,808	7,811	678	2,177	3,486	9,988
Wines	"	1,608	1,737			1,608	1,737
Metals, N.O.P	$		134				134
Musical instruments—							
Organs	No.	1	75			1	75
Pianos	"	1	200			1	200
Oil cake	Cwt.	16	16			16	16
Oils, N.E.S	Galls.	12,612	4,730			12,612	4,730
Paper—Wall	Rolls.	4,907	343			4,907	343
" N.E.S	$		9,436				9,436
Photographs	"		10				10
Sails	"		854				854
Soap	Lbs.	964,429	36,857			964,429	36,857
Stone, ornamental:—Granite, marble, &c	$		444				444
Sugar of all kinds, N.E.S	Lbs.	31,461	1,279			31,461	1,279
Tar	$		14				14
Tobacco—							
Cigars	M.	5	111			5	111
Cigarettes	"	30	30			30	30
All other	Lbs.	2,044	1,165			2,044	1,165
Vehicles—							
Carriages	No.	70	6,136			70	6,136
Parts of	$		347				347
Carts	No.	1	25			1	25
All other	$		17				17
Wood—							
Barrels, empty	No.	424	368			424	368
Household furniture	$		7,455				7,455
Doors, sashes and blinds	"		1,005				1,005
Matches and match splints	"		159				159
Mouldings, &c	"		35				35
Pails, tubs, &c	"		5				5
Other manufactures of wood	"		12,670				12,670

No. 17.—Statement of Goods Exported to British and Foreign West Indies—*Con.*

Articles.		To British West Indies and British Guiana.		To Foreign West Indies and Foreign Guiana.		Total to West Indies and Guiana.	
		Quantity.	Value.	Quantity.	Value.	Quantity.	Value.
MANUFACTURES—*Con.*			$		$		$
Woollens	$	....	664	....	....	....	664
Other articles	"	....	27,887	....	34	....	27,921
Total, manufactures		....	358,382	....	4,226	....	362,608
MISCELLANEOUS.							
Coffee	Lbs.	19	5	....	....	19	5
Dried fruits, N.E.S	"	33,454	1,650	128	6	33,582	1,656
Rice	"	1,892	41	....	....	1,892	41
Tea	"	3,868	842	60	18	3,928	860
Other miscellaneous articles	$	....	128	....	....	....	128
Total, miscellaneous articles		....	2,666	....	24	....	2,690
Grand total		....	2,847,381	....	57,137	....	2,904,518

No. 18.—STATEMENT showing the Total Value of the Imports and Exports of the Dominion of Canada, from and to each Country during the Fiscal Year 1906.

COUNTRY.	Imports.			Exports.		
	Dutiable Goods.	Free Goods.	Total.	Produce of Canada.	Foreign Produce.	Total.
BRITISH EMPIRE.	$	$	$	$	$	$
[illegible]eat Britain	52,7[illegible]022	16,550,128	69,317,150	127,456,465	5,636,106	133,092,571
Australia	31,100	195,097	226,197	2,072,702	9,517	2,082,219
Bermuda	....	....	....	389,249	9,445	398,694
British [illegible]ica	282,998	14,661	[illegible]059	1,756,439	3,280	1,759,719
" East Indies	912,150	2,508,304	3,420,454	19,612	1,942	21,554
" West Indies	4,351,727	1,102,267	5,453,994	2,337,746	21,976	2,359,722
" Guiana	2,065,870	1,496	2,067,366	481,118	6,541	4[illegible]659
" Honduras	....	....	....	5,613	....	5,613
" Possessions, all [illegible]ther	654	400	1,054	34,135	....	3[illegible]435
Fiji Islands	454,380	72	454,452	59,151	86	59,237
[illegible]tar	51	....	51	2,700	....	2,700
Hong Kong	149,242	18,304	167,546	36,519	332	36,851
Malta	....	....	....	17,423	....	17,423
Newfoundland	6,056	1,752,751	1,758,807	3,023,047	190,562	3,213,609
New Zealand	[illegible],431	294,644	302,075	729,303	4,751	734,054
Total, British Empire	61,028,681	22,438,124	83,466,805	138,421,222	5,884,538	144,305,760
OTHER COUNTRIES.						
[illegible]ia	147	15,663	15,810	....	....	....
Argentina	6,177	1,488,113	1,[illegible]290	1,881,983	6,849	1,888,832
Austria-Hungary	742,036	52,317	794,353	5,055	729	5,784
Azores	....	....	....	3	....	3
Belgium	1,943,473	379,589	2,323,062	1,187,950	377,216	1[illegible]166
Bolivia	....	....	....	445	....	445
Brazil	11,069	327,683	338,752	649,228	149	9[illegible]377
[illegible]l American States	33,287	106,976	140,263	66,358	48	66,406
Chili	....	109,262	[illegible]262	[illegible]991	160	239,151
China	281,612	259,140	540,752	839,468	16,290	855,758
Corea	11	....	11	501	....	501
Cuba	385,624	59,476	5[illegible]100	1,217,410	4,356	1,[illegible]766
Denmark	7,908	22,122	30,030	143,575	....	143,575
Danish West Indies	....	....	....	16,604	105	16,709

Country						
Dutch East Indies	596,694	1,611	598,305	628	....	628
Dutch West Indies	....	....	....	768	....	768
Dutch Guiana	....	....	....	21,327	34	21,361
Ecuador	316	....	316	2,823	....	2,823
Egypt	22,728	6,885	29,613	19,364	60	19,424
France	6,240,402	1,457,645	7,698,047	2,110,444	9,647	2,120,091
French Africa	....	14,548	14,548	7,028	....	7,028
French West Indies	....	350	350	18,299	....	18,299
Germany	5,046,778	1,993,313	7,040,091	1,690,907	181,650	1,872,557
Greece	289,250	29	289,279	1,045	....	1,045
Hawaii	198	15,779	15,977	6,252	249	6,501
Hayti	....	....	....	33,441	2	33,443
Holland	589,214	571,027	1,160,241	636,943	187,825	824,768
Iceland	68	2,235	2,303	270	....	270
Italy	526,752	54,212	580,964	215,599	256	[illegible]855
Japan	1,036,084	626,845	1,662,929	492,275	1,677	[illegible]952
Madeira	....	....	....	31,359	....	31,359
Mexico	64,372	223,144	287,516	256,381	2,991	259,372
Norway	74,307	20,079	94,386	159,890	....	159,890
Panama	....	....	....	58,654	756	59,410
Persia	8,434	....	8,434	....	....	....
Peru	70,143	....	70,143	40,080	....	40,080
Philippines	8,207	50	8,257	4,686	....	4,686
Porto Rico	211,174	457	211,631	514,055	585	514,640
Portuguese Africa	....	....	....	3,889	....	3,889
Portugal	122,267	15,381	137,648	89,598	....	89,598
Roumania	173	1,215	1,388	41,916	....	41,916
Russia	61,893	198,068	259,961	222,040	375	222,415
San Domingo	....	....	....	4,670	....	4,670
St. Pierre	18,737	3,561	22,298	146,687	5,360	152,047
Spain	886,815	44,427	931,242	55,686	....	[illegible]686
Spanish Africa	....	....	....	24,105	....	24,105
Sweden	83,913	9,761	93,674	91,120	68	91,188
Switzerland	1,982,529	49,527	2,032,056	29,809	421	30,230
Turkey	211,791	152,021	363,812	12,307	34,028	46,335
Uruguay	....	173,893	173,893	161,293	1,752	[illegible]045
U. S. of Colombia	....	....	....	42,110	667	42,777
United States	94,196,820	86,529,291	180,726,111	83,546,306	4,455,003	[illegible]309
Alaska	248	71,864	72,112	21,109	....	21,109
Total, other countries	115,761,651	95,057,559	210,819,210	97,062,734	5,289,308	102,352,042
Coin and bullion:—To United States, bullion, $5,172, coin, $9,800,071; to China, bullion, $80,146, coin, $37,246; to Great Britain, coin, $2,366; to Newfoundland, coin, $247; to Hong Kong, coin, $3,430; to Japan, coin, $150	....	....	....	....	9,928,828	9,928,828
Grand total	176,790,332	117,495,683	294,286,015	235,483,956	21,102,674	256,586,630

No. 19.—Abstract by Countries

Countries.	Imports.				
	Dutiable.	Free.	Total.	General Tariff.	
	Value.	Value.	Value.	Value.	Duty.
	$	$	$	$	$ cts.
Great Britain	52,767,022	16,550,128	69,317,150	6,054,931	3,254,684 36
Australia	31,100	195,097	226,197	28,383	9,104 08
British Africa	282,998	14,661	297,659	17,827	1,964 93
" East Indies	912,150	2,508,304	3,420,454	15,550	4,491 36
" West Indies	4,351,727	1,102,267	5,453,994	44,400	61,832 96
" Guiana	2,065,870	1,496	2,067,366	15,148	131,726 08
Fiji Islands	454,380	72	454,452	47	6 32
Gibraltar	51	....	51	51	21 64
Hong Kong	149,242	18,304	167,546	150,172	98,166 63
Newfoundland	6,056	1,752,751	1,758,807	5,649	1,092 68
New Zealand	7,431	294,644	302,075	244	81 95
British Possessions, other	654	400	1,054	693	1,301 70
Total, British Empire	61,028,681	22,438,124	83,466,805	6,333,095	3,564,474 69
Arabia	147	15,663	15,810	276	87 75
Argentina	6,177	1,488,113	1,494,290	3,553	556 66
Austria-Hungary	742,036	52,317	794,353	733,173	205,202 59
Belgium	1,943,473	379,589	2,323,062	2,214,508	508,247 32
Brazil	11,069	327,683	338,752	11,083	1,248 60
Central American States	33,287	106,976	140,263	75,230	22,825 83
Chili	....	109,262	109,262	....	....
China	281,612	259,140	540,752	284,815	169,043 69
Corea	11	....	11	11	1 10
Cuba	385,624	59,476	445,100	380,578	391,889 20
Denmark	7,908	22,122	30,030	5,330	1,260 30
Danish West Indies	....	....	....	39	197 20
Dutch East Indies	596,694	1,611	598,305	838,379	230,495 79
Ecuador	316	....	316	316	94 80
Egypt	22,728	6,885	29,613	21,073	30,010 95
France	6,240,402	1,457,645	7,698,047	6,181,635	2,509,884 10
French Africa	....	14,548	14,548	75	32 75
French West Indies	....	350	350	....	....
Germany	5,046,778	1,993,313	7,040,091	101,806	25,067 83
Greece	289,250	29	289,279	300,845	88,824 99
Hawaii	198	15,779	15,977	198	46 53
Hayti	....	....	....	....	....
Holland	589,214	571,027	1,160,241	612,791	1,620,478 12
Iceland	68	2,235	2,303	68	31 55
Italy	526,752	54,212	580,964	499,420	118,675 97
Japan	1,036,084	626,845	1,662,929	1,046,026	317,533 26
Madeira	....	....	....	44	33 90
Mexico	64,372	223,144	287,516	64,193	19,263 10
Norway	74,307	20,079	94,386	67,944	18,686 05
Persia	8,434	....	8,434	8,434	2,193 70
Peru	70,143	....	70,143	188,852	74,719 57
Philippines	8,207	50	8,257	10,541	33,236 25
Porto Rico	211,174	457	211,631	272,011	19,778 90
Portugal	122,267	15,381	137,648	113,203	44,716 82
Roumania	173	1,215	1,388	173	118 20
Russia	61,893	198,068	259,961	59,752	12,186 75
St. Pierre	18,737	3,561	22,298	1,742	474 91
Spain	886,815	44,427	931,242	883,454	289,363 62
Sweden	83,913	9,761	93,674	83,456	18,725 80
Switzerland	1,982,529	49,527	2,032,056	1,959,323	545,566 89
Turkey	211,791	152,021	363,812	189,452	49,540 43
United States	94,196,820	86,529,291	180,726,111	89,391,824	22,133,014 68

SESSIONAL PAPER No. 11

DUTIABLE AND FREE.

ENTERED FOR CONSUMPTION.

Preferential Tariff.		Surtax Tariff.		Total Dutiable.	Total Free.	Grand Total.	
Value.	Duty.	Value.	Duty.	Value.	Value.	Value.	Duty.
$	$ cts.	$	$	$	$	$	$ cts.
45,723,019	9,380,210 11	837,775	309,354 88	52,615,725	16,578,863	69,194,588	12,944,249 35
				28,383	195,796	224,179	9,104 08
142,867	25,419 95			160,694	14,661	175,355	27,384 88
830,131	121,706 60			845,681	2,508,394	3,353,985	126,197 96
4,715,920	1,057,383 06	51	20 40	4,760,371	1,102,739	5,863,110	1,119,236 42
2,477,559	504,040 09			2,492,707	1,502	2,494,209	635,766 17
269,080	69,385 43			269,127	72	269,199	69,391 75
				51		51	21 64
				150,172	18,304	168,476	98,166 63
				5,649	1,752,776	1,758,425	1,092 68
5,526	707 90			5,770	295,587	301,357	789 85
				693	400	1,093	1,301 70
54,164,102	11,158,853 14	837,826	309,375 28	61,335,023	22,469,004	83,804,027	15,032,703 11
				276	15,663	15,939	87 75
				3,553	1,488,113	1,491,666	556 66
		11,721	4,553 53	744,894	52,317	797,211	209,756 12
		15,975	3,337 34	2,230,483	379,589	2,610,072	511,584 66
				11,083	327,683	338,766	1,248 60
				75,230	106,976	182,206	22,825 83
					109,262	109,262	
		20	6 67	284,835	259,140	543,975	169,050 36
				11		11	1 10
				380,578	58,462	439,040	391,889 20
				5,330	22,122	27,452	1,260 30
				39		39	197 20
				838,379	4,130	842,509	230,495 79
				316		316	94 80
				21,073	7,061	28,134	30,010 95
		23,977	10,150 87	6,205,612	1,462,375	7,667,987	2,520,034 97
				75	14,548	14,623	32 75
					350	350	
		4,899,916	1,827,470 64	5,001,722	1,985,592	6,987,314	1.852,538 47
				300,845	74	300,919	88,824 99
				198	15,779	15,977	46 53
		604	233 60	613,395	566,497	1,179,892	1,620,711 72
				68	2,235	2,303	31 55
		123	49 20	499,543	54,212	553,755	118,725 17
				1,046,026	627,516	1,673,542	317,533 26
				44		44	33 90
				64,193	223,144	287,337	19,263 10
		86	22 94	68,030	20,079	88,109	18,708 99
				8,434		8,434	2,193 70
				188,852		188,852	74,719 57
				10,541	138	10,679	33,236 25
				272,011	556	272,567	19,778 90
				113,203	15,401	128,604	44,716 82
				173	1,215	1,388	118 20
		415	83 00	60,167	198,068	258,235	12,269 75
				1,742	3,566	5,308	474 91
				883,454	45,337	928,791	289,363 62
		1	0 40	83,457	9,761	93,218	18,726 20
		3,122	1,334 74	1,962,745	49,660	2,012,405	546,901 63
				189,452	152,021	341,473	49,540 43
		148,952	54,088 26	89,540,776	86,321,295	175,862,071	22,187,102 94

No. 19.—Abstract by Countries

Countries.	Imports.			General Tariff.	
	Dutiable.	Free.	Total.		
	Value.	Value.	Value.	Value.	Duty.
	$	$	$	$	$ cts.
Uruguay	....	173,893	173,893	....	....
Venezuela	248	71,864	72,112	248	49 60
Total, other oountries	115,761,651	95,057,559	210,819,210	106,605,874	29,503,406 05
Duty on articles lower than home trade price	....	....	....	....	74,409 28
Additional duties	....	....	....	....	159,251 55
Grand Total	176,790,332	117,495,683	294,286,015	112,938,969	33,301,541 57

SESSIONAL PAPER No. 11

DUTIABLE AND FREE—*Concluded.*

Entered for Consumption.							
Preferential Tariff.		Surtax Tariff.		Total Dutiable.	Total Free.	Grand Total.	
Value.	Duty.	Value.	Duty.	Value.	Value.	Value.	Duty.
$	$ cts.	$	$ cts.	$	$	$	$ cts.
....	....	....	....	....	173,893	173,893	....
....	....	....	....	248	71,864	72,112	49 60
....	....	5,105,212	1,901,331 19	111,711,086	94,845,694	206,556,780	31,404,737 24
....	....	....	....	....	....	....	74,409 28
....	....	....	....	....	....	....	159,251 55
54,164,102	11,158,853 14	5,943,038	2,210,706 47	173,046,109	117,314,698	290,360,807	46,671,101 18

No. 20.—ABSTRACT of the Total Value of Goods Exported from the

Number.	COUNTRIES.	THE MINE.		THE FISHERIES.		THE FOREST.		ANIMALS AND THEIR PRODUCE.	
		Produce.	Not Produce.	Produce.	Not Produce.	Produce.	Not Produce.	Produce.	Not Produce.
	BRITISH EMPIRE.	$	$	$	$	$	$	$	$
1	Great Britain	1,475,839	23	6,139,577	1,550	12,498,738	134,689	57,758,417	217,776
2	Australia	5,927		247,127		336,305		15,384	
3	Bermuda	71,609		35,470		12,974		86,069	26
4	British Africa	18,452		16,177		88,881		289,972	
5	" East Indies			5,793				20	
6	" West Indies	7,394	28	1,186,970	10,444	160,592	1,540	133,362	324
7	" Guiana	15		239,616	477	31,064	3,300	17,939	160
8	" Honduras			150					
9	" Posses. all other			250		16,360			
10	Fiji Islands			18,635		24,789			
11	Gibraltar			2,700					
12	Hong Kong	280				28,527		2,269	
13	Malta								
14	Newfoundland	468,383	27,358	47,021		19,517	271	283,705	41,054
15	New Zealand	398		69,951		22,949		2,995	
	Total, British Empire	2,048,297	27,409	8,009,437	12,471	13,240,696	139,800	58,590,132	259,340
	OTHER COUNTRIES.								
16	Argentina			12,340		1,501,108			
17	Austria Hungary	4,950							
18	Azores								
19	Belgium	91,885	746	52,939		22,432		29,734	54
20	Bolivia								
21	Brazil			611,805		14,040			
22	Central American States	2,000		27,328				1,955	
23	Chili					168,478		45	
24	China	114,270		13,532		34,915		6,207	
25	Corea							58	
26	Cuba	12,253		406,307		258,182	1,517	4,421	
27	Denmark			22,982		3,010		432	
28	Danish West Indies			7,951	81	32		6,616	
29	Dutch East Indies			540					
30	Dutch West Indies								
31	Dutch Guiana			19,787				43	
32	Ecuador								
33	Egypt								
34	France	56,447		952,467	1	50,784		181,679	154
35	French Africa			500					
36	French West Indies					99			
37	Germany	124,257		52,932		33,123		219,622	8,842
38	Greece								
39	Hawaii			2,836					
40	Hayti			31,455		231			
41	Holland	1,506		6,941		4,450		82,015	
42	Iceland								
43	Italy	24,907		114,913					
44	Japan	81,185		153,733		61,776		16,132	
45	Madeira			10,499		20,860			
46	Mexico	11,235		7,189		34,551		3,579	
47	Norway	450		600		6,555		2,011	
48	Panama			32,870	57	180		1,476	
49	Peru					31,972			
50	Philippines								
51	Porto Rico			435,434		75,357		170	
52	Portuguese Africa			525					
53	Portugal			57,727		26,573			
54	Roumania								
55	Russia								

Dominion of Canada during the Fiscal Year ended June 30, 1906.

Agricultural Products.		Manufactures.		Miscellaneous Articles.		Totals.		Grand Totals.	Number.
Produce.	Not Produce.	Produce.	Not Produce.	Produce.	Not Produce.	Produce.	Not Produce.		
$	$	$	$	$	$	$	$	$	
42,305,048	5,065,848	7,233,232	135,846	45,614	80,374	127,456,465	5,636,106	133,092,571	1
53,274		1,414,685	9,517			2,072,702	9,517	2,082,219	2
119,432	731	62,457	715	1,238	7,973	389,249	9,445	398,694	3
800,659	800	541,994	2,480	304		1,756,439	3,280	1,759,719	4
4,540		9,259	1,942			19,612	1,942	21,554	5
531,380	2,567	317,940	4,565	108	2,508	2,337,746	21,976	2,359,722	6
159,161		33,303	2,574	20	30	481,118	6,541	487,659	7
		5,463				5,613		5,613	8
7,449		10,076				34,135		34,135	9
4,494	36	11,233	50			59,151	86	59,237	10
						2,700		2,700	11
3,488	30	1,955	302			36,519	332	36,851	12
17,423						17,423		17,423	13
1,384,056	12,660	805,409	78,526	14,956	30,693	3,023,047	190,562	3,213,609	14
35,722		597,288	4,751			729,303	4,751	734,054	15
45,426,126	5,082,672	11,044,294	241,268	62,240	121,578	138,421,222	5,884,538	144,305,760	
1,580		366,955	6,849			1,881,983	6,849	1,888,832	16
		105	729			5,055	729	5,784	17
		3				3		3	18
449,591	368,507	541,289	7,423	80		1,187,950	377,216	1,565,166	19
		445				445		445	20
2,500		20,883	149			649,228	149	649,377	21
		35,075	48			66,358	48	66,406	22
2,326		68,142	160			238,991	160	239,151	23
7,059		663,485	16,272		18	839,468	16,290	855,758	23
15		388		40		501		501	25
439,889	1,528	96,348	1,175	10	136	1,217,410	4,356	1,221,766	26
97,833		19,318				143,575		143,575	27
269		1,736			24	16,604	105	16,709	28
		88				628		628	29
		768				768		768	30
590		907	34			21,327	34	21,361	31
		2,823				2,823		2,823	32
8		19,356	60			19,364	60	19,424	33
475,604	1	391,763	7,971	1,700	1,520	2,110,444	9,647	2,120,091	34
1,913		4,615				7,028		7,028	35
17,419		781				18,299		18,299	36
677,115	159,828	583,855	12,507	3	473	1,690,907	181,650	1,872,557	37
		1,045				1,045		1,045	38
		3,416	249			6,252	249	6,501	39
25		1,730	2			33,441	2	33,443	40
352,945	186,169	188,686	1,556	400	100	636,943	187,825	824,768	41
		270				270		270	42
184		75,595	256			215,599	256	215,855	43
65,760		113,689	1,397		280	492,275	1,677	493,952	44
						31,359		31,359	45
51,190		148,637	2,936		55	256,381	2,991	259,372	46
128,191		22,003		80		159,890		159,890	47
1,737		22,391	699			58,654	756	59,410	48
		8,108				40,080		40,080	49
		4,686				4,686		4,686	50
2,734		360	585			514,055	585	514,640	51
2,664		700				3,889		3,889	52
		5,298				89,598		89,598	53
		41,916				41,916		41,916	54
35,104		186,936	375			222,040	375	222,415	55

No. 20.—ABSTRACT of the Total Value of Goods Exported from the

Number.	Countries.	The Mine. Produce.	The Mine. Not Produce.	The Fisheries. Produce.	The Fisheries. Not Produce.	The Forest. Produce.	The Forest. Not Produce.	Animals and their Produce. Produce.	Animals and their Produce. Not Produce.
	Other Countries—*Con.*	$	$	$	$	$	$	$	$
56	San Domingo			2,787					
57	St. Pierre	26,985	411	5,198		4,820	585	48,489	90
68	Spain			18,821		13,135			
59	Spanish Africa					24,105			
60	Sweden			38,150		8,412			
61	Switzerland								
62	Turkey			650					
63	Uruguay					97,779			
64	U. S. of Colombia			34,243	667			1,815	
65	United States	32,869,004	207,833	4,880,407	10,277	23,085,040	9,471	7,259,329	461,249
66	Venezuela			15		1,475			
	Total, other countries	33,421,334	208,990	8,016,403	11,083	25,583,474	11,573	7,865,828	470,875
	Grand totals	35,469,631	236,399	16,025,840	23,554	38,824,170	151,373	66,455,960	730,215

To United States : Bullion, $5,172; Coin, $9,800,071: To China, Bullion, $80,146 : Coin, $37,246 : To Hong Kong, Coin, $3,430 : To Japan, Coin, $150 ....

Grand Total Exports ....

Dominion of Canada during the Fiscal Year ended June 30, 1906—*Concluded.*

Agricultural Products.		Manufactures.		Miscellaneous Articles.		Totals.		Grand Totals.	Number.
Produce.	Not Produce.	Produce.	Not Produce.	Produce.	Not Produce.	Produce.	Not Produce.		
$	$	$	$	$	$	$	$	$	
		1,883				4,670		4,670	56
36,896	457	24,180	2,616	119	1,201	146,687	5,360	152,047	57
135		23,595				55,686		55,686	58
						24,105		24,105	59
4,838		39,720	68			91,120	68	91,188	60
		29,809	421			29,809	421	30,230	61
83		11,574	34,028			12,307	34,028	46,335	62
		63,514	1,752			161,293	1,752	163 045	63
50		6,002				42,110	667	42,777	64
5,779,964	354,236	9,652,328	2,747,581	20,234	664,356	83,546,306	4,455,003	88,001,309	65
		19,619				21,109		21,109	66
8,636,211	1,070,726	13,516,818	2,847,898	22,666	668,163	97,062,734	5,289,308	102,352,042	
54,062,337	6,153,398	24,561,112	3,089,166	84,906	789,741	235,483,956	11,173,846	246,657,802	
Great Britain, Coin, $2,366 : To Newfoundland, Coin, $247 : To							9,928,828	9,928,828	
						235,483,956	21,102,674	256,586,630	

No. 21.—Summary Statement of Goods Exported from the Dominion of Canada, distinguishing Canadian Produce and Manufactures from those of other Countries, during the Fiscal Year ended June 30, 1906.

Articles.	Goods, the Produce of Canada.		Goods, not the Produce of Canada.		Total Exports.	
	Quantity.	Value.	Quantity.	Value.	Quantity.	Value.
Classification of the Mine.		$		$		$
Arsenic .... Lbs.	129,070	3,141			129,070	3,141
Asbestus .... Tons.	57,075	1,578,137			57,075	1,578,137
Barytes, ground and unground Cwt.	34,488	14,343			34,488	14,343
Coal .... Tons.	1,820,511	4,643,198	107,169	147,403	1,927,680	4,790,601
Chromite (chromic iron) .... "	1,808	21,293			1,808	21,293
Felspar .... "	12,516	37,615			12,516	37,615
Gold-bearing quartz, dust, nuggets, &c. .... $		12,991,916		12,627		13,004,543
Gypsum or plaster—Crude .... Tons.	404,854	446,789			404,854	446,789
Metals—						
* Copper, fine, contained in ore, matte, regulus, &c. .... Lbs.	43,835,451	7,069,123	4,010	682	43,839,461	7,069,805
Copper, black or coarse, cement copper and copper in pigs .... "	446,897	79,510	33,809	5,870	480,706	85,380
* Lead, metallic, contained in ore, &c. .... "	16,053,342	559,069			16,053,342	559,069
Lead, pig .... "	3,477,898	118,972			3,477,898	118,972
* Nickle, fine, contained in ore, matte or speiss .... "	23,959,841	2,166,936			23,959,841	2,166,936
* Platinum, contained in concentrates, or other forms .... Ozs.	97	1,966	26	559	123	2,525
* Silver, metallic, contained in ore, concentrates, &c. .... "	7,261,527	4,310,528	8,006	4,929	7,269,533	4,315,457
Mica .... Lbs.	1,329,634	335,591	34,193	10,674	1,363,827	346,265
Mineral pigment, iron oxides, ochres, &c. .... "	636,810	6,718			636,810	6,718
Mineral water .... Galls.	6,192	3,365	54	38	6,246	3 403
Oil—Mineral, coal and kerosene, crude .... "			51,234	4,629	51,234	4,629
Oil—Mineral, coal and kerosene, refined .... "	14,590	3,152	2,731	460	17,321	3,612
Total, oils	14,590	3,152	53,965	5,089	68,555	8,241
Ores, viz.—						
Antimony .... Tons.	428	6,157			428	6,157
Iron .... "	148,040	345,540	720	2,840	148,760	348,380
Manganese .... "	17	1,240			17	1,240
Other .... "	11,359	370,655	2	346	11,361	371,001
Total, ores	159,844	723,592	722	3,186	160,566	726,778
Plumbago, crude ore and concentrates .... Cwt.	3,976	4,726			3,976	4,726
Pyrites .... Tons.	20,285	49,768	1,822	4,000	22,107	53,768
Salt .... Lbs.	1,621,747	6,670	13,317,913	39,022	14,939,660	45,692
Sand and gravel .... Tons.	346,278	168,046			346,278	168,046

* These items to show the weight and value of the copper, lead, nickel, platinum and silver respectively, not the gross weight of ore, matte, concentrates, &c.

No. 21.—SUMMARY STATEMENT OF EXPORTS—*Continued.*

Articles.		Goods, the Produce of Canada.		Goods, not the Produce of Canada.		Total Exports.	
		Quantity.	Value.	Quantity.	Value.	Quantity.	Value.
THE MINES—*Con.*			$		$		$
Stone, ornamental, granite, marble, &c., unwrought	Tons.	3,147	3,145	....	....	3,147	3,145
Building, freestone, limestone, &c., unwrought	"	566	1,450	....	....	566	1,450
For manufacture of grindstones, rough	"	896	10,457	....	....	896	10,457
Total, stone, &c		4,609	15,052	....	....	4,609	15,052
Other articles	$	....	110,415	....	2,320	....	112,735
Total, mine		....	35,469,631	....	236,399	....	35,706,030
THE FISHERIES.							
Codfish, including haddock, ling and pollock, fresh	Lbs.	404,163	11,018	....	....	404,163	11,018
Dry salted	Cwt.	607,681	3,496,596	925	4,681	608,606	3,501,277
Wet salted	"	4,910	19,694	....	....	4,910	19,694
Pickled	"	6	24	....	....	6	24
Tongues and sounds	Brls.	1,794	20,680	....	....	1,794	20,680
Total, codfish		....	3,548,012	....	4,681	....	3,552,693
Mackerel, fresh	Lbs.	1,783,520	69,457	....	....	1,783,520	69,457
Canned	"	5,276	243	....	....	5,276	243
Pickled	Brls.	30,798	257,120	622	5,529	31,420	262,649
Total, mackerel		....	326,820	....	5,529	....	332,349
Halibut, fresh	Lbs.	686,085	32,237	....	....	686,085	32,237
Pickled	Brls.	352	3,164	....	....	352	3,164
Total, halibut		....	35,401	....	....	....	35,401
Herring, fresh or frozen	Lbs.	22,652,281	121,526	335,000	9,429	22,987,281	130,955
Pickled	Brls.	113,167	393,408	459	1,400	113,626	394,808
Canned	Lbs.	73,409	2,711	81	25	73,490	2,736
Smoked	"	3,859,063	98,003	....	....	3,859,063	98,003
Total, herrings		....	615,648	....	10,854	....	626,502
Sea fish, other, fresh	Lbs.	5,699,913	282,844	204	21	5,700,117	282,865
Pickled	Brls.	5,363	28,549	63	158	5,426	28,707
Preserved	Lbs.	875,142	39,973	13,766	2,026	888,908	41,999
Total, sea fish, other		....	351,366	....	2,205	....	353,571
Oysters, fresh	Brls.	328	1,959	9	105	337	2,064
Preserved in cans	Lbs.	424	156	245	73	669	229
Total, oysters		....	2,115	....	178	....	2,293
Lobsters, fresh	Brls.	42,125	497,541	1	13	42,126	497,554
Canned	Lbs.	11,144,402	3,010,203	....	....	11,144,402	3,010,203
Total, lobsters		....	3,507,744	....	13	....	3,507,757

No. 21.—SUMMARY STATEMENT OF EXPORTS—*Continued.*

Articles.	Goods, the Produce of Canada.		Goods, not the Produce of Canada.		Total Exports.	
	Quantity.	Value.	Quantity.	Value.	Quantity.	Value.
		$		$		$
THE FISHERIES—*Con.*						
Bait, fish.... Brls.	301	1,758	....	....	301	1,758
Clams or other.... "	66,204	126,270	....	....	66,204	126,270
Total, bait....	....	128,028	....	....	....	128,028
Salmon, fresh.... Lbs.	4,837,346	492,460	....	....	4,837,346	492,460
Smoked.... "	2,485	262	....	....	2,485	262
Canned.... "	45,978,123	4,943,413	335	40	45,978,458	4,943,453
Pickled.... Brls.	113,357	271,157	....	....	113,357	271,157
Total, salmon....	....	5,707,292	....	40	....	5,707,332
Salmon or lake trout.... Lbs.	249,053	9,054	....	....	249,053	9,054
Fish, all other, fresh.... $	....	1,368,616	....	....	....	3,368,616
Pickled.... Brls.	5,455	31,180	....	....	5,455	31,180
Total, fish, other....	....	1,399,796	....	....	....	1,399,796
Fish oil, cod.... Galls.	110,208	34,070	....	....	110,208	34,070
Seal.... "	15,570	4,536	127	36	15,697	4,572
Whale.... "	221,235	66,408	....	....	221,235	66,408
Other.... "	29,818	6,863	....	....	29,818	6,863
Total, fish oils....	376,831	111,877	127	36	376,958	111,913
Furs or skins, the produce of fish or marine animals.... $	....	273,730	....	....	....	273,730
Other articles.... "	....	8,957	....	18	....	8,975
Total, fisheries....	....	16,025,840	....	23,554	....	16,049,394
THE FOREST.						
Ashes, pot and pearl.... Brls.	1,119	37,860	....	....	1,119	37,860
All other.... $	....	67,716	....	68	....	67,784
Total, ashes....	....	105,576	....	68	....	105,644
Bark for tanning.... Cords	6,608	33,197	....	....	6,608	33,197
Firewood.... "	31,452	69,122	....	....	31,452	69,122
Knees and futtocks.... No.	27,435	21,837	....	....	27,435	21,837
Lathwood.... Cords	2,768	9,899	....	....	2,768	9,899
Logs—cedar, capable of being made into shingle bolts.... "	3,467	20,642	....	....	3,467	20,642
Logs, elm.... M. ft.	1,448	18,958	....	....	1,448	18,958
" hemlock.... "	4,998	31,061	....	....	4,998	31,061
" oak.... "	9	170	....	....	9	170
" pine.... "	1,782	25,549	....	....	1,782	25,549
" spruce.... "	11,760	102,817	....	6	11,760	102,823
" all other.... "	52,869	378,707	....	....	52,869	378,707
Total, logs....	....	557,262	....	6	....	557,268

No. 21.—SUMMARY STATEMENT OF EXPORTS—*Continued.*

Articles.	Goods, the Produce of Canada.		Goods, not the Produce of Canada.		Total Exports.	
	Quantity.	Value.	Quantity.	Value.	Quantity.	Value.
THE FOREST—*Con.*		$		$		$
Lumber, viz.:—Battens... $	....	29,008	....	132	....	29,140
" basswood............M. ft.	2,024	41,688	54	686	2,078	42,374
" deals, pine.........St. hund.	39,011	2,353,927	....	....	39,011	2,353,927
" " spruce and other "	188,775	6,554,612	....	....	188,775	6,554,612
" deal ends............ "	10,173	375,361	....	....	10,173	375,361
" hickory..............M. ft.	95	220	....	....	95	220
" laths................ M.	647,600	1,596,466	....	....	647,600	1,596,466
" palings............ "	151	1,526	....	....	151	1,526
" pickets............ "	21,256	145,409	....	....	21,256	145,409
" planks and boards....M. ft.	1,123,510	17,958,025	396	8,374	1,123,906	17,966,399
" joists............... "	276	3,641	....	....	276	3.641
" scantling........... "	90,531	1,042,747	....	....	90,531	1,042,747
" shingles........... M.	941,477	1,908,486	....	....	941,477	1,908,486
Shooks, box.................. No.	20,400	831	....	....	20,400	831
" other.................. $	....	366,947	....	....	....	366,947
Total, shooks................	....	367,778	....	....	....	367,778
Staves and headings .... $	....	111,856	....	....	....	111,856
All other lumber, N.E.S...... "	....	434,219	....	5,578	....	439,797
Total, lumber................	....	32,924,969	....	14,770	....	32,939,739
Match blocks................ $	....	29,926	....	....	....	29,926
Masts and spars.............. No.	1,008	8,502	2	135	1,010	8,637
Piling...................... $	....	194,073	....	....	....	194,073
Poles—hop, hoop, telegraph and other.................. "	....	100,545	....	799	....	101,344
Posts, cedar, tamarac and other "	....	14,579	....	63	....	14,642
Shingle bolts—of pine or cedar. Cords	9,115	16,126	....	....	9,115	16,126
Sleepers and railroad ties...... No.	1,261,252	328,383	....	....	1,261,252	328,383
Stave bolts.................. Cords	7,643	2,496	....	....	7,643	2,496
*Timber—square, viz :—						
Ash........................ Tons.	698	10,853	....	....	698	10,853
Birch...................... "	22,593	260,920	....	....	22,593	260,920
Elm........................ "	9,057	251,887	45	1,358	9,102	253,245
Maple...................... "	46	675	....	....	46	675
Oak........................ "	8,375	182,490	5,072	114,391	13,447	296,881
Pine, red.................. "	665	8,533	....	....	665	8,533
" white.................. "	42,164	967,293	442	15,745	42,606	983,038
All other.................. "	2,663	40,923	111	1,763	2,774	42,686
Total, timber, square.. "	86,261	1,723,574	5,670	133,257	91,931	1,856,831
Wood, blocks and other, for pulp.......................Cords.	614,286	2,649,106	....	....	614,286	2,649,106
Other articles of the forest..... "	....	14,356	....	2,275	....	16,631
Total, forest...............	....	38,824,170	....	151,373	....	38,975,543

* 2,750 superficial feet of board measurement are equal to one hundred standard deals.

No. 21.—SUMMARY STATEMENT OF EXPORTS—*Continued.*

Articles.	Goods, the Produce of Canada.		Goods, not the Produce of Canada.		Total Exports.	
	Quantity.	Value.	Quantity.	Value.	Quantity.	Value.
ANIMALS AND THEIR PRODUCE.		$		$		$
Animals—horses, one year old or less ..... No.	31	3,085	1	30	32	3,115
" horses, over one year old ..... "	2,763	521,535	1,205	372,933	3,968	894,468
" cattle, one year old or less ..... "	2,374	34,817	1	150	2,375	34,967
" cattle, over one year old ..... "	173,656	11,622,012	637	32,572	174,293	11,654,584
" swine ..... "	783	12,786	1	25	784	12,811
" sheep, one year old or less ..... "	155,414	643,293	1	25	155,415	643,318
" sheep, over one year old ..... "	88,848	529,047	76	1,640	88,924	530,687
" poultry ..... $	....	58,088	....	801	....	58,889
" other ..... "	....	41,785	....	6,713	....	48,498
Total, animals	....	13,466,448	....	414,889	....	13,881,337
Bones ..... Cwt.	304,287	43,328	....	....	304,287	43,328
Butter ..... Lbs.	34,031,525	7,075,539	49,617	10,480	34,081,142	7,086,019
Cheese ..... "	215,834,543	24,433,169	81,614	8,495	215,916,157	24,441,664
Eggs ..... Doz.	2,921,725	495,176	16,052	6,857	2,937,777	502,033
Furs—dressed ..... $	....	49,357	....	13,792	....	63,149
" undressed ..... "	....	2,414,980	....	43,076	....	2,458,056
Total, furs	....	2,464,337	....	56,868	....	2,521,205
Grease and grease scraps ..... Lbs.	2,987,699	149,500	680	63	2,988,379	149,563
Glue stock ..... $	....	6,347	....	35	....	6,382
Hair ..... "	....	123,664	....	1,538	....	125,202
Hides and skins, other than fur "	....	3,457,830	....	6,023	....	3,463,853
Horns and hoofs ..... "	....	14,629	....	100	....	14,729
Honey ..... Lbs.	39,485	3,652	3,475	150	42,960	3,802
Lard ..... "	129,524	13,039	5,955	472	135,479	13,511
Meats, viz.:—Bacon ..... "	99,125,059	11,666,707	1,372,080	148,299	100,497,139	11,815,006
" beef ..... "	2,887,962	200,718	474,801	25,063	3,362,763	225,781
" hams ..... "	3,782,829	420,161	12,249	1,730	3,795,078	421,891
" mutton ..... "	105,062	7,825	42,160	3,181	147,222	11,006
" pork ..... "	775,836	57,729	258,784	17,608	1,034,620	75,337
Poultry, dressed or undressed $	....	114,275	....	386	....	114,661
Game " " ..... "	....	3,796	....	....	....	3,796
Tongues ..... Lbs.	30,943	3,126	....	....	30,943	3,126
Canned ..... "	13,665,823	1,367,593	8,855	1,668	13,674,678	1,369,261
All other, N.E.S ..... "	1,723,294	174,383	7,186	663	1,730,480	175,046
Total, meats	....	14,016,313	....	198,598	....	14,214,911
Milk and cream, condensed ..... Lbs.	1,744,991	128,530	6,798	703	1,751,789	129,233
Oil—Lard ..... Galls.	50	23	....	....	50	23
Sheep pelts ..... No.	58,054	54,452	....	....	58,054	54,452
Tails ..... $	....	1,855	....	....	....	1,855
Tallow ..... Lbs.	519,792	23,085	....	....	519,792	23,085
Wool ..... "	1,424,795	352,636	80,589	16,043	1,505,384	368,679
Other articles ..... "	....	132,408	....	8,901	....	141,309
Total, animals	....	66,455,960	....	730,215	....	67,186,175

No. 21.—SUMMARY STATEMENT OF EXPORTS—*Continued.*

Articles.		Goods, the Produce of Canada.		Goods, not the Produce of Canada.		Total Exports.	
		Quantity.	Value.	Quantity.	Value.	Quantity.	Value.
AGRICULTURAL PRODUCTS.			$		$		$
Balsam	$	....	10,463	... ...	....	....	10,463
Cider	Galls.	60,510	9,340	201	60	60,711	9,400
Flax	Cwt.	68,847	244,629	....	....	68,847	244,629
Fruits, viz.—							
Apples, dried	Lbs.	3,651,260	212,848	200	14	3,651,460	212,862
" green or ripe	Brls.	1,217,564	4,083,482	41	288	1,217,605	4,083,770
Berries of all kinds	$	....	100,661	....	2,207	....	102,868
Canned or preserved	"	....	274,573	....	4,591	....	279,164
All other, N.E.S	"	....	144,324	....	59,321	....	203,645
Total, fruits		....	4,815,888	... .	66,421	. .. .	4,882,309
Grain and products of, viz.—							
Barley	Bush.	880,028	469,198	2,005,861	951,444	2,885,889	1,420,642
Beans	"	88,663	139,908	669	764	89,332	140,672
Buckwheat	"	487,449	275,591	916	440	488,365	276,031
Indian corn	"	45,257	24,403	4,820,829	2,611,807	4,866,086	2,636,210
Oats	"	2,700,303	1,083,347	2,366,628	774,977	5,066,931	1,858,324
Pease, whole	"	546,588	608,926	5	3	546,593	608,929
" split	"	128,292	148,392	1	3	128,293	148,395
Rye	"	4	2	146,232	92,681	146,236	92,683
Wheat	"	40,399,402	33,658,391	587,725	500,691	40,987,127	34,159,082
Other grain	"	1,980	2,239	....	....	1,980	2,239
Total, grain		45,277,966	36,410,397	9,928,866	4,932,810	55,206,832	41,343,207
Bran	Cwt.	678,221	412,913	....	....	678,221	412,913
Flour of wheat	Brls.	1,532,014	6,179,825	130	929	1,532,144	6,180,754
" rye	"	2	35	....	....	3	35
Indian meal	"	2,172	6,659	8	55	2,180	6,714
Oatmeal	"	132,944	542,281	....	....	132,944	542,281
Meal, all other	"	11,359	32,383	60	87	11,419	32,470
Total, flour and meal		1,678,492	6,761,183	198	1,071	1,678,690	6,762,254
Hay	Tons.	206,714	1,529,941	71	1,778	206,785	1,531,719
Hemp	Cwt.	40	555	9	281	49	836
Hops	Lbs.	71,641	13,271	900	103	72,541	13,374
Malt	Bush.	8,605	6,961	....	....	8,605	6,961
Maple sugar	Lbs.	1,874,651	129,177	1,128	82	1,875,779	129,259
" syrup	Galls.	84,450	9,128	664	87	85,114	9,215
Nuts	Lbs.	2,195	276	83,200	3,790	85,395	4,066
Seeds—							
Clover	Bush.	211,869	1,396,805	....	....	211,869	1,396,805
Flax	"	2,824	3,328	827,846	952,371	830,670	955,699
Grass	"	43,441	55,865	....	....	43,441	55,865
All other	$	....	22,471	... .	2,994	....	25,465
Total, seeds		....	1,478,469	....	955,365	....	2,433,834
Straw	Tons.	4,222	17,129	....	....	4,222	17,129
Tobacco, leaf	Lbs.	77,693	19,160	395,444	156,166	473,137	175,326
Trees, shrubs and plants	$	....	9,943	... .. .	438	....	10,381

No. 21.—Summary Statement of Exports—*Continued.*

Articles.	Goods, the Produce of Canada.		Goods, not the Produce of Canada.		Total Exports.	
	Quantity.	Value.	Quantity.	Value.	Quantity.	Value.
Agricultural products—*Con.*		$		$		$
Vegetables, canned or preserved $	....	33,311	....	16,399	....	49,710
Potatoes .... Bush.	1,259,169	655,904	7,727	5,056	1,266,896	660,960
Turnips .... "	1,138,300	137,527	....	....	1,138,300	137,527
All other vegetables .... $	....	78,414	....	3,833	....	82,247
Total, vegetables	....	905,156	....	25,288	....	930,444
Cereal foods of all kinds, N.E.S. $	....	1,185,183	....	2,851	....	1,188,034
Other articles .... "	....	93,175	....	6,807	....	99,982
Total, agricultural products	....	54,062,337	....	6,153,398	....	60,215,735
Manufactures.						
Acid, sulphuric .... Lbs.	59,393	770	....	....	59,393	770
Agricultural implements .... $	....	2,497,601	....	1,503	....	2,499,104
Aluminium, in bars, ingots, &c. Lbs.	3,088,122	618,499	3,875	765	3,091,997	619,264
Aluminium, mfrs. of, N.E.S. .... $	....	1,262	....	650	....	1,912
Books, pamphlets, maps, &c. .... "	....	253,024	....	72,230	....	325,254
Biscuits and bread .... Cwt.	10,502	39,216	26	242	10,528	39,458
Bricks .... M.	706	5,541	35	572	741	6,113
Buttons .... $	....	5,404	....	162	....	5,566
Candles .... Lbs.	136,672	9,758	3,641	469	140,313	10,227
Cartridges, gun, rifle and pistol. $	....	107,720	....	1,181	....	108,901
Charcoal .... "	....	53,840	....	....	....	53,840
Cement .... "	....	8,913	....	4,885	....	13,798
Cinders .... "	....	1,023	....	....	....	1,023
Clothing and wearing apparel .. "	....	92,766	....	21,898	....	114,664
Coke .... Tons.	59,541	281,663	....	....	59,541	281,663
Cordage, ropes and twine .... $	....	490,464	....	10,494	....	500,958
Cotton fabrics .... Yds.	15,152,684	1,246,734	291,801	20,978	15,444,485	1,267,712
Cottons, other .... $	....	31,590	....	11,137	....	42,727
Cotton waste .... Lbs.	1,145,466	53,388	555	44	1,146,021	53,432
Drugs, chemicals and medicines, N.E.S. .... $	....	1,172,012	....	665,286	....	1,837,298
Dye stuffs .... "	....	4,096	....	17,033	....	21,129
Electrical apparatus .... "	....	24,756	....	155,583	....	180,339
Electrotypes .... "	....	3,050	....	2,011	....	5,061
Extract of hemlock bark ...... Brls.	4,990	65,509	55	660	5,045	66,169
Explosives and fulminates N.E.S. Lbs.	725,730	205,856	135,531	47,229	861,261	253,085
Felt, manufactures of .... $	....	887	....	94	....	981
Fertilizers .... "	....	236,114	....	3,286	....	239,400
Fur, manufactures of .... "	....	24,197	....	9,150	....	33,347
Glass and glassware, N.E.S. .... "	....	10,558	....	4,284	....	14,842
Grindstones, manufactured ..... "	....	15,793	....	128	....	15,921
Gypsum or plaster, ground ..... "	....	1,603	....	....	....	1,603
Hats and caps .... "	....	7,405	....	3,693	....	11,098
Household effects, N.E.S. ...... "	....	1,646,810	....	114,839	....	1,761,649
Ice .... "	....	22,090	....	....	....	22,090
India rubber, manufactures of .. "	....	266,504	....	15,660	....	282,164
India rubber, scrap and other ... Lbs.	3,010,061	205,636	107,533	12,637	3,117,594	218,273
Iron and steel and mfrs. of, viz.—						
Stoves .... No.	1,019	11,286	47	599	1,066	11,885
Castings, N.E.S .... $	....	55,504	....	5,843	....	61,347
Pig-iron .... Tons.	697	17,858	....	....	697	17,858
Machinery, N.E.S. .... $	....	481,689	....	400,505	....	882,194
Sewing machines .... No.	967	22,525	286	12,700	1,253	35,225
Typewriters .... "	4,411	143,633	319	16,300	4,730	159,933
Scrap-iron or steel .... Cwt.	580,706	328,172	25,953	27,706	606,659	355,878

No. 21.—SUMMARY STATEMENT OF EXPORTS—*Continued.*

ARTICLES.	GOODS, THE PRODUCE OF CANADA.		GOODS, NOT THE PRODUCE OF CANADA.		TOTAL EXPORTS.	
	Quantity.	Value.	Quantity.	Value.	Quantity.	Value.
MANUFACTURES—*Con.*		$		$		$
Iron and steel—*Con.*						
Hardware, N.E.S. ... $	....	188,672	....	54,681	....	243,353
Steel and manufactures of ... "	....	347,967	....	278,766	....	626,733
Total, iron and steel ...	....	1,597,306	....	797,100	....	2,394,406
Jewellers' sweepings ... $	....	86,963	....	3,788	....	90,751
Junk ... Cwt.	596,212	483,042	4,603	17,509	600,815	500,551
Lamps and lanterns ... $	....	6,779	....	782	....	7,561
Leather, viz.—						
Sole ... Lbs.	7,605,777	1,592,631	66	82	7,605,843	1,592,713
Upper ... "	1,095,021	272,616	3,670	500	1,098,691	273,116
N.E.S. ... "	1,104,950	385,784	16,904	15,217	1,121,854	401,001
Boots and shoes ... $	....	133,792	....	12,323	....	146,115
Harness and saddlery ... "	....	6,939	....	3,499	....	10,438
Other manufactures of ... "	....	25,521	....	3,250	....	28,771
Total, leather ...	....	2,417,283	....	34,871	....	2,452,154
Lime ... $	....	73,534	....	....	....	73,534
Liquors, viz.—						
Ale and beer ... Galls.	8,330	6,520	1,630	1,950	9,960	8,470
Brandy ... "	6	25	470	2,038	476	2,063
Gin ... "	1,247	1,946	26,652	43,649	27,899	45,595
Rum ... "	....	....	5,077	1,554	5,077	1,554
Whisky ... "	286,395	943,649	10,482	28,772	296,877	972,421
Wines ... "	5,425	4,900	4,130	14,351	9,555	19,251
Other spirits, N.E.S ... "	294,245	98,755	2,213	5,016	296,458	103,771
Total, liquors ...	595,648	1,055,795	50,654	97,330	646,302	1,153,125
Metals, N.O.P. ... $	....	45,184	....	15,592	....	60,776
Molasses ... Galls.	....	....	99,229	25,640	99,229	25,640
Musical instruments, viz.—						
Organs ... No.	3,780	206,402	42	3,877	3,822	210,279
Pianos ... "	281	64,475	29	9,403	310	73,878
Other ... $	....	10,922	....	5,993	....	16,915
Total, musical instruments ...	....	281,799	....	19,273	....	301,072
Oakum ... Cwt.	19	81	8	32	27	113
Oil cake ... "	234,173	289,571	45	20	234,218	289,591
Oil, N.E.S. ... Galls.	977,449	97,824	25,059	8,363	1,002,508	106,187
Paper, wall ... Rolls.	533,445	35,535	15,099	2,732	548,544	38,267
" N.E.S. ... "	....	1,971,157	....	18,196	....	1,989,353
Photographs ... $	....	3,979	....	569	....	4,548
Plumbago, manufactures of ... "	....	2,948	....	....	....	2,948
Rags ... Lbs.	17,284,194	228,216	23,515	1,177	17,307,709	229,393
Sails ... $	....	1,014	....	....	....	1,014
Ships sold to other countries ... No. and tons.	7—3,749	30,370	1—332	32,300	8—4,081	62,670
Soap ... Lbs.	1,262,578	52,724	3,379	352	1,265,957	53,076
Starch ... "	99,726	4,937	3,545	366	103,271	5,303

No. 21.—SUMMARY STATEMENT OF EXPORTS—*Continued.*

Articles.		Goods, the Produce of Canada.		Goods, not the Produce of Canada.		Total Exports.	
		Quantity.	Value.	Quantity.	Value.	Quantity.	Value.
MANUFACTURES—*Con.*			$		$		$
Stone, ornamental, viz.—							
Granite, marble, &c., dressed	$		2,105		513		2,618
Building, viz.—Freestone, limestone, &c., dressed	"		292				292
Total, stone			2,397		513		2,910
Sugar of all kinds, N.E.S.	Lbs.	456,310	20,160	258,387	10,074	714,697	30,234
Sugar-house syrup	Galls.	279,013	15,681	238	155	279,251	15,836
Tar	$		98,477		373		98,850
Tin, manufactures of	"		22,106		9,352		31,458
Tobacco, viz.—							
Cigars	M.	120	2,700	16	431	136	3,131
Cigarettes	"	116	212	433	1,074	549	1,286
Snuff	Lbs.	7	4			7	4
Stems and cuttings	"	555,444	30,533	217,409	19,275	772,853	49,808
All other, N.E.S.	"	152,731	49,531	107,450	36,653	260,181	86,184
Total, tobacco			82,980		57,433		140,413
Tow	Cwt.	1,383	12,786			1,383	12,786
Vehicles, viz.—							
Carriages	No.	390	31,482	12	1,113	402	32,595
" parts of	$		17,598		1,526		19,124
Carts	No.	866	19,247	186	4,340	1,052	23,587
Wagons	"	94	5,177	90	4,418	184	9,595
Automobiles	"	67	63,329	49	88,768	116	152,097
Bicycles	"	2,418	62,400	32	1,027	2,450	63,427
" parts of	$		33,562		7,171		40,733
Other vehicles	"		55,380		95,038		150,418
Vinegar	Galls.	313	69	150	42	463	111
Wood, viz.—							
Barrels, empty	No.	9,953	12,344	20,110	32,789	30,063	45,133
Household furniture	$		283,606		5,635		289,241
Doors, sashes and blinds	"		163,081		1,146		164,227
Matches and match splints	"		109,112		33		109,145
Mouldings, trimmings and other house furnishings	"		5,089		60		5,149
Pails, tubs, churns and other hollow woodenware	"		7,926		442		8,368
Spool wood and spools	"		185,663		1,194		186,857
Wood pulp	"		3,478,150				3,478,150
Other manufactures of	"		367,946		21,995		389,941
Total, wood, manuf. of			4,612,917		63,294		4,676,211
Woollens	$		67,968		17,212		85,180
Other articles	"		859,303		452,542		1,311,845
Total, manufactures			24,561,112		3,089,166		27,650,278

No. 21.—SUMMARY STATEMENT OF EXPORTS—*Continued.*

Articles.		Goods, the Produce of Canada.		Goods, not the Produce of Canada.		Total Exports.	
		Quantity.	Value.	Quantity.	Value.	Quantity.	Value.
MISCELLANEOUS ARTICLES.			$		$		$
Coffee	Lbs.	3,300	485	356,175	38,860	359,475	39,345
Dried fruits, N.E.S.	"	1,543	135	225,295	8,187	226,838	8,322
Rice	"	....	....	40,262	1,296	40,262	1,296
" meal	"	2,675,200	29,930	....	....	2,675,200	29,930
Paintings in oil or water colours	$	....	21,744	....	76,028	....	97,772
Tea	Lbs.	....	....	2,387,358	562,059	2,387,358	562,059
Other miscellaneous articles	$	....	32,612	....	103,311	....	135,923
Total, miscellaneous		....	84,906	....	789,741	....	874,647
BULLION AND COIN.							
Bullion, silver	$	....	....	....	85,318	....	85,318
Gold coin	"	....	....	....	9,003,755	....	9,003,755
Silver coin	"	....	....	....	834,925	....	834,925
Copper coin	"	....	....	....	4,830	....	4,830
Total, bullion and coin		....	....	....	9,928,828	....	9,928,828

RECAPITULATION.

Articles.	Goods, the Produce of Canada.	Goods, not the Produce of Canada.	Total Exports, Produce and not Produce.
	$	$	$
Produce of the mine	35,469,631	236,399	35,706,030
" fisheries	16,025,840	23,554	16,049,394
" forest	38,824,170	151,373	38,975,543
Animals and their produce	66,455,960	730,215	67,186,175
Agricultural products	54,062,337	6,153,398	60,215,735
Manufactures	24,561,112	3,089,166	27,650,278
Miscellaneous articles	84,906	789,741	874,647
	235,483,956	11,173,846	246,657,802
Coin and bullion	....	9,928,828	9,928,828
Grand total, exports	235,483,956	21,102,674	256,586,630

No. 22.—STATEMENT showing the Value of Goods exported from Canada during the Fiscal Years 1905 and 1906 respectively; also the Value of Goods exported to Countries embraced in the 'British Empire' and to 'All other Countries' during the Fiscal Year 1906.

Articles.		Fiscal Year ended June 30, 1905.		Fiscal Year ended June 30, 1906.		Fiscal Year ended June 30, 1906.			
						British Empire.		All other Countries.	
		Quantity.	Value.	Quantity.	Value.	Quantity.	Value.	Quantity.	Value.
CLASSIFICATION OF THE MINE.			$		$		$		$
Arsenic	Lbs.	254,000	12,300	129,070	3,141	....	....	129,070	3,141
Asbestus	Tons.	41,127	1,311,535	57,075	1,578,137	8,625	263,224	48,450	1,314,913
Barytes, ground and unground	Cwt.	13,080	5.178	34,488	14,343	....	....	34,488	14,343
Coal	Tons.	1,668,761	4,018,487	1,927,680	4,790,601	229,633	592,597	1,698,047	4,198,004
Chromite (chromic iron)	"	4,080	47,223	1,808	21,293	....	....	1,808	21,293
Felspar	"	14,159	34,262	12,516	37,615	....	....	12,516	37,615
Gold-bearing quartz, dust, nuggets, &c.	$	....	15,309,419	....	13,004,543	....	2,430	....	13,002,113
Gypsum or plaster—crude	Tons.	320,213	334,769	404,854	446,789	134	529	404,720	446,260
Metals, viz.:—									
*Copper, fine, contained in ore, matte, regulus, &c.	Lbs.	38,549,248	4,856,389	43,839,461	7,069 805	3,542,446	457,384	40,297,015	6,612,421
Copper, black or coarse, cement copper and copper in pigs	"	9,224	1,196	480,706	85,380	80,895	12,538	399,811	72,842
*Lead, metallic, contained in ore, &c.	"	50,898,939	1,158,609	16,053,342	559,069	2,700	81	16,050,642	558,988
Lead, pig	"	1,090,462	28,523	3,477,898	118,972	242,275	7,264	3,235,623	111,708
*Nickle, fine, contained in ore, matte or speiss.	"	11,970,557	1,185,056	23,959,841	2,166,836	1,963,927	602,613	21,995,914	1,[illegible]623
*Platinum, contained in concentrates, or other forms	Ozs.	356	2,158	123	2,525	....	....	123	2,525
*Silver, metallic, contained in ore, concentrates, &c.	"	3,612,543	2,103,724	7,269,533	4,315,457	44,475	20,140	7,225,058	4,295,317
Mica	Lbs.	1,018,662	170,477	1,363,827	346,265	272,454	32,072	1,091,373	[illegible]193
Mineral pigment, iron oxides, ochres, &c.	"	903,592	8,294	636,810	6,718	100,000	1,297	536,810	5,421
Mineral water	Galls.	7,163	3,560	6,246	3,403	4,035	2,067	2,211	1,336
Oil—Mineral, coal and kerosene, crude	"	42,037	4,056	51,234	4,629	50,820	4,593	414	36
" " refined	"	30,139	6,500	17,321	3,612	3,525	579	13,796	3,033
Total, oils		72,176	10,556	68,555	8,241	54,345	5,172	14,210	3,069

* These items to show the weight and value of the copper, lead, nickel, platinum and silver respectively, not the gross weight of ore, matte, concentrates, &c.

Ores, viz.—									
Antimony	Tons.	399	32,366	428	6,157	428	6,157	.....	.....
Iron	"	224,908	540,909	148,760	348,380	23	125	148,737	348,255
Manganese	"	93	2,212	17	1,240	.....	.....	17	1,240
Other	"	17,100	691,010	11,361	371,001	342	43,140	11,019	327,861
Total, ores		242,500	1,266,497	160,566	726,778	793	49,422	159,773	677,356
Phosphates	Tons.	40	1,253	.....	.....	.....	.....	.....	.....
Plumbago, crude ore and concentrates	Cwt.	4,422	8,580	3,976	4,726	41	58	3,935	4,668
Pyrites	Tons.	22,561	63,729	22,107	53,768	.....	.....	22,107	53,768
Salt	Lbs.	16,509,832	51,461	14,939,660	45,692	7,480,701	20,519	7,458,959	25,173
Sand and gravel	Tons.	386,151	141,614	346,278	168,046	136	422	346,142	167,624
Stone—									
Ornamental, granite, marble, &c., unwrought	Tons.	99	726	3,147	3,145	.....	.....	3,147	3,145
Building, freestone, limestone, &c., unwrought	"	85,857	23,043	566	1,450	80	40	486	1,410
For manufacture of grindstones, rough	"	872	8,711	896	10,457	.....	.....	896	10,457
Total, stone		86,828	32,480	4,609	15,052	80	40	4,529	15,012
Other articles	$	.....	24,741	.....	112,735	.....	5,837	.....	106,898
Grand total, products of the mine		.....	32,192,070	.....	35,706,030	.....	2,075,706	.....	33,630,324
THE FISHERIES.									
Codfish, including haddock, ling and pollock—fresh	Lbs.	418,097	12,984	404,163	11,018	.....	.....	404,163	11,018
Dry salted	Cwt.	567,697	2,931,418	608,606	3,501,277	221,538	1,228,593	387,068	2,272,684
Wet salted	"	2,887	9,373	4,910	19,694	199	393	4,711	19,301
Pickled	"	3	8	6	24	5	20	1	4
Tongues and sounds	Brls.	1,017	10,289	1,794	20,680	29	122	1,765	20,558
Total, codfish		.....	2,964,072	.....	3,552,693	.....	1,229,128	.....	2,323,565
Mackerel—fresh	Lbs.	1,540,722	91,038	1,783,520	69,457	100	4	1,783,420	69,453
Canned	"	2,552	212	5,276	243	4,316	207	960	36
Pickled	Brls.	20,583	226,071	31,420	262,649	7,107	69,064	24,313	193,585
Total, mackerel		.....	317,321	.....	332,349	.....	69,275	.....	263,074
Halibut—fresh	Lbs.	1,652,843	64,383	686,085	32,237	315	20	685,770	32,217
Pickled	Brls.	1,900	11,001	352	3,164	352	3,164	.....	.....
Total, halibut		.....	75,384	.....	35,401	.....	3,184	.....	32,217

No, 22.—STATEMENT showing the Value of Goods exported from Canada during the Fiscal Year 1905 and 1906—*Continued.*

Articles.		Fiscal Year ended June 30, 1905.		Fiscal Year ended June 30, 1906.		Fiscal Year ended June 30, 1906.			
						British Empire.		All other Countries.	
		Quantity.	Value.	Quantity.	Value.	Quantity.	Value.	Quantity.	Value.
THE FISHERIES—*Con.*			$		$		$		$
Herring—fresh or frozen	Lbs.	21,868,985	154,383	22,987,281	130,955	4,000	310	22,983,281	130,645
Pickled	Brls.	104,719	360,701	113,626	394,808	53,273	236,209	60,353	158,599
Canned	Lbs.	92,575	4,421	73,490	2,736	1,175	86	72,315	2,650
Smoked	"	2,407,805	56,210	3,859,063	98,003	959,671	26,342	2,899,392	71,661
Total, herrings		....	575,715	....	626,502	....	262,947	....	363,555
Sea fish, other—fresh	Lbs.	42	2	5,700,117	282,865	....	....	5,700,117	282,865
Pickled	Brls.	1,171	2,703	5,426	28,707	3,662	21,573	1,764	7,134
Preserved	Lbs.	724,354	39,816	888,908	41,999	41,265	3,165	847,643	38,834
Total, sea fish, other		....	42,521	....	353,571	....	24,738	....	328,833
Oysters—fresh	Brls.	345	1,712	337	2,064	57	425	280	1,639
Preserved in cans	Lbs.	6,570	1,402	669	229	....	....	669	229
Total, oysters		....	3,114	....	2,293	....	425	....	1,868
Lobsters, fresh	Brls.	32,886	376,336	42,126	497,554	728	8,511	41,398	489,043
" canned	Lbs.	11,723,652	2,754,702	11,144,402	3,010,203	4,054,555	1,088,211	7,089,847	1,921,992
Total, lobsters		....	3,131,038	....	3,507,757	....	1,096,722	....	2,411,035
Bait, fish	Brls.	21	66	301	1,758	13	39	288	1,719
" clams or other	"	44,642	72,967	66,204	126,270	1	8	66,203	6,262
Total, bait	"	44,663	73,033	66,505	128,028	14	47	66,491	127,981

Article	Unit								
Salmon, fresh	Lbs.	1,464,232	151,569	4,837,346	492,460	2,268,151	286,432	2,569,195	206,028
" smoked	"	1,606	180	2,485	262	624	64	1,861	198
" canned	"	12,950,049	1,679,237	45,978,458	4,943,453	43,957,015	4,692,969	2,021,443	[illegible]
" pickled	Brls.	76,262	280,462	113,357	271,157	1,677	18,939	111,680	252,218
Total, salmon			2,111,448		5,707,332		4,998,404		708,928
Salmon or lake trout	Lbs.	1,350,018	57,109	249,053	9,054			249,053	9,054
Fish, all other, fresh	$		1,481,282		1,368,616		1,065		1,367,551
" pickled	Brls.	2,432	18,279	5,455	31,180	104	821	5,351	30,359
Total, fish, all other			1,499,561		1,399,796		1,886		1,397,910
Total, fish			10,850,316		15,654,776		7,686,756		7,968,020
Fish oil, cod	Galls.	81,595	39,663	110,208	34,070	6,811	2,098	103,397	31,972
" seal	"			15,697	4,572	15,570	4,536	127	36
" whale	"	1,408	307	221,235	66,408	216,490	64,213	4,745	2,195
" other	"	12,127	3,445	29,818	6,863	13,430	3,285	16,388	3,578
Total, fish oil		95,130	43,415	376,958	111,913	252,301	74,132	124,657	37,781
Furs or skins, the produce of fish or marine animals	$		228,743		273,730		258,318		15,412
Other articles	"		22,424		8,975		2,702		6,273
Grand total, produce of the fisheries			11,144,898		16,049,394		8,021,908		8,027,486
THE FOREST.									
Ashes, pot and pearl	Brls.	955	37,938	1,119	37,860	681	26,405	438	11,455
" all other	$		60,435		67,784				67,784
Total, ashes			98,373		105,644		26,405		79,239
Bark for tanning	Cords.	12,857	59,552	6,608	33,197			6,608	33,197
Firewood	"	34,767	84,949	31,452	69,122	5	10	31,447	69,112
Ivory nuts, vegetable	$		1,030						
Knees and futtocks	No.	19,088	16,029	27,435	21,837			27,435	21,837
Lathwood	Cords.	3,888	12,593	2,768	9,899			2,768	9,899
Logs, cedar, capable of being made into shingle bolts	"	611	2,615	3,467	20,642			3,467	20,642

No. 22.—STATEMENT showing the Value of Goods exported from Canada during the Fiscal Years 1905 and 1906—*Continued.*

Articles.		Fiscal Year ended June 30, 1905.		Fiscal Year ended June 30, 1906.		Fiscal Year ended June 30, 1906.			
						British Empire.		All other Countries.	
		Quantity.	Value.	Quantity.	Value.	Quantity.	Value.	Quantity.	Value.
THE FOREST—*Con.*			$		$		$		$
Logs, elm	M. ft.	1,964	20,355	1,448	18,958	386	6,250	1,062	12,708
" hemlock	"	1,397	10,642	4,998	31,061			4,998	31,061
" oak	"			9	170	2	80	7	90
" pine	"	2,455	38,869	1,782	25,549	117	3,550	1,665	21 [illegible]99
" spruce	"	5,025	48,000	11,760	102,823	18	184	11,742	2,639
" tamarac	"	226	3,233						
" all other	"	58,325	359,087	52,869	378,707	1,151	23,491	51,718	355,216
Total, logs		69,392	480,186	72,866	557,268	1,674	33,555	71,192	3[illegible]213
Lumber, viz.—									
Battens	$		29,918		29,140		23,803		5,337
Basswood	M. ft.	1,463	24,267	2,078	42,374	192	4,857	1,886	37,517
Butternut	"	5	116						
Deals—Pine	St. hund.	40,463	2,076,922	39,011	2,353,927	34,404	2,171,009	4,607	182,918
" spruce and other	"	207,605	6,898,769	188,775	6,554,612	170,331	5,874,808	18,444	679,804
Deal ends	"	11,673	392,527	10,173	375,361	9,855	365,466	318	9,895
[illegible]ry	M. ft.	9	296	95	220	95	220		
Laths	M.	532,149	1,072,399	647,600	1,596,466	5,262	9,989	642,338	1,586,477
Palings	"	108	1,124	151	1,526	151	1,526		
Pickets	"	15,624	139,969	21,256	145,409	2,025	33,479	[illegible]231	111,930
Planks and boards	M. ft.	922,923	13,851,669	1,123,906	17,966,399	120,137	2,091,156	1 [illegible]769	15,875,243
Joists	"	163	2,068	276	3,641			276	3,641
Scantling	"	118,649	866,573	90,531	1,042,747	36,605	384,095	53,926	658,652
Shingles	M.	799,222	1,620,567	941,477	1,908,486	22,574	33,065	[illegible]903	1,875,421
Shooks, box	No.	46,241	1,817	20,400	831	20,400	831		
" other	$		440,701		366,947		292,671		74,276
Total, shooks			442,518		367,778		293,502		74,276
Staves, standard	M.	2	11						
" other and headings	$		145,679		111,856		40,514		71,342

Articles	Unit	Quantity	Value	Quantity	Value	Quantity	Value	Quantity	Value
All other lumber, N.E.S.	"	....	384,021	....	439,797	....	145,545	....	294,252
Total, lumber		....	27,949,353	....	32,939,739	....	11,473,034	....	2 [illegible]
Match blocks	$	....	14,310	....	29,926	....	29,721	....	205
Masts and spars	No.	1,931	8,254	1,010	8,637	377	3,954	633	4,683
Piling	$	....	142,564	....	194,073	....	20	....	[illegible]
Poles—Hop, hoop, telegraph and other	"	....	46,470	....	101,344	....	2,464	....	98,880
Posts, cedar, tamarac and other	"	....	14,253	....	14,642	....	....	....	14,642
Shingle bolts, of pine or cedar	Cords.	3,091	10,793	9,115	16,126	....	....	9,115	[illegible]
Sleepers and railroad ties	No.	739,777	181,301	1,261,252	328,383	839	334	1,260,413	328,049
Stave bolts	Cords.	606	1,484	7,643	2,496	....	....	7,643	2,496
Timber—square, viz.—									
Ash	Tons.	1,166	12,333	698	10,853	679	10,521	19	332
Birch	"	14,661	162,244	22,593	260,920	20,472	240,942	2,121	19,978
Elm	"	9,115	249,661	9,102	253,245	9,001	250,173	101	3,072
Maple	"	....	....	46	675	25	400	21	275
Oak	"	6,298	147,962	13,447	296,881	13,424	296,651	23	230
Pine, red	"	835	13,410	665	8,533	385	5,624	280	[illegible]
" white	"	38,680	995,870	42,606	983,038	42,252	976,788	354	6,250
All other	"	3,316	46,090	2,774	42,686	1,445	29,860	1,329	12,826
Total, timber, square		74,071	1,627,570	91,931	1,856,831	87,683	1,810,959	4,248	45,872
Wood, blocks and other for pulp	Cords.	593,624	2,600,814	614,286	2,649,106	....	....	614,286	2,649,106
Other articles of the forest	$	....	9,560	....	16,631	....	40	....	16,591
Grand total, produce of the forest		....	33,362,053	....	38,975,543	....	13,380,496	....	25,595,047
ANIMALS AND THEIR PRODUCE.									
Animals—									
Horses, one year old or less	No.	29	2,325	32	3,115	1	60	31	3,055
" over one year old	"	3,917	751,873	3,968	894,468	643	80,998	3,325	813,470
Cattle, one year old or less	"	1,904	92,613	2,375	34,967	330	11,082	2,045	23,885
" over one year old	"	165,367	11,350,766	174,293	11,654,584	167,759	11,227,461	6,534	427,123
Swine	"	2,811	41,308	784	12,811	208	3,118	576	9,693
Sheep, one year old or less	"	181,298	686,728	155,415	643,318	5,666	32,155	149,749	611,163
" over one year old	"	107,407	718,378	88,924	530,687	41,494	263,253	47,430	267,434
Poultry	$	....	42,314	....	58,889	....	808	....	58,081
Other	"	....	29,943	....	48,498	....	1,050	....	47,448
Total, animals		....	13,646,248	....	13,881,337	....	11,619,985	....	2,261,352
Bones	Cwt.	64,099	47,414	304,287	43,328	1,098	1,500	303,189	41,828
Butter	Lbs.	31,934,506	5,972,366	34,081,142	7,086,019	33,764,333	7,006,404	316,809	79,615
Cheese	"	215,929,753	20,318,673	215,916,157	24,441,664	215,660,543	24,408,307	255,614	33,357
Eggs	Doz.	3,655,651	727,188	2,937,777	502,033	2,878,986	486,032	58,791	1601

No. 22.—STATEMENT showing the Value of Goods exported from Canada during the Fiscal Year 1905 and 1906—*Continued.*

Articles.		Fiscal Year ended June 30, 1905.		Fiscal Year ended June 30, 1906.		Fiscal Year ended June 30, 1906.			
						British Empire.		All other Countries.	
		Quantity.	Value.	Quantity.	Value.	Quantity.	Value.	Quantity.	Value.
ANIMALS AND THEIR PRODUCE—*Con.*			$		$		$		$
Furs, dressed	$	…	27,509	…	63,149	…	8,456	…	54,693
" undressed	"	…	2,421,903	…	2,458,056	…	1,061,102	…	1,396,954
Total, furs		…	2,449,412	…	2,521,205	…	1,069,558	…	1,451,647
Grease and grease scraps	Lbs.	2,585,004	121,966	2,988,379	149,563	266,555	8,937	2,721,824	140,626
Glue stock	$	…	11,837	…	6,382	…	53	…	6,329
Hair	"	…	113,717	…	125,202	…	11,034	…	4,168
Hides and skins, other than fur	"	…	2,726,598	…	3,463,853	…	23,346	…	3,440,507
Horns and hoofs	"	…	9,485	…	14,729	…	829	…	13,900
Honey	Lbs.	20,560	1,999	42,960	3,802	29,807	2,593	13,153	1,209
Lard	"	1,309,399	113,876	135,479	13,511	122,812	12,106	12,667	1,405
Meats, viz.—									
Bacon	"	117,041,661	12,222,423	100,497,139	11,815,006	99,909,127	11,751,767	588,012	63,239
Beef	"	1,850,080	121,438	3,362,763	225,781	1,682,678	105,287	1,680,085	120,494
Hams	"	2,942,463	335,652	3,795,078	421,891	3,767,489	417,999	27,589	3,892
Mutton	"	202,948	13,387	147,222	11,006	89,064	5,989	58,158	5,017
Pork	"	2,531,032	208,140	1,034,620	75,337	907,006	62,878	127,614	12,459
Poultry, dressed or undressed	$	…	115,053	…	114,661	…	95,368	…	19,293
Game	"	…	7,518	…	3,796	…	2	…	3,794
Tongues	Lbs.	49,726	4,106	30,943	3,126	14,787	1,432	16,156	1,694
Canned	"	38,417,494	3,546,050	13,674,678	1,369,261	13,652,912	1,366,419	21,766	2,842
All other, N.E.S.	"	1,661,861	118,790	1,730,480	175,046	1,419,947	140,181	310,533	34,865
Total, meats		…	16,692,557	…	14,214,911	…	13,947,322	…	267,589
Milk and cream, condensed	$	3,589,932	268,899	1,751,789	129,233	1,643,698	121,131	108,091	8,102
Oil—									
Neat's foot and other animal, N.E.S.	"	671	516	50	23	…	…	50	23
Total, oils		671	516	50	23	…	…	50	23

Sheep pelts	No.	198,347	144,579	58,054	54,452	.....	.....	58,054	54,452
Tails	$	.....	1,554	.....	1,855	.....	27	.....	1828
Tallow	Lbs.	738,131	58,062	519,792	23,085	469,597	20,824	50,195	2,261
Wool	"	2,004,559	425,939	1,505,384	368,679	273,871	50,625	1,231,513	318,054
Other articles	$	.....	128,034	.....	141,309	.....	58,859	.....	82,450
Total, animals and their produce		.....	63,980,919	.....	67,186,175	.....	58,849,472	.....	8,336,703
AGRICULTURAL PRODUCTS.									
Balsam	$	.....	11,744	.....	10,463	.....	1,602	.....	8,861
[illegible]	Galls.	33,710	5,425	60,711	9,490	59,651	9,210	1,060	190
Flax	Cwt.	131,548	410,291	68,847	244,629	.....	.....	68,847	244,629
Fruits, viz.—									
Apples, dried	Lbs.	6,057,078	268,657	3,651,460	212,862	240,295	13,239	3,411,165	199,623
" green or ripe	Brls.	1,037,813	2,629,057	1,217,605	4,083,770	1,048,762	3,536,386	168,843	547,384
Berries of all kinds	$	.....	139,072	.....	102,868	.....	43	.....	102,825
[illegible]d or preserved	"	.....	213,513	.....	279,164	.....	259,390	.....	19,774
All [illegible]er, N.E.S.	"	.....	117,445	.....	203,645	.....	33,116	.....	170,529
Total, fruits		.....	3,367,744	.....	4,882,309	.....	3,842,174	.....	1,040,135
Grain and products of, viz.—									
Barley	Bush.	1,808,575	893,480	2,885,889	1,420,642	2,752,442	1,358,140	133,447	62,502
Beans	"	237,896	305,856	89,332	140,672	20,502	32,402	68,830	108,270
Buckwheat	"	505,885	281,094	488,365	276,031	356,995	201,751	131,370	74,280
Indian corn	"	5,650,637	2,962,367	4,866,086	2,636,210	4,669,424	2,527,718	196,662	108,492
Oats	"	3,001,991	1,087,731	5,066,931	1,858,324	4,336,277	1,639,947	730,654	218,377
Pease, whole	"	676,502	617,729	546,593	608,929	411,223	383,492	135,370	225,437
" split	"	90,422	100,724	128,293	148,395	103,788	121,273	24,505	2122
Rye	"	20,426	12,700	146,236	92,683	128,801	81,874	17,435	0,309
Wheat	"	14,848,603	12,512,641	40,987,127	34,159,082	36,556,921	30,681,348	4,430,206	3,477,734
Other grain	"	56,575	9,956	1,980	2,239	1,243	1,414	737	825
Total, grain		26,897,512	18,784,278	55,206,832	41,343,207	49,337,616	37,029,359	5,869,216	4,313,848
Bran	Cwt.	897,365	570,064	678,221	412,913	217,885	186,356	460,336	226,557
Flour of wheat	Brls.	1,323,039	5,890,258	1,532,144	6,180,754	1,415,532	5,760,168	116,612	420,586
" rye	"	5	60	3	35	.....	.....	3	35
Indian meal	"	4,821	15,987	2,180	6,714	1,837	5,797	343	917
Oatmeal	"	168,607	641,233	132,944	542,281	122,023	497,584	10,921	44,697
Meal, all other	"	8,040	23,294	11,419	32,470	9,997	29,002	1,422	3,468
Total, flour and meal		1,504,512	6,570,832	1,678,690	6,762,254	1,549,389	6,292,551	129,301	469,703

No. 22—STATEMENT showing the Value of Goods exported from Canada during the fiscal year 1905 and 1906—*Continued.*

Articles.		Fiscal Year ended June 30, 1905.		Fiscal Year ended June 30, 1906.		Fiscal Year ended June 30, 1906.			
						British Empire.		All other Countries.	
		Quantity.	Value.	Quantity.	Value.	Quantity.	Value.	Quantity.	Value.
AGRICULTURAL PRODUCTS—*Con.*			$		$		$		$
Hay	Tons.	151,702	1,268,506	206,785	1,531,719	131,538	1,020,226	75,247	511,493
Hemp	Cwt.	493	2,466	49	836	....	....	49	836
Hops	Lbs.	48,548	6,263	72,541	13,374	72,541	13,374	....	....
Malt	Bush.	11,466	9,371	8,605	6,961	8,605	6,961	....	....
Maple sugar	Lbs.	1,949,578	135,784	1,875,779	129,259	14,117	1,541	1,861,662	127,718
" syrup	Galls.	2,793	2,627	85,114	9,215	1,573	1,416	83,541	7,799
Nuts	Lbs.	39,857	3,931	85,395	4,056	50,967	1,073	34,428	2,993
Seeds—									
Clover	Bush.	85,671	520,451	211,869	1,396,805	50,311	345,706	161,558	1,051,099
Flax	"	314	479	830,670	955,699	448,937	494,698	381,733	461,001
Grass	"	92,619	66,975	43,441	55,865	3,038	3,405	40,403	52,460
All other	"	....	13,740	....	25,465	....	9,612	....	15,853
Total, seeds		....	601,645	....	2,433,834	....	853,421	....	1,580,413
Straw	Tons.	3,085	13,929	4,222	17,129	390	2,853	3,832	14,276
Tobacco, leaf	Lbs.	822,582	324,998	473,137	175,326	215	16	472,922	175,310
Trees, shrubs and plants	$	....	14,991	....	10,381	....	488	....	9,893
Vegetables—									
Canned or preserved	$	....	33,349	....	49,710	....	18,728	....	30,982
Potatoes	Bush.	746,357	409,868	1,266,896	660,960	267,494	135,613	999,402	525,347
Turnips	"	1,417,955	162,767	1,138,300	137,527	23,372	4,760	1,114,928	132,767
All other vegetables	$	....	45,826	....	82,247	....	9,068	....	73179
Total, vegetables		....	651,810	....	930,444	....	168,169	....	762,275
Cereal foods, all kinds, N.E.S	$	....	1,286,164	....	1,188,034	....	1,035,264	....	152,770
Other articles	"	....	97,546	....	99,982	....	42,744	....	57,238
Grand total, agricultural products		....	34,140,409	....	60,215,735	....	50,508,798	....	9,706,937

MANUFACTURES.									
Acid, sulphuric	Lbs.	232,373	2,722	59,393	770	....	....	59,393	770
Agricultural implements	$	....	2,342,826	....	2,499,104	....	999,494	....	1,499,610
Brass in bar, bolts, sheets, &c	Lbs.	2,468,382	534,598	3,091,997	619,264	604,555	120,910	2,487,442	498,354
" manufactures of	$	....	7,004	....	1,912	....	712	....	1,200
Books, pamphlets, maps, &c.	"	....	268,266	....	325,254	....	134,566	....	[illegible]
[illegible]	Cwt.	3,422	31,724	10,528	39,458	3,726	30,102	6,802	9,356
Bricks	M.	854	6,216	741	6,113	276	2,926	465	[illegible]
Buttons	$	....	3,016	....	5,566	....	....	....	5,566
Candles	Lbs.	45,659	6,720	140,313	10,227	136,162	9,631	4,151	596
Cartridges, gun, rifle and pistol	$	....	114,979	....	108,901	....	17,918	....	90,983
Charcoal	"	....	2,651	....	53,840	....	3,000	....	50,840
Cement	"	....	7,179	....	13,798	....	4,077	....	9,721
Cigars	"	....	44	....	1,023	....	....	....	1,023
Clay, manufactures of	"	....	16,395	....	....	....	....	....	....
Clothing and wearing apparel	"	....	193,470	....	114,664	....	56,563	....	58,101
Coke	Tons.	128,258	[illegible]	59,541	281,663	....	....	59,541	281,663
Cordage, ropes and twine	$	....	350,186	....	500,958	....	100,719	....	400,239
Cotton fabrics	Yds.	13,164,613	1,083,255	15,444,485	1,267,712	3,507,916	346,502	11,936,569	921,210
Cottons, other	$	....	45,069	....	42,727	....	21,517	....	21,210
Cotton waste	Lbs.	1,724,698	69,813	1,146,021	53,432	11,126	888	1,134,895	52,544
Drugs, chemicals and medicines, N.E.S	$	....	1,401,040	....	1,837,298	....	552,073	....	1,285,225
Dye stuffs	"	....	23,733	....	21,129	....	3,083	....	18,046
Electrical apparatus	"	....	79,083	....	180,339	....	10,139	....	[illegible]
Electrotypes	"	....	8,566	....	5,061	....	599	....	4,462
Extract of hemlock bark	Brls.	4,796	57,861	5,045	66,169	4,105	56,259	940	[illegible]
Explosives and fulminates, N.E.S.	Lbs.	620,423	[illegible]	861,261	253,085	531,364	52,888	329,897	[illegible]
Felt, manufactures of	$	....	5,005	....	981	....	92	....	889
Fertilizers	"	....	230,224	....	239,400	....	11,105	....	228,295
Fur, manufactures of	"	....	21,023	....	33,347	....	15,788	....	17,559
Glass and glassware, N.E.S	"	....	24,992	....	14,842	....	7,492	....	7,350
Grindstones, manufactured	"	....	28,094	....	15,921	....	459	....	15,462
Gypsum or plaster, ground	"	....	3,132	....	1,603	....	960	....	643
Hats and caps	"	....	11,314	....	11,098	....	6,553	....	4,545
Household effects, N.E.S	"	....	[illegible]	....	1,761,649	....	121,647	....	[illegible]
Ice	"	....	11,240	....	22,090	....	....	....	22,090
India rubber, manufactures of	"	....	197,033	....	282,164	....	230,451	....	51,713
India rubber, scrap and other	Lbs.	1,906,723	[illegible]	3,117,594	218,273	45,300	714	3,072,294	[illegible]
Iron and steel and manufactures of, viz.—									
Stoves	No.	1,468	18,192	1,066	11,885	918	9,814	148	2,071
Castings, N.E.S	$	....	81,492	....	61,347	....	31,326	....	30,021
Pig-iron	Tons.	5,707	[illegible]	697	17,858	213	4,256	484	[illegible]
Machinery, N.E.S.	$	....	782,835	....	882,194	....	194,921	....	[illegible]
Sewing machines	No.	1,139	26,913	1,253	35,225	87	1,846	1,166	33,379
Type-writers	"	3,755	129,739	4,730	159,933	2,582	88,303	2,148	[illegible]
Scrap-iron or steel	Cwt.	260,126	[illegible]	606,659	355,878	9,877	9,198	596,782	346,680
Hardware, N.E.S.	$	....	221,994	....	243,353	....	150,270	....	93,083
Steel and manufactures of	"	....	[illegible]	....	626,733	....	137,204	....	489,529
Total, manufactures of iron and steel		....	2,108,688	....	2,394,406	....	627,138	....	[illegible]

No. 22.—STATEMENT showing the Value of Goods exported from Canada during the Fiscal Years 1905 and 1906—*Continued.*

Articles.		Fiscal Year ended June 30, 1905.		Fiscal Year ended June 30, 1906.		Fiscal Year ended June 30, 1906. British Empire.		All other Countries.	
		Quantity.	Value.	Quantity.	Value.	Quantity.	Value.	Quantity.	Value.
MANUFACTURES—*Con.*			$		$		$		$
Jeweller's sweepings	$		79,804		90,751		36,557		54,194
Junk	Cwt.	96,048	201,346	600,815	500,551	29,723	98,577	571,092	401,974
Lamps and lanterns	$		7,582		7,561		4,696		2,865
Leather—									
Sole	Lbs.	8,446,126	1,678,377	7,605,843	1,592,713	7,370,859	1,531,808	234,984	60,905
Upper	"	726,847	171,706	1,098,691	273,116	1,082,893	270,157	15,798	2,959
N.E.S.	"	1,362,555	295,296	1,121,854	401,001	845,861	339,768	275,993	61,233
Boots and shoes	$		176,691		146,115		98,261		47,854
Harness and saddlery	"		16,353		10,438		3,952		6,486
Other manufactures of	"		42,108		28,771		16,200		12,571
Total, leather and manufactures of			2,380,531		2,452,154		2,260,146		192,008
Lime	$		75,498		73,534		13,249		60,285
Liquors—									
Ale and beer	Galls.	23,686	15,361	9,960	8,470	1,331	517	8,629	7,953
Brandy	"	1,310	4,724	476	2,063	122	218	354	1,845
Gin	"	21,360	27,219	27,899	45,595	17	15	27,882	45,580
Rum	"	6,670	1,720	5,077	1,554	3,224	923	1,853	631
Whisky	"	240,881	650,725	296,877	972,421	12,583	40,948	284,294	931,473
Wines	"	12,743	21,825	9,555	19,251	3,217	4,831	6,338	14,420
Other spirits	"	184,163	77,721	296,458	103,771	96,381	31,191	200,077	72,580
Total, liquors		490,813	799,295	646,302	1,153,125	116,875	78,643	529,427	1,074,482
Metals, N.O.P.	$		278,344		60,776		21,619		39,157
Molasses	Galls.	43,133	12,486	99,229	25,640	61,036	17,845	38,193	7,795

Musical instruments, viz.—									
Organs	No.	4,256	233,553	3,822	210,279	3,460	1-7,755	362	22,524
Pianos	"	263	61,586	310	73,878	110	28,349	200	45,529
Other	$	....	11,790	....	16,915	....	3,934	....	12,981
Total, musical instruments		....	306,929	....	301,072	....	220,038	....	81,034
Oakum	Cwt.	44	247	27	113	25	89	2	24
Oil cake	"	90,316	101,641	234,218	289,591	188,367	237,528	45,851	52,063
Oil, N.E.S.	Galls.	448,846	55,991	1,002,508	106,187	104,923	48,405	897,585	57,782
Paper—									
Wall	Rolls.	313,986	28,837	548,544	38,267	528,984	34,764	19,560	3,503
N.E.S.	$	....	1,782,413	....	1,989,353	....	1,777,510	....	211,843
Photographs	"	....	4,710	....	4,548	....	1,048	....	3,500
Plumbago, manufactures of	"	....	1,478	....	2,948	....	285	....	2,663
Rags	Lbs.	12,697,149	214,357	17,307,709	229,393	19,993,307	79,294	15,314,402	150,099
Sails	$	....	....	....	1,014	....	1,014	....	....
Ships sold to other couutries	No. and Tons.	10 3,014	78,888	8 4,081	62,670	2 221	1,810	6 3,860	60,860
Soap	Lbs.	725,602	30,868	1,265,957	53,076	1,069,865	41,296	196,092	11,780
Starch	"	163,835	4,789	103,271	5,303	99,880	5,078	3,391	225
Stone, ornamental, viz.—									
Granite, marble, &c., dressed	$	....	3,902	....	2,618	....	1,866	....	752
Building, viz.: freestone, limestone, &c	"	....	276	....	292	....	292	....	....
Total, stone and marble		....	4,178	....	2,910	....	2,158	....	752
Sugar of all kinds, N.E.S.	Lbs.	479,145	21,435	714,697	30,234	266,634	10,361	448,063	19,873
Sugar hse syrup	Galls.	73,909	11,554	279,251	15,836	....	....	279,251	15,836
Tar	$	....	28,865	....	98,850	....	14,537	....	84,313
Tin, manufactures of	"	....	51,294	....	31,458	....	6,404	....	25,054
[illegible], viz.—									
Cigars	M.	555	8,136	136	3,131	112	2,867	24	264
Cigarettes	"	1,308	1,463	549	1,286	189	522	360	764
Snuff	Lbs.	11	5	7	4	....	....	7	4
Stems and cuttings	"	612,026	41,429	772,853	49,808	24,703	2,229	746,150	47,579
All ther, N.E.S.	"	303,931	111,015	260,181	86,184	104,278	38,121	155,903	48,063
Total, tobacco		....	162,048	....	140,413	....	43,739	....	96,674
Tow	Cwt.	4,389	26,394	1,383	12,786	....	....	1,383	12,786

No. 22.—STATEMENT showing the Value of Goods exported from Canada during the Fiscal Years 1905 and 1906—*Concluded.*

Articles.		Fiscal Year ended June 30, 1905.		Fiscal Year ended June 30, 1906.		Fiscal Year ended June 30, 1906.			
						British Empire.		All other Countries.	
		Quantity.	Value.	Quantity.	Value.	Quantity.	Value.	Quantity.	Value.
MANUFACTURES—*Con.*			$		$		$		$
Vehicles, viz.—									
Carriages	No.	421	36,019	402	32,595	348	27,074	54	5,521
" parts of	$	....	18,076	....	19,124	....	6,356	....	12,768
Carts	No.	673	14,608	1,052	23,587	12	1,010	1,040	22,577
Wagons	"	122	8,959	184	9,595	13	739	171	8,856
Automobiles	"	....	....	116	152,097	25	26,325	91	125,772
Bicycles	"	2,388	60,151	2,450	63,427	2,335	60,816	115	2,611
" parts of	$	....	31,597	....	40,733	....	37,911	....	2,822
Other vehicles	"	....	151,546	....	150,418	....	32,320	....	118,098
Vinegar	Galls.	1,424	454	463	111	313	69	150	42
Wood, viz.—									
Barrels, empty	No.	30,290	62,473	30,063	45,133	4,473	4,614	25,590	40,519
Household furniture	$	....	312,146	....	289,241	....	260,143	....	29,098
Doors, sashes and blinds	"	....	128,770	....	164,227	....	146,352	....	17,875
Matches and match splints	"	....	151,972	....	109,145	....	106,225	....	2,920
Mouldings, trimmings and other house furnishings	"	....	3,846	....	5,149	....	4,892	....	257
Pails, tubs, churns and other hollow woodenware	"	....	5,227	....	8,368	....	4,740	....	3,628
Spool wood and spools	"	....	86,973	....	186,857	....	185,375	....	1,482
Wood pulp	"	....	3,399,655	....	3,478,150	....	999,960	....	2,478,190
Other manufactures of	"	....	362,926	....	389,941	....	284,835	....	105,106
Total, wood manufactures		....	4,513,988	....	4,676,211	....	1,997,136	....	2,679,075
Woollens	$	....	75,515	....	85,180	....	63,381	....	21,799
Other articles	"	....	1,470,908	....	1,311,845	....	428,770	....	883,075
Grand total, manufactures		....	24,643,034	....	27,650,278	....	11,285,562	....	[illegible]716
MISCELLANEOUS ARTICLES.									
Coffee	Lbs.	146,604	15,819	359,475	39,345	6,944	1,414	352,531	37,931
Dried fruit, N.E.S.	"	93,513	5,942	226,838	8,322	71,585	3,276	155,253	5,046
Rice	"	552,733	11,820	40,262	1,296	16,962	358	23,300	938

Rice meal	"	2,365,760	22,030	2,675,200	29,930	2,675,200	29,930	....	....
Paintings in oil or water	$	....	....	....	97,772	....	73,606	....	24,166
Tea	Lbs.	18,921,841	442,962	2,387,358	562,059	218,050	41,774	2,169,308	520,285
Other miscellaneous articles	$	....	1,510,105	....	135,923	....	33,460	....	2,063
Total, miscellaneous articles		....	2,008,678	....	874,647	....	183,818	....	690,829
BULLION AND COIN.									
Bullion, gold / " silver / Gold coin / Silver " / Copper "	$	....	1,844,811	....	9,928,828	....	6,043	....	9,922,785
Grand total		....	203,316,872	....	256,586,630	....	144,311,803	....	112,274,827
RECAPITULATION.									
Produce of the mine		....	32,192,070	....	35,706,030	....	2,075,706	....	33,630,324
" fisheries		....	11,144,898	....	16,049,394	....	8,021,908	....	8,027,486
" forest		....	33,362,053	....	38,975,543	....	13,380,496	....	25,595,047
Animals and their produce		....	63,980,919	....	67,186,175	....	58,849,472	....	8,336,703
Agricultural products		....	34,140,409	....	60,215,735	....	50,508,798	....	9,706,937
Manufactures		....	24,643,034	....	27,650,278	....	11,285,562	....	16,364,716
Miscellaneous articles		....	2,008,678	....	874,647	....	183,818	....	690,829
Total		....	201,472,061	....	246,657,802	....	144,305,760	....	102,352,042
Bullion and coin		....	1,844,811	....	9,928,828	....	6,043	....	9,922,785
Grand total		....	203,316,872	....	256,586,630	....	144,311,803	....	112,274,827

No. 23.—STATEMENT showing the value of Merchandise Imported into and Exported from Canada through the United States from and to Foreign Countries; Distinguishing the countries whence Imported and to which Exported during the fiscal year 1906.

Countries whence Imported and to which Exported.	Value of Merchandise Imported from foreign Countries through the United States.	Value of Merchandise Exported to foreign Countries through the United States.
	$	$
Great Britain	13,283,428	31,769,234
Aden	238	6,585
Australia	22,247	1,265,869
British Africa	3,276	203,547
" East Indies	1,447,314	30,721
" Guiana	769,158	62,338
" Honduras	14,435	3,440
" West Indies	1,044,394	437,341
Cyprus	....	3,090
Gibraltar	....	2,661
Hong Kong	4,502	20
Malta	101	26,266
Newfoundland	89	9,377
New Zealand	21,110	449,268
Total, British Empire	16,610,292	34,269,757
Arabia	17,469	....
Argentina	743,746	1,398,339
Austria	266,784	9,657
Belgium	219,575	148,089
Brazil	160,017	313,608
Bulgaria	1,119	985
Central American States	38,241	52,576
Chili	4,603	83,271
China	80,523	14,746
Cuba	255,652	340,428
Denmark	9,916	143,663
Danish West Indies	....	8,466
Dutch East Indies	....	5,697
Dutch West Indies	....	5,465
Dutch Guiana	....	11,863
Ecuador	316	4,981
Egypt	10,358	6,009
France	2,579,112	639,677
French Africa	5,211	11,232
French West Indies	....	20,736
Germany	2,473,410	1,538,729
Greece	73,387	....
Hawaii	598	825
Hayti	....	29,044
Holland	66,692	510,992
Italy	218,135	187,975
Japan	281,065	41,207
Mexico	38,188	88,622
Panama	....	55,907
Paraguay	....	176
Persia	7,569	....
Peru	2,618	9,265
Philippines	....	1,506
Porto Rico	....	184,198
Portugal	21,559	8,538
Roumania	23	41,720
Russia	49,271	212,219
Samoa	....	210
San Domingo	165,218	2,897
Spain	99,147	24,854
St. Pierre	....	2,749
Sweden & Norway	27,959	204,687
Switzerland	1,064,448	8,930
Tunis	....	5,524

No. 23.—STATEMENT showing the value of Merchandise Imported into and Exported from Canada through the United States, &c.—*Concluded.*

Countries whence Imported and to which Exported.	Value of Merchandise Imported from foreign Countries through the United States.	Value of Merchandise Exported to foreign Countries through the United States.
	$	$
Turkey	179,620	8,277
U.S. of Colombia	5,012	22,694
Uruguay	98,109	99,389
Venezuela	56,158	7,583
Total, other countries	9,320,828	6,518,145
Grand total	25,936,120	40,787,902

No. 24.—COMPARATIVE STATEMENT of Goods remaining in Warehouse in 1904, 1905 and 1906.

ARTICLES.		REMAINING IN WAREHOUSE, JUNE 30, 1904.		REMAINING IN WAREHOUSE, JUNE 30, 1905.		REMAINING IN WAREHOUSE, JUNE 30, 1906.	
		Quantity.	Value.	Quantity.	Value.	Quantity.	Value.
			$		$		$
Breadstuffs—							
Wheat	Bush.	5,235	4,863	61,351	44,835	40,131	33,778
Other breadstuffs	$		150,665		382,550		183,494
Coal, bituminous	Tons.	398,067	893,944	427,904	927,550	387,138	838,471
Cotton and manufactures of	$		102,322		108,975		115,954
Drugs	"		168,979		96,683		89,420
Fancy goods	"		9,006		7,488		5,520
Fish	"		62,581		78,792		84,008
Flax and manufactures of	"		19,665		18,025		21,763
Fruits and nuts	"		346,030		162,450		170,086
Glass and manufactures of	"		10,501		4,534		10,429
Iron and steel "	"		281,776		242,853		196,428
Leather "	"		6,672		10,069		12,005
Oils	Galls.	1,992,085	218,052	1,049,560	113,148	1,003,410	115,067
Paper and manufactures of	"		26,092		25,021		28,518
Silk	"		60,865		55,594		40,917
Spirits and wines—							
Brandy	Galls.	216,142	264,820	175,733	297,792	167,063	285,721
Gin	"	280,570	122,944	280,769	139,490	246,750	115,203
Rum	"	169,274	26,343	65,915	29,613	59,143	37,318
Whisky	"	246,942	414,119	266,417	398,256	259,245	389,983
Wines of all kinds, except sparkling	"	241,890	189,062	270,045	206,153	270,804	215,403
Wines, sparkling	"		100,987		120,025		111,305
Sugar above No. 16 D.S	Lbs.	1,253,084	32,644	2,086,781	106,854	1,099,640	30,520
Sugar not above No. 16 D.S.	"	83,015,393	1,722,151	207,219,653	3,195,478	119,082,623	1,418,412
Molasses	Galls.	1,773,199	134,172	356,186	91,921	626,156	115,722
Tobacco, manufactures of—							
Cigars	Lbs.	27,667	75,543	25,478	104,285	24,934	101,280
Cigarettes	"	1,597	5,937	3,232	4,245	3,178	3,297
All other	"	300,489	99,833	43,916	20,788	66,674	29,906
Woollens	$		174,288		87,650		198,323
All other articles	"		1,412,412		1,846,850		1,509,117
Grand totals			7,137,268		8,977,947		6,497,368

No. 25.—STATEMENT of the Quantity and Value of Merchandise received from Foreign Countries for immediate transit through Canada and transhipped at the Port of Montreal for the United States and other countries during the Fiscal Year ended June 30, 1906.

Articles.	Countries.	Received from		Shipped to	
		Quantity.	Value.	Quantity.	Value.
THE MINE.			$		$
Ore and other produce of the mine	United States		4,970		9,767
	Germany		150		
	France		4,025		
	Great Britain		5,592		4,970
	Total		14,737		14,737
THE FISHERIES.					
Salmon and other articles of the fisheries	Great Britain		24,813		3,330
	Newfoundland		12,251		
	France		1,525		
	Belgium		31,590		
	British Africa				13,950
	United States		17,280		70,179
	Total		87,459		87,459
THE FOREST.		M. ft.		M. ft.	
Planks and boards	United States	5,024	143,340		
	British Africa			776	22,586
	Belgium			8	250
	Great Britain			4,240	120,504
	Total	5,024	143,340	5,024	143,340
Lumber and timber, N.E.S	United States		53,497		15,825
	British Africa				24,711
	Great Britain		19,175		32,136
	Total		72,672		72,672
Total, produce of the forest			216,012		216,012
ANIMALS AND THEIR PRODUCE.		No.		No.	
Horses	United States	396	45,975	6	1,600
	British Africa			355	32,375
	Great Britain	6	1,600	41	13,600
	Total	402	47,575	402	47,575
Cattle	United States	20,390	1,182,085		
	British Africa			1	175
	Great Britain			20,389	1,181,910
	Total	20,390	1,182,085	20,390	1,182,085
Sheep	United States	4,231	31,986		
	British Africa			389	1,640
	Great Britain			3,842	30,346
	Total	4,231	31,986	4,231	31,986

SESSIONAL PAPER No. 11

No. 25.—STATEMENT of the Quantity and Value of Merchandise received from Foreign Countries, &c.—*Continued.*

Articles.	Countries.	Received from		Shipped to	
		Quantity.	Value.	Quantity.	Value.
MEATS—*Con.*		Lbs.	$	Lbs.	$
Butter	United States	91,483	18,296	....	....
	Great Britain	....	....	91,483	18,296
	Total	91,483	18,296	91,483	18,296
Furs	United States	....	101,922	....	484
	Great Britain	....	484	....	101,922
	Total	....	102,406	....	102,406
Lard	United States	40,253,825	3,981,728	....	....
	France	....	....	190,763	19,076
	British Africa	....	....	114,695	11,469
	Belgium	....	....	278,265	27,826
	Germany	....	....	6,875	687
	Newfoundland	....	....	238,399	23,838
	Great Britain	....	....	39,424,828	3,898,832
	Total	40,253,825	3,981,728	40,253,825	3,981,728
Cheese	United States	434,315	47,184	52,585	6,053
	Belgium	47,835	5,523	....	....
	Great Britain	4,750	530	434,315	47,184
	Total	486,900	53,237	486,900	53,237
Bacon and hams	United States	8,157,296	725,071	....	....
	Newfoundland	....	....	53,800	6,250
	Great Britain	....	....	8,103,496	718,821
	Total	8,157,296	725,071	8,157,296	725,071
Pork	United States	3,020,208	284,192	....	....
	Newfoundland	....	....	2,274,557	208,921
	British Africa	....	....	447,384	44,737
	Great Britain	....	....	298,267	30,534
	Total	3,020,208	284,192	3,020,208	284,192
Meats, all other	United States	99,874,260	9,943,260	370,945	36,150
	France	101,960	10,100	55,160	5,516
	British Africa	....	....	1,497,379	149,039
	Newfoundland	....	....	1,917,303	190,209
	Germany	....	....	5,580	558
	Great Britain	268,985	26,050	96,398,838	9,597,938
	Total	100,245,205	9,979,410	100,245,205	9,979,410
Tallow	United States	365,562	35,177	....	....
	Great Britain	....	....	365,562	35,177
	Total	365,562	35,177	365,562	35,177

No. 25.—STATEMENT of the Quantity and Value of Merchandise received from Foreign Countries, &c.—*Continued.*

Articles.	Countries.	Received from		Shipped to	
		Quantity.	Value.	Quantity.	Value.
ANIMALS AND THEIR PRODUCTS—*Con.*			$		$
Other articles of the animals	United States		25,855		247,601
	France		60,252		
	Belgium		1,000		
	British Africa				25,855
	Great Britain		186,349		
	Total		273,456		273,456
Total, animals and produce			16,714,619		16,714,619
AGRICULTURAL PRODUCE.					
Fruits, all kinds	United States		151,348		31,010
	Belgium		21,530		
	B. W. Indies		305		
	France		2,375		
	Newfoundland				305
	Mexico				450
	Great Britain		7,555		151,348
	Total		183,113		183,113
Grain, other	United States		1,635		600
	Germany		600		
	Cuba				502
	Newfoundland				126
	Great Britain		126		1,133
	Total		2,361		2,361
		Brls.		Brls	
Flour of wheat	United States	203,891	837,763		
	British Africa			19,222	78,182
	Newfoundland			33,659	130,135
	Belgium			1,300	7,650
	Great Britain			149,710	621,796
	Total	203,891	837,763	203,891	837,763
Flour of meal, N.E.S	Great Britain		250		
	United States				250
	Total		250		250
		Bush.		Bush.	
Seeds, flax	United States	2,300	2,212	120	150
	British Africa			2,300	2,212
	Great Britain	120	150		
	Total	2,420	2,362	2,420	2,362

No. 25.—STATEMENT of the Quantity and Value of Merchandise received from Foreign Countries, &c.—*Continued.*

Articles.	Countries.	Received from Quantity.	Received from Value.	Shipped to Quantity.	Shipped to Value.
			$		$
AGRICULTURAL PRODUCE—*Con.*					
Other articles of agriculture	United States		1,350		47,220
	Belgium		13,025		
	Germany		1,800		
	France		16,430		
	British Africa				100
	Great Britain		20,465		5,750
	Total		53,070		53,070
Total, agricultural products			1,078,919		1,078,919
MANUFACTURES.					
Cotton and manufactures	United States		619,507		1,685
	Belgium		715		
	Great Britain		970		619,507
	Total		621,192		621,192
Drugs, dyes and chemicals	United States		43,256		72,428
	Belgium		33,237		
	Newfoundland				3,110
	British Africa				33,886
	Great Britain		39,191		6,260
	Total		115,684		115,684
Earthenware and china	United States				81,280
	Belgium		59,068		
	Germany		2,805		
	Newfoundland				300
	Great Britain		19,707		
	Total		81,580		81,580
Glass and glassware	Belgium		246,611		
	Germany		1,410		
	United States				252,696
	Great Britain		4,675		
	Total		252,696		252,696
Iron and steel	United States		62,288		59,266
	Germany		9,230		300
	Belgium		2,975		
	France		180		
	Newfoundland				668
	British Africa				22,070
	Great Britain		46,881		39,250
	Total		121,554		121,554

No. 25.—STATEMENT of the Quantity and Value of Merchandise received from Foreign Countries, &c.—*Continued.*

ARTICLES.	COUNTRIES.	RECEIVED FROM		SHIPPED TO	
		Quantity.	Value.	Quantity.	Value.
MANUFACTURES—*Con.*			$		$
Leather and manufactures	United States		130,350		621
	Great Britain		621		130,350
	Total		130,971		130,971
Oil cake	United States		256,412		
	Great Britain				11,834
	Belgium				244,578
	Total		256,412		256,412
		Galls.		Galls.	
Oils of all kinds	United States	1,325,255	191,365	213,254	124,202
	France	50	400		
	Belgium	19,500	10,195		
	Newfoundland			124,518	17,613
	Mexico			400	120
	British Africa			3,690	2,002
	Cuba			9,670	350
	Germany			21,680	10,979
	Great Britain	195,374	107,503	1,166,967	154,197
	Total	1,540,179	309,463	1,540,179	309,463
Paper and manufactures	United States		104,460		23,635
	Belgium		6,425		
	France		120		
	British Africa				3,390
	Newfoundland				320
	Great Britain		17,090		100,750
	Total		128,095		128,095
		Galls.		Galls.	
Spirits and wines	United States	1,626	3,046	196,811	486,711
	Belgium	40,588	154,763		
	Holland	3,025	5,500		
	Germany	2,713	6,182		
	Mexico			597	1,715
	Newfoundland			330	660
	France	18,942	73,571		
	Great Britain	132,231	248,592	1,387	2,568
	Total	199,125	491,654	199,125	491,654
		Lbs.		Lbs.	
Sugar	United States	3,449,000	118,640		
	Great Britain			3,449,000	118,640
	Total	3,449,000	118,640	3,449,000	118,640

No. 25.—STATEMENT of the Quantity and Value of Merchandise received from Foreign Countries, &c.—*Concluded.*

Articles.	Countries.	Received from		Shipped to	
		Quantity.	Value.	Quantity.	Value.
MANUFACTURES—*Con.*		Lbs.	$	Lbs.	$
Glucose	United States	4,925,102	119,082		
	British Africa			350,756	8,237
	Newfoundland			41,872	800
	Great Britain			4,532,474	110,045
	Total	4,925,102	119,082	4,925,102	119,082
Tobacco	United States	505,082	51,498		
	Belgium			35,915	17,957
	Newfoundland			57,741	12,624
	Great Britain			411,426	20,917
	Total	505,082	51,498	505,082	51,498
Tea	United States	4,717	471	584,358	150,688
	Great Britain	584,358	150,688	4,717	471
	Total	589,075	151,159	589,075	151,159
Wood and manufactures of	United States		145,562		20,550
	British Africa				41,605
	Belgium				1,250
	Newfoundland				3,330
	Great Britain		20,550		99,377
	Total		166,112		166,112
Other articles	United States		528,877		354,510
	Germany		17,211		
	British Africa		50		85,910
	Newfoundland		30		18,767
	Holland		1,384		
	Mexico		8,000		2,700
	France		15,988		279
	Belgium		137,943		21,193
	Cuba				100
	Great Britain		177,443		403,467
	Total		886,926		886,926
Total, manufactures			4,002,718		4,002,718

No. 25.—SUMMARY STATEMENT of the Value of Merchandise received from Foreign Montreal for the United States and other Countries during the Fiscal Year Montreal for Transhipment to

	Countries Received from.									
	Great Britain.	United States.	France.	Germany.	Newfoundland.	Belgium	B. W. Indies	Holland.	Br. Africa	Mexico.
	$	$	$	$	$	$	$	$	$	$
Produce of the mine.	5,592	4,970	4,025	150	....	....	......	......	.....	....
" fisheries.	24,813	17,280	1,525	....	12,251	31,590	......	......	....	....
" forest...	19,175	196,837	....	....	...	....	.....	... .	.....	....
Animals and their produce	215,013	16,422,731	70,352	....	.....	6,523	......	......	....	....
Agricultural products...	28,546	994,308	18,805	2,400	.....	34,555	305	.....	....	....
Manufactures.......	833,911	2,374,814	90,259	36,838	30	651,932	......	6,884	50	8,000
Total......	1,127,050	20,010,940	184,966	39,388	12,281	724,600	305	6,884	50	8,000

Total value of goods in transit through Montreal for transhipment for foreign countries :—

Fiscal year ended June 30, 1886	$	5,745,606
" " 1887		7,645,393
" " 1888		8,058,888
" 1889		10,314,396
" 1890		12,714,705
" 1891		13,202,292
" 1892		9,423,862
" 1893		9,313,904
" 1894		8,186,145
" 1895		8,027,366
" 1896		14,191,628
" 1897		11,077,825
" 1898		9,378,657
" 1899		10,485,519
" 1900		13,160,009
" 1901		10,707,369
" 1902		11,382,567
" 1903		11,689,912
" 1904		15,224,361
" 1905		14,095,449
" 1906		22,114,464

Countries for immediate Transit through Canada and transhipped at the Port of ended June 30, 1906; also Statement of Value of Goods in Transit through Foreign Countries from 1886 to 1906.

	Countries Shipped to.									
Total.	Great Britain.	United States.	British Africa.	Belgium	France.	Germany.	Newfoundland.	Mexico.	Cuba.	Total.
$	$	$ cts.	$	$	$	$	$	$	$	$
14,737	4,970	9,767	......	......	......	......	......	......	......	14,737
87,459	3,330	70,179	13,950	......	......	......	......	......	......	87,459
216,012	152,640	15,825	47,297	250	......	......	......	......	......	216,012
16,714,619	15,674,560	291,888	265,290	27,826	24,592	1,245	429,218	......	......	16,714,619
1,078,919	780,027	79,230	80,494	7,650	......	......	130,566	450	502	1,078,919
4,002,718	1,817,633	1,628,272	197,100	284,978	279	11,279	58,192	4,535	450	4,002,718
22,114,464	18,433,160	2,095,161	604,131	320,704	24,871	12,524	617,976	4,985	952	22,114,464

No. 26.—Statement showing the Value of Goods Imported and Exported Seaward into and from Canada, via St. Lawrence River; also the Value of Goods transhipped at Montreal for Foreign Countries, both Inwards and Outwards, during the Fiscal Year ended June 30, 1906.

Total imports from sea via St. Lawrence River.................... $	42,599,039
" exports for " "	86,857,711
" merchandise received at Montreal for transhipment for foreign ports..........	22,114,464
Total trade via St. Lawrence River....................	$ 151,571,214

PART II

GENERAL STATEMENTS

OF

IMPORTS, EXPORTS AND SHIPPING

OF THE

DOMINION OF CANADA

FOR THE

FISCAL YEAR ENDED JUNE 30

1906

No. 1.—GENERAL STATEMENT (by Countries) of the Total Quantities and Values of sumption and the Duties Collected thereon in the Dominion

(Abbreviations: B. E., British East; B. W., British West; F. W.,

Articles Imported.	Countries.	Total Imports.		Entered		
				General Tariff.		
		Quantity.	Value.	Quantity.	Value.	Duty.
DUTIABLE GOODS.		Galls.	$	Galls.	$	$ cts.
Ale, beer and porter, in bottles.	Great Britain...	175,290	153,779	182,183	158,146	43,723 92
	B. W. Indies..	7	5	7	5	1 68
	Newfoundland..	7	12	7	12	1 68
	Aust.-Hungary..	1,340	728	1,440	805	345 60
	Belgium........	164	55	164	55	39 36
	France.........	3	1	3	1	0 72
	Germany.......	4,347	2,784	320	269	76 80
	United States...	352,742	204,205	355,897	202,012	85,415 28
	Total	533,900	361,569	540,021	361,305	129,605 04
" " casks..	Great Britain...	9,002	3,339	8,169	3,246	1,307 04
	B. W. Indies...	36	15	36	15	5 76
	Aust.-Hungary..	4,077	1,565	2,289	986	366 24
	Germany.......	16,380	5,384	....	....	....
	United States...	197,382	40,208	193,871	37,777	31,019 36
	Total	226,877	50,511	204,365	42,024	32,698 40
Ginger ale............	Great Britain...	....	15,798	....	987	197 40
	United States...	....	373	....	373	74 60
	Total	....	16,171	....	1,360	272 00
Animals, living, viz.:—		Lbs.		Lbs.		
Hogs......................	United States...	6,585,642	386,995	124,795	7,233	1,871 93
		No.		No.		
Horned cattle	United States...	14,297	186,338	14,277	182,963	36,592 60
Horses	Great Britain...	1	25	1	25	5 00
	B. W. Indies...	1	50	1	50	10 00
	United States...	17,147	1,078,813	16,338	744,513	148,902 60
	Total	17,149	1,078,888	16,340	744,588	148,917 60
Sheep	Great Britain...	138	1,950	....	....	....
	United States...	69,985	199,962	69,985	199,962	39,992 40
	Total	70,123	201,912	69,985	199,962	39,992 40
All other, not elsewhere specified...	Great Britain...	....	294	....	167	33 40
	British Africa..	....	1	....	1	0 20
	B. W. Indies...	....	42	....	42	8 40
	France.........	....	4	....	4	0 80
	Germany.	....	186	....	....	....
	United States...	....	55,190	....	52,444	10,488 80
	Total	....	55,717	....	52,658	10,531 60

Merchandise imported; also of the Quantities and Values of the same entered for Con-
of Canada, during the Fiscal Year ended June 30, 1906.

French West; Dan. W., Danish West; N.E.S., not elsewhere specified.)

FOR HOME CONSUMPTION.

Preferential Tariff.			Surtax Tariff.			Total.		
Quantity.	Value.	Duty.	Quantity.	Value.	Duty.	Quantity.	Value.	Duty Collected.
Galls.	$	$ cts.	Galls.	$	$ cts.	Galls.	$	$ cts.
			86	61	27 52	182,269	158,207	43,751 44
						7	5	1 68
						7	12	1 68
						1,440	805	345 60
						164	55	39 36
						3	1	0 72
			3,767	2,481	1,205 47	4,087	2,750	1,282 27
			75	42	24 00	355,972	202,054	85,439 28
			3,928	2,584	1,256 99	543,949	363,889	130,862 03
						8,169	3,246	1,307 04
						36	15	5 76
						2,289	986	366 24
			16,070	5,391	3,428 31	16,070	5,391	3,428 31
			4,053	2,171	864 64	197,924	39,948	31,884 00
			20,123	7,562	4,292 95	224,488	49,586	36,991 35
	13,414	1,788 55					14,401	1,985 95
							373	74 60
	13,414	1,788 55					14,774	2,060 55
Lbs.			Lbs.			Lbs.		
						124,795	7,233	1,871 93
No.			No.			No.		
						14,277	182,963	36,592 60
						1	25	5 00
						1	50	10 00
						16,338	744,513	148,902 60
						16,340	744,588	148,917 60
						69,985	199,962	39,992 40
						69,985	199,962	39,992 40
	37	4 94		90	24 00		294	62 34
							1	0 20
							42	8 40
							4	0 80
				186	49 59		186	49 59
				102	27 20		52,546	10,516 00
	37	4 94		378	100 79		53,073	10,637 33

No. 1.—General Statement

Articles Imported.	Countries.	Total Imports.		Entered		
				General Tariff.		
		Quantity.	Value.	Quantity.	Value.	Duty.
DUTIABLE GOODS—*Con.*			$		$	$ cts.
Antiseptic surgical dressings such as absorbent cotton, cotton wool, lint, lamb's wool, tow, jute, gauzes and oakum, prepared for use as surgical dressings, plain or medicated.	Great Britain...		11,081		25	5 00
	France.........		238		238	47 60
	United States...		56,850		57,375	11,475 00
	Total		68,169		57,638	11,527 60
		No.		No.		
Bagatelle tables or boards	Great Britain...	1	17			
	United States...	615	197	615	197	68 95
	Total	616	214	615	197	68 95
Bags which contained cement..	Great Britain...		9,150			
	Belgium........		1,622		1,789	447 25
	France.........		285		285	71 25
	Germany........		579			
	United States...		160,839		157,998	39,499 50
	Total......		172,475		160,072	40,018 00
		Lbs.		Lbs.		
Baking powders..............	Great Britain...	12	8			
	United States...	378,722	106,628	491,168	138,577	29,470 08
	Total.....	378,734	106,636	491,168	138,577	29,470 08
Balls, cues and racks and cue tips for bagatelle boards and billiard tables..............	Great Britain...		1,361		6	2 10
	France.........		1,646		1,646	576 10
	United States...		5,075		5,075	1,776 25
	Total		8,082		6,727	2,354 45
Baskets of all kinds, N.E.S....	Great Britain...		4,652		752	225 60
	Australia.......		13		13	3 90
	B. W. Indies....		5		5	1 50
	Hong Kong.		28		28	8 40
	Aust.-Hungary..		705		705	211 50
	Belgium.... ...		2,316		2,316	694 80
	China		143		143	42 90
	France..		4,222		3,998	1,199 40
	Germany.....		17,889		27	8 10
	Holland........		300		161	48 30
	Japan.		9,960		8,979	2,693 70
	Spain		40		11	3 30
	Switzerland.....		38		38	11 40
	United States...		18,562		17,769	5,330 70
	Total. .. .		58,873		34,945	10,483 50

OF IMPORTS—*Continued.*

FOR HOME CONSUMPTION.

Preferential Tariff.			Surtax Tariff.			Total.		
Quantity.	Value.	Duty.	Quantity.	Value.	Duty.	Quantity.	Value.	Duty Collected.
	$	$ cts.		$	$ cts.		$	$ cts.
	11,523	1,536 58					11,548	1,541 58
							238	47 60
							57,375	11,475 00
	11,523	1,536 58					69,161	13,064 18
No.			No.			No.		
1	17	3 96				1	17	3 96
						615	197	68 95
1	17	3 96				616	214	72 91
	9,150	1,525 05					9,150	1,525 05
				171	57 00		1,960	504 25
							285	71 25
				579	192 94		579	192 94
				300	100 00		158,298	39,599 50
	9,150	1,525 05		1,050	349 94		170,272	41,892 99
Lbs.			Lbs.			Lbs.		
12	8	0 48				12	8	0 48
						491,168	138,577	29,470 08
12	8	0 48				491,180	138,585	29,470 56
	1,355	316 15					1,361	318 25
							1,643	576 10
							5,075	1,776 25
	1,355	316 15					8,082	2,670 60
	3,588	717 60		312	124 80		4,652	1,068 00
							13	3 90
							5	1 50
							28	8 40
							705	211 50
							2,316	694 80
							143	42 90
				224	89 60		4,222	1,289 00
				17,832	7,132 80		17,859	7,140 90
				139	55 60		300	103 90
							8,979	2,693 70
							11	3 30
							38	11 40
				839	335 60		18,608	5,666 30
	3,588	717 60		19,346	7,738 40		57,879	18,939 50

No. 1.—General Statement

Articles Imported.	Countries.	Total Imports.		Entered		
				General Tariff.		
		Quantity.	Value.	Quantity	Value.	Duty.
DUTIABLE GOODS—*Con.*			$		$	$ cts.
Belting of all kinds, except rubber and leather	Great Britain		46,239		657	131 40
	France		58		58	11 60
	Germany		290			
	United States		31,636		31,636	6,327 20
	Total		78,223		32,351	6,470 20
Belts, surgical, and trusses, electric belts, pessaries and suspensory bandages of all kinds	Great Britain		4 030		189	37 80
	France		416		416	83 20
	Germany		192			
	United States		20,754		20,737	4,147 40
	Total		25,392		21,342	4,268 40
Belts of all kinds, N.O.P.	Great Britain		43,435		1,647	576 45
	Hong Kong		1		1	0 35
	Aust.-Hungary		566		566	198 10
	China		9		9	3 15
	France		4,670		4,645	1,625 75
	Germany		2,008			
	Japan		83		83	29 05
	United States		38,527		38,691	13,541 85
	Total		89,299		45,642	15,974 70
Bells and gongs, N.E.S.	Great Britain		1,166		351	105 30
	Hong Kong		8		8	2 40
	Aust.-Hungary		281		281	84 30
	France		327		327	98 10
	Germany		868			
	Japan		559		559	167 70
	United States		35,505		35,516	10,654 80
	Total		38,714		37,042	11,112 60
		No.		No.		
Billiard tables	Great Britain	21	4,310	1	280	98 00
	United States	461	28,606	461	28,606	10,012 10
	Total	482	32,916	462	28,886	10,110 10
Blacking, shoe and shoemakers' ink; shoe, harness and leather dressing, N.O.P.	Great Britain		6,732		707	176 75
	Belgium		110		110	27 50
	France		709		709	177 25
	United States		79,279		79,008	19,752 00
	Total		86,830		80,534	20,133 50
Blinds of wood, metal or other material, not textile or paper.	Japan		264		264	79 20
	United States		5,238		5,238	1,571 40
	Total		5,502		5,502	1,650 60

SESSIONAL PAPER No. 11

OF IMPORTS—*Continued.*

FOR HOME CONSUMPTION.

Preferential Tariff.			Surtax Tariff.			Total.		
Quantity.	Value.	Duty.	Quantity	Value.	Duty.	Quantity.	Value.	Duty Collected.
	$	$ cts.		$	$ cts.		$	$ cts.
	43,902	5,853 73					44,559	5,985 13
							58	11 60
				290	77 33		290	77 33
							31,636	6,327 20
	43,902	5,853 73		290	77 33		76,543	12,401 26
	3,841	512 17					4,030	549 97
							416	83 20
				192	51 20		192	51 20
				17	4 53		20,754	4,151 93
	3,841	512 17		209	55 73		25,392	4,836 30
	39,565	9,232 20		245	114 32		41,457	9,922 97
							1	0 35
							566	198 10
							9	3 15
				25	11 66		4,670	1,637 41
				2,008	937 20		2,008	937 20
							83	29 05
				83	38 72		38,774	13,580 57
	39,565	9,232 20		2,361	1,101 90		87,568	26,308 80
	779	155 80		36	14 40		1,166	275 50
							8	2 40
							281	84 30
							327	98 10
				868	347 20		868	347 20
							559	167 70
							35,516	10,654 80
	779	155 80		904	361 60		38,725	11,630 00
No. 20	4,030	940 36	No.			No 21	4,310	1,038 36
						461	28,606	10,012 10
20	4,030	940 36				482	32,916	11,050 46
	5,879	979 92					6,586	1,156 67
							110	27 50
							709	177 25
							79,008	19,752 00
	5,879	979 92					86,413	21,113 42
							264	79 20
							5,238	1,571 40
							5,502	1,650 60

No. 1.—General Statement

Articles Imported.	Countries.	Total Imports. Quantity.	Total Imports. Value.	Entered — General Tariff. Quantity.	Entered — General Tariff. Value.	Entered — General Tariff. Duty.
DUTIABLE GOODS—*Con.*			$		$	$ cts.
Blueing—Laundry blueing of all kinds	Great Britain		23,299			
	United States		3,243		3,243	810 75
	Total		26,542		3,243	810 75
Boats—Open pleasure sail boats, skiffs and canoes		No.		No.		
	Great Britain	10	1,022	4	422	105 50
	Newfoundland	3	26	3	26	6 50
	United States	499	90,208	498	89,747	22,436 75
	Total	512	91,256	505	90,195	22,548 75
Bolsters and pillows	Great Britain		846		36	10 80
	France		34		34	10 20
	Roumania		8		8	2 40
	Switzerland		162		162	48 60
	United States		8,919		8,861	2,658 30
	Total		9,969		9,101	2,730 30
Books, printed; periodicals and pamphlets, N.E.S	Great Britain		228,011		12,927	1,292 70
	Newfoundland		25		25	2 50
	Belgium		1,166		1,166	116 60
Books—Novels or works of fiction, or literature of a similar character, unbound or paper bound, or in sheets, including freight rates for railways and telegraph rates, bound in book or pamphlet form, not including Christmas annuals or publications commonly known as juvenile and toy books	China		18		18	1 80
	France		45,065		46,004	4,600 40
	Germany		1,991			
	Holland		105		105	10 50
	Turkey		91		91	9 10
	United States		770,039		768,858	76,885 80
	Total		1,046,511		829,194	82,919 40
	Great Britain		19,117		713	142 60
	Belgium		72		72	14 40
	France		1,384		1,384	276 80
Bank notes, bonds, bills of exchange, cheques, promissory notes, drafts, and all similar work unsigned, and cards or other commercial blank forms printed or lithographed, or printed from steel or copper or other plates, and other printed matter, N.E.S	Germany		582			
	United States		78,168		78,227	15,645 40
	Total		99,323		80,396	16,079 20
	Great Britain		10,822		389	136 15
	Newfoundland		30			
	Hong Kong		2		2	0 70
	Aust.-Hungary		113		113	39 55
	China		23		23	8 05
	France		193		184	64 40
	Germany		4,022			
	Japan		61		61	21 35
	Switzerland		8		8	2 80
	United States		109,761		109,634	38,371 90
	Total		125,035		110,414	38,644 90

OF IMPORTS—*Continued.*

FOR HOME CONSUMPTION.

Preferential Tariff.			Surtax Tariff.			Total.		
Quantity.	Value.	Duty.	Quantity.	Value.	Duty.	Quantity.	Value.	Duty Collected.
	$	$ cts.		$	$ cts.		$	$ cts.
....	23,583	3,930 59	....	....	....	....	23,583	3,930 59
....	....	....	....	....	....	....	3,243	810 75
....	23,583	3,930 59	....	....	....	....	26,826	4,741 34
No. 6	600	100 01	No.	....	....	No. 10	1,022	205 51
....	....	....	....	....	....	3	26	6 50
....	....	....	....	....	....	498	89,747	22,436 75
6	600	100 01	....	....	....	511	90,795	22,648 76
....	810	162 00	....	....	....	....	846	172 80
....	....	....	....	....	....	....	34	10 20
....	....	....	....	....	....	....	8	2 40
....	....	....	....	....	....	....	162	48 60
....	....	....	....	....	....	....	8,861	2,658 30
....	810	162 00	....	....	....	....	9,911	2,892 30
....	212,055	14,137 84	....	1,973	263 06	....	226,955	15,693 60
....	....	....	....	....	....	....	25	2 50
....	....	....	....	....	....	....	1,166	116 60
....	....	....	....	....	....	....	18	1 80
....	....	....	....	73	9 73	....	46,077	4,610 13
....	....	....	....	1,991	265 44	....	1,991	265 44
....	....	....	....	....	....	....	105	10 50
....	....	....	....	....	....	....	91	9 10
....	....	....	....	464	61 86	....	769,322	76,947 66
....	212,055	14,137 84	....	4,501	600 09	....	1,045,750	97,657 33
....	18,474	2,463 43	....	183	48 80	....	19,370	2,654 83
....	....	....	....	....	....	....	72	14 40
....	....	....	....	....	....	....	1,384	276 80
....	....	....	....	582	155 23	....	582	155 23
....	....	....	....	....	....	....	78,227	15,645 40
....	18,474	2,463 43	....	765	204 03	....	99,635	18,746 66
....	10,258	2,393 64	....	129	60 20	....	10,776	2,589 99
....	....	....	....	....	....	....	....	....
....	....	....	....	....	....	....	2	0 70
....	....	....	....	....	....	....	113	39 55
....	....	....	....	....	....	....	23	8 05
....	....	....	....	....	....	....	184	64 40
....	....	....	....	2,530	1,180 67	....	2,530	1,180 67
....	....	....	....	....	....	....	61	21 35
....	....	....	....	....	....	....	8	2 80
....	....	....	....	285	133 00	....	109,919	38,504 90
....	10,258	2,393 64	....	2,944	1,373 87	....	123,616	42,412 41

No. 1.—GENERAL STATEMENT

ARTICLES IMPORTED.	COUNTRIES.	TOTAL IMPORTS.		ENTERED		
				General Tariff.		
		Quantity.	Value.	Quantity.	Value.	Duty.
DUTIABLE GOODS—*Con.*		Lbs.	$	Lbs.	$	$ cts.
Books—*Con.*						
Posters, advertising bills and folders..	Great Britain...	1,381	282	161	42	24 15
	France.........	300	74	300	74	45 00
	United States...	106,106	23,453	106,106	23,453	15,915 90
	Total....	107,787	23,809	106,567	23,569	15,985 05
Labels for cigar boxes, fruits, vegetables, meat, fish, confectionery and other goods: also shipping, price or other tags, tickets or labels; and railroad or other tickets whether lithographed or printed or partly printed, N.E.S....................	Great Britain...	....	10,363	....	502	175 70
	Belgium........	....	202	....	....	.. ..
	France.........	....	1,083	....	1,346	471 10
	Germany.......	.. ..	20,431	....	....	....
	Holland......	....	36	....	6	2 10
	Japan..	.. ..	67	....	67	23 45
	Spain.... .	.. . .	3	.. ....	3	1 05
	United States...	....	138,741	....	137,595	48,158 25
	Total	... .	170,926	....	139,519	48,831 65
Maps and charts, N.E.S.....	Great Britain...	....	4,940	....	88	17 60
	Aust.-Hungary..	....	14	....	14	2 80
	France...... ...	....	567	....	567	113 40
	Japan..	....	261	....	261	52 20
	United States...	....	15,120	......	15,082	3,016 40
	Total . ..	....	20,902	....	16,012	3,202 40
Newspapers, or supplemental editions or parts thereof partly printed and intended to be completed and published in Canada........ .	United States...	... .	2,874	....	2,874	718 50
Advertising pamphlets, pictorial show cards, illustrated advertising periodicals, illustrated price books, catalogues and price lists; advertising calendars and almanacs; patent medicine or other advertising circulars, fly sheets or pamphlets.	Great Britain...	59,340	13,958	12,810	2,793	1,921 50
	Australia.	75	32	75	32	11 25
	Hong Kong.....	100	6	100	6	15 00
	Aust.-Hungary..	437	528	437	528	65 55
	Belgium........	16	7	16	7	2 40
	France..........	5,060	1,280	4,353	1,089	652 95
	Germany	4,890	1,114	22	5	3 30
	Holland... ...	483	108	308	73	46 20
	Italy..	111	11	111	11	16 65
	Japan..	84	29	84	29	12 60
	Spain..........	14	5	14	5	2 10
	Switzerland. ...	276	152	219	56	32 85
	Turkey..	22	5	22	5	3 30
	United States...	600,717	143,781	582,567	141,326	87,385 05
	Total	671,625	161,016	601,138	145,965	90,170 70

OF IMPORTS—*Continued.*

FOR HOME CONSUMPTION.

Preferential Tariff.			Surtax Tariff.			Total.		
Quantity.	Value.	Duty.	Quantity.	Value.	Duty.	Quantity.	Value.	Duty Collected.
Lbs.	$	$ cts.	Lbs.	$	$ cts.	Lbs.	$	$ cts.
1,220	240	122 00	...	...	...	1,381	282	146 15
...	...	...	...	...	...	300	74	45 00
...	...	...	...	...	...	106,106	23,453	15,915 90
1,220	240	122 00	...	...	...	107,787	23,809	16,107 05
...	9,274	2,164 11	...	620	289 32	...	10,396	2,629 13
...	...	...	...	202	94 26	...	202	94 26
...	...	...	...	...	...	...	1,346	471 10
...	...	...	...	20,330	9,487 45	...	20,330	9,487 45
...	...	...	...	...	...	...	6	2 10
...	...	...	...	...	...	...	67	23 45
...	...	...	...	...	...	...	3	1 05
...	...	...	...	1,627	759 26	...	139,222	48,917 51
...	9,274	2,164 11	...	22,779	10,630 29	...	171,572	61,626 05
...	4,852	647 01	...	...	...	...	4,940	664 61
...	...	...	...	...	...	...	14	2 80
...	...	...	...	...	...	...	567	113 40
...	...	...	...	...	...	...	261	52 20
...	...	...	...	38	10 13	...	15,120	3,026 53
...	4,852	647 01	...	38	10 13	...	20,902	3,859 54
...	...	...	...	...	...	...	2,784	718 50
46,101	11,129	4,610 10	80	20	16 00	58,991	13,942	6,547 60
...	...	...	...	...	...	75	32	11 25
...	...	...	...	...	...	100	6	15 00
...	...	...	...	...	...	437	528	65 55
...	...	...	...	...	...	16	7	2 40
...	...	...	...	...	...	4,353	1,089	652 95
...	...	...	4,868	1,109	972 60	4,890	1,114	976 90
...	...	...	...	...	...	308	73	46 20
...	...	...	...	...	...	111	11	16 65
...	...	...	...	...	...	84	29	12 60
...	...	...	...	...	...	14	5	2 10
...	...	...	...	...	...	219	56	32 85
...	...	...	...	...	...	22	5	3 30
...	...	...	3,749	1,283	749 80	586,316	142,609	88,134 85
46,101	11,129	4,610 10	8,697	2,412	1,739 40	655,936	159,506	96,520 20

No. 1.—General Statement

Articles Imported.	Countries.	Total Imports.		Entered		
				General Tariff.		
		Quantity.	Value.	Quantity.	Value.	Duty.
DUTIABLE GOODS—*Con.*		Lbs.	$	Lbs.	$	$ cts.
Books—*Con.* Chromos, chromotypes, oleographs, or like work produced by any process other than hand painting or drawing, and having any advertisement or advertising matter printed, lithographed or stamped thereon, or attached thereto, or other similar artistic work, lithographed, printed or stamped on paper or cardboard for business or advertisement purposes, N.O.P.	Great Britain	20	2			
	United States	3,962	898	3,962	898	594 30
	Total	3,982	900	3,962	898	594 30
Printed music, bound or in sheets	Great Britain		20,916		1,520	152 00
	Hong Kong		2		2	0 20
	France		573		573	57 30
	Germany		1,992			
	United States		86,783		86,638	8,663 80
	Total		110,266		88,733	8,873 30
Photographs, chromos, chromotypes, artotypes, oleographs, paintings, drawings, pictures, engravings or prints, or proofs therefrom, and similar works of art, N.O.P.; blue prints and building plans	Great Britain		166,849		6,806	1,361 20
	Hong Kong		71		71	14 20
	Aust.-Hungary		2,831		651	130 20
	Belgium		2,171		2,171	434 20
	China		32		32	6 40
	France		19,481		18,362	3,672 40
	Germany		81,089		36	7 20
	Holland		274		270	54 00
	Italy		1,817		1,817	363 40
	Japan		754		754	150 80
	Switzerland		2,817		2,817	563 40
	Turkey		45		45	9 00
	United States		328,244		303,081	60,616 20
	Total		606,475		336,913	67,382 60
Boot, shoe and stay laces of any material	Great Britain		85,567		7,220	2,166 00
	Belgium		21,165		21,165	6,349 50
	France		5,176		5,404	1,621 20
	Germany		10,825			
	United States		12,784		13,072	3,921 60
	Total		135,517		46,861	14,058 30

OF IMPORTS—*Continued.*

FOR HOME CONSUMPTION.

Preferential Tariff.			Surtax Tariff.			Total.		
Quantity.	Value.	Duty.	Quantity.	Value.	Duty.	Quantity.	Value.	Duty Collected.
Lbs.	$	$ cts.	Lbs.	$	$ cts.	Lbs.	$	$ cts.
20	2	2 00	...	...	...	20	2	2 00
...	...	...	...	...	...	3,962	898	594 30
20	2	2 00	...	...	...	3,982	900	596 30
...	18,669	1,244 70	...	727	96 93	...	20,916	1,493 63
...	...	...	...	...	...	...	2	0 20
...	...	...	...	...	...	...	573	57 30
...	...	...	...	1,992	265 65	...	1,992	265 65
...	...	...	...	145	19 33	...	86,783	8,683 13
...	18,669	1,244 70	...	2,864	381 91	...	110,266	10,499 91
...	96,246	12,833 22	...	18,574	4,953 06	...	121,626	19,147 48
...	...	...	...	...	...	...	71	14 20
...	...	...	...	2,180	581 33	...	2,831	711 53
...	...	...	...	...	...	...	2,171	434 20
...	...	...	...	...	...	...	32	6 40
...	...	...	...	722	192 53	...	19,084	3,864 93
...	...	...	...	81,178	21,647 35	...	81,214	21,654 55
...	...	...	...	...	...	...	270	54 00
...	...	...	...	...	...	...	1,817	363 40
...	...	...	...	...	...	...	754	150 80
...	...	...	...	...	...	...	2,817	563 40
...	...	...	...	...	...	...	45	9 00
...	...	...	...	15,942	4,251 20	...	319,023	64,867 40
...	96,246	12,833 22	...	118,596	31,625 47	...	551,755	111,841 29
...	73,718	14,743 60	...	1,505	602 00	...	82,443	17,511 60
...	...	...	...	...	...	...	21,165	6,349 50
...	...	...	...	...	...	...	5,404	1,621 20
...	...	...	...	10,825	4,330 00	...	10,825	4,330 00
...	...	...	...	...	...	...	13,072	3,921 60
...	73,718	14,743 60	...	12,330	4,932 00	...	132,909	33,733 90

No. 1.—GENERAL STATEMENT

Articles Imported.	Countries.	Total Imports.		Entered		
				General Tariff.		
		Quantity.	Value.	Quantity.	Value.	Duty.
DUTIABLE GOODS—*Con.*			$		$	$ cts.
Boots and shoes, and slippers of all kinds, except rubber and leather	Great Britain		37,259		1,218	304 50
	Hong Kong		5,092		5,092	1,273 00
	Aust.-Hungary		500		500	125 00
	China		7,051		7,051	1,762 75
	France		7,896		7,897	1,974 25
	Germany		10,123			
	Japan		505		505	126 25
	Norway		223		223	55 75
	St. Pierre		6		6	1 50
	Switzerland		132		132	33 00
	United States		27,807		26,828	6,707 00
	Total		96,594		49,452	12,363 00
Braces or suspenders, and metal parts of	Great Britain		23,916		2,284	799 40
	China		9		9	3 15
	France		5,052		5,052	1,768 20
	Germany		43			
	United States		55,972		56,202	19,670 70
	Total		84,992		63,547	22,241 45
Brass and manufactures of—Nails, tacks, rivets and burrs or washers	Great Britain		867			
	France		45		45	13 50
	Germany		1,605			
	United States		6,828		6,828	2,048 40
	Total		9,345		6,873	2,061 90
Pumps	Great Britain		328		5	1 50
	Germany		39			
	United States		23,653		23,161	6,948 30
	Total		24,020		23,166	6,949 80
		Lbs.		Lbs.		
Wire, plain	Great Britain	23,952	3,992			
	France	7	3	7	3	0 30
	Germany	860	339			
	United States	152,034	22,953	149,357	21,615	2,161 50
	Total	176,853	27,287	149,364	21,618	2,161 80
Wire cloth, &c., N.E.S.	Great Britain		32,314		160	40 00
	France		1,274		1,274	318 50
	Germany		575			
	United States		10,662		10,662	2,665 50
	Total		44,825		12,096	3,024 00

OF IMPORTS—*Continued.*

FOR HOME CONSUMPTION.

Preferential Tariff.			Surtax Tariff.			Total.		
Quantity.	Value.	Duty.	Quantity.	Value.	Duty.	Quantity.	Value.	Duty Collected.
	$	$ cts.		$	$ cts.		$	$ cts.
	40,037	6,673 06		256	85 33		41,511	7,062 89
							5,092	1,273 00
							500	125 00
							7,051	1,762 75
							7,897	1,974 25
				10,595	3,531 66		10,595	3,531 66
							505	126 25
							223	55 75
							6	1 50
							132	33 00
							26,828	6,707 00
	40,037	6,673 06		10,851	3,616 99		100,340	22,653 05
	21,182	4,942 71		10	4 66		23,476	5,746 77
							9	3 15
							5,052	1,768 20
				43	20 07		43	20 07
							56,202	19,670 70
	21,182	4,942 71		53	24 73		84,782	27,208 89
	867	173 40					867	173 40
							45	13 50
				1,605	642 00		1,605	642 00
							6,828	2,048 40
	867	173 40		1,605	642 00		9,345	2,877 30
	323	64 60					328	66 10
				39	15 60		39	15 60
							23,161	6,948 30
	323	64 60		39	15 60		23,528	7,030 00
Lbs.			Lbs.			Lbs.		
23,952	3,992	266 19				23,952	3,992	266 19
						7	3	0 30
			860	339	45 20	860	339	45 20
			2,533	1,307	174 28	151,890	22,922	2,335 78
23,952	3,992	266 19	3,393	1,646	219 48	176,709	27,256	2,647 47
	32,154	5,358 97					32,314	5,398 97
							1,274	318 50
				575	191 67		575	191 67
							10,662	2,665 50
	32,154	5,358 97		575	191 67		44,825	8,574 64

No. 1.—GENERAL STATEMENT

Articles Imported.	Countries.	Total Imports.		Entered		
				General Tariff.		
		Quantity.	Value.	Quantity.	Value.	Duty.
DUTIABLE GOODS—*Con.*			$		$	$ cts.
Brass—*Con.*						
Manufactures of, N.O.P.	Great Britain		72,158		2,125	637 50
	Australia		340		340	102 00
	B. E. Indies		764		165	49 50
	B. W. Indies		15		15	4 50
	Hong Kong		97		97	29 10
	Aust.-Hungary		3,248		3,246	973 80
	Belgium		171		171	51 30
	China		302		302	90 60
	France		12,498		12,852	3,855 60
	Germany		15,249		42	12 60
	Holland		117		117	35 10
	Italy		58		58	17 40
	Japan		6,398		6,398	1,919 40
	Switzerland		16		16	4 80
	United States		669,409		668,089	200,426 70
	Total		780,840		694,033	208,209 90
Breadstuffs, &c., viz.:—		Lbs.		Lbs.		
Arrowroot	Great Britain	13,883	761			
	Australia	1,120	40	1,120	40	8 00
	B. W. Indies	10,193	353	2,190	88	17 60
	China	1,693	9	1,693	9	1 80
	United States	1,708	98	1,744	100	20 00
	Total	28,597	1,261	6,747	237	47 40
Biscuits of all kinds not sweetened	Great Britain	39,535	4,409	400	38	9 50
	Hong Kong	4,929	149	4,929	149	37 25
	Newfoundland	1,080	57	1,080	57	14 25
	China	4,191	166	4,191	166	41 50
	France	110	44			
	Holland	660	84	660	84	21 00
	Japan	15,988	633	15,988	633	158 25
	Turkey	2,974	64	2,974	64	16 00
	United States	205,101	12,924	202,404	12,658	3,164 50
	Total	274,568	18,530	232,626	13,849	3,462 25
Biscuits of all kinds sweetened	Great Britain	183,032	29,317	521	72	19 80
	Hong Kong	12.158	320	12,158	320	88 00
	Belgium	511	44	511	44	12 10
	China	14,928	501	14,928	501	137 78
	France	1,275	327	1,236	312	85 80
	Japan	5,847	389	5,847	389	106 97
	Turkey	716	74	716	74	20 35
	United States	37,618	4,693	37,408	4,670	1,284 51
	Total	256,085	35,665	73,325	6,382	1,755 31
Macaroni and vermicelli	Great Britain	27,393	1,137	29,893	1,225	306 25
	Hong Kong	10,234	204	10,234	204	51 00
	China	20,833	460	20,833	460	115 00
	France	772,590	35,676	820,849	36,547	9,136 75
	Italy	1,439,684	49,268	1,400,255	48,851	12,212 75
	Japan	21,404	588	21,404	588	147 00
	St. Pierre	40	5	40	5	1 25
	United States	493,157	19,243	490,671	19,188	4,797 00
	Total	2,785,335	106,581	2,793,579	107,068	26,767 00

OF IMPORTS—*Continued.*

FOR HOME CONSUMPTION.

Preferential Tariff.			Surtax Tariff.			Total.		
Quantity.	Value.	Duty.	Quantity.	Value.	Duty.	Quantity.	Value.	Duty Collected.
	$	$ cts.		$	$ cts.		$	$ cts.
	69,479	13,895 80		270	108 00		71,874	14,641 30
							340	102 00
	599	119 80					764	169 30
							15	4 50
							97	29 10
							3,246	973 80
							171	51 30
							302	90 60
							12,852	3,855 60
				15,199	6,079 60		15,241	6,092 20
							117	35 10
							58	17 40
							6,398	1,919 40
							16	4 80
				192	76 80		668,281	200,503 50
	70,078	14,015 60		15,661	6,264 40		779,772	228,489 90
Lbs.			Lbs.			Lbs.		
16,498	853	113 74				16,498	853	113 74
						1,120	40	8 00
8,003	265	35 36				10,193	353	52 96
						1,693	9	1 80
						1.744	100	20 00
24,501	1,118	149 10				31,248	1,355	196 50
39,135	4,371	728 59				39,535	4,409	738 09
						4,929	149	37 25
						1,080	57	14 25
						4,191	166	41 50
						660	84	21 00
						15,988	633	158 25
						2,974	64	16 00
						202,404	12,658	3,164 50
39,135	4,371	728 59				271,761	18,220	4,190 84
181,920	29,169	5,348 22				182,441	29,241	5,368 02
						12,158	320	88 00
						511	44	12 10
						14,928	501	137 78
						1,236	312	85 80
						5,847	389	106 97
						716	74	20 35
						37,408	4,670	1,284 51
181,920	29,169	5,348 22				255,245	35,551	7,103 53
						29,893	1,225	306 25
						10,234	204	51 00
						20,833	460	115 00
						820,849	36,547	9,136 75
						1,400,255	48,851	12,212 75
						21,404	588	147 00
						40	5	1 25
						490,071	19,188	4,797 00
						2,793,579	107,068	26,767 00

No. 1.—General Statement

Articles Imported.	Countries.	Total Imports.		Entered		
				General Tariff.		
		Quantity.	Value.	Quantity.	Value.	Duty.
DUTIABLE GOODS—*Con.*		Lbs.	$	Lbs.	$	$ cts.
Breadstuffs—*Con.*						
Rice, cleaned	Great Britain	4,292,488	97,449	235,128	7,662	2,939 10
	B. E. Indies	3,383,448	48,716	12,600	369	157 50
	B. W. Indies	189,600	4,392	....	....	....
	Hong Kong	2,229,339	45,026	2,342.667	45,310	29,283 34
	China	4,811,006	93,877	4,856,140	94,431	60,701 68
	Holland	29,932	1,040	30,832	1,083	385 40
	Japan	1,173,965	32,613	1,137,877	31,025	14,223 46
	St. Pierre	114	16	114	16	1 42
	United States	713,772	25,788	672,617	23,337	8,407 71
	Total	16,823,664	348,917	9,287,975	203,233	116,099 61
Rice, uncleaned, unhulled or paddy	Great Britain	3,699,423	55,072	366,779	9,343	1,833 84
	B. E. Indies	3,402,237	103,957	28,224	405	141 12
	Hong Kong	1,399,200	23,828	1.399,200	23,828	6,996 00
	China	236,450	4,663	236,450	4,668	1,182 25
	Japan	4,294,452	107,339	4,363,037	108,823	21,815 23
	United States	60,394	1,490	60,394	1,490	301 97
	Total	13,092,156	296,349	6,454,084	148,552	32,270 41
Rice and Sago Flour and Sago	Great Britain	520,371	8,570	....	....	....
	B. E. Indies	188,650	3,553	112,528	1,467	366 75
	Hong Kong	20,873	388	20,873	388	97 00
	China	65,130	1,183	65,130	1,183	295 75
	France	237	10	....	....	....
	Japan	4,455	202	4,455	202	50 50
	United States	40,890	1,402	39,856	1,351	337 75
	Total	840,606	15,308	242,842	4,591	1,147 75
Tapioca	Great Britain	625,476	15,152	5,660	144	36 00
	B. E. Indies	1,276,501	31,289	147,250	2,282	570 50
	China	2,510	91	2,510	91	22 75
	France	618	42	617	42	10 50
	United States	198,287	8,133	205,635	8,273	2,068 25
	Total	2,103,392	54,707	361,672	10,832	2,708 00
Grain and Products of, viz.:—		Bush.		Bush.		
Barley	Great Britain	240	263	....	....	....
	United States	1,923,755	900,325	2,785	1,632	489 60
	Total	1,923,995	900,588	2,785	1,632	489 60
Beans	Great Britain	9	21	....	....	....
	Hong Kong	894	445	894	445	134 10
	China	899	478	899	478	134 85
	France	5	26	5	26	0 75
	Germany	2	8	....	....	....
	Italy	313	496	313	496	46 95
	Japan	1,363	1,430	1,363	1,430	204 45
	St. Pierre	4	11	4	11	0 60
	Turkey	5	10	5	10	0 75
	United States	24,003	43,016	23,612	42,245	3,541 80
	Total	27,497	45,941	27,095	45,141	4,064 25

OF IMPORTS—*Continued.*

FOR HOME CONSUMPTION.

Preferential Tariff.			Surtax Tariff.			Total.		
Quantity.	Value.	Duty.	Quantity.	Value.	Duty.	Quantity.	Value.	Duty Collected.
Lbs.	$	$ cts.	Lbs.	$	$ cts.	Lbs.	$	$ cts.
4,930,719	105,188	41,089 55				5,165,847	112,850	44,028 65
1,028,872	21,599	8,573 94				1,041,472	21,968	8,731 44
282,584	5,783	2,354 87				282,584	5,783	2,354 87
						2,342,667	45,310	29,283 34
						4,856,140	94,431	60,701 68
						30,832	1,083	385 40
						1,137,877	31,025	14,223 46
						114	16	1 42
			84,000	3,450	1,400 00	756,617	26,787	9,807 71
6,242,175	132,570	52,018 36	84,000	3,450	1,400 00	15,614,150	339,253	169,517 97
6,350,689	88,934	21,168 96				6,717,468	98,277	23,002 80
6,255,200	76,114	20,850 70				6,283,424	76,519	20,991 82
						1,399,200	23,828	6,996 00
						236,450	4,663	1,182 25
						4,363,037	108,823	21,815 23
						60,394	1,490	301 97
12,605,889	165,048	42,019 66				19,059,973	313,600	74,290 07
576,635	9,262	1,543 71				576,635	9,262	1,543 71
123,090	2,629	438 16				235,618	4,096	804 91
						20,873	388	97 00
						65,130	1,183	295 75
						....	....	....
						4,455	202	50 50
						39,856	1,351	337 75
699,725	11,891	1,981 87				942,567	16,482	3,129 62
624,778	14,576	2,429 33				630,438	14,720	2,465 33
1,092,617	28,910	4,818 40				1,239,867	31,192	5,388 90
						2,510	91	22 75
						617	42	10 50
						205,635	8,273	2,068 25
1,717,395	43,486	7,247 73				2,079,067	54,318	9,955 73
Bush.			Bush.			Bush.		
240	263	52 60				240	263	52 60
						2,785	1,632	489 60
240	263	52 60				3,025	1,895	542 20
9	21	0 90				9	21	0 90
						894	445	134 10
						899	478	134 85
						5	26	0 75
			2	8	0 40	2	8	0 40
						313	496	46 95
						1,363	1,430	204 45
						4	11	0 60
						5	10	0 75
						23,612	42,245	3,541 80
9	21	0 90	2	8	0 40	27,106	45,170	4,065 55

No. 1.—GENERAL STATEMENT

Articles Imported.	Countries.	Total Imports.		Entered		
				General Tariff.		
		Quantity.	Value.	Quantity.	Value.	Duty.
DUTIABLE GOODS—*Con.*		Bush.	$	Bush.	$	$ cts
Grain and products of—*Con.* Buckwheat	United States	99	120	99	120	9 90
Indian corn for purposes of distillation	Fiji	79	45	79	45	5 92
	United States	1,898,104	1,036,981	1,349,697	721,608	101,227 37
	Total	1,898,183	1,037,026	1,349,776	721,653	101,233 29
Oats	Great Britain	1,618	1,309	....	....	....
	New Zealand	680	396	....	....	....
	United States	2,613,847	1,194,595	44,000	20,351	4,400 00
	Total	2,616,145	1,196,300	44,000	20,351	4,400 00
Pease, N.E.S	China	8	4	8	4	0 80
	France	434	206	434	206	43 40
	Japan	40	39	40	39	4 00
	St. Pierre	4	13	4	13	0 40
	Turkey	324	286	324	286	32 40
	United States	4,255	8,550	4,245	8,532	424 50
	Total	5,065	9,098	5,055	9,080	505 50
Rye	United States	170,361	107,729	24,072	15,068	2,407 20
Wheat	Turkey	18	17	18	17	2 16
	United States	676,678	579,622	64,909	49,724	7,789 08
	Total	676,696	579,639	64,927	49,741	7,791 24
Bran, mill feed, &c	Great Britain	....	6,175	....	1,366	273 20
	United States	....	66,153	....	66,218	13,243 60
	Total	....	72,328	....	67,584	13,516 80
		Lbs.		Lbs.		
uckwheat meal or flour	France	200	13	200	13	0 50
	Japan	225	12	225	12	0 56
	United States	104,477	2,865	103,577	2,841	258 95
	Total	104,902	2,890	104,002	2,866	260 01
		Brls.		Brls.		
Indian or corn meal	Great Britain	7	21	....	....	....
	United States	27,047	71,254	26,706	69,830	6,676 50
	Total	27,054	71,275	26,706	69,830	6,676 50
		Lbs.		Lbs.		
Oatmeal	Great Britain	5,513	185	1,630	43	8 60
	United States	3,236	114	27,461	700	140 00
	Total	8,749	299	29,091	743	148 60

OF IMPORTS—*Continued.*

FOR HOME CONSUMPTION.

Preferential Tariff.			Surtax Tariff.			Total.		
Quantity.	Value.	Duty.	Quantity.	Value.	Duty.	Quantity.	Value.	Duty Collected.
Bush.	$	$ cts.	Bush.	$	$ cts.	Bush.	$	$ cts.
						99	120	9
						79	45	5 92
						1,349,697	721,608	101,227 37
						1.349,776	721,653	101,233 29
1,618	1,309	107 89				1,618	1,309	107 89
680	396	45 34				680	396	45 34
						44,000	20,351	4,400 00
2,298	1,705	153 23				46,298	22,056	4,553 23
						8	4	0 80
						434	206	43 40
						40	39	4 00
						4	13	0 40
						324	286	32 40
						4,245	8,532	424 50
						5,055	9,080	505 50
						24.072	15,068	2,407 20
						18	17	2 16
						64,909	49,724	7,789 08
						64,927	49,741	7,791 24
	4,809	641 23					6,175	914 43
							66,218	13,243 60
	4,809	641 23					72,393	14,158 03
Lbs.			Lbs.			Lbs.		
						200	13	0 50
						225	12	0 56
						103,577	2,841	258 95
						104,002	2,866	260 01
Brls.			Brls.			Brls.		
7	21	1 16				7	21	1 16
						26,706	69,830	6,676 50
7	21	1 16				26,713	69,851	6,677 66
Lbs.			Lbs.			Lbs.		
3,883	142	18 93				5,513	185	27 53
						27,461	700	140 00
3,883	142	18 93				32,974	885	167 53

No. 1.—General Statement

Articles Imported.	Countries.	Total Imports.		Entered		
				General Tariff.		
		Quantity.	Value.	Quantity.	Value.	Duty.
dutiable goods—*Con.*		Lbs.	$	Lbs.	$	$ cts.
Grain and products of—*Con.* Rolled oats	United States	456,927	9,190	430,090	8,482	2,580 55
		Brls.		Brls.		
Rye flour	United States	1,837	6,313	1,820	6,235	910 00
Wheat flour	Great Britain	146	522	45	167	27 00
	Newfoundland	8	48	8	48	4 80
	China	3	7	3	7	1 80
	United States	43,806	173,502	41,755	161,543	25,053 00
	Total	43,963	174,079	41,811	161,765	25,086 60
Hominy, cracked, evaporated or dried corn	United States	....	4,949	....	4,922	984 40
Cereal foods, prepared	Great Britain	....	3,212	....	24	4 80
	Hong Kong	....	3	....	3	0 60
	France	....	18	....	18	3 60
	Japan	....	3	....	3	0 60
	United States	....	150,063	....	152,552	30,510 40
	Total	....	153,299	....	152,600	30,520 00
All other breadstuffs, N.E.S.	Great Britain	....	13,343	....	260	52 00
	Hong Kong	....	582	....	582	116 40
	Newfoundland	....	8	....	8	1 60
	China	....	463	....	463	92 60
	France	....	390	....	390	78 00
	Germany	....	28	....	....	....
	Japan	....	82	....	82	16 40
	Turkey	....	500	....	500	100 00
	United States	....	61,276	....	60,176	12,035 20
	Total	....	76,672	....	62,461	12,492 20
Grain, flour and meal, &c., of all kinds, when damaged by water *in transitu*	United States	....	657	....	657	131 40
Bricks and tiles: *See* earthenware—						
Fire brick and stove linings, N.E.S	Great Britain	....	4,879	....	297	59 40
	United States	....	47,013	....	47,013	9,402 60
	Total	....	51,892	....	47,310	9,462 00
Bath brick	Great Britain	....	1,345	....	90	18 00
	United States	....	158	....	158	31 60
	Total	....	1,503	....	248	49 60
		M.		M.		
Building brick	Great Britain	770	9,891	30	400	80 00
	Belgium	153	324	100	183	36 60
	United States	21,011	184,682	21,011	184,682	36,936 40
	Total	21,934	194,897	21,141	185,265	37,053 00

OF IMPORTS—*Continued.*

FOR HOME CONSUMPTION.

Preferential Tariff.			Surtax Tariff.			Total.		
Quantity.	Value.	Duty.	Quantity.	Value.	Duty.	Quantity.	Value.	Duty Collected.
Lbs.	$	$ cts.	Lbs.	$	$ cts.	Lbs.	$	$ cts.
						430,090	8,482	2,580 55
Brls.			Brls.			Brls. 1,820	6,235	910 00
101	355	40 40				146	522	67 40
						8	48	4 80
						3	7	1 80
						41,755	161,543	25,053 00
101	355	40 40				41,912	162,120	25,127 00
							4,922	984 40
	3,049	406 60					3,073	411 40
							3	0 60
							18	3 60
							3	0 60
							152,552	30,510 40
	3,049	406 60					155,649	30,926 60
	13,281	1,770 95					13,541	1,822 95
							582	116 40
							8	1 60
							463	92 60
							390	78 00
				28	7 46		28	7 46
							82	16 40
							500	100 00
				28	7 51		60,204	12,042 71
	13,281	1,770 95		56	14 97		75,798	14,278 12
							657	131 40
	4,582	610 99					4,879	670 39
							47,013	9,402 60
	4,582	610 99					51,892	10,072 99
	1,218	162 37					1,308	180 37
							158	31 60
	1,218	162 37					1,466	211 97
M. 740	9,491	1,265 47	M.			M. 770	9,891	1,345 47
			53	141	37 60	153	324	74 20
						21,011	184,682	36,936 40
740	9,491	1,265 47	53	141	37 60	21,934	194,897	38,356 07

No. 1.—General Statement

Articles Imported.	Countries.	Total Imports. Quantity.	Total Imports. Value.	Entered — General Tariff. Quantity.	Value.	Duty.
DUTIABLE GOODS—*Con.*		M.	$	M.	$	$ cts.
Bricks and tiles—*Con.* Paving brick	Great Britain	35	650	10	190	38 00
	United States	4,069	45,358	4,069	45,358	9,071 60
	Total	4,104	46,008	4,079	45,548	9,109 60
Drain tiles, not glazed	Great Britain		399			
	United States		4,328		4,328	865 60
	Total		4,727		4,328	865 60
Drain pipes, sewer pipes, chimney linings or vents, chimney tops, and inverted blocks, glazed or unglazed	Great Britain		19,911		673	235 55
	United States		111,442		111,442	39,004 70
	Total		131,353		112,115	39,240 25
Manufactures of Clay, N.O.P.	Great Britain		1,269		134	26 80
	Hong Kong		15		15	3 00
	China		11		11	2 20
	France		445		445	89 00
	Germany		551			
	United States		27,776		27,776	5,555 20
	Total		30,067		28,381	5,676 20
British gum, dextrine, sizing cream and enamel sizing		Lbs.		Lbs.		
	Great Britain	276,635	9,484	46,212	1,537	153 70
	Belgium	3,000	225	3,000	225	22 50
	Germany	120,255	3,525			
	Holland	208,203	6,335	213,303	6,527	652 70
	United States	1,185,746	42,034	1,178,672	41,510	4,151 00
	Total	1,793,839	61,603	1,441,187	49,799	4,979 90
Brooms and whisks	Great Britain		251		165	33 00
	Hong Kong		4		4	0 80
	China		9		9	1 80
	France		2		2	0 40
	Germany		115			
	United States		3,051		3,051	610 20
	Total		3,432		3,231	646 20
Brushes	Great Britain		32,369		5,141	1,285 25
	Hong Kong		30		30	7 50
	Aust.-Hungary		1,560		1,368	342 00
	Belgium		28		28	7 00
	China		401		401	100 25
	France		67,071		67,046	16,761 50
	Germany		23,985		16	4 00
	Holland		57		57	14 25
	Japan		24,238		24,238	6,059 50
	United States		132,866		132,832	33,208 00
	Total		282,605		231,157	57,789 25

OF IMPORTS—*Continued.*

FOR HOME CONSUMPTION.

Preferential Tariff.			Surtax Tariff.			Total.		
Quantity.	Value.	Duty.	Quantity.	Value.	Duty.	Quantity.	Value.	Duty Collected.
M.	$	$ cts.	M.	$	$ cts.	M.	$	$ cts.
25	460	61 34				35	650	99 34
						4,069	45,358	9,071 60
25	460	61 34				4,104	46,008	9,170 94
	399	53 19					399	53 19
							4,328	865 60
	399	53 19					4,727	918 79
	19,238	4,488 85					19,911	4,724 40
							111,442	39,004 70
	19,238	4,488 85					131,353	43,729 10
	1,135	151 35					1,269	178 15
							15	3 00
							11	2 20
							445	89 00
				551	146 93		551	146 93
							27,776	5,555 20
	1,135	151 35		551	146 93		30,067	5,974 48
Lbs.			Lbs.			Lbs.		
180,623	6,188	412 55	5,500	202	26 93	232,335	7,927	593 18
						3,000	225	22 50
			102,024	3,057	407 61	102,024	3,057	407 61
						213,303	6,527	652 70
			6,124	366	48 80	1,184,796	41,876	4,199 80
180,623	6,188	412 55	113,648	3,625	483 34	1,735,458	59,612	5,875 79
	86	11 50					251	44 50
							4	0 80
							9	1 80
							2	0 40
				115	30 60		115	30 60
							3,051	610 20
	86	11 50		115	30 60		3,432	688 30
	26,117	4,352 95		1,193	397 66		32,451	6,035 86
							30	7 50
							1,368	342 00
							28	7 00
							401	100 25
							67,046	16,761 50
				23,969	7,989 60		23,985	7,993 60
							57	14 25
							24,238	6,059 50
				299	99 66		133,131	33,307 66
	26,117	4,352 95		25,461	8,486 92		282,735	70,629 12

No. 1.—General Statement

Articles Imported.	Countries.	Total Imports.		Entered		
				General Tariff.		
		Quantity.	Value.	Quantity.	Value.	Duty.
dutiable goods—*Con.*		Gross.	$	Gross.	$	$ cts.
Buttons, pantaloon, wholly of metal..........	Great Britain...	54,628	3,080	856	141	35 25
	Aust.-Hungary.	95	29	95	29	7 25
	France........	100	43	100	43	10 75
	Germany......	78,924	4,201	1,100	61	15 25
	United States...	325,500	25,123	324,781	25,026	6,256 50
	Total	459,247	32,476	326,932	25,300	6,325 00
Buttons, shoe, N.E.S.	Great Britain...	10	2	....	....	....
	United States...	5,539	377	5,539	377	94 25
	Total	5,549	379	5,539	377	94 25
Buttons, all kinds, N.O.P.	Great Britain...	....	44,365	.. ..	8,891	3,111 85
	Hong Kong. ..	....	16	....	16	5 60
	Aust.-Hungary.	....	31,488	....	31,427	10,999 45
	Belgium........	....	341	... .	341	119 35
	China..........	....	11	....	11	3 85
	France.........	....	28,883	.. ..	28,664	10,032 40
	Germany.	....	27,344	....	1,580	553 00
	Italy..........	....	3,377	....	3,377	1,181 95
	Japan..	....	227	....	227	79 45
	Switzerland.....	....	184	....	134	64 40
	United States...	....	114,417	....	113,640	39,774 00
	Total	....	250,653	....	188,358	65,925 30
Candles—		Lbs.		Lbs.		
Paraffine wax.............	Great Britain...	3,944	360	12	2	0 50
	Hong Kong.....	75	4	75	4	1 00
	Germany.	300	35	....	....	....
	United States...	144,989	15,444	144,989	15,444	3,861 00
	Total	149,308	15,843	145,076	15,450	3,862 50
All other, N.E.S	Great Britain...	201,073	18,157	5,953	559	139 75
	France..........	1,563	212	2,328	280	70 00
	Germany. ...	2,308	518	....	....	....
	Japan.,........	304	17	304	17	4 25
	United States...	359,515	46,936	368,009	46,980	11,745 00
	Total	564,763	65,840	376,594	47,836	11,959 00
Cane, Reed or Rattan, split or otherwise manuf'd, N.O.P...	Great Britain...	.... .	3,163	....	312	46 80
	Hong Kong.....	....	61	....	61	9 15
	China..........	....	36	... .	36	5 40
	Germany.	.. ..	6,206	....	....	....
	Japan	....	5	....	5	0 75
	United States...	....	45,344	....	43,043	6,456 45
	Total	....	54,815	....	43,457	6,518 55

OF IMPORTS—*Continued.*

FOR HOME CONSUMPTION.

Preferential Tariff.			Surtax Tariff.			Total.		
Quantity.	Value.	Duty.	Quantity.	Value.	Duty.	Quantity.	Value.	Duty Collected.
Gross.	$	$ cts.	Gross.	$	$ cts.	Gross.	$	$ cts.
50,603	2,772	462 04	3,169	167	55 66	54,628	3,080	552 95
						95	29	7 25
						100	43	10 75
			77,824	4,140	1,379 99	78,924	4,201	1,395 24
			719	97	32 33	325,500	25,123	6,288 83
50,603	2,772	462 04	81,712	4,404	1,467 98	459,247	32,476	8,255 02
10	2	0 33				10	2	0 33
						5,539	377	94 25
10	2	0 33				5,549	379	94 58
	31,506	7,351 72		4,280	1,997 32		44,677	12,460 89
							16	5 60
							31,427	10,999 45
							341	119 35
							11	3 85
				219	102 20		28,883	10,134 60
				25,616	11,954 22		27,196	12,507 22
							3,377	1,181 95
							227	79 45
							184	64 40
				417	194 60		114,057	39,968 60
	31,506	7,351 72		30,532	14,248 34		250,396	87,525 36
Lbs.			Lbs.			Lbs.		
3,432	319	53 18				3,444	321	53 68
						75	4	1 00
			300	35	11 67	300	35	11 67
						144,989	15,444	3,861 00
3,432	319	53 18	300	35	11 67	148,808	15,804	3,927 35
149,190	13,761	2,293 59	50	5	1 66	155,193	14,325	2,435 00
						2,328	280	70 00
			2,308	518	172 69	2,308	518	172 69
						304	17	4 25
			370	24	8 00	368,379	47,004	11,753 00
149,190	13,761	2,293 59	2,728	547	182 35	528,512	62,144	14,434 94
	2,711	271 10		140	28 00		3,163	345 90
							61	9 15
							36	5 40
				6,206	1,241 20		6,206	1,241 20
							5	0 75
				2,301	460 20		45,344	6,916 65
	2,711	271 10		8,647	1,729 40		54,815	8,519 05

No. 1.—GENERAL STATEMENT.

Articles Imported.	Countries.	Total Imports.		Entered — General Tariff.		
		Quantity.	Value.	Quantity.	Value.	Duty.
DUTIABLE GOODS—*Con.*			$		$	$ cts.
Canvas, to be used for boats' and ships' sails	Great Britain...	....	7,835	....	180	9 00
Carriages and vehicles—Buggies, carriages, pleasure carts and similar vehicles, N.E.S.		No.		No.		
	Great Britain...	2	299	1	195	68 25
	United States...	1,473	106,788	1,354	94,393	33,037 55
	Total	1,475	107,087	1,355	94,588	33,105 80
Cutters	United States...	15	448	15	448	156 80
Farm wagons	Great Britain...	1	97	....	....	....
	United States...	4,451	186,184	4,451	186,184	46,546 00
	Total ...	4,452	186,281	4,451	186,184	46,546 00
Freight wagons, drays and similar vehicles	Great Britain...	1	2,093	....	....	....
	Sweden.........	1	35	1	35	8 75
	United States...	903	54,243	903	54,243	13,560 75
	Total	905	56,371	904	54,278	13,569 50
Finished parts of buggies, carriages and similar vehicles, N.E.S., including parts of cutters, children's carriages and sleds, N.O.P.	Great Britain...	....	1,992	....	97	33 95
	United States...	....	94,576	....	94,907	33,217 45
	Total	....	96,568	....	95,004	33,251 40
Railway cars, passenger	United States..	52	368,434	52	368,434	110,530 20
" tram or horse	Great Britain...	6	17,352	....	....	....
	United States...	18	8,042	18	8,042	2,412 60
	Total	24	25,394	18	8,024	2,412 60
" box and flat cars	United States.	473	297,899	473	297,899	89,369 70
" cars, parts of	Great Britain...	....	30,391	....	....	....
	Germany.......	....	70,590	....	....	....
	United States...	....	234,706	....	234,502	70,350 60
	Total	....	335,687	....	234,502	70,350 60
Railway or road scrapers	United States...	... .	81,173	....	81,160	24,348 00
Sleighs	United States...	894	17,990	892	17,880	4,470 00

OF IMPORTS—*Continued.*

FOR HOME CONSUMPTION.

Preferential Tariff.			Surtax Tariff.			Total.		
Quantity.	Value.	Duty.	Quantity.	Value.	Duty.	Quantity.	Value.	Duty Collected.
	$	$ cts.		$	$ cts.		$	$ cts.
	7,655	255 16					7,835	264 16
No.			No.			No.		
1	104	24 27				2	299	92 52
						1,354	94,393	33,037 55
1	104	24 27				1,356	94,692	33,130 07
						15	448	156 80
1	97	16 17				1	97	16 17
						4,451	186,184	46,546 00
1	97	16 17				4,452	186,281	46,562 17
1	2,093	348 84				1	2,093	348 84
						1	35	8 75
						903	54,243	13,560 75
1	2,093	348 84				905	56,371	13,918 34
	338	78 91					435	112 86
							94,907	33,217 45
	338	78 91					95,342	33,330 31
						52	368,434	110,530 20
6	17,352	3,470 40				6	17,352	3,470 40
						18	8,042	2,412 60
6	17,352	3,470 40				24	25,394	5,883 00
						473	297,899	89,369 70
	30,391	6,078 20					30,391	6,078 20
				70,590	28,236 00		70,590	28,236 00
				4	1 60		234,506	70,352 20
	30,391	6,078 20		70,594	28,237 60		335,487	104,666 40
							81,160	24,348 00
						892	17,880	4,470 00

No. 1.—General Statement

Articles Imported.	Countries.	Total Imports.		Entered		
				General Tariff.		
		Quantity.	Value.	Quantity.	Value.	Duty.
DUTIABLE GOODS—*Con.*		No.	$	No.	$	$ cts.
Carriages and vehicles—*Con.*						
Wheelbarrows and trucks and handcarts	Great Britain	2	22	....	....	....
	United States	17,493	103,796	17,440	103,662	31,098 60
	Total	17,495	103,818	17,440	103,662	31,098 60
Bicycles and tricycles	Great Britain	203	7,987	20	822	246 60
	United States	2,168	32,417	2,205	32,607	9,782 10
	Total	2,371	40,404	2,225	33,429	10,028 70
" " parts of	Great Britain	....	9,980	....	1,086	325 80
	France	....	14	....	14	4 20
	Germany	....	246	....	....	....
	St. Pierre	....	5	....	....	....
	United States	....	66,511	....	66,935	20,080 50
	Total	....	76,756	....	68,035	20,410 50
Children's carriages and sleds	Great Britain	....	375	....	99	34 65
	United States	....	58,364	....	58,344	20,420 40
	Total	....	58,739	....	58,443	20,455 05
		Yds.		Yds.		
Carpets, N.E.S. (see woollens)	Great Britain	1,556	791			
	Aust.-Hungary	100	49	100	49	17 15
	Germany	23	38	....	....	....
	United States	2	1	....	....	....
	Total	1,681	879	100	49	17 15
		No.		No.		
Carpet sweepers	United States	7,230	15,928	7,230	15,928	4,778 40
Cash registers	United States	1,631	237,834	1,631	237,834	71,350 20
Celluloid, manufactures of, N.E.S	Great Britain	....	7,630	....	1,133	226 60
	Aust.-Hungary	....	4	....	4	0 80
	France	....	13,789	....	13,789	2,757 80
	Germany	....	3,193	....	....	....
	Japan	....	115	....	115	23 00
	Switzerland	....	6	....	6	1 20
	United States	....	21,838	....	21,812	4,362 40
	Total	....	46,575	....	36,859	7,371 80
		Cwt.		Cwt.		
Cement, hydraulic or waterlime	United States	10,794	4,034	10,794	4,034	1,349 25

OF IMPORTS—*Continued.*

FOR HOME CONSUMPTION.

Preferential Tariff.			Surtax Tariff.			Total.		
Quantity.	Value.	Duty.	Quantity.	Value.	Duty.	Quantity.	Value.	Duty Collected.
No.	$	$ cts.	No.	$	$ cts.	No.	$	$ cts.
2	22	4 40				2	22	4 40
			1	5	2 00	17,441	103,667	31,100 60
2	22	4 40	1	5	2 00	17,443	103,689	31,105 00
166	5,327	1,065 40				186	6,149	1,312 00
						2,205	32,607	9,782 10
166	5,327	1,065 40				2,391	38,756	11,094 10
	8,849	1,769 80					9,935	2,095 60
							14	4 20
				11	4 40		11	4 40
				10	4 00		66,945	20,084 50
	8,849	1,769 80		21	8 40		76,905	22,188 70
	276	64 41					375	99 06
							58,344	20,420 40
	276	64 41					58,719	20,519 46
Yds.			Yds.			Yds.		
1,556	790	184 34		1	0 47	1,556	791	184 81
						100	49	17 15
			23	38	17 75	23	38	17 75
			2	1	0 47	2	1	0 47
1,556	790	184 34	25	40	18 69	1,681	879	220 18
No.			No.			No.		
						7,230	15,928	4,778 40
						1,631	237,834	71,350 20
	5,818	775 78		679	181 06		7,630	1,183 44
							4	0 80
							13,789	2,757 80
				3,193	851 58		3,193	851 58
							115	23 00
							6	1 20
				26	6 93		21,838	4,369 33
	5,818	775 78		3,898	1,039 57		46,575	9,187 15
Cwt.			Cwt.			Cwt.		
						10,794	4,034	1,349 25

No. 1.—General Statement

Articles Imported.	Countries.	Total Imports.		Entered		
				General Tariff.		
		Quantity.	Value.	Quantity.	Value.	Duty.
Dutiable goods—*Con.*		Cwt.	$	Cwt.	$	$ cts.
Cement—*Con.* Portland	Great Britain	705,565	217,753	3,933	1,150	491 62
	Belgium	172,525	45,109	184,101	47,905	23,012 62
	France	27,950	7,981	26,762	7,570	3,345 25
	Germany	20,041	7,127			
	Japan	64,032	28,252	64,032	28,252	8,004 00
	United States	1,871,303	664,905	1,842,146	652,690	230,268 37
	Total	2,861,416	971,127	2,120,974	737,567	265,121 86
N.E.S. and manufactures of, N.O.P	Great Britain		5,365		252	50 40
	France		309		309	61 80
	Germany		1,618			
	Italy		128		128	25 60
	United States		20,441		20,101	4,020 20
	Total		27,861		20,790	4,158 00
Chalk, prepared	Great Britain		1,731		72	14 40
	France		649		614	122 80
	Germany		1,650			
	Holland		65		65	13 00
	United States		19,726		19,674	3,934 80
	Total		23,821		20,425	4,085 00
Charcoal	Great Britain		14,813			
	France		36		36	7 20
	Japan		7		7	1 40
	United States		19,735		19,735	3,947 00
	Total		34,591		19,778	3,955 60
		Lbs.		Lbs.		
Chicory, raw or green	Great Britain	2,997	117			
" kiln-dried, roasted or ground	Great Britain	216,097	10,615	37,398	3,278	1,495 92
	Belgium	5,891	234	5,667	225	226 68
	Holland			1,344	53	53 76
	Iceland	620	41	620	41	24 80
	United States	26,276	1,603	26,276	1,603	1,051 04
	Total	248,884	12,493	71,305	5,200	2,852 20
Church vestments of any material	Great Britain		1,600		104	20 80
	Aust.-Hungary		142		142	28 40
	Belgium		53		53	10 60
	France		18,091		18,091	3,618 20
	Italy		1,091		1,091	218 20
	United States		2,524		2,524	504 80
	Total		23,501		22,005	4,401 00

OF IMPORTS—*Continued.*

FOR HOME CONSUMPTION.

Preferential Tariff.			Surtax Tariff.			Total.		
Quantity.	Value.	Duty.	Quantity.	Value.	Duty.	Quantity.	Value.	Duty Collected.
Cwt.	$	$ cts.	Cwt.	$	$ cts.	Cwt.	$	$ cts.
696,571	215,544	58,047 40	1,753	570	292 16	702,257	217,264	58,831 18
			2,799	810	466 50	186,900	48,715	23,479 12
			1,188	411	198 00	27,950	7,981	3,543 25
			20,041	7,127	3,340 14	20,041	7,127	3,340 14
						64,032	28,252	8,004 00
			5,256	1,810	876 00	1,847,402	654,500	231,144 37
696,571	215,544	58,047 40	31,037	10,728	5,172 80	2,848,582	963,839	328,342 06
	4,187	558 33		926	246 93		5,365	855 66
							309	61 80
				1,618	431 51		1,618	431 51
							128	25 60
				337	89 86		20,438	4,110 06
	4,187	558 33		2,881	768 30		27,858	5,484 63
	1,618	215 77		43	11 46		1,733	241 63
				35	9 33		649	132 13
				1,650	440 05		1,650	440 05
							65	13 00
				82	21 86		19,756	3,956 66
	1,618	215 77		1,810	482 70		23,853	4,783 47
	14,813	1,975 07					14,813	1,975 07
							36	7 20
							7	1 40
							19,735	3,947 00
	14,813	1,975 07					34,591	5,930 67
Lbs. 861	38	17 22	Lbs.			Lbs. 861	38	17 22
168,675	7,066	4,498 10				206,073	10,344	5,994 02
						5,667	225	226 68
						1,344	53	53 76
						620	41	24 80
						26,276	1,603	1,051 04
168,675	7,066	4,498 10				239,980	12,266	7,350 30
	1,496	199 54					1,600	220 34
							142	28 40
							53	10 60
							18,091	3,618 20
							1,091	218 20
							2,524	504 80
	1,496	199 54					23,501	4,600 54

No. 1.—GENERAL STATEMENT

Articles Imported.	Countries.	Total Imports.		Entered		
				General Tariff.		
		Quantity.	Value.	Quantity.	Value.	Duty.
DUTIABLE GOODS—*Con.*		Galls.	$	Galls.	$	$ cts.
der, clarified or refined.....	Great Britain...	120	71	60	7	6 00
	France..........	73	106	147	139	14 70
	United States. .	546	401	558	383	55 80
	Total	739	578	765	529	76 50
Cider, not clarified or refined..	St. Pierre.......	52	12	52	12	2 60
	United States...	2,020	385	1,546	349	77 30
	Total	2,072	397	1,598	361	79 90
Clocks, clock keys and clock movements	Great Britain...	....	10,660	....	1,740	435 00
	Aust.-Hungary..	... .	384	... .	384	96 00
	Belgium.	....	7	....	7	1 75
	France.........	....	15,115	....	15,016	3,754 00
	Germany.	....	40,991	... .	11	2 75
	Switzerland.....	....	801	....	801	200 25
	United States...	....	274,936	....	273,919	68,479 75
	Total . .	....	342,894	.. ..	291,878	72,969 50
		No.		No.		
Clothes wringers and parts thereof, for domestic use.....	Great Britain...	2	10	....	....	....
	France...... ...	1	67	1	67	23 45
	United States...	7,575	19,461	7,575	19,461	6,811 35
	Total	7,578	19,538	7,576	19,528	6,834 80
		Yds.		Yds.		
Cloths, not rubbered or made waterproof, whether of wool, cotton, unions, silk or ramie, sixty inches or over in width and weighing not more than seven ounces to the square yard, imported exclusively for the manufacture of mackintosh clothing...............	Great Britain...	113,713	21,609	....	....	....
		Tons.		Tons.		
Coal, bituminous..	Great Britain...	22,320	47,267	167	477	88 51
	United States...	4,742,485	8,748,496	4,475,883	8,316,150	2,372,217 99
	Total	4,764,805	8,795,763	4,476,050	8,316,627	2,372,306 50
Coal dust, N.E.S.	Great Britain..	725	1,719	....	....	....
	United States...	750,489	492,381	746,526	487,461	83,732 92
	Total	751,214	494,100	746,526	487,461	83,732 92
Cocoa carpeting, mats, rugs and matting	Great Britain...	....	3,691	....	7	1 75
	B. E. Indies....	....	705	....	317	79 25
	Belgium........	....	131	....	131	32 75
	China	....	12	....	12	3 00
	Japan	....	58	....	58	14 50
	United States...	....	250	....	250	62 50
	Total	....	4,847	....	775	193 75

OF IMPORTS—*Continued.*

FOR HOME CONSUMPTION.

Preferential Tariff.			Surtax Tariff.			Total.		
Quantity.	Value.	Duty.	Quantity.	Value.	Duty.	Quantity.	Value.	Duty Collected.
Galls.	$	$ cts.	Galls.	$	$ cts.	Galls.	$	$ cts.
90	119	6 00				150	126	12 00
						147	139	14 70
						558	383	55 80
90	119	6 00				855	648	82 50
						52	12	2 60
						1,546	349	77 30
						1,598	361	79 90
	4,560	760 04		4,363	1,454 33		10,663	2,649 37
							384	96 00
							7	1 75
				99	33 00		15,115	3,787 00
				41,215	13,738 39		41,226	13,741 14
							801	200 25
				972	324 00		274,891	68,803 75
	4,560	760 04		46,649	15,549 72		343,087	89,279 26
No.			No.			No.		
2	10	2 34				2	10	2 34
						1	67	23 45
						7,575	19,461	6,811 35
2	10	2 34				7,578	19,538	6,837 14
Yds.			Yds.			Yds.		
121,236	23,153	2,315 30				121,236	23,153	2,315 30
Tons.			Tons.			Tons.		
19,500	43,722	6,890 03				19,667	44,199	6,978 54
						4,475,883	8,316,150	2,372,217 99
19,500	43,722	6,890 03				4,495,550	8,360,349	2,379,196 53
725	1,719	62 88				725	1,719	62 88
						746,526	487,461	83,732 92
725	1,719	62 88				747,251	489,180	83,795 80
	3,692	615 36					3,699	617 11
	388	64 66					705	143 91
							131	32 75
							12	3 00
							58	14 50
							250	62 50
	4,080	680 02					4,855	873 77

No. 1.—General Statement

Articles Imported.	Countries.	Total Imports.		Entered		
				General Tariff.		
		Quantity.	Value.	Quantity.	Value.	Duty.
DUTIABLE GOODS—*Con.*		No.	$	No.	$	$ cts.
Cocoa nuts imported from place of growth by vessel direct to a Canadian port.	B. Guiana	28,783	537	....	....	....
	B. W. Indies	2,435,298	53,553	42,714	920	213 57
	Hawaii	400	6	400	6	2 00
	United States	270	12	270	12	1 35
	Total	2,464,751	54,108	43,384	938	216 92
Cocoa nuts, N.E.S.	United States	127,043	3,913	127,043	3,913	1,270 43
Cocoa nut, desiccated, sweetened or not		Lbs.		Lbs.		
	Great Britain	49,049	3,429	1,774	115	88 70
	B. E. Indies	63,170	4,538	1,980	129	99 00
	United States	4,519	508	4,679	545	233 95
	Total	116,738	8,475	8,433	789	421 65
Cocoa paste, chocolate paste, cocos and cocoa butter, N.O.P.	Great Britain	468,609	94,082	2,662	308	106 48
	France	150	20	2,004	490	80 16
	Germany	31,188	4,126	....	....	....
	Holland	97,175	22,343	97,175	22,343	3,887 00
	St. Pierre	29	7	29	7	1 16
	Switzerland	299	38	1,098	197	43 92
	United States	736,522	125,643	715,426	123,715	28,617 04
	Total	1,333,972	246,259	818,394	147,060	32,735 76
Cocoa shells and nibs, chocolate and other preparations of cocoa, N.E.S.	Great Britain	631,971	136,559	10,605	2,326	465 20
	Belgium	20	3	20	3	0 60
	China	38	2	38	2	0 40
	France	22,207	6,087	24,869	6,986	1,397 20
	Germany	402	52	....	....	....
	Holland	39,863	16,830	35,535	14,960	2,992 00
	Italy	3	3	3	3	0 60
	Switzerland	273,752	64,131	238,680	60,208	12,041 60
	United States	403,934	102,119	422,547	108,281	21,656 20
	Total	1,372,190	325,786	732,297	192,769	38,553 80
Coffee, green, N.E.S.	Great Britain	212	46	212	46	4 60
	Brazil	99,000	9,680	99,000	9,680	968 00
	Holland	1,200	163	1,200	163	16 30
	St. Pierre	220	33	220	33	3 30
	United States	387,402	46,338	395,671	47,315	4,731 50
	Total	488,034	56,260	496,303	57,237	5,723 70
Coffee, extract of, N.E.S., or substitutes therefor of all kinds	Great Britain	30,421	7,323	....	....	....
	United States	40,686	2,997	40,639	2,984	1,219 17
	Total	71,107	10,320	40,639	2,984	1,219 17

OF IMPORTS—*Continued.*

FOR HOME CONSUMPTION.

Preferential Tariff.			Surtax Tariff.			Total.		
Quantity.	Value.	Duty.	Quantity.	Value.	Duty.	Quantity.	Value.	Duty Collected.
No.	$	$ cts.	No.	$	$ cts.	No.	$	$ cts.
28,783	537	95 94				28,783	537	95 94
2,365,678	52,251	7,885 55				2,408,392	53,171	8,099 12
						400	6	2 00
						270	12	1 35
2,394,461	52,788	7,981 49				2,437,845	53,726	8,198 41
						127,043	3,913	1,270 43
Lbs.			Lbs.			Lbs.		
47,365	3,320	1,578 84				49,139	3,435	1,667 54
61,190	4,409	2,039 66				63,170	4,538	2,138 66
						4,679	545	233 95
108,555	7,729	3,618 50				116,988	8,518	4,040 15
466,710	93,206	12,445 86	336	45	17 92	469,708	93,559	12,570 26
						2,004	490	80 16
			31,188	4,126	1,663 35	31,188	4,126	1,663 35
						97,175	22,348	3,887 00
						29	7	1 16
						1,098	197	43 92
			192	66	10 24	715,618	123,781	28,627 28
466,710	93,206	12,445 86	31,716	4,237	1,691 51	1,316,820	244,503	46,873 13
646,765	137,678	18,357 13	144	94	25 06	657,514	140,098	18,847 39
						20	3	0 60
						38	2	0 40
						24,869	6,986	1,397 20
			402	52	13 86	402	52	13 86
						35,535	14,960	2,992 00
						3	3	0 60
						238,680	60,208	12,041 60
						422,547	108,281	21,656 20
646,765	137,678	18,357 13	546	146	38 92	1,379,608	330,593	56,949 85
						212	46	4 60
						99,000	9,680	968 00
						1,200	163	16 30
						220	33	3 30
						395,671	47,315	4,731 50
						496,303	57,237	5,723 70
30,341	7,242	606 84				30,341	7,242	606 84
						40,639	2,984	1,219 17
30,341	7,242	606 84				70,980	10,226	1,826 01

No. 1.—GENERAL STATEMENT

Articles Imported.	Countries.	Total Imports.		Entered		
				General Tariff.		
		Quantity.	Value.	Quantity.	Value.	Duty.
DUTIABLE GOODS—*Con.*		Lbs	$	Lbs.	$	$ cts.
Coffee, roasted or ground, when not imported direct from the country of growth and production	Great Britain...	1,745	365	230	97	14 30
	B. W. Indies ...	20	1	20	1	0 50
	France.........	570	68	570	68	18 20
	United States...	194,513	37,980	205,149	40,680	8,170 98
	Total.......	196,848	38,414	205,969	40,846	8,203 98
Coffee, roasted or ground, and imitations of and substitutes for, N.O.P.................	Great Britain...	124	14	....	....	....
	B. W. Indies....	205	41	205	41	4 10
	United States...	300,017	33,151	313,542	34,025	6,270 84
	Total.......	300,346	33,206	313,747	34,066	6,274 94
Coffee, condensed with milk...	Great Britain...	15	3	....	....	....
	United States...	147	35	147	35	10 50
	Total.......	162	38	147	35	10 50
Collars of cotton or linen, xylonite, xyolite or celluloid		Doz.		Doz.		
	Great Britain...	51,454	46,127	3,411	2,739	958 65
	Hong Kong.....	4	5	4	5	1 75
	Aust.-Hungary..	34,552	27,820	34,427	27,745	9,710 75
	Belgium.... ...	476	841	476	841	294 35
	France.........	2,661	3,276	2,661	3,276	1,146 60
	Germany......	17,477	15,496	82	92	32 20
	Japan..........	4,769	3,323	4,724	3,292	1,152 20
	Switzerland.....	15,909	11,419	15,909	11,419	3,996 65
	United States...	72,329	76,391	72,194	76,247	26,686 45
	Total......	199,631	184,698	133,888	125,656	43,979 60
Combs for dress and toilet, of all kinds....................	Great Britain...	.. ..	86,189	....	4,586	1,605 10
	Hong Kong. ...	... .	31	....	31	10 85
	Aust.-Hungary..	.. ..	318	....	340	119 00
	Belgium........	....	78	....	78	27 30
	China	....	60	....	60	21 00
	France.........	.. ..	30,597	.. ..	30,484	10,669 40
	Germany.......	... .	26,221	....	... .	....
	Italy.....	....	135	....	135	47 25
	Japan..........	....	61	....	61	21 35
	Switzerland... .	.. ..	99	....	30	10 50
	United States...	....	94,961	....	93,557	32,744 95
	Total. ..	. ...	238,750	....	129,362	45,276 70
Copper and manufactures of :— Copper nails, tacks, rivets and burrs or washers	Great Britain...	....	515	....	....	....
	United States...	....	2,945	....	2,945	883 50
	Total......	....	3,460	....	2,945	883 50

OF IMPORTS—*Continued.*

FOR HOME CONSUMPTION.

Preferential Tariff.			Surtax Tariff.			Total.		
Quantity.	Value.	Duty.	Quantity.	Value.	Duty.	Quantity.	Value.	Duty Collected.
Lbs.	$	$ cts.	Lbs.	$	$ cts.	Lbs.	$	$ cts.
1,515	268	38 08	....	....	....	1,745	365	52 38
....	....	....	....	....	....	20	1	0 50
....	....	....	....	....	....	570	68	18 20
....	....	....	....	....	....	205,149	40,680	8,170 98
1,515	268	38 08	....	....	....	207,484	41,114	8,242 06
124	14	1 66	....	....	....	124	14	1 66
....	....	....	....	....	....	205	41	4 10
....	....	....	....	....	....	313,542	34,025	6,270 84
124	14	1 66	....	....	....	513,871	34,080	6,276 60
15	3	0 60	....	....	....	15	3	0 60
....	....	....	....	....	....	147	35	10 50
15	3	0 60	....	....	....	162	38	11 10
Doz.			Doz.			Doz.		
45,658	41,106	9,591 68	2,307	2,167	1,011 27	51,376	46,012	11,561 60
....	....	....	....	....	....	4	5	1 75
....	....	....	125	75	35 00	34,552	27,820	9,745 75
....	....	....	....	....	....	476	841	294 35
....	....	....	....	....	....	2,661	3,276	1,146 60
....	....	....	17,395	15,404	7,188 67	17,477	15,496	7,220 87
....	....	....	....	....	....	4,724	3,292	1,152 20
....	....	....	....	....	....	15,909	11,419	3,996 65
....	....	....	135	144	67 20	72,329	76,391	26,753 65
45,658	41,106	9,591 68	19,962	17,790	8,302 14	199,508	184,552	61,873 42
....	81,483	19,013 06	....	110	51 33	....	86,179	20,669 49
....	....	....	....	....	....	....	31	10 85
....	....	....	....	85	39 67	....	425	158 67
....	....	....	....	....	....	....	78	27 30
....	....	....	....	....	....	....	60	21 00
....	....	....	....	....	....	....	30,484	10,669 40
....	....	....	....	26,221	12,236 51	....	26,221	12,236 51
....	....	....	....	....	....	....	135	47 25
....	....	....	....	....	....	....	61	21 35
....	....	....	....	....	....	....	30	10 50
....	....	....	....	1,255	585 67	....	94,812	33,330 62
....	81,483	19,013 06	....	27,671	12,913 18	....	238,516	77,202 94
....	515	103 00	....	....	....	....	515	103 00
....	....	....	....	....	....	....	2,945	883 50
....	515	103 00	....	....	....	....	3,460	986 50

No. 1.—General Statement

Articles Imported.	Countries.	Total Imports.		Entered		
				General Tariff.		
		Quantity.	Value.	Quantity.	Value.	Duty.
DUTIABLE GOODS—*Con.*		Lbs.		Lbs.	$	$ cts.
Copper, manufactures of—*Con.* Copper wire, plain, tinned or plated	Great Britain...	3,217	686	....	....	....
	China..	12	2	12	2	0 30
	United States...	213,565	39,446	213,269	39,393	5,908 95
	Total......	216,794	40,134	213,281	39,395	5,909 25
Copper, wire cloth, &c......	Great Britain...	....	2,660	.... . .	....	....
	United States...	....	643	....	643	160 75
	Total	....	3,303	....	643	160 75
Copper, all other manufactures of, N.O.P.	Great Britain...	....	8,260	....	83	24 90
	B. E. Indies....	....	221	......	221	66 30
	Hong Kong.....	....	1,143	....	1,143	342 90
	Aust.-Hungary .	....	6	... .	6	1 80
	China	....	516	....	516	154 80
	France	....	456	....	456	136 80
	Japan..........	....	219	....	219	65 70
	Sweden..... ...	....	310	....	310	93 00
	United States...	....	84,959	....	84,444	25,333 20
	Total	....	96,090	....	87,398	26,219 40
Cordage, cotton, of all kinds...	Great Britain...	95,035	12,243	694	136	34 00
	Sweden.........	3,628	685	3,628	685	171 25
	United States...	60,697	8,351	60,697	8,351	2,087 75
	Total. ...	159,360	21,279	65,019	9,172	2,293 00
Cordage, and twines of all kinds, N.E.S. (see Twines)..	Great Britain...	1,397,678	153,651	4,293	651	162 75
	B. E. Indies....	642	26	642	26	6 50
	Hong Kong.....	530	33	530	33	8 25
	New Zealand ...	7,804	438	....	....	....
	Aust.-Hungary .	6,572	871	6,572	871	217 75
	China..........	36	5	36	5	1 25
	France..	1,105	22	1,105	22	5 50
	Japan..........	50	3	50	3	0 75
	Russia.....	3,598	401	3,598	401	100 25
	Switzerland.....	414	196	414	196	49 00
	United States...	692,121	84,650	681,327	82,998	20,749 50
	Total......	2,110,550	240,296	698,567	85,206	21,301 50
Corks, and other manufactures of cork-wood, or cork-bark, N.O.P..........	Great Britain...	....	19,678	....	15,938	3,187 60
	Aust.-Hungary .	....	137	....	137	27 40
	Belgium	....	84	....	84	16 80
	France.........	....	277	....	748	149 60
	Germany.......	. ...	290	....	101	20 20
	Japan..........	....	1	....	1	0 20
	Portugal........	....	48,279	....	46,172	9,234 40
	Spain	....	90,910	....	86,635	17,327 00
	United States...	....	34,748	,.........	34,804	6,960 80
	Total	....	194,404	.. . .	184,620	36,924 00

OF IMPORTS—*Continued.*

FOR HOME CONSUMPTION.

Preferential Tariff.			Surtax Tariff.			Total.		
Quantity.	Value.	Duty.	Quantity.	Value.	Duty.	Quantity.	Value.	Duty Collected.
Lbs.	$	$ cts.	Lbs.	$	$ cts.	Lbs.	$	$ cts.
3,217	686	68 60				3,217	686	68 60
						12	2	0 30
			19	14	2 80	213,288	39,407	5,911 75
3,217	686	68 60	19	14	2 80	216,517	40,095	5,980 65
	2,660	443 34					2,660	443 34
							643	160 75
	2,660	443 34					3,303	604 09
	8,146	1,629 20		6	2 40		8,235	1,656 50
							221	66 30
							1,143	342 90
							6	1 80
							516	154 80
							456	136 80
							219	65 70
							310	93 00
							84,444	25,333 20
	8,146	1,629 20		6	2 40		95,550	27,851 00
94,341	12,107	2,421 40				95,035	12,243	2,455 40
						3,628	685	171 25
						60,697	8,351	2,087 75
94,341	12,107	2,421 40				159,360	21,279	4,714 40
1,431,054	155,305	31,061 00	19	3	1 00	1,435,366	155,959	31,224 75
						642	26	6 50
						530	33	8 25
7,804	438	87 60				7,804	438	87 60
						6,572	871	217 75
						36	5	1 25
						1,105	22	5 50
						50	3	0 75
						3,598	401	100 25
						414	196	49 00
						681,327	82,998	20,749 50
1,438,858	155,743	31,148 60	19	3	1 00	2,137,444	240,952	52,451 10
	3,705	493 98					19,643	3,681 58
							137	27 40
							84	16 80
							748	149 60
				189	50 40		290	70 60
							1	0 20
							46,172	9,234 40
							86,635	17,327 00
							34,804	6,960 80
	3,705	493 98		189	50 40		188,514	37,468 38

No. 1.—GENERAL STATEMENT

ARTICLES IMPORTED.	COUNTRIES.	TOTAL IMPORTS.		ENTERED		
				General Tariff.		
		Quantity.	Value.	Quantity.	Value.	Duty.
DUTIABLE GOODS—*Con.*			$		$	$ cts.
Corsets	Great Britain		2,123		243	85 05
	Aust.-Hungary		48		48	16 80
	Belgium		7,207		7,207	2,522 45
	France		2,367		2,367	828 45
	Germany		72			
	Switzerland		507		507	177 45
	United States		100,909		101,331	35,465 85
	Total		113,233		111,703	39,096 05
Corset clasps, busks, blanks and steels, and corset wires, tipped or untipped	Great Britain		212		22	7 70
	United States		2,819		2,819	986 65
	Total		3,031		2,841	994 35
Costumes and scenery, theatrical	Great Britain		97			
	Germany		36			
	United States		21,458		20,738	4,198 35
	Total		21,591		20,738	4,198 35
Cotton, manufactures of :—		Yds.	$	Yds.	$	$
Duck, gray or white, N.E.S.	Great Britain	91,389	24,311			
	United States	220,484	56,909	220,242	56,863	12,794 45
	Total	311,873	81,220	220,242	56,863	12,794 45
Embroideries, white	Great Britain		106,713		83,550	20,887 50
	Aust.-Hungary		5,903		5,903	1,475 75
	Belgium		3,696		3,696	924 00
	France		20,353		20,112	5,028 00
	Germany		5,078		562	140 50
	Japan		400		400	100 00
	Switzerland		354,879		351,229	87,807 25
	United States		39,582		39,578	9,894 50
	Total		536,604		505,030	126,257 50
Gray, unbleached cotton fabrics	Great Britain	78,649	5,650	48	4	1 00
	Aust.-Hungary	750	446	750	446	111 50
	Germany	40	4			
	United States	548,584	39,570	548,584	39,570	9,892 50
	Total	628,023	45,670	549,382	40,020	10,005 00
White or bleached cotton fabrics	Great Britain	12,823,820	1,033,769	278,819	21,409	5,352 25
	Hong Kong	60	5	60	5	1 25
	Aust.-Hungary	7,159	919	6,854	819	204 75
	Belgium	10,803	2,125	10,803	2,125	531 25
	China	360	25	360	25	6 25
	France	56,673	6,974	54,884	6,732	1,683 00
	Germany	55,467	3,529	300	37	9 25
	Japan	10,795	638	10,795	638	159 50
	Switzerland	203,999	20,136	204,599	20,413	5,103 25
	United States	2,314,860	206,520	2,302,821	204,826	51,206 50
	Total	15,483,996	1,274,640	2,870,295	257,029	64,257 25

OF IMPORTS—*Continued.*

FOR HOME CONSUMPTION.

Preferential Tariff.			Surtax Tariff.			Total.		
Quantity.	Value.	Duty.	Quantity.	Value.	Duty.	Quantity.	Value.	Duty Collected.
	$	$ cts.		$	$ cts.		$	$ cts.
	1,119	261 15		31	14 47		1,393	360 67
							48	16 80
							7,207	2,522 45
							2,367	828 45
				72	33 61		72	33 61
							507	177 45
							101,331	35,465 85
	1,119	261 15		103	48 08		112,925	39,405 28
	190	44 33					212	52 03
							2,819	986 65
	190	44 33					3,031	1,038 68
	97	20 21					97	20 21
				36	9 60		36	9 60
							20,738	4,198 35
	97	20 21		36	9 60		20,871	4,228 16
Yds.	$	$	Yds.	$	$	Yds.	$	$
93,377	24,402	3,660 35				93,377	24,402	3,660 35
						220,242	56,863	12,794 45
93,377	24,402	3,660 35				313,619	81,265	16,454 80
	21,058	3,509 66		646	215 33		105,254	24,612 49
							5,903	1,475 75
							3,696	924 00
							20,112	5,028 00
				4,516	1,505 34		5,078	1,645 84
							400	100 00
							351,229	87,807 25
				4	1 33		39,582	9,895 83
	21,058	3,509 66		5,166	1,722 00		531,254	131,489 16
78,507	5,636	939 29	32	3	1 00	78,587	5,643	941 29
						750	446	111 50
						548,584	39,570	9,892 50
78,507	5,636	939 29	32	3	1 00	627,921	45,659	10,945 29
12,595,828	1,013,911	168,987 25	6,384	1,004	334 67	12,881,031	1,036,324	174,674 17
						60	5	1 25
			305	100	33 33	7,159	919	238 08
						10,803	2,125	531 25
						360	25	6 25
			1,179	94	31 33	56,063	6,826	1,714 33
			55,958	3,833	1,277 64	56,258	3,870	1,286 89
						10,795	638	159 50
						204,599	20,413	5,103 25
			6,800	684	228 00	2,309,621	205,510	51,434 50
12,595,828	1,013,911	168,987 25	70,626	5,715	1,904 97	15,536,749	1,276,655	235,149 47

No. 1.—GENERAL STATEMENT

ARTICLES IMPORTED.	COUNTRIES.	TOTAL IMPORTS.		ENTERED		
				General Tariff.		
		Quantity.	Value.	Quantity.	Value.	Duty.
DUTIABLE GOODS—*Con.*		Yds.	$	Yds.	$	$ cts.
Cotton, mfrs. of—*Con.*						
Fabrics, printed, dyed or coloured, N.O.P.	Great Britain...	30,190,812	3,020,898	342,833	51,897	18,163 95
	Hong Kong....	762	39	762	39	13 65
	Aust.-Hungary..	12,762	1,518	7,219	867	303 45
	Belgium..	41,205	6,050	41,212	6,287	2,200 45
	China	1,050	93	1,050	93	32 55
	France.........	225,696	47,239	208,401	44,682	15,638 70
	Germany.	184,432	35,099	9,255	356	124 60
	Holland....	286	25	286	25	8 75
	Japan	32,911	3,351	32,911	3,351	1,172 85
	Switzerland.....	69,401	13,838	65,797	13,457	4,709 95
	United States...	5,500,001	480,317	5,462,689	477,305	167,056 75
	Total.	36,259,318	3,608,467	6,172,415	598,359	209,425 65
Jeans, coutilles and sateens, imported by corset and dress stay-makers for use in their own factories......	Great Britain...	13,916	1,687	....	....	....
	France..	235	112	235	112	22 40
	United States...	1,062,156	104,281	1,062,156	104,281	20,856 20
	Total. ...	1,076,307	106,080	1,062,391	104,393	20,878 60
Handkerchiefs..............	Great Britain...	....	289,114	....	8,445	2,955 75
	Aust.-Hungary.,	....	1,024	....	1,024	358 40
	Belgium.... ...	....	43	....	43	15 05
	China.....	....	35	....	35	12 25
	France.... ...	....	2,497	....	2,950	1,032 50
	Germany.	....	540	....	....	....
	Japan........ ...	....	3,537	....	3,537	1,237 95
	Mexico.......	....	125	....	125	43 75
	Switzerland.....	....	32,730	....	32,518	11,381 30
	United States...	....	6,088	....	6,092	2,132 20
		....	335,733	....	54,769	19,169 15
		Lbs.		Lbs.		
Batts, batting and sheet wadding....	Great Britain...	3,991	790	....	....	....
	Germany.......	421	110	....	....	....
	United States...	124,946	15,235	124,946	15,235	3,808 75
	Total.....	129,358	16,135	124,946	15,235	3,808 75
Knitting yarn, hosiery yarn or other cotton yarn.......	Great Britain...	71,449	17,094	3,014	805	201 25
	China	400	89	400	89	22 25
	United States...	119,624	28,461	119,624	28,461	7,115 25
	Total......	191,473	45,644	123,038	29,355	7,338 75
Cotton warps..............	Great Britain...	....	1,003	....	....	....
	United States...	....	1,238	....	1,238	309 50
	Total	....	2,241	....	1,238	309 50

OF IMPORTS—*Continued.*

FOR HOME CONSUMPTION.

Preferential Tariff.			Surtax Tariff.			Total.		
Quantity.	Value.	Duty.	Quantity.	Value.	Duty.	Quantity.	Value.	Duty Collected.
Yds.	$	$ cts.	Yds.	$	$ cts.	Yds.	$	$ cts.
29,676,367	2,950,950	688,559 11	71,373	12,914	6,026 53	30,090,573	3,015,761	712,749 59
....	....	....	....	....	....	762	39	13 65
....	....	....	5,543	651	303 80	12,762	1,518	607 25
....	....	....	....	....	....	41,212	6,287	2,200 45
....	....	....	....	....	....	1,050	93	32 55
....	....	....	9,678	1,759	820 87	218,079	46,441	16,459 57
....	....	....	175,127	34,738	16,211 13	184,382	35,094	16,335 73
....	....	....	....	....	....	286	25	8 75
....	....	....	....	....	....	32,911	3,351	1,172 85
....	....	....	2,049	245	114 33	67,846	13,702	4,824 28
....	....	....	8,410	1,045	487 67	5,471,099	478,350	167,544 42
29,676,367	2,950,950	688,559 11	272,180	51,352	23,964 33	36,120,962	3,600,661	921,949 09
13,916	1,687	224 95	....	....	....	13,916	1,687	224 95
....	....	....	....	....	....	235	112	22 40
....	....	....	....	....	....	1,062,156	104,281	20,856 20
13,916	1,687	224 95	....	....	....	1,076,307	106,080	21,103 55
....	282,069	65,816 86	....	14	6 53	....	290,528	68,779 14
....	....	....	....	....	....	....	1,024	358 40
....	....	....	....	....	....	....	43	15 05
....	....	....	....	....	....	....	35	12 25
....	....	....	....	....	....	....	2,950	1,032 50
....	....	....	....	540	252 00	....	540	252 00
....	....	....	....	....	....	....	3,537	1,237 95
....	....	....	....	....	....	....	125	43 75
....	....	....	....	....	....	....	32,518	11,381 30
....	....	....	....	....	....	....	6,092	2,132 20
....	282,069	65,816 86	....	554	258 53	....	337,392	85,244 54
Lbs.			Lbs.			Lbs.		
3,728	683	113 84	263	107	35 67	3,991	790	149 51
....	....	....	421	110	36 64	421	110	36 64
....	....	....	....	....	....	124,946	15,235	3,808 75
3,728	683	113 84	684	217	72 31	129,358	16,135	3,994 90
68,435	16,289	2,714 91	....	....	....	71,449	17,094	2,916 16
....	....	....	....	....	....	400	89	22 25
....	....	....	....	....	....	119,624	28,461	7,115 25
68,435	16,289	2,714 91	....	....	....	191,473	45,644	10,053 66
....	1,003	167 17	....	....	....	....	1,003	167 17
....	....	....	....	....	....	....	1,238	309 50
....	1,003	167 17	....	....	....	....	2,241	476 67

No. 1.—General Statement

Articles Imported.	Countries.	Total Imports.		Entered		
				General Tariff.		
		Quantity.	Value.	Quantity.	Value.	Duty.
DUTIABLE GOODS—*Con.*			$		$	$ cts.
Cotton, mfrs. of—*Con.* Seamless bags	Great Britain	....	6,195	....	819	163 80
	B. E. Indies	....	5,429	....	....	....
	B. Poss. Other	....	1	....	1	0 20
	Arabia	....	3	....	3	0 60
	Brazil	....	352	....	352	70 40
	Holland	....	4	....	4	0 80
	Mexico	....	40	....	40	8 00
	Turkey	....	3	....	3	0 60
	United States	....	7,166	....	7,164	1,432 80
	Venezuela	....	171	....	171	34 20
	Total	....	19,364	....	8,557	1,711 40
Sheets and bed quilts and damask of cotton, N.O.P.	Great Britain	....	179,902	....	3,694	1,108 20
	Hong Kong	....	48	....	48	14 40
	Aust.-Hungary	....	532	....	532	159 60
	Belgium	....	1,249	....	1,249	374 70
	China	....	220	....	220	66 00
	France	....	896	....	896	268 80
	Germany	....	937	....	13	3 90
	Japan	....	277	....	277	83 10
	Switzerland	....	749	....	749	224 70
	United States	....	18,056	....	17,831	5,349 30
	Total	....	202,866	....	25,509	7,652 70
		Doz.		Doz.		
Shirts of cotton	Great Britain	11,822	57,084	97	644	225 40
	Hong Kong	13	15	13	15	5 25
	Aust.-Hungary	1,076	4,800	1,076	4,800	1,680 00
	China	52	104	52	104	36 40
	France	333	1,615	331	1,612	564 20
	Germany	343	1,650	194	840	294 00
	Japan	64	575	64	575	201 25
	Switzerland	69	129	69	129	45 15
	United States	26,218	107,270	26,217	107,357	37,574 95
	Total	39,990	173,242	28,113	116,076	40,626 60
Sewing thread on spools	Great Britain	....	158,526	....	1,150	287 50
	Hong Kong	....	12	....	12	3 00
	Belgium	....	14,127	....	15,534	3,883 50
	China	....	17	....	17	4 25
	France	....	4,118	....	3,314	828 50
	Germany	....	1,093	....	....	....
	Japan	....	19	....	19	4 75
	United States	....	177,782	....	178,402	44,600 50
	Total	....	355,694	....	198,448	49,612 00
		Lbs.		Lbs.		
Sewing cotton thread in hanks, 3 and 6 cord	Great Britain	640,457	38[illegible],822	....	....	....
	United States	545	222	545	222	33 30
	Total	641,002	384,044	545	222	33 30

OF IMPORTS—*Continued.*

FOR HOME CONSUMPTION.

Preferential Tariff.			Surtax Tariff.			Total.		
Quantity.	Value.	Duty.	Quantity.	Value.	Duty.	Quantity.	Value.	Duty Collected.
	$	$ cts.		$	$ cts.		$	$ cts.
...	5,376	716 80	...	...	...	...	6,195	880 60
...	5,429	723 89	...	...	...	...	5,429	723 89
...	...	...	...	...	...	...	1	0 20
...	...	...	...	...	...	...	3	0 60
...	...	...	...	...	...	...	352	70 40
...	...	...	...	...	...	...	4	0 80
...	...	...	...	...	...	...	40	8 00
...	...	...	...	...	...	...	3	0 60
...	...	...	...	...	...	...	7,164	1,432 80
...	...	...	...	...	...	...	171	34 20
...	10,805	1,440 69	...	...	...	...	19,362	3,152 09
...	176,420	35,284 00	...	54	21 60	...	180,168	36,413 80
...	...	...	...	...	...	...	48	14 40
...	...	...	...	...	...	...	532	159 60
...	...	...	...	...	...	...	1,249	374 70
...	...	...	...	...	...	...	220	66 00
...	...	...	...	...	...	...	896	268 80
...	...	...	...	924	369 60	...	937	373 50
...	...	...	...	...	...	...	277	83 10
...	...	...	...	...	...	...	749	224 70
...	...	...	...	...	...	...	17,831	5,349 30
...	176,420	35,284 00	...	978	391 20	...	202,907	43,327 90
Doz.			Doz.			Doz.		
11,550	55,959	13,057 58	131	262	122 27	11,778	56,865	13,405 25
...	...	...	...	...	...	13	15	5 25
...	...	...	...	...	...	1,076	4,800	1,680 00
...	...	...	...	...	...	52	104	36 40
...	...	...	...	...	...	331	1,612	564 20
...	...	...	149	810	378 00	343	1,650	672 00
...	...	...	...	...	...	64	575	201 25
...	...	...	...	...	...	69	129	45 15
...	...	...	50	95	44 32	26,267	107,452	37,619 27
11,550	55,959	13,057 58	330	1,167	544 59	39,993	173,202	54,228 77
...	157,071	26,178 62	...	267	89 00	...	158,488	26,555 12
...	...	...	...	...	...	...	12	3 00
...	...	...	...	...	...	...	15,534	3,883 50
...	...	...	...	...	...	...	17	4 25
...	...	...	...	...	...	...	3,314	828 50
...	...	...	...	1,093	364 30	...	1,093	364 30
...	...	...	...	...	...	...	19	4 75
...	...	...	...	137	45 67	...	178,539	44,646 17
...	157,071	26,178 62	...	1,497	498 97	...	357,016	76,289 59
Lbs.			Lbs.			Lbs.		
640,651	383,887	38,388 70	...	...	...	640,651	383,887	38,388 70
...	...	...	...	...	...	545	222	33 30
640,651	383,887	38,388 70	...	...	...	641,196	384,109	38,422 00

No. 1.—GENERAL STATEMENT

Articles Imported.	Countries.	Total Imports.		Entered		
				General Tariff.		
		Quantity.	Value.	Quantity.	Value.	Duty.
DUTIABLE GOODS—*Con.*			$		$	$ cts.
Cotton, manufactures of—*Con.* Crochet cotton thread, on spools or tubes or in balls..	Great Britain...		11,485		30	7 50
	Germany.......		35			
	United States...		9,439		9,439	2,359 75
	Total		20,959		9,469	2,367 25
		Lbs.		Lbs.		
All other cotton thread, N.E.S.	Great Britain...	1,730	211			
	United States...	917	313	917	313	78 25
	Total	2,647	524	917	313	78 25
Clothing, N.E.S...	Great Britain...		248,645		11,297	3,953 95
	B. E. Indies....		50		50	17 50
	Hong Kong.....		637		637	222 95
	Aust.-Hungary..		2,643		735	257 25
	Belgium.......		411		411	143 85
	China..........		1,379		1,379	482 65
	France		16,192		16,610	5,813 50
	Germany.......		19,990		428	149 80
	Japan..........		4,006		4,006	1,402 10
	St. Pierre.......		12		12	4 20
	Switzerland.....		8,479		8,479	2,967 65
	United States...		370,319		370,052	129,518 20
	Total		672,763		414,096	144,933 60
Blouses and shirt waists.....	Great Britain...		5,729		624	218 40
	France		918		949	332 15
	Germany.......		1,391			
	Japan..........		164		164	57 40
	Switzerland.....		427		427	149 45
	United States...		79,320		79,057	27,669 95
	Total		87,949		81,221	28,427 35
Cotton bags made up by the use of the needle, not otherwise provided for	Great Britain...		7,083		3	1 05
	Hong Kong.....		10		10	3 50
	France		30		45	15 75
	United States...		56,266		56,385	19,734 75
	Total......		63,389		56,443	19,755 05
Lampwicks.	Great Britain...		5,164		22	5 50
	Hong Kong.....		17		17	4 25
	Belgium........		1		1	0 25
	China..........		16		16	4 00
	France		242		242	60 50
	Germany.......		23			
	Japan..........		2		2	0 50
	United States...		5,429		5,398	1,349 50
	Total		10,894		5,698	1,424 50

OF IMPORTS—*Continued.*

FOR HOME CONSUMPTION.

Preferential Tariff.			Surtax Tariff.			Total.		
Quantity.	Value.	Duty.	Quantity.	Value.	Duty.	Quantity.	Value.	Duty Collected.
	$	$ cts.		$	$ cts.		$	$ cts.
	11,455	1,909 19					11,485	1,916 69
				35	11 66		35	11 66
							9,439	2,359 75
	11,455	1,909 19		35	11 66		20,959	4,288 10
Lbs.			Lbs.			Lbs.		
1,730	211	35 16				1,730	211	35 16
						917	313	78 25
1,730	211	35 16				2,647	524	113 41
	232,894	54,343 34		4,530	2,114 00		248,721	60,411 29
							50	17 50
							637	222 95
				1,443	673 40		2,178	930 65
							411	143 85
							1,379	482 65
				47	21 93		16,657	5,835 43
				19,584	9,139 14		20,012	9,288 94
							4,006	1,402 10
							12	4 20
							8,479	2,967 65
				725	338 33		370,777	129,856 53
	232,894	54,343 34		26,329	12,286 80		673,319	211,563 74
	4,801	1,121 29		304	141 87		5,729	1,481 56
							949	332 15
				1,391	649 12		1,391	649 12
							164	57 40
							427	149 45
							79,057	27,669 95
	4,801	1,121 29		1,695	790 99		87,717	30,339 63
	7,080	1,652 02					7,083	1,653 07
							10	3 50
							45	15 75
							56,385	19,734 75
	7,080	1,652 02					63,523	21,407 07
	5,143	857 38					5,165	862 88
							17	4 25
							1	0 25
							16	4 00
							242	60 50
				23	7 67		23	7 67
							2	0 50
				12	4 00		5,410	1,353 50
	5,143	857 38		35	11 67		10,876	2,293 55

No. 1.—General Statement

Articles Imported.	Countries.	Total Imports.		Entered — General Tariff.		
		Quantity.	Value.	Quantity.	Value.	Duty.
DUTIABLE GOODS—*Con.*			$		$	$ cts.
Cotton, manufactures of—*Con.* Shawls	Great Britain	....	1,792	....	74	22 20
	Germany	....	78	....	....	....
	United States	....	11	....	11	3 30
	Total	....	1,881	....	85	25 50
		Doz. prs.		Doz. prs.		
Socks and stockings	Great Britain	94,242	127,760	1,658	2,105	736 75
	Hong Kong	72	55	72	55	19 25
	China	96	63	96	63	22 05
	France	2,477	2,920	1,859	2,045	715 75
	Germany	119,389	155,869	141	125	43 75
	Japan	20	10	20	10	3 50
	Switzerland	324	473	120	159	55 65
	United States	30,474	27,218	29,391	25,540	8,939 00
	Total	247,094	314,368	33,357	30,102	10,535 70
Tape, not dyed or coloured	Great Britain	....	49,533	....	1,656	414 00
	France	....	288	....	288	72 00
	Germany	....	2,006	....	....	....
	Switzerland	....	272	....	272	68 00
	United States	....	10,223	....	10,222	2,555 50
	Total	....	62,322	....	12,438	3,109 50
Tape, dyed or coloured	Great Britain	....	24,914	....	5,877	2,056 95
	France	....	8	....	8	2 80
	Germany	....	1,553	....	....	....
	Switzerland	....	293	....	293	102 55
	United States	....	5,762	....	5,432	1,901 20
	Total	....	32,530	....	11,610	4,063 50
Towels	Great Britain	....	96,649	....	974	292 20
	Aust.-Hungary	....	24	....	24	7 20
	France	....	131	....	131	39 30
	Germany	....	569	....	....	....
	United States	....	1,010	....	957	287 10
	Total	....	98,383	....	2,086	625 80
Undershirts and drawers	Great Britain	....	14,096	....	720	252 00
	France	....	12,156	....	12,156	4,254 60
	Germany	....	1,205	....	128	44 80
	Japan	....	71	....	71	24 85
	Switzerland	....	1,920	....	1,920	672 00
	United States	....	70,576	....	70,564	24,697 40
	Total	....	100,024	....	85,559	29,945 65

OF IMPORTS—*Continued.*

FOR HOME CONSUMPTION.

Preferential Tariff.			Surtax Tariff.			Total.		
Quantity.	Value.	Duty.	Quantity.	Value.	Duty.	Quantity.	Value.	Duty Collected.
	$	$ cts.		$	$ cts.		$	$ cts.
	1,713	342 60		5	2 00		1,792	366 80
				78	31 20		78	31 20
							11	3 30
	1,713	342 60		83	33 20		1,881	401 30
Doz. prs.			Doz. prs.			Doz. prs.		
74,778	104,633	24,414 77	17,687	21,275	9,928 33	94,123	128,013	35,079 85
						72	55	19 25
						96	63	22 05
			618	875	408 33	2,477	2,920	1,124 08
			119,310	155,781	72,697 88	119,451	155,906	72,741 63
						20	10	3 50
			204	314	146 53	324	473	202 18
			1,035	1,515	707 00	30,426	27,055	9,646 00
74,778	104,633	24,414 77	138,854	179,760	83,888 07	246,989	314,495	118,838 54
	46,805	7,800 95		1,071	357 00		49,532	8,571 95
							288	72 00
				2,006	668 63		2,006	668 63
							272	68 00
				1	0 33		10,223	2,555 83
	46,805	7,800 95		3,078	1,025 96		62,321	11,936 41
	18,186	4,243 41		851	397 13		24,914	6,697 49
							8	2 80
				1,553	724 68		1,553	724 68
							293	102 55
				330	154 00		5,762	2,055 20
	18,186	4,243 41		2,734	1,275 81		32,530	9,582 72
	94,721	18,944 20		138	55 20		95,833	19,291 60
							24	7 20
							131	39 30
				569	227 60		569	227 60
				53	21 20		1,010	308 30
	94,721	18,944 20		760	304 00		97,567	19,874 00
	13,223	3,085 52		153	71 40		14,096	3,408 92
							12,156	4,254 60
				1,077	502 64		1,205	547 44
							71	24 85
							1,920	672 00
				12	5 60		70,576	24,703 00
	13,223	3,085 52		1,242	579 64		100,024	33,610 81

No. 1.—General Statement

Articles Imported.	Countries.	Total Imports.		Entered		
				General Tariff.		
		Quantity.	Value.	Quantity.	Value.	Duty.
DUTIABLE GOODS—*Con.*		Yds.	$	Yds.	$	$ cts.
Cotton, mfrs. of—*Con.* Uncoloured cotton fabrics, bleached, viz.:—Scrims and window scrims, cambric cloths, muslin apron checks, brilliants, cords, piques, diapers, lenos, mosquito nettings, Swiss, jaconet and cambric muslins, and plain, striped or checked lawns .	Great Britain...	1,947,767	164,568	28,609	3,975	993 75
	France.........	27,324	3,242	27,867	3,374	843 50
	Japan.........	386	72	386	72	18 00
	Switzerland.....	70,073	10,720	69,630	10,588	2,647 00
	United States...	138,767	7,953	138,767	7,953	1,988 25
	Total	2,184,317	186,555	265,259	25,962	6,490 50
Velvets, velveteens and plush fabrics, N.E.S............	Great Britain...	1,448,311	348,638	55,160	15,419	4,625 70
	Aust.-Hungary .	4,253	927	4,253	927	278 10
	France.........	37,309	12,215	36,567	12,128	3,638 40
	Germany	90,634	29,786	....	....	....
	Holland........	712	477	712	477	143 10
	Japan.........	4	1	4	1	0 30
	Switzerland.....	3,022	863	3,022	863	258 90
	United States...	257,901	76,874	256,183	75,894	22,768 20
	Total	1,842,146	469,779	355,901	105,709	31,712 70
Other articles made by the seamstress from cotton fabrics, N.O.P.	Great Britain...	....	59,229	....	4,720	1,652 00
	Hong Kong.....	....	136	....	136	47 60
	Aust.-Hungary..	....	665	....	665	232 75
	Belgium........	....	469	....	469	164 15
	China..........	....	67	....	67	23 45
	France.........	....	8,158	....	7,695	2,693 25
	Germany........	....	2,650	....	29	10 15
	Holland........	....	15	....	15	5 25
	Japan.....	....	1,189	....	1,189	416 15
	Sweden.........	....	15	....	15	5 25
	Switzerland.....	....	4,107	....	3,877	1,356 95
	Turkey.........	....	383	....	....	....
	United States...	....	114,570	....	112,799	39,479 65
	Total.......	....	191,653	....	131,676	46,086 60
Crapes, black.......	Great Britain...	....	10,484	.... .	123	24 60
	China....	....	15	....	15	3 00
	France.........	....	2,323	....	2,323	464 60
	Germany.......	....	8	....	....	....
	United States...	....	473	....	473	94 60
	Total.......	....	13,303	....	2.934	586 80

OF IMPORTS—*Continued.*

FOR HOME CONSUMPTION.

Preferential Tariff.			Surtax Tariff.			Total.		
Quantity.	Value.	Duty.	Quantity.	Value.	Duty.	Quantity.	Value.	Duty Collected.
Yds.	$	$ cts.	Yds.	$	$ cts.	Yds.	$	$ cts.
1,938,584	160,868	26,812 32	7	1	0 33	1,967,200	164,844	27,806 40
....	....	....	....	....	....	27,867	3,374	843 50
....	....	....	....	....	....	386	72	18 00
....	....	....	....	....	....	69,630	10,588	2,647 00
....	....	....	....	....	....	138,767	7,953	1,988 25
1,938,584	160,868	26,812 32	7	1	0 33	2,203,850	186,831	33,303 15
1,330,969	315,218	63,043 60	62,261	18,229	7,291 60	1,448,390	348,866	74,960 90
....	....	....	....	....	....	4,253	927	278 10
....	....	....	742	85	34 00	37,309	12,213	3,672 40
....	....	....	90,139	29,812	11,924 80	90,139	29,812	11,924 80
....	....	....	....	....	....	712	477	143 10
....	....	....	....	....	....	4	1	0 30
....	....	....	....	....	....	3,022	863	258 90
....	....	....	3,206	1,166	466 40	259,389	77,060	23,234 60
1,330,969	315,218	63,043 60	156,348	49,292	19,716 80	1,843,218	470,219	114,473 10
....	53,605	12,507 31	....	1,346	628 13	....	59,671	14,787 44
....	....	....	....	....	....	....	136	47 60
....	....	....	....	....	....	....	665	232 75
....	....	....	....	....	....	....	469	164 15
....	....	....	....	....	....	....	67	23 45
....	....	....	....	156	72 80	....	7,851	2,766 05
....	....	....	....	2,521	1,176 52	....	2,550	1,186 67
....	....	....	....	....	....	....	15	5 25
....	....	....	....	....	....	....	1,189	416 15
....	....	....	....	....	....	....	15	5 25
....	....	....	....	....	....	....	3,877	1,356 95
....	....	....	....	....	....	....	....	....
....	....	....	....	131	61 13	....	112,930	39,540 78
....	53,605	12,507 31	....	4,154	1,938 58	....	189,435	60,532 49
....	9,986	1,331 52	....	375	100 00	....	10,484	1,456 12
....	....	....	....	....	....	....	15	3 00
....	....	....	....	....	....	....	2,323	464 60
....	....	....	....	8	2 11	....	8	2 11
....	....	....	....	....	....	....	473	94 60
....	9,986	1,331 52	....	383	102 11	....	13,303	2,020 43

No. 1.—General Statement

Articles Imported.	Countries.	Total Imports.		Entered		
				General Tariff.		
		Quantity.	Value.	Quantity.	Value.	Duty.
DUTIABLE GOODS—*Con.*		Pairs.	$	Pairs.	$	$ cts.
Cuffs of cotton, linen, xylonite, xyolite or celluloid....	Great Britain...	6,522	861	38	10	3 50
	Aust.-Hungary..	28,153	2,959	28,153	2,959	1,035 65
	Germany......	651	75	....	....	....
	Japan.........	512	84	512	84	29 40
	Switzerland.....	3,850	448	3,850	448	156 80
	United States...	5,877	724	5,877	724	253 40
	Total.......	45,565	5,151	38,430	4,225	1,478 75
Curtains and shams when made up, trimmed or untrimmed..	Great Britain...	....	435,905	....	33,144	11,600 40
	Hong Kong....	....	22	....	22	7 70
	Aust.-Hungary.	....	4,391	....	4,391	1,536 85
	Belgium........	....	3,466	....	3,466	1,213 10
	China.........	....	26	....	26	9 10
	France.........	....	41,937	....	42,377	14,831 95
	Germany.......	....	483	....	103	36 05
	Japan.......	....	584	....	584	204 40
	Switzerland.....	....	71,800	....	72,339	25,318 65
	Turkey.........	....	34	....	34	11 90
	United States...	....	75,343	....	75,248	26,336 80
	Total.......	....	633,991	....	231,734	81,106 90
Cyclometers and pedometers...	Great Britain...	....	267	....	13	3 25
	United States...	....	1,416	....	1,143	285 75
	Total.......	....	1,683	....	1,156	289 00
Drugs, dyes, chemicals and medicines—						
Acids—Acetic and pyroligneous, N.E.S., not exceeding proof strength.........		Galls.		Galls.		
	United States...	61	42	61	42	9 15
Acetic and pyroligneous in excess of the strength of proof..	Great Britain...	7,554	5,862	208	189	315 86
	France.........	....	....	10	32	13 50
	Germany........	4	9	....	....	....
	United States...	390	340	390	340	579 51
	Total.......	7,948	6,211	608	561	908 87
Acid, acetic and pyroligneous, crude, of any strength, not exceeding 30 per cent........	Great Britain...	55	4	....	....	....
	United States...	49,890	2,860	49,890	2,860	715 00
	Total.......	49,945	2,864	49,890	2,860	715 00
		Lbs.		Lbs.		
Acid phosphate, N.O.P......	Great Britain...	1,160	74	1,000	40	10 00
	United States...	331,363	19,418	331,363	19,418	4,854 50
	Total	332,523	19,492	332,363	19,458	4,864 50
Acids, mixed, N.E.S.... ...	Great Britain...	374	70	70	3	0 60
	United States...	297,270	7,805	297,270	7,805	1,561 00
	Total... ..	297,644	7,875	297,340	7,808	1,561 60

OF IMPORTS—*Continued.*

FOR HOME CONSUMPTION.

Preferential Tariff.			Surtax Tariff.			Total.		
Quantity.	Value.	Duty.	Quantity.	Value.	Duty.	Quantity.	Value.	Duty Collected.
Pairs.	$	$ cts.	Pairs.	$	$ cts.	Pairs.	$	$ cts.
6,484	851	198 60				6,522	861	202 10
						28,153	2,959	1,035 65
			651	75	35 00	651	75	35 00
						512	84	29 40
						3,850	448	156 80
						5,877	724	253 40
6,484	851	198 60	651	75	35 00	45,565	5,151	1,712 35
	401,347	93,648 36		740	345 33		435,231	105,594 09
							22	7 70
							4,391	1,536 85
							3,466	1,213 10
							26	9 10
							42,377	14,831 95
				345	161 00		448	197 05
							584	204 40
							72,339	25,318 65
							34	11 90
				25	11 68		75,273	26,348 48
	401,347	93,648 36		1,110	518 01		634,191	175,273 27
	254	42 33					267	45 58
							1,143	285 75
	254	42 33					1,410	331 33
Galls.			Galls.			Galls.		
						61	42	9 15
7,942	6,201	7,239 79				8,150	6,390	7,555 65
						10	32	13 50
			4	9	10 77	4	9	10 77
						390	340	579 51
7,942	6,201	7,239 79	4	9	10 77	8,554	6,771	8,159 43
55	4	0 66				55	4	0 66
						49,890	2,860	715 00
55	4	0 66				49,945	2,864	715 66
Lbs.			Lbs.			Lbs.		
160	34	5 67				1,160	74	15 67
						331,363	19,418	4,854 50
160	34	5 67				332,523	19,492	4,870 17
304	67	8 93				374	70	9 53
						297,270	7,805	1,561 00
304	67	8 93				297,644	7,875	1,570 53

No. 1.—General Statement

Articles Imported.	Countries.	Total Imports.		Entered		
				General Tariff.		
		Quantity.	Value.	Quantity.	Value.	Duty.
DUTIABLE GOODS—*Con.*		Lbs.	$	Lbs.	$	$ cts.
Drugs, dyes, &c.—*Con.*						
Acids—Muriatic and nitric...	Great Britain...	2,403	288	....	....	....
	Germany.......	10	56	....	....	....
	United States...	107,462	3,588	107,737	3,540	708 00
	Total......	109,875	3,932	107,737	3,540	708 00
Sulphuric	Great Britain...	5,015	99	4,398	81	20 25
	France.........	....	....	600	12	3 00
	United States. .	818,195	8,485	816,970	8,447	2,111 75
	Total	823,210	8,584	821,968	8,540	2,135 00
Others, N.E.S........	Great Britain...	177,739	28,763	42,016	2,364	472 80
	Belgium........	776	35	776	35	7 00
	France..........	2,500	362	3,060	476	95 20
	Germany.... ..	38,230	4,959	....	....	....
	United States...	285,281	12,785	283,656	12,360	2,472 00
	Total ...	504,526	46,904	329,508	15,235	3,047 00
Aniline dyes, in packages of less than 1 lb. weight. .. .	Germany.......	250	590	....	....	....
	United States...	1,748	132	1,748	132	26 40
	Total	1,998	722	1,748	132	26 40
Gelatine and isinglass.......	Great Britain...	48,257	16,664	3,614	979	244 75
	Aust.-Hungary..	6,860	972	6,360	944	236 00
	China	10	3	10	3	0 75
	France..........	29,813	4,762	37,995	5,951	1,487 75
	Germany.......	27,675	7,207	....	....	....
	Japan..........	5,556	1,058	2,230	317	79 25
	Switzerland....	9,686	1,611	10,236	1,688	422 00
	United States...	88,911	30,760	85,577	29,607	7,401 75
	Total.....	216,768	63,037	146,022	39,489	9,872 25
Glue, powdered or sheet... .	Great Britain...	726,420	58,728	115,180	12,527	3,131 75
	Aust.-Hungary..	344,013	17,235	223,200	13,041	3,260 25
	Belgium........	4,000	822	6,234	984	246 00
	France....... ...	275,113	22,667	267,109	21,447	5,361 75
	Germany.....	708,122	46,292	....	....	....
	Holland........	24,535	1,192	64,638	2,619	654 75
	Italy.	....	....	13,126	592	148 00
	Russia.........	169,598	8,514	230,015	10,120	2,530 00
	United States...	560,149	63.555	559,033	63,497	15,874 25
	Total	2,811,950	219,005	1,478,535	124,827	31,206 75
Glue, liquid	Great Britain...	....	800	....	312	78 00
	Aust.-Hungary..	....	....	....	25	6 25
	China.........	....	1	....	1	0 25
	Germany.......	....	52	....	....	....
	United States...	....	13,806	....	13,806	3,451 50
	Total	....	14,659	....	14,144	3,536 00

OF IMPORTS—*Continued.*

FOR HOME CONSUMPTION.

Preferential Tariff.			Surtax Tariff.			Total.		
Quantity.	Value.	Duty.	Quantity.	Value.	Duty.	Quantity.	Value.	Duty Collected.
Lbs.	$	$ cts.	Lbs.	$	$ cts.	Lbs.	$	$ cts.
2,403	288	38 40				2,403	288	38 40
			10	56	14 93	10	56	14 93
						107,737	3,540	708 00
2,403	288	38 40	10	56	14 93	110,150	3,884	761 33
617	18	3 01				5,015	99	23 26
						600	12	3 00
						816,970	8,447	2,111 75
617	18	3 01				822,585	8,558	2,138 01
130,270	25,213	3,361 80	1,330	497	132 53	173,616	28,074	3,967 13
						776	35	7 00
						3,060	476	95 20
			38,230	4,959	1,322 48	38,230	4,959	1,322 48
			1,625	425	113 33	285,281	12,785	2,585 33
130,270	25,213	3,361 80	41,185	5,881	1,568 34	500,963	46,329	7,977 14
			250	590	157 33	250	590	157 33
						1,748	132	26 40
			250	590	157 33	1,998	722	183 73
42,832	15,323	2,553 85	20	12	4 00	46,466	16,314	2,802 60
			500	28	9 33	6,860	972	245 33
						10	3	0 75
						37,995	5,951	1,487 75
			31,727	7,631	2,543 65	31,727	7,621	2,543 65
						2,230	317	79 25
						10,236	1,688	422 00
			730	515	171 67	86,307	30,122	7,573 42
42,832	15,323	2,553 85	32,977	8,186	2,728 65	221,831	62,998	15,154 75
616,125	47,707	7,951 31	2,240	180	60 00	733,545	60,414	11,143 06
						223,200	13,041	3,260 25
						6,234	984	246 00
						267,109	21,447	5,361 75
			654,793	42,760	14,253 34	654,793	42,760	14,253 34
						64,638	2,619	654 75
						13,126	592	148 00
						230,015	10,120	2,530 00
			888	44	14 67	559,921	63,541	15,888 92
616,125	47,707	7,951 31	657,921	42,984	14,328 01	2,752,581	215,518	53,486 07
	488	81 38					800	159 38
							25	6 25
							1	0 25
				52	17 34		52	17 34
							13,806	3,451 50
	488	81 38		52	17 34		14,684	3,634 72

No. 1.—General Statement

Articles Imported.	Countries.	Total Imports.		Entered		
				General Tariff.		
		Quantity.	Value.	Quantity.	Value.	Duty.
DUTIABLE GOODS—*Con*		Lbs.	$	Lbs.	$	$ cts.
Drugs, dyes, &c.—*Con.*						
Glycerine, N.E.S	Great Britain	1,269,898	108,664	1,100	127	25 40
	France	200	63	200	63	12 60
	United States	65,061	7,271	65,061	7,271	1,454 20
	Total	1,335,159	115,998	66,361	7,461	1,492 20
Glycerine, imported by manufacturers of explosives for use in the manufacture thereof in their own factories	Great Britain	2,066,732	198,714	....	....	....
	Mexico	225,741	19,634	225,744	19,634	1,963 40
	United States	92,751	9,600	120,485	12,651	1,265 10
	Total	2,385,224	227,948	346,229	32,285	3,228 50
Gums—						
Camphor	Great Britain	10,354	7,716	....	....	....
	Hong Kong	240	123	240	123	24 60
	Newfoundland	200	124	200	124	24 80
	Japan	15,200	9,721	17,100	10,712	2,142 40
	United States	6,776	5,014	7,286	5,476	1,095 20
	Total	32,770	22,698	24,826	16,435	3,287 00
Opium (crude)	Great Britain	5,839	22,062	1,074	2,046	1,074 00
	B. E. Indies	62,145	244,996	....	....	....
	France	250	487	250	487	250 00
	Germany	5	12	....	....	....
	Turkey	200	414	200	414	200 00
	United States	7,213	17,346	3,246	6,975	3,246 00
	Total	75,652	285,317	4,770	9,922	4,770 00
Other, N.E.S	Great Britain	254	49	254	49	9 80
	United States	12,288	2,280	12,288	2,280	456 00
	Total	12,542	2,329	12,542	2,329	465 80
Liquorice, in paste, rolls and sticks	Great Britain	219,319	14,940	185,088	12,494	2,498 80
	Holland	1,150	96	1,150	96	19 20
	Italy	2,691	396	2,691	396	79 20
	Russia	74,841	5,984	85,644	6,605	1,321 00
	Turkey	955,273	62,309	618,865	42,300	8,460 00
	United States	1,303,050	108,493	1,302,750	108,466	21,693 20
	Total	2,556,324	192,218	2,196,188	170,357	34,071 40
Magnesia	Great Britain	59,819	3,980	560	93	18 60
	United States	206,735	4,747	205,773	4,735	947 00
	Total	266,554	8,727	206,333	4,828	965 60
Milk food, and other similar preparations	Great Britain	....	39,374	....	....	....
	Belgium	....	264	....	264	79 20
	France	....	31	....	31	9 30
	Switzerland	....	12,189	....	9,832	2,949 60
	United States	....	38,282	....	40,803	12,240 90
	Total	....	90,140	....	50,930	15,279 00

OF IMPORTS—*Continued.*

FOR HOME CONSUMPTION.

Preferential Tariff.			Surtax Tariff.			Total.		
Quantity.	Value.	Duty.	Quantity.	Value.	Duty.	Quantity.	Value.	Duty Collected.
Lbs.	$	$ cts.	Lbs.	$	$ cts.	Lbs.	$	$ cts.
1,262,930	105,532	14,071 02				1,264,030	105,659	14,096 42
						200	63	12 60
						65,061	7,271	1,454 20
1,262,930	105,532	14,071 02				1,329,291	112,993	15,563 22
2,065,104	200,729	13,382 01				2,065,104	200,729	13,382 01
						225,744	19,634	1,963 40
						120,485	12,651	1,265 10
2,065,104	200,729	13,382 01				2,411,333	233,014	16,610 51
11,417	7,582	1,010 94				11,417	7,582	1,010 94
						240	123	24 60
						200	124	24 80
						17,100	10,712	2,142 40
						7,286	5,476	1,095 20
11,417	7,582	1,010 94				36,243	24,017	4,297 94
4,920	19,090	3,280 00				5,994	21,136	4,354 00
58,837	232,919	39,224 67				58,837	232,919	39,224 67
						250	487	250 00
			5	12	6 67	5	12	6 67
						200	414	200 00
						3,246	6,975	3,246 00
63,757	252,009	42,504 67	5	12	6 67	68,532	261,943	47,281 34
						254	49	9 80
						12,288	2,280	456 00
						12,542	2,329	465 80
53,027	4,236	564 90				238,115	16,730	3,063 70
						1,150	96	19 20
						2,691	396	79 20
						85,644	6,605	1,321 00
						618,865	42,300	8,460 00
						1,302,750	108,466	21,693 20
53,027	4,236	564 90				2,249,215	174,593	34,636 30
30,139	2,496	332 79	29,120	1,391	370 94	59,819	3,980	722 33
			962	12	3 20	206,735	4,747	950 20
30,139	2,496	332 79	30,082	1,403	374 14	266,554	8,727	1,672 53
	39,414	7,882 80					39,414	7,882 80
							264	79 20
							31	9 30
							9,832	2,949 60
							40,803	12,240 90
	39,414	7,882 80					90,344	23,161 80

No. 1.—General Statement

Articles Imported.	Countries.	Total Imports.		Entered		
				General Tariff.		
		Quantity.	Value.	Quantity.	Value.	Duty.
DUTIABLE GOODS—*Con.*		Ozs.	$	Ozs.	$	$ cts.
Drugs, dyes, &c.—*Con.* Morphine	Great Britain	5,120	5,770	8	10	2 00
	United States	321	661	321	661	132 20
	Total	5,441	6,431	329	671	134 20
		Lbs.		Lbs.		
Opium, powdered	Great Britain	181	482	63	169	85 05
	Belgium	141	423	....	....	....
	Germany	11,006	34,694	....	....	....
	Turkey	200	356	....	....	....
	United States	20	71	20	71	27 00
	Total	11,548	36,026	83	240	112 05
Proprietary medicines, in liquid form, containing alcohol	Great Britain	....	4,200	....	3,859	1,929 50
	France	....	8,707	....	7,922	3,961 00
	Germany	....	1,194	....	....	....
	Italy	....	....	....	386	193 00
	Switzerland	....	111	....	111	55 50
	United States	....	58,958	....	60,206	30,103 00
	Total	....	73,170	....	72,484	36,242 00
Proprietary medicines, not otherwise provided for	Great Britain	....	125,360	....	4,039	1,009 75
	Australia	....	39	....	39	9 75
	Hong Kong	....	1,484	....	1,484	371 00
	Aust.-Hungary	....	41	....	41	10 25
	Belgium	....	....	....	58	14 50
	China	....	2,810	....	2,636	659 00
	France	....	36,984	....	36,984	9,246 00
	Germany	....	4,208	....	140	35 00
	Holland	....	1,223	....	1,257	314 25
	Iceland	....	27	....	27	6 75
	Japan	....	1,160	....	740	185 00
	Switzerland	....	428	....	428	107 00
	United States	....	270,813	....	276,604	69,151 00
	Total	....	444,541	....	324,477	81,119 25
Potash or potassa, bicarbonate of	Great Britain	912	227	28	3	0 60
	United States	6,240	503	6,240	503	100 60
	Total	7,152	730	6,268	506	101 20
Salts, glauber	Great Britain	187,950	717	24,860	94	18 80
	United States	45,973	315	42,758	283	56 60
	Total	233,923	1,032	67,618	377	75 40
Soda, bicarbonate of	Great Brirain	4,509,311	40,326	....	....	....
	Aust.-Hungary	82,414	682	82,414	682	136 40
	United States	497,204	5,611	494,201	5,371	1,074 20
	Total	5,088,929	46,619	576,615	6,053	1,210 60

OF IMPORTS—*Continued.*

FOR HOME CONSUMPTION.

Preferential Tariff.			Surtax Tariff.			Total.		
Quantity.	Value.	Duty.	Quantity.	Value.	Duty.	Quantity.	Value.	Duty Collected.
Ozs.	$	$ cts.	Ozs.	$	$ cts.	Ozs.	$	$ cts.
5,112	5,760	768 02				5,120	5,770	770 02
						321	661	132 20
5,112	5,760	768 02				5,441	6,431	902 22
Lbs.			Lbs.			Lbs.		
118	313	106 20				181	482	191 25
						20	71	27 00
118	313	106 20				201	553	218 25
							3,859	1,929 50
							7,922	3,961 00
				3,192	2,127 98		3,192	2,127 98
							386	193 00
							111	55 50
							60,206	30,103 00
				3,192	2,127 98		75,676	38,369 98
	122,836	20,473 55		427	142 33		127,302	21,625 63
							39	9 75
							1,484	371 00
							41	10 25
							58	14 50
							2,636	659 00
				11	3 67		36,995	9,249 67
				4,120	1,373 40		4,260	1,408 40
							1,257	314 25
							27	6 75
							740	185 00
							428	107 00
				63	21 00		276,667	69,172 00
	122,836	20,473 55		4,621	1,540 40		451,934	103,133 20
884	224	29 88				912	227	30 48
						6,240	503	100 60
884	224	29 88				7,152	730	131 08
163,090	623	83 07				187,950	717	101 87
			3,215	32	8 54	45,973	315	65 14
163,090	623	83 07	3,215	32	8 54	233,923	1,032	167 01
4,509,311	40,326	5,376 86				4,509,311	40,326	5,376 86
						82,414	682	136 40
						494,201	5,371	1,074 20
4,509,311	40,326	5,376 86				5,085,926	46,379	6,587 46

No. 1.—General Statement

Articles Imported.	Countries.	Total Imports.		Entered		
				General Tariff.		
		Quantity.	Value.	Quantity.	Value.	Duty.
DUTIABLE GOODS—*Con.*			$		$	$ cts.
Drugs, dyes, &c.—*Con.*						
Sodium, hyposulphite	Great Britain	...	2,060	...	...	...
	Aust.-Hungary	...	3,940	...	3,940	788 00
	Belgium	...	172	...	172	34 40
	Germany	...	200	...	...	...
	United States	...	4,906	...	4,906	981 20
	Total	...	11,278	...	9,018	1,803 60
		Lbs.		Lbs.		
Sulphuric ether, chloroform and solutions of peroxides of hydrogen	Great Britain	13,526	8,980	680	470	117 50
	Aust.-Hungary	4,100	1,017	4,850	1,274	318 50
	France	327	97	27	4	1 00
	Germany	32,952	7,365	3,746	632	158 00
	United States	132,506	14,949	133,223	14,782	3,695 50
	Total	183,411	32,408	142,526	17,162	4,290 50
Thorium nitrate	United States	...	29	...	...	...
Vaseline and all similar preparations of petroleum, for toilet, medicinal or other purposes	Total					
	Great Britain	...	16	...	14	3 50
	France	...	22	...	22	5 50
	Germany	...	32	...	...	...
	United States	...	14,238	...	14,208	3,552 00
	Total	...	14,308	...	14,244	3,561 00
Yeast cakes	United States	3,681	366	3,616	359	216 96
Yeast, compressed, in packages weighing less than 50 lbs	United States	870	178	870	178	52 20
Yeast, compressed, in bulk or mass of not less than 50 lbs	United States	226,329	48,072	226,329	48,072	6,789 87
All other drugs, dyes and chemicals, &c., N.O.P.	Great Britain	...	194,227	...	11,513	2,302 60
	B. Guiana	...	...	...	...	...
	Hong Kong	...	59	...	59	11 80
	Aust.-Hungary	...	2,678	...	2,678	535 60
	Belgium	...	3,989	...	4,057	811 40
	China	...	92	...	92	18 40
	France	...	19,983	...	19,617	3,923 40
	Germany	...	54,108	...	51	10 20
	Holland	...	1,517	...	1,517	303 40
	Italy	...	357	...	382	76 40
	Japan	...	696	...	439	87 80
	Switzerland	...	12,415	...	12,839	2,567 80
	Turkey	...	10	...	10	2 00
	United States	...	320,577	...	315,625	63,125 00
	Total	...	610,708	...	368,879	73,775 80

OF IMPORTS—*Continued.*

FOR HOME CONSUMPTION.

Preferential Tariff.			Surtax Tariff.			Total.		
Quantity.	Value.	Duty.	Quantity.	Value.	Duty.	Quantity.	Value.	Duty Collected.
	$	$ cts.		$	$ cts.		$	$ cts.
	2,060	274 67					2,060	274 67
							3,940	788 00
							172	34 40
				200	53 33		200	53 33
							4,906	981 20
	2,060	274 67		200	53 33		11,278	2,131 60
Lbs.			Lbs.			Lbs.		
10,887	7,446	1,241 01	1,643	528	176 00	13,210	8,444	1,534 51
						4,850	1,274	318 50
						27	4	1 00
			42,456	6,578	2,192 71	46,202	7,210	2,350 71
			275	134	44 67	133,498	14,916	3,740 17
10,887	7,446	1,241 01	44,374	7,240	2,413 38	197,787	31,848	7,944 89
				29	7 74		29	7 74
	2	0 34					16	3 84
							22	5 50
				32	10 67		32	10 67
				30	10 00		14,238	3,562 00
	2	0 34		62	20 67		14,308	3,582 01
						3,616	359	216 96
						870	178	52 20
						226,329	48,072	6,789 87
	179,761	23,969 14		4,819	1,285 07		196,093	27,556 81
	65	8 67					65	8 67
							59	11 80
							2,678	535 60
							4,057	811 40
							92	18 40
				102	27 20		19,719	3,950 60
				53,418	14,244 98		53,469	14,255 18
							1,517	303 40
							382	76 40
							439	87 80
							12,839	2,567 80
							10	2 00
				5,165	1,377 33		320,790	64,502 33
	179,826	23,977 81		63,504	16,934 58		612,209	114,688 19

No. 1.—General Statement

Articles Imported.	Countries.	Total Imports. Quantity.	Total Imports. Value.	Entered — General Tariff. Quantity.	Entered — General Tariff. Value.	Entered — General Tariff. Duty.
DUTIABLE GOODS.			$		$	$ cts.
Earthen and chinaware—(See brick and tiles.)						
Baths, tubs and washstands of earthenware, stone, cement or clay, or of other material, N.O.P.	Great Britain		15,939		192	57 60
	China		8		8	2 40
	Germany		19			
	United States		52,187		51,862	15,558 60
	Total		68,153		52,062	15,618 60
Brown or coloured earthen and stoneware, and Rockingham ware	Great Britain		3,698		352	105 60
	France		373		373	111 90
	Japan		427		427	128 10
	United States		3,868		3,865	1,159 50
	Total		8,366		5,017	1,505 10
Decorated, printed or sponged, and all earthenware, N.E.S.	Great Britain		126,128		3,623	1,086 90
	Hong Kong		34[illegible]		346	103 80
	Aust.-Hungary		2,67[illegible]		2,678	803 40
	China		2[illegible]		289	86 70
	Denmark		1[illegible]8		198	59 40
	France		7,9[illegible]		7,988	2,396 40
	Germany		14,3[illegible]		755	226 50
	Italy		3[illegible]		32	9 60
	Japan		5,76[illegible]		5,690	1,707 00
	United States		33,26[illegible]		33,092	9,927 60
	Total		191,083		54,691	16,407 30
Demijohns, churns or crocks.	Great Britain		997		27	8 10
	Newfoundland		3		3	0 90
	Aust.-Hungary		101		71	21 30
	Belgium		20		20	6 00
	France		56		56	16 80
	Germany		62			
	Holland		121		121	36 30
	Turkey				1	0 30
	United States		8,912		8,912	2,673 60
	Total		10,272		9,211	2,763 30
White granite or ironstone ware, C.C. or cream coloured ware	Great Britain		38,573		1,026	307 80
	Aust.-Hungary		29		29	8 70
	Japan		188		188	56 40
	United States		7,494		7,494	2,248 20
	Total		46,284		8,737	2,621 10

OF IMPORTS—*Continued.*

FOR HOME CONSUMPTION.

Preferential Tariff.			Surtax Tariff.			Total.		
Quantity.	Value.	Duty.	Quantity.	Value.	Duty.	Quantity.	Value.	Duty Collected.
	$	$ cts.		$	$ cts.		$	$ cts.
	15,747	3,149 40					15,939	3,207 00
							8	2 40
				19	7 60		19	7 60
							51,862	15,558 60
	15,747	3,149 40		19	7 60		67,828	18,775 60
	3,346	669 20					3,698	774 80
							373	111 90
							427	128 10
							3,865	1,159 50
	3,346	669 20					8,363	2,174 30
	122,668	24,533 60		451	180 40		126,742	25,800 90
							346	103 80
							2,678	803 40
							289	86 70
							198	59 40
							7,988	2,396 40
				13,566	5,426 40		14,321	5,652 90
							32	9 60
							5,690	1,707 00
				176	70 40		33,268	9,998 00
	122,668	24,533 60		14,193	5,677 20		191,552	46,618 10
	1,205	241 00					1,232	249 10
							3	0 90
				30	12 00		101	33 30
							20	6 00
							56	16 80
				62	24 80		62	24 80
							121	36 30
							1	0 30
							8,912	2,673 60
	1,205	241 00		92	36 80		10,508	3,041 10
	39,223	7,844 60					40,249	8,152 40
							29	8 70
							188	56 40
							7,494	2,248 20
	39,223	7,844 60					47,960	10,465 70

No. 1.—General Statement

Articles Imported.	Countries.	Total Imports. Quantity.	Total Imports. Value.	Entered — General Tariff. Quantity.	Value.	Duty.
Dutiable goods—*Con.*			$		$	$ cts.
Earthen and chinaware—*Con.*						
Tableware of china, porcelain or other clay	Great Britain		699,416		5,264	1,579 20
	Hong Kong		284		284	85 20
	Aust.-Hungary		20,601		20,552	6,165 60
	Belgium		171		171	51 30
	China		1,445		1,445	433 50
	Denmark		203		203	60 90
	France		41,388		41,388	12,416 40
	Germany		101,413		4,857	1,457 10
	Holland		5,648		5,648	1,694 40
	Italy		32		32	9 60
	Japan		50,904		50,904	15,271 20
	St. Pierre		15		15	4 50
	United States		23,035		22,631	6,789 30
	Total		944,555		153,394	46,018 20
China and porcelain ware, N.E.S	Great Britain		40,113		5,607	1,682 10
	Hong Kong		505		505	151 50
	Aust.-Hungary		25,680		26,166	7,849 80
	Belgium		10		10	3 00
	China		1,089		1,089	326 70
	Denmark		24		24	7 20
	France		20,663		20,931	6,279 30
	Germany		72,890		283	84 90
	Holland		387		387	116 10
	Italy		476		476	142 80
	Japan		37,563		37,575	11,272 50
	United States		11,005		10,389	3,116 70
	Total		210,405		103,442	31,032 60
Earthenware tiles	Great Britain		28,822		303	106 05
	Belgium		228		228	79 80
	France		754		754	263 90
	Germany		19			
	Holland		1		1	0 35
	United States		48,000		48,065	16,822 75
	Total		77,824		49,351	17,272 85
Manufactures of earthenware, N.E.S	Great Britain		18,137		1,311	393 30
	Aust.-Hungary		2,669		2,683	804 90
	China		129		129	38 70
	France		4,680		4,680	1,404 00
	Germany		3,126		360	108 00
	Italy		169		169	50 70
	Japan		927		927	278 10
	Switzerland		39		39	11 70
	United States		87,999		87,817	26,345 10
	Total		117,875		98,115	29,434 50
		Doz.		Doz.		
Eggs	Australia	710	92	710	92	21 30
	Hong Kong	14,672	799	14,672	799	440 16
	China	20,918	1,169	20,918	1,169	627 54
	United States	448,929	92,172	426,369	86,877	12,791 07
	Total	485,229	94,232	462,669	88,937	13,880 07

OF IMPORTS—*Continued.*

FOR HOME CONSUMPTION.

Preferential Tariff.			Surtax Tariff.			Total.		
Quantity.	Value.	Duty.	Quantity.	Value.	Duty.	Quantity.	Value.	Duty Collected.
	$	$ cts.		$	$ cts.		$	$ cts.
....	705,415	105,812 25	....	473	189 20	....	711,152	107,580 65
....	....	....	....	....	....	....	284	85 20
....	....	....	....	288	115 20	....	20,840	6,280 80
....	....	....	....	....	....	....	171	51 30
....	....	....	....	....	....	....	1,445	433 50
....	....	....	....	....	....	....	203	60 90
....	....	....	....	....	....	....	41,388	12,416 40
....	....	....	....	96,090	38,436 00	....	100,947	39,893 10
....	....	....	....	....	....	....	5,648	1,694 40
....	....	....	....	....	....	....	32	9 60
....	....	....	....	....	....	....	50,904	15,271 20
....	....	....	....	....	....	....	15	4 50
....	....	....	....	404	161 60	....	23,035	6,950 90
....	705,415	105,812 25	....	97,255	38,902 00	....	956,064	190,732 45
....	34,715	6,943 00	....	448	179 20	....	40,770	8,804 30
....	....	....	....	....	....	....	505	151 50
....	....	....	....	391	156 40	....	26,557	8,006 20
....	....	....	....	....	....	....	10	3 00
....	....	....	....	....	....	....	1,089	326 70
....	....	....	....	....	....	....	24	7 20
....	....	....	....	....	....	....	20,931	6,279 30
....	....	....	....	74,401	29,760 40	....	74,684	29,845 30
....	....	....	....	....	....	....	387	116 10
....	....	....	....	....	....	....	476	142 80
....	....	....	....	....	....	....	37,575	11,272 50
....	....	....	....	616	246 40	....	11,005	3,363 10
....	34,715	6,943 00	....	75,856	30,342 40	....	214,013	68,318 00
....	28,877	6,737 96	....	....	....	....	29,180	6,844 01
....	....	....	....	....	....	....	228	79 80
....	....	....	....	....	....	....	754	263 90
....	....	....	....	19	8 87	....	19	8 87
....	....	....	....	....	....	....	1	0 35
....	....	....	....	....	....	....	48,065	16,822 75
....	28,877	6,737 96	....	19	8 87	....	78,247	24,019 68
....	16,788	3,357 60	....	119	47 60	....	18,218	3,798 50
....	....	....	....	....	....	....	2,683	804 90
....	....	....	....	....	....	....	129	38 70
....	....	....	....	....	....	....	4,680	1,404 00
....	....	....	....	2,766	1,106 40	....	3,126	1,214 40
....	....	....	....	....	....	....	169	50 70
....	....	....	....	....	....	....	927	278 10
....	....	....	....	....	....	....	39	11 70
....	....	....	....	36	14 40	....	87,853	26,359 50
....	16,788	3,357 60	....	2,921	1,168 40	....	117,824	33,960 50
Doz,			Doz.			Doz.		
....	....	....	....	....	....	710	92	21 30
....	....	....	....	....	....	14,672	799	440 16
....	....	....	....	....	....	20,918	1,169	627 54
....	....	....	....	....	....	426,369	86,877	12,791 07
....	....	....	....	....	....	462,669	88,937	13,880 07

No. 1.—GENERAL STATEMENT

ARTICLES IMPORTED.	COUNTRIES.	TOTAL IMPORTS.		ENTERED		
				General Tariff.		
		Quantity.	Value.	Quantity.	Value.	Duty.
						$ cts.
DUTIABLE GOODS—*Con.*						
Elastic, round or flat, including garter elastic	Great Britain		91,468		154	53 90
	Hong Kong		1		1	0 35
	France		2,215		2,215	775 25
	Germany		104			
	United States		24,574		24,574	8,600 90
	Total		118,362		26,944	9,430 40
		M.		M.		
Electric light carbons and carbon points, of all kinds, N.E.S.	Aust.-Hungary	83	1,196	72	1,011	353 85
	France	151	1,091	151	1,091	381 85
	Germany	512	7,180			
	United States	4,915	38,597	4,691	35,806	12,532 10
	Total	5,661	48,064	4,914	37,908	13,267 80
		No.		No.		
Electric carbons over 6 inches in circumference	United States	120	71	120	71	10 65
Electric apparatus, N.E.S., insulators of all kinds, &c., electric and galvanic batteries; telegraph and telephone instruments	Great Britain		68,718		1,962	490 50
	Aust.-Hungary		1,505		1,452	363 00
	Belgium		194		194	48 50
	Denmark		3,431			
	France		7,579		7,579	1,894 75
	Germany		8,438			
	Holland				1,090	272 50
	Italy		155		155	38 75
	Sweden		500		500	125 00
	Switzerland		1,689		1,689	422 25
	United States		2,369,517		2,367,497	591,874 25
	Total		2,461,726		2,382,118	595,529 50
Electric motors, generators, dynamos and sockets	Great Britain		12,583		4,851	1,212 75
	Aust.-Hungary		260		260	65 00
	France		652		652	163 00
	Holland		5,937		5,937	1,484 25
	Sweden		271		271	67 75
	Switzerland		1,151		1,151	287 75
	United States		982,999		981,097	245,274 25
	Total		1,003,853		994,219	248,554 75
Embroideries, not otherwise provided for	Great Britain		24,548		9,496	3,323 60
	Aust.-Hungary		1,675		1,675	586 25
	China		209		209	73 15
	France		6,988		6,562	2,296 70
	Germany		6,365			
	Japan		3,282		3,282	1,148 70
	Switzerland		33,899		33,566	11,748 10
	United States		9,322		8,364	2,927 40
	Total		86,288		63,154	22,103 90

OF IMPORTS—*Continued.*

FOR HOME CONSUMPTION.

Preferential Tariff.			Surtax Tariff.			Total.		
Quantity.	Value.	Duty.	Quantity.	Value.	Duty.	Quantity.	Value.	Duty Collected.
	$	$ cts.		$	$ cts.		$	$ cts.
....	91,314	21,306 85	....	....	....	....	91,468	21,360 75
....	....	....	....	....	....	....	1	0 35
....	....	....	....	....	....	....	2,215	775 25
....	....	....	....	104	48 53	....	104	48 53
....	....	....	....	....	....	....	24,574	8,600 90
....	91,314	21,306 85	....	104	48 53	....	118,362	30,785 78
M.			M.			M.		
....	....	....	....	....	....	72	1,011	353 85
....	....	....	....	....	....	151	1,091	381 85
....	....	....	512	7,180	3,350 65	512	7,180	3,350 65
....	....	....	244	3,058	1,427 07	4,935	38,864	13,959 17
....	....	....	756	10,238	4,777 72	5,670	48,146	18,045 52
No.			No.			No.		
....	....	....	....	....	....	120	71	10 65
....	66,213	11,035 63	....	54	18 00	....	68,229	11,544 13
....	....	....	....	53	17 67	....	1,505	380 67
....	....	....	....	....	....	....	194	48 50
....	....	....	....	....	....	....	....	....
....	....	....	....	....	....	....	7,579	1,894 75
....	....	....	....	8,438	2,812 69	....	8,438	2,812 69
....	....	....	....	....	....	....	1,090	272 50
....	....	....	....	....	....	....	155	38 75
....	....	....	....	....	....	....	500	125 00
....	....	....	....	....	....	....	1,689	422 25
....	....	....	....	538	179 33	....	2,368,035	592,053 58
....	66,213	11,035 63	....	9,083	3,027 69	....	2,457,414	609,592 82
....	7,732	1,288 67	....	....	....	....	12,583	2,501 42
....	....	....	....	....	....	....	260	65 00
....	....	....	....	....	....	....	652	163 00
....	....	....	....	....	....	....	5,937	1,484 25
....	....	....	....	....	....	....	271	67 75
....	....	....	....	....	....	....	1,151	287 75
....	....	....	....	166	55 33	....	981,263	245,329 58
....	7,732	1,288 67	....	166	55 33	....	1,002,117	249,898 75
....	12,053	2,812 48	....	2,970	1,386 00	....	24,519	7,522 08
....	....	....	....	....	....	....	1,675	586 25
....	....	....	....	....	....	....	209	73 15
....	....	....	....	296	138 13	....	6,858	2,434 83
....	....	....	....	6,464	3,016 53	....	6,464	3,016 53
....	....	....	....	....	....	....	3,282	1,148 70
....	....	....	....	....	....	....	33,566	11,748 10
....	....	....	....	45	21 00	....	8,409	2,948 40
....	12,053	2,812 48	....	9,775	4,561 66	....	84,982	29,478 04

No. 1.—General Statement

Articles Imported.	Countries.	Total Imports.		Entered		
				General Tariff.		
		Quantity.	Value.	Quantity.	Value.	Duty.
DUTIABLE GOODS—*Con.*			$		$	$ cts.
Emery wheels and manufactures of Emery	Great Britain		271			
	Germany		183			
	Switzerland		6			
	United States		41,626		41,626	10,406 50
	Total		42,086		41,626	10,406 50
Express parcels of small value	Great Britain		3,643		223	44 07
	Newfoundland		307		307	63 67
	Germany		140			
	United States		1,061,290		1,061,285	277,222 97
	Total		1,065,380		1,061,815	277,330 71
Fancy Goods, viz.: Alabaster, spar, amber, terra cotta, or composition ornaments	Great Britain		437		182	63 70
	Aust.-Hungary		40		40	14 00
	France		309		309	108 15
	Germany		439			
	Italy		3		3	1 05
	Japan		20		20	7 00
	United States		2,636		2,636	922 60
	Total		3,884		3,190	1,116 50
Bead ornaments and statuettes, N.E.S	Great Britain		4,486		2,976	1,041 60
	Aust.-Hungary		3,729		3,822	1,337 70
	Belgium		53		53	18 55
	China		51		51	17 85
	France		33,088		33,987	11,895 45
	Germany		16,062		1,156	404 60
	Holland		3		3	1 05
	Italy		1,575		1,575	551 25
	Japan		278		278	97 30
	Switzerland		619		619	216 65
	Turkey		867		867	303 45
	United States		15,422		15,392	5,387 20
	Total		76,233		60,779	21,272 65
Boxes, fancy, ornamental cases and writing desks, &c.	Great Britain		32,525		2,032	711 20
	B. Africa		10		10	3 50
	Hong Kong		24		24	8 40
	Aust.-Hungary		563		563	197 05
	Belgium		401		103	36 05
	China		105		105	36 75
	France		1,809		1,745	610 75
	Germany		35,412		6	2 10
	Japan		4,392		4,392	1,537 20
	Switzerland		99		99	34 65
	Turkey		88		88	30 80
	United States		63,203		62,816	21,985 60
	Total		138,631		71,983	25,194 05

OF IMPORTS—*Continued.*

FOR HOME CONSUMPTION.

Preferential Tariff.			Surtax Tariff.			Total.		
Quantity.	Value.	Duty.	Quantity.	Value.	Duty.	Quantity.	Value.	Duty Collected.
	$	$ cts.		$	$ cts.		$	$ cts.
....	271	45 17	....	....	....	....	271	45 17
....	....	....	....	183	61 01	....	183	61 01
....	....	....	....	....	....	....	....	....
....	....	....	....	....	....	....	41,626	10,406 50
....	271	45 17	....	183	61 01	....	42,080	10,512 68
....	3,420	795 67	....	....	....	....	3,643	839 74
....	....	....	....	....	....	....	307	63 67
....	....	....	....	140	46 86	....	140	46 86
....	....	....	....	5	2 33	....	1,061,290	277,225 30
....	3,420	795 67	....	145	49 19	....	1,065,380	278,175 57
....	227	52 97	....	28	13 07	....	437	129 74
....	....	....	....	....	....	....	40	14 00
....	....	....	....	....	....	....	309	108 15
....	....	....	....	439	204 88	....	439	204 88
....	....	....	....	....	....	....	3	1 05
....	....	....	....	....	....	....	20	7 00
....	....	....	....	....	....	....	2,636	922 60
....	227	52 97	....	467	217 95	....	3,884	1,387 42
....	521	121 62	....	989	461 53	....	4,486	1,624 75
....	....	....	....	....	....	....	3,822	1,337 70
....	....	....	....	....	....	....	53	18 55
....	....	....	....	....	....	....	51	17 85
....	....	....	....	34	15 87	....	34,021	11,911 32
....	....	....	....	14,480	6,757 34	....	15,636	7,161 94
....	....	....	....	....	....	....	3	1 05
....	....	....	....	....	....	....	1,575	551 25
....	....	....	....	....	....	....	278	97 30
....	....	....	....	....	....	....	619	216 65
....	....	....	....	....	....	....	867	303 45
....	....	....	....	34	15 87	....	15,426	5,403 07
....	521	121 62	....	15,537	7,250 61	....	76,837	28,644 88
....	27,829	6,493 80	....	2,461	1,148 47	....	32,322	8,353 47
....	....	....	....	....	....	....	10	3 50
....	....	....	....	....	....	....	24	8 40
....	....	....	....	....	....	....	563	197 05
....	....	....	....	298	139 06	....	401	175 11
....	....	....	....	....	....	....	105	36 75
....	....	....	....	64	29 87	....	1,809	640 62
....	....	....	....	35,400	16,520 22	....	35,406	16,522 32
....	....	....	....	....	....	....	4,392	1,537 20
....	....	....	....	....	....	....	99	34 65
....	....	....	....	....	....	....	88	30 80
....	....	....	....	424	197 87	....	63,240	22,183 47
....	27,829	6,493 80	....	38,647	18,035 49	....	138,459	49,723 34

No. 1.—General Statement

Articles Imported.	Countries.	Total Imports.		Entered		
				General Tariff.		
		Quantity.	Value.	Quantity.	Value.	Duty.
DUTIABLE GOODS—*Con.*			$		$	$ cts.
Fancy goods—*Con.*						
Braids, bracelets, cords, fringes, tassels, &c.	Great Britain		136,366		32,504	11,376 40
	Hong Kong		12		12	4 20
	Aust.-Hungary		4,098		4,098	1,434 30
	Belgium		3,730		3,730	1,305 50
	China		46		46	16 10
	France		43,393		42,863	15,002 05
	Germany		132,889		1,528	534 80
	Italy		33		33	11 55
	Japan		103		103	36 05
	Switzerland		11,587		10,944	3,830 40
	United States		122,622		122,112	42,739 20
	Total		454,879		217,973	76,290 55
Casket gimps and fringes, and embroideries or chiffon imported by manufacturers of burial caskets for robes for such manufacture	Great Britain		339		311	31 10
	France		1,419		1,419	141 90
	Germany		249			
	Switzerland		1,874		1,874	187 40
	United States		6,011		6,011	601 10
	Total		9,892		9,615	961 50
Cases for jewellery, watches, silver ware, plated ware and cutlery	Great Britain		2,693		96	33 60
	Aust.-Hungary		97		97	33 95
	France		218		218	76 30
	Germany		3,692			
	United States		13,307		13,298	4,654 30
	Total		20,007		13,709	4,798 15
Fancy manufactures of bone, shell, horn and ivory, N.E.S.	Great Britain		151			
	China		9		9	3 15
	Germany		118			
	Japan		100		100	35 00
	United States		223		223	78 05
	Total		601		332	116 20
Fans	Great Britain		838		798	279 30
	Hong Kong		111		111	38 85
	Aust.-Hungary		1,175		1,175	411 25
	Belgium		126		126	44 10
	China		320		320	112 00
	France		2,142		2,209	773 15
	Germany		1,871		194	67 90
	Italy		79		79	27 65
	Japan		1,898		1,790	626 50
	Spain		151		151	52 85
	Switzerland		237		237	82 95
	United States		3,130		3,130	1,095 50
	Total		12,078		10,320	3,612 00

OF IMPORTS—*Continued.*

FOR HOME CONSUMPTION.

Preferential Tariff.			Surtax Tariff.			Total.		
Quantity.	Value.	Duty.	Quantity.	Value.	Duty.	Quantity.	Value.	Duty Collected.
	$	$ cts.		$	$ cts.		$	$ cts.
....	71,834	16,762 24	....	31,839	14,858 20	....	136,177	42,996 84
....	....	....	....	....	....	....	12	4 20
....	....	....	....	....	....	....	4,098	1,434 30
....	....	....	....	....	....	....	3,730	1,305 50
....	....	....	....	....	....	....	46	16 10
....	....	....	....	530	247 33	....	43,393	15,249 38
....	....	....	....	131,284	61,265 99	....	132,812	61,800 79
....	....	....	....	....	....	....	33	11 55
....	....	....	....	....	....	....	103	36 05
....	....	....	....	662	308 93	....	11,606	4,139 33
....	....	....	....	632	294 93	....	122,744	43,034 13
....	71,834	16,762 24	....	164,947	76,975 38	....	454,754	170,028 17
....	28	1 87	....	....	....	....	[illegible]39	32 97
....	....	....	....	....	....	....	1,419	141 90
....	....	....	....	249	33 20	....	249	33 20
....	....	....	....	....	....	....	1,874	187 40
....	....	....	....	....	....	....	6,011	601 10
....	28	1 87	....	249	33 20	....	9,892	[illegible]96 57
....	2,346	547 42	....	321	149 80	....	2,763	730 82
....	....	....	....	....	....	....	97	33 95
....	....	....	....	....	....	....	218	76 30
....	....	....	....	3,692	1,722 93	....	3,692	1,722 93
....	....	....	....	9	4 20	....	13,307	4,658 50
....	2,346	547 42	....	4,022	1,876 93	....	20,077	7,222 50
....	39	9 10	....	112	52 27	....	151	61 37
....	....	....	....	....	....	....	9	3 15
....	....	....	....	43	20 06	....	43	20 06
....	....	....	....	....	....	....	100	35 00
....	....	....	....	....	....	....	223	78 05
....	39	9 10	....	155	72 33	....	526	197 63
....	40	9 34	....	....	....	....	838	288 64
....	....	....	....	....	....	....	111	38 85
....	....	....	....	....	....	....	1,175	411 25
....	....	....	....	....	....	....	126	44 10
....	....	....	....	....	....	....	320	112 00
....	....	....	....	33	15 40	....	2,242	788 55
....	....	....	....	1,677	782 58	....	1,871	850 48
....	....	....	....	....	....	....	79	27 65
....	....	....	....	....	....	....	1,790	626 50
....	....	....	....	....	....	....	151	52 85
....	....	....	....	....	....	....	237	8[illegible] 95
....	....	....	....	....	....	....	3,130	1,095 50
....	40	9 34	....	1,710	797 98	....	12,070	4,419 32

No. 1.—General Statement

Articles Imported.	Countries.	Total Imports.		Entered		
				General Tariff.		
		Quantity.	Value.	Quantity.	Value.	Duty.
DUTIABLE GOODS—*Con.*			$		$	$ cts.
Fancy goods—*Con.* Flowers, artificial	Great Britain		86,361		17,092	4,273 00
	Hong Kong		141		141	35 25
	Aust.-Hungary		3,918		3,918	979 50
	Belgium		641		641	160 25
	China		153		153	38 25
	France		58,602		56,487	14,121 75
	Germany		28,192		1,422	355 50
	Japan		151		151	37 75
	Switzerland		148		124	31 00
	Turkey		134		134	33 50
	United States		86,308		85,242	21,310 50
	Total		264,749		165,505	41,376 25
Feathers, fancy, undressed	Great Britain		504		50	10 00
	France		283		283	56 60
	Germany		88			
	United States		4,186		4,186	837 20
	Total		5,061		4,519	903 80
" " N.E.S.	Great Britain		150,395		14,887	4,466 10
	British Africa		24		24	7 20
	Aust.-Hungary		670		670	201 00
	Belgium		542		542	162 60
	China		4		4	1 20
	France		48,631		48,050	14,415 00
	Germany		20,879			
	Italy		38		38	11 40
	Japan		3		3	0 90
	Switzerland		9		9	2 70
	United States		50,995		50,392	15,117 60
	Total		272,190		114,619	34,385 70
Feathers, ostrich and vulture, dressed	Great Britain		20,144		1,158	347 40
	Aust.-Hungary		295		295	88 50
	France		1,815		1,787	536 10
	Germany		207			
	United States		144		144	43 20
	Total		22,605		3,384	1,015 20
Ivory or bone dice, draughts, chessmen, &c.	Great Britain		47		10	2 00
	Hong Kong		3		3	0 60
	China		65		65	13 00
	France		128		128	25 60
	Germany		28			
	Japan		153		153	30 60
	United States		367		367	73 40
	Total		791		726	145 20

OF IMPORTS—*Continued.*

FOR HOME CONSUMPTION.

Preferential Tariff.			Surtax Tariff.			Total.		
Quantity.	Value.	Duty.	Quantity.	Value.	Duty.	Quantity.	Value.	Duty Collected.
	$	$ cts.		$	$ cts.		$	$ cts.
	62,176	10,362 95		7,093	2,364 33		86,361	17,000 28
							141	35 25
							3,918	979 50
							641	160 25
							153	38 25
				2,059	686 33		58,546	14,808 08
				26,770	8,923 29		28,192	9,278 79
							151	37 75
				24	8 00		148	39 00
							134	33 50
				1,181	393 67		86,423	21,704 17
	62,176	10,362 95		37,127	12,375 62		264,808	64,114 82
	454	60 53					504	70 53
							283	56 60
				88	23 47		88	23 47
							4,186	837 20
	454	60 53		88	23 47		5,061	987 80
	127,339	25,467 80		8,185	3,274 00		150,411	33,207 90
							24	7 20
							670	201 00
							542	162 60
							4	1 20
				581	232 40		48,631	14,647 40
				20,879	8,351 60		20,879	8,351 60
							38	11 40
							3	0 90
							9	2 70
				603	241 20		50,995	15,358 80
	127,339	25,467 80		30,248	12,099 20		272,206	71,952 70
	18,941	3,788 20		45	18 00		20,144	4,153 60
							295	88 50
				28	11 20		1,815	547 30
				207	82 80		207	82 80
							144	43 20
	18,941	3,788 20		280	112 60		22,605	4,915 40
	37	4 93					47	6 93
							3	0 60
							65	13 00
							128	25 60
				28	7 47		28	7 47
							153	30 60
							367	73 40
	37	4 93		28	7 47		791	157 60

No. 1.—General Statement

Articles Imported.	Countries.	Total Imports.		Entered		
				General Tariff.		
		Quantity.	Value.	Quantity.	Value.	Duty.
DUTIABLE GOODS—*Con.*			$		$	$ cts.
Fancy goods—*Con.*						
Laces, lace collars and similar goods, lace nets and nettings of cotton, linen, silk or other material	Great Britain		1,011,486		182,615	63,915 25
	B. E. Indies		151		151	52 85
	Hong Kong		41		41	14 35
	B. Poss. Other		185		185	64 75
	Aust.-Hungary		3,657		3,586	1,255 10
	Belgium		26,438		26,446	9,256 10
	China		2		2	0 70
	Denmark		129		129	45 15
	France		195,228		193,299	67,654 65
	Germany		313,291		1,728	604 80
	Greece		19		19	6 65
	Holland		146		146	51 10
	Japan		908		908	317 80
	Russia		190		190	66 50
	Switzerland		74,030		75,333	26,366 55
	United States		78,791		76,687	26,840 45
	Total		1,704,692		561,465	196,512 75
Millinery not elsewhere provided for	Great Britain		150		81	28 35
	France		89		89	31 15
	United States		57		57	17 95
	Total		296		227	77 45
Toys and dolls of all kinds	Great Britain		32,807		1,312	459 20
	Hong Kong		37		37	12 95
	Aust.-Hungary		7,466		7,253	2,538 55
	Belgium		679		679	237 65
	China		98		98	34 30
	France		13,981		14,258	4,990 30
	Germany		183,892		429	150 15
	Holland		94		94	32 90
	Italy		2		2	0 70
	Japan		7,665		7,414	2,594 90
	Roumania		8		8	2 80
	Switzerland		592		592	207 20
	United States		115,119		113,517	39,730 95
	Total		362,440		145,693	50,992 55
All other, N.E.S.	Great Britain		4,391		1,178	412 30
	Aust.-Hungary		65		65	22 75
	Belgium		128		128	44 80
	China		34		34	11 90
	France		901		901	315 35
	Germany		1,604			
	Japan		2,255		2,255	789 25
	United States		8,767		8,668	3,033 80
	Total		18,145		13,229	4,630 15

OF IMPORTS—*Continued.*

FOR HOME CONSUMPTION.

Preferential Tariff.			Surtax Tariff.			Total.		
Quantity.	Value.	Duty.	Quantity.	Value.	Duty.	Quantity.	Value.	Duty Collected.
	$	$ cts.		$	$ cts.		$	$ cts.
	745,823	174,027 54		83,144	38,800 53		1,011,582	276,743 32
							151	52 85
							41	14 35
							185	64 75
				71	33 13		3,657	1,288 23
							26,446	9,256 10
							2	0 70
							129	45 15
				729	340 20		194,028	67,994 85
				309,391	144,383 39		311,119	144,988 19
							19	6 65
							146	51 10
							908	317 80
							190	66 50
				160	74 67		75,493	26,441 22
				2,114	986 53		78,801	27,826 98
	745,823	174,027 54		395,609	184,618 45		1,702,897	555,158 74
	69	15 57					150	43 92
							89	31 15
							57	17 95
	69	15 57					296	93 02
	26,842	6,263 71		3,671	1,713 13		31,825	8,436 04
							37	12 95
				213	99 40		7,466	2,637 95
							679	237 65
							98	34 30
							14,258	4,990 30
				184,833	86,256 09		185,262	86,406 24
							94	32 90
							2	0 70
							7,414	2,594 90
							8	2 80
							592	207 20
				1,332	621 60		114,849	40,352 55
	26,842	6,263 71		190,049	88,690 22		362,584	145,946 48
	2,794	652 02		419	195 53		4,391	1,259 85
							65	22 75
							128	44 80
							34	11 90
							901	315 35
				1,604	748 62		1,604	748 62
							2,255	789 25
				99	46 20		8,767	3,080 00
	2,794	652 02		2,122	990 35		18,145	6,272 52

No. 1.—General Statement

Articles Imported.	Countries.	Total Imports.		Entered		
				General Tariff.		
		Quantity.	Value.	Quantity.	Value.	Duty.
DUTIABLE GOODS.			$		$	$ cts.
Feathers, bed and other, undressed, N.O.P.	Great Britain		48			
	France		5,792		6,665	1,333 00
	Germany		302			
	United States		20,836		20,836	4,167 20
	Total		26,978		27,501	5,500 20
Feathers, bed and other, dressed N.O.P.	Great Britain		130		46	13 80
	United States		76		76	22 80
	Total		206		122	36 60
Feathers, all other, N.E.S.	Great Britain		127		13	3 90
	United States		14		14	4 20
	Total		141		27	8 10
Featherbone in coils	Great Britain		12			
	United States		443		443	88 60
	Total		455		443	88 60
Fertilizers, compounded or manufactured	Great Britain		7,848		53	5 30
	Germany		2,194			
	United States		157,471		157,466	15,746 60
	Total		167,513		157,519	15,751 90
Fibre, Kartavert, indurated fibre, vulcanized fibre and like material and manufactures of, N.E.S.	Great Britain		322		26	6 50
	United States		44,248		44,235	11,058 75
	Total		44,570		44,261	11,065 25
Fireworks, firecrackers and torpedoes, all kinds	Great Britain				58	14 50
	Hong Kong		1,605		1,605	401 25
	China		7,697		7,697	1,924 25
	Japan		2,112		2,112	528 00
	United States		18,025		18,025	4,506 25
	Total		29,439		29,497	7,374 25
Fish—		Lbs.		Lbs.		
Cod, haddock, ling and pollock—fresh, imported otherwise than in barrels, &c.	Great Britain	543	29	227	17	1 14
	United States	1,490,033	53,657	1,490,033	53,657	7,450 25
	Total	1,490,576	53,686	1,490,260	53,674	7,451 39

OF IMPORTS—*Continued.*

FOR HOME CONSUMPTION.

Preferential Tariff.			Surtax Tariff.			Total.		
Quantity.	Value.	Duty.	Quantity.	Value.	Duty.	Quantity.	Value.	Duty Collected.
	$	$ cts.		$	$ cts.		$	$ cts.
	48	6 41					48	6 41
							6,665	1,333 00
				302	80 54		302	80 54
							20,836	4,167 20
	48	6 41		302	80 54		27,851	5,587 15
	84	16 80					130	30 60
							76	22 80
	84	16 80					206	53 40
	48	9 60		66	26 40		127	39 90
							14	4 20
	48	9 60		66	26 40		141	44 10
	12	1 60					12	1 60
							443	88 60
	12	1 60					455	90 20
	7,795	519 71					7,848	525 01
				2,194	292 53		2,194	292 53
							157,466	15,746 60
	7,795	519 71		2,194	292 53		167,508	16,564 14
	296	49 35					322	55 85
				13	4 33		44,248	11,063 08
	296	49 35		13	4 33		44,570	11,118 93
							58	14 50
							1,605	401 25
							7,697	1,924 25
							2,112	528 00
							18,025	4,506 25
							29,497	7,374 25
Lbs.			Lbs.			Lbs.		
316	12	1 05				543	29	2 19
						1,490,033	53,657	7,450 25
316	12	1 05				1,490,576	53,686	7,452 44

No. 1.—General Statement

Articles Imported.	Countries.	Total Imports.		Entered		
				General Tariff.		
		Quantity.	Value.	Quantity.	Value.	Duty.
DUTIABLE GOODS—*Con.*		Lbs.	$	Lbs.	$	$ cts.
Fish—*Con.*						
Cod, haddock, ling and pollock—dry salted........	Great Britain...	1,790	76	1,790	76	8 95
	Hong Kong.....	42,562	977	42,562	977	212 81
	China..........	91,269	3,191	90,269	3,179	451 35
	Italy...........	520	46	520	46	2 60
	Japan..........	38,430	2,707	38,430	2,707	192 15
	St. Pierre.......	334,502	17,150	....	....	....
	United States...	106,858	5,417	104,754	5,313	523 82
	Total.....	615,931	29,564	278,325	12,298	1,391 68
Cod, haddock, ling and pollock—wet salted..........	Italy...........	137	25	137	25	0 69
	United States..	1,295	76	1,295	76	6 48
	Total.....	1,432	101	1,432	101	7 17
Cod, haddock, ling and pollock—smoked............	China..........	48	1	48	1	0 48
	United States...	42,408	2,523	42,538	2,531	425 38
	Total.....	42,456	2,524	42,586	2,532	425 86
Cod, haddock, ling and pollock—pickled, in barrels...	United States...	3,350	96	3,350	96	33 50
Halibut, fresh, not in barrels.	China..........	400	5	400	5	2
	United States...	1,174,198	53,439	1,173,945	53,417	5,869 83
	Total.....	1,174,598	53,444	1,174,345	53,422	5,871 83
Halibut, pickled, in barrels..	United States...	129	12	129	12	1 29
Herrings, fresh, not in barrels	United States...	13,965	508	12,365	449	61 83
Herrings, pickled or salted..	Great Britain...	170,462	6,117	7,175	232	35 88
	China..........	240	13	240	13	1 20
	France.........	464	28	464	28	2 32
	Germany.......	6,054	244	....	....	....
	Holland........	137,250	6,613	137,250	6,613	686 25
	Italy...........	4,749	267	4,749	267	23 75
	Norway........	70,000	3,126	70,000	3,126	350 00
	United States...	126,178	7,254	126,428	7,276	632 14
	Total.....	515,397	23,662	346,306	17,555	1,731 54
Herrings, smoked..........	Great Britain...	18	1	....	....	....
	United States...	4,067	355	4,067	355	40 67
	Total.....	4,085	356	4,067	355	40 67
Mackerel, fresh.............	United States...	15,031	1,626	14,931	1,614	149 31
Mackerel, pickled..........	United States...	199,552	8,764	3,566	300	35 66
Sea fish, other, fresh, not in barrels..............	United States...	27,806	1,578	27,806	1,578	139 04

OF IMPORTS—*Continued.*

FOR HOME CONSUMPTION.

Preferential Tariff.			Surtax Tariff.			Total.		
Quantity.	Value.	Duty.	Quantity.	Value.	Duty.	Quantity.	Value.	Duty Collected.
Lbs.	$	$ cts.	Lbs.	$	$ cts.	Lbs.	$	$ cts.
						1,790	76	8 95
						42,562	977	212 81
						90,269	3,179	451 35
						520	46	2 60
						38,430	2,707	192 15
						104,754	5,313	523 82
						278,325	12,298	1,391 68
						137	25	0 69
						1,295	76	6 48
						1,432	101	7 17
						48	1	0 48
						42,538	2,531	425 38
						42,586	2,532	425 86
						3,350	96	33 50
						400	5	2 00
						1,173,945	53,417	5,869 83
						1,174,345	53,422	5,871 83
						129	12	1 29
						12,365	449	61 83
163,287	5,885	544 31				170,462	6,117	580 19
						240	13	1 20
						464	28	2 32
			6,054	244	40 35	6,054	244	40 35
						137,250	6,613	686 25
						4,749	267	23 75
						70,000	3,126	350 00
						126,428	7,276	632 14
163,287	5,885	544 31	6,054	244	40 35	515,647	23,684	2,316 20
18	1	0 12				18	1	0 12
						4,067	355	40 67
18	1	0 12				4,085	356	40 79
						14,931	1,614	149 31
						3,566	300	35 66
						27,806	1,578	139 04

No. 1.—General Statement

Articles Imported.	Countries.	Total Imports.		Entered		
				General Tariff.		
		Quantity.	Value.	Quantity.	Value.	Duty.
DUTIABLE GOODS—*Con.*		Lbs.	$	Lbs.	$	$ cts.
Fish—*Con.* Sea fish, pickled, in barrels..	United States...	204,432	3,384	832	46	8 32
Sea fish, other, preserved, N.E.S....................	Great Britain...	9,990	848	....	....	....
	Hong Kong.....	60	5	60	5	1 25
	United States...	4,666	560	4,666	560	140 00
	Total ...	14,716	1,413	4,726	565	141 25
		Brls.		Brls.		
Oysters, fresh, in shell.......	United States...	3,507	21,606	3,497	21,528	5,382 00
		Galls.		Galls.		
Oysters, shelled, in bulk.....	United States...	219,504	278,555	219,504	278,555	21,950 40
		Cans.		Cans.		
Oysters, canned, in cans not over one pint	United States...	15,866	1,775	15,770	1,768	473 10
Oysters, canned, in cans over one pint and not over one quart	United States...	17,853	8,958	16,089	7,990	804 45
Oysters, canned, in cans exceeding one quart.........	United States...	....	....	38	77	7 60
		Lbs.		Lbs.		
Oysters, prepared or preserved, N.E.S	Great Britain...	38,750	1,668	3,500	165	41 25
	Hong Kong.....	4,298	339	4,298	339	84 75
	China	5,087	460	5,087	460	115 00
	Japan..........	663	67	663	67	16 75
	United States...	435,558	35,421	468,455	39,752	9,938 00
	Total	484,356	37,955	482,003	40,783	10,195 75
		Brls.		Brls.		
Lobsters, fresh (not alive)....	United States...	22	231	22	231	57 75
		Lbs.		Lbs.		
Lobsters, canned, N.E.S.....	United States...	519	88	300	44	11 00
Bait fish, fresh, not in barrels	United States...	16,000	560	.. ..	....	....
Salmon, fresh, not in barrels.	United States...	665,278	15,813	665,278	15,813	3,326 40
Salmon, smoked	United States...	8,652	981	7,532	905	75 32
Salmon, canned, prepared or preserved, N.E.S.	Great Britain...	72	13	....	....	....
	United States...	1,900	90	1,180	131	32 75
	Total	1,972	103	1,180	131	32 75

OF IMPORTS—*Continued.*

FOR HOME CONSUMPTION.

Preferential Tariff.			Surtax Tariff.			Total.		
Quantity.	Value.	Duty.	Quantity.	Value.	Duty.	Quantity.	Value.	Duty Collected.
Lbs.	$	$ cts.	Lbs.	$	$ cts.	Lbs.	$	$ cts.
....	....	....	....	....	....	832	46	8 32
9,735	814	135 72	....	....	....	9,735	814	135 72
....	....	....	....	....	....	60	5	1 25
....	....	....	....	....	....	4,666	560	140 00
9,735	814	135 72	....	....	....	14,461	1,379	276 97
Brls.			Brls.			Brls.		
....	....	....	....	....	....	3,497	21,528	5,382 00
Galls.			Galls.			Galls.		
....	....	....	....	....	....	219,504	278,555	21,950 40
Cans.			Cans.			Cans.		
....	....	....	....	....	....	15,770	1,768	473 10
....	....	....	....	....	....	16,089	7,990	804 45
....	....	....	....	....	....	38	77	7 60
Lbs.			Lbs.			Lbs.		
....	....	....	....	....	....	3,500	165	41 25
....	....	....	....	....	....	4,298	339	84 75
....	....	....	....	....	....	5,087	460	115 00
....	....	....	....	....	....	663	67	16 75
....	....	....	....	....	....	468,455	39,752	9,938 00
....	....	....	....	....	....	482,003	40,783	10,195 75
Brls.			Brls.			Brls.		
....	....	....	....	....	....	22	231	57 75
Lbs.			Lbs.			Lbs.		
....	....	....	....	....	....	300	44	11 00
....	....	....	....	....	....	....	....	....
....	....	....	....	....	....	665,278	15,813	3,326 40
....	....	....	....	....	....	7,532	905	75 32
72	13	2 17	....	....	....	72	13	2 17
....	....	....	....	....	....	1,180	131	32 75
72	13	2 17	....	....	....	1,252	144	34 92

No. 1.—General Statement

Articles Imported.	Countries.	Total Imports.		Entered — General Tariff.		
		Quantity.	Value.	Quantity.	Value.	Duty.
DUTIABLE GOODS—*Con.*		Lbs.	$	Lbs.	$	$ cts.
Fish—*Con.* Salmon, pickled or salted....	United States...	1,437	77	1,437	77	14 37
Fish smoked, and boneless fish, N.E.S.	Great Britain...	12	1	12	1	0 12
	Hong Kong....	14,161	789	14,161	789	141 61
	China	1,911	54	1,911	54	19 11
	Japan.........	1,786	128	1,786	128	17 86
	United States...	24,172	1,395	24,124	1,391	241 24
	Total	42,042	2,367	41,994	2,363	419 94
Anchovies and sardines, packed in oil or otherwise, in tin boxes measuring not more than 5 inches long, 4 inches wide and 3½ inches deep...		Boxes.		Boxes.		
	Great Britain...	12	4	....	....	....
	France.........	41	7	66	10	3 30
	United States...	94	22	94	22	4 70
	Total	147	33	160	32	8 00
Anchovies and sardines in half boxes, measuring not more than 5 in. long, 4 in. wide and 1⅝ in. deep.......		½ Boxes.		½ Boxes.		
	Great Britain...	27,390	3,478	16,954	2,477	423 85
	China..........	20	2	20	2	0 50
	France.........	37,089	5,493	26,530	4,509	663 26
	Holland........	1,000	100	1,000	100	25 00
	Norway	17,420	1,654	18,320	1,746	458 00
	Sweden.........	234	16	234	16	5 85
	United States...	6,169	892	6,233	905	155 83
	Total	89,322	11,635	69,291	9,755	1,732 29
Anchovies and sardines in quarter boxes, measuring not more than 4¾ in. long, 3½ in. wide and 1¼ in. deep.		¼ Boxes.		¼ Boxes.		
	Great Britain...	491,065	29,126	425,364	28,151	8,507 28
	Belgium........	7,000	413	7,000	413	140 00
	Denmark........	1,000	55	11,000	511	220 00
	France.........	588,820	57,511	626,340	49,246	12,526 80
	Holland........	1,500	89	1,500	89	30 00
	Italy..........	....	....	200	10	4 00
	Japan..........	96	6	96	6	1 92
	Norway.........	393,880	24,204	376,680	21,341	7,533 60
	Portugal.......	229,250	11,390	184,500	9,043	3,690 00
	Spain.	8,000	663	8,000	663	160 00
	Sweden	7,500	447	9,500	544	190 00
	United States...	116,746	9,229	130,796	10,130	2,615 92
	Total	1,844,857	133,133	1,780,976	120,147	35,619 52
Anchovies and sardines, imported in any other form ..	Great Britain...	....	2,753	....	257	77 10
	Hong Kong.....	....	2	....	2	0 60
	Denmark.	....	16	....	16	4 80
	France.........	....	1,042	....	989	296 70
	Germany	....	27	....	....	....
	Italy	....	377	....	377	113 10
	Norway	....	314	....	314	94 20
	St. Pierre......	....	7	....	7	2 10
	Sweden.........	....	117	....	117	35 10
	United States...	....	548	....	548	164 40
	Total	....	5,203	....	2,627	788 10

of Imports—*Continued.*

for Home Consumption.

Preferential Tariff.			Surtax Tariff.			Total.		
Quantity.	Value.	Duty.	Quantity.	Value.	Duty.	Quantity.	Value.	Duty Collected.
Lbs.	$	$ cts.	Lbs.	$	$ cts.	Lbs.	$	$ cts.
						1,437	77	14 37
						12	1	0 12
						14,161	789	141 61
						1,911	54	19 11
						1,786	128	17 86
						24,124	1,391	241 24
						41,994	2,363	419 94
Boxes.			Boxes.			Boxes.		
12	4	0 40				12	4	0 40
						66	10	3 30
						94	22	4 70
12	4	0 40				172	36	8 40
½ Boxes.			½ Boxes.			½ Boxes.		
236	60	3 93				17,190	2,537	427 78
						20	2	0 50
						26,530	4,509	663 26
						1,000	100	25 00
						18,320	1,746	458 00
						234	16	5 85
						6,233	905	155 83
236	60	3 93				69,527	9,815	1,736 22
¼ Boxes.			¼ Boxes.			¼ Boxes.		
42,602	1,980	568 01				467,966	30,131	9,075 29
						7,000	413	140 00
						11,000	511	220 00
						626,340	49,246	12,526 80
						1,500	89	30 00
						200	10	4 00
						96	6	1 92
						376,680	21,341	7,533 60
						184,500	9,043	3,690 00
						8,000	663	160 00
						9,500	544	190 00
						130,796	10,130	2,615 92
42,602	1,980	568 01				1,823,578	122,127	36,187 53
	2,352	470 40					2,609	547 50
							2	0 60
							16	4 80
							989	296 70
				27	10 80		27	10 80
							377	113 10
							314	94 20
							7	2 10
							117	35 10
							548	164 40
	2,352	470 40		27	10 80		5,006	1,269 30

No. 1.—GENERAL STATEMENT

ARTICLES IMPORTED.	COUNTRIES.	TOTAL IMPORTS.		ENTERED		
				General Tariff.		
		Quantity.	Value.	Quantity	Value.	Duty.
DUTIABLE GOODS—*Con.*			$		$	$ cts.
Fish—*Con.*						
Fish preserved in oil, except anchovies and sardines....	Great Britain...	....	14,622	....	206	61 80
	Hong Kong.....	....	474	....	474	142 20
	China	....	510	....	510	153 00
	Denmark.......	....	1	....	920	276 00
	France........	....	5,120	....	3,936	1,180 8C
	Germany.......	....	61	....	....	....
	Holland........	....	676	....	676	202 80
	Italy	....	142	....	142	42 60
	Japan..........	....	54	....	54	16 20
	Norway	....	990	....	913	273 90
	United States...	....	1,538	....	1,543	462 90
	Total	....	24,188	....	9,374	2,812 20
		Lbs.		Lbs.		
Fish, all other, not in barrels or half barrels, fresh.......	Great Britain...	8,550	474	2,550	255	12 75
	China..........	642	38	642	38	3 21
	United States...	401,290	23,550	401,290	23,550	2,006 54
	Total	410,482	24,062	404,482	23,843	2,022 50
" " " pickled..	Great Britain...	112	8	.. ....	....	....
	China	4,186	323	4,186	323	20 93
	Japan..........	1,139	69	1,139	69	5 69
	United States...	7,109	441	7,109	441	35 55
	Total	12,546	841	12,434	833	62 17
Fish, fresh or dried, N.E.S., imported in barrels or half barrels..................	China..........	1,677	69	1,677	69	16 77
	Japan	568	69	568	69	5 68
	United States...	241,425	10,091	27,425	2,274	274 25
	Total	243,670	10,229	29,670	2,412	296 70
Fish, all other, pickled or salted, in barrels.....	China.........	1,000	14	1,000	14	10 00
	United States...	20,518	693	6,918	353	69 18
	Total	21,518	707	7,918	367	79 18
Fish prepared or preserved, N.E.S....	Great Britain...	305,344	26,363	25,155	2,590	647 50
	Hong Kong.....	26,623	1,440	26,623	1,440	360 00
	China....	43,878	2,683	43,878	2,683	670 75
	France..	1,626	334	1,215	170	42 50
	Germany........	170	18	170	18	4 50
	Japan.........	54,742	4,103	54,742	4,103	1,025 75
	Norway..... ..	11,882	1,349	9,542	747	186 75
	Sweden.........	300	266	....	....	....
	United States...	225,988	20,823	195,994	19,345	4,836 25
	Total.......	670,553	57,379	357,319	31,096	7,774 00

OF IMPORTS—*Continued.*

FOR HOME CONSUMPTION.

Preferential Tariff.			Surtax Tariff.			Total.		
Quantity.	Value.	Duty.	Quantity.	Value.	Duty.	Quantity.	Value.	Duty Collected.
	$	$ cts.		$	$ cts.		$	$ cts.
	12,990	2,598 00					13,196	2,659 80
							474	142 20
							510	153 00
							920	276 00
							3,936	1,180 80
				61	24 40		61	24 40
							676	202 80
							142	42 60
							54	16 20
							913	273 90
							1,543	462 90
	12,990	2,598 00		61	24 40		22,425	5,434 60
Lbs.			Lbs.			Lbs.		
6,000	219	20 00				8,550	474	32 75
						642	38	3 21
						401,290	23,550	2,006 54
6,000	219	20 00				410,482	24,062	2,042 50
112	8	0 37				112	8	0 37
						4,186	323	20 93
						1,139	69	5 69
						7,109	441	35 55
112	8	0 37				12,546	841	62 54
						1,677	69	16 77
						568	69	5 68
						27,425	2,274	274 25
						29,670	2,412	296 70
						1,000	14	10 00
						6,918	353	69 18
						7,918	367	79 18
276,162	22,275	3,712 71				301,317	24,865	4,360 21
						26,623	1,440	360 00
						43,878	2,683	670 75
						1,215	170	42 50
						170	18	4 50
						54,742	4,103	1,025 75
						9,542	747	186 75
						195,994	19,345	4,836 25
276,162	22,275	3,712 71				633,481	53,371	11,486 71

No. 1.—GENERAL STATEMENT

ARTICLES IMPORTED.	COUNTRIES.	TOTAL IMPORTS.		ENTERED		
				General Tariff.		
		Quantity.	Value.	Quantity.	Value.	Duty.
DUTIABLE GOODS.		Galls.	$	Galls.	$	$ cts.
Fish—*Con.*						
Fish oil—cod, N.E.S.	Great Britain	....	......	200	161	32 20
	Norway	973	624	495	338	67 60
	United States	1,113	426	1,113	426	85 20
	Total	2,086	1,050	1,808	925	185 00
Fish oil—cod-liver	Great Britain	1,237	971	1,503	1,739	347 80
	China	....	....	25	23	4 60
	Norway	16,320	10,745	12,936	8,602	1,720 40
	United States	11,085	2,822	10,982	2,756	551 20
	Total	28,642	14,538	25,446	13,120	2,624 00
Whale and spermaceti, N.E.S.	Great Britain	102	65	....	....	....
	United States	3,707	2,296	3,707	2,296	459 20
	Total	3,809	2,361	3,707	2,296	459 20
Other N.E.S.	United States	36,781	10,512	36,781	10,512	2,102 40
Packages containing oysters or other fish not otherwise provided for	Great Britain	....	25	....	....	....
	Hong Kong	....	46	....	46	11 50
	China	....	169	....	167	41 75
	Holland	....	355	....	355	88 75
	Japan	....	37	....	37	9 25
	Norway	....	400	....	400	100 00
	United States	....	11,197	....	10,087	2,521 75
	Total	....	12,229	....	11,092	2,773 00
Other articles, the produce of the fisheries, not specially provided for	Great Britain	....	32	....	....	....
	Newfoundland	....	10	....	10	2 00
	United States	....	14,055	....	14,055	2,811 00
	Total	....	14,097	....	14,065	2,813 00
Flax, hemp and jute—manufactures of, viz:—						
Bags or sacks of hemp, linen or jute	Great Britain	....	11,291	....	631	126 20
	B. E. Indies	....	73,051	....	....	....
	France	....	9	....	9	1 80
	Germany	....	70	....	....	....
	United States	....	34,832	....	34,824	6,964 80
	Total	....	119,253	....	35,464	7,092 80
Carpeting, rugs, matting, and mats of hemp or jute	Great Britain	....	61,284	....	448	112 00
	B. E. Indies	....	32	....	....	....
	Aust.-Hungary	....	11,280	....	11,493	2,873 25
	China	....	119	....	119	29 75
	France	....	4,529	....	2,677	669 25
	Germany	....	392	....	14	3 50
	Japan	....	12,177	....	12,177	3,044 25
	United States	....	3,181	....	3,179	794 75
	Total	....	92,994	....	30,107	7,526 75

SESSIONAL PAPER No. 11

OF IMPORTS—*Continued.*

FOR HOME CONSUMPTION.

Preferential Tariff.			Surtax Tariff.			Total.		
Quantity.	Value.	Duty.	Quantity.	Value.	Duty.	Quantity.	Value.	Duty Collected.
Galls.	$	$ cts.	Galls.	$	$ cts.	Galls.	$	$ cts.
....	....	....	....	....	....	200	161	32 20
....	....	....	....	....	....	495	338	67 60
....	....	....	....	....	....	1,113	426	85 20
....	....	....	....	....	....	1,808	925	185 00
22	29	3 87	....	....	....	1,525	1,768	351 67
....	....	....	....	....	....	25	23	4 60
....	....	....	200	86	22 94	13,136	8,688	1,743 34
....	....	....	....	....	....	10,982	2,756	551 20
22	29	3 87	200	86	22 94	25,668	13,235	2,650 81
102	65	8 67	....	....	....	102	65	8 67
....	....	....	....	....	....	3,707	2,296	459 20
102	65	8 67	....	....	....	3,809	2,361	467 87
....	....	....	....	....	....	36,781	10,512	2,102 40
....	25	4 16	....	....	....	....	25	4 16
....	....	....	....	....	....	....	46	11 50
....	....	....	....	....	....	....	167	41 75
....	....	....	....	....	....	....	355	88 75
....	....	....	....	....	....	....	37	9 25
....	....	....	....	....	....	....	400	100 00
....	....	....	....	....	....	....	10,087	2,521 75
....	25	4 16	....	....	....	....	11,117	2,777 16
....	32	4 27	....	....	....	....	32	4 27
....	....	....	....	....	....	....	10	2 00
....	....	....	....	....	....	....	14,055	2,811 00
....	32	4 27	....	....	....	....	14,097	2,817 27
....	10,660	1,421 37	....	....	....	....	11,291	1,547 57
....	71,060	9,474 76	....	....	....	....	71,060	9,474 76
....	....	....	....	....	....	....	9	1 80
....	....	....	....	70	18 67	....	70	18 67
....	....	....	....	....	....	....	34,824	6,964 80
....	81,720	10,896 13	....	70	18 67	....	117,254	18,007 60
....	61,579	10,263 56	....	15	5 00	....	62,042	10,380 56
....	32	5 33	....	....	....	....	32	5 33
....	....	....	....	....	....	....	11,493	2,873 25
....	....	....	....	....	....	....	119	29 75
....	....	....	....	....	....	....	2,677	669 25
....	....	....	....	378	126 00	....	392	129 50
....	....	....	....	....	....	....	12,177	3,044 25
....	....	....	....	2	0 67	....	3,181	795 42
....	61,611	10,268 89	....	395	131 67	....	92,113	17,927 31

No. 1.—General Statement

Articles Imported.	Countries.	Total Imports.		Entered		
				General Tariff.		
		Quantity.	Value.	Quantity.	Value.	Duty.
DUTIABLE GOODS—*Con.*			$		$	$ cts.
Flax, hemp and jute—*Con.* Carpet linings and stair pads.	Great Britain...	....	655	....	9	2 25
	United States...	....	4,393	....	4,652	1,163 00
	Total...	....	5,048	....	4,661	1,165 25
Sail twine of flax or hemp to be used for boats and ships' sails		Lbs.		Lbs.		
	Great Britain...	13,195	2,646	....	....	....
	Aust.-Hungary.	250	45	250	45	2 25
	United States...	317	72	317	72	3 60
	Total......	13,762	2,763	567	117	5 85
Damask of linen, stair linen, diaper, napkins, doylies, table and tray cloths, quilts, and like articles of linen, N.O.P.	Great Britain...	....	639,633	....	23,601	7,080 30
	B. E. Indies...	....	26	....	26	7 80
	Hong Kong....	....	248	....	248	74 40
	Aust.-Hungary.	....	15,719	....	15,241	4,572 30
	Belgium........	....	1,519	....	1,519	455 70
	China..........	....	88	....	88	26 40
	France.........	....	8,487	....	8,487	2,546 10
	Germany.......	....	14,600	....	696	208 80
	Holland........	....	554	....	554	166 20
	Italy...........	....	617	....	617	185 10
	Japan..........	....	34,025	....	34,016	10,204 80
	Mexico.........	....	75	....	75	22 50
	Switzerland.....	....	3,920	....	3,920	1,176 00
	United States...	....	9,957	....	9,675	2,902 50
	Total......	....	729,468	....	98,763	29,628 90
Handkerchiefs................	Great Britain...	....	195,108	....	4,740	1,659 00
	B. E. Indies....	....	9	....	9	3 15
	Hong Kong.....	....	5	....	5	1 75
	Aust.-Hungary.	....	5	....	5	1 75
	Belgium........	....	2,775	....	2,775	971 25
	China..........	....	6	....	6	2 10
	France.........	....	1,622	....	1,735	607 25
	Germany.......	....	148	....	....	....
	Japan..........	....	10,864	....	6,789	2,376 15
	Switzerland.....	....	7,602	....	7,602	2,660 70
	United States...	....	1,482	....	1,502	525 70
	Total....	....	219,626	....	25,168	8,808 80
Horse clothing, shaped or otherwise manufactured........	Great Britain...	....	1,049	....	....	....
	United States...	....	1,287	....	1,127	338 10
	Total....	....	2,336	....	1,127	338 10
Towels....................	Great Britain...	....	170,261	....	3,570	1,071 00
	Aust.-Hungary.	....	2,042	....	2,042	612 60
	France.........	....	933	....	933	279 90
	Germany.......	....	5,551	....	284	85 20
	Japan..........	....	29	....	29	8 70
	Switzerland.....	....	2	....	2	0 60
	United States...	....	809	....	821	246 30
	Total...	....	179,627	....	7,681	2,304 30

OF IMPORTS—*Continued.*

FOR HOME CONSUMPTION.

Preferential Tariff.			Surtax Tariff.			Total.		
Quantity.	Value.	Duty.	Quantity.	Value.	Duty.	Quantity.	Value.	Duty Collected.
	$	$ cts.		$	$ cts.		$	$ cts.
	646	107 67					655	109 92
							4,652	1,163 00
	646	107 67					5,307	1,272 92
Lbs. 13,195	2,646	88 21	Lbs.			Lbs. 13,195	2,646	88 21
						250	45	2 25
						317	72	3 60
13,195	2,646	88 21				13,762	2,763	94 06
	604,167	120,833 40		3,721	1,488 40		631,489	129,402 10
							26	7 80
							248	74 40
							15,241	4,572 30
							1,519	455 70
							88	26 40
							8,487	2,546 10
				13,970	5,588 00		14,666	5,796 80
							554	166 20
							617	185 10
							34,016	10,204 80
							75	22 50
							3,920	1,176 00
				847	338 80		10,522	3,241 30
	604,167	120,833 40		18,538	7,415 20		721,468	157,877 50
	190,814	44,524 31		62	28 93		195,616	46,212 24
							9	3 15
							5	1 75
							5	1 75
							2,775	971 25
							6	2 10
							1,735	607 25
				148	69 06		148	69 06
							6,789	2,376 15
							7,602	2,660 70
							1,502	525 70
	190,814	44,524 31		210	97 99		216,192	53,431 10
	1,049	209 80					1,049	209 80
							1,127	338 10
	1,049	209 80					2,176	547 90
	166,327	33,265 40		540	216 00		170,437	34,552 40
							2,042	612 60
							933	279 90
				5,267	2,106 80		5,551	2,192 00
							29	8 70
							2	0 60
							821	246 30
	166,327	33,265 40		5,807	2,322 80		179,815	37,892 50

No. 1.—General Statement

Articles Imported.	Countries.	Total Imports.		Entered		
				General Tariff.		
		Quantity.	Value.	Quantity.	Value.	Duty.
DUTIABLE GOODS—*Con.*		Yds.	$	Yds.	$	$ cts.
Flax, hemp and jute—*Con.*						
Sheets and sheetings	Great Britain...	9,172	1,990	2,810	391	117 30
	France..........	340	68	340	68	20 40
	United States...	4	1	4	1	0 30
	Total......	9,516	2,059	3,154	460	138 00
Linens, brown or bleached	Great Britain...	668,267	72,296	4,269	693	173 25
	Hong Kong......	558	133	558	133	33 25
	Aust.-Hungary .	603	44	603	44	11 00
	Belgium	2,234	593	2,234	593	148 25
	France..........	468	135	468	135	33 75
	Germany.......	72	6	....	....	....
	Japan	80	34	80	34	8 50
	United States...	568	75	568	75	18 75
	Total......	672,850	73,316	8,780	1,707	426 75
Linen duck, canvas, huckabacks or other manufactures of flax, N.E.S.....................	Great Britain...	....	650,694	....	6,523	1,630 75
	B. W. Indies ...	....	4	....	4	1 00
	Aust.-Hungary .	....	72	....	72	18 00
	Belgium........	....	852	....	852	213 00
	China	....	56	....	56	14 00
	France..........	....	2,543	....	2,543	635 75
	Germany........	....	5,533	....	363	90 75
	Italy...........	....	46	....	46	11 50
	Japan.... ...	....	22	....	22	5 50
	Russia..........	....	355	....	355	88 75
	Switzerland.....	....	204	....	204	51 00
	United States...	....	28,652	....	28,644	7,161 00
	Total. . ..	....	689,033	....	39,684	9,921 00
Linen clothing, N.E.S.......	Great Britain...	....	9,455	....	413	144 55
	France...	....	717	....	717	250 95
	Germany.......	....	26	....	....	....
	Japan..........	....	377	....	377	131 95
	United States...	....	4,053	....	4,053	1,418 55
	Total......	....	14,628	....	5,560	1,946 00
" blouses and shirt waists..	Great Britain...	....	769	....	359	125 65
	Japan..........	....	46	....	46	16 10
	United States...	....	116	....	116	40 60
	Total......	....	931	....	521	182 35
		Lbs.		Lbs.		
" thread.	Great Britain...	253,347	164,223	1,249	315	78 75
	France..........	683	415	671	404	101 00
	United States...	5,869	3,145	5,869	3,145	786 25
	Total......	259,899	167,783	7,789	3,864	966 00
		Doz.		Doz.		
Shirts of linen..	Great Britain...	267	2,896	22	296	103 60
	United States...	262	2,071	262	2,071	724 85
	Total......	529	4,967	284	2,367	828 45

OF IMPORTS—*Continued.*

FOR HOME CONSUMPTION.

Preferential Tariff.			Surtax Tariff.			Total.		
Quantity.	Value.	Duty.	Quantity	Value.	Duty.	Quantity.	Value.	Duty Collected.
Yds.	$	$ cts.	Yds.	$	$ cts.	Yds.	$	$ cts.
6,362	1,599	319 80				9,172	1,990	437 10
						340	68	20 40
						4	1	0 30
6,362	1,599	319 80				9,516	2,059	457 80
649,214	71,347	11,891 67	646	70	23 33	654,129	72,110	12,088 25
						558	133	33 25
						603	44	11 00
						2,234	593	148 25
						468	135	33 75
			72	6	2 00	72	6	2 00
						80	34	8 50
						568	75	18 75
649,214	71,347	11,891 67	718	76	25 33	658,712	73,130	12,343 75
	642,578	107,098 19		275	91 67		649,376	108,820 61
							4	1 00
							72	18 00
							852	213 00
							56	14 00
							2,543	635 75
				7,397	2,465 71		7,760	2,556 46
							46	11 50
							22	5 50
							355	88 75
							204	51 00
				8	2 67		28,652	7,163 67
	642,578	107,098 19		7,680	2,560 05		689,942	119,579 24
	9,347	2,181 19					9,760	2,325 74
							717	250 95
				26	12 13		26	12 13
							377	131 95
							4,053	1,418 55
	9,347	2,181 19		26	12 13		14,933	4,139 32
	410	95 67					769	221 32
							46	16 10
							116	40 60
	410	95 67					931	278 02
Lbs.			Lbs.			Lbs.		
252,050	163,923	27,321 10	8	10	33	253,307	164,248	27,403 18
			12	11	6 67	683	415	104 67
						5,869	3,145	786 25
252,050	163,923	27,321 10	20	21	7 00	259,859	167,808	28,294 10
Doz.			Doz.			Doz.		
255	2,759	643 81				277	3,055	747 41
						262	2,071	724 85
255	2,759	643 81				539	5,126	1,472 26

No. 1.—General Statement

Articles Imported.	Countries.	Total Imports.		Entered		
				General Tariff.		
		Quantity.	Value.	Quantity.	Value.	Duty.
DUTIABLE GOODS—*Con.*		Lbs.	$	Lbs.	$	$ cts.
Flax, hemp and jute—*Con.*						
Yarn, singles, flax, hemp and jute, N.E.S.	Great Britain	11,550	2,085	....	....	....
	United States	7,196	638	7,196	638	159 50
	Total	18,746	2,723	7,196	638	159 50
Tapestry, jute	Great Britain	....	100	....	47	11 75
		Yds.		Yds.		
Jute cloth, not otherwise finished than bleached or calendered	Great Britain	6,078,795	263,460	64,662	3,361	336 10
	B. E. Indies	7,338,661	286,503	110,000	3,808	380 80
	United States	191,686	6,882	191,686	6,882	688 20
	Total	13,609,142	556,845	366,348	14,051	1,405 10
Other articles made by the seamstress from linen fabrics, N.O.P	Great Britain	....	7,261	....	1,298	454 30
	Hong Kong	....	131	....	131	45 85
	Belgium	....	124	....	124	43 40
	France	....	15	....	15	5 25
	Germany	....	1,838	....	....	....
	Japan	....	1,101	....	1,101	385 35
	Switzerland	....	14	....	14	4 90
	United States	....	4,532	....	4,565	1,597 75
	Total	....	15,016	....	7,248	2,536 80
Other manufactures of hemp or jute, N.E.S., or of flax, hemp and jute combined	Great Britain	....	193,050	....	1,116	279 00
	Belgium	....	540	....	540	135 00
	France	....	1,666	....	1,666	416 50
	Germany	....	332	....	....	....
	Japan	....	16	....	16	4 00
	Switzerland	....	4,519	....	4,519	1,129 75
	United States	....	13,448	....	13,448	3,362 00
	Total	....	213,571	....	21,305	5,326 25
Foundry facings of all kinds	Great Britain	....	6,667	....	....	....
	United States	....	14,481	....	14,481	3,620 25
	Total	....	21,148	....	14,481	3,620 25
Fruits, including nuts, viz.:		Lbs.		Lbs.		
Dried apples	United States	34,409	2,868	32,109	2,610	652 50
Currants	Great Britain	261,813	8,108	256,235	7,944	2,562 35
	France	7,680	309	11,329	418	113 29
	Greece	8,211,360	269,498	8,415,840	280,032	84,158 40
	Spain	282,295	8,345	328,407	9,663	3,284 07
	Turkey	53,164	1,449	64,784	2,349	647 84
	United States	981,256	37,484	1,111,561	41,440	11,115 61
	Total	9,797,568	325,193	10,188,156	341,846	101,881 56

OF IMPORTS—*Continued.*

FOR HOME CONSUMPTION.

Preferential Tariff.			Surtax Tariff.			Total.		
Quantity.	Value.	Duty.	Quantity.	Value.	Duty.	Quantity.	Value.	Duty Collected.
Lbs.	$	$ cts.	Lbs.	$	$ cts.	Lbs.	$	$ cts.
11,550	2,085	347 51				11,550	2,085	347 51
						7,196	638	159 50
11,550	2,085	347 51				18,746	2,723	507 01
	53	8 84					100	20 59
Yds.			Yds.			Yds.		
6,014,133	260,099	17,340 00				6,078,795	263,460	17,676 10
7,228,661	282,695	18,846 43				7,338,661	286,503	19,227 23
						191,686	6,882	688 20
13,242,794	542,794	36,186 43				13,609,142	556,845	37,591 53
	5,963	1,391 56					7,261	1,845 86
							131	45 85
							124	43 40
							15	5 25
				1,838	857 73		1,838	857 73
							1,101	385 35
							14	4 90
							4,565	1,597 75
	5,963	1,391 56		1,838	857 73		15,049	4,786 09
	192,901	32,150 51		150	50 00		194,167	32,479 51
							540	135 00
							1,666	416 50
				332	110 67		332	110 67
							16	4 00
							4,519	1,129 75
							13,448	3,362 00
	192,901	32,150 51		482	160 67		214,688	37,637 43
	6,667	1,111 18					6,667	1,111 18
							14,481	3,620 25
	6,667	1,111 18					21,148	4,731 43
Lbs.			Lbs.			Lbs.		
						32,109	2,610	652 50
643	24	4 29				256,878	7,968	2,566 64
						11,329	418	113 29
						8,415,840	280,032	84,158 40
						328,407	9,663	3,284 07
						64,784	2,349	647 84
						1,111,561	41,440	11,115 61
643	24	4 29				10,188,799	341,870	101,885 85

No. 1.—General Statement

Articles Imported.	Countries.	Total Imports.		Entered		
				General Tariff.		
		Quantity.	Value.	Quantity.	Value.	Duty.
DUTIABLE GOODS—*Con.*		Lbs.	$	Lbs.	$	$ cts.
Fruits, including nuts—*Con.*						
" Dates	Great Britain	386,064	8,392	337,543	7,314	1,828 50
	Hong Kong	205	4	205	4	1 00
	Arabia	2,865	102	8,315	223	55 75
	China	124	4	124	4	1 00
	Egypt	39,600	754	39,600	754	188 50
	France	1,250	109	1,250	109	27 25
	Greece	....	....	1,000	38	9 50
	Persia	325,137	7,279	325,137	7,279	1,819 75
	Spain	1,674	63	1,674	63	15 75
	Turkey	1,147,154	18,883	1,119,335	18,580	4,645 00
	United States	324,697	9,883	280,268	8,178	2,044 50
	Total	2,228,770	45,473	2,114,451	42,546	10,636 50
" Figs	Great Britain	280,136	6,491	280,028	6,485	1,621 25
	Hong Kong	60	2	60	2	0 50
	France	2,408	844	2,744	881	220 25
	Greece	2,598	147	2,598	147	36 75
	Italy	619	55	619	55	13 75
	Persia	22,500	303	22,500	303	75 75
	Portugal	523,855	10,992	575,373	11,011	2,752 75
	Spain	117,162	2,372	121,601	2,456	614 00
	Turkey	1,448,725	58,886	1,381,787	58,782	14,695 50
	United States	486,733	23,921	486,600	23,852	5,963 00
	Total	2,884,796	104,013	2,873,910	103,974	25,993 50
" Prunes	Great Britain	252	8	5,852	127	39 85
	Aust.-Hungary	297,273	9,026	297,273	9,026	1,981 83
	France	205,098	7,000	198,802	6,906	1,453 99
	Spain	3,500	125	3,500	125	35 00
	St. Pierre	15	3	15	3	0 15
	United States	6,301,978	236,615	6,486,815	242,991	64,868 15
	Total	6,808,116	252,777	6,992,257	259,178	68,378 97
" Raisins	Great Britain	843,225	28,150	783,710	26,451	7,837 10
	France	17,107	466	43,453	1,350	434 53
	Greece	100,550	3,335	106,527	3,477	1,065 27
	Japan	....	....	5,600	288	56 00
	St. Pierre	25	1	25	1	0 25
	Spain	10,784,037	381,115	10,920,152	385,337	109,201 52
	Turkey	1,274,512	40,888	1,258,199	39,889	12,581 99
	United States	3,526,851	220,977	3,735,722	226,886	37,357 22
	Total	16,546,307	674,932	16,853,388	683,679	168,533 88
All other, N.E.S.	Great Britain	3,387	188	17	4	1 00
	Hong Kong	30,490	852	30,490	852	213 00
	China	39,610	1,229	39,610	1,229	307 25
	France	4,730	307	4,730	307	76 75
	Japan	1,791	41	1,791	41	10 25
	Spain	1,500	142	1,500	142	35 50
	United States	2,297,434	161,890	2,317,000	162,626	40,656 50
	Total	2,378,942	164,649	2,395,138	165,201	41,300 25

OF IMPORTS—*Continued.*

FOR HOME CONSUMPTION.

Preferential Tariff.			Surtax Tariff.			Total.		
Quantity.	Value.	Duty.	Quantity.	Value.	Duty.	Quantity.	Value.	Duty Collected.
Lbs.	$	$ cts.	Lbs.	$	$ cts.	Lbs.	$	$ cts.
						337,543	7,314	1,828 50
						205	4	1 00
						8,315	223	55 75
						124	4	1 00
						39,600	754	188 50
						1,250	109	27 25
						1,000	38	9 50
						325,137	7,279	1,819 75
						1,674	63	15 75
						1,119,335	18,580	4,645 00
						280,268	8,178	2,044 50
						2,114,451	42,546	10,636 50
108	6	1 00				280,136	6,491	1,622 25
						60	2	0 50
						2,744	881	220 25
						2,598	147	36 75
						619	55	13 75
						22,500	303	75 75
						575,373	11,011	2,752 75
						121,601	2,456	614 00
						1,381,787	58,782	14,695 50
						486,600	23,852	5,963 00
108	6	1 00				2,874,018	103,980	25,994 50
						5,852	127	39 85
						297,273	9,026	1,981 83
						198,802	6,906	1,453 99
						3,500	125	35 00
						15	3	0 15
						6,486,815	242,991	64,868 15
						6,992,257	259,178	68,378 97
						783,710	26,451	7,837 10
						43,453	1,350	434 53
						106,527	3,477	1,065 27
						5,600	288	56 00
						25	1	0 25
						10,920,152	385,337	109,201 52
						1,258,199	39,889	12,581 99
						3,735,722	226,886	37,357 22
						16,853,388	683,679	168,533 88
542	47	7 84				559	51	8 84
						30,490	852	213 00
						39,610	1,229	307 25
						4,730	307	76 75
						1,791	41	10 25
						1,500	142	35 50
						2,317,000	162,626	40,656 50
542	47	7 84				2,395,680	165,248	41,308 09

No. 1.—General Statement

Articles Imported.	Countries.	Total Imports.		Entered		
				General Tariff.		
		Quantity.	Value.	Quantity.	Value.	Duty.
DUTIABLE GOODS—*Con.*		Lbs.	$	Lbs.	$	$ cts.
Fruits—*Con.*						
Almonds, shelled	Great Britain	37,434	7,707	16,646	3,234	558 57
	Hong Kong	795	39	795	39	39 75
	China	2,285	343	2,285	343	114 25
	France	137,947	22,867	131,783	21,992	4,393 10
	Italy	5,642	906	4,062	772	203 10
	Spain	670,442	116,715	659,303	114,110	22,642 50
	United States	33,639	7,338	33,909	7,390	1,257 73
	Total	888,184	155,915	848,783	147,880	29,209 00
" not shelled	Great Britain	22,946	1,696	20,627	1,533	448 91
	China	718	31	718	31	21 54
	France	338,369	24,829	252,881	18,177	5,057 62
	Italy	210	18	210	18	6 30
	Portugal	6,050	539	8,114	686	243 42
	Spain	458,178	34,928	466,553	35,700	9,359 06
	United States	103,171	9,582	119,698	10,799	2,839 10
	Total	929,642	71,623	868,801	66,944	17,975 95
Brazil nuts, not shelled	Great Britain	4,378	416	4,378	416	131 34
	France	....	....	520	36	10 40
	Italy	1,881	167	376	33	11 28
	Spain	2,111	160	704	53	21 12
	United States	220,145	17,370	211,928	16,712	6,297 36
	Total	228,515	18,113	217,906	17,256	6,471 50
Pecans, not shelled and shelled peanuts, N.E.S.	Great Britain	500	35	500	35	15 00
	Hong Kong	746	22	746	22	22 38
	China	1,153	37	1,153	37	34 59
	France	37,998	1,640	38,366	1,677	767 32
	Italy	2,068	191	2,068	191	62 04
	Japan	3,858	157	3,858	157	115 74
	Spain	77,581	3,253	77,581	3,253	2,015 30
	United States	504,565	31,988	498,742	33,037	14,855 86
	Total	628,469	37,323	623,014	38,409	17,888 23
Walnuts, not shelled	Great Britain	28,749	2,069	31,129	2,149	651 78
	Hong Kong	1,056	58	1,056	58	31 68
	China	59	4	59	4	1 77
	France	717,065	75,085	802,248	73,336	16,453 90
	Italy	550	37	550	37	16 50
	Japan	4,480	151	4,480	151	134 40
	Spain	65,718	4,732	81,185	6,160	1,623 70
	United States	163,288	17,237	162,596	16,429	4.063 53
	Total	985,965	99,373	1,083,303	98,324	22,977 26

OF IMPORTS—*Continued.*

FOR HOME CONSUMPTION.

Preferential Tariff.			Surtax Tariff.			Total.		
Quantity.	Value.	Duty.	Quantity.	Value.	Duty.	Quantity.	Value.	Duty Collected.
Lbs.	$	$ cts.	Lbs.	$	$ cts.	Lbs.	$	$ cts.
1,852	408	61 73				18,498	3,642	620 30
						795	39	39 75
						2,285	343	114 25
						131,783	21,992	4,393 10
						4,062	772	203 10
						659,303	114,110	22,642 50
						33,909	7,390	1,257 73
1,852	408	61 73				850,635	148,288	29,270 73
						20,627	1,533	448 91
						718	31	21 54
						252,881	18,177	5,057 62
						210	18	6 30
						8,114	686	243 42
						466,553	35,700	9,359 06
						119,698	10,799	2,839 10
						868,801	66,944	17,975 95
						4,378	416	131 34
						520	36	10 40
						376	33	11 28
						704	53	21 12
						211,928	16,712	6,297 36
						217,906	17,250	6,471 50
						500	35	15 00
						746	22	22 38
						1,153	37	34 59
						38,366	1,677	767 32
						2,068	191	62 04
						3,858	157	115 74
						77,581	3,253	2,015 30
						498,742	33,037	14,855 86
						623,014	38,409	17,888 23
						31,129	2,149	651 78
						1,056	58	31 68
						59	4	1 77
						802,248	73,336	16,453 90
						550	37	16 50
						4,480	151	134 40
						81,185	6,160	1,623 70
						162,596	16,429	4,063 53
						1,083,303	98,324	22,977 26

No. 1.—GENERAL STATEMENT

Articles Imported.	Countries.	Total Imports.		Entered		
				General Tariff.		
		Quantity.	Value.	Quantity.	Value.	Duty.
DUTIABLE GOODS—*Con.*		Lbs.	$	Lbs.	$	$ cts.
Fruits, including nuts—*Con.* All other nuts, N.O.P......	Great Britain...	34,166	1,481	28,580	1,246	571 60
	Hong Kong. ...	15,938	330	15,938	330	318 76
	China........	17,998	476	21,195	660	423 90
	France........	84,028	7,815	104,781	6,963	2,095 62
	Italy........	600,833	30,428	521,333	27,343	10,426 66
	Japan	314,054	10,530	225,779	7,804	4,515 58
	Spain.	173,461	6,946	152,649	8,390	3,052 98
	Turkey.	2,291	160	10,979	553	219 58
	United States...	4,794,143	218,161	4,791,326	225,075	95,826 52
	Total...	6,036,912	276,327	5,872,560	278,364	117,451 20
" shelled	Great Britain...	18,018	1,419	8,988	814	251 16
	Hong Kong.....	50	16	50	16	2 50
	China	213	5	213	5	10 65
	France.........	710,841	111,890	818,776	118,016	17,451 35
	Italy....... ..	1,316	187	1,316	187	65 80
	Spain......	62,214	5,346	57,650	5,171	1,513 39
	Turkey.........	519	63	519	63	25 95
	United States...	63,877	15,416	65,148	15,505	2,283 69
	Total...	857,048	134,342	952,660	139,777	21,604 49
		Brls.		Brls.		
Green—Apples............	Australia.......	89	659	39	270	15 60
	United States...	20,151	89,985	20,033	89,288	8,013 20
	Total...	20,240	90,644	20,072	89,558	8,028 80
		Lbs.		Lbs.		
Blackberries, gooseberries, raspberries and strawberries, N.E.S	United States...	1,485,586	138,937	1,484,833	138,824	29,696 66
Cherries.....	United States...	121,613	18,024	120,986	17,937	2,419 72
		Bush.		Bush.		
Cranberries.......	United States...	15,100	39,184	15,091	39,160	9,790 00
		Lbs.		Lbs.		
Currants.......	United States...	610	37	610	37	12 20
Grapes	Great Britain....	809,662	59,842	793,926	58,515	15,878 52
	Australia.......	5,570	487	5,570	487	111 40
	Italy....	16,960	1,833	16,960	1,833	339 20
	Japan	4,500	300	4,500	300	90 00
	Spain.....	176,832	16,020	168,122	15,197	3,362 44
	St. Pierre..... ..	97	9	97	9	1 94
	United States...	1,014,633	64,460	1,012,833	64,275	20,256 66
	Total.	2,028,254	142,951	2,002,008	140,616	40,040 16

OF IMPORTS—*Continued.*

FOR HOME CONSUMPTION.

Preferential Tariff.			Surtax Tariff.			Total.		
Quantity.	Value.	Duty.	Quantity.	Value.	Duty.	Quantity.	Value.	Duty Collected.
Lbs.	$	$ cts.	Lbs.	$	$ cts.	Lbs.	$	$ cts.
675	84	9 00				29,255	1,330	580 60
						15,938	330	318 76
						21,195	660	423 90
						104,781	6,963	2,095 62
						521,333	27,343	10,426 66
						225,779	7,804	4,515 58
						152,649	8,390	3,052 98
						10,979	553	219 58
						4,791,326	225,075	95,826 52
675	84	9 00				5,873,235	278,448	117,460 20
14,530	1,164	484 33				23,518	1,978	735 49
						50	16	2 50
						213	5	10 65
						818,776	118,016	17,451 35
						1,316	187	65 80
						57,650	5,171	1,513 39
						519	63	25 95
						65,148	15,505	2,283 69
14,530	1,164	484 33				967,190	140,941	22,088 82
Brls.			Brls.					
						39	270	15 60
						20,033	89,288	8,013 20
						20,072	89,558	8,028 80
Lbs.			Lbs.					
						1,484,833	138,824	29,696 66
						120,986	17,937	2,419 72
Bush.			Bush.					
						15,091	39,160	9,790 00
Lbs.			Lbs.					
						610	37	12 20
						793,926	58,515	15,878 52
						5,570	487	111 40
						16,960	1,833	339 20
						4,500	300	90 00
						168,122	15,197	3,362 44
						97	9	1 94
						1,012,833	64,275	20,256 66
						2,002,008	140,616	40,040 16

No. 1.—GENERAL STATEMENT

Articles Imported.	Countries.	Total Imports.		Entered		
				General Tariff.		
		Quantity.	Value.	Quantity.	Value.	Duty.
DUTIABLE GOODS—*Con.*		Boxes.	$	Boxes.	$	$ cts.
Fruits—*Con.*						
Oranges, lemons and limes, in boxes of capacity not exceeding 2½ cubic feet......	Great Britain....	4,379	6,436	4,414	6,455	1,103 50
	B. W. Indies ...	3,828	5,204	574	800	143 50
	Hong Kong.....	152	143	152	143	38 00
	China	57	36	57	36	14 25
	Greece..........	144	262	144	262	36 00
	Italy..........	105,638	203,317	104,604	178,352	26,151 00
	Mexico.........	8,929	11,727	8,929	11,727	2,232 25
	Spain..........	1,690	2,985	1,790	3,121	447 50
	United States...	491,524	1,200,150	490,715	1,197,821	122,678 75
	Total.	616,341	1,430,260	611,379	1,398,717	152,844 75
Oranges, lemons and limes, in ½ boxes of capacity not exceeding 1¼ cubic feet....		½ boxes.		½ boxes.		
	Australia.......	100	150	100	150	13 00
	B. W. Indies...	48	35	1	1	0 13
	Italy..........	16,287	19,957	16,477	16,538	2,142 00
	United States...	8,867	13,398	8,867	13,398	1,152 71
	Total.. ...	25,302	33,540	25,445	30,087	3,307 84
Oranges, lemons and limes, in cases or other packages, N.E.S................		Cu. ft. Holding capacity.		Cu. ft. Holding capacity.		
	Great Britain...	175,842	108,009	177,071	108,839	17,707 10
	Australia......	12	6	12	6	1 20
	B. W. Indies ...	223	196	3	30	0 30
	Hong Kong.....	41	13	41	13	4 10
	China.......	1,128	534	1,128	534	112 80
	Italy..........	1,977	1,565	2,167	1,657	216 70
	Japan	21,301	10,980	21,301	10,980	2,130 10
	Spain	4,714	3,079	4,714	3,079	471 40
	United States...	19,301	16,589	19,301	16,589	1,930 10
	Total......	224,539	140,971	225,738	141,727	22,573 80
Oranges, lemons and limes, in bulk.....................		No.		No.		
	United States...	4,528	102	4,528	102	6 79
Oranges, lemons and limes, in barrels, not exceeding the capacity of flour barrels....		Brls.		Brls.		
	B. W. Indies...	18,289	49,381	1,176	2,615	646 80
	United States...	2,894	10,631	2,894	10,631	1,591 70
	Total....	21,183	60,012	4,070	13,276	2,238 50
		Lbs.		Lbs.		
Peaches, N.O.P............	United States...	3,582,669	90,835	3,531,224	89,994	35,312 24
		Bush.		Bush.		
Plums....................	United States...	46,659	62,559	56,647	62,522	15,630 50

OF IMPORTS—*Continued.*

FOR HOME CONSUMPTION.

Preferential Tariff.			Surtax Tariff.			Total.		
Quantity.	Value.	Duty.	Quantity.	Value.	Duty.	Quantity.	Value.	Duty Collected.
Boxes.	$	$ cts.	Boxes.	$	$ cts.	Boxes.	$	$ cts.
						4,414	6,455	1,103 50
3,254	4,404	542 42				3,828	5,204	685 92
						152	143	38 00
						57	36	14 25
						144	262	36 00
						104,604	178,352	26,151 00
						8,929	11,727	2,232 25
						1,790	3,121	447 50
						490,715	1,197,821	122,678 75
3,254	4,404	542 42				614,633	1,403,121	153,387 17
½ boxes.			½ boxes.			½ boxes.		
						100	150	13 00
47	34	4 08				48	35	4 21
						16,477	16,538	2,142 00
						8,867	13,398	1,152 71
47	34	4 08				25,492	30,121	3,311 92
Cu. ft. Holding capacity.			Cu. ft. Holding capacity.			Cu. ft. Holding capacity.		
						177,071	108,839	17,707 10
						12	6	1 20
220	166	14 65				223	196	14 95
						41	13	4 10
						1,128	534	112 80
						2,167	1,657	216 70
						21,301	10,980	2,130 10
						4,714	3,079	471 40
						19,301	16,589	1,930 10
220	166	14 65				225,958	141,893	22,588 45
No.			No.			No.		
						4,528	102	6 79
Brls.			Brls.			Brls.		
17,113	46,736	6,274 88				18,289	49,381	6,921 68
						2,894	10,631	1,591 70
17,113	46,736	6,274 88				21,183	60,012	8,513 38
Lbs.			Lbs.			Lbs.		
						3,531,224	89,994	35,312 24
Bush.			Bush.			Bush.		
						56,647	62,522	15,630 50

No. 1.—General Statement

Articles Imported.	Countries.	Total Imports.		Entered		
				General Tariff.		
		Quantity.	Value.	Quantity.	Value.	Duty.
DUTIABLE GOODS—*Con.*		Bush.	$	Bush.	$	$ cts.
Fruits—*Con.* Quinces	United States	170	399	170	399	99 75
All other, N.E.S.	Great Britain		2			
	Australia		58		58	11 60
	Hong Kong		118		118	23 60
	China		1		1	0 20
	Hawaii		5		5	1 00
	United States		69,545		69,283	13,856 60
	Total		69,729		69,465	13,893 00
		Lbs.		Lbs.		
Fruits in air-tight cans or other packages	Great Britain	560,778	26,409	17,685	1,584	397 91
	B. E. Indies	590,176	24,424	35,706	1,671	803 39
	B. W. Indies	47,271	3,764	30,770	2,634	692 33
	Hong Kong	13,547	308	13,547	308	304 81
	Newfoundland	60	7	60	7	1 35
	China	24,095	565	24,095	565	542 14
	France	114,435	10,311	115,846	9,880	2,606 54
	Germany	145	17			
	Hawaii	282	32	282	32	6 35
	Italy	7,704	1,100	7,704	1,100	173 34
	Japan	314	13	314	13	7 07
	St Pierre	46	6	46	6	1 04
	Spain	2,205	78	2,205	78	49 61
	United States	856,102	49,889	790,583	48,545	17,788 32
	Total	2,217,160	116,923	1,038,843	66,423	23,374 20
		Galls.		Galls.		
Fruits preserved in brandy or preserved in other spirits	Great Britain			41	81	82 00
	France	1,466	243	67	173	134 00
	United States	54	255	71	304	142 00
	Total	1,520	498	179	558	358 00
Furniture—House, office, cabinet or store furniture of wood, iron or other material, in parts or finished	Great Britain		41,263		7,815	2,344 50
	B. E. Indies		100		75	22 50
	Hong Kong		1.793		1,793	537 90
	Newfoundland		17		17	5 10
	Aust.-Hungary		8,888		9,074	2,722 20
	Belgium		587		506	151 80
	China		1,384		1,328	398 40
	France		13,298		12,683	3,804 90
	Germany		4,021			
	Italy		818		818	245 40
	Japan		7,491		7,400	2,220 00
	Switzerland		61		61	18 30
	Turkey		66		66	19 80
	United States		673,802		664,867	199,460 10
	Total		753,589		706,503	211,950 90

OF IMPORTS—*Continued.*

FOR HOME CONSUMPTION.

Preferential Tariff.			Surtax Tariff.			Total.		
Quantity.	Value.	Duty.	Quantity.	Value.	Duty.	Quantity.	Value.	Duty Collected.
Bush.	$	$ cts.	Bush.	$	$ cts.	Bush.	$	$ cts.
...	...	...	...	...	...	170	399	99 75
...	2	0 27	...	...	...	...	2	0 27
...	...	...	...	...	...	...	58	11 60
...	...	...	...	...	...	...	118	23 60
...	...	...	...	...	...	...	1	0 20
...	...	...	...	...	...	...	5	1 00
...	...	...	...	...	...	...	69,283	13,856 60
...	2	0 27	...	...	...	...	69,467	13,893 27
Lbs.			Lbs.			Lbs.		
479,854	21,076	7,197 81	240	31	7 20	497,779	22,691	7,602 92
535,685	22,124	8,035 33	...	...	...	571,391	23,795	8,838 72
21,644	1,532	324 66	...	...	...	52,414	4,166	1,016 99
...	...	...	...	...	...	13,547	308	304 81
...	...	...	...	...	...	60	7	1 35
...	...	...	...	...	...	24,095	565	542 14
...	...	...	...	...	...	115,846	9,880	2,606 54
...	...	...	145	17	4 35	145	17	4 35
...	...	...	...	...	...	282	32	6 35
...	...	...	...	...	...	7,704	1,100	173 34
...	...	...	...	...	...	314	13	7 07
...	...	...	...	...	...	46	6	1 04
...	...	...	...	...	...	2,205	78	49 61
...	...	...	...	...	...	790,583	48,545	17,788 32
1,037,183	44,732	15,557 80	385	48	11 55	2,076,411	111,203	38,943 55
Galls.			Galls.			Galls.		
...	...	...	...	...	...	41	81	82 00
...	...	...	...	...	...	67	173	134 00
...	...	...	...	...	...	71	304	142 00
...	...	...	...	...	...	179	558	358 00
...	32,521	6,504 20	...	453	181 20	...	40,789	9,029 90
...	25	5 00	...	...	...	...	100	27 50
...	...	...	...	...	...	...	1,793	537 90
...	...	...	...	...	...	...	17	5 10
...	...	...	...	...	...	...	9,074	2,722 20
...	...	...	...	...	...	...	506	151 80
...	...	...	...	...	...	...	1,328	398 40
...	...	...	...	...	...	...	12,683	3,804 90
...	...	...	...	4,011	1,604 40	...	4,011	1,604 40
...	...	...	...	...	...	...	818	245 40
...	...	...	...	...	...	...	7,400	2,220 00
...	...	...	...	...	...	...	61	18 30
...	...	...	...	...	...	...	66	19 80
...	...	...	...	237	94 80	...	665,104	199,554 90
...	32,546	6,509 20	...	4,701	1,880 40	...	743,750	220,310 50

OF IMPORTS—*Continued.*

Articles Imported.	Countries.	Total Imports.		Entered		
				General Tariff.		
		Quantity.	Value.	Quantity.	Value.	Duty.
DUTIABLE GOODS—*Con.*			$		$	$ cts.
Furs and manufactures of, viz.: Fur skins wholly or partially dressed, N.E.S.	Great Britain	....	404,557	....	115,637	17,345 55
	Aust.-Hungary	....	1,246	....	1,246	186 90
	Belgium	....	7,327	....	7,288	1,093 20
	China	....	15,288	....	15,288	2,293 20
	France	....	168,333	....	163,252	24,487 80
	Germany	....	312,332	....	27,126	4,068 90
	Japan	....	25	....	25	3 75
	Russia	....	41,281	....	36,910	5,536 50
	United States	....	192,506	....	191,113	28,666 95
	Total	....	1,142,895	....	557,885	83,682 75
Caps, hats, muffs, tippets, capes, coats, cloaks and other manufactures of fur, N.O.P.	Great Britain	....	157,601	....	9,716	2,914 80
	Hong Kong	....	5	....	5	1 50
	Aust.-Hungary	....	6,562	....	6,562	1,968 60
	Belgium	....	19,762	....	19,762	5,928 60
	China	....	10	....	10	3 00
	France	....	3,208	....	3,208	962 40
	Germany	....	3,105	....	255	76 50
	Japan	....	16	....	16	4 80
	Russia	....	1,515	....	1,515	454 50
	United States	....	95,939	....	96,035	28,810 50
	Total	....	287,723	....	137,084	41,125 20
Fuses, N.O.P.	Great Britain	....	44,247	....	....	....
	Germany	....	310	....	....	....
	United States	....	19,305	....	19,660	3,932 00
	Total	....	63,862	....	19,660	3,932 00
Glass and manufactures of— Bulbs for electric lights		Doz.		Doz.		
	Great Britain	230	16	....	....	....
	Aust.-Hungary	18,234	1,874	18,234	1,874	187 40
	Germany	4,200	465	....	....	....
	United States	193,296	38,254	193,296	38,254	3,825 40
	Total	215,960	40,609	211,530	40,128	4,012 80
Glass carboys and demijohns, empty or filled, bottles, decanters, flasks and phials	Great Britain	....	33,543	....	1,792	537 60
	B. W. Indies	....	1	....	1	0 30
	Aust.-Hungary	....	6,123	....	6,193	1,857 90
	Belgium	....	1,732	....	1,732	519 60
	China	....	6	....	6	1 80
	France	....	4,606	....	4,648	1,394 40
	Germany	....	104,462	....	101	30 30
	Holland	....	43,026	....	43,031	12,909 30
	Italy	....	10	....	....	....
	Japan	....	9	....	9	2 70
	Sweden	....	27,434	....	27,324	8,197 20
	Switzerland	....	....	....	1	0 30
	United States	....	121,754	....	119,344	35,803 20
	Total	....	342,706	....	204,182	61,254 60

OF IMPORTS—*Continued.*

FOR HOME CONSUMPTION.

Preferential Tariff.			Surtax Tariff.			Total.		
Quantity.	Value.	Duty.	Quantity.	Value.	Duty.	Quantity.	Value.	Duty Collected.
	$	$ cts.		$	$ cts.		$	$ cts.
	228,461	22,846 10		34,014	6,802 80		378,112	46,994 45
							1,246	186 90
							7,288	1,093 20
							15,288	2,293 20
							163,252	24,487 80
				286,643	57,328 60		313,769	61,397 50
							25	3 75
				415	83 00		37,325	5,619 50
				2,826	565 20		193,939	29,232 15
	228,461	22,846 10		323,898	64,779 60		1,110,244	171,308 45
	145,847	29,169 40		874	349 60		156,437	32,433 80
							5	1 50
							6,562	1,968 60
							19,762	5,928 60
							10	3 00
							3,208	962 40
				2,850	1,140 00		3,105	1,216 50
							16	4 80
							1,515	454 50
							96,035	28,810 50
	145,847	29,169 40		3,724	1,489 60		286,655	71,784 20
	42,932	5,724 35					42,932	5,724 35
				310	82 66		310	82 66
							19,660	3,932 00
	42,932	5,724 35		310	82 66		62,902	9,739 01
Doz. 230	16	1 06	Doz.			Doz. 230	16	1 06
						18,234	1,874	187 40
			4,200	465	62 00	4,200	465	62 00
						193,296	38,254	3,825 40
230	16	1 06	4,200	465	62 00	215,960	40,609	4,075 86
	31,001	6,200 20		795	318 00		33,588	7,055 80
							1	0 30
				4	1 60		6,197	1,859 50
							1,732	519 60
							6	1 80
							4,848	1,394 40
				104,327	41,730 80		104,428	41,761 10
							43,031	12,909 30
							9	2 70
							27,324	8,197 20
							1	0 30
				2,427	970 80		121,771	36,774 00
	31,001	6,200 20		107,553	43,021 20		342,736	110,476 00

No. 1.—GENERAL STATEMENT

ARTICLES IMPORTED.	COUNTRIES.	TOTAL IMPORTS.		ENTERED		
				General Tariff.		
		Quantity.	Value.	Quantity.	Value.	Duty.
DUTIABLE GOODS—*Con.*			$		$	$ cts
Glass and mfrs. of—*Con.*						
Glass jars and glass balls, and cut, pressed or moulded, crystal or glass table ware, decorated or not	Great Britain		26,531		13,706	4,111 80
	Gibraltar		10		10	3 00
	Aust.-Hungary		33,904		33,975	10,192 50
	Belgium		16,718		17,003	5,100 90
	China		7		7	2 10
	France		10,040		10,033	3,009 90
	Germany		13,035		3,281	984 30
	Holland		2,013		2,013	603 90
	Italy		293		293	87 90
	Japan		23		23	6 90
	Sweden		672		781	234 30
	United States		227,223		227,142	68,142 60
	Total		330,469		308,267	92,480 10
Lamp chimneys, glass shades or globes, and blown glass table ware	Great Britain		1,083		312	93 60
	Hong Kong		27		27	8 10
	Aust.-Hungary		16,197		15,382	4,614 60
	Belgium		22		22	6 60
	China		128		128	38 40
	France		868		868	260 40
	Germany		21,774		401	120 30
	Holland		179		179	53 70
	Japan		48		48	14 40
	United States		95,708		93,454	28,036 20
	Total		136,034		110,821	33,246 30
Ornamental, figured and enamelled coloured glass and memorial or other ornamental window glass, N.O.P.	Great Britain		47,875		385	115 50
	Belgium		2,137		2,137	641 10
	France		3,357		3,357	1,007 10
	Germany		90		90	27 00
	United States		8,297		8,297	2,489 10
	Total		61,756		14,266	4,279 80
Painted or vitrified, chipped, figured, enamelled and obscured white glass		Sq. ft.		Sq. ft.		
	Great Britain	105,205	4,231	1,320	104	31 20
	Belgium	29,500	2,676	29,500	2,676	802 80
	France	643	58	643	58	17 40
	United States	32,770	2,343	32,770	2,343	702 90
	Total	168,118	9,308	64,233	5,181	1,554 30
Common and colourless window glass	Great Britain	14,956,487	340,183	453,634	10,927	1,639 05
	Belgium	22,730,982	581,127	22,641,722	578,279	86,741 85
	France	355,892	10,594	355,892	10,594	1,589 10
	Sweden	4,000	97	4,000	97	14 55
	United States	576,472	18,900	576,472	18,900	2,835 00
	Total	38,623,833	950,901	24,031,720	618,797	92,819 55

OF IMPORTS—*Continued.*

FOR HOME CONSUMPTION.

Preferential Tariff.			Surtax Tariff.			Total.		
Quantity.	Value.	Duty.	Quantity.	Value.	Duty.	Quantity.	Value.	Duty Collected.
	$	$ cts.		$	$ cts.		$	$ cts.
	11,457	2,291 40		1,389	555 60		26,552	6,958 80
							10	3 00
				9	3 60		33,984	10,196 10
							17,003	5,100 90
							7	2 10
							10,033	3,009 90
				8,945	3,578 00		12,226	4,562 30
							2,013	603 90
							293	87 90
							23	6 90
				1	0 40		782	234 70
				397	158 80		227,539	68,301 40
	11,457	2,291 40		10,741	4,296 40		330,465	99,067 90
	452	90 40		81	32 40		845	216 40
							27	8 10
				42	16 80		15,424	4,631 40
							22	6 60
							128	38 40
							868	260 40
				20,802	8,320 80		21,203	8,441 10
							179	53 70
							48	14 40
				339	135 60		93,793	28,171 80
	452	90 40		21,264	8,505 60		132,537	41,842 30
	47,440	9,488 00					47,825	9,603 50
							2,137	641 10
							3,357	1,007 10
							90	27 00
							8,297	2,489 10
	47,440	9,488 00					61,706	13,767 80
Sq. ft.			Sq. ft.			Sq. ft.		
103,885	4,127	825 40				105,205	4,231	856 60
						29,500	2,676	802 80
						643	58	17 40
						32,770	2,343	702 90
103,885	4,127	825 40				168,118	9,308	2,379 70
14,502,853	329,256	24,693 93				14,956,487	340,183	26,332 98
						22,641,722	578,279	86,741 85
						355,892	10,594	1,589 10
						4,000	97	14 55
						576,472	18,900	2,835 00
14,502,853	329,256	24,693 93				38,534,573	948,053	117,513 48

No. 1.—GENERAL STATEMENT

Articles Imported.	Countries.	Total Imports.		Entered		
				General Tariff.		
		Quantity.	Value.	Quantity.	Value.	Duty.
DUTIABLE GOODS—*Con.*		Sq. ft.	$	Sq. ft.	$	$ cts.
Glass and mfrs. of—*Con.*						
Plain, coloured, opaque, stained or tinted or muffled glass in sheets	Great Britain	320,611	26,620	29,290	2,185	437 00
	Aust.-Hungary	2,918	552	2,918	552	110 40
	Belgium	160,890	11,383	158,820	11,245	2,249 00
	France	340	20	340	20	4 00
	United States	336,927	27,473	336,820	27,445	5,489 00
	Total	821,686	66,048	528,188	41,447	8,289 40
Plate glass, not bevelled, in sheets or panes, not exceeding 7 sq. ft. each, N.O.P.	Great Britain	219,885	34,652	758	201	20 10
	Belgium	389,649	70,799	389,649	70,799	7,079 90
	France	102,995	20,276	102,995	20,276	2,027 60
	United States	29,917	5,892	29,917	5,892	589 20
	Total	742,446	131,619	523,319	97,168	9,716 80
Plate glass, not bevelled, in sheets or panes exceeding 7 sq. ft. each, and not exceeding 25 sq. ft. each, N.O.P.	Great Britain	303,912	58,376	1,090	304	76 00
	Belgium	402,265	59,190	402,265	59,190	14.797 50
	France	42,471	9,361	42,471	9,361	2,340 25
	United States	16,202	3,038	16,202	3,038	759 50
	Total	764,850	129,965	462,028	71,893	17,973 25
" " N.E.S.	Great Britain	502,921	108,163	2,592	625	218 75
	Belgium	336.449	66,628	334,895	66,205	23,171 75
	France	46,734	7,224	46,734	7,224	2,528 40
	Holland	12,023	2,770	12,023	2,770	969 50
	United States	19,371	4,352	19,371	4,352	1,523 20
	Total	917,498	189,137	415,615	81,176	28,411 60
" " bevelled, N.O.P.	Great Britain	10,361	1,974	50	9	3 15
	Belgium	13,615	3,153	13,615	3,153	1,103 55
	United States	2,155	543	2,155	543	190 05
	Total	26,131	5,670	15,820	3,705	1,296 75
" " rough rolled	Great Britain	268,805	18,413	1,000	40	12 00
	Belgium	19,512	3,179	19,512	3,179	953 70
	United States	45,730	4,779	45,730	4,779	1,433 70
	Total	334,047	26,371	66,242	7,998	2,399 40
German looking glass (thin plate), unsilvered or for silvering	Aust.-Hungary		960		960	192 00
	Germany		329			
	United States		1,271		1,271	254 20
	Total		2,560		2,231	446 20

OF IMPORTS—*Continued.*

FOR HOME CONSUMPTION.

Preferential Tariff.			Surtax Tariff.			Total.		
Quantity.	Value.	Duty.	Quantity.	Value.	Duty.	Quantity.	Value.	Duty Collected.
Sq. ft.	$	$ cts.	Sq. ft.	$	$ cts.	Sq. ft.	$	$ cts.
291,421	24,435	3,258 10	....	....	....	320,711	26,620	3,695 10
....	....	....	....	....	....	2,918	552	110 40
....	....	....	2,070	138	36 80	160,890	11,383	2,285 80
....	....	....	....	....	....	340	20	4 00
....	....	....	107	28	7 47	336,927	27,473	5,496 47
291,421	24,435	3,258 10	2,177	166	44 27	821,786	66,048	11,591 77
219,127	34,451	2,296 87	....	....	....	219,885	34,652	2,316 97
....	....	....	....	....	....	389,649	70,799	7,079 90
....	....	....	....	....	....	102,995	20,276	2,027 60
....	....	....	....	....	....	29,917	5,892	589 20
219,127	34,451	2,296 87	....	....	....	742,446	131,619	12,013 67
302,822	58,072	9,678 75	....	....	....	303,912	58,376	9,754 75
....	....	....	....	....	....	402,265	59,190	14,797 50
....	....	....	....	....	....	42,471	9,361	2,340 25
....	....	....	....	....	....	16,202	3,038	759 50
302,822	58,072	9,678 75	....	....	....	764,850	129,965	27,652 00
500,329	107,538	25,092 51	....	....	....	502,921	108,163	25,311 26
....	....	....	....	....	....	334,895	66,205	23,171 75
....	....	....	....	....	....	46,734	7,224	2,528 40
....	....	....	....	....	....	12,023	2,770	969 50
....	....	....	....	....	....	19,371	4,352	1,523 20
500,329	107,538	25,092 51	....	....	....	915,944	188,714	53,504 11
10,311	1,965	458 48	....	....	....	10,361	1,974	461 63
....	....	....	....	....	....	13,615	3,153	1,103 55
....	....	....	....	....	....	2,155	543	190 05
10,311	1,965	458 48	....	....	....	26,131	5,670	1,755 23
267,805	18,373	3,674 60	....	....	....	268,805	18,413	3,686 60
....	....	....	....	....	....	19,512	3,179	953 70
....	....	....	....	....	....	45,730	4,779	1,433 70
267,805	18,373	3,674 60	....	....	....	334,047	26,371	6,074 00
....	....	....	....	....	....	....	960	192 00
....	....	....	....	329	87 74	....	329	87 74
....	....	....	....	....	....	....	1,271	254 20
....	....	....	....	329	87 74	....	2,560	533 94

No. 1.—General Statement

Articles Imported.	Countries.	Total Imports.		Entered		
				General Tariff.		
		Quantity.	Value.	Quantity.	Value.	Duty.
DUTIABLE GOODS—*Con.*			$		$	$ cts.
Glass and mfrs.—*Con.*						
Silvered glass, bevelled or not, framed or not framed	Great Britain		30,412		1,051	367 85
	Hong Kong		7		7	2 45
	Aust.-Hungary		2,257		2,257	789 95
	Belgium		912		912	319 20
	China		6		6	2 10
	France		9,254		9,254	3,238 90
	Germany		13,952		6	2 10
	Italy		15		15	5 25
	Japan		6		6	2 10
	United States		23,208		22,317	7,810 95
	Total		80,029		35,831	12,540 85
Stained glass windows	Great Britain		101			
	France		154		154	46 20
	Germany		355			
	Total		610		154	46 20
All other glass and manufactures of glass, not otherwise provided for, including bent plate or other sheet glass	Great Britain		26,231		6,386	1,277 20
	Hong Kong		3		3	0 60
	Aust.-Hungary		19,033		19,001	3,800 20
	Belgium		1,561		1,561	312 20
	Denmark		28		28	5 60
	France		8,472		8,472	1,694 40
	Germany		14,380		5,858	1,171 60
	Holland		72		72	14 40
	Italy		2,151		2,151	430 20
	Japan		6		6	1 20
	Turkey		18		18	3 60
	United States		95,651		95,029	19,005 80
	Total		167,606		138,585	27,717 00
Gloves and mitts of all kinds	Great Britain		436,233		75,275	26,346 25
	Aust.-Hungary		43,248		43,041	15,064 35
	Belgium		3,372		3,372	1,180 20
	France		341,739		341,073	119,375 55
	Germany		168,660		6,403	2,241 05
	Holland		589		589	206 15
	Italy		9,389		9,389	3,286 15
	Japan		99		99	34 65
	Switzerland		9,819		9,546	3,341 10
	United States		153,946		138,089	48,331 15
	Total		1,167,094		626,876	219,406 60
Gold and silver, mfrs. of—						
Gold, silver and aluminium leaf, Dutch or schlag metal leaf	Great Britain		1,578		22	5 50
	Aust.-Hungary		3,456		3,456	864 00
	France		2,570		2,570	642 50
	Germany		30,971			
	United States		7,266		7,242	1,810 50
	Total		45,841		13,290	3,322 50

OF IMPORTS—*Continued.*

FOR HOME CONSUMPTION.

Preferential Tariff.			Surtax Tariff.			Total.		
Quantity.	Value.	Duty.	Quantity.	Value.	Duty.	Quantity.	Value.	Duty Collected.
	$	$ cts.		$	$ cts.		$	$ cts.
....	28,526	6,656 10	....	826	385 47	....	30,403	7,409 42
....	....	....	....	....	....	....	7	2 45
....	....	....	....	....	....	....	2,257	789 95
....	....	....	....	....	....	....	912	319 20
....	....	....	....	....	....	....	6	2 10
....	....	....	....	....	....	....	9,254	3,238 90
....	....	....	....	13,950	6,510 11	....	13,956	6,512 21
....	....	....	....	....	....	....	15	5 25
....	....	....	....	....	....	....	6	2 10
....	....	....	....	891	415 80	....	23,208	8,226 75
....	28,526	6,656 10	....	15,667	7,311 38	....	80,024	26,508 33
....	101	20 20	....	....	....	....	101	20 20
....	....	....	....	....	....	....	154	46 20
....	....	....	....	355	142 00	....	355	142 00
....	101	20 20	....	355	142 00	....	610	208 40
....	18,504	2,467 48	....	894	238 40	....	25,784	3,983 08
....	....	....	....	....	....	....	3	0 60
....	....	....	....	89	23 74	....	19,090	3,823 94
....	....	....	....	....	....	....	1,561	312 20
....	....	....	....	....	....	....	28	5 60
....	....	....	....	....	....	....	8,472	1,694 40
....	....	....	....	8,448	2,252 86	....	14,306	3,424 46
....	....	....	....	....	....	....	72	14 40
....	....	....	....	....	....	....	2,151	430 20
....	....	....	....	....	....	....	6	1 20
....	....	....	....	....	....	....	18	3 60
....	....	....	....	622	165 87	....	95,651	19,171 67
....	18,504	2,467 48	....	10,053	2,680 87	....	167,142	32,865 35
....	326,411	76,163 60	....	34,414	16,059 77	....	436,100	118,569 62
....	....	....	....	207	96 60	....	43,248	15,160 95
....	....	....	....	....	....	....	3,372	1,180 20
....	....	....	....	867	404 60	....	341,940	119,780 15
....	....	....	....	161,642	75,432 90	....	168,045	77,673 95
....	....	....	....	....	....	....	589	206 15
....	....	....	....	....	....	....	9,389	3,286 15
....	....	....	....	....	....	....	99	34 65
....	....	....	....	273	127 40	....	9,819	3,468 50
....	....	....	....	14,946	6,974 80	....	153,035	55,305 95
....	326,411	76,163 60	....	212,349	99,096 07	....	1,165,636	394,666 27
....	1,531	255 20	....	25	8 34	....	1,578	269 04
....	....	....	....	....	....	....	3,456	864 00
....	....	....	....	....	....	....	2,570	642 50
....	....	....	....	30,978	10,326 00	....	30,978	10,326 00
....	....	....	....	24	8 00	....	7,266	1,818 50
....	1,531	255 20	....	31,027	10,342 34	....	45,848	13,920 04

No. 1.—General Statement

Articles Imported.	Countries.	Total Imports. Quantity.	Total Imports. Value.	Entered — General Tariff. Quantity.	Entered — General Tariff. Value.	Entered — General Tariff. Duty.
DUTIABLE GOODS—*Con.*					$	$ cts.
Gold and silver—*Con.* Manufactures of gold, N.E.S.	Great Britain...	....	837	....	301	90 30
	France..........	....	227	....	227	68 10
	Germany.......	....	12	....	....	....
	United States...	....	13,665	....	13,665	4,099 50
	Total	....	14,741	....	14,193	4,257 90
Electro-plated ware and gilt ware of all kinds, N.E.S...	Great Britain...	....	104,326	....	3,125	937 50
	Hong Kong.....	....	15	....	15	4 50
	Aust.-Hungary.	....	1,583	....	1,597	479 10
	China......	....	20	....	20	6 00
	France........	....	2,224	....	2,230	669 00
	Germany.......	....	11,697	....	52	15 60
	Holland......	....	136	....	....	....
	Italy..........	....	151	....	151	45 30
	Japan..........	....	2,687	....	2,687	806 10
	Switzerland.....	....	6	....	6	1 80
	United States...	....	215,004	....	214,914	64,474 20
	Total ..	....	337,849	....	224,797	67,439 10
Sterling or other silverware..	Great Britain...	....	103,053	....	4,636	1,390 80
	B. E. Indies....	....	29	....	29	8 70
	Aust.-Hungary.	....	726	....	726	217 80
	China..........	....	1,225	....	1,225	367 50
	France..........	....	3,107	....	3,097	929 10
	Germany.......	....	2,829	....	....	....
	Holland......	....	1,001	....	1,001	300 30
	Italy..........	....	97	....	97	29 10
	Japan..........	....	139	....	139	41 70
	United States...	....	68,741	....	63,786	19,135 80
	Total	....	180,947	....	74,736	22,420 80
		Lbs.		Lbs.		
Grease, axle	Great Britain...	21,949	1,174	605	36	7 20
	Belgium.....	560	17	560	17	3 40
	Germany......	474	55	....	....	....
	Turkey.........	505	23	505	23	4 60
	United States...	1,609,229	63,391	1,606,279	63,246	12,649 20
	Total	1,632,717	64,660	1,607,949	63,322	12,664 40
Gunpowder and other explosives, &c.— Gun, rifle, sporting and cannister powder............	Great Britain...	27,426	6,879	5,693	1,200	170 79
	United States...	59,536	18,832	59,061	18,769	1,771 83
	Total	86,962	25,711	64,754	20,029	1,942 62
Blasting and mining powder.	Great Britain...	674,200	76,972	....	....	....
	United States...	274,835	12,268	274,835	12,268	5,496 70
	Total	949,035	89,240	274,835	12,268	5,496 70
Giant powder, nitro, nitro-glycerine and other explosives	Great Britain...	53,968	30,374	....	....	....
	United States...	489,177	64,118	107,527	14,109	3,225 81
	Total	543,145	94,492	107,527	14,109	3,225 81

OF IMPORTS—*Continued.*

FOR HOME CONSUMPTION.

Preferential Tariff.			Surtax Tariff.			Total.		
Quantity.	Value.	Duty.	Quantity.	Value.	Duty.	Quantity.	Value.	Duty Collected.
	$	$ cts.		$	$ cts.		$	$ cts.
	536	107 20					837	197 50
							227	68 10
				12	4 80		12	4 80
							13,665	4,099 50
	536	107 20		12	4 80		14,741	4,369 90
	101,244	20,248 80		276	110 40		104,645	21,296 70
							15	4 50
							1,597	479 10
							20	6 00
							2,230	669 00
				11,645	4,658 00		11,697	4,673 60
				136	54 40		136	54 40
							151	45 30
							2,687	806 10
							6	1 80
				61	24 40		214,975	64,498 60
	101,244	20,248 80		12,118	4,847 20		338,159	92,535 10
	78,296	15,659 20		118	47 20		83,050	17,097 20
							29	8 70
							726	217 80
							1,225	367 50
							3,097	929 10
				2,829	1,131 60		2,829	1,131 60
							1,001	300 30
							97	29 10
							139	41 70
							63,786	19,135 80
	78,296	15,659 20		2,947	1,178 80		155,979	39,258 80
Lbs.			Lbs.			Lbs.		
21,344	1,138	151 73				21,949	1,174	158 93
						560	17	3 40
			474	55	14 66	474	55	14 66
						505	23	4 60
						1,606,279	63,246	12,649 20
21,344	1,138	151 73	474	55	14 66	1,629,767	64,515	12,830 79
21,733	5,619	434 66				27,426	6,879	605 45
						59,061	18,769	1,771 83
21,733	5,619	434 66				86,487	25,648	2,377 28
674,200	76,972	8,989 37				674,200	76,972	8,989 37
						274,835	12,268	5,496 70
674,200	76,972	8,989 37				949,035	89,240	14,486 07
64,350	24,440	1,287 00				64,350	24,440	1,287 00
						107,527	14,109	3,225 81
64,350	24,440	1,287 00				171,877	38,549	4,512 81

No. 1.—General Statement

Articles Imported.	Countries.	Total Imports.		Entered		
				General Tariff.		
		Quantity.	Value.	Quantity.	Value.	Duty.
DUTIABLE GOODS—*Con.*			$		$	$ cts.
Gunpowder, &c.—*Con.*						
Gun, rifle and pistol cartridges or other ammunitions N. O. P.	Great Britain	....	225,562	....	1,638	491 40
	Hong Kong	....	8	....	8	2 40
	Aust.-Hungary	....	31	....	31	9 30
	Belgium	....	449	....	449	134 70
	France	....	182	....	182	54 60
	United States	....	166,278	....	165,917	49,775 10
	Total	....	392,510	....	168,225	50,467 50
Gun wads, percussion caps, primers and cartridge cases	Great Britain	....	12,805	....	....	....
	Belgium	....	906	....	906	271 80
	Germany	....	180	....	....	....
	United States	....	15,379	....	14,463	4,338 90
	Total	....	29,270	....	15,369	4,610 70
Gun or pistol covers or cases, game bags, loading tools and cartridge belts of any material	Great Britain	....	1,083	....	177	53 10
	France	....	15	....	15	4 50
	United States	....	14,951	....	14,950	4,485 00
	Total	....	16,049	....	15,142	4,542 60
Gutta percha and India-rubber, manufactures of—						
Boots and shoes	Great Britain	....	263	....	10	2 50
	Hong Kong	....	18	....	18	4 50
	China	....	177	....	157	39 25
	United States	....	179,173	....	142,763	35,690 75
	Total	....	179,631	....	142,948	35,737 00
Belting	Great Britain	....	19	....	....	....
	United States	....	40,418	....	40,241	10,060 25
	Total	....	40,437	....	40,241	10,060 25
Clothing, and clothing made waterproof with India-rubber	Great Britain	....	34,156	....	362	126 70
	Aust.-Hungary	....	168	....	....	....
	United States	....	16,046	....	16,717	5,850 95
	Total	....	50,370	....	17,079	5,977 65
Hose, including cotton or linen, lined with rubber	Great Britain	....	980	....	....	....
	Germany	....	109	....	....	....
	United States	....	51,900	....	50,173	17,560 55
	Total	....	52,989	....	50,173	17,560 55
Packing, mats and matting	Great Britain	....	3,234		1,819	636 65
	Germany	....	144	....	....	....
	United States	....	70,110	....	68,795	24,078 25
	Total	....	73,488	....	70,614	24,714 90

OF IMPORTS—*Continued.*

FOR HOME CONSUMPTION.

Preferential Tariff.			Surtax Tariff.			Total.		
Quantity.	Value.	Duty.	Quantity.	Value.	Duty.	Quantity.	Value.	Duty Collected.
	$	$ cts.		$	$ cts.		$	$ cts.
....	229,888	45,977 60	....	....	....	....	231,526	46,469 00
....	....	....	....	....	....	....	8	2 40
....	....	....	....	....	....	....	31	9 30
....	....	....	....	....	....	....	449	134 70
....	....	....	....	....	....	....	182	54 60
....	....	....	....	....	....	....	165,917	49,775 10
....	229,888	45,977 60	....	....	....	....	398,113	96,445 10
....	12,968	2,593 60	....	13	5 20	....	12,981	2,598 80
....	....	....	....	....	....	....	906	271 80
....	....	....	....	180	72 00	....	180	72 00
....	....	....	....	46	18 40	....	14,509	4,357 30
....	12,968	2,593 60	....	239	95 60	....	28,576	7,299 90
....	906	181 20	....	....	....	....	1,083	234 30
....	....	....	....	....	....	....	15	4 50
....	....	....	....	....	....	....	14,950	4,485 00
....	906	181 20	....	....	....	....	16,048	4,723 80
....	253	42 17	....	....	....	....	263	44 67
....	....	....	....	....	....	....	18	4 50
....	....	....	....	20	6 67	....	177	45 92
....	....	....	....	....	....	....	142,763	35,690 75
....	253	42 17	....	20	6 67	....	143,221	35,785 84
....	19	3 17	....	....	....	....	19	3 17
....	....	....	....	....	....	....	40,241	10,060 25
....	19	3 17	....	....	....	....	40,260	10,063 42
....	33,445	7,804 09	....	....	....	....	33,807	7,930 79
....	....	....	....	....	....	....	16,717	5,850 95
....	33,445	7,804 09	....	....	....	....	50,524	13,781 74
....	935	218 18	....	45	21 00	....	980	239 18
....	....	....	....	109	50 87	....	109	50 87
....	....	....	....	....	....	....	50,173	17,560 55
....	935	218 18	....	154	71 87	....	51,262	17,850 60
....	1,364	318 27	....	51	23 80	....	3,234	978 72
....	....	....	....	144	67 20	....	144	67 20
....	....	....	....	42	19 60	....	68,837	24,097 85
....	1,364	318 27	....	237	110 60	....	72,215	25,143 77

No. 1.—GENERAL STATEMENT

Articles Imported.	Countries.	Total Imports.		Entered		
				General Tariff.		
		Quantity.	Value.	Quantity.	Value.	Duty.
DUTIABLE GOODS—*Con.*			$		$	$ cts.
Gutta percha, &c.—*Con.*						
All other, not otherwise provided for	Great Britain		61,043		3,455	863 75
	Aust.-Hungary		6,095		6,099	1,524 75
	Belgium		200		200	50 00
	China		3		3	0 75
	France		3,225		3,192	798 00
	Germany		21,463		83	20 75
	Russia		432		432	108 00
	United States		322,367		321,006	80,251 50
	Total		414,828		334,470	83,617 50
Hair and manufactures of, not otherwise provided for—						
Braids, chains or cords	United States		1,117		1,117	390 95
		Lbs.		Lbs.		
Curled or dyed	Great Britain	336	551			
	Germany	1,006	204			
	United States	3,894	5,537	3,894	5,537	1,107 40
	Total	5,236	6,292	3,894	5,537	1,107 40
Hair cloth of all kinds	Great Britain		11,894		2,761	828 30
	Germany		28			
	United States		33		33	9 90
	Total		11,955		2,794	838 20
Other manufactures of, N.E.S.	Great Britain		1,249		452	158 20
	Hong Kong		9		9	3 15
	Aust.-Hungary		1,186		1,186	415 10
	China		7		7	2 45
	France		94		94	32 90
	Germany		708		52	18 20
	Japan		5		5	1 75
	United States		9,045		9,045	3,165 75
	Total		12,303		10,850	3,797 50
Hats, caps and bonnets, N.E.S—						
Beaver, silk or felt	Great Britain		698,073		12,055	3,616 50
	Aust.-Hungary		1,633		1,633	489 90
	China		5		5	1 50
	France		12,197		12,097	3,629 10
	Germany		165			
	Italy		25,313		25,202	7,560 60
	United States		564,478		564,624	169,387 20
	Total		1,301,864		615,616	184,684 80

OF IMPORTS—*Continued.*

FOR HOME CONSUMPTION.

Preferential Tariff.			Surtax Tariff.			Total.		
Quantity.	Value.	Duty.	Quantity.	Value.	Duty.	Quantity.	Value.	Duty Collected.
	$	$ cts.		$	$ cts.		$	$ cts.
	56,317	9,386 46		1,149	383 00		60,921	10,633 21
							6,099	1,524 75
							200	50 00
							3	75
				33	11 00		3,225	809 00
				21,200	7,066 66		21,283	7,087 41
							432	108 00
				1,244	414 67		322,250	80,666 17
	56,317	9,386 46		23,626	7,875 33		414,413	100,879 29
							1,117	390 95
Lbs.			Lbs.			Lbs.		
336	551	73 52				336	551	73 52
			1,006	204	54 40	1,006	204	54 40
						3,894	5,537	1,107 40
336	551	73 52	1,006	204	54 40	5,236	6,292	1,235 32
	9,119	1,823 80					11,880	2,652 10
				28	11 20		28	11 20
							33	9 90
	9,119	1,823 80		28	11 20		11,941	2,673 20
	777	181 33		20	933		1,249	348 86
							9	3 15
							1,186	415 10
							7	2 45
							94	32 90
				656	306 13		708	324 33
							5	1 75
							9,045	3,165 75
	777	181 33		676	315 46		12,303	4,294 29
	684,642	136,928 40		14	5 60		696,711	140,550 50
							1,633	489 90
							5	1 50
				100	40 00		12,197	3,669 10
				165	66 00		165	66 00
							25,202	7,560 60
				1	40		564,625	169,387 60
	684,642	136,928 40		280	112 00		1,300,538	321,725 20

No. 1.—General Statement

Articles Imported.	Countries.	Total Imports.		Entered		
				General Tariff.		
		Quantity.	Value.	Quantity.	Value.	Duty.
DUTIABLE GOODS—*Con.*			$		$	$ cts.
Hats, caps and bonnets—*Con.* Straw, grass, chip or other material, N.E.S.	Great Britain		357,654		25,832	7,749 60
	B. W. Indies		70		19	5 70
	Hong Kong		58		58	17 40
	Aust.-Hungary		176		176	52 80
	Belgium		264		264	79 20
	China		66		66	19 80
	Ecuador		316		316	94 80
	France		37,490		37,490	11,247 00
	Germany		627			
	Italy		15,592		15,592	4,677 60
	Japan		502		502	150 60
	Philippines		20		20	6 00
	Switzerland		1,316		1,316	394 80
	United States		520,935		518,875	155,662 50
	Total		935,086		600,526	180,157 80
Hat, cap and bonnet shapes	Great Britain		24,069		808	242 40
	France		102		102	30 60
	Germany		43			
	United States		19,315		19,315	5,794 50
	Total		43,529		20,225	6,067 50
		Tons.		Tons.		
Hay	United States	7,025	99,317	7,014	99,215	14,028 00
		Lbs.		Lbs.		
Honey, in the comb or otherwise, and imitations thereof	Great Britain	4,699	131	68	4	2 04
	Australia	2,368	113	2,368	113	71 04
	B. W. Indies	17,579	459			
	Hong Kong	1,759	49	1,759	49	52 77
	China	491	12	491	12	14 73
	Greece	144	40	144	40	4 32
	United States	56,594	6,752	54,436	6,592	1,633 08
	Total	83,634	7,556	59,266	6,810	1,777 98
Hops	Great Britain	296,844	45,926	49,268	6,786	2,956 08
	Aust.-Hungary	115,900	27,528	113,751	27,114	6,825 06
	Belgium	30,790	5,407	30,790	5,407	1,847 40
	Germany	56,928	13,852	2,870	741	172 20
	Russia	360	79	360	79	21 60
	United States	482,954	92,105	509,303	100,279	30,558 18
	Total	983,776	184,897	706,342	140,406	42,380 52
Ink, writing	Great Britain		14,511		232	46 40
	Hong Kong		18		18	3 60
	Belgium		11		11	2 20
	China		19		19	3 80
	France		2,416		2,416	483 20
	Germany		137			
	Holland		70		70	14 00
	Japan		23		23	4 60
	United States		37,754		37,937	7,587 40
	Total		54,959		40,726	8,145 20

OF IMPORTS—*Continued.*

FOR HOME CONSUMPTION.

Preferential Tariff			Surtax Tariff.			Total.		
Quantity.	Value.	Duty.	Quantity.	Value.	Duty.	Quantity.	Value.	Duty Collected.
	$	$ cts.		$	$ cts.		$	$ cts.
...	330,946	66,189 20	...	1,130	452 00	...	357,908	74,390 80
...	...	...	...	51	20 40	...	70	26 10
...	...	...	...	...	...	...	58	17 40
...	...	...	...	...	...	...	176	52 80
...	...	...	...	...	...	...	264	79 20
...	...	...	...	...	...	...	66	19 80
...	...	...	...	...	...	...	316	94 80
...	...	...	...	...	...	...	37,490	11,247 00
...	...	...	...	627	250 80	...	627	250 80
...	...	...	...	...	...	...	15,592	4,677 60
...	...	...	...	...	...	...	502	150 60
...	...	...	...	...	...	...	20	6 00
...	...	...	...	...	...	...	1,316	394 80
...	...	...	...	85	34 00	...	518,960	155,696 50
...	330,946	66,189 20	...	1,893	757 20	...	933,365	247,104 20
...	23,261	4,652 20	...	...	...	...	24,069	4,894 60
...	...	...	...	...	...	...	102	30 60
...	...	...	...	43	17 20	...	43	17 20
...	...	...	...	...	...	...	19,315	5,794 50
...	23,261	4,652 20	...	43	17 20	...	43,529	10,736 90
Tons.			Tons.			Tons.		
...	...	...	...	...	...	7,014	99,215	14,028 00
Lbs.			Lbs.			Lbs.		
4,631	127	92 62	...	...	...	4,699	131	94 66
...	...	...	...	...	...	2,368	113	71 04
20,657	552	413 14	...	...	...	20,657	552	413 14
...	...	...	...	...	...	1,759	49	52 77
...	...	...	...	...	...	491	12	14 73
...	...	...	...	...	...	144	40	4 32
...	...	...	...	...	...	54,436	6,592	1,633 08
25,288	679	505 76	...	...	...	84,554	7,489	2,283 74
251,366	38,406	10,054 64	2,249	562	179 92	302,883	45,754	13,190 64
...	...	...	1,367	356	109 36	115,118	27,470	6,934 42
...	...	...	...	...	...	30,790	5,407	1,847 40
...	...	...	52,748	13,866	4,219 84	55,618	14,607	4,392 04
...	...	...	...	...	...	360	79	21 60
...	...	...	6,193	1,846	495 44	515,496	102,125	31,053 62
251,366	38,406	10,054 64	62,557	16,630	5,004 56	1,020,265	195,442	57,439 72
...	14,279	1,904 05	...	...	...	...	14,511	1,950 45
...	...	...	...	...	...	...	18	3 60
...	...	...	...	...	...	...	11	2 20
...	...	...	...	...	...	...	19	3 80
...	...	...	...	...	...	...	2,416	483 20
...	...	...	...	137	36 54	...	137	36 54
...	...	...	...	...	...	...	70	14 00
...	...	...	...	...	...	...	23	4 60
...	...	...	...	...	...	...	37,937	7,587 40
...	14,279	19,04 05	...	137	36 54	...	55,142	10,085 79

No. 1.—General Statement

Articles Imported.	Countries.	Total Imports.		Entered		
				General Tariff.		
		Quantity.	Value.	Quantity.	Value.	Duty.
dutiable goods—*Con.*			$		$	$ cts.
Ink, printing	Great Britain	....	10,381	....	87	17 40
	China	....	1	....	1	0 20
	France	....	3,123	....	3,123	624 60
	Germany	....	152	....	....	....
	United States	....	86,634	....	86,705	17,341 00
		....	100,291	....	89,916	17,983 20
Iron and manufactures of, steel and manufactures of, or both combined.						
Agricultural implements, N.E.S., viz. :—		No.		No.		
Cultivators and weeders	Great Britain	3	137	1	25	5 00
	United States	3,826	26,257	3,826	26,257	5,251 40
		3,829	26,394	3,827	26,282	5,256 40
Drills, grain seed	United States	2,835	117,233	2,835	117,233	23,446 60
Farm road or field rollers	United States	10	206	10	204	51 00
Forks, pronged	Great Britain	280	144	....	....	....
	United States	8,285	5,105	8,285	5,105	1,276 25
		8,565	5,249	8,285	5,105	1,276 25
Harrows	Great Britain	4	52	1	16	3 20
	United States	4,383	66,180	4,382	66,150	13,230 00
		4,387	66,232	4,383	66,166	13,233 20
Harvesters, self-binding	Australia	5	910	....	....	....
	United States	927	95,846	927	95,846	19,169 20
		932	96,756	927	95,846	19,169 20
Hay loaders	United States	582	26,435	582	26,435	6,608 75
Hay tedders	United States	815	34,076	815	34,076	8,519 00
Hoes	Great Britain	537	130	....	....	....
	United States	4,365	743	4,365	743	185 75
		4,902	873	4,365	743	185 75
Horse rakes	United States	872	20,639	929	21,587	4,317 40
Knives, hay or straw	Great Britain	5	7	5	7	1 75
	United States	1,260	53	1,260	53	13 25
		1,265	60	1,265	60	15 00

OF IMPORTS—*Continued.*

FOR HOME CONSUMPTION.

Preferential Tariff.			Surtax Tariff.			Total.		
Quantity.	Value.	Duty.	Quantity.	Value.	Duty.	Quantity.	Value.	Duty Collected.
	$	$ cts.		$	$ cts.		$	$ cts.
	10,228	1,363 82		58	15 46		10,373	1,396 68
							1	0 20
							3,123	624 60
				152	40 53		152	40 53
							86,705	17,341 00
	10,228	1,363 82		210	55 99		100,354	19,403 01
No.			No.			No.		
1	15	2 00				2	40	7 00
						3,826	26,257	5,251 40
1	15	2 00				3,828	26,297	5,258 40
						2,835	117,233	23,446 60
						10	204	51 00
280	144	24 02				280	144	24 02
						8,285	5,105	1,276 25
280	144	24 02				8,565	5,249	1,300 27
3	36	4 80				4	52	8 00
						4,382	66,150	13,230 00
3	36	4 80				4,386	66,202	13,238 00
						927	95,846	19,169 20
						927	95,846	19,169 20
						582	26,435	6,608 75
						815	34,076	8,519 00
537	130	21 66				537	130	21 66
						4,365	743	185 75
537	130	21 66				4,902	873	207 41
						929	21,587	4,317 40
						5	7	1 75
						1,260	53	13 25
						1,265	60	15 00

No. 1.—General Statement

Articles Imported.	Countries.	Total Imports.		Entered		
				General Tariff.		
		Quantity.	Value.	Quantity.	Value.	Duty.
DUTIABLE GOODS—*Con.*		No.	$	No.	$	$ cts.
Iron and mfrs. of—*Con.*						
Agricultural implem'ts—*Con.*						
Lawn mowers	Great Britain	5	108	....	....	....
	United States	2,692	13,296	2,692	13,296	4,653 60
		2,697	13,404	2,692	13,296	4,653 60
Manure spreaders	United States	1,133	108,054	1,133	108,054	21,610 80
Mowing machines	United States	766	24,692	766	24,692	4,938 40
Ploughs	Great Britain	2	56	....	....	....
	Australia	1	44	....	....	....
	France	1	35	1	35	7 00
	United States	17,030	477,612	17,030	477,612	95,522 40
		17,034	477,747	17,031	477,647	95,529 40
Post hole diggers	United States	1,485	1,326	1,485	1,326	331 50
Potato diggers	Great Britain	14	880	....	....	....
	United States	212	6,604	212	6,604	1,651 00
	Total	226	7,484	212	6,604	1,651 00
Rakes, N.E.S.	Great Britain	12	3	....	....	....
	United States	9,608	1,819	9,608	1,819	454 75
	Total	9,620	1,822	9,608	1,819	454 75
Reapers	United States	284	13,872	284	13,872	2,774 40
		Doz.		Doz.		
Scythes	Great Britain	536	2,420	....	....	....
	Aust.-Hungary	12	41	12	41	10 25
	United States	1,452	7,582	1,452	7,582	1,895 50
	Total	2,000	10,043	1,464	7,623	1,905 75
Sickles or reaping hooks	Great Britain	36	170	....	....	....
	United States	5	15	5	15	3 75
	Total	41	185	5	15	3 75
Spades and shovels and spade and shovel blanks, and iron or steel cut to shape for the same	Great Britain	15,391	24,079	32	214	74 90
	United States	4,252	22,958	4,222	22,683	7,939 05
	Total	19,643	47,037	4,254	22,897	8,013 95

OF IMPORTS—*Continued.*

FOR HOME CONSUMPTION.

Preferential Tariff.			Surtax Tariff.			Total.		
Quantity.	Value.	Duty.	Quantity.	Value.	Duty.	Quantity.	Value.	Duty Collected.
No.	$	$ cts.	No.	$	$ cts.	No.	$	$ cts.
5	108	25 20	....	....	....	5	108	25 20
....	....	....	....	....	....	2,692	13,296	4,653 60
5	108	25 20	....	....	....	2,697	13,404	4,678 80
....	....	....	....	....	....	1,133	108,054	21,610 80
....	....	....	....	....	....	766	24,692	4,938 40
2	56	7 47	....	....	....	2	56	7 47
....	....	....	....	....	....	....	....	....
....	....	....	....	....	....	1	35	7 00
....	....	....	....	....	....	17,030	477,612	95,522 40
2	56	7 47	....	....	....	17,033	477,703	95,536 87
....	....	....	....	....	....	1,485	1,326	331 50
14	880	146 67	....	....	....	14	880	146 67
....	....	....	....	....	....	212	6,604	1,651 00
14	880	146 67	....	....	....	226	7,484	1,797 67
12	3	0 50	....	....	....	12	3	0 50
....	....	....	....	....	....	9,608	1,819	454 75
12	3	0 50	....	....	....	9,620	1,822	455 25
....	....	....	....	....	....	284	13,872	2,774 40
Doz.			Doz.			Doz.		
536	2,420	403 35	....	....	....	536	2,420	403 35
....	....	....	....	....	....	12	41	10 25
....	....	....	....	....	....	1,452	7,582	1,895 50
536	2,420	403 35	....	....	....	2,000	10,043	2,309 10
36	170	28 34	....	....	....	36	170	28 34
....	....	....	....	....	....	5	15	3 75
36	170	28 34	....	....	....	41	185	32 09
10,859	23,865	5,568 64	....	....	....	10,891	24,079	5,643 54
....	....	....	....	....	....	4,222	22,683	7,939 05
10,859	23,865	5,568 64	....	....	....	15,113	46,762	13,582 59

No. 1.—GENERAL STATEMENT

ARTICLES IMPORTED.	COUNTRIES.	TOTAL IMPORTS.		ENTERED		
				General Tariff.		
		Quantity.	Value.	Quantity.	Value.	Duty.
DUTIABLE GOODS—*Con.*			$		$	$ cts.
Iron and mfrs. of—*Con.*						
Agricultural implem'ts—*Con.*						
Parts of agricultural implements paying 20 p.c.	Great Britain		7,561		7,163	1,432 60
	Australia		12		62	12 40
	United States		465,270		465,148	93,029 60
	Total		472,843		472,373	94,474 60
All other agricultural implements, N.E.S.	Great Britain		3,921		151	37 75
	France		15		15	3 75
	Germany		732			
	United States		37,793		37,793	9,448 25
	Total		42,461		37,959	9,489 75
Anvils and vices	Great Britain		20,860		1,675	502 50
	Germany		306			
	United States		29,626		29,626	8,887 80
	Total		50,792		31,301	9,390 30
Cart or wagon skeins or boxes		Lbs.		Lbs.		
	Great Britain	16,764	364			
	United States	150,690	9,040	150,690	9,040	2,712 00
	Total	167,454	9,404	150,690	9,040	2,712 00
Springs, axles, axle bars, N.E.S., and axle blanks and parts thereof, of iron or steel, for railway or tramway or other vehicles		Cwt.		Cwt.		
	Great Britain	14,116	34,054	210	1,119	391 65
	United States	55,832	109,820	55,832	109,820	38,437 00
	Total	69,948	143,874	56,042	110,939	38,828 65
Bar iron or steel rolled whether in coils, bundles, rods or bars, comprising rounds, ovals, squares and flats, and rolled shapes, N.O.P.	Great Britain	331,634	509,147	9,432	14,652	3,301 20
	Belgium	12,556	14,623	12,556	14,623	4,394 60
	France	1,276	1,268	1,276	1,268	446 60
	Germany	95	122	85	102	29 75
	Norway	304	608	304	608	106 40
	Sweden	6,175	11,691	6,175	11,691	2,161 25
	United States	634,421	1.004,587	635,289	1,004,270	222,351 15
	Total	986,461	1,542,046	665,117	1,047,214	232,790 95
Butts and hinges, N.E.S.	Great Britain		1,121		49	14 70
	United States		91,585		91,585	27,475 50
	Total		92,706		91,634	27,490 20
Castings, iron or steel, in the rough, N.E.S.	Great Britain		16,952		236	59 00
	Newfoundland		119			
	United States		370,622		368,840	92,210 00
	Total		387,693		369,076	92,269 00

OF IMPORTS—*Continued.*

FOR HOME CONSUMPTION.

Preferential Tariff.			Surtax Tariff.			Total.		
Quantity.	Value.	Duty.	Quantity.	Value.	Duty.	Quantity.	Value.	Duty Collected.
	$	$ cts.		$	$ cts.		$	$ cts.
	398	53 08					7,561	1,485 68
							62	12 40
							465,148	93,029 60
	398	53 08					472,771	94,527 68
	3,693	615 50					3,844	653 25
							15	3 75
				732	243 96		732	243 96
							37,793	9,448 25
	3,693	615 50		732	243 96		42,384	10,349 21
	19,185	3,837 00					20,860	4,339 50
				306	122 40		306	122 40
							29,626	8,887 80
	19,185	3,837 00		306	122 40		50,792	13,349 70
Lbs. 16,764	364	72 80	Lbs.			Lbs. 16,764	364	72 80
						150,690	9,040	2,712 00
16,764	364	72 80				167,454	9,404	2,784 80
Cwt. 13,906	32,935	7,684 96	Cwt.			Cwt. 13,116	34,054	8,076 61
						55,832	109,820	38,437 00
13,906	32,935	7,684 96				68,948	143,874	46,513 61
322,302	494,495	75,204 56				331,734	509,147	78,505 76
						12,556	14,623	4,394 60
						1,276	1,268	446 60
			10	20	4 66	95	122	34 41
						304	608	106 40
						6,175	11,691	2,161 25
						635,289	1,004,270	222,351 15
322,302	494,495	75,204 56	10	20	4 66	987,429	1,541,729	308,000 17
	1,022	204 40					1,071	219 10
							91,585	27,475 50
	1,022	204 40					92,656	27,694 60
	16,716	2,786 02					16,952	2,845 02
							368,840	92,210 00
	16,716	2,786 02					385,792	95,055 02

No. 1.—General Statement

Articles Imported.	Countries.	Total Imports.		Entered		
				General Tariff.		
		Quantity.	Value.	Quantity.	Value.	Duty.
DUTIABLE GOODS—*Con.*		Cwt.	$	Cwt.	$	$ cts.
Iron and mfrs. of—*Con.*						
Canada plates; Russia iron; terne plate, and rolled sheets of iron or steel coated with zinc, spelter or other metal, of all widths or thickness, N.O.P.	Great Britain	258,383	573,009	323	1,651	82 55
	Belgium	102	278	102	278	13 90
	United States	45,250	126,457	45,250	126,457	6,322 85
	Total	303,735	699,744	45,675	128,386	6,419 30
Cast iron pipe of every description	Great Britain	300,109	356,427	1,369	1,732	547 60
	United States	43,295	91,023	43,295	91,023	17,318 00
	Total	343,404	447,450	44,664	92,755	17,865 60
		Tons.		Tons.		
Cast scrap iron	Great Britain	2,384	26,321	....	....	....
	St. Pierre	21	170	21	170	52 50
	United States	2,461	33,595	2,461	33,595	6,152 50
	Total	4,866	60,086	2,482	33,765	6,205 00
		Cwt.		Cwt.		
Chains, coil chain, chain links and chain shackles, of iron or steel, 5/16th of an inch in diam. and over	Great Britain	14,103	46,507	840	2,815	140 75
	Norway	25	86	25	86	4 30
	United States	26,548	95,469	26,489	95,046	4,752 30
	Total	40,676	142,062	27,354	97,947	4,897 35
Chain, malleable sprocket or link belting, for binders	United States	....	43,992	....	43,988	8,797 60
Chains, N.E.S.	Great Britain	....	17,694	....	2,128	638 40
	Aust.-Hungary	....	342	....	342	102 60
	France	....	304	....	304	91 20
	Germany	....	3,766	....	....	....
	United States	....	77,040	....	76,963	23,088 90
	Total	....	99,146	....	79,737	23,921 10
		Lbs.		Lbs.		
Tacks, shoe	Great Britain	140	5	....	....	....
	France	15	2	15	2	0 70
	United States	20,731	2,435	20,731	2,435	852 25
	Total	20,886	2,442	20,746	2,437	852 95
Cut tacks, brads sprigs, or shoe nails, double pointed, and other tacks of iron and steel, N.O.P.	Great Britain	634	39	....	....	....
	Germany	2,536	37	....	....	....
	United States	73,560	4,782	73,960	4,782	1,673 70
	Total	76,730	4,858	73,960	4,782	1,673 70

OF IMPORTS—*Continued.*

FOR HOME CONSUMPTION.

Preferential Tariff.			Surtax Tariff.			Total.		
Quantity.	Value.	Duty.	Quantity.	Value.	Duty.	Quantity.	Value.	Duty Collected.
Cwt.	$	$ cts.	Cwt.	$	$ cts.	Cwt.	$	$ cts.
258,060	571,358	19,045 48				258,383	573,009	19,128 03
						102	278	13 90
						45,250	126,457	6,322 85
258,060	571,358	19,045 48				303,735	699,744	25,464 78
298,740	354,695	79,664 10				300,109	356,427	80,211 70
						43,295	91,023	17,318 00
298,740	354,695	79,664 10				343,404	447,450	97,529 70
Tons.			Tons.			Tons.		
2,384	26,321	3,973 35				2,384	26,321	3,973 35
						21	170	52 50
						2,461	33,595	6,152 50
2,384	26,321	3,973 35				4,866	60,086	10,178 35
Cwt.			Cwt.			Cwt.		
13,263	43,692	1,456 58				14,103	46,507	1,597 33
						25	86	4 30
						26,489	95,046	4,752 30
13,263	43,692	1,456 58				40,617	141,639	6,353 93
							43,988	8,797 60
	15,557	3,111 40		9	3 60		17,694	3,753 40
							342	102 60
							304	91 20
				3,808	1,523 20		3,808	1,523 20
				77	30 80		77,040	23,119 70
	15,557	3,111 40		3,894	1,557 60		99,188	28,590 10
Lbs.			Lbs.			Lbs.		
140	5	1 17				140	5	1 17
						15	2	0 70
						20,731	2,435	852 25
140	5	1 17				20,886	2,442	854 12
634	39	9 11				634	39	9 11
			2,536	37	17 26	2,536	37	17 26
						73,960	4,782	1,673 70
634	39	9 11	2,536	37	17 26	77,130	4,858	1,700 07

No. 1.—General Statement

Articles Imported.	Countries.	Total Imports.		Entered		
				General Tariff.		
		Quantity.	Value.	Quantity.	Value.	Duty.
DUTIABLE GOODS—*Con.*		No.	$	No.	$	$ cts.
Iron and mfrs. of—*Con.*						
Engines, locomotives for railways, N.E.S.	Great Britain		80		80	28 00
	United States	85	338,099	85	338,099	118,334 65
	Total	85	338,179	85	338,179	118,362 65
Fire engines	United States	6	7,150	5	4,150	1,452 50
Fire extinguishing machines	Great Britain		31		22	7 70
	United States		53,267		53,267	18,643 45
	Total		53,298		53,289	18,651 15
Gasoline engines	Great Britain	2	1,219			
	United States	2,066	404,104	2,066	404,104	101,026 00
	Total	2,068	405,323	2,066	404,104	101,026 00
Steam engines and boilers	Great Britain	98	135,735	47	14,548	3,637 00
	United States	1,604	462,075	1,600	460,564	115,141 00
	Total	1,702	597,810	1,647	475,112	118,778 00
Fittings, iron or steel, for iron or steel pipe		Lbs.		Lbs.		
	Great Britain	147,989	5,492	1,280	101	30 30
	France	100	30	100	30	9 00
	United States	6,550,106	381,493	6,548,503	381,312	114,393 60
	Total	6,698,195	387,015	6,549,883	381,443	114,432 90
Ferro-silicon, spiegeleisen and ferro-manganese		Tons.		Tons.		
	Great Britain	12,291	363,686	3,174	68,140	3,407 00
	Belgium	49	3,977	49	3,977	198 85
	Germany	366	10,687			
	United States	2,317	84,389	2,317	84,389	4,219 45
	Total	15,023	462,739	5,540	156,506	7,825 30
Forgings of iron or steel, of whatever shape or size, or in whatever stage of manufacture, N.E.S., and steel shafting, turned, compressed or polished; and hammered iron or steel bars or shapes, N.O.P.		Lbs.		Lbs.		
	Great Britain	108,237	4,427			
	Germany	33,935	534			
	United States	3,970,129	166,315	3,955,775	165,309	49,592 70
	Total	4,112,301	171,276	3,955,775	165,309	49,592 70
Hardware, viz.: Builders', cabinetmakers', upholsterers', harnessmakers', saddlers' and carriage hardware, including curry combs and horse boots, N.E.S.	Great Britain		81,046		1,874	562 20
	Newfoundland		20			
	Belgium		17		17	5 10
	France		3,668		3,668	1,100 40
	Germany		1,003			
	Japan		115		115	34 50
	United States		665,990		665,775	199,732 50
	Total		751,859		671,449	201,434 70

OF IMPORTS—*Continued.*

FOR HOME CONSUMPTION.

Preferential Tariff.			Surtax Tariff.			Total.		
Quantity.	Value.	Duty.	Quantity.	Value.	Duty.	Quantity.	Value.	Duty Collected.
No.	$	$ cts.	No.	$	$ cts.	No.	$	$ cts.
							80	28 00
						85	338,099	118,334 65
						85	338,179	118,362 65
						5	4,150	1,452 50
	9	2 10					31	9 80
							53,267	18,643 45
	9	2 10					53,298	18,653 25
2	1,219	203 19				2	1,219	203 19
						2,066	404,104	101,026 00
2	1,219	203 19				2,068	405,323	101,229 19
51	121,187	20,197 86				98	135,735	23,834 86
						1,600	460,564	115,141 00
51	121,187	20,197 86				1,698	596,299	138,975 86
Lbs.			Lbs.			Lbs.		
146,709	5,391	1,078 20				147,989	5,492	1,108 50
						100	30	9 00
						6,548,503	381,312	114,393 60
146,709	5,391	1,078 20				6,696,592	386,834	115,511 10
Tons.			Tons.			Tons.		
9,117	295,546	9,851 52				12,291	363,686	13,258 52
						49	3,977	198 85
			366	10,687	712 47	366	10,687	712 47
						2,317	84,389	4,219 45
9,117	295,546	9,851 52	366	10,687	712 47	15,023	462,739	18,389 29
Lbs.			Lbs.			Lbs.		
108,237	4,427	885 40				108,237	4,427	885 40
			33,935	534	213 60	33,935	534	213 60
			164	56	22 40	3,955,939	165,365	49,615 10
108,237	4,427	885 40	34,099	590	236 00	4,098,111	170,326	50,714 10
	79,410	15,882 00		18	7 20		81,302	16,451 40
							17	5 10
							3,668	1,100 40
				1,003	401 20		1,003	401 20
							115	34 50
				230	92 00		666,005	199,824 50
	79,410	15,882 00		1,251	500 40		752,110	217,817 10

No. 1.—General Statement

Articles Imported.	Countries.	Total Imports.		Entered		
				General Tariff.		
		Quantity.	Value.	Quantity.	Value.	Duty.
Dutiable goods—*Con.*			$		$	$ cts.
Iron and mfrs. of—*Con.* Horse, mule and ox shoes....	United States...	....	14,360	....	14,125	4,237 50
Iron or steel ingots, cogged ingots, blooms, slabs, billets puddled bars, and loops or other forms, N.O.P., less finished than iron or steel bars, but more advanced than pig iron, except castings....	Great Britain...	Cwt. 150,983	173,353	Cwt. 45,238	44,027	4,523 80
	Belgium........	97,307	91,566	97,307	91,566	9,730 70
	Germany.......	11,120	11,733	....	....	....
	United States...	391,533	387,142	391,533	387,142	39,153 30
	Total	650,943	663,794	534,078	522,735	53,407 80
Iron or steel bridges or parts thereof; iron or steel structural work, columns, shapes or sections, drilled, punched or in any further stage of manufacture than as rolled or cast, N.E.S....	Great Britain...	946	1,871	119	474	165 90
	France..	3,500	6,000	3,500	6,000	2,100 00
	United States...	181,232	500,475	181,232	500,475	175,166 25
	Total	185,678	508,346	184,851	506,949	177,432 15
		Tons.		Tons.		
Iron in pigs....	Great Britain...	35,897	454,703	47	1,045	117 50
	United States...	62,647	940,302	61,045	946,922	152,612 50
	Total	98,544	1,395,005	61,092	947,967	152,730 00
Locks of all kinks.	Great Britain...	....	7,723	....	1,029	308 70
	Belgium	....	21	....	....	....
	China'	....	3	....	3	0 90
	France.........	....	439	....	439	131 70
	Germany.. ...	....	1,778	....	....	....
	United States...	....	273,491	....	273,491	82,047 30
	Total	....	283,455	....	274,962	82,488 60
Machines, machinery, &c.:— Automobiles....	Great Britain...	No. 63	110,630	No. 21	37,962	13,286 70
	France.........	30	60,727	32	58,826	20,589 10
	Germany.	....	11,723	....	....	....
	United States...	367	489,048	352	450,777	157,273 25
	Total	460	672,128	405	547,565	191,149 05
Fanning Mills....	United States...	267	3,144	267	3,144	786 00
Grain crushers....	United States...	1	71	1	71	17 75

OF IMPORTS—*Continued.*

FOR HOME CONSUMPTION.

Preferential Tariff.			Surtax Tariff.			Total.		
Quantity.	Value.	Duty.	Quantity.	Value.	Duty.	Quantity.	Value.	Duty Collected.
	$	$ cts.		$	$ cts.		$	$ cts.
....	....	....	....	212	84 80	....	14,337	4,322 30
Cwt.			Cwt.			Cwt.		
75,743	100,533	5,049 65	30,002	28,793	4,000 20	150,983	173,353	13,573 65
....	....	....	....	....	....	97,307	91,566	9,730 70
....	....	....	11,120	11,733	1,482 60	11,120	11,733	1,482 60
....	....	....	....	....	....	391,533	387,142	39,153 30
75,743	100,533	5,049 65	41,122	40,526	5,482 80	650,943	663,794	63,940 25
827	1,397	325 99	....	....	....	946	1,871	491 89
....	....	....	....	....	....	3,500	6,000	2,100 00
....	....	....	....	....	....	181,232	500,475	175,166 25
827	1,397	325 99	....	....	....	185,678	508,346	177,758 14
Tons.			Tons.			Tons.		
35,703	453,011	59,505 16	2	69	6 67	35,752	454,125	59,629 33
....	....	....	....	....	....	61,045	946,922	152,612 50
35,703	453,011	59,505 16	2	69	6 67	96,797	1,401,047	212,241 83
....	6,349	1,269 80	....	196	78 40	....	7,574	1,656 90
....	....	....	....	21	8 40	....	21	8 40
....	....	....	....	....	....	....	3	0 90
....	....	....	....	....	....	....	439	131 70
....	....	....	....	1,778	711 20	....	1,778	711 20
....	....	....	....	....	....	....	273,491	82,047 30
....	6,349	1,269 80	....	1,995	798 00	....	283,306	84,556 40
No.			No.			No.		
42	73,883	17,239 36	....	252	117 60	63	112,097	30,643 66
....	....	....	1	4,825	2,251 67	33	63,651	22,840 77
....	....	....	....	10,436	4,870 15	....	10,436	4,870 15
....	....	....	....	8,910	4,158 00	352	459,687	161,431 25
42	73,883	17,239 36	1	24,423	11,397 42	448	645,871	219,785 83
....	....	....	....	....	....	267	3,144	786 00
....	....	....	....	....	....	1	71	17 75

No. 1.—General Statement

Articles Imported.	Countries.	Total Imports.		Entered		
				General Tariff.		
		Quantity.	Value.	Quantity.	Value.	Duty.
DUTIABLE GOODS.		No.	$	No.	$	$ cts.
Iron and mfrs.—*Con.*						
Wind mills..	United States...	909	41,934	909	41,934	10,483 50
Ore crushers and rock crushers stamp mills, cornish and belted rolls, rock drills, air compressors, cranes, derricks, and percussion coal cutters.	Great Britain...	....	54,793	....	....	....
	Germany.	....	489	....	....	....
	United States...	....	151,387	....	151,113	37,778 25
	Total	....	206,669	....	151,113	37,778 25
Portable Machines:						
Fodder or feed cutters.......	Great Britain...	1	146	....	....	....
	United States...	26	558	26	558	139 50
	Total	27	704	26	558	139 50
Horse, powers....	United States...	11	556	11	556	139 00
Portable engines.	United States...	626	712,895	638	717,785	179,446 25
Portable saw mills and planing mills....	United States...	73	31,382	73	31,382	7,845 50
Threshers and separators....	Australia.	1	170	....	....	....
	United States...	647	358,315	652	359,986	89,996 50
	Total	648	358,485	652	359,986	89,996 50
All other portable machines.	Great Britain...	45	771	8	91	22 75
	United States...	877	100,857	880	101,362	25,340 50
	Total	922	101,628	888	101,453	25,363 25
Parts of above articles.......	United States...	....	142,124	....	142,124	35,531 00
Sewing machines, and parts of....	Great Britain...	659	14,120	2	24	7 20
	France.........	1	96	1	96	28 80
	Germany.......	24	694	....	....	....
	United States...	13,627	271,325	13,453	269,214	80,764 20
	Total	14,311	286,235	13,456	269,334	80,800 20
Slot machines..............	United States...	2,389	41,628	2,388	41,603	10,400 75
Machines, type-writing......	Great Britain...	7	426	....	....	....
	Newfoundland..	3	60	....	....	....
	United States...	4,962	284,520	4,926	282,897	70,724 25
	Total	4,972	285,006	4,926	282,897	70,724 25

OF IMPORTS—*Continued.*

FOR HOME CONSUMPTION.

Preferential Tariff.			Surtax Tariff.			Total.		
Quantity.	Value.	Duty.	Quantity.	Value.	Duty.	Quantity.	Value.	Duty Collected.
No.	$	$ cts.	No.	$	$ cts.	No.	$	$ cts.
...	...	...	...	...	...	909	41,934	10,483 50
...	52,511	8,751 89	...	2,282	760 67	...	54,793	9,512 56
...	...	...	...	489	163 00	...	489	163 00
...	...	...	...	198	66 00	...	151,311	37,844 25
...	52,511	8,751 89	...	2,969	989 67	...	206,593	47,519 81
1	146	24 34	...	...	...	1	146	24 34
...	...	...	...	...	...	26	558	139 50
1	146	24 34	...	...	...	27	704	163 84
...	...	...	...	...	...	11	556	139 00
...	...	...	...	...	...	638	717,785	179,446 25
...	...	...	...	...	...	73	31,382	7,845 50
...	...	...	...	...	...	...	...	...
...	...	...	...	...	...	652	359,986	89,996 50
...	...	...	...	...	...	652	359,986	89,996 50
37	680	113 33	...	...	...	45	771	136 08
...	...	...	...	...	...	880	101,362	25,340 50
37	680	113 33	...	...	...	925	102,133	25,476 58
...	...	...	...	...	...	...	142,124	35,531 00
642	13,954	2,790 80	15	142	56 80	659	14,120	2,854 80
...	...	...	...	...	...	1	96	28 80
...	...	...	24	694	277 60	24	694	277 60
...	...	...	1	65	26 00	13,454	269,279	80,790 20
642	13,954	2,790 80	40	901	360 40	14,138	284,189	83,951 40
...	...	...	...	...	...	2,388	41,603	10,400 75
7	426	71 00	...	...	...	7	426	71 00
...	...	...	...	...	...	...	...	...
...	...	...	...	...	...	4,926	282,897	70,724 25
7	426	71 00	...	...	...	4,933	283,323	70,795 25

No. 1.—General Statement

Articles Imported.	Countries.	Total Imports.		Entered		
				General Tariff.		
		Quantity.	Value.	Quantity.	Value.	Duty.
DUTIABLE GOODS—*Con.*			$		$	$ cts.
Iron and mfrs. of—*Con.*						
All other machinery composed wholly or in part of iron, or steel, N.O.P	Great Britain		317,611		49,343	12,335 75
	Newfoundland		200		200	50 00
	Aust.-Hungary				686	171 50
	Belgium		19		19	4 75
	Denmark		464		464	116 00
	France		27,505		27,505	6,876 25
	Germany		108,501			
	Japan		154		154	38 50
	Sweden		397		397	99 25
	Switzerland		1,789		1,186	296 50
	United States		4,879,029		4,864,559	1,216,139 75
	Total		5,335,669		4,944,513	1,236,128 25
Malleable iron castings and iron or steel castings, N.E.S	United States	Cwt. 4,957	16,819	Cwt. 4,957	16,819	4,204 75
Nails and spikes, composition and sheathing nails	Great Britain	Lbs. 4,600	788	Lbs.		
	United States	6,559	559	6,559	559	83 85
	Total	11,159	1,347	6,559	559	83 85
Nails and spikes, wrought and pressed, trunk, clout, coopers, cigar box, Hungarian, horse shoe and other nails, N.E.S	Great Britain	83,408	3,250	40	2	0 60
	United States	125,579	10,873	123,951	10,814	3,244 20
	Total	208,987	14,123	123,991	10,816	3,244 80
Nails and spikes, cut, and railway spikes	Great Britain	30,065	719			
	United States	2,050,010	37,594	2,108,010	38,559	10,540 05
	Total	2,080,075	38,313	2,108,010	38,559	10,540 05
Nails, wire, of all kinds, N.O.P	Great Britain	1,092	29	420	10	2 52
	United States	531,883	18,360	529,183	18,289	3,174 99
	Total	532,975	18,389	529,603	18,299	3,177 51
Mould boards, or shaves or plough plates, land sides and other plates for agricultural implements, cut to shape from rolled plates of steel but not moulded, punched, polished or otherwise manufactured	Great Britain	Cwt. 634	926	Cwt. 624	903	45 15
	Belgium	4,357	5,548	4,357	5,548	277 40
	United States	62,854	182,853	62,854	182,853	9,142 65
	Total	67,845	189,327	67,835	189,304	9,465 20
Pumps, N.E.S	Great Britain		8,744			
	Denmark		590			
	Germany		5,823			
	United States		246,488		246,653	61,663 25
	Total		261,645		246,653	61,663 25

OF IMPORTS—*Continued.*

FOR HOME CONSUMPTION.

Preferential Tariff.			Surtax Tariff.			Total.		
Quantity.	Value.	Duty.	Quantity.	Value.	Duty.	Quantity.	Value.	Duty Collected.
	$	$ cts.		$	$ cts.		$	$ cts.
	265,191	44,199 14		3,055	1,018 33		317,589	57,553 22
							200	50 00
							686	171 50
							19	4 75
							464	116 00
							27,505	6,876 25
				108,501	36,167 00		108,501	36,167 00
							154	38 50
							397	99 25
				603	201 00		1,789	497 50
				9,851	3,283 63		4,874,410	1,219,423 38
	265,191	44,199 14		122,010	40,669 96		5,331,714	1,320,997 35
Cwt.			Cwt.			Cwt. 4,957	16,819	4,204 75
Lbs. 4,600	760	76 00	Lbs.			Lbs. 4,600	760	76 00
						6,559	559	83 85
4,600	760	76 00				11,159	1,319	159 85
83,368	3,248	649 60				83,408	3,250	650 20
			288	51	20 40	124,239	10,865	3,264 60
83,368	3,248	649 60	288	51	20 40	207,647	14,115	3,914 80
30,065	719	100 22				30,065	719	100 22
						2,108,010	38,559	10,540 05
30,065	719	100 22				2,138,075	39,278	10,640 27
672	19	2 69				1,092	29	5 21
						529,183	18,289	3,174 99
672	19	2 69				530,275	18,318	3,180 20
Cwt. 10	23	0 77	Cwt.			Cwt. 634	926	45 92
						4,357	5,548	277 40
						62,854	182,853	9,142 65
10	23	0 77				67,845	189,327	9,465 97
	8,180	1,363 32		564	188 00		8,744	1,551 32
				5,823	1,940 96		5,823	1,940 96
							246,653	61,663 25
	8,180	1,363 32		6,387	2,128 96		261,220	65,155 53

No. 1.—General Statement

Articles Imported.	Countries.	Total Imports.		Entered		
				General Tariff.		
		Quantity.	Value.	Quantity.	Value.	Duty.
DUTIABLE GOODS—*Con.*		Tons.		Tons.		$ cts.
Iron and mfrs. of—*Con.* Iron or steel railway bars or rails of any form, punched or not punched, N.E.S. for railways, which term for the purposes of this item shall include all kinds of railways, street railways and tramways, even although the same are used for private purposes only, and even although they are not used or intended to be used in connection with the business of common carrying of goods or passengers.	Great Britain...	28,988	659,264	27	583	189 00
	Belgium........	1	27	1	27	7 00
	Germany........	283	6,435	....	....	....
	United States...	19,790	531,444	20,606	548,822	144,242 00
	Total	49,062	1,197,170	20,634	549,432	144,438 00
Railway fish-plates and tie plates..................	Great Britain...	875	28,024	....	....	....
	United States...	3,462	143,162	3,512	144,243	28,096 00
	Total	4,337	171,186	3,512	144,243	28,096 00
Rolled iron or steel angles, tees, beams, channels, joists, girders, zees, stars or rolled shapes, or trough, bridge, building or structural rolled sections, or shapes, not punched, drilled or further manufactured than rolled, N.E.S., and flat eye bar blanks not punched or drilled..................		Cwt.		Cwt.		
	Great Britain...	201,013	266,768	2,066	2,598	259 80
	Belgium........	52,526	57,163	45,495	49,628	4,962 80
	France..........	3,008	4,780	3,008	4,780	478 00
	Germany.. ...	244,256	239,352	....	....	....
	United States...	565,850	863,936	565,850	863,936	86,393 60
	Total	1,066,653	1,431,999	616,419	920,942	92,094 20
Rolled iron or steel hoop, band, scroll or strip, 8 in. or less in width, No. 18 gauge and thicker, N.E.S.. ...	Great Britain...	17,996	27,787	2,128	2,868	744 80
	Belgium........	2,252	2,888	1,754	2,402	613 90
	Germany......	217	228	....	....	....
	United States...	42,831	78,627	42,831	78,627	14,990 85
	Total	63,296	109,530	46,713	83,897	16,349 55
Rolled iron or steel hoop, band, scroll or strip, thinner than No. 18 gauge, N.E.S..	Great Britain...	17,490	37,738	735	1,812	90 60
	Belgium........	960	1,575	541	823	41 15
	Germany.......	1,312	2,485	....	....	....
	United States...	37,201	89,768	37,117	89,600	4,480 00
	Total.......	56,963	131,566	38,393	92,235	4,611 75

OF IMPORTS—*Continued.*

FOR HOME CONSUMPTION.

Preferential Tariff.			Surtax Tariff.			Total.		
Quantity.	Value.	Duty.	Quantity.	Value.	Duty.	Quantity.	Value.	Duty Collected.
Tons.	$	$ cts.	Tons.	$	$ cts.	Tons.	$	$ cts
28,623	650,953	133,574 06	338	7,728	3,154 67	28,988	659,264	136,917 73
....	....	....	....	....	....	1	27	7 00
....	....	....	283	6,435	2,641 33	283	6,435	2,641 33
....	....	....	....	....	....	20,606	548,822	144,242 00
28,623	650,953	133,574 06	621	14,163	5,796 00	49,878	1,214,548	283,808 06
875	28,024	4,666 67	....	....	....	875	28,024	4,666 67
....	....	....	....	....	....	3,512	144,243	28,096 00
875	28,024	4,666 67	....	....	....	4,387	172,267	32,762 67
Cwt.			Cwt.			Cwt.		
112,238	162,359	10,824 00	86,709	101,811	13,574 80	201,013	266,768	24,658 60
....	....	....	7,031	7,535	1,004 56	52,526	57,163	5,967 36
....	....	....	....	....	....	3,008	4,780	478 00
....	....	....	244,256	239,352	31,913 60	244,256	239,352	31,913 60
....	....	....	....	....	....	565,850	863,936	86,393 60
112,238	162,359	10,824 00	337,996	348,698	46,492 96	1,066,653	1,431,999	149,411 16
15,868	24,919	3,702 81	....	....	....	17,996	27,787	4,447 61
....	....	....	498	486	232 40	2,252	2,888	846 30
....	....	....	217	228	101 27	217	228	101 27
....	....	....	....	....	....	42,831	78,627	14,990 85
15,868	24,919	3,702 81	715	714	333 67	63,296	109,530	20,386 03
16,344	35,300	1,176 77	411	626	41 73	17,490	37,738	1,309 10
....	....	....	419	752	50 13	960	1,575	91 28
....	....	....	1,312	2,485	165 66	1,312	2,485	165 66
....	....	....	79	152	10 13	37,196	89,752	4,490 13
16,344	35,300	1,176 77	2,221	4,015	267 65	56,958	131,550	6,056 17

No. 1.—General Statement

Articles Imported.	Countries.	Total Imports.		Entered		
				General Tariff.		
		Quantity.	Value.	Quantity.	Value.	Duty.
DUTIABLE GOODS—*Con.*		Cwt.	$	Cwt.	$	$ cts.
Iron and mfrs. of—*Con.*						
Rolled iron or steel angles, tees, beams, channels, girders and other rolled shapes or sections, weighing less than 35 lbs. per lineal yard, not punched, drilled or further manufactured than rolled, N.O.P.	Great Britain	163,028	221,876	3,125	3,480	1,093 75
	Belgium	12,253	13,814	12,253	13,814	4,288 55
	Germany	2,211	2,371	...	...	...
	United States	199,200	301,952	199,194	301,945	69,717 90
	Total	376,692	540,013	214,572	319,239	75,100 20
Rolled iron or steel plates or sheets, sheared or unsheared, and skelp iron or steel, sheared or rolled in grooves, N.E.S.	Great Britain	95,801	140,033	15,684	20,600	5,489 40
	Belgium	27,255	35,914	27,123	35,707	9,493 05
	France	18	26	18	26	6 30
	Germany	38	56	...	...	...
	United States	133,136	218,273	133,123	218,245	46,593 06
	Total	256,248	394,302	175,948	274,578	61,581 81
Rolled iron or steel plates, not less than 30 inches in width and not less than ¼ inch in thickness, N.O.P.	Great Britain	100,271	139,768	5,244	6,841	684 10
	Belgium	7,495	9,536	7,495	9,536	953 60
	Germany	238	216	...	...	...
	United States	481,147	754,732	481,147	754,732	75,473 20
	Total	589,151	904,252	493,886	771,109	77,110 90
Rolled iron or steel sheets, No. 17 gauge and thinner, N.O.P.	Great Britain	202,040	403,520	7,865	11,737	586 85
	Belgium	14,021	22,749	14,021	22,749	1,137 45
	France	6	9	6	9	0 45
	Russia	78	528	78	528	26 40
	United States	126,703	292,367	126,705	292,374	14,618 70
	Total	342,848	719,173	148,675	327,397	16,369 85
Rolls of chilled iron or steel	Great Britain	344	1,290	...	...	...
	United States	10,152	32,882	10,152	32,882	9,864 60
	Total	10,496	34,172	10,152	32,882	9,864 60
Sad or smoothing, hatters' and tailors' irons, plated wholly or in part or not	Great Britain	...	615	...	100	25 00
	France	...	14	...	14	3 50
	Germany	...	65	...	...	...
	United States	...	16,053	...	16,024	4,006 00
	Total	...	16,747	...	16,138	4,034 50
Safes, doors for safes and vaults	Great Britain	...	159	...	...	...
	United States	...	113,972	...	113,972	34,191 60
	Total	...	114,131	...	113,972	34,191 60

OF IMPORTS—*Continued.*

FOR HOME CONSUMPTION.

Preferential Tariff.			Surtax Tariff.			Total.		
Quantity.	Value.	Duty.	Quantity.	Value.	Duty.	Quantity.	Value.	Duty Collected.
Cwt.	$	$ cts.	Cwt.	$	$ cts.	Cwt.	$	$ cts.
158,494	217,069	36,982 21	1,409	1,327	657 53	163,028	221,876	38,733 49
...	...	...	...	...	...	12,253	13,814	4,288 55
...	...	...	2,211	2,371	1,031 81	2,211	2,371	1,031 81
...	...	...	6	7	2 80	199,200	301,952	69,720 70
158,494	217,069	36,982 21	3,626	3,705	1,692 14	376,692	540,013	113,774 55
80,117	119,433	18,694 29	...	...	...	95,801	140,033	24,183 69
...	...	...	132	207	61 61	27,255	35,914	9,554 66
...	...	...	...	...	...	18	26	6 30
...	...	...	38	56	17 73	38	56	17 73
...	...	...	...	...	...	133,123	218,245	46,593 06
80,117	119,433	18,694 29	170	263	79 34	256,235	394,274	80,355 44
95,027	132,927	8,861 93	...	...	...	100,271	139,768	9,546 03
...	...	...	...	...	...	7,495	9,536	953 60
...	...	...	238	216	28 80	238	216	28 80
...	...	...	...	...	...	481,147	754,732	75,473 20
95,027	132,927	8,861 93	238	216	28 80	589,151	904,252	86,001 63
194,175	391,783	13,059 64	...	...	...	202,040	403,520	13,646 49
...	...	...	...	...	...	14,021	22,749	1,137 45
...	...	...	...	...	...	6	9	0 45
...	...	...	...	...	...	78	528	26 40
...	...	...	...	...	...	126,705	292,374	14,618 70
194,175	391,783	13,059 64	...	...	...	342,850	719,180	29,429 49
344	1,290	258 00	...	...	...	344	1,290	258 00
...	...	...	...	...	...	10,152	32,882	9,864 60
344	1,290	258 00	...	...	...	10,496	34,172	10,122 60
...	515	85 85	...	...	...	...	615	110 85
...	...	...	...	...	...	...	14	3 50
...	...	...	...	65	21 67	...	65	21 67
...	...	...	...	...	...	...	16,024	4,006 00
...	515	85 85	...	65	21 67	...	16,718	4,142 02
...	159	31 80	...	...	...	...	159	31 80
...	...	...	...	...	...	...	113,972	34,191 60
...	159	31 80	...	...	...	...	114,131	34,223 40

No. 1.—General Statement

Articles Imported.	Countries.	Total Imports. Quantity.	Total Imports. Value.	Entered — General Tariff. Quantity.	Value.	Duty.
DUTIABLE GOODS—*Con.*		Gross.	$	Gross.	$	$ cts.
Iron and mfrs. of—*Con.*						
Screws, iron and steel, commonly called 'wood screws,' N.E.S.	Great Britain	3,919	1,038	....	....	....
	Italy	40	7	40	7	2 45
	United States	204,871	28,438	204,864	28,436	9,952 60
	Total	208,830	29,483	204,904	28,443	9,955 05
Scales, balances, weighing beams and strength testing machines	Great Britain	....	4,034	....	847	254 10
	Aust.-Hungary	....	104	....	104	31 20
	Belgium	....	141	....	141	42 30
	China	....	6	....	6	1 80
	France	....	387	....	387	116 10
	Germany	....	573	....	....	....
	Holland	....	75	....	75	22 50
	United States	....	129,157	....	128,939	38,681 70
	Total	....	134,477	....	130,499	39,149 70
		Cwt.		Cwt.		
Sheets, flat, of galvanized iron or steel	Great Britain	215,466	621,331	1,394	4,521	226 05
	United States	154,114	479,797	154,114	479,797	23,989 85
	Total	369,580	1,101,128	155,508	484,318	24,215 90
Sheets, iron or steel, corrugated, galvanized	Great Britain	1,451	3,672	....	....	....
	United States	1,845	5,848	1,845	5,848	1,462 00
	Total	3,296	9,520	1,845	5,848	1,462 00
Sheets, iron or steel, corrugated, not galvanized	Great Britain	332	780	....	....	....
	United States	555	1,411	555	1,411	423 30
	Total	887	2,191	555	1,411	423 30
		Prs.		Prs.		
Skates, of all kinds and parts thereof	Great Britain	1,706	1,071	....	....	....
	Germany	76,641	36,533	....	....	....
	Norway	25	44	25	44	15 40
	Sweden	11	19	11	19	6 65
	United States	11,724	13,888	9,968	12,872	4,505 20
	Total	90,107	51,555	10,004	12,935	4,527 25
		Cwt.		Cwt.		
Skelp iron or steel, sheared or rolled in grooves, imported by manufacturers of wrought iron or steel pipe for use only in the manufacture of wrought iron or steel pipe in their own factories	Great Britain	10,561	17,655	3,178	2,127	106 35
	Germany	569	850	569	850	42 50
	United States	669,599	869,752	669,599	869,752	43,487 60
	Total	680,729	888,257	673,346	872,729	43,636 45

OF IMPORTS—*Continued.*

FOR HOME CONSUMPTION.

Preferential Tariff.			Surtax Tariff.			Total.		
Quantity.	Value.	Duty.	Quantity.	Value.	Duty.	Quantity.	Value.	Duty Collected.
Gross.	$	$ cts.	Gross.	$	$ cts.	Gross.	$	$ cts.
3,919	1,038	242 20				3,919	1,038	242 20
						40	7	2 45
						204,864	28,436	9,952 60
3,919	1,038	242 20				208,823	29,481	10,197 25
	3,112	622 40		75	30 00		4,034	906 50
							104	31 20
							141	42 30
							6	1 80
							387	116 10
				573	229 20		573	229 20
							75	22 50
				142	56 80		129,081	38,738 50
	3,112	622 40		790	316 00		134,401	40,088 10
Cwt.			Cwt.			Cwt.		
214,072	616,810	20,560 69				215,466	621,331	20,786 74
						154,114	479,797	23,989 85
214,072	616,810	20,560 69				369,580	1,101,128	44,776 59
1,451	3,672	612 00				1,451	3,672	612 00
						1,845	5,848	1,462 00
1,451	3,672	612 00				3,296	9,520	2,074 00
332	780	156 00				332	780	156 00
						555	1,411	423 30
332	780	156 00				887	2,191	579 30
Prs.			Prs.			Prs.		
181	160	37 33				181	160	37 33
			76,641	36,533	17,048 71	76,641	36,533	17,048 71
						25	44	15 40
						11	19	6 65
						9,968	12,872	4,505 20
181	160	37 33	76,641	36,533	17,048 71	86,826	49,628	21,613 29
Cwt.			Cwt.			Cwt.		
7,383	15,528	517 61				10,561	17,655	623 96
						569	850	42 50
						669,599	869,752	43,487 60
7,383	15,528	517 61				680,729	888,257	44,154 06

No. 1.—GENERAL STATEMENT

Articles Imported.	Countries.	Total Imports. Quantity.	Total Imports. Value.	Entered — General Tariff. Quantity.	Entered — General Tariff. Value.	Entered — General Tariff. Duty.
DUTIABLE GOODS—*Con.*			$		$	$ cts.
Iron and mfrs. of—*Con.*						
Stoves of all kinds and parts thereof, N.E.S.	Great Britain		2,390		455	113 75
	Newfoundland		99		24	6 00
	France		127		127	31 75
	Germany		2,883			
	Japan		1		1	0 25
	United States		467,922		467,534	116,883 50
	Total		473,422		468,141	117,035 25
Swedish rolled iron and Swedish rolled steel nail rods under half an inch in diameter for the manufacture of horseshoe nails		Cwt.		Cwt.		
	Sweden	14,077	26,743	14,077	26,743	4,011 45
	United States	6,382	15,686	6,382	15,686	2,352 90
	Total	20,459	42,429	20,459	42,429	6,364 35
Switches, frogs, crossings and intersections for railways	Great Britain	224	2,470			
	United States	13,522	52,650	13,522	52,650	15,795 00
	Total	13,746	55,120	13,522	52,650	15,795 00
Tubing—						
Boiler tubes of wrought iron or steel, including flues and corrugated tubes for marine boilers	Great Britain		80,246		1,316	65 80
	Aust.-Hungary		27,605		27,605	1,380 25
	Belgium		2,692		2,692	134 60
	Germany		1,872			
	United States		360,439		360,105	18,005 25
	Total		472,854		391,718	19,585 90
Tubes of rolled steel, seamless, not joined or welded, not more than 1½ in. in diameter	Great Britain		45			
	United States		4,154		4,154	415 40
	Total		4,199		4,154	415 40
Tubes, seamless steel, for bicycles	Great Britain		484			
	United States		9,730		9,730	973 00
	Total		10,214		9,730	973 00
Tubing, wrought iron or steel, plain or galvanized, threaded and coupled or not, over 2 inches in diameter, N.E.S.	Great Britain		4,327			
	Aust.-Hungary		1,280		1,280	192 00
	Germany		735		735	110 25
	United States		551,787		548,071	82,210 65
	Total		558,129		550,086	82,512 90
Tubing, wrought iron or steel, plain or galvanized, threaded and coupled or not, 2 inches or less in diameter, N.E.S.	Great Britain		19,982			
	United States		90,568		89,693	31,392 55
	Total		110,550		89,693	31,392 55

OF IMPORTS—*Continued.*

FOR HOME CONSUMPTION.

Preferential Tariff.			Surtax Tariff.			Total.		
Quantity.	Value.	Duty.	Quantity.	Value.	Duty.	Quantity.	Value.	Duty Collected.
	$	$ cts.		$	$ cts.		$	$ cts.
	1,932	322 02		3	1 00		2,390	436 77
							24	6 00
							127	31 75
				2,883	961 00		2,883	961 00
							1	0 25
				22	7 32		467,556	116,890 82
	1,932	322 02		2,908	969 32		472,981	118,326 59
Cwt.			Cwt.			Cwt.		
						14,077	26,743	4,011 45
						6,382	15,686	2,352 90
						20,459	42,429	6,364 35
224	2,470	494 00				224	2,470	494 00
						13,522	52,650	15,795 00
224	2,470	494 00				13,746	55,120	16,289 00
	78,930	2,631 15					80,246	2,696 95
							27,605	1,380 25
							2,692	134 60
				1,872	124 80		1,872	124 80
				248	16 53		360,353	18,021 78
	78,930	2,631 15		2,120	141 33		472,768	22,358 38
	45	3 00					45	3 00
							4,154	415 40
	45	3 00					4,199	418 40
	484	32 27					484	32 27
							9,730	973 00
	484	32 27					10,214	1,005 27
	4,373	437 30					4,373	437 30
							1,280	192 00
							735	110 25
							548,071	82,210 65
	4,373	437 30					554,459	82,950 20
	19,9 2	4,662 55					19,982	4,662 55
							89,693	31,392 55
	19,982	4,662 55					109,675	36,055 10

No. 1.—General Statement

Articles Imported.	Countries.	Total Imports.		Entered		
				General Tariff.		
		Quantity.	Value.	Quantity.	Value.	Duty.
Dutiable Goods—*Con.*			$		$	$ cts.
Iron and mfrs. of—*Con.*						
Tubing—*Con.*						
Other iron or steel tubes or pipes, N.O.P.	Great Britain		4,383		255	76 50
	United States		54,653		54,653	16,395 90
	Total		59,036		54,908	16,472 40
Ware—Galvanized sheet iron or of galvanized sheet steel, manufactures, N.O.P.	Great Britain		1,198		3	0 75
	Germany		438			
	United States		26,185		26,185	6,546 25
	Total		27,821		26,188	6,547 00
Ware—Agate, granite or enamelled iron or steel hollow ware	Great Britain		12,588		5,284	1,849 40
	Hong Kong		3		3	1 05
	Aust.-Hungary		16,201		16,201	5,670 35
	France		682		668	233 80
	Germany		22,504		677	236 95
	Holland		259		259	90 65
	United States		23,767		23,783	8,324 05
	Total		76,004		46,875	16,406 25
Ware—Enamelled iron or steel ware, N.E.S.; iron or steel hollow ware, plain black, tinned or coated; and nickel and aluminium kitchen or household hollow ware, N.E.S.	Great Britain		7,019		263	78 90
	Aust.-Hungary		552		552	165 60
	China		8		8	2 40
	France		221		221	66 30
	Germany		6,087			
	Japan		25		25	7 50
	Sweden		484		484	145 20
	United States		153,350		152,863	45,858 90
	Total		167,746		154,416	46,324 80
		Bdls. of 250		Bdls. of 250		
Wire bale ties.	United States	3,743	4,932	3,743	4,932	1,479 60
		Lbs.		Lbs.		
Wire cloth or wove wire and netting of iron or steel	Great Britain	895,225	48,121	18,340	790	237 00
	Belgium	1,200	468	1,200	468	140 40
	France	5,310	472	5,310	472	141 60
	Germany	290	26			
	United States	230,195	18,726	230,195	18,726	5,617 80
	Total	1,132,220	67,813	255,045	20,456	6,136 80
Wire screens, doors and windows	Great Britain		2,185			
	China		5		5	1 50
	United States		3,760		3,760	1,128 00
	Total		5,950		3,765	1,129 50

OF IMPORTS—*Continued.*

FOR HOME CONSUMPTION.

Preferential Tariff.			Surtax Tariff.			Total.		
Quantity.	Value.	Duty.	Quantity.	Value.	Duty.	Quantity.	Value.	Duty Collected.
	$	$ cts.		$	$ cts.		$	$ cts.
	4,128	825 60					4,383	902 10
							54,653	16,395 90
	4,128	825 60					59,036	17,298 00
	1,195	199 22					1,198	199 97
				438	146 00		438	146 00
							26,185	6,546 25
	1,195	199 22		438	146 00		27,821	6,892 22
	6,423	1,498 78		799	372 87		12,506	3,721 05
							3	1 05
							16,201	5,670 35
							668	233 80
				21,827	10,185 93		22,504	10,422 88
							259	90 65
				11	5 13		23,794	8,329 18
	6,423	1,498 78		22,637	10,563 93		75,935	28,468 96
	6,795	1,359 00		33	13 20		7,091	1,451 10
							552	165 60
							8	2 40
							221	66 30
				6,087	2,434 80		6,087	2,434 80
							25	7 50
							484	145 20
				502	200 80		153,365	46,059 70
	6,795	1,359 00		6,622	2,648 80		167,833	50,332 60
Bdls. of 250			Bdls. of 250			Bdls. of 250		
						3,743	4,932	1,479 60
Lbs.			Lbs.			Lbs.		
876,885	47,331	9,466 20				895,225	48,121	9,703 20
						1,200	468	140 40
						5,310	472	141 60
			290	26	10 40	290	26	10 40
						230,195	18,726	5,617 80
876,885	47,331	9,466 20	290	26	10 40	1,132,220	67,813	15,613 40
	2,185	437 00					2,185	437 00
							5	1 50
							3,760	1,128 00
	2,185	437 00					5,950	1,566 50

No. 1.—GENERAL STATEMENT

Articles Imported.	Countries.	Total Imports.		Entered		
				General Tariff.		
		Quantity.	Value.	Quantity.	Value.	Duty.
DUTIABLE GOODS—*Con.*		Lbs.	$	Lbs.	$	$ cts.
Iron and steel—*Con.*						
Wire fencing, woven, buckthorn strip, and wire fencing of iron or steel, N.E.S.	Great Britain...	65,892	2,998	....	....	....
	United States...	1,692,040	70,070	1,692,040	70,070	10,510 50
	Total.....	1,758,022	73,068	1,692,040	70,070	10,510 50
Wire single or several covered with cotton, linen, silk rubber or other material, &c., N.E.S..............	Great Britain...	276,126	35,243	59,547	4,493	1,347 90
	Belgium........	1,120	23	1,120	23	6 90
	France..........	2,470	361	2,470	361	108 30
	Germany.......	4,867	1,122	....	....	....
	Italy......	4,684	174	4,684	174	52 20
	Switzerland.....	12	5	....	....	....
	United States...	1,938,273	319,643	1,934,213	318,890	95,667 00
	Total.......	2,227,552	356,571	2,002,034	323,941	97,182 30
Wire of all kinds, N.O.P....	Great Britain...	1,618,723	36,834	76,794	1,499	299 80
	Belgium	6,080	136	6,080	136	27 20
	Denmark.	500	24	500	24	4 80
	France..........	540	106	540	106	21 20
	Germany.......	2,448,019	47,902	....	....	....
	United States...	6,620,831	160,576	6,613,611	160,334	32,066 80
	Total.......	10,694,693	245,578	6,697,525	162,099	32,419 80
Wire rope, stranded or twisted wire, clothes lines, picture or other twisted wire and wire cables, N.E.S. ..	Great Britain...	2,309,530	151,694	11,472	1,303	325 75
	France..........	1,159	216	1,159	216	54 00
	Germany........	9,747	968	....	....	....
	United States...	754,539	66,349	696,246	57,692	14,423 00
	Total......	3,074,975	219,227	708,877	59,211	14,802 75
Iron or steel nuts, washers, rivets and bolts with or without threads, and nut, bolt and hinges blanks, and T and strap hinges of all kinds, N.E.S.	Great Britain...	228,804	5,937	6,638	190	545 35
	Germany.......	714	73	....	....	....
	United States...	2,769,429	112,199	2,776,529	112,347	48,463 21
	Total.......	2,998,947	118,209	2,783,167	112,537	49,008 56
Iron or steel scrap, wrought, being waste or refuse, including punchings, cuttings and clippings of iron or steel plates or sheets, having been in actual use; crop ends of tin plate bars, blooms and rails, the same not having been in actual use		Cwt.		Cwt.		
	Great Britain...	224,611	167,830	....	....	....
	British Africa..	13,000	10,400	13,000	10,400	650 00
	British Guiana..	328	84	....	....	....
	B. W. Indies....	167	102	....	....	....
	Newfoundland..	3,757	2,008	3,757	2,008	187 85
	Belgium........	9,000	7,538	9,000	7,538	450 00
	Germany.. . .	8,940	7,143	8,940	7,143	447 00
	St. Pierre.......	863	450	863	450	43 15
	United States...	161,470	129,816	161,470	129,816	8,073 51
	Total..... .	422,136	325,371	197,030	157,355	9,851 51

OF IMPORTS—*Continued.*

FOR HOME CONSUMPTION.

Preferential Tariff.			Surtax Tariff.			Total.		
Quantity.	Value.	Duty.	Quantity.	Value.	Duty.	Quantity.	Value.	Duty Collected.
Lbs.	$	$ cts.	Lbs.	$	$ cts.	Lbs.	$	$ cts.
65,892	2,998	299 80				65,892	2,998	299 80
						1,692,040	70,070	10,510 50
65,892	2,998	299 80				1,757,932	73,068	10,810 30
215,930	30,621	6,124 20	699	152	60 80	276,176	35,266	7,532 90
						1,120	23	6 90
						2,470	361	108 30
			4,867	1,122	448 80	4,867	1,122	448 80
						4,684	174	52 20
			12	5	2 00	12	5	2 00
						1,934,213	318,890	95,667 00
215,930	30,621	6,124 20	5,578	1,279	511 60	2,223,542	355,841	103,818 10
1,541,929	35,335	4,711 39				1,618,723	36,834	5,011 19
						6,080	136	27 20
						500	24	4 80
						540	106	21 20
			2,448,019	47,902	12,773 86	2,448,019	47,902	12,773 86
			2,220	107	28 53	6,615,831	160,441	32,095 33
1,541,929	35,335	4,711 39	2,450,239	48,009	12,802 39	10,689,693	245,443	49,933 58
2,266,008	148,741	24,790 39	20,696	754	251 33	2,298,176	150,798	25,367 47
						1,159	216	54 00
			9,747	968	322 66	9,747	968	322 66
						696,246	57,692	14,423 00
2,266,008	148,741	24,790 39	30,443	1,722	573 99	3,005,328	209,674	40,167 13
222,166	5,747	2,068 75				228,804	5,937	2,614 10
			714	73	31 46	714	73	31 46
						2,776,529	112,347	48,463 21
222,166	5,747	2,068 75	714	73	31 46	3,006,047	118,357	51,108 77
Cwt.			Cwt.			Cwt.		
224,611	167,830	7,486 88				224.611	167,830	7,486 88
						13,000	10,400	650 00
328	84	10 93				328	84	10 93
						3,757	2,008	187 85
						9,000	7,538	450 00
						8,940	7,143	447 00
						863	450	43 15
						161,470	129,816	8,073 51
224,939	167,914	7,497 81				421,969	325,269	17,349 32

No. 1.—General Statement

Articles Imported.	Countries.	Total Imports.		Entered		
				General Tariff.		
		Quantity.	Value.	Quantity.	Value.	Duty.
DUTIABLE GOODS—*Con.*			$		$	$ cts.
Iron and mfrs. of—*Con.*						
Pen knives, jack knives, and pocket knives of all kinds..	Great Britain...	....	102,629	....	1,195	358 50
	Aust.-Hungary .	....	1,071	....	1,071	321 30
	France........	....	214	....	204	61 20
	Germany......	....	37,191	... .	....	....
	United States...	....	1,538	....	1,453	435 90
	Total.	....	142,643	....	3,923	1,176 90
Table cutlery, all kinds, N.O.P.	Great Britain...	.. ..	220,417	....	2,048	614 40
	Hong Kong.....	....	2	....	2	0 60
	Aust.-Hungary .	....	355	....	355	106 50
	France.........	....	4,152	....	3,829	1,148 70
	Germany.... ...	....	9,837	....	....	....
	Holland........	....	3	... .	3	0 90
	United States...	....	25,198	....	25,211	7,563 30
	Total.......	....	259,964	....	31,448	9,434 40
All other cutlery, N.E.S.....	Great Britain....	....	96,157	....	1,868	560 40
	Hong Kong	....	3	....	3	0 90
	Aust.-Hungary .	.. ..	231	... .	317	95 10
	Belgium.... ...	. ...	1,256	....	235	70 50
	China..........	....	26	... .	26	7 80
	France.........	....	2,189	....	2,164	649 20
	Germany.	....	116,153	....	....	....
	Japan....	....	23	....	23	6 90
	Sweden.........	....	492	.. ..	492	147 60
	Switzerland.....	....	210	....	210	63 00
	United States...	....	119,262	....	118,434	35,530 20
	Total.	....	336,002	....	123,772	37,131 60
Guns, rifles, including air guns and air rifles (not being toys), muskets, cannons, pistols, revolvers, or other firearms.	Great Britain...	....	31,052	....	4,675	1,402 50
	Australia.....	....	61	....	61	18 30
	Newfoundland..	....	17	....	17	5 10
	Aust.-Hungary ..	. ....	162	....	162	48 60
	Belgium.... ...	....	72,260	....	72,764	21,829 20
	China...........	... .	16	....	16	4 80
	France..........	....	5,855	....	5,855	1,756 50
	Germany......	....	1,273	....	648	194 40
	United States...	....	324,791	....	323,269	96,980 70
	Total	....	435,487	....	407,467	122,240 10
Bayonets, swords, fencing foils and masks	Great Britain...	....	218	....	24	7 20
	France..........	....	305	....	305	91 50
	Germany.......	....	695	....	....	....
	Japan..........	....	10	....	10	3 00
	United States...	....	1,259	. ...	1,259	377 70
	Total	....	2,487	....	1,598	479 40

OF IMPORTS—*Continued.*

FOR HOME CONSUMPTION.

Preferential Tariff.			Surtax Tariff.			Total.		
Quantity.	Value.	Duty.	Quantity.	Value.	Duty.	Quantity.	Value.	Duty Collected.
	$	$ cts.		$	$ cts.		$	$ cts.
	101,042	20,208 40		448	179 20		102,685	20,746 10
							1,071	321 30
				10	4 00		214	65 20
				37,042	14,816 80		37,042	14,816 80
				85	34 00		1,538	469 90
	101,042	20,208 40		37,585	15,034 00		142,550	36,419 30
	218,517	43,703 40		108	43 20		220,673	44,361 00
							2	0 60
							355	106 50
							3,829	1,148 70
				10,323	4,129 20		10,323	4,129 20
							3	0 90
				7	2 80		25,218	7,566 10
	218,517	43,703 40		10,438	4,175 20		260,403	57,313 00
	92,184	18,436 80		2,144	857 60		96,196	19,854 80
							3	0 90
							317	95 10
				1,021	408 40		1,256	478 90
							26	7 80
				38	15 20		2,202	664 40
				115,788	46,315 20		115,788	46,315 20
							23	6 90
							492	147 60
							210	63 00
				795	318 00		119,229	35,848 20
	92,184	18,436 80		119,786	47,914 40		335,742	103,482 80
	26,372	5,274 40					31,047	6,676 90
							61	18 30
							17	5 10
							162	48 60
							72,764	21,829 20
							16	4 80
							5,855	1,756 50
				625	250 00		1,273	444 40
				210	84 00		323,479	97,064 70
	26,372	5,274 40		835	334 00		434,674	127,848 50
	187	37 40		7	2 80		218	47 40
							305	91 50
				695	278 00		695	278 00
							10	3 00
							1,259	377 70
	187	37 40		702	280 80		2,487	797 60

No. 1.—General Statement

Articles Imported.	Countries.	Total Imports.		Entered		
				General Tariff.		
		Quantity.	Value.	Quantity.	Value.	Duty.
DUTIABLE GOODS—*Con.*			$		$	$ cts.
Iron and mfrs. of—*Con.*						
Needles, of any material or kind, N.O.P.	Great Britain	....	42,278	....	635	190 50
	Aust.-Hungary	....	178	....	178	53 40
	China	....	4	....	4	1 20
	France	....	201	....	201	60 30
	Germany	....	3,633	....	....	....
	Switzerland	....	17	....	....	....
	United States	....	35,153	....	34,840	10,452 00
	Total	....	81,464	....	35,858	10,757 40
		Cwt.		Cwt.		
Steel—chrome steel	United States	5,275	24,614	5,275	24,614	3,692 10
Steel plate, universal mill or rolled edge bridge plates imported by manufacturers of bridges	Great Britain	1,494	1,933	136	167	16 70
	Belgium	981	1,024	981	1,024	102 40
	United States	241,293	344,403	241,293	344,403	34,410 30
	Total	243,768	347,360	242,410	345,594	34,559 40
Steel in bars, bands, hoops, scroll or strips, sheets or plates, of any size, thickness or width when of greater value than 2½c. per lb., N.O.P.	Great Britain	42,214	284,917	528	6,117	305 85
	France	154	2,978	·154	2,978	148 90
	Germany	652	6,051	....	....	....
	Sweden	320	1,437	320	1,437	71 85
	United States	130,064	561,648	129,894	560,863	28,043 15
	Total	173,404	857,031	130,896	571,395	28,569 75
Tools and implements—Adzes, cleavers, hatchets, wedges, sledges, hammers, crowbars, cant dogs and track tools; picks, mattocks and eyes or poles for the same	Great Britain	....	5,108	....	2,048	614 40
	France	....	434	....	434	130 20
	Germany	....	2,572	....	....	....
	Sweden	....	562	....	562	168 60
	United States	....	79,106	....	78,349	23,504 70
	Total	....	87,782	....	81,393	24,417 90
		Doz.		Doz.		
Axes	United States	6,055	35,116	6,051	35,123	8,780 75
Saws	Great Britain	....	2,554	....	1,320	396 00
	France	....	749	....	749	224 70
	Germany	....	1,310	....	....	....
	United States	....	201,915	....	201,705	60,511 50
	Total	....	206,528	....	203,774	61,132 20
Files and rasps, N.E.S.	Great Britain	....	9,316	....	474	142 20
	France	....	629	....	629	188 70
	Germany	....	3,035	....	....	....
	Switzerland	....	566	....	566	169 80
	United States	....	74,665	....	74,663	22,398 90
	Total	....	88,211	....	76,332	22,899 60

SESSIONAL PAPER No. 11

OF IMPORTS—*Continued.*

FOR HOME CONSUMPTION.

Preferential Tariff.			Surtax Tariff.			Total.		
Quantity.	Value.	Duty.	Quantity.	Value.	Duty.	Quantity.	Value.	Duty Collected.
	$	$ cts.		$	$ cts.		$	$ cts.
....	41,563	8,312 60	....	31	12 40	....	42,229	8,515 50
....	....	....	....	....	....	....	178	53 40
....	....	....	....	....	....	....	4	1 20
....	....	....	....	....	....	....	201	60 30
....	....	....	....	3,633	1,453 20	....	3,633	1,453 20
....	....	....	....	17	6 80	....	17	6 80
....	....	....	....	313	125 20	....	35,153	10,577 20
....	41,563	8,312 60	....	3,994	1,597 60	....	81,415	20,667 60
Cwt.			Cwt.			Cwt.		
....	....	....	....	....	....	5,275	24,614	3,692 10
1,358	1,766	117 73	....	....	....	1,494	1,933	134 43
....	....	....	....	....	....	981	1,024	102 40
....	....	....	....	....	....	241,293	344,403	34,440 30
1,358	1,766	117 73	....	....	....	243,768	347,360	34,677 13
41,685	278,796	9,293 38	1	4	0 26	42,214	284,917	9,599 49
....	....	....	....	....	....	154	2,978	148 90
....	....	....	652	6,051	403 39	652	6,051	403 39
....	....	....	....	....	....	320	1,437	71 85
....	....	....	6	108	7 20	129,900	560,971	28,050 35
41,685	278,796	9,293 38	659	6,163	410 85	173,240	856,354	38,273 98
....	3,060	612 00	....	....	....	....	5,108	1,226 40
....	....	....	....	....	....	....	434	130 20
....	....	....	....	2,572	1,028 80	....	2,572	1,028 80
....	....	....	....	....	....	....	562	163 60
....	....	....	....	....	....	....	78,349	23,504 70
....	3,060	612 00	....	2,572	1,028 80	....	87,025	26,058 70
Doz.			Doz.			Doz.		
....	....	....	....	....	....	6,051	35,123	8,780 75
....	1,130	226 00	....	104	41 60	....	2,554	663 60
....	....	....	....	....	....	....	749	224 70
....	....	....	....	1,310	524 00	....	1,310	524 00
....	....	....	....	210	84 00	....	201,915	60,595 50
....	1,130	226 00	....	1,624	649 60	....	206,528	62,007 80
....	8,828	1,765 60	....	14	5 60	....	9,316	1,913 40
....	....	....	....	....	....	....	629	188 70
....	....	....	....	3,035	1,214 00	....	3,035	1,214 00
....	....	....	....	....	....	....	566	169 80
....	....	....	....	2	0 80	....	74,665	22,399 70
....	8,828	1,765 60	....	3,051	1,220 40	....	88,211	25,885 60

No. 1.—General Statement

Articles Imported.	Countries.	Total Imports.		Entered — General Tariff.		
		Quantity.	Value.	Quantity.	Value.	Duty.
DUTIABLE GOODS—*Con.*			$		$	$ cts.
Iron and mfrs. of—*Con.* Tools and implements—*Con.* Tools, hand or machine, of all kinds, N.O.P.	Great Britain		64,322		4,476	1,342 80
	Newfoundland		50			
	New Zealand		71		71	21 30
	Aust.-Hungary		286		286	85 80
	Belgium		412		49	14 70
	France		4,578		1,340	402 00
	Germany		45,879		178	53 40
	Japan		71		71	21 30
	United States		904,722		903,660	271,098 00
	Total		1,020,391		910,131	273,039 30
Knife blades, or blanks, and forks of iron or steel, in the rough, not handled, filed, ground or otherwise manufactured	Great Britain		70			
Manufactures, articles or wares not specially enumerated or provided for, composed wholly or in part of iron or steel, and whether partly or wholly manufactured	Great Britain		238,146		14,309	4,292 70
	B. E. Indies				80	24 00
	Hong Kong		169		169	50 70
	Aust.-Hungary		1,842		1,821	546 30
	Belgium		984		922	276 60
	China		202		202	60 60
	Denmark		29		29	8 70
	France		8,621		8,437	2,531 10
	Germany		44,818		613	183 90
	Holland		81		81	24 30
	Japan		1,325		1,325	397 50
	Sweden		235		235	70 50
	United States		2,727,594		2,719,859	815,957 70
	Total		3,024,046		2,748,082	824,424 60
Ivory manufactures of, not otherwise provided for	Great Britain		105		37	7 40
	Hong Kong		7		7	1 40
	China		57		57	11 40
	France		66		66	13 20
	Italy		53		53	10 60
	Japan		81		81	16 20
	United States		861		861	172 20
	Total		1,230		1,162	232 40

OF IMPORTS—*Continued.*

FOR HOME CONSUMPTION.

Preferential Tariff.			Surtax Tariff.			Total.		
Quantity.	Value.	Duty.	Quantity.	Value.	Duty.	Quantity.	Value.	Duty Collected.
	$	$ cts.		$	$ cts.		$	$ cts.
	57,969	11,593 80		1,691	676 40		64,136	13,613 00
							71	21 30
							286	85 80
				363	145 20		412	159 90
				3,238	1,295 20		4,578	1,697 20
				45,720	18,288 00		45,898	18,341 40
							71	21 30
				549	219 60		904,209	271,317 60
	57,969	11,593 80		51,561	20,624 40		1,019,661	305,257 50
	70	4 67					70	4 67
	221,104	44,220 80		1,383	553 20		236,796	49,066 70
							80	24 00
							169	50 70
				21	8 40		1,842	554 70
				62	24 80		984	301 40
							202	60 60
							29	8 70
							8,437	2,531 10
				45,863	18,345 20		46,476	18,529 10
							81	24 30
							1,325	397 50
							235	70 50
				1,386	554 40		2,721,245	816,512 10
	221,104	44,220 80		48,715	19,486 00		3,017,901	888,131 40
	68	9 06					105	16 46
							7	1 40
							57	11 40
							66	13 20
							53	10 60
							81	16 20
							861	172 20
	68	9 06					1,230	241 46

No. 1.—General Statement

Articles Imported.	Countries.	Total Imports.		Entered		
				General Tariff.		
		Quantity.	Value.	Quantity.	Value.	Duty.
dutiable goods—*Con.*		Lbs.	$	Lbs.	$	$ cts.
Jellies, jams and preserves, N.E.S.	Great Britain	1,736,491	128,758	11,911	817	387 11
	Australia	6,840	420	5,121	327	166 43
	British Guiana	7,296	401	....	....	....
	B. W. Indies	300	53	132	22	4 29
	Hong Kong	48	1	48	1	1 56
	Belgium	10	1	10	1	0 33
	China	2,092	43	2,092	43	68 00
	France	3,208	495	3,208	495	104 26
	Germany	460	72	....	....	....
	Japan	136	7	136	7	4 42
	United States	65,312	7,404	62,682	7,384	2,037 39
	Total	1,822,193	137,655	85,340	9,097	2,773 79
Jewellery, N.O.P.	Great Britain	....	92,523	....	11,919	3,575 70
	Australia	....	184	....	184	55 20
	Hong Kong	....	214	....	214	64 20
	Newfoundland	....	40	....	40	12 00
	Aust.-Hungary	....	12,589	....	12,320	3,696 00
	Belgium	....	67	....	67	20 10
	China	....	400	....	400	120 00
	France	....	21,290	....	21,189	6,356 70
	Germany	....	66,499	....	1,263	378 90
	Italy	....	204	....	81	24 30
	Japan	....	247	....	247	74 10
	Roumania	....	115	....	115	34 50
	Switzerland	....	1,083	....	906	271 80
	Turkey	....	5	....	5	1 50
	United States	....	692,459	....	692,294	207,688 20
	Total	....	887,919	....	741,244	222,373 20
Knitted goods of every description, N.E.S.	Great Britain	....	1,446	....	44	15 40
	France	....	45	....	45	15 75
	United States	....	448	....	448	156 80
	Total	....	1,939	....	537	187 95
Lead and manufactures of—		Cwt.		Cwt.		
Old, scrap, pig and block	Great Britain	82,236	269,937	1,128	4,047	607 05
	B. W. Indies	435	840	384	778	116 70
	Newfoundland	11	48	11	48	7 20
	St. Pierre	2	7	2	7	1 05
	United States	45	273	45	273	40 95
	Total	82,729	271,105	1,570	5,153	772 95
Bars and in sheets	Great Britain	14,320	49,302	....	....	....
	United States	1,788	7,888	1,786	7,883	1,970 75
	Total	16,108	57,190	1,786	7,883	1,970 75
		Lbs.		Lbs.		
Pipe	Great Britain	25,965	1,406	....	....	....
	United States	58,684	4,015	61,779	4,011	1,403 85
	Total	84,649	5,421	61,779	4,011	1,403 85

SESSIONAL PAPER No. 11

OF IMPORTS—*Continued.*

FOR HOME CONSUMPTION.

Preferential Tariff.			Surtax Tariff.			Total.		
Quantity.	Value.	Duty.	Quantity.	Value.	Duty.	Quantity.	Value.	Duty Collected.
Lbs.	$	$ cts.	Lbs.	$	$ cts.	Lbs.	$	$ cts.
1,751,078	129,330	37,940 43				1,762,989	130,147	38,327 54
						5,121	327	166 43
168	31	3 64				300	53	7 93
						48	1	1 56
						10	1	0 33
						2,092	43	68 00
						3,208	495	104 26
			460	72	19 93	460	72	19 93
						136	7	4 42
						62,682	7,384	2,037 39
1,751,246	129,361	37,944 07	460	72	19 93	1,837,046	138,530	40,737 79
	78,084	15,616 80		2,701	1,080 40		92,704	20,272 90
							184	55 20
							214	64 20
							40	12 00
				120	48 00		12,440	3,744 00
							67	20 10
							400	120 00
				104	41 60		21,293	6,398 30
				65,065	26,026 00		66,328	26,404 90
				123	49 20		204	73 50
							247	74 10
							115	34 50
				177	70 80		1,083	342 60
							5	1 50
				1,261	504 40		693,555	208,192 60
	78,084	15,616 80		69,551	27,820 40		888,879	265,810 40
	1,355	316 19		47	21 93		1,446	353 52
							45	15 75
							448	156 80
	1,355	316 19		47	21 93		1,939	526 07
Cwt.			Cwt.			Cwt.		
81,108	265,890	26,589 00				82,236	269,937	27,196 05
51	62	6 20				435	840	122 90
						11	48	7 20
						2	7	1 05
						45	273	40 95
81,159	265,952	26,595 20				82,729	271,105	27,368 15
14,320	49,302	8,217 15				14,320	49,302	8,217 15
						1,786	7,883	1,970 75
14,320	49,302	8,217 15				16,106	57,185	10,187 90
Lbs.			Lbs.			Lbs.		
25,965	1,406	328 06				25,965	1,406	328 06
						61,779	4,011	1,403 85
25,965	1,406	328 06				87,744	5,417	1,731 91

No. 1.—General Statement

Articles Imported.	Countries.	Total Imports.		Entered		
				General Tariff.		
		Quantity.	Value.	Quantity.	Value.	Duty.
Dutiable Goods—*Con.*		Lbs.	$	Lbs.	$	$ cts.
Lead and mfrs. of—*Con.*						
Shot and bullets	Great Britain	66,044	2,405	....	....	....
	United States	7,881	537	6,806	466	163 10
	Total	73,925	2,942	6,806	466	163 10
Manufactures of, N.O.P.	Great Britain	....	13,168	....	5,597	1,679 10
	Hong Kong	....	6	....	6	1 80
	Aust.-Hungary	....	8,663	....	8,663	2,598 90
	Belgium	....	36	....	36	10 80
	China	....	14	....	14	4 20
	France	....	14,512	....	14,620	4,386 00
	Germany	....	789	....	16	4 80
	Holland	....	5,977	....	5,973	1,791 90
	Japan	....	54	....	54	16 20
	Spain	....	291	....	291	87 30
	Sweden	....	344	....	344	103 20
	United States	....	31,563	....	31,563	9,468 90
	Total	....	75,417	....	67,177	20,153 10
Leather and manufactures of—						
Sole leather, all kinds	Great Britain	227,039	55,126	2,800	576	86 40
	United States	240,273	63,466	240,273	63,466	9,519 90
	Total	467,312	118,592	243,073	64,042	9,606 30
Leather, belting leather of all kinds	Great Britain	303,783	106,326	4,204	1,431	214 65
	United States	3,608	1,292	3,608	1,292	193 80
	Total	307,391	107,618	7,812	2,723	408 45
Upper leather, not dressed, waxed or glazed	United States	896	371	896	371	55 65
Calf, kid or goat, lamb and sheep skins, tanned	Great Britain	823	673	....	....	....
	United States	4,908	1,468	3,308	1,390	208 50
	Total	5,731	2,141	3,308	1,390	208 50
Calf, kid or goat, lamb and sheep skins, dressed, waxed or glazed	Great Britain	74,687	68,077	4,207	2,470	432 25
	France	45,815	31,049	45,815	31,049	5,433 57
	Germany	280	340	....	....	....
	Japan	7	9	7	9	1 57
	United States	300,080	284,009	284,240	267,093	46,742 03
	Total	420,869	383,484	334,269	300,621	52,609 42
Glove leathers, tanned or dressed, coloured or uncoloured, imported by glove manufacturers for use in their own factories in the manufacture of gloves	Great Britain	3,084	2,927	....	....	....
	Germany	11,234	11,845	....	....	....
	United States	665,101	368,793	665,021	368,684	36,868 40
	Total	679,419	383,565	665,021	368,684	36,868 40

OF IMPORTS—*Continued.*

FOR HOME CONSUMPTION.

Preferential Tariff.			Surtax Tariff.			Total.		
Quantity.	Value.	Duty.	Quantity.	Value.	Duty.	Quantity.	Value.	Duty Collected.
Lbs.	$	$ cts.	Lbs.	$	$ cts.	Lbs.	$	$ cts.
66,044	2,405	561 16				66,044	2,405	561 16
						6,806	466	163 10
66,044	2,405	561 16				72,850	2,871	724 26
	7,668	1,533 60		1	0 40		13,266	3,213 10
							6	1 80
							8,663	2,598 90
							36	10 80
							14	4 20
							14,620	4,386 00
				773	309 20		789	314 00
							5,973	1,791 90
							54	16 20
							291	87 30
							344	103 20
							31,563	9,468 90
	7,668	1,533 60		774	309 60		75,619	21,996 30
224,239	54,550	5,455 00				227,039	55,126	5,541 40
						240,273	63,466	9,519 90
224,239	54,550	5,455 00				467,312	118,592	15,061 30
317,845	108,588	10,858 80				322,049	110,019	11,073 45
						3,608	1,292	193 80
317,845	108,588	10,858 80				325,657	111,311	11,267 25
						896	371	55 65
823	673	67 30				823	673	67 30
			1,600	78	15 60	4,908	1,468	224 10
823	673	67 30	1,600	78	15 60	5,731	2,141	291 40
70,480	65,607	7,654 34				74,687	68,077	8,086 59
						45,815	31,049	5,433 57
			280	340	79 33	280	340	79 33
						7	9	1 57
			1,190	990	231 00	285,430	268,083	46,973 03
70,480	65,607	7,654 34	1,470	1,330	310 33	406,219	367,558	60,574 09
3,084	2,927	195 20				3,084	2,927	195 20
			11,234	11,845	1,579 32	11,234	11,845	1,579 32
			80	109	14 53	665,101	368,793	36,882 93
3,084	2,927	195 20	11,314	11,954	1,593 85	679,419	383,565	38,657 45

No. 1.—General Statement

Articles Imported.	Countries.	Total Imports.		Entered		
				General Tariff.		
		Quantity.	Value.	Quantity.	Value.	Duty.
DUTIABLE GOODS—*Con*		Lbs.	$	Lbs.	$	$ cts.
Leather and mfrs. of—*Con.*						
Harness leather............	Great Britain...	24,444	11,003	203	130	22 75
	United States...	2,288	1,050	2,288	1,050	183 77
	Total......	26,732	12,053	2,491	1,180	206 52
Tanners' scrap leather.......	Great Britain...	120	191	....	.... .	....
	Newfoundland..	....	227	.. ..	227	34 05
Upper leather, including dongola, cordovan, kangaroo, alligator and chamois skins, or other upper leather, N.E.S., dressed, waxed or glazed....................	United States...	143,855	4,847	143,855	4,847	727 05
	Total......	143,975	5,265	143,855	5,074	761 10
	Great Britain...	65,478	46,382	3,256	2,240	392 00
	Newfoundland..	....	150	....	150	26 25
	France..........	33,459	22,738	33,459	22,738	3,979 15
	Germany	1,478	1,901	... .	.... ..	....
	Japan..........	730	557	730	557	97 48
	United States...	119,989	113,100	113,229	103,394	18,094 49
	Total......	221,132	184,828	150,674	129,079	22,589 37
Japanned, patent or enamelled leather and Morocco leather...................	Great Britain...	5,477	4,189	15	15	3 75
	France...... ...	58	140	58	140	35 00
	Germany... ...	2,120	2,641	....	.. ..	....
	United States..	71,977	83,143	70,487	81,038	20,259 50
	Total.....	79,632	90,113	70,560	81,193	20,298 25
Skins for Morocco leather, tanned, but not further manufactured......... ...	Great Britain...	6,992	2,325	....	....	....
	United States...	570	234	570	234	35 10
	Total......	7,562	2,559	570	234	35 10
All other leather and skins, N.O.P..................	Great Britain...	148,885	51,971	721	216	32 40
	France..........	1,626	3,183	1,626	3,183	477 45
	United States...	79,916	21,864	79,916	21,864	3,279 60
	Total.....	230,427	77,018	82,266	25,263	3,789 45
All other leather and skins, dressed, waxed or glazed, &c., N.E.S..............	Great Britain...	7,599	5,817	301	448	78 40
	United States...	32,780	15,532	32,780	15,532	2,718 22
	Total......	40,379	21,349	33,081	15,980	2,796 62
Boots and shoes........	Great Britain...	....	66,629	....	3,577	894 25
	Hong Kong.....	.. ..	75	..... .	75	18 75
	Aust.-Hungary..	....	1,191	... .	1,191	297 75
	China	....	332	....	332	83 00
	France..........	....	307	....	307	76 75
	Germany	....	41	....	....	....
	Japan..........	....	36	....	36	9 00
	Turkey..........	....	40	....	40	10 00
	United States...	....	1,216,003	... .	1,214,353	303,588 25
	Total.... ..	....	1,284,654	....	1,219,911	304,977 75

OF IMPORTS—*Continued.*

FOR HOME CONSUMPTION.

Preferential Tariff.			Surtax Tariff.			Total.		
Quantity.	Value.	Duty.	Quantity.	Value.	Duty.	Quantity.	Value.	Duty Collected.
Lbs.	$	$ cts.	Lbs.	$	$ cts.	Lbs.	$	$ cts.
24,241	10,873	1,268 54				24,444	11,003	1,291 29
						2,288	1,050	183 77
24,241	10,873	1,268 54				26,732	12,053	1,475 06
120	191	19 10				120	191	19 10
							227	34 05
						143,855	4,847	727 05
120	191	19 10				143,975	5,265	780 20
62,247	44,185	5,155 04				65,503	46,425	5,547 04
							150	26 25
						33,459	22,738	3,979 15
			1,478	1,901	443 56	1,478	1,901	443 56
						730	557	97 48
						113,229	103,394	18,094 49
62,247	44,185	5,155 04	1,478	1,901	443 56	214,399	175,165	28,187 97
5,437	4,157	692 84	25	17	5 66	5,477	4,189	702 25
						58	140	35 00
			2,120	2,641	880 33	2,120	2,641	880 33
			1,490	2,105	701 67	71,977	83,143	20,961 17
5,437	4,157	692 84	3,635	4,763	1,587 66	79,632	90,113	22,578 75
6,992	2,325	232 50				6,992	2,325	232 50
						570	234	35 10
6,992	2,325	232 50				7,562	2,559	267 60
150,929	52,650	5,265 00				151,653	52,866	5,297 40
						1,626	3,183	477 45
						79,916	21,864	3,279 60
150,929	52,650	5,265 00				233,195	77,913	9,054 45
7,298	5,369	626 44				7,599	5,817	704 84
						32,780	15,532	2,718 22
7,298	5,369	626 44				40,379	21,349	3,423 06
	63,052	10,508 85					66,629	11,403 10
							75	18 75
							1,191	297 75
							332	83 00
							307	76 75
				41	13 67		41	13 67
							36	9 00
							40	10 00
							1,214,353	303,588 25
	63,052	10,508 85		41	13 67		1,283,004	315,500 27

No. 1.—General Statement

Articles Imported.	Countries.	Total Imports.		Entered		
				General Tariff.		
		Quantity.	Value.	Quantity.	Value.	Duty.
DUTIABLE GOODS.			$		$	$ cts.
Leather and mfrs. of—*Con.*						
Harness and saddlery, N.E.S.	Great Britain		23,926		2,018	605 40
	France		62		62	18 60
	Japan		17		17	5 10
	Sweden		22		22	6 60
	United States		67,065		64,462	19,338 60
	Total		91,092		66,581	19,974 30
Leather belting	Great Britain		23,890		65	13 00
	France		29		29	5 80
	United States		30,900		30,885	6,177 00
	Total		54,819		30,979	6,195 80
All other manufactures of leather and raw hide, not otherwise provided for	Great Britain		27,008		1,400	350 00
	Aust.-Hungary		119		119	29 75
	France		564		564	141 00
	Germany		4,121			
	Holland		16		16	4 00
	Italy		3		3	0 75
	Japan		62		62	15 50
	Switzerland		16		16	4 00
	United States		180,139		178,839	44,709 75
	Total		212,048		181,019	45,254 75
		Brls.		Brls.		
Lime	United States	134,334	93,630	134,334	93,630	18,726 00
		Galls.		Galls.		
Lime juice, and fruit juices fortified with or containing not more than twenty-five per cent of proof spirits	Great Britain	30	27			
	United States	330	660	313	625	187 80
	Total	360	687	313	625	187 80
Lime juice, and fruit juices containing more than twenty-five per cent of proof spirits	France			6	32	12 00
	United States	52	100	70	261	140 00
	Total	52	100	76	293	152 00
Lime juice and other fruit syrups and fruit juices, N.O.P.	Great Britain	10,179	10,474	119	218	43 60
	B. W. Indies	1,410	820	600	313	62 60
	France	683	1,411	964	1,858	371 60
	Germany	3	4			
	Holland			44	90	18 00
	Switzerland	2	2	2	2	0 40
	United States	7,156	9,511	7,411	9,947	1,989 40
	Total	19,433	22,222	9,140	12,428	2,485 60

OF IMPORTS—*Continued.*

FOR HOME CONSUMPTION.

Preferential Tariff.			Surtax Tariff.			Total.		
Quantity.	Value.	Duty.	Quantity.	Value.	Duty.	Quantity.	Value.	Duty Collected.
	$	$ cts.		$	$ cts.		$	$ cts.
	22,197	4,439 40					24,215	5,044 80
							62	18 60
							17	5 10
							22	6 60
							64,462	19,338 60
	22,197	4,439 40					88,778	24,413 70
	21,294	2,839 26					21,359	2,852 26
							29	5 80
							30,885	6,177 00
	21,294	2,839 26					52,273	9,035 06
	25,345	4,224 43		283	94 33		27,028	4,668 76
							119	29 75
							564	141 00
				4,121	1,373 66		4,121	1,373 66
							16	4 00
							3	0 75
							62	15 50
							16	4 00
				651	217 00		179,490	44,926 75
	25,345	4,224 43		5,055	1,684 99		211,419	51,164 17
Brls.			Brls.			Brls.		
						134,334	93,630	18,726 00
Galls.			Galls.			Galls.		
						313	625	187 80
						313	625	187 80
						6	32	12 00
						70	261	140 00
						76	293	152 00
10,133	10,512	1,401 79				10,252	10,730	1,445 39
810	507	67 60				1,410	820	130 20
						964	1,858	371 60
			3	4	1 07	3	4	1 07
						44	90	18 00
						2	2	0 40
						7,411	9,947	1,989 40
10,943	11,019	1,469 39	3	4	1 07	20,086	23,451	3,956 06

No. 1.—GENERAL STATEMENT

Articles Imported.	Countries.	Total Imports.		Entered		
				General Tariff.		
		Quantity.	Value.	Quantity.	Value.	Duty.
DUTIABLE GOODS—*Con.*			$		$	$ cts.
Lithographic presses and type making accessories therefor..	Great Britain...	....	8,431	....	....	....
	France..........	....	18	....	18	1 80
	United States...	....	56,361	....	53,235	5,323 50
	Total....	....	64,810	....	53,253	5,325 30
Lithographic stones, not engraved	Great Britain...	....	36	....	....	....
	Germany.......	....	1,991	....	....	....
	United States...	....	4,745	....	1,309	261 80
	Total	....	6,772	....	1,309	261 80
Machine card clothing........	Great Britain...	....	28,526	....	583	145 75
	Belgium........	....	587	....	587	146 75
	France.........	....	93	....	93	23 25
	Germany......	....	991	....	....	....
	United States...	....	5,549	....	5,549	1,387 25
	Total	....	35,746	....	6,812	1,703 00
Magic lanterns and slides therefor	Great Britain...	....	1,533	....	273	68 25
	France.........	....	149	....	149	37 25
	Germany.......	....	2,552	....	....	....
	Japan..........	....	81	....	81	20 25
	United States...	....	7,413	....	7,413	1,853 25
	Total	....	11,728	....	7,916	1,979 00
		Bush.		Bush.		
Malt..........................	Great Britain...	1,016	2,370	....	....	....
	United States...	93,136	65,870	93,136	65,870	13,970 40
	Total	94,152	68,240	93,136	65,870	13,970 40
Malt, extract of (non-alcoholic), for medicinal and baking purposes.........	Great Britain...	....	1,013	....	....	....
	United States...	....	9,774	....	9,690	2,422 50
	Total	....	10,787	....	9,690	2,422 50
Marble and manufactures of—Marble, sawn only........	Great Britain...	....	406	....	17	3 40
	Italy...........	....	29,904	....	29,904	5,980 80
	United States...	....	78,408	....	78,408	15,681 60
	Total	....	108,718	....	108,329	21,665 80
Rough, not hammered or chiselled	Great Britain...	....	3,044	....	3,044	456 60
	France.........	....	70	....	70	10 50
	Holland........	....	59	....	59	8 85
	Italy...........	....	111	....	111	16 65
	United States...	....	3,543	....	3,543	531 45
	Total	....	6,827	....	6,827	1,024 05

OF IMPORTS—*Continued.*

FOR HOME CONSUMPTION.

Preferential Tariff.			Surtax Tariff.			Total.		
Quantity.	Value.	Duty.	Quantity.	Value.	Duty.	Quantity.	Value.	Duty Collected.
	$	$ cts.		$	$ cts.		$	$ cts.
	8,431	562 07					8,431	562 07
							18	1 80
							53,235	5,323 50
	8,431	562 07					61,684	5,887 37
				36	9 60		36	9 60
				1,991	530 93		1,991	530 93
				3,436	916 26		4,745	1,178 06
				5,463	1,456 79		6,772	1,718 59
	27,263	4,543 89		241	80 33		28,087	4,769 97
							587	146 75
							93	23 25
				991	330 33		991	330 33
							5,549	1,387 25
	27,263	4,543 89		1,232	410 66		35,307	6,657 55
	1,237	206 23		23	7 67		1,533	282 15
							149	37 25
				2,594	864 66		2,594	864 66
							81	20 25
							7,413	1,853 25
	1,237	206 23		2,617	872 33		11,770	3,057 56
Bush.			Bush.			Bush.		
1,016	2,370	101 60				1,016	2,370	101 60
						93,136	65,870	13,970 40
1,016	2,370	101 60				94,152	68,240	14,072 00
	1,013	168 84					1,013	168 84
							9,690	2,422 50
	1,013	168 84					10,703	2,591 34
	389	51 89					406	55 29
							29,904	5,980 80
							78,408	15,681 60
	389	51 89					108,718	21,717 69
							3,044	456 60
							70	10 50
							59	8 85
							111	16 65
							3,543	531 45
							6,827	1,024 05

No. 1.—General Statement

Articles Imported.	Countries.	Total Imports.		Entered		
				General Tariff.		
		Quantity.	Value.	Quantity.	Value.	Duty.
DUTIABLE GOODS—*Con.*			$		$	$ cts.
Marble and mfrs. of—*Con.* Manufactures of, N.O.P.	Great Britain		3,102		501	175 35
	B. E. Indies		40		40	14 00
	Hong Kong		3		3	1 05
	Aust.-Hungary		55			
	Belgium		6		6	2 10
	France		798		798	279 30
	Germany		2			
	Italy		2,362		2,362	826 70
	Japan		61		61	21 35
	United States		68,070		67,666	23,683 10
	Total		74,499		71,437	25,002 95
Mattresses, including hair, spring and other	Great Britain		556		85	25 50
	Japan		6		6	1 80
	United States		6,489		6,246	1,873 80
	Total		7,051		6,337	1,901 10
Mats and rugs, including door and carriage, N.E.S.	Great Britain		302,793		36,241	12,684 35
	B. E. Indies		1,014		1,014	354 90
	B. W. Indies		30		30	10 50
	Aust.-Hungary		7,820		7,441	2,604 35
	Belgium		135		135	47 25
	China		9		9	3 15
	Egypt		450		450	157 50
	France		4,145		4,230	1,480 50
	Germany		8,634		15	5 25
	Japan		393		393	137 55
	Russia		300		300	105 00
	Sweden		36		36	12 60
	Turkey		11,685		11,685	4,089 75
	United States		27,308		27,254	9,538 90
	Total		364,752		89,233	31,231 55
Metal, N.E.S., and manufactures of— Aluminium, manufactures of N.O.P.	Great Britain		660		51	12 75
	France		4,101		4,101	1,025 25
	Germany		1,501		76	19 00
	Italy		4		4	1 00
	Japan		57		57	14 25
	United States		17,242		17,316	4,329 00
	Total		23,565		21,605	5,401 25
Babbit metal	Great Britain		19,284		625	62 50
	United States		40,383		40,378	4,037 80
	Total		59,667		41,003	4,100 30
Britannia metal, manufactures of, not plated	Great Britain		5,467			
	Germany		1,632			
	United States		22,259		22,259	5,564 75
	Total		29,358		22,259	5,564 75

OF IMPORTS—*Continued.*

FOR HOME CONSUMPTION.

Preferential Tariff.			Surtax Tariff.			Total.		
Quantity.	Value.	Duty.	Quantity.	Value.	Duty.	Quantity.	Value.	Duty Collected.
	$	$ cts.		$	$ cts.		$	$ cts.
	2,599	606 48		2	0 93		3,102	782 76
							40	14 00
							3	1 05
							6	2 10
							798	279 30
				2	0 93		2	0 93
							2,362	826 70
							61	21 35
				4	1 88		67,670	23,684 98
	2,599	606 48		8	3 74		74,044	25,613 17
	471	94 20					556	119 70
							6	1 80
							6,246	1,873 80
	471	94 20					6,808	1,995 30
	263,834	61,562 39		2,085	973 00		302,160	75,219 74
							1,014	354 90
							30	10 50
				26	12 14		7,467	2,616 49
							135	47 25
							9	3 15
							450	157 50
							4,230	1,480 50
				8,619	4,022 20		8,634	4,027 45
							393	137 55
							300	105 00
							36	12 60
							11,685	4,089 75
							27,254	9,538 90
	263,834	61,562 39		10,730	5,007 34		363,797	97,801 28
	416	69 35		193	64 34		660	146 44
				1,425	475 00		5,526	1,500 25
							76	19 00
							4	1 00
							57	14 25
							17,316	4,329 00
	416	69 35		1,618	539 34		23,639	6,009 94
	18,659	1,243 94					19,284	1,306 44
							40,378	4,037 80
	18,659	1,243 94					59,662	5,344 24
	5,467	911 19					5,467	911 19
				1,632	544 02		1,632	544 02
							22,259	5,564 75
	5,467	911 19		1,632	544 02		29,358	7,019 96

No. 1.—GENERAL STATEMENT

Articles Imported.	Countries.	Total Imports.		Entered		
				General Tariff.		
		Quantity.	Value.	Quantity.	Value.	Duty.
DUTIABLE GOODS—*Con.*			$		$	$ cts.
Metals, N.E.S.—*Con.*						
Bronze statuettes or ornaments	Great Britain		93		41	14 35
	Aust.-Hungary		111		10	3 50
	France		3,060		3,060	1,071 00
	Germany		381			
	Holland		55		55	19 25
	Italy		98		98	34 30
	Japan		8		8	2 80
	United States		1,519		1,519	531 65
	Total		5,325		4,791	1,676 85
Buckles of iron, steel, brass or copper, of all kinds, N.O.P. (not being jewellery)	Great Britain		4,735		1,075	322 50
	France		1,459		1,459	437 70
	Germany		5,178		228	68 40
	Japan		25		25	7 50
	United States		27,207		26,983	8,094 90
	Total		38,604		29,770	8,931 00
Cages—Bird, parrot, squirrel and rat, of wire, and metal parts thereof	Japan		3		3	1 05
	United States		5,257		5,257	1,839 95
	Total		5,260		5,260	1,841 00
Composition metal for the manufacture of jewellery and filled gold watch cases.	France		68		68	6 80
	United States		6,235		6,235	623 50
	Total		6,303		6,303	630 30
Frames, clasps and fasteners for purses and chatelaine bags or reticules, not more than seven inches in width, imported by the manufacturers of purses and chatelaine bags or reticules for use in their factories	Great Britain		365			
	Germany		336			
	United States		16,684		16,684	3,336 80
	Total		17,385		16'684	3,336 80
Furniture springs	Great Britain		42			
	United States		11,635		11,635	3,490 50
	Total		11,677		11,635	3,490 50
Phosphor tin and phosphor bronze, in blocks, bars, plates, sheets and wire	Great Britain		727			
	Germany		208			
	United States		11,803		11,803	1,180 30
	Total		12,738		11,803	1,180 30
Garden or lawn sprinklers	United States		1,050		1,050	315 00

OF IMPORTS—*Continued.*

FOR HOME CONSUMPTION.

Preferential Tariff.			Surtax Tariff.			Total.		
Quantity.	Value.	Duty.	Quantity.	Value.	Duty.	Quantity.	Value.	Duty Collected.
	$	$ cts.		$	$ cts.		$	$ cts.
	52	12 14					93	26 49
				101	47 13		111	50 63
							3,060	1,071 00
				381	177 80		381	177 80
							55	19 25
							98	34 30
							8	2 80
							1,519	531 65
	52	12 14		482	224 93		5,325	1,913 92
	3,628	725 60		32	12 80		4,735	1,060 90
							1,459	437 70
				4,950	1,980 00		5,178	2,048 40
							25	7 50
				165	66 00		27,148	8,160 90
	3,628	725 60		5,147	2,058 80		38,545	11,715 40
							3	1 05
							5,257	1,839 95
							5,260	1,841 00
							68	6 80
							6,235	623 50
							6,303	630 30
				365	97 33		365	97 33
				336	89 60		336	89 60
							16,684	3,336 80
				701	186 93		17,385	3,523 73
	125	25 00					125	25 00
							11,635	3,490 50
	125	25 00					11,760	3,515 50
	727	48 48					727	48 48
				208	27 73		208	27 73
							11,803	1,180 30
	727	48 48		208	27 73		12,738	1,256 51
							1,050	315 00

No. 1.—General Statement

Articles Imported.	Countries.	Total Imports.		Entered		
				General Tariff.		
		Quantity.	Value.	Quantity.	Value.	Duty.
DUTIABLE GOODS—*Con.*			$		$	$ cts.
Metals, N.E.S.—*Con.*						
Gas, coal or other oil and electric light fixtures or parts thereof of metal, including lava or other tips, burners, collars, galleries, shades and shade holders..	Great Britain...		13,470		1,824	547 20
	Hong Kong.....		4		4	1 20
	Aust.-Hungary .		1,432		1,391	417 30
	France......		6,676		6,358	1,907 40
	Germany......		3,022		153	45 90
	Holland.......		11		11	3 30
	Italy.........		353		353	105 90
	Japan.......		5		5	1 50
	United States...		318,045		319,779	95,933 70
	Total.....		343,018		320,878	98,963 40
Gas mantels and incandescent gas burners...............	Great Britain...		472		13	3 90
	Germany		298			
	United States...		39,121		39,400	11,820 00
	Total......		39,891		39,413	11,823 90
		No.		No.		
Gas meters..	Great Britain...	654	6,721			
	United States...	1,812	34,055	1,812	34,055	11,919 25
	Total......	2,466	40,776	1,812	34,055	11,919 25
German, Nevada and nickel silver, manufactures of, not plated....................	Great Britain...		6,293		283	70 75
	France.......		270		270	67 50
	Germany......		265		187	46 75
	United States...		23,422		23,422	5,855 50
	Total		30,250		24,162	6,040 50
Lamp springs	United States...		2,727		2,727	272 70
Lamps, side lights, head lights, and lanterns	Great Britain...		11,038		1,104	331 20
	Hong Kong.....		425		425	127 50
	Newfoundland..		20		20	6 00
	Aust.-Hungary..		17,565		17,402	5,220 60
	China........		75		75	22 50
	France........		3,247		3,599	1,079 70
	Germany.......		6,752			
	Holland........		71		71	21 30
	Italy..........		125		125	37 50
	Japan.......		566		566	169 80
	United States...		326,661		326,181	97,854 30
	Total		366,545		349,568	104,870 40

OF IMPORTS—*Continued.*

FOR HOME CONSUMPTION.

Preferential Tariff.			Surtax Tariff.			Total.		
Quantity.	Value.	Duty.	Quantity.	Value.	Duty.	Quantity.	Value.	Duty Collected.
	$	$ cts.		$	$ cts.		$	$ cts.
	11,347	2,269 40		138	55 20		13,309	2,871 80
							4	1 20
				41	16 40		1,432	433 70
							6,358	1,907 40
				2,869	1,147 60		3,022	1,193 50
							11	3 30
							353	105 90
							5	1 50
				329	131 60		320,108	96,065 30
	11,347	2,269 40		3,377	1,350 80		344,602	102,583 60
	409	81 80		50	20 00		472	105 70
				298	119 20		298	119 20
							39,400	11,820 00
	409	81 80		348	139 20		40,170	12,044 90
No. 654	6,721	1,568 21	No.			No. 654	6,721	1,568 21
						1,812	34,055	11,919 25
654	6,721	1,568 21				2,466	40,776	13,487 46
	5,992	998 68		18	6 00		6,293	1,075 43
							270	67 50
				78	26 00		265	72 75
							23,422	5,855 50
	5,992	998 68		96	32 00		30,250	7,071 18
							2,727	272 70
	9,166	1,833 20		404	161 60		10,674	2,326 00
							425	127 50
							20	6 00
				163	65 20		17,565	5,285 80
							75	22 50
							3,599	1,079 70
				6,526	2,610 40		6,526	2,610 40
							71	21 30
							125	37 50
							566	169 80
				213	85 20		326,394	97,939 50
	9,166	1,833 20		7,306	2,922 40		366,040	109,626 00

No. 1.—General Statement

Articles Imported.	Countries.	Total Imports.		Entered		
				General Tariff.		
		Quantity.	Value.	Quantity.	Value.	Duty.
DUTIABLE GOODS—*Con.*			$		$	$ cts.
Metals, N.E.S—*Con.*						
Nickel-plated ware, N.E.S. . .	Great Britain . . .	. . . .	13,231	. . . .	835	250 50
	Aust.-Hungary . .	. . . .	379	. . . .	163	48 90
	France	. . . .	1,494	. . . .	1,340	402 00
	Germany	. . . .	4,149	. . . .	81	24 30
	Italy	. . . .	9	. . . .	9	2 70
	Japan	. . . .	374	. . . .	374	112 20
	Turkey	. . . .	9	. . . .	9	2 70
	United States . . .	. . . .	137,602	. . . .	137,464	41,239 20
	Total	. . . .	157,247	. . . .	140,275	42,082 50
Nickel anodes	Germany	. . . .	168	. . . .	. . . .	. . . .
	United States . . .	. . . .	15,808	. . . .	15,808	1,580 80
	Total	. . . .	15,976	. . . .	15,808	1,580 80
Patterns of brass, iron, steel or other metal	United States . . .	. . . .	4,436	. . . .	4,436	1,330 80
Pins, N.O.P.	Great Britain . . .	. . . .	65,749	. . . .	1,626	487 80
	Hong Kong	. . . .	6	. . . .	6	1 80
	Aust.-Hungary . .	. . . .	886	. . . .	603	180 90
	Belgium	. . . .	70	. . . .	70	21 00
	China	. . . .	7	. . . .	7	2 10
	France	. . . .	2,039	. . . .	2,036	610 80
	Germany	. . . .	7,133	. . . .	95	28 50
	Japan	. . . .	42	. . . .	42	12 60
	Switzerland	. . . .	302	. . . .	27	8 10
	United States . . .	. . . .	30,615	. . . .	30,556	9,166 80
	Total	. . . .	106,849	. . . .	35,068	10,520 40
Screws, brass or other metal, except iron or steel, N.O.P.	Great Britain . . .	. . . .	209	. . . .	. . . .	. . . .
	United States . . .	. . . .	6,094	. . . .	6,094	2,132 90
	Total	. . . .	6,303	. . . .	6,094	2,132 90
Stereotypes, electrotypes and celluloids for almanacs, calendars, illustrated pamphlets, newspaper advertisements or engravings, and all other like work for commercial, trade or other purposes, N.E.S., and matrices or copper shells for the same		Sq. in.		Sq. in.		
	Great Britain . . .	25,387	803	2,033	64	30 50
	France	192	11	192	11	2 87
	Germany	346	28	. . . .	. . . .	. . . .
	United States . . .	392,524	14,875	392,112	14,840	5,881 80
	Total	418,449	15,717	394,337	14,915	5,915 17
Stereotypes, electrotypes, and celluloids of newspaper columns, and bases for the same, composed wholly or partly of metal or celluloid	United States . . .	516,639	4,175	516,639	4,175	1,291 61
Stereotypes, matrices or copper shells for the same	United States . . .	706	50	706	50	10 59

OF IMPORTS—*Continued.*

FOR HOME CONSUMPTION.

Preferential Tariff.			Surtax Tariff.			Total.		
Quantity.	Value.	Duty.	Quantity.	Value.	Duty.	Quantity.	Value.	Duty Collected.
	$	$ cts.		$	$ cts.		$	$ cts.
....	12,034	2,406 80	....	362	144 80	....	13,231	2,802 10
....	....	....	....	216	86 40	....	379	135 30
....	....	....	....	....	....	....	1,340	402 00
....	....	....	....	4,068	1,627 20	....	4,149	1,651 50
....	....	....	....	....	....	....	9	2 70
....	....	....	....	....	....	....	374	112 20
....	....	....	....	....	....	....	9	2 70
....	....	....	....	151	60 40	....	137,615	41,299 60
....	12,034	2,406 80	....	4,797	1,918 80	....	157,106	46,408 10
....	....	....	....	168	22 40	....	168	22 40
....	....	....	....	....	....	....	15,808	1,580 80
....	....	....	....	168	22 40	....	15,976	1,603 20
....	....	....	....	....	....	....	4,436	1,330 80
....	63,587	12,717 40	....	597	238 80	....	65,810	13,444 00
....	....	....	....	....	....	....	6	1 80
....	....	....	....	283	113 20	....	886	294 10
....	....	....	....	....	....	....	70	21 00
....	....	....	....	....	....	....	7	2 10
....	....	....	....	3	1 20	....	2,039	612 00
....	....	....	....	7,020	2,808 00	....	7,115	2,836 50
....	....	....	....	....	....	....	42	12 60
....	....	....	....	275	110 00	....	302	118 10
....	....	....	....	59	23 60	....	30,615	9,190 40
....	63,587	12,717 40	....	8,237	3,294 80	....	106,892	26,532 60
....	209	48 77	....	....	....	....	209	48 77
....	....	....	....	....	....	....	6,094	2,132 90
....	209	48 77	....	....	....	....	6,303	2,181 67
Sq. in.			Sq. in.			Sq. in.		
23,354	739	233 54	....	....	....	25,387	803	264 04
....	....	....	....	....	....	192	11	2 87
....	....	....	346	28	6 92	346	28	6 92
....	....	....	26	2	0 52	392,138	14,842	5,882 32
23,354	739	233 54	372	30	7 44	418,063	15,684	6,156 15
....	....	....	....	....	....	516,639	4,175	1,291 61
....	....	....	....	....	....	706	50	10 59

No. 1.—General Statement

Articles Imported.	Countries.	Total Imports.		Entered		
				General Tariff.		
		Quantity.	Value.	Quantity.	Value.	Duty.
DUTIABLE GOODS—*Con.*			$		$	$ cts.
Metals, N.E.S.—*Con.*						
Type for printing, including chases, quoins and slugs of all kinds	Great Britain	.....	42,682	.....	158	31 60
	France	.....	92	.....	92	18 40
	Germany	.....	160	.....	.....	.....
	Japan	.....	35	.....	35	7 00
	United States	.....	72,113	.....	71,661	14,332 20
	Total	.....	115,082	.....	71,946	14,389 20
Type metal	Great Britain	.....	2,389	.....	248	24 80
	Newfoundland	.....	64	.....	64	6 40
	United States	.....	6,222	.....	6,222	622 20
	Total	.....	8,675	.....	6,534	653 40
Pewter, platina and metal composition, N.E.S	Great Britain	.....	489	.....	.....	.....
	Germany	.....	46	.....	.....	.....
	Japan	.....	137	.....	137	41 10
	United States	.....	2,044	.....	2,044	613 20
	Total	.....	2,716	.....	2,181	654 30
		Lbs.		Lbs.		
Wire of all kinds, N.O.P	Great Britain	4,307	736	.....	.....	.....
	France	132	194	132	194	38 80
	Germany	8,581	290	.....	.....	.....
	United States	52,676	11,831	50,999	11,528	2,305 60
	Total	65,696	13,051	51,131	11,722	2,344 40
Wire, twisted, &c., except iron or steel, N.E.S	Great Britain	.....	154	.....	.....	.....
	United States	.....	125	.....	125	31 25
	Total	.....	279	.....	125	31 25
Milk, condensed	Great Britain	83,056	2,345	1,836	337	59 67
	New Zealand	606	37	606	37	19 70
	Belgium	480	29	480	29	15 60
	Switzerland	3,573	216	2,233	138	72 55
	United States	100,534	7,195	69,723	4,828	2,265 91
	Total	188,249	9,822	74,878	5,369	2,433 43
Mineral substances, not otherwise provided for—						
Asbestus, in any form other than crude, and all manufactures of	Great Britain	.....	8,007	.....	249	62 25
	Aust.-Hungary	.....	821	.....	821	205 25
	France	.....	231	.....	231	57 75
	Germany	.....	6,250	.....	.....	.....
	United States	.....	122,691	.....	122,672	30,668 00
	Total	.....	138,000	.....	123,973	30,993 25

OF IMPORTS—*Continued.*

FOR HOME CONSUMPTION.

Preferential Tariff.			Surtax Tariff.			Total.		
Quantity.	Value.	Duty.	Quantity.	Value.	Duty.	Quantity.	Value.	Duty Collected.
	$	$ cts.		$	$ cts.		$	$ cts.
....	43,517	5,802 26	....	54	14 40	....	43,729	5,848 26
....	....	....	....	....	....	....	92	18 40
....	....	....	....	160	42 67	....	160	42 67
....	....	....	....	....	....	....	35	7 00
....	....	....	....	....	....	....	71,661	14,332 20
....	43,517	5,802 26	....	214	57 07	....	115,677	20,248 53
....	2,141	142 74	....	....	....	....	2,389	167 54
....	....	....	....	....	....	....	64	6 40
....	....	....	....	....	....	....	6,222	622 20
....	2,141	142 74	....	....	....	....	8,675	796 14
....	172	34 40	....	317	126 80	....	489	161 20
....	....	....	....	46	18 40	....	46	18 40
....	....	....	....	....	....	....	137	41 10
....	....	....	....	....	....	....	2,044	613 20
....	172	34 40	....	363	145 20	....	2,716	833 90
Lbs.			Lbs.			Lbs.		
4,307	736	98 16	....	....	....	4,307	736	98 16
....	....	....	....	....	....	132	194	38 80
....	....	....	8,581	290	77 35	8,581	290	77 35
....	....	....	47	30	8 00	51,046	11,558	2,313 60
4,307	736	98 16	8,628	320	85 35	64,066	12,778	2,527 91
....	154	25 67	....	....	....	....	154	25 67
....	....	....	....	....	....	....	125	31 25
....	154	25 67	....	....	....	....	279	56 92
37,627	2,618	815 29	....	....	....	39,463	2,955	874 96
....	....	....	....	....	....	606	37	19 70
....	....	....	....	....	....	480	29	15 60
....	....	....	....	....	....	2,233	138	72 55
....	....	....	....	....	....	69,723	4,828	2,265 91
37,627	2,618	815 29	....	....	....	112,505	7,987	3,248 72
....	7,697	1,282 93	....	....	....	....	7,946	1,345 18
....	....	....	....	....	....	....	821	205 25
....	....	....	....	....	....	....	231	57 75
....	....	....	....	6,250	2,083 33	....	6,250	2,083 33
....	....	....	....	54	18 00	....	122,726	30,686 00
....	7,697	1,282 93	....	6,304	2,101 33	....	137,974	34,377 51

No. 1.—General Statement

Articles Imported.	Countries.	Total Imports.		Entered		
				General Tariff.		
		Quantity.	Value.	Quantity	Value.	Duty.
DUTIABLE GOODS—*Con.*			$		$	$ cts.
Mineral substances—*Con.* Blacklead	Great Britain		8,370		560	140 00
	United States		25,634		25,575	6,393 75
	Total		34,004		26,135	6,533 75
Mineral and bituminous substances, not otherwise provided for	Great Britain		13,735		670	134 00
	B. E. Indies		49		49	9 80
	Aust.-Hungary		120		120	24 00
	Belgium		539		539	107 80
	Denmark		69		69	13 80
	France				3	0 60
	Germany		7,671			
	Japan		29		29	5 80
	United States		55,219		55,345	11,069 00
	Total		77,431		56,824	11,364 80
Plumbago, not ground or otherwise manufactured	Aust.-Hungary		609		609	60 90
	United States		2,182		2,182	218 20
	Total		2,791		2,791	279 10
Plumbago, ground, and manufactures of, N.E.S.	Great Britain		3,139			
	United States		15,935		16,009	4,002 25
	Total		19,074		16,009	4,002 25
Mineral and aerated waters, N.E.S.	Great Britain		19,528		1,665	333 00
	Australia				36	7 20
	Aust.-Hungary		4,138		3,951	790 20
	Belgium		1,066		423	84 60
	Denmark		1		1	0 20
	France		56,866		54.539	10,907 80
	Germany		21,376		454	90 80
	Holland		482		15	3 00
	Italy		23		23	4 60
	Japan		563		600	120 00
	Spain		507		103	20 60
	Sweden		2		2	0 40
	United States		73,531		75,260	15,052 00
	Total		178,083		137,072	27,414 40
Mosaic flooring of any material	Great Britain		389			
	France		104		206	61 80
	Italy		348		348	104 40
	United States		11,648		11,741	3,522 30
	Total		12,489		12,295	3,688 50
Mucilage	Great Britain		1,059		11	2 75
	France		2		2	0 50
	United States		22,853		22,853	5,713 25
	Total		23,914		22,866	5,716 50

OF IMPORTS—*Continued.*

FOR HOME CONSUMPTION.

Preferential Tariff.			Surtax Tariff.			Total.		
Quantity.	Value.	Duty.	Quantity.	Value.	Duty.	Quantity.	Value.	Duty Collected.
	$	$ cts.		$	$ cts.		$	$ cts.
	7,772	1,295 40					8,332	1,435 40
							25,575	6,393 75
	7,772	1,295 40					33,907	7,829 15
	12,539	1,671 90		511	136 27		13,720	1,942 17
							49	9 80
							120	24 00
							539	107 80
							69	13 80
							3	0 60
				7,671	2,045 62		7,671	2,045 62
							29	5 80
				149	39 73		55,494	11,108 73
	12,539	1,671 90		8,331	2,221 62		77,694	15,258 32
							609	60 90
							2,182	218 20
							2,791	279 10
	3,049	508 16					3,049	508 16
							16,009	4,002 25
	3,049	508 16					19,058	4,510 41
	9,557	1,274 34		8,754	2,334 40		19,976	3,941 74
							36	7 20
				187	49 87		4,138	840 07
				129	34 40		552	119 00
							1	0 20
							54,539	10,907 80
				21,171	5,645 62		21,625	5,736 42
							15	3 00
							23	4 60
							600	120 00
							103	20 60
							2	0 40
				15	4 00		75,275	15,056 00
	9,557	1,274 34		30,256	8,068 29		176,885	36,757 03
	389	77 80					389	77 80
							206	61 80
							348	104 40
							11,741	3,522 30
	389	77 80					12,684	3,766 30
	1,062	177 04					1,073	179 79
							2	0 50
							22,853	5,713 25
	1,062	177 04					23,928	5,893 54

No. 1.—GENERAL STATEMENT

Articles Imported.	Countries.	Total Imports.		Entered		
				General Tariff.		
		Quantity.	Value.	Quantity.	Value.	Duty.
DUTIABLE GOODS—*Con.*			$		$	$ cts.
Musical instruments, viz.—						
Brass band instruments	Great Britain...	....	13,081	....	449	112 25
	Australia..	....	7	... .	7	1 75
	Hong Kong.....	....	6	....	6	1 50
	Aust.-Hungary.	....	3,847	....	4,188	1,047 00
	Belgium........	....	69	....	69	17 25
	France.........	....	9,196	....	9,148	2,287 00
	Germany.......	....	1,785	....	137	34 25
	United States...	.. ..	10,543	....	10,469	2,617 25
	Total......	....	38,534	....	24,473	6,118 25
		No.		No.		
Cabinet organs............	Great Britain...	3	78	2	41	12 30
	Germany.......	5	327	....	....	....
	United States...	276	18,024	276	18,024	5,407 20
	Total......	284	18,429	278	18,065	5,419 50
Pipe organs.................	United States...	1	750	1	750	225 00
Parts of organs	Great Britain...	....	563	....	35	8 75
	United States...	....	21,979	....	21,979	5,494 75
	Total......	... .	22,542	....	22,014	5,503 50
Pianofortes	Great Britain...	30	4,572	12	2,130	639 00
	Germany.......	4	1,022	....	....	....
	United States...	782	168,734	781	168,634	50,590 20
	Total.. ...	816	174,328	793	170,764	51,229 20
Pianos, parts of....	Great Britain...	....	882	.... . .	882	220 50
	France.........	....	1,483	....	1,483	370 75
	Germany.......	....	5,390	.... ..	....	....
	United States...	....	144,002	....	143,991	35,997 75
	Total	....	151,757	....	146,356	36,589 00
Other musical instruments, N.E.S....................	Great Britain...	....	6,694	.. ..	2,287	686 10
	Australia.......	....	9	....	9	2 70
	British Africa..	....	3	....	3	0 90
	Hong Kong.....	... .	153	....	153	45 90
	Aust.-Hungary.	....	3,594	....	2,877	863 10
	Belgium........	....	3	....	3	0 90
	China	....	146	....	146	43 80
	France.........	....	2,737	....	2,602	780 60
	Germany.......	.. ..	63,772	.. . .	695	208 50
	Italy...........	....	101	....	101	30 30
	Japan	....	141	. ...	141	42 30
	United States...	....	49,695	....	48,504	14,551 20
	Total	....	127,048	....	57,521	17,256 30

OF IMPORTS—*Continued.*

FOR HOME CONSUMPTION.

Preferential Tariff.			Surtax Tariff.			Total.		
Quantity.	Value.	Duty.	Quantity.	Value.	Duty.	Quantity.	Value.	Duty Collected.
	$	$ cts.		$	$ cts.		$	$ cts.
....	11,517	1,919 56	....	231	77 00	....	12,197	2,108 81
....	....	....	....	....	....	....	7	1 75
....	....	....	....	....	....	....	6	1 50
....	....	....	....	....	....	....	4,188	1,047 00
....	....	....	....	....	....	....	69	17 25
....	....	....	....	48	16 00	....	9,196	2,303 00
....	....	....	....	1,665	555 00	....	1,802	589 25
....	....	....	....	34	11 34	....	10,503	2,628 59
....	11,517	1,919 56	....	1,978	659 34	....	37,968	8,697 15
No.			No.			No.		
1	37	7 40	....	....	....	3	78	19 70
....	....	....	5	327	130 80	5	327	130 80
....	....	....	....	....	....	276	18,024	5,407 20
1	37	7 40	5	327	130 80	284	18,429	5,557 70
....	....	....	....	....	....	1	750	225 00
....	528	88 00	....	....	....	....	563	96 75
....	....	....	....	....	....	....	21,979	5,494 75
....	528	88 00	....	....	....	....	22,542	5,591 50
16	1,921	384 20	1	321	128 40	29	4,372	1,151 60
....	....	....	4	1,022	408 80	4	1,022	408 80
....	....	....	....	....	....	781	168,634	50,590 20
16	1,921	384 20	5	1,343	537 20	814	174,028	52,150 60
....	....	....	....	....	....	....	882	220 50
....	....	....	....	....	....	....	1,483	370 75
....	....	....	....	5,390	1,796 66	....	5,390	1,796 66
....	....	....	....	11	3 67	....	144,002	36,001 42
....	....	....	....	5,401	1,800 33	....	151,757	38,389 33
....	2,643	528 60	....	1,764	705 60	....	6,694	1,920 30
....	....	....	....	....	....	....	9	2 70
....	....	....	....	....	....	....	3	0 90
....	....	....	....	....	....	....	153	45 90
....	....	....	....	1,137	454 80	....	4,014	1,317 90
....	....	....	....	....	....	....	3	0 90
....	....	....	....	....	....	....	146	43 80
....	....	....	....	135	54 00	....	2,737	834 60
....	....	....	....	65,549	26,219 60	....	66,244	26,428 10
....	....	....	....	....	....	....	101	30 30
....	....	....	....	....	....	....	141	42 30
....	....	....	....	1,001	400 40	....	49,505	14,951 60
....	2,643	528 60	....	69,586	27,834 40	....	129,750	45,619 30

No. 1.—General Statement

Articles Imported.	Countries.	Total Imports.		Entered		
				General Tariff.		
		Quantity.	Value.	Quantity.	Value.	Duty.
DUTIABLE GOODS—*Con.*		Lbs.	$	Lbs.	$	$ cts.
Mustard, ground	Great Britain	364,939	91,040	436	104	26 00
	France	708	42	708	42	10 50
	United States	262,922	15,695	264,194	15,842	3,960 50
	Total	628,569	106,777	265,338	15,988	3,997 00
Mustard, French, liquid	Great Britain	....	89	....	89	31 15
	France	....	588	....	581	203 35
	United States	....	7,405	....	6,920	2,422 00
Oils— Mineral—	Total	....	8,082	....	7,590	2,656 50
Coal and kerosene, distilled, purified or refined, naphtha, and petroleum, N.E.S		Galls.		Galls.		
	Great Britain	8,557	1,936	1,829	257	45 72
	United States	9,217,004	806,661	9,246,643	810,290	231,166 85
	Total	9,225,561	808,597	9,248,472	810,547	231,212 57
Products of petroleum, N.E.S	Great Britain	2,713	763	25	15	0 67
	Belgium	849	342	849	342	21 22
	United States	1,727,336	180,824	1,629,772	175,984	40,744 42
	Total	1,730,898	181,929	1,630,646	176,341	40,766 31
Crude petroleum, gas oils other than benzine and gasoline	United States	21,383	1,405	19,680	1,282	295 21
Illuminating oils composed wholly or in part of the products of petroleum, coal, shale or lignite, costing more than thirty cents per gallon	Great Britain	179	103	....	....	....
	France	229	158	229	158	31 60
	United States	3,361	1,336	3,128	1,229	245 80
	Total	3,769	1,597	3,357	1,387	277 40
Animal— Lard oil	United States	12,829	6,420	12,600	6,337	1,584 25
Neatsfoot	Great Britain	31	23	....	....	....
	United States	23,282	17,714	23,282	17,714	4,428 50
	Total	23,313	17,737	23,282	17,714	4,428 50
Other animal oil, N.E.S	Great Britain	12	21	....	....	....
	Norway	250	177	250	177	35 40
	United States	5,358	2,434	5,182	2,414	482 80
	Total	5,620	2,632	5,432	2,591	518 20
Vegetable— Castor	Great Britain	87,544	40,291	711	483	96 60
	France	494	414	392	349	69 80
	Italy	1,243	1,053	1,391	1,150	230 00
	United States	1,743	1,004	1,654	922	184 40
	Total	91,024	42,762	4,148	2,904	580 80

OF IMPORTS—*Continued.*

FOR HOME CONSUMPTION.

Preferential Tariff.			Surtax Tariff.			Total.		
Quantity.	Value.	Duty.	Quantity.	Value.	Duty.	Quantity.	Value.	Duty Collected.
Lbs.	$	$ cts.	Lbs.	$	$ cts.	Lbs.	$	$ cts.
373,233	93,986	15,664 51				373,669	94,090	15,690 51
						708	42	10 50
						264,194	15,842	3,960 50
373,233	93,986	15,664 51				638,571	109,974	19,661 51
							89	31 15
							581	203 35
							6,920	2,422 00
							7,590	2,656 50
Galls.			Galls.			Galls.		
6,728	1,679	112 16				8,557	1,936	157 88
						9,246,643	810,290	231,166 85
6,728	1,679	112 16				9,255,200	812,226	231,324 73
2,663	728	44 39				2,688	743	45 06
						849	342	21 22
						1,629,772	175,984	40,744 42
2,663	728	44 39				1,633,309	177,069	40,810 70
						19,680	1,282	295 21
179	103	13 73				179	103	13 73
						229	158	31 60
						3,128	1,229	245 80
179	103	13 73				3,536	1,490	291 13
						12,600	6,337	1,584 25
31	23	3 83				31	23	3 83
						23,282	17 714	4,428 50
31	23	3 83				23,313	17,737	4,432 33
12	21	2 80				12	21	2 80
						250	177	35 40
						5,182	2,414	482 80
12	21	2 80				5,444	2,612	521 00
87,361	40,000	5,333 42				88,072	40,483	5,430 02
						392	349	69 80
						1,391	1,150	230 00
						1,654	922	184 40
87,361	40,000	5,333 42				91,509	42,904	5,914 22

No. 1.—General Statement

Articles Imported.	Countries.	Total Imports.		Entered		
				General Tariff.		
		Quantity.	Value.	Quantity.	Value.	Duty.
DUTIABLE GOODS—*Con.*		Galls.	$	Galls.	$	$ cts.
Oils—*Con.*						
Vegetable—*Con.*						
Cotton seed	Great Britain	24,586	7,874	....	....	....
	China	30	43	30	43	8 60
	Italy	4,835	1,915	4,835	1,915	383 00
	Norway	625	475	625	475	95 00
	United States	1,092,101	310,268	1,070,445	309,444	61,888 80
	Total	1,122,177	320,575	1,075,935	311,877	62,375 40
Flaxseed or linseed, raw or boiled	Great Britain	1,058,312	392,797	15,879	5,827	1,456 75
	United States	126,403	51,640	126,403	51,640	12,910 00
	Total	1,184,715	444,437	142,282	57,467	14,366 75
Olive, N.E.S.	Great Britain	11,179	16,543	2,182	2,173	434 60
	Belgium	360	351	365	411	82 20
	China	26	21	26	21	4 20
	France	31,659	35,139	31,000	33,950	6,790 00
	Greece	36	35	36	35	7 00
	Holland	2	3	2	3	0 60
	Italy	10,687	10,977	12,951	12,902	2,580 40
	Spain	625	1,006	475	631	126 20
	Turkey	186	104	186	104	20 80
	United States	13,089	11,690	13,330	11,511	2,302 20
	Total	67,849	75,869	60,553	61,741	12,348 20
Sesame seed	Hong Kong	89	29	89	29	7 25
	China	108	41	108	41	10 25
	Japan	45	31	45	31	7 75
	United States	410	342	410	342	85 50
	Total	652	443	652	443	110 75
Vegetable oil, not otherwise specified	Great Britain	9,460	6,211	1,046	631	126 20
	Australia	480	286	480	286	57 20
	Hong Kong	12,191	8,900	12,191	8,900	1,780 00
	Belgium	900	661	900	661	132 20
	China	36,751	22,491	36,751	22,491	4,498 20
	France	200	106	200	106	21 20
	Germany	78	49	....	....	....
	Japan	472	241	472	241	48 20
	Switzerland	30	22	30	22	4 40
	United States	34,303	13,153	30,636	12,098	2,419 60
	Total	94,865	52,120	82,706	45,436	9,087 20
Lubricating oils composed wholly or in part of petroleum and costing less than 25 cts. per gallon	Great Britain	8,281	1,500	8,281	1,500	207 03
	United States	1,907,861	248,518	1,898,748	247,438	47,469 16
	Total	1,916,142	250,018	1,907,029	248,938	47,676 19

OF IMPORTS—*Continued.*

FOR HOME CONSUMPTION.

Preferential Tariff.			Surtax Tariff.			Total.		
Quantity.	Value.	Duty.	Quantity.	Value.	Duty.	Quantity.	Value.	Duty Collected.
Galls.	$	$ cts.	Galls.	$	$ cts.	Galls.	$	$ cts.
24,729	7,939	1,058 54				24,729	7,939	1,058 54
						30	43	8 60
						4,835	1,915	383 00
						625	475	95 00
						1,070,445	309,444	61,888 80
24,729	7,939	1,058 54				1,100,664	319,816	63,433 94
1,027,730	381,470	63,578 44				1,043,609	387,297	65,035 19
						126,403	51,640	12,910 00
1,027,730	381,470	63,578 44				1,170,012	438,937	77,945 19
8,506	13,132	1,751 27				10,688	15,305	2,185 87
						365	411	82 20
						26	21	4 20
						31,000	33,950	6,790 00
						36	35	7 00
						2	3	0 60
						12,951	12,902	2,580 40
						475	631	126 20
						186	104	20 80
						13,330	11,511	2,302 20
8,506	13,132	1,751.27				69,059	74,873	14,099 47
						89	29	7 25
						108	41	10 25
						45	31	7 75
						410	342	85 50
						652	443	110 75
8,109	5,400	720 06				9,155	6,031	846 26
						480	286	57 20
						12,191	8,900	1,780 00
						900	661	132 20
						36,751	22,491	4,498 20
						200	106	21 20
			78	49	13 07	78	49	13 07
						472	241	48 20
						30	22	4 40
			3,152	844	225 07	33,788	12,942	2,644 67
8,109	5,400	720 06	3,230	893	238 14	94,045	51,729	10,045 40
						8,281	1,500	207 03
						1,898,748	247,438	47,469 16
						1,907,029	248,938	47,676 19

No. 1.—General Statement

Articles Imported.	Countries.	Total Imports.		Entered		
				General Tariff.		
		Quantity.	Value.	Quantity.	Value.	Duty.
DUTIABLE GOODS—*Con.*		Galls.		Galls.	$	$ cts.
Oils—Con.						
All other lubricating oils, N.E.S.	Great Britain	44,304	16,337	1,865	602	120 40
	Belgium	38	82	38	82	16 40
	Germany	169	86	....	....	....
	United States	341,156	127,999	319,136	120,215	24,043 00
	Total	385,667	144,504	321,039	120,899	24,179 80
		Lbs.		Lbs.		
Essential	Great Britain	8,301	7,846	3,335	2,610	261 00
	B. E. Indies	1,108	359	1,108	359	35 90
	Hong Kong	1	1	1	1	0 10
	Belgium	75	218	75	218	21 80
	China	462	42	462	42	4 20
	France	3,347	7,232	3,348	7,236	723 60
	Germany	3,350	2,226	....	....	....
	Italy	6,128	4,188	6,128	4,188	418 80
	Japan	65	65	65	C5	6 50
	Spain	260	130	260	130	13 00
	Switzerland	1,726	1,291	1,201	1,153	115 30
	United States	137,376	106,282	132,510	103,772	10,377 20
	Total	162,199	129,880	148,493	119,774	11,977 40
		Galls.		Galls.		
All other oils, not elsewhere specified	Great Britain	7,585	3,183	....	....	....
	China	9,981	4,697	9,981	4,697	939 40
	France	9	13	9	13	2 60
	Germany	3,598	2,028	....	....	....
	United States	36,870	14,977	36,266	14,827	2,965 40
	Total	58,043	24,898	46,256	19,537	3,907 40
Oiled silk and cloth, and tape or other textile, india-rubbered, flocked or coated, N.O.P.	Great Britain	....	20,518	....	1,255	376 50
	France	....	194	....	194	58 20
	Germany	....	186	....	....	....
	United States	....	156,402	....	156,477	46,943 10
	Total	....	177,300	....	157,926	47,377 80
		Sq. yds.		Sq. yds.		
Oil cloth, enamelled carriage, floor, shelf and table oil cloth, cork matting or carpets and linoleum	Great Britain	2,331,931	708,134	5,028	2,235	670 50
	Belgium	2,924	299	3,069	373	111 90
	Germany	333	244	....	....	....
	United States	151,306	27,129	150,385	26,730	8,019 00
	Total	2,486,494	735,806	158,482	29,338	8,801 40
Optical, philosophical, photographic and mathematical instruments, N.E.S.	Great Britain	....	38,052	....	3,323	830 75
	Aust.-Hungary	....	88	....	86	21 50
	Belgium	....	24	....	....	....
	France	....	28,932	....	28,916	7,229 00
	Germany	....	15,604	....	....	....
	Holland	....	221	....	221	55 25
	Japan	....	10	....	10	2 50
	Switzerland	....	457	....	457	114 25
	United States	....	209,742	....	206,343	51,585 75
	Total	....	293,130	....	239,356	59,839 00

SESSIONAL PAPER No. 11

OF IMPORTS—*Continued.*

FOR HOME CONSUMPTION.

Preferential Tariff.			Surtax Tariff.			Total.		
Quantity.	Value.	Duty.	Quantity.	Value.	Duty.	Quantity.	Value.	Duty Collected.
Galls.	$	$ cts.	Galls.	$	$ cts.	Galls.	$	$ cts.
17,936	6,780	904 09				19,801	7,382	1,024 49
						38	82	16 40
			169	86	22 93	169	86	22 93
						319,136	120,215	24,043 00
17,936	6,780	904 09	169	86	22 93	339,144	127,765	25,106 82
Lbs.			Lbs.			Lbs.		
4,386	4,514	300 93	580	722	96 27	8,301	7,846	658 20
						1,108	359	35 90
						1	1	0 10
						75	218	21 80
						462	42	4 20
						3,348	7,236	723 60
			3,350	2,226	296 80	3,350	2,226	296 80
						6,128	4,188	418 80
						65	65	6 50
						260	130	13 00
						1,201	1,153	115 30
			4,864	2,410	321 38	137,374	106,182	10,698 58
4,386	4,514	300 93	8,794	5,358	714 45	161,673	129,646	12,992 78
Galls.			Galls.			Galls.		
7,333	3,145	419 35				7,333	3,145	419 35
						9,981	4,697	939 40
						9	13	2 60
			3,598	2,028	540 80	3,598	2,028	540 80
						36,266	14,827	2,965 40
7,333	3,145	419 35	3,598	2,028	540 80	57,187	24,710	4,867 55
	19,241	3,848 20		22	8 80		20,518	4,233 50
							194	58 20
				186	74 40		186	74 40
				67	26 80		156,544	46,969 90
	19,241	3,848 20		275	110 00		177,442	51,336 00
Sq. yds.			Sq. yds.			Sq. yds.		
2,323,172	707,899	141,579 80	450	165	66 00	2,328,650	710,299	142,316 30
						3,069	373	111 90
			333	244	97 60	333	244	97 60
						150,385	26,730	8,019 00
2,323,172	707,899	141,579 80	783	409	163 60	2,482,437	737,646	150,544 80
	33,298	5,549 99		1,278	426 00		37,899	6,806 74
				2	0 66		88	22 16
				24	8 00		24	8 00
				6	2 00		28,922	7,231 00
				15,602	5,200 70		15,602	5,200 70
							221	55 25
							10	2 50
							457	114 25
				1,737	579 00		208,080	52,164 75
	33,298	5,549 99		18,649	6,216 36		291,303	71,605 35

No. 1.—General Statement

Articles Imported.	Countries.	Total Imports.		Entered		
				General Tariff.		
		Quantity.	Value.	Quantity.	Value.	Duty.
DUTIABLE GOODS—*Con.*			$		$	$ cts.
Optical, &c.—*Con.*						
Spectacles and eye-glasses ...	Great Britain...		258		214	64 20
	Aust.-Hungary.		32		32	9 60
	China		3		3	0 90
	France		1,694		1,694	508 20
	Germany		297			
	Japan		1		1	0 30
	United States...		12,994		12,991	3,897 30
	Total		15,279		14,935	4,480 50
" " frames and metal parts of	Great Britain...		12		12	2 40
	France		250		250	50 00
	United States...		46,695		46,639	9,327 80
	Total		46,957		46,901	9,380 20
Packages	Great Britain		308,092		230,465	46,093 00
	Australia		314		293	58 60
	B. E. Indies...		1,038		106	21 20
	B. W. Indies		4,100		1,783	356 60
	British Guiana..		2,688		3,122	624 40
	Fiji		2		2	0 40
	Hong Kong		6,974		6,988	1,397 60
	Newfoundland..		5		5	1 00
	New Zealand		109			
	Arabia		42		42	8 40
	Aust.-Hungary		1,353		1,555	311 00
	Belgium		221		218	43 60
	Brazil		1,037		1,051	210 20
	Cent. Am. States		260		266	53 20
	China		8,778		8,880	1,776 00
	Cuba		6		23	4 60
	Dan. W. Indies.				2	0 40
	Denmark		2		12	2 40
	Dutch E. Indies		10		8	1 60
	Egypt		9		9	1 80
	France		134,407		130,567	26,113 40
	Germany		3,280		281	56 20
	Greece		15,264		16,146	3,229 20
	Hawaii		54		54	10 80
	Holland		159,201		166,696	33,339 20
	Italy		2,154		2,284	456 80
	Japan		6,153		5,926	1,185 20
	Mexico		19		19	3 80
	Norway		119		89	17 80
	Peru		2		2	0 40
	Portugal		26		76	15 20
	Roumania		6		6	1 20
	Russia		17		20	4 00
	Spain		38,469		38,822	7,764 40
	St. Pierre		63		68	13 60
	Sweden		120		111	22 20
	Switzerland		97		84	16 80
	Turkey		2,775		2,893	578 60
	United States..		248,394		240,357	48,071 40
	Venezuela		77		77	15 40
	Total		945,737		859,408	171,881 60

OF IMPORTS—*Continued.*

FOR HOME CONSUMPTION.

Preferential Tariff			Surtax Tariff.			Total.		
Quantity.	Value.	Duty.	Quantity.	Value.	Duty.	Quantity.	Value.	Duty Collected.
	$	$ cts.		$	$ cts.		$	$ cts.
	50	10 00					264	74 20
							32	9 60
							3	0 90
							1,694	508 20
				297	118 80		297	118 80
							1	0 30
				3	1 20		12,994	3,898 50
	50	10 00		300	120 00		15,285	4,610 50
							12	2 40
							250	50 00
				56	14 94		46,695	9,342 74
				56	14 94		46,957	9,395 14
	66,261	8,836 05		4	1 07		296,730	54,930 12
							293	58 60
	885	118 00					991	139 20
	1,842	245 60					3,625	602 20
	2	0 27					3,124	624 67
							2	0 40
							6,988	1,397 60
							5	1 00
	115	15 33					115	15 33
							42	8 40
				3	0 80		1,558	311 80
							218	43 60
							1,051	210 20
							266	53 20
							8,880	1,776 00
							23	4 60
							2	0 40
							12	2 40
							8	1 60
							9	1 80
				2	0 53		130,569	26,113 93
				3,347	892 57		3,628	948 77
							16,146	3,229 20
							54	10 80
							166,696	33,339 20
							2,284	456 80
							5,926	1,185 20
							19	3 80
							89	17 80
							2	0 40
							76	15 20
							6	1 20
							20	4 00
							38,822	7,764 40
							68	13 60
							111	22 20
							84	16 80
							2,893	578 60
				328	87 50		240,685	48,158 90
							77	15 40
	69,105	9,215 25		3,684	982 47		932,197	182,079 32

No. 1.—General Statement

Articles Imported.	Countries.	Total Imports.		Entered		
				General Tariff.		
		Quantity.	Value.	Quantity.	Value.	Duty.
DUTIABLE GOODS—*Con.*			$		$	$ cts.
Paints and colours—						
Brocade and bronze powders and gold liquid paint	Great Britain...	....	1,448	....	18	4 50
	China........	....	6	....	6	1 50
	Germany......	....	26,636	....	15	3 75
	United States...	....	14,324	....	11,560	2,890 00
	Total......	....	42,414	....	11,599	2,899 75
		Lbs.		Lbs.		
Colours, dry, N.E.S.........	Great Britain...	321,143	23,275	16,886	1,407	281 40
	Aust.-Hungary.	628	132	628	132	26 40
	France.........	7,610	599	7,610	599	119 80
	Germany.......	258,120	8,234	....	....	....
	Holland.......	4,154	1,109	3,855	679	135 80
	Switzerland.....	373	725	373	725	145 00
	United States...	1,822,452	105,635	1,809,255	104,819	20,963 80
	Total.......	2,414,480	139,709	1,838,607	108,361	21,672 20
Dry white lead.	Great Britain...	4,981,186	214,071	200	11	0 65
	Belgium........	367,885	12,678	288,600	9,664	574 91
	France.........	2,257	101	2,257	101	6 00
	Germany.......	1,687,539	49,939	....	....	....
	United States...	1,209,190	59,353	1,209,190	59,353	3,538 14
	Total.......	8,248,057	336,142	1,500,247	69,129	4,119 70
White lead ground in oil	Great Britain..	253,741	11,650	4,125	229	80 15
	United States...	17,179	883	17,179	883	309 05
	Total	270,920	12,533	21,304	1,112	389 20
Red lead and orange mineral	Great Britain...	842,546	34,947	21,266	544	27 20
	Belgium........	65,880	3,143	65,880	3,143	157 15
	Germany.......	707,976	16,065	....	....	....
	United States...	277,512	14,614	274,212	14,449	722 45
	Total.......	1,893,914	68,769	361,358	18,136	906 80
Ochres, ochrey earths and raw siennas..	Great Britain...	298,754	5,282	53,791	575	115 00
	France.........	371,609	3,348	371,609	3,348	669 60
	Germany.......	30,266	685	....	....	....
	Italy..........	1,713	95	1,713	95	19 00
	United States...	1,060,340	14,380	1,060,340	14,380	2,876 00
	Total.....	1,762,682	23,790	1,487,453	18,398	3,679 60
Zinc white........	Great Britain...	962,459	31,727	233,160	11,116	555 80
	Aust.-Hungary..	119,850	5,970	119,850	5,970	298 50
	Belgium........	423,844	18,622	423,844	18,622	931 10
	Germany......	599,978	25,850	....	....	....
	Holland........	84,810	4,143	84,810	4,143	207 15
	United States...	2,713,363	111,751	2,710,712	111,545	5,577 25
	Total.....	4,904,304	198,063	3,572,376	151,396	7,569 80

OF IMPORTS—*Continued.*

FOR HOME CONSUMPTION.

Preferential Tariff.			Surtax Tariff.			Total.		
Quantity.	Value.	Duty.	Quantity.	Value.	Duty.	Quantity.	Value.	Duty Collected.
	$	$ cts.		$	$ cts.		$	$ cts.
...	1,342	223 68	...	88	29 34	...	1,448	257 52
...	...	...	...	...	...	...	6	1 50
...	...	...	...	26,823	8,941 00	...	26,838	8,944 75
...	...	...	...	2,577	859 00	...	14,137	3,749 00
...	1,342	223 68	...	29,488	9,829 34	...	42,429	12,952 77
Lbs. 303,512	21,728	2,897 13	Lbs. 745	140	37 33	Lbs. 321,143	23,275	3,215 86
...	...	...	...	...	...	628	132	26 40
...	...	...	...	...	...	7,610	599	119 80
...	...	...	247,694	7,503	2,000 80	247,694	7,503	2,000 80
...	...	...	...	...	...	3,855	679	135 80
...	...	...	...	...	...	373	725	145 00
...	...	...	13,197	816	217 63	1,822,452	105,635	21,181 43
303,512	21,728	2,897 13	261,636	8,459	2,255 76	2,403,755	138,548	26,825 09
4,980,986	214,060	37,829 51	...	...	...	4,981,186	214,071	37,830 16
...	...	...	79,285	3,014	271 26	367,885	12,678	846 17
...	...	...	...	...	...	2,257	101	6 00
...	...	...	1,687,539	49,939	4,363 61	1,687,539	49,939	4,363 61
...	...	...	...	...	...	1,209,190	59,353	3,538 14
4,980,986	214,060	37,829 51	1,766,824	52,953	4,634 87	8,248,057	336,142	46,584 08
249,616	11,421	2,638 78	...	...	...	253,741	11,650	2,718 93
...	...	...	...	...	...	17,179	883	309 05
249,616	11,421	2,638 78	...	...	...	270,920	12,533	3,027 98
818,580	34,185	1,139 46	2,700	218	14 53	842,546	34,947	1,181 19
...	...	...	...	...	...	65,880	3,143	157 15
...	...	...	707,976	16,065	1,071 00	707,976	16,065	1,071 00
...	...	...	3,300	165	11 00	277,512	14,614	733 45
818,580	34,185	1,139 46	713,976	16,448	1,096 53	1,893,914	68,769	3,142 79
244,963	4,707	627 64	...	...	...	298,754	5,282	742 64
...	...	...	...	...	...	371,609	3,348	669 60
...	...	...	30,266	685	182 65	30,266	685	182 65
...	...	...	...	...	...	1,713	95	19 00
...	...	...	...	...	...	1,060,340	14,380	2,876 00
244,963	4,707	627 64	30,266	685	182 65	1,762,682	23,790	4,489 89
729,309	20,611	687 06	...	...	...	962,469	31,727	1,242 86
...	...	...	...	...	...	119,850	5,970	298 50
...	...	...	...	...	...	423,844	18,622	931 10
...	...	...	599,978	25,850	1,723 33	599,978	25,850	1,723 33
...	...	...	...	...	...	84,810	4,143	207 15
...	...	...	2,651	206	13 70	2,713,363	111,751	5,590 95
729,309	20,611	687 06	602,629	26,056	1,737 03	4,904,314	198,063	9,993 89

No. 1.—GENERAL STATEMENT

Articles Imported.	Countries.	Total Imports.		Entered		
				General Tariff.		
		Quantity.	Value.	Quantity.	Value.	Duty.
DUTIABLE GOODS—*Con.*		Lbs.	$	Lbs.	$	$ cts.
Paints and colours—*Con.* Oxides, fire proofs, umbers and burnt siennas, N.E.S.	Great Britain	896,035	18,229	86,317	2,986	746 50
	France	776	179	776	179	44 75
	Germany	68,383	1,176	6,760	330	82 50
	Italy	12,270	142	12,270	142	35 50
	United States	1,583,325	13,878	1,581,384	13,881	3,470 25
	Total	2,560,789	33,604	1,687,507	17,518	4,379 50
Paints and colours, and rough stuff and fillers, anti-corrosive and anti-fouling paints commonly used for ships' hulls, and ground and liquid paints, N.E.S.	Great Britain	729,089	56,884	20,698	3,182	795 50
	Newfoundland	200	12	200	12	3 00
	Belgium	380	174	....	....	....
	France	11,114	1,233	11,294	1,288	322 00
	Germany	24,770	3,313	760	24	6 00
	Holland	503	395	503	395	98 75
	United States	3,953,009	214,730	3,951,201	214,172	53,543 00
	Total	4,719,065	276,741	3,984,656	219,073	54,768 25
Paris green, dry	Great Britain	155,223	34,537	....	....	....
	United States	1,525	121	1,525	121	12 10
	Total	156,748	34,658	1,525	121	12 10
Paints and colours ground in spirits, and all spirit varnishes and lacquers		Galls.		Galls.		
	Great Britain	37	130	1	5	1 13
	France	3	19	3	19	3 37
	United States	809	2,616	809	2,616	910 20
	Total	849	2,765	813	2,640	914 70
		Lbs.		Lbs.		
Putty	Great Britain	8,022	101	....	....	....
	France	44	4	44	4	0 80
	United States	238,914	3,757	238,914	3,757	751 40
	Total	246,980	3,862	238,958	3,761	752 20
Paper, and manufactures of, not otherwise specified— Albumenized and other papers and films chemically prepared for photographers' use	Great Britain	....	13,417	....	54	16 20
	Germany	....	479	....	....	....
	United States	....	110,898	....	110,818	33,245 40
	Total	....	124,794	....	110,872	33,261 60
Bags or sacks, printed or not	Great Britain	....	1,185	....	83	20 75
	France	....	54	....	77	19 25
	Germany	....	1,420	....	....	....
	United States	....	30,963	....	30,895	7,723 75
	Total	....	33,622	....	31,055	7,763 75

OF IMPORTS—*Continued.*

FOR HOME CONSUMPTION.

Preferential Tariff.			Surtax Tariff.			Total.		
Quantity.	Value.	Duty.	Quantity.	Value.	Duty.	Quantity.	Value.	Duty Collected.
Lbs.	$	$ cts.	Lbs.	$	$ cts.	Lbs.	$	$ cts.
809,718	15,243	2,540 50				896,035	18,229	3,287 00
						776	179	44 75
			61,623	846	282 00	68,383	1,176	364 50
						12,270	142	35 50
						1,581,384	13,881	3,470 25
809,718	15,243	2,540 50	61,623	846	282 00	2,558,848	33,607	7,202 00
723,735	53,148	8,858 35	85	12	4 00	744,518	56,342	9,657 85
						200	12	3 00
			380	174	58 00	380	174	58 00
						11,294	1,288	322 00
			24,010	3,289	1,096 51	24,770	3,313	1,102 51
						503	395	98 75
			45	7	2 19	3,951,246	214,179	53,545 19
723,735	53,148	8,858 35	24,520	3,482	1,160 70	4,732,911	275,703	64,787 30
155,223	34,537	2,302 47				155,223	34,537	2,302 47
						1,525	121	12 10
155,223	34,537	2,302 47				156,748	34,658	2,314 57
Galls.			Galls.			Galls.		
36	125	27 03				37	130	28 16
						3	19	3 37
						809	2,616	910 20
36	125	27 03				849	2,765	941 73
Lbs.			Lbs.			Lbs.		
8,022	101	13 49				8,022	101	13 49
						44	4	0 80
						238,914	3,757	751 40
8,022	101	13 49				246,980	3,862	765 69
	13,357	2,671 40		6	2 40		13,417	2,690 00
				479	191 60		479	191 60
				46	18 40		110,864	33,263 80
	13,357	2,671 40		531	212 40		124,760	36,145 40
	984	164 02		99	33 00		1,166	217 77
							77	19 25
				1,420	473 33		1,420	473 33
				68	22 68		30,963	7,746 43
	984	164 02		1,587	529 01		33,626	8,456 78

No. 1.—General Statement

Articles Imported.	Countries.	Total Imports.		Entered — General Tariff.		
		Quantity.	Value.	Quantity.	Value.	Duty.
DUTIABLE GOODS—*Con.*		Packs.	$	Packs.	$	$ cts.
Paper and mfrs.—*Con.* Cards for playing	Great Britain	248,901	31,317	11,646	2,600	698 76
	China	415	13	415	13	24 90
	France	1,000	100	1,000	100	60 00
	Japan	100	10	100	10	6 00
	United States	337,332	35,739	336,603	35,525	20,196 18
	Total	587,748	67,179	349,764	38,248	20,985 84
Card board, paste board, in sheets or cut to size, N.E.S.	Great Britain		9,644		469	164 15
	Hong Kong		10		10	3 50
	Aust.-Hungary		1		1	0 35
	France		346		346	121 10
	Germany		2,001		135	47 25
	Holland		248		248	86 80
	Japan		2		2	0 70
	United States		67,274		67,230	23,530 50
	Total		79,526		68,441	23,954 35
		M.		M.		
Envelopes	Great Britain	9,660	13,856	43	129	45 15
	Hong Kong	23	9	23	9	3 15
	China	18	7	18	7	2 45
	France	176	449	176	449	157 15
	Germany	781	1,057			
	Japan	30	23	30	23	8 05
	Switzerland	23	67	23	67	23 45
	United States	59,586	49,318	58,877	48,194	16,867 90
	Total	70,297	64,786	59,190	48,878	17,107 30
Paper, felt or straw board	Great Britain		1,604			
	Belgium		130		130	32 50
	United States		237,189		237,285	59,321 25
	Total		238,923		237,415	59,353 75
		Rolls.		Rolls.		
Hangings or wall paper, including borders	Great Britain	99,211	25,125	4,226	1,465	512 75
	France	14,781	3,938	14,218	3,563	1,247 05
	Germany	77,109	8,153			
	Japan	2,743	2,432	2,746	2,432	851 20
	Switzerland	240	40			
	United States	2,115,596	177,519	2,182,464	178,831	62,590 85
	Total	2,309,680	217,207	2,203,654	186,291	65,201 85
Leather board, leatheroid and manufactures of	Great Britain		291		189	47 25
	United States		35,737		35,737	8,934 25
	Total		36,028		35,926	8,981 50

OF IMPORTS—*Continued.*

FOR HOME CONSUMPTION.

Preferential Tariff.			Surtax Tariff.			Total.		
Quantity.	Value.	Duty.	Quantity.	Value.	Duty.	Quantity.	Value.	Duty Collected.
Packs.	$	$ cts.	Packs.	$	$ cts.	Packs.	$	$ cts.
237,783	28,953	9,511 32				249,429	31,553	10,210 08
						415	13	24 90
						1,000	100	60 00
						100	10	6 00
			1,944	144	155 52	338,547	35,669	20,351 70
237,783	28,953	9,511 32	1,944	144	155 52	589,491	67,345	30,652 68
	9,001	2,100 29		151	70 47		9,621	2,334 91
							10	3 50
							1	0 35
							346	121 10
				1,866	870 82		2,001	918 07
							248	86 80
							2	0 70
				44	20 53		67,274	23,551 03
	9,001	2,100 29		2,061	961 82		79,503	27,016 46
M.			M.			M.		
9,753	14,094	3,288 94	5	14	6 53	9,801	14,237	3,340 62
						23	9	3 15
						18	7	2 45
						176	449	157 15
			781	1,057	493 28	781	1,057	493 28
						30	23	8 05
						23	67	23 45
			94	112	52 27	58,971	48,306	16,920 17
9,753	14,094	3,288 94	880	1,183	552 08	69,823	64,155	20,948 32
	1,604	267 33					1,604	267 33
							130	32 50
							237,285	59,321 25
	1,604	267 33					239,019	59,621 08
Rolls.			Rolls.			Rolls.		
90,067	22,276	5,197 78	488	188	87 73	94,781	23,929	5,798 26
			320	81	37 80	14,538	3,644	1,284 85
			77,109	8,153	3,804 73	77,109	8,153	3,804 73
						2,746	2,432	851 20
			240	40	18 67	240	40	18 67
			5,935	774	361 21	2,188,399	179,605	62,932 06
90,067	22,276	5,197 78	84,092	9,236	4,310 14	2,377,813	217,803	74,709 77
	102	17 00					291	64 25
							35,737	8,934 25
	102	17 00					36,028	8,998 50

No. 1.—GENERAL STATEMENT

Articles Imported.	Countries.	Total Imports.		Entered		
				General Tariff.		
		Quantity.	Value.	Quantity.	Value.	Duty.
DUTIABLE GOODS—*Con.*						$ cts.
Paper and mfrs. of—*Con.* Mill board, not straw board	Great Britain		1,619			
	France		1,800		1,800	180 00
	Germany		20			
	United States		41,341		41,341	4,134 10
	Total		44,780		43,141	4,314 10
Union collar cloth paper, in rolls or sheets, not glossed or finished	United States		1,108		1,108	166 20
Union collar cloth paper, in rolls or sheets, glossed or finished	Great Britain		12			
	Germany		125			
	United States		263		263	52 60
	Total		400		263	52 60
Pads not printed, papier maché ware N.O.P., and manufactures of paper, N.E.S	Great Britain		146,697		17,467	6,113 45
	Australia		134		134	46 90
	Hong Kong		1,054		1,054	368 90
	Aust.-Hungary		3,245		1,675	586 25
	Belgium		4,174		4,174	1,460 90
	China		1,459		1,459	510 65
	Cuba				2	0 70
	France		16,410		16,320	5,712 00
	Germany		42,000		519	181 65
	Holland		303		303	106 05
	Japan		5,051		5,034	1,761 90
	Switzerland		1		1	0 35
	Turkey		78		78	27 30
	United States		523,328		519,215	181,725 25
	Total		743,934		567,435	198,602 25
		Lbs.		Lbs.		
Printing paper of not greater value than 2¼ per lb. O.C.	United States	244,638	5,594	244,638	5,594	839 10
Printing paper, N.E.S	Great Britain	2,497,316	148,700	47,103	2,870	717 50
	Aust.-Hungary	800	132	800	132	33 00
	China	1,700	103	1,700	103	25 75
	France	3,000	229			
	Germany	73,514	5,749	946	490	122 50
	Holland	18,024	1,194	17,128	1,133	283 25
	Japan	1,104	255	1,104	255	63 75
	United States	5,930,899	359,434	5,927,520	358,940	89,735 00
	Total	8,526,357	515,796	5,996,301	363,923	90,980 75

OF IMPORTS—*Continued.*

FOR HOME CONSUMPTION.

Preferential Tariff.			Surtax Tariff.			Total.		
Quantity.	Value.	Duty.	Quantity.	Value.	Duty.	Quantity.	Value.	Duty Collected.
	$	$ cts.		$	$ cts.		$	$ cts
....	1,619	107 99	....	....	....	....	1,619	107 99
....	....	....	....	....	....	....	1,800	180 00
....	....	....	....	20	2 67	....	20	2 67
....	....	....	....	....	....	....	41,341	4,134 10
....	1,619	107 99	....	20	2 67	....	44,780	4,424 76
....	....	....	....	....	....	....	1,108	166 20
....	12	1 61	....	....	....	....	12	1 61
....	....	....	....	125	33 33	....	125	33 33
....	....	....	....	....	....	....	263	52 60
....	12	1 61	....	125	33 33	....	400	87 54
....	126,828	29,594 00	....	2,570	1,199 33	....	146,865	36,906 78
....	....	....	....	....	....	....	134	46 90
....	....	....	....	....	....	....	1,054	368 90
....	....	....	....	1,455	679 03	....	3,130	1,265 28
....	....	....	....	....	....	....	4,174	1,460 90
....	....	....	....	....	....	....	1,459	510 65
....	....	....	....	....	....	....	2	0 70
....	....	....	....	73	34 07	....	16,393	5,746 07
....	....	....	....	41,249	19,249 57	....	41,768	19,431 22
....	....	....	....	....	....	....	303	106 05
....	....	....	....	....	....	....	5,034	1,761 90
....	....	....	....	....	....	....	1	0 35
....	....	....	....	....	....	....	78	27 30
....	....	....	....	2,021	943 13	....	521,236	182,668 38
....	126,828	29,594 00	....	47,368	22,105 13	....	741,631	250,301 38
Lbs.			Lbs.			Lbs.		
....	....	....	....	....	....	244,638	5,594	839 10
2,439,504	145,480	24,246 72	4,953	382	127 33	2,491,560	148,732	25,091 55
....	....	....	....	....	....	800	132	33 00
....	....	....	....	....	....	1,700	103	25 75
....	....	....	3,000	229	76 33	3,000	229	76 33
....	....	....	72,568	5,259	1,753 00	73,514	5,749	1,875 50
....	....	....	896	61	20 33	18,024	1,194	303 58
....	....	....	....	....	....	1,104	255	63 75
....	....	....	635	221	73 65	5,928,155	359,161	89,808 65
2,439,504	145,480	24,246 72	82,052	6,152	2,050 64	8,517,857	515,555	117,278 11

No. 1.—General Statement

Articles Imported.	Countries.	Total Imports.		Entered		
				General Tariff.		
		Quantity.	Value.	Quantity.	Value.	Duty.
DUTIABLE GOODS—*Con.*			$		$	$ cts.
Paper and mfrs. of—*Con.* Ruled, border and coated papers and papeteries and boxed papers	Great Britain	....	43,254	....	774	270 90
	Hong Kong	....	20	....	20	7 00
	Aust.-Hungary	....	42	....	42	14 70
	Belgium	....	17,802	....	17,560	6,146 00
	China	....	92	....	92	32 20
	France	....	5,191	....	5,191	1,816 85
	Germany	....	3,621	....	....	....
	Italy	....	158	....	158	55 30
	Japan	....	....	....	1	0 35
	Sweden	....	119	....	119	41 65
	Switzerland	....	437	....	437	152 95
	United States	....	141,959	....	141,457	49,509 95
	Total	....	212,695	....	165,851	58,047 85
		Lbs.		Lbs.		
Straw board, in sheets or rolls	Belgium	5,800	82	5,800	82	20 50
	France	21,500	240	21,500	240	60 00
	Holland	27,500	718	27,500	718	179 50
	Japan	6,000	92	6,000	92	23 00
	United States	363,464	7,499	363,464	7,499	1,874 75
	Total	424,264	8,631	424,264	8,631	2,157 75
Window blinds of paper of all kinds	Great Britain	....	309	....	....	....
	United States	....	67	....	67	23 45
	Total	....	376	....	67	23 45
Wrapping	Great Britain	258,463	12,792	33,553	1,873	468 25
	Hong Kong	9,032	202	9,032	202	50 50
	Aust.-Hungary	43,590	551	43,590	551	137 75
	Belgium	12,044	564	12,044	564	141 00
	China	8,374	201	8,374	201	50 25
	France	110	6	110	6	1 50
	Germany	28,876	1,439	....	....	....
	Holland	21,603	832	21,603	832	208 00
	Japan	1,210	53	1,210	53	13 25
	Norway	124,402	3,893	124,402	3,893	973 25
	Sweden	76,543	1,781	76,543	1,781	445 25
	United States	1,228,238	39,330	1,227,087	39,254	9,813 50
	Total	1,812,485	61,644	1,557,548	49,210	12,302 50

OF IMPORTS—*Continued.*

FOR HOME CONSUMPTION.

Preferential Tariff.			Surtax Tariff.			Total.		
Quantity.	Value.	Duty.	Quantity.	Value.	Duty.	Quantity.	Value.	Duty Collected.
	$	$ cts.		$	$ cts.		$	$ cts.
	42,845	9,997 38		130	60 67		43,749	10,328 95
							20	7 00
							42	14 70
				242	112 93		17,802	6,258 93
							92	32 20
							5,191	1,816 85
				3,621	1,689 80		3,621	1,689 80
							158	55 30
							1	0 35
							119	41 65
							437	152 95
				456	212 80		141,913	49,722 75
	42,845	9,997 38		4,449	2,076 20		213,145	70,121 43
Lbs.			Lbs.			Lbs.		
						5,800	82	20 50
						21,500	240	60 00
						27,500	718	179 50
						6,000	92	23 00
						363,464	7,499	1,874 75
						424,264	8,631	2,157 75
	309	72 10					309	72 10
							67	23 45
	309	72 10					376	95 55
241,984	11,508	1,918 07				275,537	13,381	2,386 32
						9,032	202	50 50
						43,590	551	137 75
						12,044	564	141 00
						8,374	201	50 25
						110	6	1 50
			28,876	1,439	479 68	28,876	1,439	479 68
						21,603	832	208 00
						1,210	53	13 25
						124,402	3,893	973 25
						76,543	1,781	445 25
			1,151	76	25 33	1,228,238	39,330	9,838 83
241,984	11,508	1,918 07	30,027	1,515	505 01	1,829,559	62,233	14,725 58

No. 1.—General Statement

Articles Imported.	Countries.	Total Imports.		Entered		
				General Tariff.		
		Quantity.	Value.	Quantity.	Value.	Duty.
DUTIABLE GOODS—*Con.*			$		$	$ cts.
Paper and mfrs. of—*Con.* All kinds, N.E.S.	Great Britain		164,099		7,242	1,810 50
	Hong Kong		12		12	3 00
	Aust.-Hungary		535		535	133 75
	Belgium		28,415		28,415	7,103 75
	China		241		241	60 25
	France		12,562		12,768	3,192 00
	Germany		8,894		322	80 50
	Holland		5,001		4,822	1,205 50
	Italy		515		515	128 75
	Japan		3,999		4,263	1,065 75
	Norway		3,197		3,197	799 25
	Sweden		1,908		1,908	477 00
	Switzerland		210		210	52 50
	United States		462,373		459,177	114,794 25
	Total		691,961		523,627	130,906 75
Pencils, lead, in wood or otherwise	Great Britain		30,299		22,551	5,637 75
	Hong Kong		5		5	1 25
	Aust.-Hungary		249		86	21 50
	France		259		259	64 75
	Germany		41,338			
	Japan		6		6	1 50
	United States		103,591		103,281	25,820 25
	Total		175,747		126,188	31,547 00
Pens, penholders and rulers, of all kinds	Great Britain		38,915		476	119 00
	Hong Kong		36		36	9 00
	Aust.-Hungary		152		152	38 00
	China		54		54	13 50
	France		1,031		1,031	257 75
	Germany		2,350		134	33 50
	Japan		4		4	1 00
	Turkey		7		7	1 75
	United States		137,654		137,623	34,405 75
	Total		180,203		139,517	34,879 25
Perfumery, non-alcoholic, viz.—Hair oil, tooth and other powders and washes, pomatums, pastes, and all other perfumed preparations, N.O.P., used for the hair, mouth or skin.	Great Britain		16,710		2,207	662 10
	Hong Kong		13		13	3 90
	Aust.-Hungary		9			
	China		14		14	4 20
	France		26,546		26,825	8,047 50
	Germany		295			
	Japan		557		557	167 10
	United States		78,310		78,422	23,526 60
	Total		122,454		108,038	32,411 40
Photographic dryplates	Great Britain		11,871		6	1 80
	France				192	57 60
	Germany		480			
	United States		44,891		45,066	13,519 80
	Total		57,242		45,264	13,579 20

OF IMPORTS—*Continued.*

FOR HOME CONSUMPTION.

Preferential Tariff.			Surtax Tariff.			Total.		
Quantity.	Value.	Duty.	Quantity.	Value.	Duty.	Quantity.	Value.	Duty Collected.
	$	$ cts.		$	$ cts.		$	$ cts.
	157,866	26,311 53		352	117 33		165,460	28,239 36
							12	3 00
							535	133 75
							28,415	7,103 75
							241	60 25
							12,768	3,192 00
				8,638	2,879 34		8,960	2,959 84
				179	59 67		5,001	1,265 17
							515	128 75
							4,263	1,065 75
							3,197	799 25
							1,908	477 00
							210	52 50
				1,804	601 33		460,981	115,395 58
	157,866	26,311 53		10,973	3,657 67		692,466	160,875 95
	4,357	726 28		3,528	1,176 00		30,436	7,540 03
							5	1 25
				163	54 33		249	75 83
							259	64 75
				41,338	13,779 32		41,338	13,779 32
							6	1 50
				310	103 33		103,591	25,923 58
	4,357	726 28		45,339	15,112 98		175,884	47,386 26
	38,337	6,389 97		102	34 00		38,915	6,542 97
							36	9 00
							152	38 00
							54	13 50
							1,031	257 75
				2,216	738 66		2,350	772 16
							4	1 00
							7	1 75
				31	10 33		137,654	34,416 08
	38,337	6,389 97		2,349	782 99		180,203	42,052 21
	14,110	2,822 00		283	113 20		16,600	3.597 30
							13	3 90
				9	3 60		9	3 60
							14	4 20
							26,825	8,047 50
				295	118 00		295	118 00
							557	167 10
				63	25 20		78,485	23,551 80
	14,110	2,822 00		650	260 00		122,798	35,493 40
	11,865	2,373 00					11,871	2,374 80
							192	57 60
				480	191 00		480	191 00
							45,066	13,519 80
	11,865	2,373 00		480	191 00		57,609	16,143 20

No. 1.—GENERAL STATEMENT

Articles Imported.	Countries.	Total Imports.		Entered		
				General Tariff.		
		Quantity.	Value.	Quantity.	Value.	Duty.
DUTIABLE GOODS—*Con.*			$		$	$ cts.
Picture and photograph frames of any material	Great Britain	....	11,534	....	2,861	858 30
	Hong Kong	....	9	....	9	2 70
	Aust.-Hungary	....	198	....	148	44 40
	Belgium	....	100	....	100	30 00
	China	....	24	....	24	7 20
	France	....	2,457	....	2,451	735 30
	Germany	....	8,802	....	4	1 20
	Holland	....	313	....	305	91 50
	Italy	....	437	....	437	131 10
	Japan	....	342	....	342	102 60
	Spain	....	11	....	11	3 30
	Turkey	....	11	....	11	3 30
	United States	....	76,867	....	75,074	22,522 20
	Total	....	101,105	....	81,777	24,533 10
Pickles, in bottles, jars or similar vessels		Galls.		Galls.		
	Great Britain	176,231	155,624	1,112	1,121	392 35
	Hong Kong	280	33	280	33	11 55
	Belgium	137	72	137	72	25 20
	China	685	186	685	186	65 10
	France	3,062	2,947	2,986	2,982	1,043 20
	Germany	40	49	....	....	....
	Greece	11	3	11	3	1 05
	Italy	329	132	329	132	46 70
	Japan	248	59	248	59	20 65
	Spain	2,835	1,998	2,320	1,864	652 40
	Turkey	172	63	172	63	22 05
	United States	46,214	42,979	46,723	44,580	15,603 00
	Total	230,244	204,145	55,003	51,095	17,883 25
Pickles, in bulk	Great Britain	1,372	911	320	229	80 15
	Hong Kong	83	16	83	16	5 60
	China	1,899	245	1,899	245	85 75
	France	....	....	10	20	7 00
	Greece	2,505	552	2,505	552	193 20
	Japan	16,249	1,034	16,249	1,034	361 90
	Spain	12,808	7,388	12,368	7,230	2,530 50
	Turkey	640	229	640	229	80 15
	United States	69,018	20,246	68,168	19,696	6,893 60
	Total	104,574	30,621	102,242	29,251	10,237 85
Plants and trees, viz.—		No.		No.		
Apple trees	Great Britain	1,032	227	104	16	3 12
	United States	202,486	14,878	202,486	14,878	6,074 58
	Total	203,518	15,105	202,590	14,894	6,077 70
Cherry trees	Great Britain	11	6	....	....	....
	United States	48,838	7,998	48,838	7,998	1,465 14
	Total	48,849	8,004	48,838	7,998	1,465 14
Currant bushes	United States	57,869	1,208	57,869	1,208	241 60

OF IMPORTS—*Continued.*

FOR HOME CONSUMPTION.

Preferential Tariff.			Surtax Tariff.			Total.		
Quantity.	Value.	Duty.	Quantity.	Value.	Duty.	Quantity.	Value.	Duty Collected.
	$	$ cts.		$	$ cts.		$	$ cts.
....	8,064	1,612 80	....	605	242 00	....	11,530	2,713 10
....	....	....	....	....	....	....	9	2 70
....	....	....	....	50	20 00	....	198	64 40
....	....	....	....	....	....	....	100	30 00
....	....	....	....	....	....	....	24	7 20
....	....	....	....	....	....	....	2,451	735 30
....	....	....	....	8,798	3,519 20	....	8,802	3,520 40
....	....	....	....	8	3 20	....	313	94 70
....	....	....	....	....	....	....	437	131 10
....	....	....	....	....	....	....	342	102 60
....	....	....	....	....	....	....	11	3 30
....	....	....	....	....	....	....	11	3 30
....	....	....	....	31	12 40	....	75,105	22,534 60
....	8,064	1,612 80	....	9,492	3,796 80	....	99,333	29,942 70
Galls.			Galls.			Galls.		
175,034	151,378	35,322 60	....	....	....	176,146	152,499	35,714 95
....	....	....	....	....	....	280	33	11 55
....	....	....	....	....	....	137	72	25 20
....	....	....	....	....	....	685	186	65 10
....	....	....	....	....	....	2,986	2,982	1,043 20
....	....	....	40	49	22 87	40	49	22 87
....	....	....	....	....	....	11	3	1 05
....	....	....	....	....	....	329	132	46 70
....	....	....	....	....	....	248	59	20 65
....	....	....	....	....	....	2,320	1,864	652 40
....	....	....	....	....	....	172	63	22 05
....	....	....	....	....	....	46,723	44,580	15,603 00
175,034	151,378	35,322 60	40	49	22 87	230,077	202,522	53,228 72
1,086	726	169·42	....	....	....	1,406	955	249 57
....	....	....	....	....	....	83	16	5 60
....	....	....	....	....	....	1,899	245	85 75
....	....	....	....	....	....	10	20	7 00
....	....	....	....	....	....	2,505	552	193 20
....	....	....	....	....	....	16,249	1,034	361 90
....	....	....	....	....	....	12,368	7,230	2,530 50
....	....	....	....	....	....	640	229	80 15
....	....	....	....	....	....	68,168	19,696	6,893 60
1,086	726	169 42	....	....	....	103,328	29,977	10,407 27
No.			No.			No.		
928	211	18 56	....	....	....	1,032	227	21 68
....	....	....	....	....	....	202,486	14,878	6,074 58
928	211	18 56	....	....	....	203,518	15,105	6,096 26
11	6	0 22	....	....	....	11	6	0 22
....	....	....	....	....	....	48,838	7,998	1,465 14
11	6	0 22	....	....	....	48,849	8,004	1,465 36
....	....	....	....	....	....	57,869	1,208	241 60

No. 1.—GENERAL STATEMENT

ARTICLES IMPORTED.	COUNTRIES.	TOTAL IMPORTS.		ENTERED		
				General Tariff.		
		Quantity.	Value.	Quantity.	Value.	Duty.
DUTIABLE GOODS—*Con.*			$		$	$ cts.
Plants and trees—*Con.* Fruit, shade, lawn and ornamental trees, shrubs and plants, N.E.S.	Great Britain	....	2,384	....	987	197 40
	Aust.-Hungary	....	144	....	144	28 80
	Belgium	....	3,387	....	3,387	677 40
	Denmark	....	362	....	362	72 40
	France	....	2,351	....	2,351	470 20
	Germany	....	99	....	84	16 80
	Holland	....	5,655	....	5,655	1,131 00
	Italy	....	26	....	26	5 20
	Japan	....	78	....	78	15 60
	United States	....	47,367	....	47,367	9,473 40
	Total	....	61,853	....	60,441	12,088 20
		No.		No.		
Gooseberry bushes	Great Britain	14,500	411	10,000	268	53 60
	United States	45,056	1,126	45,056	1,126	225 20
	Total	59,556	1,537	55,056	1,394	278 80
Grape vines	United States	58,145	781	58,145	781	156 20
Peach trees	United States	210,070	11,926	210,070	11,926	6,302 10
Pear trees	United States	11,962	1,082	11,962	1,082	358 86
Plum trees	France	110	25	110	25	3 30
	United States	45,659	4,640	45,659	4,640	1,369 77
	Total	45,769	4,665	45,769	4,665	1,373 07
Raspberry bushes	Great Britain	4,448	67	....	....	....
	France	50	2	50	2	0 40
	United States	176,343	987	176,343	987	197 40
	Total	180,841	1,056	176,393	989	197 80
Rose bushes	Great Britain	8,661	775	600	78	15 60
	Aust. Hungary	1,000	30	1,000	30	6 00
	France	2,672	580	2,672	580	116 00
	Germany	40	8	....	....	....
	Holland	12,310	1,072	12,310	1,072	214 40
	United States	18,636	1,888	18,636	1,888	377 60
	Total	43,319	4,353	35,218	3,648	729 60
Quince trees	United States	643	101	643	101	19 29
		Brls.		Brls.		
Plaster of Paris, or gypsum, ground, not calcined	Great Britain	9	38	9	38	5 70
	United States	6,553	1,761	6,553	1,761	264 15
	Total	6,562	1,799	6,562	1,799	269 85

OF IMPORTS—*Continued.*

FOR HOME CONSUMPTION.

Preferential Tariff.			Surtax Tariff.			Total.		
Quantity.	Value.	Duty.	Quantity.	Value.	Duty.	Quantity.	Value.	Duty Collected.
	$	$ cts.		$	$ cts.		$	$ cts.
	1,397	186 28					2,384	383 68
							144	28 80
							3,387	677 40
							362	72 40
							2,351	470 20
				15	4 00		99	20 80
							5,655	1,131 00
							26	5 20
							78	15 60
							47,367	9,473 40
	1,397	186 28		15	4 00		61,853	12,278 48
No.			No.			No.		
4,500	143	19 07				14,500	411	72 67
						45,056	1,126	225 20
4,500	143	19 07				59,556	1,537	297 87
						58,145	781	156 20
						210,070	11,926	6,302 10
						11,962	1,082	358 86
						110	25	3 30
						45,659	4,640	1,369 77
						45,769	4,665	1,373 07
4,448	67	8 94				4,448	67	8 94
						50	2	0 40
						176,343	987	197 40
4,448	67	8 94				180,841	1,056	206 74
8,061	697	92 97				8,661	775	108 57
						1,000	30	6 00
						2,672	580	116 00
			40	8	2 13	40	8	2 13
						12,310	1,072	214 40
						18,636	1,888	377 60
8,061	697	92 97	40	8	2 13	43,319	4,353	824 70
						643	101	19 29
Brls.			Brls.			Brls.		
						9	38	5 70
						6,553	1,761	264 15
						6,562	1,799	269 85

No. 1.—General Statement

Articles Imported.	Countries.	Total Imports.		Entered		
				General Tariff.		
		Quantity.	Value.	Quantity.	Value.	Duty.
DUTIABLE GOODS—*Con.*		Cwt.	$	Cwt.	$	$ cts.
Plaster of Paris, or gypsum, calcined or manufactured....	Great Britain...	35	13			
	United States...	128,632	43,753	128,630	43,729	16,078 78
	Total	128,667	43,766	128,630	43,729	16,078 78
Plates, engraved on wood, steel or on other metal and transfers taken from the same, including engravers' plates, of steel polished, engraved or for engraving thereon.....	United States...		14,887		14,811	2,962 20
Pocket-books, purses, reticules and musical instrument cases.	Great Britain...		40,669		2,396	718 80
	Hong Kong......		5		5	1 50
	Aust.-Hungary..		2,790		2,655	796 50
	Belgium........		218		218	65 40
	China..........		17		17	5 10
	France.........		8,386		8,127	2,438 10
	Germany......		20,629			
	Holland........		93		93	27 90
	Japan..........		1,909		1,909	572 70
	Switzerland.....		337		337	101 10
	Turkey.........		10		10	3 00
	United States...		127,998		127,957	38,387 10
	Total		203,061		143,724	43,117 20
Polish or composition, knife and other, N.O.P.	Great Britain...		5,647		989	247 25
	Belgium........		47		45	11 25
	France.........		630		351	87 75
	Germany.		1,033			
	United States...		61,102		60,513	15,128 25
	Total		68,459		61,898	15,474 50
Pomades, French or flower odours, &c., imported in tins of not less than ten pounds each....		Lbs.		Lbs.		
	France.........	1,293	1,774	1,293	1,774	266 10
	United States...	3,141	4,082	3,141	4,082	612 30
	Total	4,434	5,856	4,434	5,856	878 40
" all other.............	Great Britain...	10	6	1	3	0 90
	France.........	21	44	21	44	13 20
	United States...	31	15	31	15	4 50
	Total	62	65	53	62	18 60
Post office parcels and packages.	Great Britain...		144,015		11,753	3,448 68
	Aust.-Hungary..		2		2	0 40
	France.........		710		710	172 44
	Germany.		129		70	21 66
	Italy....		5		5	1 16
	Switzerland.....		17		17	5 39
	United States...		462,874		462,804	112,156 63
	Total		607,752		475,361	115,806 36

OF IMPORTS—*Continued.*

FOR HOME CONSUMPTION.

Preferential Tariff.			Surtax Tariff.			Total.		
Quantity.	Value.	Duty.	Quantity.	Value.	Duty.	Quantity.	Value.	Duty Collected.
Cwt.	$	$ cts.	Cwt.	$	$ cts.	Cwt.	$	$ cts.
35	13	2 91				35	13	2 91
						128,630	43,729	16,078 78
35	13	2 91				128,665	43,742	16,081 69
				76	20 27		14,887	2,982 47
	36,227	7,245 40		2,168	867 20		40,791	8,831 40
							5	1 50
				135	54 00		2,790	850 50
							218	65 40
							17	5 10
							8,127	2,438 10
				20,656	8,262 40		20,656	8,262 40
							93	27 90
							1,909	572 70
							337	101 10
							10	3 00
				51	20 40		128,008	38,407 50
	36,227	7,245 40		23,010	9,204 00		202,961	59,566 60
	4,252	708 71		50	16 67		5,291	972 63
							45	11 25
				279	93 00		630	180 75
				1,033	344 32		1,033	344 32
				162	54 00		60,675	15,182 25
	4,252	708 71		1,524	507 99		67,674	16,691 20
Lbs.			Lbs.			Lbs.		
						1,293	1,774	266 10
						3,141	4,082	612 30
						4,434	5,856	878 40
9	3	0 60				10	6	1 50
						21	44	13 20
						31	15	4 50
9	3	0 60				62	65	19 20
	130,218	30,601 76		2,044	747 64		144,015	34,798 08
							2	0 40
							710	172 44
				59	21 25		129	42 91
							5	1 16
							17	5 39
				70	27 68		462,874	112,184 31
	130,218	30,601 76		2,173	796 57		607,752	147,204 69

No. 1.—General Statement

Articles Imported.	Countries.	Total Imports. Quantity.	Total Imports. Value.	Entered — General Tariff. Quantity.	General Tariff. Value.	General Tariff. Duty.
DUTIABLE GOODS—*Con.*			$		$	$ cts.
Precious stones, N.E.S., polished, but not set, pierced or otherwise manufactured, and imitations thereof.	Great Britain...	....	18,533	....	2,843	284 30
	Aust.-Hungary..	....	2,067	....	2,067	206 70
	Belgium...	....	126	....	126	12 60
	France.........	....	21,614	....	21,614	2,161 40
	Germany.......	....	8,230	....	1,793	179 30
	Italy.	....	104	....	104	10 40
	United States...	....	35,203	....	35,203	3,520 30
	Total	....	85,877	....	63,750	6,375 00
Printing presses, printing machines, folding machines bookbinders' bookbinding, ruling, embossing and paper cutting machines, N.E.S............	Great Britain...	....	51,590	....	4,356	435 60
	France.........	....	122	....	122	12 20
	Germany.......	....	9,058	....	....	....
	United States...	....	326,659	....	326,161	32,616 10
	Total	....	387,429	....	330,639	33,063 90
Provisions, not otherwise specified—		Lbs.		Lbs.		
Butter......	Great Britain...	21,356	4,633	120	38	4 80
	Australia......	1,176	239	1,176	239	47 04
	New Zealand....	21,616	5,148	....	....	....
	France..	25	9	25	9	1 00
	Italy..........	253	59	253	59	10 12
	Turkey.........	50	5	50	5	2 00
	United States...	247,736	54,426	103,923	25,810	4,156 92
	Total.....	292,212	64,519	105,547	26,160	4,221 88
Cheese	Great Britain...	17,954	4,230	2,908	563	87 24
	France..	42,580	7,593	43,328	7,904	1,299 84
	Germany. .. .	50	20	....	....	....
	Greece.........	110	3	110	3	3 30
	Holland.......	6,124	942	6,722	976	201 66
	Italy..........	93,674	16,337	90,725	15,528	2,721 75
	Norway	10	2	10	2	0 30
	St. Pierre.......	66	10	66	10	1 98
	Sweden.........	6,303	1,096	5,035	876	151 05
	Switzerland. ...	41,452	7,030	42,043	7,104	1,261 29
	Turkey.........	1,060	157	1,060	157	31 80
	United States...	300,033	45,904	162,989	28,838	4,889 67
	Total.	509,416	83,324	354,996	61,961	10,649 88
Lard	Great Britain...	5,548	518	5,124	471	102 48
	United States...	7,656,347	652,526	7,524,075	644,449	150,481 50
	Total	7,661,895	653,044	7,529,199	644,920	150,583 98
Lard compound and similar substances, cottolene and animal stearine of all kinds, N.E.S..........	Great Britain...	203,427	16,949	....	....	....
	Germany.......	224	28	....	....	....
	United States...	212,460	18,818	225,186	16,129	4,503 72
	Total	416,111	35,795	225,186	16,129	4,503 72

OF IMPORTS—*Continued.*

FOR HOME CONSUMPTION.

Preferential Tariff.			Surtax Tariff.			Total.		
Quantity.	Value.	Duty.	Quantity.	Value.	Duty.	Quantity.	Value.	Duty Collected.
	$	$ cts.		$	$ cts.		$	$ cts.
	15,517	1,034 50		173	23 07		18,533	1,341 87
							2,067	206 70
							126	12 60
							21,614	2,161 40
				6,437	858 22		8,230	1,037 52
							104	10 40
							35,203	3,520 30
	15,517	1,034 50		6,610	881 29		85,877	8,290 79
	42,706	2,847 06		4,528	603 72		51,590	3,886 38
							122	12 20
				9,058	1,207 73		9,058	1,207 73
				480	64 00		326,641	32,680 10
	42,706	2,847 06		14,066	1,875 45		387,411	37,786 41
Lbs.			Lbs.			Lbs.		
22,392	5,082	597 12				22,512	5,120	601 92
						1,176	239	47 04
15,512	3,702	413 63				15,512	3,702	413 63
						25	9	1 00
						253	59	10 12
						50	5	2 00
						103,923	25,810	4,156 92
37,904	8,784	1,010 75				143,451	34,944	5,232 63
13,585	3,328	271 71				16,493	3,891	358 95
						43,328	7,904	1,299 84
			50	20	2 00	50	20	2 00
						110	3	3 30
						6,722	976	201 66
						90,725	15,528	2,721 75
						10	2	0 30
						66	10	1 98
						5,035	876	151 05
						42,043	7,104	1,261 29
						1,060	157	31 80
						162,989	28,838	4,889 67
13,585	3,328	271 71	50	20	2 00	368,631	65,309	10,923 59
424	47	5 66				5,548	518	108 14
						7,524,075	644,449	150,481 50
424	47	5 66				7,529,623	644,967	150,589 64
203,427	16,949	2,712 39				203,427	16,949	2,712 39
			224	28	5 97	224	28	5 97
						225,186	16,129	4,503 72
203,427	16,949	2,712 39	224	28	5 97	428,837	33,106	7,222 08

No. 1.—General Statement

Articles Imported.	Countries.	Total Imports.		Entered		
				General Tariff.		
		Quantity.	Value.	Quantity.	Value.	Duty.
DUTIABLE GOODS—*Con.*		Lbs.	$	Lbs.	$	$ cts.
Meats, viz.—						
Bacon and hams, shoulders and sides	Great Britain	3,397	576	100	10	00
	Australia	3,711	514	3,711	514	22
	Hong Kong	1,694	101	1,694	101	2 88
	China	362	25	362	25	[illegible] 24
	United States	7,131,205	782,330	7,073,978	775,226	141,479 56
	Total	7,140,369	783,546	7,079,845	775,876	141,596 90
Beef, salted, in barrels	Great Britain	14,996	992	14,996	992	299 92
	Newfoundland	1,450	109	1,450	109	29 00
	United States	3,462,419	159,848	2,358,069	110,761	47,161 38
	Total	3,478,865	160,949	2,374,515	111,862	47,490 30
Canned meats and canned poultry and game	Great Britain	44,976	7,344	11,952	1,807	451 75
	Australia	52,515	3,909	43,426	3,026	756 50
	Hong Kong	3,186	187	3,186	187	46 75
	New Zealand	5,412	494	240	24	6 00
	Belgium	548	85	548	85	21 25
	China	12,316	912	12,316	912	228 00
	France	11,953	2,580	12,630	2,902	725 50
	Germany	910	342	....	....	....
	Japan	655	69	655	69	17 25
	Norway	5,910	355	510	102	25 50
	St. Pierre	3	3	3	3	0 75
	United States	679,532	82,805	632,268	78,146	19,536 50
	Total	817,916	99,085	717,734	87,263	21,815 75
Extracts of meats and fluid beef not medicated, and soups	Great Britain	....	20,310	....	14,459	3,614 75
	Australia	....	158	....	230	57 50
	China	....	11	....	11	2 75
	France	....	401	....	460	115 00
	Germany	....	260	....	....	....
	Japan	....	2	....	2	0 50
	United States	....	64,081	....	65,174	16,293 50
	Total	....	85,223	....	80,336	20,084 00
		Lbs.		Lbs.		
Mutton and lamb, fresh	Australia	354,575	17,380	354,575	17,380	6,083 00
	United States	21,743	2,178	48,667	3,982	1,393 70
	Total	376,318	19,558	403,242	21,362	7,476 70
Pork, barrelled, in brine	Great Britain	70,450	5,158	70,450	5,158	1,409 00
	Hong Kong	290	19	290	19	5 80
	Newfoundland	800	60	800	60	16 00
	United States	11,143,780	816,416	10,654,569	780,668	213,091 38
	Total	11,215,320	821,653	10,726,109	785,905	214,522 18

OF IMPORTS—*Continued.*

FOR HOME CONSUMPTION.

Preferential Tariff.			Surtax Tariff.			Total.		
Quantity.	Value.	Duty.	Quantity.	Value.	Duty.	Quantity.	Value.	Duty Collected.
Lbs.	$	$ cts.	Lbs.	$	$ cts.	Lbs.	$	$ cts.
3,297	566	43 98				3,397	576	45 98
						3,711	514	74 22
						1,694	101	33 88
						362	25	7 24
						7,073,978	775,226	141,479 56
3,297	566	43 98				7,083,142	776,442	141,640 88
						14,996	992	299 92
						1,450	109	29 00
						2,358 069	110,761	47,161 38
						2,374,515	111,862	47,490 30
30,558	4,824	804 00	408	52	17 33	42,918	6,683	1,273 08
						43,426	3,026	756 50
						3,186	187	46 75
3,417	249	41 62				3,657	273	47 62
						548	85	21 25
						12,316	912	228 00
			450	105	35 00	13,080	3,007	760 50
			310	68	22 66	310	68	22 66
						655	69	17 25
						510	102	25 50
						3	3	0 75
			131	25	8 35	632,399	78,171	19,544 85
33,975	5,073	845 62	1,299	250	83 34	753,008	92,586	22,744 71
	6,441	1,073 54		4	1 33		20,904	4,689 62
							230	57 50
							11	2 75
							460	115 00
				252	84 00		252	84 00
							2	0 50
				40	13 36		65,214	16,306 86
	6,441	1,073 54		296	98 69		87,073	21,256 23
Lbs.			Lbs.			Lbs.		
						354,575	17,380	6,083 00
						48,667	3,982	1,393 70
						403,242	21,362	7,476 70
						70,450	5,158	1,409 00
						290	19	5 80
						800	60	16 00
						10,654,569	780,668	213,091 38
						10,726,109	785,905	214,522 18

No. 1.—General Statement

Articles Imported.	Countries.	Total Imports.		Entered		
				General Tariff.		
		Quantity.	Value.	Quantity.	Value.	Duty.
DUTIABLE GOODS—*Con.*			$		$	$ cts.
Meats—*Con.*						
Poultry and game, N.O.P...	Great Britain...	....	379	....	156	31 20
	Hong Kong.....	....	539	....	539	107 80
	China..........	....	194	....	194	38 80
	United States..	....	38,481	....	38,679	7,735 80
	Total......	....	39,593	....	39,568	7,913 60
Dried or smoked meats, and meats preserved in any other way than salted or pickled, N.E.S............		Lbs.		Lbs.		
	Great Britain...	1,093	239	342	145	6 84
	Hong Kong.....	25,010	1,968	25,010	1,968	500 20
	China..........	58,537	4,835	58,537	4,835	1,170 74
	France.........	55	21	55	21	1 10
	Italy....	200	18	200	18	4 00
	Japan..	219	16	219	16	4 38
	United States...	1,344,981	155,288	1,348,803	154,741	26,976 06
	Total......	1,430,095	162,385	1,433,166	161,744	28,663 32
Other meats, fresh..... ...	United States...	269,628	29,605	246,094	28,044	7,382 82
Other meats, salted, N.E.S..	Great Britain...	624	29	600	24	12 00
	Hong Kong.....	2,055	148	2,055	148	41 10
	China....... ..	6,986	522	6,986	522	139 72
	United States...	578,894	50,254	568,675	49,639	11,373 50
	Total......	588,559	50,953	578,316	50,333	11,566 32
Regalia and badges..........	Great Britain...	....	2,082	....	81	28 35
	France.........	....	578	....	578	202 30
	United States...	....	8,762	....	8,762	3,066 70
	Total......	....	11,422	....	9,421	3,297 35
Ribbons....	Great Britain...	....	456,872	....	420,651	147,227 85
	Hong Kong.....	....	19	....	19	6 65
	Aust.-Hungary..	....	7,937	....	7,881	2,758 35
	Belgium........	....	17,042	....	17,042	5,964 70
	China	....	16	....	16	5 60
	France........	....	212,662	....	212,040	74,214 00
	Germany......	....	37,264	....	2,253	788 55
	Italy..........	....	3,066	....	3,066	1,073 10
	Japan....	....	90	....	90	31 50
	Switzerland....	....	343,219	....	335,869	117,554 15
	United States...	....	79,699	....	79,342	27,769 70
	Total......	....	1,157,886	....	1,078,269	377,394 15
Railway or travelling rugs and lap dusters of all kinds.....	Great Britain...	....	41,188	... .	4,020	1,206 00
	Aust.-Hungary..	....	349	... .	349	
	Belgium........	....	24	....	24	104 70
	France.........	....	295	....	295	7 20
	Germany.... ..	....	449	. . ...	... ...	88 50
	United States...	. . ....	9,197	....	9,197	....
	Total......	....	51,502	....	13,885	4,165 50

OF IMPORTS—*Continued.*

FOR HOME CONSUMPTION.

Preferential Tariff.			Surtax Tariff.			Total.		
Quantity.	Value.	Duty.	Quantity.	Value.	Duty.	Quantity.	Value.	Duty Collected.
	$	$ cts.		$	$ cts.		$	$ cts.
	223	29 74					379	60 94
							539	107 80
							194	38 80
							38,679	7,735 80
	223	29 74					39,791	7,943 34
Lbs.			Lbs.			Lbs.		
751	94	10 02				1,093	239	16 86
						25,010	1,968	500 20
						58,537	4,835	1,170 74
						55	21	1 10
						200	18	4 00
						219	16	4 38
						1,348,803	154,741	26,976 06
751	94	10 02				1,433,917	161,838	28,673 34
						246,094	28,044	7,382 82
24	5	0 32				624	29	12 32
						2,055	148	41 10
						6,986	522	139 72
						568,675	49,639	11,373 50
24	5	0 32				578,340	50,338	11,566 64
	1,962	457 85		39	18 20		2,082	504 40
							578	202 30
							8,762	3,066 70
	1,962	457 85		39	18 20		11,422	3,773 40
	11,225	2,619 31		24,882	11,611 60		456,758	161,458 76
							19	6 65
							7,881	2,758 35
							17,042	5,964 70
							16	5 60
				367	171 28		212,407	74,385 28
				35,011	16,338 47		37,264	17,127 02
							3,066	1,073 10
							90	31 50
				178	83 08		333,047	117,637 23
				400	186 68		79,742	27,956 38
	11,225	2,619 31		60,838	28,391 11		1,150,332	408,404 57
	36,415	7,283 00		829	331 60		41,264	8,820 60
							349	104 70
							24	7 20
							295	88 50
				449	179 60		449	179 60
							9,197	2,759 10
	36,415	7,283 00		1,278	511 20		51,578	11,959 70

No. 1.—General Statement

Articles Imported.	Countries.	Total Imports.		Entered		
				General Tariff.		
		Quantity.	Value.	Quantity.	Value.	Duty.
dutiable goods—*Con.*			$		$	$ cts.
Sails for boats and ships	Great Britain		762		140	35 00
	United States		1,934		1,934	483 50
	Total		2,696		2,074	518 50
		Lbs.		Lbs.		
Salt, coarse, N.E.S.	United States	14,900,108	33,627	14,900,108	33,627	7,450 06
Salt, fine, in bulk	United States	2,797,950	7,983	2,797,950	7,983	1,398 98
Salt, N.E.S., in bags, barrels or other packages	Holland	1,100	23	1,100	23	0 83
	United States	3,673,327	18,198	3,666,906	18,172	2,750 34
	Total	3,674,427	18,221	3,668,006	18,195	2,751 17
Sand paper, glass, flint, emery paper and emery cloth	Great Britain		2,232		528	132 00
	France		39		39	9 75
	Germany		57			
	United States		104,002		104,002	26,000 50
	Total		106,330		104,569	26,142 25
		Galls.		Galls.		
Sauces and catsups, in bottles	Great Britain	51,530	77,890	568	508	177 80
	B. E. Indies	74	47	14	13	4 55
	Hong Kong	1,644	366	1,644	366	128 10
	China	3,074	632	3,074	632	221 20
	France	380	426	289	396	138 60
	Germany	60	4	60	4	1 40
	Italy	37	80	37	80	28 00
	Japan	54	51	54	51	17 85
	United States	31,491	37,432	31,779	35,014	12,254 90
	Total	88,344	116,928	37,519	37,064	12,972 40
Sauces and catsups, in bulk	Great Britain	2,848	1,409			
	Hong Kong	2,251	449	2,251	449	157 15
	China	2,987	599	2,987	599	209 65
	Japan	2,087	409	2,087	409	143 15
	United States	18,539	4,398	19,651	5,668	1,983 80
	Total	28,712	7,264	26,976	7,125	2,493 75
Sauces—Soy	Hong Kong	2,419	491	2,419	491	171 85
	China	7,083	1,224	7,083	1,224	428 40
	Japan	19,431	5,067	19,446	5,070	1,774 50
	United States	231	87	231	87	30 45
	Total	29,164	6,869	29,179	6,872	2,405 20
Sausage casings, N.E.S	Great Britain		22,534		479	95 80
	Australia		598		598	119 60
	Holland		215		215	43 00
	United States		59,550		60,072	12,014 40
	Total		82,897		61,364	12,272 80

OF IMPORTS—*Continued.*

FOR HOME CONSUMPTION.

Preferential Tariff.			Surtax Tariff.			Total.		
Quantity.	Value.	Duty.	Quantity.	Value.	Duty.	Quantity.	Value.	Duty Collected.
	$	$ cts.		$	$ cts.		$	$ cts.
	622	103 67					762	138 67
							1,934	483 50
	622	103 67					2,696	622 17
Lbs.			Lbs.			Lbs.		
						14,900,108	33,627	7,450 06
						2,797,950	7,983	1,398 98
						1,100	23	0 83
						3,666,906	18,172	2,750 34
						3,668,006	18,195	2,751 17
	1,704	284 04					2,232	416 04
							39	9 75
				57	19 01		57	19 01
							104,002	26,000 50
	1,704	284 04		57	19 01		106,330	26,445 30
Galls.			Galls.			Galls.		
48,971	72,517	16,921 04				49,539	73,025	17,098 84
60	34	7 94				74	47	12 49
						1,644	366	128 10
						3,074	632	221 20
						289	396	138 60
						60	4	1 40
						37	80	28 00
						54	51	17 85
						31,779	35,014	12,254 90
49,031	72,551	16,928 98				86,550	109,615	29,901 38
2,424	1,048	244 59				2,424	1,048	244 59
						2,251	449	157 15
						2,987	599	209 65
						2,087	409	143 15
						19,651	5,668	1,983 80
2,424	1,048	244 59				29,400	8,173	2,738 34
						2,419	491	171 85
						7,083	1,224	428 40
						19,446	5,070	1,774 50
						231	87	30 45
						29,179	6,872	2,405 20
	22,055	2,940 68					22,534	3,036 48
							598	119 60
							215	43 00
							60,072	12,014 40
	22,055	2,940 68					83,419	15,213 48

No. 1.—General Statement

Articles Imported.	Countries.	Total Imports.		Entered		
				General Tariff.		
		Quantity.	Value.	Quantity.	Value.	Duty.
DUTIABLE GOODS—*Con.*			$		$	$ cts.
Seeds, viz.—						
Garden, field and other seeds for agricultural or other purposes, N.O.P., when in bulk or in large parcels....	Great Britain...	....	13,040	....	6,988	698 80
	Hong Kong...	... .	134	... .	134	13 40
	New Zealand....	....	29	... .	29	2 90
	Argentina.......	....	1,829	....	1,829	182 90
	China	....	280	....	280	28 00
	Corea..........	....	11	....	11	1 10
	Denmark......	....	1,935	....	1,935	193 50
	France.........	....	7,825	....	7,825	782 50
	Germany	....	4,671	....	575	57 50
	Holland........	....	1,495	....	1,495	149 50
	Japan.....	....	73	....	73	7 30
	Turkey..........	....	6,812	....	5,128	512 80
	United States...	....	336,840	....	337,708	33,770 80
	Total	....	374,974	....	364,010	36,401 00
Garden, field and other seeds for agricultural or other purposes, N.O.P., when in small papers or parcels	Great Britain...	....	2,369	....	88	22 00
	France.........	....	8	....	8	2 00
	United States...	....	4,441	.... ..	4,444	1,111 00
	Total	. ....	6,821	......	4,540	1,135 00
Bulbous roots, N.O.P..	Great Britain...	....	1,418	....	1,137	227 40
	Holland........	....	546	... .	546	109 20
	United States...	....	12,424	....	12,424	2,484 80
	Total	... .	14,388	....	14,107	2,821 40
Ships, foreign built British on applying for Canadian coasting license.............	France.........	... .	875	....	875	218 75
	Norway	....	19,954	... .	19,954	4,988 50
	United States...	....	157,621	.. . ...	157,621	39,405 25
	Total	....	178,450	. ....	178,450	44,612 50
Ships and vessels, repairs on...	United States...	.. ...	415	....	415	103 75
Signs of any material, framed or not, and letters of any material for signs or similar use........	Great Britain...	....	6,273	....	912	273 60
	Hong Kong.....	....	2	... .	2	0 60
	China	.. ..	55	... .	55	16 50
	France..........	....	393	....	387	116 10
	Germany.......	....	703	....	....	....
	Holland........	....	2	....	2	0 60
	Norway	....	129	....	129	38 70
	Spain....... ...	....	4	.. ....	4	1 20
	Switzerland.....	.... .	303	....	303	90 90
	United States...	....	58,369	....	58,205	17,461 50
	Total	....	66,233	....	59,999	17,999 70

OF IMPORTS—*Continued.*

FOR HOME CONSUMPTION.

Preferential Tariff.			Surtax Tariff.			Total.		
Quantity.	Value.	Duty.	Quantity.	Value.	Duty.	Quantity.	Value.	Duty Collected.
	$	$ cts.		$	$ cts.		$	$ cts.
	5,579	371 98		274	36 53		12,841	1,107 31
							134	13 40
							29	2 90
							1,829	182 90
							280	28 00
							11	1 10
							1,935	193 50
							7,825	782 50
				3,340	445 32		3,915	502 82
							1,495	149 50
							73	7 30
							5,128	512 80
				306	40 80		338,014	33,811 60
	5,579	371 98		3,920	522 65		373,509	37,295 63
	2,281	380 23					2,369	402 23
							8	2 00
							4,444	1,111 00
	2,281	380 23					6,821	1,515 23
	281	37 47					1,418	264 87
							546	109 20
							12,424	2,484 80
	281	37 47					14,388	2,858 87
							875	218 75
							19,954	4,988 50
							157,621	39,405 25
							178,450	44,612 50
							415	103 75
	5,293	1,058 60		91	36 40		6,296	1,368 60
							2	0 60
							55	16 50
							387	116 10
				703	281 20		703	281 20
							2	0 60
							129	38 70
							4	1 20
							303	90 90
				151	60 40		58,356	17,521 90
	5,293	1,058 60		945	378 00		66,237	19,436 30

No. 1.—General Statement

Articles Imported.	Countries.	Total Imports.		Entered		
				General Tariff.		
		Quantity.	Value.	Quantity.	Value.	Duty.
DUTIABLE GOODS—*Con.*			$		$	$ cts.
Silk and manufactures of— Fabrics, N.E.S.	Great Britain		1,267,714		885,961	265,738 30
	B. E. Indies		14		14	4 20
	Hong Kong		2,332		2,332	699 60
	Aust.-Hungary		16,228		15,725	4,717 50
	Belgium		4,239		4,239	1,271 70
	China		18,392		18,392	5,517 60
	France		539,303		544,911	163,473 30
	Germany		46,310		1,417	425 10
	Italy		45,660		45,660	13,698 00
	Japan		350,378		359,831	107,949 30
	Switzerland		494,367		486,615	145,984 50
	United States		94,779		93,024	27,907 20
	Total		2,879,716		2,458,121	737,436 30
Silk cloth, including satin, imported by manufacturers of burial caskets or burial robes for use in such manufacture	Great Britain		356		313	31 30
	France		7,362		7,362	736 20
	Germany		4,766		689	68 90
	Switzerland		4,757		4,757	475 70
	United States		742		742	74 20
	Total		17,983		13,863	1,386 30
Silk when imported by manufacturers of men's neckties for use exclusively in the manufacture of such neckties in their own factories	Great Britain		103,023		24,194	2,419 40
	Aust.-Hungary		16,151		16,039	1,603 90
	Belgium		898		898	89 80
	France		57,842		58,984	5,898 40
	Germany		98,277		1,223	122 30
	Italy		8,984		8,984	898 40
	Japan		507		507	50 70
	Switzerland		100,802		103,479	10,347 90
	United States		107,374		105,942	10,594 20
	Total		493,858		320,250	32,025 00
Handkerchiefs	Great Britain		46,413		16,748	5,861 80
	Hong Kong		1,095		1,095	383 25
	Belgium		318		318	111 30
	China		3,144		3,144	1,100 40
	France		895		895	313 25
	Germany		70			
	Japan		67,164		76,019	26,606 65
	Switzerland		847		847	296 45
	United States		1,650		1,660	581 00
	Total		121,596		100,726	35,254 10
Blouses and shirt waists	Great Britain		30,964		1,549	542 15
	Aust.-Hungary		413		413	144 55
	Belgium		129		129	45 15
	France		6,098		6,098	2,134 30
	Germany		1,291			
	Japan		1,120		1,120	392 00
	Switzerland		294		294	102 90
	United States		15,440		15,393	5,387 55
	Total		55,749		24,996	8,748 60

OF IMPORTS—*Continued.*

FOR HOME CONSUMPTION.

Preferential Tariff.			Surtax Tariff.			Total.		
Quantity.	Value.	Duty.	Quantity.	Value.	Duty.	Quantity.	Value.	Duty Collected.
	$	$ cts.		$	$ cts.		$	$ cts.
....	363,991	72,798 20	....	15,842	6,336 80	....	1,265,794	344,923 30
....	....	....	....	....	....	....	14	4 20
....	....	....	....	....	....	....	2,332	699 60
....	....	....	....	....	....	....	15,725	4,717 50
....	....	....	....	....	....	....	4,239	1,271 70
....	....	....	....	....	....	....	18,392	5,517 60
....	....	....	....	122	48 80	....	545,033	163,522 10
....	....	....	....	44,264	17,705 60	....	45,681	18,130 70
....	....	....	....	....	....	....	45,660	13,698 00
....	....	....	....	....	....	....	359,831	107,949 30
....	....	....	....	....	....	....	486,615	145,984 50
....	....	....	....	214	85 60	....	93,238	27,992 80
....	363,991	72,798 20	....	60,442	24,176 80	....	2,882,554	834,411 30
....	43	2 87	....	....	....	....	356	34 17
....	....	....	....	....	....	....	7,362	736 20
....	....	....	....	4,077	543 60	....	4,766	612 50
....	....	....	....	....	....	....	4,757	475 70
....	....	....	....	....	....	....	742	74 20
....	43	2 87	....	4,077	543 60	....	17,983	1,932 77
....	66,110	4,407 33	....	12,881	1,717 47	....	103,185	8,544 20
....	....	....	....	267	35 60	....	16,306	1,639 50
....	....	....	....	....	....	....	898	89 80
....	....	....	....	....	....	....	58,984	5,898 40
....	....	....	....	99,764	13,301 86	....	100,987	13,424 16
....	....	....	....	....	....	....	8,984	898 40
....	....	....	....	....	....	....	507	50 70
....	....	....	....	234	31 20	....	103,713	10,379 10
....	....	....	....	1,432	190 93	....	107,374	10,785 13
....	66,110	4,407 33	....	114,578	15,277 06	....	500,938	51,709 39
....	29,117	6,794 13	....	20	9 34	....	45,885	12,665 27
....	....	....	....	....	....	....	1,095	383 25
....	....	....	....	....	....	....	318	111 30
....	....	....	....	....	....	....	3,144	1,100 40
....	....	....	....	....	....	....	895	313 25
....	....	....	....	70	32 66	....	70	32 66
....	....	....	....	....	....	....	76,019	26,606 65
....	....	....	....	....	....	....	847	296 45
....	....	....	....	....	....	....	1,660	581 00
....	29,117	6,794 13	....	90	42 00	....	129,933	42,090 23
....	27,881	6,505 74	....	657	306 60	....	30,087	7,354 49
....	....	....	....	....	....	....	413	144 55
....	....	....	....	....	....	....	129	45 15
....	....	....	....	....	....	....	6,098	2,134 30
....	....	....	....	1,291	602 50	....	1,291	602 50
....	....	....	....	....	....	....	1,120	392 00
....	....	....	....	....	....	....	294	102 90
....	....	....	....	47	21 87	....	15,440	5,409 42
....	27,881	6,505 74	....	1,995	930 97	....	54,872	16,185 31

No. 1.—GENERAL STATEMENT

Articles Imported.	Countries.	Total Imports.		Entered		
				General Tariff.		
		Quantity.	Value.	Quantity.	Value.	Duty.
DUTIABLE GOODS—*Con.*			$		$	$ cts.
Silk and mfrs. of—*Con.* Clothing	Great Britain		169,676		14,836	5,192 60
	Hong Kong		1,159		1,159	405 65
	Aust.-Hungary		512		248	86 80
	Belgium		195		195	68 25
	China		1,383		1,383	484 05
	France		12,795		12,500	4,375 00
	Germany		7,240		14	4 90
	Japan		23,513		23,857	8,349 95
	Switzerland		2,345		2,345	820 75
	United States		35,717		33,207	11,622 45
	Total		254,535		89,744	31,410 40
Silk in the gum or spun, not more advanced than singles, tram and thrown organzine, not coloured		Lbs.		Lbs.		
	Great Britain	15,565	30,286			
	United States	2,390	2,752	2,390	2,752	412 80
	Total	17,955	33,038	2,390	2,752	412 80
Sewing and embroidery silk and silk twist	Great Britain		24,519		969	242 25
	Hong Kong		77		77	19 25
	China		71		71	17 75
	Germany		172			
	Japan		7		7	1 75
	Switzerland		42		42	10 50
	United States		15,299		15,297	3,824 25
	Total		40,187		16,463	4,115 75
Shawls	Great Britain		1,660		181	54 30
	Hong Kong		145		145	43 50
	China		142		142	42 60
	France		264		264	79 20
	Germany		1,663			
	Italy		1,159		1,159	347 70
	Japan		565		565	169 50
	Switzerland		2,077		2,187	656 10
	United States		917		917	275 10
	Total		8,592		5,560	1,668 00
Shirts		Doz.		Doz.		
	Great Britain	165	2,044	1	8	2 80
	Hong Kong	3	27	3	27	9 45
	France	30	210	30	210	73 50
	Japan	15	199	15	199	69 65
	United States		3		3	1 05
	Total	213	2,483	49	447	156 45

OF IMPORTS—*Continued.*

FOR HOME CONSUMPTION.

Preferential Tariff.			Surtax Tariff.			Total.		
Quantity.	Value.	Duty.	Quantity.	Value.	Duty.	Quantity.	Value.	Duty Collected.
	$	$ cts.		$	$ cts.		$	$ cts.
	148,468	34,643 35		2,276	1,062 13		165,580	40,898 08
							1,159	405 65
				264	123 22		512	210 02
							195	68 25
							1,383	484 05
				295	137 68		12,795	4,512 68
				7,124	3,324 46		7,138	3,329 36
							23,857	8,349 95
							2,345	820 75
				39	18 20		33,246	11,640 65
	148,468	34,643 35		9,998	4,665 69		248,210	70,719 44
Lbs.			Lbs.			Lbs.		
15,565	30,286	3,028 60				15,565	30,286	3,028 60
						2,390	2,752	412 80
15,565	30,286	3,028 60				17,955	33,038	3,441 40
	23,206	3,867 93		69	23 00		24,244	4,133 18
							77	19 25
							71	17 75
				172	57 33		172	57 33
							7	1 75
							42	10 50
				2	0 67		15,299	3,824 92
	23,206	3,867 93		243	81 00		39,912	8,064 68
	1,405	281 00		74	29 60		1,660	364 90
							145	43 50
							142	42 60
							264	79 20
				1,663	665 20		1,663	665 20
							1,159	347 70
							565	169 50
							2,187	656 10
							917	275 10
	1,405	281 00		1,737	694 80		8,702	2,643 80
Doz.			Doz.			Doz.		
164	2,036	475 10				165	2,044	477 90
						3	27	9 45
						30	210	73 50
						15	199	69 65
							3	1 65
164	2,036	475 10				213	2,483	631 55

No. 1.—GENERAL STATEMENT

Articles Imported.	Countries.	Total Imports.		Entered		
				General Tariff.		
		Quantity.	Value.	Quantity.	Value.	Duty.
DUTIABLE GOODS—*Con.*			$		$	$ cts
Silk and mfrs. of—*Con.*						
Silk and all manufactures of, not otherwise provided for, or of which silk is the component part of chief value, N.E.S.	reat Britain		49,641		14,127	4,944 45
	Hong Kong		353		353	123 55
	Aust.-Hungary		27		27	9 45
	Belgium		107		107	37 45
	China		1,064		1,064	372 40
	France		8,894		8,919	3,121 65
	Germany		5,517		27	9 45
	Italy		123		123	43 05
	Japan		28,101		27,749	9,712 15
	Switzerland		1,557		1,557	544 95
	Turkey		626		626	219 10
	United States		18,511		18,288	6,400 80
	Total		114,521		72,967	25,538 45
		Doz. prs.		Doz. prs.		
Socks and stockings	Great Britain	840	5,679	16	159	55 65
	France	14	200	14	200	70 00
	Germany	577	2,571			
	United States	23	305	21	283	99 05
	Total	1,454	8,755	51	642	224 70
Undershirts and drawers	Great Britain		6,157		252	88 20
	Japan		11		11	3 85
	United States		381		381	133 35
	Total		6,549		644	225 40
		Yds.		Yds.		
Velvets, velveteens, plush fabrics, N.E.S	Great Britain	315,386	191,253	34,138	25,226	7,567 80
	Aust.-Hungary	798	900	798	900	270 00
	Belgium	761	774	761	774	232 20
	France	64,726	44,399	64,561	44,153	13,245 90
	Germany	41,881	26,050	221	176	52 80
	Italy	6	10	6	10	3 00
	Switzerland	3,248	3,685	3,248	3,685	1,105 50
	United States	21,932	15,199	20,410	14,197	4,259 10
	Total	448,738	282,270	124,143	89,121	26,736 30
Slate and manufactures of—		Sq.		Sq.		
Roofing slate	United States	15,373	60,054	15,373	60,054	11,351 00
School writing slates	Great Britain		7			
	France		341		341	85 25
	Germany		917			
	United States		19,259		19,259	4,814 75
	Total		20,524		19,600	4,900 00

OF IMPORTS—*Continued.*

FOR HOME CONSUMPTION.

Preferential Tariff.			Surtax Tariff.			Total.		
Quantity.	Value.	Duty.	Quantity.	Value.	Duty.	Quantity.	Value.	Duty Collected.
	$	$ cts.		$	$ cts.		$	$ cts.
	32,815	7,657 27		2,575	1,201 67		49,517	13,803 39
							353	123 55
							27	9 45
							107	37 45
							1,064	372 40
							8,919	3,121 65
				5,573	2,600 78		5,600	2,610 23
							123	43 05
							27,749	9,712 15
							1,557	544 95
							626	219 10
				246	114 80		18,534	6,515 60
	32,815	7,657 27		8,394	3,917 25		114,176	37,112 97
Doz. prs.			Doz. prs.			Doz. prs.		
704	4,796	1,119 13	120	724	337 87	840	5,679	1,512 65
						14	200	70 00
			577	2,571	1,199 80	577	2,571	1,199 80
			2	22	10 27	23	305	109 32
704	4,796	1,119 13	699	3,317	1,547 94	1,454	8,755	2,891 77
	5,905	1,377 93					6,157	1,466 13
							11	3 85
							381	133 35
	5,905	1,377 93					6,549	1,603 33
Yds.			Yds.			Yds.		
243,370	142,910	28,582 00	40,383	23,801	9,520 40	317,891	191,937	45,670 20
						798	900	270 00
						761	774	232 20
						64,561	44,153	13,245 90
			43,168	26,331	10,532 40	43,389	26,507	10,585 20
						6	10	3 00
						3,248	3,685	1,105 50
			1,604	1,084	433 60	22,014	15,281	4,692 70
243,370	142,910	28,582 00	85,155	51,216	20,486 40	452,668	283,247	75,804 70
Sq.			Sq.			Sq.		
						15,373	60,054	11,351 00
	7	1 17					7	1 17
							341	85 25
				928	309 35		928	309 35
							19,259	4,814 75
	7	1 17		928	309 35		20,535	5,210 52

No. 1.—GENERAL STATEMENT

Articles Imported.	Countries.	Total Imports.		Entered		
				General Tariff.		
		Quantity.	Value.	Quantity.	Value.	Duty.
DUTIABLE GOODS—*Con.*			$		$	$ cts.
Slate and mfrs. of—*Con.*						
Slate pencils	Great Britain	....	20	....	20	5 00
	Aust.-Hungary	....	48	....	48	12 00
	Germany	....	1,950	....	....	....
	United States	....	1,532	....	1,532	383 00
	Total	....	3,550	....	1,600	400 00
Slate and mfrs. of, N.E.S.	Great Britain	....	817	....	817	245 10
	France	....	9	....	9	2 70
	United States	....	28,197	....	28,197	8,459 10
	Total	....	29,023	....	29,023	8,706 90
Soap—		Lbs.		Lbs.		
Common or laundry	Great Britain	37,188	1,616	7,393	418	73 93
	Australia	3,480	175	3,480	175	34 80
	Aust.-Hungary	783	84	783	84	7 83
	France	3,533	174	3,533	174	35 33
	Italy	22,903	939	22,903	939	229 03
	Turkey	5,276	257	5,276	257	52 76
	United States	1,665,381	92,906	1,608,255	89,360	16,082 55
	Total	1,738,544	96,151	1,651,623	91,407	16,516 23
Castile, mottled or white	Great Britain	16,076	857	17,754	934	198 19
	France	1,361,267	64,990	1,406,806	65,461	14,317 90
	Italy	58,850	3,841	59,002	3,853	1,180 04
	United States	59,951	4,797	59,951	4,797	914 56
	Total	1,496,144	74,485	1,543,513	75,045	16,610 69
Common soft and liquid	Great Britain	73,406	2,181	16,205	493	172 55
	Germany	712	86	....	....	....
	United States	63,637	2,338	63,637	2,338	818 30
	Total	137,755	4,605	79,842	2,831	990 85
Harness	Great Britain	3,043	390	458	41	10 25
	United States	13,909	1,852	13,909	1,852	463 00
	Total	16,952	2,242	14,367	1,893	473 25
Toilet	Great Britain	....	39,077	....	1,294	452 90
	Aust.-Hungary	....	137	....	....	....
	China	....	1	....	1	0 35
	France	....	7,520	....	7,611	2,663 85
	Germany	....	1,479	....	....	....
	Japan	....	152	....	152	53 20
	Turkey	....	14	....	14	4 90
	United States	....	134,923	....	132,341	46,319 35
	Total	....	183,303	....	141,413	49,494 55

OF IMPORTS—*Continued.*

FOR HOME CONSUMPTION.

Preferential Tariff.			Surtax Tariff.			Total.		
Quantity.	Value.	Duty.	Quantity.	Value.	Duty.	Quantity.	Value.	Duty Collected.
	$	$ cts.		$	$ cts.		$	$ cts.
....	....	....	....	....	....	....	20	5 00
....	....	....	....	....	....	....	48	12 00
....	....	....	....	1,729	576 36	....	1,729	576 36
....	....	....	....	....	....	....	1,532	383 00
....	....	....	....	1,729	576 36	....	3,329	976 36
....	....	....	....	....	....	....	817	245 10
....	....	....	....	....	....	....	9	2 70
....	....	....	....	....	....	....	28,197	8,459 10
....	....	....	....	....	....	....	29,023	8,706 90
Lbs.			Lbs.			Lbs.		
37,075	1,633	247 20	....	....	....	44,468	2,051	321 13
....	....	....	....	....	....	3,480	175	34 80
....	....	....	....	....	....	783	84	7 83
....	....	....	....	....	....	3,533	174	35 33
....	....	....	....	....	....	22,903	939	229 03
....	....	....	....	....	....	5,276	257	52 76
....	....	....	....	....	....	1,608,255	89,360	16,082 55
37,075	1,633	247 20	....	....	....	1,688,698	93,040	16,763 43
122	6	1 62	....	....	....	17,876	940	199 81
....	....	....	....	....	....	1,406,806	65,461	14,317 90
....	....	....	....	....	....	59,002	3,853	1,180 04
....	....	....	....	....	....	59,951	4,797	914 56
122	6	1 62	....	....	....	1,543,635	75,051	16,612 31
57,201	1,688	393 93	....	....	....	73,406	2,181	566 48
....	....	....	712	86	40 13	712	86	40 13
....	....	....	....	....	....	63,637	2,338	818 30
57,201	1,688	393 93	712	86	40 13	137,755	4,605	1,424 91
2,585	349	58 18	....	....	....	3,043	390	68 43
....	....	....	....	....	....	13,909	1,852	463 00
2,585	349	58 18	....	....	....	16,952	2,242	531 43
....	37 514	8,753 59	....	143	66 76	....	38,951	9,273 25
....	....	....	....	....	....	....	....	....
....	....	....	....	....	....	....	1	0 35
....	....	....	....	....	....	....	7,611	2,663 85
....	....	....	....	1,479	690 20	....	1,479	690 20
....	....	....	....	....	....	....	152	53 20
....	....	....	....	....	....	....	14	4 90
....	....	....	....	6	2 80	....	132,347	46,322 15
....	37,514	8,753 59	....	1,628	759 76	....	180,555	59,007 90

No. 1.—General Statement

Articles Imported.	Countries.	Total Imports.		Entered		
				General Tariff.		
		Quantity.	Value.	Quantity.	Value.	Duty.
DUTIABLE GOODS—*Con.*		Lbs.	$	Lbs.	$	$ cts.
Soap, N. E. S., including pumice, silver and mineral soaps, sapolio and like articles....................	Great Britain...	4,869	456	110	14	4 90
	China...........	800	5	800	5	1 75
	France..........	633	100	633	100	35 00
	Japan	90	4	90	4	1 40
	United States...	632,392	54,025	577,955	48,744	17,060 40
	Total.....	638,784	54,590	579,588	48,867	17,103 45
Pearline and other soap powders....	Great Britain...	2,172	153	....	....	....
	China...	60	7	60	7	2 10
	France....	20	1	20	1	0 30
	United States...	2,355,796	95,904	2,329,933	94,499	28,349 70
	Total......	2,358,048	96,065	2,330,013	94,507	28,352 10
Spices— Ginger and spices of all kinds, N.E.S., unground.........	Great Britain...	1,029,982	109,152	110,479	9,253	1,156 62
	B. Africa.......	1,000	25	1,000	25	3 13
	B. E. Indies....	1,194,059	74,499	20,928	2,372	296 50
	B. W. Indies....	80,124	4,207	11,056	451	56 38
	Hong Kong.....	7,125	516	7,125	516	64 50
	China...........	60,334	2,903	60,334	2,903	362 87
	Dutch E. Indies	6,300	1,032	6,300	1,032	129 00
	Italy..........	995	40	995	40	5 00
	Japan..........	65,701	4,078	65,701	4,078	509 75
	United States...	591,834	52,372	602,015	52,485	6,561 28
	Total......	3,037,454	248,824	885,933	73,155	9,145 03
" " ground..........	Great Britain...	60,076	8,012	10,082	367	91 75
	B. E. Indies....	50	8	50	8	2 00
	B. W. Indies....	61	25	....	....	....
	Hong Kong.....	804	9	804	9	2 25
	China...........	1,425	110	1,425	110	27 50
	France..........	12	2	12	2	0 50
	Holland........	1,800	164	1,800	164	41 00
	Japan...... ...	93	5	93	5	1 25
	United States...	237,794	18,151	238,724	18,070	4,517 50
	Total......	302,118	26,486	252,990	18,735	4,683 75
Ginger, preserved...........	Great Britain...	22,278	2,188	16,299	1,153	345 90
	B. W. Indies....	4	1	4	1	0 30
	Hong Hong.....	15,546	883	15,546	883	264 90
	China....... ...	83,386	4,516	77,397	4,516	1,354 80
	Italy...........	382	80	382	80	24 00
	Japan..........	11,017	428	11,017	428	128 40
	United States...	8,784	721	8,784	721	216 30
	Total......	143,397	8,817	129,429	7,782	2,334 60

OF IMPORTS—*Continued.*

FOR HOME CONSUMPTION.

Preferential Tariff.			Surtax Tariff.			Total.		
Quantity.	Value.	Duty.	Quantity.	Value.	Duty.	Quantity.	Value.	Duty Collected.
Lbs.	$	$ cts.	Lbs.	$	$ cts.	Lbs.	$	$ cts.
3,909	319	74 44				4,019	333	79 34
						800	5	1 75
						633	100	35 00
						90	4	1 40
						577,955	48,744	17,060 40
3,909	319	74 44				583,497	49,186	17,177 89
922	70	14 00				922	70	14 00
						60	7	2 10
						20	1	0 30
						2,329,933	94,499	28,349 70
922	70	14 00				2,330,935	94,577	28,366 10
917,767	99,167	8,263 95				1,028,246	108,420	9,420 57
						1,000	25	3 13
1,166,876	71,521	5,960 38				1,187,804	73,893	6,256 88
65,675	3,609	300 75				76,731	4,060	357 13
						7,125	516	64 50
						60,334	2,903	362 87
						6,300	1,032	129 00
						995	40	5 00
						65,701	4,078	509 75
						602,015	52,485	6,561 28
2,150,318	174,297	14,525 08				3,036,251	247,452	23,670 11
52,143	7,677	1,279 80				62,225	8,044	1,371 55
477	56	9 34				527	64	11 34
						804	9	2 25
						1,425	110	27 50
						12	2	0 50
						1,800	164	41 00
						93	5	1 25
						238,724	18,070	4,517 50
52,620	7,733	1,289 14				305,610	26,468	5,972 89
5,885	995	199 00				22,184	2,148	544 90
						4	1	0 30
						15,546	883	264 90
						77,397	4,516	1,354 80
						382	80	24 00
						11,017	428	128 40
						8,784	721	216 30
5,885	995	199 00				135,314	8,777	2,533 60

No. 1.—General Statement

Articles Imported.	Countries.	Total Imports.		Entered		
				General Tariff.		
		Quantity.	Value.	Quantity.	Value.	Duty.
DUTIABLE GOODS—*Con.*		Lbs.	$	Lbs.	$	$ cts.
Spices—*Con.*						
Nutmegs and mace..........	Great Britain...	112,107	18,754	6,709	939	234 75
	B. E. Indies....	8,892	783	....	....	....
	B. W. Indies....	1,238	125	454	54	13 50
	Holland........	996	321	996	321	80 25
	United States...	30,463	4,063	30,463	4,063	1,015 75
	Total......	153,696	24,046	38,622	5,377	1,344 25
Spirits and wines, viz.—						
Amyl alcohol or fusel oil, or any substance known as potato spirit or potato oil..	United States...	Galls. 3	8	3	Galls. 8	7 20
Ethyl alcohol, or the substance known as alcohol, hydrated oxide of ethyl, or spirits of wine......................	Germany.......	115	105	....	....	....
	United States...	308,750	58,880	115,661	23,155	277,586 40
	Total......	308,865	58,985	115,661	23,155	277,586 40
Methyl alcohol, wood alcohol, wood naphtha, pyroxylic spirits, wood spirits, or methylated spirits	Germany......	2	3	....	....	....
	United States...	18	28	18	28	43 20
	Total......	20	31	18	28	43 20
Absinthe......................	Great Britain...	380	534	251	451	602 40
	France..........	2,421	3,660	2,581	3,642	6,194 40
	St. Pierre.......	2	9	....	....	....
	Switzerland.....	200	345	214	313	513 60
	United States...	....	....	36	64	86 40
	Total......	3,003	4,548	3,082	4,470	7,396 80
Arrack or palm spirit........	Aust.-Hungary .	11	10	11	10	26 40
	Italy...........	78	175	32	69	76 80
	Turkey.........	133	284	261	371	626 40
	United States...	300	361	300	361	720 00
	Total......	522	830	604	811	1,449 60
Brandy, including artificial brandy and imitations of brandy	Great Britain...	12,953	18,909	13,408	23,648	32,179 20
	Australia......	122	311	72	201	172 80
	B. Guiana......	....	....	4	3	9 60
	Aust.-Hungary .	170	105	356	154	854 40
	Egypt.........	35	26	35	26	84 00
	France.........	340,872	518,206	326,850	526,696	784,440 00
	Greece.........	13	9	20	8	48 00
	Holland........	....	....	8	5	19 20
	Italy..........	165	230	194	286	465 60
	Spain	185	263	373	758	895 20
	St. Pierre......	12	54	12	54	28 80
	Turkey........	29	14	29	14	69 60
	United States...	655	1,535	393	1,249	943 20
	Total.......	355,211	539,662	341,754	553,102	820,209 60

OF IMPORTS—*Continued.*

FOR HOME CONSUMPTION.

Preferential Tariff.			Surtax Tariff.			Total.		
Quantity.	Value.	Duty.	Quantity.	Value.	Duty.	Quantity.	Value.	Duty Collected.
Lbs.	$	$ cts.	Lbs.	$	$ cts.	Lbs.	$	$ cts.
103,132	17,777	2,962 89				109,841	18,716	3,197 64
8,892	783	130 51				8,892	783	130 51
784	71	11 84				1,238	125	25 34
						996	321	80 25
						30,463	4,063	1,015 75
112,808	18,631	3,105 24				151,430	24,008	4,449 49
Galls.			Galls.			Galls.		
						3	8	7 20
			115	105	368 00	115	105	368 00
						115,661	23,155	277,586 40
			115	105	368 00	115,776	23,260	277,954 40
			2	3	6 40	2	3	6 40
						18	28	43 20
			2	3	6 40	20	31	49 60
						251	451	602 40
						2,581	3,642	6,194 40
						214	313	513 60
						36	64	86 40
						3,082	4,470	7,396 80
						11	10	26 40
						32	69	76 80
						261	371	626 40
						300	361	720 00
						604	811	1,449 60
						13,408	23,648	32,179 20
						72	201	172 80
						4	3	9 60
						356	154	854 40
						35	26	84 00
						326,850	526,696	784,440 00
						20	8	48 00
						8	5	19 20
						194	286	465 60
						373	758	895 20
						12	54	28 80
						29	14	69 60
						393	1,249	943 20
						341,754	553,102	820,209 60

No. 1.—General Statement

Articles Imported.	Countries.	Total Imports.		Entered		
				General Tariff.		
		Quantity.	Value.	Quantity.	Value.	Duty.
		Galls.	$	Galls.	$	$ cts.
Dutiable goods—*Con.*						
Spirits and wines—*Con.*						
Cordials and liqueurs of all kinds, N.E.S.; mescal, pulque, rum shrub, schiedam and other schnapps; tafia, angostura and similar alcoholic bitters or beverages..................	Great Britain...	4,493	11,322	4,407	13,314	10,576 80
	B. W. Indies...	....	....	12	92	28 80
	B. Guiana......	19	85	19	85	45 60
	Hong Kong.....	8,812	6,346	8,960	6,638	21,504 00
	Aust.-Hungary .	....	....	13	68	31 20
	Belgium.......	10	24	11	32	26 40
	China..........	4,272	2,824	4,252	2,851	10,204 80
	Denmark.......	....	....	20	58	48 00
	France.........	16,888	57,098	14,319	45,559	34,365 60
	Germany.......	180	270	....	....	....
	Holland........	960	1,739	653	1,684	1,567 20
	Italy...........	409	848	452	1,011	1,084 80
	Norway........	301	609	189	408	453 60
	Russia.........	8	26	8	26	19 20
	St. Pierre......	4	33	4	33	9 60
	Spain..........	130	868	93	437	223 20
	Sweden........	52	115	25	57	60 00
	Switzerland....	....	....	2	4	4 80
	United States...	1,809	9,151	1,928	9,917	4,627 20
	Total.......	38,347	91,358	35,367	82,274	84,880 80
Gin of all kinds, N.E.S......	Great Britain...	102,777	113,081	82,747	88,864	198,592 80
	France.........	11	28	43	59	103 20
	Germany.......	....	....	....	....	....
	Holland........	568,987	264,226	644,303	280,841	1,546,327 20
	St. Pierre......	11	28	11	28	26 40
	Spain..........	....	....	68	70	163 20
	United States...	177	165	325	165	780 00
	Total.......	671,963	377,528	727,497	370,027	1,745,992 80
Rum..........................	Great Britain...	34,322	20,683	34,700	19,899	83,280 00
	B. Guiana......	37,111	10,081	54,496	11,069	130,790 40
	B. W. Indies...	20,123	11,608	21,171	10,368	50,810 40
	Aust.-Hungary..	115	39	....	....	....
	Dan. W. Indies.	....	....	82	37	196 80
	France.........	17,323	17,100	17,342	17,451	41,620 80
	St. Pierre......	29	61	29	61	69 60
	United States...	4,644	1,926	5,426	2,219	13,022 40
	Total.......	113,667	61,498	133,246	61,104	319,790 40
Whisky.......................	Great Britain...	639,817	1,012,799	581,037	919,533	1,394,488 80
	B. W. Indies...	2,000	1,433	350	390	840 00
	Hong Kong.....	3	12	3	12	7 20
	China..........	17	6	44	25	105 60
	France.........	239	455	328	635	787 20
	Germany.......	192	456	29	68	69 60
	St. Pierre......	3	9	3	9	7 20
	United States...	4,272	9,423	4,366	9.162	10,478 40
	Total.......	646,543	1,024.593	586,160	929,834	1,406,784 00

OF IMPORTS—*Continued.*

FOR HOME CONSUMPTION.

Preferential Tariff.			Surtax Tariff.			Total.		
Quantity.	Value.	Duty.	Quantity.	Value.	Duty.	Quantity.	Value.	Duty Collected.
Galls.	$	$ cts.	Galls.	$	$ cts.	Galls.	$	$ cts.
			11	31	35 20	4,418	13,345	10,612 00
						12	92	28 80
						19	85	45 60
						8,960	6,638	21,504 00
						13	68	31 20
						11	32	26 40
						4,252	2,851	10,204 80
						20	58	48 00
						14,319	45,559	34,365 60
			129	203	412 80	129	203	412 80
						653	1,684	1,567 20
						452	1,011	1,084 80
						189	408	453 60
						8	26	19 20
						4	33	9 60
						93	437	223 20
						25	57	60 00
						2	4	4 80
			22	66	70 40	1,950	9,983	4,697 60
			162	300	518 40	35,529	82,574	85,399 20
						82,747	88,864	198,592 80
						43	59	103 20
			55	38	176 00	55	38	176 00
						644,303	280,841	1,546,327 20
						11	28	26 40
						68	70	163 20
						325	165	780 00
			55	38	176 00	727,552	370,065	1,746,168 80
						34,700	19,899	83,280 00
						54,496	11,069	130,790 40
						21,171	10,368	50,810 40
						82	37	196 80
						17,342	17,451	41,620 80
						29	61	69 60
						5,426	2,219	13,022 40
						133,246	61,104	319,790 40
						581,037	919,533	1,394,488 80
						350	390	840 00
						3	12	7 20
						44	25	105 60
						328	635	787 20
			226	523	723 20	255	591	792 80
						3	9	7 20
						4,366	9,162	10,478 40
			226	523	723 20	586,386	930,357	1,407,507 20

No. 1.—General Statement

Articles Imported.	Countries.	Total Imports.		Entered		
				General Tariff.		
		Quantity.	Value.	Quantity.	Value.	Duty.
DUTIABLE GOODS—*Con.*		Galls.	$	Galls.	$	$ cts.
Spirits and wines—*Con.* All spirituous or alcoholic liquors, N.O.P...	Great Britain...	104	231	48	116	115 20
	Hong Kong.....	3,601	2,427	3,522	2,361	8,452 80
	Aust.-Hungary .	545	172	200	59	480 00
	China..........	13,067	8,432	12,870	8,357	30,888 00
	France.........	54	260	28	30	67 20
	Germany.	21	20	....	....	....
	Italy.	....	....	10	26	24 00
	Japan.........	199	112	199	112	477 60
	United States...	489	627	458	535	1,099 20
	Total......	18,080	12,281	17,335	11,596	41,604 00
Spirits and strong waters of any kind, mixed with any ingredient or ingredients, as being or known or designated as anodynes, elixirs, essences, extracts, lotions, tinctures or medicines, or medicinal wines (so called), or ethereal and spirituous fruit essences, N.E.S.......	Great Britain...	1,203	5,140	1,186	5,025	4,353 90
	Aust.-Hungary .	1	7	1	7	4 50
	China	33	21	33	21	85 50
	France.........	221	2,571	182	2,014	1,041 00
	Germany.	79	112	....	....	....
	United States...	884	7,244	880	7,197	4,271 10
	Total......	2,421	15,095	2,282	14,264	9,756 00
Medicinal or medicated wines containing not more than 40 per cent of proof spirit...	Great Britain...	29	167	29	167	43 50
	Aust.-Hungary..	....	....	14	95	21 00
	France.........	3,219	9,406	3,071	8,310	4,606 50
	United States...	5	25	5	25	7 50
	Total......	3,253	9,598	3,119	8,597	4,678 50
Alcoholic perfumes and perfumed spirits, bay rum, cologne and lavender waters, hair, tooth and skin washes, and other toilet preparations containing spirits of any kind in bottles or flasks containing not more than 4 ounces each..	Great Britain...	399	8,661	387	8,536	4,268 00
	B. E. Indies....	12	42	12	42	21 00
	Hong Kong. ...	....	1	....	1	0 50
	Aust.-Hungary..	150	918	148	839	419 50
	France.	2,042	27,613	2,091	28,261	14,130 50
	Germany.	337	3,024	....	....	....
	Holland..	2	4	2	4	2 00
	United States...	989	13,840	998	14,086	7,043 00
	Total.....	3,931	54,103	3,638	51,769	25,884 50
Alcoholic perfumes and perfumed spirits in bottles, flasks or other packages containing more than 4 ounces each....	Great Britain. ..	155	3,356	128	3,018	1,514 40
	B. W. Indies....	91	140	41	69	126 00
	Aust.-Hungary .	5	30	....	....	....
	France.	2,494	36,065	2,570	36,510	20,772 00
	Germany.	77	570	....	....	....
	United States...	656	13,235	648	13,203	6,836 40
	Total... .	3,478	53,396	3,387	52,800	29,248 80

OF IMPORTS—*Continued.*

FOR HOME CONSUMPTION.

Preferential Tariff.			Surtax Tariff.			Total.		
Quantity.	Value.	Duty.	Quantity.	Value.	Duty.	Quantity.	Value.	Duty Collected.
Galls.	$	$ cts.	Galls.	$	$ cts.	Galls.	$	$ cts.
....	....	....	....	....	....	48	116	115 20
....	....	....	....	....	....	3,522	2,361	8,452 80
....	....	....	....	....	....	200	59	480 00
....	....	....	....	....	....	12,870	8,357	30,888 00
....	....	....	....	....	....	28	30	67 20
....	....	....	21	20	67 20	21	20	67 20
....	....	....	....	....	....	10	26	24 00
....	....	....	....	....	....	199	112	477 60
....	....	....	....	....	....	458	535	1,099 20
....	....	....	21	20	67 20	17,356	11,616	41,671 20
....	....	....	....	....	....	1,186	5,025	4,353 90
....	....	....	....	....	....	1	7	4 50
....	....	....	....	....	....	33	21	85 50
....	....	....	6	7	22 00	188	2,021	1,063 00
....	....	....	57	78	213 60	57	78	213 60
....	....	....	....	....	....	880	7,197	4,271 10
....	....	....	63	85	235 60	2,345	14,349	9,991 60
....	....	....	....	....	....	29	167	43 50
....	....	....	....	....	....	14	95	21 00
....	....	....	....	....	....	3,071	8,310	4,606 50
....	....	....	....	....	....	5	25	7 50
....	....	....	....	....	....	3,119	8,597	4,678 50
....	....	....	14	81	54 00	401	8,617	4,322 00
....	....	....	....	....	....	12	42	21 00
....	....	....	....	....	....	....	1	0 50
....	....	....	3	86	57 33	151	925	476 83
....	....	....	....	....	....	2,091	28,261	14,130 50
....	....	....	340	3,083	2,055 33	340	3,083	2,055 33
....	....	....	....	....	....	2	4	2 00
....	....	....	1	20	13 30	999	14,106	7,056 30
....	....	....	358	3,270	2,179 96	3,996	55,039	28,064 46
....	....	....	....	....	....	128	3,018	1,514 40
....	....	....	....	....	....	41	69	126 00
....	....	....	5	30	32 00	5	30	32 00
....	....	....	....	....	....	2,570	36,510	20,772 00
....	....	....	81	602	580 27	81	602	580 27
....	....	....	8	32	42 64	656	13,235	6,879 04
....	....	....	94	664	654 91	3,481	53,464	29,903 71

No. 1.—General Statement

Articles Imported.	Countries.	Total Imports.		Entered		
				General Tariff.		
		Quantity.	Value.	Quantity.	Value.	Duty.
DUTIABLE GOODS—*Con.*		Galls.	$	Galls.	$	$ cts.
Spirits and wines—*Con.*						
Vermouth containing not more than 36 per cent of proof spirits	Great Britain	440	538	1,171	1,392	1,053 90
	France	13,283	16,549	11,382	13,294	10,243 80
	Italy	4,988	5,318	4,622	4,752	4,159 80
	St. Pierre	8	19	8	19	7 20
	Spain	77	80	3	2	2 70
	United States	569	849	523	788	470 70
	Total	19,365	23,353	17,709	20,247	15,938 10
Vermouth containing more than 36 per cent of proof spirits	Great Britain	60	90	30	40	72 00
	France	....	....	21	25	50 40
	Italy	126	136	29	32	69 60
	Total	186	226	80	97	192 00
Nitrous ether, sweet spirits of nitre and aromatic spirits of ammonia	Great Britain	381	863	367	814	1,125 00
	Germany	151	272	48	82	139 80
	United States	151	685	151	685	567 90
	Total	683	1,820	566	1,581	1,832 70
Wines, ginger, containing not more than 26 per cent of proof spirits	Great Britain	2,116	1,675	2,016	1,581	1,814 40
	France	5	9	5	9	4 50
	St. Pierre	8	22	4	11	3 60
	Total	2,129	1,706	2,025	1,601	1,822 50
Wines, ginger, containing more than 26 per cent of proof spirits	Hong Kong	35	10	35	10	84 00
	China	96	115	96	115	230 40
	United States	1	4	1	4	2 40
	Total	132	129	132	129	316 80
Wines of all kinds, except sparkling wines, including orange, lemon, strawberry, raspberry, elder and currant wines:—						
Containing 26 p.c. or less of spirits	Great Britain	2,912	4,291	2,808	4,378	1,090 20
	Australia	4	6	4	6	2 80
	Gibraltar	6	7	6	7	3 60
	Aust.-Hungary	119	46	119	46	43 55
	Belgium	11	21	11	21	9 05
	China	33	9	33	9	10 95
	Egypt	27	13	27	13	10 65
	France	155,605	119,192	151,040	119,426	38,579 00
	French Africa	....	....	131	75	32 75
	Germany	7,633	12,948	51	52	25 95
	Greece	37	5	37	5	10 75
	Holland	24	81	....	....	....
	Italy	3,430	2,222	6,350	4,026	2,786 00
	Japan	601	452	601	452	285 85
	Portugal	274	288	368	278	123 50
	St. Pierre	332	422	441	597	149 55
	Spain	146,018	55,232	138,351	52,157	34,852 95
	Turkey	79	58	79	58	37 15
	United States	19,364	10,278	20,053	10,867	8,170 75
	Total	336,509	205,571	320,510	192,473	86,225 00

OF IMPORTS—*Continued.*

FOR HOME CONSUMPTION.

Preferential Tariff.			Surtax Tariff.			Total.		
Quantity.	Value.	Duty.	Quantity.	Value.	Duty.	Quantity.	Value.	Duty Collected.
Galls.	$	$ cts.	Galls.	$	$ cts.	Galls.	$	$ cts.
....	....	....	....	....	....	1,171	1,392	1,053 90
....	....	....	....	....	....	11,382	13,294	10,243 80
....	....	....	....	....	....	4,622	4,752	4,159 80
....	....	....	....	....	....	8	19	7 20
....	....	....	....	....	....	3	2	2 70
....	....	....	....	....	....	523	788	470 70
....	....	....	....	....	....	17,709	20,247	15,938 10
....	....	....	....	....	....	30	40	72 00
....	....	....	....	....	....	21	25	50 40
....	....	....	....	....	....	29	32	69 60
....	....	....	....	....	....	80	97	192 00
....	....	....	....	....	....	367	814	1,125 00
....	....	....	150	269	587 60	198	351	727 40
....	....	....	....	....	....	151	685	567 90
....	....	....	150	269	587 60	716	1,850	2,420 30
....	....	....	....	....	....	2,016	1,581	1,814 40
....	....	....	....	....	....	5	9	4 50
....	....	....	....	....	....	4	11	3 60
....	....	....	....	....	....	2,025	1,601	1,822 50
....	....	....	....	....	....	35	10	84 00
....	....	....	....	....	....	96	115	230 40
....	....	....	....	....	....	1	4	2 40
....	....	....	....	....	....	132	129	316 80
....	....	....	46	220	103 30	2,854	4,598	1,193 50
....	....	....	....	....	....	4	6	2 80
....	....	....	....	....	....	6	7	3 60
....	....	....	....	....	....	119	46	43 55
....	....	....	....	....	....	11	21	9 05
....	....	....	....	....	....	33	9	10 95
....	....	....	....	....	....	27	13	10 65
....	....	....	2	7	3 47	151,042	119,433	38,582 47
....	....	....	....	....	....	131	75	32 75
....	....	....	6,297	10,215	6,185 00	6.348	10,267	6,210 95
....	....	....	....	....	....	37	5	10 75
....	....	....	24	81	40 40	24	81	40 40
....	....	....	....	....	....	6,350	4,026	2,786 00
....	....	....	....	....	....	601	452	285 85
....	....	....	....	....	....	368	278	123 50
....	....	....	....	....	....	441	597	149 55
....	....	....	....	....	....	138,351	52,157	34,852 95
....	....	....	....	....	....	79	58	37 15
....	....	....	....	....	....	20,053	10,867	8,170 75
....	....	....	6,369	10,523	6,332 17	326,879	202,996	92,557 17

No. 1.—General Statement

Articles Imported.	Countries.	Total Imports.		Entered		
				General Tariff.		
		Quantity.	Value.	Quantity.	Value.	Duty.
Dutiable Goods—*Con*		Galls.	$	Galls.	$	$ cts.
Spirits and wines—*Con.* Wines of all kinds, except sparkling wines—*Con.*						
Containing over 26 p.c. and not over 27 p.c....	Great Britain...	693	623	604	499	318 82
	China	235	50	235	50	80 80
	France..... ...	113	157	479	344	237 32
	Italy	4,241	1,392	5,450	1,976	2,118 80
	Japan	628	286	850	385	353 50
	Portugal.......	130	91	72	101	50 46
	Spain.....	1,444	1,309	1,851	1,503	969 18
	United States...	126	197	73	58	37 84
	Total.	7,610	4,105	9,614	4,916	4,166 72
Containing over 27 p.c. and not over 28 p.c....	Great Britain...	98	257	210	456	201 90
	Hong Kong.....	298	93	298	93	120 28
	China	1,529	282	1,529	282	558 59
	France	499	490	513	723	375 93
	Italy	1,279	496	1,734	787	773 64
	Japan	4,892	2,480	4,705	2,327	2,156 65
	Portugal........	524	418	603	498	336 33
	Spain.	3,399	2,932	2,695	1,848	1,389 85
	United States...	105	109	186	212	121 26
	Total.......	12,623	7,557	12,473	7,226	6,034 43
Containing over 28 p.c. and not over 29 p.c....	Great Britain...	1,372	1,464	872	956	583 28
	Hong Kong.....	1,107	214	1,107	214	440 58
	China	6,103	1,191	6,103	1,191	2,432 32
	France.........	544	574	588	695	408 42
	Italy.	1,618	839	2,600	1,298	1,273 40
	Japan..........	8,010	3,781	7,616	3,572	3,661 04
	Portugal	....	....	192	190	122 28
	Spain..........	4,608	3,775	3,651	2,857	2,098 44
	United States...	653	730	676	745	453 34
	Total.......	24,015	12,568	23,405	11,718	11,473 10
Containing over 29 p.c. and not over 30 p.c....	Great Britain...	774	1,220	619	1,139	570 73
	Hong Kong.....	1,556	318	1,556	318	671 12
	China..........	6,728	1,357	6,831	1,397	2,946 57
	France.........	258	332	322	502	269 74
	Italy...........	21	13	718	410	388 66
	Japan	7,599	3,404	6,859	3,223	3,504 73
	Portugal........	1,306	1,466	1,348	1,363	907 66
	Spain...........	6,403	6,282	6,557	6,456	4,362 89
	United States...	1,166	1,255	1,112	1,156	758 24
	Total	25,811	15,647	25,922	15,964	14,380 34

OF IMPORTS—*Continued.*

FOR HOME CONSUMPTION.

Preferential Tariff.			Surtax Tariff.			Total.		
Quantity.	Value.	Duty.	Quantity.	Value.	Duty.	Quantity.	Value.	Duty Collected.
Galls.	$	$ cts.	Galls.	$	$ cts.	Galls.	$	$ cts.
....	....	....	....	....	....	604	499	318 82
....	....	....	....	....	....	235	50	80 80
....	....	....	....	....	....	479	344	237 32
....	....	....	....	....	....	5,450	1,976	2,118 80
....	....	....	....	....	....	850	385	353 50
....	....	....	....	....	....	72	101	50 46
....	....	....	....	....	....	1,851	1,503	969 18
....	....	....	....	....	....	73	58	37 84
....	....	....	....	....	....	9,614	4,916	4,166 72
....	....	....	....	....	....	210	456	201 90
....	....	....	....	....	....	298	93	120 28
....	....	....	....	....	....	1,529	282	558 59
....	....	....	....	....	....	513	723	375 93
....	....	....	....	....	....	1,734	787	773 64
....	....	....	....	....	....	4,705	2,327	2,156 65
....	....	....	....	....	....	603	498	336 33
....	....	....	....	....	....	2,695	1,848	1,389 85
....	....	....	....	....	....	186	212	121 26
....	....	....	....	....	....	12,473	7,226	6,034 43
....	....	....	....	....	....	872	956	583 28
....	....	....	....	....	....	1,107	214	440 58
....	....	....	....	....	....	6,103	1,191	2,432 32
....	....	....	....	....	....	588	695	408 42
....	....	....	....	....	....	2,600	1,298	1,273 40
....	....	....	....	....	....	7,616	3,572	3,661 04
....	....	....	....	....	....	192	190	122 28
....	....	....	....	....	....	3,651	2,857	2,098 44
....	....	....	....	....	....	676	745	453 34
....	....	....	....	....	....	23,405	11,718	11,473 10
....	....	....	....	....	....	619	1,139	570 73
....	....	....	....	....	....	1,556	318	671 12
....	....	....	....	....	....	6,831	1,397	2,946 57
....	....	....	....	....	....	322	502	269 74
....	....	....	....	....	....	718	410	388 66
....	....	....	....	....	....	6,859	3,223	3,504 73
....	....	....	....	....	....	1,348	1,363	907 66
....	....	....	....	....	....	6,557	6,456	4,362 89
....	....	....	....	....	....	1,112	1,156	758 24
....	....	....	....	....	....	25,922	15,964	14,380 34

No. 1.—GENERAL STATEMENT

Articles Imported.	Countries.	Total Imports.		Entered		
				General Tariff.		
		Quantity.	Value.	Quantity.	Value.	Duty.
DUTIABLE GOODS—*Con.*		Galls.	$	Galls.	$	$ cts.
Spirits and wines—*Con.* Wines of all kinds, except sparkling wines—*Con.* Containing over 30 p.c. and not over 31 p.c.	Great Britain	1,576	2,173	1,394	1,696	1,066 40
	Hong Kong	2,432	420	2,463	471	1,126 50
	China	5,754	1,218	5,769	1,226	2,675 40
	France	95	247	226	344	193 60
	Holland	....	....	5	14	6 20
	Italy	....	....	194	176	130 40
	Japan	1,500	680	1,180	532	631 60
	Portugal	921	1,478	1,495	2,234	1,268 20
	Spain	9,446	11,040	9,844	10,941	7,219 90
	United States	1,083	749	1,130	780	686 00
	Total	22,807	18,005	23,700	18,414	15,004 20
Containing over 31 p.c. and not over 32 p.c.	Great Britain	3,818	3,462	1,692	2,334	1,427 76
	Hong Kong	2,880	529	2,804	516	1,360 52
	China	3,283	677	3,310	699	1,633 00
	France	506	596	974	1,141	761 12
	Japan	313	135	313	135	175 09
	Portugal	5,436	5,431	4,243	4,815	3,268 99
	Spain	14,518	14,587	17,288	16,812	12,477 46
	United States	2,717	1,914	2,557	1,820	1,645 51
	Total	33,471	27,331	33,181	28,272	22,749 45
Containing over 32 p.c. and not over 33 p.c.	Great Britain	1,383	2,581	1,627	2,680	1,552 42
	Gibraltar	6	13	6	13	6 66
	Hong Kong	3,283	639	3,283	639	1,701 88
	Newfoundland	27	125	27	125	49 92
	China	1,796	342	1,822	378	951 52
	France	577	973	753	1,068	666 78
	Italy	....	....	10	9	7 30
	Madeira	....	....	45	44	33 90
	Portugal	5,862	8,585	5,259	7,718	4,734 54
	Spain	15,172	17,341	13,883	17,287	11,572 28
	United States	3,386	1,952	3,311	1,911	2,096 36
	Total	31,492	32,551	30,026	31,872	23,373 56
Containing over 33 p.c. and not over 34 p.c.	Great Britain	2,335	4,413	1,728	3,621	1,933 02
	Hong Kong	1,656	332	1,656	332	911 04
	Newfoundland	26	126	26	126	50 54
	China	1,716	370	1,654	335	910 96
	France	486	787	588	833	538 02
	Italy	53	69	....	....	....
	Japan	90	17	90	17	49 20
	Portugal	7,056	9,569	8,170	11,236	7,374 10
	Spain	14,678	18,416	12,895	16,592	11,296 16
	United States	2.153	1,343	2,596	1,617	1,757 14
	Total	30,249	35,442	29,403	34,709	24,820 18

OF IMPORTS—*Continued.*

FOR HOME CONSUMPTION.

Preferential Tariff.			Surtax Tariff.			Total.		
Quantity.	Value.	Duty.	Quantity.	Value.	Duty.	Quantity.	Value.	Duty Collected.
Galls.	$	$ cts.	Galls.	$	$ cts.	Galls.	$	$ cts.
						1,394	1,696	1,066 40
						2 463	471	1,126 50
						5,769	1,226	2,675 40
						226	344	193 60
						5	14	6 20
						194	176	130 40
						1,180	532	631 60
						1,495	2,234	1,268 20
						9,844	10,941	7,219 90
						1,130	780	686 00
						23,700	18,414	15,004 20
						1,692	2,334	1,427 76
						2,804	516	1,360 52
						3,310	699	1,633 00
						974	1,141	761 12
						313	135	175 09
						4,243	4,815	3,268 99
						17,288	16,812	12,477 46
						2,557	1,820	1,645 51
						33,181	28,272	22,749 45
						1,627	2,680	1,552 42
						6	13	6 66
						3,283	639	1,701 88
						27	125	49 92
						1,822	378	951 52
						753	1,068	666 78
						10	9	7 30
						45	44	33 90
						5,259	7,718	4,734 54
						13,883	17,287	11,572 28
						3,311	1,911	2,096 36
						30,026	31,872	23,373 56
						1,728	3,621	1,933 02
						1,656	332	911 04
						26	126	50 54
						1,654	335	910 96
						588	833	538 02
						....	....	....
						90	17	49 20
						8,170	11,236	7,374 10
						12,895	16,592	11,296 16
						2,596	1,617	1,757 14
						29,403	34,709	24,820 18

No. 1.—GENERAL STATEMENT

Articles Imported.	Countries.	Total Imports.		Entered — General Tariff.		
		Quantity.	Value.	Quantity.	Value.	Duty.
DUTIABLE GOODS—*Con.*			$		$	$ cts.
Spirits and wines—*Con.* Wines of all kinds, except sparkling wines—*Con.*						
Containing over 34 p.c. and not over 35 p.c....	Great Britain...	3,414	5,391	2,654	4,952	2,865 68
	Gibraltar......	4	21	4	21	8 38
	Hong Kong.....	316	65	316	65	183 82
	Newfoundland..	51	262	64	326	131 08
	China..........	279	50	304	61	176 38
	France.........	814	1,171	614	1,148	663 68
	Italy..........	....	....	29	68	35 48
	Portugal.......	4,814	8,388	4,536	7,748	4,683 12
	Spain.........	8,158	11,085	8,183	11,330	7,654 16
	United States...	897	621	961	661	698 02
	Total.....	18,747	27,054	17,665	26,380	17,099 80
Containing over 35 p.c. and not over 36 p.c...	Great Britain...	1,288	2,786	1,873	4,142	2,272 75
	Hong Kong.....	207	40	207	40	125 85
	Newfoundland..	33	145	29	130	54 95
	China.........	159	41	159	41	99 75
	France.........	37	112	100	306	146 80
	Portugal......	5,269	9,739	3,873	6,781	4,164 45
	Spain..........	4,385	6,791	4,167	6,927	4,369 95
	United States...	258	298	378	685	413 40
	Total.....	11,636	19,952	10,786	19,052	11,647 90
Containing over 36 p.c. and not over 37 p.c....	Great Britain...	776	1,599	939	1,784	1,079 82
	China..........	45	13	45	13	36 00
	France.........	55	100	81	139	88 68
	Germany......	58	58	....	....	....
	Portugal.......	1,607	3,248	1,143	2,470	1,403 94
	Spain.........	684	1,217	811	1,349	875 08
	United States...	283	275	283	275	246 64
	Total...	3,508	6,510	3,302	6,030	3,724 16
Containing over 37 p.c. and not over 38 p.c....	Great Britain...	....	....	31	52	34 51
	Hong Kong.....	24	9	24	9	17 34
	Newfoundland..	112	342	112	342	170 92
	China..........	48	12	48	12	32 88
	France.........	14	17	24	61	32 94
	Portugal.......	539	2,340	178	783	343 48
	Spain..........	163	297	165	305	192 15
	United States...	....	....	2	3	2 12
	Total......	900	3,017	584	1,567	826 34
Containing over 38 p.c. and not over 39 p.c....	Great Britain...	6	97	6	97	32 94
	China..........	177	79	177	79	136 98
	Spain..........	100	468	100	213	127 90
	Total......	283	644	283	389	297 82
Containing over 39 p.c. and not over 40 p.c....	Hong Kong.....	45	10	45	10	33 15
	China.........	701	189	701	189	526 37
	Total....	746	199	746	199	559 52

OF IMPORTS—*Continued.*

FOR HOME CONSUMPTION.

Preferential Tariff.			Surtax Tariff.			Total.		
Quantity.	Value.	Duty.	Quantity.	Value.	Duty.	Quantity.	Value.	Duty Collected.
	$	$ cts.		$	$ cts.		$	$ cts.
						2,654	4,952	2,865 68
						4	21	8 38
						316	65	183 82
						64	326	131 08
						304	61	176 38
						614	1,148	663 68
						29	68	35 48
						4,536	7,748	4,683 12
						8,183	11,330	7,654 16
						961	661	698 02
						17,665	26,380	17,099 80
						1,873	4,142	2,272 75
						207	40	125 85
						29	130	54 95
						159	41	99 75
						100	306	146 80
						3,873	6,781	4,164 45
						4,167	6,927	4,369 95
						378	685	413 40
						10,786	19,052	11,647 90
						939	1,784	1,079 82
						45	13	30 00
						81	139	88 68
			58	58	68 05	58	58	68 05
						1,143	2,470	1,403 94
						811	1,349	875 08
						283	275	246 64
			58	58	68 05	3,360	6,088	3,792 21
						31	52	34 51
						24	9	17 34
						112	342	170 92
						48	12	32 88
						24	61	32 94
						178	783	343 48
						165	305	192 15
						2	3	2 12
						584	1,567	826 34
						6	97	32 94
						177	79	136 98
						100	213	127 90
						283	389	297 82
						45	10	33 15
						701	189	526 37
						746	199	559 52

No. 1.—GENERAL STATEMENT

ARTICLES IMPORTED.	COUNTRIES.	TOTAL IMPORTS.		ENTERED		
				General Tariff.		
		Quantity.	Value.	Quantity.	Value.	Duty.
DUTIABLE GOODS—*Con.*		Doz.	$	Doz.	$	$ cts.
Spirits and wines—*Con.* Champagne and all other sparkling wines— In bottles containing each not more than a quart but more than a pint, old wine measure	Great Britain	604	10,504	544	9,541	1,873 50
	Belgium	2	29	2	29	15 30
	France	7,287	95,231	7,335	96,310	24,552 60
	Germany	217	1,666	....	....	....
	Italy	15	104	27	149	133 80
	Spain	2	15	7	37	27 60
	United States	116	1,634	128	1,819	734 40
	Total	8,243	109,183	8,043	107,885	27,337 20
In bottles containing not more than a pint but more than half a pint, old wine measure	Great Britain	632	5,641	593	5,295	998 85
	Belgium	6	31	6	31	19 20
	France	26,234	181,526	25,559	167,360	42,409 95
	Germany	284	1,217	20	102	33 00
	Spain	....	....	20	36	33 00
	United States	1,004	8,266	778	4,872	1,354 80
	Total	28,160	196,681	26,976	177,696	44,848 80
In bottles containing one-half pint each or less	Great Britain	14	49	18	53	14 76
	France	1,635	4,718	1,227	2,903	1,006 14
	Spain	....	....	20	48	16 40
	United States	22	104	34	135	31 18
	Total	1,671	4,871	1,299	3,139	1,068 48
		Doz. Galls.		Doz. Galls.		
In bottles containing more than one quart each	Great Britain	6 12	225	2 3	66	11 55
	France	5 15	251	3 6	101	19 80
	Total	11 27	476	5 9	167	31 35
Sponges	Great Britain	....	12,068	....	1,819	363 80
	B. W. Indies	....	2,569	....	358	71 60
	Cuba	....	1,940	....	2,409	481 80
	France	....	220	....	252	50 40
	Germany	....	167	....	....	....
	Greece	....	78	....	78	15 60
	Russia	....	160	....	160	32 00
	United States	....	34,319	....	34,976	6,995 20
	Total	....	51,521	....	40,052	8,010 40

OF IMPORTS—*Continued.*

FOR HOME CONSUMPTION.

Preferential Tariff.			Surtax Tariff.			Total.		
Quantity.	Value.	Duty.	Quantity.	Value.	Duty.	Quantity.	Value.	Duty Collected.
	$	$ cts.	Doz.	$	$ cts.	Doz.	$	$ cts.
			7	69	58 40	551	9,610	1,931 90
						2	29	15 30
						7,335	96,310	24,552 60
			169	1,323	1,272 80	169	1,323	1,272 80
						27	149	133 80
						7	37	27 60
						128	1,819	734 40
			176	1,392	1,331 20	8,219	109,277	28,668 40
			2	7	7 20	595	5,302	1,006 05
						6	31	19 20
						25,559	167,360	42,409 95
			218	910	843 60	238	1,012	876 60
						20	36	33 00
						778	4,872	1,354 80
			220	917	850 80	27,196	178,613	45,699 60
						18	53	14 76
						1,227	2,903	1,006 14
						20	48	16 40
						34	135	31 18
						1,299	3,139	1,068 48
						Doz. Galls.		
						2 3	66	11 55
						3 6	101	19 80
						5 9	167	31 35
	12,197	1,626 21		95	25 33		14,111	2,015 34
	1,517	206 27					1,905	277 87
							2,409	481 80
							252	50 40
				167	44 52		167	44 52
							78	15 60
							160	32 00
							34,976	6,995 20
	13,744	1,832 48		262	69 85		54,058	9,912 73

No. 1.—General Statement

Articles Imported.	Countries.	Total Imports.		Entered		
				General Tariff.		
		Quantity.	Value.	Quantity.	Value.	Duty.
Dutiable Goods—*Con.*		Lbs.	$	Lbs.	$	$ cts.
Starch, including farina, corn starch, &c., &c.	Great Britain	263,042	14,361	3,103	141	46 62
	Hong Kong	66,737	1,126	66,737	1,126	1,001 05
	Aust.-Hungary	35,309	986	35,309	986	529 63
	Belgium	14,420	555	9,800	373	147 00
	China	33,192	471	33,192	471	497 88
	France	2,290	114	2,990	141	44 85
	Germany	40,751	1,088	38,571	968	578 57
	Holland	22,000	481	22,000	481	330 00
	Japan	2,016	51	2,016	51	30 24
	United States	544,951	21,342	544,078	21,279	8,161 05
	Total	1,024,708	40,575	757,801	26,017	11,366 89
Stearic acid	Great Britain	59,680	6,778	....	....	....
	United States	119,371	10,272	119,371	10,272	2,054 40
	Total	179,051	17,050	119,371	10,272	2,054 40
Stockinettes for the manufacture of rubber boots and shoes, imported by manufacturers of rubber boots and shoes, for use exclusively in the manufacture thereof in their own factories	Great Britain	....	14,112	....	....	....
	United States	....	58,522	....	58,522	8,778 30
	Total	....	72,634	....	58,522	8,778 30
Stone and manufactures of—Flagstones, granite, rough freestone, sandstone, and all building stone, not hammered or chiselled		Tons.		Tons.		
	Great Britain	248	2,143	52	692	103 80
	France	84	262	84	262	39 30
	United States	14,392	64,589	14,392	64,589	9,688 35
	Total	14,724	66,994	14,528	65,543	9,831 45
Granite and freestones, dressed; all other building stone dressed, except marble	Great Britain	35	372	....	....	....
	United States	11,346	64,762	11,346	64,762	12,952 40
	Total	11,381	65,134	11,346	64,762	12,952 40
Granite, sawn only	Great Britain	4	239	....	....	....
	United States	9,491	32,077	9,491	32,077	6,415 40
	Total	9,495	32,316	9,491	32,077	6,415 40
Granite, manufactures of, N.O.P.	Great Britain	....	87,815	....	1,143	400 05
	Italy	....	146	....	146	51 10
	United States	....	6,756	....	6,756	2,364 60
	Total	....	94,717	....	8,045	2,815 75
Grindstones, not mounted and not less than 36 inches in diameter	Great Britain	....	5,453	....	1,225	183 75
	United States	....	43,230	....	43,230	6,484 50
	Total	....	48,683	....	44,455	6,668 25

OF IMPORTS—*Continued.*

FOR HOME CONSUMPTION.

Preferential Tariff.			Surtax Tariff.			Total.		
Quantity.	Value.	Duty.	Quantity	Value.	Duty.	Quantity.	Value.	Duty Collected.
Lbs.	$	$ cts.	Lbs.	$	$ cts.	Lbs.	$	$ cts.
248,050	13,898	2,480 50	13,263	369	265 27	264,421	14,408	2,792 39
						66,737	1,126	1,001 05
						35,309	986	529 63
						9,800	373	147 00
						33,192	471	497 88
						2,990	141	44 85
			2,180	120	43 60	40,751	1,088	622 17
						22,000	481	330 00
						2,016	51	30 24
			8,811	282	176 22	552,889	21,561	8,337 27
248,050	13,893	2,480 50	24,254	771	485 09	1,030,105	40,686	14,332 48
59,680	6,778	903 74				59,680	6,778	903 74
						119,371	10,272	2,054 40
59,680	6,778	903 74				179,051	17,050	2,958 14
	14,112	1,411 20					14,112	1,411 20
							58,522	8,778 30
	14,112	1,411 20					72,634	10,189 50
Tons.			Tons.			Tons.		
196	1,451	145 10				248	2,143	248 90
						84	262	39 30
						14,392	64,589	9,688 35
196	1,451	145 10				14,724	66,994	9,976 55
35	372	49 61				35	372	49 61
						11,346	64,762	12,952 40
35	372	49 61				11,381	65,134	13,002 01
4	239	31 87				4	239	31 87
						9,491	32,077	6,415 40
4	239	31 87				9,495	32,316	6,447 27
	86,672	20,224 13					87,815	20,624 18
							146	51 10
							6,756	2,364 60
	86,672	20,224 13					94,717	23,039 88
	3,182	318 20		1,046	209 20		5,453	711 15
							43,230	6,484 50
	3,182	318 20		1,046	209 20		48,683	7,195 65

No. 1.—General Statement

Articles Imported.	Countries.	Total Imports.		Entered		
				General Tariff.		
		Quantity.	Value.	Quantity.	Value.	Duty.
DUTIABLE GOODS—*Con.*			$		$	$ cts.
Stone and mfrs. of—*Con.* Grindstones, N.E.S.	Great Britain		114			
	China		5		5	1 25
	United States		10,825		10,825	2,706 25
	Total		10,944		10,830	2,707 50
Paving blocks	Great Britain		5,676			
	United States		19,141		19,141	3,828 20
	Total		24,817		19,141	3,828 20
Manufactures of stone, N.O.P	Great Britain		729		9	2 70
	Hong Kong		9		9	2 70
	Aust.-Hungary		22		22	6 60
	Belgium		331		331	99 30
	China		32		32	9 60
	France		343		343	102 90
	Germany		1,036		86	25 80
	Japan		38		38	11 40
	United States		24,045		23,894	7,168 20
	Total		26,585		24,764	7,429 20
		Tons.		Tons.		
Straw	United States	127	941	127	941	188 20
Straw carpeting, rugs, mats and matting	Great Britain		169		28	7 00
	B. E. Indies		46			
	Hong Kong		136		136	34 00
	Belgium		44		44	11 00
	China		3,651		3,651	912 75
	Germany		77			
	Japan		35,133		35,909	8,977 25
	United States		7,055		7,032	1,758 00
	Total		46,311		46,800	11,700 00
Straw, manufactures of, not otherwise provided for	Great Britain		155		87	17 40
	Belgium		127		127	25 40
	China		27		27	5 40
	France		642		686	137 20
	Germany		12,452		245	49 00
	Holland		4,657		4,613	922 60
	Japan		172		172	34 40
	Sweden		1,421		1,421	284 20
	United States		1,002		875	175 00
	Total		20,655		8,253	1,650 60

OF IMPORTS—*Continued.*

FOR HOME CONSUMPTION.

Preferential Tariff.			Surtax Tariff.			Total.		
Quantity.	Value.	Duty.	Quantity.	Value.	Duty.	Quantity.	Value.	Duty Collected.
	$	$ cts.		$	$ cts.		$	$ cts.
	114	19 00					114	19 00
							5	1 25
							10,825	2,706 25
	114	19 00					10,944	2,726 50
	5,676	756 80					5,676	756 80
							19,141	3,828 20
	5,676	756 80					24,817	4,585 00
	666	133 20		54	21 60		729	157 50
							9	2 70
							22	6 60
							331	99 30
							32	9 60
							343	102 90
				950	380 00		1,036	405 80
							38	11 40
				151	60 40		24,045	7,228 60
	666	133 20		1,155	462 00		26,585	8,024 40
Tons.			Tons.			Tons.		
						127	941	188 20
	113	18 84		28	9 34		169	35 18
	46	7 67					46	7 67
							136	34 00
							44	11 00
							3,651	912 75
				77	25 64		77	25 64
							35,909	8,977 25
				23	7 68		7,055	1,765 68
	159	26 51		128	42 66		47,087	11,769 17
	68	9 07					155	26 47
							127	25 40
							27	5 40
							686	137 20
				12,207	3,255 20		12,452	3,304 20
							4,613	922 60
							172	34 40
							1,421	284 20
				127	33 91		1,002	208 91
	68	9 07		12,334	3,289 11		20,655	4,948 78

No. 1.—General Statement

Articles Imported.	Countries.	Total Imports.		Entered		
				General Tariff.		
		Quantity.	Value.	Quantity.	Value.	Duty.
DUTIABLE GOODS.		Lbs.	$	Lbs.	$	$ cts.
Sugars, syrups and molasses—Sugar, above No. 16 D.S. in colour, and all refined sugars of whatever kinds, grades or standards	Great Britain	26,201,319	777,295	1,191,563	37,934	14,904 69
	British Guiana	43,587	1,430	....	....	....
	B.W. Indies	165,036	4,543	200	8	2 50
	Hong Kong	105,678	3,867	117,678	4,314	1,472 95
	Aust.-Hungary	77,845	2,070	125,480	4,106	1,569 50
	Belgium	148,745	4,923	112,000	3,346	1,400 00
	China	15,489	297	100,989	3,447	1,263 36
	Japan	136	2	136	2	1 70
	United States	328,302	14,225	208,365	9,216	2,605 64
	Total	27,086,137	808,652	1,856,411	62,367	23,220 34
Sugar, N.E.S., not above No. 16 D.S. in colour, sugar drainings, or pumpings drained in transit, melado or concentrated melado, tank bottoms and sugar concrete	Great Britain	297,480	6,911	74,320	1,724	569 62
	British Africa	10,807,896	272,535	284,672	7,364	1,300 00
	British Guiana	96,655,257	2,050,342	36,789	758	233 88
	B.E. Indies	305,535	5,432	....	....	....
	B.W. Indies	220,126,593	4,195,995	1,065,940	19,960	5,847 11
	Fiji Islands	13,095,152	454,333	....	....	....
	Hong Kong	12,116	223	12,116	223	46 05
	Argentina	153,958	4,348	58,400	1,724	373 76
	Belgium	17,675,648	392,541	26,096,257	678,075	188,783 28
	Cent. Am. States	1,395,700	33,027	3,159,265	74,964	22,772 63
	China	3,223	64	3,223	64	29 77
	Dutch E. Indies	24,847,946	595,652	32,565,128	837,339	230,365 19
	Mexico	1,541,375	30,889	1,541,375	30,889	11,945 65
	Peru	3,451,092	70,141	10,687,446	188,850	74,719 17
	United States	477,249	9,502	478,249	9,532	2,384 39
	Total	390,846,220	8,121,935	76,063,180	1,851,466	539,370 50
Syrups and molasses of all kinds, N.O.P., the product of the sugar cane or beet, N.E.S., and all imitations thereof or substitutes therefor	Great Britain	96,631	3,304	4,000	438	30 00
	Australia	1,680	92	1,680	92	12 60
	B.W. Indies	167,412	1,822	....	....	....
	China	321	8	321	8	2 41
	Japan	564	18	564	18	4 23
	United States	3,331,374	51,553	3,025,826	46,868	22,693 70
	Total	3,597,982	56,797	3,032,391	47,424	22,742 94
Molasses produced in the process of the manufacture of cane sugar from the juice of the cane without any admixture with any other ingredient, when imported in the original package in which it was placed at the point of production and not afterwards subjected to any process of treating or mixing—		Galls.		Galls.		
Testing by polariscope, forty degreess or over	Great Britain	572	11	....	....	....
	B.W. Indies	....	....	....	....	....
	Newfoundland	1,626	574	1,630	597	28 52
	Cuba	92,663	9,163	94,840	7,119	1,659 70
	Porto Rico	945,237	211,174	1,130,232	272,011	19,778 90
	United States	130,860	32,997	108,892	30,007	1,905 59
	Total	1,170,958	253,919	1,335,594	309,734	23,372 71

OF IMPORTS—*Continued.*

FOR HOME CONSUMPTION.

Preferential Tariff.			Surtax Tariff.			Total.		
Quantity.	Value.	Duty.	Quantity.	Value.	Duty.	Quantity.	Value.	Duty Collected.
Lbs.	$	$ cts.	Lbs.	$	$ cts.	Lbs.	$	$ cts.
26,503,811	834,632	221,647 31	336	15	5 57	27,695,710	872,581	236,557 57
6,179	183	51 60				6,179	183	51 60
166,066	4,572	1,311 65				166,266	4,580	1,314 15
						117,678	4,314	1,472 95
			110	3	1 84	125,590	4,103	1,571 34
						112,000	3,346	1,400 00
						100,989	3,447	1,263 36
						136	2	1 70
						208,365	9,216	2,605 64
26,676,056	839,387	223,010 56	446	18	7 41	28,532,913	901,772	246,238 31
						74,320	1,724	569 62
5,591,845	142,867	25,419 95				5,876,517	150,231	26,719 95
105,242,994	2,476,688	503,872 68				105,279,783	2,477,446	504,106 56
430,253	7,874	2,252 03				430,253	7,874	2,252 03
218,345,718	4,587,417	1,036,531 68				219,411,658	4,607,377	1,042,378 79
14,755,620	269,080	69,385 43				14,755,620	269,080	69,385 43
						12,116	223	46 05
						58,400	1,724	373 76
						26,096,257	678,075	188,783 28
						3,159,265	74,964	22,772 63
						3,223	64	29 77
						32,565,128	837,339	230,365 19
						1,541,375	30,889	11,945 65
						10,687,446	188,850	74,719 17
						478,249	9,532	2,384 39
344,366,430	7,483,926	1,637,461 77				420,429,610	9,335,392	2,176,832 27
92,343	2,879	461 70				96,343	3,317	491 70
						1,680	92	12 60
34,454	604	172 24				34,454	604	172 24
						321	8	2 41
						564	18	4 23
						3,025,826	46,868	22,693 70
126,797	3,483	633 94				3,159,188	50,907	23,376 88
Galls.			Galls.			Gals.		
976	102	11 40				976	102	11 40
1,425	339	16 63				1,425	339	16 63
						1,630	597	28 52
						94,840	7,119	1,659 70
						1,130,232	272,011	19,778 90
						108,892	30,007	1,905 59
2,401	441	28 03				1,337,995	310,175	23,400 74

No. 1.—General Statement

Articles Imported.	Countries.	Total Imports.		Entered		
				General Tariff.		
		Quantity.	Value.	Quantity.	Value.	Duty.
dutiable goods—*Con.*		Galls.	$	Galls.	$	$ cts.
Sugar, &c.—Con. Molasses, &c., 39 degrees....	United States...	729	226	2,008	430	55 22
" " 37 "	United States...	243	70	243	70	11 54
Sugar candy, brown or white, and confectionery, including sweetened gums, candied peel and pop corn.....		Lbs.		Lbs.		
	Great Britain...	1,363,407	159,926	37,781	4,606	1,801 00
	Hong Kong.....	25,035	748	25,035	748	386 98
	New Zealand....	1,440	41	1,440	41	21 55
	Belgium........	6,124	237	7,310	274	132 45
	China..........	44,982	1,251	44,982	1,251	662 76
	France.........	55,564	10,425	55,614	10,447	3,934 52
	Hawaii.........	246	20	246	20	8 23
	Holland........	6,093	740	6,093	740	289 47
	Italy..........	22,237	1,922	14,100	1,295	523 75
	Japan..........	2,513	151	2,513	151	65 42
	Spain..........	2,016	164	2,016	164	67 48
	St. Pierre......	13	1	13	1	0 42
	Switzerland.....	554	209	617	198	72 39
	Turkey.........	9,897	763	9,897	763	316 54
	United States...	756,701	127,907	747,820	126,786	48,114 22
	Total......	2,296,822	304,505	955,477	147,485	56,397 18
Glucose or grape sugar, glucose syrup and corn syrup or any syrups containing any admixture thereof....	Great Britain...	9,520	431	....	....	....
	Turkey.........	1,180	43	1,180	43	8 86
	United States...	2,225,062	40,596	2,225,062	40,596	16,687 97
	Total.......	2,235,762	41,070	2,226,242	40,639	16,696 83
Saccharine or any product containing over one-half per cent thereof...	Great Britain...	150	45	....	....	....
	Aust.-Hungary..	50	77	50	77	15 40
	France.........	618	471	618	471	94 20
	Switzerland.....	692	747	692	747	149 40
	United States...	607	591	607	591	118 20
	Total.......	2,117	1,931	1,967	1,886	377 20
Sugar, maple, and maple syrup......	Great Britain...	24,900	1,782	....	....	....
	United States...	68,819	6,784	27,043	2,999	599 80
	Total.......	93,719	8,566	27,043	2,999	599 80
Tallow.....................	Great Britain...	15,062	1,557	9,121	962	192 40
	United States...	68,888	3,673	68,888	3,673	734 60
	Total.......	83,950	5,230	78,009	4,635	927 00

SESSIONAL PAPER No. 11

OF IMPORTS—*Continued.*

FOR HOME CONSUMPTION.

Preferential Tariff.			Surtax Tariff.			Total.		
Quantity.	Value.	Duty.	Quantity.	Value.	Duty.	Quantity.	Value.	Duty Collected.
Galls.	$	$ cts.	Galls.	$	$ cts.	Galls.	$	$ cts.
						2,008	430	55 22
						243	70	11 54
Lbs.			Lbs.			Lbs.		
1,342,472	156,471	40,985 23				1,380,253	161,077	42,786 23
						25,035	748	386 98
						1,440	41	21 55
						7,310	274	132 45
						44,982	1,251	662 76
						55,614	10,447	3,934 52
						246	20	8 23
						6,093	740	289 47
						14,100	1,295	523 75
						2,513	151	65 42
						2,016	164	67 48
						13	1	0 42
						617	198	72 39
						9,897	763	316 54
						747,820	126,786	48,114 22
1,342,472	156,471	40,985 23				2,297,949	303,956	97,382 41
9,520	431	47 60				9,520	431	47 60
						1,180	43	8 86
						2,225,062	40,596	16,687 97
9,520	431	47 60				2,235,762	41,070	16,744 43
150	45	6 00				150	45	6 00
						50	77	15 40
						618	471	94 20
						692	747	149 40
						607	591	118 20
150	45	6 00				2,117	1,931	383 20
24,954	1,793	239 07				24,954	1,793	239 07
						27,043	2,999	599 80
24,954	1,793	239 07				51,997	4,792	838 87
5,941	595	79 35				15,062	1,557	271 75
						68,888	3,673	734 60
5,941	595	79 35				83,950	5,230	1,006 35

No. 1.—GENERAL STATEMENT

ARTICLES IMPORTED.	COUNTRIES.	TOTAL IMPORTS.		ENTERED		
				General Tariff.		
		Quantity.	Value.	Quantity	Value.	Duty.
DUTIABLE GOODS—*Con.*			$		$	$ cts.
Tape lines of any material	Great Britain	....	11,384	....	82	20 50
	Belgium	....	1	....	....	....
	France	....	50	....	50	12 50
	Germany	....	761	....	....	....
	United States	....	16,321	....	16,252	4,063 00
	Total	....	28,517	....	16,384	4,096 00
		Lbs.		Lbs.		
Tea of Ceylon, black	Great Britain	1,478	376	108	49	4 90
	United States	30,230	4,589	30,290	4,605	460 50
	Total	31,708	4,965	30,398	4,654	465 40
Tea of Ceylon, green	United States	4,307	439	4,307	439	43 90
Tea of India, black	Great Britain	7,796	1,412	7,796	1,412	141 20
	United States	17,773	1,656	2,880	272	27 20
	Total	25,569	3,068	10,676	1,684	168 40
Tea of China, black	United States	30,080	6,468	29,358	6,322	632 20
Tea of China, green	United States	6,795	1,410	4,292	1,160	116 00
Tea of Japan, green	United States	40,962	6,265	77,041	9,937	993 70
" other countries, black	China	200	33	200	33	3 30
	United States	4,857	1,523	4,932	1,482	148 20
	Total	5,057	1,556	5,132	1,515	151 50
" " green	United States	23,740	4,317	9,577	1,235	123 50
Tinware, plain, japanned, or lithographed, and all manufactures of tin, N.E.S.	Great Britain	....	29,673	....	1,724	431 00
	B. E. Indies	....	44	....	44	11 00
	Hong Kong	....	44	....	44	11 00
	Aust.-Hungary	....	199	....	192	48 00
	Belgium	....	120	....	120	30 00
	China	....	65	....	65	16 25
	France	....	5,031	....	5,028	1,257 00
	Germany	....	5,983	....	103	25 75
	Holland	....	217	....	217	54 25
	Japan	....	63	....	63	15 75
	Sweden	....	123	....	123	30 75
	United States	....	187,409	....	187,303	46,825 75
	Total	....	228,971	....	195,026	48,756 50

OF IMPORTS—*Continued.*

FOR HOME CONSUMPTION.

Preferential Tariff.			Surtax Tariff.			Total.		
Quantity.	Value.	Duty.	Quantity.	Value.	Duty.	Quantity.	Value.	Duty Collected.
	$	$ cts.		$	$ cts.		$	$ cts.
	11,273	1,878 99		29	9 68		11,384	1,909 17
				1	0 17		1	0 17
							50	12 50
				759	253 14		759	253 14
							16,252	4,063 00
	11,273	1,878 99		789	262 99		28,446	6,237 98
Lbs.			Lbs.			Lbs.		
1,370	327	21 80				1,478	376	26 70
						30,290	4,605	460 50
1,370	327	21 80				31,768	4,981	487 20
						4,307	439	43 90
						7,796	1,412	141 20
						2,880	272	27 20
						10,676	1,684	168 40
						29,358	6,322	632 20
						4,292	1,160	116 00
						77,041	9,937	993 70
						200	33	3 30
						4,932	1,482	148 20
						5,132	1,515	151 50
						9,577	1,235	123 50
	25,889	4,315 19		1,814	604 67		29,427	5,350 86
							44	11 00
							44	11 00
				7	2 33		199	50 33
							120	30 00
							65	16 25
							5,028	1,257 00
				5,526	1,842 00		5,629	1,867 75
							217	54 25
							63	15 75
							123	30 75
				176	58 66		187,479	46,884 41
	25,889	4,315 19		7,523	2,507 66		228,438	55,579 35

No. 1.—General Statement

Articles Imported.	Countries.	Total Imports.		Entered		
				General Tariff.		
		Quantity.	Value.	Quantity.	Value.	Duty.
DUTIABLE GOODS—*Con.*		Lbs.	$	Lbs.	$	$ cts.
Tobacco and manufactures of—Cigarettes	Great Britain	17,114	38,866	14,489	34,178	52,011 50
	B. Poss., other	346	468	342	477	1,145 25
	Hong Kong	62	8	....	......	....
	Arabia	......	....	7	8	23 00
	Aust.-Hungary	30	30	30	30	97 50
	Cuba	168	168	164	166	533 50
	Egypt	8,967	21,266	8,205	19,613	29,518 25
	France	768	143	18	17	58 25
	Germany	78	181	26	62	93 50
	Philippines	....	....	40	30	127 50
	Russia	5	3	5	3	15 75
	St. Pierre	6	10	6	10	20 50
	Turkey	6	27	6	27	24 75
	United States	820	2,143	755	1,985	2,761 25
	Total	28,370	63,313	24,093	56,606	86,430 50
Cigars	Great Britain	607	2,300	857	2,911	3,298 75
	B. E. Indies	252	115	269	158	846 50
	B. Poss., other	....	....	28	30	91 50
	B. W. Indies	326	1,097	390	1,250	1,482 50
	Hong Kong	265	190	265	190	842 50
	Aust.-Hungary	8	12	8	12	27 00
	Belgium	226	216	261	247	844 75
	China	160	321	160	321	560 25
	Cuba	101,440	374,267	98,754	370,715	388,940 75
	France	3	49	3	49	21 25
	Germany	596	902	3	8	11 00
	Holland	137	148	159	171	519 75
	Mexico	945	1,788	873	1,609	3,021 25
	Philippines	7,963	8,187	10,160	10,491	33,102 75
	Spain	104	256	104	256	376 00
	Switzerland	207	295	206	295	691 75
	United States	2,965	12,495	4,005	15,241	15,825 25
	Total	116,204	402,638	116,505	403,954	450,503 50
Tobacco, cut	Great Britain	98,453	76,156	104,320	81,336	57,376 00
	Australia	500	167	500	167	275 00
	Hong Kong	8,259	1,401	8,169	1,388	4,492 95
	Aust.-Hungary	3,258	1,572	3,258	1,572	1,791 90
	Belgium	16	12	16	12	8 80
	China	14,305	2,263	14,755	2,309	8,115 25
	Cuba	374	69	474	132	260 70
	Egypt	35	84	35	84	19 25
	France	1,592	2,158	1,049	625	576 95
	Germany	1,647	879	1,597	802	878 35
	Japan	176	25	176	25	96 80
	Roumania	136	36	136	36	74 80
	Russia	3,191	2,099	3,191	2,099	1,755 05
	Turkey	371	133	371	133	204 05
	United States	196,803	102,204	183,336	93,140	100,834 80
	Total	329,116	189,258	321,383	183,860	176,760 65

OF IMPORTS—*Continued.*

OR HOME CONSUMPTION.

Preferential Tariff.			Surtax Tariff.			Total.		
Quantity.	Value.	Duty.	Quantity.	Value.	Duty.	Quantity.	Value.	Duty Collected.
Lbs.	$	$ cts.	Lbs.	$	$ cts.	Lbs.	$	$ cts.
						14,489	34,178	52,011 50
						342	477	1,145 25
						7	8	23 00
						30	30	97 50
						164	166	533 50
						8,205	19,613	29,518 25
						18	17	58 25
			26	57	123 00	52	119	216 50
						40	30	127 50
						5	3	15 75
						6	10	20 50
						6	27	24 75
						755	1,985	2,761 25
			26	57	123 00	24,119	56,663	86,553 50
						857	2,911	3,298 75
						269	158	846 50
						28	30	91 50
						390	1,250	1,482 50
						265	190	842 50
						8	12	27 00
						261	247	844 75
						160	321	560 25
						98,754	370,715	388,940 75
						3	49	21 25
			593	894	2,670 01	596	902	2,681 01
						159	171	519 75
						873	1,609	3,021 25
						10,160	10,491	33,102 75
						104	256	376 00
						206	295	691 75
						4,005	15,241	15,825 25
			593	894	2,670 01	117,098	404,848	453,173 51
						104,320	81,336	57,376 00
						500	167	275 00
						8,169	1,388	4,492 95
						3,258	1,572	1,791 90
						16	12	8 80
						14,755	2,309	8,115 25
						474	132	260 70
						35	84	19 25
						1,049	625	576 95
						1,597	802	878 35
						176	25	96 80
						136	36	74 80
						3,191	2,099	1,755 05
						371	133	204 05
						183,336	93,140	100,834 80
						321,383	183,860	176,760 65

No. 1.—General Statement

Articles Imported.	Countries.	Total Imports.		Entered		
				General Tariff.		
		Quantity.	Value.	Quantity.	Value.	Duty.
		Lbs.	$	Lbs.	$	$ cts.
DUTIABLE GOODS—*Con.*						
Tobacco and mfrs. of—*Con.*						
Snuff	Great Britain	2,245	883	2,245	883	1,122 50
	France	1,058	450	838	359	419 00
	Germany	88	21			
	Roumania	5		5		2 50
	Turkey	28	7	28	7	14 00
	United States	38,969	17,297	39,598	16,899	19,799 00
	Total	42,393	18,658	42,714	18,148	21,357 00
All other manufactures of tobacco, N.E.S.	Great Britain	14,401	5,732	13,198	5,293	6,599 00
	Newfoundland	6	2	6	2	3 00
	China	90	13	90	13	45 00
	United States	148,141	62,511	103,912	46,469	51,956 00
	Total	162,638	68,258	117,206	51,777	58,603 00
Foreign raw leaf tobacco, samples, unstemmed	Great Britain	11	11	11	11	4 40
	Cuba			9	1	3 60
	United States	22,735	11,866			
	Total	22,746	11,877	20	12	8 00
Tobacco pipes of all kinds, pipe mounts, cigar and cigarette holders and cases for same, smokers' sets and cases therefor and tobacco pouches	Great Britain		253,139		150,525	52,683 75
	Hong Kong		244		244	85 40
	Aust.-Hungary		36,421		35,722	12,502 70
	Belgium		187		187	65 45
	China		183		183	64 05
	Cuba		11		11	3 85
	France		86,196		86,335	30,217 25
	Germany		28,284		1,989	696 15
	Holland		3		3	1 05
	Italy		59		59	20 65
	Japan		717		717	250 95
	Switzerland		30		30	10 50
	Turkey		1		1	0 35
	United States		37,548		36,771	12,869 85
	Total		443,023		312,777	109,471 95
Trawls, trawling spoons, fly hooks, sinkers, swivels, and sportsman's fishing bait, and fish hooks, N.E.S.	Great Britain		25,278		275	82 50
	Japan		4		4	1 20
	United States		24,236		23,795	7,138 50
	Total		49,518		24,074	7,222 20
Trunks, valises, hat-boxes, carpet bags, satchels, tool bags or baskets, portmanteaus, fly-books and parts thereof, N.O.P.	Great Britain		17,868		805	241 50
	Hong Kong		42		42	12 60
	Aust.-Hungary		29		29	8 70
	China		60		60	18 00
	France		666		662	198 60
	Germany		2,446		133	39 90
	Japan		806		806	241 80
	Switzerland		12		12	3 60
	United States		80,694		80,013	24,003 90
	Total		102,623		82,562	24,768 60

OF IMPORTS—*Continued.*

FOR HOME CONSUMPTION.

Preferential Tariff.			Surtax Tariff.			Total.		
Quantity.	Value.	Duty.	Quantity.	Value.	Duty.	Quantity.	Value.	Duty Collected.
Lbs.	$	$ cts.	Lbs.	$	$ cts.	Lbs.	$	$ cts.
						2,245	883	1,122 50
						838	359	419 00
			88	21	58 67	88	21	58 67
						5		2 50
						28	7	14 00
						39,598	16,899	19,799 00
			88	21	58 67	42,802	18,169	21,415 67
						13,198	5,293	6,599 00
						6	2	3 00
						90	13	45 00
						103,912	46,469	51,956 00
						117,206	51,777	58,603 00
						11	11	4 40
						9	1	3 60
						20	12	8 00
	97,099	22,656 75		4,318	2,015 07		251,942	77,355 57
							244	85 40
				84	39 20		35,806	12,541 90
							187	65 45
							183	64 05
							11	3 85
				55	25 67		86,390	30,242 92
				25,881	12,077 80		27,870	12,773 95
							3	1 05
							59	20 65
							717	250 95
							30	10 50
							1	0 35
				83	38 78		36,854	12,908 63
	97,099	22,656 75		30,421	14,196 52		440,297	146,325 22
	25,003	5,000 60					25,278	5,083 10
							4	1 20
				31	12 40		23,826	7,150 90
	25,003	5,000 60		31	12 40		49,108	12,235 20
	16,864	3,372 80		174	69 60		17,843	3,683 90
							42	12 60
							29	8 70
							60	18 00
							662	198 60
				2,313	925 20		2,446	965 10
							806	241 80
							12	3 60
				376	150 40		80,389	24,154 30
	16,864	3,372 80		2,863	1,145 20		102,289	29,286 60

No. 1.—General Statement

Articles Imported.	Countries.	Total Imports.		Entered		
				General Tariff.		
		Quantity.	Value.	Quantity.	Value.	Duty.
Dutiable goods—*Con.*		Galls.	$	Galls.	$	$ cts.
Turpentine, spirits of..........	Great Britain...	10,007	5,329	7,370	4,001	200 05
	United States...	888,093	597,730	888,093	597,730	29,886 50
	Total.......	898,100	603,059	895,463	601,731	30,086 55
Twine, manufactures of, viz.: hammocks and lawn tennis nets, sportsmans fish nets and other articles, N.O.P........	Great Britain...	....	1,612	....	394	118 20
	Belgium	....	37	....	37	11 10
	France....... .	....	513	....	513	153 90
	United States...	....	31,035	....	31,035	9,310 50
	Total.......	....	33,197	. ...	31,979	9,593 70
Umbrellas, parasols and sunshades, of all kinds and materials........	Great Britain...	....	42,131	....	281	98 35
	France....... .	....	857	....	857	299 95
	Germany...... .	....	374	....	....	....
	Japan	.. ..	679	....	679	237 65
	United States...	....	9,081	....	9,145	3,200 75
	Total.......	... .	53,122	....	10,962	3,836 70
Unenumerated articles...	Great Britain...	....	27,791	....	5,718	1,143 60
	Australia......	....	350	. ...	350	70 00
	British Guiana .	....	222	....	111	22 20
	B. W. Indies....	....	357	....	262	52 40
	Hong Kong.....	... .	377	....	377	75 40
	Newfoundland..	....	282	....	282	56 40
	Aust.-Hungary..	....	7	.. ..	7	1 40
	Belgium........	....	2	... .. .	2	0 40
	China....	....	457	....	276	55 20
	France	. . ....	7,745	.. ..	7,742	1,548 40
	Germany........	.. ..	1,515	....	100	20 00
	Hawaii.........	....	42	....	42	8 40
	Holland...	... .	31	....	31	6 20
	Italy..........	....	223	... .	223	44 60
	Japan.........	....	944	....	944	188 80
	Turkey.........	....	11	....	11	2 20
	United States...	....	84,646	....	84,950	16,990 00
	Total.......	....	125,002	....	101,428	20,285 60
Varnish, lacquers, japans, japan dryers, liquid dryers, and oil finish, not elsewhere specified.		Galls.		Galls.		
	Great Britain...	23,992	58,076	705	1,577	456 40
	Hong Kong.....	12	9	12	9	4 20
	France.........	109	331	109	331	88 00
	Germany.. . ..	38	39	....	... .	....
	United States...	64,755	110,532	64,357	109,784	34,828 20
	Total.......	88,906	168,987	65,183	111,701	35,376 80
Vegetables, viz.—		No.		No.		
Melons......	United States...	507,523	35,139	505,689	35,087	8,771 75

OF IMPORTS—*Continued.*

FOR HOME CONSUMPTION.

Preferential Tariff.			Surtax Tariff.			Total.		
Quantity.	Value.	Duty.	Quantity.	Value.	Duty.	Quantity.	Value.	Duty Collected.
Galls.	$	$ cts.	Galls.	$	$ cts.	Galls.	$	$ cts.
1,594	785	26 19	1,043	528	35 20	10,007	5,314	261 44
						888,093	597,730	29,886 50
1,594	785	26 19	1,043	528	35 20	898,100	603,044	30,147 94
	1,548	309 60					1,942	427 80
							37	11 10
							513	153 90
							31,035	9,310 50
	1,548	309 60					33,527	9,903 30
	41,817	9,757 55					42,098	9,855 90
							857	299 95
				374	174 53		374	174 53
							679	237 65
				21	9 80		9,166	3,210 55
	41,817	9,757 55		395	184 33		53,174	13,778 58
	21,705	2,894 20		136	36 28		27,559	4,074 08
							350	70 00
							111	22 20
	217	28 93					479	81 33
							377	75 40
							282	56 40
							7	1 40
							2	0 40
							276	55 20
							7,742	1,548 40
				1,415	377 33		1,515	397 33
							42	8 40
							31	6 20
							223	44 60
							944	188 80
							11	2 20
				151	40 27		85,101	17,030 27
	21,922	2,923 13		1,702	453 88		125,052	23,662 61
Galls.			Galls.			Galls.		
23,331	56,605	10,658 29				24,036	58,182	11,114 69
						12	9	4 20
						109	331	88 00
			38	39	20 53	38	39	20 53
						64,357	109,784	34,828 20
23,331	56,605	10,658 29	38	39	20 53	88,552	168,345	46,055 62
No.			No.			No.		
						505,689	35,087	8,771 75

No. 1.—General Statement

Articles Imported.	Countries.	Total Imports.		Entered		
				General Tariff.		
		Quantity.	Value.	Quantity.	Value.	Duty.
DUTIABLE GOODS—*Con.*		Bush.	$	Bush.	$	$ cts.
Vegetables—*Con.*						
Potatoes	Great Britain	14,396	5,712	43	21	6 45
	B. E. Indies	3	2	3	2	0 45
	China	17	6	17	6	2 55
	Japan	34	8	34	8	5 10
	United States	227,155	126,163	222,142	123,078	33,321 31
	Total	241,605	131,891	222,239	123,115	33,335 86
Potatoes sweet and yams	Great Britain	15	14	....	....	....
	B. W. Indies	50	23	....	....	....
	Hong Kong	583	217	583	217	58 30
	China	1,040	365	1,040	365	104 00
	Japan	48	25	48	25	4 80
	United States	28,199	24,768	28,140	24,670	2,814 00
	Total	29,935	25,412	29,811	25,277	2,981 10
Tomatoes, fresh	B. W. Indies	11	33	11	33	5 50
	United States	51,475	116,901	51,443	116,553	21,943 90
	Total	51,486	116,934	51,454	116,586	21,949 40
Tomatoes and other vegetables, including corn and baked beans in cans or other packages, N.E.S.		Lbs.		Lbs.		
	Great Britain	30,986	2,412	24,158	1,462	362 37
	Hong Kong	55,984	1,148	55,984	1,148	839 76
	Belgium	21,510	1,418	47,271	3,083	709 07
	China	117,473	3,075	114,393	2,611	1,715 90
	France	742,691	60,501	702,791	57,789	10,541 86
	Germany	821	144	....	....	....
	Italy	6,819	352	6,819	352	102 28
	Japan	28,588	1,665	29,663	1,668	444 95
	Norway	10,080	465	10,080	465	151 20
	St. Pierre	60	8	60	8	0 90
	Turkey	550	8	550	8	8 25
	United States	1,488,798	58,309	1,681,188	63,077	25,217 82
	Total	2,504,360	129,505	2,672,957	131,671	40,094 36
Fresh or dry salted, N.O.P.	Great Britain	....	52,118	....	51,438	12,859 50
	Australia	....	2,608	....	2,353	588 25
	B. W. Indies	....	398	....	152	38 00
	Hong Kong	....	5,120	....	5,120	1,280 00
	New Zealand	....	668	....	42	10 50
	Aust.-Hungary	....	149	....	149	37 25
	Belgium	....	42	....	42	10 50
	China	....	10,277	....	10,277	2,569 25
	Egypt	....	126	....	124	31 00
	France	....	513	....	513	128 25
	Germany	....	10,435	....	33	8 25
	Hawaii	....	39	....	39	9 75
	Italy	....	630	....	630	157 50
	Japan	....	6,933	....	6,933	1,733 25
	Spain	....	6,346	....	6,346	1,586 50
	Turkey	....	42	....	42	10 50
	United States	....	267,088	....	263,909	65,977 25
	Total	....	363,532	....	348,142	87,035 50

OF IMPORTS—*Continued.*

FOR HOME CONSUMPTION.

Preferential Tariff			Surtax Tariff.			Total.		
Quantity.	Value.	Duty.	Quantity.	Value.	Duty.	Quantity.	Value.	Duty Collected.
Bush.	$	$ cts.	Bush.	$	$ cts.	Bush.	$	$ cts.
1,400	528	140 00				1,443	549	146 45
						3	2	0 45
						17	6	2 55
						34	8	5 10
						222,142	123,078	33,321 31
1,400	528	140 00				223,639	123,643	33,475 86
15	14	3 33				15	14	3 33
50	23	1 00				50	23	1 00
						583	217	58 30
						1,040	365	104 00
						48	25	4 80
						28,140	24,670	2,814 00
65	37	4 33				29,876	25,314	2,985 43
						11	33	5 50
						51,443	116,553	21,943 90
						51,454	116,586	21,949 40
Lbs.			Lbs.			Lbs.		
19,498	1,350	194 99				43,656	2,812	557 36
						55,984	1,148	839 76
						47,271	3,083	709 07
						114,393	2,611	1,715 90
						702,791	57,789	10,541 86
			821	144	16 41	821	144	16 41
						6,819	352	102 28
						29,663	1,668	444 95
						10,080	465	151 20
						60	8	0 90
						550	8	8 25
						1,681,188	63,077	25,217 82
19,498	1,350	194 99	821	144	16 41	2,693,276	133,165	40,305 76
	835	139 18		49	16 33		52,322	13,015 01
							2,353	588 25
	246	41 00					398	79 00
							5,120	1,280 00
	626	104 38					668	114 88
							149	37 25
							42	10 50
							10,277	2,569 25
							124	31 00
							513	128 25
				2,709	903 00		2,742	911 25
							39	9 75
							630	157 50
							6,933	1,733 25
							6,346	1,586 50
							42	10 50
				92	30 67		264,001	66,007 92
	1,707	284 56		2,850	950 00		352,699	88,270 06

No. 1.—General Statement

Articles Imported.	Countries.	Total Imports.		Entered		
				General Tariff.		
		Quantity.	Value.	Quantity.	Value.	Duty.
DUTIABLE GOODS—*Con.*		Galls.	$	Galls.	$	$ cts.
Vinegar, of any strength not exceeding strength of proof...	Great Britain...	54,650	18,550	1,070	233	160 50
	Hong Kong.....	1,305	121	370	63	55 50
	Aust.-Hungary..	42	10	42	10	6 30
	China..........	865	129	865	129	129 75
	France.....	2,170	693	3,559	911	533 85
	Germany.......	10,458	712	....	....	....
	Japan..........	20	3	20	3	3 00
	St. Pierre.......	3	2	3	2	0 45
	United States...	24,170	2,859	23,636	2,715	3,545 40
	Total......	93,683	23,079	29,565	4,066	4,434 75
Vinegar above strength of proof	Great Britain...	3,631	2,859	10	18	7 30
	France..........	810	104	1,157	177	212 95
	United States...	4,576	2,917	3,498	2,011	652 92
	Total......	9,017	5,880	4,665	2,206	873 17
Watches.........	Great Britain...	....	12,892	....	10,681	2,670 25
	Newfoundland..	....	160	....	35	8 75
	Aust.-Hungary..	....	505	....	505	126 25
	Belgium.......	....	29	....	....	....
	France..........	....	8,765	....	7,782	1,945 50
	Germany . . .	....	1,363	....	23	5 75
	Italy..... . .	....	20	....	20	5 00
	Switzerland.....	....	25,907	....	25,907	6,476 75
	United States...	....	32,782	....	32,778	8,194 50
	Total ..	....	82,423	....	77,731	19,432 75
Watch cases.................	Great Britain...	....	1,703	....	1,348	404 40
	Aust.-Hungary..	....	193	....	193	57 90
	France.........	....	2,679	....	2,661	798 30
	Germany.	....	269	....	....	....
	Japan...	....	2	....	2	0 60
	Switzerland.....	....	10,185	....	10,185	3,055 50
	United States...	....	59,057	....	59,057	17,717 10
	Total......	....	74,088	....	73,446	22,033 80
Watch actions and movements.	Great Britain...	....	7,779	....	6,698	669 80
	Aust.-Hungary .	....	2,330	....	2,330	233 00
	France.........	....	25,352	....	25,306	2,530 60
	Germany.	....	2,201	....	100	10 00
	Switzerland.....	....	128,626	....	128,419	12,841 90
	United States...	....	601,549	....	601,530	60,153 00
	Total	....	767,837	....	764,383	76,438 30
Watch glasses and watch keys.	Great Britain...	....	4,836	....	1,755	438 75
	France.........	....	1,603	....	1,603	400 75
	Germany.	....	2,416	....	6	1 50
	Switzerland.....	....	621	....	621	155 25
	United States...	....	2,330	....	2,327	581 75
	Total	....	11,806	....	6,312	1,578 00

SESSIONAL PAPER No. 11

OF IMPORTS—*Continued.*

FOR HOME CONSUMPTION.

Preferential Tariff.			Surtax Tariff.			Total.		
Quantity.	Value.	Duty.	Quantity.	Value.	Duty.	Quantity.	Value.	Duty Collected.
Galls.	$	$ cts.	Galls.	$	$ cts.	Galls.	$	$ cts.
53,624	18,863	5,362 40	33	12	6 60	54,727	19,108	5,529 50
						370	63	55 50
						42	10	6 30
						865	129	129 75
						3,559	911	533 85
			10,458	712	2,091 60	10,458	712	2,091 60
						20	3	3 00
						3	2	0 45
						23,636	2,715	3,545 40
53,624	18,863	5,362 40	10,491	724	2,098 20	93,680	23,653	11,895 35
4,802	3,517	3,898 68				4,812	3,535	3,905 98
						1,157	177	212 95
						3,498	2,011	652 92
4,802	3,517	3,898 68				9,467	5,723	4,771 85
	1,105	184 23		1,066	355 33		12,852	3,209 81
							35	8 75
							505	126 25
				983	327 65		8,765	2,273 15
				1,340	446 65		1,363	452 40
							20	5 00
							25,907	6,476 75
							32,778	8,194 50
	1,105	184 23		3,389	1,129 63		82,225	20,746 61
	123	24 60		164	65 60		1,635	494 60
							193	57 90
				18	7 20		2,679	805 50
				269	107 60		269	107 60
							2	0 60
							10,185	3,055 50
							59,057	17,717 10
	123	24 60		451	180 40		74,020	22,238 80
	503	33 54		78	10 40		7,279	713 74
							2,330	233 00
				46	6 13		25,352	2,536 73
				2,101	280 13		2,201	290 13
				207	27 60		128,626	12,869 50
				19	2 54		601,549	60,155 54
	503	33 54		2,451	326 80		767,337	76,798 64
	576	96 00		2,505	835 00		4,836	1,369 75
							1,603	400 75
				2,410	803 33		2,416	804 83
							621	155 25
				3	1 00		2,330	582 75
	576	96 00		4,918	1,639 33		11,806	3,313 33

No. 1.—General Statement

Articles Imported.	Countries.	Total Imports.		Entered		
				General Tariff.		
		Quantity.	Value.	Quantity.	Value.	Duty.
DUTIABLE GOODS—*Con.*		Lbs.	$	Lbs.	$	$ cts.
Wax, bees	Great Britain	428	113	70	26	2 60
	United States	31,519	11,061	31,519	11,061	1,106 10
	Total	31,947	11,174	31,589	11,087	1,108 70
Wax, paraffine	Great Britain	8,041	470	3	1	0 25
	China	68	11	68	11	2 75
	France	375	73	375	73	18 25
	United States	104,128	9,167	103,750	9,101	2,275 25
	Total	112,612	9,721	104,196	9,186	2,296 50
Wax and manufactures of, N.E.S	Great Britain	....	28,754	....	16,221	3,244 20
	Hong Kong	....	7	....	7	1 40
	Aust.-Hungary	....	1,170	....	1,170	234 00
	Belgium	....	39	....	39	7 80
	China	....	83	....	83	16 60
	France	....	728	....	728	145 60
	Germany	....	1,479	....	382	76 40
	Japan	....	218	....	218	43 60
	United States	....	51,131	....	50,823	10,164 60
	Total	....	83,609	....	69,671	13,934 20
Webbing, elastic and non-elastic	Great Britain	....	64,226	....	1,976	395 20
	Belgium	....	316	....	316	63 20
	France	....	2,000	....	2,000	400 00
	Germany	....	2,334	....	....	....
	United States	....	134,710	....	134,710	26,942 00
	Total	....	203,586	....	139,002	27,800 40
Whips of all kinds, including thongs and lashes	Great Britain	....	3,923	....	447	156 45
	France	....	39	....	39	13 65
	Germany	....	4	....	....	....
	United States	....	4,377	....	4,377	1,531 95
	Total	....	8,343	....	4,863	1,702 05
Window cornices and cornice poles of all kinds	Great Britain	....	907	....	13	3 90
	United States	....	11,589	....	11,589	3,476 70
	Total	....	12,496	....	11,602	3,480 60
Window shade or blind rollers	Great Britain	....	271	....	....	....
	United States	....	34,345	....	34,345	12,020 75
	Total	....	34,616	....	34,345	12,020 75

OF IMPORTS—*Continued.*

FOR HOME CONSUMPTION.

Preferential Tariff.			Surtax Tariff.			Total.		
Quantity.	Value.	Duty.	Quantity.	Value.	Duty.	Quantity.	Value.	Duty Collected.
Lbs.	$	$ cts.	Lbs.	$	$ cts.	Lbs.	$	$ cts.
358	87	5 80	....	....	....	428	113	8 40
....	....	....	....	....	....	31,519	11,061	1,106 10
358	87	5 80	....	....	....	31,947	11,174	1,114 50
8,038	469	78 17	....	....	....	8,041	470	78 42
....	....	....	....	....	....	68	11	2 75
....	....	....	....	....	....	375	73	18 25
....	....	....	378	66	22 00	104,128	9,167	2,297 25
8,038	469	78 17	378	66	22 00	112,612	9,721	2,396 67
....	10,853	1,447 08	....	20	5 32	....	27,094	4,696 60
....	....	....	....	....	....	....	7	1 40
....	....	....	....	....	....	....	1,170	234 00
....	....	....	....	....	....	....	39	7 80
....	....	....	....	....	....	....	83	16 60
....	....	....	....	....	....	....	728	145 60
....	....	....	....	311	82 93	....	693	159 33
....	....	....	....	....	....	....	218	43 60
....	....	....	....	307	81 86	....	51,130	10,246 46
....	10,853	1,447 08	....	638	170 11	....	81,162	15,551 39
....	61,740	8,232 08	....	510	136 00	....	64,226	8,763 28
....	....	....	....	....	....	....	316	63 20
....	....	....	....	....	....	....	2,000	400 00
....	....	....	....	2,334	622 39	....	2,334	622 39
....	....	....	....	....	....	....	134,710	26,942 00
....	61,740	8,232 08	....	2,844	758 39	....	203,586	36,790 87
....	3,476	811 16	....	....	....	....	3,923	967 61
....	....	....	....	....	....	....	39	13 65
....	....	....	....	4	1 87	....	4	1 87
....	....	....	....	....	....	....	4,377	1,531 95
....	3,476	811 16	....	4	1 87	....	8,343	2,515 08
....	894	178 80	....	....	....	....	907	182 70
....	....	....	....	....	....	....	11,589	3,476 70
....	894	178 80	....	....	....	....	12,496	3,659 40
....	271	63 24	....	....	....	....	271	63 24
....	....	....	....	....	....	....	34,345	12,020 75
....	271	63 24	....	....	....	....	34,616	12,083 99

No. 1.—GENERAL STATEMENT

Articles Imported.	Countries.	Total Imports.		Entered		
				General Tariff.		
		Quantity.	Value.	Quantity.	Value.	Duty.
DUTIABLE GOODS—*Con.*		Sq. yds.	$	Sq. yds.	$	$ cts.
Window shades in the piece or cut and hemmed or mounted on rollers, N.E.S.	Great Britain	52,388	7,561	960	191	66 85
	France	350	82	350	82	28 70
	Switzerland	35	9	35	9	3 15
	United States	35,685	4,443	35,685	4,443	1,555 05
	Total	88,458	12,095	37,030	4,725	1,653 75
Wood and manufactures of—						
Barrels containing petroleum or its products, or any mixture of which petroleum forms a part, when such contents are chargeable with a specific duty		No.		No.		
	Great Britain	205	205	....	....	....
	United States	36,560	37,089	36,191	36,719	7,238 20
	Total	36,765	37,294	36,191	36,719	7,238 20
Fishing rods	Great Britain	....	2,054	....	69	20 70
	Japan	....	3	....	3	0 90
	United States	....	10,137	....	10,137	3,041 10
	Total	....	12,194	....	10,209	3.062 70
Handles of all kinds, hickory.	Great Britain	....	118	....	....	....
	United States	....	38,830	....	39,092	9,773 00
	Total	....	38,948	....	39,092	9,773 00
Handles of all kinds, ash	Great Britain	....	18	....	....	....
	United States	....	18,546	....	18,546	4,636 50
	Total	....	18,564	....	18,546	4,636 50
Caskets and coffins and metal parts thereof	United States	....	23,869	....	23,869	5,967 25
Lasts of wood	United States	....	29,056	....	29,056	7,264 00
Mouldings, plain, gilded or otherwise further manufactured	Great Britain	....	456	....	88	22 00
	Germany	....	15	....	....	....
	United States	....	70,381	....	70,399	17,599 75
	Total	....	70,852	....	70,487	17,621 75
		No.		No.		
Rakes, hay	United States	27,916	3,313	27,916	3,313	828 25
Show cases and metal parts thereof	Great Britain	228	1,119	10	84	29 40
	Hong Kong	11	46	11	46	16 10
	Belgium	....	5	....	....	....
	France	2	20	2	20	7 00
	Germany	17	37	....	....	....
	Japan	1	6	1	6	2 10
	United States	2,028	28,339	2,028	28,339	9,918 65
	Total	2,287	29,572	2,052	28,495	9,973 25

OF IMPORTS—*Continued.*

FOR HOME CONSUMPTION.

Preferential Tariff.			Surtax Tariff.			Total.		
Quantity.	Value.	Duty.	Quantity.	Value.	Duty.	Quantity.	Value.	Duty Collected.
Sq. yds.	$	$ cts.	Sq. yds.	$	$ cts.	Sq. yds.	$	$ cts.
51,428	7,370	1,719 66				52,388	7,561	1,786 51
						350	82	28 70
						35	9	3 15
						35,685	4,443	1,555 05
51,428	7,370	1,719 66				88,458	12,095	3,373 41
No.			No.			No.		
205	205	27 34				205	205	27 34
						36,191	36,719	7,238 20
205	205	27 34				36,396	36,924	7,265 54
	1,985	397 00					2,054	417 70
							3	0 90
							10,137	3,041 10
	1,985	397 00					12,194	3,459 70
	118	19 67					118	19 67
							39,092	9,773 00
	118	19 67					39,210	9,792 67
	18	3 00					18	3 00
							18,546	4,636 50
	18	3 00					18,564	4,639 50
							23,869	5,967 25
							29,056	7,264 00
	368	61 32					456	83 32
				15	5 00		15	5 00
							70,399	17,599 75
	368	61 32		15	5 00		70,870	17,688 07
No.			No.			No. 27,916	3,313	828 25
238	1,052	245 53				248	1,136	274 93
						11	46	16 10
				5	2 33		5	2 33
						2	20	7 00
			17	37	17 27	17	37	17 27
						1	6	2 10
						2,028	28,339	9,918 65
238	1,052	245 53	17	42	19 60	2,307	29,589	10,238 38

No. 1.—General Statement

Articles Imported.	Countries.	Total Imports.		Entered		
				General Tariff.		
		Quantity.	Value.	Quantity.	Value.	Duty.
DUTIABLE GOODS—*Con.*			$		$	$ cts.
Wood and mfrs. of—*Con.*						
Woodenware, churns, wash-boards, pounders and rolling-pins	Great Britain		36			
	United States		10,165		10,214	2,042 80
	Total		10,201		10,214	2,042 80
Woodenware, pails and tubs	Great Britain		21			
	China		4		4	1 00
	France		2		2	0 50
	Japan		1		1	0 25
	United States		27,068		27,136	6,784 00
	Total		27,096		27,143	6,785 75
Manufactures of wood, N.O.P.	Great Britain		29,485		2,801	700 25
	Australia		13		13	3 25
	B. E. Indies		49		49	12 25
	B. W. Indies		6		6	1 50
	Hong Kong		376		376	94 00
	Aust.-Hungary		1,131		1,071	267 75
	Belgium		1,074		1,072	268 00
	China		487		487	121 75
	France		2,648		2,647	661 75
	Germany		10,243		229	57 25
	Holland		1,230		1,230	307 50
	Italy		97		97	24 25
	Japan		1,995		1,964	491 00
	Norway		565		565	141 25
	Russia		9		9	2 25
	Spain		8		8	2 00
	St. Pierre		45		45	11 25
	Sweden		930		930	232 50
	Turkey		114		114	28 50
	United States		858,543		854,992	213,748 00
	Total		909,048		868,705	217,176 25
Sawed boards, planks, deals, planed or dressed on one or both sides, when the edges thereof are jointed or tongued and grooved	United States	M. ft. 7,610	126,527	M. ft. 7,610	126,513	31,628 25
Lumber and timber manufactured, N.E.S.	Great Britain	M. ft.	9	M. ft.		
	United States	1,735	25,988	1,735	25,988	5,197 60
	Total	1,735	25,997	1,735	25,988	5,197 60
Umbrella, parasol and sunshade sticks or handles, N.E.S.	Great Britain		2,056		167	33 40
	Aust.-Hungary		399		399	79 80
	France		55		55	11 00
	Germany		1,216		46	9 20
	United States		10,460		10,460	2,092 00
	Total		14,186		11,127	2,225 40

OF IMPORTS—*Continued.*

FOR HOME CONSUMPTION.

Preferential Tariff.			Surtax Tariff.			Total.		
Quantity.	Value.	Duty.	Quantity.	Value.	Duty.	Quantity.	Value.	Duty Collected.
	$	$ cts.		$	$ cts.		$	$ cts.
	36	4 80					36	4 80
							10,214	2,042 80
	36	4 80					10,250	2,047 60
	21	3 50					21	3 50
							4	1 00
							2	0 50
							1	0 25
							27,136	6,784 00
	21	3 50					27,164	6,789 25
	25,655	4,276 20		840	280 00		29,296	5,256 45
							13	3 25
							49	12 25
							6	1 50
							376	94 00
				60	20 00		1,131	287 75
							1,072	268 00
							487	121 75
							2,647	661 75
				10,227	3,409 00		10,456	3,466 25
							1,230	307 50
							97	24 25
							1,964	491 00
							565	141 25
							9	2 25
							8	2 00
							45	11 25
							930	232 50
							114	28 50
				214	71 32		855,206	213,819 32
	25,655	4,276 20		11,341	3,780 32		905,701	225,232 77
M. ft.			M. ft.			M. ft.		
						7,610	126,513	31,628 25
M. ft.			M. ft.			M. ft.		
	9	1 20					9	1 20
						1,735	25,988	5,197 60
	9	1 20				1,735	25,997	5,198 80
	1,728	230 42		161	42 93		2,056	306 75
							399	79 80
							55	11 00
				1,170	312 00		1,216	321 20
							10,460	2,092 00
	1,728	230 42		1,331	354 93		14,186	2,810 75

No. 1.—GENERAL STATEMENT

Articles Imported.	Countries.	Total Imports.		Entered		
				General Tariff.		
		Quantity.	Value.	Quantity.	Value.	Duty.
DUTIABLE GOODS—*Con.*			$		$	$ cts.
Wood and mfrs. of—*Con.* Veneers of wood, not over $\frac{3}{32}$ of an inch in thickness	Great Britain		85		47	3 52
	France		26		26	1 95
	United States		181,487		181,487	13,612 01
	Total		181,598		181,560	13,617 48
Walking sticks and canes of all kinds, N.E.S.	Great Britain		6,577		117	35 10
	Aust.-Hungary		369		369	110 70
	France		524		524	157 20
	Germany		16			
	Japan		12		12	3 60
	United States		11,965		11,904	3,571 20
	Total		19,463		12,926	3,877 80
Wood pulp	Great Britain		878			
	Germany		31			
	United States		50,670		50,670	12,667 50
	Total		51,579		50,670	12,667 50
Willow or osier wares and all manufactures of like material not otherwise provided for	Great Britain		23			
	Sweden		2,118		2,118	529 50
	United States		6,475		6,475	1,618 75
	Total		8,616		8,593	2,148 25
Wool, manufactures of—		Lbs.		Lbs.		
Blankets	Great Britain	351,224	100,332	21,486	4,529	1,585 15
	Hong Kong	10	11	10	11	3 85
	Aust.-Hungary	5,900	1,249	5,900	1,249	437 15
	France	10	12	10	12	4 20
	Germany	3,868	2,009			
	United States	13,566	5,156	13,086	4,928	1,724 80
	Total	374,578	108,769	40,492	10,729	3,755 15
Cassimeres, cloths and doeskins		Yds.		Yds.		
	Great Britain	2,938,552	1,921,707	42,613	28,459	9,960 65
	Hong Kong	27	13	27	13	4 55
	Aust.-Hungary	175	102	284	183	64 05
	Belgium	4,977	4,421	4,304	3,824	1,338 40
	France	76,898	43,166	76,603	42,857	14,999 95
	Germany	39,978	23,646			
	Holland	99	126	99	126	44 10
	Japan	10	13	10	13	4 55
	Spain	101	61	101	61	21 35
	Switzerland	584	461	584	461	161 35
	United States	13,827	9,445	13,722	9,205	3,221 75
	Total	3,075,228	2,003,161	138,347	85,202	29,820 70

OF IMPORTS—*Continued.*

FOR HOME CONSUMPTION.

Preferential Tariff.			Surtax Tariff.			Total.		
Quantity.	Value.	Duty.	Quantity.	Value.	Duty.	Quantity.	Value.	Duty Collected.
	$	$ cts.		$	$ cts.		$	$ cts.
	38	1 90					85	5 42
							26	1 95
							181,487	13,612 01
	38	1 90					181,598	13,619 38
	6,387	1,277 40		73	29 20		6,577	1,341 70
							369	110 70
							524	157 20
				16	6 40		16	6 40
							12	3 60
				61	24 40		11,965	3,595 60
	6,387	1,277 40		150	60 00		19,463	5,215 20
	878	146 33					878	146 33
				31	10 33		31	10 33
							50,670	12,667 50
	878	146 33		31	10 33		51,579	12,824 16
				23	7 67		23	7 67
							2,118	529 50
							6,475	1,618 75
				23	7 67		8,616	2,155 92
Lbs. 339,236	98,669	23,023 12	Lbs. 214	83	38 73	Lbs. 360,936	103,281	24,647 00
						10	11	3 85
						5,900	1,249	437 15
						10	12	4 20
			3,868	2,009	937 55	3,868	2,009	937 55
						13,086	4,928	1,724 80
339,236	98,669	23,023 12	4,082	2,092	976 28	383,810	111,490	27,754 55
Yds. 2,828,325	1,853,932	556,179 60	Yds. 20,772	14,686	6,853 47	Yds. 2,891,710	1,897,077	572,993 72
						27	13	4 55
						284	183	64 05
						4,304	3,824	1,338 40
						76,603	42,857	14,999 95
			39,283	23,238	10,844 37	39,283	23,238	10,844 37
						99	126	44 10
						10	13	4 55
						101	61	21 35
						584	461	161 35
			240	151	70 47	13,962	9,356	3,292 22
2,828,325	1,853,932	556,179 60	60,295	38,075	17,768 31	3,026,967	1,977,209	603,768 61

No. 1.—General Statement

Articles Imported.	Countries.	Total Imports.		Entered		
				General Tariff.		
		Quantity.	Value.	Quantity.	Value.	Duty.
Dutiable Goods—*Con.*		Yds.		Yds.	$	$ cts.
Wool and mfrs. of—*Con.* Coatings and overcoatings...	Great Britain...	1,803,700	1,138,218	20,838	13,770	4,819 50
	Belgium........	1,988	2,586	1,988	2,586	905 10
	France	6,497	2,536	9,637	3,723	1,303 05
	Germany........	25,320	22,946	....	....	....
	Holland........	537	658	537	658	230 30
	United States...	19	10	19	10	3 50
	Total	1,838,061	1,166,954	33,019	20,747	7,261 45
Tweeds	Great Britain...	3,890,123	2,062,157	62,718	27,843	9,745 05
	Aust.-Hungary..	348	131	....	....	....
	Belgium........	5,343	4,278	4,992	4,453	1,558 55
	France..........	41,763	16,024	41,763	16,024	5,608 40
	Germany........	22,484	9,007	....	....	....
	Holland........	809	275	809	275	96 25
	United States...	1,720	687	474	282	98 70
	Total......	3,962,590	2,092,559	110,756	48,877	17,106 95
Felt cloth, N.E.S...........	Great Britain...	12,539	11,185	61	170	59 50
	France..........	1,535	2,044	1,535	2,044	715 40
	Germany........	1,282	1,078	....	....	....
	United States...	14,200	18,281	14,200	18,281	6,398 35
	Total......	29,556	32,588	15,796	20,495	7,173 25
Flannels....................	Great Britain...	628,173	107,552	43,311	9,734	3,406 90
	Aust.-Hungary..	5,556	1,128	5,556	1,128	394 80
	France..........	41,658	9,127	42,870	9,366	3,278 10
	Germany........	63,358	13,117	7,225	933	326 55
	United States...	7,322	1,424	7,322	1,424	498 40
	Total......	746,067	132,348	106,284	22,585	7,904 75
Knitted goods, including knitted underwear, N.E.S.	Great Britain...	....	297,755	....	11,687	4,090 45
	Newfoundland..	....	15	....	15	5 25
	Aust.-Hungary..	....	1,020	....	1,020	357 00
	Belgium........	....	1,096	....	917	320 95
	China..........	....	5	....	5	1 75
	Denmark........	....	347	....	347	121 45
	France..........	....	5,493	....	5,478	1,917 30
	Germany........	....	48,149	....	....	....
	Switzerland......	....	2,753	....	2,745	960 75
	United States...	....	50,426	....	49,535	17,337 25
	Total......	....	407,059	....	71,749	25,112 15
Bed comforters and counterpanes		No.		No.		
	Great Britain..	6,042	13,728	123	442	154 70
	Hong Kong.....	2	7	2	7	2 45
	France.........	4	18	4	18	6 30
	United States...	1,643	2,274	1,643	2,274	795 90
	Total......	7,691	16,027	1,772	2,741	959 35

OF IMPORTS—*Continued.*

FOR HOME CONSUMPTION.

Preferential Tariff.			Surtax Tariff.			Total.		
Quantity.	Value.	Duty.	Quantity.	Value.	Duty.	Quantity.	Value.	Duty Collected.
Yds.	$	$ cts.	Yds.	$	$ cts.	Yds.	$	$ cts.
1,758,644	1,116,122	334,836 60	4,901	3,956	1,845 93	1,784,383	1,133,848	341,502 03
						1,988	2,586	905 10
						9,637	3,723	1,303 05
			25,339	24,104	11,248 72	25,339	24,104	11,248 72
						537	658	230 30
						19	10	3 50
1,758,644	1,116,122	334,836 60	30,240	28,060	13,094 65	1,821,903	1,164,929	355,192 70
3,708,900	2,008,409	602,522 70	10,712	6,755	3,152 45	3,782,330	2,043,007	615,420 20
			348	131	60 89	348	131	60 89
						4,99[illegible]	4,453	1,558 55
						41,763	16,024	5,608 40
			22,732	9,149	4,269 63	22,732	9,149	4,269 63
						809	275	96 25
			1,246	455	189 00	1,720	687	287 70
3,708,900	2,008,409	602,522 70	35,038	16,440	7,671 97	3,854,694	2,073,726	627,301 62
12,376	10,973	3,291 90	102	42	19 60	12,539	11,185	3,371 00
						1,535	2,044	715 40
			1,282	1,078	503 06	1,282	1,078	503 06
						14,200	18,281	6,398 35
12,376	10,973	3,291 90	1,384	1,120	522 66	29,556	32,588	10,987 81
562,193	93,429	21,800 75	9,499	2,754	1,285 20	615,003	105,917	26,492 85
						5,556	1,128	394 80
			3,142	747	348 60	46,012	10,113	3,626 70
			55,963	12,159	5,674 23	63,188	13.092	6,000 78
						7,322	1,424	498 40
562,193	93,429	21,800 75	68,604	15,660	7,308 03	737,081	131,674	37,013 53
	258,100	60,224 68		25,502	11,900 98		295,289	76,216 11
							15	5 25
							1,020	357 00
				179	83 53		1,096	404 48
							5	1 75
							347	121 45
				15	7 00		5,493	1,924 30
				48,149	22,469 73		48,149	22,469 73
				8	3 73		2,753	964 48
				325	151 67		49,860	17,488 92
	258,100	60,224 68		74,178	34,616 64		404,027	119,953 47
No.			No.			No.		
5,919	13,286	3,100 13				6,042	13,728	3,254 83
						2	7	2 45
						4	18	6 30
						1,643	2,274	795 90
5,919	13,286	3,100 13				7,691	16,027	4,059 48

Articles Imported.	Countries.	Total Imports.		Entered		
				General Tariff.		
		Quantity.	Value.	Quantity.	Value.	Duty.
DUTIABLE GOODS—*Con.*			$		$	$ cts.
Wool and mfrs. of—*Con.*						
Shawls	Great Britain		87,704		1,965	589 50
	Aust.-Hungary		153		151	45 30
	Belgium		39		39	11 70
	China		10		10	3 00
	France		560		560	168 00
	Germany		19,456			
	Japan		10		10	3 00
	Mexico		75		75	22 50
	Switzerland		498		498	149 40
	United States		1,477		1,370	411 00
	Total		109,982		4,678	1,403 40
		Doz.		Doz.		
Shirts of wool	Great Britain	3,318	26,279	42	316	110 60
	France	3	42	3	42	14 70
	Germany	285	1,016			
	United States	540	3,728	540	3,728	1,304 80
	Total	4,146	31,065	585	4,086	1,430 10
Socks and stockings of wool, worsted, the hair of the alpaca goat, &c., &c.		Doz. pairs.		Doz. pairs.		
	Great Britain	572,697	1,035,048	1,810	3,604	1,261 40
	Hong Kong	5	6	5	6	2 10
	China	35	16	35	16	5 60
	France	1,699	3,523	1,699	3,523	1,233 05
	Germany	38,716	65,777			
	Switzerland	67	329	67	329	115 15
	United States	13,532	15,997	13,355	15,777	5,521 95
	Total	626,751	1,120,696	16,971	23,255	8,139 25
Undershirts and drawers	Great Britain		165,207		8,496	2,973 60
	Belgium		1,184		1,184	414 40
	France		3,738		3,775	1,321 25
	Germany		5,772		452	158 20
	Sweden		672		672	235 20
	Switzerland		1,397		1,397	488 95
	United States		45,002		43,957	15,384 95
	Total		222,972		59,933	20,976 55
Yarns costing 30c. per lb. and over, imported on the cop, tube or in the hank by manufacturers of woollen goods for use in their products		Lbs.		Lbs.		
	Great Britain	1,529,566	738,251	3,011	2,352	470 40
	Belgium	22,193	13,383	22,193	13,383	2,676 60
	France	195	199	195	199	39 80
	United States	2,570	1,635	2,570	1,635	327 00
	Total	1,554,524	753,468	27,969	17,569	3,513 80
Yarns, N.E.S.	Great Britain	203,490	119,219	7,612	2,199	659 70
	Belgium	35	41	35	41	12 30
	France	1,077	780	800	605	181 50
	Germany	79,183	39,350			
	Spain	2	2	2	2	0 60
	United States	1,632	710	1,632	710	213 00
	Total	285,419	160,102	10,081	3,557	1,067 10

OF IMPORTS—*Continued.*

FOR HOME CONSUMPTION.

Preferential Tariff.			Surtax Tariff.			Total.		
Quantity.	Value.	Duty.	Quantity.	Value.	Duty.	Quantity.	Value.	Duty Collected.
	$	$ cts.		$	$ cts.		$	$ cts.
	77,544	15,508 80		7,801	3,120 40		87,310	19,218 70
				2	0 80		153	46 10
							39	11 70
							10	3 00
							560	168 00
				18,986	7,594 40		18,986	7,594 40
							10	3 00
							75	22 50
							498	149 40
				107	42 80		1,477	453 80
	77,544	15,508 00		26,896	10,758 40		109,118	27,670 60
Doz. 3,221	25,566	5,965 58	Doz. 55	397	185 27	Doz. 3,318	26,279	6,261 45
						3	42	14 70
			285	1,016	474 13	285	1,016	474 13
						540	3,728	1,304 80
3,221	25,566	5,965 58	340	1,413	659 40	4,146	31,065	8,055 08
Doz. pairs. 560,490	1,012,426	236,234 91	Doz. pairs. 10,349	17,527	8,179 29	Doz. pairs. 572,649	1,033,557	245,675 60
						5	6	2 10
						35	16	5 60
						1,699	3,523	1,233 05
			38,649	65,647	30,635 34	38,649	65,647	30,635 34
						67	329	115 15
			262	426	198 80	13,617	16,203	5,720 75
560,490	1,012,426	236,234 91	49,260	83,600	39,013 43	626,721	1,119,281	283,387 59
	155,989	36,397 67		912	425 60		165,397	39,796 87
							1,184	414 40
							3,775	1,321 25
				5,320	2,482 68		5,772	2,640 88
							672	235 20
							1,397	488 95
				21	9 80		43,978	15,394 75
	155,989	36,397 67		6,253	2,918 08		222,175	60,292 30
Lbs. 1,548,680	745,008	99,335 03	Lbs. 19	9	2 40	Lbs. 1,551,710	747,369	99,807 83
						22,193	13,383	2,676 60
						195	199	39 80
						2,570	1,635	327 00
1,548,680	745,008	99,335 03	19	9	2 40	1,576,668	762,586	102,851 23
170,974	102,892	20,578 40	7,275	5,571	2,228 40	185,861	110,662	23,466 50
						35	41	12 30
			277	175	70 00	1,077	780	251 50
			79,183	39,350	15,740 00	79,183	39,350	15,740 00
						2	2	0 60
						1,632	710	213 00
170,974	102,892	20,578 40	86,735	45,096	18,038 40	267,790	151,545	39,683 90

No. 1.—General Statement

Articles Imported.	Countries.	Total Imports. Quantity.	Total Imports. Value.	Entered — General Tariff. Quantity.	General Tariff. Value.	General Tariff. Duty.
			$		$	$ cts.
DUTIABLE GOODS—*Con.*						
Wool, mfrs. of—*Con.*						
All fabrics and manufactures composed wholly or in part of wool, worsted, &c., N.E.S.	Great Britain		4,693,473		520,502	182,175 70
	Newfoundland		41		41	14 35
	Aust.-Hungary		9,200		9,182	3 213 70
	Belgium		27,162		26,644	9,325 40
	China		3		3	1 05
	France		985,961		983.813	344,334 55
	Germany		127,894		5,644	1,975 40
	Holland		265		265	92 75
	Japan		157		157	54 95
	Persia		852		852	298 20
	Switzerland		55,759		55,982	19,593 70
	Turkey		156		156	54 60
	United States		55,770		55.562	19,446 72
	Total		5,956,693		1,658,803	580,581 07
Women's and children's dress goods, coat linings, Italian cloths, alpacas, orleans, cashmeres, henriettas, serges, buntings, nun's cloth, bengalines, whip cords, twills, plains or jasquards of similar fabrics, composed wholly or in part of wool, worsted, the hair of the camel, alpaca, goat or like animal, not exceeding in weight six ounces to the square yard, imported in the gray or unfinished state for the purpose of being dyed or finished in Canada		Sq. yds.		Sq. yds.		
	Great Britain	406,394	70,564	1,363	198	49 50
	France	89,529	20,860	103,123	23,254	5,813 50
	Switzerland	3,299	1,186	4,543	1,461	365 25
	Total	499,222	92,610	109,029	24,913	6,228 25
Clothing, women's and children's outside garments	Great Britain		171,876		2,947	1,031 45
	France		2,912		2,593	907 55
	Germany		209,832		7	2 45
	Italy		230		230	80 50
	United States		103,674		102,685	35,939 75
	Total		488,524		108,462	37,961 70
Clothing, ready-made and wearing apparel, N.E.S., composed wholly or in part of wool, worsted, &c., N.E.S.	Great Britain		411,605		21,729	7,605 15
	Hong Kong		155		155	54 25
	Aust.-Hungary		622		622	217 70
	Belgium		761		761	266 35
	China		1,527		1.527	534 45
	France		9,248		8,958	3,135 30
	Germany		99,665		....	....
	Italy		214		214	74 90
	Japan		383		383	134 05
	Sweden		181		181	63 35
	Switzerland		763		763	267 05
	United States		263,680		262,316	91,810 60
	Total		788,804		297,609	104,163 15

OF IMPORTS—*Continued.*

FOR HOME CONSUMPTION.

Preferential Tariff.			Surtax Tariff.			Total.		
Quantity.	Value.	Duty.	Quantity.	Value.	Duty.	Quantity.	Value.	Duty Collected.
	$	$ cts.		$	$ cts.		$	$ cts
...	4,107,222	1,232,166 60	...	77,665	36,243 51	...	4,705,389	1,450,585 81
...	...	...	...	...	...	...	41	14 35
...	...	...	...	18	8 40	...	9,200	3,222 10
...	...	...	...	...	...	...	26,644	9,325 40
...	...	...	...	...	...	...	3	1 05
...	...	...	...	1,084	505 87	...	984,897	344,840 42
...	...	...	...	120,680	56,317 03	...	126,324	58,292 43
...	...	...	...	...	...	...	265	92 75
...	...	...	...	...	...	...	157	54 95
...	...	...	...	...	...	...	852	298 20
...	...	...	...	...	...	...	55,982	19,593 70
...	...	...	...	...	...	...	156	54 60
...	...	...	...	176	82 13	...	55,738	19,528 85
...	4,107,222	1,232,166 60	...	199,623	93,156 94	...	5,965,648	1,905,904 61
Sq. yds.			Sq. yds.			Sq, yds.		
361,776	63,369	10,561 51	...	...	...	363,139	63,567	10,611 01
...	...	...	...	...	...	103,123	23,254	5,813 50
...	...	...	...	...	...	4,543	1,461	365 25
361,776	63,369	10,561 51	...	...	...	470,805	88,282	16,789 76
...	141,231	42,369 30	...	28,018	13,075 07	...	172,196	56,475 82
...	...	...	...	288	134 40	...	2,881	1,041 95
...	...	...	...	211,523	98,710 60	...	211,530	98,713 05
...	...	...	...	...	...	...	230	80 50
...	...	...	...	989	461 53	...	103,674	36,401 28
...	141,231	42,369 30	...	240,818	112,381 60	...	490,511	192,712 60
...	377,999	113,399 70	...	14,092	6,576 30	...	413,820	127,581 15
...	...	...	...	...	...	...	155	54 25
...	...	...	...	...	...	...	622	217 70
...	...	...	...	...	...	...	761	266 35
...	...	...	...	...	...	...	1,527	534 45
...	...	...	...	290	135 34	...	9,248	3,270 64
...	...	...	...	98,431	45,934 67	...	98,431	45,934 67
...	...	...	...	...	...	...	214	74 90
...	...	...	...	...	...	...	383	134 05
...	...	...	...	...	...	...	181	63 35
...	...	...	...	...	...	...	763	267 05
...	...	...	...	1,095	511 00	...	263,411	92,321 60
...	377,999	113,399 70	...	113,908	53,157 31	...	789,516	270,720 16

No. 1.—GENERAL STATEMENT

Articles Imported.	Countries.	Total Imports. Quantity.	Total Imports. Value.	Entered — General Tariff. Quantity.	General Tariff. Value.	General Tariff. Duty.
DUTIABLE GOODS—*Con.*		Yds.	$	Yds.	$	$ cts.
Wool and mfrs. of—*Con.* Carpets, Brussels	Great Britain	641,503	454,730	2,123	1,474	515 90
	Aust.-Hungary	426	417	426	417	145 95
	France	1,211	737	1,211	737	257 95
	Germany	6,638	3,346	....	....	....
	United States	1,450	1,554	1,450	1,554	543 90
	Total	651,228	460,784	5,210	4,182	1,463 70
" tapestry	Great Britain	1,576,118	561,931	6,459	2,248	786 80
	Aust.-Hungary	1,572	656	1,572	656	229 60
	France	1,692	654	1,692	654	228 90
	Germany	336	347	....	....	....
	United States	1,531	587	1,531	587	205 45
	Total	1,581,249	564,175	11,254	4,145	1,450 75
" wool, N.E.S.	Great Britain	722,690	527,387	8,266	11,113	3,889 55
	Aust.-Hungary	1,721	1,126	1,690	1,099	384 65
	France	4,483	2,893	4,483	2,893	1,012 55
	Germany	9,886	6,092	....	....	....
	Holland	245	49	245	49	17 15
	Japan	420	79	420	79	27 65
	Turkey	1,021	1,117	1,021	1,117	390 95
	United States	5,827	3,610	5,827	3,362	1,176 70
	Total	746,302	542,353	21,952	19,712	6,899 20
Felt, pressed, of all kinds, not filled or covered by or with any woven fabric		Lbs.		Lbs.		
	Great Britain	50,160	19,809	311	166	33 20
	Aust.-Hungary	232,538	71,438	249,127	76,728	15,345 60
	France	12,869	7,117	12,869	7,117	1,423 40
	Germany	158,118	50,917	....	....	....
	United States	357,982	40,893	357,982	40,893	8,178 60
	Total	811,667	190,174	620,289	124,904	24,980 80
Shoddy	Great Britain	428,142	40,151	2,474	237	47 40
	United States	16,316	552	16,316	552	110 40
	Total	444,458	40,703	18,790	789	157 80
Zinc, manufactures of, N.O.P.	Great Britain	....	962	....	61	15 25
	Aust.-Hungary	....	12	....	12	3 00
	Belgium	....	214	....	214	53 50
	France	....	571	....	571	142 75
	Germany	....	97	....	....	....
	United States	....	11,061	....	11,061	2,765 25
	Total	....	12,917	....	11,919	2,979 75

OF IMPORTS—*Continued.*

FOR HOME CONSUMPTION.

Preferential Tariff.			Surtax Tariff.			Total.		
Quantity.	Value.	Duty.	Quantity.	Value.	Duty.	Quantity.	Value.	Duty Collected.
Yds.	$	$ cts.	Yds.	$	$ cts.	Yds.	$	$ cts.
649,602	460,335	107,412 28	131	159	74 20	651,856	461,968	108,002 38
						426	417	145 95
						1,211	737	257 95
			6,638	3,346	1,561 47	6,638	3,346	1,561 47
						1,450	1,554	543 90
649,602	460,335	107,412 28	6,769	3,505	1,635 67	661,581	468,022	110,511 65
1,567,191	560,093	130,689 16	20	14	6 53	1,573,670	562,355	131,482 49
						1,572	656	229 60
						1,692	654	228 90
			336	347	161 93	336	347	161 93
						1,531	587	205 45
1,567,191	560,093	130,689 16	356	361	168 46	1,578,801	564,599	132,308 37
725,011	515,439	120,269 73	384	324	151 20	733,661	526,876	124,310 48
			31	27	12 60	1,721	1,126	397 25
						4,483	2,893	1,012 55
			9,886	6,092	2,842 92	9,886	6,092	2,842 92
						245	49	17 15
						420	79	27 65
						1,021	1,117	390 95
						5,827	3,362	1,176 70
725,011	515,439	120,269 73	10,301	6,443	3,006 72	757,264	541,594	130,175 65
Lbs.			Lbs.			Lbs.		
48,325	18,955	2,527 50	981	427	113 86	49,617	19,548	2,674 56
			644	315	84 00	249,771	77,043	15,429 60
						12,869	7,117	1,423 40
			158,118	50,917	13,577 86	158,118	50,917	13,577 86
						357,982	40,893	8,178 60
48,325	18,955	2,527 50	159,743	51,659	13.775 72	828,357	195,518	41,284 02
425,668	39,914	5,321 89				428,142	40,151	5,369 29
						16,316	552	110 40
425,668	39,914	5,321 89				444,458	40,703	5,479 69
	901	150 18					962	165 43
							12	3 00
							214	53 50
							571	142 75
				97	32 33		97	32 33
							11,061	2,765 25
	901	150 18		97	32 33		12,917	3,162 26

No. 1.—GENERAL STATEMENT

Articles Imported.	Countries.	Total Imports.		Entered		
				General Tariff.		
		Quantity.	Value.	Quantity.	Value.	Duty.
DUTIABLE GOODS—*Con.*			$		$	$ cts.
Damaged goods, under sections 49 to 53 of Rev. Stat., cap. 32	Great Britain...	....	1,882	....	665	137 14
	B. W. Indies...	....	3,814	....	704	148 11
	Hong Kong....	....	33	....	33	6 60
	Belgium......	....	143	....	143	50 05
	France.	....	17	.. ....	17	3 40
	Germany.	.. ..	602	....	....	....
	United States...	....	12,337	.... .	12,337	2,791 77
	Total.....	... .. .	18,828	.... . .	13,899	3,137 07
Prepaid postal packages. Duty received by Customs from Post Office Department.....	Great Britain...	....	18,399	....	18,399	3,680 15
Special duty on articles shipped to Canada at lower than usual home trade price	....	....	....	....	....	74,409 28
Additional duties, post entries over collections, &c.........	....	.... ..	....	....	....	159,251 55
	Total, dutiable goods.......	. ...	176,790,332	....	112,938,969	33,301,541 57

OF IMPORTS—*Continued.*

FOR HOME CONSUMPTION.

Preferential Tariff.			Surtax Tariff.			Total.		
Quantity.	Value.	Duty.	Quantity.	Value.	Duty.	Quantity.	Value.	Duty Collected.
	$	$ cts.		$	$ cts.		$	$ cts.
....	1,217	193 74	....	....	....	....	1,882	330 88
....	3,110	588 42	....	....	....	....	3,814	736 53
....	....	....	....	....	....	....	33	6 60
....	....	....	....	....	....	....	143	50 05
....	....	....	....	....	....	....	17	3 40
....	....	....	....	602	141 39	....	602	141 39
....	....	....	....	....	....	....	12,337	2,791 77
....	4,327	782 16	....	602	141 39	....	18,828	4,060 62
....	....	....	....	....	....	....	18,399	3,680 15
....	....	....	....	....	....	....	....	74,409 28
....	....	....	....	....	....	....	....	159,251 55
....	54,164,102	11,158,953 14	....	5,943,038	2,210,706 47	....	173,046,109	46,671,101 18

No. 1.—General Statement of Imports—*Continued.*

Articles Imported.	Countries.	Imported.		Entered for Home Consumption.	
		Quantity.	Value.	Quantity.	Value.
FREE GOODS.		No.	$	No.	$
THE MINE.					
Burrstones in blocks, rough or unmanufactured, not bound up or prepared for binding into mill stones	France	1,724	2,158	1,724	2,158
	Germany	6	314	6	314
	United States	16	189	16	189
	Total	1,746	2,661	1,746	2,661
Chalk stone, China or Cornwall stone, Cliff stone, and felspar, ground or unground	Great Britain	....	1,429	....	1,429
	United States	....	7,624	....	7,624
	Total	....	9,053	....	9,053
Clays, viz.—		Cwt.		Cwt.	
China clay	Great Britain	118,654	37,431	118,654	37,431
	United States	57,430	28,478	57,430	28,478
	Total	176,084	65,909	176,084	65,909
Fire clay	Great Britain	....	22,342	....	22,342
	United States	....	108,788	....	108,788
	Total	....	131,130	....	131,130
Pipe clay	Great Britain	....	364	....	364
	United States	....	969	....	969
	Total	....	1,333	....	1,333
Clays, all other, N.E.S.	Great Britain	....	3,954	....	3,954
	United States	....	18,178	....	18,178
	Total	....	22,132	....	22,132
		Tons.		Tons.	
Coal, anthracite, and anthracite coal dust.	Great Britain	48,247	162,953	48,247	162,953
	United States	2,152,616	10,141,350	2,152,616	10,141,350
	Total	2,200,863	10,304,303	2,200,863	10,304,303
Emery, in bulk, crushed or ground	Great Britain	....	1,744	....	1,744
	Germany	....	14	....	14
	United States	....	20,023	....	20,023
	Total	....	21,781	....	21,781
		Cwt.		Cwt.	
Flint, flints and ground flint stones.	Great Britain	4,720	3,754	4,720	3,754
	France	3,207	1,499	3,207	1,499
	United States	23,181	14,082	23,181	14,082
	Total	31,108	19,335	31,108	19,335

No. 1.—General Statement of Imports—*Continued.*

Articles Imported.	Countries.	Imported.		Entered for Home Consumption.	
		Quantity.	Value.	Quantity.	Value.
FREE GOODS—THE MINE—*Con.*			$		$
Fossils	United States	....	15	....	15
Fuller's earth in bulk only, not prepared for toilet and other purposes	Great Britain	....	963	....	963
	United States	....	3,681	....	3,681
	Total	....	4,644	....	4,644
		Cwt.		Cwt.	
Gannister	Great Britain	10,564	2,336	10,564	2,336
	United States	2,239	783	2,239	783
	Total	12,803	3,119	12,803	3,119
		Tons.		Tons.	
Gravels and sand	Great Britain	8,099	38,873	8,099	38,873
	Belgium	28	73	28	73
	France	6,229	12,285	6,229	12,285
	Germany	200	122	200	122
	United States	101,944	122,374	101,944	122,374
	Total	116,500	173,727	116,500	173,727
Gypsum, crude (sulphate of lime)	Great Britain	29	455	29	455
	United States	6,303	21,553	6,303	21,553
	Total	6,332	22,008	6,332	22,008
Pumice and pumice stone, ground or unground	Great Britain	....	543	....	543
	France	....	67	....	67
	Germany	....	8	....	8
	Italy	....	777	....	777
	United States	....	7,658	....	7,658
	Total	....	9,053	....	9,053
		Cwt.		Cwt.	
Minerals, viz.: Alumina or oxide of aluminum	Great Britain	6,680	20,319	6,680	20,319
	Belgium	5,351	18,592	5,351	18,592
	Germany	13,907	52,045	13,907	52,045
	United States	50,136	103,127	50,136	103,127
	Total	76,074	194,083	76,074	194,083
Cryolite or kryolite	Germany	60	324	60	324
	United States	3,994	22,469	3,994	22,469
	Total	4,054	22,793	4,054	22,793
Litharge	Great Britain	6,937	25,685	6,937	25,685
	Germany	1,851	7,018	1,851	7,018
	Holland	8	33	8	33
	United States	1,369	7,100	1,369	7,100
	Total	10,165	39,836	10,165	39,836

No. 1.—General Statement of Imports—*Continued.*

Articles Imported.	Countries.	Imported.		Entered for Home Consumption.	
		Quantity.	Value	Quantity.	Value.
FREE GOODS—THE MINE—*Con.*		Galls.	$	Galls.	$
Mineral waters, natural, not in bottle....	United States.....	8,285	1,754	8,285	1,754
Mineralogical specimens..........	Germany..........	....	207	....	207
	Norway..........	....	100	....	100
	United States.....	....	419	....	419
	Total........	....	726	....	726
Ores of metals, all kinds, including cobalt ore..............................		Cwt.		Cwt.	
	Great Britain.....	570	456	570	456
	Australia.........	420	310	420	310
	Newfoundland...	8,982,622	460,501	8,982,622	460,501
	Norway..........	184,380	13,829	184,380	13,829
	Spain...........	228,620	27,400	228,620	27,400
	United States.....	8,282,079	1,767,540	8,282,079	1,767,540
	Total........	17,678,691	2,270,036	17,678,691	2,270,036
Phosphate rock (fertilizer)..........	Great Britain.....	....	960	....	960
	United States.....	....	19,537	....	19,537
	Total	....	20,497	....	20,497
Precious stones in the rough......... ...	Great Britain.....	....	215,691	....	215,691
	B. E. Indies	....	5,000	....	5,000
	Denmark.........	....	4,901	....	4,901
	France............	....	49,477	....	49,477
	Germany.........	....	20,709	....	20,709
	Holland..........	....	52	....	52
	United States.....	....	10,083	....	10,083
	Total........	....	305,913	....	305,913
Diamonds, unset, diamond dust or bort, and black diamonds for borers.........	Great Britain.....	....	351,980	....	351,980
	Br. Africa	....	1,352	....	1,352
	Aust.-Hungary....	....	40,697	....	40,697
	Belgium.........	....	47,895	....	47,895
	France..........	....	249,414	....	249,414
	Germany.........	....	53,222	....	53,222
	Holland..........	....	342,879	....	342,879
	Italy..........	....	1,030	....	1,030
	United States.....	....	121,286	....	121,286
	Total.........	....	1,209,755	....	1,209,755
Salt, imported from the United Kingdom, or any British Possession, or imported for the use of the Sea or Gulf fisheries..		Cwt.		Cwt.	
	Great Britain.....	1,497,033	296,487	1,497,033	296,487
	Australia	1,547	880	1,547	880
	B. W. Indies	104,705	14,187	104,705	14,187
	Newfoundland....	15,700	2,050	15,700	2,050
	Fr. W. Indies....	2,427	330	2,427	330
	Italy	196,242	12,514	196,242	12,514
	Portugal..........	6,800	1,725	6,800	1,725
	St. Pierre.........	3,425	713	3,425	713
	Spain.............	171,702	16,462	171,702	16,462
	United States.....	31,219	6,866	31,219	6,866
	Total.........	2,030,800	352,214	2,030,800	352,214

No. 1.—GENERAL STATEMENT OF IMPORTS—*Continued.*

Articles Imported.	Countries.	Imported.		Entered for Home Consumption.	
		Quantity.	Value.	Quantity.	Value.
FREE GOODS—THE MINE—*Con.*		Cwt.	$	Cwt.	$
Silex or crystallized quartz	United States	7,465	8,347	7,465	8,347
Tufa, calcareous	United States	600	30	600	30
Whiting or whitening, gilders' whiting and Paris white	Great Britain	148,311	37,164	148,311	37,164
	United States	11,719	7,712	11,719	7,712
	Total	160,030	44,876	160,030	44,876
THE FISHERIES.					
Ambergris	United States	....	141	....	141
Fish offal or refuse and fish skins	United States	....	203	... .	203
Fur skins, undressed, the produce of marine animals	Newfoundland	....	16,020	.. ....	16,020
Pearl, mother of, unmanufactured	Great Britain	....	355	....	355
	United States	... .	3,554	....	3,554
	Total	....	3,909	....	3,909
Tortoise and other shells	Great Britain	....	94	....	94
	B. W. Indies	....	54	....	54
	United States	....	2,841	....	2,841
	Total	....	2,989	.. . .	2,989
Turtles	B. W. Indies	....	28	....	28
	United States	....	765	....	765
	Total	... .	793	....	793
Whalebone, unmanufactured	United States	Lbs. 7	59	Lbs. 7	59
Seed and breeding oysters, imported for the purpose of being planted in Canadian waters	United States	....	525	... .	525
Special from Newfoundland.					
Fish— Cod, haddock, ling and pollock—fresh	Newfoundland	Lbs. 2,610	109	Lbs. 2,610	109
" " " dry salted—or smoked	Newfoundland	Cwt. 180,781	812,344	Cwt. 180,781	812,344
" " " pickled	Newfoundland	2,465	11,464	2,465	11,464
Halibut, fresh	Newfoundland	Lbs. 8,750	544	Lbs. 8,750	544

No. 1.—General Statement of Imports—Continued.

Articles Imported.	Countries.	Imported.		Entered Home Consumption.	
		Quantity.	Value.	Quantity.	Value.
FREE GOODS—THE FISHERIES—*Con.*			$		$
Fish—*Con.* Herring, fresh	Newfoundland	Lbs. 2,075,600	36,162	Lbs. 2,075,600	36,162
" pickled	Newfoundland	11,146,710	183,171	11,146,710	183,171
" smoked	Newfoundland	1,640	54	1,640	54
Lobsters, fresh in cans	Newfoundland	30	13	30	13
" preserved in cans	Newfoundland	244,255	58,760	244,255	58,760
Salmon, fresh	Newfoundland	121,441	10,974	121,441	10,974
" smoked	Newfoundland	200	31	200	31
" canned	Newfoundland	528	85	528	85
" pickled	Newfoundland	640,874	33,993	640,874	33,993
Fish, all other, fresh	Newfoundland	....	2,828	....	2,828
" pickled	Newfoundland	54,784	1,721	54,784	1,721
Fish Oil, viz.:— Cod	Newfoundland	Galls. 102,500	33,959	102,500	Galls. 33,959
Seal	Newfoundland	42,341	13,431	42,341	13,431
Other	Newfoundland	37,839	10,196	37,839	10,196
Other articles, produce of the fisheries, N.E.S.	Newfoundland	....	85	....	85
THE FOREST.					
Cork-wood	Great Britain	....	5,421	....	5,421
	Belgium	....	19	....	19
	France	....	436	....	436
	Portugal	....	12,452	....	12,452
	Spain	....	174	....	174
	United States	....	56,750	....	56,750
	Total	....	75,252	....	75,252
Barks, viz.: Cork-wood	France	....	94	....	94

No. 1.—General Statement of Imports—*Continued.*

Articles Imported.	Countries.	Imported.		Entered for Home Consumption.	
		Quantity.	Value.	Quantity.	Value.
FREE GOOD—THE FOREST—*Con.*		Cords.	$	Cords.	$
Bark—*Con.*					
Hemlock	United States	36	171	36	171
Oak and tanners'	United States	....	283	....	283
(D) Shovel handles wholly of wood	Great Britain	....	1,650	....	1,650
	United States	....	34,025	....	34,025
	Total	....	35,675	....	35,675
Felloes of hickory wood, rough sawn to shape only, or rough sawn and bent to shape, not planed, smoothed or otherwise manufactured	United States	....	26,744	....	26,744
Handle, heading, stave and shingle bolts	United States	....	43,356	....	43,356
Hickory billets	United States	....	9,833	....	9,833
Hickory sawn to shape for spokes of wheels	United States	....	6,681	....	6,681
Hickory spokes rough turned, not tenoned, mitred, throated, faced, sized, cut to length, round tenoned or polished	United States	....	108,100	....	108,100
Hubs for wheels, posts, last blocks, wagon, oar, gun, heading and all like blocks or sticks, rough hewn or sawed only	United States	....	14,359	....	14,359
Ivory nuts (vegetable)	United States	....	27,009	....	27,009
Fence posts and railroad ties	Newfoundland	....	20	....	20
	United States	....	508,676	....	508,676
	Total	....	508,696	....	508,696
Logs, and round unmanufactured timber	Australia	....	1,521	....	1,521
	Belgium	....	50	....	50
	United States	....	888,000	....	888,000
	Total	....	889,571	....	889,571
Lumber and timber, planks and boards, when not otherwise manufactured than rough sawn or split or creosoted, vulcanized, or treated by any other preserving process, viz. :—		Feet.		Feet.	
Boxwood	United States	5,560	430	5,560	430
Cherry, chestnut, gumwood and hickory and whitewood	Great Britain	39	16	39	16
	Australia	193,070	8,731	193,070	8,731
	United States	9,467,720	411,777	9,467,720	411,777
	Total	9,660,829	420,524	9,660,829	420,524

No. 1.—General Statement of Imports—*Continued.*

Articles Imported.	Countries.	Imported.		Entered for Home Consumption.	
		Quantity.	Value.	Quantity.	Value.
THE FOREST—*Con.*		Feet.	$	Feet.	$
Lumber and timber—*Con.*					
Mahogany	Great Britain	187,142	17,233	187,142	17,233
	Australia	25,009	1,251	25,009	1,251
	United States	1,540,265	178,992	1,540,265	178,992
	Total	1,752,416	197,476	1,752,416	197,476
Oak	Great Britain	384	40	384	40
	Australia	7,921	716	7,921	716
	United States	32,843,918	1,238,503	32,843,918	1,238,503
	Total	32,852,223	1,239,259	32,852,223	1,239,259
Pitch pine	United States	22,576,299	565,474	22,576,299	565,474
Red wood	United States	72,840	2,658	72,840	2,658
Rose wood	Australia	54,010	4,396	54,010	4,396
	United States	1,079	378	1,079	378
	Total	55,089	4,774	55,089	4,774
Sandal wood	United States	517	56	517	56
Spanish cedar	Australia	1,963	198	1,963	198
	United States	37,424	7,190	37,424	7,190
	Total	39,387	7,388	39,387	7,388
Sycamore	United States	24,951	556	24,951	556
Walnut	United States	1,003,318	43,246	1,003,318	43,246
White ash	United States	1,715,091	72,034	1,715,091	72,034
African teak, black heart ebony, lignum vitæ, red cedar and satin-wood	Great Britain		2,427		2,427
	Australia		256		256
	B. W. Indies		19		19
	Hong Kong		275		275
	China		72		72
	Porto Rico		20		20
	United States		26,766		26,766
	Total		29,835		29,835
Timber hewn or sawed, squared or sided, or creosoted	Great Britain		4		4
	Australia		2,27		2,276
	United States		187,138		187,138
	Total		189,418		189,418

No. 1.—General Statement of Imports—*Continued.*

Articles Imported.	Countries.	Imported.		Entered for Home Consumption.	
		Quantity.	Value.	Quantity.	Value.
FREE GOODS—THE FOREST—*Con.*		M. ft.	$	M. ft.	$
Lumber and timber, &c.—*Con.*					
Sawed or split boards, planks, deals, and other lumber, when not further manufactured than dressed on one side only or creosoted, vulcanized or treated by any preserving process	Australia	80	3,610	80	3,610
	Newfoundland	544	5,867	544	5,867
	United States	51,777	1,115,161	51,777	1,115,161
	Total	52,401	1,124,638	52,401	1,124,638
Pine and spruce clapboards	United States	323	2,860	323	2,860
		M.		M.	
Laths	Newfoundland	1	2	1	2
	United States	467	1,432	467	1,432
	Total	468	1,434	468	1,434
Shingles	United States	10,301	21,311	10,301	21,311
Staves, not listed or jointed, of wood of all kinds	United States	6,622	198,835	6,622	198,835
Sawdust of the following woods:—Amaranth, cocoboral, boxwood, cherry, chestnut, walnut, gumwood, mahogany, pitch pine, rosewood, sandalwood, sycamore, Spanish cedar, oak, hickory, whitewood, African teak, black heart ebony, lignum vitæ, red cedar, redwood, satin-wood, white ash, persimmon and dogwood	Great Britain	....	412	....	412
	United States	....	3,211	....	3,211
	Total	....	3,623	....	3,623
		Cords.		Cords.	
Wood for fuel	United States	38,991	96,021	38,991	96,021
ANIMALS AND THEIR PRODUCE.					
Animals for improvement of stock, viz.—		No.		No.	
Horses	Great Britain	805	358,279	805	358,279
	Belgium	16	13,896	16	13,896
	France	29	19,935	30	20,135
	United States	616	428,569	631	432,069
	Total	1,466	820,679	1,482	824,379
Cattle	Great Britain	119	12,741	119	12,741
	United States	423	44,768	423	44,768
	Total	542	57,509	542	57,509

No. 1.—General Statement of Imports—*Continued.*

Articles Imported.	Countries.	Imported. Quantity.	Imported. Value.	Entered for Home Consumption. Quantity.	Entered for Home Consumption. Value.
FREE GOODS— ANIMALS AND THEIR PRODUCE—*Con.*		No.	$	No.	$
Animals for improvement of stock—*Con.* Sheep	Great Britain	318	8,236	318	8,236
	United States	16	452	16	452
	Total	334	8,688	334	8,688
Swine	Great Britain	58	1,755	58	1,755
	United States	30	609	30	609
	Total	88	2,364	88	2,364
Dogs	Great Britain	45	2,433	45	2,433
	United States	298	8,640	298	8,640
	Total	343	11,073	343	11,073
Goats	Belgium	17	51	17	51
	United States	5	45	5	45
	Total	22	96	22	96
Fowls, domestic, pure bred	Great Britain	118	567	118	567
	United States	3,597	8,136	3,597	8,136
	Total	3,715	8,703	3,715	8,703
Animals brought into Canada, temporarily, and for a period not exceeding three months, for the purpose of exhibition or competition for prizes offered by any agricultural or other association, viz.— Horses	United States	1,476	378,492	....	....
Cattle	United States	25	6,125	....	....
Sheep	United States	39	260	....	....
All others, N.E.S.	United States	....	3,310	....	....
Bees	United States	....	596	....	596
Bones, crude, not manufactured, burned, calcined, ground or steamed		Cwt.		Cwt.	
	Great Britain	18	518	18	518
	Newfoundland	31,633	19,956	31,633	19,956
	China	1	3	1	3
	Germany	1	61	1	61
	United States	1,772	4,990	1,772	4,990
	Total	33,425	25,528	33,425	25,528

No. 1.—GENERAL STATEMENT OF IMPORTS—*Continued.*

Articles Imported.	Countries.	Imported.		Entered for Home Consumption.	
		Quantity.	Value.	Quantity.	Value.
FREE GOODS. ANIMALS AND THEIR PRODUCE—*Con.*		Cwt.	$	Cwt.	$
Bone dust, bone black or charred bone and bone ash	Great Britain	11	10	11	10
	Newfoundland	963	723	963	723
	United States	35,235	51,631	35,235	51,631
	Total	36,209	52,364	36,209	52,364
		Lbs.		Lbs.	
Bristles	Great Britain	55,728	51,374	55,728	51,374
	China	100	112	100	112
	France	4,200	4,264	4,200	4,264
	Germany	6,206	6,323	6,206	6,323
	United States	67,462	50,715	67,462	50,715
	Total	133,696	112,788	133,696	112,788
Cat-gut or worm-gut unmanufactured, for whip and other cord	Great Britain		359		359
	Germany		52		52
	United States		178		178
	Total		589		589
Egg yolk	Germany		2,816		2,816
	United States		3,424		3,424
	Total		6,240		6,240
Fur skins, of all kinds, not dressed in any manner, N.E.S	Great Britain		286,099		286,099
	Australia		13,000		13,000
	B. E. Indies		5,839		5,839
	B. W. Indies		2		2
	Newfoundland		14,223		14,223
	China		2,376		2,376
	France		57,077		57,077
	Germany		774,697		774,697
	Philippines		50		50
	Russia		169,080		169,080
	United States		1,984,782		1,984,782
	Total		3,307,225		3,307,225
Grease, degras and oleostearine	Great Britain	211,023	7,004	211,023	7,004
	Belgium	1,552	56	1,552	56
	Germany	362,507	7,683	362,507	7,683
	United States	1,204,698	62,067	1,204,698	62,067
	Total	1,779,780	76,810	1,779,780	76,810
Grease, rough, the refuse of animal fat, for the manufacture of soap and oils only	B. W. Indies	400	8	400	8
	Germany	462	19	462	19
	United States	6,495,809	303,880	6,495,809	303,880
	Total	6,496,671	303,907	6,496,671	303,907

No. 1.—General Statement of Imports—*Continued.*

Articles Imported.	Countries.	Imported. Quantity.	Imported. Value.	Entered for Home Consumption. Quantity.	Entered for Home Consumption. Value.
FREE GOODS—ANIMALS AND THEIR PRODUCE—*Con.*		Cwt.	$	Cwt.	$
Guano and other animal manures	Great Britain	112	143	112	143
	France	248	1,352	248	1,352
	Turkey	340	954	340	954
	United States	3,425	9,191	3,425	9,191
	Total	4,125	11,640	4,125	11,640
		Lbs.		Lbs.	
Hair, cleaned or uncleaned, but not curled, dyed or otherwise manufactured	Great Britain	26,772	2,286	26,772	2,286
	New Zealand	2,274	208	2,274	208
	France	74,705	4,656	74,705	4,656
	Germany	4,816	1,637	4,816	1,637
	United States	310,367	51,047	310,367	51,047
	Total	418,934	59,834	418,934	59,834
Horse hair, not further manufactured than simply cleaned and dipped or dyed, for use in the manufacture of horse hair cloth	Great Britain	14,933	19,165	14,933	19,165
	China	717	296	717	296
	France	10	3	10	3
	Germany	5,001	7,001	5,001	7,001
	United States	34,762	25,306	34,762	25,306
	Total	55,423	51,771	55,423	51,771
Hatters' furs, not on the skin	Great Britain		11,602		11,602
	Belgium		2,032		2,032
	Germany		593		593
	United States		44,297		44,297
	Total		58,524		58,524
Hides and skins raw, whether dry salted or pickled, and tails undressed	Great Britain		1,903,096		1,903,096
	Australia		17,068		17,068
	British Africa		2,779		2,779
	B. E. Indies		191,145		191,145
	B. W. Indies		170,180		170,180
	Hong Kong		3,165		3,165
	Newfoundland		6,851		6,851
	New Zealand		35,791		35,791
	Argentina		1,415,388		1,415,388
	Belgium		46,186		46,186
	Brazil		16,219		16,219
	China		54,793		54,793
	Denmark		5,328		5,328
	France		329,259		329,259
	French Africa		14,548		14,548
	Germany		129,131		129,131
	Holland		26,391		26,391
	Mexico		144,450		144,450
	Russia		22,805		22,805
	St. Pierre		564		564
	Sweden		2,224		2,224
	Turkey		146,314		146,314
	United States		1,694,751		1,694,751
	Uruguay		173,893		173,893
	Total		6,552,319		6,552,319

No. 1.—General Statement of Imports—*Continued.*

Articles Imported.	Countries.	Imported.		Entered for Home Consumption.	
		Quantity.	Value.	Quantity.	Value.
FREE GOODS—ANIMALS AND THEIR PRODUCE—*Con.*			$		$
Hoofs, horn strips, horn and horn tips, in the rough, not polished or otherwise manufactured than cleaned	Great Britain		156		156
	British Africa		50		50
	Newfoundland		50		50
	France		4		4
	Germany		2,711		2,711
	Italy		728		728
	Norway		4,620		4,620
	United States		10,674		10,674
	Total		18,993		18,993
		Lbs.		Lbs.	
Ivory, unmanufactured	Great Britain	32	125	32	125
	Germany	10	43	10	43
	United States	1,256	6,665	1,256	6,665
	Total	1,298	6,833	1,298	6,833
Leeches	United States		247		247
		Oz.		Oz.	
Musk in pods or in grains	Great Britain	1	19	1	19
	United States	255	2,246	255	2,246
	Total	256	2,265	256	2,265
Pelts, raw	Great Britain		205,930		205,930
	New Zealand		5,957		5,957
	France		234		234
	St. Pierre		189		189
	United States		27,645		27,645
	Total		239,955		239,955
Pigeons, homing and messenger, pheasants and quails	Great Britain		25		25
	United States		3,048		3,048
	Total		3,073		3,073
Quills in their natural state or unplumed	United States		2,461		2,461
Rennet, raw and prepared	Great Britain		378		378
	Denmark		11,280		11,280
	Germany		8,038		8,038
	Holland		1,850		1,850
	Sweden		1,861		1,861
	United States		41,887		41,887
	Total		65,294		65,294

No. 1.—General Statement of Imports—*Continued.*

Articles Imported.	Countries.	Imported.		Entered for Home Consumption.	
		Quantity.	Value.	Quantity.	Value.
FREE GOODS. ANIMALS AND THEIR PRODUCE—*Con.*		Lbs.	$	Lbs.	$
Silk, raw or as reeled from the cocoon, not being doubled, twisted or advanced in manufacture in any way	China	1,729	6,485	1,729	6,485
	Japan	5,249	19,776	5,249	19,776
	United States	113,229	425,446	113.229	425,446
	Total	120,207	451,707	120,207	451,707
Silk in the gum or spun, imported by manufacturers of silk underwear for such manufactures in their own factories	Great Britain	86	222	86	222
	United States	362	1,051	362	1,051
	Total	448	1,273	448	1,273
Silk cocoons and silk waste	Great Britain	....	2,636	....	2,636
	Australia	....	190	....	190
	United States	....	254	....	254
	Total	....	3,080	....	3,080
Sausage skins or casings, not cleaned	Great Britain	....	219	....	219
	Germany	....	117	....	117
	Holland	....	39	....	39
	Japan	....	21	....	21
	United States	....	29	....	29
	Total	....	425	....	425
Wool not further prepared than washed, N.E.S.	Great Britain	2,779,872	651,943	2,779,872	651,943
	Australia	280,645	63,580	280,645	63,580
	British Africa	83,732	9,727	83,732	9,727
	B. E. Indies	10,104	1,409	10,104	1,409
	B. W. Indies	4,220	276	4,220	276
	New Zealand	754,632	183,588	754,632	183,588
	Argentina	186,642	43,699	186,642	43,699
	Belgium	7,419	2,167	7,419	2,167
	Chili	14,928	2,349	14,928	2,349
	China	39,008	4,886	39,008	4,886
	France	520,420	174,073	520,420	174,073
	Holland	1,306	596	1,306	596
	Italy	40,650	8,384	40,650	8,384
	Russia	5,625	984	5,625	984
	Turkey	25,426	3,360	25,426	3,360
	United States	1,557,208	338,247	1,557,208	338,247
	Total	6,311,837	1,489,268	6,311,837	1,489,268

No. 1.—General Statement of Imports—*Continued.*

Articles Imported.	Countries.	Imported.		Entered for Home Consumption.	
		Quantity.	Value.	Quantity.	Value.
FREE GOODS. AGRICULTURAL PRODUCTS.			$		$
Bamboo-reeds, not further manufactured than cut into suitable lengths for walking sticks or canes, or for sticks for umbrellas, parasols or sunshades, and bamboos unmanufactured	Great Britain	....	67	....	67
	B. E. Indies	....	11	....	11
	China	....	8	....	8
	Japan	....	1,868	....	1,868
	United States	....	4,112	....	4,112
	Total	....	6,066	....	6,066
Broom corn	United States	....	196,084	....	196,084
Cane and rattans not manufactured	Great Britain	....	2,658	....	2,658
	B. E. Indies	....	9	....	9
	Germany	....	149	....	149
	Holland	....	412	....	412
	United States	....	8,066	....	8,066
	Total	....	11,294	....	11,294
Cocoa beans, not roasted, crushed or ground		Lbs		Lbs.	
	Great Britain	241,419	33,525	241,419	33,525
	B. E. Indies	33,800	4,319	33,800	4,319
	B. W. Indies	465,452	48,249	465,452	48,249
	British Guiana	2,400	304	2,400	304
	Holland	66,013	10,907	66,013	10,907
	Portugal	11,202	1,204	11,202	1,204
	United States	936,505	115,871	936,505	115,871
	Total	1,756,791	214,379	1,756,791	214,379
Esparto, or Spanish grass, and other grasses and pulp of, including fancy grasses dried, but not coloured or otherwise manufactured		Cwt.		Cwt.	
	Great Britain	4	48	4	48
	United States	71	453	71	453
	Total	75	501	75	501
Fibre, Mexican, Istle, or Tampico	Great Britain	240	2,832	240	2,832
	Belgium	123	1,521	123	1,521
	France	52	573	52	573
	Germany	11	99	11	99
	United States	2,427	26,800	2,427	26,800
	Total	2,853	31,825	2,853	31,825
Fibre flax and flax tow	Great Britain	411	3,463	411	3,463
	United States	540	2,515	540	2,515
	Total	951	5,978	951	5,978

No. 1.—General Statement of Imports—*Continued.*

Articles Imported.	Countries.	Imported. Quantity.	Imported. Value.	Entered for Home Consumption. Quantity.	Entered for Home Consumption. Value.
FREE GOODS. AGRICULTURAL PRODUCTS—*Con.*		Cwt.	$	Cwt.	$
Fibre vegetable, N.E.S.	Great Britain	219	1,677	219	1,677
	B. E. Indies	216	642	216	642
	Belgium	48	358	48	358
	Germany	94	894	94	894
	United States	4,843	24,766	4,843	24,766
	Total	5,420	28,337	5,420	28,337
Florist stock, viz.— Palms, bulbs, corms, tubes, rhizomes, arucaria, spiræ and lilies of the valley	Great Britain		4,136		4,136
	B. W. Indies		61		61
	Hong Kong		383		383
	Newfoundland		23		23
	Aust.-Hungary		42		42
	Belgium		7,590		7,590
	China		543		543
	France		4,951		4,951
	Germany		13,524		13,524
	Holland		40,622		40,622
	Italy		34		34
	Japan		3,505		3,505
	United States		33,298		33,298
	Total		108,712		108,712
Fruit, green, viz.—		Bunches.		Bunches.	
Bananas	B. W. Indies	55,092	46,350	55,092	46,350
	Cent. Am. States	650	650	650	650
	Hawaii	326	233	326	233
	United States	1,144,466	1,124,154	1,144,466	1,124,154
	Total	1,200,534	1,171,387	1,200,534	1,171,387
		No.		No.	
Pineapples	Australia	13,566	1,614	13,566	1,614
	B. W. Indies	35,223	2,899	35,223	2,899
	Fiji	500	72	500	72
	Hawaii	13,306	1,823	13,306	1,823
	United States	2,178,622	186,859	2,178,622	186,859
	Total	2,241,217	193,267	2,241,217	193,267
Guavas, mangoes, plantains, pomegranates, and shaddocks	Great Britain		85		85
	Australia		24		24
	B. W. Indies		6,100		6,100
	China		110		110
	United States		17,436		17,436
	Total		23,755		23,755
Berries, viz.: Wild blueberries, wild strawberries and wild raspberries	United States		1,642		1,642
Foot grease, the refuse of the cotton seed after the oil has been pressed out, but not when treated with alkalies		Cwt.		Cwt.	
	Great Britain	8	42	8	42
	United States	1,627	6,835	1,627	6,835
	Total	1,635	6,877	1,635	6,877

No. 1.—General Statement of Imports—*Continued.*

Articles Imported.	Countries.	Imported.		Entered for Home Consumption.	
		Quantity.	Value.	Quantity.	Value.
FREE GOODS. AGRICULTURAL PRODUCTS—*Con.*		Cwt.	$	Cwt.	$
Hemp, undressed	Great Britain	58,881	455,496	58,881	455,496
	Australia	3,052	18,722	3,052	18,722
	New Zealand	9,491	60,034	9,491	60,034
	Germany	130	760	130	760
	United States	52,303	379,370	52,303	379,370
	Total	123,857	914,382	123,857	914,382
		Bush.		Bush.	
Indian corn, N.E.S	Great Britain	11	13	11	13
	Australia	1,673	1,202	1,673	1,202
	United States	10,130,812	5,544,552	9,964,737	5,457,080
	Total	10,132,496	5,545,767	9,966,421	5,458,295
		Cwt.		Cwt.	
Jute butts and jute	Great Britain	3,894	17,349	3,894	17,349
	United States	2,144	8,305	2,144	8,305
	Total	6,038	25,654	6,038	25,654
		Lbs.		Lbs.	
Locust beans and locust bean meal	Great Britain	2,240	43	2,240	43
	United States	15,429	695	15,429	695
	Total	17,669	738	17,669	738
		Cwt.		Cwt.	
Manilla grass	Great Britain	22,131	202,795	22,131	202,795
	Mexico	7,123	48,281	7,123	48,281
	United States	86,990	555,575	66,990	555,575
	Total	96,244	806,651	96,244	806,651
Osiers or willows, unmanufactured	Great Brtain	....	1,004	....	1,004
	United States	....	319	....	319
	Total	....	1,323	....	1,323
Palm leaf, unmanufactured	United States	....	253	....	253
Seedling stock for grafting, viz.: Plum, pear, peach and other fruit trees	Great Britain	....	5	....	5
	France	....	3,017	....	3,017
	Holland	....	107	....	107
	United States	....	2,594	....	2,594
	Total	....	5,723	....	5,723
		Lbs.		Lbs.	
Seeds, viz.: Annato	Great Britain	25	46	25	46
	France	1,512	83	1,512	83
	United Statas	3,907	306	3,907	306
	Total	5,444	435	5,444	435

No. 1.—GENERAL STATEMENT OF IMPORTS—*Continued.*

Articles Imported.	Countries.	Imported.		Entered for Home Consumption.	
		Quantity.	Value.	Quantity.	Value.
FREE GOODS. AGRICULTURAL PRODUCTS—*Con.*		Lbs.	$	Lbs.	$
Seeds—*Con.*					
Beet and mangold	Great Britain	78,388	6,580	78,388	6,580
	Denmark	2,000	283	2,000	283
	France	207,292	13,497	207,292	13,497
	Germany	232,278	15,643	232,278	15,643
	Holland	701	67	701	67
	United States	40,284	3,433	40,284	3,433
	Total	560,943	39,503	560,943	39,503
Carrot	Great Britain	10,267	1,705	10,267	1,705
	France	12,455	1,923	12,455	1,923
	Germany	75	8	75	8
	Holland	915	61	915	61
	United States	8,259	1,470	8,259	1,470
	Total	31,971	5,167	31,971	5,167
Flax	Great Britain	2,250	90	2,250	90
	Belgium	10,330	274	10,330	274
	Holland	14,400	652	14,400	652
	United States	76,922,226	1,646,178	76,922,226	1,646,178
	Total	76,949,206	1,647,194	76,949,206	1,647,194
Turnip	Great Britain	138,591	11,184	138,591	11,184
	France	104,323	7,246	104,323	7,246
	Germany	56	18	56	18
	Holland	100	7	100	7
	United States	1,080	182	1,080	182
	Total	244,150	18,637	244,150	18,637
Mustard	Great Britain	113,862	5,539	113,862	5,539
	France	2,200	95	2,200	95
	United States	12,873	509	12,873	509
	Total	128,935	6,143	128,935	6,143
Beans (seed) from Great Britain	Great Britain	7,785	460	7,785	460
Pease " "	Great Britain	107,739	4,263	107,739	4,263
Rape seed, sowing	Great Britain	39,929	1,278	39,929	1,278
	Holland	139,620	4,003	139,620	4,003
	United States	64,853	1,968	64,853	1,968
	Total	214,402	7,249	244,402	7,249

No. 1.—GENERAL STATEMENT OF IMPORTS—*Continued.*

Articles Imported.	Countries.	Imported.		Entered for Home Consumption.	
		Quantity.	Value.	Quantity.	Value.
FREE GOODS. AGRICULTURAL PRODUCTS—*Con.*			$		$
Mushroom spawn	Great Britain	....	605	....	605
	France	....	11	....	11
	United States	....	364	....	364
	Total	....	980	....	980
Tobacco, unmanufactured, for excise purposes, under conditions of the Inland Revenue Act		Lbs.		Lbs.	
	Great Britain	11,284	1,945	11,851	1,947
	Cuba	186,387	58,812	225,630	57,108
	Dutch E. Indies	....	....	2,519	2,519
	Germany	97,044	11,479	29,457	3,160
	Holland	92,761	16,610	64,327	11,769
	United States	14,215,879	2,580,379	14,185,874	2,633,590
	Total	14,603,355	2 669,225	14,519,658	2,710,093
Trees, N.E.S.	Great Britain	....	52	....	52
	France	....	216	....	216
	Holland	....	103	....	103
	United States	....	2,775	....	2,775
	Total	....	3,146	....	3,146
MANUFACTURED AND PARTLY MANUFACTURED ARTICLES.					
Admiralty charts	Great Britain	....	854	....	854
	United States	....	337	....	337
	Total	....	1,191	....	1,191
Album insides, made of paper	Great Britain	....	33	....	33
	United States	....	4	....	4
	Total	....	37	....	37
Artificial limbs	United States	....	21,225	....	21,225
Artificial teeth	Great Britain	....	26,775	....	26,775
	United States	....	78,419	....	78,419
	Total	....	105,194	....	105,194
Ash, pot and pearl, in packages of not less than 25 lbs	Great Britain	3,327	304	3,327	304
	Hong Kong	2,200	8	2,200	8
	Belgium	50,221	1,733	50,221	1,733
	Germany	4,956	165	4,956	165
	United States	226,907	10,210	226,907	10,210
	Total	287,611	12,420	287,611	12,420
Asphaltum or asphalt		Cwt.		Cwt.	
	Great Britain	465	918	465	918
	B. W. Indies	850	850	850	850
	United States	156,958	170,873	156,958	170,873
	Total	158,273	172,641	158,273	172,641

No. 1.—General Statement of Imports—*Continued.*

Articles Imported.	Countries.	Imported.		Entered for Home Consumption.	
		Quantity.	Value.	Quantity.	Value.
FREE GOODS. MANUFACTURED ARTICLES—*Con.*			$		$
Astrachan or Russian hair skins and China-goat plates or rugs, wholly or partially dressed but not dyed........	Great Britain.....	....	5,066	....	5,066
	China........	....	20,419	....	20,419
	France........	....	309	....	309
	Germany........	....	10,452	....	10,452
	United States.....	....	26,307	....	26,307
	Total........	....	62,553	....	62,553
Bells, imported for the use of churches..	Great Britain.....	....	7,208	....	7,208
	France........	....	42,864	....	42,864
	United States.....	....	20,332	....	20,332
	Total........	....	70,404	....	70,404
Binder twine of hemp, jute, manilla or sisal, and of manilla and sisal mixed..		Lbs.		Lbs.	
	Great Britain.....	192,915	21,818	192,915	21,818
	United States.....	14,569,630	1,628,923	14,569,630	1,628,923
	Total........	14,762,545	1,650,741	14,762,545	1,650,741
Binder twine, articles for the manufacture of........	Great Britain.....	....	5,689	....	5,689
	United States.....	....	61,889	....	61,889
	Total........	....	67,578	....	67,578
Blanc fixe and satin white........	Great Britain.....	79,336	1,038	79,336	1,038
	Belgium........	4,337	50	4,337	50
	United States.....	320,353	3,640	320,353	3,640
	Total........	404,026	4,728	404,026	4,728
Blanketing and lapping and discs or mills for engraving copper rollers, imported by cotton manufacturers, calico printers and wall paper manufacturers for use in their own factories only....	Great Britain.....	....	8,195	....	8,195
	France........	....	503	....	503
	United States.....	....	2,196	....	2,196
	Total........	......	10,894	....	10,894
Blast furnace slag........	Great Britain.....	....	16,831	....	16,831
	United States.....	....	2,174	....	2,174
	Total........	....	19,005	....	19,005
Bolting cloth, not made up........	Great Britain.....	....	97	....	97
	France........	....	216	....	216
	Germany........	....	124	....	124
	Switzerland.....	....	122	....	122
	United States....	....	17,034	....	17,034
	Total........	....	17,593	....	17,593

No. 1.—General Statement of Imports—*Continued.*

Articles Imported.	Countries.	Imported. Quantity.	Imported. Value.	Entered for Home Consumption. Quantity.	Entered for Home Consumption. Value.
FREE GOODS. MANUFACTURED ARTICLES—*Con.*			$		$
Bone pitch, crude only	United States		718		718
Books, viz.: Bibles, prayer books, psalm and hymn books and religious tracts, &c	Great Britain		123,294		123,294
	Aust.-Hungary		237		237
	Belgium		18,610		18,610
	France		23,758		23,758
	Germany		2,773		2,773
	Holland		144		144
	Italy		30		30
	Russia		48		48
	Switzerland		180		180
	Turkey		15		15
	United States		69,566		69,566
	Total		238,655		238,655
Books, printed by or for any government or by any association for the promotion of science or letters and official annual reports of religious or benevolent associations and issued in the course of the proceedings of said associations, to their members, and not for the purpose of sale or trade	Great Britain		772		772
	British Africa		60		60
	Belgium		24		24
	France		210		210
	United States		1,829		1,829
	Total		2,895		2,895
Books, embossed, for the blind, and books for the instruction of the deaf and dumb and blind	Great Britain		143		143
	France		45		45
	United States		152		152
	Total		340		340
Books, not printed or reprinted in Canada, which are included or used as text books in the curriculum of any university, incorporated college or normal school in Canada; books specially imported for the bona fide use of incorporated mechanics' institutes, public libraries, libraries or universities, colleges and schools, or for the library of any incorporated medical, law, literary, scientific or art association or society, and being the property of the organized authorities of such library, and not in any case the property of individuals	Great Britain		58,711		58,711
	Hong Kong		35		35
	Newfoundland		40		40
	Aust.-Hungary		12		12
	Belgium		257		257
	China		138		138
	France		17,319		17,319
	Germany		4,041		4,041
	Italy		323		323
	Japan		316		316
	United States		180,981		180,981
	Total		262,173		262,173

No. 1.—General Statement of Imports—*Continued.*

Articles Imported.	Countries.	Imported. Quantity.	Imported. Value.	Entered for Home Consumption. Quantity.	Entered for Home Consumption. Value.
FREE GOODS. MANUFACTURED ARTICLES—*Con.*			$		$
Books, bound or unbound, which have been printed and manufactured more than twelve years	Great Britain		10,909		10,909
	Belgium		102		102
	France		3,162		3,162
	Germany		558		558
	Holland		495		495
	United States		5,548		5,548
	Total		20,774		20,774
Books, viz.:—Books on the application of science to industries of all kinds, including books on agriculture, horticulture, forestry, fish and fishing, mining, metallurgy, architecture, electric and other engineering, carpentry, shipbuilding, mechanism, dyeing, bleaching, tanning, weaving and other mechanic arts, and similar industrial books; also books printed in any language other than the English and French languages, or in any two languages not being English and French, or in any three or more languages	Great Britain		6,015		6,015
	Hong Kong		38		38
	Aust.-Hungary		183		183
	Belgium		1,327		1,327
	China		126		126
	Denmark		5		5
	France		8,311		8,311
	Germany		716		716
	Greece		25		25
	Iceland		2,235		2,235
	Italy		122		122
	Japan		100		100
	Russia		66		66
	Turkey		10		10
	United States		93,149		93,149
	Total		112,428		112,428
Manuscript and insurance maps	Great Britain		120		120
	United States		3,995		3,995
	Total		4,115		4,115
Bookbinders' cloth	Great Britain		26,424		26,424
	Germany		2,014		2,014
	United States		16,005		16,005
	Total		44,443		44,443
Brick, fire, for use in process of manufactures		M.		M.	
	Great Britain	8,749	121,533	8,749	121,533
	Germany	10	158	10	158
	United States	16,216	418,271	16,216	418,271
	Total	24,975	539,962	24,975	539,962

No. 1.—General Statement of Imports—*Continued.*

Articles Imported.	Countries.	Imported. Quantity.	Imported. Value.	Entered for Home Consumption. Quantity.	Entered for Home Consumption. Value.
FREE GOODS. MANUFACTURED ARTICLES—*Con.*		Yds.	$	Yds.	$
Buckram, for the manufacture of hat and bonnet shapes	Great Britain	13,495	2,621	13,495	2,621
	France	280	191	280	191
	Germany	17,874	2,359	17,874	2,359
	United States	45,865	6,612	45,865	6,612
	Total	77,514	11,783	77,514	11,783
Bullion or gold fringe	Great Britain	....	310	....	310
	France	....	3,490	....	3,490
	United States	....	182	....	182
	Total	....	3,982	....	3,982
		Gross.		Gross.	
Buttons, shoe, papier maché	Great Britain	18,611	532	18,611	532
	France	300	10	300	10
	United States	69,322	1,956	69,322	1,956
	Total	88,233	2,498	88,233	2,498
Canvas or fabric, not frictionized, for the manufacture of bicycle tires, imported by the manufacturers of bicyles for use exclusively in the manufacture of bicycle tires in their own factories	United States	....	17,125	....	17,125
Caplins, unfinished leghorn hats	Great Britain	....	571	....	571
	France	....	281	....	281
	Italy	....	85	....	85
	United States	....	1,162	....	1,162
	Total	....	2,099	....	2,099
		No.		No.	
Carbons over 6 inches in circumference, for use in Canadian manufactures	Great Britain	2,466	111	2,466	111
	France	6,533	555	6,533	555
	Sweden	2,000	435	2,000	435
	United States	342,841	69,439	342,841	69,439
	Total	353,840	70,540	353,840	70,540
Catgut or gut cord for musical instruments	Great Britain	....	582	....	582
	Aust.-Hungary	....	60	....	60
	Belgium	....	11	....	11
	France	....	143	....	143
	Germany	....	4,499	....	4,499
	United States	....	1,795	....	1,795
	Total	....	7,090	....	7,090
Celluloid, xylonite, or xyolite, in sheets and in lumps, blocks or balls in the rough	Great Britain	....	13,114	....	13,114
	Germany	....	4,290	....	4,290
	United States	....	48,088	....	48,088
	Total	....	65,492	....	65,492

No. 1.—General Statement of Imports—*Continued.*

Articles Imported.	Countries.	Imported.		Entered for Home Consumption.	
		Quantity.	Value.	Quantity.	Value.
FREE GOODS. MANUFACTURED ARTICLES—*Con.*			$		$
Chronometers and compasses for ships....	Great Britain.....	....	3,202	....	3,202
	Aust.-Hungary....	....	188	....	188
	France....	....	5	....	5
	Switzerland.......	....	129	....	129
	United States.....	....	8,815	....	8,815
	Total	....	12,339	....	12,339
Citron, lemon and orange rinds, in brine .	Great Britain.....	....	1,732	....	1,732
	United States. ...	....	161	....	161
	Total	....	1,893	....	1,893
		Galls.		Galls.	
Coal tar and coal pitch..................	Great Britain.....	512,202	22,669	512,202	22,669
	United States.....	2,282,485	131,959	2,282,485	131,959
	Total	2,794,687	154,628	2,794,687	154,628
		Tons.		Tons.	
Coke..................................	Great Britain.. ..	6,014	31,311	6,014	31,311
	United States.....	474,208	1,280,064	474,208	1,280,064
	Total	480,222	1,311,375	480,222	1,311,375
Colours, metallic, viz.:—Oxides of cobalt, tin and copper. N.E.S................		Lbs.		Lbs.	
	Great Britain.....	4,281	1,110	4,281	1,110
	France...........	440	495	440	495
	Germany.........	46,545	15,155	46,545	15,155
	United States.....	162,754	50,167	162,754	50,167
	Total	214,020	66,927	214,020	66,927
Communion plate, imported for the use of churches.............................	Great Britain.....	....	476	....	476
	Aust.-Hungary....	....	40	....	40
	Belgium..........	....	361	....	361
	France..	....	15,967	....	15,967
	Germany.........	....	39	....	39
	Holland..	....	30	....	30
	Italy............	....	143	....	143
	United States. ...	....	5,533	....	5,533
	Total	....	22,589	....	22,589
Coir and coir yarns......................	Great Britain.....	8,186	428	8,186	428
	United States.....	300,466	13,495	300,466	13,495
	Total	308,652	13,923	308,652	13,923
Cotton waste, not dyed, &c	Great Britain.....	1,211,913	72,722	1,211,913	72,722
	Newfoundland. ..	1,060	69	1,060	69
	Belgium..........	26,190	1,664	26,190	1,664
	Germany.........	218,231	9,813	218,231	9,813
	United States.....	8,091,064	528,832	8,091,064	528,832
	Total	9,548,458	613,100	9,548,458	613,100

No. 1.—General Statement of Imports—*Continued.*

Articles Imported.	Countries.	Imported.		Entered for Home Consumption.	
		Quantity.	Value.	Quantity.	Value.
FREE GOODS—MANUFACTURED ARTICLES—*Con.*		Lbs.	$	Lbs.	$
Cotton wool or raw cotton	Great Britain	7,665	1,185	7,665	1,185
	China	211,790	22,876	211,790	22,876
	Egypt	37,854	5,835	37,854	5,835
	United States	67,743,738	7,596,729	67,743,738	7,596,729
	Total	68,001,047	7,626,625	68,001,047	7,626,625
Crucibles, clay or plumbago	Great Britain		6,741		6,741
	Germany		664		664
	United States		25,545		25,545
	Total		32,950		32,950
		No.		No.	
Curling stones	Great Britain	1,476	7,755	1,476	7,755
	United States	990	4,140	990	4,140
	Total	2,466	11,895	2,466	11,895
Diamond drills for prospecting for minerals not to include motive power	United States	26	40,620	26	40,620
Drugs, dyes, chemicals and medicines—		Lbs.		Lbs.	
Acid, boracic	Great Britain	191,477	9,875	191,477	9,875
	France	120	12	120	12
	Germany	615	48	615	48
	Italy	2,000	200	2,000	200
	United States	5,929	417	5,929	417
	Total	200,141	10,552	200,141	10,552
Acid, hydro-fluo-silicic	Great Britain	10,080	504	10,080	504
	United States	246,104	6,559	246,104	6,559
	Total	256,184	7,063	256,184	7,063
Acid, oxalic	Great Britain	19,112	1,178	19,112	1,178
	Belgium	46,014	2,284	46,014	2,284
	Germany	12,416	582	12,416	582
	Switzerland	2,073	219	2,073	219
	United States	78,647	4,213	78,647	4,213
	Total	158,262	8,476	158,262	8,476
Acid, tannic and blood albumen	Great Britain		1,457		1,457
	France		471		471
	Germany		721		721
	United States		8,084		8,084
	Total		10,733		10,733

No. 1.—General Statement of Imports—*Continued.*

Articles Imported.	Countries.	Imported.		Entered for Home Consumption.	
		Quantity.	Value.	Quantity.	Value.
FREE GOODS—MANUFACTURED ARTICLES—*Con.*		Lbs.	$	Lbs.	$
Drugs, dyes, &c.—*Con.*					
Alazarine and artificial alazarine	Great Britain	4,650	640	4,650	640
	Germany	2,700	835	2,700	835
	United States	22,822	4,446	22,822	4,446
	Total	30,172	5,921	30,172	5,921
Alum, in bulk only, ground or unground, and alum cake	Great Britain	906,453	9,825	906,453	9,825
	Belgium	21,922	330	21,922	330
	Germany	38,773	340	38,773	340
	United States	3,801,631	41,419	3,801,631	41,419
	Total	4,768,779	51,914	4,768,779	51,914
Alumina, sulphate of	Great Britain	2,910,194	17,091	2,910,194	17,091
	Belgium	32,700	332	32,700	332
	Germany	57,933	541	57,933	541
	United States	750,045	10,183	750,045	10,183
	Total	3,750,872	28,147	3,750,872	28,147
Ammonia, nitrate of	Great Britain	44,748	3,337	44,748	3,337
	Germany	2,112	147	2,112	147
	United States	19,423	869	19,423	869
	Total	66,283	4,353	66,283	4,353
Ammonia, sulphate of	Great Britain	208,166	6,032	208,166	6,032
	Belgium	626	33	626	33
	United States	159,326	5,443	159,326	5,443
	Total	368,118	11,508	368,118	11,508
Aniline dyes and coal tar dyes, in bulk or packages of not less than 1 lb.	Great Britain	107,107	27,413	107,107	27,413
	Aust.-Hungary	2,497	480	2,497	480
	Belgium	26,663	5,042	26,663	5,042
	France	8,614	2,459	8,614	2,459
	Germany	571,653	137,923	571,653	137,923
	Switzerland	128,735	32,546	128,735	32,546
	United States	581,944	163,109	581,944	163,109
	Total	1,427,213	368,972	1,427,213	368,972
Aniline salts and arseniate of aniline	Great Britain	138,682	11,462	138,682	11,462
	France	25	17	25	17
	Germany	27,334	2,137	27,334	2,137
	United States	19,845	1,883	19,845	1,883
	Total	185,886	15,499	185,886	15,499
Aniline oil, crude	Great Britain	9,643	838	9,643	838
	United States	5,454	520	5,454	520
	Total	15,097	1,358	15,097	1,358

No. 1.—General Statement of Imports—*Continued.*

Articles Imported.	Countries.	Imported.		Entered for Home Consumption.	
		Quantity	Value.	Quantity.	Value.
FREE GOODS. MANUFACTURED ARTICLES—*Con.*		Lbs.	$	Lbs.	$
Drugs, dyes, &c.—*Con.*					
Annatto, liquid or solid	Great Britain	724	83	724	83
	Germany	30	4	30	4
	United States	88,647	12,420	88,647	12,420
	Total	89,401	12,507	89,401	12,507
Antimony, or regulus of, not ground, pulverized or otherwise manufactured	Great Britain	212,559	29,142	212,559	29,142
	Belgium	7,070	1,050	7,070	1,050
	Germany	1,569	241	1,569	241
	United States	95,080	12,084	95,080	12,084
	Total	316,278	42,517	316,278	42,517
Antimony salts	Great Britain	59,664	10,438	59,664	10,438
	Belgium	8,200	1,159	8,200	1,159
	Germany	10,431	996	10,431	996
	United States	9,345	1,187	9,345	1,187
	Total	87,640	13,780	87,640	13,780
Argols or argal	Great Britain	1,202	124	1,202	124
	United States	167,011	7,191	167,011	7,191
	Total	168,213	7,315	168,213	7,315
Arsenic	Great Britain	12,629	799	12,629	799
	Aust.-Hungary	11,022	700	11,022	700
	France	1,179	44	1,179	44
	Germany	32,307	1,880	32,307	1,880
	United States	389,838	15,746	389,838	15,746
	Total	446,975	19,169	446,975	19,169
Beans, viz.: Nux vomica, crude only	United States	163	4	163	4
Tonquin, crude only	Great Britain	28	16	28	16
	B. W. Indies	240	124	240	124
	United States	3,814	2,229	3,814	2,229
	Total	4,082	2,369	4,082	2,369
Vanilla, crude only	Great Britain	237	361	237	361
	France	55	87	55	87
	United States	15,772	29,241	15,772	29,241
	Total	16,064	29,689	16,064	29,689
Borax, ground or unground, in bulk of not less than 25 lbs	Great Britain	2,443,667	76,202	2,443,667	76,202
	United States	49,829	2,075	49,829	2,075
	Total	2,493,496	78,277	2,493,496	78,277

No. 1.—General Statement of Imports—*Continued.*

Articles Imported.	Countries.	Imported.		Entered for Home Consumption.	
		Quantity.	Value.	Quantity.	Value.
FREE GOODS—MANUFACTURED ARTICLES—*Con.*		Lbs.	$	Lbs.	$
Drugs, dyes, &c.—*Con.*					
Brimstone, crude, or in roll or flour, and sulphur crude in roll or flour	Great Britain	14,698,027	141,102	14,698,027	141,102
	France	67,173	1,730	67,173	1,730
	Italy	880,530	11,187	880,530	11,187
	Japan	2,366,222	18,703	2,366,222	18,703
	United States	25,035,720	263,434	25,035,720	263,434
	Total	43,047,672	436,156	43,047,672	436,156
Bromine	Germany	28	12	28	12
	United States	605	200	605	200
	Total	633	212	633	212
Burgundy pitch	United States	4,920	113	4,920	113
Camwood and sumac and extract thereof	Great Britain	222,560	5,552	222,560	5,552
	Germany	2,669	59	2,669	59
	Italy	337,768	5,880	337,768	5,880
	United States	219,256	5,586	219,256	5,586
	Total	782,253	17,077	782,253	17,077
Chloralum or chloride of aluminium	United States	50	21	50	21
Chloride of lime in packages of not less than 25 lbs	Great Britain	3,838,633	38,023	3,838,633	38,023
	Belgium	413,337	4,316	413,337	4,316
	Germany	304,876	3,319	304,876	3,319
	United States	1,274,337	13,657	1,274,337	13,657
	Total	5,831,183	59,315	5,831,183	59,315
Cochineal	Great Britain	3,741	1,754	3,741	1,754
	United States	4,060	550	4,060	550
	Total	7,801	2,304	7,801	2,304
Copper, precipitate of, crude	Great Britain	1,878	302	1,878	302
	United States	3,110	316	3,110	316
	Total	4,988	618	4,988	618
Cream of Tartar in crystals	Great Britain	81,872	14,154	81,872	14,154
	France	1,076,745	162,362	1,076,745	162,362
	Germany	8,276	1,958	8,276	1,958
	United States	203,328	34,780	203,328	34,780
	Total	1,370,221	213,254	1,370,221	213,254

No. 1.—General Statement of Imports—*Continued.*

Articles Imported.	Countries.	Imported.		Entered for Home Consumption.	
		Quantity.	Value.	Quantity.	Value.
FREE GOODS—MANUFACTURED ARTICLES—*Con.*		Lbs.	$	Lbs.	$
Drugs, dyes, &c.—*Con.*					
Cyanide of potassium	Great Britain	61,164	10,852	61,164	10,852
	France	50	12	50	12
	Germany	177	27	177	27
	United States	51,470	9,548	51,470	9,548
	Total	112,861	20,439	112,861	20,439
Dragon's blood	Great Britain	3	2	3	2
	France	35	23	35	23
	United States	357	232	357	232
	Total	395	257	395	257
Dyes, patent prepared	Great Britain	3,800	355	3,800	355
	France	7,095	1,046	7,095	1,046
	Germany	16,425	1,562	16,425	1,562
	United States	11,631	2,269	11,631	2,269
	Total	38,951	5,232	38,951	5,232
Dyeing or tanning articles in a crude state used in dyeing or tanning, N.E.S.	Great Britain	134,163	3,808	134,163	3,808
	Belgium	29,150	948	29,150	948
	France	2,395	284	2,395	284
	Germany	60	37	60	37
	United States	698,449	16,820	698,449	16,820
	Total	864,217	21,897	864,217	21,897
Extract of logwood, fustic, oak, and of oak bark and quebracho	Great Britain	3,185,122	96,077	3,185,122	96,077
	B. W. Indies	21,190	2,437	21,190	2,437
	Belgium	82,035	1,938	82,035	1,938
	France	36,085	2,903	36,085	2,903
	Germany	46,616	999	46,616	999
	United States	13,910,237	309,451	13,910,237	309,451
	Total	17,281,285	413,805	17,281,285	413,805
Ferment cultures to be used in butter making	United States	....	36	....	36
Flowers, leaves and roots—					
Roots, medicinal, viz.: Alkanet, crude, crushed or ground, aconite, calumba, foliæ digitalis, gentian, ginseng, jalap, ipecacuanha, iris, orris root, liquorice, sarsaparilla, squills, taraxacum, rhubarb and valerian, unground	Great Britain	....	250	....	250
	Aust.-Hungary	....	237	....	237
	China	....	45	....	45
	France	....	1,713	....	1,713
	Germany	....	9	....	9
	United States	....	16,277	....	16,277
	Total	....	18,531	....	18,531

No. 1.—General Statement of Imports—*Continued.*

Articles Imported.	Countries.	Imported.		Entered for Home Consumption.	
		Quantity.	Value.	Quantity.	Value.
FREE GOODS. MANUFACTURED ARTICLES—*Con.*		Lbs.	$	Lbs.	$
Drugs, dyes, &c.—*Con.*					
Gums, viz.—					
Amber, Arabic, Australian, copal, damar, elemy, kaurie, mastic, sandarac, Senegal, shellac; and white shellac in gum or flake, for manufacturing purposes; and gum tragacanth, gum gedda and gum barberry......	Great Britain.....	97,224	16,143	97,224	16,143
	B. E. Indies.....	11,839	3,267	11,839	3,267
	New Zealand......	19,283	3,741	19,283	3,741
	France............	176	46	176	46
	Germany	377	130	377	130
	United States.....	1,787,029	330,380	1,787,029	330,380
	Total......	1,915,928	353,707	1,915,928	353,707
Chicle or Sappato gum, crude........	Cent. Am. States..	34,560	6,476	34,560	6,476
	United States.. ..	4,179,699	1,042,611	4,179,699	1,042,611
	Total.......	4,214,259	1,049,087	4,214,259	1,049,087
Hemp bleaching compound when imported by manufacturers of rope to be used in their own factories for the manufacture of rope, O.C., Feb. 13, 1902........................	Great Britain.....	....	533	....	533
	Germany	....	256	....	256
	United States....	....	12,151	....	12,151
	Total........	....	12,940	....	12,940
Indigo	United States.....	54,407	9,092	54,407	9,092
Indigo auxiliary or zinc dust...	Great Britain.....	25	3	25	3
	Belgium....	5,543	280	5,543	280
	France...........	300	52	300	52
	Germany	2,933	648	2,933	648
	United States...	120,868	4,710	120,868	4,710
	Total......	129,669	5,693	129,669	5,693
Indigo, paste and extract of	United States.....	47,981	9,032	47,981	9,032
Iodine, crude...	Great Britain.....	1,748	3,672	1,748	3,672
	Japan....	9,435	2,886	9,435	2,886
	United States.....	3,012	7,777	3,012	7,777
	Total..	14,195	14,335	14,195	14,335
Iron liquor, solutions of acetate or nitrate of iron for dyeing and calico printing.	Great Britain.....	....	367	....	367
	Germany.........	....	11	....	11
	United States....	....	3,156	....	3,156
	Total........	....	3,534	....	3,534

No. 1.—GENERAL STATEMENT OF IMPORTS—*Continued.*

Articles Imported.	Countries.	Imported.		Entered for Home Consumption.	
		Quantity.	Value.	Quantity.	Value.
FREE GOODS. MANUFACTURED ARTICLES—*Con.*		Lbs.	$	Lbs.	$
Drugs, dyes, &c.—*Con.*					
Kainite, or German potash salts for fertilizers	Great Britain	33,600	189	33,600	189
	Germany	293,328	1,473	293,328	1,473
	United States	347,469	1,749	347,469	1,749
	Total	674,397	3,411	674,397	3,411
Lac, crude, seed, button, stick and shell	United States	233	80	233	80
Lead, nitrate and acetate of, not ground	Great Britain	377,964	19,728	377,964	19,728
	Belgium	45,618	2,527	45,618	2,527
	Germany	14,753	784	14,753	784
	United States	13,717	1,334	13,717	1,334
	Total	452,052	24,373	452,052	24,373
Litmus and all lichens, prepared and not prepared	United States	20	5	20	5
Logwood and fustic, ground, and ground oak bark	Great Britain	32,624	600	32,624	600
	Germany	4,817	145	4,817	145
	United States	277,136	4,287	277,136	4,287
	Total	314,577	5,032	314,577	5,032
Madder and munjeet, or Indian madder, ground or prepared and all extracts of	Great Britain	....	689	....	689
	United States	....	2	....	2
	Total	....	691	....	691
Manganese, oxide of	Great Britain	13,747	358	13,747	358
	Germany	53,148	537	53,148	537
	United States	177,725	4,613	177,725	4,613
	Total	244,620	5,508	244,620	5,508
Moss, Iceland and other mosses	Great Britain	262	69	262	69
	Belgium	811	9	811	9
	China	567	34	567	34
	France	712	14	712	14
	Germany	2,015	113	2,015	113
	Japan	439	29	439	29
	United States	632,043	37,036	632,043	37,036
	Total	636,849	37,304	636,849	37,304
Nut galls and extracts thereof	Great Britain	4,725	1,087	4,725	1,087
	United States	6,145	1,071	6,145	1,071
	Total	10,870	2,158	10,870	2,158

No. 1.—General Statement of Imports—*Continued.*

Articles Imported.	Countries.	Imported.		Entered for Home Consumption.	
		Quantity.	Value.	Quantity.	Value.
FREE GOODS. MANUFACTURED ARTICLES—*Con.*		Oz.	$	Oz.	$
Drugs, dyes, &c.—*Con.*					
Ottar or attar of roses, and oil of roses..	Great Britain.....	139	350	139	350
	United States.....	2,016	7,045	2,016	7,045
	Total........	2,155	7,395	2,155	7,395
		Lbs.		Lbs.	
Persis, or extract of archill and cudbear.	Great Britain.....	2,254	144	2,254	144
	United States.....	1,770	234	1,770	234
	Total........	4,024	378	4,024	378
Phosphorus.	Great Britain.....	10	8	10	8
	France...........	1,000	380	1,000	380
	Germany.........	10	1	10	1
	United States. ...	595	282	595	282
	Total..	1,615	671	1,615	671
Potash, caustic	Great Britain.....	6,139	368	6,139	368
	Belgium....	80,047	2,691	80,047	2,691
	France..	3,768	140	3,768	140
	Germany.........	4,541	357	4,541	357
	United States.....	135,302	7,471	135,302	7,471
	Total........	229,797	11,027	229,797	11,027
		Lbs.		Lbs.	
Potash, chlorate of, not further prepared than ground, and free from admixture with any other substance	Great Britain. ...	44,843	3,119	44,843	3,119
	Belgium....	6,615	446	6,615	446
	France..........	10,080	642	10,080	642
	Germany.........	50	10	50	10
	United States.....	347,366	24,548	347,366	24,548
	Total........	408,954	28,765	408,954	28,765
Potash, German mineral.	Belgium....... ..	5,594	185	5,594	185
	United States....	43,314	765	43,314	765
	Total........	48,908	950	48,908	950
Potash, muriate and bichromate of, crude....	Great Britain.....	558,200	33,630	558,200	33,630
	France...........	6,615	331	6,615	331
	Germany..	831,520	17,483	831,520	17,483
	United States....	777,587	15,322	777,587	15,322
	Total........	2,173,922	66,766	2,173,922	66,766
Potash, red and yellow prussiate of.. .	Great Britain.....	21,000	2,013	21,000	2,013
	Belgium	16,355	1,505	16,355	1,505
	Germany.	6,341	604	6,341	604
	United States....	1,398	215	1,398	215
	Total........	45,094	4,337	45,094	4,337

No. 1.—General Statement of Imports—*Continued.*

Articles Imported.	Countries.	Imported.		Entered for Home Consumption.	
		Quantity.	Value.	Quantity.	Value.
FREE GOODS. MANUFACTURED ARTICLES—*Con.*		Lbs.	$	Lbs.	$
Drugs, dyes, &c.—*Con.*					
Quicksilver	Great Britain	655	353	655	353
	United States	149,709	69,152	149,709	69,152
	Total	150,364	69,505	150,364	69,505
		Ozs.		Ozs.	
Quinine, salts of	Great Britain	68,628	13,014	68,628	13,014
	France	10	3	10	3
	Germany	8,584	1,875	8,584	1,875
	United States	14,487	3,066	14,487	3,066
	Total	91,709	17,958	91,709	17,958
Red liquor, a crude acetate of aluminum prepared from pyroligneous acid for dyeing and calico printing	Great Britain	....	162	....	162
	United States	....	247	....	247
	Total	....	409	....	409
Safety bate, and tannin preserver when imported by tanners for use exclusively in their own tanneries in tanning leather, O.C., March 1, 1899	United States	....	457	....	457
		Lbs.		Lbs.	
Saffron and safflower and extract of, and saffron cake	Great Britain	10	74	10	74
	United States	551	848	551	848
	Total	561	922	561	922
Sal ammoniac	Great Britain	327,455	11,578	327,455	11,578
	Belgium	3,131	155	3,131	155
	Germany	17,119	997	17,119	997
	United States	115,000	3,340	115,000	3,340
	Total	462,705	16,070	462,705	16,070
Saltpetre	Great Britain	241,523	10,269	241,523	10,269
	B. E. Indies	2,240	105	2,240	105
	Newfoundland	1,500	75	1,500	75
	Belgium	9,680	499	9,680	499
	China	200	3	200	3
	France	52	7	52	7
	Germany	500,998	22,295	500,998	22,295
	United States	1,760,579	75,752	1,760,579	75,752
	Total	2,516,772	109,005	2,516,772	109,005
Seeds, aromatic, crude, not edible, viz.—Anise, anise-star, caraway, coriander, cardamon, cumin, fenugreek and fennel	Great Britain	14,240	1,077	14,240	1,077
	France	3,440	322	3,440	322
	Holland	18,290	1,126	18,290	1,126
	United States	86,873	6,485	86,873	6,485
	Total	122,843	9,010	122,843	9,010

No. 1.—General Statement of Imports—*Continued.*

Articles Imported.	Countries.	Imported.		Entered for Home Consumption.	
		Quantity.	Value.	Quantity.	Value.
FREE GOODS—MANUFACTURED ARTICLES—*Con.*		Lbs.	$	Lbs.	$
Drugs, dyes, &c.—*Con.*					
Soda, ash	Great Britain	13,070,729	99,942	13,070,729	99,942
	United States	6,216,968	50,007	6,216,968	50,007
	Total	19,287,697	149,949	19,287,697	149,949
Soda, bichromate	Great Britain	149,524	6,754	149,524	6,754
	Belgium	26,460	1,309	26,460	1,309
	Germany	21,535	917	21,535	917
	United States	61,510	769	61,510	769
	Total	259,029	9,749	259,029	9,749
Soda, bisulphite of	Great Britain	110,768	1,088	110,768	1,088
	United States	516,517	5,209	516,517	5,209
	Total	627,285	6,297	627,285	6,297
Soda, caustic	Great Britain	7,883,818	148,322	7,883,818	148,322
	Belgium	32,644	1,030	32,644	1,030
	Germany	163	26	163	26
	United States	1,623,991	31,736	1,623,991	31,736
	Total	9,540,616	181,114	9,540,616	181,114
Soda, chlorate of	Great Britain	2,240	143	2,240	143
	United States	34,272	2,327	34,272	2,327
	Total	36,512	2,470	36,512	2,470
Soda, nitrate of	Great Britain	82,531	2,172	82,531	2,172
	Argentina	1,388,800	29,026	1,388,800	29,026
	Belgium	8,766	411	8,766	411
	Chili	5,070,214	106,913	5,070,214	106,913
	Germany	138,878	4,825	138,878	4,825
	United States	16,393,245	373,520	16,393,245	373,520
	Total	23,082,434	516,867	23,082,434	516,867
Soda, nitrite of	Great Britain	200	12	200	12
	Belgium	4,516	238	4,516	238
	United States	973	92	973	92
	Total	5,689	342	5,689	342

No. 1.—General Statement of Imports—*Continued.*

Articles Imported.	Countries.	Imported.		Entered for Home Consumption.	
		Quantity.	Value.	Quantity.	Value.
FREE GOODS— MANUFACTURED ARTICLES—*Con.*		Lbs.	$	Lbs.	$
Drugs, dyes, &c.—*Con.*					
Soda, sal	Great Britain	3,865,814	23,633	3,865,814	23,633
	Germany	214	8	214	8
	United States	6,056,209	55,051	6,056,209	55,051
	Total	9,922,237	78,692	9,922,237	78,692
Soda, silicate of, in crystal or in solution	Great Britain	881,961	5,601	881,961	5,601
	United States	2,007,644	20,763	2,007,644	20,763
	Total	2,889,605	26,364	2,889,605	26,364
Soda, sulphate of, crude, known as salt cake	Great Britain	1,600	13	1,600	13
	United States	515,672	2,661	515,672	2,661
	Total	517,272	2,674	517,272	2,674
Sodium, sulphide of, arseniate, binarseniate, chloride and stannate of soda.	Great Britain	7,247	239	7,247	239
	Belgium	62,301	704	62,301	704
	Germany	150,350	1,744	150,350	1,744
	United States	649,166	7,851	649,166	7,851
	Total	869,064	10,538	869,064	10,538
Sulphate of iron (copperas)	Great Britain	116,913	453	116,913	453
	Germany	7,277	202	7,277	202
	United States	238,725	1,838	238,725	1,838
	Total	362,915	2,493	362,915	2,493
Sulphate of copper (blue vitriol)	Great Britain	151,617	7,877	151,617	7,877
	Germany	30	2	30	2
	United States	1,710,420	87,170	1,710,420	87,170
	Total	1,862,067	95,049	1,862,067	95,049
Tartar emetic and gray tartar	Germany	24,644	3,799	24,644	3,799
	United States	5,710	1,065	5,710	1,065
	Total	30,354	4,864	30,354	4,864
Tartaric acid crystals	Great Britain	31,645	6,691	31,645	6,691
	Aust.-Hungary	4,570	965	4,570	965
	France	17,938	3,736	17,938	3,736
	Germany	42,887	8,444	42,887	8,444
	United States	50,333	10,652	50,333	10,652
	Total	147,373	30,488	147,373	30,488

No. 1.—General Statement of Imports—*Continued.*

Articles Imported.	Countries.	Imported.		Entered for Home Consumption.	
		Quantity.	Value.	Quantity.	Value.
FREE GOODS—MANUFACTURED ARTICLES—*Con.*		Lbs.	$	Lbs.	$
Drugs, dyes, &c—*Con.* Terra japonica, gambier or cutch.....	Great Britain.....	120,329	5,538	120,329	5,538
	B. E. Indies	5,600	153	5,600	153
	United States.....	855,160	39,157	855,160	39,157
	Total........	981,089	44,848	981,089	44,848
Tin crystals..................	Great Britain.....	....	891	... ...	891
	United States.....	....	1,743	.. ..	1,743
	Total	....	2,634	....	2,634
Turmeric............................	Great Britain....	14,889	679	14,889	679
	United States.....	29,396	1,842	29,396	1,842
	Total........	44,285	2,521	44,285	2,521
Ultramarine blue, dry or in pulp.... ..	Great Britain.....	22,331	1,315	22,331	1,315
	Germany.........	106,104	6,584	106,104	6,584
	United States.....	250,261	14,286	250,261	14,286
	Total........	378,696	22,185	378,696	22,185
Verdigris, or sub-acetate of copper, dry.	Great Britain.....	112	17	112	17
	United States.....	750	125	750	125
	Total........	862	142	862	142
Zinc, salts of..........................	Great Britain. ...	33,133	774	33,133	774
	Belgium..........	3,052	31	3,052	31
	Germany.	11,051	108	11,051	108
	United States. ...	72,929	3,673	72,929	3,673
	Total	120,165	4,586	120,165	4,586
Drugs, crude, such as barks, flowers, roots, beans, berries, balsams, bulbs, fruits, insects, grains, gums and gum resins, herbs, leaves, nuts, fruit and stem seeds which are not edible and which are in a crude state and not advanced in value by refining or grinding or any other process of manufacture and not otherwise provided for.................. ...	Great Britain.....	....	6,724	... .	6,724
	British Africa.....	....	138	....	138
	Hong Kong.......	....	147	....	147
	Belgium..........	....	49	... .	49
	China	....	239	....	239
	France......	....	1,174	... .	1,174
	Germany..... ...	....	690	....	690
	Holland..........	....	272	....	272
	Italy.	....	24	....	24
	Japan	....	14	....	14
	United States.. ..	....	57,829	....	57,829
	Total........	....	67,300	....	67,300

No. 1.—General Statement of Imports—*Continued.*

Articles Imported.	Countries.	Exported.		Entered for Home Consumption.	
		Quantity.	Value.	Quantity.	Value.
FREE GOODS—MANUFACTURED ARTICLES—*Con.*			$		$
Duck for belting and hose, imported by manufacturers of such articles for use in the manufacture thereof in their own factories	Great Britain		168		168
	United States		118,169		118,169
	Total		118,337		118,337
Fashion plates, tailors', milliners' and mantle makers'	Great Britain		430		430
	France		174		174
	United States		3,549		3,549
	Total		4,153		4,153
Felt, adhesive, for sheathing vessels	Great Britain		318		318
	United States		89		89
	Total		407		407
Fertilizers uncompounded or unmanufactured, N.E.S.	Great Britain		469		469
	Newfoundland		84		84
	United States		6,323		6,323
	Total		6,876		6,876
Fillets of cotton and rubber, not exceeding 7 inches wide, imported by and for the use and manufacture of card clothing	Great Britain		86		86
Fisheries for the use of, viz.—					
Fish hooks for deep sea or lake fishing, not smaller in size than No. 2 0, not including hooks commonly used for sportsman's purposes	Great Britain		13,992		13.992
	Newfoundland		75		75
	Norway		981		981
	Sweden		83		83
	United States		2,151		2,151
	Total		17,282		17,282

No. 1.—GENERAL STATEMENT OF IMPORTS—*Continued.*

Articles Imported.	Countries.	Exported.		Entered for Home Consumption.	
		Quantity.	Value.	Quantity.	Value.
FREE GOODS—MANUFACTURED ARTICLES—*Con.*			$		$
Fisheries—*Con.* Bank, cod, pollock and mackerel fish lines; and mackerel, herring, salmon, seal, seine, mullet, net and trawl twine in hanks or coil, barked or not,—in variety of sizes and threads,—including gilling thread in balls, and head ropes, barked marine, and net morsels of cotton, hemp or flax, and deep sea fishing nets or seines, when used exclusively for the fisheries, and not including lines or nets commonly used for sportsman's purposes........	Great Britain.....	....	298,918	....	298,918
	Newfoundland....	....	2,547	....	2,547
	Aust.-Hungary....	....	1,260	....	1,260
	Germany.........	....	224	....	224
	Japan...........	....	6,527	....	6,527
	Norway	....	512	....	512
	United States.....	....	367,145	....	367,145
	Total.........	....	677,133	....	677,133
Glass cut to size for manufacture of dry plates for photographic purposes when imported by the manufacturers of such dry plates for use exclusively in the manufacture thereof in their own factories..................	Great Britain.....	....	3,344	....	3,344
	Belgium..........	....	2,710	....	2,710
	France...........	....	1,796	....	1,796
	Germany.........	....	949	....	949
	United States.....	....	77	....	77
	Total.........	....	8,876	....	8.876
Glove fasteners, metal, eyelet hooks and eyelets, and shoe lace wire fasteners....	Great Britain. ...	....	9,588	....	9,588
	Aust.-Hungary....	....	49	....	49
	France...........	....	3,348	....	3,348
	Germany........	....	3,130	....	3,130
	Switzerland.......	....	28	....	28
	United States.....	....	135,430	....	135,430
	Total.........	....	151,573	....	151,573
Globes, geographical, topographical and astronomical............................	Great Britain.....	....	166	....	166
	France...........	....	257	....	257
	United States.....	....	3,456	....	3,456
	Total.	....	3,879	....	3,879
Gold beaters' moulds and gold beaters' skins...........................	United States....	....	1,434	....	1,434
Gold and silver sweepings......	United States.....	....	974	....	974

No. 1.—General Statement of Imports—*Continued.*

Articles Imported.	Countries.	Imported.		Entered for Home Consumption.	
		Quantity.	Value.	Quantity.	Value.
FREE GOODS. MANUFACTURED ARTICLES—*Con.*		Lbs.	$	Lbs.	$
Gutta percha	United States	825	971	825	971
Hatters' bands (not cords), bindings, tips and sides, hat sweats and linings, both tips and sides, imported by hat and cap manufacturers, for use in the manufacture of these articles only in their own factories	Great Britain		84,340		84,727
	Aust.-Hungary		28		28
	France		5,803		5,803
	Germany		22,534		22,738
	Italy		34		34
	Japan		4,586		4,586
	Switzerland		1,736		1,869
	United States		55,193		55,464
	Total		174,254		175,249
Hatters' plush of silk or cotton	Great Britain		739		739
	France		944		944
	Germany		60		60
	United States		1,227		1,227
	Total		2,970		2,970
Hemp paper, made on four cylinder machines and calendered to between ·006 and ·008 inch thickness, for the manufacture of shot shells; primers for shot shells and cartridges, and felt board sized and hydraulic pressed and covered with paper or uncovered, for the manufacture of gunwads, imported by manufacturers of shot shells, cartridges and gun wads, to be used for these purposes only in their own factories	Germany		16,986		16,986
	United States		6,998		6,998
	Total		23,984		23,984
Ingot moulds	Great Britain		52,141		52,141
	United States		101,415		101,415
	Total		153,556		153,556
Iron sand or globules or iron shot and dry putty for polishing glass or granite		Lbs.		Lbs.	
	Great Britain	82,330	1,372	82,330	1,372
	United States	360,373	3,298	360,373	3,298
	Total	442,703	4,670	442,703	4,670
Ivories, piano key	Great Britain		25,162		25,162
	Newfoundland		1,675		1,675
	Germany		49,236		49,236
	United States		35,006		35,006
	Total		111,079		111,079

No. 1.—GENERAL STATEMENT OF IMPORTS—*Continued.*

Articles Imported.	Countries.	Imported. Quantity.	Imported. Value.	Entered for Home Consumption. Quantity.	Entered for Home Consumption. Value.
FREE GOODS. MANUFACTURED ARTICLES—*Con.*		Cwt.	$	Cwt.	$
Junk, old, and oakum	Great Britain	6,243	28,486	6,243	28,486
	B. W. Indies	41	187	41	187
	Newfoundland	170	209	170	209
	Germany	40	47	40	47
	St. Pierre	279	402	279	402
	United States	9,635	21,481	9,635	21,481
	Total	16,408	50,812	16,408	50,812
Jute cloth as taken from the loom, not coloured, cropped, mangled, pressed, calendered nor finished in any way		Yds.		Yds.	
	Great Britain	12,449,339	619,673	12,449,339	619,673
	B. E. Indies	5,650,264	197,141	5,650,264	197,141
	United States	597,238	27,036	597,238	27,036
	Total	18,696,841	843,850	18,696,841	843,850
Jute, flax or hemp yarn, plain, dyed or coloured, jute canvas, not pressed or calendered, imported by manufacturers of carpets, rugs and mats, jute webbing or jute cloth, hammocks, twines and floor oil cloth, for use in the manufacture of any of these articles only, in their own factories		Lbs.		Lbs.	
	Great Britain	2,906,274	258,807	2,906,274	258,807
	United States	407,003	32,085	407,003	32,085
	Total	3,313,277	290,892	3,313,277	290,892
Kelp, sea grass and sea weed, N.E.S.		Cwt.		Cwt.	
	China	2	19	2	19
	Germany	5	37	5	37
	Japan	88	389	88	389
	United States	320	376	320	376
	Total	415	821	415	821
Lampblack and ivery black		Lbs.		Lbs.	
	Great Britain	6,584	411	6,584	411
	B. W. Indies	4,650	653	4,650	653
	Germany	17,910	690	17,910	690
	Sweden	10,380	259	10,380	259
	United States	577,300	28,993	577,300	28,993
	Total	616,824	31,006	616,824	31,006
Lime juice, crude only		Galls.		Galls.	
	Great Britain	108	135	108	135
	B. W. Indies	26,587	4,889	26,587	4,889
	United States	1,920	886	1,920	886
	Total	28,615	5,910	28,615	5,910
Lastings, mohair cloth or other manufactures of cloth, imported by manufacturers of buttons for use in their own factories, and woven or made in patterns of such size, shape or form, or cut in such manner as to be fit for covering buttons exclusively	Great Britain	....	271	....	271
	Germany	....	2,871	....	2,871
	United States	....	2,184	....	2,184
	Total	....	5,326	....	5,326

No. 1.—General Statement of Imports—*Continued.*

Articles Imported.	Countries.	Imported.		Entered for Home Consumption.	
		Quantity.	Value.	Quantity.	Value.
FREE GOODS—MANUFACTURED ARTICLES—*Con.*			$		$
Manilla hoods	United States	....	74	....	74
Medals of gold, silver or copper, and other metallic articles, actually bestowed as trophies or prizes and received and accepted as honorary distinctions, and cups or other prizes won in *bona fide* competitions	Great Britain	....	1,012	....	1,012
	France	....	103	....	103
	Germany	....	29	....	29
	United States	....	1,022	....	1,022
	Total	....	2,166	....	2,166
Mexican saddle trees and stirrups of wood	Great Britain	....	559	....	559
	United States	....	8,879	....	8,879
	Total	....	9,438	....	9,438
Metals, viz.—					
Aluminium in ingots, blocks or bars, strips, sheets or plates		Lbs.		Lbs.	
	Germany	2,597	900	2,597	900
	United States	718,126	167,505	718,126	167,505
	Total	720,723	168,405	720,723	168,405
Anchors		Cwt.		Cwt.	
	Great Britain	2,987	9,701	2,987	9,701
	B. W. Indies	9	5	9	5
	Newfoundland	2	12	2	12
	United States	1,797	8,325	1,797	8,325
	Total	4,795	18,043	4,795	18,043
Bismuth, metallic, in its natural state		Lbs.		Lbs.	
	Great Britain	261	533	261	533
	United States	268	416	268	416
	Total	529	949	529	949
Brass cups, being rough blanks, for the manufacture of paper shells or cartridges, when imported by manufacturers of brass and paper shells and cartridges, for use in their own factories	Great Britain	....	38,089	....	38,089
	United States	....	27,030	....	27,030
	Total	....	65,119	....	65,119
Brass, old and scrap or in blocks		Cwt.		Cwt.	
	Great Britain	853	12,742	853	12,742
	B. W. Indies	115	906	115	906
	Newfoundland	35	264	35	264
	France	111	2,555	111	2,555
	Germany	80	884	80	884
	Holland	275	2,739	275	2,739
	United States	19,180	238,697	19,180	238,697
	Total	20,649	258,787	20,649	258,787

No. 1.—General Statement of Imports—*Continued.*

Articles Imported.	Countries.	Imported. Quantity.	Imported. Value.	Entered for Home Consumption. Quantity.	Entered for Home Consumption. Value.
FREE GOODS. MANUFACTURED ARTICLES—*Con.*		Cwt.	$	Cwt.	$
Metals—*Con.*					
Brass in bolts, bars and rods in coils or otherwise, in lengths not less than 6 feet, unmanufactured	Great Britain	127	2,313	127	2,313
	United States	10,462	181,548	10,462	181,548
	Total	10,589	183,861	10,589	183,861
Brass in strips, sheets or plates, not polished, planished or coated	Great Britain	437	7,254	437	7,254
	Germany	124	3,043	124	3,043
	United States	10,351	189,968	10,351	189,968
	Total	10,912	200,265	10,912	200,265
Brass, tubing, not bent or otherwise manufactured, in lengths not less than 6 feet		Lbs.		Lbs.	
	Great Britain	309,201	58,793	309,201	58,793
	Hong Kong	11,250	4,665	11,250	4,665
	Belgium	1,124	260	1,124	260
	United States	531,798	128,529	531,798	128,529
	Total	853,373	192,247	853,373	192,247
		Cwt.		Cwt.	
Britannia metal, in pigs, block or bars	United States	307	11,104	307	11,104
Copper, old and scrap or in blocks	B. W. Indies	82	607	82	607
	Newfoundland	92	854	92	854
	St. Pierre	39	400	39	400
	United States	4,239	61,904	4,239	61,904
	Total	4,452	63,765	4,452	63,765
Copper in pigs or ingots	Great Britain	149	2,130	149	2,130
	United States	21,676	375,959	21,676	375,959
	Total	21,825	378,089	21,825	378,089
Copper in bolts, bars and rods in coils or otherwise in lengths not less than 6 feet, unmanufactured	Great Britain	121	2,317	121	2,317
	United States	112,155	1,919,754	112,155	1,919,754
	Total	112,276	1,922,071	112,276	1,922,071
Copper, in strips, sheets or plates, not planished or coated, &c	Great Britain	574	11,479	574	11,479
	Belgium	43	753	43	753
	United States	24,855	507,576	24,855	507,576
	Total	25,472	519,808	25,472	519,808
Copper tubing in lengths not less than 6 feet, and not polished, bent or otherwise manufactured		Lbs.		Lbs.	
	Great Britain	57,442	13,642	57,442	13,642
	France	1,810	540	1,810	540
	United States	203,509	55,137	203,509	55,137
	Total	262,761	69,319	262,761	69,319

No. 1.—General Statement of Imports—*Continued.*

Articles Imported.	Countries.	Imported.		Entered for Home Consumption.	
		Quantity.	Value.	Quantity.	Value.
FREE GOODS. MANUFACTURED ARTICLES—*Con.*			$		$
Metals—*Con.*					
Copper rollers, for use in calico printing imported by calico printers for use in their own factories	Great Britain	....	311	....	311
	United States	....	6,386	....	6,386
	Total	....	6,697	....	6,697
Cream separators and steel bowls for	Great Britain	....	205,670	....	205,670
	Germany	....	8,915	....	8,915
	Sweden	....	3,852	....	3,852
	United States	....	407,073	....	407,073
	Total	....	625,510	....	625,510
Cream separators, articles for the construction or manufacture of—when imported by manufacturers of cream separators to be used in their own factories for the manufacture of cream separators, O.C., Feb. 12, 1902	Great Britain	....	2,553	....	2,553
	United States	....	93,025	....	93,025
	Total	....	95,578	....	95,578
Iron or steel, rolled round wire rods, in the coil, not over ⅜-inch in diameter, imported by wire manufacturers for use in making wire in the coil in their factories		Cwt.		Cwt.	
	Great Britain	66,036	85,899	66,036	85,899
	Belgium	4,770	5,184	4,770	5,184
	Germany	5,604	6,998	5,604	6,998
	Sweden	232	421	232	421
	United States	299,578	380,489	299,578	380,489
	Total	376,220	478,991	376,220	478,991
Iron or steel masts, or parts of	United States	18	367	18	367
Rolled iron tubes not welded, or joined, under 1½-inch in diameter, angle iron 9 and 10 gauge, not over 1½-inch wide, iron tubing lacquered or brass covered, not over 1¼-inch diameter, all of which are to be cut to lengths for the manufacture of bedsteads, and to be used for no other purpose, and brass trimmings, for bedsteads, imported for the manufacture of iron or brass bedsteads	Great Britain	....	58,154	....	58,154
	United States	....	154,186	....	154,186
	Total	....	212,340	....	212,340
Scrap iron and scrap steel, old, and fit only to be re-manufactured, being part of or recovered from any vessel wrecked in waters subject to the jurisdiction of Canada	Great Britain	2,500	1,220	2,500	1,220
Iron or steel beams, sheets, plates, angles, knees and cable chains for wooden, iron, steel or composite ships or vessels	Great Britain	35,708	64,898	35,708	64,898
	Newfoundland	22	55	22	55
	United States	175,023	250,711	175,023	250,711
	Total	210,753	315,664	210,753	315,664

No. 1.—General Statement of Imports—*Continued.*

Articles Imported.	Countries.	Imported. Quantity.	Imported. Value.	Entered for Home Consumption. Quantity.	Entered for Home Consumption. Value.
FREE GOODS—MANUFACTURED ARTICLES—*Con.*		Cwt.	$	Cwt.	$
Metals—*Con.*					
Locomotive and car wheel tires of steel in the rough	Great Britain	612	1,726	612	1,726
	Belgium	1,648	2,883	1,648	2,883
	Germany	64,507	124,725	64,507	124,725
	United States	13,598	32,580	13,598	32,580
	Total	80,365	161,914	80,365	161,914
Manufactured articles of iron or steel or brass which at the time of their importation are of a class or kind not manufactured in Canada, imported for use in the construction or equipment of ships or vessels	Great Britain	....	35,154	....	35,154
	United States	....	50,073	....	50,073
	Total	....	85,227	....	85,227
		Lbs.		Lbs.	
Lead, tea	Great Britain	973,827	41,344	973,827	41,344
	Spain	2,688	164	2,688	164
	United States	928,572	38,378	928,572	38,378
	Total	1,905,087	79,886	1,905,087	79,886
Machinery, viz.: Mining, smelting and reducing, coal-cutting machines except percussion coal cutters, coal heading machines, coal augers and rotary coal drills, core drills, miners' safety lamps, coal washing machinery, coke-making machinery, ore drying machinery, ore roasting machinery, electric or magnetic machines for separating or concentrating iron ores, blast furnace water jackets, converters for metallurgical processes in iron or copper briquette making machines, ball and rock emery grinding machines, copper plates, plated or not, machinery for extraction of precious metals, by the chlorination or cyanide processes, monitors, giants and elevators for hydraulic mining, amalgam safes, automatic ore samplers, automatic feeders, jigs, classifiers, separators, retorts, buddles, vanners, mercury pumps, pyrometers, bullion furnaces, amalgam cleaners, gold mining slime tables, blast-furnace blowing engines, wrought iron tubing, butt or lap-welded, threaded or coupled or not, not less than 2½ inches diameter, imported for use exclusively in mining, smelting, reducing or refining	Great Britain	....	36,302	....	36,385
	Belgium	....	1,268	....	1,268
	Germany	....	13,905	....	13,905
	United States	....	816,629	....	827,658
	Total	....	868,104	....	879,216
" And appliances of a kind not made in Canada, for use exclusively in alluvial gold mining	New Zealand	....	4,610	....	4,610
	United States	....	65,322	....	65,322
	Total	....	69,932	....	69,932

No. 1.—General Statement of Imports—*Continued.*

Articles Imported.	Countries.	Imported.		Entered for Home Consumption.	
		Quantity.	Value.	Quantity.	Value.
FREE GOODS. MANUFACTURED ARTICLES—*Con.*			$		$
Metals—*Con.*					
Machinery, viz.: Of a class or kind not made in Canada for the manufacture of linen	Great Britain		3,404		3,404
	Belgium		193		193
	United States		1,160		1,160
	Total		4,757		4,757
" Of a class or kind not made in Canada for the manufacture of brass goods such as are mentioned in tariff item 492, viz.: Brass in bolts, blocks, bars, rods, strips, sheets and plates and brass tubing	United States		4,983		4,983
" Well digging and apparatus of a class or kind not made in Canada, for drilling for water and oil, not to include motive power	Great Britain		877		877
	United States		101,006		101,006
	Total		101,883		101,883
" Charcoal making	United States		39,836		39,836
" And tools not manufactured in Canada necessary for any factory to be established in Canada for the manufacture of rifles for the Government of Canada	Great Britain		1,498		1,498
	United States		12,559		12,559
	Total		14,057		14,057
" All materials or parts in the rough and unfinished, and screws, nuts, bands and springs, to be used in rifles to be manufactured at any such factory for the Government of Canada	Great Britain		31,939		31,939
	United States		38,314		38,314
	Total		70.253		70,253
Machinery of every kind and structural iron and steel, when imported for use in the construction and equipment of factories for the manufacture of sugar from beet root	United States		7,043		7,043
Platinum wire and platinum in bars, strips, sheets or plates: platinum retorts, pans, condensers, tubing and pipe, imported by manufacturers of sulphuric acid for use in their works	Great Britain		1,348		1,348
	Germany		4		4
	United States		53,142		53,142
	Total		54,494		54,494

No. 1.—General Statement of Imports—*Continued.*

Articles Imported.	Countries.	Imported.		Entered for Home Consumption.	
		Quantity.	Value.	Quantity.	Value.
FREE GOODS—MANUFACTURED ARTICLES—*Con.*			$		$
Metals—*Con.*					
Ribs of brass, iron or steel, runners, rings, caps, notches, ferrules, mounts and sticks or canes in the rough, or not further manufactured than cut into lengths suitable for umbrella, parasol or sunshade or walking sticks, imported by manufacturers of umbrellas, parasols and sunshades for use in their factories in the manufacture of umbrellas, parasols, sunshades or walking sticks	Great Britain		44,488		44,488
	Aust.-Hungary		5,678		5,678
	France		104		104
	Germany		17,524		17,524
	Switzerland		136		136
	United States		75,851		75,851
	Total		143,781		143,781
Sewing machine attachments	Great Britain		3		3
	United States		48,138		48,138
	Total		48,141		48,141
Silver, German silver, and nickel silver, in ingots, blocks, bars, strips, sheets or plates, unmanufactured		Lbs.		Lbs.	
	Great Britain	3,350	801	3,350	801
	United States	203,903	53,244	203,903	53,244
	Total	207,253	54,045	207,253	54,045
Silver tubing, when imported by manufacturers of silverware to be used in their own factories in the manufacture of silverware, O.C., Feb. 12, 1902	United States		722		722
Steel for saws and straw cutters, cut to shape but not further manufactured		Cwt.		Cwt.	
	Great Britain	280	2,290	280	2,290
	France	6	51	6	51
	United States	11,525	129,058	11,525	129,058
	Total	11,811	131,399	11,811	131,399
Steel strip and flat steel wire imported by manufacturers of buckthorn and plain strip fencing, for use in their own factories in the manufacture thereof	United States	80	277	80	277
Steel wire, Bessemer soft drawn spring, of Nos. 10, 12 and 13 gauge, respectively, and homo steel spring wire of Nos. 11 and 12 gauge, respectively, imported by manufacturers of wire mattresses, to be used in their own factories in the manufacture of such articles	Great Britain	1,018	2,442	1,018	2,442
	United States	2,657	6,744	2,657	6,744
	Total	3,675	9,186	3,675	9,186

No. 1.—General Statement of Imports—*Continued.*

Articles Imported.	Countries.	Imported.		Entered for Home Consumption.	
		Quantity.	Value.	Quantity.	Value.
FREE GOODS. MANUFATURED ARTICLES—*Con.*		Cwt.	$	Cwt.	$
Metals—*Con.*					
Crucible sheet steel, 11 to 16 gauge, 2½ to 18 inches wide imported by manufacturers of mower and reaper knives for manufacture of such knives in their own factories	Great Britain	2,304	10,152	2,304	10,152
	United States	8,033	32,550	8,033	32,550
	Total	10,337	42,702	10,337	42,702
Steel of No. 20 gauge and thinner, but not thinner than No. 30 gauge, for the manufacture of corset steels, clock springs and shoe shanks, imported by the manufacturers of such articles for exclusive use in the manufacture thereof in their own factories	Great Britain	50	148	50	148
	United States	10	130	10	130
	Total	60	278	60	278
Flat steel wire, of No. 16 gauge or thinner, imported by the manufacturers of crinoline or corset wire and dress stays, for use in the manufacture of such articles in their own factories	Great Britain	650	2,025	650	2,025
	United States	3,235	20,426	3,235	20,426
	Total	3,885	22,451	3,885	22,451
Steel valued at 2½ cents per pound and upwards, imported by the manufacturers of skates, for use exclusively in the manufacture thereof in their own factories	Great Britain	1,947	8,170	1,947	8,170
	United States	1,645	7,837	1,645	7,837
	Total	3,592	16,007	3,592	16,007
Steel, under ½ inch in diameter, or under ½ inch square, imported by the manufacturers of cutlery, or of knobs, or of locks, for use exclusively in the manufacture of such articles in their own factories	Great Britain	920	2,249	920	2,249
	United States	2,175	5,452	2,175	5,452
	Total	3,095	7,701	3,095	7,701
Steel for the manufacture of cutlery when imported by manufacturers of cutlery to be used in their own factories in the manufacture of such articles, O.C., Feb. 13, 1902	United States	271	637	271	637
Steel of No 12 gauge and thinner, but not thinner than No. 30 gauge for the manufacture of buckle clasps, bed fasts, furniture casters and ice creepers, imported by the manufacturers of such articles, for use exclusively in the manufacture thereof in their own factories	Great Britain	201	523	201	523
	United States	1,898	4,856	1,898	4,856
	Total	2,099	5,379	2,099	5,379
Steel of No. 24 and 17 gauge, in sheets sixty-three inches long, and from 18 inches to 32 inches wide, imported by the manufacturers of tubular bow sockets for use in the manufacture of such articles in their own factories	United States	1,174	2,349	1,174	2,349

No. 1.—General Statement of Imports—*Continued.*

Articles Imported.	Countries.	Imported.		Entered for Home Consumption.	
		Quantity.	Value.	Quantity.	Value.
FREE GOODS—MANUFACTURED ARTICLES—*Con.*		Cwt.	$	Cwt.	$
Metals—*Con.*					
Steel for the manufacture of bicycle chain, imported by the manufacturers of bicycle chain for use in the manufacture thereof in their own factories..	United States.....	178	680	178	680
Steel for the manufacture of files, augers, auger bits, hammers, axes, hatchets, scythes, reaping hooks, hoes, hand-rakes, hay or straw knives, wind mills and agricultural or harvesting forks imported by the manufacturers of such or any of such articles for use exclusively in the manufacture thereof in their own factories....	Great Britain.....	16,183	38,686	16,183	38,686
	Belgium....	1,256	2,295	1,256	2,295
	United States	81,960	157,989	81,960	157,989
	Total..	99,399	198,970	99,399	198,970
Steel springs for the manufacture of surgical trusses imported by the manufacturers for use exclusively in the manufacture thereof in their own factories...............		Lbs.		Lbs.	
	United States.....	980	443	980	443
Flat spring steel, steel billets and steel axle bars, imported by manufacturers of carriage springs and carriage axles for use exclusively in the manufacture of springs and axles for carriages or vehicles other than railway or tramway, in their own factories...........		Cwt.		Cwt.	
	Great Britain... .	8,183	14,117	8,183	14,117
	United States.....	84,942	112,988	84,942	112,988
	Total........	93,125	127,105	93,125	127,105
Spiral spring steel for spiral springs for railways, imported by the manufacturers of railway springs for use exclusively in the manufacture of railway spiral springs in their own factories..	Great Britain.....	2,094	3,529	2,094	3,529
	United States.....	71,023	119,931	71,023	119,931
	Total........	73,117	123,460	73,117	123,460
Stereotypes, electrotypes and celluloids of newspaper columns in any language other than French and English, and of books, and bases and matrices and copper shells for the same, whether composed wholly or in part of metal or celluloid............		Sq. in.		Sq. in.	
	Great Britain.....	45,176	1,516	45,176	1,516
	United States.....	555,329	14,308	555,329	14,308
	Total	600,505	15,824	600,505	15,824
		Cwt.		Cwt.	
Spelter, zinc, in blocks and pigs... . ..	Great Britain.....	11,202	65,168	11,202	65,168
	Belgium.....	3,788	21,427	3.788	21,427
	Germany....... ..	3,914	22,417	3,914	22.417
	United States.....	31,233	181,674	31,233	181,674
	Total........	50,137	290,686	50,137	290,686

No. 1.—General Statement of Imports—*Continued.*

Articles Imported.	Countries.	Imported.		Entered for Home Consumption.	
		Quantity.	Value.	Quantity.	Value.
FREE GOODS—MANUFACTURED ARTICLES—*Con.*		Cwt.	$	Cwt.	$
Metals—*Con.*					
Tagging metal, plain, japanned or coated, in coils, not over 1½ in. wide, imported by manufacturers of shoe and corset laces for use in their factories..	Germany.........	2	31	2	31
	United States.....	37	618	37	618
	Total	39	649	39	649
Tin in blocks, pigs and bars............	Great Britain.....	10,815	371,471	10,815	371,471
	Australia.........	951	38,876	951	38,876
	B. E. Indies	4,401	161,365	4,401	161,365
	Germany.........	23	789	23	789
	Holland.........	11	308	11	308
	United States.....	17,216	598,760	17,216	598,760
	Total........	33,417	1,171,569	33,417	1,171,569
Tin plates and sheets................	Great Britain	350,397	1,134,492	350,397	1,134,492
	Belgium.........	45	1,341	45	1,341
	United States.....	254,740	733,167	254,740	733,167
	Total........	605,182	1,869,000	605,182	1,869,000
		Lbs.		Lbs.	
Tin-foil...........................	Great Britain.....	4,923	2,062	4,923	2,062
	France..........	107	54	107	54
	Germany.........	18,875	6,493	18,875	6,493
	United States. ...	537,718	56,698	537,718	56,698
	Total......	561,623	65,307	561,623	65,307
		Cwt.		Cwt.	
Barbed fencing wire of iron and steel...	Great Britain.....	2,696	5,771	2,696	5,771
	Belgium	2,239	4,745	2,239	4,745
	Germany........	244	546	244	546
	United States.....	441,033	918,598	441,033	918,598
	Total........	446,212	929,660	446,212	929,660
		Lbs.		Lbs.	
Wire, crucible cast steel.	Great Britain	2,162,489	85,220	2,162,489	85,220
	Germany.........	57,186	14,780	57,186	14,780
	United States.....	207,731	15,541	207,731	15,541
	Total........	2,427,406	115,541	2,427,406	115,541
Wire of brass, zinc, iron or steel, screwed or twisted, or flattened and corrugated, for use in connection with nailing machines for the manufacture of boots and shoes.........................	United States...	89,142	30,800	89,142	30,800
		Cwt.		Cwt.	
Galvanized iron or steel wire Nos. 9, 12, and 13 gauge.........................	Great Britain.....	7,432	16,370	7,432	16,370
	Belgium	1,327	2,410	1,327	2,410
	Germany.........	19,700	40,320	19,700	40,320
	United States.....	516,880	1,017,489	516,880	1,017,489
	Total........	545,339	1,076,589	545,339	1,076,589

No. 1.—GENERAL STATEMENT OF IMPORTS—*Continued.*

Articles Imported.	Countries.	Imported.		Entered for Home Consumption.	
		Quantity.	Value.	Quantity.	Value.
FREE GOODS—MANUFACTURED ARTICLES—*Con.*		Cwt.	$	Cwt.	$
Metals—*Con*					
Wire rigging for ships and vessels	Great Britain.....	3,873	16,769	3,913	16,984
	United States.. ..	386	2,286	386	2,286
	Total.......	4,259	19,055	4,299	19,270
Yellow metal, in bars, bolts and for sheathing.	Great Britain.....	1,800	26,628	1,800	26,628
	B. W. Indies.....	33	300	33	300
	Germany.........	227	2,762	227	2,762
	United States.. ..	18	305	18	305
	Total	2,078	29,995	2,078	29,995
Zinc in blocks, pigs, sheets and plates..	Great Britain. ...	8,420	56,385	8,420	56,385
	Belgium..........	7,222	45,839	7,222	45,839
	France...........	33	218	33	218
	Germany.........	2,928	18,225	2,928	18,225
	St. Pierre.........	60	200	60	200
	United States.....	5,799	37,571	5,799	37,571
	Total........	24,462	158,438	24,462	158,438
		Lbs.		Lbs.	
Zinc, seamless drawn tubing.....	United States....	71	12	71	12
		Galls.		Galls.	
Molasses, the produce of any British country entitled to the benefits of the British Preferential Tariff, when produced from sugar cane and imported direct by vessel from the country of production in the original package in which it was placed at the point of production and not afterwards subjected to any process of treating or mixing, but not for distillation........................	B. W. Indies.....	4,136,408	778,360	4,137,291	778,564
	B. Guiana.......	6,899	1,172	6,899	1,172
	Total........	4,143,307	779,532	4,144,190	779,736
		Lbs.		Lbs.	
Syrup or molasses of cane or beet testing under 35 degrees by the Polar scope, for use in the manufacture of compressed food for live stock, when imported by the manufactures of such food, to be used for such manufacture only in their factories, O.C. Aug. 19, 1899..........	United States.....	533,646	5,881	533,646	5,881
Newspapers, and quarterly, monthly and semi-monthly magazines, and weekly literary papers, unbound.....	Great Britain...	....	53,036	....	53,036
	France.....	....	1,279	....	1,279
	Japan...........	. .. .	30	....	30
	United States....	....	260,018	....	260,018
	Total........	....	314,363	....	314,363

No. 1.—General Statement of Imports—*Continued.*

Articles Imported.	Countries.	Imported.		Entered for Home Consumption.	
		Quantity.	Value.	Quantity.	Value.
FREE GOODS—MANUFACTURED ARTICLES—*Con.*			$		$
Noils, being the short wool which falls from the combs in worsted factories; and worsted tops, N.E.S.	Great Britain	....	201,072	....	201,072
	Belgium	....	7,612	....	7,612
	France	....	21,391	....	21,391
	Germany	....	2,777	....	2,777
	United States	....	58,275	....	58,275
	Total	....	291,127	....	291,127
Oil cake and oil cake meal, cotton seed cake and meal, palm nut cake and meal.		Cwt.		Cwt.	
	Great Britain	111	218	111	218
	United States	20,500	26,566	20,500	26,566
	Total	20,611	26,784	20,611	26,784
Oils, viz.—		Galls.		Galls.	
Carbolic or heavy oil	Great Britain	56,020	5,512	56,020	5,512
	Germany	2,000	545	2,000	545
	United States	29,177	4,365	29,177	4,365
	Total	87,197	10,422	87,197	10,422
Cotton seed imported by manufacturers of liquid annatto, O.C., January 15, 1898	Great Britain	440	156	440	156
	United States	7,349	2,418	7,349	2,418
	Total	7,789	2,574	7,789	2,574
Cocoa nut and palm in their natural state	Great Britain	153,395	86,870	153,395	86,870
	Australia	19,785	11,555	19,785	11,555
	B. E. Indies	16,142	8,779	16,142	8,779
	United States	70,007	47,979	70,007	47,979
	Total	259,329	155,183	259,329	155,183
Cotton seed for canning fish, O.C., June 4, 1902	United States	6,071	1,972	6,071	1,972
Palm bleached, for use as material in Canadian manufactures	United States	160	101	160	101
Olive, for manufacturing soap or tobacco or for canning fish	Great Britain	1,299	733	1,299	733
	Germany	125	79	125	79
	Italy	40	58	40	58
	United States	25,011	12,349	25,011	12,349
	Total	26,475	13,219	26,475	13,219
Petroleum crude, fuel and gas oils (·8233 specific gravity)	United States	19,805,656	667,172	19,805,656	667,172
Rosin oil	Great Britain	....	4,344	....	4,344
	United States	....	30,437	....	30,437
	Total	....	34,781	....	34,781

No. 1.—General Statement of Imports—*Continued.*

Articles Imported.	Countries.	Imported.		Entered for Home Consumption.	
		Quantity.	Value.	Quantity.	Value.
FREE GOODS—MANUFACTURED ARTICLES—*Con.*			$		$
Paper tubes and cones, when imported by manufacturers of cotton yarns or fabrics, to be used in winding yarns thereon, O.C., March 9, 1904	Great Britain		63		63
	United States		5,467		5,467
	Total		5,530		5,530
Paper, photographic, plain basic, baryta coated, for albumenizing or sensitizing, when imported by manufacturers of sensitized paper	Great Britain		264		264
	Belgium		682		682
Philosophical and scientific apparatus, utensils, instruments and preparations, including boxes and bottles containing the same, of a class or kind not manufactured in Canada, when specially imported in good faith for use and by order of any society or institution incorporated or established solely for religious, philosophical, educational, scientific or literary purposes, or for the encouragement of the fine arts, or for the use or by order of any college, academy, school or seminary of learning in Canada, and not for sale	France		621		621
	Germany		7,496		7,496
	United States		13,341		13,341
	Total		22,404		22,404
	Great Britain		13,185		13,185
	France		1,749		1,749
	Germany		15,056		15,056
	Holland		145		145
	United States		36,523		36,523
	Total		66,658		66,658
Photographs, not exceeding three, sent by friends and not for purpose of sale	Great Britain		5		5
	United States		194		194
Piano and organ parts:—Key pins, damper springs, jack springs, regulating spoons, bridle wires, damper wires, back check wires, dowel wires, German centre pins, rail hooks, brass brackets, plates, damper rod nuts, damper sockets and screws, shell, brass sapstan screws, brass flange plates and screws, hammer wires, felt, butt felt, damper felt, hammer rail cloth, back check felt, catch felt, thin damper felt, whip cloth, bushing cloth, hammer felt, back hammer felt, bridle leather and buckskin, when imported by manufacturers of piano-keys, actions, hammers, base dampers and organ keys, to be used exclusively for the manufacture of such articles in their own factories, O.C., June 6, 1901	Total		199		199
	Great Britain		6,900		6,900
	Aust.-Hungary		76		76
	Germany		28,325		28,325
	United States		33,102		33,102
	Total		68,403		68,403
Pictorial illustrations of insects, &c., when imported for the use of colleges and schools, scientific and literary societies	France		23		23

No. 1.—General Statement of Imports—*Continued.*

Articles Imported.	Countries.	Imported.		Entered for Home Consumption.	
		Quantity.	Value.	Quantity.	Value.
FREE GOODS—MANUFACTURED ARTICLES—*Con.*		Galls.	$	Galls.	$
Pitch and tar (pine) in packages of not less than 15 gallons	Great Britain	34,286	1,745	34,286	1,745
	United States	103,570	12,287	103,570	12,287
	Total	137,856	14,032	137,856	14,032
Plaits, plain, chip, manilla, cotton, mohair, straw, tuscan and grass	Great Britain	....	35,791	....	35,791
	Aust.-Hungary	....	49	....	49
	Belgium	....	565	....	565
	France	....	11,018	....	11,018
	Germany	....	5,315	....	5,315
	Holland	....	48	....	48
	Italy	....	7,667	....	7,667
	Japan	....	4,335	....	4,335
	Switzerland	....	14,290	....	14,290
	United States	....	81,578	....	81,578
	Total	....	160,656	....	160,656
Printing presses (rotary) of a class or kind not made in Canada		No.		No.	
	United States	97	398,187	97	398,187
Prunella	Great Britain	....	1,333	....	1,333
Rags of cotton, linen, jute, hemp and woollen; paper waste clippings, and waste of any kind, except mineral		Cwt.		Cwt.	
	Great Britain	61,835	93,711	61,835	93,711
	Hong Kong	1	3	1	3
	Newfoundland	112	537	112	537
	Belgium	2,842	2,893	2,842	2,893
	France	3,260	5,136	3,260	5.136
	Germany	19,438	34,357	19,438	34,357
	United States	1,610,313	225,085	1,610,313	225,085
	Total	1,697,801	361,722	1,697,801	361,722
Resin or rosin in packages of not less than 100 lbs.	Great Britain	1,048	2,616	1,048	2,616
	Germany	6	67	6	67
	United States	187,698	346,432	187,698	346,432
	Total	188,752	349,115	188,752	349,115
Rubber, crude caoutchouc or India rubber unmanufactured		Lbs.		Lbs.	
	Great Britain	4,191	1,775	4,191	1,775
	B. E. Indies	1,000	1,426	1,000	1,426
	France	250	280	250	280
	United States	2,485,315	2,391,347	2,485,315	2,391,347
	Total	2,490,756	2,394,828	2,490,756	2,394,828
Rubber, recovered, and rubber substitute and hard rubber in sheets	Great Britain	1,046	90	1,046	90
	B. W. Indies	1,900	57	1,900	57
	Newfoundland	1,196	54	1,196	54
	Germany	2,605	1,893	2,605	1,893
	St. Pierre	900	40	900	40
	United States	3,061,541	355,246	3,061,541	355,246
	Total	3,069,188	357,380	3,069,188	357,380

No. 1.—General Statement of Imports—*Continued.*

Articles Imported.	Countries.	Imported. Quantity.	Imported. Value.	Entered for Home Consumption. Quantity.	Entered for Home Consumption. Value.
FREE GOODS—MANUFACTURED ARTICLES—*Con.*		Lbs.	$	Lbs.	$
Rubber, powdered, and rubber waste	United States	330,272	22,543	330,272	22,543
Rubber thread, elastic	United States	1,255	2,171	1,255	2,171
Soap, whale oil	Great Britain	19,554	441	19,554	441
	United States	6,357	247	6,357	247
	Total	25,911	688	25,911	688
Spurs and stilts used in the manufacture of earthenware	United States	....	880	....	880
Square or round reeds and raw hide centres, textile leather or rubber heads, thumbs and tips, and steel, iron or nickel caps for whip ends, imported by whip manufacturers for use in the manufacture of whips in their own factories	Great Britain	....	106	....	106
	United States	....	23,956	....	23,956
	Total	....	24,062	....	24,062
Surgical and dental instruments and surgical needles	Great Britain	....	19,395	....	19,395
	Aust.-Hungary	....	74	....	74
	China	....	1	....	1
	France	....	3,986	....	3,986
	Germany	....	13,003	....	13,003
	United States	....	161,599	....	161,382
	Total	....	198,058	....	197,841
Teasels	Great Britain	....	423	....	423
	United States	....	304	....	304
	Total	....	727	....	727
		Lbs.		Lbs.	
Turpentine, raw or crude	United States	53,474	3,688	53,474	3,688
Vaccine points, articles for the manufacture, viz.: Glass caps, shells, containers and capillary tubes: rubber bulbs, boxes or corks; only when imported by manufacturers of vaccine points. (O.C., 13th July, 1901)	United States	....	10	....	10
		Galls.		Galls.	
Varnish, black and bright, for ships use	Great Britain	50	93	50	93
	United States	898	475	898	475
	Total	948	568	948	568

No. 1.—General Statement of Imports—*Continued.*

Articles Imported.	Countries.	Imported.		Entered for Home Consumption.	
		Quantity.	Value.	Quantity.	Value.
FREE GOODS—MANUFACTURED ARTICLES—*Con.*		Lbs.	$	Lbs.	$
Yarn, Botany yarn single, in numbers 30 and finer, on mule cops, dry spun on what is known as the French and Belgian system, not doubled or twisted, in white only, when imported by manufacturers of cashmere socks and stockings, to be used exclusively for the manufacture of such articles in their own factories, O.C., June 6, 1901	Great Britain	150,121	91,810	150,121	91,810
Yarn, cotton, No. 40 and finer	Great Britain	981,937	304,979	981,937	304,979
	France	1,711	5,345	1,711	5,345
	Germany	1,919	771	1,919	771
	United States	182,756	70,922	182,756	70,922
	Total	1,168,323	382,017	1,168,323	382,017
Yarn, cotton, polished or glazed, when imported by manufacturers of shoe laces, for the manufacture of such goods in their own factories, O.C., March 1, 1899	Germany	23,737	4,637	23,737	4,637
	United States	575	1,499	575	1,499
	Total	24,312	6,136	24,312	6,136
Yarn, of jute, flax or hemp for the manufacture of towels, when imported by the manufacturers of jute linen or union towels to be used in their own factories in the manufacture of such articles, O.C., April 14, 1902	Great Britain	93,253	14,170	93,253	14,170
	United States	3,000	258	3,000	258
	Total	96,253	14,428	96,253	14,428
Yarn, mohair	Great Britain	1,369	1,243	1,369	1,243
	United States	221	157	221	157
	Total	1,590	1,400	1,590	1,400
Yarn, spun from the hair of the alpaca or of the angora goat, imported by manufacturers of braid for use exclusively in their factories in the manufacture of such braids only	Great Britain	102	63	102	63
	France	90	386	90	386
	Total	192	449	192	449
Yarn, wool or worsted, genapped, dyed or finished, imported by manufacturers of braids, cords, tassels and fringes	Great Britain	48,340	21,323	48,340	21,323
	France	10	10	10	10
	United States	4,766	3,709	4,766	3,709
	Total	53,116	25,042	53,116	25,042
MISCELLANEOUS ARTICLES.					
Anatomical preparations and skeletons or parts thereof	France	....	438	....	438
	Germany	....	102	....	102
	United States	....	1,584	....	1,584
	Total	....	2,124	....	2,124

No. 1.—General Statement of Imports—*Continued.*

Articles Imported.	Countries.	Imported.		Entered for Home Consumption.	
		Quantity.	Value.	Quantity.	Value.
FREE GOODS—MISCELLANEOUS ARTICLES—*Con.*			$		$
Apparel, wearing, and other personal and household effects, not merchandise, of British subjects dying abroad, but domiciled in Canada; books, pictures, family plate or furniture, personal effects and heirlooms left by bequest	Great Britain		3,038		3,038
	B. W. Indies		100		100
	Japan		200		200
	United States		816		816
	Total		4,154		4,154
Articles the growth, produce or manufacture of Canada, returned after having been exported	Great Britain		103,900		103,900
	Australia		262		262
	B. E. Indies		105		105
	B. W. Indies		1,363		1,363
	Newfoundland		2,631		2,631
	Belgium		543		543
	Cuba		370		370
	France		2,873		2,873
	Germany		2,017		2,017
	Holland		1,044		1,044
	St. Pierre		55		55
	United States		669,291		669,291
	Total		784,454		784,454
Articles for the use of the Governor General	Great Britain		7,442		7,645
	B. Africa		120		120
	France		74		323
	Germany		15		15
	Japan		75		75
	United States		4,699		4,699
	Total		12,425		12,877
Articles for the personal or official use of Consuls General who are natives or citizens of the country they represent, and who are not engaged in any other business or profession	Great Britain		105		105
	Aust.-Hungary		89		89
	Belgium		22		22
	Cuba		289		289
	Egypt				37
	France		156		659
	Germany		99		99
	Japan		413		413
	Norway		27		27
	Russia		5		5
	Sweden		15		15
	Spain				7
	United States		1,540		1,540
	Total		2,760		3,307

No. 1.—GENERAL STATEMENT OF IMPORTS—*Continued.*

ARTICLES IMPORTED.	COUNTRIES.	IMPORTED.		ENTERED FOR HOME CONSUMPTION.	
		Quantity.	Value.	Quantity.	Value.
FREE GOODS—MISCELLANEOUS ARTICLES—*Con.*			$		$
Articles imported by, or for the use of, the Dominion Government, or any of the Departments thereof, or by and for the Senate and House of Commons, &c.	Great Britain		794,407		794,707
	Hong Kong		81		81
	Newfoundland		450		450
	Belgium		3,681		3,681
	France		128,304		128,304
	Germany		75,390		75,390
	Greece		4		4
	Spain		7		7
	Sweden		611		611
	Switzerland		22		22
	United States		828,515		829,551
	Total		1,831,472		1,832,808
Articles for the use of the Army and Navy, viz.:— Arms, military or naval clothing, musical instruments for bands, military stores, and munitions of war; also articles consigned direct to officers and men on board vessels of His Majesty's navy, for their own personal use	Great Britain		5,782		5,782
	B. E. Indies		10		10
	Newfoundland		300		300
	B. Poss., other		163		163
	United States		1,550		1,689
	Total		7,805		7,944
Articles ex-warehoused for ships' stores.	Great Britain				27,545
	Australia				699
	B. Guiana				6
	B. W. Indies				268
	Newfoundland				25
	New Zealand				943
	Cuba				690
	Egypt				139
	France				3,778
	Germany				394
	Greece				45
	Holland				311
	Japan				671
	Philippines				88
	Porto Rico				99
	Portugal				20
	St. Pierre				5
	Spain				903
	United States				361,423
	Total				398,052
Articles ex-warehoused for excise purposes to be manufactured in bond, not elsewhere specified	United States				3,007
Articles for the Anglo-American Telegraph Co.	Great Britain		8		8
	United States		35		35
	Total		43		43

No. 1.—GENERAL STATEMENT OF IMPORTS—*Continued.*

Articles Imported.	Countries.	Imported. Quantity.	Imported. Value.	Entered for Home Consumption. Quantity.	Entered for Home Consumption. Value.
FREE GOODS—MISCELLANEOUS ARTICLES—*Con.*			$		$
Bacteriological products or serums for subcutaneous injections	Great Britain		3,213		3,213
	France		4,117		4,117
	Japan		5		5
	United States		37,965		37,965
	Total		45,300		45,300
Barrels or packages of Canadian manufacture which have been exported filled with Canadian products, when returned, or exported empty and returned filled with foreign products	Great Britain		360		360
	B. W. Indies		22		22
	Newfoundland		130		130
	Belgium		110		110
	Germany		29		29
	Holland		23		23
	St. Pierre		12		12
	United States		28,546		28,546
	Total		29,232		29,232
Bird skins and skins of animals not native to Canada, for taxidermic purposes, not further manufactured than prepared for preservation	Great Britain		560		560
	United States		100		100
	Total		660		660
Botanical specimens	Great Britain		10		10
	United States		11		11
	Total		21		21
Cabinets of coins, collections of medals, and of other antiquities, including collections of postage stamps	Great Britain		12,452		12,452
	Australia		15		15
	Aust.-Hungary		366		366
	Belgium		890		890
	Egypt		1,000		1,000
	France		455		455
	Germany		150		150
	Holland		971		971
	Italy		10		10
	United States		4,392		4,392
	Total		20,701		20,701
Casts as models for the use of schools of design	United States		43		43
Clothing, and books, donations of, for charitable purposes	Great Britain		3,682		3,682
	B. E. Indies		15		15
	Newfoundland		3		3
	France		35		35
	Italy		50		50
	St. Pierre		4		4
	United States		6,265		6,265
	Total		10,054		10,054

No. 1.—General Statement of Imports—*Continued.*

Articles Imported.	Countries.	Imported. Quantity.	Imported. Value.	Entered for Home Consumption. Quantity.	Entered for Home Consumption. Value.
FREE GOODS—MISCELLANEOUS ARTICLES—*Con.*		Lbs.	$	Lbs.	$
Coffee, green, imported direct from the country of growth and production or purchased in bond in the United Kingdom	Great Britain	954,548	124,544	954,548	124,544
	B. E. Indies	44,400	5,117	44,400	5,117
	B. W. Indies	192,184	16,808	192,184	16,808
	B. Poss. other	1,680	237	1,680	237
	Arabia	115,850	15,663	115,850	15,663
	Brazil	3,763,459	311,464	3,763,459	311,464
	Cent. Am. States	774,081	99,850	774,081	99,850
	Cuba	50	5	50	5
	Dutch E. Indies	10,000	1,611	10,000	1,611
	Hawaii	119,834	13,593	119,834	13,593
	Holland	616	165	616	165
	Mexico	236,327	30,413	236,327	30,413
	Porto Rico	3,475	437	3,475	437
	Venezuela	679,663	71,864	679,663	71,864
	Turkey	8,400	1,368	8,400	1,368
	Total	6,904,567	693,139	6,904,567	693,139
Entomological specimens	Great Britain		62		62
	United States		184		184
	Total		246		246
Ice	United States		5,049		5,049
Models of inventions and of other improvements in the arts, but no article shall be deemed a model which can be fitted for use	Great Britain		162		162
	Australia		49		49
	Belgium		237		237
	United States		16,953		16,953
	Total		17,401		17,401
Paintings in oil, or water colours by artists of well-known merit, or copies of the old masters by such artists	Great Britain		406,565		406,565
	Newfoundland		50		50
	Aust.-Hungary		267		267
	Belgium		660		660
	Denmark		300		300
	France		3,204		3,204
	Germany		4,176		4,176
	Holland		117,656		117,656
	Italy		4,832		4,832
	Switzerland		79		79
	United States		289,936		289,936
	Total		827,725		827,725
Paintings in oil or water colours, the production of Canadian artists	Great Britain		20		20
	France		250		250
	Italy		100		100
	United States		343		343
	Total		713		713

No. 1.—General Statement of Imports—*Continued.*

Articles Imported.	Countries.	Imported. Quantity.	Imported. Value.	Entered for Home Consumption. Quantity.	Entered for Home Consumption. Value.
			$		$
FREE GOODS—MISCELLANEOUS ARTICLES—*Con.*					
Passover bread, O.C.	United States	....	15,044	....	15,044
Settlers' effects	Great Britain	....	1,949,485	....	1,949,485
	Australia	....	4,795	....	4,795
	B. Africa	....	435	....	435
	B. E. Indies	....	572	....	572
	B. Guiana	....	20	....	20
	B. W. Indies	....	2,665	....	2,665
	Hong Kong	....	6,355	....	6,355
	Newfoundland	....	6,427	....	6,427
	New Zealand	....	715	....	715
	Aust.-Hungary	....	540	....	540
	Belgium	....	75,986	....	75,986
	China	....	2,480	....	2,480
	Denmark	....	25	....	25
	Egypt	....	50	....	50
	France	....	14,006	....	14,006
	Fr. W. Indies	....	20	....	20
	Germany	....	11,421	....	11,421
	Hawaii	....	130	....	130
	Holland	....	470	....	470
	Japan	....	750	....	750
	Norway	....	10	....	10
	Roumania	....	1,215	....	1,215
	Russia	....	5,080	....	5,080
	St. Pierre	....	982	....	982
	Spain	....	220	....	220
	Switzerland	....	40	....	40
	United States	....	7,169,617	....	7,169,617
	Total	....	9,254,511	....	9,254,511
Specimens, models and wall diagrams for illustration of natural history for universities and public museums	Great Britain	....	278	....	278
	France	....	129	....	129
	Germany	....	325	....	325
	United States	....	602	....	602
	Total	....	1,334	....	1,334
		Lbs.		Lbs.	
Tea of India, black, imported direct, or purchased in bond in United Kingdom.	Great Britain	2,317,012	349,245	2,317,012	349,245
	B. E. Indies	6,063,380	784,120	6,063,380	784,120
	Total	8,380,392	1,133,365	8,380,392	1,133,365
Tea of India, green, imported direct, or purchased in bond in United Kingdom.	Great Britain	75,028	9,902	75,028	9,902
	B. E. Indies	423,292	52,561	423,292	52,561
	Total	498,320	62,463	498,320	62,463
Tea of Ceylon, black, imported direct, or purchased in bond in United Kingdom.	Great Britain	3,341,236	560,015	3,341,236	560,015
	B. E. Indies	6,700,282	931,770	6,700,282	931,770
	Total	10,041,518	1,491,785	10,041,518	1,491,785
Tea of Ceylon, green, imported direct, or purchased in bond in United Kingdom.	Great Britain	338,467	47,887	338,467	47,887
	B. E. Indies	1,141,856	153,424	1,141,856	153,424
	Total	1,480,323	201,311	1,480,323	201,311

No. 1.—GENERAL STATEMENT OF IMPORTS—*Continued.*

Articles Imported.	Countries.	Imported.		Entered for Home Consumption.	
		Quantity.	Value.	Quantity.	Value.
FREE GOODS—MISCELLANEOUS ARTICLES—*Con.*		Lbs.	$	Lbs.	$
Tea of China, black, imported direct, or purchased in bond in United Kingdom.	Great Britain	155,255	23,629	155,255	23,629
	Hong Kong	18,343	2,571	18,343	2,571
	China	572,236	80,405	572,236	80,405
	Total	745,834	106,605	745,834	106,605
Tea of China, green, imported direct, or purchased in bond in United Kingdom.	Great Britain	59,241	8,101	59,241	8,101
	Hong Kong	1,140	179	1,140	179
	China	420,687	62,646	420,687	62,646
	Total	481,068	70,926	481,068	70,926
Tea of Japan, green, imported direct, or purchased in bond in United Kingdom.	Great Britain	64,711	9,736	64,711	9,736
	Japan	3,768,310	562,317	3,768,310	562,317
	Total	3,833,021	572,053	3,833,021	572,053
Vaccine and ivory vaccine points	United States	....	5,018	....	5,018
Coins, gold and silver, except U. S. silver coin	Great Britain	....	10,673	....	10,673
	B. W. Indies	....	3,521	....	3,521
	Hong Kong	....	399	....	399
	United States	....	6,256,413	....	6,256,413
	Total	....	6,271,006	....	6,271,006
Gold bullion, in bars, blocks, ingots, drops, sheets or plates, unmanufactured	China	....	25	....	25
	France	....	290	....	290
	United States	....	349,206	....	349,206
	Total	....	349,521	....	349,521
Silver bullion, in bars, blocks, ingots, drops, sheets or plates, unmanufactured.	United States	....	458,076	....	458,076
Menageries	United States	....	51,036	....	....
Paintings for exhibition	United States	....	114,200	....	....
Other articles	Great Britain	....	766	....	766
	France	....	400	....	400
	Germany	....	470	....	470
	United States	....	17,371	....	17,371
	Total	....	19,007	....	19,007
	Total free goods	....	117,495,683	....	117,314,698

No. 1.—General Statement of Imports—*Concluded.*

RECAPITULATION, 1905-6.

Totals.	Provinces.	Imported.	Entered for Home Consumption.							
			General Tariff.		Preferential Tariff.		Surtax Tariff.		Total.	
		Value.	Value.	Duty.	Value.	Duty.	Value.	Duty.	Value.	Duty.
		$	$	$ cts.	$	$ cts.	$	$ cts.	$	$ cts.
Total Dutiable Goods........	Ontario....	76,563,813	54,848,093	14,651,501 35	16,802,108	3,533,227 83	2,499,025	981,913 12	74,149,226	19,[illegible]642 30
	Quebec........	57,971,616	28,719,170	9,382,368 98	25,036,655	5,111,121 37	2,838,973	980,578 47	56,594,798	15,[illegible]68 82
	Nova Scotia ...	7,878,257	3,320,659	1,251,898 70	4,600,273	947,550 93	115,697	46,506 89	8,036,629	2,245,956 52
	New Brunswick.	4,403,141	2,785,764	1,091,921 41	1,498,582	309,683 98	151,066	56,410 73	4,435,412	1,458,016 12
	Manitoba.......	14,145,065	11,154,862	3,158,203 51	2,841,196	600,327 67	210,685	91,348 50	14,206,743	3,849,879 68
	B. Columbia....	11,632,172	8,253,893	2,702,100 14	3,074,395	589,830 39	105,660	44,875 13	11,433,948	3,336,805 66
	P. E. Island....	268,616	166,980	76,125 57	99,717	20,060 81	5,448	2,464 87	272,145	98,651 25
	N.W. Territories	2,880,283	2,678,549	701,731 04	206,772	46,014 27	14,663	5,933 71	2,899,984	753,679 02
	Yukon	1,028,970	992,600	282,010 72	4,404	1,035 89	1,821	675 05	998,825	283,721 66
Prepaid British postal packages.................. ..	....	18,399	18,399	3,680 15	....	....	....	....	18,399	3,680 15
		176,790,332	112,938,969	33,301,541 57	54,164,102	11,158,853 14	5,943,038	2,210,706 47	173,046,109	46,671,101 18
Free Goods....	Ontario.........	52,090,454	....	....	....	....	. .....	....	51,915,291	.. . .
	Quebec.........	41,900,615	....	..	....	....	....	....	41,797,414	....
	Nova Scotia	6,225,799	....	....	....	....	....	....	6,275,735	....
	New Brunswick.	4,445,523	....	....	....	....	....	....	4,450,997	....
	Manitoba.......	4,932,442	....	....	....	....	....	....	4,910,483	....
	B. Columbia ...	4,086,407	....	....	....	....	....	....	4,150,472	....
	P. E. Island....	266,640	....	....	....	....	....	....	266,672	....
	N.W. Territories	3,265,153	....	....	....	....	....	....	3,263,853	....
	Yukon..... ..	282,650	....	....	....	....	....	....	283,781	....
		117,495,683	....	....	....	....	....	....	117,314,698	. ...

Grand Totals....	Ontario...	128,654,267	54, [illegible]	14,651,501 35	16, [illegible]	3,533,227 83	2,499,025	981,913 12	126,064,517	....
	Quebec.........	99,872,231	28,719,170	9,382,368 98	25,036,655	5,111,121 37	2,838,973	980,578 47	98,392,212	....
	Nova Scotia	14,104,056	3,320,659	1,251,898 70	4, [illegible]273	947,550 93	5[illegible]	46,506 89	14,312,364	....
	N[illegible]w Brunswick.	8,848,664	2,785,764	i, [illegible]921 41	1,498,582	309,683 98	151,066	56,410 73	8,886,409	....
	Manitoba.......	19,077,507	11,154,862	3,158,203 51	2,841,196	600,327 67	210,685	91,348 50	19,117,226	....
	B. [illegible]a....	15,718,579	8,253,893	2,702,100 14	3, [illegible]95	539,830 39	105,660	44,875 13	15,584,420	....
	P. E. Island....	535,256	[illegible]	76,125 57	99,717	20,060 81	5,448	2,464 87	538,817	....
	N.W. Territories	[illegible]36	2,673,549	[illegible]31 04	206,772	46,014 27	14,663	5,933 71	6,163,837	....
Prepaid British postal packages...	Yukon..........	1, [illegible]20	[illegible]	282,010 72	1,404	1,035 89	1,821	675 05	1,282,606	....
	....	18,399	18,399	3,680 15	....	....	....	....	18,399	....
		294,286,015	112,938,969	33,301,541 57	54,164,102	11,158,853 14	5,943,038	2,210,706 47	290,360,807	46,671,101 18

No. 2.—Abstract by Countries,

Countries.	Imports.			General Tariff.		
	Dutiable.	Free.	Total.			
	Value.	Value.	Value.	Value.	Duty.	
	$	$	$	$	$	cts.
Great Britain	52,767,022	16,550,128	69,317,150	6,054,931	3,254,684	36
Australia	31,100	195,097	226,197	28,383	9,104	08
British Africa	282,998	14,661	297,659	17,827	1,964	93
" East Indies	912,150	2,508,304	3,420,454	15,550	4,491	36
" West Indies	4,351,727	1,102,267	5,453,994	44,400	61,832	96
" Guiana	2,065,870	1,496	2,067,366	15,148	131,726	08
Fiji Islands	454,380	72	454,452	47	6	32
Gibraltar	51	....	51	51	21	64
Hong Kong	149,242	18,304	167,546	150,172	98,166	63
Newfoundland	6,056	1,752,751	1,758,807	5,649	1,092	68
New Zealand	7,431	294,644	302,075	244	81	95
British Possessions, other	654	400	1,054	693	1,301	70
Total, British Empire	61,028,681	22,438,124	83,466,805	6,333,095	3,564,474	69
Arabia	147	15,663	15,810	276	87	75
Argentina	6,177	1,488,113	1,494,290	3,553	556	66
Austria-Hungary	742,036	52,317	794,353	733,173	205,202	59
Belgium	1,943,473	379,589	2,323,062	2,214,508	508,247	32
Brazil	11,069	327,683	338,752	11,083	1,248	60
Central American States	33,287	106,976	140,263	75,230	22,825	83
Chili	....	109,262	109,262	....	....	
China	281,612	259,140	540,752	284,815	169,043	69
Corea	11	....	11	11	1	10
Cuba	385,624	59,476	445,100	380,578	391,889	20
Denmark	7,908	22,122	30,030	5,330	1,260	30
Danish West Indies	....	....	....	39	197	20
Dutch East Indies	596,694	1,611	598,305	838,379	230,495	79
Ecuador	316	....	316	316	94	80
Egypt	22,728	6,885	29,613	21,073	30,010	95
France	6,240,402	1,457,645	7,698,047	6,181,635	2,509,884	10
French Africa	....	14,548	14,548	75	32	75
French West Indies	....	350	350	....	....	
Germany	5,046,778	1,993,313	7,040,091	101,806	25,067	83
Greece	289,250	29	289,279	300,845	88,824	99
Hawaii	198	15,779	15,977	198	46	53
Holland	589,214	571,027	1,160,241	612,791	1,620,478	12
Iceland	68	2,235	2,303	68	31	55
Italy	526,752	54,212	580,964	499,420	118,673	97
Japan	1,036,084	626,845	1,662,929	1,046,026	317,533	26
Madeira	....	....	....	44	33	90
Mexico	64,372	223,144	287,516	64,193	19,263	10
Norway	74,307	20,079	94,386	67,944	18,686	05
Persia	8,434	....	8,434	8,434	2,193	70
Peru	70,143	....	70,143	188,852	74,719	57
Philippines	8,207	50	8,257	10,541	33,236	25
Porto Rico	211,174	457	211,631	272,011	19,778	90
Portugal	122,267	15,381	137,648	113,203	44,716	82
Roumania	173	1,215	1,388	173	118	20
Russia	61,893	198,068	259,961	59,752	12,186	75
St. Pierre	18,737	3,561	22,298	1,742	474	91

DUTIABLE AND FREE.

ENTERED FOR CONSUMPTION.

Preferential Tariff.		Surtax Tariff.		Total Dutiable.	Total Free.	Grand Total.	
Value.	Duty.	Value.	Duty.	Value.	Value.	Value.	Duty.
$	$ cts.	$	$ cts.	$	$	$	$ cts.
45,723,019	9,380,210 11	837,775	309,354 88	52,615,725	16,578,863	69,194,588	12,944,249 35
....	....	....	....	28,383	195,796	224,179	9,104 08
142,867	25,419 95	....	....	160,694	14,661	175,355	27,384 88
830,131	121,706 60	....	....	845,681	2,508,304	3,353,985	126,197 96
4,715,920	1,057,383 06	51	20 40	4,760,371	1,102,739	5,863,110	1,119,236 42
2,477,559	504,040 09	....	....	2,492,707	1,502	2,494,209	635,766 17
269,080	69,385 43	....	....	269,127	72	269,199	69,391 75
....	....	....	....	51	....	51	21 64
....	....	....	....	150,172	18,304	168,476	98,166 63
....	....	....	....	5,649	1,752,776	1,758,425	1,092 68
5,526	707 90	....	....	5,770	295,587	301,357	789 85
....	....	....	....	693	400	1,093	1,301 70
54,164,102	11,158,853 14	837,826	309,375 28	61,335,023	22,469,004	83,804,027	15,032,703 11
....	....	....	....	276	15,663	15,939	87 75
....	....	....	....	3,553	1,488,113	1,491,666	556 66
....	....	11,721	4,553 53	744,894	52,317	797,211	209,756 12
....	....	15,975	3,337 34	2,230,483	379,589	2,610,072	511,584 66
....	....	....	....	11,083	327,683	338,766	1,248 60
....	....	....	....	75,230	106,976	182,206	22,825 83
....	....	....	....	....	109,262	109,262	....
....	....	20	6 67	284,835	259,140	543,975	169,050 36
....	....	....	....	11	....	11	1 10
....	....	....	....	380,578	58,462	439,040	391,889 20
....	....	....	....	5,330	22,122	27,452	1,260 30
....	....	....	....	39	....	39	197 20
....	....	....	....	838,379	4,130	842,509	230,495 79
....	....	....	....	316	....	316	94 80
....	....	....	....	21,073	7,061	28,134	30,010 95
....	....	23,977	10,150 87	6,205,612	1,462,375	7,667,987	2,520,034 97
....	....	....	....	75	14,548	14,623	32 75
....	....	....	....	....	350	350	....
....	....	4,899,916	1,827,470 64	5,001,722	1,985,592	6,987,314	1,852,538 47
....	....	....	....	300,845	74	300,919	88,824 99
....	....	....	....	198	15,779	15,977	46 53
....	....	604	233 60	613,395	566,497	1,179,892	1,620,711 72
....	....	....	....	68	2,235	2,303	31 55
....	....	123	49 20	499,543	54,212	553,755	118,725 17
....	....	....	....	1,046,026	627,516	1,673,542	317,533 26
....	....	....	....	44	....	44	33 90
....	....	....	....	64,193	223,144	287,337	19,263 10
....	....	86	22 94	68,030	20,079	88,109	18,708 99
....	....	....	....	8,434	....	8,434	2,193 70
....	....	....	....	188,842	....	188,852	74,719 57
....	....	....	....	10,541	138	10,679	33,236 25
....	....	....	....	272,011	556	272,567	19,778 90
....	....	....	....	113,203	15,401	128,604	44,716 82
....	....	....	....	173	1,215	1,388	118 20
....	....	415	83 00	60,167	198,068	258,235	12,269 75
....	....	....	....	1,742	3,566	5,308	474 91

No. 2—Abstract by Countries,

Countries.	Imports.			General Tariff.	
	Dutiable.	Free.	Total.		
	Value.	Value.	Value.	Value.	Duty.
	$	$	$	$	$ cts.
Spain	886,815	44,427	931,242	883,454	289,363 62
Sweden	83,913	9,761	93,674	83,456	18,725 80
Switzerland	1,982,529	49,527	2,032,056	1,959,323	545,566 89
Turkey	211,791	152,021	363,812	189,452	49,540 43
United States	94,196,820	86,529,291	180,726,111	89,391,824	22,133,014 68
Uruguay	....	173,893	173,893	....	....
Venezuela	248	71,864	72,112	248	49 60
Total, Other Countries	115,761,651	95,057,559	210,819,210	106,605,874	29,503,406 05
Duty on articles lower than home trade price	....	....	....	....	74,409 28
Additional duties	....	....	....	....	159,251 55
Grand Totals	176,790,332	117,495,683	294,286,015	112,938,969	33,301,541 57

DUTIABLE AND FREE.—*Concluded.*

ENTERED FOR CONSUMPTION.

Preferential Tariff.		Surtax Tariff.		Total Dutiable.	Total Free.	Grand Total.	
Value.	Duty.	Value.	Duty.	Value.	Value.	Value.	Duty.
$	$ cts.	$	$ cts.	$	$ cts.	$	$ cts.
....	....	....	....	883,454	45,337	928,791	289,363 62
....	....	1	0 40	83,457	9,761	93,218	18,726 20
....	....	3,422	1,334 74	1,962,745	49,660	2,012,405	546,901 63
....	....	....	....	189,452	152,021	341,473	49,540 43
....	....	148,952	54,088 26	89,540,776	86,321,295	175,862,071	22,187,102 94
....	....	....	....	....	173,893	173,893	....
....	....	....	....	248	71,864	72,112	49 60
....	....	5,105,212	1,901,331 19	111,711,086	94,845,694	206,556,780	31,404,737 24
....	....	....	....	....	....	....	74,409 28
....	....	....	....	....	....	....	159,251 55
54,164,102	11,158,853 14	5,943,038	2,210,706 47	173,046,109	117,314,698	290,360,807	46,671,101 18

No. 3.—General Statement by Countries of the Total Quantities and Values of Merchandise exported from the Dominion of Canada, Distinguishing Canadian Produce and Manufactures from those of other Countries, during the Fiscal Year ended June 30, 1906.

Articles Exported.	Countries.	Goods, the Produce of Canada.		Goods, not the Produce of Canada.		Total Exports.	
		Quantity.	Value.	Q'ty.	Value.	Quantity.	Value.
THE MINE.		Lbs.	$	Lbs.	$	Lbs.	$
Arsenic	United States	129,070	3,141	....	....	129,070	3,141
		Tons.		Tons.		Tons.	
Asbestus	Great Britain	8,614	262,774	....	....	8,614	262,774
	Australia	10	300	....	....	10	300
	Newfoundland	1	150	....	....	1	150
	Aust.-Hungary	165	4,950	....	....	165	4,950
	Belgium	2,692	87,635	....	....	2,692	87,635
	France	1,746	49,620	....	....	1,746	49,620
	Germany	4,344	111,617	....	....	4,344	111,617
	Italy	592	23,993	....	....	592	23,993
	Norway	15	450	....	....	15	450
	United States	38,896	1,036,648	....	....	38,896	1,036,648
	Total	57,075	1,578,137	....	....	57,075	1,578,137
		Cwt.		Cwt.		Cwt.	
Barytes, ground and unground	United States	34,488	14,343	....	....	34,488	14,343
		Tons.		Tons.		Tons.	
Coal	Great Britain	15,412	29,014	....	....	15,412	29,014
	Bermuda	17,382	70,907	....	....	17,382	70,907
	British Africa	7,000	17,600	....	....	7,000	17,600
	B. W. Indies	1,620	6,750	....	....	1,620	6,750
	Newfoundland	187,767	465,443	452	2,883	188,219	468,326
	Cent. Am. States	700	2,000	....	....	700	2,000
	Cuba	2,700	10,013	....	....	2,700	10,013
	France	441	1,712	....	....	441	1,712
	Germany	579	1,872	....	....	579	1,872
	Holland	532	1,506	....	....	532	1,506
	Italy	300	900	....	....	300	900
	Mexico	3,867	11,032	....	....	3,867	11,032
	St. Pierre	8,978	26,982	60	400	9,038	27,382
	United States	1,573,233	3,997,467	106,657	144,120	1,679,890	4,141,587
	Total	1,820,511	4,643,198	107,169	147,403	1,927,680	4,790,601
Chromite (chromic iron)	United States	1,808	21,293	....	....	1,808	21,293
Felspar	United States	12,516	37,615	....	....	12,516	37,615
Gold-bearing quartz, dust, nuggets, &c	Great Britain	....	2,150	....	....	....	2,150
	Hong Kong	....	280	....	....	....	280
	China	....	1,944	....	....	....	1,944
	United States	....	12,987,542	....	12,627	....	13,000,169
	Total	....	12,991,916	....	12,627	....	13,004,543

No. 3.—General Statement of Exports—*Continued.*

Articles Exported.	Countries.	Goods, the Produce of Canada.		Goods not the Produce of Canada.		Total Exports.	
		Quantity.	Value.	Q'ty.	Value.	Quantity.	Value.
THE MINE—*Con.*		Tons.	$	Tons.	$	Tons.	$
Gypsum or plaster—crude.	B. W. Indies....	11	96	....	....	11	96
	B. Africa.......	13	95	....	....	13	95
	Bermuda	10	60	....	....	10	60
	Newfoundland..	100	278	....	....	100	278
	St. Pierre......	2	3	....	....	2	3
	United States...	404,718	446,257	....	....	404,718	446,257
	Total......	404,854	446,789	....	....	404,854	446,789
Metals, viz.:—							
Copper, fine, contained in ore, matte, regulus, &c......		Lbs.		Lbs.		Lbs.	
	Great Britain...	3,542,446	457,384	....	....	3,542,446	457,384
	United States...	40,293,005	6,611,739	4,010	682	40,297,015	6,612,421
	Total......	43,835,451	7,069,123	4,010	682	43,839,461	7,069,805
Copper, black or coarse, cement copper and copper in pigs........	Great Britain...	80,895	12,538	....	....	80,895	12,538
	Belgium........	....	....	5,007	746	5,007	746
	Germany	26,017	3,876	....	....	26,017	3,876
	United States...	339,985	63,096	28,802	5,124	368,787	68,220
	Total......	446,897	79,510	33,809	5,870	480,706	85,380
Lead, metallic, contained in ore, &c...		Lbs.		Lbs.		Lbs.	
	Newfoundland..	2,700	81	....	....	2,700	81
	Germany	23,600	856	....	....	23,600	856
	United States...	16,027,042	558,132	....	....	16,027,042	558,132
	Total......	16,053,342	559,069	....	....	16,053,342	559,069
Lead pig	Australia.......	236,975	5,627	....	....	236,975	5,627
	Newfoundland..	5,300	1,637	....	....	5,300	1,637
	China	785,436	27,264	....	....	785,436	27,264
	Japan..........	2,339,574	81,185	....	....	2,339,574	81,185
	United States...	110,613	3,259	....	....	110,613	3,259
	Total......	3,477,898	118,972	....	....	3,477,898	118,972
Nickle, fine, contained in ore, matte or speiss.	Great Britain...	1,963,927	602,613	....	....	1,963,927	602,613
	United States...	21,995,914	1,564,323	....	....	21,995,914	1,564,323
	Total.....	23,959,841	2,166,936	....	....	23,959,841	2,166,936
Platinum, contained in concentrates, or other forms................	United States...	Ozs. 97	1,966	Ozs. 26	559	Ozs. 123	2,525
Silver, metallic, contained in ore, concentrates, &c.	Great Britain ..	44,475	20,140	....	....	44,475	20,140
	China	155,680	85,062	....	....	155,680	85,062
	United States...	7,061,372	4,205,326	8,006	4,929	7,069,378	4,210,255
	Total......	7,261,527	4,310,528	8,006	4,929	7,269,533	4,315,457

No. 3.—GENERAL STATEMENT OF EXPORTS—*Continued.*

Articles Exported.	Countries.	Goods, the Produce of Canada. Quantity.	Goods, the Produce of Canada. Value.	Goods, not the Produce of Canada. Q'ty.	Goods, not the Produce of Canada. Value.	Total Exports. Quantity.	Total Exports. Value.
THE MINE—*Con.*		Lbs.	$	Lbs.	$	Lbs.	$
Mica	Great Britain	272,454	32,072			272,454	32,072
	France	18,615	3,150			18,615	3,150
	Mexico	100	200			100	200
	United States	1,038,465	300,169	34,193	10,674	1,072,658	310,843
	Total	1,329,634	335,591	34,193	10,674	1,363,827	346,265
Mineral pigment, iron oxides, ochres, &c	Great Britain	100,000	1,297			100,000	1,297
	United States	536,810	5,421			536,810	5,421
	Total	636,810	6,718			636,810	6,718
		Galls.		Galls.		Galls.	
Mineral water	Great Britain	2,031	1,200	16	18	2,047	1,218
	B. Guiana	33	15			33	15
	Bermuda	1,247	633			1,247	633
	B. W. Indies	300	56			300	56
	Newfoundland	408	145			408	145
	Italy	28	14			28	14
	United States	2,145	1,302	38	20	2,183	1,322
	Total	6,192	3,365	54	38	6,246	3,403
Oil— Mineral, coal and kerosene, crude	Newfoundland			50,820	4,593	50,820	4,593
	St. Pierre			134	11	134	11
	United States			280	25	280	25
	Total			51,234	4,629	51,234	4,629
Mineral, coal and kerosene, refined	Newfoundland	839	128	2,686	451	3,525	579
	United States	13,751	3,024	45	9	13,796	3,033
	Total	14,590	3,152	2,731	460	17,321	3,612
Ores, viz.—		Tons.		Tons.		Tons.	
Antimony	Great Britain	428	6,157			428	6,157
Iron	Great Britain	23	125			23	125
	United States	148,017	345,415	720	2,840	148,737	348,255
	Total	148,040	345,540	720	2,840	148,760	348,380
Manganese	United States	17	1,240			17	1,240
Other	Great Britain	342	43,140			342	43,140
	Belgium	41	4,130			41	4,130
	France	5	1,275			5	1,275
	Germany	49	5,636			49	5,636
	United States	10,922	316,474	2	346	10,924	316,820
	Total	11,359	370,655	2	346	11,361	371,001

No. 3.—General Statement of Exports—*Continued.*

Articles Exported.	Countries.	Goods, the Produce of Canada.		Goods, not the Produce of Canada.		Total Exports.	
		Quantity.	Value.	Qt'y.	Value.	Quantity.	Value.
THE MINE—*Con.*		Cwt.	$		$	Cwt.	$
Plumbago, crude ore and concentrates	Great Britain	41	58			41	58
	United States	3,935	4,668			3,935	4,668
	Total	3,976	4,726			3,976	4,726
		Tons.		Tons.		Tons.	
Pyrites	United States	20,285	49,768	1,822	4,000	22,107	53,768
		Lbs.		Lbs.		Lbs.	
Salt	Bermuda	700	9			700	9
	B. Africa	263,200	757			263,200	757
	Newfoundland	748	46	7,140,053	19,431	7,140,801	19,477
	New Zealand	76,000	276			76,000	276
	Mexico	200	3			200	3
	United States	1,280,899	5,579	6,177,860	19,591	7,458,759	25,170
	Total	1,621,747	6,670	13,317,913	39,022	14,939,660	45,692
		Tons.				Tons.	
Sand and gravel	Newfoundland	100	300			100	300
	New Zealand	36	122			36	122
	United States	346,142	167,624			346,142	167,624
	Total	346,278	168,046			346,278	168,046
Stone—ornamental, granite, marble, &c., unwrought	Cuba	224	2,240			224	2,240
	United States	2,923	905			2,923	905
	Total	3,147	3,145			3,147	3,145
" building, freestone, limestone, &c., unwrought	Newfoundland	80	40			80	40
	United States	486	1,410			486	1,410
	Total	566	1,450			566	1,450
" for manufacture of grindstones, rough	United States	896	10,457			896	10,457
Other articles	Great Britain		5,177		5		5,182
	B. W. Indies		492		28		520
	Newfoundland		135				135
	Belgium		120				120
	France		690				690
	Germany		400				400
	United States		103,401		2,287		105,688
	Total		110,415		2,320		112,735

No. 3.—General Statement of Exports—*Continued.*

Articles Exported.	Countries.	Goods, the Produce of Canada.		Goods, not the Produce of Canada.		Total Exports.	
		Quantity.	Value.	Q'ty.	Value.	Quantity.	Value.
THE FISHERIES.		Lbs.	$	Lbs.	$	Lbs.	$
Codfish, including haddock, ling and pollock, fresh	United States	404,163	11,018	....	....	404,163	11,018
		Cwt.		Cwt.		Cwt.	
Codfish, dry salted	Great Britain	18,552	87,093	....	....	18,552	87,093
	Australia	226	1,399	....	....	226	1,399
	Bermuda	4 375	27,024	....	....	4,375	27,024
	B. Africa	25	150	....	....	25	150
	B. W. Indies	146,559	855,734	925	4,681	147,484	860,415
	B. Guiana	41,844	208,314	....	....	41,844	208,314
	B. Honduras	25	150	....	....	25	150
	Gibraltar	600	2,700	....	....	600	2,700
	Newfoundland	8,407	41,348	....	....	8,407	41,348
	Argentina	1,280	7,000	....	....	1,280	7,000
	Brazil	93,097	611,062	....	....	93,097	611,062
	Cent. Am. States	3,694	23,574	....	....	3,694	23,574
	Cuba	72,123	394,508	....	....	72,123	394,508
	Denmark	153	1,068	....	....	153	1,068
	Dan. W. Indies	814	4,676	....	....	814	4,676
	Dutch Guiana	4,216	18,800	....	....	4,216	18,800
	France	20	120	....	....	20	120
	Hawaii	448	2,780	....	....	448	2,780
	Hayti	4,987	29,740	....	....	4,987	29,740
	Italy	21,485	114,913	....	....	21,485	114,913
	Japan	609	3,430	....	....	609	3,430
	Maderia	1,568	10,449	....	....	1,568	10,449
	Mexico	1,070	5,596	....	....	1,070	5,596
	Panama	4,174	25,099	....	....	4,174	25,099
	Porto Rico	70,374	416,699	....	....	70,374	416,699
	Portugal	8,754	57,727	....	....	8,754	57,727
	San Domingo	544	2,787	....	....	544	2,787
	Spain	4,442	18,621	....	....	4,442	18,621
	U. S. Colombia	4,448	28,649	....	....	4,448	28,649
	United States	88,766	495,371	....	....	88,766	495,371
	Venezuela	2	15	....	....	2	15
	Total	607,681	3,496,596	925	4,681	608,606	3,501,277
" wet salted	B. W. Indies	196	388	....	....	196	388
	B. Guiana	3	5	....	....	3	5
	United States	4,711	19,301	....	....	4,711	19,301
	Total	4,910	19,694	....	....	4,910	19,694
" pickled	B. W. Indies	5	20	....	....	5	20
	United States	1	4	....	....	1	4
	Total	6	24	....	....	6	24
		Brls.		Brls.		Brls.	
" tongues and sounds	Bermuda	15	101	....	....	15	101
	B. W. Indies	14	21	....	....	14	21
	Cuba	42	504	....	....	42	504
	United States	1,723	20,054	....	....	1,723	20,054
	Total	1,794	20,680	....	....	1,794	20,680

No. 3.—General Statement of Exports—*Continued.*

Articles Exported.	Countries.	Goods, the Produce of Canada.		Goods, not the Produce of Canada.		Total Exports.	
		Quantity.	Value.	Q'ty.	Value.	Quantity.	Value.
THE FISHERIES—*Con.*		Lbs.	$	Lbs.	$	Lbs.	$
Mackrel, fresh	B. W. Indies	100	4	....	....	100	4
	United States	1,783,420	69,453	....	....	1,783,420	69,453
	Total	1,783,520	69,457	....	....	1,783,520	69,457
" canned	Great Britain	4,316	207	....	....	4,316	207
	Mexico	960	36	....	....	960	36
	Total	5,276	243	....	....	5,276	243
		Brls.		Brls.		Brls.	
Mackerel, pickled	Bermuda	154	1,716	....	....	154	1,716
	B. W. Indies	5,008	49,500	465	4,091	5,473	53,591
	B. Guiana	1,427	13,280	53	477	1,480	13,757
	Brazil	5	60	....	....	5	60
	Cent. Am. States	271	2,848	....	....	271	2,848
	Cuba	188	1,933	....	....	188	1,933
	Dan. W. Indies	38	475	8	81	46	556
	Dutch Guiana	4	35	....	....	4	35
	Hayti	275	1,715	....	....	275	1,715
	Mexico	15	148	....	....	15	148
	Panama	638	6,663	6	57	644	6,720
	Porto Rico	60	523	....	....	60	523
	U. S. Colombia	471	4,398	72	667	543	5,065
	United States	22,244	173,826	18	156	22,262	173,982
	Total	30,798	257,120	622	5,529	31,420	262,649
		Lbs.		Lbs.		Lbs.	
Halibut, fresh	Australia	315	20	....	....	315	20
	United States	685,770	32,217	....	....	685,770	32,217
	Total	686,085	32,237	....	....	686,085	32,237
		Brls.		Brls.		Brls.	
" pickled	Great Britain	352	3,164	....	....	352	3,164
		Lbs		Lbs.		Lbs.	
Herring, fresh or frozen	Australia	4,000	310	....	....	4,000	310
	United States	22,648,281	121,216	335,000	9,429	22,983,281	130,645
	Total	22,652,281	121,526	335,000	9,429	22,987,281	130,955
		Brls.		Brls.		Brls.	
" pickled	Great Britain	100	425	....	....	100	425
	Australia	53	297	....	....	53	297
	Bermuda	21	94	....	....	21	94
	B. W. Indies	49,889	222,290	459	1,400	50,348	223,690
	B. Guiana	2,725	11,600	....	....	2,725	11,600
	Newfoundland	26	103	....	....	26	103
	Brazil	60	270	....	....	60	270
	Cent. Am. States	38	202	....	....	38	202
	China	1,697	5,067	....	....	1,697	5,067
	Cuba	931	4,421	....	....	931	4,421
	Dan. W. Indies	397	1,965	....	....	397	1,965
	Dutch Guiana	48	241	....	....	48	241
	France	150	750	....	....	150	750

No. 3.—General Statement of Exports—*Continued.*

Articles Exported.	Countries.	Goods, the Produce of Canada.		Goods, not the Produce of Canada.		Total Exports.	
		Quantity.	Value.	Q'ty.	Value.	Quantity.	Value.
THE FISHERIES—*Con.*		Brls.	$	Brls.	$	Brls.	$
Herring, pickled—*Con.*....	French Africa ..	100	500	....	....	100	500
	Japan	10,465	21,128	....	....	10,465	21,128
	Hawaii.........	5	46	....	....	5	46
	Mexico.........	20	112	....	....	20	112
	Panama...	56	151	....	....	56	151
	Porto Rico......	3,988	16,795	....	....	3,988	16,795
	St. Pierre	3,300	3,300	....	....	3,300	3,300
	U. S. Colombia..	22	80	....	....	22	80
	United States...	39,076	103,571	....	....	39,076	103,571
	Total	113,167	393,408	459	1,400	113,626	394,808
		Lbs.		Lbs.		Lbs.	
" canned......	Great Britain...	....	....	81	25	81	25
	Australia.......	400	22	....	....	400	22
	Bermuda.......	474	29	....	....	474	29
	B. W. Indies.. .	220	10	....	....	220	10
	United States...	72,315	2,650	....	....	72,315	2,650
	Total	73,409	2,711	81	25	73,490	2,736
Herring—smoked...	Great Britain...	34,930	1,245	....	....	34,930	1,245
	Australia.......	1,000	55	....	....	1,000	55
	Bermuda........	52,062	1,729	....	....	52,062	1,729
	B. W. Indies....	779,897	21,114	....	....	779,897	21,114
	B. Guiana.....	76,962	1,838	....	....	76,962	1,838
	Newfoundland.	13,970	337	....	....	13,970	337
	New Zealand....	850	24	....	....	850	24
	Brazil.........	2,100	43	....	....	2,100	43
	Cent. Am. States	3,700	87	....	....	3,700	87
	Cuba...	71,600	1,340	....	....	71,600	1,340
	Dan. W. Indies..	13,566	324	....	....	13,566	324
	Dutch Guiana ..	11,500	289	....	....	11,500	289
	Madeira........	2,500	50	....	....	2,500	50
	Mexico.........	1,000	22	....	....	1,000	22
	Panama.......	3,070	89	....	....	3,070	89
	Porto Rico.	11,500	285	....	....	11,500	285
	St. Pierre	2,056	50	....	....	2,056	50
	U. S. Colombia.	2,000	48	....	....	2,000	48
	United States...	2,774,800	69,034	....	....	2,774,800	69,034
	Total	3,859,063	98,003	....	....	3,859,063	98,003
Sea fish, other—fresh.... ..	France..	....	....	4	1	4	1
	United States...	5,699,913	282,844	200	20	5,700,113	282,864
	Total	5,699,913	282,844	204	21	5,700,117	282,865

No. 3.—GENERAL STATEMENT OF EXPORTS—*Continued.*

Articles Exported.	Countries.	Goods, the produce of Canada.		Goods, not the Produce of Canada.		Total Exports.	
		Quantity.	Value.	Q'ty.	Value.	Quantity.	Value.
THE FISHERIES—*Con.*		Brls.	$	Brls.	$	Brls.	$
Sea fish, other—pickled...	B. Guiana......	35	151	....	....	35	151
	Bermuda........	1	4	....	....	1	4
	B. W. Indies....	3,563	21,260	63	158	3,626	21,418
	Cent. Am. States	3	30	....	....	3	30
	China........	202	680	....	....	202	680
	Cuba.........	20	120	....	....	20	120
	Dan. W. Indies.	61	361	....	....	61	361
	Dutch Guiana ..	16	101	....	....	16	101
	Japan	716	2,430	....	....	716	2,430
	Panama........	1	5	....	....	1	5
	United States...	745	3,407	....	....	745	3,407
	Total	5,363	28,549	63	158	5,426	28,707
		Lbs.		Lbs.		Lbs.	
" preserved	Great Britain...	855	65	9,662	1,485	10,517	1,550
	Australia.......	300	22	....	....	300	22
	Bermuda........	6,899	404	....	....	6,899	404
	B. W. Indies ...	11,637	588	1,396	114	13,033	702
	B. Guiana......	1,414	61	....	....	1,414	61
	Newfoundland..	9,102	426	....	....	9,102	426
	China..........	44,000	2,500	....	....	44,000	2,500
	Cuba..........	9,903	336	....	....	9,903	336
	Dan. W. Indies.	1,075	52	....	....	1,075	52
	Mexico.........	5,690	292	....	....	5,690	292
	United States...	784,267	35,227	2,708	427	786,975	35,654
	Total	875,142	39,973	13,766	2,026	888,908	41,999
		Brls.		Brls.		Brls.	
Oysters—fresh.......	Great Britain...	43	317	....	....	43	317
	B. Africa......	12	102	....	....	12	102
	Newfoundland..	2	6	....	....	2	6
	St. Pierre.....	13	52	....	....	13	52
	United States...	258	1,482	9	105	267	1,587
	Total	328	1,959	9	105	337	2,064
		Lbs.		Lbs.		Lbs.	
" preserved in cans.	United States...	424	156	245	73	669	229
		Brls.		Brls.		Brls.	
Lobsters—fresh	Great Britain...	728	8,511	....	....	728	8,511
	United States...	41,397	489,030	1	13	41,398	489,043
	Total	42,125	497,541	1	13	42,126	497,554

No. 3.—General Statement of Exports—*Continued.*

Articles Exported.	Countries.	Goods, the Produce of Canada.		Goods, not the Produce of Canada.		Total Exports.	
		Quantity.	Value.	Qt'y.	Value.	Quantity.	Value.
THE FISHERIES—*Con.*			Lbs.		Lbs.		Lbs.
Lobsters, canned..........	Great Britain...	4,008,680	1,076,332	......	......	4,008,680	1,076,332
	Australia......	12,912	4,631	......	......	12,912	4,631
	Bermuda........	6,038	1,543	......	......	6,038	1,543
	B. Africa... ...	700	125	......	......	700	125
	B. E. Indies	336	84	......	......	336	84
	B. Guiana......	6,595	1,493	......	......	6,595	1,493
	B. W. Indies...	18,326	3,797	......	......	18,326	3,797
	Fiji Islands	8	2	......	......	8	2
	New Zealand....	960	204	......	......	960	204
	Argentina.......	21,360	5,340	......	......	21,360	5,340
	Belgium	192,763	50,964	......	......	192,763	50,964
	Cuba.	7,675	454	......	......	7,675	454
	Denmark. ...	61,944	15,713	......	......	61,944	15,713
	France..	3,317,427	935,188	......	......	3,317,427	935,188
	Germany......	170,818	45,323	......	......	170,818	45,323
	Holland........	28,760	6,941	......	......	28,760	6,941
	Norway	2,400	600	......	......	2,400	600
	St. Pierre.......	5,600	1,516	......	......	5,600	1,516
	Sweden.........	143,640	37,837	......	......	143,640	37,837
	Turkey........	3,500	650	......	......	3,500	650
	United States...	3,133,960	821,466	......	......	3,133,960	821,466
	Total......	11,144,402	3,010,203	......	......	11,144,402	3,010,203
		Brls.		Brls.		Brls.	
Bait, fish	Newfoundland.	13	39	......	......	13	39
	St. Pierre.	2	4	......	......	2	4
	United States...	286	1,715	......	......	286	1,715
	Total	301	1,758	......	......	301	1,758
Clams or other...	Newfoundland..	1	8	......	......	1	8
	St. Pierre.......	52	247	......	......	52	247
	United States...	66,151	126,015	......	......	66,151	126,015
	Total	66,204	126,270	......	......	66,204	126,270
		Lbs.			Lbs.		Lbs.
Salmon, fresh..	Great Britain...	2,103,616	277,332	......	......	2,103,616	277,332
	Australia. ...	136,280	5,554	......	......	136,280	5,554
	B. Africa.......	27,640	3,495	......	......	27,640	3,495
	Fiji Islands.....	430	46	......	......	430	46
	New Zealand....	185	5	......	......	185	5
	China	12,000	625	......	......	12,000	625
	Germany.......	27,922	2,792	......	......	27,922	2,792
	United States...	2,529,273	202,611	......	......	2,529,273	202,611
	Total.....	4,837,346	492,460	......	......	4,837,346	492,460
" smoked..........	Great Britain...	50	7	......	......	50	7
	Australia.	270	25	......	......	270	25
	Bermuda........	200	20	......	......	200	20
	B. W. Indies....	104	12	......	......	104	12
	Dutch Guiana...	53	8	......	......	53	8
	United States...	1,808	190	......	......	1,808	190
	Total......	2,485	262	......	......	2,485	262

No. 3.—General Statement of Exports—*Continued.*

Articles Exported.	Countries.	Goods, the Produce of Canada.		Goods, not the Produce of Canada.		Total Exports.	
		Quantity.	Value.	Q'ty.	Value.	Quantity.	Value.
THE FISHERIES—*Con.*		Lbs.	$	Lbs.	$	Lbs.	$
Salmon—*Con.*							
Canned	Great Britain	40,801,698	4,353,379	335	40	40,802,033	4,353,419
	Australia	2,054,534	230,227			2,054,534	230,227
	Bermuda	14,841	2,386			14,841	2,386
	B. Africa	152,128	11,760			152,128	11,760
	B. E. Indies	54,432	5,709			54,432	5,709
	B. W. Indies	16,452	1,504			16,452	1,504
	B. Guiana	704	64			704	64
	B. Poss., other	2,880	210			2,880	210
	Fiji Islands	239,118	18,572			239,118	18,572
	New Zealand	619,893	69,118			619,893	69,118
	Belgium	16,800	1,975			16,800	1,975
	China	16,800	840			16,800	840
	Cuba	5,620	563			5,620	563
	Dutch E. Indies	10,800	540			10,800	540
	France	161,470	15,062			161,470	15,062
	Germany	1,038	56			1,038	56
	Japan	236,121	8,148			236,121	8,148
	Mexico	11,418	917			11,418	917
	Panama	1,200	95			1,200	95
	Port'gse Africa	8,400	525			8,400	525
	St. Pierre	288	29			288	29
	Spain	1,920	200			1,920	200
	United States	1,549,568	221,534			1,549,568	221,534
	Total	45,978,123	4,943,413	335	40	45,978,458	4,943,453
		Brls.		Brls.		Brls.	
Pickled	Great Britain	95	1,290			95	1,290
	Australia	361	3,528			361	3,528
	Bermuda	42	420			42	420
	B. Africa	39	545			39	545
	B. W. Indies	849	10,171			849	10,171
	B. Guiana	266	2,810			266	2,810
	New Zealand	25	175			25	175
	Brazil	25	370			25	370
	Cent. Am. States	41	587			41	587
	Cuba	8	118			8	118
	Denmark	210	4,200			210	4,200
	Dan. W. Indies	10	98			10	98
	Dutch Guiana	24	313			24	313
	France	30	450			30	450
	Germany	1	16			1	16
	Hawaii	2	10			2	10
	Japan	31,793	115,505			31,793	115,505
	Mexico	5	66			5	66
	Panama	64	768			64	768
	U.S. of Colombia	84	1,068			84	1,068
	United States	79,383	128,649			79,383	128,649
	Total	113,357	271,157			113,357	271,157
		Lbs.				Lbs.	
Salmon or lake trout	United States	249,053	9,054			249,053	9,054
Fish, all other—fresh	Great Britain		613				613
	Australia		437				437
	Fiji Islands		15				15
	Germany		27				27
	United States		1,367,524				1,367,524
	Total		1,368,616				1,368,616

No. 3.—General Statement of Exports—*Continued.*

Articles Exported.	Countries.	Goods, the Produce of Canada. Quantity.	Goods, the Produce of Canada. Value.	Goods, not the Produce of Canada. Q'ty.	Goods, not the Produce of Canada. Value.	Total Exports. Quantity.	Total Exports. Value.
THE FISHERIES—*Con.*		Brls.	$	Brls.	$	Brls.	$
Fish, all other—pickled...	Great Britain...	17	134	....	....	17	134
	Australia.....	31	440	....	....	31	440
	B. W. Indies....	49	207	....	....	49	207
	B. Poss., other..	7	40	....	....	7	40
	China	1,407	3,820	....	....	1,407	3,820
	Cuba..........	202	1,408	....	....	202	1,408
	Denmark.......	139	2,001	....	....	139	2,001
	Germany......	664	4,718	....	....	664	4,718
	Japan.........	1,101	3,092	....	....	1,101	3,092
	Sweden.......	12	233	....	....	12	233
	United States..	1,826	15,087	....	....	1,826	15,087
	Total......	5,455	31,180	....	....	5,455	31,180
Fish oil—		Galls.		Galls.		Galls.	
Cod	Great Britain...	1,237	351	....	....	1,237	351
	B. W. Indies....	1,004	318	....	....	1,004	318
	Newfoundland..	4,570	1,429	....	....	4,570	1,429
	Cuba..........	2,004	602	....	....	2,004	602
	Porto Rico......	4,357	1,132	....	....	4,357	1,132
	United States...	97,036	30,238	....	....	97,036	30,238
	Total......	110,208	34,070	....	....	110,208	34,070
Seal............	Great Britain...	15,570	4,536	....	....	15,570	4,536
	United States...	....	....	127	36	127	36
	Total.......	15,570	4,536	127	36	15,697	4,572
Whale..........	Great Britain...	216,490	64,213	....	....	216,490	64,213
	United States...	4,745	2,195	....	....	4,745	2,195
	Total......	221,235	66,408	....	....	221,235	66,408
Other	Great Britain...	11,123	2,500	....	....	11,123	2,500
	Australia.......	514	160	....	....	514	160
	B. W. Indies....	80	25	....	....	80	25
	New Zealand....	1,713	600	....	....	1,713	600
	United States...	16,388	3,578	....	....	16,388	3,578
	Total......	29,818	6,863	....	....	29,818	6,863
Furs or skins, the produce of fish or marine animals	Great Britain...	....	255,168	....	....	....	255,168
	Newfounland....	....	3,150	....	....	....	3,150
	United States...	....	15,412	....	....	....	15,412
	Total......	....	273,730	....	....	....	273,730
Other articles	Great Britain...	....	2,695	....	....	....	2,695
	B. W Indies....	....	7	....	....	....	7
	France.........	....	897	....	....	....	897
	Sweden........	....	80	....	....	....	80
	United States...	....	5,278	....	18	....	5,296
	Total......	....	8,957	....	18	....	8,975

No. 3.—GENERAL STATEMENT OF EXPORTS—*Continued.*

Articles.	Countries.	Goods, the Produce of Canada. Quantity.	Goods, the Produce of Canada. Value.	Goods, not the Produce of Canada. Q'ty.	Goods, not the Produce of Canada. Value.	Total Exports. Quantity.	Total Exports. Value.
THE FOREST.		Brls.	$		$	Brls.	$
Ashes—pot and pearl	Great Britain	671	26,028	....	....	671	26,028
	New Zealand	10	377	....	....	10	377
	Belgium	16	649	....	....	16	649
	France	91	3,282	....	....	91	3,282
	United States	331	7,524	....	....	331	7,524
	Total	1,119	37,860	....	....	1,119	37,860
All other	St. Pierre	....	42	....	....	....	42
	United States	....	67,674	....	68	....	67,742
	Total	....	67,716	....	68	....	67,784
Bark for tanning	United States	Cords. 6,608	33,197	....	....	Cords. 6,608	33,197
Firewood	Newfoundland	5	10	....	....	5	10
	St. Pierre	73	231	....	....	73	231
	United States	31,374	68,881	....	....	31,374	68,881
	Total	31,452	69,122	....	....	31,452	69,122
Knees and futtocks	United States	No. 27,435	21,837	....	....	No. 27,435	21,837
Lathwood	United States	Cords. 2,768	9,899	....	....	Cords. 2,768	9,899
Logs:—							
Cedar, capable of being made into shingle bolts	United States	3,467	20,642	....	....	3,467	20,642
Elm	Great Britain	M ft. 386	6,250	....	....	M ft. 386	6,250
	United States	1,062	12,708	....	....	1,062	12,708
	Total	1,448	18,958	....	....	1,448	18,958
Hemlock	United States	4,998	31,061	....	....	4,998	31,061
Oak	Great Britain	2	80	....	....	2	80
	United States	7	90	....	....	7	90
	Total	9	170	....	....	9	170
Pine	Great Britain	117	3,550	....	....	117	3,550
	United States	1,665	21,999	....	....	1,665	21,999
	Total	1,782	25,549	....	....	1,782	25,549
Spruce	Great Britain	8	80	....	....	8	80
	Newfoundland	10	104	....	....	10	104
	United States	11,742	102,633	....	6	11,742	102,639
	Total	11,760	102,817	....	6	11,760	102,823

No. 3.—General Statement of Exports—*Continued.*

Articles Exported.	Countries.	Goods, the Produce of Canada.		Goods, not the Produce of Canada.		Total Exports.	
		Quantity.	Value.	Qty.	Value.	Quantity.	Value.
THE FOREST.		M. Ft.	$	M. Ft.	$	M. Ft.	$
Logs—All other	Great Britain	1,018	22,266			1,018	22,266
	Newfoundland	133	1,225			133	1,225
	France	4	80			4	80
	St. Pierre	8	85			8	85
	United States	51,706	355,051			51,706	355,051
	Total	52,869	378,707			52,869	378,707
Lumber, viz.—Battens	Great Britain		23,803				23,803
	Sweden		5,205				5,205
	United States				132		132
	Total		29,008		132		29,140
Basswood	Great Britain	192	4,857			192	4,857
	France	160	5,545			160	5,545
	United States	1,672	31,286	54	686	1,726	31,972
	Total	2,024	41,688	54	686	2,078	42,374
		Std. Hnd.		S. Hnd.		Std. Hnd.	
Deals—Pine	Great Britain	34,335	2,166,525			34,335	2,166,525
	Australia	31	2,059			31	2,059
	B. Africa	37	2,400			37	2,400
	Newfoundland	1	25			1	25
	Belgium	51	4,126			51	4,126
	Brazil	5	880			5	880
	France	33	1,800			33	1,800
	Germany	12	1,930			12	1,930
	Norway	4	210			4	210
	Spain	21	1,187			21	1,187
	United States	4,481	172,785			4,481	172,785
	Total	39,011	2,353,927			39,011	2,353,927
Spruce and other	Great Britain	169,105	5,827,309			169,105	5,827,309
	Australia	1,161	42,044			1,161	42,044
	B. Poss. other	55	5,160			55	5,160
	Newfoundland	10	295			10	295
	Argentina	616	24,530			616	24,530
	Belgium	25	864			25	864
	Brazil	337	13,160			337	13,160
	France	795	26,798			795	26,798
	Germany	5	299			5	299
	Norway	190	6,345			190	6,345
	Portugal	876	25,856			876	25,856
	Spain	290	11,672			290	11,672
	Uruguay	30	680			30	680
	United States	15,280	569,600			15,280	569,600
	Total	188,775	6,554,612			188,775	6,554,612

No. 3.—General Statement of Exports—*Continued.*

Articles Exported.	Countries.	Goods, the Produce of Canada.		Goods, not the Produce of Canada.		Total Exports.	
		Quantity.	Value.	Q'ty.	Value.	Quantity.	Value.
THE FOREST—*Con.*		Std. Hnd.	$	S. Hnd.		Std. Hnd.	$
Lumber—*Con.*							
Deal ends	Great Britain	9,810	364,252			9,810	364,252
	Australia	45	1,214			45	1,214
	France	30	840			30	840
	Portugal	25	717			25	717
	Spain	10	276			10	276
	United States	253	8,062			253	8,062
	Total	10,173	375,361			10,173	375,361
		M. Ft.		M. Ft.		M. Ft.	
Hickory	Great Britain	95	220			95	220
		M.				M.	
Laths	Great Britain	150	337			150	337
	Australia	2,633	5,506			2,633	5,506
	Bermuda	1,302	1,387			1,302	1,387
	B. W. Indies	627	1,344			627	1,344
	Newfoundland	1	3			1	3
	New Zealand	549	1,412			549	1,412
	Chili	441	638			441	638
	St. Pierre	11	33			11	33
	Spanish Africa	355	710			355	710
	United States	641,531	1,585,096			641,531	1,585,096
	Total	647,600	1,596,466			647,600	1,596,466
Palings	Great Britain	151	1,526			151	1,526
Pickets	Great Britain	1,751	30,371			1,751	30,371
	Australia	224	2,353			224	2,353
	B. Africa	40	600			40	600
	New Zealand	10	155			10	155
	United States	19,231	111,930			19,231	111,930
	Total	21,256	145,409			21,256	145,409
		M. ft				M. ft	
Planks and boards	Great Britain	81,176	1,499,438	47	2,375	81,223	1,501,813
	Australia	17,061	276,748			17,061	276,748
	Bermuda	21	405			21	405
	B. Africa	6,327	81,583			6,327	81,583
	B. W. Indies	7,287	110,754			7,287	110,754
	B. Guiana	1,817	30,678	205	3,300	2,022	33,978
	Fiji Islands	1,801	23,458			1,801	23,458
	Hong Kong	2,396	28,527			2,396	28,527
	Newfoundland	817	12,890			817	12,890
	New Zealand	1,182	21,000			1,182	21,000
	Argentina	64,039	1,367,774			64,039	1,367,774
	Belgium	611	16,793			611	16,793
	Chili	12,192	165,260			12,192	165,260
	China	2,257	34,915			2,257	34,915
	Cuba	14,938	248,067	90	1,517	15,028	249,584
	Denmark	100	3,010			100	3,010
	Dan. W. Indies	2	32			2	32
	France	75	1,700			75	1,700
	Fr. W. Indies	9	99			9	99
	Germany	982	24,500			982	24,500

No. 3.—General Statement of Exports—*Continued.*

Articles Exported.	Countries.	Goods, the Produce of Canada.		Goods, not the Produce of Canada.		Total Exports.	
		Quantity.	Value.	Q'ty.	Value.	Quantity.	Value.
THE FOREST—*Con.*		M. ft.	$		$	M. ft.	$
Lumber—*Con.* Planks and boards—*Con.*	Hayti........	16	231	....	....	16	231
	Holland........	173	4,450	....	....	173	4,450
	Japan........	3,700	61,771	....	....	3,700	61,771
	Madeira........	986	20,842	....	....	986	20,842
	Mexico........	614	8,060	....	....	614	8,060
	Panama	12	180	....	....	12	180
	Peru........	2,487	31,972	....	....	2,487	31,972
	Porto Rico........	5,074	74,950	....	....	5,074	74,950
	St. Pierre........	188	2,243	....	....	188	2,243
	Spanish Africa..	1,098	21,225	....	....	1,098	21,225
	Uruguay........	4,792	83,281	....	....	4,792	83,281
	United States...	889,268	13,700,968	54	1,182	889,322	13,702,150
	Venezuela	12	221	....	....	12	221
	Total........	1,123,510	17,958,025	396	8,374	1,123,906	17,966,399
Joists........	United States...	276	3,641	....	....	276	3,641
Scantling........	Great Britain...	36,086	379,933	....	....	36,086	379,933
	Bermuda........	9	146	....	....	9	146
	B. Africa........	12	180	....	....	12	180
	B. W. Indies....	477	3,467	....	....	477	3,467
	B. Guiana........	13	240	....	....	13	240
	Newfoundland..	8	129	....	....	8	129
	Argentina........	6,036	93,486	....	....	6,036	93,486
	Cuba........	40	880	....	....	40	880
	St. Pierre........	12	120	....	....	12	120
	Uruguay........	693	11,245	....	....	693	11,245
	United States...	47,145	552,921	....	....	47,145	552,921
	Total	90,531	1,042,747	....	....	90,531	1,042,747
		M.				M.	
Shingles........	Great Britain...	395	990	....	....	395	990
	B. W. Indies....	21,437	30,814	....	....	21,437	30,814
	Newfoundland..	742	1,261	....	....	742	1,261
	Cuba........	50	85	....	....	50	85
	Porto Rico........	233	347	....	....	233	347
	St. Pierre........	477	740	....	....	477	740
	United States...	918,143	1,874,249	....	....	918,143	1,874,249
	Total........	941,477	1,908,486	....	....	941,477	1,908,486
		No.				No.	
Shooks, box........	Fiji Islands........	20,400	831	....	....	20,400	831
Shooks, other........	Great Britain...	....	268,550	....	....	....	268,550
	B. Africa........	....	72	....	....	....	72
	Bermuda........	....	10,786	....	....	....	10,786
	B. W. Indies...	....	12,071	....	....	....	12,071
	B. Guiana........	....	82	....	....	....	82
	Fiji Islands........	....	500	....	....	....	500
	Newfoundland..	....	610	....	....	....	610
	Argentina........	....	13,337	....	....	....	13,337
	Cuba........	....	500	....	....	....	500
	Germany........	....	6,119	....	....	....	6,119

No. 3.—General Statement of Exports—*Continued.*

Articles Exported.	Countries.	Goods, the Produce of Canada.		Goods, not the Produce of Canada.		Total Exports.	
		Quantity.	Value.	Q'ty.	Value.	Quantity.	Value.
THE FOREST—*Con.*			$		$		$
Lumber—*Con.*							
Shooks, other—*Con.*	Mexico		19,907				19,907
	St. Pierre		215				215
	Uruguay		2,573				2,573
	United States		31,625				31,625
	Total		366,947				366,947
Staves—other and headings	Great Britain		35,198				35,198
	Australia		4,795				4,795
	B. W. Indies		178				178
	Newfoundland		343				343
	St. Pierre		190				190
	Sweden		3,207				3,207
	United States		67,945				67,945
	Total		111,856				111,856
All other lumber, N.E.S.	Great Britain		137,389		50		137,439
	Australia		1,171				1,171
	B. Africa		4,000				4,000
	B. W. Indies		120		1,540		1,660
	B. Guiana		64				64
	Newfoundland		1,010		201		1,211
	Argentina		1,981				1,981
	Cuba		6,600				6,600
	Japan		5				5
	Mexico		4,452				4,452
	St. Pierre		147				147
	United States		276,764		3,787		280,551
	Venezuela		516				516
	Total		434,219		5,578		439,797
Match blocks	Great Britain		29,721				29,721
	United States		205				205
	Total		29,926				29,926
		No.		No.		No.	
Masts and spars	Australia	52	410			52	410
	Bermuda	5	250			5	250
	B. W. Indies	261	1,844			261	1,844
	Newfoundland	58	1,380	1	70	59	1,450
	Cuba	83	1,128			83	1,128
	Madeira	6	18			6	18
	Porto Rico	4	50			4	50
	St. Pierre	20	411	1	65	21	476
	Spanish Africa	90	2,170			90	2,170
	United States	429	841			429	841
	Total	1,008	8,502	2	135	1,010	8,637
Piling	Newfoundland		20				20
	United States		194,053				194,053
	Total		194,073				194,073

No. 3.—General Statement of Exports—*Continued.*

Articles Exported.	Countries.	Goods, the Produce of Canada.		Goods, not the Produce of Canada.		Total Exports.	
		Quantity.	Value.	Q'ty.	Value.	Quantity.	Value.
THE FOREST—*Con.*			$		$		$
Poles—Hop, hoop, telegraph and other	Great Britain		2,374				2,374
	B. Africa		12				12
	Newfoundland		78				78
	Cuba		48				48
	Chili		2,580				2,580
	Porto Rico		10				10
	St. Pierre		10		520		530
	United States		95,433		279		95,712
	Total		100,545		799		101,344
Posts, cedar, tamarack and other	United States		14,579		63		14,642
Shingle bolts—of pine or cedar	United States	Cords. 9,115	16,126	Cords.		Cords. 9,115	16,126
Sleepers and railroad ties	Great Britain	779	300			779	300
	B. Africa	60	34			60	34
	Cuba	1,241	577			1,241	577
	Mexico	4,291	2,132			4,291	2,132
	United States	1,254,881	325,340			1,254,881	325,340
	Total	1,261,252	328,383			1,261,252	328,383
Stave bolts	United States	Cords. 7,643	2,496	Cords.		Cords. 7,643	2,496
Timber, square, viz.: Ash	Great Britain	Tons. 679	10,521	Tons.		Tons. 679	10,521
	France	19	332			19	332
	Total	698	10,853			698	10,853
Timber, square, viz.: Birch	Great Britain	20,472	240,942			20,472	240,942
	France	351	4,815			351	4,815
	United States	1,770	15,163			1,770	15,163
	Total	22,593	260,920			22,593	260,920
Elm	Great Britain	8,705	241,070	45	1,358	8,750	242,428
	B. Poss., other	251	7,745			251	7,745
	France	81	2,865			81	2,865
	United States	20	207			20	207
	Total	9,057	251,887	45	1,358	9,102	253,245
Maple	Great Britain	25	400			25	400
	Germany	21	275			21	275
	Total	46	675			46	675

No. 3.—GENERAL STATEMENT OF EXPORTS—*Continued.*

Articles Exported.	Countries.	Goods, the Produce of Canada.		Goods, not the Produce of Canada.		Total Exports.	
		Quantity.	Value.	Q'ty.	Value.	Quantity.	Value.
THE FOREST—*Con.*		Tons.	$	Tons.	$	Tons.	$
Timber—*Con.*							
Oak	Great Britain...	8,352	182,260	5,072	114,391	13,424	296,651
	United States...	23	230	....	....	23	230
	Total.. ..	8,375	182,490	5,072	114,391	13,447	296,881
Pine, red	Great Britain...	385	5,624	....	....	385	5,624
	United States...	280	2,909	....	....	280	2,909
	Total......	665	8,533	....	....	665	8,533
Pine, white	Great Britain...	41,685	957,588	442	15,745	42,127	973,333
	B. Poss., other..	125	3,455	....	....	125	3,455
	Cuba.....	30	296	....	... ...	30	296
	France..	76	2,220	....	....	76	2,220
	United States...	200	2,996	....	....	200	2,996
	Venezuela......	48	738	....	....	48	738
	Total......	42,164	967,293	442	15,745	42,606	983,038
All other.....	Great Britain...	1,393	28,956	21	770	1,414	29,726
	Newfoundland..	31	134	....	....	31	134
	France..	12	507	....	....	12	507
	St. Pierre.... ..	40	162	....	....	40	162
	United States...	1,187	11,164	90	993	1,277	12,157
	Total.	2,663	40,923	111	1,763	2,774	42,686
Wood, blocks and other, for pulp..........	United States...	Cords. 614,286	2,649,106	Cords.	....	Cords. 614,286	2,649,106
Other articles of the forest	Great Britain..	....	30	....	....	.. ....	30
	Australia... ..	....	5	....	....	....	5
	Newfoundland..	.. ..	5	....	....	....	5
	Cuba..........	....	1	....	....	....	1
	St. Pierre......	....	191	....	....	....	191
	United States...	....	14,124	....	2,275	....	16,399
	Total.......	....	14,356	....	2,275	....	16,631
ANIMALS, ETC.		No.		No.		No.	
Horses, one year old or less	Newfoundland..	1	60	... .	....	1	60
	United States...	30	3,025	1	30	31	3,055
	Total.....	31	3,085	1	30	32	3,115
" over one year old..	Great Britain...	249	42,230	2	275	251	42,505
	Bermuda........	66	7,350	....	.. ....	66	7,350
	B. Africa.	108	10,800	....	....	108	10,800
	B. W. Indies...	34	4,110	....	....	34	4,110
	Newfoundland..	184	16,233	....	....	184	16,233
	St. Pierre......	5	640	..... .	......	5	640
	United States...	2,117	440,172	1,203	372,658	3,320	812,830
	Total......	2,763	521,535	1,205	372,933	3,968	894,468

No. 3.—General Statement of Exports—*Continued.*

Articles Exported.	Countries.	Goods, the Produce of Canada.		Goods, not the Produce of Canada.		Total Exports.	
		Quantity.	Value.	Qt'y.	Value.	Quantity.	Value.
Animals, etc.—*Con.*		No.	$	No.	$	No.	$
Cattle, one year old or less........	Great Britain...	90	1,215	....	....	90	1,215
	B. Africa......	136	4,370	....	....	136	4,370
	B. Guiana	14	1,400	....	....	14	1,400
	Newfoundland..	90	4,097	....	....	90	4,097
	St. Pierre.......	101	224	....	....	101	224
	United States...	1,943	23,511	1	150	1,944	23,661
	Total......	2,374	34,817	1	150	2,375	34,967
" over one year old.	Great Britain...	163,904	11,044,248	599	29,950	164,503	11,074,198
	Bermuda........	29	1,475	....	....	29	1,475
	B. Africa.	667	48,350	....	....	667	48,350
	B. W. Indies....	8	455	....	....	8	455
	Newfoundland..	2,532	101,783	....	....	2,532	101,783
	New Zealand....	20	1,200	....	....	20	1,200
	France........ .	2,267	164,330	....	....	2,267	164,330
	Holland........	830	58,100	....	....	830	58,100
	Japan	42	5,900	....	....	42	5,900
	Mexico.........	20	600	....	....	20	600
	St. Pierre	554	12,980	....	....	554	12,980
	United States...	2,783	182,591	38	2,622	2,821	185,213
	Total	173,656	11,622,012	637	32,572	174,293	11,654,584
Swine.....	Great Britain...	150	2,700	....	....	150	2,700
	B. Guiana	4	80	....	....	4	80
	Hong Kong.....	1	20	....	....	1	20
	Newfoundland..	53	318	....	....	53	318
	St. Pierre.... ..	133	1,269	....	....	133	1,269
	United States...	442	8,399	1	25	443	8,424
	Total.. .	783	12,786	1	25	784	12,811
Sheep, one year old or less	Great Britain...	5,063	29,800	....	....	5,063	29,800
	Bermuda	74	392	....	....	74	392
	B. W. Indies....	96	559	....	....	96	559
	Newfoundland..	433	1,404	....	....	433	1,404
	St. Pierre.......	192	485	....	....	192	485
	United States...	149,556	610,653	1	25	149,557	610,678
	Total......	155,414	643,293	1	25	155,415	643,318
" over one year old.	Great Britain...	37,717	244,053	....	....	37,717	244,053
	B. Africa.......	669	5,133	....	....	669	5,133
	Bermuda.... ...	152	902	....	....	152	902
	B. Guiana	17	102	....	....	17	102
	B. W. Indies...	546	3,201	....	....	546	3,201
	Newfoundland..	2,393	9,862	....	....	2,393	9,862
	St. Pierre.......	754	2,335	....	....	754	2,335
	United States...	46,600	263,459	76	1,640	46,676	265,099
	Total	88,848	529,047	76	1,640	88,924	530,687

No. 3.—General Statement of Exports—*Continued.*

Articles Exported.	Countries.	Goods, the Produce of Canada.		Goods, not the Produce of Canada.		Total Exports.	
		Quantity.	Value.	Q'ty.	Value.	Quantity.	Value.
ANIMALS, ETC.—*Con.*			$		$		$
Poultry	Great Britain		118				118
	Bermuda		456				456
	B. Africa		25				25
	B. W. Indies		167				167
	B. Guiana		10				10
	Hong Kong		20				20
	Newfoundland		12				12
	Cuba		4				4
	Mexico		50				50
	St. Pierre		800				800
	United States		56,426		801		57,227
	Total		58,088		801		58,889
Other	Great Britain		70				70
	B. Africa		960				960
	Newfoundland		20				20
	United States		40,735		6,713		47,448
	Total		41,785		6,713		48,498
		Cwt.		Cwt.		Cwt.	
Bones	Great Britain	1,098	1,500			1,098	1,500
	Belgium	195	400			195	400
	United States	302,994	41,428			302,994	41,428
	Total	304,287	43,328			304,287	43,328
		Lbs.		Lbs.		Lbs.	
Butter	Great Britain	32,904,990	6,802,003	41,040	8,148	32,946,030	6,810,151
	Bermuda	193,901	47,045			193,901	47,045
	B. Africa	9,215	2,056			9,215	2,056
	B. W. Indies	329,618	87,085			329,618	87,085
	B. Guiana	43,958	11,654			43,958	11,654
	Newfoundland	240,910	48,283	701	130	241,611	48,413
	Cen. Am. States	6,620	1,955			6,620	1,955
	China	2,724	761			2,724	761
	Cuba	968	285			968	285
	Dan. W. Indies	21,270	4,560			21,270	4,560
	Dutch Guiana	150	30			150	30
	France	20,794	4,155			20,794	4,155
	Japan	37,399	9,373			37,399	9,373
	Mexico	6,010	1,268			6,010	1,268
	Panama	5,246	1,476			5,246	1,476
	Porto Rico	568	170			568	170
	St. Pierre	87,962	17,668			87,962	17,668
	U. S. Colombia	5,964	1,747			5,964	1,747
	United States	113,258	33,965	7,876	2,202	121,134	36,167
	Total	34,031,525	7,075,539	49,617	10,480	34,081,142	7,086,019
Cheese	Great Britain	214,877,077	24,300,908	79,992	8,188	214,957,069	24,309,096
	Australia	16,739	5,350			16,739	5,350
	Bermuda	106,407	14,033			106,407	14,033
	B. Africa	118,094	16,623			118,094	16,623
	B. E. Indies	147	20			147	20
	B. W. Indies	163,618	25,509			163,618	25,509
	B. Guiana	27,560	3,860			27,560	3,860

No. 3.—General Statement of Exports—*Continued.*

Articles Exported.	Countries.	Goods, the Produce of Canada.		Goods, not the Produce of Canada.		Total Exports.	
		Quantity.	Value.	Q'ty.	Value.	Quantity.	Value.
Animals, etc.—*Con.*		Lbs.	$	$	$	Lbs.	$
Cheese—*Con.*	Hong Kong	4,506	1,029			4,506	1,029
	Newfoundland	260,759	30,992			260,759	30,992
	New Zealand	5,644	1,795			5,644	1,795
	Belgium	2,224	287			2,224	287
	China	9,171	2,195			9,171	2,195
	Cuba	6,808	811			6,808	811
	Dan. W. Indies	15,420	2,056			15,420	2,056
	Dutch Guiana	100	13			100	13
	France	72,540	7,203			72,540	7,203
	Holland	527	97			527	97
	Japan	3,922	775			3,922	775
	Mexico	12,539	1,594			12,539	1,594
	Norway	8,641	994			8,641	994
	St. Pierre	7,585	875			7,585	875
	U.S. of Colombia	492	68			492	68
	United States	114,023	16,082	1,622	307	115,645	16,389
	Total	215,834,543	24,433,169	81,614	8,495	215,916,157	24,441,664
		Doz.		Doz.		Doz.	
Eggs	Great Britain	2,688,977	448,463			2,688,977	448,463
	Bermuda	38,197	8,643			38,197	8,643
	B. Africa	124,250	23,345			124,250	23,345
	B. W. Indies	169	36			169	36
	Newfoundland	27,393	5,545			27,393	5,545
	Cuba	158	33			158	33
	Japan	50	50			50	50
	Mexico	150	33			150	33
	St. Pierre	24,042	3,961			24,042	3,961
	United States	18,339	5,067	16,052	6,857	34,391	11,924
	Total	2,921,725	495,176	16,052	6,857	2,937,777	502,033
Furs—Dressed	Great Britain		2,078		6,378		8,456
	Belgium		125		540		665
	Germany				3,526		3,526
	United States		47,154		3,348		50,502
	Total		49,357		13,792		63,149
" undressed	Great Britain		1,058,936		1,846		1,060,782
	Australia		120				120
	Newfoundland				200		200
	France		3,652		29		3,681
	Belgium		45				45
	Germany		1,500		5,316		6,816
	United States		1,350,727		35,685		1,386,412
	Total		2,414,980		43,076		2,458,056
		Lbs.		Lbs.		Lbs.	
Grease and grease scraps	Great Britain	226,085	7,492			226,085	7,492
	Australia	7,530	114			7,530	114
	Newfoundland	32,940	1,331			32,940	1,331
	Belgium	82,114	3,733			82,114	3,733
	France	61,456	2,007			61,456	2,007
	Germany	1,163,419	76,567			1,163,419	76,567
	Holland	347,776	23,818			347,776	23,818
	United States	1,066,379	34,438	680	63	1,067,059	34,501
	Total	2,987,699	149,500	680	63	2,988,379	149,563

No. 3.—General Statement of Exports—*Continued.*

Articles Exported.	Countries.	Goods, the Produce of Canada.		Goods, not the Produce of Canada.		Total Exports.	
		Quantity.	Value.	Q'ty.	Value.	Quantity.	Value.
Animals, etc.—*Con.*			$		$		$
Glue stock	Great Britain		32				32
	B. W. Indies		6				6
	Newfoundland		15				15
	United States		6,294		35		6,329
	Total		6,347		35		6,382
Hair	Great Britain		11,034				11,034
	Germany		238				238
	United States		112,392		1,538		113,930
	Total		123,664		1,538		125,202
Hides and skins, other than fur	Great Britain		16,969				16,969
	Bermuda		900				900
	B. W. Indies		45				45
	Newfoundland		5,432				5,432
	Belgium		12,008				12,008
	France		5		125		130
	Germany		1,250				1,250
	Norway		1,017				1,017
	United States		3,420,204		5,898		3,426,102
	Total		3,457,830		6,023		3,463,853
Horns and hoofs	Great Britain		829				829
	France		50				50
	United States		13,750		100		13,850
	Total		14,629		100		14,729
		Lbs.		Lbs.		Lbs.	
Honey	Great Britain	26,987	2,424	2,090	70	29,077	2,494
	Newfoundland	730	99			730	99
	France	9	1			9	1
	United States	11,759	1,128	1,385	80	13,144	1,208
	Total	39,485	3,652	3,475	150	42,960	3,802
Lard	Great Britain	116,720	11,666			116,720	11,666
	Bermuda	80	10	100	5	180	15
	B. W. Indies			133	10	133	10
	Newfoundland	1,740	166	4,039	249	5,779	415
	St. Pierre	120	5			120	5
	United States	10,864	1,192	1,683	208	12,547	1,400
	Total	129,524	13,039	5,955	472	135,479	13,511
Meats, viz.: Bacon	Great Britain	98,173,242	11,563,619	1,365,384	147,211	99,538,626	11,710,830
	Bermuda	8,590	1,146			8,590	1,146
	B. Africa	353,208	38,545			353,208	38,545
	B. W. Indies	1,810	295			1,810	295
	Newfoundland	6,893	951			6,893	951
	Belgium	68,150	6,365			68,150	6,365
	Cuba	1,652	224			1,652	224
	France	484	96			484	96
	St. Pierre	441	55	158	19	599	74
	United States	510,589	55,411	6,538	1,069	517,127	56,480
	Total	99,125,059	11,666,707	1,372,080	148,299	100,497,139	11,815,006

No. 3.—General Statement of Exports—*Continued.*

Articles Exported.	Countries.	Goods, the Produce of Canada.		Goods, not the Produce of Canada.		Total Exports.	
		Quantity.	Value.	Q'ty.	Value.	Quantity.	Value.
ANIMALS—*Con.*		Lbs.	$	Lbs.	$	Lbs.	$
Meats—*Con.*							
Beef	Great Britain	763,169	47,839	6,400	264	769,569	48,103
	Bermuda	456	48			456	48
	B. Africa	55,360	6,643			55,360	6,643
	B. W. Indies	25,879	1,545	5,500	265	31,379	1,810
	B. Guiana	2,800	120	2,200	160	5,000	280
	Newfoundland	398,303	26,894	422,611	21,509	820,914	48,403
	Belgium	22,198	1,856			22,198	1,856
	Germany	1,557,176	109,287			1,557,176	109,287
	St. Pierre	34,643	3,145	1,004	65	35,647	3,210
	United States	27,978	3,341	37,086	2,800	65,064	6,141
	Total	2,887,962	200,718	474,801	25,063	3,362,763	225,781
Hams	Great Britain	3,683,563	408,369	5,300	605	3,688,863	408,974
	Bermuda	15,609	2,096			15,609	2,096
	B. Africa	59,362	6,503			59,362	6,503
	B. W. Indies	1,271	187			1,271	187
	Newfoundland	2,384	239			2,384	239
	Cuba	3,692	596			3,692	596
	France	737	146			737	146
	St. Pierre	611	79			611	79
	United States	15,600	1,946	6,949	1,125	22,549	3,071
	Total	3,782,829	420,161	12,249	1,730	3,795,078	421,891
Mutton	Great Britain	8,197	529			8,197	529
	Bermuda	133	14			133	14
	B. W. Indies	17,856	525			17,856	525
	Newfoundland	20,898	1,758	41,980	3,163	62,878	4,921
	St. Pierre	4,693	432			4,693	432
	United States	53,285	4,567	180	18	53,465	4,585
	Total	105,062	7,825	42,160	3,181	147,222	11,006
Pork	Great Britain	338,008	32,916			338,008	32,916
	Bermuda	3,400	472			3,400	472
	B. Africa	6,000	396			6,000	396
	B. W. Indies	138,850	4,283	700	49	139,550	4,332
	B. Guiana	4,440	223			4,440	223
	Newfoundland	186,183	8,759	229,425	15,780	415,608	24,539
	Cuba	600	68			600	68
	Denmark	8,640	432			8,640	432
	St. Pierre	31,131	2,548			31,131	2,548
	United States	58,584	7,632	28,659	1,779	87,243	9,411
	Total	775,836	57,729	258,784	17,608	1,034,620	75,337
Poultry, dressed or undressed	Great Britain		79,670				79,670
	Bermuda		561				561
	B. Africa		6,142				6,142
	B. W. Indies		125				125
	Newfoundland		8,870				8,870
	St. Pierre		308				308
	United States		18,599		386		18,985
	Total		114,275		386		114,661

No. 3.—General Statement of Exports—*Continued.*

Articles Exported.	Countries.	Goods, the Produce of Canada. Quantity.	Value.	Goods, not the Produce of Canada. Q'ty.	Value.	Total Exports. Quantity.	Value.
ANIMALS, ETC.—*Con.*			$		$		$
Poultry—*Con.* Game, dressed or undressed	B. W. Indies		2				2
	St. Pierre		9				9
	United States		3,785				3,785
	Total		3,796				3,796
		Lbs.		Lbs.		Lbs.	
Tongues	Great Britain	14,787	1,432			14,787	1,432
	Germany	16,108	1,689			16,108	1,689
	St. Pierre	48	5			48	5
	Total	30,943	3,126			30,943	3,126
Canned	Great Britain	13,503,781	1,349,880	5,595	1,295	13,509,376	1,351,175
	Bermuda	720	90			720	90
	B. Africa	136,637	14,352			136,637	14,352
	B. W. Indies	2,785	286			2,785	286
	B. Guiana	144	15			144	15
	Newfoundland	3,035	478	215	23	3,250	501
	Corea	600	58			600	58
	France	200	20			200	20
	Japan	240	34			240	34
	United States	17,681	2,380	3,045	350	20,726	2,730
	Total	13,665,823	1,367,593	8,855	1,668	13,674,678	1,369,261
All other, N.E.S.	Great Britain	1,341,126	131,190	2,688	96	1,343,814	131,286
	Bermuda	1,181	147			1,181	147
	B. Africa	50,960	6,621			50,960	6,621
	B. W. Indies	7,796	574			7,796	574
	Newfoundland	16,196	1,553			16,196	1,553
	Belgium	33,356	2,970			33,356	2,970
	Germany	78,496	4,762			78,496	4,762
	St. Pierre	580	49	53	6	633	55
	United States	193,603	26,517	4,445	561	198,048	27,078
	Total	1,723,294	174,383	7,186	663	1,730,480	175,046
Milk and cream, condensed	Great Britain	142,802	9,140	960	140	143,762	9,280
	Bermuda	2,885	245			2,885	245
	B. Africa	1,309,250	99,086			1,309,250	99,086
	B. W. Indies	66,794	4,363			66,794	4,363
	B. Guiana	9,600	475			9,600	475
	Hong Kong	15,600	1,200			15,600	1,200
	Newfoundland	95,807	6,482			95,807	6,482
	Chili	550	45			550	45
	China	40,000	3,251			40,000	3,251
	Cuba	40,000	2,400			40,000	2,400
	Mexico	183	34			183	34
	St. Pierre	4,520	326			4,520	326
	United States	17,000	1,483	5,838	563	22,838	2,046
	Total	1,744,991	128,530	6,798	703	1,751,789	129,233
		Galls.		Galls.		Galls.	
Oil—Lard	United States	50	23			50	23

No. 3.—General Statement of Exports—*Continued.*

Articles Exported.	Countries.	Goods, the Produce of Canada.		Goods, not the Produce of Canada.		Total Exports.	
		Quantity.	Value.	Q'ty.	Value.	Quantity.	Value.
Animals, etc.—*Con.*		No.	$	No.		No.	$
Sheep pelts	United States	58,054	54,452			58,054	54,452
Tails	Great Britain		27				27
	United States		1,828				1,828
	Total		1,855				1,855
		Lbs.		Lbs.		Lbs.	
Tallow	Great Britain	453,287	20,009			453,287	20,009
	B. W. Indies	45	4			45	4
	Newfoundland	16,265	811			16,265	811
	Belgium	43,958	1,890			43,958	1,890
	France	200	7			200	7
	St. Pierre	4,820	291			4,820	291
	United States	1,217	73			1,217	73
	Total	519,792	23,085			519,792	23,085
Wool	Great Britain	206,039	37,616	67,051	12,794	273,090	50,410
	Newfoundland	781	215			781	215
	United States	1,217,975	314,805	13,538	3,249	1,231,513	318,054
	Total	1,424,795	352,636	80,589	16,043	1,505,384	368,679
Other articles	Great Britain		47,413		516		47,929
	Australia		9,800				9,800
	Bermuda		44		21		65
	B. Africa		22				22
	Newfoundland		1,043				1,043
	Belgium		55				55
	France		7				7
	Germany		24,329				24,329
	United States		49,695		8,364		58,059
	Total		132,408		8,901		141,309
Agricultural Products							
Balsam	Great Britain		1,602				1,602
	Germany		138				138
	United States		8,723				8,723
	Total		10,463				10,463
		Galls.		Galls.		Galls.	
Cider	Great Britain	59,601	9,204			59,601	9,204
	Newfoundland	50	6			50	6
	China	12	18			12	18
	Mexico	180	12			180	12
	United States	667	100	201	60	868	160
	Total	60,510	9,340	201	60	60,711	9,400

No. 3.—General Statement of Exports—*Continued.*

Articles Exported.	Countries.	Goods, the Produce of Canada.		Goods, not the Produce of Canada.		Total Exports.	
		Quantity.	Value.	Q'ty.	Value.	Quantity.	Value.
Agricultural Products—*Con.*		Cwt.	$	Cwt.	$	Cwt.	$
Flax	United States	68,847	244,629			68,847	244,629
		Lbs.		Lbs.		Lbs.	
Fruits, viz.: Apples, dried	Great Britain	221,994	12,254			221,994	12,254
	Bermuda	201	17			201	17
	Newfoundland	17,900	954	200	14	18,100	968
	Germany	1,327,390	75,504			1,327,390	75,504
	Holland	2,013,353	119,701			2,013,353	119,701
	Mexico	4,731	335			4,731	335
	Sweden	5,000	200			5,000	200
	United States	60,691	3,883			60,691	3,883
	Total	3,651,260	212,848	200	14	3,651,460	212,862
		Brls.		Brls.		Brls.	
Apples, green or ripe	Great Britain	1,029,418	3,475,825			1,029,418	3,475,825
	Australia	156	1,176			156	1,176
	Bermuda	1,066	2,987			1,066	2,987
	British Africa	6,769	22,534			6,769	22,534
	British Guiana	34	102			34	102
	B. W. Indies	118	368			118	368
	Fiji	26	214			26	214
	Hong Kong	7	35			7	35
	Newfoundland	11,095	32,690			11,095	32,690
	New Zealand	73	455			73	455
	Belgium	110	289			110	289
	China	23	120			23	120
	Cuba	767	3,114			767	3,114
	Denmark	772	2,241			772	2,241
	France	55,862	209,131			55,862	209,131
	Germany	63,221	197,001			63,221	197,001
	Holland	3,473	10,359			3,473	10,359
	Mexico	204	774			204	774
	St. Pierre	169	476			169	476
	Norway	150	600			150	600
	United States	44,051	122,991	41	288	44,092	123,279
	Total	1,217,564	4,083,482	41	288	1,217,605	4,083,770
Berries of all kinds	Great Britain		4				4
	Bermuda		24				24
	Newfoundland		15				15
	Cuba		123				123
	St. Pierre		5				5
	United States		100,490		2,207		102,697
	Total		100,661		2,207		102,868
Canned or preserved	Great Britain		248,619		50		248,669
	Australia		8				8
	Bermuda		1,707				1,707
	B. Africa		503				503
	B. E. Indies		40				40
	B. W. Indies		230		24		254
	B. Guiana		27				27
	Fiji		185				185
	Hong Kong		47		30		77
	Newfoundland		5,344		2,576		7,920

No. 3.—General Statement of Exports—*Continued.*

Articles Exported.	Countries.	Goods, the Produce of Canada.		Goods, not the Produce of Canada.		Total Exports.	
		Quantity.	Value.	Q'ty.	Value.	Quantity.	Value.
Agricultural Products—*Con.*			$		$		$
Fruits—*Con.*							
Canned or preserved....	China	....	228	....	....	....	228
	Cuba	....	5	....	....	....	5
	Egypt	....	8	....	....	....	8
	France	....	713	....	....	....	713
	Germany	....	2,718	....	....	....	2,718
	Holland	....	700	....	....	....	700
	Japan	....	13	....	....	....	13
	Mexico	....	869	....	....	....	869
	St. Pierre	....	2	....	5	....	7
	U. S. Colombia	....	16	....	....	....	16
	United States	....	12,591	....	1,906	....	14,497
	Total	....	274,573	....	4,591	....	279,164
All other, N.E.S.	Great Britain	....	18,788	....	1,964	....	20,752
	Australia	....	13	....	....	....	13
	Bermuda	....	7	....	....	....	7
	B. Africa	....	1,952	....	800	....	2,752
	B. Guiana	....	5	....	....	....	5
	B. W. Indies	....	136	....	29	....	165
	Fiji	....	32	....	....	....	32
	Hong Kong	....	27	....	....	....	27
	Newfoundland	....	3,193	....	6,170	....	9,363
	Belgium	....	1,300	....	....	....	1,300
	Cuba	....	26	....	....	....	26
	France	....	3,578	....	....	....	3,578
	Germany	....	43,333	....	2,400	....	45,733
	Holland	....	49,146	....	....	....	49,146
	St. Pierre	....	672	....	333	....	1,005
	United States	....	22,116	....	47,625	....	69,741
	Total	....	144,324	....	59,321	....	203,645
Grain and products, viz.—		Bush.		Bush.		Bush.	
Barley.	Great Britain	790,804	426,917	1,961,530	931,119	2,752,334	1,358,036
	Bermuda	48	47	....	....	48	47
	B. W. Indies	58	55	....	....	58	55
	Newfoundland	2	2	....	....	2	2
	Belgium	33,890	17,239	41,114	18,829	75,004	36,068
	Germany	5,581	2,285	3,100	1,426	8,681	3,711
	Holland	2,400	1,008	....	....	2,400	1,008
	United States	47,245	21,645	117	70	47,362	21,715
	Total	880,028	469,198	2,005,861	951,444	2,885,889	1,420,642
Beans..............	Great Britain	18,241	28,763	....	....	18,241	28,763
	Bermuda	454	843	....	....	454	843
	B. Africa	50	100	....	....	50	100
	B. Guiana	38	67	....	....	38	67
	B. W. Indies	438	791	4	9	442	800
	Newfoundland	788	1,205	489	624	1,277	1,829
	Chili	1,161	2,326	....	....	1,161	2,326
	Cuba	5,351	11,494	....	....	5,351	11,494
	Dan. W. Indies	8	12	....	....	8	12
	France	49,798	72,321	....	....	49,798	72,321
	Fr. W. Indies	733	1,027	....	....	733	1.027
	Panama	4	7	....	....	4	7
	United States	11,599	20,952	176	131	11,775	21,083
	Total	88,663	139,908	669	764	89,332	140,672

No. 3.—General Statement of Exports—*Continued.*

Articles Exported.	Countries.	Goods, the Produce of Canada.		Goods, not the Produce of Canada.		Total Exports.	
		Quantity.	Value.	Q'ty.	Value.	Quantity.	Value.
Agricultural Products—*Con.*		Bush.	$	Bush.	$	Bush.	$
Grain—*Con.*							
Buckwheat	Great Britain	349,178	198,131	916	440	350,094	198,571
	B. Africa	6,901	3,180			6,901	3,180
	Belgium	77,539	43,998			77,539	43,998
	Germany	13,520	7,144			13,520	7,144
	Holland	21,606	12,827			21,606	12,827
	United States	18,705	10,311			18,705	10,311
	Total	487,449	275,591	916	440	488,365	276,031
Indian corn	Great Britain	43,253	23,554	4,624,404	2,503,475	4,667,657	2,527,029
	Bermuda	1,200	450			1,200	450
	B. W. Indies	4	3			4	3
	Newfoundland	563	236			563	236
	Belgium			94,234	47,117	94,234	47,117
	Germany			101,191	60,715	101,191	60,715
	Mexico	10	5			10	5
	St. Pierre	200	125			200	125
	United States	27	30	1,000	500	1,027	530
	Total	45,257	24,403	4,820,829	2,611,807	4,866,086	2,636,210
Oats	Great Britain	1,885,166	762,503	1,927,740	662,602	3,812,906	1,425,105
	Bermuda	63,609	27,114	1,379	625	64,988	27,739
	B. Africa	512	315			512	315
	B. Guiana	38,327	15,672			38,327	15,672
	B. W. Indies	189,037	73,266	3,265	1,323	192,302	74,589
	Newfoundland	227,242	96,527			227,242	96,527
	Belgium	124,292	43,655			124,292	43,655
	Cuba	6,782	3,420			6,782	3,420
	Dan. W. Indies	48	25			48	25
	Dutch Guiana	1,143	500			1,143	500
	France	1,500	435			1,500	435
	Germany	6,555	2,066			6,555	2,066
	Holland	1,514	424			1,514	424
	Mexico	142	58			142	58
	Porto Rico	196	94			196	94
	St Pierre	1,636	660			1,636	660
	United States	152,602	56,613	434,244	110,427	586,846	167,040
	Total	2,700,303	1,083,347	2,366,628	774,977	5,066,931	1,858,324
Pease, whole	Great Britain	352,080	324,037			352,080	324,037
	Bermuda	18	20			18	20
	B. Africa	3,919	3,108			3,919	3,108
	B. Guiana	6,031	5,850			6,031	5,850
	B. W. Indies	24,018	23,836			24,018	23,836
	Newfoundland	25,157	26,641			25,157	26,641
	Dan. W. Indies	56	70			56	70
	France	38,768	102,125			38,768	102,125
	Holland	1,000	1,100			1,000	1,100
	Mexico	66	75			66	75
	Panama	8	10			8	10
	St. Pierre	16	28			16	28
	United States	95,451	122,026	5	3	95,456	122,029
	Total	546,588	608,926	5	3	546,593	608,929

No. 3.—GENERAL STATEMENT OF EXPORTS—*Continued.*

ARTICLES EXPORTED.	COUNTRIES.	GOODS, THE PRODUCE OF CANADA.		GOODS, NOT THE PRODUCE OF CANADA.		TOTAL EXPORTS.	
		Quantity.	Value.	Q'ty.	Value.	Quantity.	Value.
AGRICULTURAL PRODUCTS—*Con.*		Bush.	$	Bush.	$	Bush.	$
Grain—*Con.*							
Pease, split	Great Britain	10,214	8,821			10,214	8,821
	Bermuda	4,871	5,100			4,871	5,100
	B. Africa	1,795	2,279			1,795	2,279
	B. Guiana	38,785	45,367			38,785	45,367
	B. W. Indies	46,819	58,057			46,819	58,057
	Newfoundland	1,304	1,649			1,304	1,649
	Cuba	127	170			127	170
	Dan. W. Indies	122	158			122	158
	Germany	933	793			933	793
	Holland	660	560			660	560
	Mexico	20	30			20	30
	Panama	350	480			350	480
	U. S. Colombia	23	34			23	34
	United States	22,269	24,894	1	3	22,270	24,897
	Total	128,292	148,392	1	3	128,293	148,395
Rye	Great Britain			128,789	81,865	128,789	81,865
	Newfoundland			12	9	12	9
	Belgium			17,431	10,807	17,431	10,807
	United States	4	2			4	2
	Total	4	2	146,232	92,681	146,236	92,683
Wheat	Great Britain	36,027,692	30,234,611	459,249	389,213	36,486,941	30,623,824
	Australia	200	105			200	105
	B. Africa	69,780	57,419			69,780	57,419
	Belgium	352,407	291,892	20,000	17,000	372,407	308,892
	China	6	6			6	6
	France	68,836	60,049			68,836	60,049
	Germany	17,182	9,206	108,476	94,478	125,658	103,684
	Holland	1,050	800			1,050	800
	Mexico	30,261	22,695			30,261	22,695
	United States	3,831,988	2,981,608			3,831,988	2,981,608
	Total	40,399,402	33,658,391	587,725	500,691	40,987,127	34,159,082
Other grain	B. W. Indies	1,063	1,306			1,063	1,306
	Newfoundland	180	108			180	108
	United States	737	825			737	825
	Total	1,980	2,239			1,980	2,239
		Cwt.		Cwt.		Cwt.	
Bran	Great Britain	184,565	155,298			184,565	155,298
	Bermuda	8,981	8,568			8,981	8,568
	B. Africa	560	558			560	558
	B. Guiana	410	350			410	350
	B. W. Indies	11,134	9,678			11,134	9,678
	Newfoundland	12,235	11,904			12,235	11,904
	Belgium	55,726	28,445			55,726	28,445
	Denmark	18,190	5,534			18,190	5,534
	France	1,780	1,674			1,780	1,674
	Germany	110,472	47,864			110,472	47,864
	Holland	42,188	23,752			42,188	23,752
	Norway	11,650	4,737			11,650	4,737
	Porto Rico	55	58			55	58
	St. Pierre	109	182			109	182
	United States	220,166	114,311			220,166	114,311
	Total	678,221	412,913			678,221	412,913

No. 3.—General Statement of Exports—*Continued.*

Articles Exported.	Countries.	Goods, the Produce of Canada.		Goods, not the Produce of Canada.		Total Exports.	
		Quantity.	Value.	Qt'y.	Value.	Quantity.	Value.
AGRICULTURAL PRODUCTS—*Con.*		Brls.	$	Brls.	$	Brls.	$
Grain, &c.—*Con.*							
Flour of wheat	Great Britain	943,777	3,656,938	....	....	943,777	3,656,938
	Australia	6,281	23,943	....	....	6,281	23,943
	Bermuda	6,241	26,556	....	....	6,241	26,556
	B. Africa	119,766	553,899	....	....	119,766	553,899
	B. E. Indies	1,226	4,495	....	....	1,226	4,495
	B. Guiana	14,083	54,333	....	....	14,083	54,333
	B. W. Indies	76,112	302,861	....	....	76,112	302,861
	Fiji	385	847	....	....	385	847
	Hong Kong	725	1,944	....	....	725	1,944
	Malta	5,146	17,423	....	....	5,146	17,423
	Newfoundland	240,040	1,109,480	....	....	240,040	1,109,480
	B. Poss., other	1,750	7,449	....	....	1,750	7,449
	Belgium	225	770	....	....	225	770
	China	1,768	6,280	....	....	1,768	6,280
	Brazil	500	2,000	....	....	500	2,000
	Corea	2	15	....	....	2	15
	Cuba	2,593	12,220	....	....	2,593	12,220
	Denmark	8,659	30,924	....	....	8,659	30,924
	France	1,406	6,348	....	....	1,406	6,348
	French Africa	365	1,913	....	....	365	1,913
	Fr. W. Indies	4,261	16,392	....	....	4,261	16,392
	Germany	449	1,726	....	....	449	1,726
	Hayti	5	25	....	....	5	25
	Italy	32	129	....	....	32	129
	Holland	22,958	70,855	....	....	22,958	70,855
	Japan	20,232	64,131	....	....	20,232	64,131
	Mexico	82	405	....	....	82	405
	Norway	16,495	54,433	....	....	16,495	54,433
	Portug'se Africa	660	2,664	....	....	660	2,664
	Russia	4,462	14,878	....	....	4,462	14,878
	St. Pierre	4,656	21,176	....	....	4,656	21,176
	Sweden	888	3,808	....	....	888	3,808
	Turkey	12	77	....	....	12	77
	United States	25,772	108,488	130	929	25,902	109,417
	Total	1,532,014	6,179,825	130	929	1,532,144	6,180,754
Flour of rye	United States	3	35	....	....	3	35
Indian meal	Great Britain	797	2,342	....	....	797	2,342
	B. W. Indies	267	1,281	....	....	267	1,281
	Newfoundland	773	2,174	....	....	773	2,174
	St. Pierre	131	330	....	....	131	330
	United States	204	532	8	55	212	587
	Total	2,172	6,659	8	55	2,180	6,714
Oatmeal	Great Britain	120,744	492,084	....	....	120,744	492,084
	B. Africa	65	304	....	....	65	304
	B. Guiana	275	1,070	....	....	275	1,070
	Newfoundland	939	4,126	....	....	939	4,126
	Denmark	2,820	11,465	....	....	2,820	11,465
	Germany	213	1,128	....	....	213	1,128
	Holland	2,916	11,476	....	....	2,916	11,476
	Norway	3,616	15,292	....	....	3,616	15,292
	Russia	440	1,858	....	....	440	1,858
	United States	916	3,478	....	....	916	3,478
	Total	132,944	542,281	....	....	132,944	542,281

No. 3.—General Statement of Exports—*Continued.*

Articles Exported.	Countries.	Goods, the Produce of Canada.		Goods, not the Produce of Canada.		Total Exports.	
		Quantity.	Value.	Q'ty.	Value.	Quantity.	Value.
Agricultural Products—*Con.*		Brls.	$	Brls.	$	Brls.	$
Grain, &c.—*Con.*							
Meal, all other	Great Britain	8,229	22,089			8,229	22,089
	Bermuda	102	410			102	410
	B. Africa	227	789			227	789
	Newfoundland	1,379	5,627	60	87	1,439	5,714
	Holland	749	1,193			749	1,193
	Sweden	275	560			275	560
	United States	398	1,715			398	1,715
	Total	11,359	32,383	60	87	11,419	32,470
		Tons.		Tons.		Tons.	
Hay	Great Britain	124,947	952,728	29	170	124,976	952,898
	Bermuda	1,127	12,404			1,127	12,404
	B. Africa	549	5,816			549	5,816
	B. Guiana	118	1,278			118	1,278
	B. W. Indies	997	10,524			997	10,524
	Hong Kong	5	100			5	100
	Newfoundland	3,766	37,206			3,766	37,206
	Cuba	3,956	31,548			3,956	31,548
	Dutch Guiana	9	90			9	90
	France	339	2,911			339	2,911
	Holland	175	1,666			175	1,666
	Mexico	1,456	15,553			1,456	15,553
	Panama	17	200			17	200
	Porto Rico	40	577			40	577
	Russia	155	1,714			155	1,714
	St. Pierre	517	6,077			517	6,077
	United States	68,541	449,549	42	1,608	68,583	451,157
	Total	206,714	1,529,941	71	1,778	206,785	1,531,719
		Cwt.		Cwt.		Cwt.	
Hemp	United States	40	555	9	281	49	836
		Lbs.		Lbs.		Lbs.	
Hops	Great Britain	66,423	12,306			66,423	12,306
	Australia	2,890	495			2,890	495
	New Zealand	2,286	460			2,286	460
	Newfoundland	42	10	900	103	942	113
	Total	71,641	13,271	900	103	72,541	13,374
		Bush.		Bush.		Bush.	
Malt	B. W. Indies	72	87			72	87
	Newfoundland	8,533	6,874			8,533	6,874
	Total	8,605	6,961			8,605	6,961
		Lbs.		Lbs.		Lbs.	
Maple sugar	Great Britain	12,634	1,379			12,634	1,379
	B. E. Indies	50	5			50	5
	New Zealand	1,033	114			1,033	114
	Newfoundland	400	43			400	43
	Belgium	83	9			83	9
	France	673	68			673	68
	Mexico	5,243	468			5,243	468
	United States	1,854,535	127,091	1,128	82	1,855,663	127,173
	Total	1,874,651	129,177	1,128	82	1,875,779	129,259

No. 3.—GENERAL STATEMENT OF EXPORTS—*Continued.*

Articles Exported.	Countries.	Goods, the Produce of Canada. Quantity.	Goods, the Produce of Canada. Value.	Goods, not the Produce of Canada. Q'ty.	Goods, not the Produce of Canada. Value.	Total Exports. Quantity.	Total Exports. Value.
AGRICULTURAL PRODUCTS—*Con.*		Galls.	$	Galls.	$	Galls.	$
Maple syrup	Great Britain	1,244	1,138			1,244	1,138
	B. Africa	184	154			184	154
	B. W. Indies	6	3			6	3
	Newfoundland	139	121			139	121
	France	123	82			123	82
	Mexico	54	39			54	39
	United States	82,700	7,591	664	87	83,364	7,678
	Total	84,450	9,128	664	87	85,114	9,215
		Lbs.		Lbs.		Lbs.	
Nuts	Great Britain			14,750	236	14,750	236
	B. W. Indies			35,463	764	35,463	764
	Bermuda			214	15	214	15
	Newfoundland	60	8	480	50	540	58
	Cuba			250	24	250	24
	St. Pierre			125	13	125	13
	United States	2,135	268	31,918	2,688	34,053	2,956
	Total	2,195	276	83,200	3,790	85,395	4,066
		Bush.		Bush.		Bush.	
Seeds— Clover	Great Britain	42,763	312,217			42,763	312,217
	Newfoundland	16	147			16	147
	New Zealand	7,532	33,342			7,532	33,342
	Argentina	42	377			42	377
	Denmark	4,515	32,177			4,515	32,177
	France	986	6,900			986	6,900
	Germany	40,152	276,998			40,152	276,998
	Holland	660	4,177			660	4,177
	Norway	462	3,300			462	3,300
	Turkey	1	6			1	6
	United States	114,740	727,164			114,740	727,164
	Total	211,869	1,396,805			211,869	1,396,805
Flax	Great Britain			448,937	494,698	448,937	494,698
	Belgium			219,283	274,104	219,283	274,104
	Holland			159,626	183,569	159,626	183,569
	United States	2,824	3,328			2,824	3,328
	Total	2,824	3,328	827,846	952,371	830,670	955,699
Grass	Great Britain	2,979	3,260			2,979	3,260
	Newfoundland	29	78			29	78
	New Zealand	30	67			30	67
	Argentina	43	32			43	32
	Denmark	100	258			100	258
	Germany	2,930	4,779			2,930	4,779
	Holland	240	140			240	140
	St. Pierre	2	6			2	6
	United States	37,088	47,245			37,088	47,245
	Total	43,441	55,865			43,441	55,865

No. 3.—General Statement of Exports—*Continued.*

Articles Exported.	Countries.	Goods, the Produce of Canada.		Goods, not the Produce of Canada.		Total Exports.	
		Quantity.	Value.	Q'ty.	Value.	Quantity.	Value.
AGRICULTURAL PRODUCTS—*Con.*			$		$		$
Seeds—*Con.*							
All other	Great Britain		8,915				8,915
	Australia		207				207
	Bermuda		85				85
	B. Africa		71				71
	B. W. Indies				180		180
	Newfoundland		150		4		154
	Argentina		91				91
	Germany		15				15
	Italy		55				55
	St. Pierre		3				3
	United States		12,879		2,810		15,689
	Total		22,471		2,994		25,465
		Tons.		Tons.		Tons.	
Straw	Great Britain	294	2,122			294	2,122
	Bermuda	27	205			27	205
	B. Africa	4	32			4	32
	B. W. Indies	17	152			17	152
	Newfoundland	48	342			48	342
	United States	3,832	14,276			3,832	14,276
	Total	4,222	17,129			4,222	17,129
		Lbs.		Lbs.		Lbs.	
Tobacco, leaf	Great Britain			215	16	215	16
	Belgium	52,819	10,369	4,500	650	57,319	11,019
	France	28	7			28	7
	Germany			5,391	809	5,391	809
	Holland			1,324	470	1,324	470
	United States	24,846	8,784	384,014	154,221	408,860	163,005
	Total	77,693	19,160	395,444	156,166	473,137	175,326
Trees, shrubs and plants	Great Britain		110				110
	Newfoundland		378				378
	China		45				45
	St. Pierre		92				92
	United States		9,318		438		9,756
	Total		9,943		438		10,381
Vegetables, canned or preserved	Great Britain		9,295				9,295
	Bermuda		3,418				3,418
	B. Africa		5,150				5,150
	B. W. Indies		175		88		263
	Newfoundland		532		10		542
	New Zealand		60				60
	France		8,160				8,160
	Mexico		1,385				1,385
	St. Pierre		119				119
	United States		5,017		16,301		21,318
	Total		33,311		16,399		49,710

No. 3.—General Statement of Exports—*Continued.*

Articles Exported.	Countries.	Goods, the Produce of Canada.		Goods, not the Produce of Canada.		Total Exports.	
		Quantity.	Value.	Q'ty.	Value.	Quantity.	Value.
Agricultural Products—*Con.*		Bush.	$	Bush.	$	Bush.	$
Potatoes	Great Britain	9	5			9	5
	Australia	1,756	1,455			1,756	1,455
	Bermuda	46,142	26,175			46,142	26,175
	B. Africa	51	20			51	20
	B. Guiana	64,825	34,978			64,825	34,978
	B. W. Indies	76,498	47,585			76,498	47,585
	Fiji	3,138	2,845	55	23	3,193	2,868
	Hong Kong	22	10			22	10
	Newfoundland	74,998	22,517			74,998	22,517
	Cuba	482,825	375,636	4,068	1,504	486,893	377,140
	Dan. W. Indies	5	4			5	4
	Mexico	9,136	7,753			9,136	7,753
	Panama	1,867	1,040			1,867	1,040
	Porto Rico	2,837	1,946			2,837	1,946
	St. Pierre	21,821	5,572	4	2	21,825	5,574
	United States	473,239	128,363	3,600	3,527	476,839	131,890
	Total	1,259,169	655,904	7,727	5,056	1,266,896	660,960
Turnips	Bermuda	1,086	488			1,086	488
	B. Guiana	158	51			158	51
	B. W. Indies	41	18			41	18
	Newfoundland	22,087	4,203			22,087	4,203
	St. Pierre	2,632	454			2,632	454
	United States	1,112,296	132,313			1,112,296	132,313
	Total	1,138,300	137,527			1,138,300	137,527
All other vegetables	Great Britain		600				600
	Australia		528				528
	Bermuda		1,681		91		1,772
	B. Africa		142				142
	B. Guiana		11				11
	B. W. Indies		846		150		996
	Fiji		364		13		377
	Newfoundland		4,597		45		4,642
	Cuba		2,109				2,109
	Mexico		88				88
	Porto Rico		59				59
	St. Pierre		907		104		1,011
	United States		66,482		3,430		69,912
	Total		78,414		3,833		82,247
Cereal foods, all kinds, N.E.S.	Great Britain		860,363				860,363
	Australia		25,344				25,344
	Bermuda		1,064				1,064
	B. Africa		142,334				142,334
	B. W. Indies		122				122
	Fiji		7				7
	Newfoundland		4,638		168		4,806
	New Zealand		1,224				1,224
	Argentina		1,080				1,080
	Belgium		11,625				11,625
	Denmark		15,234				15,234
	France		1,070				1,070
	Germany		3,675				3,675
	Holland		42,069		2,130		44,199

No. 3.—General Statement of Exports—*Continued.*

Articles Exported.	Countries.	Goods, the Produce of Canada.		Goods, not the Produce of Canada.		Total Exports.	
		Quantity.	Value.	Q'ty.	Value.	Quantity.	Value.
AGRICULTURAL PRODUCTS—*Con.*			$		$		$
Cereal foods—*Con.*	Japan		8				8
	Mexico		21				21
	Norway		49,829				49,829
	Russia		16,654				16,654
	Spain		135				135
	St. Pierre		10				10
	Sweden		270				270
	United States		8,407		553		8,960
	Total		1,185,183		2,851		1,188,034
Other articles	Great Britain		38,226				38,226
	Bermuda		62				62
	Hong Kong		1,325				1,325
	Newfoundland		331		2,800		3,131
	Brazil		500				500
	China		362				362
	Cuba		24				24
	France		32		1		33
	Germany		742				742
	Holland		992				992
	Japan		1,608				1,608
	Mexico		625				625
	United States		48,346		4,006		52,352
	Total		93,175		6,807		99,982
MANUFACTURES.							
		Lbs.		Lbs.		Lbs.	
Acid, sulphuric	United States	59,393	770			59,393	770
Agricultural implements	Great Britain		236,955				236,955
	Australia		523,030		484		523,514
	Bermuda		10				10
	B. Africa		94,042				94,042
	B. Poss., other		264				264
	B. W. Indies		330				330
	Hong Kong		18				18
	Newfoundland		1,057				1,057
	New Zealand		143,304				143,304
	Argentina		256,006				256,006
	Belgium		9,652				9,652
	Brazil		121				121
	Cent. Am. States		133				133
	Chili		30,457				30,457
	Cuba		217				217
	Denmark		8,398				8,398
	France		293,536				293,536
	Fr. Africa		1,084				1,084
	Germany		443,703				443,703
	Holland		100,102				100,102
	Italy		23,004				23,004
	Mexico		40				40
	Norway		600				600
	Peru		78				78
	Roumania		41,916				41,916
	Russia		180,175				180,175
	Spain		21,695				21,695
	Sweden		16,870				16,870
	Turkey		1,383				1,383

No. 3.—General Statement of Exports—*Continued.*

Articles Exported.	Countries.	Goods, the Produce of Canada.		Goods, not the Produce of Canada.		Total Exports.	
		Quantity.	Value.	Q'ty.	Value	Quantity.	Value.
MANUFACTURES—*Con.*			$		$		$
Agricultural implements—*Con.*	Uruguay		2,397				2,397
	United States		67,024		1,019		68,043
	Total		2,497,601		1,503		2,499,104
Aluminium, in bars, ingots, etc.		Lbs.		Lbs.		Lbs.	
	Great Britain	604,555	120,910			604,555	120,910
	Belgium	1,750,969	350,240	3,875	765	1,754,844	351,005
	Holland	220,438	44,087			220,438	44,087
	United States	512,160	103,262			512,160	103,262
	Total	3,088,122	618,499	3,875	765	3,091,997	619,264
Aluminium manufactures, in other forms	Great Britain		8				8
	Australia		507				507
	B. Africa		12				12
	New Zealand		185				185
	Mexico		6				6
	United States		544		650		1,194
	Total		1,262		650		1,912
Books, pamphlets, maps, etc.	Great Britain		95,658		3,771		99,429
	Australia		2,608		91		2,699
	Bermuda		2,427				2,427
	B. Africa		3,322				3,322
	B. E. Indies		931		98		1,029
	B. Guiana		250				250
	B. W. Indies		7,741		428		8,169
	B. Honduras		24				24
	Fiji		79				79
	Hong Kong		45				45
	Newfoundland		12,740		2,558		15,298
	New Zealand		1,795				1,795
	Argentina		233				233
	Belgium		7,173				7,173
	Cent. Am. States		29				29
	Chili		50				50
	China		866				866
	Cuba		2,620		18		2,638
	Egypt		296				296
	France		2,193		1,178		3,371
	Germany		238		18		256
	Hawaii		20				20
	Hayti		50				50
	Holland		7,744				7,744
	Italy		1,997				1,997
	Japan		1,440				1,440
	Mexico		1,134		10		1,144
	Norway		180				180
	Porto Rico		133				133
	San Domingo		30				30
	St. Pierre		468		10		478
	Spain		19				19
	Sweden		108		8		116
	Switzerland		50		50		100
	United States		98,323		63,992		162,325
	Total		253,024		72,230		325,254

No. 3.—General Statement of Exports—*Continued.*

Articles Exported.	Countries.	Goods, the Produce of Canada. Quantity.	Goods, the Produce of Canada. Value.	Goods, not the Produce of Canada. Q'ty.	Goods, not the Produce of Canada. Value.	Total Exports. Quantity.	Total Exports. Value.
MANUFACTURES—*Con.*		Cwt.	$	Cwt.	$	Cwt.	$
Biscuits and bread	Great Britain	24	179			24	179
	Bermuda	401	2,946			401	2,946
	B. Africa	20	254			20	254
	B. Guiana	170	2,015			170	2,015
	B. W. Indies	2,030	18,559			2,030	18,559
	Newfoundland	1,081	6,149			1,081	6,149
	Argentina	20	200			20	200
	Dutch Guiana	2	16			2	16
	Dutch W. Indies	5	85			5	85
	St. Pierre	76	573			76	573
	United States	6,673	8,240	26	242	6,699	8,482
	Total	10,502	39,216	26	242	10,528	39,458
		M.		M.		M.	
Bricks	Bermuda	9	61			9	61
	B. Guiana	1	5			1	5
	B. W. Indies	1	5			1	5
	Newfoundland	250	2,661	15	194	265	2,855
	Azores		3				3
	United States	445	2,806	20	378	465	3,184
	Total	706	5,541	35	572	741	6,113
Buttons	United States		5,404		162		5,566
		Lbs.		Lbs.		Lbs.	
Candles	Newfoundland	160	15			160	15
	New Zealand	136,002	9,616			136,002	9,616
	United States	510	127	3,641	469	4,151	596
	Total	136,672	9,758	3,641	469	140,313	10,227
Cartridges—gun, rifle and pistol	Great Britain		8,447		198		8,645
	Australia		7,939				7,939
	Newfoundland		446		330		776
	New Zealand		558				558
	Argentina		135				135
	Chili		302				302
	Cuba		714				714
	Mexico		5,711				5,711
	United States		83,468		653		84,121
	Total		107,720		1,181		108,901
Charcoal	Great Britain		3,000				3,000
	Cuba		3				3
	Mexico		8				8
	United States		50,829				50,829
	Total		53,840				53,840
Cement	Great Britain		1,239				1,239
	Bermuda		18				18
	B. Guiana		4				4
	B. W. Indies		23				23
	Newfoundland		2,769		24		2,793
	Panama		120				120
	United States		4,740		4,861		9,601
	Total		8,913		4,885		13,798

No. 3.—General Statement of Exports—*Continued.*

Articles Exported.	Countries.	Goods, the Produce of Canada.		Goods, not the Produce of Canada.		Total Exports.	
		Quantity.	Value.	Q'ty.	Value.	Quantity.	Value.
MANUFACTURES—*Con.*			$		$	$	$
Cinders	United States		1,023				1,023
Clothing and wearing apparel	Great Britain		16,123		4,019		20,142
	Australia		4,972				4,972
	Bermuda		749				749
	B. Africa		257				257
	B. Guiana		90				90
	B. E. Indies				30		30
	B. W. Indies		1,047				1,047
	Fiji		30				30
	Hong Kong		79				79
	Newfoundland		29,087		18		29,105
	New Zealand		62				62
	Belgium		3				3
	Chili		78				78
	China		2,735				2,735
	Cuba		121				121
	France		1,486		110		1,596
	Germany		85		300		385
	Japan		105		15		120
	Mexica		6,923		987		7,910
	St. Pierre		19				19
	Switzerland		15				15
	United States		28,700		16,419		45,119
	Total		92,766		21,898		114,664
		Tons.				Tons.	
Coke	Mexico	130	910			130	910
	United States	59,411	280,753			59,411	280,753
	Total	59,541	281,663			59,541	281,663
Cordage, ropes and twine	Great Britain		52,047		1,000		53,047
	Bermuda		3,964				3,964
	B. Africa		180				180
	B. Guiana		5,633				5,633
	B. W. Indies		30,342				30,342
	Newfoundland		3,128		4,095		7,223
	New Zealand		330				330
	Argentina		17,082				17,082
	Belgium		450				450
	China		110				110
	Germany		223				223
	Mexico		13,231				13,231
	St. Pierre		39				39
	United States		363,705		5,399		369,104
	Total		490,464		10,494		500,958
		Yds.		Yds.		Yds.	
Cotton fabrics	Great Britain	226,401	33,624	13,681	1,638	240,082	35,262
	Australia	1,239,074	99,279			1,239,074	99,279
	Bermuda	300	75			300	75
	B. Africa	1,216,543	99,401			1,216,543	99,401
	B. W. Indies	21,692	2,852			21,692	2,852
	B. Honduras	7,632	1,670			7,632	1,670
	B. Poss., other	75,000	3,562			75,000	3,562
	Newfoundland	263,528	45,511			263,528	45,511
	New Zealand	444,065	58,890			444,065	58,890

No. 3.—General Statement of Exports—*Continued.*

Articles Exported.	Countries.	Goods, the Produce of Canada.		Goods, not the Produce of Canada.		Total Exports.	
		Quantity.	Value.	Q'ty.	Value.	Quantity.	Value.
MANUFACTURES—*Con.*		Yds.	$	Yds.	$	Yds.	$
Cotton fabrics—*Con*	Argentina	56,823	12,290			56,823	12,290
	Bolivia	2,138	445			2,138	445
	Brazil	58,508	13,718			58,508	13,718
	Cent. Am. States	35,556	9,229			35,556	9,229
	Chili	68,850	16,620			68,850	16,620
	China	9,624,602	635,611	250,000	16,040	9,874,602	651,651
	Corea	1,505	300			1,505	300
	Cuba	684	43			684	43
	Denmark	5,995	1,822			5,995	1,822
	Dan. W. Indies	1,561	480			1,561	480
	Dutch Guiana	2,271	315			2,271	315
	Ecuador	23,355	2,198			23,355	2,198
	Egypt	130,310	8,109			130,310	8,109
	Fr. W. Indies	12,500	781			12,500	781
	Germany	74,104	17,472			74,104	17,472
	Hayti	6,470	1,680			6,470	1,680
	Holland	13,610	2,384			13,610	2,384
	Japan	344,481	26,889			344,481	26,889
	Mexico	155,414	35,640			155,414	35,640
	Norway	90,660	18,830			90,660	18,830
	Panama	116,230	16,632			116,230	16,632
	Peru	1,271	330			1,271	330
	Portugal	1,370	422			1,370	422
	Russia	12,877	3,130			12,877	3,130
	San Domingo	7,126	1,611			7,126	1,611
	St. Pierre	12,724	3,219			12,724	3,219
	Turkey	134,766	8,108			134,766	8,108
	Uruguay	12,778	3,747			12,778	3,747
	U. S. Colombia	17,758	3,401			17,758	3,401
	United States	561,424	39,315	28,120	3,300	589,544	42,615
	Venezuela	70,728	17,099			70,728	17,099
	Total	15,152,684	1,246,734	291,801	20,978	15,444,485	1,267,712
Cottons other	Great Britain		6,021		1,404		7,425
	Australia		632				632
	B. Africa		972				972
	Newfoundland		12,177		10		12,187
	New Zealand		301				301
	Brazil		1,289				1,289
	Denmark		1,000				1,000
	Ecuador		121				121
	Germany		529				529
	Japan		275				275
	Mexico		1,712				1,712
	Portugal		163				163
	San Domingo		219				219
	St Pierre		90				90
	Uruguay		1,045				1,045
	U. S. Colombia		159				159
	United States		4,588		9,723		14,311
	Venezuela		297				297
	Total		31,590		11,137		42,727
		Lbs.		Lbs.			Lbs.
Cotton waste	Great Britain	4,800	384			4,800	384
	Newfoundland	5,721	459	555	44	6,276	503
	Aust.-Hungary	50	1			50	1
	Belgium	197,981	3,960			197,981	3,960
	United States	936,914	48,584			936,914	48,584
	Total	1,145,46[illegible]	53,388	555	44	1,146,021	53,432

No. 3.—General Statement of Exports—*Continued.*

Articles Exported.	Countries.	Goods, the Produce of Canada.		Goods, not the Produce of Canada.		Total Exports.	
		Quantity.	Value.	Q'ty.	Value.	Quantity.	Value.
Manufactures—*Con.*			$		$		$
Drugs, chemicals and medicines, N.E.S.	Great Britain		323,309		11,700		335,009
	Australia		26,245				26,245
	Bermuda		14,531		62		14,593
	B. Africa		4,812				4,812
	B. E. Indies		308				308
	B. Guiana		10,107				10,107
	B. W. Indies		122,687		76		122,763
	B. Honduras		26				26
	Hong Kong		200		302		502
	Newfoundland		32,181		5,479		37,660
	New Zealand		48				48
	Argentina		2,466				2,466
	Belgium		38,333				38,333
	Cent. Am. States		1,022				1,022
	Chili		179				179
	China		9,004		141		9,145
	Cuba		16,669				16,669
	Dan. W. Indies		49				49
	Dutch Guiana		26				26
	Ecuador		152				152
	France		650		607		1,257
	Germany		18,244		540		18,784
	Holland		10,667				10,667
	Japan		8,719				8,719
	Mexico		7,636				7,636
	Panama		287				287
	Peru		1,224				1,224
	Porto Rico		145				145
	San Domingo		23				23
	St. Pierre		306		76		382
	Turkey				34,028		34,028
	U. S. Colombia		328				328
	United States		521,411		612,275		1,133,686
	Venezuela		18				18
	Total		1,172,012		665,286		1,837,298
Dye stuffs	Newfoundland		3,083				3,083
	United States		1,013		17,033		18,046
	Total		4,096		17,033		21,129
Electrical apparatus	Great Britain		3,400		118		3,518
	Australia		1,092		568		1,660
	Bermuda		10				10
	B. W. Indies		86				86
	Fiji		3,735				3,735
	Newfoundland		1,118		12		1,130
	Argentina		850				850
	France		50		900		950
	Japan				150		150
	Mexico		75				75
	Porto Rico		60				60
	St. Pierre		180		63		243
	United States		14,100		153,772		167,872
	Total		24,756		155,583		180,339

No. 3.—General Statement of Exports—*Continued.*

Articles Exported.	Countries.	Goods, the Produce of Canada.		Goods, not the Produce of Canada.		Total Exports.	
		Quantity.	Value.	Q'ty.	Value.	Quantity.	Value.
Manufactures—*Con.*			$		$		$
Electrotypes	Great Britain		591		6		597
	B. W. Indies		2				2
	Belgium		21				21
	United States		2,436		2,005		4,441
	Total		3,050		2,011		5,061
		Brls.		Brls.		Brls.	
Extract of hemlock bark	Great Britain	3,774	52,513			3,774	52,513
	B. Africa	100	1,160			100	1,160
	Newfoundland	176	1,926	55	660	231	2,586
	France	330	3,960			330	3,960
	United States	610	5,950			610	5,950
	Total	4,990	65,509	55	660	5,045	66,169
		Lbs.		Lbs.		Lbs.	
Explosives and fulminates, N.E.S.	Great Britain			85,000	1,700	85,000	1,700
	B. W. Indies	24	3			24	3
	Newfoundland	434,000	50,812	12,340	373	446,340	51,185
	Panama	1,750	265			1,750	265
	United States	289,956	154,776	38,191	45,156	328,147	199,932
	Total	725,730	205,856	135,531	47,229	861,261	253,085
Felt, manufactures of	Great Britain				60		60
	Newfoundland				32		32
	United States		887		2		889
	Total		887		94		981
Fertilizers	Great Britain		7,930				7,930
	Newfoundland		118				118
	New Zealand		3,057				3,057
	Cuba		20				20
	Japan		24,242				24,242
	United States		200,747		3,286		204,033
	Total		236,114		3,286		239,400
Fur, manufactures of	Great Britain		12,876		1,208		14,084
	Australia		50				50
	Newfoundland		1,564		90		1,654
	Belgium		77				77
	France		125				125
	Germany		125		410		535
	St. Pierre		6				6
	United States		9,374		7,442		16,816
	Total		24,197		9,150		33,347

No. 3.—General Statement of Exports—*Continued.*

Articles Exported.	Countries.	Goods, the Produce of Canada.		Goods, not the Produce of Canada.		Total Exports.	
		Quantity.	Value.	Q'ty.	Value.	Quantity.	Value.
			$		$		
Manufactures—*Con.*							
Glass and glassware, N.E.S	Great Britain		860		66		926
	Australia		10		7		17
	Bermuda		11				11
	B. W. Indies		152				152
	B. Guiana		10				10
	Newfoundland		5,964		255		6,219
	New Zealand		157				157
	Aust.-Hungary				2		2
	Belgium		20				20
	China		33				33
	Germany		11				11
	St. Pierre		131		4		135
	United States		3,199		3,950		7,149
	Total		10,558		4,284		14,842
Grindstones, manufactured	Newfoundland		459				459
	Cuba		1,217				1,217
	Panama		35				35
	United States		14,082		128		14,210
	Total		15,793		128		15,921
Gypsum or plaster, ground	Great Britain		12				12
	B. Africa		825				825
	Newfoundland		123				123
	United States		643				643
	Total		1,603				1,603
Hats and caps	Great Britain		1,019		549		1,568
	Bermuda		70				70
	Newfoundland		4,915				4,915
	Italy				6		6
	St. Pierre		200				200
	United States		1,201		3,138		4,339
	Total		7,405		3,693		11,098
Household effects, N.E.S.	Great Britain		97,377		4,290		101,667
	Australia		603				603
	Bermuda		685				685
	B. Africa		991				991
	B. E. Indies				800		800
	B. W. Indies		1,760				1,760
	B. Guiana		30				30
	Fiji		3,200				3,200
	Hong Kong		7				7
	Newfoundland		10,691		740		11,431
	New Zealand		473				473
	Argentina		207				207
	Belgium		125				125
	China		879				879
	Corea		28				28
	Cuba		5,952				5,952
	Egypt		3,500				3,500
	France		1,960				1,960
	Greece		500				500

No. 3.—GENERAL STATEMENT OF EXPORTS—*Continued.*

Articles Exported.	Countries.	Goods, the Produce of Canada. Quantity.	Goods, the Produce of Canada. Value.	Goods, not the Produce of Canada. Q'ty.	Goods, not the Produce of Canada. Value.	Total Exports. Quantity.	Total Exports. Value.
MANUFACTURES—*Con.*			$		$		$
Household effects—*Con.*	Germany		1,789		50		1,839
	Holland		100				100
	Hawaii		1,530				1,530
	Italy		100				100
	Japan		3,260				3,260
	Mexico		2,705				2,705
	Panama		1,450				1,450
	St. Pierre		29				29
	United States		1,506,879		108,959		1,615,838
	Total		1,646,810		114,839		1,761,649
Ice	United States		22,090				22,090
India rubber, manufactures of	Great Britain		91,540		1,821		93,361
	Australia		45,872				45,872
	Bermuda		81				81
	B. Africa		100				100
	B. W. Indies		68		22		90
	B. Guiana		342				342
	Newfoundland		20,045		55		20,100
	New Zealand		70,505				70,505
	Argentina		264				264
	Chili		2,120				2,120
	China		1,007				1,007
	Denmark		636				636
	France		495		231		726
	Germany		600				600
	Italy		10,552				10,552
	St. Pierre		30				30
	Sweden		82				82
	Turkey		16				16
	United States		22,149		13,531		35,680
	Total		266,504		15,660		282,164
		Lbs.		Lbs.		Lbs.	
India rubber, scrap and other	Great Britain	45,300	714			45,300	714
	United States	2,964,761	204,922	107,533	12,637	3,072,294	217,559
	Total	3,010,061	205,636	107,533	12,637	3,117,594	218,273
Iron and steel and manufactures of, viz.—		No.		No.		No.	
Stoves	Great Britain	27	554			27	554
	Bermuda	21	166			21	166
	B. Africa	27	225			27	225
	B. W. Indies	8	138			8	138
	B. Guiana	2	15			2	15
	Fiji	1	87			1	87
	Newfoundland	832	8,629			832	8,629
	China	6	117			6	117
	France	1	25			1	25
	St. Pierre	33	361			33	361
	United States	61	969	47	599	108	1,568
	Total	1,019	11,286	47	599	1,066	11,885

No. 3.—General Statement of Exports—*Continued.*

Articles Exported.	Countries.	Goods, the Produce of Canada.		Goods, not the Produce of Canada.		Total Exports.	
		Quantity.	Value.	Q'ty.	Value.	Quantity.	Value.
MANUFACTURES—*Con.*			$		$		$
Iron—*Con.*							
Castings, N.E.S.	Great Britain		16,940				16,940
	B. Africa		1,938				1,938
	B. W. Indies		30				30
	Newfoundland		5,691		302		5,993
	New Zealand		6,425				6,425
	China		10				10
	Japan		432				432
	Mexico		32				32
	St. Pierre		31				31
	Sweden		8				8
	United States		23,967		5,541		29,508
	Total		55,504		5,843		61,347
		Tons.		Tons.		Tons.	
Pig-iron	Great Britain	213	4,256			213	4,256
	France	140	3,750			140	3,750
	United States	344	9,852			344	9,852
	Total	697	17,858			697	17,858
Machinery, N.E.S.	Great Britain		39,415		8,753		48,168
	Australia		47,683		347		48,030
	Bermuda		60				60
	B. Africa		25,184		366		25,550
	B. E. Indies		1,452		318		1,770
	B. W. Indies		3,713				3,713
	B. Guiana		130				130
	B Poss., other		2,467				2,467
	Fiji Islands		520				520
	Newfoundland		48,670		14,049		62,719
	New Zealand		1,794				1,794
	Argentina		23,082		2,585		25,667
	Belgium		2,405		1,100		3,505
	Brazil		3,639		149		3,788
	Cent. Am. States		350				350
	Chili		11,743		144		11,887
	China		791				791
	Cuba		1,447		355		1,802
	France		200				200
	French Africa		3,016				3,016
	Germany		5,236		80		5,316
	Holland		300				300
	Italy		2,415				2,415
	Japan		5,330				5,330
	Mexico		6,742		969		7,711
	Panama		2,380				2,380
	Peru		2,851				2,851
	Portugal		4,713				4,713
	Russia		550				550
	Spain		791				791
	Sweden		3,613		60		3,673
	Switzerland		3,520		56		3,576
	Uruguay		56,214		1,752		57,966
	United States		169,273		369,422		538,695
	Total		481,689		400,505		882,194

No. 3.—General Statement of Exports—*Continued.*

Articles Exported.	Countries.	Goods, the Produce of Canada.		Goods, not the Produce of Canada.		Total Exports.	
		Quantity.	Value.	Q'ty.	Value.	Quantity.	Value
MANUFACTURES—*Con.*		No.	$	No.	$	No.	$
Iron and steel—*Con.*							
Sewing machines	Great Britain	51	956			51	956
	Australia	15	250			15	250
	Bermuda			1	25	1	25
	Newfoundland	18	525	1	50	19	575
	New Zealand	1	40			1	40
	Mexico	300	4,988			300	4,988
	Uruguay	1	16			1	16
	United States	581	15,750	284	12,625	865	28,375
	Total	967	22,525	286	12,700	1,253	35,225
Type-writers	Great Britain	2,564	87,616	1	12	2,565	87,628
	B. W. Indies	1	50			1	50
	Hong Kong	2	150			2	150
	Newfoundland	14	475			14	475
	Belgium	538	16,236			538	16,236
	Brazil	2	104			2	104
	Cent. Am. States	10	562			10	562
	China	3	142			3	142
	Denmark	37	1,110			37	1,110
	Ecuador	1	52			1	52
	France	386	11,661			386	11,661
	Germany	233	5,800			233	5,800
	Holland	252	7,560	1	48	253	7,608
	Italy	257	7,732			257	7,732
	Japan	1	60			1	60
	Sweden	48	1,440			48	1,440
	United States	62	2,883	317	16,240	379	19,123
	Total	4,411	143,633	319	16,300	4,730	159,933
		Cwt.		Cwt.		Cwt.	
Scrap-iron or steel	Great Britain	9,794	9,107	23	16	9,817	9,123
	B. W. Indies	60	75			60	75
	Holland	10	171			10	171
	United States	570,842	318,819	25,930	27,690	596,772	346,509
	Total	580,706	328,172	25,953	27,706	606,659	355,878
Hardware, N.E.S	Great Britain		37,631		470		38,101
	Australia		12,356				12,356
	Bermuda		116				116
	B. Africa		2,553				2,553
	B. W. Indies		1,218		48		1,266
	B. Guiana		210		56		266
	Fiji				50		50
	Newfoundland		56,679		4,556		61,235
	New Zealand		34,327				34,327
	Argentina		4,607		66		4,673
	Belgium		3		2		5
	Cent. Am. States		42				42
	China		608				608
	Cuba		75				75
	Denmark		267				267
	Dutch W. Indies		263				263
	Ecuador		167				167
	France				210		210
	Germany		4,337		20		4,357

No. 3.—General Statement of Exports—*Continued.*

Articles Exported.	Countries.	Goods, the Produce of Canada.		Goods, not the Produce of Canada.		Total Exports.	
		Quantity.	Value.	Q'ty.	Value.	Quantity.	Value.
MANUFACTURES—*Con.*			$		$		$
Iron and steel—*Con.* Hardware—*Con.*	Holland		3,386				3,386
	Italy		1				1
	Iceland		95				95
	Japan		1,195				1,195
	Mexico		125				125
	Norway		463				463
	St. Pierre		932		175		1,107
	Spain		290				290
	Sweden		1,662				1,662
	Uruguay		28				28
	United States		25,036		49,028		74,064
	Total		188,672		54,681		243,353
Steel and mfrs. of	Great Britain		37,546		3,959		41,505
	Australia		20,948				20,948
	Bermuda		314				314
	B. Africa		27,197		5		27,202
	B. E. Indies		191		561		752
	B. W. Indies		2,923		62		2,985
	B. Guiana		106				106
	Fiji		731				731
	Newfoundland		28,027		3,015		31,042
	New Zealand		11,619				11,619
	Argentina		3,710		1,000		4,710
	Aust.-Hungary				294		294
	Belgium		302		150		452
	Cent. Am. States		97				97
	China		3,153		40		3,193
	Cuba		2,775				2,775
	Egypt		70				70
	France		7,884				7,884
	Germany		809		350		1,159
	Holland		385				385
	Italy		25				25
	Japan		2,345		2		2,347
	Mexico		2,160				2,160
	Philippines		387				387
	Russia		15				15
	St. Pierre		759		732		1,491
	Sweden		96				96
	Switzerland				238		238
	Turkey		184				184
	Uruguay		67				67
	United States		193,142		268,358		461,500
	Total		347,967		278,766		626,733
Jeweller's sweepings	Great Britain		36,557				36,557
	Mexico		113				113
	United States		50,293		3,788		54,081
	Total		86,963		3,788		90,751

No. 3.—General Statement of Exports—*Continued.*

Articles Exported.	Countries.	Goods, the Produce of Canada.		Goods, not the Produce of Canada.		Total Exports.	
		Quantity.	Value.	Q'ty.	Value.	Quantity.	Value.
MANUFACTURES—*Con.*		Cwt.	$	Cwt.	$	Cwt.	$
Junk	Great Britain	29,423	97,677			29,423	97,677
	Australia	300	900			300	900
	Belgium	3,978	3,890			3,978	3,890
	Germany	964	571			964	571
	Holland	2,911	1,616			2,911	1,616
	Italy	478	6,214			478	6,214
	United States	558,158	372,174	4,603	17,509	562,761	389,683
	Total	596,212	483,042	4,603	17,509	600,815	500,551
Lamps and lanterns	Great Britain		2,129		98		2,227
	Australia		306				306
	B. Africa		448				448
	Newfoundland		1,345				1,345
	New Zealand		370				370
	France		1				1
	Mexico		4				4
	St. Pierre		20				20
	United States		2,156		684		2,840
	Total		6,779		782		7,561
		Lbs.		Lbs.		Lbs.	
Leather, sole	Great Britain	7,175,287	1,488,106			7,175,287	1,488,106
	B. Africa	48,255	10,525			48,255	10,525
	B. W. Indies	23,736	5,374			23,736	5,374
	B. Guiana	2,257	502			2,257	502
	Newfoundland	111,334	24,306			111,334	24,306
	New Zealand	9,990	2,995			9,990	2,995
	Belgium	142,500	40,753			142,500	40,753
	Germany	15,457	3,569			15,457	3,569
	Greece	2,400	545			2,400	545
	Holland	910	197			910	197
	Norway	5,550	1,170			5,550	1,170
	St. Pierre	46	13			46	13
	Turkey	2,770	624			2,770	624
	United States	65,285	13,952	66	82	65,351	14,034
	Total	7,605,777	1,592,631	66	82	7,605,843	1,592,713
Leather, upper	Great Britain	1,052,835	265,797			1,052,835	265,797
	B. Africa	2,023	430			2,023	430
	Newfoundland	27,935	3,910			27,935	3,910
	B. W. Indies	100	20			100	20
	Belgium	2,100	350			2,100	350
	Switzerland	1,500	450			1,500	450
	United States	8,528	1,659	3,670	500	12,198	2,159
	Total	1,095,021	272,616	3,670	500	1,098,691	273,116
Leather, N.E.S.	Great Britain	666,509	292,934	248	163	666,757	293,097
	Australia	5,245	1,045			5,245	1,045
	B Africa	23,500	5,170			23,500	5,170
	B. W. Indies	2,777	586			2,777	586
	B. Guiana	257	53			257	53
	B. Poss., other	8,940	1,833			8,940	1,833
	Newfoundland	131,857	36,451			131,857	36,451
	New Zealand	6,528	1,533			6,528	1,533

No. 3.—General Statement of Exports—*Continued.*

Articles Exported.	Countries.	Goods, the Produce of Canada.		Goods, not the Produce of Canada.		Total Exports.	
		Quantity.	Value.	Q'ty.	Value.	Quantity.	Value.
Manufactures—*Con.*		Lbs.	$	Lbs.	$	Lbs.	$
Leather, N.E.S.—*Con*....	Aust.-Hungary..	600	45	....	....	600	45
	Belgium........	2,101	2,131	....	....	2,101	2,131
	France.........	613	945	....	....	613	945
	Germany.......	5,300	452	200	131	5,500	583
	Japan..........	9,650	2,423	....	....	9,650	2,423
	Switzerland.....	15,000	2,792	....	....	15,000	2,792
	Turkey	475	335	....	....	475	335
	United States...	225,598	37,056	16,456	14,923	242,054	51,979
	Total	1,104,950	385,784	16,904	15,217	1,121,854	401,001
Boots and shoes..........	Great Britain...	....	6,656	....	....	....	6,656
	Australia.	....	1,575	....	....	....	1,575
	Bermuda........	....	1,636	....	....	....	1,636
	B. Africa.	....	2,769	....	....	....	2,769
	B. W. Indies....	....	12,922	....	....	....	12,922
	B. Guiana......	....	2,597	....	....	....	2,597
	Fiji	....	6	....	....	....	6
	Newfoundland..	....	52,360	....	36	....	52,396
	New Zealand....	....	17,704	....	....	....	17,704
	Aust.-Hungary..	....	10	....	....	....	10
	Belgium........	....	2,721	....	12	....	2,733
	France.........	....	1,473	....	....	....	1,473
	Germany	....	8	....	....	....	8
	St. Pierre......	....	6,529	....	....	....	6,529
	Switzerland.....	....	1	....	....	....	1
	Turkey.........	....	19	....	....	....	19
	United States...	....	24,806	....	12,275	....	37,081
	Total	....	133,792	....	12,323	....	146,115
Harness and saddlery...	Great Britain...	....	1,180	....	103	....	1,283
	Australia.	....	283	....	....	....	283
	B. Africa.......	....	134	....	....	....	134
	Bermuda........	....	208	....	....	....	208
	B. W. Indies ...	....	120	....	....	....	120
	Newfoundland..	....	1,824	....	....	....	1,824
	New Zealand....	....	100	....	....	....	100
	China	....	30	....	....	....	30
	Egypt..........	....	26	....	....	....	26
	France.........	....	30	....	....	....	30
	United States...	....	3,004	....	3,396	....	6,400
	Total	....	6,939	....	3,499	....	10,438
Other manufactures of..	Great Britain...	....	14,141	....	154	....	14,295
	B. Africa.......	....	40	....	....	....	40
	B. W. Indies ...	....	603	....	....	....	603
	Newfoundland..	....	936	....	206	....	1,142
	New Zealand....	....	120	....	....	....	120
	France.........	....	2	....	....	....	2
	Germany.......	....	17	....	....	....	17
	Mexico.........	....	154	....	....	....	154
	Norway.........	....	264	....	....	....	264
	United States...	....	9,244	....	2,890	....	12,134
	Total	....	25,521	....	3,250	....	28,771

No. 3.—General Statement of Exports—*Continued.*

Articles Exported.	Countries.	Goods, the Produce of Canada.		Goods, not the Produce of Canada.		Total Exports.	
		Quantity.	Value.	Qt'y.	Value.	Quantity.	Value.
Manufactures—*Con.*			$		$		$
Lime	Great Britain		13,140				13,140
	Fiji		68				68
	Newfoundland		41				41
	Hawaii		796				796
	St. Pierre		48				48
	United States		59,441				59,441
	Total		73,534				73,534
		Galls.		Galls.		Galls.	
Liquors—Ale and beer	Great Britain	870	352			870	352
	B. W. Indies	432	143			432	143
	Newfoundland	29	22			29	22
	Belgium	18	15			18	15
	Mexico	300	215			300	215
	St. Pierre	18	23			18	23
	United States	6,663	5,750	1,630	1,950	8,293	7,700
	Total	8,330	6,520	1,630	1,950	9,960	8,470
Brandy	Great Britain			3	26	3	26
	Newfoundland			119	192	119	192
	France			19	58	19	58
	Mexico			12	36	12	36
	United States	6	25	317	1,726	223	1,751
	Total	6	25	470	2,038	476	2,063
Gin	Newfoundland			17	15	17	15
	Mexico	30	45			30	45
	St. Pierre			8	11	8	11
	United States	1,217	1,901	26,627	43,623	27,844	45,524
	Total	1,247	1,946	26,652	43,649	27,899	45,595
Rum	Great Britain			26	76	26	76
	Newfoundland			3,198	847	3,198	847
	St. Pierre			1,768	395	1,768	395
	United States			85	236	85	236
	Total			5,077	1,554	5,077	1,554
Whisky	Great Britain	3,313	10,925	528	920	3,841	11,845
	Australia	2,481	8,573			2,481	8,573
	Bermuda	14	38			14	38
	B. Africa	1,573	6,615			1,573	6,615
	B. E. Indies	422	1,313			422	1,313
	B. W. Indies	2,808	7,811			2,808	7,811
	B. Honduras	1,137	3,743			1,137	3,743
	Newfoundland	208	708	20	40	228	748
	New Zealand	79	262			79	262
	Argentina	1,042	3,000			1,042	3,000
	Belgium	1,097	2,188			1,097	2,188
	Brazil	162	372			162	372
	Cent. Am. States	7,215	23,145			7,215	23,145
	Chili	1,823	6,043			1,823	6,043
	China	570	936			570	936

No. 3.—GENERAL STATEMENT OF EXPORTS—*Continued.*

Articles Exported.	Countries.	Goods, the Produce of Canada.		Goods, not the Produce of Canada.		Total Exports.	
		Quantity.	Value.	Q'ty.	Value.	Quantity.	Value.
MANUFACTURES—*Con.*		Galls.	$	Galls.	$	Galls.	$
Liquor—*Con.* Whisky—*Con.*	Cuba	2,103	6,681			2,103	6,681
	Dan. W. Indies	396	1,207			396	1,207
	Dutch W. Indies	126	420			126	420
	Dutch Guiana	156	550			156	550
	Egypt	2,207	7,355			2,207	7,355
	Ecuador	33	113			33	113
	France	1,106	3,701			1,106	3,701
	Germany	571	1,358	5	10	576	1,368
	Hawaii	299	1,050	89	249	388	1,299
	Italy	408	1,375			408	1,375
	Japan	72	281			72	281
	Mexico	6,853	20,039	240	672	7,093	20,711
	Norway	195	493			195	493
	Panama	238	787			238	787
	Peru	425	1,418			425	1,418
	Philippines	1,042	3,675			1,042	3,675
	St. Pierre			85	162	85	162
	Sweden	117	234			117	234
	U.S. of Colombia	636	2,114			636	2,114
	United States	244,923	813,310	9,515	26,719	254,438	840,029
	Venezuela	545	1,816			545	1,816
	Total	286,395	943,649	10,482	28,772	296,877	972,421
Wines	Great Britain	247	439	199	632	446	1,071
	Bermuda	533	423			533	423
	B. W. Indies	1,084	1,345			1,084	1,345
	B. Guiana	524	392			524	392
	Hong Kong	78	69			78	69
	Newfoundland	120	190	432	1,341	552	1,531
	Belgium			1	3	1	3
	Chili			43	16	43	16
	France			4	23	4	23
	Mexico	24	60	3	6	27	66
	United States	2,815	1,982	3,448	12,330	6,263	14,312
	Total	5,425	4,900	4,130	14,351	9,555	19,251
Other spirits, N.E.S.	Great Britain	95,791	30,748	8	76	95,799	30,824
	Newfoundland	575	352	7	15	582	367
	Belgium	25,000	7,500			25,000	7,500
	Germany	150,000	45,000			150,000	45,000
	Holland	4	5			4	5
	St. Pierre	8	28	4	22	12	50
	United States	22,867	15,122	2,194	4,903	25,061	20,025
	Total	294,245	98,755	2,213	5,016	296.458	103,771
Metals, N.O.P.	Great Britain		13,322		1,103		14,425
	Australia		2,074				2,074
	Bermuda		9				9
	B. W. Indies		134				134
	Newfoundland		4,448		258		4,706
	New Zealand		272				272
	Argentina		438				438
	Belgium		184				184
	Brazil		250				250
	Corea		45				45
	Cuba		145				145
	France		400		200		600
	Germany				247		247

No. 3.—General Statement of Exports—*Continued.*

Articles Exported.	Countries.	Goods, the Produce of Canada.		Goods, not the Produce of Canada.		Total Exports.	
		Quantity.	Value.	Q'ty.	Value.	Quantity.	Value.
MANUFACTURES—*Con.*			$		$		$
Metals, N.O.P.—*Con.*	Mexico		896				896
	Porto Rico		22		585		607
	St. Pierre				15		15
	United States		22,545		13,184		35,729
	Total		45,184		15,592		60,776
				Galls.		Galls.	
Molasses	Great Britain			70	21	70	21
	Bermuda			70	24	70	24
	Newfounland			60,896	17,800	60,896	17,800
	St. Pierre			2,025	519	2,025	519
	United States			36,168	7,276	36,168	7,276
	Total			99,229	25,640	99,229	25,640
Musical instruments, viz.—		No.		No.		No.	
Organs	Great Britain	2,857	149,854	1	1,850	2,858	151,704
	Australia	114	9,650	37	1,600	151	11,250
	Bermuda	1	50			1	50
	B. Africa	206	10,645			206	10,645
	B. W. Indies	1	75			1	75
	Newfoundland	46	2,740			46	2,740
	New Zealand	197	11,291			197	11,291
	Argentina	6	400			6	400
	Belgium	1	70			1	70
	Germany	184	10,230			184	10,230
	Holland	72	3,850			72	3,850
	Italy	7	450	1	250	8	700
	Iceland	1	175			1	175
	Russia	4	450			4	450
	United States	83	6,472	3	177	86	6,649
	Total	3,780	206,402	42	3,877	3,822	210,279
Pianos	Great Britain	25	8,515			25	8,515
	Australia	67	15,224			67	15,224
	Bermuda	2	600			2	600
	B. Africa	5	1,410			5	1,410
	B. W. Indies	1	200			1	200
	Newfoundland	9	2,150			9	2,150
	New Zealand	1	250			1	250
	Argentina	2	800			2	800
	China	2	485			2	485
	Mexico	1	300			1	300
	United States	166	34,541	29	9,403	195	43,944
	Total	281	64,475	29	9,403	310	73,878
Other	Great Britain		818		136		954
	Australia		1,970				1,970
	B. Africa				375		375
	Newfoundland		255				255
	New Zealand		230		150		380
	China		100				100
	Denmark		540				540
	France				39		39
	Germany		2				2
	United States		7,007		5,293		12,300
	Total		10,922		5,993		16,915

No. 3.—General Statement of Exports—*Continued.*

Articles Exported.	Countries.	Goods, the Produce of Canada.		Goods, not the Produce of Canada.		Total Exports.	
		Quantity.	Value.	Q'ty.	Value.	Quantity.	Value.
MANUFACTURES—*Con.*		Cwt.	$	Cwt.	$	Cwt.	$
Oakum	Newfoundland	17	57	8	32	25	89
	United States	2	24			2	24
	Total	19	81	8	32	27	113
Oil cake	Great Britain	188,329	237,462			188,329	237,462
	B. W. Indies	16	16			16	16
	Newfoundland	22	50			22	50
	Belgium	30,345	36,582			30,345	36,582
	Germany	11,130	11,130			11,130	11,130
	United States	4,331	4,331	45	20	4,376	4,351
	Total	234,173	289,571	45	20	234,218	289,591
		Galls.		Galls.		Galls.	
Oil, N.E.S	Great Britain	47,477	31,190			47,477	31,190
	Australia	25,130	7,246	3,000	975	28,130	8,221
	Bermuda			270	103	270	103
	B. E. Indies	6,150	621			6,150	621
	B. W. Indies	50	28	5,652	2,184	5,702	2,212
	B. Guiana	358	111	6,552	2,407	6,910	2,518
	Newfoundland	6,226	2,238	4,058	1,302	10,284	3,540
	Belgium	23,006	2,301			23,006	2,301
	Germany	39,973	5,990			39,973	5,990
	St. Pierre	40	18	90	23	130	41
	United States	829,039	48,081	5,437	1,369	834,476	49,450
	Total	977,449	97,824	25,059	8,363	1,002,508	106,187
		Rolls.		Rolls.		Rolls.	
Paper, wall	Great Britain	650	136			650	136
	Australia	63,885	7,785	250	148	64,135	7,933
	Bermuda	200	30			200	30
	B. Africa	750	132			750	132
	B. W. Indies	4,907	343			4,907	343
	Newfoundland	316,078	10,159			316,078	10,159
	New Zealand	142,264	16,031			142,264	16,031
	China	100	22			100	22
	United States	4,611	897	14,849	2,584	19,460	3,481
	Total	533,445	35,535	15,099	2,732	548,544	38,267
Paper, N.E.S	Great Britain		1,149,403		1,110		1,150,513
	Australia		383,167				383,167
	Bermuda		3,381				3,381
	B. Africa		53,270				53,270
	B. W. Indies		8,604		75		8,679
	B. Guiana		757				757
	Newfoundland		44,316		5,479		49,795
	New Zealand		127,948				127,948
	Argentina		12,327				12,327
	Belgium		35				35
	Cent. Am. States		441				441
	Cuba		10,547				10,547
	France		712				712
	French Africa		515				515
	Italy		97				97
	Japan		12,491				12,491

No. 3.—General Statement of Exports—*Continued.*

Articles Exported.	Countries.	Goods, the Produce of Canada.		Goods, not the Produce of Canada.		Total Exports.	
		Quantity.	Value.	Q'ty.	Value.	Quantity.	Value.
			$		$		$
Manufactures—*Con.*							
Paper, N.E S.—*Con*	Mexico........	....	2,369	....	... ...	... .	2,369
	Peru....	. ...	2,207	....	....	... .	2,207
	Philippines.....	....	607	....	....	....	607
	St. Pierre.. . ..	....	82	....	....	....	82
	United States...	... .	157,577	....	11,532	....	169,109
	Venezuela..	.. ..	304	....	....	....	304
	Total......	....	1,971,157	.... . .	18,196	....	1,989,353
Photographs..	Great Britain. .	....	876	....	2	....	878
	Australia. .. .	... .	6	....	....	....	6
	B. W. Indies....	... .	10	....	....	.. ..	10
	Newfoundland..	....	154	....	... .	....	154
	Aust.-Hungary .	....	7	....	....	....	7
	Belgium........	... .	25	....	....	....	25
	Cuba....	....	55	.. ....	....	....	55
	Ecuador	... .	20	....	....	....	20
	France........	....	44	....	....	....	44
	Germany..	....	24	....	.... ..	.. ... .	24
	Italy.....	....	20	....	....	....	20
	Japan..........	....	18	. .....	. . .	....	18
	St. Pierre.......	....	7	....	....	....	7
	Sweden........	....	1	....	....	....	1
	United States...	. .. .	2,712	....	567	....	3,279
	Total......	....	3,979	....	569	....	4,548
Plumbago, manufactures of....................	Great Britain...	. ...	267	....	.. ....	....	267
	Newfoundland..	....	18	......	... .	. .. .	18
	United States...	....	2,663	....	....	....	2,663
	Total	....	2,948	....	....	....	2,948
		Lbs.		Lbs.		Lbs.	
Rags....	Great Britain...	1,993,307	79,294	....	... ...	1,993,307	79,294
	France.........	5,365	97	12,000	960	17,365	1,057
	United States...	15,285,522	148,825	11,515	217	15,297,037	149,042
	Total	17,284,194	228,216	23,515	1,177	17,307,709	229,393
Sails.	B. W. Indies ...	....	854	....	....	....	854
	Newfoundland..	. .. .	160	....	....	....	160
	Total.....	....	1,014	....	....	.. .. ..	1,014
		No. / Tons.		No. / Tons.		No. / T's.	
Ships sold to other countries............	Newfoundland..	2 / 221	1,810	....	....	2 / 221	1,810
	France.........	1 / 1,350	3,000	....	....	1 / 1,350	3,000
	Mexico.........	1 / 20	300	. .....	....	1 / 20	300
	Sweden........	1 / 394	9,500	....	....	1 / 394	9,500
	United States...	2 / 1,764	15,760	1 / 332	32,300	3 / 2,096	48,060
	Total......	7 / 3,749	30,370	1 / 332	32,300	8 / 4,081	62,670

SESSIONAL PAPER No. 11

No. 3.—General Statement of Exports—*Continued.*

Articles Exported.	Countries.	Goods, the Produce of Canada.		Goods, not the Produce of Canada.		Total Exports.	
		Quantity.	Value.	Q'ty.	Value.	Quantity.	Value
manufactures—*Con.*		Lbs.	$	Lbs.	$	Lbs.	$
Soap..	Great Britain...	21,760	848	....	....	21,760	848
	Australia.....	3,650	399	....	....	3,650	399
	Bermuda........	2,900	114	....	....	2,900	114
	B. W. Indies....	944,267	36,191	....	....	944,267	36,191
	B. Guiana......	20,162	666	....	....	20,162	666
	Newfoundland..	74,163	2,637	258	81	74,421	2,718
	New Zealand....	2,705	360	....	....	2,705	360
	Japan........	159,722	9,828	....	....	159,722	9,828
	Mexico........	50	4	140	8	190	12
	United States...	33,199	1,677	2,981	263	36,180	1,940
	Total......	1,262,578	52,724	3,379	352	1,265,957	53,076
Starch........	Great Britain...	85,560	4,134	....	....	85,560	4,134
	Newfoundland..	14,050	796	270	148	14,320	944
	St. Pierre.......	100	5	....	....	100	5
	United States...	16	2	3,275	218	3,291	220
	Total	99,726	4,937	3,545	366	103,271	5,303
Stone, ornamental, viz.—Granite, marble, &c., dressed...	Great Britain...	....	975	....	50	....	1,025
	Bermuda......	....	80	....	....	....	80
	B. W. Indies...	....	444	....	....	....	444
	Newfoundland..	....	296	....	21	....	317
	St. Pierre.......	....	....	....	45	....	45
	United States...	....	310	....	397	....	707
	Total ...	....	2,105	....	513	....	2,618
Building, viz:—Freestone, limestone, &c, dressed.	Newfoundland..	....	292	....	....	....	292
Sugar of all kind, N.E.S..	Great Britain...	25,750	895	122,750	4,667	148,500	5,562
	Bermuda........	....	....	200	9	200	9
	B. W. Indies....	17,507	648	13,954	631	31,461	1,279
	Fiji	15	6	....	....	15	6
	Newfoundland..	60	3	86,398	3,502	86,458	3,505
	Japan.........	18,000	832	....	....	18,000	832
	Corea........	190	15	....	....	190	15
	Panama........	....	....	27,013	699	27,013	699
	United States...	394,788	17,761	8,072	566	402,860	18,327
	Total	456,310	20,160	258,387	10,074	714,697	30,234
Sugar house syrup.......	Japan.........	48	8	....	....	48	8
	United States...	278,965	15,673	238	155	279,203	15,828
	Total....	279,013	15,681	238	155	279,251	15,836
Tar..........	Great Britain ..	....	1,595	....	....	....	1,595
	B. Africa......	....	8,724	....	....	....	8,724
	B. W. Indies....	....	14	....	....	....	14
	Newfoundland..	....	4,169	....	35	....	4,204
	Italy..........	....	17,041	....	....	....	17,041
	Mexico......	....	18	....	....	....	18
	St. Pierre.. ..	....	6	....	....	....	6
	Switzerland.....	....	22,777	....	....	....	22,777
	United States...	....	44,133	....	338	....	44,471
	Total......	....	98,477	....	373	....	98,850

No. 3.—General Statement of Exports—*Continued.*

Articles Exported.	Countries.	Goods, the Produce of Canada.		Goods, not the Produce of Canada.		Total Exports.	
		Quantity.	Value.	Q'ty.	Value.	Quantity.	Value.
MANUFACTURES—*Con.*			$		$		$
Tin, manufacturers of.....	Great Britain...	....	87	......	40	....	127
	B. Africa.......	.. ..	29	.... ..	......	....	29
	Bermuda..	....	41	.... ..	... ..	....	41
	Newfoundland..	....	4,923	....	1,284	....	6,207
	Brazil	....	1,200	....	....	....	1,200
	Holland...	... .	147	....	....	.. ....	147
	Mexico.	....	79	......	....	....	79
	St. Pierre......	... .	89	.. .. ..	171	....	260
	United States...	....	15,511	....	7,857	....	23,368
	Total	....	22,106	....	9,352	....	31,458
		M.		M.		M.	
Tobacco, viz.: Cigars.....	Great Britain...	35	1,373	.. ..	....	35	1,373
	Bermuda........	1	25	....	. . ..	1	25
	B. W. Indies...	... .	....	5	111	5	111
	Newfoundland..	51	795	....	.... ..	51	795
	New Zealand...	10	263	10	300	20	563
	Holland	1	10	..... .	....	1	10
	St. Pierre.......	21	217	... . ..	....	21	217
	United States...	1	17	1	20	2	37
	Total......	120	2,700	16	431	136	3,131
Cigarettes.....	Great Britain...	8	41	......	....	8	41
	Bermuda	....	. .. .	8	45	8	45
	B. W. Indies ...	30	30	....	....	30	30
	Hong Kong.....	62	8	....	....	62	8
	Newfoundland..	16	133	65	265	81	398
	Japan..	....	... .	357	689	357	689
	United States...	....	....	3	75	3	75
	Total......	116	212	433	1,074	549	1,286
		Lbs.		Lbs.		Lbs.	
Snuff	United States...	7	4	....	....	7	4
Stems and cuttings....	Great Britain...	18,670	1,566	....	.. ..	18,670	1,566
	Australia.......	....	..:..	8,033	663	8,033	663
	Belgium.... ..	73,642	8,948	48,342	4,412	121,984	13,360
	Germany.......	55,566	1,771	17,716	1,324	73,282	3,095
	Holland	17,205	1,276	8,574	941	25,779	2,217
	United States...	390,361	16,972	134,744	11,985	525,105	28,907
	Total	555,444	30,533	217,409	19,275	772,853	49,808
All other, N.E.S.	Great Britain...	67,556	18,447	2,112	887	69,668	19,334
	Australia... ...	4,961	1,423	....	....	4,961	1,423
	B. Africa... ...	75	22	....	....	75	22
	B. Guiana.. ...	1,794	1,054	250	111	2,044	1,165
	Newfoundland..	25,333	15,666	2,197	511	27,530	16,177
	Belgium........	2,746	211	... ...	....	2,746	211
	France	2,010	623	. .. ...	....	2,010	623
	Germany......	....	....	2,996	200	2,996	200
	Holland	....	....	6,076	474	6,076	474
	St. Pierre.......	21,937	6,480	612	128	22,549	6,608
	United States...	26,319	5,605	93,207	34,342	119,526	39,947
	Total......	152,731	49,531	107,450	36,653	260,181	86,184

No. 3.—GENERAL STATEMENT OF EXPORTS—*Continued.*

Articles Exported.	Countries.	Goods, the Produce of Canada.		Goods, not the Produce of Canada.		Total Exports.	
		Quantity.	Value.	Q'ty.	Value.	Quantity.	Value.
MANUFACTURES—*Con.*		Cwt.	$		$	Cwt.	$
Tow	United States	1,383	12,786			1,383	12,786
Vehicles, viz.—		No.		No.		No.	
Carriages	Great Britain	18	3,012			18	3,012
	Australia	1	110			1	110
	Bermuda	3	270			3	270
	B. Africa	171	14,142			171	14,142
	B. Guiana	2	180			2	180
	B. W. Indies	68	5,956			68	5,956
	Newfoundland	58	2,586			58	2,586
	New Zealand	27	818			27	818
	United States	42	4,408	12	1,113	54	5,521
	Total	390	31,482	12	1,113	402	32,595
" parts of	Great Britain		568		15		583
	Australia		2,811				2,811
	B. Africa		56				56
	Bermuda		110				110
	B. W. Indies		317		30		347
	Newfoundland		1,476		196		1,672
	New Zealand		777				777
	Argentina		1,151				1,151
	Switzerland		143				143
	United States		10,189		1,285		11,474
	Total		17,598		1,526		19,124
Carts	Great Britain	10	960			10	960
	B. W. Indies	1	25			1	25
	Newfoundland	1	25			1	25
	Argentina	814	16,833	150	3,000	964	19,833
	United States	40	1,404	36	1,340	76	2,744
	Total	866	19,247	186	4,340	1,052	23,587
Wagons	Great Britain	1	75			1	75
	B. Africa	4	385			4	385
	Newfoundland	4	78			4	78
	New Zealand	4	201			4	201
	Argentina	12	700			12	700
	St. Pierre	1	50			1	50
	United States	68	3,688	90	4,418	158	8,106
	Total	94	5,177	90	4,418	184	9,595
Automobiles	Great Britain	1	1,750	5	9,483	6	11,233
	Australia	2	2,500			2	2,500
	B. Poss., Other	2	1,600			2	1,600
	New Zealand	15	10,992			15	10,992
	Argentina	2	1,762			2	1,762
	Belgium	1	800			1	800
	China	1	2,700			1	2,700
	Cuba	1	825			1	825
	Denmark	3	4,420			3	4,420
	Germany			1	5,000	1	5,000
	Holland	3	2,560			3	2,560
	Italy	2	4,170			2	4,170
	Portuguese Afr.	1	700			1	700

No. 3.—GENERAL STATEMENT OF EXPORTS—*Continued.*

Articles Exported.	Countries.	Goods, the Produce of Canada.		Goods, not the Produce of Canada.		Total Exports.	
		Quantity.	Value.	Q'ty.	Value.	Quantity.	Value.
MANUFACTURES—*Con.*		No.	$	No.	$	No.	$
Automobiles—*Con*	Russia	3	2,245			3	2,245
	Mexico	5	4,060			5	4,060
	Spain	1	800			1	800
	Sweden	5	6,080			5	6,080
	United States	19	15,365	43	74,285	62	89,650
	Total	67	63,329	49	88,768	116	152.097
Bicycles	Great Britain	16	598	1	15	17	613
	Australia	1,850	47,444			1,850	47,444
	Bermuda	2	50			2	50
	B. E. Indies	6	100			6	100
	Newfoundland	2	55			2	55
	New Zealand	452	12,305	6	249	458	12,554
	France	1	40			1	40
	Japan	29	551			29	551
	United States	60	1,257	25	763	85	2,020
	Total	2,418	62,400	32	1,027	2,450	63,427
Bicycles, parts of	Great Britain		68				68
	Australia		26,615		2,830		29,445
	B. E. Indies				25		25
	New Zealand		4,657		3,716		8,373
	Argentina		10				10
	Belgium		123				123
	Japan		1,934		160		2,094
	St. Pierre				5		5
	United States		155		435		590
	Total		33,562		7,171		40,733
Other vehicles	Great Britain		13,659		5,000		18,659
	Australia		6,075				6,075
	Bermuda		23				23
	B. Africa		4,708				4,708
	B. W. Indies		17				17
	Newfoundland		914				914
	New Zealand		1,924				1,924
	Argentina		2,185				2,185
	Cuba		2,190				2,190
	Holland		1,520				1,520
	United States		22,165		90,038		112,203
	Total		55,380		95,038		150,418
		Galls.		Galls.		Galls.	
Vinegar	Bermuda	313	69			313	69
	United States			150	42	150	42
	Total	313	69	150	42	463	111

No. 3.—General Statement of Exports—*Continued.*

Articles Exported.	Countries.	Goods, the Produce of Canada.		Goods, not the Produce of Canada.		Total Exports.	
		Quantity.	Value.	Q'ty.	Value.	Quantity.	Value.
MANUFACTURES—*Con.*		No.	$	No.	$	No.	$
Wood, viz.—							
Barrels, empty........	Great Britain...	722	1,636	675	1,677	1,397	3,313
	B. W. Indies...	17	26	407	342	424	368
	Newfoundland..	2,402	827	250	106	2,652	933
	Belgium.......	155	233	100	100	255	333
	Germany......	....	....	299	544	299	544
	United States...	6,657	9,622	18,379	30,020	25,036	39,642
	Total.....	9,953	12,344	20,110	32,789	30,063	45,133
Household furniture....	Great Britain...	....	122,913	....	113	....	123,026
	Australia.......	....	31,134	....	900	....	32,034
	Bermuda.......	....	5,187	....	55	....	5,242
	B. Africa.......	....	60,329	....	333	....	60,662
	B. E. Indies....	....	44	....	....	....	44
	B. W. Indies...	....	7,311	....	....	....	7,311
	B. Guiana......	....	144	....	....	....	144
	Fiji...........	....	82	....	....	....	82
	Newfoundland..	....	21,405	....	....	....	21,405
	New Zealand...	....	10,098	....	95	....	10,193
	Argentina.......	....	4,153	....	198	....	4,351
	Aust-Hungary..	....	36	....	....	....	36
	Belgium........	....	35	....	....	....	35
	China.........	....	203	....	....	....	203
	Cuba..........	....	4,298	....	336	....	4,634
	France.........	....	800	....	3	....	803
	Germany......	....	136	....	....	....	136
	Mexico.........	....	697	....	20	....	717
	Philippines.....	....	17	....	....	....	17
	St. Pierre......	....	8	....	....	....	8
	United States...	....	14,576	....	3,582	....	18,158
	Total.....	....	283,606	....	5,635	....	289,241
Doors, sashes and blinds	Great Britain...	....	84,651	....	....	....	84,651
	Bermuda.......	....	50	....	....	....	50
	B. Africa......	....	60,525	....	20	....	60,545
	B. W. Indies...	....	1,005	....	....	....	1,005
	Newfoundland..	....	21	....	....	....	21
	New Zealand....	....	80	....	....	....	80
	France.........	....	50	....	....	....	50
	Holland.......	....	20	....	....	....	20
	St. Pierre......	....	90	....	....	....	90
	United States...	....	16,589	....	1,126	....	17,715
	Total.....	....	163,081	....	1,146	....	164,227
Matches and match splints.............	Great Britain...	....	105,314	....	....	....	105,314
	Bermuda.......	....	614	....	....	....	614
	B. W. Indies...	....	159	....	....	....	159
	Newfoundland..	....	138	....	....	....	138
	France.........	....	357	....	....	....	357
	Mexico.........	....	295	....	....	....	295
	St. Pierre......	....	103	....	....	....	103
	United States...	....	2,132	....	33	....	2,165
	Total.....	....	109,112	....	33	....	109,145

No. 3.—General Statement of Exports—*Continued.*

Articles Exported.	Countries.	Goods, the Produce of Canada.		Goods, not the Produce of Canada.		Total Exports.	
		Quantity.	Value.	Q'ty.	Value.	Quantity.	Value.
			$		$		$
MANUFACTURES—*Con.*							
Wood—*Con.*							
Mouldings, trimmings and other house furnishings	Great Britain		388				388
	B. Africa		390				390
	Bermuda		84				84
	B. Guiana		25				25
	B. W. Indies		10				10
	Newfoundland		3,902				3,902
	New Zealand		93				93
	United States		197		60		257
	Total		5,089		60		5,149
Pails, tubs, churns and other hollow wooden-ware	Great Britain		3,221				3,221
	Bermuda		6				6
	B. Africa		458				458
	B. W. Indies		5				5
	Newfoundland		42				42
	New Zealand		1,008				1,008
	Belgium		875				875
	France		500				500
	Russia				375		375
	United States		1,811		67		1,878
	Total		7,926		442		8,368
Spool wood and spools	Great Britain		184,779		596		185,375
	United States		884		598		1,482
	Total		185,663		1,194		186,857
Wood pulp	Great Britain		998,702				998,702
	New Zealand		1,258				1,258
	France		46,337				46,337
	Japan		5,329				5,329
	Mexico		6,896				6,896
	United States		2,419,628				2,419,628
	Total		3,478,150				3,478,150
Other manufactures of	Great Britain		170,866		5,424		176,290
	Australia		38,238		783		39,021
	Bermuda		4,046				4,046
	B. Africa		15,817				15,817
	B. Guiana		615				615
	B. W. Indies		12,055				12,055
	Fiji		2,548				2,548
	Hong Kong		40				40
	Newfoundland		13,171		123		13,294
	New Zealand		20,935		174		21,109
	Argentina		375				375
	Belgium		1,137				1,137
	China		384				384
	Cuba		5,928		466		6,3[illegible]4
	Denmark		545				545
	France		726		1,395		2,121
	Germany		1,113				1,113
	Holland		50				50

No. 3.—General Statement of Exports—*Continued.*

Articles Exported.	Countries.	Goods, the Produce of Canada.		Goods, not the Produce of Canada.		Total Exports.	
		Quantity.	Value.	Q'ty.	Value.	Quantity.	Value.
Manufactures—*Con.*		No.	$	No.	$	No.	$
Wood—*Con.*							
Other mfrs. of—*Con.*	Italy		233				233
	Japan		805				805
	Mexico		694		27		721
	Panama		75				75
	Switzerland		6				6
	St. Pierre		434				434
	United States		77,110		13,603		90,713
	Total		367,946		21,995		389,941
Woollens	Great Britain		4,222		14,381		18,603
	Bermuda		157				157
	B. Africa		1,050				1,050
	B. E. Indies		8				8
	B. W. Indies		574				574
	B. Guiana		90				90
	Newfoundland		41,732		334		42,066
	New Zealand		833				833
	Belgium				485		485
	China		17				17
	France		43				43
	Mexico		950				950
	St. Pierre		60				60
	United States		18,232		2,012		20,244
	Total		67,968		17,212		85,180
Other articles	Great Britain		173,214		40,270		213,484
	Australia		24,056		121		24,177
	Bermuda		18,862		392		19,254
	B. Africa		20,346		1,381		21,727
	B. E. Indies		4,291		110		4,401
	B. Guiana		7,170				7,170
	B. W. Indies		20,161		556		20,717
	Br. poss. other		350				350
	Fiji		141				141
	Hong Kong		1,339				1,339
	Newfoundland		100,433		7,416		107,849
	New Zealand		8,094		67		8,161
	Argentina		1,689				1,689
	Austria		6		433		439
	Belgium		1,182		394		1,576
	Brazil		190				190
	Cen. Am. States		25		48		73
	Chili		550				550
	China		3,542		51		3,593
	Cuba		33,806				33,806
	Denmark		580				580
	Dutch E. Indies		88				88
	Dutch Guiana				34		34
	Egypt				60		60
	France		3,907		2,057		5,964
	Germany		3,283		3,283		6,566
	Hawaii		20				20
	Hayti				2		2
	Holland		549		93		642
	Italy		169				169
	Japan		4,897		381		5,278
	Mexico		20,671		201		20,872
	Norway		3				8

No. 3.—General Statement of Exports—*Continued.*

Articles Exported.	Countries.	Goods, the Produce of Canada.		Goods, not the Produce of Canada.		Total Exports.	
		Quantity.	Value.	Q'ty.	Value.	Quantity.	Value.
MANUFACTURES—*Con.*			$		$		$
Other articles—*Con.*	Panama		360				360
	Russia		371				371
	St. Pierre		2,497		60		2,557
	Sweden		26				26
	Switzerland		55		77		132
	Turkey		905				905
	United States		401,390		395,055		796,445
	Venezuela		85				85
	Total		859,303		452,542		1,311,845
MISCELLANEOUS ARTICLES.		Lbs.		Lbs.		Lbs.	
Coffee	Great Britain	144	44			144	44
	B. Africa	240	60			240	60
	Bermuda	1,605	191	365	61	1,970	252
	B. W. Indies			19	5	19	5
	Newfoundland	342	55	4,229	998	4,571	1,053
	Japan			1,000	280	1,000	280
	St. Pierre	869	109	351	57	1,220	166
	United States	100	26	350,211	37,459	350,311	37,485
	Total	3,300	485	356,175	38,860	359,475	39,345
Dried fruits, N.E.S	Great Britain	678	64	2,780	191	3,458	255
	Bermuda			13,640	559	13,640	559
	B. W. Indies			33,454	1,650	33,454	1,650
	Newfoundland			21,033	812	21,033	812
	Dan. W. Indies			128	6	128	6
	St. Pierre			882	46	882	46
	United States	865	71	153,378	4,923	154,243	4,994
	Total	1,543	135	225,295	8,187	226,838	8,322
Rice	B. W. Indies			1,892	41	1,892	41
	Newfoundland			15,070	317	15,070	317
	United States			23,300	938	23,300	938
	Total			40,262	1,296	40,262	1,296
Rice meal	Great Britain	2,675,200	29,930			2,675,200	29,930
Paintings in oil or water colours	Great Britain		11,936		61,670		73,606
	Belgium		80				80
	France		200		1,520		1,720
	Holland		400		100		500
	Norway		80				80
	United States		9,048		12,738		21,786
	Total		21,714		76,028		97,772

No. 3.—General Statement of Exports—*Continued.*

Articles Exported.	Countries.	Goods, the Produce of Canada.		Goods, not the Produce of Canada.		Total Exports.	
		Quantity.	Value.	Q'ty.	Value.	Quantity.	Value.
MISCELLANEOUS—*Con.*			$		$		$
Tea	Great Britain			29,054	5,246	29,054	5,246
	Bermuda			37,428	7,353	37,428	7,353
	B. Guiana			120	30	120	30
	B. W. Indies			3,748	812	3,748	812
	Newfoundland			147,700	28,333	147,700	28,333
	Cuba			400	136	400	136
	Dan. W. Indies			60	18	60	18
	Germany			9,458	473	9,458	473
	Mexico			132	55	132	55
	St. Pierre			8,068	1,098	8,068	1,098
	United States			2,151,190	518,505	2,151,190	518,505
	Total			2,387,358	562,059	2,387,358	562,059
Other miscellaneous articles	Great Britain		3,640		13,267		16,907
	B. Africa		244				244
	Bermuda		1,047				1,047
	B. Guiana		20				20
	B. W. Indies		108				108
	Newfoundland		14,901		233		15,134
	Germany		3				3
	China				18		18
	Cuba		10				10
	Corea		40				40
	France		1,500				1,500
	St. Pierre		10				10
	United States		11,089		89,793		100,882
	Total		32,612		103,311		135,923
COIN AND BULLION.							
Silver	China				80,146		80,146
	United States				5,172		5,172
	Total				85,318		85,318
Gold coin	Hong Kong				3,430		3,430
	China				37,246		37,246
	Japan				150		150
	United States				8,962,929		8,962,929
	Total				9,003,755		9,003,755
Silver coin	Great Britain				2,000		2,000
	Newfoundland				247		247
	United States				832,678		832,678
	Total				834,925		834,925
Copper coin	Great Britain				366		366
	United States				4,464		4,464
	Total				4,830		4,830
Grand total exports			235,483,956		21,102,674		256,586,630

No. 4.—Abstract of the total Value of Exports by Countries.

Countries.	Canadian Produce.	Foreign Produce.	Total.
	$	$	$
Great Britain	127,456,465	5,636,106	133,092,571
Australia	2,072,702	9,517	2,082,219
Bermuda	389,249	9,445	398,694
British Africa	1,756,439	3,280	1,759,719
" East Indies	19,612	1,942	21,554
" West Indies	2,337,746	21,976	2,359,722
" Guiana	481,118	6,541	487,659
" Honduras	5,613	....	5,613
" possessions, all other	34,135	....	34,135
Fiji Islands	59,151	86	59,237
Gibraltar	2,700	....	2,700
Hong Kong	36,519	332	36,851
Malta	17,423	....	17,423
Newfoundland	3,023,047	190,562	3,213,609
New Zealand	729,303	4,751	734,054
Total, British Empire	138,421,222	5,884,538	144,305,760
Argentina	1,881,983	6,849	1,888,832
Austria, Hungary	5,055	729	5,784
Azores	3	....	3
Belgium	1,187,950	377,216	1,565,166
Bolivia	445	....	445
Brazil	649,228	149	649,377
Central American States	66,358	48	66,406
Chili	238,991	160	239,151
China	839,468	16,290	855,758
Corea	501	....	501
Cuba	1,217 410	4,356	1,221,766
Denmark	143,575	....	143,575
Danish West Indies	16,604	105	16,709
Dutch East Indies	628	....	628
Dutch West Indies	768	....	768
Dutch Guiana	21,327	34	21,361
Ecuador	2,823	....	2,823
Egypt	19,364	60	19,424
France	2,110,444	9,647	2,120,091
French Africa	7,028	....	7,028
French West Indies	18,299	....	18,299
Germany	1,690,907	181.650	1,872,557
Greece	1,045	....	1,045
Hawaii	6,252	249	6,501
Hayti	33,441	2	33,443
Holland	636,943	187,825	824,768
Iceland	270	....	270
Italy	215,599	256	215,855
Japan	492,275	1,677	493,952
Madeira	31,359	....	31,359
Mexico	256,381	2,991	259,372
Norway	159,890	....	159,890
Panama	58,654	756	59,410
Peru	40,080	....	40,080
Philippines	4,686	....	4,686
Porto Rico	514,055	585	514,640
Portuguese Africa	3,889	....	3,889
Portugal	89,598	....	89,598
Roumania	41,916	....	41,916
Russia	222,040	375	222,415
San Domingo	4,670	....	4,670
St. Pierre	146,687	5,360	152,047

No. 4.—ABSTRACT of the total Value of Exports by Countries—*Continued.*

Countries.	Canadian Produce.	Foreign Produce.	Total.
		$	$
Spain	55,686	....	55,686
Spanish Africa	24,105	....	24,105
Sweden	91,120	68	91,188
Switzerland	29,809	421	30,230
Turkey	12,307	34,028	46,335
Uruguay	161,293	1,752	163,045
U. S. of Colombia	42,110	667	42,777
United States	83,546,306	4,455,003	88,001,309
Venezuela	21,109	....	21,109
Total, other countries	97,062,734	5,289,308	102,352,042
To United States: bullion, $5,172, coin, $9,800,071; to China, bullion, $80,146, coin, $37,246; to Great Britain, coin, $2,366; to Newfoundland, coin, $247; to Hong Kong, coin, $3,430; to Japan, coin, $150	....	9,928,828	9,928,828
Grand total, exports	235,483,956	21,102,674	256,586,630

No. 5.—STATEMENT of Vessels, British, Canadian and Foreign, entered inwards,

Number.	PORTS AND OUTPORTS.	WITH CARGOES.									
		BRITISH.					CANADIAN.				
		Number of Vessels.	Tons Register.	Quantity of Freight.		Crew Number.	Number of Vessels.	Tons Register.	Quantity of Freight.		Crew Number.
				Tons Weight.	Tons Measurement.				Tons Weight.	Tons Measurement.	
1	Advocate Harbor, N.S.										
2	Alberton .... P.E.I.						1	83	112		5
3	Alma.......... N.B.										
4	Amherst ...... N.S.						1	397	8		7
5	Annapolis Royal. "						9	1,145	1,544	1,688	47
6	Apple River...... "										
7	Arichat........ "						75	2,250			350
8	Aspey Bay....... "										
9	Baddeck......... "						1	267			2
10	Baie Verte .... N.B.										
11	Barrington....... N.S.						1	89	147		4
12	Barton .... "						9	793	329		52
13	Bathurst ...... N.B										
14	Bayfield......... N.S.										
15	Bear River ..... "						26	2,001	304		98
16	Belliveau's Cove.. "						7	928	294		40
17	Bridgetown...... "						3	291	453	310	12
18	Bridgewater ..... "	1	1,737	2,740		18	9	1,388	1,588		51
19	Buctouche..... N.B.										
20	Campbellton .... "										
21	Campobello ..... "						98	1,295	70		218
22	Canning......... N S.						1	108			5
23	Canso .... "	11	7,389	11,150		338	15	1,492	1,912		107
24	Caraquet .... N.B.										
25	Cardigan. ... P.E.I.										
26	Charlottetown ... "	5	5,204	1,588		163	48	43,951	6,180	466	1,533
27	Chatham .... N.B.	1	1,950	200		24	2	244	398		9
28	Chemainus ..... B C.						24	5,217	7,901		152
29	Chester.......... N.S.						5	262	405		27
30	Cheticamp...... "						9	291	81		27
31	Cheverie ...... "						2	248	4		9
32	Chicoutimi....... Que.	2	3,604	1,442		57					
33	Church Point .. N.S.						6	613	280		31
34	Clark's Harbor... "										
35	Clementsport .. "						14	1,402	181	248	81
36	Comox......... B.C.										
37	Crofton .... "	1	1,262	967		23	8	2,162	3,330		54
38	Dalhousie .... N.B										
39	Dawson .... Y.T.						3	1,533	980		37
40	Digby .... N.S.						5	485	763		24
41	Dorchester ..... N.B.	1	298		6,841	8	7	2,096		39,971	59
42	Douglas .... B.C.										
43	Economy .... N.S.										
44	Five Islands..... "										
45	Fredericton...... N.B.						5	496	1,019		24
46	Freeport ..... N.S.						2	135	144		8
47	Gabarouse....... "										
48	Gaspé .... Que.						3	316	390		20
49	Georgetown .. P.E.I.						7	277	209		33
50	Halifax.......... N S.	357	630,097	170,937		17,968	564	81,958	56,485		6,139
51	Hantsport ...... "						1	695	224		9
52	Harvey......... N.B.										
53	Hillsboro'...... "										
54	Isaacs Harbour... N.S.						1	99	201		5
55	Jordan Bay ..... "										
56	Kentville....... "						3	254			12
57	Kingsport...... "						2	393			11
58	Ladner .... B.C.										
59	Ladysmith ...... "						41	5,222	5,003		374

from Sea, at each Port and Outport, during the Fiscal Year ended June 30, 1906.

Foreign.					In Ballast.									
					British.			Canadian.			Foreign.			
Number of Vessels.	Tons Register.	Quantity of Freight. Tons Weight.	Quantity of Freight. Tons Measurement.	Crew Number.	Number of Vessels.	Tons Register.	Crew Number.	Number of Vessels.	Tons Register.	Crew Number.	Number of Vessels.	Tons Register.	Crew Number.	Number.
....	....	....	....	....	....	....	....	8	2,353	56	4	1,204	27	1
....	....	....	....	....	....	....	....	....	....	....	....	....	....	2
....	....	....	....	....	....	....	....	....	....	....	1	56	4	3
....	....	....	....	....	....	....	....	....	....	....	2	1,390	30	4
....	....	....	....	....	1	1,079	18	5	1,033	31	9	2,612	62	5
....	....	....	....	....	....	....	....	10	1,744	54	24	5,230	131	6
....	....	....	....	....	....	....	....	2	198	10	15	180	45	7
....	....	....	....	....	....	....	....	2	68	6	....	....	....	8
....	....	....	....	....	....	....	....	....	....	....	....	....	....	9
1	461	400	....	10	1	1,172	21	....	....	....	7	4,768	90	10
....	....	....	....	....	....	....	....	1	42	4	27	1,579	397	11
....	....	....	....	....	....	....	....	53	5,377	288	3	282	15	12
....	....	....	....	....	3	5,566	74	2	610	15	9	6,992	125	13
....	....	....	....	....	....	....	....	6	594	35	....	....	....	14
....	....	....	....	....	....	....	....	....	....	....	4	1,525	27	15
....	....	....	....	....	....	....	....	11	1,211	58	....	....	....	16
....	....	....	....	....	....	....	....	1	95	6	....	....	....	17
....	....	....	....	....	2	3,331	53	18	7,139	143	12	8,017	135	18
....	....	....	....	....	....	....	....	....	....	....	2	818	20	19
....	....	....	....	....	5	6,363	115	....	....	....	1	549	7	20
285	6,894	35	....	884	....	....	....	166	22,006	1,003	334	8,501	1,119	21
....	....	....	....	....	....	....	....	1	322	7	....	....	....	22
....	....	....	....	....	....	....	....	194	17,931	3,249	277	23,219	5,006	23
1	248	....	....	7	....	....	....	....	....	....	....	....	....	24
....	....	....	....	....	....	....	....	4	323	19	....	....	....	25
15	13,590	1,976	8	686	2	96	10	14	1,306	200	....	....	....	26
2	1,046	795	....	21	10	13,580	240	....	....	....	17	15,803	261	27
1	47	132	....	8	12	20,604	265	22	3,618	202	22	12,304	270	28
2	164	36	....	43	....	....	....	1	432	7	1	73	17	29
....	....	....	....	....	....	....	....	....	....	....	....	....	....	30
....	....	....	....	....	....	....	....	16	11,385	83	17	10,556	112	31
....	....	....	....	....	2	4,577	60	....	....	....	10	14,305	232	32
....	....	....	....	....	....	....	....	9	1,009	51	....	....	....	33
....	....	....	....	....	....	....	....	....	....	....	8	263	42	34
....	....	....	....	....	....	....	....	8	760	47	....	....	....	35
....	....	....	....	....	57	151,369	3,071	58	18,537	532	69	75,956	1,873	36
....	....	....	....	....	....	....	....	6	275	34	....	....	....	37
....	....	....	....	....	5	1,473	31	....	....	....	45	34,036	576	38
25	12,959	2,194	....	882	....	....	....	....	....	....	....	....	....	39
....	....	....	....	....	....	....	....	9	2,025	60	20	1,928	130	40
....	....	....	....	....	....	....	....	4	371	19	....	....	....	41
4	34	13	....	10	....	....	....	9	528	69	24	246	78	42
....	....	....	....	....	....	....	....	4	333	17	....	....	....	43
....	....	....	....	....	....	....	....	4	302	15	....	....	....	44
....	....	....	....	....	....	....	....	....	....	....	1	91	5	45
....	....	....	....	....	....	....	....	....	....	....	....	....	....	46
....	....	....	....	....	....	....	....	2	106	22	1	79	18	47
1	346	600	....	10	....	....	....	2	476	13	12	10,733	172	48
2	352	75	381	25	7	288	31	3	248	15	2	365	33	49
165	88,400	42,151	....	4,248	45	50,522	2,534	28	9,861	247	43	28,192	799	50
1	266	500	....	7	9	521	118	25	13,034	146	65	24,451	842	51
....	....	....	....	....	1	1,617	19	15	3,526	102	4	2,672	42	52
....	....	....	....	....	5	11,091	123	23	6,846	143	92	59,760	1,169	53
....	....	....	....	....	....	....	....	....	....	....	11	1,010	221	54
....	....	....	....	....	....	....	....	2	146	37	....	....	....	55
....	....	....	....	....	....	....	....	1	69	3	....	....	....	56
1	407	....	....	7	....	....	....	3	866	21	4	1,037	23	57
....	....	....	....	....	2	137	15	....	....	....	....	....	....	58
3	4,804	14	....	97	21	31,372	536	103	36,132	2,078	73	90,658	2,957	59

No. 5.—STATEMENT of Vessels, British, Canadian and Foreign, entered

Number.	Ports and Outports.	WITH CARGOES. British. Number of Vessels.	Tons Register.	Quantity of Freight. Tons Weight.	Quantity of Freight. Tons Measurement.	Crew Number.	Canadian. Number of Vessels.	Tons Register.	Quantity of Freight. Tons Weight.	Quantity of Freight. Tons Measurement.	Crew Number.
60	La Have .... N.S						117	9,747	5,391		1,614
61	L'Ardoise...... "	42	1,902	331		167					
62	Liscombe....... "										
63	Liverpool........ "						12	2,248	1,850	420	74
64	Lockeport....... "						25	1,505	2,155		214
65	Lords Cove...... N.B.						27	1,055	11		100
66	Louisburg ..... N.S.	14	16,701	25,875		268	9	1,164	1,651		49
67	Lunenburg ...... "	8	624	730		47	245	23,061	18,386		3,359
68	Magdalen Islands. Que.										
69	Mahone Bay..... N.S.						39	2,674	2,997		544
70	Main-a-dieu ..... "										
71	Maitland .... "										
72	Matane........ Que.										
73	Meteghan........ N.S.						12	1,105	19[illegible]	6	63
74	Middleton........ "	2	120			12					
75	Moncton .... N.B						7	1,339	2,649		43
76	Montague ...... P.E.I.						4	278	258	5	20
77	Montreal .... Que	336	1,243,543	483,168	132,408	30,573	21	14,543	1,728		465
78	Murray Harbour P.E.I.						21	465	205		123
79	Musquash ...... N.B.										
80	Nanaimo. .... B.C.	2	2,534	3		47	2	137	60		14
81	New Campbellton N.S.	2	93	40		8					
82	Newcastle....... N.B.										
83	New London ... P.E.I.						4	67	9		19
84	New Westminster B.C.						38	2,727	1,753		203
85	North East Harbo'r N.S						15	789	769	10	87
86	North Head.. .. N.B.						123	22,068	16		950
87	Northport ...... N.S.										
88	North Sydney... "	112	37,361	5,397		3,482	16	3,830	3,960		176
89	Parrsboro........ "										
90	Paspebiac ...... Que.	1	241	300		8	10	1,367	1,583		59
91	Percé .... "						3	259	120		41
93	Pictou .... N.S.	11	1,387	1,812		52					
94	Port Greville..... "										
95	Port Hastings.... "						5	1,251			40
96	Port Hawkesbury. "	5	4,095			169	110	35,050			2,107
97	Port Hood... ... "										
98	Port la Tour ... "										
99	Port Medway..... "						3	297	331		34
100	Port Morien...... "										
101	Port Mulgrave.... "										
102	Port Simpson..... B.C.										
103	Port Williams.... N.S.										
104	Pubnico .... "						36	938	1,010		510
105	Pugwash .... "										
106	Quebec .... Que.	271	1,069,538	53,131	4,222	28,621	30	3,445	1,767		365
107	Richibucto....... N.B.						1	149		292	5
108	Rimouski .... Que.										
109	River Bourgeois.. N.S.						53	1,464	274		423
110	River Hebert..... "						3	295	192		13
111	Rivière du Loup.. Que.										
112	Rustico .... P.E.I.						1	10	1		5
113	St. Andrews...... N.B.						14	1,579	2,533		61
114	St. Ann's...... N.S.										
115	St. George....... N.B.						6	134	50	4	14
116	St. John.......... "	175	476,513	136,264	58,123	11,253	294	29,103	29,851	8,211	2,315
117	St. Martin's. ... "						1	80		3	4
118	St. Peter's...... N.S.						4	58	14		14
119	St. Stephen...... N.B.						35	975	956		80

Inwards, *from Sea*, at each Port and Outport, &c.—*Continued.*

Foreign.					In Ballast.									
					British.			Canadian.			Foreign.			
Number of Vessels.	Tons Register.	Quantity of Freight. Tons Weight.	Quantity of Freight. Tons Measurement.	Crew Number.	Number of Vessels.	Tons Register.	Crew Number.	Number of Vessels.	Tons Register.	Crew Number.	Number of Vessels.	Tons Register.	Crew Number.	Number.
...	...	...	...	...	...	...	...	23	3,103	131	3	801	47	60
...	...	...	...	...	...	...	...	...	...	...	...	...	...	61
...	...	...	...	...	...	...	...	...	...	...	36	2,960	655	62
91	7,303	6,080	...	1,600	...	...	...	26	3,469	150	18	860	81	63
29	1,324	498	...	261	...	...	...	...	...	...	...	...	...	64
14	149	13	...	28	...	...	...	111	2,640	336	245	3,278	586	65
6	4,086	7,590	...	107	79	131,581	1,992	54	18,812	365	174	138,983	3,217	66
1	78	10	...	22	...	...	...	20	2,202	188	5	561	82	67
...	...	...	...	...	1	275	20	...	...	...	15	951	160	68
...	...	...	...	...	...	...	...	5	464	41	...	...	...	69
...	...	...	...	...	...	...	...	1	13	3	...	...	...	70
...	...	...	...	...	...	...	...	7	940	36	...	...	...	71
...	...	...	...	...	1	1,782	23	...	...	...	5	7,042	113	72
...	...	...	...	...	...	...	...	21	2,108	94	2	363	10	73
...	...	...	...	...	...	...	...	...	...	...	...	...	...	74
...	...	...	...	...	...	...	...	5	486	24	2	187	8	75
...	...	...	...	...	3	112	14	2	156	10	...	...	...	76
16	22,458	33,511	4,413	366	21	45,765	681	1	78	10	4	6,222	88	77
...	...	...	...	...	...	...	...	...	...	...	...	...	...	78
...	...	...	...	...	...	...	...	17	1,341	65	45	5,884	164	79
19	30,531	370	102	446	2	5,173	91	29	5,127	261	61	41,703	1,75[illegible]	80
...	...	...	...	...	5	216	73	...	...	...	...	...	...	81
...	...	...	...	...	9	13,517	223	3	750	21	18	14,491	240	82
...	...	...	...	...	...	...	...	...	...	...	...	...	...	83
...	...	...	...	...	1	1,047	17	96	4,463	422	19	1,978	53	84
4	270	37	...	78	...	...	...	2	32	8	6	249	60	85
4	110	...	...	10	...	...	...	27	2,861	132	41	701	155	86
...	...	...	...	...	...	...	...	...	...	...	4	4.563	62	87
29	46,436	85,605	...	669	375	63,186	4,952	133	32,800	1,649	373	49,098	6,069	88
...	...	...	...	...	22	19,472	403	122	28,674	630	41	31,417	659	89
2	1,158	540	...	21	2	416	15	5	2,3[illegible]	38	7	4,454	80	90
12	950	250	...	215	...	...	...	...	...	...	6	5,696	85	91
2	2,535	2,250	...	34	2	2,358	28	...	...	...	4	4,468	85	93
...	...	...	...	...	...	...	...	48	15,961	353	...	...	...	94
1	398	...	...	18	...	...	...	...	...	...	...	...	...	95
60	17,967	...	...	1,430	...	...	...	...	...	...	...	...	...	96
2	183	35	...	36	...	...	...	...	...	...	...	...	...	97
...	...	...	...	...	...	...	...	...	...	...	3	228	41	98
...	...	...	...	...	...	...	...	1	98	5	3	1,341	52	99
...	...	...	...	...	...	...	...	4	1,404	56	1	652	17	100
...	...	...	...	...	...	...	...	23	2,647	303	16	1,143	185	101
13	377	...	14	68	...	...	...	59	29,709	2,024	12	1,245	78	102
...	...	...	...	...	...	...	...	1	299	7	...	...	...	103
53	2,670	1,014	...	911	...	...	...	...	...	...	...	...	...	104
...	...	...	...	...	3	4,655	63	...	...	...	3	3,553	60	105
8	10,499	3,191	190	170	18	38,478	635	14	2,647	287	4	5,387	84	106
...	...	...	...	...	...	...	...	...	...	...	8	2,285	67	107
...	...	...	...	...	2	3,564	48	...	...	...	13	16,168	258	108
...	...	...	...	...	...	...	...	...	...	...	...	...	...	109
2	554	2	...	10	...	...	...	37	4,453	165	18	3,804	93	110
...	...	...	...	...	1	1,774	24	...	...	...	1	229	8	111
...	...	...	...	...	...	...	...	1	74	5	...	...	...	112
203	27,072	1,631	2	1,972	...	...	...	6	558	18	334	9,799	1,215	113
...	...	...	...	...	7	461	81	...	...	...	14	5,026	122	114
4	249	414	1	12	...	...	...	31	1,075	89	207	6,672	453	115
191	302,414	23,136	10,544	2,4[illegible]6	28	51,692	897	364	30,397	1,491	402	54,059	1,64[illegible]	116
...	...	...	...	...	...	...	...	26	2,477	122	3	79	10	117
4	565	325	...	50	...	...	...	...	...	...	3	231	58	118
18	2,096	4,218	...	73	...	...	...	122	10,256	631	199	3,000	503	119

No. 5.—Statement of Vessels, British, Canadian and Foreign entered

Number.	PORTS AND OUTPORTS.	WITH CARGOES. British. Number of Vessels.	Tons Register.	Quantity of Freight. Tons Weight.	Tons Measurement.	Crew, Number.	Canadian. Number of Vessels.	Tons Register.	Quantity of Freight. Tons Weight.	Tons Measurement.	Crew, Number.
120	Sackville.... ...N.B.	....	....	....	....	....	34	4,970	....	....	176
121	Salmon River....N.S.	....	....	....	....	....	27	1,037	347	....	161
122	Sandy Cove...... "	....	....	....	....	....	1	168	174	....	6
123	Shediac..........N.B.	....	....	....	....	....	....	....	....	....	....
124	Sheet Harbour...N.S.	....	....	....	....	....	1	37	....	....	6
125	Shelburne.... .. "	2	2,907	2,500	800	59	56	2,941	2,293	7	524
126	Sherbrooke...... "	....	....	....	....	....	....	....	....	....	....
127	Shippegan.......N.B.	....	....	....	....	....	2	198	....	....	13
128	Souris... ...P...E.I.	....	....	....	....	....	10	808	64	....	70
129	Stikeen..........B.C.	....	....	....	....	....	7	1,865	339	....	149
130	Summerside... P.E.I.	....	....	....	....	....	3	343	269	....	15
131	Sydney .........N.S.	27	44,109	66,343	....	822	22	11,735	17,437	....	661
132	Thorne's Cove... "	....	....	....	....	....	13	1,397	237	316	70
133	Three Rivers.....Que.	1	2,016	3,000	....	35	....	....	....	....	....
134	Tidnish..........N.S.	....	....	....	....	....	....	....	....	....	....
135	Tignish.. . ...P.E.I.	....	....	....	....	....	1	99	150	....	5
136	Truro ....N.S.	....	....	....	....	....	....	....	....	....	....
137	Tusket .... "	....	....	....	....	....	1	99	25	....	5
138	Tusket Wedge... "	....	....	....	....	....	28	314	292	....	102
139	Vancouver ......B.C.	174	240,377	75,167	79,721	18,459	77	24,232	4,824	1,424	1,605
140	Victoria.......... "	150	156,634	11,489	2,623	13,913	232	103,556	9,298	257	7,556
141	Walton..........N.S.	....	....	....	....	....	1	310	1	....	7
142	Westport .... "	....	....	....	....	....	1	99	91	....	4
143	Weymouth ...... "	....	....	....	....	....	6	1,006	383	....	35
144	Windsor... ..... "	5	591	788	....	29	12	4,166	1,478	....	65
145	Wolfville......... "	....	....	....	....	....	10	1,850	....	....	58
146	Yarmouth........ "	86	61,180	1,793	567	6,020	288	85,908	11,986	923	7,815
	Total	1805	4,014,037	1,057,155	285,395	132,643	3197	573,270	223,356	54,561	42,991

Inwards, *from Sea*, at each Port and Outport, &c.—*Continued.*

					IN BALLAST.									
FOREIGN.					BRITISH.			CANADIAN.			FOREIGN.			
Number of Vessels.	Tons Register.	Quantity of Freight. Tons Weight.	Quantity of Freight. Tons Measurement.	Crew, Number.	Number of Vessels.	Tons Register.	Crew, Number.	Number of Vessels.	Tons Register.	Crew, Number.	Number of Vessels.	Tons Register.	Crew, Number.	Number.
4	739	....	....	22	....	....	....	2	230	10	....	....	....	120
....	....	....	....	....	....	....	....	1	31	3	....	....	....	121
....	....	....	....	....	....	....	....	....	....	....	....	....	....	122
2	1,110	....	2,220	23	....	....	....	....	....	....	6	3,343	67	123
....	....	....	....	....	....	....	....	....	....	....	1	1,754	18	124
104	8,006	1,743	....	1,933	....	....	....	12	1,340	125	81	7,499	1,369	125
....	....	....	....	....	....	....	....	1	191	5	7	3,958	86	126
....	....	....	....	....	....	....	....	2	243	13	....	....	....	127
2	411	667	....	14	2	401	19	2	192	10	....	....	....	128
....	....	....	....	....	....	....	....	....	....	....	....	....	....	129
1	217	371	....	6	....	....	....	....	....	....	....	....	....	130
81	176,913	397,493	....	2,134	46	37,667	768	28	23,518	624	63	66,453	1,206	131
....	....	....	....	....	....	....	....	1	98	5	1	52	18	132
....	....	....	....	....	29	62,784	1,083	5	7,618	130	1	1,070	20	133
....	....	....	....	....	....	....	....	....	....	....	1	909	14	134
....	....	....	....	....	....	....	....	....	....	....	....	....	....	135
....	....	....	....	....	....	....	....	2	263	10	....	....	....	136
9	700	550	....	158	....	....	....	2	201	9	26	2,887	442	137
4	451	385	....	88	4	2,699	48	....	....	....	6	5,962	80	138
294	243,536	29,453	10,586	12,803	32	72,298	1,899	190	48,311	3,289	84	52,339	3,266	139
289	334,994	12,239	8,962	15,371	69	135,495	7,864	101	18,446	1,330	213	251,048	12,006	140
....	....	....	....	....	2	946	18	33	15,142	216	11	4,491	68	141
....	....	....	....	....	....	....	....	1	148	6	7	78	17	142
....	....	....	....	....	....	....	....	10	1,985	64	15	8,573	149	143
1	315	535	....	7	....	....	....	42	30,618	183	57	52,654	481	144
....	....	....	....	....	....	....	....	....	....	....	....	....	....	145
54	3,214	525	....	752	1	1,723	25	59	3,444	462	164	26,408	2,723	146
2142	1,382,856	663,632	37,423	51,359	948	1,004,295	29,338	2796	540,163	36,111	4,394	1,380,732	58,601	

No. 6.—STATEMENT of Vessels, British, Canadian and Foreign entered Inwards

ABSTRACT BY

Number.	COUNTRIES WHENCE ARRIVED.	WITH CARGOES.									
		BRITISH.					CANADIAN.				
		Number of Vessels.	Tons Register.	Quantity of Freight. Tons Weight.	Quantity of Freight. Tons Measurement.	Crew, Number.	Number of Vessels.	Tons Register.	Quantity of Freight. Tons Weight.	Quantity of Freight. Tons Measurement.	Crew, Number.
1	Great Britain	851	3,006,920	703,016	198,998	77,056	1	612	100		32
2	Australia	25	60,290	10,982	4,674	2,513					
3	British Africa	5	13,823	7,869	5,075	214					
4	British Guiana	29	41,955	54,565		1,154					
5	British West Indies	63	84,673	59,475	4,453	2,211	78	12,215	15,848	3	546
6	Newfoundland	227	88,895	15,923		5,316	186	41,125	28,060		1,841
7	New Zealand	1	2,284	87	100	36					
8	Argentina										
9	Azores, Madeira and Cape Verde Islands										
10	Belgium	46	218,471	40,310	1,312	4,098					
11	Brazil										
12	Central American States										
13	Chili	2	4,506	1,300		54					
14	China										
15	Cuba and Porto Rico						35	5,772	6,913		226
16	Denmark										
17	Dutch East Indies	1	2,851	5,677		35					
18	Dutch West Indies										
19	France	19	49,621	5,188	898	1,532	1	9			7
20	French West Indies						1	99	208		7
21	Germany	2	5,626	870	672	66					
22	Greenland						1	[illegible]	[illegible]		10
23	Hawaii										
24	Holland	4	8,495	6,401		124					
25	Iceland										
26	Italy	5	8,252	12,504		158					
27	Japan	28	89,531	28,125	59,084	5,062					
28	Mediterranean ports	1	1,951	300		34					
29	Mexico	10	18,286	10,230		382					
30	Norway and Sweden	1	2,165			29					
31	Panama										
32	Peru										
33	Portugal						4	395	390		25
34	Russia										
35	Sea	2	1,968	2,000		160					
36	Sea fisheries	45	2,234	660		207	1,373	65,706	22,449	140	15,370
37	South Sea seal fisheries						3	277			57
38	Spain	11	18,758	23,501		276	5	651	920		33
39	Spanish Africa										
40	St. Pierre						26	8,079	341		215
41	United States	427	282,482	68,172	10,039	31,926	1,483	442,614	117,277	54,418	24,622
42	Uruguay										
	Total	1,805	4,014,037	1,057,155	285,305	132,643	3,197	573,270	223,356	54,561	42,991

from Sea, in the Dominion of Canada, during the Fiscal Year ended June 30, 1906.

COUNTRIES.

Foreign.					In Ballast. British.			In Ballast. Canadian.			In Ballast. Foreign.			
Number of Vessels.	Tons Register.	Quantity of Freight. Tons Weight.	Quantity of Freight. Tons Measurement.	Crew, Number.	Number of Vessels.	Tons Register.	Crew, Number.	Number of Vessels.	Tons Register.	Crew, Number.	Number of Vessels.	Tons Register.	Crew, Number.	Number.
21	20,994	21,642	2,220	338	127	240,734	4,133	30	14,707	286	150	133,898	2,465	1
....	....	....	....	....	1	1,888	101	....	....	....	....	....	....	2
....	....	....	....	....	2	5,677	85	....	....	....	7	5,607	91	3
2	2,513	5,600	....	42	....	....	....	....	....	....	....	....	....	4
46	29,466	17,837	1,640	808	3	4,560	85	3	2,153	54	7	4,998	94	5
106	210,856	468,298	....	2,670	354	61,935	4,403	179	67,332	2,545	46	23,062	582	6
....	....	....	....	....	....	....	....	....	....	....	....	....	....	7
....	....	....	....	....	....	....	....	....	....	....	1	1,232	16	8
....	....	....	....	....	1	1,916	27	....	....	....	....	....	....	9
....	....	....	....	....	1	4,206	54	....	....	....	3	3,267	54	10
....	....	....	....	....	8	1,809	63	1	632	11	9	8,130	130	11
....	....	....	....	....	....	....	....	....	....	....	1	1,399	19	12
....	....	....	....	....	6	11,159	138	....	....	....	4	6,200	77	13
15	68,573	2,484	3,969	1,473	27	77,152	4,794	....	....	....	2	3,937	32	14
....	....	....	....	....	....	....	....	5	1,159	33	2	1,364	31	15
....	....	....	....	....	....	....	....	....	....	....	1	147	6	16
....	....	....	....	....	....	....	....	....	....	....	1	1,165	15	17
....	....	....	....	....	....	....	....	1	166	7	....	....	....	18
6	8,424	8,781	20	151	....	....	....	....	....	....	24	13,351	322	19
....	....	....	....	....	....	....	....	....	....	....	....	....	....	20
8	12,590	5,474	4,573	188	....	....	....	....	....	....	10	8,545	141	21
....	....	....	....	....	....	....	....	....	....	....	....	....	....	22
....	....	....	....	....	....	....	....	2	3,310	37	....	....	....	23
1	2,418	4,941	....	29	....	....	....	....	....	....	1	836	13	24
....	....	....	....	....	....	....	....	....	....	....	2	408	13	25
1	1,547	3,600	....	23	....	....	....	....	....	....	1	1,484	12	26
13	50,297	239	1,919	1,454	10	21,401	301	....	....	....	4	8,115	139	27
....	....	....	....	....	....	....	....	....	....	....	....	....	....	28
....	....	....	....	....	3	7,150	98	1	1,770	20	1	2,115	27	29
4	5,773	10,211	....	96	....	....	....	....	....	....	66	64,-32	1,013	30
....	....	....	....	....	5	9,968	161	....	....	....	....	....	....	31
2	4,815	1,007	....	112	5	6,934	113	....	....	....	1	1,395	17	32
....	....	....	....	....	4	7,020	105	....	....	....	1	1,035	16	33
....	....	....	....	....	....	....	....	....	....	....	1	2,088	27	34
....	....	....	....	....	22	24,711	1,803	....	....	....	6	5,752	360	35
401	31,705	12,509	247	8,079	86	5,153	1,228	323	25,763	4,618	821	63,694	14,508	36
....	....	....	....	....	....	....	....	....	....	....	....	....	....	37
10	8,735	16,425	....	153	2	4,066	64	1	470	10	1	353	8	38
....	....	....	....	....	1	1,795	27	....	....	....	2	2,012	33	39
7	2,259	250	8	128	5	402	38	39	4,650	429	69	7,677	635	40
1499	922,391	84,334	22,827	35,615	275	504,659	11,517	2,210	417,952	18,052	3,149	1,002,634	37,705	41
....	....	....	....	....	....	....	....	1	99	9	....	....	....	42
2,142	1,382,856	663,632	37,423	51,359	948	1,004 295	29,338	2,796	540,163	26,111	4,394	1,380,732	58,601	

No. 6.—STATEMEMT of Vessels, British, Canadian and Foreign,

RECAPITU

—	Number of Vessels.	Tons Register.	Quantity of Freight.		Crew, Number.
			Tons Weight.	Tons Measurement.	
With Cargo—					
British	1,805	4,014,037	1,057,155	285,305	132,643
Canadian	3,197	573,270	223,356	54,561	42,991
Foreign	2,142	1,382,856	663,632	37,423	51,359
Total	7,144	5,970,163	1,944,143	377,289	226,993
Grand total	.....	.....	.....	.....	.....

entered Inwards, *from Sea*, by Ports and Outports, &c.—*Concluded.*

LATION.

—	Number of Vessels.	Tons Register	Quantity of Freight.		Crew, Number.
			Tons Weight.	Tons Measurement.	
In Ballast—					
British	948	1,004,295	...	...	29,338
Canadian	2,796	540,163	...	...	26,111
Foreign	4,394	1,380,732	...	...	58,601
...	8,138	2,925,190	...	...	114,050
...	15,282	8,895,353	1,944,143	377,239	341,043

No. 7.—STATEMENT of Vessels, British, Canadian and Foreign, entered Outwards,

Number.	PORTS AND OUTPORTS.	WITH CARGOES.									
		British.					Canadian.				
		Number of Vessels.	Tons Register.	Quantity of Freight. Tons Weight.	Quantity of Freight. Tons Measurement.	Crew, Number.	Number of Vessels.	Tons Register.	Quantity of Freight. Tons Weight.	Quantity of Freight. Tons Measurement.	Crew Number.
1	Advocate Harbour, N.S.						10	2,471	4,795		65
2	Alberton.........P.E.I.						3	280	279		18
3	Alma.... ....N.B.						1	90	275		5
4	Amherst..........N.S.						1	397	660		7
5	Annapolis Royal ... "						25	5,579	13,996	16,764	163
6	Apple River .. ... "						21	3,840	6,733		116
7	Arichat..... ....., "						2	198			10
8	Aspey Bay........ "						2	68		40	6
9	Baddeck .. .. "						7	1,699	130		136
10	Baie Verte........N.B.	1	1,172		3,820	21					
11	Barrington........N.S.										
12	Barton .... "						58	5,780		11,175	309
13	Bathurst.... .....N.B.	3	5,566			75	8	1,335			45
14	Bayfield .. ..N.S.						7	693	276		40
15	Bear River.... ... "						35	6,299		23,214	232
16	Belliveau's Cove... "						22	2,471	17	4,579	118
17	Bridgetown.... .. "	1	95	150	110	6					
18	Bridgewater.... .. "	1	1,722	3,013		27	67	15,747	27,643		434
19	Buctouche.........N.B.										
20	Campbellton...... "	6	8,511			137	4	1,069			26
21	Campobello....... "						65	497	109		132
22	Canning..........N.S.						4	991			24
23	Canso .... "	4	11,922	37,000		448	8	806	1,075		44
24	Cardigan .... ..P,E.I.						9	834	1,175	8	50
25	Charlottetown ... "	6	3,912	1,393	2	156	86	58,978	9,507	941	2,418
26	Chatham..........N.B.	17	26,063		72,719	407	17	2,362		5,794	95
27	Chemainus........B.C.	13	23,675		40,671	336	2	1,830	131	2,987	25
28	Chester ....N.S						2	610	1,067		12
29	Cheticamp.. ..... "						11	372	105		33
30	Cheverie ... . "						14	2,063	2,625		70
31	Chicoutimi .. . ..Que.	6	12,796	18,359		177					
32	Church Point ....N.S.						15	1,718		2,905	85
33	Clark's Harbour... "										
34	Clementsport ..... "						25	2,493	4,874	6,499	145
35	Comox..........	57	141,212	76,992		2,884	50	15,802	25,386		538
36	Crapaud ....P.E.I.	1	75	96		6	3	283	425		15
37	Dalhousie	3	809		1,008	23	5	1,450		2,753	38
38	Dawson										
39	Digby............						9	1,081	23	3,255	52
40	Dorchester........N.B.						15	1,540		81,409	73
41	Douglas.... ... ..N.B.						9	376	1,244		52
42	Economy ... .N.S.						1	98		115	3
43	Five Islands ..... "						11	1,488	2,633		54
45	Fredericton........N.B.						4	397		840	19
46	Freeport .........N.S.	1	46	38		4					
47	Gabarouse......... "										
48	Gaspe......... . Que.	3	2,057	2,100		37	15	2,697	810	3,320	106
49	Georgetown......P.E.I.	6	259	290		27	1	99	192		6
50	Grand River..... "	2	89	74		8					
51	Halifax.......... N.S.	364	657,056	274,375		18,971	598	94,220	53,517		7,135
52	Hantsport......... "						27	4,381	7,728		127
53	Harvey.. ....N.B.	1	1,617	3,234	2,935	19	17	5,400	10,844	8,209	124
54	Hillsboro'.... .... "	5	11,091	18,000		125	23	6,846	8,328		185
55	Ingonish ..........N.S.										
56	Isaac's Harbor..... "										

for Sea, at each Port and Outport, during the Fiscal Year ended June 30, 1906.

Foreign.					In Ballast.									
					British.			Canadian.			Foreign.			
Number of Vessels.	Tons Register.	Quantity of Freight. Tons Weight.	Quantity of Freight. Tons Measurement.	Crew, Number.	Number of Vessels.	Tons Register.	Crew, Number.	Number of Vessels.	Tons Register.	Crew, Number.	Number of Vessels.	Tons Register.	Crew, Number.	Number.
5	1,403	2,675	....	34	....	....	....	....	....	....	....	....	....	1
....	....	....	....	....	....	....	....	....	....	....	....	....	....	2
1	56	170	....	4	....	....	....	....	....	....	....	....	....	4
2	1,390	2,300	....	30	....	....	....	....	....	....	....	....	....	4
13	4,189	7,750	9,297	91	....	....	....	....	....	....	....	....	....	5
23	5,079	9,485	....	126	....	....	....	....	....	....	....	....	....	6
....	....	....	....	....	....	....	....	83	2,490	498	16	1,247	298	7
....	....	....	....	....	....	....	....	....	....	....	....	....	....	8
1	50	30	....	4	....	....	....	....	....	....	....	....	....	9
10	6,072	....	15,010	128	....	....	....	....	....	....	....	....	....	10
....	....	....	....	....	....	....	....	4	108	29	26	1,536	391	11
....	....	....	....	....	....	....	....	....	....	....	....	....	....	12
11	7,575	....	....	112	....	....	....	....	....	....	....	....	....	13
....	....	....	....	....	....	....	....	....	....	....	....	....	....	14
6	2,142	....	5,028	41	....	....	....	....	....	....	....	....	....	15
....	....	....	....	....	....	....	....	....	....	....	....	....	....	16
....	....	....	....	....	....	....	....	....	....	....	....	....	....	17
8	3,696	6,580	....	343	1	1,737	23	3	54	18	....	....	....	18
3	1,248	....	....	25	....	....	....	....	....	....	....	....	....	19
22	13,315	....	....	237	....	....	....	....	....	....	....	....	....	20
108	2,858	274	1,175	367	....	....	....	6	55	12	28	799	83	21
....	....	....	....	....	....	....	....	....	....	....	....	....	....	22
13	824	1,050	....	123	2	1,520	100	223	19,418	3,545	278	23,209	5,020	23
....	....	....	....	....	....	....	....	....	....	....	1	42	11	24
18	16,532	1,067	6	823	....	....	....	2	96	10	....	....	....	26
26	24,550	....	52,255	365	....	....	....	....	....	....	....	....	....	27
5	9,032	....	15,785	102	....	....	....	9	632	45	17	1,671	178	28
....	....	....	....	....	....	....	....	1	15	5	2	155	39	29
....	....	....	....	....	....	....	....	....	....	....	....	....	....	30
16	9,013	14,698	....	113	....	....	....	....	....	....	....	....	....	31
15	22,080	41,184	4,708	328	....	....	....	....	....	....	....	....	....	22
....	....	....	....	....	....	....	....	....	....	....	....	....	....	32
7	228	32	....	22	....	....	....	....	....	....	1	83	18	33
....	....	....	....	....	....	....	....	....	....	....	....	....	....	34
58	61,940	72,897	....	1,614	....	....	....	8	1,504	84	14	15,609	261	35
....	....	....	....	....	....	....	....	....	....	....	....	....	....	36
25	18,997	....	35,491	301	....	....	....	....	....	....	....	....	....	37
....	....	....	....	....	....	....	....	1	639	80	....	....	....	38
11	234	33	200	30	....	....	....	....	....	....	5	507	58	39
....	....	....	....	....	....	....	....	....	....	....	....	....	....	40
21	235	1,224	....	69	....	....	....	....	....	....	10	82	28	41
....	....	....	....	....	....	....	....	....	....	....	....	....	....	42
....	....	....	....	....	....	....	....	....	....	....	....	....	....	43
1	91	....	220	5	....	....	....	1	98	5	....	....	....	45
....	....	....	....	....	....	....	....	....	....	....	....	....	....	46
....	....	....	....	....	....	....	....	2	106	22	2	154	36	47
15	12,542	....	18,880	182	....	....	....	....	....	....	....	....	....	48
1	72	113	....	6	....	....	....	8	343	44	3	451	51	49
....	....	....	....	....	....	....	....	....	....	....	....	....	....	50
197	108,791	70,930	....	4,438	9	12,182	272	1	40	4	1	377	15	51
8	2,696	4,625	....	49	8	848	109	1	491	7	31	6,453	534	52
9	6,243	12,322	11,058	96	....	....	....	....	....	....	....	....	....	53
92	59,760	115,160	....	1,135	....	....	....	....	....	....	....	....	....	54
....	....	....	....	....	....	....	....	1	11	2	....	....	....	55
....	....	....	....	....	....	....	....	....	....	....	5	481	103	56

No. 7.—STATEMENT of Vessels, British, Canadian and Foreign, entered Outwards,

Number.	PORTS AND OUTPORTS.	WITH CARGOES.									
		BRITISH.					CANADIAN.				
		Number of Vessels.	Tons Register.	Quantity of Freight. Tons Weight.	Quantity of Freight. Tons Measurement.	Crew, Number.	Number of Vessels.	Tons Register.	Quantity of Freight. Tons Weight.	Quantity of Freight. Tons Measurement.	Crew, Number.
57	Jordan Bay..........N.S.						11	1,145		1,763	62
58	Kentville.......... "						4	240			14
59	Kingsport.......... "						6	1,885			43
60	Ladner..........B.C.						1	88	54		9
61	Ladysmith.......... "	19	29,910	5,448		507	84	15,316	13,656		841
62	LaHave..........N.S.						10	1,500	2,636		59
63	L'Ardoise.......... "										
64	Liscombe.......... "						1	191	180		6
65	Liverpool.......... "						50	6,630	5,058	6,685	270
66	Lockeport.......... "						27	1,653	1,129		266
67	Lord's Cove..........N.B						80	1,243	1,419		215
68	Louisburg..........N.S.	95	191,015	397,288		2,703	21	13,304	22,159		352
69	Lunenburg.......... "						49	6,344	11,258		310
70	Magdalen Islands..Que.	1	275	100		6					
71	Mahone Bay..........N.S.						15	1,612	2,842		99
72	Main à Dieu.......... "										
73	Maitland.......... "						11	1,915	2,800		61
74	Malpeque..........P.E.I.	1	57	17		4					
75	Matane..........Que.										
76	Meteghan..........N.S.						32	3,107	380	5,714	160
77	Murray Harbour.P.E.I.										
78	Musquash..........N.B.						17	1,929	4	4,544	72
79	Montreal..........Que.	353	1,284,957	1,286,331	101,801	3,0 89	45	33,578	30,215	14	996
80	Moncton..........N.B.						17	1,676	3,390		82
81	Montague..........P.E.I.	5	265	260		23	10	916	1,282	45	58
82	Nanaimo..........B.C.	10	16,489	16,570		300	64	8,196	8,511		397
83	Newcastle..........N.B.	8	13,234		27,100	201	15	2,921		6,200	92
84	New Campbellton..N.S.	6	609	997		32					
85	New London.....P.E.I.										
86	New Westminster..B.C.	2	3,157	5,847		50	72	4,175	5,679		320
87	Northeast Harbour.N.S.						4	169	20	100	34
88	North Head..........N.B.						28	5,108	109		140
89	Northport..........N.S.										
90	North Sydney..........N.S.	261	68,673	31,413		6,140	88	17,890	26,648		901
91	Parrsboro'.......... "	24	23,485	50,730		452	83	23,855	39,441		426
92	Paspebiac..........Que.	4	898	837	250	31	34	7,786	1,527	17,003	243
93	Percé.......... "						2	160	40		34
94	Pictou..........N.S	1	2,259	2,259		23	14	1,438	510		216
95	Port Greville.......... "						60	18,057	35,025		429
96	Port Hastings.......... "						9	3,598			110
97	Port Hawksbury.......... "						122	34,747			2.404
98	Port Hood.......... "										
99	Port La Tour.......... "										
100	Port Medway.......... "						1	68		254	5
101	Port Morien.......... "	3	1,305	2,350		39	1	671	1,434		16
102	Port Mulgrave.......... "						13	1,841	1,400		92
103	Port Simpson..........B.C.										
104	Port Williams..........N.S.						4	874			27
105	Pubnico.......... "						27	1,357	115		365
106	Pugwash.......... "	2	3,388		6,747	46	1	99		190	5
107	Quebec..........Que.	124	430,956	98,661	58,140	11,454	17	1,625	1,536		108
108	Rimouski.......... "	2	3,564			42					
109	River Bourgeoise...N.S.										
110	Richibucto..........N.B.						16	1,694			81
111	River Hebert..........N.S.						69	8,371		10,060	312

for Sea, at each Port and Outport, &c.—*Continued.*

Foreign.					In Ballast.									
					British.			Canadian.			Foreign.			
Number of Vessels.	Tons Register.	Quantity of Freight. Tons Weight.	Quantity of Freight. Tons Measurement.	Crew, Number.	Number of Vessels.	Tons Register.	Crew, Number.	Number of Vessels.	Tons Register.	Crew, Number.	Number of Vessels.	Tons Register.	Crew, Number.	Number.
1	325		425	6				2	196	39	2	146	37	57
														58
3	847			18										59
								1	98	7	1	63	1	60
67	93,092	146,954		2,007	1	1,267	23	62	23,968	1,661	9	2,370	108	61
1	626	1,095		12				47	3,644	696	1	87	18	62
								46	1,925	294				63
4	2,111	192		72							30	2,635	609	64
106	8,391	6,210	800	1,748				1	190	6	4	355	29	65
24	1,223	672		273										66
185	3,112	3,296		566				20	2,063	161	8	140	18	67
87	156,624	346,322		1,867	9	555	122	46	2,753	397	106	8,770	1,695	68
1	231	400		6				208	16,311	3,077	8	673	155	69
12	839	1,596		63										70
								15	996	196				71
								2	50	20				72
														73
														74
2	3,243			98										75
4	417	15	900	17										76
											15	347	82	77
45	5,834	6	12,019	169				12	209	42	1	8	2	78
14	18,008	21,846	90	307	1	3,126	46	1	78	10				79
1	103	205		4										80
								1	15	4				81
87	79,010	158,555	1,200	2,883	1	1,945	27	16	1,542	127	42	6,334	931	82
17	12,756		25,910	201										83
														84
								4	59	17				85
16	5,039	9,165		83				72	3,698	418	5	196	15	86
7	309	50		84				11	160	54	3	210	54	87
32	411	318		47				127	22,717	1,003	15	475	102	88
6	6,049		11,388	86										89
29	20,788	14,427		410	102	24,803	1,795	60	28,273	1,121	342	66,754	6,973	90
41	30,962	64,017		652										91
12	6,696		14,555	129										92
19	7,764	250	7,700	314										93
3	2,948	2,948		52										94
														95
1	398			19										96
62	18,511			1,619							7	368	35	97
2	183	35		36										98
											3	228	41	99
1	1,177	2,068	104	16							2	164	36	100
								1	99	17				101
								1	97	12	3	205	50	102
								49	26,570	1,786	28	2,546	190	103
														104
52	3,813	951		960										105
4	4,867		6,170	74										106
23	34,741	25,991	15,786	517	3	5,945	196	3	681	18	3	2,955	41	107
14	17,272			92										108
								90	1,713	630				109
13	4,023			99										110
22	4,959		5,575	115										111

No. 7.—STATEMENT of Vessels, British, Canadian and Foreign, entered Outwards,

Number.	PORTS AND OUTPORTS.	WITH CARGOES.									
		BRITISH.					CANADIAN.				
		Number of Vessels.	Tons Register.	Quantity of Freight. Tons Weight.	Quantity of Freight. Tons Measurement.	Crew, Number.	Number of Vessels.	Tons Register.	Quantity of Freight. Tons Weight.	Quantity of Freight. Tons Measurement.	Crew, Number.
112	Rivière du Loup ... Que.	8	14,100	....	24,325	209	1	199	....	400	7
113	Rustico ..... P.E.I.	....	....	....	....	....	1	74	125	....	5
114	St. Andrews ...... N.B	....	....	....	....	....	3	133	127	87	8
115	St. Ann's .... "	....	....	....	....	....	....	....	....	....	....
116	St. George .... "	....	....	....	....	....	24	674	81	1,036	54
117	St. John .... "	99	266,301	201,504	218,847	5,682	449	48,757	8,630	115,451	1,817
118	St. Martin's .... "	....	....	....	....	....	41	4,052	....	11,036	189
119	St. Peter's .... "	....	....	....	....	....	....	....	....	....	....
120	St. Stephen ...... "	....	....	....	....	....	76	1,447	332	....	153
121	Sackville .... "	....	....	....	....	....	14	1,685	....	....	68
122	Salmon River ...... N.S.	....	....	....	....	....	11	759	....	2,315	53
123	Shediac .... N.B.	....	....	....	....	....	....	....	....	....	....
124	Sheet Harbour ..... N.S.	....	....	....	....	....	8	1,873	2,557	....	52
125	Shelburne .... "	....	....	....	....	....	28	4,614	3,623	2,960	194
126	Sherbrooke .... "	....	....	....	....	....	3	636	650	....	19
127	Shippegan .... "	2	246	....	....	12	2	298	....	....	13
128	Souris .... P.E.I.	3	497	742	....	25	22	2,151	1,654	281	187
129	Stikeen .... B.C.	....	....	....	....	....	7	1,865	3	....	149
130	Summerside ...... P.E.I.	3	469	393	....	23	12	5,281	705	....	200
131	Sydney .... N.S.	207	79,304	129,422	....	2,005	69	36,125	53,504	....	1,043
132	Three Rivers. ..... Que.	31	76,877	....	23,814	1,225	....	....	....	....	....
133	Thorne's Cove ..... N.S.	....	....	....	....	....	5	379	875	1,092	22
134	Truro .... "	....	....	....	....	....	4	581	612	....	20
135	Tusket .... "	....	....	....	....	....	14	1,948	4,534	....	76
136	Tusket Wedge ..... "	1	1,723	771	....	25	37	1,825	1,930	....	139
137	Vancouver .... B.C.	119	227,187	101,529	124,243	13,131	107	45,624	34,229	10,715	2,350
138	Vernon River Bridge .... P.E.I.	1	25	23	....	5	2	179	296	....	11
139	Victoria .... B.C.	102	81,789	5,021	1,114	9,976	211	111,378	5,207	1,969	7,477
140	Walton .... N.S.	2	946	....	1,500	18	52	23,653	20,868	14,869	349
141	Westport .... "	....	....	....	....	....	8	116	10	....	20
142	Weymouth .... "	....	....	....	....	....	25	4,449	....	10,933	158
143	Windsor .... "	....	....	....	....	....	74	49,550	77,802	3,820	325
144	Wolfville .... "	....	....	....	....	....	1	335	....	....	7
145	Yarmouth .... "	82	59,333	4,160	274	5,695	159	85,049	20,041	1,551	6,528
	Total	2082	3,793,038	2,777,787	709,420	115,067	4024	932,389	645,454	405,894	45,815

for Sea, at each Port and Outport, &c.—*Concluded.*

Foreign.					In Ballast. British.			In Ballast. Canadian.			In Ballast. Foreign.			
Number of Vessels.	Tons Register.	Quantity of Freight. Tons Weight.	Quantity of Freight. Tons Measurement.	Crew, Number.	Number of Vessels.	Tons Register.	Crew, Number.	Number of Vessels.	Tons Register.	Crew, Number.	Number of Vessels.	Tons Register.	Crew, Number.	Number.
1	229	....	550	8	....	....	....	....	....	....	....	....		112
....	....	....	....	....	....	....	....	2	20	10	....	....	....	113
392	20,412	3,187	1,559	1,901	....	....	....	7	259	20	131	13,874	1,110	114
4	2,903	3,200	....	70	5	371	74	....	....	....	10	467	134	115
180	6,291	7,366	3,930	436	....	....	....	7	133	21	28	590	111	116
559	326,037	9,771	150,826	12,873	....	....	....	194	7,856	1,717	31	27,681	873	117
4	498	....	1,298	16	....	....	....	....	....	....	1	11	2	118
1	90	21	....	8	....	....	....	6	119	29	3	274	59	119
159	2,357	2,066	180	557	....	....	....	59	9,380	453	42	2,384	159	120
3	619	....	....	17	....	....	....	....	....	....	....	....	....	121
....	....	....	....	....	....	....	....	12	217	81	....	....	....	122
10	5,660	....	11,320	106	....	....	....	....	....	....	....	....	....	123
1	796	1,000	....	13	....	....	....	....	....	....	....	....	....	124
106	8,042	1,751	....	1,928	....	....	....	56	1,808	509	72	6,028	1,348	125
8	2,937	950	....	74	....	....	....	....	....	....	....	....	....	126
....	....	....	....	....	....	....	....	....	....	....	....	....	....	127
1	61	99	....	5	....	....	....	2	36	7	....	....	....	128
....	....	....	....	....	....	....	....	....	....	....	....	....	....	129
1	652	3	....	15	....	....	....	....	....	....	....	....	....	130
63	29,065	46,322	....	681	7	5,183	201	3	1,308	41	96	211,392	2,731	131
4	6,531	....	7,832	86	....	....	....	....	....	....	1	1,485	20	132
....	....	....	....	....	....	....	....	....	....	....	....	....	....	133
....	....	....	....	....	....	....	....	....	....	....	....	....	....	134
12	1,645	1,806	....	178	....	....	....	....	....	....	23	1,942	419	135
9	4,550	4,565	....	150	....	....	....	....	....	....	....	....	....	136
237	238,503	35,566	33,543	11,267	27	54,489	1,964	175	33,993	2,489	139	58,486	5,023	137
....	....	....	....	....	....	....	....	....	....	....	....	....	....	138
246	205,061	3,637	672	11,875	93	134,112	9,884	137	32,508	2,776	239	311,504	12,290	139
12	4,972	5,253	2,850	71	....	....	....	....	....	....	....	....	....	140
....	....	....	....	....	....	....	....	....	....	....	....	....	....	141
16	7,761	....	16,387	141	....	....	....	....	....	....	....	....	....	142
82	70,883	126,368	3,190	720	....	....	....	....	....	....	....	....	....	143
....	....	....	....	....	....	....	....	....	....	....	....	....	....	144
14	10,193	12,974	....	156	....	....	....	272	7,278	2,037	185	13,060	3,334	145
3896	1,917,383	1,438,088	505,872	70,418	269	248,083	14,836	2184	259,120	26,413	2079	798,063	45,963	

No. 8—STATEMENT of Vessels, British, Canadian and Foreign, Entered Outwards,

ABSTRACT BY

Number.	COUNTRIES TO WHICH DEPARTED.	WITH CARGOES.									
		BRITISH.					CANADIAN.				
		No. of Vessels.	Tons Register.	Quantity of Freight. Tons Weight.	Quantity of Freight. Tons Measurement.	Crew, Number.	No. of Vessels.	Tons Register.	Quantity of Freight. Tons Weight.	Quantity of Freight. Tons Measurement.	Crew, Number.
1	Great Britain	790	2,467,368	1,796,259	541,106	58,352	7	7,340	10,960	6,909	95
2	Australia	31	68,333	21,467	36,583	2,457	1	1,769	....	2,987	19
3	British Africa	24	65,343	78,634	19,438	993	....	....	....	....	....
4	British Guiana	....	....	....	....	....	2	365	354	150	13
5	British West Indies	39	42,026	44,250	729	1,431	61	10,440	7,926	11,826	456
6	Fiji Islands	....	....	....	....	....	....	....	....	....	....
7	Newfoundland	539	138,038	82,267	....	9,066	453	151,399	143,642	410	5,676
8	New Zealand	6	10,785	6,757	4,047	172	....	....	....	....	....
9	British Possessions, other	....	....	....	....	....	1	377	685	....	8
10	Argentina	....	....	....	....	....	22	12,819	12,948	19,922	232
11	Azores, Madeira and Cape Verde Islands	....	....	....	....	....	5	1,087	1,136	800	34
12	Belgium	12	54,155	63,130	6,504	1,026	....	....	....	....	....
13	Brazil	5	1,073	1,292	....	38	6	1,344	1,820	....	46
14	Chili	6	12,848	....	22,328	166	....	....	....	....	....
15	China	6	19,317	8,112	4,357	613	....	....	....	....	....
16	Cuba and Porto Rico	3	5,539	5,700	....	78	78	17,820	19,732	20,185	514
17	France	5	13,045	426	1,101	424	....	....	....	....	....
18	Germany	1	1,913	3,000	....	24	....	....	....	....	....
19	Holland	3	7,212	12,868	....	116	....	....	....	....	....
20	Italy	3	5,335	5,387	....	90	....	....	....	....	....
21	Japan	30	86,033	38,833	39,864	4,650	....	....	....	....	....
22	Mexico	20	36,491	40,913	....	828	....	....	....	....	....
23	Norway and Sweden	....	....	....	....	....	....	....	....	....	....
24	Panama	....	....	....	....	....	1	99	150	....	7
25	Peru	3	5,044	5,340	9,297	67	....	....	....	....	....
26	Portugal	1	99	150	....	6	1	99	156	....	7
27	Russia	1	1,716	700	....	33	1	2,804	1,050	....	48
28	Sea	3	10,938	27,000	....	368	....	....	....	....	....
29	Sea fisheries	2	203	110	....	34	515	27,754	1,752	....	5,644
30	Spain	3	2,535	5,341	....	48	1	386	853	1,023	8
31	St. Pierre	22	1,301	2,262	....	101	74	7,692	3,871	655	764
32	United States	524	736,348	527,589	24,066	33,886	2,794	688,337	437,956	341,027	32,234
33	Uruguay	....	....	....	....	....	1	458	463	....	10
	Total	2,082	3,793,038	2,777,787	709,420	115,067	4,024	932,389	645,454	405,894	45,815

for Sea, in the Dominion of Canada, during the Fiscal Year ended June 30, 1906.

BY COUNTRIES.

Foreign.					In Ballast.										
					British.			Canadian.			Foreign.				
No. of Vessels.	Tons Register.	Quantity of Freight. Tons Weight.	Quantity of Freight. Tons Measurement.	Crew, Number.	No. of Vessels.	Tons Register.	Crew, Number.	No. of Vessels.	Tons Register.	Crew, Number.	No. of Vessels.	Tons Register.	Crew, Number.	Number.
285	260,377	151,460	274,709	4,105	9	18,840	427	...	...	...	6	9,075	132	1
4	6,520	2,190	12,409	79	3	7,146	247	1	2,048	22	1	1,575	16	2
2	3,068	2,400	5,474	37	...	...	...	...	...	...	...	...	...	3
...	...	...	...	...	...	...	...	...	...	...	...	...	...	4
37	24,559	22,334	1,250	635	...	...	...	1	249	6	...	...	...	5
1	520	...	1,340	10	...	...	...	...	...	...	...	...	...	6
53	41,312	36,654	...	806	30	8,691	628	75	28,830	1,118	127	209,663	3,050	7
...	...	...	...	...	1	2,284	36	...	...	...	...	...	...	8
...	...	...	...	...	...	...	...	1	377	8	...	...	...	9
22	18,786	19,210	16,647	302	...	...	...	...	...	...	...	...	...	10
1	320	560	...	8	...	...	...	...	...	...	...	...	...	11
...	...	...	...	...	...	...	...	...	...	...	...	...	...	12
1	1,035	...	1,564	16	...	...	...	...	...	...	...	...	...	13
3	4,658	6,930	5,560	61	1	2,242	29	...	...	...	...	...	...	14
...	...	...	...	...	19	60,228	3,698	...	...	...	...	...	...	15
15	7,877	6,618	10,231	143	...	...	...	...	...	...	1	377	15	16
6	5,829	6,493	1,520	159	...	...	...	...	...	...	1	1,456	21	17
11	32,004	17,666	2,117	673	...	...	...	...	...	...	1	1,289	19	18
...	...	...	...	...	...	...	...	...	...	...	1	1,785	25	19
2	5,097	3,000	...	149	...	...	...	...	...	...	...	...	...	20
1	923	...	2,350	17	...	...	...	...	...	...	7	27,051	745	21
1	376	...	1,200	9	2	3,975	59	...	...	...	...	...	...	22
18	20,809	2,223	2,164	202	...	...	...	...	...	...	...	...	...	23
...	...	...	...	...	1	2,973	43	...	...	...	...	...	...	24
1	1,547	2,400	...	19	...	...	...	...	...	...	...	...	...	25
1	851	...	728	15	...	...	...	...	...	...	...	...	...	26
1	2,088	808	...	27	...	...	...	...	...	...	...	...	...	27
...	...	...	...	...	1	1,472	95	...	...	...	...	...	...	28
429	35,416	11,288	...	9,138	86	5,334	1,270	1,354	66,694	14,615	1,152	91,589	22,790	29
3	856	2,000	300	34	...	...	...	...	...	...	2	5,196	60	30
59	7,880	9,377	6	448	1	184	20	9	1,419	156	4	1,247	76	31
2,938	1,433,543	1,133,392	166,303	53,310	115	134,714	8,284	743	159,503	10,488	776	447,760	19,014	32
1	1,132	1,085	...	16	...	...	...	...	...	...	...	...	...	33
3,896	1,917,383	1,438,088	505,872	70,418	269	248,083	14,836	2,184	259,120	26,413	2,079	798,063	45,963	

No. 8.—Statement of Vessels, British, Canadian and Foreign, entered Outwards, *for*

RECAPITU

—	Number of Vessels.	Tons Register.	Quantity of Freight.		Crew, Number.
			Tons Weight.	Tons Measurement.	
With cargo—					
British	2,082	3,793,038	2,777,787	709,420	115,067
Canadian	4,024	932,389	645,454	405,894	45,815
Foreign	3,896	1,917,383	1,438,088	505,872	70,418
Total	10,002	6,642,810	4,861,329	1,621,186	231,300
Grand total	....	....	....	....	....

Sea, in the Dominion of Canada, during the Fiscal Year ended June 30, 1906.

LATION.

—	Number of Vessels.	Tons Register.	Quantity of Freight.		Crew, Number.
			Tons Weight.	Tons Measurement.	
In ballast—					
British	269	248,083	....	....	14,836
Canadian	2,184	259,120	....	....	26,413
Foreign	2,079	798,063	....	....	45,963
	4,532	1,305,266	....	....	87,212
	14,534	7,948,076	4,861,329	1,621,186	318,512

No. 9.—SUMMARY STATEMENT of Sea-going Vessels, entered and cleared at each Port during the Fiscal Year, 1906.

RECAPITULATION BY PORTS AND OUTPORTS.

PORTS AND OUTPORTS.	VESSELS ARRIVED.						VESSELS DEPARTED.					
	British.		Foreign.		Total.		British.		Foreign.		Total.	
	No.	Tons.	No.	Tons.	No.	Tons.	No.	Tons.	No.	Tons.	No.	Tons.
[illegible]te Harbour, N.S.	8	2,353	4	1,204	12	3,557	10	2,471	5	1,403	15	3,874
[illegible]n, P.E.I.	1	83	....	....	1	83	3	280	....	....	3	280
Alma, N.B.	....	....	1	56	1	56	1	90	1	56	2	146
Amherst, N.S.	1	397	2	1,390	3	1,787	1	397	2	1,390	3	1,787
Annapolis Royal, N.S	15	3,257	9	2,612	24	5,869	25	5,579	13	4,189	38	9,768
Apple [illegible]r, N.S.	10	1,744	24	5,230	34	6,974	21	3,840	23	5,079	44	8,919
Arichat, N.S.	77	2,448	15	180	92	2,628	85	2,688	16	1,247	101	3,935
Aspy Bay, N.S.	2	68	....	....	2	68	2	68	....	....	2	68
Baddeck, N.S.	1	267	....	....	1	267	7	1,699	1	50	8	1,749
Baie Verte, N.B.	1	1,172	8	5,229	9	6,401	1	1,172	10	6,072	11	7,244
Barrington, N.S.	2	131	27	1,579	29	1,710	4	108	26	1,536	30	1,644
Barton, N.S.	62	6,170	3	282	65	6,452	58	5,780	....	....	58	5,780
Bathurst, N.B.	5	6,176	9	6,992	14	13,168	11	6,901	11	7,575	22	14,476
Bayfield, N.S.	6	594	....	....	6	594	7	693	....	....	7	693
Bear River, N.S	26	2,001	4	1,525	30	3,526	35	6,299	6	2,142	41	8,441
Belliveau's [illegible]ve, N.S.	18	2,139	....	....	18	2,139	22	2,471	....	....	22	2,471
Bridgetown, N.S.	4	386	....	....	4	386	1	95	....	....	1	95
Bridgewater, N.S	30	13,595	12	8,017	42	21,612	72	9,260	8	3,696	80	22,956
[illegible]e, N.S.	....	....	2	818	2	818	....	....	3	1,248	3	1,248
[illegible]n, N.B	5	6,363	1	549	6	6,912	10	9,580	22	13,315	32	22,895
Campobello, N.B.	264	23,301	619	15,395	883	38,696	71	552	136	3,657	207	4,209
[illegible]g, N.S.	2	430	....	....	2	430	4	991	....	....	4	991
[illegible]o, N.S	220	26,812	277	23,219	497	50,031	237	33,666	291	24,033	528	57,699
Caraquet, N.B.	....	....	1	248	1	248	....	....	....	....	....	....
Cardigan, P.E.I.	4	323	....	....	4	323	9	834	1	42	10	876
[illegible]n, P.E.I.	69	50,557	15	13,590	84	64,147	94	62,986	18	16,532	112	79,518
[illegible], N.B.	13	15,774	19	16,849	32	32,623	34	28,425	26	24,550	60	52,975
[illegible]s, B.C	58	29,439	23	12,351	81	41,790	24	26,137	22	10,703	46	36,840
[illegible]er, N.S.	6	694	3	237	9	931	3	625	2	155	5	780
[illegible]p, N.S	9	291	....	....	9	291	11	372	....	....	11	372
Cheverie, N.S.	18	11,633	17	10,556	35	22,189	14	2,063	16	9,013	30	11,076
[illegible]i, Que.	4	8,181	10	14,305	14	22,486	6	12,796	15	22,080	21	34,876
Church [illegible]t, N.S	15	1,622	....	....	15	1,622	15	1,718	....	....	15	1,718
Clark's Harbour, N.S.	....	....	8	263	8	263	....	....	8	311	8	311
[illegible]rt, N.S.	22	2,162	....	....	22	2,162	25	2,493	....	....	25	2,493
[illegible]k, B.C.	115	169,906	69	75,956	184	245,862	115	158,518	72	77,549	187	236,067
Crofton, B.C.	15	3,699	....	....	15	3,699	4	358	....	....	4	358

Dalhousie, N.B.	5	1,473	45	34,036	50	35,509	8	2,259	25	18,997	33	21,256
Dawson, Y.T.	3	1,533	25	12,959	28	14,492	1	639			1	639
Digby, N.S.	14	2,510	20	1,928	34	4,438	9	1,081	16	741	25	1,822
Dorchester, N.B.	12	2,765			12	2,765	15	1,540			15	1,540
Douglas, B.C.	9	528	28	280	37	808	9	376	31	317	40	693
[illegible]y, N.S.	4	333			4	333	1	98			1	98
Five Islands, N.S.	4	302			4	302	11	1,488			11	1,488
[illegible]n, N.B.	5	496	1	91	6	587	5	495	1	91	6	586
Freeport, N.S.	2	135			2	135	1	46			1	46
Gabarouse, N.S.	2	106	1	79	3	185	2	106	2	154	4	260
Gaspé, Que.	5	792	13	11,079	18	11,871	18	4,754	15	12,542	33	17,296
Georgetown, P.E.I.	17	813	4	717	21	1,530	15	701	4	523	19	1,224
[illegible]d [illegible]r, P.E.I.							2	89			2	89
Halifax, N.S.	994	772,438	208	116,592	1,202	889,030	972	763,498	198	109,168	1,170	872,666
Hantsport, N.S.	35	14,250	66	24,717	101	8,967	36	5,720	39	9,149	75	14,869
[illegible]y, N.B.	16	5,143	4	2,672	20	7,815	18	7,017	9	6,243	27	13,260
Hillsboro', N.B.	28	17,937	92	59,760	120	77,697	28	27,937	92	59,760	120	77,697
[illegible]h, N.S.							1	11			1	11
Isaacs Harbour, N.S.	1	99	11	1,010	12	1,109			5	481	5	481
Jordan Bay, N.S.	2	146			2	146	13	1,341	3	471	16	812
Kentville, N.S.	4	323			4	323	4	240			4	240
Kingsport, N.S.	5	1,259	5	1,444	10	2,703	6	1,885	3	847	9	2,732
Ladner, B.C.	2	137			2	137	2	186	1	63	3	249
[illegible]th, B.C.	165	72,726	76	95,462	241	168,188	166	70,461	76	95,462	242	165,923
La [illegible]e, N.S.	140	12,850	3	801	143	13,651	57	5,144	2	713	59	5,857
L'Ardoise, N.S.	42	1,902			42	1,902	46	1,925			46	1,925
Liscombe, N.S.			36	2,960	36	2,960	1	191	34	4,746	35	4,937
[illegible]l, N.S.	38	5,717	109	8,163	147	13,880	51	6,820	110	8,746	161	15,566
Lockeport, N.S.	25	1,505	29	1,324	54	2,829	27	1,653	24	1,223	51	2,876
Lord's Cove, N.B.	138	3,695	259	3,427	397	7,122	100	3,306	193	3,252	293	6,558
[illegible]burg, N.S.	147	168,258	180	143,069	327	311,327	171	207,627	193	165,394	364	373,021
Lunenburg, N.S.	273	25,887	6	639	279	26,526	257	22,655	9	904	266	23,559
Magdalen Islands, Que.	1	275	15	951	16	1,226	1	275	12	839	13	1,114
[illegible]e Bay, N.S.	44	3,138			44	3,138	30	2,608			30	2,608
Main à Dieu, N.S.	1	13			1	13	2	50			2	50
Maitland, N.S.	7	940			7	940	11	1,915			11	1,915
[illegible]e, P.E.I.							1	57			1	57
[illegible]e, Que.	1	1,782	5	7,042	6	8,824			2	3,243	2	3,243
Meteghan, N.S.	33	3,213	2	363	35	3,576	32	3,107	4	417	36	3,524
Middleton, N.S.	2	120			2	120						
M[illegible]ton, N.B.	12	1,825	2	187	14	2,012	17	1,676	1	103	18	1,779
Montague, P.E.I.	9	546			9	546	16	1,196			16	1,196
Montreal, Que.	379	1,330,029	20	2,580	399	1,332,609	400	1,321,739	14	18,008	414	1,339,747
Murray Harbour, P.E.I.	21	465			21	465			15	347	15	347
Musquash, N.B.	17	1,341	45	5,884	62	7,225	29	2,138	46	5,842	75	7,980
Nanaimo, B.C.	35	12,971	80	72,234	115	85,205	91	28,172	129	85,344	220	113,516
New Campbellton, N.S.	7	309			7	309	6	609			6	609
N[illegible]le, N.B.	12	14,267	18	14,494	30	28,761	23	16,155	17	12,756	40	28,911
New London, P.E.I.	4	67			4	67	4	59			4	59
New Westminster, B.C.	135	8,237	19	1,978	154	10,215	146	11,030	21	5,235	167	16,265

No. 9.—SUMMARY STATEMENT of Sea-going Vessels, entered and cleared at each Port during the Fiscal Year, 1906.

RECAPITULATION BY PORTS AND OUTPORTS.

PORTS AND OUTPORTS.	Vessels Arrived.						Vessels Departed.					
	British.		Foreign.		Total.		British.		Foreign.		Total.	
	No.	Tons.	No.	Tons.	No.	Tons.	No.	Tons.	No.	Tons.	No.	Tons.
[illegible] East [illegible]bour, N.S.	17	821	10	519	27	1,340	15	329	10	519	25	848
North [illegible]d, N.B.	150	24,929	45	811	195	25,740	155	27,825	47	886	202	28,711
[illegible]t, N.S.	....	....	4	4,563	4	4,563	....	....	6	6,049	6	6,049
[illegible]th Sydney, N.S.	636	[illegible]	402	95,534	1,038	232,711	511	139,639	371	87,542	882	227,181
Parrsboro', N.S.	144	[illegible]	41	31,417	185	79,563	107	47,340	41	0,962	148	78,302
[illegible]c, Que.	18	4,357	9	5,612	27	9,969	38	8,684	12	[illegible]	50	15,380
Percé, Que.	3	259	18	6,646	21	6,905	2	160	19	7,764	21	7,924
Pictou, N.S.	13	3,745	6	7,003	19	0,748	15	3,[illegible]7	3	2,948	18	6,645
Port [illegible]e, N.S.	48	15,961	....	....	48	5,[illegible]61	60	18,057	....	....	60	18,057
[illegible]t Hastings, N.S.	5	1,251	1	398	6	1,649	9	[illegible]98	1	398	10	[illegible]06
[illegible]t Hawkesbury, N.S.	115	39,145	60	17,967	175	5[illegible]12	122	34,747	69	18,879	191	5[illegible]26
[illegible]t [illegible]l, N.S.	....	....	2	183	2	183	....	....	2	183	2	183
Port La [illegible]r, N.S.	....	....	3	228	3	228	....	....	3	228	3	228
Port Medway, N.S.	4	395	3	1,341	7	1,736	1	68	3	1,341	4	1,409
Port Morien, N.S.	4	1,404	1	652	5	2,056	5	2,075	....	....	5	2,075
[illegible]t [illegible], N.S.	23	2,647	16	1,143	39	3,790	14	1,938	3	205	17	2,143
[illegible]t Simpson, B.C.	59	29,709	25	1,622	84	31,331	49	2[illegible]0	28	2,546	77	29,116
[illegible]t Williams, N.S.	1	299	....	....	1	299	4	874	....	....	4	874
Pubnico, N.S.	36	938	53	2,670	89	3,608	27	1,357	52	3,813	79	5,170
Pugwash, N.S.	3	4,655	3	3,553	6	8,208	3	3,487	4	4,867	7	8,354
Quebec, Que.	333	1,[illegible]108	12	15,886	345	1,129,994	147	9[illegible]307	26	37,696	173	476,903
Richibucto, N.B.	1	149	8	2,285	9	2,434	16	1,694	13	4,023	29	5,717
Rimouski, Que.	2	3,564	13	16,168	15	19,732	2	3,564	14	17,272	16	20,836
[illegible]er Bourgeoise, N.S.	53	1,464	....	....	53	1,464	90	1,713	....	....	90	1,713
River [illegible]t, N.S.	40	4,748	20	4,358	60	9,106	69	8,371	22	4,959	91	13,330
Rivière du Loup, Que.	1	1,774	1	229	2	2,003	9	4,[illegible]99	1	229	10	14,528
[illegible]o, P.E.I.	2	84	....	....	2	84	3	94	....	....	3	94
St. [illegible]s, N.B.	20	2,137	557	36,871	557	39,008	10	392	523	34,286	533	34,678
St. Ann's, N.S.	7	461	14	3,026	21	3,487	5	371	14	3,370	19	3,741
St. George, N.B.	37	1,209	211	6,921	248	8,130	31	807	208	6,881	239	7,688
St. John, N.B.	861	587,705	593	356,473	1,454	944,178	742	322,914	590	353,718	1,332	676,632
St. Martin's, N.B.	27	2,557	3	79	30	2,636	41	4,052	5	509	46	4,561
St. Peters, N.S.	4	58	7	596	11	654	6	119	4	364	10	483
St. [illegible]n, N.B.	157	11,231	217	5,096	374	[illegible]27	135	0,[illegible]27	201	4,741	336	15,568
Sackville, N.B.	36	5,200	4	739	40	5,939	14	1,685	3	619	17	2,304
Salmon River, N.S.	28	[illegible]8	....	....	28	1,068	23	976	....	....	23	976
Sandy Cove, N.S.	1	168	....	....	1	168	....	....	....	....	....	....

Shediac, N.P	....	....	8	4,453	8	4,453	....	....	10	5,660	10	5,660
Sheet Harbour, N.S	1	37	1	1,754	2	1,791	8	1,873	1	796	9	2,669
Shelburne, N.S	70	7,188	185	15,505	255	22,693	84	6,422	178	14,070	262	20,492
Sherbrooke, N.S	1	191	7	3,958	8	4,149	3	636	8	2,937	11	3,573
Shippegan, N.B	4	441	....	....	4	441	4	544	....	....	4	544
Souris, P.E.I	14	1,401	2	411	16	1,812	27	2,684	1	61	28	2,745
Stikeen, B.C	7	1,865	....	....	7	1,865	7	1,865	....	....	7	1,865
Summerside, P.E.I	3	343	1	217	4	560	15	5,750	1	652	16	6,402
Sydney, N.S	123	71,029	144	243,366	267	314,395	286	121,920	159	240,457	445	362,377
Thornes Cove, N.S	14	1,495	1	52	15	1,547	5	379	....	....	5	379
Three Rivers, Que	35	72,448	1	1,070	36	73,518	31	76,877	5	8,016	36	84,893
Tidnish, N.S	....	....	1	909	1	909	....	....	....	....	....	....
Tignish, P.E.I	1	99	....	....	1	99	....	....	....	....	....	....
Truro, N.S	2	263	....	....	2	263	4	581	....	....	4	581
Tusket, N.S	3	300	35	3,587	38	3,887	14	1,948	35	3,587	49	5,535
Tusket Wedge, N.S	32	3,013	10	6,413	42	9,426	38	3,548	9	4,550	47	8,098
Vancouver, B.C	473	385,218	378	295,875	851	681,093	428	361,293	376	296,989	804	658,282
Vernon River Bridge, B.E.I	....	....	....	....	....	....	3	204	....	....	3	204
Victoria, B.C	552	414,131	502	586,042	1,054	1,000,173	543	359,787	485	516,565	1,028	876,352
Walton, N.S	36	16,398	11	4,491	47	20,889	54	24,599	12	4,972	66	29,571
Westport, N.S	2	247	7	78	9	325	8	116	....	....	8	116
Weymouth, N.S	16	2,991	15	8,573	31	11,564	25	4,449	16	7,761	41	12,210
Windsor, N.S	59	35,375	58	52,969	117	88,344	74	49,550	82	70,883	156	120,433
Wolfville, N.S	10	1,850	....	....	10	1,850	1	335	....	....	1	335
Yarmouth, N.S	434	152,255	218	29,622	652	181,877	513	151,660	199	23,253	712	174,913
Total	8,746	6,131,765	6,536	2,763,588	15,282	8,895,353	8,559	5,232,630	5,975	2,715,446	14,534	7,948,076

No. 10.—STATEMENT of Nationalities of Sea-going Vessels entered and cleared, during the Fiscal Year, 1906.

ABSTRACT BY NATIONALITIES.

Arrived.			Departed.		
Under the Flag of	No.	Tons.	Under the Flag of	No.	Tons.
Great Britain	8,746	[illegible]365	Great Britain	8,559	5,[illegible]30
Austria-Hungary	1	316	Chili	1	1,338
Belgium	4	369	Denmark	34	27,920
Chili	2	3,010	France	205	21,735
Denmark	31	31,919	Germany	39	96,184
France	216	24,275	Holland	6	4,308
Germany	36	9[illegible]50	Italy	17	16,790
Holland	6	4,309	Japan	20	77,351
Italy	15	15,262	Norway-Sweden	729	940,343
Japan	20	7,[illegible]43	Russia	22	14,928
Mexico	1	145	Spain	3	856
Norway-Sweden	726	934,228	United States	4,899	1,513,693
Russia	23	15,540			
Spain	1	149			
St. Pierre	1	34			
United States	5,452	[illegible]36			
Uruguay	1	703			
Total	15,282	8,895,353	Total	14,534	7,948,076

DESCRIPTION OF VESSELS.

	Arrived.							Departed.					
—	Steamers.		Sailing Vessels.		Total.		—	Steamers.		Sailing Vessels.		Total.	
	No.	Tons.	No.	Tons.	No.	Tons.		No.	Tons.	No.	Tons.	No.	Tons.
British.......	3,981	5,541,713	4,765	590,052	8,746	6,131,765	British.......	3,619	4,633,600	4,940	599,030	8,559	5,232,630
Foreign	3,056	2,205,182	3,480	558,406	6,536	2,763,588	Foreign......	2,551	2,158,794	3,424	556,652	5,975	2,715,446
Total......	7,037	7,746,895	8,245	1,148,458	15,282	8,895,353	Total.....	6,170	6,792,394	8,364	1,155,682	14,534	7,948,076

No. 11.—Summary Statement of Sea-going Vessels entered Inwards and Outwards in the Dominion of Canada during the Fiscal Year ended June 30, 1906.

Nationalities.	Sea-going Vessels, Inwards.					Sea-going Vessels, Outwards.					Total Sea-going Vessels, Inwards and Outwards.				
	Number of Vessels.	Tons Register.	Quantity of Freight.		Crew, Number.	Number of Vessels.	Tons Register.	Quantity of Freight.		Crew, Number.	Number of Vessels.	Tons Register.	Quantity of Freight.		Crew, Number.
			Tons Weight.	Tons Measurement.				Tons Weight.	Tons Measurement.				Tons Weight.	Tons Measurement.	
British	2,753	5,018,332	1,057,155	285,305	161,981	2,351	4,041,121	2,777,787	709,420	129,903	5,104	9,059,453	3,834,942	994,725	291,884
Canadian	5,993	1,113,433	223,356	54,561	69,102	6,208	1,191,509	645,454	405,894	72,228	12,201	2,304,942	868,810	460,455	141,330
Foreign	6,536	2,733,588	663,632	37,423	109,960	5,975	2,715,446	1,438,088	505,872	116,381	12,511	5,479,034	2,101,720	543,295	226,341
Total	15,282	8,895,353	1,944,143	377,289	341,043	14,534	7,948,076	4,861,329	1,621,186	318,512	29,816	16,843,429	6,805,472	1,998,475	659,555

No. 12.—SUMMARY STATEMENT of Vessels arrived and departed (exclusive of Coasting Vessels) during the Fiscal Year ended June 30, 1906.

	Sea-going Vessels, Inwards and Outwards.			Vessels of the Inland Waters, between Canada and the United States.			Total Shipping (exclusive of Coasting Vessels) Inwards and Outwards.		
	Number of Vessels.	Tons Register.	Crew Number.	Number of Vessels.	Tons Register.	Crew Number.	Number of Vessels.	Tons Register.	Crew Number.
British	5,104	9,059,453	291,884	....	....	....	5,104	9,059,453	291,884
Canadian	12,201	2,304,942	141,330	20,038	8,936,973	396,634	32,239	11,241,915	537,964
Foreign	12,511	5,479,034	226,341	25,133	8,951,770	264,243	37,644	14,430,804	490,584
Total	29,816	16,843,429	659,555	45,171	17,888,743	660,877	74,987	34,732,172	1,320,432

TRADE WITH EACH COUNTRY

No. 13.—STATEMENT of the Number and Tonnage of Sailing and Steam Vessels entered Foreign Countries, distinguishing the Nationality of the Vessels employed in

Ports and Outports and Countries whence Arrived.	Nationality									
	British.		United States.		Norwegian and Swedish.		Austrian.		Belgian.	
	Vessels.	Tons Register.	Vessels.	Tons Register.	Vessels.	Tons Register.	Vessels.	Tons Register.	Vessels.	Tons Register.
Advocate Harbor, N.S.—										
United States......... Sail.	8	2,353	4	1,204						
Alberton, P.E.I.—										
Newfoundland........ Sail.	1	83								
Alma, N.B.—										
United States......... Sail.			1	56						
Amherst, N.S.—										
United States ....Steam.					2	1,390				
" .... Sail.	1	397								
Total................	1	397			2	1,390				
Annapolis Royal, N.S.—										
Cuba and Porto Rico..... Sail.										
Germany........... "					1	985				
Norway and Sweden .. "					1	968				
Portugal.............. "	1	1,079								
United States......... "	14	2,178	6	510						
Total................	15	3,257	6	510	2	1,953				
Apple River, N.S.—										
United States......... Sail.	10	1,744	24	5,230						
Arichat, N.S.—										
Saint Pierre........... Sail.	2	198								
United States......... "			15	180						
Sea Fisheries.......... "	75	2,250								
Total................	77	2,448	15	180						
Aspy Bay, N.S.—										
Saint Pierre........... Sail.	2	68								
Baddeck, N.S.—										
Newfoundland........Steam.	1	267								
Baie Verte, N.B.—										
Great Britain.........Steam.	1	1,172			8	5,229				
Barrington, N.S.—										
United States......... Sail.	1	89	10	554						
Sea Fisheries.......... "	1	42	17	1,025						
Total................	2	131	27	1,579						
Barton, N.S.—										
United States......... Sail.	62	6,170	3	282						
Bathurst, N.B.—										
Great Britain.........Steam.	3	5,566								
" .... Sail.					4	2,762				
British W. Indies...... "					1	795				
Germany............ "					1	578				
Norway and Sweden... "					2	1,524				
United States......... "	2	610								
Total................	5	6,176			8	5,659				
Bayfield, N.S.—										
Newfoundland......... Sail.	6	594								

AND NATIONALITY OF VESSELS.

Inwards from Sea at each of the undermentioned Ports and Outports in Canada from the trade with each Country, during the Fiscal Year ended June 30, 1906.

OF VESSELS.

Danish.		French.		German.		Italian.		Russian.		Other Nationalities.			Total.	
Vessels.	Tons Register.	Vessels.	Tons Register.	Vessels.	Tons Register.	Vessels.	Tons Register.	Vessels.	Tons Register.	Names.	Vessels.	Tons Register.	Vessels.	Tons Register.
													12	3,557
													1	83
													1	56
													2	1,390
													1	397
													3	1,787
										Spanish.	1	149	1	149
													1	985
													1	968
													1	1,079
													20	2,688
											1	149	24	5,869
													34	6,974
													2	198
													15	180
													75	2,250
													92	2,628
													2	68
													1	267
													9	6,401
													11	643
													18	1,067
													29	1,710
													65	6,452
1	1,333												4	6,890
													4	2,762
													1	795
													1	578
													2	1,524
													2	610
1	1,333												14	13,168
													6	594

No. 15.—Statement of the Number and Tonnage of Sailing

Ports and Outports and Countries for which Departed.	Nationality									
	British.		United States.		Norwegian and Swedish.		Austrian.		Belgian.	
	Vessels.	Tons Register.	Vessels	Tons Register.	Vessels.	Tons Register.	Vessels.	Tons Register.	Vessels.	Tons Register.
Bear River, N.S.—										
United States......... Sail.	26	2,001	3	1,127	....	....	....	....	....	....
Dutch W. Indies....... "	....	....	....	....	....	....	....	....	....	....
Total................	26	2,001	3	1,127	....	....	....	....	....	....
Belliveau's Cove, N.S.—										
British W. Indies...... Sail.	1	149	....	....	....	....	....	....	....	....
Cuba & Porto Rico.... "	1	149	....	....	....	....	....	....	....	....
United States......... "	16	1,841	....	....	....	....	....	....	....	....
Total................	18	2,139	....	....	....	....	....	....	....	....
Bridgetown, N.S.—										
United States......... Sail.	4	386	....	....	....	....	....	....	....	....
Bridgewater, N.S.—										
Great Britain.........Steam.	2	3,459	....	....	....	....	....	....	....	....
" .... Sail.	....	....	....	....	2	1,921	....	....	....	....
British W. Indies...... "	....	....	1	320	2	1,490	....	....	....	....
Cuba & Porto Rico.... "	2	633	....	....	....	....	....	....	....	....
Norway and Sweden... "	....	....	....	....	1	704	....	....	....	....
United States ....Steam.	1	1,609	....	....	....	....	....	....	....	....
" .... Sail.	25	7,894	4	1,938	1	547	....	....	....	....
B. Africa............. "	....	....	....	....	1	1,097	....	....	....	....
Total................	30	13,595	5	2,258	7	5,759	....	....	....	....
Buctouche, N.B.— —										
Great Britain......... Sail.	....	....	....	....	2	818	....	....	....	....
Campbellton, N.B.—										
Great Britain.........Steam.	3	3,172	....	....	....	....	....	....	....	....
United States......... "	2	3,191	....	....	....	....	....	....	....	....
" .... Sail.	....	....	1	549	....	....	....	....	....	....
Total................	5	6,363	1	549	....	....	....	....	....	....
Campobello, N.B.—										
United States.........Steam.	130	22,572	556	12,801	....	....	....	....	....	....
" .... Sail.	134	729	63	2,594	....	....	....	....	....	....
Total................	264	23,301	619	15,395	....	....	....	....	....	....
Canning, N.S.—										
United States......... Sail.	2	430	....	....	....	....	....	....	....	....
Canso, N.S.—										
Great Britain.........Steam.	1	4,977	....	....	....	....	....	....	....	....
Newfoundland......... Sail.	18	1,335	....	....	....	....	....	....	....	....
United States......... "	6	675	58	4,923	....	....	....	....	....	....
Sea Fisheries..........Steam.	2	1,968	....	....	....	....	....	....	....	....
" .... Sail.	193	17,857	219	18,296	....	....	....	....	....	....
Total................	220	26,812	277	23,219	....	....	....	....	....	....
Caraquet, N.B.—										
Spain................ Sail.	....	....	....	....	....	....	....	....	....	....
Cardigan, P.E.I.—										
United States......... Sail.	1	103	....	....	....	....	....	....	....	....
Sea Fisheries......... "	3	220	....	....	....	....	....	....	....	....
Total................	4	323	....	....	....	....	....	....	....	....

and Steam Vessels entered Inwards *from Sea, &c.—Continued.*

OF VESSELS.

Danish.		French.		German.		Italian.		Russian.		Other Nationalities.			Total.	
Vessels.	Tons Register.	Vessels.	Tons Register.	Vessels.	Tons Register.	Vessels.	Tons Register.	Vessels.	Tons Register.	Names.	Vessels.	Tons Register.	Vessels.	Tons Register.
													29	3,128
										Holland....	1	398	1	398
											1	398	30	3,526
													1	149
													1	149
													16	1,841
													18	2,139
													4	386
													2	3,459
													2	1,921
													3	1,810
													2	633
													1	704
													1	1,609
													30	10,379
													1	1,097
													42	21,612
													2	818
													3	3,172
													2	3,191
													1	549
													6	6,912
													686	35,373
													197	3,323
													883	38,696
													2	430
													1	4,977
													18	1,335
													64	5,598
													2	1,968
													412	36,153
													497	50,031
								1	248				1	248
													1	103
													3	220
													4	323

No. 13.—STATEMENT of the Number and Tonnage of Sailing

Ports and Outports and Countries whence Arrived.		Nationality									
		British.		United States.		Norwegian and Swedish.		Austrian.		Belgian.	
		Vessels.	Tons Register.	Vessels.	Tons Register.	Vessels.	Tons Register.	Vessels.	Tons Register.	Vessels.	Tons Register.
Charlottetown, P.E.I.—											
Great Britain	Steam.	2	2,324			1	997				
British W. Indies	Sail.	4	545								
Newfoundland	Steam.	11	1,133								
"	Sail.	2	96								
Saint Pierre	Steam.	1	103								
"	Sail.										
United States	Steam.	29	42,922	12	12,312						
"	Sail.	16	3,324	1	165						
Sea Fisheries	"	4	110								
Total		69	50,557	13	12,477	1	997				
Chatham, N.B.—											
Great Britain	Steam.	10	13,898			2	2,114				
"	Sail.					7	5,235				
Brazil	"					1	539				
Norway and Sweden	"					3	2,992				
Portugal	"										
Spain	"					1	450				
United States	Steam.	1	1,632			3	4,028				
"	Sail.	2	244								
Total		13	15,774			17	15,358				
Chemainus, B.C.—											
United States	Steam.	45	7,065	17	1,708						
"	Sail.	6	9,189	2	2,981						
China	"	2	4,014	1	1,469						
Japan	"	1	1,642								
Mexico	"	1	1,770								
Chili	"	3	5,759								
Total		58	29,439	20	6,158						
Chester, N.S.—											
United States	Sail.	3	625								
Sea Fisheries	"	3	69	3	237						
Total		6	694	3	237						
Cheticamp, N.S.—											
Saint Pierre	Sail.	9	291								
Cheverie, N.S.—											
United States	Sail.	18	11,633	17	10,556						
Chicoutimi, P.Q.—											
Great Britain	Steam.	4	8,181			7	9.167				
Church Point, N.S.—											
British W. Indies	Sail.	1	122								
United States	Sail.	14	1,500								
Total		15	1,622								
Clark's Harbour, N.S.—											
United States	Sail.			7	214						
Sea Fisheries	"			1	49						
Total				8	263						
Clementsport, N.S.—											
United States	Sail.	22	2,162								

and Steam Vessels entered Inwards *from Sea, &c.—Continued.*

OF VESSELS.

Danish.		French.		German.		Italian.		Russian.		Other Nationalities.			Total.	
Vessels.	Tons Register.	Vessels.	Tons Register.	Vessels.	Tons Register.	Vessels.	Tons Register.	Vessels.	Tons Register.	Names.	Vessels.	Tons Register.	Vessels.	Tons Register.
...	...	...	...	...	...	...	...	...	...	...	...	...	3	3,321
...	...	...	...	...	...	...	...	...	...	...	...	...	4	545
...	...	...	...	...	...	...	...	...	...	...	...	...	11	1,133
...	...	...	...	...	...	...	...	...	...	...	...	...	2	96
...	...	...	...	...	...	...	...	...	...	...	...	...	1	103
...	...	1	116	...	...	...	...	...	...	...	...	...	1	116
...	...	...	...	...	...	...	...	...	...	...	...	...	41	55,234
...	...	...	...	...	...	...	...	...	...	...	...	...	17	3,489
...	...	...	...	...	...	...	...	...	...	...	...	...	4	110
...	...	1	116	...	...	...	...	...	...	...	...	...	84	64,147
...	...	...	...	...	...	...	...	...	...	...	...	...	12	16,012
...	...	...	...	...	...	...	...	...	...	...	...	...	7	5,235
...	...	...	...	...	...	...	...	...	...	...	...	...	1	539
...	...	...	...	...	...	...	...	1	456	...	...	...	4	3,448
...	...	...	...	1	1,035	...	...	...	...	...	...	...	1	1,035
...	...	...	...	...	...	...	...	...	...	...	...	...	1	450
...	...	...	...	...	...	...	...	...	...	...	...	...	4	5,660
...	...	...	...	...	...	...	...	...	...	...	...	...	2	244
...	...	...	...	1	1,035	...	...	1	456	...	...	...	32	32,623
...	...	...	...	...	...	...	...	...	...	...	...	...	62	8,773
...	...	...	...	1	2,053	...	...	...	...	...	...	...	9	14,223
...	...	...	...	1	2,468	...	...	...	...	...	...	...	4	7,951
...	...	...	...	...	...	...	...	...	...	...	...	...	1	1,642
...	...	...	...	...	...	...	...	...	...	...	...	...	1	1,770
...	...	...	...	...	...	...	...	...	...	Chilian	1	1,672	4	7,431
...	...	...	...	2	4,521	...	...	...	...	...	1	1,672	81	41,790
...	...	...	...	...	...	...	...	...	...	...	...	...	3	625
...	...	...	...	...	...	...	...	...	...	...	...	...	6	306
...	...	...	...	...	...	...	...	...	...	...	...	...	9	931
...	...	...	...	...	...	...	...	...	...	...	...	...	9	291
...	...	...	...	...	...	...	...	...	...	...	...	...	35	22,189
3	5,138	...	...	...	...	...	...	...	...	...	...	...	14	22,486
...	...	...	...	...	...	...	...	...	...	...	...	...	1	122
...	...	...	...	...	...	...	...	...	...	...	...	...	14	1,500
...	...	...	...	...	...	...	...	...	...	...	...	...	15	1,622
...	...	...	...	...	...	...	...	...	...	...	...	...	7	214
...	...	...	...	...	...	...	...	...	...	...	...	...	1	49
...	...	...	...	...	...	...	...	...	...	...	...	...	8	263
...	...	...	...	...	...	...	...	...	...	...	...	...	22	2,162

No. 13.—STATEMENT of the Number and Tonnage of Sailing

PORTS AND OUTPORTS AND COUNTRIES WHENCE ARRIVED.	NATIONALITY									
	British.		United States.		Norwegian and Swedish.		Austrian.		Belgian.	
	Vessels.	Tons Register.	Vessels.	Tons Register.	Vessels.	Tons Register.	Vessels.	Tons Register.	Vessels.	Tons Register.
Comox, B.C.—										
Russia................Steam.					1	2,088				
United States.......... "	109	157,061	37	18,674	10	21,435				
" .... Sail.	1	1,564	12	12,359						
Japan................Steam.	5	11,281								
Total................	115	169,906	49	31,033	11	23,523				
Crofton, B.C.—										
United States..........Steam.	11	3,137								
" .... Sail.	4	562								
Total................	15	3,699								
Dalhousie, N.B.—										
Great Britain.......... Sail.	2	1,129			15	11,966				
British W. Indies...... "					1	878				
Belgium.............. "					1	1,020				
France.............. "					2	1,098				
Germany.............. "					3	2,329				
Norway and Sweden... "					10	9,032				
Spain................ "										
United States.......... "	3	344								
Denmark.............. "										
British Africa.......... "					2	2,207				
Iceland.............. "										
Brazil................ "					1	1,149				
Total................	5	1,473			35	29,679				
Dawson, Y.T.—										
United States..........Steam.	1	408	20	11,574						
" .... Sail.	2	1,125	5	1,385						
Total................	3	1,533	25	12,959						
Digby, N.S.—										
Great Britain.......... Sail.					1	1,148				
Cuba and Porto Rico.... "	1	168								
United States..........Steam.			5	435						
" .... Sail.	12	2,176	14	345						
Dutch W. Indies....... "	1	166								
Total................	14	2,510	19	780	1	1,148				
Dorchester, N.B.—										
United States.......... Sail.	12	2,765								
Douglas, B.C.—										
United States..........Steam.	9	528	28	280						
Economy, N.S.—										
United States.......... Sail.	4	333								
Five Islands, N.S.—										
United States.......... Sail.	4	302								
Fredericton, N.B.—										
United States.......... Sail.	5	496	1	91						
Freeport, N.S.—										
United States.......... Sail.	2	135								
Gabarouse, N.S.—										
Sea Fisheries.......... Sail.	2	106	1	79						

and Steam Vessels entered Inwards *from Sea*, &c.—*Continued.*

OF VESSELS.

Danish.		French.		German.		Italian.		Russian.		Other Nationalities.			Total.	
Vessels.	Tons Register.	Vessels.	Tons Register.	Vessels.	Tons Register.	Vessels.	Tons Register.	Vessels.	Tons Register.	Names.	Vessels.	Tons Register.	Vessels.	Tons Register.
...	...	...	...	...	...	...	...	...	...	...	...	...	1	2,088
...	...	...	...	9	21,400	...	...	...	...	...	...	...	165	218,570
...	...	...	...	...	...	...	...	...	...	...	...	...	13	13,923
...	...	...	...	...	...	...	...	...	...	...	...	...	5	11,281
...	...	...	...	9	21,400	...	...	...	...	...	...	...	184	245,862
...	...	...	...	...	...	...	...	...	...	...	...	...	11	3,137
...	...	...	...	...	...	...	...	...	...	...	...	...	4	562
...	...	...	...	...	...	...	...	...	...	...	...	...	15	3,699
...	...	...	...	...	...	...	...	5	3,311	...	...	...	22	16,406
...	...	...	...	...	...	...	...	...	...	...	...	...	1	878
...	...	...	...	...	...	...	...	...	...	...	...	...	1	1,020
...	...	...	...	...	...	...	...	...	...	...	...	...	2	1,098
...	...	...	...	...	...	...	...	...	...	...	...	...	3	2,329
...	...	...	...	...	...	...	...	...	...	...	...	...	10	9,032
1	353	...	...	...	...	...	...	...	...	...	...	...	1	353
...	...	...	...	...	...	...	...	...	...	...	...	...	3	344
1	147	...	...	...	...	...	...	...	...	...	...	...	1	147
2	365	...	...	...	...	...	...	...	...	...	...	...	4	2,572
1	181	...	...	...	...	...	...	...	...	...	...	...	1	181
...	...	...	...	...	...	...	...	...	...	...	...	...	1	1,149
5	1,046	...	...	...	...	...	...	5	3,311	...	...	...	50	35,509
...	...	...	...	...	...	...	...	...	...	...	...	...	21	11,982
...	...	...	...	...	...	...	...	...	...	...	...	...	7	2,510
...	...	...	...	...	...	...	...	...	...	...	...	...	28	14,492
...	...	...	...	...	...	...	...	...	...	...	...	...	1	1,148
...	...	...	...	...	...	...	...	...	...	...	...	...	1	168
...	...	...	...	...	...	...	...	...	...	...	...	...	5	435
...	...	...	...	...	...	...	...	...	...	...	...	...	26	2,521
...	...	...	...	...	...	...	...	...	...	...	...	...	1	166
...	...	...	...	...	...	...	...	...	...	...	...	...	34	4,438
...	...	...	...	...	...	...	...	...	...	...	...	...	12	2,765
...	...	...	...	...	...	...	...	...	...	...	...	...	37	808
...	...	...	...	...	...	...	...	...	...	...	...	...	4	333
...	...	...	...	...	...	...	...	...	...	...	...	...	4	302
...	...	...	...	...	...	...	...	...	...	...	...	...	6	587
...	...	...	...	...	...	...	...	...	...	...	...	...	2	135
...	...	...	...	...	...	...	...	...	...	...	...	...	3	185

No. 13.—STATEMENT of the Number and Tonnage of Sailing

Ports and Outports and Countries whence Arrived.		Nationality									
		British.		United States.		Norwegian and Swedish.		Austrian.		Belgian.	
		Vessels.	Tons Register.	Vessels.	Tons Register.	Vessels.	Tons Register.	Vessels.	Tons Register.	Vessels.	Tons Register.
Gaspé, P.Q.—											
Great Britain	Sail.					7	6,154				
British W. Indies	"	1	99								
Newfoundland	"	1	92								
Brazil	"					2	2,315				
Germany	"					1	1,228				
Norway and Sweden	"					2	1,036				
Spain	"	1	99								
United States	"	2	502								
Total		5	792			12	10,733				
Georgetown, P.E.I.—											
Newfoundland	Sail.	7	288								
Saint Pierre	"	2	156								
United States	Steam.			1	287						
"	Sail.	2	191	1	266						
Sea Fisheries	"	6	178	2	164						
Total		17	813	4	717						
Halifax, N.S.—											
Great Britain	Steam.	146	382,946			3	2,860				
"	Sail.					8	5,522				
British W. Indies	Steam.	17	15,235			32	21,080				
"	Sail.	19	3,481								
Newfoundland	Steam.	56	54,311								
"	Sail.	139	10,525	2	135						
Belgium	Steam.	11	63,393								
Brazil	Sail.	3	715			1	891				
Cuba & Porto Rico	Steam.					1	1,215				
"	Sail.	13	2,439								
France	Steam.	2	5,399								
"	Sail.					4	2,380				
British Guiana	Steam.	26	35,319			2	2,513				
Holland	Sail.										
Italy	Steam.	1	1,758								
Norway and Sweden	Steam.	1	2,165								
"	Sail.					5	3,395				
Portugal	"	2	197								
Mediterranean Ports	Steam.	1	1,951								
Saint Pierre	"	7	1,869								
"	Sail.	1	78								
Spain	Steam.	1	1,649								
"	Sail.					1	441	1	316		
United States	Steam.	103	119,680	19	15,465	2	2,033				
"	Sail.	125	26,569	65	10,406						
Sea Fisheries	Steam.	21	23,727								
Canary Islands	Sail.										
Cape Verde Islands	Steam.	1	1,916								
South Sea Fisheries	Sail.	3	277								
Br. Poss. S. Africa	Sail.					1	996				
Mexico	Steam.	4	7,387								
Uruguay	Sail.	1	99								
Sea Fisheries	Steam.	7	117								
"	Sail.	283	9,236	32	2,587						
Total		994	772,438	118	28,593	60	43,326	1	316		
Hantsport, N.S.—											
United States	Steam.	8	48	30	6,290	10	6,989				
"	Sail.	27	14,202	26	11,438						
Total		35	14,250	56	17,728	10	6,989				

'and Steam Vessels entered Inwards *from Sea, &c.—Continued.*

OF VESSELS.

Danish.		French.		German.		Italian.		Russian.		Other Nationalities.			Total.	
Vessels.	Tons Register.	Vessels.	Tons Register.	Vessels.	Tons Register.	Vessels.	Tons Register.	Vessels.	Tons Register.	Names.	Vessels.	Tons Register.	Vessels.	Tons Register.
													7	6,154
													1	99
													1	92
													2	2,315
													1	1,228
													2	1,036
								1	346				2	445
													2	502
								1	346				18	11,871
													7	288
													2	156
													1	287
													3	457
													8	342
													21	1,530
													149	385,806
													8	5,522
													49	36,315
													19	3,481
													56	54,311
1	323							1	159				143	11,142
													11	63,393
													4	1,606
													1	1,215
													13	2,439
													2	5,399
													4	2,380
													28	37,832
						1	836						1	836
1	1,547												2	3,305
													1	2,165
													5	3,395
													2	197
													1	1,951
		5	2,000										12	3,869
		3	375										4	453
1	1,991												2	3,640
1	324									Uruguay...	1	703	4	1,784
1	588			6	30,129								131	167,895
						1	1,144						191	38,119
		5	3,890										26	27,617
								1	348				1	348
													1	1,916
													3	277
													1	996
													4	7,387
													1	99
													7	117
													315	11,823
5	4,773	13	6,265	6	30,129	2	1,980	2	507		1	703	1,202	889,030
													48	13,327
													53	25,640
													101	38,967

No. 13.—STATEMENT of the Number and Tonnage of Sailing

Ports and Outports and Countries whence Arrived.	Nationality									
	British.		United States.		Norwegian and Swedish.		Austrian.		Belgian.	
	Vessels.	Tons Register.	Vessels.	Tons Register.	Vessels.	Tons Register.	Vessels.	Tons Register.	Vessels.	Tons Register.
Harvey, N.B.—										
Great Britain.......... Sail.	1	1,617								
British W. Indies...... "	1	1,351								
France.............. "					1	1,427				
United States ....Steam.	3	161								
" .... Sail.	11	2,014	2	307						
Total................	16	5,143	2	307	1	1,427				
Hillsboro, N.B.—										
Great Britain.........Steam.	1	2,255			6	3,919				
" .... Sail.	23	6,846								
United States.........Steam.	4	8,836			55	38,446				
" .... Sail.			31	17,395						
Total................	28	17,937	31	17,395	61	42,365				
Isaacs Harbour, N.S.—										
United States .... Sail.	1	99	8	748						
Sea Fisheries.......... "			3	262						
Total................	1	99	11	1,010						
Jordan Bay, N.S.—										
United States......... Sail.	2	146								
Kentville, N.S.—										
United States......... Sail.	4	323								
Kingsport, N.S.—										
United States .... Sail.	5	1,259	5	1,444						
Ladner, B.C.—										
United States ....Steam.	2	137								
Ladysmith, B.C.—										
United States ....Steam.	153	70,944	43	29,380	28	56,801				
" .... Sail.	12	1,782	3	4,131						
Total................	165	72,726	46	33,511	28	56,801				
La Have, N.S.—										
British W. Indies...... Sail.	3	312								
Newfoundland......... "	1	99								
Brazil................ "	1	632								
Cuba & Porto Rico.... "	3	297								
Spain................ "	1	114								
United States .... "	25	2,788			1	626				
Sea Fisheries.......... "	106	8,608	2	175						
Total................	140	12,850	2	175	1	626				
L'Ardoise, N.S.—										
Sea Fisheries .... Sail.	42	1,902								
Liscombe, N.S.—										
United States .... Sail.			11	990						
Sea Fisheries .... "			25	1,970						
Total................			36	2,960						
Liverpool, N.S.—										
Newoundland.......... Sail.			4	308						
United States .... "	37	5,091	53	3,633						
Greenland............ "	1	626								
Sea Fisheries .... "			52	4,222						
Total................	38	5,717	109	8,163						

'and Steam Vessels entered Inwards *from Sea, &c.—Continued.*

OF VESSELS.

Danish.		French.		German.		Italian.		Russian.		Other Nationalities.			Total.	
Vessels.	Tons Register.	Vessels.	Tons Register.	Vessels.	Tons Register.	Vessels.	Tons Register.	Vessels.	Tons Register.	Names.	Vessels.	Tons Register.	Vessels.	Tons Register.
...	...	...	...	...	...	...	...	...	...	...	...	...	1	1,617
...	...	...	...	...	...	...	...	...	...	...	...	...	1	1,351
...	...	...	...	...	...	...	...	...	...	...	...	...	1	1,427
...	...	...	...	...	...	...	...	...	...	...	...	...	3	161
...	...	...	...	...	...	1	938	...	...	...	...	...	14	3,259
...	...	...	...	...	...	1	938	...	...	...	...	...	20	7,815
...	...	...	...	...	...	...	...	...	...	...	...	...	7	6,174
...	...	...	...	...	...	...	...	...	...	...	...	...	23	6,846
...	...	...	...	...	...	...	...	...	...	...	...	...	59	47,282
...	...	...	...	...	...	...	...	...	...	...	...	...	31	17,395
...	...	...	...	...	...	...	...	...	...	...	...	...	120	77,697
...	...	...	...	...	...	...	...	...	...	...	...	...	9	847
...	...	...	...	...	...	...	...	...	...	...	...	...	3	262
	...	...	...	...	...	...	...	...	...	...	...	...	12	1,109
...	...	...	...	...	...	...	...	...	...	...	...	...	2	146
...	...	...	...	...	...	...	...	...	...	...	...	...	4	323
...	...	...	...	...	...	...	...	...	...	...	...	...	10	2,703
...	...	...	...	...	...	...	...	...	...	...	...	...	2	137
...	...	...	...	2	5,150	...	...	...	...	...	...	...	226	162,275
...	...	...	...	...	...	...	...	...	...	...	...	...	15	5,913
...	...	...	...	2	5,150	...	...	...	...	...	...	...	241	168,188
...	...	...	...	...	...	...	...	...	...	...	...	...	3	312
...	...	...	...	...	...	...	...	...	...	...	...	...	1	99
...	...	...	...	...	...	...	...	...	...	...	...	...	1	632
...	...	...	...	...	...	...	...	...	...	...	...	...	3	297
...	...	...	...	...	...	...	...	...	...	...	...	...	1	114
...	...	...	...	...	...	...	...	...	...	...	...	...	26	3,414
...	...	...	...	...	...	...	...	...	...	...	...	...	108	8,783
...	...	...	...	...	...	...	...	...	...	...	...	...	143	13,651
...	...	...	...	...	...	...	...	...	...	...	...	...	42	1,902
...	...	...	...	...	...	...	...	...	...	...	...	...	11	990
...	...	...	...	...	...	...	...	...	...	...	...	...	25	1,970
...	...	...	...	...	...	...	...	...	...	...	...	...	36	2,960
...	...	...	...	...	...	...	...	...	...	...	...	...	4	308
...	...	...	...	...	...	...	...	...	...	...	...	...	90	8,724
...	...	...	...	...	...	...	...	...	...	...	...	...	1	626
...	...	...	...	...	...	...	...	...	...	...	...	...	52	4,222
...	...	...	...	...	...	...	...	...	...	...	...	...	147	13,880

No. 13.—STATEMENT of the Number and Tonnage of Sailing

PORTS AND OUTPORTS AND COUNTRIES WHENCE ARRIVED.	NATIONALITY									
	British.		United States.		Norwegian and Swedish.		Austrian.		Belgian.	
	Vessels.	Tons Register.	Vessels.	Tons Register.	Vessels.	Tons Register.	Vessels.	Tons Register.	Vessels.	Tons Register.
Lockeport, N.S.—										
British W. Indies...... Sail.	4	393								
Newfoundland......... "	2	197								
United States......... "	3	296	23	973						
Sea Fisheries.......... "	16	619	6	351						
Total.................	25	1,505	29	1,324						
Lord's Cove, N.B.—										
United States.........Steam.	37	2,459	91	806						
" .... Sail.	101	1,236	168	2,621						
Total.................	138	3,695	259	3,427						
Louisburg, N.S.—										
Great Britain.........Steam.					1	2,522				
British W. Indies...... "	1	1,506								
Newfoundland......... "	21	16,522			5	5,487				
" .... Sail.	15	1,283	7	653						
Brazil................ "	1	248								
France...............Steam.	1	1,855								
" .... Sail.										
Norway and Sweden...Steam.					1	1,646				
Saint Pierre........... "										
" .... Sail.	4	328								
Spain...............Steam.	5	8,793								
United States......... "	59	135,413	1	·86	52	121,818				
" .... Sail.	7	836	15	1,235						
Laspalmas...........Steam.					1	1,664				
Sea Fisheries......... Sail.	33	1,474	80	6,664						
Total.................	147	168,258	103	8,638	60	133,137				
Lunenburg, N.S.—										
British W. Indies...... Sail.	15	2,574								
Newfoundland......... "	17	1,503								
Cuba and Porto Rico.... "	5	645								
Portugal.............. "	1	99								
United States......... "	32	3,891	1	231						
Sea Fisheries.......... "	203	17,175	5	408						
Total.................	273	25,887	6	639						
Magdalen Islands, P.Q.—										
Newfoundland.........Steam.	1	275								
Saint Pierre........... Sail.										
United States......... "			10	696						
Total.................	1	275	10	696						
Mahone Bay, N.S.—										
British W. Indies...... Sail.	5	496								
United States......... "	8	889								
Sea Fisheries.......... "	31	1,753								
Total.................	44	3,138								
Main-à-Dieu, N.S.—										
Sea Fisheries.......... Sail.	1	13								
Maitland, N.S.—										
United States......... Sail.	7	940								
Matane, P.Q.—										
Great Britain.........Steam.	1	1,782								
Norway and Sweden... "					4	5,943				
" ... Sail.					1	1,099				
Total.................	1	1,782			5	7,042				

and Steam Vessels entered Inwards *from Sea, &c.*—*Continued.*

OF VESSELS.

Danish.		French.		German.		Italian.		Russian.		Other Nationalities.			Total.	
Vessels.	Tons Register.	Vessels.	Tons Register.	Vessels.	Tons Register.	Vessels.	Tons Register.	Vessels.	Tons Register.	Names.	Vessels.	Tons Register.	Vessels.	Tons Register.
													4	393
													2	197
													26	1,269
													22	970
													54	2,829
													128	3,265
													269	3,857
													397	7,122
													1	2,522
													1	1,506
													26	22,009
													22	1,936
													1	248
													1	1,855
		4	253										4	253
													1	1,646
		1	400										1	400
		8	493										12	821
													5	8,793
													112	257,317
													22	2,071
													1	1,664
		4	148										117	8,286
		17	1,294										327	311,327
													15	2,574
													17	1,503
													5	645
													1	99
													33	4,122
													208	17,583
													279	36,526
													1	275
		5	255										5	255
													10	696
		5	255										16	1,226
													5	496
													8	889
													31	1,753
													44	3,138
													1	13
													7	940
													1	1,782
													4	5,943
													1	1,099
													6	8,824

No. 13.—STATEMENT of the Number and Tonnage of Sailing

Ports and Outports and Countries whence Arrived.	Nationality									
	British.		United States.		Norwegian and Swedish.		Austrian.		Belgian.	
	Vessels.	Tons Register.	Vessels.	Tons Register.	Vessels.	Tons Register.	Vessels.	Tons Register.	Vessels.	Tons Register.
Meteghan, N.S.—										
Cuba and Porto Rico .. Sail.	3	554								
United States......... "	30	2,659	2	363						
Total................	33	3,213	2	363						
Middleton, N.S.—										
United States......... Sail.	2	120								
Moncton, N.B.—										
United States......... Sail.	12	1,825	2	187						
Montague, P.E.I.—										
Newfoundland......... Sail.	3	112								
Saint Pierre........... "	2	156								
United States......... "	3	263								
Sea Fisheries.......... "	1	15								
Total................	9	546								
Montreal, P.Q.—										
Great Britain.........Steam.	317	1,198,781			3	4,337				
" ....Sail.					1	1,345				
British W. Indies......Steam.	9	17,123								
" ......Sail.	1	185								
Newfoundland.........Steam.	21	14,543			2	1,304				
Belgium.............. "	8	27,204								
France............... "	2	5,486			2	3,340				
Germany.............. "	1	2,813								
Holland.............. "	2	4,248			1	2,418				
Italy................ "	4	6,494								
Norway and Sweden... "					1	1,426				
Portugal............. "	2	4,146								
United States......... "	3	3,429			1	2,788				
" ....Sail.					1	796				
British Africa.........Steam.	2	5,754								
" ....Sail.										
British Guiana........Steam.	2	4,634								
Mexico............... "	5	9,089								
Total................	379	1,303,929			12	17,754				
Murray Harbour, P.E.I.—										
Sea Fisheries.......... Sail.	21	465								
Musquash, N.B.—										
United States......... Sail.	17	1,341	45	5,884						
Nanaimo, B.C.—										
United States.........Steam.	34	12,840	52	12,996	25	54,905				
" ....Sail.	1	131	2	1,147						
Japan................Steam.										
Total................	35	12,971	54	14,143	25	54,905				
New Campbellton, N.S.—										
Newfoundland......... Sail.	7	309								
Newcastle, N.B.—										
Great Britain.........Steam.	7	10,165			1	1,667				
" ....Sail.					11	7,790				
Norway and Sweden...Steam.					1	997				
" ...Sail.					4	3,285				
Spain................Steam.	1	2,202								
United States......... "	1	1,150								
" ....Sail.	3	750								
Total................	12	14,267			17	13,739				

and Steam Vessels entered Inwards *from Sea*, &c.—*Continued.*

OF VESSELS.

Danish.		French.		German.		Italian.		Russian.		Other Nationalities.			Total.	
Vessels.	Tons Register.	Vessels.	Tons Register.	Vessels.	Tons Register.	Vessels.	Tons Register.	Vessels.	Tons Register.	Names.	Vessels.	Tons Register.	Vessels.	Tons Register.
													3	554
													32	3,022
													35	3,576
													2	120
													14	2,012
													3	112
													2	156
													3	263
													1	15
													9	546
								1	1,147				321	1,204,265
													1	1,345
													9	17,123
													1	185
													23	15,847
													8	27,204
								2	2,542				6	11,368
3	5,006			1	1,289								5	9,108
													3	6,666
													4	6,494
													1	1,426
													2	4,146
													4	6,217
													1	796
													2	5,754
								1	942				1	942
													2	4,634
													5	9,089
3	5,006			1	1,289			4	4,631				399	1,332,609
													21	465
													62	7,225
													111	80,741
													3	1,278
		1	3,186										1	3,186
		1	3,186										115	85,205
													7	309
													8	11,832
						1	755						12	8,545
													1	997
													4	3,285
													1	2,202
													1	1,150
													3	750
						1	755						30	28,761

No. 13.—STATEMENT of the Number and Tonnage of Sailing

Ports and Outports and Countries whence Arrived.		Nationality									
		British.		United States.		Norwegian and Swedish.		Austrian.		Belgian.	
		Vessels.	Tons Register.	Vessels.	Tons Register.	Vessels.	Tons Register.	Vessels.	Tons Register.	Vessels.	Tons Register.
New London, P.E.I.—											
Sea Fisheries	Sail.	4	67								
New Westminster, B.C.—											
Chili	Sail.					1	1,547				
United States	Steam.	124	7,037	18	431						
"	Sail.	1	1,047								
Sea Fisheries	Steam.	6	81								
"	Sail.	4	72								
Total		135	8,237	18	431	1	1,547				
North East Harbour, N.S.—											
Cuba and Porto Rico	Sail.	1	148								
United States	"	2	422	3	39						
Sea Fisheries	"	14	251	7	480						
Total		17	821	10	519						
North Head, N.B.—											
United States	Steam.	136	24,598	3	29						
"	Sail.	14	331	42	782						
Total		150	24,929	45	811						
Northport, N.S.—											
Great Britain	Sail.					4	4,563				
North Sydney, N.S.—											
Great Britain	Steam.	3	4,459			7	8,074				
"	Sail.					2	823				
British W. Indies	Steam.	2	2,805			1	633				
"	Sail.	1	199								
Newfoundland	Steam.	225	87,761			24	38,183				
"	Sail.	282	24,779	8	717					4	369
Brazil	"	2	430								
Norway and Sweden	Steam.					1	2,303				
"	Sail.					1	464				
Saint Pierre	Steam.	19	3,022								
"	Sail.	8	638								
Spain	Steam.	2	3,936			2	3,916				
United States	"	5	3,872			5	5,028				
"	Sail.	9	697	7	806						
Sea "	Steam.					1	1,862				
" Fisheries	Sail.	78	4,579	185	15,790						
Total		636	137,177	200	17,313	44	61,286			4	369
Parrsboro', N.S.—											
Great Britain	Steam.	1	2,343								
"	Sail.					1	499				
United States	Steam.	21	17,129			40	30,918				
"	Sail.	122	28,674								
Total		144	48,146			41	31,417				
Paspebiac, P.Q.—											
Great Britain	Sail.	1	241			4	2,374				
British W. Indies	"	5	733								
Brazil	"	2	416								
France	"					3	1,909				
Norway and Sweden	"					2	1,329				
Saint Pierre	"	1	148								
Spain	"	2	339								
United States	"	7	2,480								
Total		18	4,357			9	5,612				

and Steam Vessels entered Inwards *from Sea,* &c.—*Continued.*

OF VESSELS.

Danish.		French.		German.		Italian.		Russian.		Other Nationalities.			Total.	
Vessels.	Tons Register.	Vessels.	Tons Register.	Vessels.	Tons Register.	Vessels.	Tons Register.	Vessels.	Tons Register.	Names.	Vessels.	Tons Register.	Vessels.	Tons Register.
...	...	...	...	...	...	...	...	...	...	...	...	...	4	67
...	...	...	...	...	...	...	...	...	...	...	...	...	1	1,547
...	...	...	...	...	...	...	...	...	...	...	...	...	142	7,468
...	...	...	...	...	...	...	...	...	...	...	...	...	1	1,047
...	...	...	...	...	...	...	...	...	...	...	...	...	6	81
...	...	...	...	...	...	...	...	...	...	...	...	...	4	72
...	...	...	...	...	...	...	...	...	...	...	...	...	154	10,215
...	...	...	...	...	...	...	...	...	...	...	...	...	1	148
...	...	...	...	...	...	...	...	...	...	...	...	...	5	461
...	...	...	...	...	...	...	...	...	...	...	...	...	21	731
...	...	...	...	...	...	...	...	...	...	...	...	...	27	1,340
...	...	...	...	...	...	...	...	...	...	...	...	...	139	24,627
...	...	...	...	...	...	...	...	...	...	...	...	...	56	1,113
...	...	...	...	...	...	...	...	...	...	...	...	...	195	25,740
...	...	...	...	...	...	...	...	...	...	...	...	...	4	4,563
...	...	...	...	...	...	...	...	...	...	...	...	...	10	12,533
...	...	...	...	...	...	...	...	1	382	...	...	...	3	i,205
...	...	...	...	...	...	...	...	...	...	...	...	...	3	3,438
...	...	...	...	...	...	...	...	...	...	...	...	...	1	199
...	...	...	...	...	...	...	...	...	...	Dutch......	3	2,443	252	128,387
...	...	1	55	...	...	...	...	...	...	"	1	169	296	26,089
...	...	...	...	...	...	...	...	...	...	...	...	...	2	430
...	...	...	...	...	...	...	...	...	...	...	...	...	1	2,303
...	...	...	...	...	...	...	...	...	...	...	...	...	1	464
...	...	6	2,400	...	...	...	...	...	...	...	...	...	25	5,422
...	...	28	2,651	...	...	...	...	...	...	...	...	...	36	3,289
...	...	...	...	...	...	...	...	...	...	...	...	...	4	7,852
2	2,319	...	...	...	...	...	...	...	...	...	...	...	12	11,219
...	...	...	...	...	...	...	...	...	...	...	...	...	16	1,503
...	...	...	...	...	...	...	...	...	...	...	...	...	1	1,862
...	...	112	6,147	...	...	...	...	...	...	...	...	...	375	26,516
2	2,319	147	11,253	...	...	...	...	1	382	...	4	2,612	1,038	232,711
...	...	...	...	...	...	...	...	...	...	...	...	...	1	2,343
...	...	...	...	...	...	...	...	...	...	...	...	...	1	499
...	...	...	...	...	...	...	...	...	...	...	...	...	61	48,047
...	...	...	...	...	...	...	...	...	...	...	...	...	122	28,674
...	...	...	...	...	...	...	...	...	...	...	...	...	185	79,563
...	...	...	...	...	...	...	...	...	...	...	...	...	5	2,615
...	...	...	...	...	...	...	...	...	...	...	...	...	5	733
...	...	...	...	...	...	...	...	...	...	...	...	...	2	416
...	...	...	...	...	...	...	...	...	...	...	...	...	3	1,909
...	...	...	...	...	...	...	...	...	...	...	...	...	2	1,329
...	...	...	...	...	...	...	...	...	...	...	...	...	1	148
...	...	...	...	...	...	...	...	...	...	...	...	...	2	339
...	...	...	...	...	...	...	...	...	...	...	...	...	7	2,480
...	...	...	...	...	...	...	...	...	...	...	...	...	27	9,969

No. 13.—STATEMENT of the Number and Tonnage of Sailing

Ports and Outports and Countries whence Arrived.	Nationality — British. Vessels.	British. Tons Register.	United States. Vessels.	United States. Tons Register.	Norwegian and Swedish. Vessels.	Norwegian and Swedish. Tons Register.	Austrian. Vessels.	Austrian. Tons Register.	Belgian. Vessels.	Belgian. Tons Register.
Percé, P.Q.—										
Great Britain.......... Sail.	....	....	....	....	1	1,453	....	....	....	....
British W. Indies...... "	1	99	....	....	....	....	....	....	....	....
Newfoundland......... "	....	....	....	....	1	891	....	....	....	....
France............... "	....	....	....	....	1	672	....	....	....	....
Norway and Sweden... "	....	....	....	....	3	2,680	....	....	....	....
Sea Fisheries.......... "	2	160	12	950	....	....	....	....	....	....
Total................	3	259	12	950	6	5,696	....	....	....	....
Pictou, N.S.—										
Great Britain.........Steam.	....	....	....	....	3	4,882	....	....	....	....
France............... Sail.	....	....	....	....	1	627	....	....	....	....
United States.........Steam.	1	2,259	....	....	1	1,215	....	....	....	....
" .... Sail.	12	1,486	1	279	....	....	....	....	....	....
Total................	13	3,745	1	279	5	6,724	....	....	....	....
Port Greville, N.S.—										
United States......... Sail.	48	15,961	....	....	....	....	....	....	....	....
Port Hastings, N.S.—										
Newfoundland.........Steam.	1	872	....	....	....	....	....	....	....	....
Norway and Sweden... "	....	....	....	....	1	398	....	....	....	....
United States......... Sail.	4	379	....	....	....	....	....	....	....	....
Total................	5	1,251	....	....	1	398	....	....	....	....
Port Hawkesbury, N.S.—										
British W. Indies......Steam.	1	603	....	....	....	....	....	....	....	....
" ...... Sail.	5	652	....	....	....	....	....	....	....	....
Newfoundland......... "	8	698	....	....	....	....	....	....	....	....
Cuba and Porto Rico... "	1	99	....	....	....	....	....	....	....	....
France............... "	1	99	....	....	....	....	....	....	....	....
Portugal............. "	1	99	....	....	....	....	....	....	....	....
Saint Pierre.......... "	1	98	....	....	....	....	....	....	....	....
United States.........Steam.	30	30,977	16	14,364	....	....	....	....	....	....
" .... Sail.	9	1,485	9	916	....	....	....	....	....	....
Sea Fisheries.......... "	58	4,335	33	2,570	....	....	....	....	....	....
Total................	115	39,145	58	17,850	....	....	....	....	....	....
Port Hood, N.S.—										
Sea Fisheries.......... Sail.	....	....	2	183	....	....	....	....	....	....
Port La Tour, N.S.—										
United States......... Sail.	....	....	1	61	....	....	....	....	....	....
Sea Fisheries.......... "	....	....	2	167	....	....	....	....	....	....
Total................	....	....	3	228	....	....	....	....	....	....
Port Medway, N.S.—										
Belgium.............. Sail.	....	....	....	....	1	1,177	....	....	....	....
United States......... "	2	197	2	164	....	....	....	....	....	....
French W. Indies...... "	1	99	....	....	....	....	....	....	....	....
Sea Fisheries.......... "	1	99	....	....	....	....	....	....	....	....
Total................	4	395	2	164	1	1,177	....	....	....	....
Port Morien, N.S.—										
Newfoundland.........Steam.	1	435	....	....	1	652	....	....	....	....
United States......... "	2	870	....	....	....	....	....	....	....	....
Sea Fisheries.......... Sail.	1	99	....	....	....	....	....	....	....	....
Total................	4	1,404	....	....	1	652	....	....	....	....

and Steam Vessels entered Inwards *from Sea*, &c.—*Continued.*

OF VESSELS.

Danish.		French.		German.		Italian.		Russian.		Other Nationalities.			Total.	
Vessels.	Tons Register.	Vessels.	Tons Register.	Vessels.	Tons Register.	Vessels.	Tons Register.	Vessels.	Tons Register.	Names.	Vessels.	Tons Register.	Vessels.	Tons Register.
													1	1,453
													1	99
													1	891
													1	672
													3	2,680
													14	1,110
													21	6,905
													3	4,882
													1	627
													2	3,474
													13	1,765
													19	10,748
													48	15,961
													1	872
													1	398
													4	379
													6	1,649
													1	603
													5	652
													8	698
													1	99
													1	99
													1	99
													1	98
													46	48,341
													18	2,401
		2	117										93	7,022
		2	117										175	57,112
													2	183
													1	61
													2	167
													3	228
													1	1,177
													4	361
													1	99
													1	99
													7	1,736
													2	1,087
													2	870
													1	99
													5	2,056

No. 13.—STATEMENT of the Number and Tonnage of Sailing

Ports and Outports and Countries whence arrived.	Nationality — British. Vessels.	British. Tons Register.	United States. Vessels.	United States. Tons Register.	Norwegian and Swedish. Vessels.	Norwegian and Swedish. Tons Register.	Austrian. Vessels.	Austrian. Tons Register.	Belgian. Vessels.	Belgian. Tons Register.
Port Mulgrave, N.S.—										
British W. Indies......Steam.	1	603								
Newfoundland......... Sail.	5	528								
Saint Pierre........... "	3	234								
United States.........Steam.	1	82	1	94						
" .... Sail.			12	877						
Sea Fisheries.......... "	13	1,200	2	138						
Total.................	23	2,647	15	1,109						
Port Simpson, B.C.—										
United States.........Steam.	58	29,702	24	851						
" .... Sail.	1	7	1	771						
Total.................	59	29,709	25	1,622						
Port Williams, N.S.—										
United States......... Sail.	1	299								
Pubnico, N.S.—										
United States......... Sail.	3	150	26	773						
Sea Fisheries.......... "	33	788	27	1,897						
Total.................	36	938	53	2,670						
Pugwash, N.S.—										
Great Britain.........Steam.	1	1,267			1	1,486				
Norway and Sweden... Sail.					1	768				
United States.........Steam.	2	3,388								
Total.................	3	4,655			2	2,254				
Quebec, P.Q.—										
Great Britain.........Steam.	232	913,307			1	1,581				
" .... Sail.					1	545				
British W. Indies .....Steam.	3	7,898								
" ..... Sail.	2	578								
Newfoundland.........Steam.	1	155								
Belgium...............Steam.	28	132,080								
Cuba & Porto Rico.... Sail.	2	379								
France................Steam.	14	36,881			1	1,477				
Germany..............Steam.	1	2,813								
Holland.............. "	2	4,247								
Spain................. "	3	4,990								
United States.........Steam.	3	5,419								
Sea Fisheries .... "	21	4,021								
" .... Sail.	21	1,340								
Total.................	333	1,114,108			3	3,603				
Richibucto, N.B.—										
Great Britain......... Sail.					1	167				
France................ "										
Norway and Sweden... "					2	697				
United States......... "	1	149								
Total.................	1	149			3	864				
Rimouski, P.Q.—										
Great Britain.........Steam.	2	3,564								
Germany.............. Sail.										
Norway and Sweden...Steam.					7	10,139				
" .. Sail.					5	4,994				
Total.................	2	3,564			12	15,133				

and Steam Vessels entered Inwards *from Sea,* &c.—*Continued.*

OF VESSELS.

Danish.		French.		German.		Italian.		Russian.		Other Nationalities.			Total.	
Vessels.	Tons Register.	Vessels.	Tons Register.	Vessels.	Tons Register.	Vessels.	Tons Register.	Vessels.	Tons Register.	Names.	Vessels.	Tons Register.	Vessels.	Tons Register.
...	...	...	...	...	...	...	...	...	...	...	...	...	1	603
...	...	...	...	...	...	...	...	...	...	...	...	...	5	528
...	...	...	...	...	...	...	...	...	...	...	...	...	3	234
...	...	...	...	...	...	...	...	...	...	...	...	...	2	176
...	...	...	...	...	...	...	...	...	...	...	...	...	12	877
...	...	...	...	...	...	...	...	...	...	Saint Pierre..	1	34	16	1,372
...	...	...	...	...	...	...	...	...	...	...	1	34	39	3,790
...	...	...	...	...	...	...	...	...	...	...	...	...	82	30,553
...	...	...	...	...	...	...	...	...	...	...	...	...	2	778
...	...	...	...	...	...	...	...	...	...	...	...	...	84	31,331
...	...	...	...	...	...	...	...	...	...	...	...	...	1	299
...	...	...	...	...	...	...	...	...	...	...	...	...	29	923
...	...	...	...	...	...	...	...	...	...	...	...	...	60	2,685
...	...	...	...	...	...	...	...	...	...	...	...	...	89	3,608
...	...	...	...	...	...	...	...	...	...	Dutch.......	1	1,299	3	4,052
...	...	...	...	...	...	...	...	...	...	...	...	...	1	768
...	...	...	...	...	...	...	...	...	...	...	...	...	2	3,388
...	...	...	...	...	...	...	...	...	...	...	1	1,299	6	8,208
...	...	...	...	...	...	...	...	...	...	...	...	...	233	914,888
...	...	...	...	...	...	...	...	...	...	...	...	...	1	545
...	...	...	...	...	...	...	...	...	...	...	...	...	3	7,898
...	...	...	...	...	...	...	...	...	...	...	...	...	2	578
...	...	...	...	...	...	...	...	...	...	...	...	...	1	155
...	...	...	...	...	...	...	...	...	...	...	...	...	28	132,080
...	...	...	...	...	...	...	...	...	...	...	...	...	2	379
...	...	...	...	...	...	...	...	2	2,542	...	...	...	17	40,900
3	5,006	...	...	1	1,289	...	...	...	...	...	...	...	5	9,108
...	...	...	...	...	...	...	...	...	...	...	...	...	2	4,247
...	...	...	...	...	...	...	...	...	...	...	...	...	3	4,990
2	3,365	...	...	...	...	...	...	...	...	...	...	...	5	8,784
1	81	...	...	...	...	...	...	...	...	...	...	...	21	4,021
...	...	...	...	...	...	...	...	...	...	...	...	...	22	1,421
6	8,452	...	...	1	1,289	...	...	2	2,542	...	...	...	345	1,129,994
1	252	...	...	...	...	...	...	2	659	...	...	...	4	1,078
1	286	...	...	...	...	...	...	1	224	...	...	...	2	510
...	...	...	...	...	...	...	...	...	...	...	...	...	2	697
...	...	...	...	...	...	...	...	...	...	...	...	...	1	149
2	538	...	...	...	...	...	...	3	883	...	...	...	9	2,434
...	...	...	...	...	...	...	...	...	...	...	...	...	2	3,564
...	...	...	...	1	1,035	...	...	...	...	...	...	...	1	1,035
...	...	...	...	...	...	...	...	...	...	...	...	...	7	10,139
...	...	...	...	...	...	...	...	...	...	...	...	...	5	4,994
...	...	...	...	1	1,035	...	...	...	...	...	...	...	15	19,732

No. 13.—STATEMENT of the Number and Tonnage of Sailing

Ports and Outports and Countries whence Arrived.	Nationality									
	British.		United States.		Norwegian and Swedish.		Austrian.		Belgian.	
	Vessels.	Tons Register.	Vessels.	Tons Register.	Vessels.	Tons Register.	Vessels.	Tons Register.	Vessels.	Tons Register.
River Bourgeois, N.S.—										
Sea Fisheries.......... Sail.	53	1,464								
River Hebert, N.S.—										
United States......... Sail.	40	4,748	20	4,358						
Riviere du Loup, P.Q.—										
Great Britain ....Steam.	1	1,774								
" .... Sail.					1	229				
Total................	1	1,774			1	229				
Rustico, P.E.I.—										
United States......... Sail.	1	74								
Sea Fisheries.......... "	1	10								
Total................	2	84								
St. Andrews, N.B.—										
United States ....Steam.	2	364	337	33,756						
" .... Sail.	18	1,773	200	3,115						
Total................	20	2,137	537	36,871						
St. Annes, N.S.—										
Great Britain......... Sail.										
Newfoundland......... "	7	461								
Saint-Pierre. .... "										
United States.........Steam.					4	2,646				
Total................	7	461			4	2,646				
St. George, N.B.—										
United States ....Steam.	7	520	12	190						
" .... Sail.	30	689	199	6,731						
Total................	37	1,209	211	6,921						
St. John, N.B.—										
Great Britain.........Steam.	163	465,184			1	1,426				
" .... Sail.					3	1,782				
British W. Indies......Steam.	26	36,748			13	8,066				
" .. Sail.	7	1,263	1	320	1	882				
Cuba & Porto Rico.... "	8	1,420								
Germany............. "					2	1.538				
Norway and Sweden... "					1	1,046				
Portugal.............Steam.	1	1,795								
United States ....Steam.	20	15,866	243	283,773	1	1,376				
" .... Sail.	474	48,928	321	50,733						
British S. Africa ......Steam.	3	8,559								
Spanish Poss. in Africa. "	1	1,795								
Iceland............... Sail.										
Sea Fisheries.......... Sail.	158	6,147								
Total................	861	587,705	565	334,826	22	16,116				
St. Martins, N.B.—										
United States .... Sail.	27	2,557	3	79						
St. Peters, N.S.—										
Sea Fisheries .... Sail.	4	58	7	596						
St. Stephen, N.B.—										
United States ....Steam.	47	9,212	36	619						
" .... Sail.	110	2,019	181	4 477						
Total................	157	11,231	217	5,096						
Sackville, NB.—										
United States .... Sail.	36	5,200	4	739						

and Steam Vessels entered Inwards *from Sea, &c.—Continued.*

OF VESSELS.

Danish.		French.		German.		Italian.		Russian.		Other Nationalities.			Total.	
Vessels.	Tons Register.	Vessels.	Tons Register.	Vessels.	Tons Register.	Vessels.	Tons Register.	Vessels.	Tons Register.	Names.	Vessels.	Tons Register.	Vessels.	Tons Register.
													53	1,464
													60	9,106
													1	1,774
													1	229
													2	2,003
													1	74
													1	10
													2	84
													339	34,120
													218	4,888
													557	39,008
		8	318										8	318
													7	461
		2	62										2	62
													4	2,646
		10	380										21	3,487
													19	710
													229	7,420
													248	8,130
2	2,926												166	469,536
													3	1,782
													39	44,814
													9	2,465
													8	1,420
								1	852				3	2,390
													1	1,046
													1	1,795
													264	301,015
						2	1,526						797	101,187
													3	8,559
													1	1,795
1	227												1	227
													158	6,147
3	3,153					2	1,526	1	852				1,454	944,178
													30	2,636
													11	654
													83	9,831
													291	6,496
													374	16,327
													40	5,939

No. 13.—STATEMENT of the Number and Tonnage of Sailing

Ports and Outports and Countries whence Arrived.	Nationality									
	British.		United States.		Norwegian and Swedish.		Austrian.		Belgian.	
	Vessels.	Tons Register.	Vessels.	Tons Register.	Vessels.	Tons Register.	Vessels.	Tons Register.	Vessels.	Tons Register.
Salmon River, N.S.—										
United States .... Sail.	11	741								
Sea Fisheries .... "	17	327								
Total................	28	1,068								
Sandy Cove, N.S.—										
United States .... Sail.	1	168								
Shediac, N.B.—										
Great Britain......... Sail.					3	1,836				
France............... Sail.					4	2,029				
Norway and Sweden .. "					1	588				
Total................					8	4,453				
Street Harbour, N.S.—										
United States .... Sail.										
Sea Fisheries .... "	1	37								
Total................	1	37								
Shelburne, N.S.—										
Great Britain.........Steam.	1	2,434								
" .... Sail.					1	1,260				
British W. Indies...... "	4	494								
Newfoundland......... "			1	57						
United States .... "	12	2,141	79	6,135						
Sea Fisheries .... "	53	2,119	104	8,053						
Total........................	70	7,188	184	14,245	1	1,260				
Sherbrooke, N.S.—										
Great Britain......... Sail.					2	923				
Newfoundland.........Steam.					2	1,948				
United States......... Sail.	1	191	1	230						
Total................	1	191	1	230	4	2,871				
Shippigan, N.B.—										
Great Britain......... Sail.	2	243								
British W. Indies...... "	1	99								
Spain................ "	1	99								
Total................	4	441								
Souris, P.E.I.—										
Great Britain......... Sail.										
Newfoundland.........Steam.	1	372								
" .... Sail.	2	125								
Saint Pierre.......... "	7	664								
United States......... "	1	96	1	99						
Sea Fisheries......... "	3	144								
Total................	14	1,401	1	99						
Stickeen, B.C.—										
United States.........Steam.	7	1.865								
Summerside, P.E.I.—										
United States......... Sail.	3	343	1	217						

and Steam Vessels entered Inwards *from Sea*, &c.—*Continued.*

OF VESSELS.

Danish.		French.		German.		Italian.		Russian.		Other Nationalities.			Total.	
Vessels.	Tons Register.	Vessels.	Tons Register.	Vessels.	Tons Register.	Vessels.	Tons Register.	Vessels.	Tons Register.	Names.	Vessels.	Tons Register.	Vessels.	Tons Register.
...	...	...	...	...	...	...	...	...	...	...	...	...	11	741
...	...	...	...	...	...	...	...	...	...	...	...	...	17	327
...	...	...	...	...	...	...	...	...	...	...	...	...	28	1,068
...	...	...	...	...	...	...	...	...	...	...	...	...	1	168
...	...	...	...	...	...	...	...	...	...	...	...	...	3	1,836
...	...	...	...	...	...	...	...	...	...	...	...	...	4	2,029
...	...	...	...	...	...	...	...	...	...	...	...	...	1	588
...	...	...	...	...	...	...	...	...	...	...	...	...	8	4,453
...	...	...	...	...	...	1	1,754	...	...	...	...	...	1	1,754
...	...	...	...	...	...	...	...	...	...	...	...	...	1	37
...	...	...	...	...	...	1	1,754	...	...	...	...	...	2	1,791
...	...	...	...	...	...	...	...	...	...	...	...	...	1	2,434
...	...	...	...	...	...	...	...	...	...	...	...	...	1	1,260
...	...	...	...	...	...	...	...	...	...	...	...	...	4	494
...	...	...	...	...	...	...	...	...	...	...	...	...	1	57
...	...	...	...	...	...	...	...	...	...	...	...	...	91	8,276
...	...	...	...	...	...	...	...	...	...	...	...	...	157	10,172
...	...	...	...	...	...	...	...	...	...	...	...	...	255	22,693
1	161	...	...	...	...	...	...	...	...	...	...	...	3	1,084
...	...	...	...	...	...	...	...	...	...	...	...	...	2	1,948
...	...	...	...	...	...	1	696	...	...	...	...	...	3	1,117
1	161	...	...	...	...	1	696	...	...	...	...	...	8	4,149
...	...	...	...	...	...	...	...	...	...	...	...	...	2	243
...	...	...	...	...	...	...	...	...	...	...	...	...	1	99
...	...	...	...	...	...	...	...	...	...	...	...	...	1	99
...	...	...	...	...	...	...	...	...	...	...	...	...	4	441
...	...	...	...	...	...	...	...	1	312	...	...	...	1	312
...	...	...	...	...	...	...	...	...	...	...	...	...	1	372
...	...	...	...	...	...	...	...	...	...	...	...	...	2	125
...	...	...	...	...	...	...	...	...	...	...	...	...	7	664
...	...	...	...	...	...	...	...	...	...	...	...	...	2	195
...	...	...	...	...	...	...	...	...	...	...	...	...	3	144
...	...	...	...	...	...	...	...	1	312	...	...	...	16	1,812
...	...	...	...	...	...	...	...	...	...	...	...	...	7	1,865
...	...	...	...	...	...	...	...	...	...	...	...	...	4	560

No. 13.—Statement of the Number and Tonnage of Sailing

Ports and Outports and Countries whence Arrived.	Nationality									
	British.		United States.		Norwegian and Swedish.		Austrian.		Belgian.	
	Vessels.	Tons Register.	Vessels.	Tons Register.	Vessels.	Tons Register.	Vessels.	Tons Register.	Vessels.	Tons Register.
Sydney, N.S.—										
Great Britain.........Steam.	10	18,785	...	...	9	19,305	...	...	...	...
British W. Indies...... "	4	6,737	...	...	...	...	...	...	...	...
Newfoundland......... "	45	36,380	...	...	84	180,065	...	...	...	...
" .... Sail.	28	2,002	...	...	...	...	...	...	...	...
Norway and Sweden...Steam.	...	...	...	...	2	4,426	...	...	...	...
Saint Pierre........... Sail.	1	80	...	...	...	...	...	...	...	...
Spain.................Steam.	1	1,254	...	...	...	...	...	...	...	...
United States......... "	24	42,962	...	...	27	37,658	...	...	...	...
" .... Sail.	6	1,335	1	383	...	...	...	...	...	...
Mexico................Steam.	2	3,638	...	...	...	...	...	...	...	...
British Africa......... "	1	2,872	...	...	...	...	...	...	...	...
Sea.................. "	1	984	...	...	...	...	...	...	...	...
Sea Fisheries.......... "	...	...	1	120	...	...	...	...	...	...
Total................	123	117,029	2	503	122	241,434	...	...	...	...
Thorne's Cove, N.S.—										
United States......... Sail.	14	1,495	1	52	...	...	...	...	...	...
Three Rivers, P.Q.—										
Great Britain.........Steam.	34	71,104	...	...	...	...	...	...	...	...
" .... Sail.	1	1344	...	...	...	...	...	...	...	...
Belgium..............Steam.	...	...	...	...	...	...	...	...	...	...
Total................	35	72,448	...	...	...	...	...	...	...	...
Tidnish, N.S.—										
Great Britain......... Sail.	...	...	...	...	1	909	...	...	...	...
Tignish, P.E.I.—										
United States......... Sail.	1	99	...	...	...	...	...	...	...	...
Truro, N.S.—										
United States......... Sail.	2	263	...	...	...	...	...	...	...	...
Tusket, N.S.—										
United States......... Sail.	3	300	26	2,887	...	...	...	...	...	...
Sea Fisheries.......... "	...	...	9	700	...	...	...	...	...	...
Total................	3	300	35	3,587	...	...	...	...	...	...
Tusket Wedge, N.S.—										
Great Britain.........Steam.	1	1,723	...	...	...	...	...	...	...	...
France............... Sail.	...	...	...	...	...	...	...	...	...	...
Norway and Sweden... "	...	...	...	...	1	1,132	...	...	...	...
United States......... "	3	976	4	675	2	2,129	...	...	...	...
Sea Fisheries.......... "	28	314	1	124	...	...	...	...	...	...
Total................	32	3,013	5	799	3	3,261	...	...	...	...
Vancouver, B.C.—										
Great Britain.........Steam.	9	45,095	...	...	...	...	...	...	...	...
" .... Sail.	5	8,957	...	...	...	...	...	...	...	...
British Guiana........Steam.	1	2,002	...	...	...	...	...	...	...	...
British Africa......... Sail.	1	2,315	...	...	...	...	...	...	...	...
Chili................. "	2	3,451	...	...	...	...	...	...	...	...
Guatemala............. "	...	...	...	...	...	...	...	...	...	...
Hawaiian Islands...... "	1	2,048	...	...	...	...	...	...	...	...
Panama..............Steam.	1	2,072	...	...	...	...	...	...	...	...
" .... Sail.	1	1,391	...	...	...	...	...	...	...	...
United States.........Steam.	353	165,270	299	264,347	2	2,418	...	...	...	...
" .... Sail.	48	20,118	10	4,914	...	...	...	...	...	...
Australia.............Steam.	13	31,089	...	...	...	...	...	...	...	...
Japan................ "	28	89,531	...	...	1	1,209	...	...	...	...
" .... Sail.	1	1,533	...	...	...	...	...	...	...	...
Peru.................Steam.	1	71	...	...	...	...	...	...	...	...
" .... Sail.	3	4,793	...	...	...	...	...	...	...	...
Java.................Steam.	1	2,851	...	...	...	...	...	...	...	...
" .... Sail.	...	...	...	...	...	...	...	...	...	...

and Steam Vessels entered Inwards *from Sea, &c.—Continued.*

OF VESSELS.

Danish.		French.		German.		Italian.		Russian.		Other Nationalities.			Total.	
Vessels.	Tons Register.	Vessels.	Tons Register.	Vessels.	Tons Register.	Vessels.	Tons Register.	Vessels.	Tons Register.	Names.	Vessels.	Tons Register.	Vessels.	Tons Register.
													19	38,090
													4	6,737
													129	216,445
													28	2,002
													2	4,426
		17	1,184										18	1,264
													1	1,254
													51	80,620
													7	1,718
													2	3,638
													1	2,872
													1	984
		3	225										4	345
		20	1,409										267	360,395
													15	1,547
													34	71,104
													1	1,344
								1	1,070				1	1,070
								1	1,070				36	73,518
													1	909
													1	99
													2	263
													29	3,187
													9	700
													38	3,887.
													1	1,723
						1	969						1	969
													1	1,132
						1	1384						10	5,164
													29	438
						2	2,353						42	9,426
													9	45,095
													5	8,957
													1	2,002
													1	2,315
										Chilian	1	1,338	3	4,789
				1	1,399								1	1,399
													1	2,048
													1	2,072
													1	1,391
				2	5,041								656	437,076
													58	25,032
													13	31,089
													29	90,740
				2	3,720								3	5,253
				2	4,315								3	4,386
													3	4,793
													1	2,851
				1	1,165								1	1,165

No. 13.—STATEMENT of the Number and Tonnage of Sailing

Ports and Outports and Countries whence Arrived.		Nationality									
		British.		United States.		Norwegian and Swedish.		Austrian.		Belgian.	
		Vessels.	Tons Register.	Vessels.	Tons Register.	Vessels.	Tons Register.	Vessels.	Tons Register.	Vessels.	Tons Register.
Vancouver—*Con.*											
Sea Fisheries	Steam.	2	203	57	6,009	....	....	....	....	....	....
"	Sail.	1	144	....	....	....	....	....	....	....	....
New Zealand	Steam.	1	2,284	....	....	....	....	....	....	....	....
Total		473	385,218	366	275,270	3	3,627	....	....	....	....
Victoria, B.C.—											
Great Britain	Steam.	13	64,576	....	....	....	....	....	....	....	....
"	Sail.	4	6,580	....	....	....	....	....	....	....	....
Australia	Steam.	13	31,089	....	....	....	....	....	....	....	....
Japan	"	3	6,945	....	....	....	....	....	....	....	....
China	"	25	73,138	15	68,573	....	....	....	....	....	....
Chili	"	2	4,506	....	....	....	....	....	....	....	....
"	Sail.	1	1,949	....	....	....	....	....	....	....	....
Peru	"	1	2,070	....	....	1	1,395	....	....	....	....
Mexico	"	2	5,322	....	....	....	....	....	....	....	....
United States	Steam.	457	202,335	449	419,282	3	5,528	....	....	....	....
"	Sail.	3	6,061	8	2,114	....	....	....	....	....	....
Hawaiian Islands	"	1	1,262	....	....	....	....	....	....	....	....
Panama	Steam.	3	6,505	....	....	....	....	....	....	....	....
Sea Fisheries	Sail.	24	1,793	....	....	....	....	....	....	....	....
Total		552	414,131	472	489,969	4	6,923	....	....	....	....
Walton, N.S.—											
United States	Sail.	36	16,398	11	4,491	....	....	....	....	....	....
Westport, N.S.—											
United States	Sail.	2	247	7	78	....	....	....	....	....	....
Weymouth, N.S.—											
Great Britain	Sail.	....	....	....	....	1	720	....	....	....	....
Brazil	"	....	....	....	....	4	3,236	....	....	....	....
Spain	"	1	470	....	....	....	....	....	....	....	....
United States	"	15	2,521	7	2,225	....	....	....	....	....	....
Total		16	2,991	7	2,225	5	3,956	....	....	....	....
Windsor, N.S.—											
Great Britain	Steam.	....	....	....	....	1	699	....	....	....	....
Newfoundland	Sail.	8	956	....	....	....	....	....	....	....	....
United States	Steam.	....	....	....	....	15	10,136	....	....	....	....
"	Sail.	51	34,419	42	42,134	....	....	....	....	....	....
Total		59	35,375	42	42,134	16	10,835	....	....	....	....
Wolfville, N.S.—											
United States	Sail.	10	1,850	....	....	....	....	....	....	....	....
Yarmouth, N.S.—											
Great Britain	Steam.	1	1,723	....	....	3	2,896	....	....	....	....
British W. Indies	Sail.	4	715	....	....	....	....	....	....	....	....
Italy	"	....	....	....	....	....	....	....	....	....	....
Norway and Sweden	"	....	....	....	....	5	5,138	....	....	....	....
United States	Steam.	188	136,048	....	....	....	....	....	....	....	....
"	Sail.	46	6,974	5	3,107	....	....	....	....	....	....
Argentine Republic	"	....	....	....	....	1	1,232	....	....	....	....
Sea Fisheries	"	195	6,795	202	14,381	....	....	....	....	....	....
Total		434	152,255	207	17,488	9	9,266	....	....	....	....

and Steam Vessels entered Inwards *from Sea, &c.- Continued.*

OF VESSELS.

Danish.		French.		German.		Italian.		Russian.		Other Nationalities.			Total.	
Vessels.	Tons Register.	Vessels.	Tons Register.	Vessels.	Tons Register.	Vessels.	Tons Register.	Vessels.	Tons Register.	Names.	Vessels.	Tons Register.	Vessels.	Tons Register.
													59	6,212
													1	144
													1	2,284
				8	15,640						1	1,338	851	681,093
													13	64,576
													4	6,580
													13	31,089
										Japanese.....	13	50,297	16	57,242
													40	141,711
													2	4,506
				1	1,643								2	3,592
													2	3,465
				1	2,115								3	7,437
				3	7,904					Japanese.....	7	27,046	919	662,095
										Mexican....	1	145	12	8,320
													1	1,262
													3	6,505
													24	1,793
				5	11,662						21	77,488	1,054	1,000,173
													47	20,889
													9	325
						1	994						2	1,714
													4	3,236
													1	470
						2	1,398						24	6,144
						3	2,392						31	11,564
													1	699
													8	956
													15	10,136
													93	76,553
													117	88,344
													10	1,850
													4	4,619
													4	715
						1	1,484						1	1,484
													5	5,138
													188	136,048
						1	1,384						52	11,465
													1	1,232
													397	21,176
						2	2,868						652	181,877

No. 14.—SUMMARY STATEMENT of the Nationality of Sea-going Vessels entered

Countries from which arrived.	Nationality											
	British.		United States.		Norwegian and Swedish.		Austrian.		Belgian.		Danish.	
	Vessels.	Tons Register.	Vessels.	Tons Register.	Vessels.	Tons Register.	Vessels.	Tons Register.	Vessels.	Tons Register.	Vessels.	Tons Register.
Great Britain	1,009	3,262,973			142	135,905					8	9,810
Australia	26	62,178										
British Africa	7	19,500			4	4,300					2	365
British Guiana	29	41,955			2	2,513						
British West Indies	147	103,601	2	640	51	33,824						
Newfoundland	946	259,287	22	1,870	119	228,530			4	369	1	323
New Zealand	1	2,284										
Argentina					1	1,232						
Azores, Madeira and Cape Verde Islands	1	1,916										
Belgium	47	222,677			2	2,197						
Brazil	9	2,441			9	8,130						
Central Am. States												
Chili	8	15,665			1	1,547						
China	27	77,152	16	70,042								
Cuba and Porto Rico	40	6,931			1	1,215						
Denmark											1	147
Dutch East Indies	1	2,851										
Dutch West Indies	1	166										
France	20	49,720			19	14,959					1	286
French West Indies	1	99										
Germany	2	5,626			8	6,658					6	10,012
Greenland	1	626										
Hawaii	2	3,310										
Holland	4	8,495			1	2,418						
Iceland											2	408
Italy	5	8,252									1	1,547
Japan	38	110,932			1	1,209						
Mediterranean Ports	1	1,951										
Mexico	14	27,206										
Norway and Sweden	1	2,165			69	70,149						
Panama	5	9,968										
Peru	5	6,934			1	1,395						
Portugal	8	7,415										
Russia					1	2,088						
Sea	24	26,679			1	1,862						
Sea Fisheries	1,827	98,856	1,099	88,647							1	81
South Sea Seal Fish'ies	3	277										
Spain	19	23,945			4	4,807	1	316			3	2,668
Spanish Africa	1	1,795			1	1,664						
St. Pierre	70	8,131										
United States	4,395	1,647,707	4,313	1,401,637	288	407,626					5	6,272
Uruguay	1	99										
Total	8,746	6,131,765	5,452	1,562,836	726	934,228	1	316	4	369	31	31,919

Inwards *from Sea* from each Country, during the Fiscal year ending June 30, 1906.

OF VESSELS.

French.		German.		Italian.		Russian.		Other Nationalities.			Total.	
Vessels.	Tons Register.	Vessels.	Tons Register.	Vessels.	Tons Register.	Vessels.	Tons Register.	Names.	Vessels.	Tons Register.	Vessels.	Tons Register.
8	318			2	1,749	10	5,811	Dutch	1	1,299	1,180	3,417,865
											26	62,178
						1	942				14	25,107
											31	44,468
											200	138,065
1	55					1	159	Dutch	4	2,612	1,098	493,205
											1	2,284
											1	1,232
											1	1,916
						1	1,070				50	225,944
											18	10,571
		1	1,399								1	1,399
		1	1,643					Chilian	2	3,010	12	21,865
		1	2,468								44	149,662
								Spanish	1	149	42	8,295
											1	147
		1	1,165								2	4,016
											1	166
4	253			1	969	5	5,308				50	71,495
											1	99
		3	3,613			1	852				20	26,761
											1	626
											2	3,310
				1	836						6	11,749
											2	408
				1	1,484						7	11,283
1	3,186	2	3,720					Japanese	13	50,297	55	169,344
											1	1,951
		1	2,115								15	29,321
						1	456				71	72,770
											5	9,968
		2	4,315								8	12,644
		1	1,035								9	8,450
											1	2,088
5	3,890										30	32,431
121	6,637							St. Pierre	1	34	3,049	194,255
											3	277
						2	594	Uruguay	1	703	30	33,033
						1	348				3	3,807
76	9,936										146	18,067
		23	71,677	10	10,224			Dutch Mexican Japanese	1 1 7	398 145 27,046	9,043	3,572,732
											1	99
[216	24,275	36	93,150	15	15,262	23	15,540		32	85,693	15,282	8,895,353

TRADE WITH EACH COUNTRY

No. 15.—STATEMENT of the Number and Tonnage of Sailing and Steam Vessels in Canada for foreign countries distinguishing the Nationality the Fiscal Year ending

Ports, and Outports and Countries for which Departed.	NATIONALITY									
	British.		United States.		Norwegian and Swedish.		Austrian.		Belgian.	
	Vessels.	Tons Register.	Vessels.	Tons Register.	Vessels.	Tons Register.	Vessels.	Tons Register.	Vessels.	Tons Register.
Advocate Harbour, N.S.—										
United States........... Sail.	10	2,471	5	1,403						
Alberton, P.E.I.—										
British W. Indies...... Sail.	1	99								
Newfoundland......... "	1	83								
United States......... "	1	98								
Total................	3	280								
Alma, N.B.—										
United States......... Sail.	1	90	1	56						
Amherst, N.S.—										
United States ....Steam.					2	1,390				
" .... Sail.	1	397								
Total................	1	397			2	1,390				
Annapolis Royal, N.S.—										
British W. Indies...... Sail.	5	1,101								
Cuba & Porto Rico.... "	11	2,917	2	853						
Spain................ "	1	386								
United States......... "	7	578	7	86						
Argentine Republic.... "	1	597			3	3,101				
Total................	25	5,579	9	939	3	3,101				
Apple River, N.S.—										
United States......... Sail.	21	3,840	23	5,079						
Arichat, N.S.—										
Saint Pierre.......... Sail.	2	198								
Sea Fisheries.......... "	83	2,490	16	1,247						
Total................	85	2,688	16	1,247						
Aspy Bay, N.S.—										
Saint Pierre........... Sail.	2	68								
Baddeck, N.S.—										
Newfoundland.........Steam.	6	1,602								
Saint Pierre........... Sail.										
United States......... "	1	97								
Total................	7	1,699								
Baie Verte, N.B.—										
Great Britain.........Steam.	1	1,172			1	1,326				
" .... Sail.					9	4,746				
Total................	1	1,172			10	6,072				
Barrington, N.S.—										
United States .... Sail.			6	258						
Sea Fisheries.......... "	4	108	20	1,278						
Total................	4	108	26	1,536						
Barton, N.S.—										
United States......... Sail.	58	5,780								

AND NATIONALITY OF VESSELS.

entered outwards, *for Sea*, at each of the undermentioned Ports and Outports of the Vessels employed in the trade with each country, during June 30, 1906.

OF VESSELS.

Danish.		French.		German.		Italian.		Russian.		Other Nationalities.			Total.	
Vessels.	Tons Register.	Vessels.	Tons Register.	Vessels.	Tons Register.	Vessels.	Tons Register.	Vessels.	Tons Register.	Names.	Vessels.	Tons Register.	Vessels.	Tons Register.
													15	3,874
													1	99
													1	83
													1	98
													3	280
													2	146
													2	1,390
													1	397
													3	1,787
													5	1,101
													13	3,770
										Spanish.	1	149	2	535
													14	664
													4	3,698
											1	149	38	9,768
													44	8,919
													2	198
													99	3,737
													101	3,935
													2	68
													6	1,602
		1	50										1	50
													1	97
		1	50										8	1,749
													2	2,498
													9	4,746
													11	7,244
													6	258
													24	1,386
													30	1,644
													58	5,780

No. 15.—STATEMENT of the Number and Tonnage of Sailing

Ports and Outports and Countries for which Departed.		Nationality									
		British.		United States.		Norwegian and Swedish.		Austrian.		Belgian.	
		Vessels.	Tons Register.	Vessels.	Tons Register.	Vessels.	Tons Register.	Vessels.	Tons Register.	Vessels.	Tons Register.
Bathurst, N.B.—											
Great Britain	Steam.	3	5,566	....	....	....	....	....	....	....	....
"	Sail.	....	....	....	....	9	6,075	....	....	....	....
United States	"	8	1,335	1	167	....	....	....	....	....	....
Total		11	6,901	1	167	9	6,075	....	....	....	....
Bayfield, N.S.—											
Newfoundland	Sail.	7	693	....	....	....	....	....	....	....	....
Bear River, N.S.—											
British W. Indies	Sail.	....	....	....	....	....	....	....	....	....	....
Cuba & Porto Rico	"	4	1,486	3	1,321	....	....	....	....	....	....
United States	"	30	4,416	2	423	....	....	....	....	....	....
Argentina	"	1	397	....	....	....	....	....	....	....	....
Total		35	6,299	5	1,744	....	....	....	....	....	....
Belliveau's Cove, N.S.—											
British W. Indies	Sail.	1	158	....	....	....	....	....	....	....	....
Cuba & Porto Rico	"	1	149	....	....	....	....	....	....	....	....
United States	"	20	2,164	....	....	....	....	....	....	....	....
Total		22	2,471	....	....	....	....	....	....	....	....
Bridgetown, N.S.—											
United States	Sail.	1	95	....	....	....	....	....	....	....	....
Bridgewater, N.S.—											
Great Britain	Steam.	1	1,722	....	....	....	....	....	....	....	....
British W. Indies	Sail.	1	199	....	....	....	....	....	....	....	....
Cuba & Porto Rico	"	7	1,983	....	....	....	....	....	....	....	....
United States	Steam.	1	1,737	....	....	....	....	....	....	....	....
"	Sail.	52	10,639	4	1,509	....	....	....	....	....	....
Madeira	"	3	647	1	320	....	....	....	....	....	....
Argentina	"	4	2,279	1	668	2	1,199	....	....	....	....
Sea Fisheries	"	3	54	....	....	....	....	....	....	....	....
Total		72	19,260	6	2,497	2	1,199	....	....	....	....
Buctouche, N.B.—											
Great Britain	Sail.	....	....	....	....	3	1,248	....	....	....	....
Campbellton, N.B.—											
Great Britain	Steam.	6	8,511	....	....	....	....	....	....	....	....
"	Sail.	....	....	....	....	12	9,071	....	....	....	....
United States	"	4	1,069	2	1,183	....	....	....	....	....	....
Total		10	9,580	2	1,183	12	9,071	....	....	....	....
Campobello, N.B.—											
United States	Steam.	....	....	93	3,015	....	....	....	....	....	....
"	Sail.	71	552	43	642	....	....	....	....	....	....
Total		71	552	136	3,657	....	....	....	....	....	....
Canning, N.S.—											
Cuba and Porto Rico	Sail.	3	923	....	....	....	....	....	....	....	....
United States	Sail.	1	68	....	....	....	....	....	....	....	....
Total		4	991	....	....	....	....	....	....	....	....

and Steam Vessels entered Outwards *for Sea, &c.*—*Continued.*

OF VESSELS.

Danish.		French.		German.		Italian.		Russian.		Other Nationalities.			Total.	
Vessels.	Tons Register.	Vessels.	Tons Register.	Vessels.	Tons Register.	Vessels.	Tons Register.	Vessels.	Tons Register.	Names.	Vessels.	Tons Register.	Vessels.	Tons Register.
1	1,333	...	...	...	...	...	...	...	...	...	...	...	4	6,899
...	...	...	...	...	...	...	...	...	...	...	...	...	9	6,075
...	...	...	...	...	...	...	...	...	...	...	...	...	9	1,502
1	1,333	...	...	...	...	...	...	...	...	...	...	...	22	14,476
...	...	...	...	...	...	...	...	...	...	...	...	...	7	693
...	...	...	...	...	...	...	...	...	...	Dutch	1	398	1	398
...	...	...	...	...	...	...	...	...	...	...	...	...	7	2,807
...	...	...	...	...	...	...	...	...	...	...	...	...	32	4,839
...	...	...	...	...	...	...	...	...	...	...	...	...	1	397
...	...	...	...	...	...	...	...	...	...	...	1	398	41	8,441
...	...	...	...	...	...	...	...	...	...	...	...	...	1	158
...	...	...	...	...	...	...	...	...	...	...	...	...	1	149
...	...	...	...	...	...	...	...	...	...	...	...	...	20	2,164
...	...	...	...	...	...	...	...	...	...	...	...	...	22	2,471
...	...	...	...	...	...	...	...	...	...	...	...	...	1	95
...	...	...	...	...	...	...	...	...	...	...	...	...	1	1,722
...	...	...	...	...	...	...	...	...	...	...	...	...	1	199
...	...	...	...	...	...	...	...	...	...	...	...	...	7	1,983
...	...	...	...	...	...	...	...	...	...	...	...	...	1	1,737
...	...	...	...	...	...	...	...	...	...	...	...	...	56	12,148
...	...	...	...	...	...	...	...	...	...	...	...	...	4	967
...	...	...	...	...	...	...	...	...	...	...	...	...	7	4,146
...	...	...	...	...	...	...	...	...	...	...	...	...	3	54
...	...	...	...	...	...	...	...	...	...	...	...	...	80	22,956
...	...	...	...	...	...	...	...	...	...	...	...	...	3	1,248
...	...	...	...	1	1,426	...	...	...	...	...	...	...	7	9,937
5	1,063	...	...	...	...	...	...	2	572	...	...	...	19	10,706
...	...	...	...	...	...	...	...	...	...	...	...	...	6	2,252
5	1,063	...	...	1	1,426	...	...	2	572	...	...	...	32	22,895
...	...	...	...	...	...	...	...	...	...	...	...	...	93	3,015
...	...	...	...	...	...	...	...	...	...	...	...	...	114	1,194
...	...	...	...	...	...	...	...	...	...	...	...	...	207	4,209
...	...	...	...	...	...	...	...	...	...	...	...	...	3	923
...	...	...	...	...	...	...	...	...	...	...	...	...	1	68
...	...	...	...	...	...	...	...	...	...	...	...	...	4	991

No. 15.—STATEMENT of the Number and Tonnage of Sailing

Ports and Outports and Countries for which Departed.	Nationality									
	British.		United States.		Norwegian and Swedish.		Austrian.		Belgian.	
	Vessels.	Tons Register.	Vessels.	Tons Register.	Vessels.	Tons Register.	Vessels.	Tons Register.	Vessels.	Tons Register.
Canso, N.S.—										
Newfoundland .... Steam.	1	984								
" .... Sail.	3	245								
Saint Pierre .... "	1	78								
United States .... "	7	728	13	824						
Sea .... Steam.	4	12,410								
Sea Fisheries .... Sail.	221	19,221	278	23,209						
Total	237	33,666	291	24,033						
Cardigan, P.E.I.—										
Saint Pierre .... Sail.	3	220								
United States .... "	6	614								
Sea Fisheries .... "			1	42						
Total	9	834	1	42						
Charlottetown, P.E.I.—										
Newfoundland .... Steam.	54	31,410			3	2,052				
" .... Sail.	3	127								
Saint Pierre .... "	2	156								
United States .... Steam.	29	30,442	14	14,364						
" .... Sail.	4	520								
British Guiana .... "	1	266								
Sea Fisheries .... "	1	65								
Total	94	62,986	14	14,364	3	2,052				
Chatham, N.B.—										
Great Britain .... Steam.	16	25,467			6	7,751				
" .... Sail.	1	596			14	13,222				
Norway and Sweden ... "										
United States .... Steam					1	1,434				
" .... Sail.	12	2,298	2	561						
Sea Fisheries .... "	5	64								
Total	34	28,425	2	561	21	22,407				
Chemainus, B.C.—										
Great Britain .... Sail.	1	1,642								
United States .... Steam.	10	693	17	1,671						
New Zealand .... Sail.	1	1,119								
Australia .... Steam.	1	2,072								
" .... Sail.	3	4,111	2	3,041						
British Africa .... "	2	3,652	1	1,469						
Chili .... "	6	12,848								
Total	24	26,137	20	6,181						
Chester, N.S.—										
Cuba and Porto Rico .. Sail.	1	188								
United States .... "	1	422								
Sea Fisheries .... "	1	15	2	155						
Total	3	625	2	155						
Cheticamp, N.S.—										
Saint Pierre .... Sail.	11	372								
Cheverie, N.S.—										
United States .... Sail.	14	2,063	16	9,013						
Chicoutimi, Que.—										
Great Britain .... Steam.	6	12,796			9	12,467				

and Steam Vessels entered Outwards *for Sea, &c.—Continued.*

OF VESSELS.

Danish.		French.		German.		Italian.		Russian.		Other Nationalities.			Total.	
Vessels.	Tons Register.	Vessels.	Tons Register.	Vessels.	Tons Register.	Vessels.	Tons Register.	Vessels.	Tons Register.	Names.	Vessels.	Tons Register.	Vessels.	Tons Register.
													1	984
													3	245
													1	78
													20	1,552
													4	12,410
													499	42,430
													528	57,699
													3	220
													6	614
													1	42
													10	876
													57	33,462
													3	127
		1	116										3	272
													43	44,806
													4	520
													1	266
													1	65
		1	116										112	79,518
													22	33,218
								1	456				16	14,274
		2	1,126										2	1,126
													1	1,434
													14	2,859
													5	64
		2	1,126					1	456				60	52,975
				1	2,054								2	3,696
													27	2,364
													1	1,119
													1	2,072
				1	2468								6	9,620
													3	5,121
													6	12,848
				2	4,522								46	36,840
													1	188
													1	422
													3	170
													5	780
½													11	372
													30	11,076
6	9,613												21	34,876

No. 15.—STATEMENT of the Number and Tonnage of Sailing

Ports and Outports and Countries for which Departed.		Nationality									
		British.		United States.		Norwegian and Swedish.		Austrian.		Belgian.	
		Vessels.	Tons Register.	Vessels.	Tons Register.	Vessels.	Tons Register.	Vessels.	Tons Register.	Vessels.	Tons Register.
Church Point, N.S.—											
British W. Indies......	Sail.	1	162								
Cuba and Porto Rico ..	"	1	162								
United States.........	"	13	1,394								
Total.................		15	1,718								
Clark's Harbour, N.S.—											
United States.........	Sail.			7	228						
Sea Fisheries..........	"			1	83						
Total.................				8	311						
Clementsport, N.S.—											
United States.........	Sail.	25	2,493								
Comox, B.C.—											
Italy.................	Steam.	1	2,110								
Russia...............	"					1	2,088				
United States.........	"	106	135,335	32	39,794						
"	Sail.	1	1,564	12	12,359						
Japan................	Steam.	6	16,856								
China................	"	1	2,653								
Sea Fisheries..........	"			18	1,908						
Total.................		115	158,518	62	54,061	1	2,088				
Crapaud, P.E.I.—											
United States.........	Sail.	4	358								
Dalhousie, N.B.—											
Great Britain.........	Steam.					1	1,426				
"	Sail.	2	1,129			18	15,126				
British W. Indies......	"	2	395								
United States.........	"	4	735	2	649						
Total.................		8	2,259	2	649	19	16,552				
Dawson, Y.T. —											
United States.........	Steam.	1	639								
Digby, N.S.—											
Cuba and Porto Rico...	Sail.	1	272								
United States.........	"	8	809	16	741						
Total.................		9	1,081	16	741						
Dorchester, N.B.—											
United States.........	Sail.	15	1,540								
Douglas, B.C.—											
United States.........	Steam.	9	376	31	317						
Economy, N.S.—											
United States.........	Sail.	1	98								
Five Islands, N.S.—											
United States.........	Sail.	11	1,488								
Fredericton, N.B.—											
United States.........	Sail.	5	495	1	91						
Freeport, N.S.—											
United States.........	Sail.	1	46								
Gabarouse, N.S.—											
Sea Fisheries.........	Sail.	2	106	2	154						

and Steam Vessels entered Outwards *for Sea, &c.—Continued.*

OF VESSELS.

Danish.		French.		German.		Italian.		Russian.		Other Nationalities.			Total.	
Vessels.	Tons Register.	Vessels.	Tons Register.	Vessels.	Tons Register.	Vessels.	Tons Register.	Vessels.	Tons Register.	Names.	Vessels.	Tons Register.	Vessels.	Tons Register.
													1	162
													1	162
													13	1,394
													15	1,718
													7	228
													1	83
													8	311
													25	2,493
													1	2,110
													1	2,088
				9	21,400								147	196,529
													13	13,923
													6	16,856
													1	2,653
													18	1,908
				9	21,400								187	236,067
														358
													1	1,426
1	147							3	1,649				24	18,051
													2	395
													6	1,384
1	147							3	1,649				33	21,256
													1	639
													1	272
													24	1,550
													25	1,822
													15	1,540
													40	693
													1	98
													11	1,488
													6	586
													1	46
													4	260

No. 15.—STATEMENT of the Number and Tonnage of Sailing

Ports and Outports and Countries for which Departed.		Nationality									
		British.		United States.		Norwegian and Swedish.		Austrian.		Belgian.	
		Vessels.	Tons Register.	Vessels.	Tons Register.	Vessels.	Tons Register.	Vessels.	Tons Register.	Vessels.	Tons Register.
Gaspé, Que.—											
Great Britain	Sail.	1	147			14	12,26				
British W. Indies	"	2	398								
Newfoundland	"	1	99								
Brazil	"	1	199								
Cuba and Porto Rico	"	1	1,811								
Portugal	"	1	99								
Saint Pierre	"	1	99								
United States	"	10	1,902	1	279						
Total		18	4,754	1	279	14	[illegible]				
Georgetown, P.E.I.—											
Newfoundland	Sail.	6	259								
United States	Steam.			1	287						
"	Sail.	1	99	1	72						
Sea Fisheries	"	8	343	2	164						
Total		15	701	4	523						
Grand River, P.E.I.—											
Newfoundland	Sail.	2	89								
Halifax, N.S.—											
Great Britain	Steam.	124	329,619			4	4,625				
"	Sail.	1	1,333			20	13,099				
British W. Indies	Steam.	39	42,349			34	23,465				
"	Sail.	2	295								
Newfoundland	Steam.	53	48,816								
"	Sail.	153	12,035	3	184						
Brazil	"	2	416								
Cuba and Porto Rico	Steam.	1	1,815			3	2,807				
"	Sail.	2	448								
France	Steam.										
Germany	"										
Italy	"										
Norway and Sweden	Sail.					2	1,307				
Portugal	"	1	99								
Saint Pierre	Steam.	7	1,869								
"	Sail.	1	78								
Spain	"										
United States	Steam.	150	261,232	20	15,526						
"	Sail.	90	19,838	12	4,119						
Republic of Panama	"	1	99								
Mexico	Steam.	12	21,936								
British Africa	"	1	2,794								
Sea Fisheries	"	8	455								
"	Sail.	324	17,972	78	6,639						
Total		972	763,498	113	26,468	63	45,303				
Hantsport, N.S.—											
Cuba and Porto Rico	Sail.	1	440	2	912						
United States	Steam.	8	848	31	6,453						
"	Sail.	27	4,432	6	1,784						
Total		36	5,720	39	9,149						
Harvey, N.B.—											
Great Britain	Sail.	3	4,597			3	3,004				
United States	Steam.	2	112								
"	Sail.	13	2,308	4	862						
Total		18	7,017	4	862	3	3,004				

and Steam Vessels entered Outwards *for Sea, &c.—Continued.*

OF VESSELS.

Danish.		French.		German.		Italian.		Russian.		Other Nationalities.			Total.	
Vessels.	Tons Register.	Vessels.	Tons Register.	Vessels.	Tons Register.	Vessels.	Tons Register.	Vessels.	Tons Register.	Names.	Vessels.	Tons Register.	Vessels.	Tons Register.
													15	12,410
													2	398
													1	99
													1	199
													1	1,811
													1	99
													1	99
													11	2,181
													33	17,296
													6	259
													1	287
													2	171
													10	507
													19	1,224
													2	89
													128	334,244
1	324					2	1,974						24	16,730
													73	65,814
													2	295
													53	48,816
													156	12,219
													2	416
1	588												5	5,210
													2	448
		1	976										1	976
				3	18,405								3	18,405
				1	3,176								1	3,176
													2	1,307
													1	99
		5	2,000										12	3,869
		3	375										4	453
										Spanish.	2	707	2	707
				2	8,548								172	285,306
1	324												103	24,281
													1	99
													12	21,936
													1	2,794
													8	455
													402	24,611
3	1,236	9	3,351	6	30,129	2	1,974				2	707	1,170	872,666
													3	1,352
													39	7,301
													33	6,216
													75	14,869
						2	2,377						8	9,978
													2	112
													17	3,170
						2	2,377						27	13,260

No. 15.—STATEMENT of the Number and Tonnage of Sailing

Ports and Outports and Countries for which Departed.	Nationality									
	British.		United States.		Norwegian and Swedish.		Austrian.		Belgian.	
	Vessels.	Tons Register.	Vessels.	Tons Register.	Vessels.	Tons Register.	Vessels.	Tons Register.	Vessels.	Tons Register.
Hillsboro, N.B.—										
Great Britain.........Steam.	5	11,091	....	....	....	....	....	....	....	....
" ....Sail.	1	736	....	....	....	....	....	....	....	....
United States.........Steam.	....	....	....	....	61	42,365	....	....	....	....
" ....Sail.	22	6,110	31	17,395	....	....	....	....	....	....
Total................	28	17,937	31	17,395	61	42,365	....	....	....	....
Ingonish, N.S.—										
Newfoundland......... Sail.	1	11	....	....	....	....	....	....	....	....
Isaac's Harbour, N.S.—										
Sea Fisheries .... Sail.	....	....	5	481	....	....	....	....	....	....
Jordan Bay, N.S.—										
United States......... Sail.	11	1,145	1	325	....	....	....	....	....	....
Sea Fisheries.......... "	2	196	2	146	....	....	....	....	....	....
Total................	13	1,341	3	471	....	....	....	....	....	....
Kentville, N.S.—										
United States......... Sail.	4	240	....	....	....	....	....	....	....	....
Kingsport, N.S.—										
Cuba & Porto Rico.... Sail.	3	1,082	....	....	....	....	....	....	....	....
United States......... "	3	803	3	847	....	....	....	....	....	....
Total................	6	1,885	3	847	....	....	....	....	....	....
Ladner, B.C.—										
United States.........Steam.	2	186	1	63	....	....	....	....	....	....
Ladysmith, B.C.—										
United States.........Steam.	154	68,801	46	30,422	25	55,609	....	....	....	....
" .... Sail.	12	1,660	3	4,131	....	....	....	....	....	....
Total................	166	70,461	49	34,553	25	55,609	....	....	....	....
La Have, N.S.—										
British W. Indies...... Sail.	3	297	....	....	....	....	....	....	....	....
Newfoundland.......... "	2	175	....	....	....	....	....	....	....	....
Cuba & Porto Rico.... "	2	198	....	....	....	....	....	....	....	....
United States......... "	4	373	....	....	....	....	....	....	....	....
Argentina............. "	1	632	....	....	1	626	....	....	....	....
Sea Fisheries.......... "	45	3,469	1	87	....	....	....	....	....	....
Total................	57	5,144	1	87	1	626	....	....	....	....
L'Ardoise, N.S.—										
Sea Fisheries .... Sail.	46	1,925	....	....	....	....	....	....	....	....
Liscombe, N.S.—										
Great Britain.........Steam.	....	....	....	....	2	1,948	....	....	....	....
Newfoundland......... Sail.	....	....	1	100	....	....	....	....	....	....
United States......... "	1	191	2	163	....	....	....	....	....	....
Sea Fisheries.......... "	....	....	29	2,535	....	....	....	....	....	....
Total................	1	191	32	2,798	2	1,948	....	....	....	....
Liverpool, N.S.—										
Great Britain......... Sail.	....	....	....	....	1	478	....	....	....	....
British W. Indies ..... "	5	963	....	....	....	....	....	....	....	....
Newfoundland......... "	5	759	4	355	....	....	....	....	....	....
Cuba & Porto Rico.... "	1	349	....	....	....	....	....	....	....	....
United States......... "	37	4,210	23	1,281	....	....	....	....	....	....
British Guiana........ "	1	99	....	....	....	....	....	....	....	....
Madeira.............. "	2	440	....	....	....	....	....	....	....	....
Sea Fisheries .... "	....	....	82	6,632	....	....	....	....	....	....
Total................	51	6,820	109	8,268	1	478	....	....	....	....

and Steam Vessels entered Outwards *for Sea, &c.—Continued.*

OF VESSELS.

Danish.		French.		German.		Italian.		Russian.		Other Nationalities.			Total.	
Vessels.	Tons Register.	Vessels.	Tons Register.	Vessels.	Tons Register.	Vessels.	Tons Register.	Vessels.	Tons Register.	Names.	Vessels.	Tons Register.	Vessels.	Tons Register.
...	...	...	...	...	...	...	...	...	...	...	...	...	5	11,091
...	...	...	...	...	...	...	...	...	...	...	...	...	1	736
...	...	...	...	...	...	...	...	...	...	...	...	...	61	42,365
...	...	...	...	...	...	...	...	...	...	...	...	...	53	23,505
...	...	...	...	...	...	...	...	...	...	...	...	...	120	77,697
...	...	...	...	...	...	...	...	...	...	...	...	...	1	11
...	...	...	...	...	...	...	...	...	...	...	...	...	5	481
...	...	...	...	...	...	...	...	...	...	...	...	...	12	1,470
...	...	...	...	...	...	...	...	...	...	...	...	...	4	342
...	...	...	...	...	...	...	...	...	...	...	...	...	16	1,812
...	...	...	...	...	...	...	...	...	...	...	...	...	4	240
...	...	...	...	...	...	...	...	...	...	...	...	...	3	1,082
...	...	...	...	...	...	...	...	...	...	...	...	...	6	1,650
...	...	...	...	...	...	...	...	...	...	...	...	...	9	2,732
...	...	...	...	...	...	...	...	...	...	...	...	...	3	249
...	...	...	...	2	5.300	...	...	...	...	...	...	...	227	160,132
...	...	...	...	...	...	...	...	...	...	...	...	...	15	5,791
...	...	...	...	2	5,300	...	...	...	...	...	...	...	242	165,923
...	...	...	...	...	...	...	...	...	...	...	...	...	3	297
...	...	...	...	...	...	...	...	...	...	...	...	...	2	175
...	...	...	...	...	...	...	...	...	...	...	...	...	2	198
...	...	...	...	...	...	...	...	...	...	...	...	...	4	373
...	...	...	...	...	...	...	...	...	...	...	...	...	2	1,258
...	...	...	...	...	...	...	...	...	...	...	...	...	46	3,556
...	...	...	...	...	...	...	...	...	...	...	...	...	59	5,857
...	...	...	...	...	...	...	...	...	...	...	...	...	46	1,925
...	...	...	...	...	...	...	...	...	...	...	...	...	2	1,948
...	...	...	...	...	...	...	...	...	...	...	...	...	1	100
...	...	...	...	...	...	...	...	...	...	...	...	...	3	354
...	...	...	...	...	...	...	...	...	...	...	...	...	29	2,535
...	...	...	...	...	...	...	...	...	...	...	...	...	35	4,937
...	...	...	...	...	...	...	...	...	...	...	...	...	1	478
...	...	...	...	...	...	...	...	...	...	...	...	...	5	963
...	...	...	...	...	...	...	...	...	...	...	...	...	9	1,114
...	...	...	...	...	...	...	...	...	...	...	...	...	1	349
...	...	...	...	...	...	...	...	...	...	...	...	...	60	5,491
...	...	...	...	...	...	...	...	...	...	...	...	...	1	99
...	...	...	...	...	...	...	...	...	...	...	...	...	2	440
...	...	...	...	...	...	...	...	...	...	...	...	...	82	6,632
...	...	...	...	...	...	...	...	...	...	...	...	...	161	15,566

No. 15.—STATEMENT of the Number and Tonnage of Sailing

Ports and Outports and countries for which Departed.		Nationality									
		British.		United States.		Norwegian and Swedish.		Austrian.		Belgian.	
		Vessels.	Tons Register.	Vessels.	Tons Register.	Vessels.	Tons Register.	Vessels.	Tons Register.	Vessels.	Tons Register.
Lockeport, N.S.—											
British W. Indies	Sail.	4	393								
Newfoundland	"	2	197								
United States	"	2	197	9	267						
Sea Fisheries	"	19	866	15	956						
Total		27	1,653	24	1,223						
Lord's Cove, N.B.—											
United States	Steam.	20	2,047	68	755						
"	Sail.	80	1,259	125	2,497						
Total		100	3,306	193	3,252						
Louisburg, N.S.—											
Great Britain	Steam.	8	13,702			2	2,802				
Newfoundland	"	15	10,931			4	2,581				
"	Sail.	32	2,756	8	667						
Germany	Steam.					1	2,881				
Italy	"	1	1,969			1	1,921				
Saint Pierre	"	1	267								
"	Sail.	1	99								
United States	Steam.	69	165,057			70	145,972				
"	Sail.	1	97	13	1,159						
British Africa	Steam.	4	10,927								
Sea Fisheries	"	2	344								
"	Sail.	37	1,478	75	5,992						
Total		171	207,627	96	7,818	78	156,157				
Lunenburg, N.S.—											
British W. Indies	Sail.	4	427								
Newfoundland	"	15	1,446								
Cuba & Porto Rico	"	20	3,019								
United States	"	11	1,067	1	231						
Argentina	"	1	583								
Sea Fisheries	"	206	16,113	8	673						
Total		257	22,655	9	904						
Magdalen Islands, Que.—											
Newfoundland	Steam.	1	275								
Saint Pierre	Sail.			1	95						
United States	"			11	744						
Total		1	275	12	839						
Mahone Bay, N.S.—											
British W. Indies	Sail.	3	299								
Newfoundland	"	2	199								
Cuba & Porto Rico	"	3	297								
United States	"	7	817								
Sea Fisheries	"	15	996								
Total		30	2,608								
Main-à-Dieu, N.S.—											
Sea Fisheries	Sail.	2	50								
Maitland, N.S.—											
United States	Sail.	11	1,915								
Malpeque, P.E.I.—											
Newfoundland	Sail.	1	57								
Matane, Que.—											
Norway and Sweden	Sail.					2	3,243				

and Steam Vessels entered Outwards *for Sea, &c.—Continued.*

OF VESSELS.

Danish.		French.		German.		Italian.		Russian.		Other Nationalities.			Total.	
Vessels.	Tons Register.	Vessels.	Tons Register.	Vessels.	Tons Register.	Vessels.	Tons Register.	Vessels.	Tons Register.	Names.	Vessels.	Tons Register.	Vessels.	Tons Register.
...	...	...	...	...	...	...	...	...	...	...	...	...	4	393
...	...	...	...	...	...	...	...	...	...	...	...	...	2	197
...	...	...	...	...	...	...	...	...	...	...	...	...	11	464
...	...	...	...	...	...	...	...	...	...	...	...	...	34	1,822
...	...	...	...	...	...	...	...	...	...	...	...	...	51	2,876
...	...	...	...	...	...	...	...	...	...	...	...	...	88	2,802
...	...	...	...	...	...	...	...	...	...	...	...	...	205	3,756
...	...	...	...	...	...	...	...	...	...	...	...	...	293	6,558
...	...	...	...	...	...	...	...	...	...	...	...	...	10	16,504
...	...	...	...	...	...	...	...	...	...	...	...	...	19	13,512
...	...	...	...	...	...	...	...	...	...	...	...	...	40	3,423
...	...	...	...	...	...	...	...	...	...	...	...	...	1	2,881
...	...	...	...	...	...	...	...	...	...	...	...	...	2	3,890
...	...	1	400	...	...	...	...	...	...	...	...	...	2	667
...	...	4	281	...	...	...	...	...	...	...	...	...	5	380
...	...	...	...	...	...	...	...	...	...	...	...	...	139	311,029
...	...	...	...	...	...	...	...	...	...	...	...	...	14	1,256
...	...	...	...	...	...	...	...	...	...	...	...	...	4	10,927
...	...	...	...	...	...	...	...	...	...	...	...	...	2	344
...	...	14	738	...	...	...	...	...	...	...	...	...	126	8,208
...	...	19	1,419	...	...	...	...	...	...	...	...	...	364	373,021
...	...	...	...	...	...	...	...	...	...	...	...	...	4	427
...	...	...	...	...	...	...	...	...	...	...	...	...	15	1,446
...	...	...	...	...	...	...	...	...	...	...	...	...	20	3,019
...	...	...	...	...	...	...	...	...	...	...	...	...	12	1,298
...	...	...	...	...	...	...	...	...	...	...	...	...	1	583
...	...	...	...	...	...	...	...	...	...	...	...	...	214	16,786
...	...	...	...	...	...	...	...	...	...	...	...	...	266	23,559
...	...	...	...	...	...	...	...	...	...	...	...	...	1	275
...	...	...	...	...	...	...	...	...	...	...	...	...	1	95
...	...	...	...	...	...	...	...	...	...	...	...	...	11	744
...	...	...	...	...	...	...	...	...	...	...	...	...	13	1,114
...	...	...	...	...	...	...	...	...	...	...	...	...	3	299
...	...	...	...	...	...	...	...	...	...	...	...	...	2	199
...	...	...	...	...	...	...	...	...	...	...	...	...	3	297
...	...	...	...	...	...	...	...	...	...	...	...	...	7	817
...	...	...	...	...	...	...	...	...	...	...	...	...	15	996
...	...	...	...	...	...	...	...	...	...	...	...	...	30	2,608
...	...	...	...	...	...	...	...	...	...	...	...	...	2	50
...	...	...	...	...	...	...	...	...	...	...	...	...	11	1,915
...	...	...	...	...	...	...	...	...	...	...	...	...	1	57
...	...	...	...	...	...	...	...	...	...	...	...	...	2	3,243

No. 15.—STATEMENT of the Number and Tonnage of Sailing

Ports and Outports and Countries for which Departed.	Nationality									
	British.		United States.		Norwegian and Swedish.		Austrian.		Belgian.	
	Vessels.	Tons Register.	Vessels.	Tons Register.	Vessels.	Tons Register.	Vessels.	Tons Register.	Vessels.	Tons Register.
Meteghan, N.S.—										
British W. Indies...... Sail.	1	98								
Cuba & Porto Rico.... "	4	750								
United States......... "	27	2,259	4	417						
Total..........	32	3,107	4	417						
Moncton, N.B.—										
United States......... Sail.	17	1,676	1	103						
Montague, P.E.I.—										
Newfoundland......... Sail.	5	265								
Saint Pierre........... "	3	243								
United States......... "	7	673								
Sea Fisheries.......... "	1	15								
Total.................	16	1,196								
Montreal, Que.—										
Great Britain.........Steam.	325	1,198,401			2	4,243				
" .... Sail.					1	1,344				
British W. Indies...... "	1	249								
Newfoundland.........Steam.	45	33,578			5	4,211				
Belgium............. "	11	48,815								
France.............. "										
Germany............. "					1	2,418				
Holland............. "	2	4,966								
United States......... "	2	3,204								
British Africa......... "	7	19,798								
Republic of Mexico.... "	7	12,728								
Total.................	400	1,321,739			9	12,216				
Murray Harbour, P.E.I.—										
Sea Fisheries.......... Sail.			15	347						
Musquash, N.B.—										
United States......... Sail.	16	1,232	46	5,842						
Argentine Republic.... "	1	697								
Sea Fisheries.......... "	12	209								
Total.................	29	2,138	46	5,842						
Nanaimo, B.C.—										
Russia...............Steam.	2	4,520								
United States......... "	81	19,766	33	12,856	27	57,473				
" .... Sail.	5	688	1	771						
Mexico.............. "			1	376						
China................Steam.	1	2,995								
Sea Fisheries.......... "	2	203	65	7,601						
Total.................	91	28,172	100	21,604	27	57,473				
New Campbellton, N.S.—										
Newfoundland.........Steam.	1	279								
" .... Sail.	5	330								
Total.................	6	609								
Newcastle, N.B.—										
Great Britain.........Steam.	8	13,234			1	997				
" .... Sail.					14	10,657				
France.............. "										
United States......... "	15	2,921								
Total.................	23	16,155			15	11,654				
New London, P.E.I.—										
Sea Fisheries.......... Sail.	4	59								

and Steam Vessels entered Outwards *for Sea,* &c.—*Continued.*

OF VESSELS.

Danish.		French.		German.		Italian.		Russian.		Other Nationalities.			Total.	
Vessels.	Tons Register.	Vessels.	Tons Register.	Vessels.	Tons Register.	Vessels.	Tons Register.	Vessels.	Tons Register.	Names.	Vessels.	Tons Register.	Vessels.	Tons Register.
...	...	...	...	...	...	...	...	...	...	...	...	...	1	98
...	...	...	...	...	...	...	...	...	...	...	...	...	4	750
...	...	...	...	...	...	...	...	...	...	...	...	...	31	2,676
...	...	...	...	...	...	...	...	...	...	...	...	...	36	3.524
...	...	...	...	...	...	...	...	...	...	...	...	...	18	1.779
...	...	...	...	...	...	...	...	...	...	...	...	...	5	265
...	...	...	...	...	...	...	...	...	...	...	...	...	3	243
...	...	...	...	...	...	...	...	...	...	...	...	...	7	673
...	...	...	...	...	...	...	...	...	...	...	...	...	1	15
...	...	...	...	...	...	...	...	...	...	...	...	...	16	1,196
...	...	...	...	...	...	...	...	2	2,542	...	...	...	329	1,205,186
...	...	...	...	...	...	...	...	...	...	...	...	...	1	1,344
...	...	...	...	...	...	...	...	...	...	...	...	...	1	249
1	814	...	...	...	...	...	...	...	...	...	...	...	51	38,603
...	...	...	...	...	...	...	...	...	...	...	...	...	11	48,815
...	...	...	...	...	...	...	...	1	1,147	...	...	...	1	1,147
...	...	...	...	1	1,289	...	...	...	...	...	...	...	2	3,707
...	...	...	...	...	...	...	...	...	...	...	...	...	2	4,966
...	...	...	...	...	...	...	...	...	...	...	...	...	2	3,204
...	...	...	...	...	...	...	...	...	...	...	...	...	7	19,798
...	...	...	...	...	...	...	...	...	...	...	...	...	7	12,728
1	814	...	...	1	1,289	...	...	3	3,689	...	...	...	414	1,339,747
...	...	...	...	...	...	...	...	...	...	...	...	...	15	347
...	...	...	...	...	...	...	...	...	...	...	...	...	62	7,074
...	...	...	...	...	...	...	...	...	...	...	...	...	1	697
...	...	...	...	...	...	...	...	...	...	...	...	...	12	209
...	...	...	...	...	...	...	...	...	...	...	...	...	75	7,980
...	...	...	...	...	...	...	...	...	...	...	...	...	2	4,520
...	...	1	3,186	1	3,081	...	...	...	...	...	...	...	143	96,362
...	...	...	...	...	...	...	...	...	...	...	...	...	6	1,459
...	...	...	...	...	...	...	...	...	...	...	...	...	1	376
...	...	...	...	...	...	...	...	...	...	...	...	...	1	2,995
...	...	...	...	...	...	...	...	...	...	...	...	...	67	7,804
...	...	1	3,186	1	3,081	...	...	...	...	...	...	...	220	113,516
...	...	...	...	...	...	...	...	...	...	...	...	...	1	279
...	...	...	...	...	...	...	...	...	...	...	...	...	5	330
...	...	...	...	...	...	...	...	...	...	...	...	...	6	609
...	...	...	...	...	...	...	...	...	...	...	...	...	9	14,231
...	...	...	...	...	...	...	...	1	347	...	...	...	15	11,004
...	...	...	...	...	...	1	755	...	...	...	...	...	1	755
...	...	...	...	...	...	...	...	...	...	...	...	...	15	2,921
...	...	...	...	...	...	1	755	1	347	...	...	...	40	28,911
...	...	...	...	...	...	...	...	...	...	...	...	...	4	59

No. 15.—STATEMENT of the Number and Tonnage of Sailing

Ports and Outports and Countries for which Departed.	Nationality									
	British.		United States.		Norwegian and Swedish.		Austrian.		Belgian.	
	Vessels.	Tons Register.	Vessels.	Tons Register.	Vessels.	Tons Register.	Vessels.	Tons Register.	Vessels.	Tons Register.
New Westminster, B.C.—										
New Zealand.......... Steam.	1	2,110								
" .... Sail.	1	1,047								
Chili.................. "										
Peru.................. "					1	1,547				
United States.......... Steam.	134	7,720	18	433	1	1,612				
Sea Fisheries.......... "	6	81								
" .... Sail.	4	72								
Total................	146	11,030	18	433	2	3,159				
North East Harbour, N.S.—										
United States.......... Sail.	1	71	3	39						
Sea Fisheries.......... "	14	258	7	480						
Total................	15	329	10	519						
North Head, N.B.—										
United States.......... Steam.	140	24,796	3	29						
" .... Sail.	15	3,029	44	857						
Total................	155	27,825	47	886						
Northport, N.S.—										
Great Britain.......... Sail.					6	6,049				
North Sydney, N.S.—										
Great Britain.......... Steam.	5	8,630			5	7,590				
Newfoundland.......... "	234	97,315			28	43,893				
" .... Sail.	166	19,462	8	1,101						
France.......... Steam.					1	1,456				
Germany.......... "										
Saint Pierre.......... "	16	2,304								
" .... Sail.	6	365								
United States.......... Steam.	4	6,211			2	3,594				
" .... Sail.	2	196	4	522						
British Poss. (other)... "	1	377								
Sea Fisheries.......... "	77	4,779	192	16,410						
Total................	511	139,639	204	18,033	36	56,533				
Parrsboro', N.S.—										
Great Britain.......... Steam.	6	11,803			3	3,383				
" .... Sail.					1	499				
United States.......... Steam.	18	11,682			35	24,783				
" .... Sail.	83	23,855	1	743						
Total................	107	47,340	1	743	39	28,665				
Paspebiac, Que.—										
Great Britain.......... Sail.					9	5,732				
British W. Indies...... "	7	879								
Brazil.......... "	7	1,603								
United States.......... Steam.	3	2,179								
" .... Sail.	21	4,023	2	579						
Total................	38	8,684	2	579	9	5,732				
Percé, Que.—										
Great Britain.......... Sail.					7	6,814				
Sea Fisheries.......... "	2	160	12	950						
Total................	2	160	12	950	7	6,814				

and Steam Vessels entered Outwards *for Sea, &c.—Continued.*

OF VESSELS.

Danish.		French.		German.		Italian.		Russian.		Other Nationalities.			Total.	
Vessels.	Tons Register.	Vessels.	Tons Register.	Vessels.	Tons Register.	Vessels.	Tons Register.	Vessels.	Tons Register.	Names.	Vessels.	Tons Register.	Vessels.	Tons Register.
													1	2,110
													1	1,047
				1	1,643								1	1,643
													1	1,547
													153	9,765
													6	81
													4	72
				1	1,643								167	16,265
													4	110
													21	738
													25	848
													143	24,825
													59	3,886
													202	28,711
													6	6,049
													10	16,220
										Dutch	2	1,628	264	142,836
4	396							2	318	"	1	169	181	21,446
													1	1,456
				1	1,289								1	1,289
		3	1,200										19	3,504
		7	1,168										13	1,533
										Dutch	1	814	7	10,619
													6	718
													1	377
		110	5,994										379	27,183
4	396	120	8,362	1	1,289			2	318		4	2,611	882	227,181
													9	15,186
						1	1,554						2	2,053
													53	36,465
													84	24,598
						1	1,554						148	78,302
								1	385				10	6,117
													7	879
													7	1,603
													3	2,179
													23	4,602
								1	385				50	15,380
													7	6,814
													14	1,110
													21	7,924

No. 15.—STATEMENT of the Number and Tonnage of Sailing

PORTS AND OUTPORTS AND COUNTRIES FOR WHICH DEPARTED.	NATIONALITY									
	British.		United States.		Norwegian and Swedish.		Austrian.		Belgian.	
	Vessels.	Tons Register.	Vessels.	Tons Register.	Vessels.	Tons Register.	Vessels.	Tons Register.	Vessels.	Tons Register.
Pictou, N.S.—										
Great Britain.........Steam.	1	2,259			1	984				
" .... Sail.					1	749				
Saint Pierre...........Steam.	12	1,236								
United States......... "					1	1,215				
" .... Sail.	2	202								
Total................	15	3,697			3	2,948				
Port Greville, N.S.—										
United States......... Sail.	60	18,057								
Port Hastings, N.S.—										
British W. Indies......Steam.	1	603								
Newfoundland......... Sail.	1	68								
Saint Pierre........... "	1	30								
United States.........Steam.	3	2,616			1	398				
" .... Sail.	3	281								
Total................	9	3,598			1	398				
Port Hawkesbury, N.S.—										
British W. Indies...... Sail.	4	492								
Newfoundland......... "	3	283								
Saint Pierre........... "	1	78								
United States ....Steam.	28	27,275	14	14,358	2	596				
" .... Sail.	13	1,690	10	858						
Sea Fisheries .... "	73	4,929	36	2,699						
Total................	122	34,747	60	17,915	2	596				
Port Hood, N.S.—										
Sea Fisheries .... Sail.			2	183						
Port La Tour, N.S.—										
United States......... Sail.			1	85						
Sea Fisheries. .... "			2	143						
Total................			3	228						
Port Medway, N.S.—										
Great Britain......... Sail.					1	1,177				
United States .... "	1	68	2	164						
Total................	1	68	2	164	1	1,177				
Port Morien, N.S.—										
United States.........Steam.	4	1,976								
Sea Fisheries .... Sail.	1	99								
Total................	5	2,075								
Port Mulgrave, N.S.—										
Newfoundland......... Sail.	12	1,319								
United States.........Steam.	1	522								
Sea Fisheries.......... Sail.	1	97	3	205						
Total................	14	1,938	3	205						
Port Simpson, B.C.—										
United States ....Steam.	49	26,570	27	1,775						
" .... Sail.			1	771						
Total................	49	26,570	28	2,546						
Port Williams, N.S.—										
Cuba & Porto Rico.... Sail.	4	874								

and Steam Vessels entered Outwards *for Sea, &c.—Continued.*

OF VESSELS.

Danish.		French.		German.		Italian.		Russian.		Other Nationalities.			Total.	
Vessels.	Tons Register.	Vessels.	Tons Register.	Vessels.	Tons Register.	Vessels.	Tons Register.	Vessels.	Tons Register.	Names.	Vessels.	Tons Register.	Vessels.	Tons Register.
...	...	...	...	...	...	...	...	...	...	...	...	...	2	3,243
...	...	...	...	...	...	...	...	...	...	...	...	...	1	749
...	...	...	...	...	...	...	...	...	...	...	...	...	12	1,236
...	...	...	...	...	...	...	...	...	...	...	...	...	1	1,215
...	...	...	...	...	...	...	...	...	...	...	...	...	2	202
...	...	...	...	...	...	...	...	...	...	...	...	...	18	6,645
...	...	...	...	...	...	...	...	...	...	...	...	...	60	18,057
...	...	...	...	...	...	...	...	...	...	...	...	...	1	603
...	...	...	...	...	...	...	...	...	...	...	...	...	1	68
...	...	...	...	...	...	...	...	...	...	...	...	...	1	30
...	...	...	...	...	...	...	...	...	...	...	...	...	4	3,014
...	...	...	...	...	...	...	...	...	...	...	...	...	3	281
...	...	...	...	...	...	...	...	...	...	...	...	...	10	3,996
...	...	...	...	...	...	...	...	...	...	...	...	...	4	492
...	...	...	...	...	...	...	...	...	...	...	...	...	3	283
...	...	...	...	...	...	...	...	...	...	...	...	...	1	78
...	...	...	...	...	...	...	...	...	...	...	...	...	44	42,229
...	...	...	...	...	...	...	...	...	...	...	...	...	23	2,548
...	...	7	368	...	...	...	...	...	...	...	...	...	116	7,996
...	...	7	368	...	...	...	...	...	...	...	...	...	191	53,626
...	...	...	...	...	...	...	...	...	...	...	...	...	2	183
...	...	...	...	...	...	...	...	...	...	...	...	...	1	85
...	...	...	...	...	...	...	...	...	...	...	...	...	2	143
...	...	...	...	...	...	...	...	...	...	...	...	...	3	228
...	...	...	...	...	...	...	...	...	...	...	...	...	1	1,177
...	...	...	...	...	...	...	...	...	...	...	...	...	3	232
...	...	...	...	...	...	...	...	...	...	...	...	...	4	1,409
...	...	...	...	...	...	...	...	...	...	...	...	...	4	1,976
...	...	...	...	...	...	...	...	...	...	...	...	...	1	99
...	...	...	...	...	...	...	...	...	...	...	...	...	5	2,075
...	...	...	...	...	...	...	...	...	...	...	...	...	12	1,319
...	...	...	...	...	...	...	...	...	...	...	...	...	1	522
...	...	...	...	...	...	...	...	...	...	...	...	...	4	302
...	...	...	...	...	...	...	...	...	...	...	...	...	17	2,143
...	...	...	...	...	...	...	...	...	...	...	...	...	76	28,345
...	...	...	...	...	...	...	...	...	...	...	...	...	1	771
...	...	...	...	...	...	...	...	...	...	...	...	...	77	29,116
...	...	...	...	...	...	...	...	...	...	...	...	...	4	874

No. 15.—Statement of the Number and Tonnage of Sailing

Ports and Outports and Countries for which Departed.	Nationality									
	British.		United States.		Norwegian and Swedish.		Austrian.		Belgian.	
	Vessels.	Tons Register.	Vessels.	Tons Register.	Vessels.	Tons Register.	Vessels.	Tons Register.	Vessels.	Tons Register.
Pubnico, N.S.—										
United States .... Sail.	1	50	9	797						
Sea Fisheries .... "	26	1,307	43	3,016						
Total................	27	1,357	52	3,813						
Pugwash, N.S.—										
Great Britain.........Steam.	2	3,388			1	1,426				
" .... Sail.					2	2,142				
Newfoundland......... "	1	99								
Total................	3	3,487			3	3,568				
Quebec, Que.—										
Great Britain.........Steam.	117	416,419			13	2,889				
" .... Sail.					1	545				
British W. Indies...... "	1	249								
Newfoundland.........Steam.	2	695			1	1,785				
Belgium.............. "	1	5,340								
Brazil................ Sail.										
France...............Steam.	5	13,045			1	1,456				
Holland.............. "					1	1,785				
Saint Pierre.......... "	1	184								
Spain................ "	1	1,218								
United States .... Sail.	1	398	1	1,132						
Br. Poss. (all other) Malta.............. Sail.	1	377								
Sea Fisheries .... "	17	1,282								
Total................	147	439,207	1	1,132	17	26,460				
Richibucto, N.B.—										
Great Britain......... Sail.					5	1,857				
United States .... "	16	1,694			1	341				
Total................	16	1,694			6	2,198				
Rimouski, Que.—										
Great Britain.........Steam.	2	3,564								
Germany.............. "										
Norway and Sweden .. "					7	10,140				
" .. Sail.					5	4,993				
Total................	2	3,564			12	15,133				
River Bourgeois, N.S.—										
Sea Fisheries .... Sail.	90	1,713								
River Hebert, N.S.—										
United States .... Sail.	69	8,371	22	4,959						
Riviere du Loup, Que.—										
Great Britain.........Steam.	8	14,100								
" .... Sail.					1	229				
United States .... "	1	199								
Total................	9	14,299			1	229				
Rustico, P.E.I.—										
United States .... Sail.	1	74								
Sea Fisheries .... "	2	20								
Total................	3	94								
St. Andrews, N.B.—										
United States ....Steam.	1	182	332	32,526						
" .... Sail.	9	210	191	1,760						
Total................	10	392	523	34,286						

and Steam Vessels entered Outwards *for Sea, &c.—Continued.*

OF VESSELS.

Danish.		French.		German.		Italian.		Russian.		Other Nationalities.			Total.	
Vessels.	Tons Register.	Vessels.	Tons Register.	Vessels.	Tons Register.	Vessels.	Tons Register.	Vessels.	Tons Register.	Names.	Vessels.	Tons Register.	Vessels.	Tons Register.
...	...	...	...	...	...	...	...	...	...	...	...	...	10	847
...	...	...	...	...	...	...	...	...	...	...	...	...	69	4,323
...	...	...	...	...	...	...	...	...	...	...	...	...	79	5,170
...	...	...	...	...	...	...	...	...	...	Dutch......	1	1,299	4	6,113
...	...	...	...	...	...	...	...	...	...	...	...	...	2	2,142
...	...	...	...	...	...	...	...	...	...	...	...	...	1	99
...	...	...	...	...	...	...	...	...	...	...	1	1,299	7	8,354
3	5,620	...	...	...	...	...	...	1	1,271	...	...	...	134	444,199
...	...	...	...	...	...	...	...	...	...	...	...	...	1	545
...	...	...	...	...	...	...	...	...	...	...	...	...	1	249
1	38	...	...	...	...	...	...	...	...	...	...	...	4	2,518
...	...	...	...	...	...	...	...	...	...	...	...	...	1	5,340
...	...	...	...	1	1,035	...	...	...	...	...	...	...	1	1,035
...	...	...	...	...	...	...	...	...	...	...	...	...	6	14,501
...	...	...	...	1	1,289	...	...	...	...	...	...	...	1	1,289
...	...	...	...	...	...	...	...	...	...	...	...	...	1	1,785
...	...	...	...	1	851	...	...	...	...	...	...	...	1	851
...	...	...	...	...	...	...	...	...	...	...	...	...	1	184
...	...	...	...	...	...	...	...	...	...	...	...	...	1	1,218
...	...	...	...	...	...	...	...	...	...	...	...	...	2	1,530
...	...	...	...	...	...	...	...	...	...	...	...	...	1	377
...	...	...	...	...	...	...	...	...	...	...	...	...	17	1,282
4	5,658	...	...	3	3,175	...	...	1	1,271	...	...	...	173	476,903
3	762	...	...	...	...	...	...	4	1,063	...	...	...	12	3,682
...	...	...	...	...	...	...	...	...	...	...	...	...	17	2,035
3	762	...	...	...	...	...	...	4	1,063	...	...	...	29	5,717
...	...	...	...	...	...	...	...	...	...	...	...	...	2	3,564
...	...	...	...	2	2,139	...	...	...	...	...	...	...	2	2,139
...	...	...	...	...	...	...	...	...	...	...	...	...	7	10,140
...	...	...	...	...	...	...	...	...	...	...	...	...	5	4,993
...	...	...	...	2	2,139	...	...	...	...	...	...	...	16	20,836
...	...	...	...	...	...	...	...	...	...	...	...	...	90	1,713
...	...	...	...	...	...	...	...	...	...	...	...	...	91	13,330
...	...	...	...	...	...	...	...	...	...	...	...	...	8	14,100
...	...	...	...	...	...	...	...	...	...	...	...	...	1	229
...	...	...	...	...	...	...	...	...	...	...	...	...	1	199
...	...	...	...	...	...	...	...	...	...	...	...	...	10	14,528
...	...	...	...	...	...	...	...	...	...	...	...	...	1	74
...	...	...	...	...	...	...	...	...	...	...	...	...	2	20
...	...	...	...	...	...	...	...	...	...	...	...	...	3	94
...	...	...	...	...	...	...	...	...	...	...	...	...	333	32,708
...	...	...	...	...	...	...	...	...	...	...	...	...	200	1,970
...	...	...	...	...	...	...	...	...	...	...	...	...	533	34,678

No. 15.—STATEMENT of the Number and Tonnage of Sailing

Ports and Outports and Countries for which Departed.	Nationality									
	British.		United States.		Norwegian and Swedish.		Austrian.		Belgian.	
	Vessels.	Tons Register.	Vessels.	Tons Register.	Vessels.	Tons Register.	Vessels.	Tons Register.	Vessels.	Tons Register.
St. Anns, N.S.—										
Newfoundland......... Sail.	5	371	2	152						
United States.........Steam.					4	2,903				
Total................	5	371	2	152	4	2,903				
Saint George, N.B.—										
United States ....Steam.	1	86	33	625						
" .... Sail.	27	698	174	6,181						
Sea Fisheries.......... "	3	23	1	75						
Total................	31	807	208	6,881						
Saint John, N.B.—										
Great Britain.........Steam.	80	218,088			2	2,802				
" .... Sail.					5	3,319				
British W. Indies...... "	6	1,633								
Cuba and Porto Rico... "	1	533	1	279						
United States.........Steam.	27	36,324	185	285,130	2	2,573				
" .... Sail.	445	43,331	383	49,122						
Argentine Republic.... "	3	2,569								
British Possessions in South Africa........Steam.	5	14,140								
Sea Fisheries.......... Sail.	175	6,296	2	130						
Total................	742	322,914	571	334,661	9	8,694				
Saint Martins, N.B.—										
Cuba and Porto Rico... Sail.	1	318								
United States......... "	40	3,734	5	509						
Total................	41	4,052	5	509						
St. Peters, N.S.—										
United States.........Steam.			4	364						
Sea Fisheries.......... Sail.	6	119								
Total................	6	119	4	364						
St. Stephen, N.B.—										
United States.........Steam.	53	9,208	32	537						
" .... Sail.	82	1,619	169	4,204						
Total................	135	10,827	201	4,741						
Sackville, N.B.—										
United States......... Sail.	14	1,685	3	619						
Salmon River, N.S.—										
United States......... Sail.	11	759								
Sea Fisheries.......... "	12	217								
Total................	23	976								
Shediac, N.B.—										
Great Britain......... Sail.					10	5,660				
Sheet Harbour, N.S.—										
Great Britain......... Sail.	1	1,333			1	796				
Newfoundland......... "	1	97								
United States......... "	3	346								
Sea Fisheries.......... "	3	97								
Total................	8	1,873			1	796				

and Steam Vessels entered Outwards *for Sea, &c.—Continued.*

OF VESSELS.

Danish.		French.		German.		Italian.		Russian.		Other Nationalities.			Total.	
Vessels.	Tons Register.	Vessels.	Tons Register.	Vessels.	Tons Register.	Vessels.	Tons Register.	Vessels.	Tons Register.	Names.	Vessels.	Tons Register.	Vessels.	Tons Register.
		8	315										15	838
													4	2,903
		8	315										19	3,741
													34	711
													201	6,879
													4	98
													239	7,688
4	6,463												86	227,353
2	435					3	2,613	1	852				11	7,219
													6	1,633
													2	812
													214	324,027
													828	92,453
													3	2,569
													5	14,140
													177	6,426
6	6,898					3	2,613	1	852				1,332	676,632
													1	318
													45	4,243
													46	4,561
													4	364
													6	119
													10	483
													85	9,745
													251	5,823
													336	15,568
													17	2,304
													11	759
													12	217
													23	976
													10	5,660
													2	2,129
													1	97
													3	346
													3	97
													9	2,669

No. 15.—STATEMENT of the Number and Tonnage of Sailing

Ports and Outports and Countries for which Departed.	Nationality									
	British.		United States.		Norwegian and Swedish.		Austrian.		Belgian.	
	Vessels.	Tons Register.	Vessels.	Tons Register.	Vessels.	Tons Register.	Vessels.	Tons Register.	Vessels.	Tons Register.
Shelburne, N.S.—										
British W. Indies...... Sail.	3	312	....	....	....	....	....	....	....	....
Newfoundland.........Steam.	....	....	1	98	....	....	....	....	....	....
" .... Sail.	....	....	1	100	....	....	....	....	....	....
United States.........Steam.	....	....	1	198	....	....	....	....	....	....
" .... Sail.	22	4,123	12	790	....	....	....	....	....	....
Sea Fisheries.......... "	59	1,987	163	12,884	....	....	....	....	....	....
Total.................	84	6,422	178	14,070	....	....	....	....	....	....
herbrooke, N.S.—										
Great Britain......... Sail.	....	....	....	....	4	1,450	....	....	....	....
France............... "	....	....	....	....	....	....	....	....	....	....
United States.........Steam.	....	....	....	....	1	633	....	....	....	....
" .... Sail.	3	636	2	506	....	....	....	....	....	....
Total.................	3	636	2	506	5	2,083	....	....	....	....
Shippigan, N.B.—										
Great Britain......... Sail.	2	246	....	....	....	....	....	....	....	....
Brazil................ "	1	199	....	....	....	....	....	....	....	....
Spain................ "	1	99	....	....	....	....	....	....	....	....
Total.................	4	544	....	....	....	....	....	....	....	....
Souris, P.E.I.—										
Newfoundland.........Steam.	1	372	....	....	....	....	....	....	....	....
" .... Sail.	3	160	....	....	....	....	....	....	....	....
Saint Pierre...........Steam.	6	618	....	....	....	....	....	....	....	....
" .... Sail.	8	764	....	....	....	....	....	....	....	....
United States......... "	7	734	1	61	....	....	....	....	....	....
Sea Fisheries.......... "	2	36	....	....	....	....	....	....	....	....
Total.................	27	2,684	1	61	....	....	....	....	....	....
ſ tickeen, B.C.—										
United States.........Steam.	7	1,865	....	....	....	....	....	....	....	....
Summerside, P.E.I.—										
Newfoundland.........Steam.	11	5,488	....	....	1	652	....	....	....	....
" .... Sail.	3	163	....	....	....	....	....	....	....	....
United States......... "	1	99	....	....	....	....	....	....	....	....
Total.................	15	5,750	....	....	1	652	....	....	....	....
Sydney, N.S.—										
Great Britain.........Steam.	19	31,545	....	....	5	6,548	....	....	....	....
Newfoundland......... "	55	42,856	....	....	88	189,195	....	....	....	....
" .... Sail.	176	10,485	3	171	....	....	....	....	....	....
France...............Steam.	....	....	....	....	1	1,147	....	....	....	....
Germany............ "	1	1,913	....	....	1	2,418	....	....	....	....
Holland............. "	1	2,246	....	....	....	....	....	....	....	....
Italy................. "	1	1,256	....	....	....	....	....	....	....	....
Saint Pierre.......... "	1	103	....	....	....	....	....	....	....	....
" .... Sail.	19	1,167	....	....	....	....	....	....	....	....
Spain...............Steam.	1	1,218	....	....	2	5,196	....	....	....	....
United States......... "	5	11,359	1	157	19	31,959	....	....	....	....
Cuba................. "	1	1,913	....	....	....	....	....	....	....	....
British Africa......... "	5	14,032	....	....	....	....	....	....	....	....
Mexico.............. "	1	1,827	....	....	....	....	....	....	....	....
Sea Fisheries.......... Sail.	....	....	2	224	....	....	....	....	....	....
Total.................	286	121,920	6	552	116	236,463	....	....	....	....
Thorne's Cove, N.S.—										
United States......... Sail.	5	379	....	....	....	....	....	....	....	....

and Steam Vessels entered Outwards *for Sea,* &c.—*Continued.*

OF VESSELS.

Danish.		French.		German.		Italian.		Russian.		Other Nationalities.			Total.	
Vessels.	Tons Register.	Vessels.	Tons Register.	Vessels.	Tons Register.	Vessels.	Tons Register.	Vessels.	Tons Register.	Names.	Vessels.	Tons Register.	Vessels.	Tons Register.
													3	312
													1	98
													1	100
													1	198
													34	4,913
													222	14,871
													262	20 492
													4	1,450
								1	348				1	348
													1	633
													5	1,142
								1	348				11	3,573
													2	246
													1	199
													1	99
													4	544
													1	372
													3	160
													6	618
													8	764
													8	795
													2	36
													28	2,745
													7	1,865
													12	6,140
													3	163
													1	99
													16	6,402
													24	38,093
													143	232,051
													179	10,656
													1	1,147
													2	4,331
													1	2,246
													1	1,256
													1	103
		37	3,442										56	4,609
													3	6,414
													25	43,475
													1	1,913
													5	14,032
													1	1,827
													2	224
		37	3,442										445	362,377
													5	379

No. 15.—STATEMENT of the Number and Tonnage of Sailing

Ports and Outports and Countries for which Departed.	Nationality									
	British.		United States.		Norwegian and Swedish.		Austrian.		Belgian.	
	Vessels.	Tons Register.	Vessels.	Tons Register.	Vessels.	Tons Register.	Vessels.	Tons Register.	Vessels.	Tons Register.
Three Rivers, Que.—										
Great Britain.........Steam.	31	76,877	....	....	2	2,694	....	....	....	....
" ....Sail.	....	....	....	....	1	1,344	....	....	....	....
Total................	31	76,877	....	....	3	4,038	....	....	....	....
Truro, N.S.—										
United States......... Sail.	4	581	....	....	....	....	....	....	....	....
Tusket, N.S.—										
United States......... Sail.	14	1,948	12	1,645	....	....	....	....	....	....
Sea Fisheries.......... "	....	....	23	1,942	....	....	....	....	....	....
Total................	14	1,948	35	3,587	....	....	....	....	....	....
Tusket Wedge, N.S.—										
Great Britain.........Steam.	1	1,723	....	....	....	....	....	....	....	....
" .... Sail.	....	....	....	....	....	....	....	....	....	....
British W. Indies...... "	....	....	1	348	....	....	....	....	....	....
Uruguay............. "	1	458	....	....	1	1,132	....	....	....	....
Argentine Republic.... "	1	470	....	....	1	894	....	....	....	....
Cuba and Porto Rico... "	1	99	....	....	....	....	....	....	....	....
United States......... "	1	419	3	544	....	....	....	....	....	....
Sea Fisheries..........Steam.	2	12	....	....	....	....	....	....	....	....
" .... Sail.	31	367	2	248	....	....	....	....	....	....
Total................	38	3,548	6	1,140	2	2,026	....	....	....	....
Vancouver, B.C.—										
Great Britain.........Steam.	11	50,342	....	....	....	....	....	....	....	....
" .... Sail.	2	3,838	....	....	....	....	....	....	....	....
Chili................ "	....	....	....	....	....	....	....	....	....	....
Germany.............. "	....	....	....	....	....	....	....	....	....	....
Peru................. "	3	5,044	....	....	....	....	....	....	....	....
Fiji Islands........... "	....	....	1	520	....	....	....	....	....	....
United States.........Steam.	305	164,042	296	261,640	3	3,626	....	....	....	....
" .... Sail.	60	14,630	4	2,328	....	....	....	....	....	....
Japan................Steam.	24	69,177	....	....	....	....	....	....	....	....
" .... Sail.	....	....	1	923	....	....	....	....	....	....
China................Steam.	3	9,716	....	....	....	....	....	....	....	....
Australia............. "	14	32,705	1	1,011	....	....	....	....	....	....
" .... Sail.	3	5,290	....	....	....	....	....	....	....	....
New Zealand..........Steam.	3	6,509	....	....	....	....	....	....	....	....
Sea Fisheries.......... "	....	....	60	6,927	....	....	....	....	....	....
South Africa.......... Sail.	....	....	....	....	....	....	....	....	....	....
Total................	428	361,293	363	273,349	3	3,626	....	....	....	....
Vernon River Bridge, P.E.I.—										
Newfoundland......... Sail.	1	25	....	....	....	....	....	....	....	....
United States......... "	2	179	....	....	....	....	....	....	....	....
Total................	3	204	....	....	....	....	....	....	....	....
Victoria, B.C.—										
Great Britain.........Steam.	3	14,676	....	....	....	....	....	....	....	....
" .... Sail.	1	1,533	....	....	....	....	....	....	....	....
Australia.............Steam.	13	31,088	....	....	....	....	....	....	....	....
" .... Sail.	2	4,030	1	1,575	....	....	....	....	....	....
New Zealand..........Steam.	1	2,284	....	....	....	....	....	....	....	....
Japan................ "	....	....	....	....	....	....	....	....	....	....
China................ "	20	64,181	....	....	....	....	....	....	....	....
Chili................ Sail.	1	2.242	....	....	....	....	....	....	....	....
Mexico...............Steam.	2	3,975	....	....	....	....	....	....	....	....
United States......... "	469	223,136	458	431,711	1	1,612	....	....	....	....
" .... Sail.	4	7,729	3	806	1	1,395	....	....	....	....
Panama..............Steam.	1	2,973	....	....	....	....	....	....	....	....
Sea Fisheries.......... Sail.	26	1,940	....	....	....	....	....	....	....	....
Total................	543	359,787	462	434,092	2	3,007	....	....	....	....

and Steam Vessels entered Outwards *for Sea, &c.—Continued.*

OF VESSELS.

Danish.		French.		German.		Italian.		Russian.		Other Nationalities.			Total.	
Vessels.	Tons Register.	Vessels.	Tons Register.	Vessels.	Tons Register.	Vessels.	Tons Register.	Vessels.	Tons Register.	Names.	Vessels.	Tons Register.	Vessels.	Tons Register.
								2	3,978				35	83,549
													1	1,344
								2	3,978				36	84,893
													4	581
													26	3,593
													23	1,942
													49	5,535
													1	1,723
						1	1,384						1	1,384
													1	348
													2	1,590
													2	1,364
													1	99
													4	963
													2	12
													33	615
						1	1,384						47	8,098
													11	50,342
				1	1,916								3	5,754
				1	1,677					Chilian	1	1,338	2	3,015
				1	1,165								1	1,165
													3	5,044
													1	520
				5	12,319								609	441,627
													64	16,958
													24	69,177
													1	923
													3	9,716
													15	33,716
													3	5,290
													3	6,509
													60	6,927
				1	1,599								1	1,599
				9	18,676						1	1,338	804	658,282
													1	25
													2	179
													3	204
													3	14,676
													1	1,533
													13	31,088
													3	5,605
													1	2,284
													7	27,051
													20	64,181
													1	2,242
													2	3,975
				1	2,115								941	706,759
													9	12,045
													1	2,973
													26	1,940
				1	2,115								1,028	876,352

No. 15.—Statement of the Number and Tonnage of Sailing

Ports and Outports and Countries for which Departed.		Nationality									
		British.		United States.		Norwegian and Swedish.		Austrian.		Belgian.	
		Vessels.	Tons Register.	Vessels.	Tons Register.	Vessels.	Tons Register.	Vessels.	Tons Register.	Vessels.	Tons Register.
Walton, N.S.—											
United States	Sail.	54	24,599	12	4,972	....	....	....	....	....	....
Westport, N.S.—											
United States	Sail.	8	116	....	....	....	....	....	....	....	....
Weymouth, N.S.											
Cuba and Porto Rico	Sail.	5	998	4	1,494	....	....	....	....	....	....
United States	"	18	2,482	5	964	....	....	....	....	....	....
Argentina	"	2	969	....	....	2	1,553	....	....	....	....
Total		25	4,449	9	2,458	2	1,553	....	....	....	....
Windsor, N.S.—											
United States	Steam.	....	....	....	....	25	17,126	....	....	....	....
"	Sail.	74	49,550	57	53,757	....	....	....	....	....	....
Total		74	49,550	57	53,757	25	17,126	....	....	....	....
Wolfville, N.S.—											
Cuba and Porto Rico	Sail.	1	335	....	....	....	....	....	....	....	....
Yarmouth, N.S											
Great B[illegible]n	Sail.	1	1,723	....	....	....	....	....	....	....	....
British W Indies	"	4	665	1	348	....	....	....	....	....	....
United States	Steam.	184	133,222	....	....	....	....	....	....	....	....
"	Sail.	45	5,146	5	1,466	....	....	....	....	....	....
Argentine Republic	"	7	3,626	....	....	6	5,996	....	....	....	....
Sea Fisheries	"	272	7,278	185	13,060	....	....	....	....	....	....
Total		513	151,660	191	14,874	6	5,996	....	....	....	....

and Steam Vessels entered Outwards *for Sea, &c.—Continued.*

OF VESSELS.

Danish.		French.		German.		Italian.		Russian.		Other Nationalities.			Total.	
Vessels.	Tons Register.	Vessels.	Tons Register.	Vessels.	Tons Register.	Vessels.	Tons Register.	Vessels.	Tons Register.	Names.	Vessels.	Tons Register.	Vessels.	Tons Register.
...	...	...	...	...	...	...	...	...	...	...	...	...	66	29,571
...	...	...	...	...	...	...	...	...	...	...	...	...	8	116
...	...	...	...	...	...	...	...	...	...	...	...	...	9	2,492
...	...	...	...	...	...	...	...	...	...	...	...	...	23	3,446
...	...	...	...	...	...	5	3,750	...	...	...	...	...	9	6,272
...	...	...	...	...	...	5	3,750	...	...	...	...	...	41	12,210
...	...	...	...	...	...	...	...	...	...	...	...	...	25	17,126
...	...	...	...	...	...	...	...	...	...	...	...	...	131	103,307
...	...	...	...	...	...	...	...	...	...	...	...	...	156	120,433
...	...	...	...	...	...	...	...	...	...	...	...	...	1	335
...	...	...	...	...	...	1	1,384	...	...	...	...	...	2	3,107
...	...	...	...	...	...	...	...	...	...	...	...	...	5	1,013
...	...	...	...	...	...	...	...	...	...	...	...	...	184	133,222
...	...	...	...	...	...	...	...	...	...	...	...	...	50	6,612
...	...	...	...	...	...	1	999	...	...	...	...	...	14	10,621
...	...	...	...	...	...	...	...	...	...	...	...	...	457	20,338
...	...	...	...	...	...	2	2,383	...	...	...	...	...	712	174,913

No. 16.—SUMMARY STATEMENT of the Nationality of Sea-going Vessels ending June

Number.	Countries to which Departed.	Nationality of									
		British.		United States.		Norwegian and Swedish.		Austrian.		Belgian.	
		Vessels.	Tons Register.	Vessels.	Tons Register.	Vessels.	Tons Register.	Vessels.	Tons Register.	Vessels.	Tons Register.
1	Great Britain	806	2,493,548	....	....	233	212,596	....	....	....	....
2	Australia	36	79,296	4	5,627	....	....	....	....	....	....
3	British Africa	24	65,343	1	1,469	....	....	....	....	....	....
4	British Guiana	2	365	....	....	....	....	....	....	....	....
5	British West Indies	101	52,715	2	696	34	23,465	....	....	....	....
6	Fiji Islands	....	....	1	520	....	....	....	....	....	....
7	Newfoundland	1,097	326,958	31	2,928	130	244,369	....	....	....	....
8	New Zealand	7	13,069	....	....	....	....	....	....	....	....
9	British Possessions, other	2	754	....	....	....	....	....	....	....	....
10	Argentina	22	12,819	1	668	15	13,369	....	....	....	....
11	Azores, Madeira and Cape Verde Islands	5	1,087	1	320	....	....	....	....	....	....
12	Belgium	12	54,155	....	....	....	....	....	....	....	....
13	Brazil	11	2,417	....	....	....	....	....	....	....	....
14	Chili	7	15,090	....	....	....	....	....	....	....	....
15	China	25	79,545	....	....	....	....	....	....	....	....
16	Cuba and Porto Rico	81	23,359	12	4,859	3	2,807	....	....	....	....
17	France	5	13,045	....	....	3	4,059	....	....	....	....
18	Germany	1	1,913	....	....	3	7,717	....	....	....	....
19	Holland	3	7,212	....	....	1	1,785	....	....	....	....
20	Italy	3	5,335	....	....	1	1,921	....	....	....	....
21	Japan	30	86,033	1	923	....	....	....	....	....	....
22	Mexico	22	40,466	1	376	....	....	....	....	....	....
23	Norway and Sweden	....	....	....	....	16	19,683	....	....	....	....
24	Panama	2	8,072	....	....	....	....	....	....	....	....
25	Peru	3	5,044	....	....	1	1,547	....	....	....	....
26	Portugal	2	198	....	....	....	....	....	....	....	....
27	Russia	2	4,520	....	....	1	2,088	....	....	....	....
28	Sea	4	12,410	....	....	....	....	....	....	....	....
29	Sea Fisheries	1,957	99,985	1,450	119,905	....	....	....	....	....	....
30	Spain	4	2,921	....	....	2	5,196	....	....	....	....
31	St. Pierre	106	10,596	1	95	....	....	....	....	....	....
32	United States	4,176	1,718,902	3,393	1,375,307	285	398,609	....	....	....	....
33	Uruguay	1	458	....	....	1	1,132	....	....	....	....
	Total	8,559	5,232,630	4,899	1,513,693	729	940,343	....	....	....	....

entered Outwards, *for Sea*, for each Country, during the Fiscal Year 30, 1906.

Vessels (Flag).

Danish.		French.		German.		Italian.		Russian.		Other Nationalities.			Total.		
Vessels.	Tons Register.	Vessels.	Tons Register.	Vessels.	Tons Register.	Vessels.	Tons Register.	Vessels.	Tons Register.	Name of Flag.	Vessels.	Tons Register.	Vessels.	Tons Register.	Number.
26	25,760			3	5,396	10	11,286	18	13,115	Dutch....	1	1,299	1,097	2,763,000	1
				1	2,468								41	87,391	2
				1	1,599								26	68,411	3
													2	365	4
										Dutch....	1	398	138	77,274	5
													1	520	6
6	1,248	8	315					2	318	Dutch....	3	1,797	1,277	577,933	7
													7	13,069	8
													2	754	9
						6	4,749						44	31,605	10
													6	1,407	11
													12	54,155	12
				1	1,035								12	3,452	13
				2	3,320					Chilian...	1	1,338	10	19,748	14
													25	79,545	15
1	588												97	31,613	16
		1	976			1	755	2	1,495				12	20,330	17
				9	25,576								13	35,206	18
													4	8,997	19
				1	3,176								5	10,432	20
										Japanese..	7	27,051	38	114,007	21
													23	40,842	22
		2	1,126										18	20,809	23
													2	3,072	24
													4	6,591	25
				1	851								3	1,049	26
													3	6,608	27
													4	12,410	28
		131	7,100										3,538	226,990	29
										Spanish ..	3	856	9	8,973	30
		62	9,032										169	19,723	31
1	324	1	3,186	20	52,763					Dutch ... Japanese .	1 13	814 50,300	7,890	3,600,205	32
													2	1,590	33
34	27,920	205	21,735	39	96,184	17	16,790	22	14,928		30	83,853	14,534	7,948,076	

No. 17.—STATEMENT showing the Description, Number and Tonnage of Canadian and United States Vessels trading on the Rivers and Lakes between Canada and the United States (exclusive of Ferriage) which arrived at each Port and Outport during the Fiscal Year ending June 30, 1906.

VESSELS ARRIVED.

Numbers.	Ports and Outports.		Canadian.						United States.					
			Steam.			Sail.			Steam.			Sail.		
			Number of Vessels.	Tons Register.	Number of Crew.	Number of Vessels.	Tons Register.	Number of Crew.	Number of Vessels.	Tons Register.	Number of Crew.	Number of Vessels.	Tons Register.	Number of Crew.
1	Algoma Mills	Ont.	25	11,982	517	3	1,667	21	101	43,932	1,368	130	56,863	907
2	Amherstburg	"	54	5,229	321	70	1,029	264	789	180,922	7,239	144	35,257	641
3	Bath	"	54	25,652	1,650	2	353	11						
4	Belleville	"	41	17,371	888	37	8,827	210						
5	Bowmanville	"	4	1,492	100	10	1,664	59						
6	Bridgeburg	"							330	10,629	996	607	241,836	1,069
7	Brighton	"	82	41,722	2,679	5	268	21						
8	Brockville	"	228	192,229	11,595	2	979	12	603	88,583	5,016	62	19,792	370
9	Bruce Mines	"	33	22,503	973				15	7,266	213	7	2,645	49
10	Cardinal	"	10	674	61	4	677	17	7	752	43	3	578	13
11	Chatham	"	117	24,531	1,446	7	1,197	42	15	2,499	120	20	4,579	101
12	Chicoutimi	Que.										1	281	4
13	Chippawa	Ont.				3	264	12	11	359	37			
14	Clarenceville	Que.	5	535	30							1	98	2
15	[illegible]	Ont.	116	55,770	4,002	8	1,659	48						
16	[illegible]rn Islands	"	11	2,074	138	4	860	38	5	1,306	56	4	989	26
17	Colborne	"	2	746	50	3	343	14						
18	Collingwood	"	50	3366	1,446				29	20,655	396	6	3,240	48
19	[illegible]ll	"	669	201,425	14,746									
20	Courtright	"							30	1,225	255			
21	[illegible]ler	"	12	3,909	190	2	617	14	60	24,118	797	49	21,822	341
22	Dawson	Y.T.	7	1,873	137	1	177	1	25	9,348	868	6	1,206	6
23	Deseronto	Ont.	204	71,947	3,934	44	11,071	255	11	1,610	99	22	5,079	124
24	Dunnville	"	23	393	134				2	1,076	54			

No.	Port												
25	Fort Francis .... "	8	197	38				2	56	13			
26	Fort William .... "	95	[illegible]	2,040	5	4,656	42	263	564,782	5,206	18	25,726	146
27	Forty Mile .... Y.T.	5	1,300	91	1	177	1	8	4,281	367	1	80	1
28	Gananoque .... Ont.	392	58,023	3,785	25	3,700	129	283	17,436	1,804	23	1,310	72
29	Goderich .... "	12	5,073	384	1	261	7	20	7,881	506	12	4,183	67
30	Hamilton .... "	7	3,689	141	4	927	24						
31	Hope .... "	115	61,952	3,895	5	2,006	35						
32	Iroquois .... "	4	360	38				156	18,520	760	3	613	16
33	Kenora .... "	24	2,334	260				33	394	202			
34	Kincardine .... "	6	2,992	180	2	254	10	6	1,524	110	4	895	24
35	Kingston .... "	633	480,432	24,481	214	50,248	1,964	367	35,696	2,368	195	16,724	730
36	Kingsville .... "	5	1,555	45				2	736	21			
37	Leamington .... "							52	2,288	408			
38	Little Current .... "	20	4,550	260	2	608	14	38	16,310	549	23	9,866	157
39	Meaford .... "	3	3,889	56				6	1,306	85	4	1,280	30
40	Michipicoten .... "	28	13,140	570	2	6,616	18	4	8,233	75			
41	Midland .... "	45	36,181	676	18	5,933	105	37	42,889	602	14	6,300	98
42	Montreal .... Que.	116	46,977	2,169	103	49,709	622	120	113,987	2,113	263	46,154	762
43	Morrisburg .... Ont.	553	19,217	1,751	1	187	4	92	9,617	415	2	445	13
44	Napanee .... "	5	295	37	22	2,938	114						
45	Niagara .... "	741	[illegible]	21,848									
46	Nicolet .... Que.										6	590	12
47	[illegible]h Portal .... N.W.T.							14	672	98	42	2,000	84
48	Oakville .... Ont.	4	840	24									
49	[illegible]a .... "				1	294	6						
50	[illegible]wa .... "	86	11,263	923							5	501	10
51	[illegible]en Sound .... "	609	367,639	14,057	4	2,870	28	42	37,163	622	35	18,897	272
52	Parry Sound .... "	81	35,933	1,682	11	3,107	74	129	197,577	2,346	47	21,488	312
53	Penetanguishene .... "	3	560	32				2	894	21			
54	Philipsburg .... Que.	4	428	24							15	1,492	30
55	Picton .... Ont.	79	28,697	1,832	22	3,336	122				6	1,200	32
56	Point Edward .... "	188	114,182	3,058	6	835	28	153	41,868	935	20	6,431	105
57	Port Arthur .... "	369	446,490	12,177	2	418	10	291	161,796	5,820	17	12,002	136
58	Port Burwell .... "	31	735	154				37	1,059	181			
59	Port Colborne .... "	100	5,841	540				34	17,798	601	69	19,495	113
60	Port Dalhousie .... "							1	171	2			
61	Port Dover .... "	2	504	20				4	1,173	77			
62	Port Lambton .... "	2	128	13				170	88,332	6,487	6	1,355	23
63	Port Stanley .... "	26	18,875	886				495	649,377	15,740			
64	Prescott .... "	166	80,603	5,727	10	4,317	40	260	74,666	2,551	41	13,887	246
65	Quebec .... Que.	26	9,565	287	24	11,245	128	9	5,611	102	231	27,067	494
66	Queenston .... Ont.	13	7,902	418									
67	Rockport .... "	131	34,383	2,618	1	91	3	18	254	45	34	686	68
68	Rondeau .... "	20	2,173	215				170	132,885	3,104			
69	Rykerts .... B.C.	2	86	8				8	144	24			
70	Sarnia .... Ont.	330	76,492	3,388	59	26,129	249	773	431,313	29,358	119	43,075	607
71	Sault Ste. Marie .... "	1,100	388,357	17,293	24	54,026	184	215	73,845	2,034	47	24,839	326
72	Smith's Falls .... "	58	4,538	344									
73	Sorel .... Que.										128	13,046	297
74	St. J[illegible] .... "	10	917	66	121	9,842	337	95	7,527	810	1,054	108,701	2,143

No. 17.—Statement showing the Description, Number and Tonnage of Canadian and United States Vessels trading on the Rivers and Lakes, &c.—*Continued.*

VESSELS ARRIVED.

Number.	Ports and Outports.		Canadian.						United States.					
			Steam.			Sail.			Steam.			Sail.		
			Number of Vessels.	Tons Register.	Number of Crew.	Number of Vessels.	Tons Register.	Number of Crew.	Number of Vessels.	Tons Register.	Number of Crew.	Number of Vessels.	Tons Register.	Number of Crew.
75	Stratford	Ont.	139	20,081	1,407	....	....	....	2	515	26	....	....	....
76	Thessalon	"	19	6,303	292	2	919	14	23	8,328	280	32	10,884	213
77	Three Rivers	Que.	1	157	11	15	1,705	32	2	799	24	627	55,515	1,210
78	Toronto	Ont.	878	635,141	34,077	109	34,940	613	75	16,951	671	12	2,451	70
79	Trenton	"	21	8,042	385	5	336	22	....	....	....	....	....	....
80	Valleyfield	Que.	23	695	95	23	4,350	92	....	....	....	....	....	....
81	Walkerville	Ont.	95	41,925	1,813	2	1,055	23	177	90,954	4,722	35	11,183	138
82	Wallaceburg	"	78	10,428	466	12	1,589	64	81	11,822	573	18	2,935	52
83	West Dock	"	23	2,318	181	13	585	48	166	11,411	1,108	21	1,159	79
84	Whitby	"	1	373	25	6	1,478	34	....	....	....	....	....	....
85	Windsor	"	164	76,678	3,009	7	2,164	38	690	276,694	6,002	162	55,881	536
	Total		9,446	4,474,653	215,329	1,089	328,493	6,317	7,658	3,584,806	117,525	4,453	964,701	13,425

No. 17.—SUMMARY STATEMENT of Canadian and United States Vessels trading on The Rivers and Lakes, which arrived at Canadian ports during the Fiscal Year ended June 30, 1906.

RECAPITULATION.

—	Number of Vessels.	Tons Register.	Crew Number.
Canadian—Steam	9,446	4,474,653	215,329
Sail	1,089	328,493	6,317
United States—Steam	7,658	3,584,806	117,525
Sail	4,453	964,701	13,425
Total	22,646	9,352,653	352,596

DESCRIPTION OF VESSELS.

—	Number of Vessels.	Tons Register.
Steam—Screw	13,474	5,488,998
Paddle	3,571	2,552,987
Stern wheel	59	17,474
Sail—Schooners	2,009	642,898
Sloops	104	1,281
Barges	3,429	649,015
Total	22,646	9,352,653

No. 18.—STATEMENT showing the Description, Number and Tonnage of Canadian and United States Vessels trading on the Rivers and Lakes between Canada and the United States (exclusive of Ferriage) which DEPARTED from each Port or Outport during the Fiscal Year ended June 30, 1906.

VESSELS DEPARTED.

Number.	PORTS AND OUTPORTS.	Canadian.						United States.					
		Steam.			Sail.			Steam.			Sail.		
		Number of Vessels.	Tons Register.	Crew, Number.	Number of Vessels.	Tons Register.	Crew, Number.	Number of Vessels.	Tons Register.	Crew, Number.	Number of Vessels.	Tons Register.	Crew, Number.
1	Algoma Mills, Ont	24	11,825	527	3	1,667	21	102	43,974	1,380	130	56,863	909
2	Amherstburg, Ont	54	5,229	321	70	4,029	264	789	180,922	7,239	144	35,257	641
3	Bath, Ont.	6	930	70	1	155	5						
4	[illegible]e, Ont	17	5,135	257	36	8,962	207						
5	Bowmanville, Ont.	4	1,492	100	8	1,268	44						
6	Bridgeburg, Ont.							372	12,293	1,161	636	250,737	1,134
7	Brighton, Ont	86	43,481	2,780	4	224	17						
8	Brockville, Ont.	223	199,341	11,260	2	579	12	712	112,599	5,151			
9	Bruce Mines	23	14,327	613				15	7,266	211	7	2,645	48
10	Cardinal, Ont.	10	674	61	4	677	17	7	752	43	3	578	13
11	[illegible]m, Ont	123	23,873	1,425	8	1,391	46	12	1,447	98	21	4,833	102
12	Chippawa, Ont				5	532	25	10	380	37			
13	Clarenceville, Que	10	1,070	60							1	98	2
14	Cobourg, Ont	46	23,274	1,571	9	1,564	51						
15	Cockburn Island, Ont	11	2,074	138	4	860	38	5	1,306	56	4	989	26
16	Colbourne, Ont	2	598	50	3	343	14						
17	Collingwood, Ont	100	61,402	2,746				28	20,655	396	5	2,681	36
18	Cornwall, Ont	310	7,608	1,051									
19	Courtright, Ont							32	3,714	360	9	1,064	28
20	Cutler, Ont	10	3,208	109	6	2,927	42	60	24,118	797	49	21,822	341
21	a[illegible]n, Y.T	7	1,874	130	2	211	2	38	16,980	1,606	13	2,890	15
22	Deseronto, Ont	133	26,289	1,393	55	13,468	355	13	1,975	125	21	4,511	115
23	Dunville, Ont.	22	416	140				2	1,076	54			
24	Fort Francis, Ont	8	197	38				2	56	13			

25	Fort William, Ont.	123	202,647	3,671	4	6,445	33	262	564,632	5,284	18	25,726	146
26	Forty Mile, Y.T	1	165	15				3	1,482	117			
27	Gananoque, Ont.	301	12,323	1,125	27	3,624	129	292	17,509	1,815	20	1,075	64
28	[illegible]h, Ont.	12	7,370	201				20	7,881	506	12	4,183	67
29	Hamilton, Ont	17	16,531	413	5	988	27						
30	Hope, Ont.	115	57,479	3,947	5	1,105	31						
31	[illegible]s, Ont.	3	267	24				156	17,836	612	1	128	6
32	Kenora, Ont	27	2,358	284				30	389	183			
33	Kincardine, Ont.				[illegible]	254	10	6	1,524	110	4	895	24
34	Kingston, Ont.	779	484,716	28,472	268	57,931	1,316	391	40,429	2,498	112	9,056	422
35	Kingsville, Ont.	5	1,555	45				2	736	21			
36	Leamington, Ont							52	2,288	408			
37	Little Current, Ont.	19	4,490	253	1	276	7	39	[illegible]	549	23	9,866	157
38	Meaford, Ont.	1	1,201	18				6	3,926	84	2	654	15
39	Michipicoten, Ont.	21	19,712	416	8	22,272	68	4	8,233	75			
40	Midland, Ont.	36	37,250	618	22	7,916	151	40	46,706	631	14	6,196	99
41	Montreal, Que.	116	46,977	2,169	103	49,709	622	121	[illegible]	2,351	271	44,816	904
42	Morrisburg, Ont.	554	19,438	1,773				94	[illegible]	423	3	787	17
43	Napanee, Ont.	4	236	29	18	2,243	85						
44	Niagara, Ont.	337	34,970	8,156									
45	[illegible]t, Que										6	590	12
46	North Portal, N.W.T.							14	672	98	42	2,000	84
47	Oakville, Ont.	4	840	24									
48	Oshawa, Ont.				1	294	6						
49	a[illegible]a, Ont.	25	2,981	227				2	288	5	158	15,272	316
50	[illegible]en Sound, Ont	556	385,425	1,448	4	2,870	28	44	32,373	650	35	[illegible]	247
51	Parry Sound, Ont.	46	32,999	887	6	2,465	43	129	199,782	2,389	49	22,209	306
52	Penetanguishene, Ont.	3	560	32				1	354	7			
53	[illegible], Que.	4	428	24							15	1,492	30
54	Picton, Ont.	29	9,467	575	27	4,865	143				6	[illegible]	32
55	Point Edward, Ont	234	166,058	4,736	3	384	14	144	24,152	941	18	4,744	89
56	Port Arthur, Ont	84	111,888	2,940	2	418	10	291	161,796	5,093	17	12,002	136
57	Port Burwell, Ont.	29	909	156				34	554	107			
58	Port [illegible]e, Ont.	61	10,596	332	7	1,527	26	33	8,360	306	67	20,234	177
59	[illegible] Dalhousie, Ont.							1	171	2			
60	Port Dover, Ont.	2	504	20				5	[illegible]	79			
61	Port, [illegible]n, Ont.	4	234	31	1	135	5	173	88,798	6,557	5	1,711	23
62	Port Stanley, Ont	19	11,401	520				493	642,662	15,724			
63	Prescott, Ont.	173	78,687	5,598	40	16,180	193	266	74,076	2,742	46	15,634	260
64	[illegible]c, [illegible]	32	12,602	387	62	26,912	352	12	10,086	196	296	42,517	682
65	Queenston, Ont.	247	173,737	9,058									
66	Rockport, Ont.	55	3,478	266				18	254	45	34	686	68
67	Rondeau, Ont.	20	2,064	209				169	13,255	3,115			
68	Rykerts, B.C.	2	86	8				8	144	24			
69	Sarnia, Ont.	308	73,875	2,340	55	25,056	240	800	428,944	29,292	125	44,486	645
70	Sault Ste. Marie, Ont.	1,170	492,436	21,474	18	37,514	144	215	73,845	2,034	47	24,839	326
71	Smith's Falls, Ont.	55	4,420	329									
72	Sorel, Que.										122	12,077	249
73	Southampton, Ont.	1	60	7									
74	St. John's, Que.	10	1,018	71	149	11,125	403	99	7,810	840	1,591	157,944	3,165

No. 18.—STATEMENT showing the Description, Number and Tonnage of Canadian and United States Vessels trading on the Rivers and Lakes, &c.—*Continued.*

VESSELS DEPARTED.

Number.	PORTS AND OUTPORTS.	Canadian.						United States.					
		Steam.			Sail.			Steam.			Sail.		
		Number of Vessels.	Tons Register.	Number of Crew.	Number of Vessels.	Tons Register.	Number of Crew.	Number of Vessels.	Tons Register.	Number of Crew.	Number of Vessels.	Tons Register.	Number of Crew.
75	Stratford, Ont.	143	20,636	1,476				1	218	6			
76	[illegible]	14	2,894	137	2	919	14	23	8,328	280	32	10,884	213
77	Three Rivers, Que.	1	157	11	14	1,587	30	3	963	36	628	55,921	1,225
78	Toronto, [illegible]	880	652,825	33,181	109	34,328	722	75	20,515	566	11	2,283	65
79	Trenton, Ont.	14	4,862	231	7	635	32						
80	[illegible]e, Ont.	28	15,003	585	2	102	7	168	103,187	5,397	28	9,341	112
81	Wallaceburg, Ont.	74	9,237	439	12	1,707	63	81	11,822	573	18	2,935	52
82	West Dock, Ont.	23	2,318	181	13	585	48	166	11,411	1,108	21	1,159	79
83	[illegible]y, Ont.	1	373	25	5	1,123	28						
84	Windsor, Ont.	224	99,619	4,324	6	2,797	35	688	159,264	6,236	209	65,401	527
	[illegible]	8,275	3,768,679	168,763	1,228	365,148	6,225	7,873	3,369,274	118,842	5,149	1,032,989	14,451

No. 18.—SUMMARY STATEMENT of Canadian and United States Vessels trading on Rivers and Lakes, which departed from Canadian ports during the Fiscal Year ending June 30, 1906.

RECAPITULATION.

—	Number of Vessels.	Tons Register.	Number of Crew.
Canadian—Steam	8,275	3,768,679	168,763
" Sail	1,228	365,148	6,225
United States—Steam	7,873	3,369,274	118,842
" Sail	5,149	1,032,989	14,451
Total	22,525	8,536,090	308,281

DESCRIPTION OF VESSELS.

—	Number of Vessels.	Tons Register.
Steam—Screw	12,890	4,943,224
" Paddle	3,195	2,173,556
" Stern wheel	63	21,173
Sail—Schooners	1,920	649,510
" Sloops	213	3,785
" Barges	4,244	744,842
Total	22,525	8,536,090

No. 19.—STATEMENT showing the Description, Number and Tonnage of Canadian and United States Vessels trading on the Rivers and Lakes between Canada and the United States (exclusive of Ferriage), which arrived and departed during the Fiscal Year ending June 30, 1906.

—	Canadian.			United States.			Total.		
	Number of Vessels.	Tons Register.	Number of Crew.	Number of Vessels.	Tons Register.	Number of Crew.	Number of Vessels.	Tons Register.	Number of Crew.
Arrived	10,535	4,803,146	221,646	12,111	4,549,507	130,950	22,646	9,352,653	352,596
Departed	9,503	4,133,827	174,988	13,022	4,402,263	133,293	22,525	8,536,090	308,281
Total	20,038	8,936,973	396,634	25,133	8,951,770	264,243	45,171	17,888,743	660,877

No 20.—STATEMENT of Vessels, British and Foreign, employed in the Coasting Trade of the Dominion of Canada, which arrived at, or departed from, the undermentioned Ports and Outports, during the Fiscal Year ended June 30, 1906.

STEAMERS.

PORTS AND OUTPORTS.	VESSELS ARRIVED.						VESSELS DEPARTED.					
	British.			Foreign.			British.			Foreign.		
	Number of Vessels.	Tons Register.	Crew, Number.	Number of Vessels.	Tons Register.	Crew, Number.	Number of Vessels.	Tons Register.	Crew, Number.	Number of Vessels.	Tons Register.	Crew, Number.
Algoma [illegible]s, Ont.	55	26,950	1,520				55	2[illegible]50	1,505			
Amherstburg, Ont.	59	3,209	264				68	3,914	307			
Annapolis Royal, N.S	58	2,898	395				58	2,898	395			
[illegible]nish, N.S.	26	1,092	104				26	1,092	104			
[illegible]e River, N.S	25	2[illegible]0	125				2[illegible]	1.056	110			
Arichat, NS	812	4[illegible]32	7,684				764	4,[illegible]52	6,112			
Baddeck, N.S	37	9841	595	1	267	20	35	9,303	577	2	538	41
Barrington, N.S	491	76,054	6,015				491	76,054	6,007			
Bath, Ont.	419	81,525	6,854				3	247	27			
Bathurst, N.B	4	[illegible]96	20				5	245	25			
Bear River, N.S.	47	3,106	229				44	2,890	212			
Bellevilie, Ont	391	147,320	10,514				99	12,308	1,065			
Bowmanville, Ont	174	83,892	1,321				174	83,892	4,321			
Bridgewater, N.S	1[illegible]5	10,748	1,018				106	12 [illegible]93	1,057			
Pridgeburg, Ont	21	945	126				21	945	126			
Bridgetown, N.S.	1	49	7				1	49	7			
Prighton, Ont	229	1[illegible]207	8,010				100	47,400	2,960			
Brockville, Ont.	[illegible]49	442,966	[illegible]400				330	286,096	17,063			
Bruce [illegible]s, Ont	328	9[illegible]602	6,297				338	146,978	6,657			
Burlington, Ont	24	2,655	165				24	2,655	165			
Campbellton, N.B	64	31,484	1,681	1	1,426	24	67	[illegible]2,545	1,740			
Campobello, N.B.	42	7,498	337				6	111	17			
[illegible]g, N.S	65	4,680	520				65	1,680	520			
Canso, N.S	781	[illegible]763	8,763				781	9[illegible]69	8,560			
Cardigan, [illegible].I	21	966	168				19	874	131			
Cardinal, [illegible]	6	382	36				6	382	6			
[illegible]n, P.E.I.	633	208,405	3,[illegible]65				664	3[illegible]59	14,164	7	3,645	104
[illegible]m, N.B.	26	11,554	283	4	4,502	75	32	7,507	261			

Chatham, Ont.	93	15,152	835				123	22,182	1,236			
Chemainus, B.C.	102	7,505	723				131	7,311	616			
Chester, N.S.	155	12,293	951				15	12,293	951			
[illegible]p, N.S.	64	4,922	614				71	5,437	694			
Cheverie, N.S.										1	344	14
Clark's Harbour, N.S.	207	11,759	1,749				204	11,780	1,735			
[illegible]e, Que.	27	2,889	69				29	3,101	116			
Clementsport, N.S.	11	732	56				11	732	56			
Cocagne, N.B.	1	12	3				1	12	3			
Cobourg, Ont.	200	105,839	7,282				117	58,581	3,853			
Colborne, Ont.	44	17,076	1,200				33	12,309	825			
Collingwood, Ont.	324	122,219	6,851				279	96,903	5,501			
[illegible]x, B.C.	457	73,655	5,458				477	7[illegible]05	5,678			
[illegible]ll, Ont.	6	1,651	38	12	2,125	81	6	1,651	38	12	2,125	81
Courtright, Ont.	114	101,343	2,265				82	7[illegible]59	1,675			
Crapaud, P.E.I.	47	13,818	470				46	3,[illegible]24	460			
Crofton, B.C.	103	11,475	843				114	14,612	952			
Cutler, Ont.	104	45,936	2,529				106	46,637	2,585			
Dalhousie, N.B.	6	374	24	1	1,426	24	6	374	24			
Dawson, Y. T.	180	68,559	3,656				180	6[illegible]43	3,654			
Deseronto, Ont.	319	133,537	9,586				30	6,084	267			
Digby, N.S.	285	158,437	9,622				288	155,645	9,482			
Dorchester, N.B.	3	147	18				3	147	18			
Douglas, B.C.	2	124	15				5	361	41			
Dunville, Ont.	2	734	25				3	934	27			
English [illegible]ay, Que.	18	2,418	259				18	2,602	277	1	256	54
Esquimaux Point, Que.	28	9,156	616				28	9,156	616			
Fortymile, Y.T.	38	11,656	536				38	11,656	540			
Fort William, Ont.	477	612,288	13,840				451	571,399	12,167			
Freeport, N.S.	33	1,616	229				31	1,519	217			
Gabarouse, N.S.	34	3,269	282				3	3,269	282	3	672	44
Gananoque, Ont.	412	146,280	9,653				93	7,121	588			
Gaspé, [illegible]	106	71,518	2,927				106	71,518	2,927			
[illegible], P.E.I.	325	47,977	5,812				334	48,754	5,942			
Glace Bay, N.S.	7	2,288	93				7	2,288	93			
Goderich, Ont.	55	30,977	1,133				60	28,184	1,314			
[illegible]d Harbour, N.B.	2	64	4				2	64	4			
[illegible]nd River, P.E.I.	24	1,104	146				25	1,150	172			
Guysborough, N.S.	241	22,759	2,184				242	22,930	2,195			
Halifax, N.S.	1,202	439,422	18,477	35	27,661	1,024	1,111	4[illegible]627	20,259	44	37,296	1,531
Hamilton, Ont.	1,085	517,548	33,400				1,072	481,846	33,050			
Hantsport, N.S.	2	58	5				1	29	2	10	6,989	155
Harvey, N.B.	23	1,155	125				24	1,204	130			
Hillsboro', N.B.	32	1,343	160				26	1,150	143			
Isaac's Harbour, N.S.	177	24,935	2,589				176	24,945	2,568			
Inverness, N.S.	10	645	71				10	645	71			
Iroquois, Ont.	226	122,027	7,785				226	[illegible]027	7,785			
Jordon Bay, N.S.	3	198	21				3	198	21			
Kaslo, B.C.	709	174,268	1[illegible]284				709	4[illegible]268	12,784			
Kincardine, Ont.	37	15,052	958				41	1[illegible]755	1,064			

No. 20.—STATEMENT of Vessels, British and Foreign, employed in the Coasting Trade, &c.—*Continued.*

STEAMERS—*Continued.*

PORTS AND OUTPORTS.	VESSELS ARRIVED.						VESSELS DEPARTED.					
	British.			Foreign.			British.			Foreign.		
	Number of Vessels.	Tons Register.	Crew, Number.	Number of Vessels	Tons Register.	Crew, Number.	Number of Vessels.	Tons Register.	Crew, Number.	Number of Vessels.	Tons Register.	Crew, Number.
Kenora, Ont	63	9,195	738				65	9,431	766			
Kingsport, N.S.	11	792	88				11	792	88			
Kingston, Ont	996	293,910	23,568				533	117,259	5,929			
Kingsville, Ont	7	3,089	98				3	779	30			
Ladner, B.C.	B1	11,227	1,055				137	11,112	1,087			
Ladysmith, B.C	836	115,770	7,990				836	117,368	8,103			
La Have, N.S	192	20,225	1,893				192	20,534	1,911			
Liscombe, NS	7	2,270	82				2	900	27			
Liverpool, N.S	162	64,150	3,225				164	64,300	3,237			
Lile [illegible]t, Ont.	396	191,551	10,224				396	191,551	10,224			
Lockeport, N.S	132	60,641	3,097				132	60,641	3,097			
Lord's Cove, N.B	142	11,280	906				124	9,760	812			
Louisburg, N.S	171	116,370	3,293	47	40,051	823	161	98,297	2,720	39	23,952	605
Lunenburg, N.S	133	61,858	3,112				135	62,422	3,144			
Mabou, N.S	45	1,504	198	4	1,444	56	44	1,446	191	3	1,083	42
Magdalen Islands, Que	66	7,017	393				65	6,914	1,054			
Mahone Bay, N.S	84	6,636	504				84	6,636	504			
Main-à-Dieu, N.S	11	360	56				12	388	61			
[illegible]land, N. S	16	1,152	1[illegible]				14	1,008	112			
[illegible]le [illegible]n, N.S	130	130,867	2,280				130	130,867	2,250			
Margaree, N.S	46	3,094	359				50	3,310	375			
Meaford, Ont	257	147,892	6,537				184	92,706	4,620			
Michipicoten, Ont	69	48,658	1,288				76	43,216	1,522			
Midland, N.B	147	82,735	2,175				146	82,391	2,151			
Moncton, N.B	18	864	90				18	864	90			
Montague, P.E.I	1[illegible]0	7,800	1,000				97	7,566	970			
Montreal, Que	3,558	1,587,834	69,599	177	336,302	4,516	3,555	1,580,950	69,538	162	315,002	4,368
Morrisburg, Ont	432	231,755	14,868				432	231,755	14,868			
Murray Harbour, P.E.I.	63	4,914	630				61	4,758	610			
Musquash, N.B	25	1,145	114				31	1,433	142			

Nanaimo, B.C	1,351	380,223	18,262				1,329	380,398	17,586			
Napanee, Ont	14	1,262	131				15	1,321	149			
Nelson, B.C	2,886	931,465	56,780				2,886	931,465	56,780			
Newcastle, N.B							1	1,930	25			
New Glasgow, N.S	7	294	35				7	294	35			
New Westminster, B.C	686	94,402	7,812	1	1,612	26	842	93,472	6,978			
Niagara, Ont	468	297,074	15,586				424	261,303	14,133			
Northeast Harbour, N.S	101	5,771	861				101	5,771	861			
North Head N.B	1	182	8				1	96	8			
[illegible]th Sydney, N.S	356	114,425	4,856	59	66,641	1,200	364	107,357	4,945	67	70,592	1,331
Oakville, Ont	33	7,578	330				33	7,578	330			
Oshawa, Ont	157	60,701	3,325				157	60,701	3,325			
[illegible]a, Ont	225	26,252	2,379	1	92	2	293	31,694	2,863			
Owen Sound, Ont	575	348,081	13,391				556	385,425	14,218			
Parrsboro', N.S	103	13,107	1,029				108	15,179	1,012			
Parry Sound, Ont	890	309,945	17,123				890	286,096	16,750			
Paspebiac, Que	128	66,827	2,705				126	64,918	2,679			
Penetanguishene, Ont	18	3,818	231	2	894	21	18	3,818	231	2	894	21
Percé, Que	92	68,336	2,624				92	68,336	2,624			
Philipsburg, Ont	4	428	24				4	428	24			
Picton, Ont	407	158,788	10,877				143	18,374	1,563			
Pictou, N.S	553	101,613	9,532	24	29,669	525	549	101,156	9,398	26	33,566	572
Point Edward, Ont	62	77,763	1,713				60	64,871	1,576			
Port Arthur, Ont	432	574,560	13,392				715	908,744	22,619			
[illegible]Burwell, Ont	24	1,164	124				20	1,123	104			
Port [illegible]e, Ont	88	77,412	1,167				22	11,743	213			
Port Credit, Ont	1	401	18				1	401	18			
Port Dalhousie, Ont	507	167,392	7,743				512	160,202	7,497			
[illegible]Dover, Ont	9	1,081	54	2	24	6	10	860	51	2	24	6
Port Hastings, N.S	57	27,624	779				54	26,348	776			
Port Hawkesbury, N.S	168	26,307	2,695				175	27,886	2,701			
Port Hood, N.S	146	10,575	1,237				143	9,863	1,197			
Port Hope, Ont	206	111,084	7,546				206	111,256	7,546			
[illegible]Latour, N.S	148	7,131	1,201				146	7,206	1,201			
Port [illegible]y, N.S	11	567	41				9	540	33			
Port Morien, N.S	30	13,980	400	5	3,355	80	30	13,980	400	5	3,355	80
Port Mulgrave, N.S	833	65,389	6,320				942	68,998	6,712			
Port Simpson, B.C	200	7,700	4,747				198	76,097	4,649			
[illegible]Stanley, Ont	22	724	106				27	4,831	299			
Prescott, Ont	530	394,946	24,658				396	253,938	14,692			
Pubnico, N.S	103	9,092	981									
Pugwash, N.S	1	40	2				1	40	2			
[illegible]ec, Que	651	903,131	34,256	43	66,181	963	810	1,557,388	50,784	33	46,975	738
Queenston, Ont	246	158,054	8,936									
Rainy River, Ont	80	9,280	792				80	9,280	792			
River Herbert, N.S	34	1,598	172				26	1,216	132			
Rivière du Loup, Que	2	3,401	50									
Rockport, Ont	173	26,664	1,445				124	35,457	2,346			
Rondeau and Blenheim, Ont	2	145	16				4	522	43			
Rykerts, B.C	2	86	8	8	144	24	2	86	8	8	144	24

No. 20.—STATEMENT of Vessels, British and Foreign, employed in the Coasting Trade, &c.—*Continued.*

STEAMERS—*Continued.*

PORTS AND OUTPORTS.	VESSELS ARRIVED.						VESSELS DEPARTED.					
	BRITISH.			FOREIGN.			BRITISH.			FOREIGN.		
	Number of Vessels.	Tonnage.	Crew, Number.	Number of Vessels.	Tonnage.	Crew, Number.	Number of Vessels.	Tonnage.	Crew, Number.	Number of Vessels.	Tonnage.	Crew, Number.
Sackville, N.B	3	145	16				3	145	16			
Sandy [illegible]e, N.S	56	1,909	229				26	830	140			
Sarnia, Ont	263	[illegible]	4,225				237	91,177	3,173			
Sault Ste. Marie, Ont	950	786,035	25,956				888	684,013	21,968			
Shediac, N.B	208	108,054	6,596				208	[illegible]	6,596			
Sheet [illegible]r, N.S	59	6,835	1,003				52	6,054	893			
Shelburne, N.S	127	64,554	3,268	1	198	14	128	[illegible]	[illegible]			
[illegible]ke, N.S	50	5,138	437				49	6,421	449			
Smith's Falls, Ont	104	18,931	1,392				51	8,762	637			
Souris, P.E.I	124	9,401	1,403				117	11,553	1,737			
Southampton, Ont	31	11,949	810				30	12,468	814			
Stratford, Ont	139	[illegible]	1,407	2	515	26	143	20.636	1,476	1	218	6
St. Andrews, N.B	30	3,567	164				25	3,736	191			
St. George, N.B	18	1,244	97				26	1,902	145			
St. John, N.B	856	263,648	[illegible]	5	7,651	108	980	533,740	22,714	17	13,173	317
St. John's, Que	60	8,472	573				61	8,579	593			
St. Martins, N.B	14	651	61				12	594	55			
St. Peters, N.S	25	[illegible]	474				25	6,433	474			
St. [illegible]n, N.B	148	12,628	906				147	[illegible]	881			
Summerside, P.E.I	292	[illegible]	7,973				279	[illegible]	7,722			
Sydney, N.S	532	413,341	11,104	207	375,186	5,197	541	424,331	11,342	215	392,085	5,447
Thessalon, Ont	239	113,474	5,096				247	[illegible]	5,273			
Thorne's [illegible]e, N.S	1	42	5				1	42	7			
Three Rivers, [illegible]e	562	800,133	[illegible]	4	5,969	87	546	[illegible]	21,373	5	7,422	110
Toronto, Ont	1,870	688,861	43,577				1,761	609,279	40,104			
[illegible]ie, N.B	27	1,797	114				25	1,569	[illegible]			
Trenton, Ont	193	104,611	6,988				11	1,334	86			
Truro, N.S	36	2,592	288				36	2,592	288			
Tusket Wedge, N.S	1	49	10				1	49	10			
Vancouver, B.C	3,929	[illegible]	[illegible]				4,115	[illegible]	61,727			

Vernon River Bridge, P.E.I.	29	8,526	290				29	8,526	290			
Victoria, B.C.	2,241	585,194	56,769	1	2,088	27	2,268	[illegible]862	56,674	3	7,687	148
Walkerville, Ont.	69	41,624	1,260				118	54,360	1,995			
Wallaceburg, Ont.	123	21,544	684				135	15,310	656			
West Bay, N.S.	63	6,615	441				63	6,615	141			
West Dock, Ont.	32	4,859	252				21	3,190	171			
Westport, N.S.	160	7,775	1,120				136	6,661	952			
Weymouth, N.S.	56	2,633	336				56	2,633	386			
Whitby, Ont.	255	64,463	3,432				106	6,039	369			
White Horse, Y.T.	125	52,616	2,799				129	52,639	2,861			
Whycocomagh, N.S.	26	6,994	234				26	2,994	234			
Windsor, N.S.	1	15	2	9	6,290	140	1	15	2			
Windsor, Ont.	327	140,226	5,173				205	98,282	3,210			
Wolfville, N.S.	32	2,304	256				32	2,304	256			
Yarmouth, N.S.	427	86,848	5,696	7	2,408	98	420	89,208	5,868	7	2,408	98
Total	50,960	19,107,821	1,013,423	663	984,121	15,187	47,799	18,385,954	931,734	675	970,445	15,937

SAILING.

Advocate Harbour, N.S.	54	3,420	169				49	2,747	158			
Alberton, P.E.I.	66	3,541	279				63	3,324	255			
Alma, N.B.	33	2,527	124				32	2,417	117			
Amherstburg, Ont.	66	2,849	236				53	2,172	93			
[illegible]is Royal, N.S.	113	8,905	400	3	1,557	25	98	5,513	336			
Antigonish, N.S.	10	370	31				10	370	31			
Apple River, N.S.	46	4,116	174				40	2,422	140			
[illegible]at, N.S.	344	17,200	2,064	15	1,125	180	336	16,800	1,680	15	1,125	180
Baddeck, N.S.	8	588	38				6	487	25	2	147	9
Baie Verte, N.B.	23	656	50	1	464	10	25	659	55			
Barrington, N.S.	121	4,470	423	1	30	2	137	4,838	475	2	47	4
Bath, Ont.	10	259	20				10	259	20			
Bathurst, N.B.	57	3,218	216				55	2,536	205			
Bayfield, N.S.	7	267	24				6	168	18			
Bear River, N.S.	28	3,128	118	3	1,104	12	20	1,132	65			
Belleville, Ont.	78	3,035	181				87	1,242	223			
Belliveau's Cove, N.S.	55	2,279	173				55	2,367	168			
Bowmanville, Ont.	2	396	12				2	396	12			
Bridgetown, N.S.	42	2,182	148				45	2,382	159			
Bridgewater, N.S.	143	15,770	704				106	8,463	458			
Brighton, Ont.	2	327	11				2	299	9			
Brockville, Ont.	2	1,263	27				2	1,263	27			
Bruce Mines, Ont.	3	822	20				3	822	20			
Campbellton, N.B.	46	3,971	195	30	24,009	384	40	2,713	159			
Campobello, N.B.	102	1,939	237				97	1,914	229			
Canning, N.S.	38	2,152	110				37	1,928	107			
Canso, N.S.	834	38,855	4,171				830	34,717	3,722			
[illegible]quet, N.B.	68	2,211	254				74	2,608	273			

No. 20.—STATEMENT of Vessels, British and Foreign, employed in the Coasting Trade, &c.—*Continued.*

SAILING—*Continued.*

PORTS AND OUTPORTS.	VESSELS ARRIVED.						VESSELS DEPARTED.					
	BRITISH.			FOREIGN.			BRITISH.			FOREIGN.		
	Number of Vessels.	Tons Register.	Crew, Number.	Number of Vessels.	Tons Register.	Crew, Number.	Number of Vessels.	Tons Register.	Crew, Number.	Number of Vessels.	Tons Register.	Crew, Number.
Cardigan, P.E.I.	19	1,141	87				15	873	63			
Cardinal, Ont	2	461	10				2	461	10			
[illegible]n, P.E.I	705	41,211	2,292				726	42,956	2,364			
Chatham, N.B	320	19,533	1,101				303	[illegible]867	1,011	1	1,036	16
Chatham, Ont	30	5,537	178				33	5,870	195			
Chester, N.S	140	7,105	492				143	7,212	515			
Cheticamp, N.S	50	1,644	197				49	1,662	140			
[illegible]e, N.S	34	1,507	92	2	1,176	14	37	11,609	111	5	5,014	24
Church Point, N.S	12	633	64				10	594	45			
Clarenceville, Que	21	165	43				16	135	34			
Clark's Harbour, N.S	154	[illegible]98	[illegible]89	3	130	22	194	6,296	633	2	53	6
Clementsport, N.S	16	1,025	60				11	485	38			
Cobourg, Ont	7	1,144	37				6	1,078	33			
Cocagne, N.B	5	79	11				5	79	11			
Colborne, Ont	3	124	10				3	124	10			
Collingwood, Ont	3	184	10				2	150	6			
Comox, B.C	57	40[illegible]84	335				52	41,371	301			
[illegible]t, [illegible]	16	4,584	105				15	4,378	97			
Crapaud, P.E.I	68	3,729	229				62	3,277	207			
Crofton, B.C	63	38,257	[illegible]09				63	38,257	209			
[illegible]r, Ont	6	3,334	42				2	1,024	14			
Dalhousie, N.B	65	3,853	241	3	1,136	24	61	3,221	221	27	23,199	363
Dawson, Y.T	37	[illegible]072	37				38	6,612	38			
Deseronto, Ont	93	6,649	254				90	5,860	236			
[illegible]by, N.S	307	4,[illegible]19	2,417	17	2,232	234	315	15,302	2,574	14	1,469	165
Dorchester, N.B	26	4,145	127				27	4,467	138			
Economy, N.S	34	1,981	99				34	1,981	98			
Esquimaux [illegible]t, Que	17	920	95				16	907	85			
Five Islands, N.S	63	3,530	206				55	2,324	165			
Fortymile, Y.T	4	1,704	4				5	2,213	5			
Fort William, Ont	20	19,058	154				20	15,855	146			
Freeport, N.S	198	5,454	1,003				202	6,450	1,271			

Fredericton, N.B.	3	155	11	1	24	4	3	155	11	1	24	4
Gabarouse, N.S.	86	6,517	367									
Gananoque, Ont.	20	3,230	70				17	1,084	52			
Gaspé, Que.	114	0,152	617				108	9,501	640			
[illegible]n, P.E.I.	148	7,842	532				153	8,321	551			
Glace Bay, N.S.	203	11,734	626				214	12,021	760			
[illegible]h, [illegible]	14	1,824	76				15	2,029	83			
Grand Harbour, N.B.	206	5,155	489				196	4,986	457			
[illegible]d Narrows, N.S.	21	459	59				21	460	61			
Grand River, P.E.I.	45	1,986	144				45	1,915	143			
Guysboro', N.S.	41	2,368	145				45	2,600	162			
Halifax, N.S.	2,870	147,767	12,673	9	3,918	80	2,614	156,509	9,981	9	4,672	77
Hamilton, Ont.	2	116	6				1	58	3			
Hantsport, N.S.	22	2,259	80	3	681	17	24	11,421	113	19	8,945	118
Harbour au Bouche, N.S.	29	1,080	91				29	1,080	91			
[illegible]y, N.B.	23	1,544	79	2	555	11	23	1,428	75			
Hillsboro', N.B.	7	721	37				9	679	36			
Ingonish, N.S.	4	[illegible]60	15				4	160	15			
Inverness, N.S.	1	23	2				1	23	2			
Isaac's Harbour, N.S.	104	7,147	423				106	7,040	421			
Jordan Bay, N.S.	33	2,249	163	1	325	4	20	932	65			
Kentville, N.S.	54	1,540	132				55	1,535	138			
Kincardine, Ont.	41	3,474	152				41	3,470	153			
Kingsport, N.S.	29	2,458	91				28	1,514	80			
Kingston, Ont.	305	6[illegible]42	1,895				380	130,314	1,717			
Kingsville, Ont.	1	45	4									
Ladysmith, B.C.	41	40,558	114				44	41,864	121			
La Have, N.S.	64	4,986	369				157	13,060	1,044			
L'[illegible], N.S.	42	1,902	153				47	1,925	158			
Liscombe, N.S.	29	2,093	116				30	1,818	133			
Little Bras d'Or, N.S.	22	474	54				33	460	61			
Little Current, Ont.	4	1,246	25				5	1,578	32			
Liverpool, N.S.	211	16,572	920				214	15,800	901			
Lockeport, N.S.	72	4,370	290				79	4,717	322			
Londonderry, N.S.	14	786	43				14	786	43			
Lord's Cove, N.B.	50	1,714	141				54	1,452	152			
Louisburg, N.S.	335	59,049	1,503	2	150	38	336	59,393	1,500			
Lunenburg, N.S.	440	29,006	2,368				480	32,522	2,591			
Mabou, N.S.	21	950	66				21	941	68			
Magdalen Islands, Que.	117	6,112	553	21	1,582	337	123	6,146	540	27	1,858	471
Mahone Bay, N.S.	116	7,986	521				131	9,361	796			
[illegible]n à Dieu, N.S.	28	792	79				28	792	79			
Maitland, N.S.	28	1,598	84				27	1,610	81			
[illegible]que, P.E.I.	20	1,380	90				20	1,330	89			
Marble [illegible]n, N.S.	90	4,752	296				90	4,752	296			
Margaree, N.S.	15	564	47				17	621	56			
[illegible]e, N.S.	40	1,760	119				41	1,803	134			
Meteghan, N.S.	88	3,434	275	3	2,000	23	88	3,613	310	2	1,973	19
Michipicoten, Ont.	8	18,080	66				2	2,424	14			
Midland, Ont.	16	4,431	[illegible]06				16	5,174	105			

No. 20.—STATEMENT of Vessels, British and Foreign, employed in the Coasting Trade, &c.—*Continued.*

SAILING—*Continued.*

Ports and Outports.	Vessels Arrived. British. Number of Vessels.	Vessels Arrived. British. Tons Register.	Vessels Arrived. British. Crew, Number.	Vessels Arrived. Foreign. Number of Vessels.	Vessels Arrived. Foreign. Tons Register.	Vessels Arrived. Foreign. Crew, Number.	Vessels Departed. British. Number of Vessels.	Vessels Departed. British. Tons Register.	Vessels Departed. British. Crew, Number.	Vessels Departed. Foreign. Number of Vessels.	Vessels Departed. Foreign. Tons* Register.	Vessels Departed. Foreign. Crew, Number.
Moncton, N.B.	44	2,446	143				42	2,506	142			
Montague, P.E.I.	137	7,927	485				131	7,669	476			
Montreal, Que.	2,216	[illegible]	9,085				2,237	560,986	9,178			
Murray Harbour, P.E.I.	52	2,025	149				54	2,037	152			
Musquash, N.B.	82	2,224	239				64	1,749	162			
Nanaimo, B.C.	17	234	34				20	648	57			
Napanee, Ont.	16	661	41				22	1,244	64			
Nelson, B.C.	1,425	724,130	2,850				1,425	724,130	2,850			
Newcastle, N.B.	100	6,983	388				67	3,499	237			
New Campbellton, N.S.	1	85	4				1	85	4			
New Glasgow, N.S.	26	910	74				26	910	74			
New London, P.E.I.	24	1,269	89				26	1,394	100			
New Westminster, B.C.	72	17,550	168	1	1,643	21	72	[illegible]	114			
North East Harbour, N.S.	49	2,270	199	2	26	4	53	2,783	205	2	26	4
North Head, N.B.	135	4,414	363				152	4,825	417			
Northport, N.S.	16	464	38				17	484	40			
North Sydney, N.S.	573	4,823	2,477	2	604	14	705	50,845	2,965	30	4,975	202
Ottawa, Ont.	386	58,361	1,468	231	22,893	448	536	83,977	2,123	109	11,353	213
Owen Sound, Ont.	4	2,870	28				4	2,870	28			
Parrsboro', N.S.	511	[illegible]	1,416				547	78,658	1,551			
Parry Sound, Ont.	48	[illegible]	321				55	14,518	362			
Paspebiac, Que.	198	14,391	1,039	1	488	11	171	10,010	722	3	1,463	32
Percé, Que.	62	5,183	533				42	2,778	190			
Philipsburg, Que.				15	1,492	30				15	1,492	30
[illegible], Ont.	56	4,111	213				43	1,859	133			
[illegible], N.S.	433	25,176	1,443				444	25,650	1,601			
Point Edward, Ont.	17	3,714	104				21	4,430	124			
Port [illegible], Ont.	15	344	31				20	478	43			
[illegible], N.S.	20	972	59				24	1,246	71			
Port [illegible], N.S.	74	5,262	241				88	7,632	293			

Port Hastings, N.S.	505	27,609	1,825				506	27,542	1,791			
Port Hawkesbury, N.S.	357	25,363	1,668				339	20,941	1,514			
Port Hill, P.E.I.	1	91	5				1	91	5			
Port Hood, N.S.	98	5,781	379				97	5,528	364			
Port Hope, Ont.	2	505	13				2	515	13			
Port Latour, N.S.	57	1,554	261				54	1,456	241			
Port Lorne, N.S.	16	400	34				14	350	30			
Port Medway, N.S.	47	2,941	188				47	2,822	184			
Port Morien, N.S.	81	7,000	360				81	7,000	360			
Port Mulgrave, N.S.	83	4,253	496				98	5,607	706			
Port Simpson, B.C.	10	110	55				14	171	77			
Port Stanley, Ont.	4	1,187	27				2	463	17			
Port Williams, N.S.	30	2,026	100				28	1,707	87			
Prescott, Ont.	7	3,329	42				6	3,588	36			
Pubnico, N.S.	113	3,606	372				124	3,545	449			
Pugwash, N.S.	87	3,593	236				88	3,573	240			
Quebec, Que.	785	76,479	2,519	73	11,142	180	731	55,602	2,284	18	4,139	51
River Bourgeois, N.S.	85	1,538	203				90	1,713	355			
River Hebert, N.S.	134	11,681	504				110	8,975	363			
River John, N.S.	5	160	10				5	160	10			
Rivière du Loup, Que.	1	199	7									
Rustico, P.E.I.	24	1,330	79				26	1,388	85			
Sackville, N.B.	28	1,771	103				48	5,271	185			
Salmon River, N.S.	7	299	22				10	423	35			
Sandy Cove, N.S.	55	1,327	140				57	1,846	177			
Sarnia, Ont.	75	19,822	452				75	20,018	453			
Sault Ste. Marie, Ont.	15	8,919	120				22	25,966	163			
Shediac, N.B.	84	3,824	255				85	3,864	254			
Sheet Harbour, N.S.	76	4,982	310				68	4,261	259	1	1,260	17
Shelburne, N.S.	130	9,496	603	4	78	10	128	8,867	614	10	1,538	45
Sherbrooke, N.S.	50	1,454	182				45	2,832	161			
Shippegan, N.B.	59	2,220	223				64	2,402	235			
Sorel, Que.				128	13,046	297				122	12,077	249
Souris, P.E.I.	92	4,687	387				95	4,840	396			
Southampton, Ont.	15	1,460	61				16	1,641	67			
St. Andrews, N.B.	145	3,220	390				161	5,913	450			
St. George, N.B.	58	2,114	195				44	1,512	122			
St. John, N.B.	1,542	140,436	5,212				1,653	137,392	5,173	1	818	14
St. John's, Que.	6	183	13				25	355	50			
St. Martin's, N.B.	40	10,168	501				130	9,158	452			
St. Peters, N.S.	116	4,850	464				129	5,550	516			
St. Stephen, N.B.	138	3,908	331				146	3,873	356			
Summerside, P.E.I.	229	13,085	792				232	13,320	663	1	217	6
Sydney, N.S.	653	55,237	2,602	27	2,803	166	507	48,023	1,976	3	834	22
Tatamagouche, N.S.	1	38	2				1	38	2			
Thessalon, Ont.	1	150	6				1	150	6			
Thorne's Cove, N.S.	20	573	65	4	160	57	28	1,742	98	5	467	56
Three Rivers, Que.	18	2,704	74				15	2,390	76			
Tidnish, N.S.	7	253	17				7	253	17			
Tignish, P.E.I.	23	1,288	124				24	1,387	130			

No. 20.—STATEMENT of Vessels, British and Foreign, employed in the Coasting Trade, &c.—*Continued.*

SAILING—*Continued.*

PORTS AND OUTPORTS.	VESSELS ARRIVED.						VESSELS DEPARTED.					
	BRITISH.			FOREIGN.			BRITISH.			FOREIGN.		
	Number of Vessels.	Tons Register.	Crew, Number.	Number of Vessels.	Tons Register.	Crew, Number.	Number of Vessels.	Tons Register.	Crew, Number.	Number of Vessels.	Tons Register.	Crew, Number.
[illegible]o, [illegible]	261	15,727	702				289	15,474	769			
Tracadie, N.B	30	941	83				33	1,024	98			
Trenton, Ont	26	1,243	68				34	1,537	88			
[illegible]o, N.S	46	3,194	135				46	3,173	135			
Tusket, N.S	17	2,185	81				5	222	15			
Tusket Wedge, N.S	15	1,166	62	1	341	6	11	619	41			
Vancouver, B.C	271	203,194	1,469				248	181,296	1,322			
Vernon River Bridge, P.E.I	33	1,791	118				32	1,743	115			
Victoria, B.C	93	23,058	356				95	29,473	406	1	1,643	21
Walkerville, Ont	42	6,213	387				42	2,230	159			
Wallace, N.S	35	1,395	86				35	1,395	86			
Wallaceburg, Ont	39	8,763	226				53	11,117	299			
Walton, N.S	80	10,878	254	2	747	11	67	3,327	166	1	266	7
West Bay, N.S	17	937	64				17	937	64			
West Dock, Ont	2	362	11				3	407	15			
Westport, N.S	189	6,156	865				179	5,146	854			
Weymouth, N.S	90	4,909	290				76	3,826	240	3	188	12
Whitby, Ont	3	448	15				4	709	21			
White Horse, Y.T	30	3,773	30				29	3,731	29			
Whycocomagh, N.S	4	197	13				4	197	13			
W[illegible]r, N.S	187	24,187	545	20	12,971	115	211	12,051	591	3	934	21
[illegible]r, Ont	70	10,775	219				83	10,444	374			
[illegible]e, N.S	61	2,695	164				67	3,720	191			
Yarmouth, N.S	231	7,277	719	1	1,446	15	330	19,351	996	1	1,446	15
Total	26,329	3,339,584	102,427	632	112,078	2,806	26,562	3,329,361	99,611	455	94,698	2,473

No. 20.—STATEMENT of Vessels, British and Foreign, employed in the Coasting Trade, &c.—*Concluded.*

RECAPITULATION.

—	Steamers.			Sailing Vessels.			Total.		
	Number of Vessels.	Tonnage.	Crew, Number.	Number of Vessels.	Tonnage.	Crew, Number.	Number of Vessels.	Tonnage.	Crew, Number.
Arrived—									
British	50,960	19,107,821	1,013,423	26,329	3,339,584	102,427	77,289	22,447,405	1,115,850
Foreign	663	984,121	15,187	632	112,078	2,806	1,295	1,096,199	17,993
Total	51,623	20,091,942	1,028,610	26,961	3,451,662	105,233	78,584	23,543,604	1,133,843
Departed—									
British	47,799	18,385,954	931,734	26,562	3,329,361	99,611	74,361	21,715,315	1,031,345
Foreign	675	970,445	15,937	455	94,698	2,473	1,130	1,065,143	18,410
Total	48,474	19,356,399	947,671	27,017	3,424,059	102,084	75,491	22,780,458	1,049,755

DESCRIPTION OF VESSELS.

—	Arrived.		Departed.		Total.	
	Number of Vessels.	Tonnage.	Number of Vessels.	Tonnage.	Number of Vessels.	Tonnage.
Steamers—						
Screw	38,725	13,132,251	38,124	13,820,836	76,849	26,953,087
Paddle	9,388	5,684,259	6,837	4,261,405	16,225	9,945,664
Sternwheel	3,510	1,275,432	3,513	1,274,158	7,023	2,549,590
Total steamers	51,623	20,091,942	48,474	19,356,399	100,097	39,448,341
Sailing vessels						
Ships	1	1,260	6	11,368	7	12,628
Barques	43	41,331	46	39,685	89	81,016
Barquentines	32	9,540	62	8,517	94	18,057
Brigs	4	2,050	5	2,229	9	4,279
Brigantines	42	8,220	47	8,849	89	17,069
Schooners	20,427	1,375,329	20,410	1,371,496	40,837	2,746,825
Sloops	1,380	68,419	1,416	69,579	2,796	137,998
Barges, canal boats, &c.	5,032	1,945,513	5,025	1,912,336	10,057	3,857,849
Total sailing	26,961	3,451,662	27,017	3,424,059	53,978	6,875,721
Grand total	78,584	23,543,604	75,491	22,780,458	154,075	46,324,062

No. 21.—STATEMENT showing the Description, Number and Tonnage of Vessels built and registered, also the Number, Tonnage and Value of Vessels sold to other Countries at each Port and Outport in the Dominion of Canada, during the Fiscal Year ended June 30, 1906.

Ports and Outports.	Built.						Registered.						Ships sold to other Countries.		
	Steam.		Sail.		Total.		Steam.		Sail.		Total.				
	No.	Tonnage.	No.	Tonnage.	No.	Tonnage.	No.	Tonnage.	No.	Tonnage.	No.	Tonnage.	No.	Tonnage.	Value.
Amherst, N.S.									2	126	2	126			
Amherstburg, Ont.							1	91			1	91			
Annapolis Royal, N.S.			1	388	1	388			1	388	1	388			
Arichat, N.S.			6	75	6	75			6	75	6	75	3	141	2,400
Barrington, N.S.	2	40	1	20	3	60	2	40	10	141	12	181			
Canso, N.S.			1	10	1	10			1	10	1	10			
Charlottetown, P.E.I.	2	10	4	155	6	165	3	622	10	466	13	1,088	6	1,066	24,725
Chatham, N.B.			7	83	7	83			7	83	7	83			
Clark's Harbour, N.S.			9	104	9	104									
Collingwood, Ont.	3	386			3	386	3	386			3	386			
Digby, N.S.	3	53	5	154	8	207	3	53			3	53			
Goderich, Ont.	2	65			2	65									
Halifax, N.S.	1	5	9	369	10	374	4	2,378	3	579	7	2,957			
Hamilton, Ont.							3	2,192			3	2,192	1	15	1,800
Kenora, Ont.	13	257			13	257	13	257			13	257			
Kingston, Ont.	7	385			7	385	7	385			7	385	1	14	2,500
Liverpool, N.S.			4	248	4	248			1	116	1	116			
Lockeport, N.S.			2	93	2	93			2	93	2	93			
Lunenburg, N.S.	1	10	38	2,543	39	2,553	1	10	40	2,643	41	2,653	28	2,163	78,500
Maitland, N.S.			1	132	1	132							1	1,215	10,000
Montreal, Que.	12	540	7	793	19	1,333	15	1,756	15	5,219	30	6,975			
Nelson, B.C.	1	1,008			1	1,008	1	537			1	537			
New Westminster, B.C.	2	182	5	435	7	617	2	182	5	435	7	617			
Ottawa, Ont.	3	48	5	637	8	685	12	988	6	501	18	1,489			
Owen Sound, Ont.	2	118	1	359	3	477	2	83	1	338	3	421			
Parrsboro, N.S.			2	809	2	809			2	809	2	809	2	3,011	18,500
Paspebiac, Que.									1	99	1	99			
Peterborough, Ont.	2	82			2	82	2	56			2	56			
Port Arthur, Ont.			1	951	1	951	5	95	2	1,460	7	1,555			
Port Dover, Ont.	1	16			1	16	1	16			1	16			

Port Hawkesbury, N.S	....	....	1	11	1	11	....	....	1	11	1	11	....	....	....
[illegible]c, Que	6	104	9	400	15	504	8	443	12	701	20	1,144	....	....	....
[illegible]e, N.S	....	....	9	480	9	480	....	....	9	480	9	480	....	....	....
St. [illegible]s, N.B	....	....	2	38	2	38	2	13	9	130	11	143	....	....	....
St. [illegible]n, N.B	5	497	2	84	7	581	7	676	4	233	11	909	1	332	32,300
Sorel, Que	4	386	5	565	9	951	4	258	5	493	9	751	....	....	....
Sydney, N.S	....	....	4	65	4	65	....	....	4	65	4	65	....	....	....
Vancouver, B.C	36	687	6	448	42	1,135	46	757	15	794	61	1,551	....	....	....
Victoria, B.C	3	39	8	750	11	789	4	2,866	2	2,406	6	5,272	....	....	....
[illegible]e, N.S	....	....	1	76	1	76	....	....	....	....	....	....	....	....	....
Weymouth, N.S	....	....	2	207	2	207	1	5	3	249	4	254	....	....	....
[illegible]ite Horse, Y.T	....	....	3	488	3	488	....	....	....	....	....	....	....	....	....
[illegible]r, N.S	1	9	1	331	2	340	1	9	2	1,469	3	1,478	2	1,530	17,000
[illegible]g, Mn	6	772	1	58	7	830	6	772	1	58	7	830	....	....	....
[illegible], N.S	3	124	39	542	42	666	3	124	76	919	79	1,043	....	....	....
Total	121	5,823	202	12,901	323	18,724	162	16,050	258	21,589	420	37,639	45	9,487	187,725

INDEX TO IMPORTS.

INDEX TO IMPORTS—*Continued.*

INDEX TO IMPORTS—*Continued.*

INDEX TO IMPORTS—*Continued.*

INDEX TO IMPORTS—*Continued.*

INDEX TO IMPORTS—*Continued.*

INDEX TO IMPORTS—*Continued.*

INDEX TO IMPORTS—*Continued.*

INDEX TO IMPORTS—*Continued.*

INDEX TO IMPORTS—*Continued.*

INDEX TO IMPORTS—*Continued.*

INDEX TO IMPORTS—*Continued.*

INDEX TO IMPORTS—*Continued.*

INDEX TO IMPORTS—*Continued.*

INDEX TO IMPORTS—*Continued.*

INDEX TO IMPORTS—*Continued.*

INDEX TO IMPORTS—*Continued.*

INDEX TO IMPORTS—*Continued.*

INDEX TO IMPORTS—*Continued.*

INDEX TO IMPORTS—*Continued.*

INDEX TO IMPORTS—*Continued.*

INDEX TO IMPORTS—*Continued.*

INDEX TO IMPORTS—*Continued.*

INDEX TO IMPORTS—*Continued.*

INDEX TO IMPORTS—*Concluded.*

INDEX TO EXPORTS

INDEX TO EXPORTS—*Continued.*

INDEX TO EXPORTS—*Continued.*

INDEX TO EXPORTS—*Continued.*

INDEX TO EXPORTS—*Continued.*

REPORT, RETURNS AND STATISTICS

OF THE

INLAND REVENUES

OF THE

DOMINION OF CANADA

FOR THE FISCAL YEAR ENDED JUNE 30

1906

PART I. EXCISE, &c.

PRINTED BY ORDER OF PARLIAMENT

OTTAWA
PRINTED BY S. E. DAWSON, PRINTER TO THE KING'S MOST
EXCELLENT MAJESTY
1906

[No. 12—1907]

To His Excellency the Right Honourable Sir Albert Henry George, Earl Grey, Viscount Howick, Baron Grey of Howick, in the County of Northumberland, in the Peerage of the United Kingdom and a Baronet; Knight Grand Cross of the Most Distinguished Order of Saint Michael and Saint George, &c., &c., Governor General of Canada.

MAY IT PLEASE YOUR EXCELLENCY:

I have the honour to transmit to Your Excellency the RETURNS AND STATISTICS of Inland Revenues of the Dominion of Canada, for the Fiscal Year ended June 30, 1906, as prepared and laid before me by the Deputy Minister of Inland Revenue.

All of which is respectfully submitted.

WM. TEMPLEMAN,
Minister of Inland Revenue.

CONTENTS

FINANCIAL.

STATISTICS (APPENDIX A.)

EXCISE.

—	Spirits.	Malt.	Malt Liquor.	Manufactured Tobacco.	Raw Leaf Tobacco.	Canada Twist Tobacco.	Cigars.	Petroleum.	Bonded Manufactures.	Acetic Acid.	Methylated Spirits.
	Pge	Pge	Pge	Pge	Pge	Pge	Pge	Pge	Pge	Pge	Pge
RETURN OF MANUFACTURES—Showing the number of Licenses issued and Fees collected, the materials used, the quantity produced, the amount of duties collected, ex-manufactory, and the amount of duties accruing upon excisable articles warehoused.......	68	76	82	84	..	....	82	....	100	108	....
COMPARATIVE STATEMENT of the above, for the years ended June 30, 1905 and 1906, respectively........	67	77	83	85	....	....	94	....	99	108	....
RETURN OF DISTILLERIES—Showing their transactions during the year ended June 30, 1906....	71	....	....	....	....	.. ..	...	....	....	...	....
RETURN OF WAREHOUSE TRANSACTIONS—Showing the quantity of excisable goods remaining in bonded warehouses of each Collection Division, respectively, from previous years; quantity placed in warehouse ex-factory during the fiscal year ended June 30, 1905, placed in warehouse from other Collection Divisions; also, quantity ex-warehoused for consumption, with duty accrued thereon; ex-warehoused to be rewarehoused in other Collection Divisions; ex-warehoused for exportation; also quantity used in bonded factories, and remaining in warehouse June 30, 1906....	72	78	....	86	88	....	96	.. .	104	109	....
COMPARATIVE STATEMENT of the above, for the years ended June 30, 1905 and 1906 respectively........	74	80	...	87	90	....	97	....	106	110	....
RETURN OF REVENUE collected from Canada Twist Tobacco..................	....	...	.. .	....	...	91	....	....	....	...	....
COMPARATIVE STATEMENT of the above, for the years ended June 30, 1905 and 1906 respectively	....	....	....	....	...	91	....	...	....	.. .	....
RETURN of Petroleum and Naphtha—Showing the quantity inspected during the year ended June 30, 1906..........	....	....	....	...	....	....	....	98	....	....	....
COMPARATIVE STATEMENT of Petroleum and Naphtha inspected during the years ended June 30, 1905 and 1906, respectively	....	....	....	....	....	....	....	99	....	....	....
METHYLATED SPIRITS—Statement showing the quantity of raw material on hand at beginning of year, raw material used, quantity produced and how disposed of...............	....	....	.. ..	....	....	....	....	....	..	....	111

HYDRAULIC AND OTHER RENTS.

35 35 (*a*)	Amount due from each Lessee or Purchaser, July 1, 1905 .... " accrued during the year ended June 30, 1906........ ... ... " paid by each Lessee or Purchaser, during the year ended June 30, 1906...... .. . . " remaining due by each Lessee or Purchaser on June 30, 1906........	112 to 117

EXPENDITURES—(Appendix B.)

REPORT

OF THE

DEPUTY MINISTER OF INLAND REVENUE

To the HON. WM. TEMPLEMAN,
Minister of Inland Revenue.

SIR,—Herewith I have the honour to submit statements of the Inland Revenues collected by this department during the fiscal year ended June 30, 1906, with the usual information as to the cost of collection and statistics respecting the sources whence these revenues were derived.

The following summary comparison shows the accrued revenue for the years ended June 30, 1902, 1903, 1904, 1905 and 1906, respectively :—

—	1902.	1903.	1904.	1905.	1906.
	$	$	$	$	$
Excise	11,257,485	12,190,123	13,126,593	12,719,191	14,201,534
Public Works	4,749	4,901	4,687	4,863	4,623
Weights and Measures, Gas and Law Stamps	88,198	109,535	110,416	114,309	125,753
Electric Light	21,062	23,895	23,457	27,810	35,100
Other Revenues	592	610	569	1,614	3,102
Methylated Spirits	66,785	72,269	68,326	68,121	65,530
Totals	11,438,871	12,401,333	13,334,048	12,935,908	14,435,642

The increase over last fiscal year being $1,499,734.

DETAILS of Excise Revenue accrued during the undermentioned years :—

—	1	2	3	4	5
	1902.	1903.	1904.	1905.	1906.
	$	$	$	$	$
Spirits................................	5,620,613	6,162,827	6,672,149	5,950,632	6,795,900
Malt Liquor..........................	6,970	9,485	9,039	9,124	10,003
Malt...................................	1,077,809	1,020,623	1,137,556	1,140,639	1,292,443
Tobacco...............................	3,563,578	3,904,617	4,127,679	4,412,374	4,842,348
Cigars.................................	897,360	998,495	1,070,823	1,103,743	1,146,936
Acetic Acid	8,862	6,128	2,701	7,694	1,656
Manufactures in bond................	45,306	45,024	45,343	51,141	56,115
Seizures..............................	1,567	2,830	4,413	2,352	3,501
Other receipts........................	35,419	40,094	56,889	41,492	52,632
Methylated spirits	66,785	72,269	68,326	68,121	65,530
Totals..............................	11,324,269	12,262,392	13,194,918	12,787,312	14,267,064

The quantity of spirits produced during the year was 6,743,244 proof gallons, as compared with 6,009,024 proof gallons produced in the previous fiscal year. The raw material used in its production being as follows :—

	Lbs.
Malt..	8,251,734
Indian corn..	77,538,818
Rye..	18,568,974
Wheat...	2,205,990
Oats...	518,085
Molasses..	7,732,144

The transactions of the several distilleries will be found stated in detail in Appendix A (Statement No. 3), pages 70 and 71.

		Proof Galls.
There was on July 1, 1905, in process of manufacture.......		256,718
Manufactured during the year..........................		6,743,244
Returned to distilleries for re-distillation—Duty paid	1,005	
" " " In bond.	1,118,568	
		1,119,573
Received into distilleries from other sources—Duty paid....		12,404
" " " In bond..................		
Total		8,131,939

This was disposed of as follows :—

	Proof Gallons.
Placed in warehouse under crown lock	7,878,966
Fusel-oil written off..................................	29,431
Deficiency arising from rectification..................	3,765
Remaining in process of manufacture, June 30, 1906, by actual stock-taking..........................	219,777
Written off..	Nil.
Total..........................	8,131,939

SPIRITS :—

The following statement shows the warehousing transactions in spirits during the year ended June 30, 1906, and the four preceding years :—

Fiscal Years.	1	2	3	4	5	6	7	8	9
	In Warehouse at beginning of year.	Warehoused during the year. Ex-distillery.	Otherwise Warehoused.	Taken for consumption.	Exported.	Used in Bonded Factories.	Otherwise accounted for.	For Re-distillation.	In Warehouse at end of year.
	Pf. Galls.	Pf. Galls.	Pf. Galls.	Pf. Galls.	Pf. Galls.	Pf. Galls.	Pf. Galls.	Pf. Galls.	Pf. Galls.
1901-1902....	10,853,570	3,068,286	187,827	2,933,183	151,799	360,235	231,641	469,417	10,563,408
1902-1903...	10,563,408	4,953,575	228,601	3,207,748	157,666	418,631	306,220	870,231	10,785,088
1903-1904....	10,785,088	6,323,439	225,329	3,481,287	180,291	405,663	193,851	748,823	12,323,941
1904-1905....	12,323,941	6,774,392	160,925	3,112,843	211,525	363,471	209,046	848,209	14,514,164
Totals	44,526,007	21,719,692	802,682	12,735,061	701,281	1,548,000	940,758	2,936,680	48,186,601
Annual average of four years ended June 30, 1905.......	11,131,502	5,429,923	200,670	3,183,765	175,320	387,000	235,190	734,170	12,046,650
1905-1906 ...	14,514,164	7,878,966	239,480	3,545,785	277,905	450,499	205,433	1,118,568	17,034,420

It will be of interest to note the gradual development of a foreign demand for Canadian distillery products.

The quantities exported being as follows :—

	Proof Gallons.
1901–1902..............................	151,799
1902–1903..............................	157,666
1903–1904..............................	180,291
1904–1905..............................	211,525
1905–1906..............................	277,905

The following statement exhibits the entire quantities upon which duties were collected during the several years recited therein. The total column will be found to accord with the figures shown in Financial Statement No. 13, page 23:—

Fiscal Years.	Canadian Spirits.		Imported Spirits used in Bonded Factories. Paid difference between Customs and Excise Duty.	Total quantities upon which duty was collected.	Memorandum of Revenue accrued including License Fees.
	Paid duty Ex-distillery.	Paid duty Ex-warehouse.			
	Pf. Gallons.	Pf. Gallons.	Pf. Gallons.	Pf. Gallons.	$
1901-1902	2,488	2,933,183	187,759	3,123,430	5,620,613
1902-1903	1,019	2,979,268	228,480	3,208,767	6,162,827
1903-1904	6,458	3,481,287	225,326	3,713,071	6,672,149
1904-1905	200	3,112,843	160,842	3,273,885	5,950,632
Totals	10,165	12,506,581	802,407	13,319,153	24,406,221
Annual average of four years ended June 30, 1905	2,541	3,126,645	200,602	3,329,788	6,101,555
1905-1906	3,765	3,545,785	239,432	3,788,982	6,795,900

MALT:

The following statement shows the transactions in Malt during the Year 1905-1906 and the four preceding years:—

Fiscal Years.	1 In Warehouse at beginning of year.	2 Manufactured during the year.	3 Increase by absorption.	4 Taken for consumption.	5 Exported.	6 Otherwise accounted for.	7 In Warehouse at end of year.	8 Memorandum of Revenue accrued, including License Fees.
	Lbs.	Lbs.	Lbs.	Lbs.	Lbs.	Lbs.	Lbs.	$
1901-1902.....	26,074,656	72,870,605 *3,600,214	835,511	71,440,519	369,230	1,314,308	30,256,929	1,077,809
1902-1903.....	30,256,929	66,492,160 *3,596,116	739,592	67,608,157	287,040	1,735,390	31,454,210	1,020,623
1903-1904.....	31,454,210	68,503,928 *4,158,218	623,592	75,430,347	376,936	2,253,306	26,679,359	1,137,556
1904-1905.....	26,679,359	75,357,218 *3,878,089	811,286	75,517,352	498,960	2,824,310	27,885,330	1,140,639
Total....	114,465,154	283,223,911 *15,232,637	3,009,981	289,996,375	1,532,166	8,127,314	116,275,828	4,376,627
Annual average of four years ended June 30, 1905	28,616,289	70,805,978 *3,808,159	752,495	72,499,094	383,041	2,031,829	29,068,957	1,094,157
1905-1906.....	27,885,330	90,089,573 *3,470,197	649,819	85,699,102	528,400	3,248,754	32,618,663	1,292,443

*Imported.

TOBACCO :

The following Statement shows the transactions during the Fiscal Years ended June 30, 1902, 1903, 1904, 1905 and 1906 respectively, in Tobacco, Snuff and Cigarettes.

Fiscal Years.	1 In Warehouse at beginning of year.	2 Manufactured during the year.	3 Taken for consumption.	4 Exported.	5 Otherwise accounted for.	6 In Warehouse at end of year.	7 Raw Leaf taken for consumption.	8 Canadian Twist taken for consumption.	9 Total Tobacco taken for consumption.	10 Duty collected thereon, including License Fees.
	Lbs.	Lbs.	Lbs.	Lbs.	Lbs.	Lbs.	Lbs.	Lbs.	Lbs.	$
1901 1902	1,298,004	12,054,467	11,900,054	222,355	53,193	1,176,869	10,704,962	72,286	22,677,302	3,563,578
1902-1903	1,176,869	13,371,321	12,983,995	141,209	79,923	1,343,063	11,615,963	53,256	24,653,214	3,904,617
1903-1904	1,343,063	13,488,306	13,160,660	163,829	69,329	1,437,551	12,139,700	47,771	25,348,131	4,127,679
1904-1905	1,437,551	14,388,104	14,164,325	181,220	68,536	1,411,574	12,387,376	32,867	26,584,568	4,412,374
Totals	5,255,487	53,302,198	52,209,034	708,613	270,981	5,369,057	46,848,001	206,180	99,263,215	16,008,248
Annual average of four years ended June 30, 1905	1,313,872	13,325,549	13,052,259	177,153	67,745	1,342,264	11,712,000	51,545	24,815,804	4,002,062
1905-1906	1,411,574	15,588,289	15,289,576	155,432	65,310	1,489,545	13,638,620	36,340	28,964,536	4,842,348

CIGARS:

The following statement shows the transactions in Cigars during the fiscal year ended June 30, 1906, and the four preceding years:—

Fiscal Years.	1	2	3	4	5	6	7	8
	In Warehouse at beginning of Year.	Manufactured during the Year.	Assessment to bring production up to Standard.	Taken for Consumption.	Exported.	Otherwise accounted for.	In Warehouse at end of Year.	Memorandum of Revenue accrued including License Fees.
	No.	No.	No.	No.	No.	No.	No.	$
1901–1902	17,048,435	156,686,795	4,096	151,780,516	128,845	7,150	21,822,815	897,360
1902–1903	21,822,815	171,996,232	84,875	168,290,422	190,920	662,450	24,760,130	998,495
1903–1904	24,760,130	183,048,907	15,745	180,485,202	278,450	123,900	26,937,230	1,070,823
1904–1905	26,937,230	188,044,370	37,887	186,110,777	162,250	26,775	28,719,685	1,103,743
Totals	90,568,610	699,776,304	142,603	686,666,917	760,465	820,275	102,239,860	4,070,421
Annual average of four years ended June 30, 1905	22,642,152	174,944,076	35,651	171,666,729	190,116	205,069	25,559,965	1,017,605
1905–1906	28,719,685	190,941,283	29,139	193,827,342	144,575	376,925	25,341,265	1,146,936

The revenue derived from goods manufactured in bond during the past five years has been as follows :—

1901–1902	$ 45,306
1902–1903	45,024
1903–1904	45,343
1904–1905	51,141
1905–1906	56,115

ACETIC ACID :

The revenue derived from acetic acid during the last five years has been as follows :—

1901–1902	$ 8,862
1902–1903	6,128
1903–1904	2,701
1904–1905	7,694
1905–1906	1,656

INSPECTION OF PETROLEUM :

The quantity of Canadian Petroleum and Naphtha inspected during the year was as follows :—

	Gallons.
Petroleum	15,740,771
Naphtha	2,893,384
Total	18,634,155

PUBLIC WORKS :

The revenue accrued from this source was as follows :—

	1904–1905.	1905–1906.
Hydraulic and other rents	$ 3,647 00	$ 3,647 00
Minor public work	1,215 75	975 50

WEIGHTS AND MEASURES, GAS AND ELECTRIC LIGHT :

The usual special reports in relation to these services have been prepared, containing full statistical information.

The aggregate revenue accrued from these services was $149,472.86.

The cost of the three services being $130,436.35.

PREVENTION OF ADULTERATION OF FOOD AND AGRICULTURAL FERTILIZERS :

The usual supplementary report in relation to this service will be submitted, containing details of the work done and the report of the analysts.

METHYLATED SPIRITS :

The quantity of methylated spirits manufactured during the year was 84,856·59 proof gallons, and the sales 85,137·55 proof gallons. A statement of details appears on pages 64, 65 and 111.

The price of this denatured alcohol has recently been reduced as follows :—

Grade No. 1 from $1.10 to 80c. per gallon.

Grade No. 2 from $1.50 to $1.25.

The Department trusts that by the use of a cheaper, but equally efficient, denaturing agent to be able to supply manufacturers with this class of spirit at a price materially less than that now charged.

Appendix A shows the consumption of, and revenue derived annually from, spirits tobacco and other goods subject to Excise, and of similar goods subject to duties of Customs, per head of the population of the Dominion.

Appendix B contains, as usual, the details concerning illicit stills seized during the year.

Appendix C shows the amount of Excise Revenue collected at each out-office and under various headings, separately.

I have the honour to be, sir,

Your obedient servant,

W. J. GERALD,
Deputy Minister.

INLAND REVENUE DEPARTMENT,
OTTAWA, August 29, 1906.

APPENDIX A

TABLE showing the Annual Consumption per head of the undermentioned articles paying Excise and Customs Duties, and the Revenue per head derived annually.

Years.	Dominion of Canada.									
	Quantity.					Duty.				
	Spirits.	Beer.	Wine.	Tobacco.	Petroleum.	Spirits.	Beer.	Wine.	Tobacco.	Petroleum.
	Galls.	Galls.	Galls.	Lbs.	Galls.	$	$	$	$	$
1869	1·124	2·290	·115	1·755	·575	·761	·092	·037	·193	·041
1870	1·434	2·163	·195	2·190	1·103	·962	·085	·049	·259	·061
1871	1·578	2·490	·259	2·052	1·591	1·059	·095	·056	·336	·077
1872	1·723	2·774	·257	2·481	1·302	1·160	·103	·070	·422	·076
1873	1·682	3·188	·238	1·999	1·387	1·135	·120	·066	·350	·084
1874	1·994	3·012	·288	2·566	1·618	1·363	·119	·086	·442	·103
1875	1·394	3·091	·149	1·995	1·589	1·127	·114	·069	·428	·098
1876	1·204	2·454	·177	2·316	1·360	1·182	·098	·075	·513	·105
1877	·975	2·322	·096	2·051	1·103	·949	·109	·057	·446	·084
1878	·960	2·169	·096	1·976	....	·927	·147	·052	·439	......
1879	1·131	2·209	·104	1·954	....	1·005	·125	·057	·449	......
1880	·715	2·248	·077	1·936	....	·772	·081	·055	·428	...
1881	·922	2·293	·099	2·035	....	·990	·081	·073	·443	......
1882	1·009	2·747	·120	2·150	....	1·084	·098	·092	·485	......
1883	1·090	2·882	·135	2·280	....	1·186	·103	·097	·473	......
1884	·998	2·924	·117	2·476	....	1·074	·104	·082	·365	......
1885	1·126	2·639	·109	2·623	....	1·198	·111	·074	·393	......
1886	·711	2·839	·110	2·052	....	1·007	·091	·074	·502	......
1887	·746	3·084	·095	2·062	....	1·045	·100	·066	·514	......
1888	·645	3·247	·094	2·093	....	·944	·110	·066	·509	......
1889	·776	3·263	·097	1·153	....	1·107	·114	·068	·529	......
1890	·883	3·360	·104	2·143	....	1·257	·121	·072	·539	......
1891	·745	3·790	·111	2·292	....	1·094	·137	·080	·590	......
1892	·701	3·516	·101	2·291	....	1·156	·211	·075	·680	......
1893	·740	3·485	·094	2·314	....	1·235	·218	·070	·691	......
1894	·742	3·722	·089	2·264	....	1·235	·205	·060	·683	......
1895	·666	3·471	·090	2·163	....	1·124	·161	·056	·645	......
1896	·623	3·528	·070	2·120	....	1·159	·164	·047	·639	......
1897	·723	3·469	·084	2·243	....	1·341	·213	·041	·671	......
1898	·536	3·808	·082	2·358	....	1·306	·126	·041	·615	......
1899	·661	3·995	·086	2·174	....	1·367	·174	·045	·841	......
1900	·701	4·364	·085	2·300	....	1·455	·185	·044	·853	......
1901	·765	4·737	·100	2·404	....	1·593	·198	·048	·875	......
1902	·796	5·102	·090	2·404	....	1·653	·214	·048	·915	......
1903	·870	4·712	·096	2·548	....	1·812	·205	·051	·992	......
1904	·952	4·918	·096	2·765	....	1·985	·225	·051	1·042	......
1905	·869	4·972	·090	2·686	....	1·842	·207	·040	1·005	......
1906	·861	5·255	·091	2·777	....	1·800	·228	·050	1·053	......
Average	·968	3·330	·121	2·222	....	1·222	·142	·062	·585	......

W. J. GERALD,
Deputy Minister.

INLAND REVENUE DEPARTMENT,
OTTAWA, August 29, 1906.

APPENDIX B

STATEMENT of Seizures of Illicit Manufactures for Fiscal Year ended June 30, 1906.

Divisions.	Nos.	Dates.	Names.	Residences.	Schedule Value.	Remarks.
					$ cts.	
Guelph.	90	Dec. 21, 1905	John McCormick	Township of Wellesley	18 00	Case dismissed by order of the court.
Montreal	02	" 27, 1905	J. R. Beauchamp	Montreal	24 74	Fine $100, imposed and paid.
"	07	" 30, 1905	W. Bousquet	"	10 60	" $100 "
"	11	Mar. 3, 1906	H. Barskey	Bordeaux	15 50	" $200 "
Quebec	62	Oct. 12, 1905	D. Coulombe	St. Marcel	20 00	
"	50	Jan. 25, 1906	N. Claisse	Portneuf	48 50	" $100 and costs, the party left the country.
"	51	" 25, 1906	P. Gervais	"	37 70	" $100, imposed and paid.
"	52	Feb. 23, 1906	J. Rousseau	"	17 50	" $100.

W. J. GERALD,
Deputy Minister.

INLAND REVENUE DEPARTMENT,
OTTAWA, August 29 1906.

APPENDIX—C.

STATEMENT showing the Amount of Excise and other Revenues collected at each of the undermentioned Out-Offices, during the Fiscal Year ended June 30, 1906.

Divisions.	Out-Offices.	Licenses.	Spirits.	Malt Liquor.	Malt.	Tobacco.	Cigars.	Manufactures in Bond.	Other Receipts.	Electric Light Inspection Fees.	Totals.
		$ cts.	$ cts.	$ cts.	$ cts.	$ cts.	$ cts.	$ cts.	$ cts.	$ cts.	$ cts.
Belleville	Deseronto	20 00	2,257 00			1,867 00					4,144 00
	Picton	20 00	1,424 32							25 00	1,469 32
	[illegible]n.	20 00	5,015 52								5,035 52
Brantford	Embro									5 00	5 00
	Ingersoll									25 00	25 00
	Norwich	50 00						1,604 59	600 00	10 00	2,264 59
	Paris									10 00	10 00
	Port [illegible]r.									5 00	5 00
	Port Rowan									5 00	5 00
	Simcoe									5 00	5 00
	Tilsonburg									10 00	10 00
	[illegible]ck.	220 00	3,593 17		1,650 30	1,582 98	3,778 65		1,124 15	25 00	11,974 25
Guelph	Berlin	445 00	60,773 03		10,485 00	9,251 38	10,430 85		1,938 47	25 00	93,348 73
	Elmira									90 00	90 00
	Galt	195 00			7,235 76	487 30	1,401 75			25 00	9,344 81
	New Hamburg	50 00			3,600 00					5 00	3,655 00
	Preston	175 00			3,778 74	702 70	2,054 40			10 00	6,720 84
	Salem	50 00			3,474 00						3,524 00
	St. [illegible]bs.									85 00	85 00
	[illegible]lo	575 00	385,429 72		37,671 00	1,582 50	6,183 00		5,686 50	25 00	437,152 72
Hamilton	Dundas	200 00			42,976 43						43,176 43
Kingston	Napanee	20 00	6,068 95							10 00	6,098 95
London	Alvinston									5 00	5 00
	[illegible]er									10 00	10 00
	Dutton									10 00	10 00
	Forest									5 00	5 00
	Lucan									5 00	5 00
	Park Hill									10 00	10 00
	Petrolea	21 00	4,729 97						40 95	25 00	4,816 92
	Sarnia	153 50	27,133 46		1,644 00	733 40	361 95		0 48	25 00	30,051 79
	St. [illegible]as.	275 00				3,995 08	12,382 70			25 00	16,677 78
	Strathroy	100 00			4,230 00				257 52	25 00	4,612 52
Owen Sound	[illegible]od	40 00	56 43			16,402 50			1 00	25 00	16,524 93
	Kincardine								101 72	10 00	111 72

	[illegible]rd	40 00	132 56			4,439 75				10 00	4,622 31
	Walkerton	100 00			4,344 00				150 75	35 00	4,629 75
Ottawa	Moose Factory	20 00				1,703 00					1,723 00
Perth	[illegible]ior	20 00	5,220 73							25 00	5,265 73
	Eganville	20 00	628 38			4,850 25					6,498 63
	Carleton Place	20 00	814 70							25 00	859 70
	[illegible]h Bay	110 00	13,879 08		6,536 59	11,464 50	36 00			25 00	32,051 17
	Pembroke	225 00	7,675 47			8,768 45	837 93			25 00	17,531 85
	Renfrew	40 00	6,833 57							35 00	6,908 57
	Sturgeon Falls	25 00	22,503 71				21 00			25 00	22,574 71
	Sudbury	40 00	14,844 78							10 00	14,894 78
Peterborough	[illegible]rg	20 00	5,765 94							45 00	5,830 94
	Port Hope	295 00	2,976 79		10,954 49					25 00	14,251 28
Port Arthur	Wabigoon	20 00	3,177 03								3,197 03
Prescott	[illegible]	195 00	1,879 72		6,049 50	651 30	2,040 00		27 00	25 00	13,867 52
	Gananoque	20 00	2,535 67							10 00	2,565 67
St. Catharines	Beamsville									5 00	5 00
	[illegible]lle	95 00	1,432 36			239 32	898 20			10 00	2,674 88
	Fort Erie									50 00	50 00
	Grimsby									5 00	5 00
	Humberstone	75 00				91 50	351 30				517 80
	Merritton								30 00	10 00	40 00
	Niagara									10 00	10 00
	Niagara Falls	75 00				301 90	951 60			25 00	1,353 50
	Port [illegible]	137 50			6,223 50	120 90	252 00				6,733 90
	Port Dalhousie									10 00	10 00
	Queenston								10 00		10 00
	[illegible]ld									10 00	10 00
	[illegible]d	75 00				108 10	559 65			10 00	752 75
Stratford	Goderich	70 00	258 71		615 00						943 71
	Listowel	125 00			4,380 00	1,004 50	3,627 00				9,136 50
	Palmerston	220 00			12,957 75				45 00		13,222 75
Toronto	Barrie	200 00			4,513 50	36 00					4,749 50
	[illegible]y	100 00			3,440 88						3,540 88
	Orillia	100 00			942 48						1,042 48
	Sault Ste. Marie	220 00	3,818 80		10,590 00	707 20	1,436 10				6,772 10
Windsor	[illegible]n	190 00	29,656 07			1,309 78	4,469 14			25 00	35,649 99
	Kingsville	102 50				143 00	711 91			10 00	967 41
	Leamington	200 00				768 20	2,293 38			10 00	3,271 58
Joliette	Berthierville	187 50	5,162 40						8,340 00		13,689 90
	L'Epiphanie	140 00				1,166 01	4,067 95				5,373 96
Montreal	St. [illegible]	60 00	28,246 09								28,306 09
	Valleyfield	40 00	40,920 92				66 00				41,026 92
Quebec	Fraserville	40 00	8,239 31							25 00	8,304 31
	Gaspé	40 00	2,309 25			1,190 00					3,539 25
	Rimouski	20 00	5,574 04								5,594 04
	Ste. Flavie	10 00	248 24								258 24
Sherbrooke	Granby	340 00				150,469 81	24,508 29				175,318 10
	Lake Megantic		2,619 30								2,619 30
St. Hyacinthe	Sorel	100 00	38,070 82							25 00	38,195 82

APPENDIX C—*Concluded.*

STATEMENT showing the Amount of Excise and other Revenues collected at each of the undermentioned Out-Offices, during the Fiscal Year ended June 30, 1906—*Concluded.*

Divisions.	Out-Offices.	Licenses.	Spirits.	Malt Liquor.	Malt.	Tobacco.	Cigars.	Manufactures in Bond.	Other Receipts.	Electric Light Inspection Fees.	Totals.
		$ cts.	$ cts.	$ cts.	$ cts.	$ cts.	$ cts.	$ cts.	$ cts.	$ cts.	$ cts.
St. Hyacinthe *Con.*	St. Johns, Que.	90 00	24,803 26					3,368 67	605 75		28,867 68
	Victoriaville	20 00	15,775 45							50 00	15,845 45
Three Rivers	Grand Mére	20 00	4,911 93								4,931 93
	Louiseville	20 00	10,334 51								10,354 51
St. John	Chatham	20 00				13,141 5				30 0	13,191 75
	Fredericton	20 00				17,463 50			4 00	25 00	17,512 50
	Moncton	40 00				15,066 00			2 00	25 00	15,133 00
	Newcastle	20 00				3,295 50				25 00	3,340 50
	Sackville	20 00				3,041 62				10 00	3,071 62
	Sussex	20 00				2,776 00			1 00	10 00	2,807 00
	St. Stephen	20 00	116 54			4,021 75			6 00	25 00	4,192 29
	W ck	40 00	669 45			2,683 00				15 00	3,407 45
Halifax.	Amherst	20 00	1,719 61			811 00				25 00	2,575 61
	Truro.	20 00				11,309 00				25 00	11,354 00
	Yarmouth	135 00				6,984 93	1,216 80			5 00	8,341 73
Pictou	Antigonish	40 00				2,170 50				10 00	2,220 50
	N Glasgow	20 00				10,012 75				25 00	10,057 75
	North Sydney	20 00				2,963 00				25 00	3,008 00
	Sy dey	77 50	9,190 69			44 00	90 90			60 00	9,463 09
Calgary	Edmonton	425 00	37,667 82		11,560 82	11,687 [illegible]	2,932 20		66 00	25 00	64,364 48
	Lethbridge	235 00	2,644 76		4,683 41	4,689 47	485 40			10 00	12,748 04
	Maple Creek	20 00	360 53								80 53
	Medicine Hat		45 54								45 54
	Pincher Creek	20 00	753 43								73 43
	Wetaskiwin	40 00	10,016 50						12 00	10 00	10,078 50
Winnipeg	Main									5 00	5 00
	Brandon	87 50	65,263 28		11,035 00	5,470 20	4,751 70		42 00	25 00	79,934 68
	Carman									10 00	10 00
	Dauphin									5 00	5 00
	Estevan									5 00	5 00
	Gr ta	20 00	1,211 42								[illegible] 42
	Indian Head		1,058 56							5 0	1,063 56
	Kenora	90 00	22,946 73		13 25	4,682 75			24 00	25 00	27,781 73
	Morden	20 00	5,083 35							10 00	5,113 35

	Minnedosa									10 00	10 00
	Moosejaw									25 00	25 00
	Neepawa									25 0	25 00
	Portage la Prairie	115 0	23,880 71			3,593 73	871 20		12 00	25 00	28,497 64
	Prince Albert	70 0	5,057 53		2,325 00					10 00	7,462 53
	Rainy River	20 00	6,627 65								6,647 65
	Regina	67 50	8,653 79			22 40	54 60			25 00	8,823 19
	Saskatoon	40 0	7,077 29								7,117 29
	Selkirk	20 00	3,147 53							10 00	3,177 53
	Virden	20 00	7,443 33								7,463 33
Vancouver	[illegible]a	50 00									50 00
	[illegible]lin	50 00									50 00
	[illegible]k	160 00	9,950 47	839 38	276 12						11,225 97
	Fernie	145 00	13,902 01	228 75	7,194 50		670 91				22,141 17
	Golden	20 00	3,027 18								3,047 18
	[illegible]d Forks	120 00	3,367 68		913 75						4,401 43
	Greenwood	70 00	14,241 76		932 40						15,244 16
	Hedley	25 00			122 58						147 58
	Kamloops	125 0		1,345 30	966 14		3,591 00				6,027 44
	Kelowna						23 40				23 40
	Michel	20 00	2,087 29								2,107 29
	Moyie	50 00									50 00
	Nelson	240 00	27,897 95	970 70	3,422 33		2,558 65				35,089 63
	New Westminster	200 00		1,653 90	3,495 83		5,426 10				0,775 83
	Phoenix	50 00			600 00						650 0
	Revelstoke	215 00	8,434 51	324 22	952 04	148 75	846 00				0,920 52
	Rossland	145 00	8,463 11	352 65	2,743 96		1,038 00				12,742 72
	Sandon	50 00			903 31						953 31
	[illegible]ut Lake	50 00			218 85						268 85
	Vernon	155 00	4,935 37	100 10	242 70		141 30				5,574 47
	Ymir	50 00									50 00
Victoria	[illegible]ith	20 00	46 83								66 83
	Nanaimo	370 0	3,820 77		8,876 12	721 00	2,064 60		13 00	25 00	5,[illegible]90 49
		11,434 50	1,132,542 03	5,815 00	242,771 03	352,941 55	110,483 51	4,973 26	19,141 29	1,820 00	1,881,922 17

W. J. GERALD,
Deputy Minister.

INLAND REVENUE DEPARTMENT,
OTTAWA, August 29, 1906.

FINANCIAL RETURNS, 1905-1906

No. 1.—GENERAL REVENUES ACCOUNT, 1905-1906.

DR. CR.

Memo. of Refunds deducted below.	Amounts deposited to the credit of the Receiver General.	Balances due June 30, 1906.	Totals.	SERVICES.	Revenues of previous years not collected July 1, 1905.	Revenues accrued, 1905-1906.	Totals.
$ cts.	$ cts.	$ cts.	$ cts.		$ cts.	$ cts.	$ cts.
253,261 38	14,201,452 48	13,554 92	14,215,007 40	Excise and Seizures, per Statement No. 3	13,473 72	14,201,533 68	14,215,007 40
....	3,608 00	27,940 17	31,548 17	Hydraulic and other rents, per Statement No. 5	27,901 17	3,647 00	31,548 17
....	965 50	12,472 16	13,437 66	Minor Public Works, per Statement No. 6	12,462 16	975 50	3,437 66
....	72,979 43	196 21	73,175 64	Weights and Measures, per Statements Nos 19(A) and 19(B)	241 78	72,933 86	73,175 64
....	41,439 25	....	41,439 25	Gas Inspection, per Statement No. 21	....	41,439 25	41,439 25
....	35,099 75	....	35,099 75	Electric Light Inspection, per Statement No. 23	....	35,099 75	35,099 75
....	11,380 80	....	11,380 80	Law Stamps, per Statements Nos. 10 and 18	....	11,380 80	11,380 80
....	....	45 04	45 04	Bill Stamps, per Statement No. 9	45 04	....	45 04
....	3,102 30	....	3,102 30	Sundry Minor Revenues, per Statement No. 11	....	3,102 30	3,102 30
....	65,530 18	....	65,530 18	Methylated Spirits, per Statement No. 25	....	65,530 18	65,530 18
253,261 38	14,435,557 69	....	14,489,766 19		....	14,435,642 32	14,489,766 19
....	253,261 38	....	253,261 38	LESS—Refunds, as per Statement No. 16	....	253,261 38	253,261 38
....	14,182,296 31	54,208 50	14,236,504 81	Totals	54,123 87	14,182,380 94	14,236,504 81

INLAND REVENUE DEPARTMENT,
OTTAWA, August 29, 1906.

W. J. GERALD,
Deputy Minister.

DR. No. 2.—GENERAL EXPENDITURES

Balances due to Collectors, &c., July 1, 1905.	Expenditures Authorized by the Department.			Balances due by Collectors, &c., June 30, 1906.	Totals.	Services.
	Salaries.	Contingencies.	Seizures.			
$ cts.	$ cts.	$ cts.	$ cts.	$ cts.	$ cts.	
49 08	376,035 42	121,400 28	552 21	343 98	498,380 97	Excise and Seizures per Statement No. 4
....	....	....	2,475 16	......	2,475 16	Excise Seizures distributed per Statement No. 4, Appendix B.
....	2,691 51	7,877 38	....	....	10,568 89	Preventive Service, per Statement No. 7
....	11,866 15	15,496 57	....	....	27,362 72	Adulteration of Food, per Statement No. 8 and Appendix B.
....	....	9 29	....	....	9 29	Sundry minor Expenditures, per Statement No. 12
....	53,967 12	7,904 67	....	16 66	61,888 45	Departmental Expenditures, per Statement No. 17
....	59,232 58	32,280 09	6 20	193 26	91,712 13	Weights and Measures, per Statements Nos. 20 (A) and 20 (B)
....	22,557 71	6,505 55	....	212 88	29,276 14	Gas Inspection, per Statement No. 22
....	4,592 12	5,262 10	....	....	9,854 22	Electric Light Inspection, per Statement No. 24
....	4,549 77	43,917 30	....	....	48,467 07	Methylated Spirits, per Statement No. 25
49 08	535,492 38	240,653 23	3,033 57	766 78	779,995 04	Totals

INLAND REVENUE DEPARTMENT,
OTTAWA, August 29, 1906.

ACCOUNT, 1905-1906. CR.

Balances due by Collectors, &c., July 1, 1905.	Amounts disbursed by the Receiver General on requisition of the Department.	Deductions from Salaries for				Balances due to Collectors, &c., June 30, 1906.	Totals.
		Superannuation.	Insurance.	Retirement.	Guarantee.		
$ cts.	$ cts.	$ cts.	$ cts.	$ cts.	$ cts.	$ cts.	$ cts.
343 98	484,562 81	4,910 52	158 16	6,511 24	1,290 47	603 79	498,380 97
....	2,475 16	....	......	....	....	....	2,475 16
....	10,563 13	....	....	....	5 76	......	10,568 89
....	27,247 76	114 96	....	....	....	....	27,362 72
....	9 29	....	....	....	....	....	9 29
16 66	60,510 41	631 29	116 40	613 69	....	......	61,888 45
193 26	91,024 30	308 86	22 33	....	163 38	....	91,712 13
212 88	28,774 95	159 44	....	5 00	123 87	....	29,276 14
....	9,846 57	....	....	....	7 65	....	9,854 22
....	48,367 03	....	....	100 04	....	......	48,467 07
766 78	763,381 41	6,125 07	296 89	7,229 97	1,591 13	603 79	779,995 04

W. J. GERALD,
Deputy Minister.

EXCISE,

No. 3.—Collection Divisions

Balances due July 1, 1905.	Amount Accrued during the Year, including License Fees.							
	Spirits.	Malt Liquor.	Malt.	Tobacco.	Cigars.	Acetic Acid.	Bonded manufactures.	Seizures.
$ cts.	$ cts.	$ cts.	$ cts.	$ cts.	$ cts.	$ cts.	$ cts.	$ cts.
	120,680 22	50 00	7,016 56	4,359 55	2,925 00			3 00
112 61	35,814 52	150 00	10,779 80	9,681 88	29,382 45		1,654 59	
	6,465 58			143 00				
	462,363 74	400 00	93,219 60	16,916 76	22,767 90		50 00	
	268,829 30	100 00	60,533 68	436,719 93	93,414 46		5,439 20	
	65,445 48	100 00	7,551 13	19,067 12	17,643 12		2,973 55	
	68,604 29	300 00	75,235 93	71,110 00	187,226 34			100 00
	304,761 75	150 00	11,758 00	38,288 25	1,694 55		309 64	270 00
	11,798 30	300 00	18,937 28	39,856 00	3,222 30			
	106,990 41	50 00	6,701 09	25,006 70	981 93		50 00	
	44,182 20	150 00	21,586 69	148 40	838 20			
	34,986 44	87 50	1,849 38	5,593 13	185 85			
	107,725 50	100 00	19,460 90	656 30	2,115 00		300 00	
	11,816 16	100 00	19,077 82	2,145 22	10,057 05			1 80
	37,337 66	200 00	19,827 02	11,648 55	11,198 40			50 00
	765,582 23	700 00	249,827 13	217,667 96	130,115 61	1,299 80	21,699 69	270 00
	122,836 69	100 00	58,774 03	15,572 68	11,184 15		500 00	
522 89								
635 50	2,876,220 47	3,037 50	682,136 04	914,581 43	524,952 31	1,299 80	32,976 67	694 80
	47,000 24			5,368 13	8,789 45			35 00
990 49	1,697,751 66		259,345 73	2,807,966 08	372,665 16	356 29	9,967 98	883 68
39 45	514,379 35	475 00	70,243 09	156,720 96	49,326 34		843 37	375 00
	169,980 21	250 00	22,463 55	165,319 95	54,219 02		300 00	
	126,158 61		1,952 20	2,799 22	17,117 58		4,515 35	55 00
	68,551 95			755 13	3,113 81			
3,295 57								
4,325 51	2,623,822 02	725 00	354,004 57	3,138,929 47	505,231 36	356 29	15,626 70	1,348 68
	154,562 54	100 00	24,120 00	105,280 04	14,956 18		2,320 96	1,250 00
1,442 62								
1,442 62	154,562 54	100 00	24,120 00	105,280 04	14,956 18		2,320 96	1,250 00
	56,230 67	150 00	41,323 66	75,163 44	3,952 86			
	9,190 69			23,501 53	128 40			
5,860 50								
5,860 50	65,421 36	150 00	41,323 66	98,664 97	4,081 26			
				54,202 18				
	658,080 11	844 80	76,514 54	355,308 89	53,458 30		3,432 36	
	109,673 91	200 00	46,152 09	50,075 72	5,830 26			
	767,754 02	1,044 80	122,666 63	405,384 61	59,288 56		3,432 36	

1905–1906.

in Account with Revenues.

Other Receipts.	Total Duties Accrued.	Total Debits.	Divisions.	Deposited to the Credit of the Receiver General.	Balances due June 30, 1906.	Total Credits.
$ cts.	$ cts.	$ cts.		$ cts.	$ cts.	$ cts.
1,671 15	136,705 48	136,705 48	..Belleville	136,705 48	....	136,705 48
640 00	88,103 24	88,215 85	. Brantford	88,103 24	112 61	88,215 85
65 00	6,673 58	6,673 58	..Cornwall	6,673 58	....	6,673 58
5,463 50	601,181 50	601,181 50	..Guelph	601,181 50	.. ..	601,181 50
3,257 70	868,294 27	868,294 27	..Hamilton	868,294 27	....	868,294 27
407 00	113,187 40	113,187 40	..Kingston	113,187 40	.. ...	113,187 40
183 16	402,759 72	402,759 72	..London	402,759 72	....	402,759 72
390 00	357,622 19	357,622 19	..Ottawa	357,622 19	.. ..	357,622 19
100 00	74,213 88	74,213 88	..Owen Sound	74,213 88	....	74,213 88
641 34	140,421 47	140,421 47	..Perth	140,421 47	....	140,421 47
100 00	67,005 49	67,005 49	..Peterborough	67,005 49	.. ..	67,005 49
210 00	42,912 30	42,912 30	..Port Arthur	42,912 30	....	42,912 30
1,534 17	131,891 87	131,891 87	..Prescott	131,891 87	....	131,891 87
80 00	43,278 05	43,278 05	..St. Catharines	43,278 05	....	43,278 05
100 00	80,361 63	80,361 63	..Stratford	80,361 63	....	80,361 63
8,867 11	1,396,029 53	1,396,029 53	..Toronto	1,396,029 53	....	1,396,029 53
11,319 87	520,287 42	520,287 42	..Windsor	520,287 42	....	520,287 42
....	....	522 89	..Suspense Account	....	522 89	522 89
35,030 00	5,070,929 02	5,071,564 52	*Ontario*	5,070,929 02	635 50	5,071,564 52
8,360 00	69,552 82	69,552 82	..Joliette	69,552 82	....	69,552 82
3,400 73	5,152,812 31	5,153,802 80	..Montreal	5,152,756 79	1,046 01	5,153,802 80
488 15	792,576 26	792,615 71	..Quebec	792,584 51	31 20	792,615 71
180 00	412,512 73	412,512 73	..Sherbrooke	412,512 73	....	412,512 73
1,105 75	153,703 71	153,703 71	..St. Hyacinthe	153,703 71	....	153,703 71
120 00	72,540 89	72,540 89	..Three Rivers	72,540 89	....	72,540 89
... .	....	3,295 57	..Suspense Account	......	3,295 57	3,295 57
13,654 63	6,653,698 72	6,658,024 23	*Quebec*	6,653,651 45	4,372 78	6,658,024 23
913 10	303,502 82	303,502 82	..St. John	303,461 39	41 43	303,502 82
....	....	1,442 62	Suspense Account	....	1,442 62	1,442 62
913 10	303,502 82	304,945 44	*New Brunswick*	303,461 39	1,484 05	304,945 44
290 00	177,110 63	177,110 63	..Halifax	177,110 63	....	177,110 63
120 00	32,940 62	32,940 62	..Pictou	32,940 62	....	32,940 62
....	....	5,860 50	..Suspense Account	....	5,860 50	5,860 50
410 00	210,051 25	215,911 75	*Nova Scotia*	210,051 25	5,860 50	215,911 75
....	54,202 18	54,202 18	..Charlottetown, P.E.I	54,202 18	....	54,202 18
1,084 00	1,148,723 00	1,148,723 00	..Winnipeg	1,148,723 00	... .	1,148,723 00
360 00	212,291 98	212,291 98	..Calgary	212,291 98	.. ..	212,291 98
1,444 00	1,361,014 98	1,361,014 98	*Manitoba and N.W.T.*	1,361,014 98	.. ..	1,361,014 98

EXCISE,

No. 3.—Collection Divisions

Balances due July 1, 1905.	Amount Accrued during the Year, including License Fees.							
	Spirits.	Malt Liquor.	Malt.	Tobacco.	Cigars.	Acetic Acid.	Bonded manufactures.	Seizures.
$ cts.	$ cts.	$ cts.	$ cts.	$ cts.	$ cts.	$ cts.	$ cts.	$ cts.
1,202 09	189,845 08	2,761 10	44,819 93	88,038 56	27,399 91	....	1,758 04	207 50
7 50	106,309 35	2,147 30	20,600 92	34,702 34	11,025 93	....	....	....
1,209 59	296,154 43	4,908 40	65,420 85	122,740 90	38,425 84	....	1,758 04	207 50
....	11,965 24	37 50	2,771 38	2,564 63	....	....	... .	....
13,473 72	6,795,900 08	10,003 20	1,292,443 13	4,842,348 23	1,146,935 51	1,656 09	56,114 73	3,500 98
....	82,826 97	....	83,027 44	86,768 81	313 16	....	25 00	.. ....
....	6,713,073 11	10,003 20	1,209,415 69	4,755,579 42	1,146,622 35	1,656 09	56,089 73	3,500 98

Inland Revenue Department,
Ottawa, August 29, 1906.

1905-1906—*Concluded.*

in Account with Revenues.

Other Receipts.	Total Duties Accrued.	Total Debits.	Divisions.	Deposited to the Credit of the Receiver General.	Balances due June 30, 1906.	Total Credits.
$ cts.	$ cts.	$ cts.		$ cts.	$ cts.	$ cts.
890 00	355,720 12	356,922 21	..Vancouver	355,720 12	1,202 09	356,922 21
200 00	174,985 84	174,993 34	..Victoria	174,993 34	... .	174,993 34
1,090 00	530,705 96	531,915 55	......*British Columbia*......	530,713 46	1,202 09	531,915 55
90 00	17,428 75	17,428 75	..Yukon	17,428 75	....	17,428 75
52,631 73	14,201,533 68	14,215,007 40	........Totals.............	14,201,452 48	13,554 92	14,215,007 40
300 00	253,261 38	253,261 38	..Less refunds as per statement No. 16..........	....	....	....
52,331 73	13,948,272 30	....	..Net Revenue	. ...	....	....

W. J. GERALD,
Deputy Minister.

EXCISE,

DR. No. 4.—COLLECTION DIVISIONS

Balances due by Collectors, July 1, 1905.	Amounts received from Department to meet Expenditures.	Deductions from Salaries for				Balances due to Collectors, June 30, 1906.	Totals.	Divisions.
		Superannuation.	Insurance.	Retirement.	Guarantee.			
$ cts.	$ cts.	$ cts.	$ cts.	$ cts.	$ cts.	$ cts.	$ cts.	
43 98	10,671 24	194 84		63 72	29 28		11,003 06	Belleville
	7,100 99	93 92		96 84	18 96		7,310 71	Brantford
	1,162 92	21 96			3 60		1,188 48	Cornwall
	19,371 28	355 38		107 19	53 95		19,887 80	Guelph
	21,980 18	272 72		333 64	68 16		22,654 70	Hamilton
	8,535 20	100 46		42 24	26 40		8,704 30	Kingston
	21,548 22	324 52	71 76	275 68	62 64	92 81	22,375 63	London
	8,570 29	81 80		227 38	29 52		8,908 99	Ottawa
	5,979 44	54 54		61 57	15 36		6,110 91	Owen Sound
	8,452 69	55 44		244 26	38 88		8,791 27	Perth
	3,881 52	30 00		112 50	12 96		4,036 98	Peterborough
	2,014 32			34 28	8 75		2,057 35	Port Arthur
	11,256 60	120 30	44 64	168 73	33 84		11,624 11	Prescott
	5,449 71	112 90		51 17	18 72		5,632 50	St. Catharines
	6,661 99	54 34		192 86	23 04		6,935 23	Stratford
	43,252 14	612 58	41 76	704 47	127 32		44,738 27	Toronto
	23,817 57	287 36		474 36	80 76	49 08	24,709 13	Windsor
	8,672 11	81 28			27 00		8,780 39	District Inspectors
43 98	218,381 41	2,854 34	158 16	3,190 89	679 14	141 89	225,449 81	*Ontario*
	8,686 81	28 44		315 83	26 85		9,057 93	Joliette
	48,233 47	533 38		1,007 71	163 25		49,937 81	Montreal
	20,198 67	177 93		259 79	49 00		20,685 39	Quebec
	7,077 18	63 05		177 85	24 48		7,342 56	Sherbrooke
	13,485 54	100 35		330 79	43 17		13,959 85	St. Hyacinthe
	3,353 15	46 78		35 50	11 56		3,446 99	Three Rivers
	5,439 96	50 00		125 00	18 00		5,632 96	District Inspectors
	106,474 78	999 93		2,252 47	336 31		110,063 49	*Quebec*
	9,276 57	153 40		33 81	31 62		9,495 40	St. John
	3,082 20	50 00			9 00		3,141 20	District Inspector
	12,358 77	203 40		33 81	40 62		12,636 60	*New Brunswick*
	12,908 10	230 99		19 96	41 76		13,200 81	Halifax
	2,869 64	21 96		71 88	9 36		2,972 84	Pictou
	15,777 74	252 95		91 84	51 12		16,173 65	*Nova Scotia*
100 00	2,387 65	33 16			6 48		2,527 29	*Charlottetown, P.E.I.*
200 00	17,958 27	219 44		315 47	54 00		18,747 18	Winnipeg
	5,485 43	47 29		82 41	16 98	461 90	6,094 01	Calgary, N.W.T
	3,934 65	50 00			9 00		3,993 65	District Inspector
200 00	27,378 35	316 73		397 88	79 98	461 90	28,834 84	*Manitoba and N.W.T.*

1905-1906.

in Account with Expenditures. CR.

Balances due to Collectors, July 1, 1905.	Expenditures Authorized by the Department.						Balances due by Collectors, June 30, 1906.	Totals.
	Salaries.	Seizures Expenditures.	Special Assistance	Rent.	Travelling Expenses.	Sundries.		
$ cts.	$ cts.	$ cts.	$ cts.	$ cts.	$ cts.	$ cts.	$ cts.	$ cts.
....	10,222 37	....	299 06	....	254 00	183 65	43 98	11,003 06
....	5,809 51	....	628 75	....	663 40	209 05	....	7,310 71
....	1,099 98	....	....	....	....	88 50	....	1,188 48
....	18,643 90	16 00	....	150 00	505 66	572 24	....	19,887 80
....	20,987 79	....	1,258 17	....	107 75	300 99	....	22,654 70
....	7,655 74	....	299 06	270 00	98 45	381 05	....	8,704 30
....	21,614 97	12 85	120 00	....	287 60	340 21	....	22,375 63
....	8,649 82	87 15	....	....	....	172 02	....	8,908 99
....	5,465 97	....	26 03	125 00	363 60	130 31	....	6,110 91
....	8,059 85	36 05	113 61	120 00	167 15	294 61	....	8,791 27
....	3,750 00	....	....	....	129 65	157 33	....	4,036 98
....	1,787 08	....	....	....	160 10	110 17	....	2,057 35
....	10,301 77	....	999 84	....	76 40	246 10	....	11,624 11
....	5,244 81	....	....	48 00	184 40	155 29	....	5,632 50
....	6,577 40	9 35	....	....	138 55	209 93	....	6,935 23
....	43,125 25	15 60	130 48	50 00	769 00	647 94	....	44,738 27
49 08	23,524 71	....	300 00	84 00	349 50	401 84	....	24,709 13
....	7,399 96	....	....	200 00	1,020 72	159 71	....	8,780 39
49 08	209,920 88	177 00	4,175 00	1,047 00	5,275 93	4,760 94	43 98	225,449 81
....	7,747 11	....	478 41	....	99 35	733 06	....	9,057 93
....	44,681 27	90 37	3,322 13	....	772 50	1,071 54	....	49,937 81
....	14,524 33	131 39	4,398 24	....	597 91	1,033 52	....	20,685 39
....	6,714 91	....	....	....	418 39	209 26	....	7,342 56
....	11,042 71	....	2,062 32	144 00	77 00	633 82	....	13,959 85
....	3,055 01	....	245 91	....	52 50	93 57	....	3,446 99
....	5,000 00	....	....	....	568 94	64 02	....	5,632 96
....	92,765 34	221 76	10,507 01	144 00	2,586 59	3,838 79	....	110,063 49
....	8,471 37	127 65	504 58	....	129 65	262 15	....	9,495 40
....	2,500 00	....	....	....	613 05	28 15	....	3,141 20
....	10,971 37	127 65	504 58	....	742 70	290 30	....	12,636 60
....	12,778 26	....	....	....	157 50	265 05	....	13,200 81
....	2,539 98	21 80	....	....	225 06	186 00	....	2,972 84
....	15,318 24	21 80	....	....	332 56	451 05	....	16,173 65
....	2,350 00	....	....	....	....	77 29	100 00	2,527 29
....	15,338 05	....	1,416 26	180 00	1,135 67	477 20	200 00	18,747 18
....	3,599 13	....	569 82	15 00	1,134 65	775 41	....	6,094 01
....	2,500 00	....	....	....	1,393 10	100 55	....	3,993 65
....	21,437 18	....	1,986 08	195 00	3,663 42	1,353 16	200 00	28,834 84

EXCISE,

No. 4.—COLLECTION DIVISIONS in

Balances due by Collectors, July 1, 1905.	Amounts received from Department to meet Expenditures.	Deductions from Salaries for				Balances due to Collectors, June 30, 1906.	Totals.	Divisions.
		Superannuation.	Insurance.	Retirement.	Guarantee.			
$ cts.	$ cts.	$ cts.	$ cts.	$ cts.	$ cts.	$ cts.	$ cts.	
....	16,612 77	67 96	......	474 43	60 46	....	17,215 62	..Vancouver..............
....	6,381 38	141 09	......	19 96	20 16	....	6,562 59	..Victoria..... ....
....	2,950 34	24 96	......	....	9 00	....	2,984 30	..District Inspector........
....	25,944 49	234 01	......	494 39	89 62	....	26,762 51	....*British Columbia*.......
....	942 84	....	.....	49 96	7 20	....	1,000 00	....*Yukon*........... .....
....	472 91	4 00	......	....	....	....	476 91	. Inspector of Bonded Factories..... ... .
....	1,159 80	6 00	......	....	....	....	1,165 80	..Inspector of Breweries and Malt Houses... ..
....	767 17	....	......	....	....	....	767 17	..Inspector of Distilleries..
....	294 00	6 00	......	....	....	....	300 00	..Inspector of Tobacco Factories.... .. ..
....	7,402 40	....	......	....	....	....	7,402 40	..General Expenditures...
....	314 00	....	......	....	....	....	314 00	..Legal Expenses. ......
....	39,000 00	....	......	....	....	....	39,000 00	..Printing Tobacco Stamps
....	19 37	....	......	....	....	....	19 37	..Technical Translation...
....	4,013 94	....	......	....	....	....	4,013 94	..Printing ....
....	1,513 81	....	......	....	....	....	1,513 81	..Stationery..... ....
....	73 00	....	......	....	....	....	73 00	..Lithographing and Engraving, &c..........
....	10,493 95	....	......	....	....	....	10,493 95	..Commission to Customs Officers.. .. ..
....	34 77	....	......	....	....	....	34 77	..Commission on sale of Stamps for Canada Twist........ ... ...
....	8,259 67	....	......	....	....	....	8,259 67	..Duty-pay to Officers in charge of most important establishments....
....	1,097 99	....	......	....	....	....	1,097 99	..Provisional Allowance...
343 98	484,562 81	4,910 52	158 16	6,511 24	1,290 47	603 79	498,380 97	....*Grand Totals*..........

INLAND REVENUE DEPARTMENT,
OTTAWA, August 29th, 1906.

1905-1906—*Concluded.*

Account with Expenditures—*Concluded.*

Balances due to Collectors, July 1, 1905.	Expenditures Authorized by the Department.						Balances due by Collectors, June 30, 1906.	Totals.
	Salaries.	Seizures Expenditures.	Special Assistance	Rent.	Travelling Expenses.	Sundries.		
$ cts.	$ cts.	$ cts.	$ cts.	$ cts.	$ cts.	$ cts.	$ cts	$ cts.
....	12,892 61	4 00	2,183 10	586 00	739 31	810 60	....	17,215 62
....	5,679 84	....	600 00	....	91 10	191 65	....	6,562 59
....	2,499 96	....	....	....	484 34	....	....	2,984 30
....	21,072 41	4 00	2,783 10	586 00	1,314 75	1,002 25	....	26,762 51
....	1,000 00	....	....	....	....	....	....	1,000 00
....	300 00	....	....	....	175 85	1 06	....	476 91
....	300 00	....	....	....	865 80	....	....	1,165 80
....	300 00	....	....	....	460 05	7 12	....	767 17
....	300 00	....	....	....	....	....	....	300 00
....	....	....	....	....	....	7,402 40	....	7,402 40
....	....	....	....	....	....	314 00	....	314 00
....	....	....	....	....	....	39,000 00	....	39,000 00
....	....	....	....	....	....	19 37	....	19 37
....	....	....	....	....	....	4,013 94	....	4,013 94
....	....	....	....	....	....	1,513 81	....	1,513 81
....	....	....	....	....	....	73 00	....	73 00
....	....	....	....	....	....	10,493 95	....	10,493 95
....	....	....	....	....	....	34 77	....	34 77
....	....	....	....	....	....	8,259 67	....	8,259 67
....	....	....	....	....	....	1,097 99	....	1,097 99
49 08	376,035 42	552 21	19,955 77	1,972 00	15,467 65	84,004 86	343 98	498,380 97

W. J. GERALD,
Deputy Minister.

HYDRAULIC AND OTHER RENTS.

No. 5.—Summary Statement of Lessees Accounts, 1905–1906.

Dr. | Cr.

Balances due July 1, 1905.	Accrued during the Year ended June 30, 1906.	Totals.	—	Deposited to the credit of the Receiver General.	Balances due June 30, 1906.	Totals.
$ cts.	$ cts.	$ cts.		$ cts.	$ cts.	$ cts.
1,931 84	3,360 00	5,291 84	Chaudière Falls and Ottawa River	3,347 00	1,944 84	5,291 84
175 00	26 00	201 00	St. Lawrence River	1 00	200 00	201 00
70 00		70 00	Rivière du Lièvre		70 00	70 00
676 00	261 00	937 00	Sundry properties	260 00	677 00	937 00
			Land Sales.			
15,573 50		15,573 50	Principal accounts		15,573 50	15,573 50
9,474 83		9,474 83	Interest		9,474 83	9,474 83
27,901 17	3,647 00	31,548 17	Totals	3,608 00	27,940 17	31,548 17

Inland Revenue Department,
Ottawa, August 29, 1906.

W. J. GERALD,
Deputy Minister.

Dr. | **No. 6.—MINOR PUBLIC WORKS, 1905–1906.** | Cr.

Balances due July 1, 1905.	Accrued during the Year ended June 30, 1906.	Totals.	——	Deposited to the credit of the Receiver General.	Balances due June 30, 1906.	Totals.
$ cts.	$ cts.	$ cts.		$ cts.	$ cts.	$ cts.
			Bridges.			
2,600 62		2,600 62	Dunnville		2,600 62	2,600 62
			Ferries.			
	15 00	15 00	Buckingham and Cumberland	15 00		15 00
30 00	10 00	40 00	Clair Station and Kent		40 00	40 00
	10 00	10 00	Courtring and St. Clair	10 00		10 00
	10 00	10 00	Cross Point and Campbellton	10 00		10 00
20 00		20 00	Edmundston and Maine		20 00	20 00
	50 00	50 00	Fort Erie and Buffalo	50 00		50 00
1,736 79		1,736 79	Hull (old lease)		1,736 79	1,736 79
	200 50	200 50	La Passe and Gower Point	200 50		200 50
	6 00	6 00	Montebello and Alfred	6 00		6 00
	30 00	30 00	Niagara and Youngstown	30 00		30 00
	1 00	1 00	Ouellette Street, Detroit	1 00		1 00
	130 00	130 00	Pembroke and Allumette Island (new lease)	130 00		130 00
1 00		1 00	" " " (old lease)		1 00	1 00
	200 00	200 00	Prescott and Ogdensburg	200 00		200 00
	10 00	10 00	Queenston and Lewiston	10 00		10 00
	70 00	70 00	Quyon	70 00		70 00
	5 00	5 00	Rockliffe and Gatineau	5 00		5 00
	1 00	1 00	Sandwich and Detroit	1 00		1 00
	100 00	100 00	Sault St. Marie	100 00		100 00
30 00		30 00	St. Leonard and Van Buren		30 00	30 00
			Sundries.			
8,000 00		8,000 00	Dundas and Waterloo Road		8,000 00	8,000 00
	2 00	2 00	Government telegraph lines	2 00		2 00
	25 00	25 00	Wiarton docks	25 00		25 00
43 75		43 75	Part of building, Portland, N.B.		43 75	43 75
	100 00	100 00	Building, Ouellette Avenue, Windsor, Ont.	100 00		100 00
12,462 16	975 50	13,437 66	Totals	965 50	12,472 16	13,437 66

Inland Revenue Department,
Ottawa, August 29, 1906.

W. J. GERALD,
Deputy Minister.

PREVENTIVE SERVICE, 1905–1906.

DR. — No. 7.—IN ACCOUNT WITH EXPENDITURES. — CR.

Amounts received from Department to meet Expenditures.	Guarantee.	Totals.		Expenditures Authorized by the Department. Salaries.	Special Assistance.	Travelling Expenses.	Sundries.	Totals.
$ cts.	$ cts.	$ cts.		$ cts.	$ cts.	$ cts.	$ cts.	$ cts.
10 00		10 00	Ottawa, Ont			10 00		10 00
13 45		13 45	Peterborough, Ont			13 45		13 45
2,140 90	5 76	2,146 66	[illegible]o, Ont	1,299 96	799 92	44 10	2 68	2,146 66
303 25		303 25	Joliette, Que		300 00	3 25		303 25
621 70		621 70	M[illegible]al, Q[illegible]		600 00	21 70		621 70
3,506 30		3,506 30	[illegible], Que		3,474 84	31 46		3,506 30
636 26		636 26	St. [illegible]e, Que		591 66	44 60		636 26
52 20		52 20	Sherbrooke, Que			52 20		52 20
1,575 61		1,575 61	St. John, N.B	1,391 55		175 33	8 73	1,575 61
217 17		217 17	Halifax, N.S		199 92	17 25		217 17
1,070 38		1,070 38	Pictou, N.S		883 33	180 60	6 45	1,070 38
415 91		415 91	[illegible]l				415 91	415 91
10,563 13	5 76	10,568 89	Totals	2,691 51	6,849 67	593 94	433 77	10,568 89

W. J. GERALD,
Deputy Minister.

INLAND REVENUE DEPARTMENT,
OTTAWA, August 29, 1906.

FOOD INSPECTION, 1905–1906.

DR. **No. 8.—In Account with Expenditures.** CR.

Amounts received from Department to meet Expenditures.	Superannuation.	Totals.	—	Expenditures Authorized by the Department.					Totals.
				Salaries.	Special Assistance.	Rent.	Travelling Expenses.	Sundries.	
$ cts.	$ cts.	$ cts.		$ cts.	$ cts.	$ cts.	$ cts.	$ cts.	$ cts.
12,052 80	103 96	12,156 76	Chief Analyst	8,897 98	1,024 70	366 67	226 95	1,640 46	12,156 76
37 02		257 02	Kingston, Ont	100 00			53 25	03 77	37 02
45 70		45 70	Ottawa, Ont	186 48			136 75	92 47	45 70
1,046 87		1,046 87	Seaforth, Ont	500 00		120 00	291 35	35 52	1,046 87
105 63		105 63	Toronto, Ont	72 28			18 55	14 80	105 63
784 09	7 00	91 09	M[illegible]l, Que	350 00			207 70	23 39	91 09
82 28		82 28	Quebec, Que	189 70			194 58	98 00	82 28
85 25		85 25	St. Hyacinthe, Que	200 00			296 73	128 52	85 25
59 29	4 00	63 29	St. [illegible]n, N.B	200 00			155 90	107 39	63 29
94 91		594 91	Halifax, N.S	350 00			165 80	79 11	594 91
319 80		39 80	[illegible], P.E.I	200 00			55 65	64 15	39 80
38 22		38 22	Calgary, Man	200 00			62 05	76 17	38 22
680 01		680 01	Winnipeg, Man	200 00			366 10	13 91	680 01
19 71		19 71	Victoria, B.C	19 71					19 71
43 78		43 78	[illegible]r, B.C	200 00			115 20	98 58	13 78
6 95 64		6,915 64	General					6,915 64	6 95 64
31 23		31 23	Stationery					31 23	31 23
1,401 59		1,401 59	Printing					1,401 59	01 59
2 00		2 00	Lithographing					2 00	2 00
11 94		11 94	[illegible]					11 94	11 94
27,247 76	114 96	27,362 72	Totals	11,866 15	1,024 70	486 67	2,346 56	11,638 64	27,362 72

W. J. GERALD,
Deputy Minister.

Inland Revenue Department,
Ottawa, August 29, 1906.

BILL STAMPS.

DR. No. 9.—BILL STAMP Distributors account with the Inland Revenue Department. CR.

Balances July 1, 1905.		Totals.		Balances, June 30, 1906.		Totals.
Stamps on hand.	Cash on hand.			Stamps on hand.	Cash on hand.	
$ cts.	$ cts.	$ cts.		$ cts.	$ cts.	$ cts.
1,372 77		1,372 77	Post Office Department	1,372 77		1,372 77
	11 54	11 54	Belleville, ex-Collector E. R. Benjamin		11 54	11 54
	33 50	33 50	Three Rivers, ex-collector B. Lasalle		33 50	33 50
160 00		160 00	McLeod, Colonel J. F., Fort McLeod	160 00		160 00
1,532 77	45 04	1,577 81	Totals	1,532 77	45 04	1,577 81

W. J GERALD,
Deputy Minister.

INLAND REVENUE DEPARTMENT,
OTTAWA, August 29, 1906.

LAW STAMPS.

DR. No. 10.—LAW STAMPS in account with the Revenue Department. CR.

Stamps on hand July 1, 1905.	Stamps received from Department.	Totals.		Commission of 5 per cent allowed by Department on stamps sold.	Deposited to the Credit of the Receiver General.	Stamps on hand June 30, 1906.	Totals.
$ cts.	$ cts.	$ cts.		$ cts.	$ cts.	$ cts.	$ cts.
....	1,700 00	1,700 00	Cameron, R., Registrar, Supreme Court	85 00	1,615 00	....	1,700 00
....	3,679 00	3,679 00	Audette, L. A., Registrar, Exchequer Court	183 95	3,495 05	....	3,679 00
16,090 25	....	16,090 25	Lithgow, J. T., Dawson, Yukon Territorial Court	....	5,517 50	10,572 75	16,090 25
2,963 25	....	2,963 25	" " " Mining Court	....	753 25	2,210 00	2,963 25
19,053 50	5,379 00	24,432 50	Totals	268 95	11,380 80	12,782 75	24,432 50

W. J. GERALD,
Deputy Minister.

INLAND REVENUE DEPARTMENT,
OTTAWA, August 29, 1906.

DR. No. 11.—SUNDRY MINOR REVENUES, 1905-1906. CR.

Accrued during the Year ended June 30, 1906.	Totals.	—	Deposited to the credit of the Receiver General.	Totals.
$ cts.	$ cts.		$ cts.	$ cts.
628 00	628 00	....Fertilizer Inspection Fees.	628 00	628 00
2,462 50	2,462 50	....Adulteration of Food Fees......................	2,462 50	2,462 50
11 80	11 80	....Casual Revenue....................................	11 80	11 80
3,102 30	3,102 30	...........Totals................................	3,102 30	3,102 30

W. J. GERALD,
Deputy Minister.

INLAND REVENUE DEPARTEMENT,
OTTAWA, August 29, 1906.

DR. No. 12.—MINOR EXPENDITURES, 1905-1906. CR.

Amount received from Department to meet Expenditures.	Totals.	—	Contingencies.	Totals.
$ cts.	$ cts.		$ cts.	$ cts.
9 29	9 29	....Minor expenditures..................	9 29	9 29

W. J. GERALD,
Deputy Minister.

INLAND REVENUE DEPARTMENT,
OTTAWA, August 29, 1906.

No. 13.—STATEMENT showing the quantities of the several articles subject to Excise and the Duty

Articles Subject to Excise Duty.	1904.			
	Quantities.			Duty.
	Ex-Manufactory.	Ex-Warehouse.	Totals.	
	Gallons.	Gallons.	Gallons.	$ cts.
Spirits	6,458	3,481,287	3,487,745	6,601,801 10
	Imported.	*225,326	225,326	67,597 85
Totals	6,458	3,706,613	3,713,071	6,669,398 95
Malt liquor, the duty being paid on malt	27,335,985	....	27,335,985	2,489 00
	Lbs.	Lbs.	Lbs.	
Malt	....	75,430,347	75,430,347	1,131,455 78
Cigars—	No.	No.	No.	
Foreign	87,942,746	82,991,404	170,934,150	1,025,625 27
Canadian	1,609,040	591,200	2,200,240	6,600 72
Combination	3,588,387	3,762,425	7,350,812	22,052 48
Totals	93,140,173	87,345,029	180,485,202	1,054,278 47
Cigarettes—				
Foreign	204,350,900	1,241,400	205,592,300	620,581 90
Canadian	....	....	....	....
Combination	4,764,650	945,091	5,709,741	8,564 62
Totals	209,115,550	2,186,491	211,302,041	629,146 52
	Lbs.	Lbs.	Lbs.	
Tobacco from Foreign Leaf	785,548	7,036,102	7,821,650	1,955,412 87
" Canadian Leaf	2,927,747	66,104	2,993,851	149,692 64
" Combination	920,698	612,497	1,533,195	76,660 00
Snuff	178,057	....	178,057	32,702 23
Canadian twist	....	47,771	47,771	2,388 58
Totals	4,812,050	7,762,474	12,574,524	2,846,002 84
Raw leaf tobacco, foreign	....	12,139,700	12,139,700	1,278,455 09
Total duties on tobacco and cigarettes	....	....	....	4,124,457 93
Vinegar	....	....	....	42,743 28
Acetic acid	....	....	....	2,600 97
Licenses, spirits	....	....	....	2,750 00
" malt liquor	....	....	....	6,550 00
" malt	....	....	....	6,100 00
" cigars	....	....	....	16,545 00
" tobacco	....	....	....	3,221 00
" bonded manufacture	....	....	....	2,600 00
" acetic acid	....	....	....	100 00
Grand total duty	....	....	....	13,065,290 38

* Spirits imported for use in the manufacture of crude fulminate, on which duty at a rate of 30 cents

INLAND REVENUE DEPARTMENT,
OTTAWA, August 29, 1906.

Duty taken for consumption, during the years ended June 30, 1904, 1905 and 1906, accrued thereon.

1905.				1906.			
Quantities.			Duty.	Quantities.			Duty.
Ex-Manufactory.	Ex-Warehouse.	Totals.		Ex-Manufactory.	Ex-Warehouse.	Totals.	
Gallons.	Gallons.	Gallons.	$ cts.	Gallons.	Gallons.	Gallons.	$ cts.
200	3,112,843	3,113,043	5,899,444 47	3,765	3,545,785	3,549,550	6,721,008 08
Imported.	*160,208 634	160,208 634	48,062 37	Imported.	239,432	239,432	71,829 50
200	3,273,051 634	3,273,251 634	5,947,506 84	3,765	3,785,217	3,788,982	6,792,837 58
30,330,370	......	30,330,370	2,499 30	33,250,637	....	33,250,657	3,578 20
Lbs. 7,542	Lbs. 75,509,810	Lbs. 75,517,352	11,134,538 70	Lbs.	Lbs. 85,699,102	Lbs. 85,699,102	1,286,093 13
No. 88,060,472 2,069,190 2,896,820	No. 88,566,145 193,210 4,324,940	No. 176,626,617 2,262,400 7,221,760	1,059,780 16 6,787 20 21,665 28	No. 95,465,362 539,580 4,426,000	No. 87,928,975 628,020 4,839,405	No. 183,394,337 1,167,600 9,265,405	1,100,388 99 3,502 80 27,796 22
93,026,482	93,084,295	186,110,777	1,088,232 64	100,430,942	93,396,400	193,827,342	1,131,688 01
240,371,687	2,138,370	242,510,057	733,140 17	259,712,200	2,671,750	262,383,950	794,794 35
3,779,900	4,570,430	8,350,330	12,525 50	3,834,500	3,116,489	6,950,989	10,426 48
244,151,587	6,708,800	250,860,387	745,665 67	263,546,700	5,788,239	269,334,939	805,220 83
Lbs. 916,571 3,044,133 1,170,234 134,901	Lbs. 7,343,707 63,694 708,504 32,867	Lbs. 8,260,278 3,107,827 1,878,738 164,901 32,867	2,065,070 08 155,391 36 93,937 17 30,256 73 1,643 35	Lbs. 1,096,486 3,142,100 1,157,181 162,844	Lbs. 8,144,033 30,366 748,561 36,340	Lbs. 9,240,519 3,172,466 1,905,742 162,844 36,340	2,310,130 15 158,623 40 95,287 28 29,911 40 1,817 00
5,295,839	3,148,772 12,387,376	13,444,611 12,387,376	3,091,964 36 1,317,186 19	5,558,611	8,959,300 13,638,620	14,517,911 13,638,620	3,400,990 06 1,437,895 67
....	....	....	4,409,150 55	....	....	....	4,838,885 73
....	....	....	48,441 53	....	....	....	53,589 73
....	....	....	7,593 61	....	....	....	1,556 09
....	....	....	3,125 00	....	....	....	3,062 50
....	....	....	6,625 00	....	....	....	6,425 00
....	....	....	6,160 00	....	....	....	6,350 00
....	....	....	15,510 00	....	....	....	15,247 50
....	....	....	3,223 50	....	....	....	3,462 50
....	....	....	2,700 00	....	....	....	2,525 00
....	....	....	100 00	....	....	....	100 00
....	....	....	12,675,346 67	....	....	....	14,145,400 97

per gallon was collected and afterwards refunded on the exportation of the fulminate.

W. J. GERALD,
Deputy Minister.

No. 14.—Amounts deposited monthly to the credit of the Honourable the Receiver General on account of Inland Revenues during the Fiscal Year ended June 30, 1906.

—	Ontario.	Quebec.	New Brunswick.	Nova Scotia.	Prince Edward Island.	Manitoba, Alberta and Saskatchewan.	British Columbia.	Yukon.	Totals.
	$ cts.	$ cts.	$ cts.	$ cts.	$ cts.	$ cts.	$ cts.	$ cts.	$ cts.
July :—									
Excise	299,513 72	474,934 25	22,346 43	14,177 69	2,642 25	81,797 16	34,694 54	612 66	[illegible]018 70
" Seizures		25 00	450 00						475 00
Hydraulic and other Rents	1 00								1 00
Minor Public Works	1 00								1 00
Weights and Measures	1,103 66	950 00					11 80		2,065 46
Gas Inspection	38 50								38 50
Electric Light	298 00								298 00
Law Stamps (Supreme Court)	95 00								95 00
" (Exchequer Court)	95 00								95 00
" (Yukon Territor'l Court)								372 00	372 00
Electric Light Fees	2,405 00	490 00	235 00	315 00	40 00	300 00	270 00	25 00	4,080 00
Adulteration of Food Fees		5 00		5 00					10 00
Methylated Spirits	3,310 37	2,636 73	44 76			92 99			6,084 85
Totals	306,861 25	479,040 98	23,076 19	14,497 69	2,682 25	82,190 15	34,976 34	1,009 66	944,334 51
August :—									
Excise	395,757 18	554,436 51	24,958 10	17,080 08	5,555 29	99,877 34	43,185 82	3,133 44	1,143,983 76
" Seizures	135 00	45 00	250 00						430 00
Hydraulic and other Rents	5 00								5 00
Weights and Measures	2,575 89	2,696 37	123 84	358 18	52 56	962 20	50 50		6,819 54
Gas Inspection	1,593 75	753 25	27 50	11 25		138 25	148 00		2,672 00
Electric Light	494 50	379 00	58 50	8 25	26 00	373 00	282 00		1,621 25
Law Stamps (Exchequer Court)	19 00								19 00
" (Yukon Territor'l Court)								1,009 00	1,009 00
" " Mining "								114 25	114 25
Electric Light Fees	300 00	150 00		40 00		20 00	50 00		560 00
Fertilizers' Fees	4 00								4 00
Adulteration of Food Fees	5 00								5 00
Methylated Spirits	2,876 12	1,547 36	43 83						4,467 31
Totals	403,765 44	560,007 49	25,461 77	17,497 76	5,633 85	101,370 79	43,716 32	4,256 69	1,161,710 11
September :—									
Excise	383,683 64	548,072 00	27,829 25	18,768 55	4,655 62	115,662 80	38,725 29	2,790 13	1,140,187 28
" Seizures	50 00								50 00
Weights and Measures	2,573 30	2,576 79	101 93	133 38	49 00	904 91	31 45		6,370 76

Gas Inspection	1,843 25	949 50	36 00	23 50		32 00	50 50		2,934 75
Electric Light	612 00	375 00	49 75	19 25	31 50	137 75	229 25		1,454 50
Law Stamps (Supreme Court	237 50								237 50
" (Exchequer Court.)	733 40								733 40
" (Yukon Territor'l Court)								547 50	547 50
" " Mining "								110 50	110 50
Electric Light Fees	40 00	55 00		30 00			5 00		130 00
Fertilizers' Fees				6 00			4 00		10 00
Adulteration of Food Fees	20 00								20 00
Methylated Spirits	3,205 79	2,139 35	43 73	103 84		97 85	104 51		5,700 07
Totals	392,998 88	554,167 64	28,065 66	19,084 52	4,736 12	116,835 31	39,150 00	3,448 13	1,158,486 26
OCTOBER :—									
Excise	424,534 39	550,589 07	23,454 26	18,819 81	4,314 12	118,824 95	45,329 22	829 34	1,189,695 16
" Seizures		200 00	100 00						300 00
Hydraulic and other Rents							1 00		1 00
Weights and Measures	4,804 42	1,796 92	195 10	224 53	105 58	1,266 69	166 85		8,560 09
" " Seizures		5 00							5 00
Gas Inspection	2,135 25	526 00	123 00	41 00	10 00	136 50	127 00		3,098 75
Electric Light	783 50	507 75	102 25	157 50	36 75	264 25	339 50		2,191 50
Law Stamps (Supreme Court)	47 50								47 50
" (Exchequer Court)	380 00								380 00
" (Yukon Territor'l Court)								684 00	684 00
" " Mining "								81 00	81 00
Electric Light Fees	5 00	30 00		5 00					40 00
Fertilizers' Fees				3 00					3 00
Adulteration of Food Fees	19 00	5 00	12 00						36 00
Methylated Spirits	3,536 80	1,963 61	49 39	124 74		130 12			5,804 66
Totals	436,245 86	555,623 35	27,036 00	19,375 58	4,466 45	120,622 51	45,963 57	1,594 34	1,210,927 66
NOVEMBER :—									
Excise	526,489 07	611,553 97	30,914 59	22,164 39	5,826 02	117,625 11	43,454 34	788 75	1,358,816 24
" Seizures	25 00	126 20	200 00						351 20
Weights and Measures	2,831 80	1,522 87	224 62	198 08	113 69	824 51	92 00		5,807 57
Gas Inspection	2,352 00	579 25	43 25	37 50	20 75	130 75	142 25		3,305 75
" Seizures	5 00								5 00
Electric Light	1,264 50	665 00	94 00	107 25	19 00	436 25	244 50		2,830 50
Law Stamps (Supreme Court)	47 50								47 50
" (Exchequer Court)	286 90								286 90
" (Yukon Territor'l Court)								230 00	230 00
Elec. Light Fees	20 00	35 00							55 00
Fertilizers' Fees				3 00					3 00
Adulteration of Food Fees	20 00								20 00
" " Penalties	733 50	309 00	9 00	66 00	111 00	162 00			1,390 50
Methylated Spirits	3,738 60	2,808 85	92 17			330 69	124 34		7,094 65
Totals	537,813 87	617,600 14	31,577 63	22,576 22	6,090 46	119,509 31	44,057 43	1,018 75	1,380,243 81

No. 14.—Amounts deposited monthly to the credit of the Honourable the Receiver General on account of Inland Revenues during the Fiscal Year ended June 30, 1906—*Continued.*

—	Ontario.	Quebec.	New Brunswick.	Nova Scotia.	Prince Edward Island.	Manitoba, Alberta and Saskatchewan.	British Columbia.	Yukon.	Totals.
	$ cts.	$ cts.	$ cts.	$ cts.	$ cts.	$ cts.	$ cts.	$ cts.	$ cts.
December:—									
Excise	485,274 42	699,182 44	26,716 15	19,112 30	5,406 85	130,009 87	42,008 86	873 77	1,408,584 66
" Seizures	50 00	273 44							323 44
Hydraulic and other Rents	300 00						25 00		325 00
Minor Public Works	50 00								50 00
Weights and Measures	3,612 33	1,033 84	401 44	208 03	57 40	757 05	51 65	112 45	6,234 19
Gas Inspection	3,022 25	719 00	25 75	14 00		104 25	112 75		3,998 00
Electric Light	1,395 50	623 75	100 75	162 00	27 25	518 00	301 00		3,128 25
Law Stamps (Supreme Court)	95 00								95 00
" (Exchequer Court)	598 50								598 50
" (Yukon Terr'l Court)								335 00	335 00
" " Mining "								149 75	149 75
Electric Light Fees	10 00			5 00					15 00
Fertilizers' Fees	171 00			1 00					172 00
Adulteration of Food, Penalties	99 00	176 75	96 00	18 00		99 00	145 50		634 25
Methylated Spirits	2,394 28	1,279 14	48 07			98 64	130 51		3,950 64
Totals	497,072 28	703,288 36	27,388 16	19,520 33	5,491 50	131,586 81	42,775 27	1,470 97	1,428,593 68
January:—									
Excise	391,225 18	482,104 10	21,417 06	17,873 74	4,253 60	110,847 95	40,008 67	961 10	1,068,691 40
" Seizures	60 00	90 52	100 00						250 52
Hydraulic and other Rents	50 00								50 00
Minor Public Works	25 00								25 00
Weights and Measures	3,046 66	875 67	148 75	157 48	17 55	400 75	155 95	144 95	4,947 76
Gas Inspection	2,428 75	571 75	82 00	67 25	11 50	130 00	160 00		3,451 25
Electric Light	1,102 25	846 75	112 75	116 25	41 00	384 25	308 50		2,911 75
Law Stamps, (Supreme Court)	332 50								332 50
" (Exchequer Court)	294 50								294 50
" (Yukon Territor'l Court)								190 00	190 00
Electric Light Fees		10 00							10 00
Fertilizers Fees	38 00	6 00	18 00	27 00					89 00
Adulteration of Food, Fees		10 00							10 00
" " Penalties		33 00					14 00		47 00
Methylated Spirits	2,859 04	1,128 60	43 18	125 79					4,156 61

Casual Revenue....	10 00								10 00
Totals	401,471 88	485,676 39	21,921 74	18,367 51	4,323 65	111,762 95	40,647 12	1,296 05	1,085,467 29
FEBRUARY :—									
Excise	388,977 62	502,391 08	19,696 44	13,883 63	3,522 30	95,096 02	38,108 85	814 10	1,062,490 04
" Seizures	100 00	92 10	100 00						292 10
Hydraulic and other Rents	2,612 00	104 00		16 00			25 00		2,757 00
Minor Public Works	52 00						1 00		53 00
Weights and Measures	1,958 07	1,423 35	145 53	197 65	22 55	698 65	153 10		4,598 90
Gas Inspection	2,113 25	656 75	22 50	20 25		109 75	181 75		3,104 25
Electric Light	1,131 75	708 25	112 75	80 25	90 50	174 00	90 00		2,387 50
Law Stamps, (Supreme Court)	95 00								95 00
" (Exchequer Court)	228 00								228 00
" (Yukon Territor'l Court)								105 00	105 00
" " Mining Court								89 25	89 25
Electric Light Fees	10 00								10 00
Fertilizers Fees	138 00		15 00	24 00					177 00
Adulteration of Food, Fees	35 00								35 00
" " Penalties	64 00					18 00	36 75		118 75
Methylated Spirits	3,256 24	2,384 12	92 83						5,733 19
Totals	400,770 93	507,759 65	20,185 05	14,221 78	3,635 35	96,096 42	38,596 45	1,008 35	1,082,273 98
MARCH :—									
Excise	434,614 77	537,186 30	23,401 26	18,423 31	6,302 92	111,553 59	45,354 74	675 86	1,177,512 75
" Seizures	38 00	213 36	50 00						301 36
Hydraulic and other Rents	1 00						13 00		14 00
Weights and Measures	1,702 68	1,354 90	58 26	30 79	22 63	221 00	163 70		3,553 96
" " Seizures		10 00							10 00
Gas inspection	1,802 50	709 50	55 25	22 00	10 50	120 00	93 00		2,812 75
Electric Light	1,349 00	773 50	132 50	49 00	25 50	86 25	315 25		2,731 00
Law Stamps, (Supreme Court)	190 00								190 00
" (Exchequer Court)	161 50								161 50
" (Yukon Territor'l Court)								225 25	225 25
" " Mining Court								46 50	46 50
Electric Light Fees	5 00	15 00					5 00		25 00
Fertilizers Fees	17 00			18 00			27 00		62 00
Adulteration of Food, Penalties		75 00							75 00
Methylated Spirits	3,446 83	2,553 77	45 82	133 72		197 20	103 58		6,480 92
Totals	443,328 28	542,891 33	23,743 09	18,676 82	6,361 55	112,178 04	46,075 27	947 61	1,194,201 99

No. 14. Amounts deposited monthly to the credit of the Honourable the Receiver General on account of Inland Revenues during the Fiscal Year ended June 30, 1906—*Concluded.*

	Ontario.	Quebec.	New Brunswick.	Nova Scotia.	Prince Edward Island.	Manitoba, Alberta and Saskatchewan.	British Columbia.	Yukon.	Totals.
	$ cts.	$ cts.	$ cts.	$ cts.	$ cts.	$ cts.	$ cts.	$ cts.	$ cts.
April:									
Excise	437,913 00	517,166 47	21,999 81	16,482 77	4,216 03	122,900 91	44,652 58	2,353 06	1,167,684 69
" Seizures	10 00	116 50					200 00		326 50
Hydraulic and other Rents							1 00		1 00
Weights and Measures	2,660 68	1,418 25	125 78	148 00	22 05	724 07	192 80		5,291 63
Gas Inspection	2,084 25	711 50	67 25	32 75	9 75	137 75	228 25		3,271 50
Electric Light	1,055 75	429 75	81 50	32 00	25 25	196 25	220 75		2,041 25
Law Stamps, (Supreme Court)	237 50								237 50
" (Exchequer Court)	147 25								147 25
" (Yukon Territor'l Court)								276 00	276 00
" " Mining Court								23 75	23 75
Electric Light Fees	185 00								185 00
Fertilizers Fees	49 00	12 00	5 00						66 00
Adulteration of Food, Fees		5 00							5 00
" " Penalties						12 00			12 00
Methylated Spirits	2,704 06	1,978 53	97 06				131 80		4,911 45
Totals	447,046 49	521,838 00	22,376 43	16,695 52	4,273 08	123,971 01	45,627 18	2,652 81	1,184,480 52
May:—									
Excise	456,247 34	591,852 69	23,869 56	16,508 27	4,579 13	109,922 50	53,461 67	1,163 78	1,257,604 94
" Seizures		85 53							85 53
Hydraulic and other Rents	41 00	1 00							42 00
Minor Public Works	615 50	75 00	10 00						700 50
Weights and Measures	2,907 39	1,861 83	174 70	283 50	16 90	554 10	110 55	81 50	5,990 47
Gas Inspection	2,441 75	933 25	77 25	39 00		129 75	151 50		3,772 50
" Seizures	5 00								5 00
Electric Light	1,117 75	804 25	115 75	71 75		436 75	88 75		2,635 00
Law Stamps, (Supreme Court)	142 50								142 50
" (Exchequer Court)	178 60								178 60
" (Yukon Territor'l Court)								475 00	475 00
Electric Light Fees						15 00			15 00
Fertilizers Fees	12 00		3 00				13 00		28 00
Adulteration of Food Fees	3 00					9 00			12 00
Methylated Spirits	3,737 47	1,767 27	46 22			98 78			5,649 74
Totals	467,449 30	597,380 82	24,296 48	16,902 52	4,596 03	111,165 88	53,825 47	1,720 28	1,277,336 78

JUNE :—									
Excise	446,003 89	582,833 89	32,608 45	16,756 71	2,928 05	146,896 75	61,521 38	2,432 76	1,291,981 88
" Seizures.	226 80	81 03					7 50		315 33
Hydraulic and other Rents	355 00	1 00		6 00			50 00		412 00
Mor Public Works	130 00	6 00							136 00
Weights and Measures	5,268 88	4,329 57	727 31	572 95	148 64	1,278 45	310 85	80 25	12,716 90
" " Seizures	7 20								7 20
Gas Inspection	5,882 75	2,189 25	235 75	69 50	9 00	268 50	309 50		8,964 25
" Seizures	5 00								5 00
Electric Light	2,039 00	1,565 50	201 00	240 50	12 00	666 00	1,020 25		5,744 25
Law Stamps, (Supreme Court)	95 00								95 00
" (Exchequer Court)	372 40								372 40
" (Yukon Territor'l Court)								1,068 75	1,068 75
" " Mining Court								138 25	138 25
Fertilizers Fees			6 00				8 00		14 00
Adulteration of Food Fees	5 00								5 00
" " Penalties						27 00			27 00
Methylated Spirits	2,928 22	2,519 80	48 07						5,496 09
Casual Revenue							1 80		1 80
Totals	463,319 14	593,526 04	33,826 58	17,645 66	3,097 69	149,136 70	63,229 28	3,720 01	1,327,501 10
Grand Totals	5,198,143 60	6,718,800 19	308,954 78	215,061 91	55,387 98	1,376,425 88	538,639 70	24,143 65	14,435,557 69

W. J. GERALD,
Deputy Minister.

INLAND REVENUE DEPARTMENT,
OTTAWA, August 29, 1906.

No. 15.—Comparative Monthly,

—	July.	August.	September.	October.	November.
	$ cts.	$ cts.	$ cts.	$ cts.	$ cts.
Spirits 1904-1905	452,271 43	482,855 75	526,215 09	550,039 12	516,996 70
Spirits 1905-1906	437,796 93	497,895 83	533,638 87	602,938 48	702,764 34
Increase, 1905-1906		15,040 08	7,423 78	52,899 36	185,767 64
Decrease, 1905-1906	14,474 50				
Malt Liquor 1904-1905	6,904 20	675 20	50 00	339 10	
Malt Liquor 1905-1906	6,138 10	254 70	282 00	20 60	272 20
Increase, 1905-1906			232 00		272 20
Decrease, 1905-1906	766 10	420 50		318 50	
Malt 1904-1905	81,615 79	82,050 19	81,626 78	88,112 60	94,868 01
Malt 1905-1906	101,101 29	108,765 53	95,949 22	96,129 65	103,773 28
Increase, 1905-1906	19,485 50	26,715 34	14,322 44	8,017 05	8,905 27
Decrease, 1905-1906					
Tobacco 1904-1905	348,172 38	393,972 84	391,235 04	388,736 99	386,835 87
Tobacco 1905-1906	401,642 50	418,559 23	408,142 92	414,506 03	436,867 66
Increase, 1905-1906	53,470 12	24,586 39	16,907 88	25,769 04	50,031 79
Decrease, 1905-1906					
Cigars 1904-1905	105,322 60	99,014 68	99,533 52	94,949 13	97,971 51
Cigars 1905-1906	108,871 98	105,812 74	96,824 36	95,704 67	100,961 94
Increase, 1905-1906	3,549 38	6,798 06		755 54	2,990 43
Decrease, 1905-1906			2,709 16		
Acetic Acid 1904-1905	1,668 79	1,545 30	1,526 17	399 56	255 96
Acetic Acid 1905-1906	100 00		1,249 80		220 37
Increase, 1905-1906					
Decrease, 1905-1906	1,568 79	1,545 30	276 37	399 56	35 59
Manufactures in bond 1904-1905	5,133 63	4,358 82	8,083 94	8,058 29	3,893 80
Manufactures in bond 1905-1906	4,631 48	7,475 77	8,140 50	7,529 37	3,831 89
Increase, 1905-1906		3,116 95	56 56		
Decrease, 1905-1906	502 15			528 92	61 91
Seizures 1904-1905	102 00	260 00	361 00	179 00	
Seizures 1905-1906	725 00	170 00	160 00	276 20	285 30
Increase, 1905-1906	623 00			97 20	285 30
Decrease, 1905-1906		90 00	201 00		
Other Receipts 1904-1905	8,732 44	1,860 50	1.553 00	2,089 25	3,277 80
Other Receipts 1905-1906	9,335 13	2,309 07	3,552 08	6,046 66	4,525 76
Increase, 1905-1906	602 69	448 57	1,999 08	3,957 41	1,247 96
Decrease, 1905-1906					
Total Revenue, 1904-1905	1,009,923 26	1,066,593 28	1,110,184 54	1,132,903 04	1,104,099 65
" " 1905-1906	1,070,342 41	1,141,242 87	1,147,939 75	1,223,151 66	1,353,502 74
Total Increase, 1905-1906	60,419 15	94,649 59	37,755 21	90,248 62	249,403 09
" Decrease, 1905-1906					

Inland Revenue Department,
Ottawa, August 29, 1906.

Statement, 1904–1905 and 1905–1906.

December.	January.	February.	March.	April.	May.	June.	Totals.
$ cts	$ cts.	$ cts.	$ cts.	$ cts.	$ cts.	$ cts.	$ cts.
721,815 44	428,398 24	420,848 01	461,377 75	426,383 32	496,572 91	466,858 08	5,950,631 84
830,8[illegible]0 26	510,438 09	508,670 34	539,092 23	549,145 80	576,885 68	505,753 23	6,795,900 08
109,064 82	82,039 85	87,822 33	77,714 48	122,762 48	80,312 77	38,895 15	845,268 24
....	....	....	....	....	....	....	....
95 60	201 20	....	275 10	196 20	79 40	308 30	9,124 30
282 90	391 20	752 50	96 20	805 30	283 80	423 70	10,003 20
187 30	190 00	752 50	....	609 10	204 40	115 40	878 90
....	....	....	178 90	....	....	....	....
98,454 93	84,937 75	85,030 44	112,812 45	102,946 56	117,611 96	110,571 24	1,140,638 70
101,715 61	108,305 15	98,661 92	121,464 36	115,806 94	123,924 50	116,845 68	1,292,443 13
3,260 68	23,367 40	13,631 48	8,651 91	12,860 38	6,312 54	6,274 44	151,804 43
....	....	....	....	....	....	....	....
323,819 34	311,667 39	336,246 31	379,899 15	352,497 41	411,982 69	387,308 64	4,412,374 05
347,718 32	373,944 72	368,675 63	410,127 84	408,378 12	450,178 46	403,606 80	4,842,348 23
23,898 98	62,277 33	32,429 32	30,228 69	55,880 71	38,195 77	16,298 16	429,974 28
....	....	....	....	....	....	....	....
91,466 37	73,072 87	71,359 33	85,428 30	85,760 19	99,032 68	100,831 46	1,103,742 64
89,828 32	79,240 05	76,757 19	90,029 22	92,557 10	104,439 33	105,908 61	1,146,935 51
....	6,167 18	5,397 86	4,600 92	6,796 91	5,406 65	5,077 15	43,192 87
1,638 05	....	....	....	....	....	....	....
....	100 92	314 91	161 19	....	....	1,720 81	7,693 61
....	36 18	40 70	9 04	....	....	....	1,656 09
....	....	....	....	....	....	....	....
....	69 74	274 21	152 15	....	....	1,720 81	6,037 62
1,879 58	940 36	1,462 84	4,405 87	4,301 39	4,970 02	3,652 99	51,141 53
1,963 13	2,030 83	1,561 77	3,060 58	5,642 81	5,379 26	4,867 34	56,114 73
83 55	1,090 47	98 93	....	1,341 42	409 24	1,214 35	4,973 20
....	....	....	1,345 29	....	....	....	....
244 75	300 20	58 00	235 00	185 00	104 14	323 15	2,352 24
363 14	225 52	270 10	504 86	120 00	311 16	89 70	3,500 98
118 39	....	212 10	269 86	....	207 02	....	1,148 74
....	74 68	....	....	65 00	....	233 45	....
3,131 40	3,883 26	3,796 03	3,711 45	3,654 14	3,176 71	2,626 60	41,492 58
3,174 94	4,651 61	4,055 42	3,451 35	2,872 60	5,455 40	3,201 71	52,631 73
43 54	768 35	259 39	....	....	2,278 69	575 11	11,139 15
....	....	....	260 10	781 54	....	....	....
1,240,907 41	903,502 19	919,115 87	1,048,306 26	975,924 21	1,133,530 51	1,074,201 27	12,719,191 49
1,375,926 62	1,079,263 35	1,059,445 57	1,167,835 68	1,175,328 67	1,266,857 59	1,140,696 77	14,201,533 68
135,019 21	175,761 16	140,329 70	119,529 42	199,404 46	133,327 08	66,495 50	1,482,342 19
....	....	....	....	....	....	....	....

W. J. GERALD,
Deputy Minister.

No. 16—Refunds of Revenue during the fiscal year ended June 30, 1906.

EXCISE.

Articles.	To whom paid.	Date.	Divisions.	Under what Authority Refunded.	Amounts.	Totals.
		1905.			$ cts.	$ cts.
Spirits	Parke, Davis & Co.	Aug. 2	Windsor	Refunded under Revised Statutes, cap. 34, sec. 238	52 14	
	" "	" 8	"	" " 34 " 238	411 97	
	McLaren, J. (Estate of)	" 8	Perth	" " 34 " 238	250 00	
	Parke, Davis & Co.	" 9	Windsor	" " 34 " 238	31 59	
	" "	" 25	"	" " 34 " 238	43 18	
	" "	" 30	"	" " 34 " 238	18 81	
	" "	Sept. 5	"	" " 34 " 238	622 08	
	" "	" 20	"	" " 34 " 238	428 30	
	" "	Oct. 4	"	" " 34 " 238	199 78	
	" "	" 7	"	" " 34 " 238	280 03	
	Heney, J. J.	" 18	Prescott	" " 34 " 238	14,504 67	
	Parke, Davis & Co.	" 20	Windsor	" " 34 " 238	118 59	
	" "	" 28	"	" " 34 " 238	286 33	
	King, H. L.	Nov. 2	"	" " 34 " 238	1,137 78	
	Parke, Davis & Co.	" 3	"	" " 34 " 238	94 18	
	Howard, G. M.	" 3	Sherbrooke	" " 34 " 238	3,792 72	
	Parke, Davis & Co.	" 11	Windsor	" " 34 " 238	88 86	
	" "	" 23	"	" " 34 " 238	451 43	
	" "	" 23	"	" " 34 " 238	35 85	
	" "	Dec. 6	"	" " 34 " 238	89 71	
	" "	" 14	"	" " 34 " 238	436 07	
	" "	" 19	"	" " 34 " 238	30 71	
	" "	" 26	"	" " 34 " 238	394 82	
	" "	" 30	"	" " 34 " 238	39 23	
		1906.				
	" "	Jan. 9	"	" " 34 " 238	682 38	
	" "	" 30	"	" " 34 " 238	108 13	
	" "	Feb. 5	"	" " 34 " 238	595 97	
	" "	" 12	"	" " 34 " 238	329 02	
	" "	" 22	"	" " 34 " 238	377 17	
	" "	Mar. 5	"	" " 34 " 238	840 91	
	" "	" 16	"	" " 34 " 238	71 91	
	" "	" 23	"	" " 34 " 238	265 73	
	" "	" 30	"	" " 34 " 238	425 72	

	Hamilton, J. S. & Co.	April	3	Brantford	"	"	34 " 238	159 46	
	Parke, Davis & Co.	"	9	Windsor	"	"	34 " 238	350 02	
	" "	"	18	"	"	"	34 " 238	75 96	
	Heney, J. J.	"	21	Prescott	"	"	34 " 238	14,401 30	
	Parke, Davis & Co.	May	5	Windsor	"	"	34 " 238	414 20	
	Eastern Township Bank The (for A. L. Howard Co.)	"	9	Sherbrooke	"	"	34 " 238	7,809 92	
	Heney, J. J.	"	11	Prescott	"	"	34 " 238	14,408 27	
	Parke, Davis & Co.	"	15	Windsor	"	"	34 " 238	230 23	
	" "	"	23	"	"	"	34 " 238	317 00	
	Heney, J. J.	"	25	[illegible]tt	"	"	34 " 238	14,387 22	
	King, H. L.	"	31	Windsor	"	"	34 " 238	1,387 62	
	Parke, Davis & Co.	"	31	"	"	"	34 " 238	231 26	
	" "	June	8	"	"	"	34 " 238	285 27	
	Gooderham, W. G.	"	13	Toronto	"	"	34 " 238	63 42	
	Parke, Davis & Co.	"	19	Windsor	"	"	34 " 238	274 22	
	" "	"	25	"	"	"	34 " 238	281 08	
	" "	July	6	"	"	"	34 " 238	169 08	
	" "	"	24	"	"	"	34 " 238	45 67	
									82,826 97
Malt	Dow, William & Co.	July	31	Montreal	"	"	29 " 78	2,942 50	
	Dawes, [illegible]w J.	"	31	"	"	"	29 " 78	2,166 29	
	Cloutier, D.	"	31	"	"	"	29 " 78	28 74	
	Canada Malting Co., Ltd.	"	34	"	"	"	29 " 78	572 73	
	Reinhardt, C. S.	"	31	"	"	"	29 " 78	290 70	
	[illegible]n, J. T.	"	31	"	"	"	29 " 78	45 00	
	Cl rke, [illegible]. H.	"	31	"	"	"	29 " 78	1,516 66	
	Oshner, R.	"	31	Calgary	"	"	29 " 78	132 75	
	Cross, A. E.	"	31	"	"	"	29 " 78	1,121 25	
	Lethbridge Brewing and [illegible]g Co., Ltd., The	"	31	"	"	"	29 " 78	143 10	
	[illegible]on, D. H.	"	31	Toronto	"	"	34 " 178	119 74	
	[illegible]y, D. J.	"	31	Prescott	"	"	34 " 178	25 94	
	Blackwood, W.	Aug.	2	Winnipeg	"	"	29 " 78	11 56	
	Brandon Brewing Co., The.	"	2	"	"	"	29 " 78	196 27	
	[illegible]a, P.	"	2	"	"	"	29 " 78	912 57	
	Elliott, Alexander	"	2	Peterborough	"	"	29 " 78	569 95	
	[illegible]n, W. H.	"	2	"	"	"	29 " 78	83 70	
	Bowie, Robert	"	2	Prescott	"	"	29 " 78	309 15	
	[illegible]D. J.	"	2	"	"	"	29 " 78	487 20	
	Lyons Bros.	"	2	Winnipeg	"	"	29 " 78	2 20	
	[illegible]a Brewing and Malting Co., The	"	2	"	"	"	29 " 78	115 50	
	[illegible] [illegible]on Brewing Co., The	"	2	"	"	"	29 " 78	97 50	
	Drewry, E. L.	"	2	"	"	"	29 " 78	1,859 13	
	Edmonton Brewing and [illegible]ing Co., Ltd., The	"	4	Vancouver	"	"	29 " 78	88 25	
	Phœnix Brewing Co.	"	8	"	"	"	29 " 78	37 32	
	Enterprise Brewing Co., The	"	8	"	"	"	29 " 78	30 73	

No. 16.—REFUNDS OF REVENUE—*Continued.*

EXCISE—*Continued.*

Articles.	To whom paid.	Date.	Divisions.	Under what Authority Refunded.	Amounts.	Totals.
		1905.			$ cts.	$ cts.
Malt—*Con*.........	Robinson, T. A	Aug. 9..	Winnipeg.........	Refunded under Revised Statutes, cap. 29, sec. 78.. ...	69 87	
	Seagram, Jos. E...........	" 11..	Guelph	" " 29 " 78	366 00	
	Proteau & Carignan.......	" 21..	Quebec............	" " 29 " 78.....	513 00	
	Northern Brewing Co......	" 25..	Vancouver.........	" " 29 " 78.....	7 50	
	Taylor, H. J......	" 30..	St. Catharines	" " 29 " 78.....	721 81	
	Shea, Patrick	Sept. 2..	Winnipeg	" " 34 " 238......	84 00	
	British Columbia Distillery Co., Ltd.	" 6..	Vancouver	" " 29 " 78....	36 00	
	Vancouver Breweries, Ltd., The......	" 6..	"	" " 29 " 78.....	63 75	
	Nelson, Nels..............	" 6..	"	" " 29 " 78	121 87	
	Carling, T. H.....	" 18..	London	" " 34 " 178......	3 32	
	Flushrer, John	" 20..	Vancouver	" " 29 " 78......	9 00	
	Carling, T. H	Oct. 2..	London	" " 34 " 178 ...	17 10	
	Halifax Breweries Co., Ltd.	" 10..	Halifax.... .	" " 34 " 238	152 34	
	Wickwire, W. N.........	" 10..	"	" " 34 " 238.. ...	1,907 07	
	Tate, Robt	" 10..	Victoria	" " 34 " 238......	191 27	
	Victoria Phœnix Brewing Co., Ltd..........	" 10..	"	" " 34 " 238......	236 06	
	Henderson, Hugh.........	" 11..	Vancouver	" " 29 " 78......	7 64	
	Vancouver Breweries, Ltd., The	" 14..	"	" " 34 " 238......	60 00	
	Victoria Phœnix Brewing Co., Ltd	" 17..	Victoria....	" " 34 " 238......	107 56	
	Labatt, John.	" 20..	London	" " 34 " 178 ..	8 41	
	Carling, T. H......	" 23..	"	" " 34 " 178	3 48	
	"	Nov. 14..	"	" " 34 " 178......	3 35	
	Vancouver Breweries, Ltd., The...............	Dec. 14..	Vancouver	" " 34 " 238......	60 00	
	Bauer, A..........	" 19..	Guelph	" " 29 " 78......	79 38	
	McCarthy, D. J	" 19..	Prescott........	" " 29 " 78......	85 31	
	Heuther, C	" 19..	Guelph	" " 29 " 78 ..	427 50	
		1906.				
	May, L. A......	Jan. 11..	Halifax	" " 34 " 238......	18 01	

Halifax Breweries, Ltd	"	11	"	"	"	34	"	238	236 25
Wickwire, W. N	"	11	"	"	"	34	"	238	1,433 87
Victoria Phœnix Brewing Co., Ltd	"	11	Victoria	"	"	34	"	238	256 34
Wilson, D. H	"	22	Toronto	"	"	34	"	178	237 81
Halifax Breweries, Ltd	"	23	Halifax	"	"	34	"	238	113 20
Labatt, John	Feb.	16	London	"	"	34	"	238	7 32
Vancouver Breweries, Ltd., The	"	20	Vancouver	"	"	34	"	238	94 50
McCarthy, D. J	"	26	Prescott	"	"	29	"	78	254 22
Victoria Phœnix Brewing Co., Ltd	April	1	Victoria	"	"	34	"	238	201 00
Wickwire, W. N	"	7	Halifax	"	"	34	"	238	108 83
Halifax Breweries, Ltd	"	7	"	"	"	34	"	238	139 79
Victoria Phœnix Brewing Co., Ltd	"	7	Victoria	"	"	34	"	238	82 11
Bixel Brewing and Malting Co., Ltd	"	9	Brantford	"	"	34	"	238	46 50
McCarthy, D. J	"	9	Prescott	"	"	34	"	238	44 10
Carling, T. H	"	25	London	"	"	34	"	238	29 30
Portman & Portman	"	27	Vancouver	"	"	34	"	238	313 60
Hartinger, Frank	"	27	"	"	"	34	"	238	306 75
Vancouver Breweries, Ltd., The	May	15	"	"	"	34	"	238	96 83
Carling, T. H	"	15	London	"	"	34	"	238	253 16
Victoria Phœnix Brewing Co., Ltd			Victoria	"	"	34	"	238	132 75
Victoria Phœnix Brewing Co., Ltd	June	22	Victoria	"	"	34	"	238	66 75
Carling, T. H	"	23	London	"	"	34	"	238	22 22
Superior Brewing & Malting Co., Ltd., The	July	16	Port Arthur	"	"	29	"	78	98 61
Vancouver Breweries, Ltd., The	"	17	Vancouver	"	"	34	"	238	94 50
Roy, J. A	"	31	Belleville	"	"	29	"	78	256 54
Corby, H	"	31	"	"	"	29	"	78	27 00
Corby, H. Distillery Co	"	31	"	"	"	29	"	78	64 78
Westbrook & Hocken	"	31	Brantford	"	"	29	"	78	107 85
Otterbein, C	"	31	"	"	"	29	"	78	82 51
Bixel, A	"	31	"	"	"	29	"	78	334 80
Grant Spring Brewery Co., Ltd	"	31	Hamilton	"	"	29	"	78	860 36
Wilson, M. S	"	31	"	"	"	29	"	78	2,148 82
Fisher, John	"	31	Kingston	"	"	29	"	78	226 48
Stevenson, R	"	31	"	"	"	29	"	78	146 07
Union Brewing Co., Ltd., The	"	31	London	"	"	29	"	78	82 20
Dwyer, P	"	31	"	"	"	29	"	78	211 50
Labatt, John	"	31	"	"	"	29	"	78	1,567 96
Carling, T. H	"	31	"	"	"	29	"	78	1,877 62

No. 16.—Refunds of Revenue—*Continued.*

EXCISE—*Continued.*

Articles.	To whom paid.	Date.	Divisions.	Under what Authority Refunded.	Amounts.	Totals.
		1906.			$ cts.	$ cts.
Malt—*Con.*	Eaton, C	July 31	Owen Sound	Refunded under Revised Statutes, cap. 29, sec. 78	228 19	
	Heisz, L	" 31	"	" " 29 " 78	129 67	
	Huether, Wm.	" 31	"	" " 29 " 78	183 38	
	Farquharson & Grainger	" 31	"	" " 29 " 78	87 52	
	Scl[illegible]n, Wm	" 31	"	" " 29 " 78	308 10	
	Superior Brewing & M. Co., Ltd., The	" 31	Port Arthur	" " 29 " 78	92 47	
	Kuntz, Barbara	" 31	Stratford	" " 29 " 78	30 75	
	Clarke, L. H	" 31	"	" " 29 " 78	647 88	
	[illegible]n, John	" 31	"	" " 29 " 78	219 00	
	Devlin, F	" 31	"	" " 29 " 78	83 71	
	Gooderham & Worts, Ltd	" 31	Toronto	" " 29 " 78	1,474 57	
	Cosgrove Brewery Co., Ltd., The	" 31	"	" " 29 " 78	1,193 90	
	Kormann Brewery Co., Ltd., The	" 31	"	" " 29 " 78	54 00	
	Copland Brewing Co., Ltd.	" 31	"	" " 29 " 78	2,029 50	
	Rocot, C	" 31	"	" " 29 " 78	529 50	
	Toronto Brewing & Malting Co., Ltd	" 31	"	" " 29 " 78	805 87	
	Davies, H. H	" 31	"	" " 29 " 78	105 15	
	O'Keefe Brewery Co., Ltd., The	" 31	"	" " 29 " 78	2,787 14	
	Brain, Mary E	" 31	"	" " 29 " 78	172 04	
	Barrie Brewing Co., Ltd., The	" 31	"	" " 29 " 78	97 20	
	Reinhardt, L	" 31	"	" " 29 " 78	1,629 00	
	Wright, A. J	" 31	"	" " 29 " 78	47 12	
	Dominion Brewery Co., Ltd., The	" 31	"	" " 29 " 78	1,271 45	
	Anderton & Co	" 31	"	" " 29 " 78	128 47	
	Irion, A. L	" 31	Windsor	" " 29 " 78	390 00	
	Hiram Walker & Sons, Ltd.	" 31	"	" " 29 " 78	2,537 35	
	Amyot & Gauvin	" 31	Quebec	" " 29 " 78	941 25	
	Proteau & Carignan	" 31	"	" " 29 " 78	561 00	
	Boswell & Bros., Ltd	" 31	"	" " 29 " 78	1,342 40	

Beauport Brewing Co ...	"	31..	"	"	"	29	"	78......	660 00	
Tellier, J. A	"	31..	St. Hyacinthe....	"	"	29	"	78 ..	97 61	
Silver Spring Brewery, Ltd	"	31..	Sherbrooke..	"	"	29	"	78	1,123 18	
Jones, Simeon, Ltd	"	31..	St. John	"	"	29	"	78......	300 00	
Ready, James.	"	31..	"	"	"	29	"	78......	906 00	
Wickwire, W. N	"	31..	Halifax	"	'	29	"	78......	1,270 50	
May, L. A	"	31..	"	"	"	29	"	78......	214 05	
Halifax Breweries, Ltd.	"	31..	"	"	"	29	"	78......	572 73	
Drewry, E. L.	"	31..	Winnipeg	"	"	29	"	78......	1,299 35	
Brandon Brewing Co., The.	"	31..	"	"	"	29	"	78......	111 75	
Robinson, Isaac A	"	31..	"	"	"	29	"	78	90 00	
Golden Lion Brewing Co., The	"	31..	"	"	"	29	"	78. ...	116 25	
aMba Brewing & Malting Co., Ltd., The.	"	31..	"	"	"	29	"	78.. ...	297 65	
Lyone Bros	"	31..	"	"	"	29	"	78......	23 77	
Shea, Patrick	"	31..	"	"	"	29	"	78......	1,159 60	
Cross, A. E.	"	31..	Calgary	"	"	29	"	78......	1,486 11	
Lethbridge Brewing & Malting Co., Ltd., The..	"	31..	"	"	"	29	"	78.....	234 17	
Ochsner, Robt	"	31..	"	"	"	29	"	78......	240 00	
Edmunton Brewing & Mng Co., Ltd., The..	"	31..	"	"	"	29	"	78 ...	327 33	
Victoria Phœnix Brewing Co., Ltd	"	31..	Victoria	"	"	29	"	78.	480 00	
Union Brewing Co., Ltd....	"	31..	"	"	"	29	"	78	308 93	
Sleeman Brewing and Malting Co., Ltd., The	"	31..	Guelph	"	"	29	"	78	608 55	
Sleeman Go. A	"	31..	"	"	"	29	"	78......	400 50	
Seagram, Jos E	"	31..	"	"	"	29	"	78......	376 24	
Bauer, A	"	31..	"	"	"	29	"	78....	1,507 31	
Lutz, W	"	31..	"	"	"	29	"	78.....	1 50	
Todd, Martin U	"	31..	"	"	"	29	"	78	360 28	
Rau Mary	"	31..	"	"	"	29	"	78......	186 00	
Andrick, C. E.	"	31.	"	"	"	29	"	78......	188 70	
Bernhardt, V. B.	"	31..	"	"	"	29	"	78	188 93	
Capital Brewing Co., The..	"	31..	Ottawa	"	"	29	"	78......	519 15	
Mt, Henry	"	31..	Peterborough.	"	"	29	"	78	387 76	
Eltt, Alex	"	31..	"	"	"	29	"	78......	549 22	
Taylor, H. J	"	31..	St. Catharines..	"	"	29	"	78......	637 72	
Dawes, A. J.	"	31.	Montreal.	"	"	29	"	78......	2,967 65	
Dow, Wm. & Co..	"	31..	"	"	"	29	"	78......	3,057 59	
Reinhardt. C. S.	"	31..	"	"	"	29	"	78......	268 05	
Mn, John T.	"	31..	"	"	"	29	"	78.....	1,804 20	
Gada Malting G., Ltd..	"	31 .	"	"	"	29	"	78......	4,719 91	
Meldrum, W. H.	Aug.	7 .	Peterborough	"	"	29	"	78.....	129 84	
Huether, C. N.	"	8..	Guelph	"	"	29	"	78....	521 25	
Holliday, T..	"	8..	"	"	"	29	"	78.....	294 70	83,027 44

No. 16.—Refunds of Revenue—*Continued*.

EXCISE—*Continued*.

Articles.	To whom paid.	Date.		Divisions.	Under what Authority Refunded.	Amounts.	Totals.
		1905.				$ cts.	$ cts.
Tobacco	Flynn, F. L	July	31	Hamilton	Refunded under Revised Statutes, cap. 34, sec. 238	97 10	
	McKenna, A	"	31	Pictou	" " 34 238	198 80	
	Geo. E. Tuckett & Son Co., Ltd., The	"	31	Hamilton	" " 34 " 238	641 99	
	Wilson, Andrew	"	31	Toronto	" " 34 " 238	276 10	
	McDonald, R. D	"	31	London	" " 34 " 238	4 50	
	Macdonald, Sir W. C	"	31	Montreal	" " 34 " 238	113 30	
	McDonald, R. D	"	31	London	" " 34 " 238	661 50	
	Hynes, Jos	Aug.	2	Hamilton	" " 34 " 238	133 70	
	Schrader, J. H	"	2	"	" " 34 " 238	117 60	
	Canley, Bryan	"	2	"	" " 34 " 238	74 60	
	Hill, John	"	2	"	" " 34 " 238	59 30	
	Blumenstiel, I	"	2	"	" " 34 " 238	121 70	
	Rosin, Louis	"	2	Toronto	" " 34 " 238	32 90	
	Kilbourne, W. P	"	2	Winnipeg	" " 34 " 238	211 50	
	Hamilton, D. J	"	2	Stratford	" " 34 " 238	109 70	
	[illegible], Eugène	"	2	Montreal	" " 34 " 238	17 50	
	American Tobacco Co. of Canada, Ltd., The	"	2	"	" " 34 " 238	165 40	
	George E. Tuckett & Son Co., Ltd., The	"	2	Hamilton	" " 34 " 238	8 05	
	Hobrecker, A	"	2	Halifax	" " 34 " 238	[illegible]09 37	
	"	"	2	"	" " 34 " 238	2 75	
	Foy, John	"	4	Hamilton	" " 34 " 238	91 70	
	Donohue, D	"	4	"	" " 34 " 238	101 50	
	Tobin & Co., John	"	4	Halifax	" " 34 " 238	10 77	
	Dooley, James	"	9	London	" " 34 " 238	117 80	
	Firstbrook, Jos	"	9	"	" " 34 " 238	72 80	
	Kimberley, G. F	"	11	St. Catharines	" " 34 " 238	37 50	
	Isaacs, A	"	12	St. John	" " 34 " 238	13 56	
	McKenna, A	"	12	Pictou	" " 34 " 238	145 36	
	Ryall, C. A	"	14	Windsor	" " 34 " 238	32 20	
	George E. Tuckett & Son Co., Ltd., The	"	16	Hamilton	" " 34 " 259	148 29	
	Bollard, Arthur	"	16	Toronto	" " 34 " 259	1 65	
	American Tobacco Co. of Canada, Ltd., The	"	16	Montreal	" " 34 " 259	1,588 47	

Fortier, J. M., Ltd	"	16	"	"	"	34	"	259	23 16
Solomon, E	"	16	"	"	"	34	"	259	8 89
Isaacs, A	"	16	St. John	"	"	34	"	259	16 45
Heinbecker, J	"	18	Winnipeg	"	"	34	"	238	145 30
Harkness, Thos	"	18	Montreal	"	"	34	"	238	24 12
Tobin & Co., John	"	21	Halifax	"	"	34	"	238	18 70
Hobrecker, A	"	21	"	"	"	34	"	238	731 22
"	"	21	"	"	"	34	"	238	6 56
Tobin, John & Co	"	22	Halifax	"	"	34	"	238	17 20
Davis, S. & Sons	"	25	Montreal	"	"	34	"	238	1 25
Davis, S. & Sons	"	25	"	"	"	34	"	238	346 50
[illegible], L. O	"	25	"	"	"	34	"	238	753 20
Inland Cigar Mfg. Co	"	25	Vancouver	"	"	34	"	238	318 00
McKenna, A	"	30	Pictou	"	"	34	"	238	61 68
Fair, T. J. & Co	"	30	Brantford	"	"	34	"	238	135 20
Billman, Chisholm & Co	Sept.	5	Halifax	"	"	34	"	238	46 82
Bauld Bros. & Co	"	5	"	"	"	34	"	238	29 92
American Tobacco Co. of Canada, Ltd. (The)	"	5	Montreal	"	"	34	"	238	157 30
Fortier, J. M., Ltd	"	5	"	"	"	34	"	238	1,068 00
Payne, J. B	"	5	Sherbrooke	"	"	34	"	238	202 60
Bryan, G. F	"	5	Winnipeg	"	"	34	"	238	182 20
Hobrecker, A	"	11	Halifax	"	"	34	"	238	78 12
Bauld Bros & Co	"	11	"	"	"	34	"	238	18 10
American Tobacco Co. of Canada, Ltd., The	"	11	Montreal	"	"	34	"	238	538 60
Rock City Cigar Co	"	11	Quebec	"	"	34	"	238	104 30
Fortier, J. M., Ltd	"	11	Montreal	"	"	34	"	238	684 00
Bollard, A	"	21	Toronto	"	"	34	"	259	1 13
G. E. Tuckett & Son Co. Ltd., The	"	21	Hamilton	"	"	34	"	259	199 31
Solomon, E	"	21	Montreal	"	"	34	"	259	9 10
Fortier, J. M., Ltd	"	21	"	"	"	34	"	259	35 30
American Tobacco Co. of Canada, Ltd., The	"	21	"	"	"	34	"	259	1,753 87
Isaacs, A	"	21	St. John	"	"	34	"	259	22 19
Hobrecker, A	"	21	Halifax	"	"	34	"	238	5 37
McKenna, A	"	21	Pictou	"	"	34	"	238	38 64
The Sherbrooke Cigar Co	"	21	Sherbrooke	"	"	34	"	238	179 90
Spilling, M. E	"	25	Toronto	"	"	34	"	238	150 70
[illegible] & Co	"	25	Montreal	"	"	34	"	238	263 20
Hobrecker, A	"	25	Halifax	"	"	34	"	238	288 95
G. C. Tuckett & Son Co., Ltd	"	25	Hamilton	"	"	34	"	238	1,409 67
McKenna, A	"	25	Pictou	"	"	34	"	238	208 64
Tobin, John & Co	"	4	Halifax	"	"	34	"	238	14 36
Holloran, M. K	"	4	Brantford	"	"	34	"	238	94 80
Tuckett Cigar Co., Ltd., The	"	12	Hamilton	"	"	34	"	238	404 50
[illegible], G	"	12	London	"	"	34	"	238	156 60
Dooley, James	"	12	"			34	"	238	236 80

No. 16.—Refunds of Revenue—*Continued*.

EXCISE—*Continued*.

[Ar]ticles.	To whom paid.	Date.		Divisions.	Under what Authority Refunded.	Amounts.	Totals.
		1906.				$ cts.	$ cts.
Con.	McDonald, R. D.	Sept.	12	London	Refunded under Revised Statutes, cap. 34, sec. 238	479 60	
	Wilson, Andrew	Oct.	12	Toronto	" " 34 " 238	402 30	
	Webster, W. R.	"	12	Sherbrooke	" " 34 " 238	326 00	
	Jacobs, A. & Co.	"	12	Montreal	" " 34 " 238	223 70	
	American Tobacco Co. of Canada, Ltd., The	"	12	"	" " 34 " 238	69 90	
	Macdonald, Sir W. C.	"	12	"	" " 34 " 238	242 00	
	McKenna, A.	"	12	Pictou	" " 34 " 238	32 00	
	[illegible]n, John & Co.	"	12	Halifax	" " 34 " 238	5 16	
	Hobrecker, A.	"	12	"	" " 34 " 238	479 64	
	Sievert, J. G.	"	12	"	" " 34 " 238	12 28	
	Hobrecker, A.	"	12	"	" " 34 " 238	4 62	
	Bollard, A.	"	16	Toronto	" " 34 " 259	1 50	
	Ateshian Carnig	"	16	Montreal	" " 34 " 259	8 97	
	Oriental [illegible]co Co.	"	16	"	" " 34 " 259	10 99	
	Goldstein, B.	"	16	"	" " 34 " 259	11 08	
	Solomon, E.	"	16	"	" " 34 " 259	9 38	
	Fortier, J. M., Ltd	"	16	"	" " 34 " 259	34 77	
	American [illegible]o Co. of [illegible]h, Ltd., The	"	16	"	" " 34 " 259	1,414 75	
	Henry, James	"	16	"	" " 34 " 259	11 22	
	Geo. E. [illegible]tt & Son Co., Ltd	"	16	Hamilton	" " 34 " 259	158 35	
	Geo. E. Tuckett & Son Co., Ltd	"	16	"	" " 29 " 78	9 10	
	Brener, A. H.	"	16	London	" " 34 " 238	85 60	
	[illegible]e, John	"	16	"	" " 34 " 238	273 80	
	Milligan, Geo	"	16	Toronto	" " 34 " 238	377 40	
	Hisch, Jacob	"	16	Montreal	" " 34 " 238	220 10	
	Grothé, L. O.	"	16	"	" " 34 " 238	717 50	
	Smith, Jos.	"	16	London	" " 34 " 238	114 10	
	Gold, Thos. F.	"	19	Victoria	" " 34 " 238	54 30	
	Hobrecker, A.	"	20	Halifax	" " 34 " 238	1 50	
	Isaacs, A.	"	20	St. John	" " 34 " 259	23 57	
	[illegible]n, John & Co.	"	25	Halifax	" " 34 " 238	17 20	
	McKenna, A.	"	25	Pictou	" " 34 " 238	81 92	

American [illegible]co Co. of [illegible]da, Ltd., The	"	25	Montreal	"	"	34	"	238	413 60
Fortier, J. M., [illegible]	"	25	"	"	"	34	"	238	891 70
Province Cigar Co.	"	25	Victoria	"	"	34	"	238	201 10
Isaacs, A.	"	28	St. John	"	"	34	"	238	9 75
Hobrecker	"	28	Halifax	"	"	34	"	238	451 48
Fair, J. D. & Co., Ltd.	Nov.	2	Brantford	"	"	34	"	238	2 30
Wilberg, B.	"	3	Vancouver	"	"	34	"	238	229 00
Hobrecker, A.	"	3	Halifax	"	"	34	"	238	1 50
Geo. E. Tuckett & Son Co., Ltd., The	"	3	Hamilton		"	34	"	238	1,321 35
McKenna, A.	"	4	Pictou		"	34	"	238	177 68
Bauld Bros. & Co.	"	11	Halifax	"	"	34	"	238	57 44
Rock City Tob. Co., Ltd., The	"	11	[illegible]ec	"	"	34	"	259	83 33
Schneter, W. J.	"	11	[illegible]h	"	"	34	"	238	82 70
Tuckett Cigar Co., Ltd., The	"	11	Hamilton	"	"	34	"	238	212 40
Henry, J	"	17	Montreal	"	"	34	"	270	20 00
Hobrecker, A.	"	17	Halifax	"	"	34	"	238	15 98
Rock City Tob. Co., Ltd., The	"	18	[illegible]c	"	"	34	"	259	5 19
Lemesurier, John	"	18	"	"	"	34	"	259	12 18
Bollard, A	"	18	Toronto	"	"	34	"	259	1 88
Geo. E. [illegible]tt & Son Co., Ltd., The	"	18	Hamilton	"	"	34	"	259	161 73
Solomon, E	"	18	Montreal	"	"	34	"	259	9 28
Fortier, J. M., Ltd	"	18	"	"	"	34	"	259	26 89
American [illegible]b. Co. of Canada, Ltd., The	"	18	"	"	"	34	"	259	1,576 61
Isaacs, A	"	18	St. John	"	"	34	"	259	3 68
McKenna, A	"	21	Pictou	"	"	34	"	238	51 92
McHugh, John	"	21	St. Catharines	"	"	34	"	259	28 60
Wilson, Andrew	"	21	Toronto	"	"	34	.	259	257 10
Dyer, W. R.	"	21	London	"	"	34	"	259	92 50
Kelley, Geo.	"	21	"	"	"	34	"	259	99 70
Firstbrook, Jos.	"	21	"	"	"	34	"	259	132 90
Dyer, Jno. J	"	21	"	"	"	34	"	259	149 70
American Tob. Co. of Canada, Ltd., The	"	23	Montreal	"	"	34	"	259	710 40
Hobrecker, A.	"	24	Halifax	"	"	34	"	259	93 75
Tobin, John & Co.	"	27	"	"	"	34	"	259	22 81
Geo. C. [illegible]tt & Son Co., Ltd	"	28	Hamilton	"	"	34	"	259	1,038 32
Payne, J. Bruce	"	28	[illegible]ke	"	"	34	"	259	336 00
McKenna, A.	Dec.	6	Montreal	"	"	34	"	259	48 24
American Tob. Co. of Can., Ltd., The	"	6	"	"	"	34	"	259	95 80
Jacobs, H. & Co.	"	6	Toronto	"	"	34	"	259	302 90
Milligan, Geo.	"	6	Windsor		"	34	"	259	396 50

No. 16.—REFUNDS OF Revenue—*Continued.*

EXCISE—*Continued.*

Articles.	To whom paid.	Date.	Divisions.	Under what Authority Refunded.	Amounts.	Totals.
		1905.			$ cts.	$ cts.
Tobacco—*Continued.*	Whaley, H. R.	Dec. 6	Windsor	Refunded under Revised Statutes, cap. 34, sec. 259	71 80	
	Hobrecker, A.	" 11	Halifax	" " 34 " 259	505 10	
	Lee, Thos.	" 11	Winnipeg	" " 34 " 259	192 10	
	Jones, Patrick	" 11	St. John	" " 34 " 259	208 00	
	[illegible]a, A	" 19	Pictou	" " 34 " 259	146 43	
	Fair, T. J. & Co.	" 19	Brantford	" " 34 " 259	122 80	
	[illegible]tt Cigar Co., Ltd., The	" 19	Hamilton	" " 34 " 259	216 60	
	Dooley, James	" 19	London	" " 34 " 259	197 50	
	Ward, W	" 19	"	" " 34 " 238	184 50	
	Bollard, A	" 19	Toronto	" " 34 " 259	1 40	
	Lemesurier, John	" 19	Quebec	" " 34 " 259	3 32	
	Rock City Tob. Co., Ltd., The	" 19	"	" " 34 " 259	23 29	
	Solomon, E.	" 19	Montreal	" " 34 " 259	10 77	
	Fortier, J. M., Ltd	" 19	"	" " 34 " 259	26 57	
	[illegible]an Tobacco Co. of Canada, Ltd., The	" 19	"	" " 34 " 259	1,460 52	
	Isaacs, A.	" 19	"	" " 34 " 259	10 38	
	Tuckett Cigar Co., Ltd., The	" 19	St. John	" " 34 " 259	161 45	
	Dooley, James	" 19	Hamilton	" " 34 " 238	3 00	
	Gignac, R. T.	" 19	London	" " 34 " 238	11 00	
	Macdonald, Sir W. C	" 26	Windsor	" " 34 " 238	299 20	
	Fortier, J. M., Ltd	" 26	Montreal	" " 34 " 238	714 10	
	Grothé, L. O.	" 26	"	" " 34 " 238	718 90	
	Berner, A. H.	" 26	"	" " 34 " 238	159 10	
	McDonald, R. D	" 26	London	" " 34 " 238	503 00	
	Hobrecker, A	" 26	Halifax	" " 34 " 238	53 43	
	[illegible]a, A.	" 26	Pictou	" " 34 " 238	272 40	
		1906.				
	Kelly, Geo.	Jan. 8	London	" " 34 " 238	3 60	
	Simon Leizer & Co., Ltd	" 9	Victoria	" " 34 " 238	53 98	
	Tobin, John & Co.	" 9	Halifax	" " 34 " 238	10 77	
	McKenna, A	" 9	Pictou	" "	160 80	
	Geo. E. Tuckett & Son Co., Ltd., The	" 9	Hamilton	" 34 " 238 " 34 " 238	746 39	

[illegible]h, Arthur	"	9	Montreal	"	"	34	"	238	40 00
[illegible] Co. of [illegible]a, Ltd., The	"	9	"	"	"	34	"	238	56 40
Hirch, J[illegible]b	"	9	"	"	"	34	"	236	240 20
Oberndorffer, Simon	"	9	Kingston	"	"	34	"	238	166 00
McGowan, G. A.	"	9	"	"	"	34	"	238	335 50
Smith, J	"	9	London	"	"	34	"	238	79 20
Bollard, A	"	19	Toronto	"	"	34	"	259	1 68
[illegible]h, A	"	19	Montréal	"	"	34	"	259	4 84
Ateshian, Carnig	"	19	"	"	"	34	"	259	12 54
[illegible]ff, Muscovetch Co.	"	19	"	"	"	34	"	259	1 60
[illegible]n, P	"	19	"	"	"	34	"	259	9 41
Solomon, E	"	19	"	"	"	34	"	259	11 02
[illegible]al Tobacco Co	"	19	"	"	"	34	"	259	8 99
[illegible]y, [illegible]s.	"	19	"	"	"	34	"	259	10 14
Fortier, J. M., Ltd	"	19	"	"	"	34	"	259	5 85
[illegible]n Tobacco Co. of Canada, Ltd., The	"	19	"	"	"	34	"	259	1,420 74
Rock City Tobacco Co., The	"	19	Quebec	"	"	34	"	259	12 27
Lemesurier, John	"	19	"	"	"	34	"	259	1 86
G. E. [illegible]tt & Son Co., Ltd	"	19	Hamilton	"	"	34	"	259	130 59
G. E. [illegible]tt & Son Co., Ltd	"	19	"	"	"	29	"	78	5 50
Fortier, J. M., Ltd	"	20	Montreal	"	"	34	"	238	63 72
McKenna, A.	"	20	Picton	"	"	34	"	238	34 24
Despond, C. R.	"	20	[illegible]h	"	"	34	"	238	36 30
[illegible]t, Jos.	"	20	"	"	"	34	"	238	90 70
Blumenstiel, T.	"	20	Hamilton	"	"	34	"	238	127 40
Milligan, Geo.	"	20	Toronto	"	"	34	"	238	433 30
Grothé, L. O.	"	20	Montreal	"	"	34	"	238	407 00
Barry, H. D	"	20	[illegible]	"	"	34	"	238	436 20
Bullman, Chisholm & Co.	"	23	Halifax	"	"	34	"	238	49 66
[illegible]tt Cigar Co., Ltd	"	23	Hamilton	"	"	34	"	238	174 00
Tuckett Cigar Co., Ltd	"	23	"	"	"	34	"	338	239 30
Dyer, Jno. J	"	23	London	"	"	34	"	238	133 60
Kelley, [illegible]	"	23	"	"	"	34	"	238	149 60
Dooley, James	"	23	"	"	"	34	"	238	74 90
Dooley, James	"	23	"	"	"	34	"	238	182 20
Nolan, J. F.	"	23	"	"	"	34	"	238	290 90
Taylor, John	"	23	Toronto	"	"	34	"	238	93 90
Wilson, Andrew	"	23	"	"	"	34	"	238	378 80
[illegible]e Cigar Co.	"	23	Sherbrooke	"	"	34	"	238	290 20
[illegible]r, W. R.	"	23	"	"	"	34	"	238	415 50
Rosin, Louis	"	30	Toronto	"	"	34	"	238	94 70
[illegible]e, [illegible]s	"	30	Winnipeg	"	"	34	"	238	159 70
Bryan, G. F.	"	30	"	"	"	34	"	238	208 80
[illegible]er, J. M., Ltd	Feb.	5	Montreal	"	"	34	"	238	1,540 00
Ban h[illegible], M.	"	5	Victoria	"	"	34	"	238	15 20
Gold, F. F	"	5	"	"	"	34	"	238	17 30

No. 16—Refunds of Revenue—*Continued.*

EXCISE—*Continued.*

Articles.	To whom paid.	Date.		Divisions.	Under what Authority Refunded.	Amounts.	Totals.
		1906.				$ cts.	$ cts.
[illegible]acco—*Con*	[illegible]ston, J. M.	Feb.	5	Victoria	Refunded under Revised Statutes, cap. 34, sec. 238	39 20	
	Donnelly, John	"	12	London	" " 34 " 238	28 50	
	[illegible]s, S. R.	"	12	"	" " 34 " 238	51 70	
	Wartig, B. J.	"	12	"	" " 34 " 238	53 80	
	[illegible]e, John	"	12	"	" " 34 " 238	290 10	
	[illegible]y, C. E.	"	12	St. Catharines	" " 34 " 238	19 90	
	Scl[illegible]er, F.	"	12	Victoria	" " 34 " 238	21 80	
	Province Cigar Co.	"	12	"	" " 34 " 238	98 30	
	Levy, J. & Sons	"	12	"	" " 34 " 238	29 75	
	[illegible]a, A.	"	12	Pictou	" " 34 " 238	17 44	
	McDonald, R. D.	"	14	London	" " 34 " 238	14 00	
	St. Louis, Clovis	"	14	Montreal	" " 34 " 238	10 70	
	[illegible]d, Sir W. C.	"	14	"	" " 34 " 238	133 40	
	[illegible]tt Cigar Co., Ltd., The	"	15	Hamilton	" " 34 " 238	7 56	
	[illegible] Tobacco Co. of Canada, Ltd., The	"	15	[illegible]al	" " 34 " 238	339 60	
	Hobrecker, A.	"	15	Halifax	" " 34 " 238	205 03	
	[illegible]rd, A.	"	16	Toronto	" " 34 " 259	93	
	Lemesurier, John	"	16	[illegible]c	" " 34 " 259	2 88	
	Rock City Tobacco Co., The	"	16	"	" " 34 " 259	26 37	
	Fortier, J. M., Ltd	"	16	Montreal	" " 34 " 259	8 92	
	Solomon, E.	"	16	"	" " 34 " 259	9 46	
	American Tobacco Co. of [illegible]a, Ltd., The	"	16	"	" " 34 " 259	1,381 75	
	George E. Tuckett & Son Co., Ltd., The	"	16	Hamilton	" " 34 " 259	131 76	
	Begg, L. H.	"	22	St. Catharines	" " 34 " 238	26 20	
	Hirsch, Jacob	"	22	Montreal	" " 34 " 238	149 60	
	Belmson, H. F. W.	"	22	Victoria	" " 34 " 238	159 00	
	Grothé, L. O.	"	24	Montreal	" " 34 " 238	889 30	
	Fortier, J. M.	"	26	"	" " 34 " 238	864 40	
	Hooker, F. D.	"	27	St. Catharines	" " 34 " 238	12 70	
	Blankstein, C.	Mar.	5	Guelph	" " 34 " 238	55 60	
	Fair, T. J. & Co., Ltd.	"	9	Brantford	" " 34 " 238	141 90	
	Smith, Joseph	"	9	London	" " 34 " 238	65 10	

Brener, A. H.	"	9	"	"	"	34	"	238	70 80
Kelly, [illegible]	"	9	"	"	"	34	"	238	107 90
Ward, W.	"	9	"	"	"	34	"	238	143 80
[illegible]n, J. F.	"	9	"	"	"	34	"	238	194 10
McDonald, R. D.	"	9	"	"	"	34	"	238	322 80
McHugh, John	"	9	St. Catharines	"	"	34	"	238	30 00
Milligan, Geo.	"	9	Toronto	"	"	34	"	238	468 70
Wilson, Andrew	"	9	"	"	"	34	"	238	343 40
Brown, H. A.	"	15	Vancouver	"	"	34	"	238	92 90
Tuckett Cigar Co., Ltd., The	"	15	Hamilton	"	"	34	"	238	242 70
[illegible]h, [illegible]	"	15	Montreal	"	"	34	"	238	40 00
[illegible] [illegible] Co. of [illegible]da, Ltd., The	"	15	"	"	"	34	"	238	306 40
Solomon, E.	"	16	"	"	"	34	"	259	8 67
Fortier, J. M., Ltd	"	16	"	"	"	34	"	259	13 14
[illegible] [illegible] Co. of Canada, Ltd., [illegible]	"	16	"	"	"	34	"	259	1,258 74
[illegible] E. Tuckett & Son Co., Ltd	"	16	Hamilton	"	"	34	"	259	135 65
Bollard, A.	"	16	Toronto	"	"	34	"	259	1 15
Lemesurier, John	"	16	[illegible]	"	"	34	"	259	1 53
Rock City [illegible] Co.	"	23	"	"	"	34	"	259	8 77
St. Louis, [illegible]	"	23	Montreal	"	"	34	"	238	120 60
Henry, James	"	23	"	"	"	34	"	238	195 90
Prozesky, Paul	"	23	Winnipeg	"	"	34	"	238	212 60
Dyer, John J.	"	23	London	"	"	34	"	238	148 00
[illegible] E. [illegible]kett & Sons Co., Ltd	"	23	Hamilton	"	"	34	"	238	1,099 81
McKenna, A	"	24	Pictou	"	"	34	"	238	126 72
Tobin & Co., John	"	26	Halifax	"	"	34	"	238	10 77
[illegible]r, A.	"	30	"	"	"	34	"	238	12 49
Tuckett Cigar Co., Ltd., The	April	9	Hamilton	"	"	34	"	238	238 30
Dooley, Jas.	"	9	London	"	"	34	"	238	160 70
Firstbrook, Jos	"	9	"	"	"	34	"	238	329 80
Jacobs, H. & Co.	"	9	Montreal	"	"	34	"	238	179 70
"	"	9	"	"	"	34	"	238	254 60
[illegible]thé, L. O	"	9	"	"	"	34	.	238	909 90
Hart, A. S.	"	9	St. John	"	"	34	"	238	111 60
Nicholson, D.	"	11	Charlottetown	"	"	34	"	238	176 30
Brener, A. H.	"	11	London	"	"	34	"	238	23 00
McDonald, D	"	11	"	"	"	34	"	238	19 10
Bauld, Bros. & Co.	"	18	Halifax	"	"	34	"	238	93 50
[illegible]r, A.	"	18	"	"	"	34	"	238	32 41
Bollard, A.	"	18	[illegible]o	"	"	34	"	259	1 70
[illegible]n, B.	"	18	Montreal	"	"	34	"	259	7 21
Henry, James	"	18	"	"	"	34	"	259	9 76
Ateshian, C.	"	18	"	"	"	34	"	259	5 88
Walsh, Arthur	"	18	"	"	"	34	"	259	8 74

No. 16.—Refunds of Revenue—*Continued*.

EXCISE—*Continued*.

Articles.	To whom paid.	Date.		Divisions.	Under what Authority Refunded.	Amounts.	Totals.
		1906.				$ cts.	$ cts.
[illegible]acco—*Con*.	Muscovetch, K.	April	18	Montreal	Refunded under Revised Statutes, cap. 34, sec. 259	1 71	
	[illegible] Tobacco Co.	"	18	"	" " 34 " 259	11 63	
	Solomon, E.	"	18	"	" " 34 " 259	9 91	
	Fortier, J. M., Ltd.	"	18	"	" " 34 " 259	18 78	
	Imperial Tobacco Co. of Canada, Ltd., The	"	18	"	" " 34 " 259	1,452 63	
	Rock City Tobacco Co.	"	18	Quebec	" " 34 " 259	19 36	
	Tuckett, George E. & Son Co., Ltd., The	"	18	Hamilton	" " 34 " 259	156 60	
	Tuckett, George E. & Son Co., Ltd., The	"	18	"	" " 29 " 78	2 00	
	American Tobacco Co. of Canada, Ltd., The	"	25	Montreal	" " 34 " 238	19 50	
	Imperial Tobacco Co. of Canada, Ltd., The	"	25	"	" " 34 " 38	593 70	
	McKenna, A.	"	25	Pictou	" " 34 " 38	175 68	
	Imperial Tobacco Co. of Canada, Ltd., The	May	5	Montreal	" " 34 " 38	14 70	
	[illegible], A.	"	8	Pictou	" " 34 " 38	19 68	
	McDonald, Sir W. C.	"	8	Montreal	" " 34 " 238	93 50	
	American Tobacco Co. of Canada, Ltd., The	"	8	"	" " 34 " 238		
	Tuckett Cigar Co., Ltd., The	"	8	"	" " 34 " 38	121 30	
	Sherbrooke Cigar Co.	"	8	Sherbrooke	" " 34 " 38	234 40	
	Fair, E. J. & Co., Ltd.	"	8	Brantford	" " 34 " 238	157 30	
	Tuckett Cigar Co., Ltd., The	"	8	Hamilton	" " 34 " 238	343 50	
	[illegible]	"	8	Guelph	" " 34 " 238	50 90	
	Manness, S. R.	"	8	London	" " 34 " 38	30 00	
	Smith, Joseph	"	8	"	" " 34 " 38	65 30	
	Kelly, George	"	8	"	" " 34 " 238	103 10	
	Nolan, J. F.	"	8	"	" " 34 " 238	129 10	
	Dooley, James	"	8	"	" " 34 " 238	138 30	
	McDonald, R. D.	"	8	"	" " 34 " 238	216 90	
	[illegible], Andrew	"	8	Toronto	" " 34 " 238	331 70	
	Milligan, Geo.	"	8	"	" " 34 " 238	478 70	

G. E. Tuckett & Son Co., Ltd.	"	11..	Hamilton	"		34	"	238	1,049 14
Tuckett Cigar Co., Ltd., The	"	11..	"	"	"	34	"	238	205 20
McNee, John	"	11..	London	"	"	34	"	238	297 10
Gignac, R. T.	"	11..	Windsor	"	"	34	"	238	128 00
[illegible], J. M.	"	11..	Montreal	"	"	34	"	238	985 40
Kurtz & Co.	"	11..	Vancouver	"	"	34	"	238	154 40
Tietzen, W.	"	11..	"	"	"	34	"	238	196 30
Bollard, A.	"	16..	Toronto	"	"	34	"	259	1 47
Lemesurier, John	"	16..	Quebec	"	"	34	"	238	5 32
Rock City Tobacco Co., Ltd., The	"	16..	"	"	"	34	"	238	10 44
Solomon, E.	"	16..	"	"	"	34	"	238	10 06
[illegible] Tobacco Co. of Canada, Ltd., The	"	16..	Montreal	"	"	34	"	238	1,436 37
G. E. Tuckett & Son Co., Ltd., The	"	16..	[illegible]	"	"	34	"	238	176 55
Fortier, J. M., Ltd	"	16..	Montreal	"	"	34	"	238	23 05
Bauld, Bros. & Co.	"	16..	Halifax	"	"	34	"	238	1 87
Walsh, [illegible]	"	23..	Montreal	"	"	34	"	238	90 00
American Tobacco Co., of Canada, Ltd., The	"	23..	"	"	"	34	"	238	615 10
Hobrecker, A.	"	23..	Halifax	"	"	34	"	238	5 16
McKenna, A.	"	23..	Pictou	"	"	34	"	238	55 07
Macdonald, Sir W. C.	"	31..	Montreal	"	"	34	"	238	92 40
[illegible] Tobacco Co. of Canada Ltd., The	June	8..	"	"	"	34	"	238	395 00
[illegible], B.	"	8..	"	"	"	34	"	238	11 00
McKenna, A.	"	8..	Pictou	"	"	34	"	238	38 24
Nicholson, D.	"	8..	Charlottetown	"	"	34	"	238	23 94
[illegible], H. F.	"	8..	Belleville	"	"	34	"	238	255 20
[illegible] Cigar Co., Ltd., The	"	8..	Hamilton	"	"	34	"	238	199 80
Wilson, [illegible]	"	8..	Toronto	"	"	34	"	238	377 00
Fortier, J. M., Ltd.	"	13..	Montreal	"	"	34	"	238	2 90
[illegible], T. J. & Co., Ltd.	"	13..	Brantford	"	"	34	"	238	5 60
McKenna, A.	"	19..	Pictou	"	"	34	"	238	33 04
[illegible], John & Co.	"	19..	Halifax	"	"	34	"	238	59 46
Sievert, J. G.	"	19..	"	"	"	34	"	238	3 84
Levy, J. & Sons	"	19..	Victoria	"	"	34	"	238	10 37
Bollard, A.	"	19..	Toronto	"	"	34	"	259	0 75
Lemesurier, John	"	19..	Quebec	"	"	34	"	259	3 15
Rock City Tobacco Co., The	"	19..	"	"	"	34	"	259	12 33
Solomon, E.	"	19..	Montreal	"	"	34	"	259	13 43
Fortier, J. M., Ltd	"	19..	"	"	"	34	"	259	20 88
[illegible] Tobacco Co. of Canada, Ltd., The	"	19..	"	"	"	34	"	259	1,809 75
Tuckett, G. E. & Son Co., Ltd., The	"	19..	Hamilton	"	"	34	"	259	213 97

No. 16.—Returns of Revenue—*Continued.*

EXCISE—*Continued.*

Articles.	To whom paid.	Date.		Divisions.	Under what Authority Refunded.	Amounts.	Totals.
		1906.				$ cts.	$ cts.
Tobacco—*Con*	Tuckett, G. E. & Son Co., Ltd. The	June	19	Hamilton	Refunded under Revised Statutes, cap. 34, sec. 238	932 01	
	Blumensteil, I	"	19	"	" " 34 " 238	209 80	
	Kelly, G	"	19	London	" " 34 " 238	149 10	
	Weis, Frank	"	19	St. Catharines	" " 34 " 238	44 00	
	Milligan, Geo	"	19	Toronto	" " 34 " 238	527 80	
	Webster, W. R	"	19	Sherbrooke	" " 34 " 238	206 80	
	Bryan, Geo. F	"	19	Winnipeg	" " 34 " 238	179 60	
	Inland Cigar Co	"	22	Vancouver	" " 34 " 238	176 40	
	Macdonald, Sir W.C	"	22	Montreal	" " 34 " 238	93 50	
	American Tobacco Co. of Canada, Ltd., The	"	22	"	" " 34 " 238	164 05	
	Grothé, L. O	July	6	"	" " 34 " 238	682 90	
	Bradley, John	"	6	Hamilton	" " 34 " 238	41 40	
	Thynes, Joseph	"	6	"	" " 34 " 238	92 70	
	Oberndorfer, S	"	6	Kingston	" " 34 " 238	115 20	
	McGowan, G. A	"	6	"	" " 34 " 238	286 60	
	Firstbrooke, Joseph	"	6	London	" " 34 " 238	138 00	
	Dyer, Jno. J	"	6	"	" " 34 " 238	147 50	
	Tobin, John & Co	"	6	Halifax	" " 34 " 238	10 77	
	McKenna, A	"	6	Pictou	" " 34 " 238	48 24	
	American Tobacco Co. of Canada, Ltd., The	"	6	Montreal	" " 34 " 238	84 80	
	American Tobacco Co. of Canada, Ltd., The	"	9	"	" " 34 " 238	108 53	
	Gardner, H. B	"	12	Brantford	" " 34 " 238	102 00	
	Dyer, Jno	"	12	London	" " 34 " 238	44 80	
	Ward, W	"	12	"	" " 34 " 238	203 00	
	Brener, A. H	"	12	"	" " 34 " 238	188 70	
	Taylor, John	"	12	Toronto	" " 34 " 238	130 40	
	Wilson, Andrew	"	12	"	" " 34 " 238	356 20	
	Spilling, M. E	"	16	"	" " 34 " 238	20 80	
	Macdonald, Sir W. C	"	16	Montreal	" " 34 " 238	75 30	
	Macdonald, Sir W. C	"	16	"	" " 34 " 238	24 08	
	McKenna, A	"	17	Pictou	" " 34 " 238	99 84	
	Fair, T. J. & Co., Ltd	"	17	Brantford	" " 34 " 238	125 50	
	Tuckett Cigar Co., Ltd., The	"	17	Hamilton	" " 34 " 238	288 50	
	Firstbrooke, Joseph	"	17	London	" " 34 " 238	47 30	

	Kelly, [illegible]eo	"	17	"	"	"	34	"	238	53 50	
	Nolan, J. F	"	17	"	"	"	34	"	238	152 10	
	Dooley, James	"	17	"	"	"	34	"	238	231 50	
	McNee, John	"	17	"	"	"	34	"	238	308 80	
	[illegible], R. D	"	17	"	"	"	34	"	238	624 80	
	Bauld Bros. & Co	"	24	Halifax	"	"	34	"	238	7 18	
	Harkness, Thos	"	24	Montreal	"	"	34	"	238	165 10	
	Tuckett Cigar Co., Ltd., The	"	24	"	"	"	34	"	238	235 40	
	Tuckett Cigar Co., Ltd., The	"	24	"	"	"	34	"	238	316 60	
	Kenny, James	"	24	"	"	"	34	"	259	14 09	
	[illegible]n, B	"	24	"	"	"	34	"	259	13 78	
	Atheshian, Carnig	"	24	"	"	"	34	"	259	0 63	
	[illegible]is, P. & G., Ltd	"	24	"	"	"	34	"	259	15 49	
	[illegible]h, A	"	24	"	"	"	34	"	259	16 99	
	Muscovetch, K	"	24	"	"	"	34	"	259	5 47	
	[illegible] Co	"	24	"	"	"	34	"	259	14 19	
	Solomon, E	"	24	"	"	"	34	"	259	13 21	
	Fortier, J. M., Ltd	"	24	"	"	"	34	"	259	24 85	
	American To[illegible]acco Co. of Ca[illegible], Ltd., The	"	24	"							
	Lemesurier, John	"	24	[illegible]c	"	"	34	"	259	1,379 63	
	Rock City Tobacco Co., The	"	24	"	"	"	34	"	259	2 50	
	[illegible]n, D	"	24	Charlottetown	"	"	34	"	259	3 39	
	Geo. E. Tuckett & Son Co., Ltd., The	"	24	[illegible]n	"	"	34	"	259	17 43	
	Geo. E. Tuckett & Son Co., Ltd., The	"	24	"	"	"	34	"	259	211 19	
	Schl[illegible]er, W. G	"	26	[illegible]h	"	"	29	"	78	1 60	
	Smith, Jos	"	26	London	"	"	34	"	238	80 80	
	Cauley, B	"	28	[illegible]n	"	"	34	"	238	71 70	
	Schwarz, John H	"	28	"	"	"	34	"	238	48 60	
	Youngs, John	"	28	Brantford	"	"	34	"	238	109 20	
	[illegible]a, A	"	28	Picton	"	"	34	"	238	82 10	
	Schrader, John H	"	28	Hamilton	"	"	34	"	238	68 32	
Cigars	Tuckett Cigar Co., Ltd. The	March	30	"	"	"	34	"	238	54 60	86,768 81
Manufactures in bond	Milligan, Geo	July	6	Toronto	"	"	34	"	238	202 65	
	The British Columbia Distillery Co	1905. Sept.	2	[illegible]r	"	"	34	"	238	110 51	313 16
Officer's salary	Allen Solomon	Nov.	2	Brantford	"	"	34	"	238		25 00
							34	"	238		300 00
											253,261 38

W. J. GERALD,
Deputy Minister.

INLAND REVENUE DEPARTMENT,
OTTAWA, August 29, 1906.

No. 17.—DEPARTMENTAL EXPENDITURES.

(For Details, see Appendix B.)

Due by sundry persons, July 1, 1905.	Disbursed by the Receiver General.	Deductions for			Totals.	—	Salaries.	Contingencies.	Due by sundry persons, June 30, 1906.	Totals.
		Superannuation.	Insurance.	Retirement.						
$ cts.	$ cts.	$ cts.	$ cts.	$ cts.	$ cts.		$ cts.	$ cts.	$ cts.	$ cts.
....	7,000 00	....	......	....	7,000 00	Minister of Inland Revenue	7,000 00	....	....	7,000 00
....	45,605 74	631 29	116 40	613 69	46,967 12	Departmental officers	46,967 12	....	....	[illegible]967 12
....	237 40	....	....	....	237 40	Subscription to newspapers	....	237 40	....	237 40
....	1,214 97	....	......	....	1,214 97	Extra clerks, &c	....	1,214 97	....	1,214 97
....	758 45	....	......	....	758 45	Telegraph companies and telephones	....	758 45	....	758 45
....	2,012 92	....	......	....	2,012 92	Stationery	....	2,012 92	....	2,012 92
....	1,616 50	....	......	....	1,616 50	Printing and lithographing	....	1,616 50	....	1,616 50
....	41 86	....	......	....	41 86	Postage	....	41 86	....	41 86
16 66	2,022 57	....	......	....	2,039 23	Sundry persons	....	2,022 57	16 66	2,039 23
16 66	60,510 41	631 29	116 40	613 69	61,888 45	Totals	53,967 12	7,904 67	16 66	1,888 45

INLAND REVENUE DEPARTMENT,
OTTAWA, August 29, 1906.

W. J. GERALD,
Deputy Minister.

WEIGHTS AND MEASURES, GAS, ELECTRIC LIGHT AND LAW STAMPS.

No. 18.—STATEMENT showing amount of Revenue accrued during Year ended June 30, 1906.

DR.

—	Weights and Measures Stamps.	Gas Stamps.	Electric Light Stamps.	Law Stamps.				Totals.
				Supreme Court.	Exchequer Court.	Yukon Territorial Court.	Yukon Mining Court.	
	$ cts.	$ cts.	$ cts.	$ cts.	$ cts.	$ cts.	$ cts.	$ cts.
To amount of stamps destroyed or returned by distributors	948 87	3 50	....	....	....	....	....	952 37
To commission allowed	....	....	....	85 00	183 95	....	....	268 95
To amount of stamps remaining in hands of distributors, June 30, 1906	64,178 78	44,102 80	42,208 50	....	....	10,572 75	2,210 00	163,272 83
To balance, being the revenue during 1905-1906	72,883 86	41,424 25	29,974 75	1,615 00	3,495 05	5,517 50	753 25	155,663 66
Totals	138,011 51	85,530 55	72,183 25	1,700 00	3,679 00	16,090 25	2,963 25	320,157 81

CR.

—	Weights and Measures Stamps.	Gas Stamps.	Electric Light Stamps.	Supreme Court.	Exchequer Court.	Yukon Territorial Court.	Yukon Mining Court.	Totals.
To amount of stamps in the hands of distributors on July 1, 1905	66,573 01	34,110 05	40,658 25	....	....	16,090 25	2,963 25	160,394 81
To stamps issued by Inland Revenue Department during the year	71,438 50	51,420 50	31,525 00	1,700 00	3,679 00	....	....	159,763 00
Totals	138,011 51	85,530 55	72,183 25	1,700 00	3,679 00	16,090 25	2,963 25	320,157 81

INLAND REVENUE DEPARTMENT,
OTTAWA, August 29, 1906.

W. J. GERALD,
Deputy Minister.

WEIGHTS AND MEASURES, 1905–1906.

DR. No. 19 (A).—INSPECTION Divisions in Account with Revenue. CR.

Balances due by Inspectors, July 1, 1905.		Stamps issued to Inspectors	Seizures and Penalties.	Other Receipts	Transfer of Stamps.	Totals.	Divisions.	Transfer of Stamps.	Stamps returned or destroyed.	Deposited to the credit of the Receiver General.	Balances due by Inspectors, June 30, 1906.		Totals.
Stamps on hand.	Cash on hand.										Stamps on hand.	Cash on hand.	
$ cts.	$ cts.	$ cts.	$ cts.	$ cts.	$ cts.	$ cts.		$ cts.	$ cts.	$ cts.	$ cts.	$ cts.	$ cts.
4,069 40		2,140 00	7 20			6,216 60	Belleville		5 40	4,252 45	1,958 75		6,216 60
5,452 49		6,486 00				11,938 49	Hamilton			7,917 18	4,021 31		11,938 49
2,241 09		5,155 00		23 50		7,419 59	Ottawa		0 50	4,574 98	2,844 11		7,419 59
6,341 68		7,275 00				13,616 68	Toronto			7,748 55	5,868 13		13,616 68
4,986 25		8,970 00				13,956 25	Windsor			10,559 80	3,396 45		13,956 25
23,090 91		30,026 00	7 20	23 50		53,147 61	*Ontario*		5 90	35,052 96	18,088 75		53,147 61
19,308 40	7 30	16,285 00	10 00			35,610 70	Montreal			13,354 60	22,256 10		35,610 70
6,231 50	11 25	3,450 00				9,692 75	Quebec		21 00	3,934 35	5,670 00	67 40	9,692 75
3,390 89		3,215 00				6,605 89	St. Hyacinthe			3,077 91	3,527 98		6,605 89
2,337 20		850 00	5 00			3,192 20	Three Rivers			1,488 50	1,703 70		3,192 20
31,267 99	18 55	23,800 00	15 00			55,101 54	*Quebec*		21 00	21,855 36	33,157 78	67 40	55,101 54
1,316 31	1 00	2,390 00				3,707 31	*St. John, N.B*		5 00	2,427 26	1,238 96	36 09	3,707 31
215 24	14 17	787 50		0 30		1,017 21	Cape Breton		43 29	746 90	227 02		1,017 21
1,335 48	13 16	150 00				1,498 64	Halifax			983 20	515 44		1,498 64
1,722 56	102 18	640 00		4 00		2,468 74	Pictou		12 23	782 47	1,674 04		2,468 74
3,273 28	129 51	1,577 50		4 30		4,984 59	*Nova Scotia*		55 52	2,512 57	2,416 50		4,984 59
586 83		630 00				1,216 83	*Charlottetown, P.E.I.*			628 55	588 28		1,216 83
3,402 30		7,125 00				10,527 30	*Winnipeg, Man.*		262 00	7,288 68	2,976 62		10,527 30

1,620 59						1,620 59	*Calgary, Alta*			1,303 70	316 89		1,620 59
		1,160 00			230 95	1,390 95	Nelson			702 15	688 80		1,390 95
		1,455 00			555 55	2,010 55	Vancouver		593 45	726 75	690 35		2,010 55
848 80						848 80	Victoria	786 50		62 30			848 80
848 80		2,615 00			786 50	4,250 30	*British Columbia*	786 50	593 45	1,491 20	1,379 15		4,250 30
1,166 00		3,275 00				4,441 00	*Dawson, Yukon*		6 00	419 15	4,015 85		4,441 00
66,573 01	149 06	71,438 50	22 20	27 80	786 50	138,997 07	Grand Totals	786 50	948 87	72,979 43	64,178 78	103 49	138,997 07

W. J. GERALD,
Deputy Minister.

INLAND REVENUE DEPARTMENT,
OTTAWA, August 29, 1906.

WEIGHTS AND MEASURES, 1905-1906.

No. 19 (B.)—Deputy Inspectors of the Old Divisions in Account with Revenue.

Dr. Cr.

Balances due July 1, 1905. — Cash on hand.	Totals.	Divisions.	Balances due June 30, 1906. — Cash on hand.	Totals.
$ cts.	$ cts.		$ cts.	$ cts.
87 10	87 10	.....Essex	87 10	87 10
5 62	5 62	..... Hull, Quebec	5 62	5 62
92 72	92 72		92 72	92 72

W. J. GERALD,
Deputy Minister.

Inland Revenue Department,
Ottawa, August 29 1906.

WEIGHTS AND MEASURES—1905-1906.

DR. No. 20 (A).—INSPECTION DIVISIONS in Account with Expenditures. CR.

Amounts received from Department to meet Expenditures.	Deductions from Salaries for: Superannuation.	Insurance.	Guarantee.	Totals.	Divisions.	Expenditures Authorized by the Department: Salaries.	Special Assistance.	Seizures.	Rent.	Travelling Expenses.	Sundries.	Totals.
$ cts.	$ cts.	$ cts.	$ cts.	$ cts.		$ cts.	$ cts.	$ cts.	$ cts.	$ cts.	$ cts.	$ cts.
6,507 47	50 72	......	11 40	6,569 59	Belleville	3,682 70	358 93	5 20	300 00	1,642 84	579 92	6,569 59
6,947 25	18 70	......	13 80	6,979 75	Hamilton	5,908 04	......	......	......	995 31	76 40	6,979 75
6,076 71	13 96	......	12 60	6,103 27	Ottawa	4,683 88	......	......	125 00	1,046 63	247 76	6,103 27
6,224 48	16 04	......	10 80	6,251 32	Toronto	4,349 84	......	......	......	1,744 15	157 33	6,251 32
6,257 79	30 00	......	9 72	6,297 51	Windsor	4,100 62	299 06	......	......	1,567 10	330 73	6,297 51
32,013 70	129 42	......	58 32	32,201 44	*Ontario*	22,725 08	657 99	5 20	425 00	6,996 03	1,392 14	32,201 44
8,655 10	48 00	......	13 50	8,716 60	Montreal	5,773 16	299 06	1 00	507 00	1,881 94	254 44	8,716 60
8,815 67	76 40	22 33	16 20	8,930 60	Quebec	6,343 95	600 00	......	300 00	1,371 50	315 15	8,930 60
3,922 94	......	......	7 95	3,930 89	St. Hyacinthe	2,540 99	299 05	......	......	994 67	96 18	3,930 89
2,307 65	......	......	5 40	2,313 05	Three Rivers	1,599 96	......	......	......	699 14	13 95	2,313 05
23,701 36	124 40	22 33	43 05	23,891 14	*Quebec*	16,258 06	1,198 11	1 00	807 00	4,947 25	679 72	23,891 14
3,584 86	15 00	......	9 00	3,608 86	*St. John, N.B.*	3,049 92	......	......	......	492 70	66 24	3,608 86
1,354 29	......	......	3 60	1,357 89	Cape Breton	849 96	......	......	37 50	395 12	75 31	1,357 89
3,332 27	......	......	5 40	3,337 67	Halifax	1,699 92	799 92	......	300 00	391 98	145 85	3,337 67
1,953 74	19 96	......	5 40	1,979 10	Pictou	1,699 96	......	......	......	203 06	76 08	1,979 10
6,640 30	19 96	......	14 40	6,674 66	*Nova Scotia*	4,249 84	799 92	......	337 50	990 16	297 24	6,674 66
1,930 92	......	......	5 40	1,936 32	*Charlottetown, P.E.I.*	1,649 88	......	......	......	223 20	63 24	1,936 32

WEIGHTS AND MEASURES—1905-1906.

Dr. No. 20 (A).—Inspection Divisions in Account with Expenditures—*Concluded.* Cr.

Amounts received from Department to meet Expenditures.	Deductions from Salaries for: Superannuation.	Insurance.	Guarantee.	Totals.	Divisions.	Expenditures Authorized by the Department: Salaries.	Special Assistance.	Seizures.	Rent.	Travelling Expenses.	Sundries.	Totals.
$ cts.	$ cts.	$ cts.	$ cts.	$ cts.		$ cts.	$ cts.	$ cts.	$ cts.	$ cts.	$ cts.	$ cts.
5,888 05	4 04	....	13 65	5,905 74	....Winnipeg..................	3,708 07	....	....	....	2,063 48	134 19	5,905 74
1,439 63	16 04	....	5 40	1,461 07	....Calgary..................	999 92	....	....	....	461 15	....	1,461 07
7,327 68	20 08	....	19 05	7,366 81	...*Manitoba and N. W. Territories*...	4,707 99	....	....	....	2,524 63	134 19	7,366 81
1,880 91	....	....	3 60	1,884 51	....Nelson..................	900 00	....	....	165 00	551 90	267 61	1,884 51
2,810 81	....	....	6 96	2,817 77	....Vancouver..................	2,091 85	....	....	330 00	73 80	322 12	2,817 77
148 61	....	....	....	148 61	....Victoria..................	....	....	....	15 00	126 36	7 25	148 61
4,840 33	....	....	10 56	4,850 89	........*British Columbia*..........	2,991 85	....	....	510 00	752 06	596 98	4,850 89
1,211 31	....	....	3 60	1,214 91	........*Dawson*..............	999 96	....	....	....	155 00	59 95	1,214 91
3,048 02	....	....	....	3,048 02	....Chief Inspector..............	2,600 00	....	....	....	199 07	248 95	3,048 02
1,994 54	....	....	....	1,994 54	....General contingencies........	....	....	....	....	....	1,994 54	1,994 54
3,138 86	....	....	....	3,138 86	....Metric system..............	....	....	....	....	....	3,138 86	3,138 86
760 67	....	....	....	760 67	....Printing..................	....	....	....	....	....	760 67	760 67
431 81	....	....	....	431 81	....Stationery..................	....	....	....	....	....	431 81	431 81
399 94	....	....	....	399 94	....Provisional allowance........	....	....	....	....	....	399 94	399 94
91,024 30	308 86	22 33	163 38	91,518 87	........Grand Totals..........	59,232 58	2,656 02	6 20	2,079 50	17,280 10	10,264 47	91,518 87

Inland Revenue Department,
Ottawa, August 29, 1906.

W. J. GERALD,
Deputy Minister.

WEIGHTS AND MEASURES—1905-06.

DR. No. 20 (B).—OLD INSPECTION DIVISIONS in Account with Expenditures. CR.

Balances due by sundry persons, July 1, 1905.	Totals.	Divisions.	Balances due by sundry persons, June 30, 1906.	Totals.
$ cts.	$ cts.		$ cts.	$ cts.
39 56	39 56	......Essex	39 56	39 56
33 53	33 53	......Waterloo	33 53	33 53
73 09	73 09	*Ontario*	73 09	73 09
0 33	0 33	.....Drummond	0 33	0 33
41 25	41 25	......Laval	41 25	41 25
26 88	26 88	......Montmorency	26 88	26 88
27 51	27 51	......Richelieu	27 51	27 51
96 17	96 17	*Quebec.*	96 17	96 17
24 00	24 00	.....Lunenburg, Nova Scotia	24 00	24 00
193 26	193 26	Totals	193 26	193 26

W. J. GERALD,
Deputy Minister.

INLAND REVENUE DEPARTMENT,
OTTAWA, August 29, 1906.

No. 21.—GAS INSPECTION, 1905-1906.

Dr. INSPECTION Districts in Account with Revenue. Cr.

Balances due by Inspectors, July 1, 1905.		Stamps issued to Inspectors.	Penalties.	Sundries.	Totals.	Districts.	Returned damaged stamps.	Deposited to the credit of the Receiver General.	Balances due by Inspectors, June 30, 1906.		Totals.
Stamps on hand.	Cash on hand.								Stamps on hand.	Cash on hand.	
$ cts.	$ cts.	$ cts.	$ cts.	$ cts.	$ cts.		$ cts.	$ cts.	$ cts.	$ cts.	$ cts.
912 00	....	475 00	....	....	1,387 00	Barrie	....	176 50	1,210 50	....	1,387 00
1,556 25	....	....	....	....	1,556 25	Belleville	....	285 0	1,271 25	....	1,556 25
879 75	....	1,300 00	....	....	2,179 75	Berlin	....	334 25	1,845 50	....	2,179 75
732 25	....	237 50	....	....	969 75	Brockville	....	345 50	624 25	....	969 75
363 00	....	75 00	....	....	438 00	Cobourg	1 00	178 00	259 00	....	438 00
320 00	....	....	....	....	320 00	Cornwall	....	47 75	272 25	....	320 00
1,078 75	....	1,375 00	....	....	2,453 75	Guelph	....	421 50	2,032 25	....	2,453 75
1,621 25	....	11,520 50	....	....	13,141 75	Hamilton	....	9,829 25	3,312 50	....	13,141 75
360 50	....	875 00	....	....	1,235 50	Kingston	....	538 25	697 25	....	1,235 50
165 50	....	....	....	....	165 50	Listowel	....	47 50	118 00	....	165 50
1,360 50	....	3,550 00	15 00	....	4,925 50	London	2 50	3,043 00	1,880 00	....	4,925 50
447 25	....	....	....	....	447 25	Napanee	....	42 00	405 25	....	447 25
1,405 50	....	8,125 00	....	....	9,530 50	Ottawa	....	971 25	8,559 25	....	9,530 50
195 75	....	275 00	....	....	470 75	Owen Sound	....	118 25	352 50	....	470 75
779 25	....	....	....	....	779 25	Peterborough	....	143 50	635 75	....	779 25
870 25	....	175 00	....	....	1,045 25	Sarnia	....	441 00	604 25	....	1,045 25
1,145 25	....	150 00	....	....	1,295 25	Stratford	....	191 00	1,104 25	....	1,295 25
5,727 80	....	8,750 00	....	....	14,477 80	Toronto	....	10,599 75	3,878 05	....	14,477 80
19,920 80	....	36,883 00	15 00	....	56,818 80	*Ontario*	3 50	27,753 25	29,062 05	....	56,818 80
2,590 00	....	8,700 00	....	....	11,290 00	Montreal	....	8,605 50	2,684 50	....	11,290 00
1,488 75	....	....	....	....	1,488 75	Quebec	....	384 50	1,104 25	....	1,488 75
545 50	....	....	....	....	545 50	Sherbrooke	....	181 00	364 50	....	545 50
1,002 75	....	75 00	....	....	1,077 75	St. Hyacinthe	....	128 00	949 75	....	1,077 75
5,627 00	....	8,775 00	....	....	14,402 00	*Quebec*	....	9,299 00	5,103 00	....	14,402 00

667 00	....	212 50	....	....	879 50	Fredericton	....	153 00	726 50	....	879 50
503 50	....	625 00	....	....	1,128 50	St. John	....	642 50	486 00	....	1,128 50
1,170 50	....	837 50	....	....	2,008 00	*New Brunswick*	....	795 50	1,212 50	....	2,008 0
1,208 25	....	400 00	....	....	1,608 25	*Halifax, N.S*	....	378 00	1,230 25	....	1,608 25
708 50	....	50 00	....	....	758 50	*Charlottetown, P.E.I*	....	71 50	687 00	....	758 50
1,143 00	....	1,725 00	....	....	2,868 00	*Winnipeg, Man*	....	1,437 50	1,430 50	....	2,868 00
707 25	....	....	....	....	707 25	Nanaimo	....	38 00	669 25	....	707 25
1,004 75	....	....	....	....	1,004 75	New Westminster	....	61 75	943 00	....	1,004 75
1,967 75	....	2,250 00	....	....	4,217 75	Vancouver	....	1,123 75	3,094 00	....	4,217 75
652 25	....	500 00	....	....	1,152 25	Victoria	....	481 00	671 25	....	1,152 25
4,332 00	....	2,750 00	....	....	7,082 00	*British Columbia*	....	1,704 50	5,377 50	....	7,082 00
34,110 05	....	51,420 50	15 00	....	85,545 55	Totals	3 50	41,439 25	44,102 80	....	85,545 55

INLAND REVENUE DEPARTMENT,
OTTAWA, August 29, 1906.

W. J. GERALD,
Deputy Minister.

GAS

DR. No. 22.—INSPECTION DISTRICTS in

Balances due by Inspectors, July 1, 1905.	Amounts received from Department to meet Expenditures.	Deductions from Salaries for — Superannuation.	Deductions from Salaries for — Retirement.	Deductions from Salaries for — Guarantee.	Totals.	Districts.
$ cts.	$ cts.	$ cts.	$ cts.	$ cts.	$ cts.	
....	94 40	2 00	....	3 60	100 00	....Barrie....................
....	536 44	7 04	....	6 48	549 96	....Belleville....................
....	148 29	....	....	3 60	151 89	...Berlin....................
....	75 86	....	....	....	75 86	...Brockville....................
....	155 55	2 00	....	3 60	161 15	....Cobourg....................
....	131 85	2 00	....	3 60	137 45	....Cornwall....................
....	205 55	4 00	....	3 60	213 15	....Guelph....................
....	3,500 80	36 00	....	8 16	3,544 96	....Hamilton....................
....	491 75	....	....	3 60	495 35	....Kingston....................
....	189 39	....	....	3 60	192 99	....Listowel....................
....	1,899 49	....	....	4 77	1,904 26	....London....................
....	30 35	....	....	....	30 35	...Napanee....................
....	2,076 72	....	....	3 69	2,080 41	....Ottawa....................
....	318 68	2 64	....	3 60	324 92	....Owen Sound....................
....	157 50	....	....	3 60	161 10	....Peterborough....................
....	12 90	....	....	....	12 90	....Sarnia....................
....	207 40	4 00	....	3 60	215 00	....Stratford....................
....	4,231 24	34 04	....	9 00	4,274 28	....Toronto....................
....	14,464 16	93 72	....	68 10	14,625 98	......*Ontario*....................
....	3,754 05	....	....	8 28	3,762 33	...Montreal....................
....	1,636 84	29 96	....	3 60	1,670 40	..Quebec....................
....	143 40	3 00	....	3 60	150 00	....Sherbrooke....................
....	98 20	....	....	1 80	100 00	....St. Hyacinthe....................
....	5,632 49	32 96	....	17 28	5,682 73	.....*Quebec*....................
....	179 96	....	....	3 30	183 26	....Fredericton....................
....	1,197 32	....	....	3 60	1,200 92	....St. John....................
....	1,377 28	....	....	6 90	1,384 18	.... *New Brunswick*....................
....	2,608 53	22 76	....	7 11	2,638 40	...Halifax....................
12 88	....	....	....	....	12 88	....Pictou....................
12 88	2,608 53	22 76	....	7 11	2,651 28	......*Nova Scotia*....................
....	446 40	....	....	3 60	450 00	......*Charlottetown, P.E.I.*.......
....	1,263 36	....	....	6 48	1,269 84	..... *Winnipeg, Man*..............
....	96 40	....	....	3 60	100 00	...Nanaimo....................
....	91 40	....	5 00	3 60	100 00	...New Westminster....................
....	671 10	6 00	....	3 60	680 70	....Vancouver....................
....	192 40	4 00	....	3 60	200 00	....Victoria....................
....	1,051 30	10 00	5 00	14 40	1,080 70	..... *British Columbia*..............
....	100 00	....	....	....	100 00	....Chief Inspector....................
200 00	....	....	....	....	200 00	...General....................
....	731 79	....	....	....	731 79	....General expenses....................
....	794 35	....	....	....	794 35	....Printing....................
....	274 89	....	....	....	274 89	....Stationery....................
....	30 40	....	....	....	30 40	....Technical translation....................
212 88	28,774 95	159 44	5 00	123 87	29,276 14	......*Grand Totals*....................

INLAND REVENUE DEPARTMENT,
OTTAWA, August 29, 1906.

INSPECTION—1905-1906.

Account with Expenditures. CR.

Expenditures Authorized by the Department.					Balances due by Inspectors, June 30, 1906.	Totals.
Salaries.	Special Assistance.	Rent.	Travelling Expenses.	Sundries.		
$ cts.	$ cts.	$ cts.	$ cts.	$ cts.	$ cts.	$ cts.
100 00						100 00
449 96		100 00				549 96
100 00			31 80	20 09		151 89
	58 31			17 55		75 86
100 00			32 15	29 00		161 15
100 00				37 45		137 45
200 00				13 15		213 15
2,920 88		120 00	376 95	127 13		3,544 96
400 00		45 00		50 35		495 35
100 00		78 00		14 99		192 99
1,591 66	24 00		213 45	75 15		1,904 26
			28 85	1 50		30 35
1,169 96	540 00	300 00		70 45		2,080 41
199 92		125 00				324 92
150 00			9 10	2 00		161 10
			6 90	6 00		12 90
200 00				15 00		215 00
4,199 84			12 60	61 84		4,274 28
11,982 22	622 31	768 00	711 80	541 65		14,625 98
3,299 88		240 00	53 25	169 20		3,762 33
1,500 00		150 00		20 40		1,670 40
150 00						150 00
100 00						100 00
5,049 88		390 00	53 25	189 60		5,682 73
183 26						183 26
1,100 00			91 06	9 86		1,200 92
1,283 26			91 06	9 86		1,384 18
1,992 39		300 00	253 41	92 60		2,638 40
					12 88	12 88
1,992 39		300 00	253 41	92 60	12 88	2,651 28
450 00						450 00
999 96			200 55	69 33		1,269 84
100 00						100 00
100 00						100 00
300 00			146 20	234 50		680 70
200 00						200 00
700 00			146 20	234 50		1,080 70
100 00						100 00
					200 00	200 00
				731 79		731 79
				794 35		794 35
				274 89		274 89
				30 40		30 40
22,557 71	622 31	1,458 00	1,456 27	2,968 97	212 88	29,276 14

W. J. GERALD,
Deputy Minister.

ELECTRIC LIGHT INSPECTION, 1905-1906.

Dr. No. 23.—Inspection Districts in Account with Revenue. Cr.

Balances, July 1, 1905.		Stamps issued to Inspectors	Registration Fees accrued.	Totals.	Districts.	Deposited to the Credit of the Receiver General.		Balances, June 30, 1906.		Totals.
Stamps on hand.	Cash on hand.					Registration Fees.	Inspection Fees.	Stamps on hand.	Cash on hand.	
$ cts.	$ cts.	$ cts.	$ cts.	$ cts.		$ cts.	$ cts.	$ cts.	$ cts.	$ cts.
3,067 00	....	1,550 00	590 00	5,207 00	Belleville	590 00	1,222 00	3,395 00	....	5,207 00
1,455 75	....	2,400 00	295 00	4,150 75	Hamilton	295 00	1,659 50	2,196 25	....	4,150 75
1,723 00	....	2,050 00	590 00	4,363 00	London	590 00	1,922 50	1,850 50	....	4,363 00
7,475 50	....	1,875 00	390 00	9,740 50	Ottawa	390 00	1,930 25	7,420 25	....	9,740 50
7,195 00	....	5,750 00	1,065 00	14,010 00	Toronto	1,065 00	5,909 25	7,035 75	....	14,010 00
20,916 25	....	13,625 00	2,930 00	37,471 25	*Ontario*	2,930 00	12,643 50	21,897 75	....	37,471 25
3,718 75	....	5,300 00	165 00	9,183 75	Montreal	165 00	6,262 00	2,756 75	....	9,183 75
2,169 00	....	750 00	165 00	3,084 00	Quebec	165 00	593 00	2,326 00	....	3,084 00
320 25	....	250 00	185 00	755 25	Sherbrooke	185 00	153 75	416 50	....	755 25
997 75	....	650 00	205 00	1,852 75	St. Hyacinthe	205 00	478 00	1,169 75	....	1,852 75
167 50	....	375 00	65 00	607 50	Three Rivers	65 00	191 75	350 75	....	607 50
7,373 25	....	7,325 00	785 00	15,483 25	*Quebec*	785 00	7,678 50	7,019 75	....	5,483 25
1,825 50	....	1,075 00	235 00	3,135 50	*St. John N. B*	235 00	1,161 50	1,739 00	....	3,135 50
2,227 25	....	1,525 00	395 00	4,147 25	*Halifax, N. S*	395 00	1,044 00	2,708 25	....	4,147 25
309 25	....	325 00	40 00	674 25	*Charlottetown, P. E. I.*	40 00	334 75	299 50	....	674 25
....	....	1,050 00	....	1,050 00	*Edmonton*	....	216 75	833 25	....	1,050 00
2,291 75	....	3,250 00	385 00	5,926 75	*Winnipeg*	385 00	3,456 00	2,085 75	....	5,926 75
3,099 50	....	2,875 00	265 00	6,239 50	Vancouver	265 00	2,797 25	3,177 25	....	6,239 50
1,265 50	....	475 00	65 00	1,805 50	Victoria	65 00	642 50	1,098 00	....	1,805 50
4,365 00	....	3,350 00	330 00	8,045 00	*British Columbia*	330 00	3,439 75	4,275 25	....	8,045 0
1,350 00	....	....	25 00	1,375 00	Dawson	25 00	....	1,350 00	....	1,375 00
40,658 25	....	31,525 00	5,125 00	77,308 25	Grand totals	5,125 00	29,974 75	42,208 50	....	77,308 25

Inland Revenue Department,
Ottawa, August 29, 1906.

W. J. GERALD,
Deputy Minister.

ELECTRIC LIGHT INSPECTION, 1905-1906.

DR. No. 24.—INSPECTION Districts in Account with Expenditures. CR.

Amounts received from Department to meet expenditures.	Guarantee.	Totals.	DISTRICTS.	Expenditures Authorized by the Department.				Totals.
				Salaries.	Special Assistance.	Travelling Expenses.	Sundries.	
$ cts.	$ cts.	$ cts.		$ cts.	$ cts.	$ cts.	$ cts.	$ cts.
550 34	0 75	551 09	..Belleville	40 16	1 49	385 20	124 24	551 09
83 08	....	83 08	..Hamilton	....	....	82 75	0 33	83 08
251 45	....	251 45	..London	....	....	249 85	1 60	251 45
129 00	....	129 00	..Ottawa	....	....	129 00	....	129 00
2 50	....	2 50	..Owen Sound	....	....	....	2 50	2 50
487 87	....	487 87	..Toronto	....	....	479 30	8 57	487 87
55 85	....	55 85	..Montreal	....	....	26 05	29 80	55 85
148 15	....	148 15	..Quebec	....	....	35 85	112 30	148 15
70 70	....	70 70	..Sherbrooke	....	....	64 30	6 40	70 70
445 50	1 80	447 30	..St. Hyacinthe	300 00	....	143 60	3 70	447 30
631 50	....	631 50	.Three Rivers	500 00	....	130 40	1 10	631 50
220 15	....	220 15	..St. John	....	....	213 44	6 71	220 15
184 31	....	184 31	..Halifax	....	....	180 74	3 57	184 31
81 19	....	81 19	..Charlottetown	....	....	40 00	41 19	81 19
43 25	....	43 25	..Victoria	....	....	35 50	7 75	43 25
55 40	....	55 40	..Winnipeg	....	....	42 30	13 10	55 40
176 89	1 50	178 39	..Edmonton	85 44	....	....	92 95	178 39
496 32	3 60	499 92	..Yukon	499 92	....	....	....	499 92
3,996 66	....	3,996 66	..Chief Electr. Engineer	3,166 60	24 44	455 00	350 62	3,996 66
1,653 75	....	1,653 75	..General	....	....	....	1,653 75	1,653 75
35 75	....	35 75	..Printing	....	....	....	35 75	35 75
46 96	....	46 96	..Stationery	....	....	....	46 96	46 96
9,846 57	7 65	9,854 22	......Totals	4,592 12	25 93	2,693 28	2,542 89	9,854 22

W. J. GERALD,
Deputy Minister.

INLAND REVENUE DEPARTMENT,
OTTAWA, August 29, 1906.

DR. No. 25.—STATEMENT showing the transactions in connection with the manufacture of Methylated Spirits, 1905-1906. CR.

——	Amounts.	Totals.
	$ cts.	$ cts.
To Stock on hand, July 1, 1905, viz		9,521 46
W od Naphtha, 5,603·62 Proof Ga'ls. =3,352·71 Std. Galls. at $1.29	4,325 00	
M [illegible]ted Spirits, 3,177·63 Proof Galls. = 1,918·88 Std. Galls., viz: 1,387·42 Std. Galls. No. 1 at $1.10, 372·56 Galls. No. 2 at $1.50, and 158·90 Galls. Special, at $1.10	2,259 79	
Alcohol, 3,550·80 Pof Galls. at 30c	1,065 24	
" 2,207·70 " at 25c	551 93	
Drums, 60 at $10	600 00	
Barrels, 239 at $3 and 1 at $2 50	719 50	
To Stock sold in 1904-05 and not paid until after July 1, 1905		1,686 00
Methylated Spirits, 1,884·85 Proof Galls. =		
941·76 Std. Galls at $1.10	1,035 93	
112·95 " 1.08	121 98	
83·39 " 1.50	125 09	
Drums, 6 at $10	60 00	
Barrels, 51 at $3 and 76 at $2.50	343 00	
To Disbursements for purchase, &c.		41,568 62
Alcohol, 50,443·55 Proof Galls. at 30c	15,133 07	
" 9,966·85 " at 25c	2,491 73	
Wood Naphtha, 22,078·16 Proof Galls. = 13,060·69 Std. Galls. at $1.29	16,848 18	
Drums, 4 at $4	16 00	
" 178 at $10	1,780 00	
" 30 at $12	360 00	
Barrels, 1,527 at $3	4,581 00	
" 182 at $2.50	455 00	
	41,664 98	
Less freight and cartage	96 36	

——	Amounts.	Totals.
	$ cts.	$ cts.
By Cash received on account of Methylated Spirits, &c.		65,530 18
Methylated Spirits, 84,364·11 Proof Galls. =		
9,895·56 Std. Galls. at $1.08	10,687 15	
35,039·69 " at $1.10	38,543 35	
6,007·87 " at $1.50	9,011 57	
Barrels, 310 at $2.50 and 1,550 at $3	5,425 00	
Drums, 185 at $10, and 1 at $7.75	1,857 75	
	65,524 82	
Add alcohol 16·50 Proof Galls. at 30c.	4 95	
Freight	0 99	
	65,530 76	
Less	0 58	
By Methylated Spirits sold and not paid up to June 30, 1906.		547 10
773·44 Proof Galls. = 39·53 Std. Galls. at $1.08	42 68	
427 66 " at $1.10	470 42	
Barrels, 8 at $3, Drum, 1 at $10	34 00	
By material used in manufacture—		
Wood Naphtha, 23,809·03 Proof Galls. = 14,133·09 Std. Galls		
Alcohol, 63,684·95 Proof Galls		
Barrels destroyed, 60		
By Stock on hand, June 30, 1906		8,318 52
Wood Naphtha, 3,872·75 Proof Galls. = 2,280·31 Std. Galls. at $1.29	2,941 60	
Methylated Spirits, 4,781·52 Proof Galls. = 2,887·77 Std. Galls., viz—		
2,154·43 Galls. No. 1, at $1.10	2,369 87	
300·47 " " 2, at $1.50	450 66	
432·87 " Special at $1.10	476 16	

	$ cts.	$ cts.		$ cts.	$ cts.
To other expenses as follows		6,898 45	Alcohol, 2,467·45 Proof Galls. at 30c	740 23	
Rent	733 33		Drums on hand, 88 at $10 and 4 at $4	896 00	
Salaries	4,449 73		Barrels, 148 at $3	444 00	
Retirement	100 04				
Freight	652 60				
Stationery	19 76				
Parliamentary publications	0 20				
Advertising	9 90				
Sundries, including rent of motor power, heating, fuel, &c	932 89				
Manufactured during the year:—Methylated Spirits, 84,856·59 Proof Galls. = 51,241·10 Std. Galls					
Net profit		14,721 27			
Total		74,395 80			74,395 80

W. J. GERALD,
Deputy Minister.

INLAND REVENUE DEPARTMENT,
OTTAWA, August 29, 1906.

No. 26—STATEMENT showing the Amounts voted, and the Expenditures authorized for each service for the Year ended June 30, 1906.

Services.	Grants.	Expenditures.	Over Expenditures.	Under Expenditures.
	$ cts.	$ cts.	$ cts.	$ cts.
Minister's salary	7,000 00	7,000 00	....	....
Departmental salaries	50,636 32	46,967 12	....	3,669 20
" contingencies	7,900 00	7,904 67	4 67	....
Excise salaries	390,718 75	376,035 42	....	14,683 33
" contingencies	62,000 00	61,939 82	....	60 18
Duty pay	7,600 00	7,549 51	....	50 49
" other than special survey	1,000 00	710 16	....	289 84
Preventive service	13,000 00	10,568 89	....	2,431 11
Tobacco stamps	39,000 00	39,000 00	....	....
Commission to Customs officers	10,500 00	10,493 95	....	6 05
Tobacco stamps commission	100 00	34 77	....	65 23
L. A. Fréchette, translation	100 00	61 71	....	38 29
Provisional allowance	2,100 00	1,497 93	....	602 07
Methylated spirits	60,000 00	48,467 07	....	11,532 93
Weights and measures, salaries	63,750 00	59,232 58	....	4,517 42
" " " water meters	1,000 00	....	....	1,000 00
" " contingencies	35,000 00	28,880 15	....	6,119 85
Gas and electric light, salaries	27,500 00	27,149 83	....	350 17
" " contingencies	12,000 00	11,737 25	....	262 75
Adulteration of food	30,000 00	27,350 78	....	2,649 22
Minor expenditure	1,000 00	9 29	....	990 71
Metric system	3,000 00	3,000 00	....	....
	824,905 07	775,590 90	4 67	49,318 84

W. J. GERALD,
Deputy Minister.

INLAND REVENUE DEPARTMENT,
OTTAWA, August 29, 1906.

APPENDIX A

STATISTICS

APPENDIX A.—SPIRITS.

No. 1.—RETURN of Manufactures for the Year ended June 30, 1906.

Divisions.	Licenses.		Grain, &c., used for Distillation.						Total Grain used for Distillation.	Proof Spirits Manufactured.	Duty Collected ex-Manufactory, on Deficiencies and Assessments.		Total Duty Collected ex-Manufactory, including License Fees.
	No.	Fees.	Malt.	Indian Corn.	Rye.	Oats.	Wheat.	Molasses.					
		$	Lbs.	Lbs.	Lbs.	Lbs.	Lbs.	Lbs.	Lbs.	Galls.	Galls.	$ cts.	$ cts.
Belleville, Ont.	2	375 00	257,556	4,444,096	1,305,118	28,300	....	....	6,035,070	345,700·46	23·06	43 81	418 81
Guelph "	1	250 00	544,175	7,125,700	1,330,645	73,610	14,670	....	9,088,800	500,869·48	32·06	60 91	310 91
Hamilton "	1	250 60	244,949	4,075,300	701,320	34,370	572,061	....	5,628,000	341,508·29	....	....	250 00
Perth "	2	500 00	415,672	....	....	....	....	....	415,672	22,594·39	....	....	500 00
Prescott "	1	250 00	289,671	5,808,572	1,040,763	32,270	39,637	....	7,210,913	5[illegible]36·10	....	....	250 00
Toronto "	1	250 00	1,877,830	26,128,775	5,060,800	198,240	....	....	33,265,645	1,[illegible]6·98	3,362·25	6,388 28	6,638 28
Windsor "	1	250 00	3,071,297	26,565,900	7,251,598	139,080	....	....	37,027,875	2,167,833·98	347·44	660 55	910 55
Totals	9	2,125 00	6,701,150	74,148,343	16,690,244	505,870	626,368	....	98,671,975	5,818,289·68	3,764·81	7,153 55	9,278 55
Joliette, Que.	1	*187 50	1,314,125	1,573,400	1,586,025	....	31,120	....	4,504,670	225,511·62	....	....	187 50
Montreal "	1	250 00	28,301	....	....	....	....	7,732,144	28,301	454,670·69	....	....	250 00
St. Hyacinthe, Q.	1	250 00	127,495	1,595,160	254,207	....	98	....	1,976,960	3[illegible]92·70	....	....	250 00
Totals	3	687 50	1,469,921	3,168,560	1,840,232	....	31,218	7,732,144	6,509,931	803,775·01	....	....	687 50
Vancouver, B.C.	1	250 00	80,663	221,915	38,493	12,215	1,548,404	....	1,901,695	121,179·15	....	....	250 00
Grand Totals	13	3,062 50	8,251,734	77,538,818	18,568,974	518,085	2,205,990	7,732,144	107,083,601	6,743,243·84	3,764·81	7,153 55	10,216 05

*For 1906-7.

INLAND REVENUE DEPARTMENT,
OTTAWA, August 29, 1906.

W. J. GERALD,
Deputy Minister.

APPENDIX A.—*Continued*—SPIRITS.

No. 2.—COMPARATIVE STATEMENT of Manufactures for the years ended June 30, 1905 and 1906.

Provinces.	Licenses.		Grain, &c., used for Distillation.						Total Grain used for Distillation.	Proof Spirits Manufactured.	Duty Collected ex-Manufactory, on Deficiencies and Assessments.		Total Duty Collected ex-Manufactory, including License Fees.
	No.	Fees.	Malt.	Indian Corn.	Rye.	Oats.	Wheat.	Molasses.					
1905.		$	Lbs.	Lbs.	Lbs.	Lbs.	Lbs.	Lbs.	Lbs.	Galls.	Galls.	$ cts.	$ cts.
Ontario	8	2,000 00	5,861,196	67,359,345	16,359,669	660,502	3,550	....	90,244,262	5,191,856·96	200·15	380 38	2,380 38
Quebec	4	1,000 00	1,493,055	3,015,006	1,716,529	....	26,500	7,105,308	6,251,090	741,286·77	....	....	1,000 00
British Columbia	1	125 00	46,840	865,820	37,007	6,685	222,803	....	1,179,155	75,880·11	....	....	125 00
Totals	13	3,125 00	7,401,091	71,240,171	18,113,205	667,187	252,853	7,105,308	97,674,507	6,009,023·84	200·15	380 38	3,505 38
1906.													
Ontario	9	2,125 00	6,701,150	74,148,343	16,690,244	505,870	626,368	....	98,671,975	5,818,289·68	3,764·81	7,153 55	9,278 55
Quebec	3	687 50	1,469,921	3,168,560	1,840,232	....	31,218	7,732,144	6,509,931	803,775·01	....	....	687 50
British Columbia	1	250 00	80,663	221,915	38,498	12,215	1,548,404	....	1,901,695	121,179·15	....	....	250 00
Totals	13	3,062 50	8,251,734	77,538,818	18,568,974	518,085	2,205,990	7,732,144	107,083,601	6,743,243·84	3,764·81	7,153 55	10,216 05

INLAND REVENUE DEPARTMENT,
OTTAWA, August 29, 1906.

W. J. GERALD,
Deputy Minister.

APPENDIX A—*Continued*—SPIRITS.

No. 3.—STATEMENT showing the transactions in the Distilleries, in

Divisions.	In process, including deficiencies brought forward.	Manufactured, including surpluses.	Returned to Distillery for Redistillation.	
			In bond.	Duty paid.
	Gallons.	Gallons.	Gallons.	Gallons.
Belleville, Ont.	2,163 94	345,700 46	5,322 97	.....
Guelph "	21,829 79	500,869 48	27,976 44	.....
Hamilton "	936 22	341,508 29	42,589 46	.....
Perth "	120 41	22,594 39	.....	.....
Prescott "	15,438 33	445,736 10	.....	.....
Toronto "	15,571 73	1,994,046 98	947,655 57	1,004 90
Windsor "	132,024 46	2,167,833 98	94,982 24	.....
Totals	188,084 88	5,818,289 68	1,118,526 68	1,004 90
Joliette, Que	10,611 17	225,511 62	.....	.....
Montreal, Que.	39,404 15	454,670 69	.....	.....
St. Hyacinthe, Que	13,899 29	123,592 70	41 27	.....
Totals	63,914 61	803,775 01	41 27	.....
Vancouver, B.C.	4,718 38	121,179 15	.....	.....
Grand Totals	256,717 87	6,743,243 84	1,118,567 95	1,004 90

INLAND REVENUE DEPARTMENT,
OTTAWA, August 29, 1906.

the Dominion of Canada, during the year ended June 30, 1906.

Received from other sources, duty paid.	Totals.	Warehoused.	Fusel oil written off.	Deficiencies on which duty was collected.	In process, including deficiencies carried forward.	Totals.
Gallons.	Gallons.	Gallons.	Gallons.	Gallons.	Gallons.	Gallons.
1,772 59	354,959 96	349,310 96	3,214 34	23 06	2,411 60	354,959 96
1,872 73	552,548 44	520,623 28	1,891 29	32 06	30,001 81	552,548 44
190 47	385,224 44	383,918 72	308 37	....	997 35	385,224 44
....	22,714 80	22,585 19	....	... .	129 61	22,714 80
1,583 52	462,757 95	422,414 53	796 17	....	39,547 25	462,757 95
5,129 51	2,963,408 69	2,935,319 12	7,253 12	3,362 25	17,474 20	2,963,408 69
1,814 75	2,396,655 43	2,327,371 29	1,414 67	347 44	67,522 03	2,396,655 43
12,363 57	7,138,269 71	6,961,543 09	14,877 96	3,764 81	158,083 85	7,138,269 71
....	236,122 79	232,627 52	....	....	3,495 27	236,122 79
....	494,074 84	445,470 41	14,456 21	... .	34,148 22	494,074 84
41 05	137,574 31	123,869 42	....	....	13,704 89	137,574 31
41 05	867,771 94	801,967 35	14,456 21		51,348 38	867,771 94
....	125,897 53	115,455 80	96 87	....	10,344 86	125,897 53
12,404 62	8,131,939 18	7,878,966 24	29,431 04	3,764 81	219,777 09	8,131,939 18

W. J. GERALD,
Deputy Minister.

APPENDIX A—*Continued*—SPIRITS.

DR. No. 4.—WAREHOUSE RETURN

Remaining in Warehouse from last year.	Warehoused	Imported.	Received from other Divisions.	Totals.	DIVISIONS.	Entered for Consumption.	
Galls.	Galls.	Galls.	Galls.	Galls.		Galls.	$ cts.
676,716·23	349,310·96	....	12,795·43	1,038,822·62	Belleville, Ont.	63,295·55	120,261 41
3,229·79	....	....	27,340·23	30,570·02	Brantford "	18,849·74	35,814 52
704·58	....	....	3,021·25	3,725·83	Cornwall "	3,402·70	6,465 58
1,054,380·07	520,623·28	....	46,390·72	1,621,394·07	Guelph "	244,135·77	462,052 83
686,410·48	383,918·72	32·33	104,457·10	1,174,818·63	Hamilton "	141,658·43	268,579 30
7,367·02	....	....	42,165·38	49,532·40	Kingston "	34,443·32	65,445 48
4,701·57	....	....	36,095·95	40,797·52	London "	36,106·83	68,604 29
28,941·46	....	....	165,606·22	194,547·68	Ottawa "	160,312·42	304,761 75
5,758·50	....	....	61,723·14	67,481·64	" Govt. Wse. "	....	....
....	....	....	75·94	75·94	" Dept. Lab. "	....	....
900·31	....	....	5,470·61	6,370·92	Owen Sound "	6,208·08	11,798 30
83,272·52	22,585·19	....	52,297·15	158,154·86	Perth "	56,455·12	106,490 41
6,158·38	....	....	24,289·51	30,442·89	Peterboro' "	23,252·67	44,182 20
4,135·48	....	....	19,581·61	23,717·09	Port Arthur "	18,402·50	34,986 44
1,060,824·55	422,414·53	192,338·21	2,369·06	1,677,946·35	Prescott "	26,197·15	107,475 50
694·89	....	....	6,250·20	6,945·09	St. Cath'ines "	6,218·97	11,816 16
2,362·27	....	....	19,334·90	21,697·17	Stratford "	19,648·44	37,337 66
3,795,721·40	2,935,319·12	....	299,830·38	7,030,870·90	Toronto "	404,065·90	758,943 95
5,274,795·97	2,327,371·29	8,417·99	44,406·30	7,654,991·55	Windsor "	222,372·30	421,926 14
12,697,070·47	6,961,543·09	200,788·53	973,501·08	20,832,903·17	..Totals......	1,485,025·89	2,866,941 92
452,702·20	232,627·52	....	20,853·45	706,183·17	Joliette, Que.	24,599·40	46,812 74
929,677·78	445,470·41	*16·20	897,007·69	2,272,172·08	Montreal "	897,819·67	1,697,501 66
32,103·33	....	....	282,855·25	314,958·58	Québec "	270,631·46	514,379 35
161,132·50	123,869·42	....	78,585·83	363,587·75	St. Hya'nthe "	66,222·22	125,908 61
7,250·42	....	38,675·46	82,767·34	128,693·22	Sherbrooke "	83,340·02	169,980 21
5,166·85	....	....	40,572·13	45,738·98	Three Rivers "	36,061·58	68,551 95
1,588,033·08	801,967·35	*16·20 38,675·46	1,402,641·69	3,831,333·78	..Totals.....	1,378,674·35	2,623,134 52
15,127·55	....	....	93,587·71	108,715·26	St. John, N.B.	31,339·17	154,562 54
7,791·91	....	....	32,906·99	40,698·90	Halifax, N.S...	29,587·01	56,230 67
500·67	....	....	5,135·77	5,636·44	Pictou " ..	4,833·62	9,190 69
8,292·58	....	....	38,042·76	46,335·34	..Totals....	34,420·63	65,421 36
51,682·56	....	....	374,565·36	426,247·92	Winnipeg, Man	346,584·39	658,080 11
11,112·45	....	....	60,890·54	72,002·99	Calgary, Alta..	57,717·04	109,673 91
112,304·61	115,455·80	....	106,524·59	334,285·00	Vancouver, B.C	99,779·24	189,595 08
19,723·21	....	....	62,731·01	82,454·22	Victoria, "	55,947·12	106,309 35
132,027·82	115,455·80	....	169,255·60	416,739·22	..Totals......	155,726·36	295,904 43
2,205·10	....	....	7,760·57	9,965·67	Dawson, Y.T..	6,297·52	11,965 24
8,612·54	....	....	....	8,612·54	Sundries....	....	....
14,514,164·15	7,878,966·24	*16·20 239,463·99	3,120,245·31	25,752,855·89	..Grand Totals.	3,545,785·35	†6,785,684 03

* Seizure.

INLAND REVENUE DEPARTMENT,
OTTAWA, August 29, 1906.

for the year ended June 30, 1906. CR.

Removed.		Free.		Exported.	Used in Bonded Factories.	Remaining in Warehouse.	Totals.
To other Divisions.	To Distillery for Re-distillation.	Legal Allowance.	Other.				
Galls.	Galls.	Galls.	Galls.	Galls.	Galls.	Galls.	Galls.
202,043·11	5,322·97	7,199·10	1,294·53	143·29	....	759,524·07	1,038,822 62
....	....	....	....	....	5,196·45	6,523·83	30,570 02
....	....	....	....	....	....	323·13	3,725 83
70,782·78	27,976·44	27,621·88	1,875·58	25,313·57	....	1,223,688·05	1,621,394 07
190,347·71	42,589·46	10,099·38	520·89	405·30	23,399·65	765,797·81	1,174,818 63
....	....	....	....	79·29	9,798·03	5,211·76	49,532 40
....	....	....	....	31.59	....	4,659 10	40,797 52
....	....	....	130·36	....	358·92	33,745·98	194,547 68
....	....	....	16·50	....	‡63,684·95	3,780·19	67,481 64
....	....	....	75·94	....	....	....	75 94
....	....	....	68·32	....	....	94·52	6,370 92
3,335·60	....	583·50	....	21·65	....	97,758·99	158,154 86
....	....	....	....	....	....	7,190·22	30,442 89
....	....	....	....	....	....	5,314·59	23,717 09
334,986·06	....	5,453·23	1,692·46	1,394·54	192,338·21	1,115,884·70	1,677,946 35
31·90	....	....	....	....	....	694·22	6,945 09
....	....	....	....	....	....	2,048·73	21,697 17
1,041,772·72	947,655·57	16,905·82	5,875·85	2,747·52	92,836·33	4,519,011·19	7,030,870 90
876,061·31	94,982·24	56,141·46	1,076·45	245,037·09	8,417·99	6,150,902·71	7,654,991 55
2,719,361·19	1,118,526·68	124,004·37	12,626·88	275,173·84	{ ‡63,684·95 332,345·58	14,702,153·79	20,832,903 17
184,926.49	....	836·45	....	....	....	495,820·83	706,183 17
158,764·35	....	3,420·23	....	122·49	33,495·72	1,178,549·62	2,272,172 08
1,268·52	....	....	619·21	....	4,928·60	37,510·79	314,958 58
28,706·56	41·27	171·74	....	....	20,720·99	247,724·97	363,587 75
....	....	....	....	....	38,675·46	6,677·74	128,693 22
1,150·95	....	....	....	....	....	8,526·45	45,738 98
374,816.87	41·27	4,428·42	619.21	122·49	97,820·77	1,974,810·40	3,831,333 78
795·72	....	....	....	14·98	9,243·46	17,321·93	108,715 26
4,519·00	....	....	....	204·58	....	6,388·31	40,698 90
....	....	....	....	....	....	802·82	5,636 44
4,519·00	....	....	....	204·58	....	7,191·13	46,335 34
8,418·77	....	....	....	18 05	2,858·46	68,368·25	426,247 92
39·60	....	....	....	....	....	14,246·35	72,002 99
5,853·47	....	....	....	132·39	8,231·18	220,288·72	334,285 00
6,440·69	....	....	68·91	2,239·09	....	17,758·41	82,454 22
12,294·16	....	....	68·91	2,371·48	8,231·18	238,047·13	416,739 22
....	....	....	....	....	....	3,668·15	9,965 67
....	....	....	....	....	....	8,612·54	8,612 54
3,120,245·31	1,118,567·95	128,432·79	13,315·00	277,905·42	{ ‡ 63,684·95 450,499·45	17,034,419·67	25,752,855 89

† This amount includes $71,829.50 collected on Imported Spirits used in bonded factories, at 30c. per gallon.

‡ Used in the manufacture of Methylated Spirits at the Government Warehouse, Ottawa.

W. J. GERALD,
Deputy Minister.

APPENDIX A—*Continued*—SPIRITS.

No. 5.—COMPARATIVE STATEMENT of Warehouse

Remaining in Warehouse from last year.	Warehoused.	Imported.	Received from other Divisions.	Totals.	Provinces.	Entered for Consumption.	
Galls.	Galls.	Galls.	Galls.	Galls.	1905.	Galls.	$ cts.
11,083,330·41	*3·36 5,991,074·59	107,467·87	804,786·52	17,986,662·75	Ontario........	1,229,229·44	2,355,598 22
1,069,238·11	712,155·77	‡79·52 52,740·07	1,404,814·41	3,239,027·88	Quebec.........	1,280,018·92	2,444,937 36
18,937·23	....	634·47	78,474·09	98,045·79	New Brunswick.	75,213·33	143,123 33
8,861·38	....	....	42,036·76	50,898·14	Nova Scotia...	37,212·87	70,731 44
47,213·44	....	....	304,213·50	351,426·94	Manitoba.......	296,582·05	562,979 62
13,404,32	....	....	37,146·53	50,550·85	N. W. Territory	39,283·51	74,651 19
68,824·57	71,161·73	....	159,053·49	299,039·79	B. Columbia....	148,275·37	281,750 16
5,518·83	....	....	3,747·80	9,266·63	Yukon Territory	7,027·85	13,355 14
8,612·54	....	....	....	8,612·54	Sundries........	....	....
12,323,940·83	*3·36 6,774,392·09	‡79·52 160,842·41	2,834,273·10	22,093,531·31	..Totals........	3,112,843·34	5,947,126 46
					1906.		
12,697,070·47	6,961,543·09	200,788·53	973,501·08	20,832,903·17	Ontario.........	1,485,025·89	2,866,941 92
1,588,033·08	801,967·35	‡16·20 38,675·46	1,402,641·69	3,831,333·78	Quebec.........	1,378,674·35	2,623,134 52
15,127·55	....	....	93,587·71	108,715.26	New Brunswick.	81,339·17	154,562 54
8,292·58	....	....	38,042·76	46,335·34	Nova Scotia....	34,420·63	65,421 36
51,682·56	....	....	374,565·36	426,247·92	Manitoba. ...	316,584·39	658,080 11
11,112·45	....	....	60,890·54	72,002·99	Alberta........	57,717·04	109,673 91
132,027·82	115,455·80	....	169,255·60	416,739·22	B. Columbia....	155,726·36	295,904·43
2,205·10	....	....	7,760·57	9,965·67	Yukon Territory	6,297·52	11,965 24
8,612·54	....	....	....	8,612·54	Sundries........	....	....
14,514,164·15	7,878,966·24	‡16·20 239,463·99	3,120,245·31	25,752;855·89	..Totals........	3,545,785.35	6,785,684 03

* Surplus. ‡ Seizure

INLAND REVENUE DEPARTMENT,
OTTAWA, August 29, 1906.

Returns for the Years ended June 30, 1905 and 1906.

Removed.		Free.		Exported.	Used in Bonded Factories.	Remaining in Warehouse.	Totals.
To other Divisions.	To Distillery for Re-distillation.	Legal Allowance.	Other.				
Galls.	Galls.	Galls.	Galls.	Galls.	Galls.	Galls.	Galls.
2,592,564·23	833,058·08	128,482·88	11,953·28	209,116·38	†64,092·05 221,095·94	12,697,070·47	17,986,662·75
219,502·62	15,151·08	2,871·68	325·95	79·68	133,044·97	1,588,033·08	3,239,027·88
915·55	....	....	....	....	6,789·36	15,127·55	98,045·79
5,175·08	....	....	....	217·61	....	8,292·58	50,898·14
3,135·54	....	....	....	26·79	....	51,682·56	351,426·94
154·89	....	....	....	....	....	11,112·45	50,550·85
12,825·19	....	....	1,319·53	2,050·62	2,541·26	132,027·82	299,039·79
....	....	....	....	33·68	....	2,205·10	9,266·63
....	....	....	....	....	....	8,612·54	8,612·54
2,834,273·10	848,209·16	131,354·56	13,598·76	211,524·76	†64,092·05 363,471·43	14,514,164·15	22,093,531·31
2,719,361·19	1,118,526·68	124,004·37	12,626·88	275,173·84	† 63,684·95 332,345·58	14,702,153·79	20,832,903·17
374,816·87	41·27	4,428·42	619·21	122·49	97,820·77	1,974,810·40	3,831,333·78
795·72	....	....	....	14·98	9,243·46	17,321·93	108,715·26
4,519·00	....	....	....	204·58	....	7,191·13	46,335·34
8,418·77	....	....	....	18·05	2,858·46	68,368·25	426,247·92
39·60	....	....	....	....	....	14,246·35	72,002·99
12,294·16	....	....	68·91	2,371·48	8,231·18	238,047·13	416,739·22
....	....	....	....	....	....	3,668·15	9,965·67
....	....	....	....	....	....	8,612·54	8,612·54
3,120,245·31	1,118,567·95	128,432·79	13,315·00	277,905·42	† 63,684·95 450,499·45	17,034,419·67	25,752,855·89

†Used in the manufacture of Methylated Spirits at the Government Warehouse, Ottawa.

	1905.	1906.
Total duty collected ex-manufactory and ex-warehouse...	$ 5,947,506 84	$ 6,792,837 58
License Fees..........	3,125 00	3,062 50
	$ 5,950,631 84	$ 6,795,900 08

W. J. GERALD,
Deputy Minister.

APPENDIX A.—*Continued*—MALT.

No. 6.—RETURN of Manufactures for the Year ended June 30, 1906.

Divisions.	Licenses.		Grain used.	Malt.		Total Dtuy Collected ex-manufactory, including License Fees.
	No.	Fees.		Manufactured.	Warehoused.	
		$	Lbs.	Lbs.	Lbs.	$ cts.
Belleville, Ont.	1	50	361,950	277,368	277,368	50 00
Brantford "	1	50	528,263	425,862	425,862	50 00
Guelph "	5	600	5,812,428	4,638,018	4,638,018	600 00
Hamilton "	2	350	5,879,200	4,709,815	4,709,815	350 00
Kingston "	2	100	396,143	309,400	309,400	100 00
London "	3	450	6,016,406	4,718,281	4,718,281	450 00
Ottawa "	1	100	741,287	589,320	589,320	100 00
Owen Sound, Ont	1	200	2,906,360	2,226,962	2,226,962	200 00
Perth "	2	100	377,539	308,775	308,775	100 00
Peterborough "	2	250	2,048,877	1,600,902	1,600,902	250 00
Prescott "	3	200	1,526,520	1,175,212	1,175,212	200 00
St. Catharines "	2	100	925,010	736,484	736,484	100 00
Stratford "	1	200	7,858,800	6,219,860	6,219,860	200 00
Toronto "	10	1,400	21,134,476	16,494,708	16,494,708	1,400 00
Windsor "	1	200	5,961,270	4,901,285	4,901,285	200 00
Totals	37	4,350	62,474,529	49,332,252	49,332,252	4,350 00
Montreal, Que	4	800	42,108,407	33,813,198	33,813,198	800 00
Quebec, Que	1	150	1,257,722	989,883	989,883	150 00
Totals	5	950	43,366,129	34,803,081	34,803,081	950 00
Halifax, N.S	1	150	631,626	503,468	503,468	150 00
Winnipeg, Man.	3	450	2,676,590	2,174,002	2,174,002	450 00
Calgary, Alberta	4	400	3,534,481	2,864,867	2,864,867	400 00
Victoria, B.C	1	50	519,386	411,903	411,903	50 00
Grand Totals	51	6,350	113,202,741	90,089,573	90,089,573	6,350 00

INLAND REVENUE DEPARTMENT,
OTTAWA, August 29, 1906.

W. J. GERALD,
Deputy Minister.

APPENDIX A.—*Continued*—MALT.

No. 7—Comparative Statement of Manufactures for the Years ended June 30, 1905 and 1906.

Provinces.	Licenses.		Grain used.	Malt.			Total Duty collected ex-Manufactory, including License Fees.
	No.	Fees.		Manufactured.	Paid Duty	Warehoused.	
1905.		$	Lbs.	Lbs.	Lbs.	Lbs.	$ cts.
Ontario.......... ...	38	4,600	68,549,489	54,617,707	....	54,617,707	4,600 00
Quebec...........	5	850	20,321,423	16,389,839	....	16,389,839	850 00
Nova Scotia.........	1	150	712,401	566,754	....	566,754	150 00
Manitoba......... ..	2	175	1,769,337	1,398,992	... .	1,398,992	175 00
N.W. Territories.....	4	325	2,960,956	2,383,926	7,542	2,376,384	438,14
Totals.........	50	6,100	94,313,606	75,357,218	7,542	75,349,676	6.213 14
1906.							
Ontario.............	37	4,350	62,474,529	49,332,252	....	49,332,252	4,350 00
Quebec....	5	950	43,366,129	34,803,081	....	34,803,081	950 00
Nova Scotia.........	1	150	631,626	503,468	... .	503,468	150 00
Manitoba..	3	450	2,676,590	2,174,002	....	2,174,002	450 00
Alberta.......	4	400	3,534,481	2,864,867	....	2,864,867	400 00
British Columbia.....	1	50	519,386	411,903	....	411,903	50 00
Totals......	51	6,350	113,202,741	90,089,573	....	90,089,573	6,350 00

INLAND REVENUE DEPARTMENT,
OTTAWA, August 29, 1906.

W. J. GERALD,
Deputy Minister.

APPENDIX A.—*Continued*—MALT.

No. 8.—Warehouse Return for

Dr.

Remaining in Warehouse from last year.	Warehoused	Increases.	Received from other Divisions.	Imported.	Totals.	Divisions.
Lbs.	Lbs.	Lbs.	Lbs.	Lbs.	Lbs.	
100,920	277,368	2,898	122,380	....	503,566	..Belleville, Ont.......
207,528	425,862	7,663	259,200	7,200	907,453	..Brantford " ....
2,874,924	4,638,018	75,506	1,986,450	35,200	9,610,098	..Guelph " ....
1,480,986	4,709,815	33,862	16,200	....	6,240,863	..Hamilton " ....
256,032	309,400	5,922	121,000	....	692,354	..Kingston " ....
2,661,526	4,718,281	58,999	109,600	....	7,548,406	..London " ....
166,118	589,320	3,062	250,000	....	1,008,500	..Ottawa " ....
1,295,475	2,226,962	464	968,330	....	4,491,231	..Owen Sound " ....
57,841	308,775	3,368	585,000	2,163	957,147	..Perth " ....
589,911	1,600,902	38,208	188,000	....	2,417,021	..Peterborough " ....
32,723	....	....	136,530	....	169,253	..Port Arthur " ....
562,458	1,175,212	26,523	40,000	....	1,804,193	..Prescott " ....
125,870	736,484	1,124	598,200	....	1,461,678	..St. Catharines " ....
1,435,700	6,219,860	13,700	325,000	....	7,994,260	..Stratford " ....
7,636,221	16,494,708	187,601	2,243,000	40,420	26,601,950	..Toronto " ....
1,598,875	4,901,285	9,709	1,194,000	1,800	7,705,669	..Windsor " ....
21,083,108	49,332,252	468,609	9,142,890	86,783	80,113,642	.......Totals...........
22,825	....	10,636	1,328,050	....	1,361,511	..Joliette, Que......
5,174,200	33,813,198	132.936	600,000	11,176	39,731,510	..Montreal " ......
40,000	989,883	....	3,683,000	....	4,712,883	..Quebec " ......
....	....	....	130,147	....	130,147	..St. Hyacinthe " ......
70,970	....	....	1,480,000	....	1,550,970	..Sherbrooke " ......
5,307,995	34,803,081	143,572	7,221,197	11,176	47,487,021	.......Totals...........
36,000	....	....	1,652,000	....	1,688,000	..St. John, N.B..........
52,714	503,468	4,404	2,229,000	1,120	2,790,706	..Halifax, N.S...........
260,924	2,174,002	18,168	2,470,000	981,800	5,904,894	.Winnipeg, Man........
706,223	2,864,867	15,066	....	....	3,586,156	..Calgary, Alta ....
256,427	....	....	1,041,430	1,973,270	3,271,127	..Vancouver. B.C........
44,830	411,903	....	648,019	311,093	1,415,845	..Victoria " ....
301,257	411,903	....	1,689,449	2,284,363	4,686,972	........Totals...........
137,109	....	....	....	104,955	242,064	..Dawson, Y.T..........
27,885,330	90,089,573	649,819	24,404,536	3,470,197	146,499,455	........Grand Totals.....

Inland Revenue Department,
Ottawa, August 29, 1906.

the Year ended 30th June, 1906.

CR.

Entered for Consumption at $1\frac{1}{2}$ cents per lb.			Removed to other Divisions.	Exported.	Written Off.	Free.	Remaining in Warehouse.	Totals
Lbs.	$	cts.	Lbs.	Lbs.	Lbs.		Lbs.	Lbs.
464,437	6,966	56	....	....	....	....	39,129	503,566
710,520	10,729	80	....	....	....	....	196,933	907,453
6,174,640	92,619	60	1,011,200	....	....	....	2,424,258	9,610,098
4,012,245	60,183	68	1,044,000	....	....	....	1,184,618	6,240,863
496,742	7,451	13	....	....	....	....	195,612	692,354
4,985,696	74,785	93	....	....	....	....	2,562,710	7,548,406
777,200	11,658	00	....	....	....	....	231,300	1,008,500
1,249,152	18,737	28	1,666,530	249,600	274,649	....	1,051,300	4,491,231
440,073	6,601	09	....	....	13,459	415,672	87,943	957,147
1,422,446	21.336	69	360,000	....	....	....	634,575	2,417,021
123,293	1,849	38	....	....	....	....	45,960	169,253
1,284,060	19,260	90	....	....	....	....	520,133	1,804,193
1,265,188	18,977	82	....	....	....	....	196,490	1,461,678
1,308,468	19,627	02	4,912,780	....	....	....	1,773,012	7,994,260
16,534,862	248,427	13	2,624,000	....	....	....	7,443,088	26,601,950
3,904,935	58,574	03	....	....	....	1,191,554	2,609,180	7,705,669
45,153,957	677,786	04	11,618,510	249,600	288,108	1,607,226	21,196,241	80,113,642
....	....		....	....	....	1,314,125	47,386	1,361,511
17,228,931	258,545	73	12,717,577	275,200	....	....	9,509,802	39,731,510
4,672,883	70,093	09	....	....	....	....	40,000	4,712,883
130,147	1,952	20	....	....	....	....	....	130,147
1,497,570	22,463	55	....	....	....	....	53,400	1,550,970
23,529,531	353,054	57	12,717,577	275,200	....	1,314,125	9,650,588	47,487,021
1,608,000	24,120	00	....	....	....	....	80,000	1,688,000
2,744,164	41,173	66	....	3,600	....	....	42,942	2,790,706
5,070,61 6	76,064	54	....	....	26,596	....	807,682	5,904,894
3.050,140	45,752	09	60,430	....	6,184	....	469,402	3,586,156
2,987,998	44,819	93	8,019	....	6,515	....	268,595	3,271,127
1,370,066	20,550	92	....	....	....	....	45,779	1,415,845
4,358,064	65,370	85	8,019	....	6,515	....	314,374	4,686,972
184,630	2,771	38	....	....	....	....	57,434	242,064
85,699,102	1,286,093	13	24,404,536	528,400	327,403	2,921,351	32,618,663	146,499,455

W. J. GERALD,
Deputy Minister.

APPENDIX A.—*Continued*—MALT.

DR. No. 9.—COMPARATIVE STATEMENT of Warehouse Returns

Remaining in Warehouse from last year.	Warehoused	Increases.	Received from other Divisions.	Imported.	Totals.	Provinces.
Lbs.	Lbs.	Lbs.	Lbs.	Lbs.	Lbs.	1905.
21,609,932	54,617,707	601,162	6,506,834	45,349	83,380,984	..Ontario..............
3,770,990	16,389,839	166,617	6,402,700	11,200	26,741,346	..Quebec..............
76,934	....	....	1,460,000	....	1,536,934	..New Brunswick........
205,223	566,754	2,835	2,230,934	....	3,005,746	..Nova Scotia...........
308,792	1,398,992	28,358	2,878,384	181,025	4,795,551	..Manitoba..............
461,991	2,376,384	12,314	120,000	81,740	3,052,429	..N. W. Territories.......
239,853	....	....	1,346,618	3,244,420	4,830,891	..British Columbia.......
5,644	....	....	....	314,355	319,999	..Yukon Territory........
26,679,359	75,349,676	811,286	20,945,470	3,878,089	127,663,880	....Grand Totals.........
						1906.
21,083,108	49,332,252	468,609	9,142,890	86,783	80,113,642	..Ontario..............
5,307,995	34,803,081	143,572	7,221,197	11,176	47,487,021	..Quebec..............
36,000	....	....	1,652,000	....	1,688,000	..New Brunswick.........
52,714	503,468	4,404	2,229,000	1,120	2,790,706	..Nova Scotia............
260,924	2,174,002	18,168	2,470,000	981,800	5,904,894	..Manitoba..............
706,223	2,864,867	15,066	....	....	3,586,156	..Alberta..............
301,257	411,903	....	1,689,449	2,284,363	4,686,972	..British Columbia.......
137,109	....	....	....	104,955	242,064	..Yukon Territory........
27,885,330	90,089,573	649,819	24,404,536	3,470,197	146,499,455	....Grand Totals.........

INLAND REVENUE DEPTARTMENT,
OTTAWA, August 29, 1906.

for the years ended of June 30, 1905 and 1906. CR.

Entered for Consumption at 1½ cents per lb.		Removed to other Divisions.	Exported.	Written of.	Free.	Remaining in Warehouse.	Totals.
Lbs.	$ cts.	Lbs.	Lbs.	Lbs.	Lbs.	Lbs.	Lbs.
44,243,519	664,021 44	16,215,122	302,000	11,689	1,525,546	21,083,108	83,380,984
15,473,546	232,215 09	4,488,730	184,000	....	1,287,075	5,307,995	26,741,346
1,500,934	22,514 01	....	....	....	....	36,000	1,536,934
2,940,072	44,101 08	....	12,960	....	....	52,714	3,005,746
1,534,627	68,019 41	....	....	....	....	260,924	4,795,551
2,104,588	31,568 83	241,618	....	....	....	706,223	3,052,429
4,529,634	68,606 23	....	....	....	....	301,257	4,830,891
182,890	3,379 47	....	....	....	....	137,109	319,999
75,509,810	1,134,425 56	20,945,470	498,960	11,689	2,812,621	27,885,330	127,663,880
45,153,957	677,786 04	11,618,510	249,600	288,108	1,607,226	21,196,241	80,113,642
23,529,531	353,054 57	12,717,577	275,200	....	1,314,125	9,650,588	47,487,021
1,608,000	24,120 00	....	....	....	....	80,000	1,688,000
2,744,164	41, 73 66	....	3,600	....	....	42,942	2,790,706
5,070,616	76,064 54	....	....	26,596	....	807,682	5,904,894
3,050,140	45,752 09	60,430	....	6,184	....	469,402	3,586,156
4,358,064	65,370 85	8,019	....	6,515	....	314,374	4,686,972
184,630	2,771 38	....	....	....	....	57,434	242,064
85,699,102	1,286,093 13	24,404,536	528,400	327,403	2,921,351	32,618,663	146,499,455

	1905.	1906.
Total duty collected, ex-manufactory and ex-warehouse.......	$ 1,134,538 70	$ 1,286,093 13
License Fees	6,100 00	6,350 00
	$ 1,140,638 70	$ 1,292,443 13

W. J. GERALD,
Deputy Minister.

APPENDIX A—*Continued*—MALT LIQUOR.

No. 10—RETURN of Manufactures for the year ended June 30, 1906.

Divisions.	Licenses.		Malt used.	Other commodities used.	Malt Liquor manufactured.	Malt Liquor exported, and used by H. M. Army and Navy.	Total Duty collected, including License Fees.
	No.	Fees.					
		$ cts.	Lbs.	Lbs.	Galls.	Galls.	$ cts.
Belleville, Ont........	1	50 00	207,369	.....	98,125	....	50 00
Brantford, "	3	150 00	711,288	....	305,255	....	150 00
Guelph, "	8	400 00	5,678,746	....	2,560,148	. ...	400 00
Hamilton, "	2	100 00	3,514,194	....	1,712,979	....	100 00
Kingston, "	2	100 00	494,114	....	148,625	. ...	100 00
London, "	6	300 00	5,422,282	....	2,164,525	2,696	300 00
Ottawa, "	3	150 00	1,205,356	....	480,820	....	150 00
Owen Sound, "	6	300 00	1,292,874	....	540,515	....	300 00
Perth, "	1	50 00	438,735	.... ..	177,870	....	50 00
Peterborough, "	3	150 00	1,411,026	....	482,330	....	150 00
Port Arthur, "	1	*a* 87 50	125,293	....	55,555	....	87 50
Prescott, "	2	100 00	971,850	....	340,837	....	100 00
St. Catharines, "	2	100 00	1,265,688	....	500,330	. ...	100 00
Stratford, "	4	200 00	604,718	....	287,150	....	200 00
Toronto, "	14	700 00	14,572,578	....	6,126,598	. . ..	700 00
Windsor, "	2	100 00	1,878,736	....	899,683	... .	100 00
Totals....	60	3,037 50	39,794,847	......	16,891,345	2,696	3,037 50
Montreal, Que.......	10	475 00	16,593,079	....	7,029,361	....	475 00
Quebec, "	4	200 00	4,617,213	....	1,865,085	....	200 00
Sherbrooke, "	1	50 00	1,507,570	....	732,294	....	50 00
Totals.............	15	725 00	22,717,862	....	9,626,740	....	725 00
St. John, N.B	2	100 00	1,621,913	....	604,824	....	100 00
Halifax, N.S.......... ...	3	150 00	2,743,836	....	959,930	124,818	150 00
Winnipeg, Man..	11	550 00	5,127,584	4,342	2,254,505	....	844 80
Calgary, Alberta	4	200 00	3,025,811	....	1,189,742	....	200 00
Vancouver, B.C....	27	1,325 00	2,912,994	14,863	1,156,892	....	2,761 10
Victoria, "	6	300 00	1,916,282	14,500	495,278	46,097	2,147 30
Totals.............	33	1,625 00	4,829,276	29,363	1,652,170	46,097	4,908 40
Dawso Y.T.............	1	*b* 37 50	184,630	....	71,381	....	37 50
Grand Totals ...	129	6,425 00	80,045,759	33,705	33,250,637	173,611	10,003 20

a Includes license fee for 1906–07.
b License Fee for 1906–07.

W. J. GERALD,
Deputy Minister

INLAND REVENUE DEPARTMENT.
OTTAWA, August 29, 1906.

APPENDIX A—*Continued*—MALT LIQUOR.

No. 11.—Comparative Statement of Manufactures for the Years ended June 30, 1905 and 1906.

Provinces.	Licenses. No.	Licenses. Fees.	Malt used.	Other commodities used.	Malt Liquor manufactured.	Malt Liquor exported, and used by H. M. Army and Navy.	Total Duty collected, including License Fees.
1905.		$ cts.	Lbs.	Lbs.	Galls.	Galls.	$ cts.
Ontario	61	3,050 00	37,479,038	....	15,886,268	2,175	3,050 00
Quebec	16	800 00	20,423,087	....	8,576,810	....	800 00
New Brunswick	2	100 00	1,491,584	....	551,821	....	100 00
Nova Scotia	3	150 00	2,919,159	....	1,022,740	213,516	150 00
Manitoba	10	450 00	4,462,857	....	1,886,372	....	450 00
N.W. Territories	4	200 00	2,091,457	....	738,589	....	200 00
British Columbia	36	1,775 00	4,458,856	22,979	1,619,200	47,592	4,274 30
Yukon Territory	2	100 00	123,953	....	48,270	....	100 00
Totals	134	6,625 00	73,449,991	22,979	30,330,070	263,283	9,124 30
1906.							
Ontario	60	3,037 50	39,794,847	....	16,891,345	2,696	3,037 50
Quebec	15	725 00	22,717,862	....	9,626,740	....	725 00
New Brunswick	2	100 00	1,621,913	....	604,824	....	100 00
Nova Scotia	3	150 00	2,743,836	....	959,930	124,818	150 00
Manitoba	11	550 00	5,127,584	4,342	2,254,505	....	844 80
Alberta	4	200 00	3,025,811	....	1,189,742	....	200 00
British Columbia	33	1,625 00	4,829,276	29,363	1,652,170	46,097	4,908 40
Yukon Territory	1	37 50	184,630	....	71,381	....	37 50
Totals	129	6,425 00	80,045,759	33,705	33,250,637	173,611	10,003 20

—	1905.	1906.
	Galls.	Galls.
Exported	2,202	2,788
Used by H. M. Army and Navy	261,081	170,823
Totals	263,283	173,611

W. J. GERALD,
Deputy Minister.

Inland Revenue Department,
Ottawa, August 29, 1906.

APPENDIX A *Continued*—TOBACCO

No. 12.—Return of Manufactures for the Year ended June 30, 1906.

Divisions.	Licenses.		Total Raw Leaf Tobacco and other materials actually used.	Foreign.			Cigarettes.			Canadian Tobacco.			Combination Tobacco.			Combination Cigarettes.			Snuff.				Total Duty collected ex-Manufactory, including License Fees.
	No.	Fees.		At 25 cents per lb.	Paid Duty.	Warehoused.	At $3 per M.	Paid Duty.	Warehoused.	At 5 cents per lb.	Paid Duty.	Warehoused.	At 5 cents per lb.	Paid Duty.	Warehoused.	At $1.50 per M.	Paid Duty	Warehoused.	At 25 cents per lb.	Paid Duty	At 18 cents per lb.	Paid Duty	
		$ cts.	Lbs.	Lbs.	Lbs.	Lbs.	No.	No.	No.	Lbs.	Lbs.	Lbs.	Lbs.	Lbs.	Lbs.	No.	No.	No.	Lbs.	Lbs.	Lbs.	Lbs.	$ cts.
Hamilton, Ont.	1	75 00	1,270,391	1,307,607	328,354	979,253	5,935,100	5,909,600	25,500														99,802 30
Toronto "	2	140 00	263,547	3,227 15/16	3,227 15/16								268,303	94,242	174,061								5,659 09
Windsor "	2	100 00	235,855							246,324	246,324												12,416 20
Totals....	5	315 00	1,769,793	1,310,834 15/16	331,581 15/16	979,253	5,935,100	5,909,600	25,500	246,324	246,324		268,303	94,242	174,061								117,907 59
Joliette, Que.	3	125 00	55,746							61,853½	61,853½												3,217 68
Montreal "	25	1,582 50	8,808,880½	8,069,286½	673,305½	7,395,981	250,818,500 *1,528,500	248,735,200 1,528,500	2,083,300	408,528	402,669	5,859	346,512	172,373	174,139				6,870	6,870	81,810	81,810	973,537 89
Quebec "	10	580 00	1,446,257½	20,530½	17,470	3,060½	3,804,200	2,312,800	1,491,400	1,026,828	998,418	28,408	366,716½	316,466½	50,250	7,161,500	3,834,500	3,327,000	20	20	38,965	38,965	90,400 62
Sherbrooke, Que.	4	215 00	2,195,039½							1,398,889½	1,398,889½		849,448½	560,524½	288,924				1,674	1,674	33,505	33,505	104,635 12
Totals	42	2,502 50	12,505,923½	8,089,817	690,775½	7,399,041½	254,622,700 *1,528,500	251,048,000 1,528,500	3,574,700	2,896,097	2,861,830	34,267	1,562,677	1,049,364	513,313	7,161,500	3,834,500	3,327,000	8,564	8,564	164,280	164,280	1,171,791 31
St. John, N.B.	1	75 00	5,991	545	545		1,629,550	1,226,100	403,450														3,889 56
Pictou, N.S.	3	190 00	55,320½	37,285 3/8	9,126 3/8	28,159				11,290	8,932	2,358	10,655	10,655									3,450 93
Charlottetown, P.E.I.	4	265 00	175,936½	150,333½	64,457	85,876½				25,014	25,014		3,637	2,920	717								17,775 95
Grand Totals	55	3,347 50	14,512,964½	9,588,815¾	1,096,485¾	8,492,330	262,187,350 *1,528,500	258,183,700 1,528,500	4,003,650	3,178,725	3,142,100	36,625	1,845,272	1,157,181	688,091	7,161,500	3,834,500	3,327,000	8,564	8,564	164,280	164,280	1,314,875 33

* Cigarettes at $8 per M.

Inland Revenue Department,
Ottawa, August 29, 1906.

W. J. GERALD,
Deputy Minister.

No. 13.—Comparative Statement of Manufactures for the Years ended June 30, 1905 and 1906.

[illegible]	Licenses		Total Raw Leaf Tobacco and other materials [illegible]	Tobacco: At 25c. per lb.	Tobacco: Paid Duty.	Tobacco: Warehoused.	Cigarettes: At $3 per M.	Cigarettes: Paid Duty.	Cigarettes: Warehoused.	Canadian Tobacco: At 5c. per lb.	Canadian Tobacco: Paid Duty.	Canadian Tobacco: Warehoused.	Combination Tobacco: At 5c. per lb.	Combination Tobacco: Paid Duty.	Combination Tobacco: Warehoused.	Combination Cigarettes: At $1.50 per M.	Combination Cigarettes: Paid Duty.	Combination Cigarettes: Warehoused.	Snuff: At 25c. per lb.	Snuff: Paid Duty	Snuff: At 5c. per lb.	Snuff: Paid Duty	Total [illegible]
1905.		$ cts.		Lbs.	Lbs.	Lbs.	No.	No.	No.	Lbs.	Lbs.	Lbs.	Lbs.	Lbs.	Lbs.	No.	No.	No.	Lbs.	Lbs.	Lbs.	Lbs.	
[illegible]	[illegible]	750 00	541	1,391,8[illegible]	292,074½	1,079,789	6,560,400	6,429,400	140,000	236,504	236,504		299,772	71,290	189,402	8,294,150	3,779,900	1,311,270	8,116	8,116	146,670	146,670	[illegible]
[illegible]	[illegible]	2,315 00	do	6,780,758	555,282½	6,245,225	232,918,287 *1,122,000	229,620,987 1,122,000	3,367,300	2,844,798	2,781,177	68,619	1,716,797	1,095,747½	621,089½								[illegible]
New Brunswick	1	75 00	916	2,[illegible]	2,294		4,739,200	3,209,300	1,530,900														
Nova Scotia	3	157 50	910	15,7[illegible]	4,411½	51				11,888	4,094	7,794	3,297	3,297									
Prince Edward Island	4	255 00	788	172,16[illegible]	92,11[illegible]	41,324				3,358	8,358												
[illegible]	1	50 00	67½			80,051																	
Totals	57	3,152 50	13,[illegible]	8,[illegible]	946,371	7,449,4[illegible]	244,207,887 *1,122,000	239,249,087 1,122,000	4,908,200	3,115,546	3,044,133	71,413	1,990,776	1,170,234½	810,541½	8,294,150	3,779,900	1,311,270	8,[illegible]	[illegible]	[illegible]	[illegible]	[illegible]
1906.																							
[illegible]	42	315 00 562 50	1 12	1,370,[illegible] 8,0[illegible]	431,[illegible] [illegible]	979,253 7,399,041	5,935,[illegible] 251,622,700	5,[illegible] 251,018,000	25,[illegible] 3,374,700	216,324 2,896,097	216,324 2,861,830	34,267	298,303 1,542,677	94,242 1,049,364	174,081 513,313	7,161,500	3,834,500	3,327,000	8,5[illegible]	8,5[illegible]	54,290	[illegible]	117,[illegible] 1,171,[illegible]
New Brunswick	1	75 00	[illegible]	545	545		*1,528,500	1,528,500															
Nova Scotia	3	190 00	[illegible]	37,[illegible]	9,[illegible]	28,[illegible]	1,629,550	1,229,100	403,450	11,290	8,502	2,338	10,655	10,655									
Prince Edward Island	4	255 00	[illegible]	170,[illegible]	64,[illegible]	85,[illegible]				25,014	25,014		3,037	2,920	717								3,[illegible] 3,[illegible] 17,[illegible]
Totals	55	1,347 50	14	9,588,[illegible]	1,066,48[illegible]	8,492,330	262,187,350 *1,528,500	258,183,700 1,528,500	4,003,650	3,178,725	3,142,100	36,625	1,845,272	1,157,181	688,091	7,161,500	3,834,500	3,327,000	8,5[illegible]	[illegible]	154,290	154,820	1,314,8[illegible]

* Cigarettes $6 per M.

INLAND REVENUE DEPARTMENT,
OTTAWA, August 22, 1906.

W. J. GERALD,
Deputy Minister.

No. 15.—COMPARATIVE STATEMENT of Warehouse Returns for the Years ended June 30, 1905 and 1906.

Dr. | Cr.

Provinces.	Entered for Consumption: Tobacco at 5c. per lb. (Lbs.)	Cigarettes ($ per M.) (No.)	Canadian Tobacco (Lbs.)	Combination Tobacco (Lbs.)	Combination Cigarettes (No.)	Duty ($ cts.)	Removed to other Divisions: Tobacco (Lbs.)	Cigarettes (No.)	Exported: Tobacco (Lbs.)	Cigarettes (No.)	Canadian Tobacco (Lbs.)
1905.											
Ontario	[illegible]	[illegible]	[illegible]	[illegible]	[illegible]	[illegible]	[illegible]	[illegible]	[illegible]	[illegible]	[illegible]
Quebec	[illegible]	[illegible]	[illegible]	[illegible]	[illegible]	[illegible]	[illegible]	[illegible]	[illegible]	[illegible]	[illegible]
New Brunswick	[illegible]	[illegible]				[illegible]		[illegible]	[illegible]	[illegible]	
Nova Scotia	[illegible]		[illegible]			[illegible]			[illegible]	[illegible]	
Prince Edward Island	[illegible]					[illegible]			[illegible]		
Manitoba	[illegible]					[illegible]					
Northwest Territories	[illegible]					[illegible]	[illegible]				
British Columbia	[illegible]					[illegible]	[illegible]				
Yukon Territory	[illegible]					[illegible]	[illegible]				
Sundries						[illegible]					
Totals	[illegible]	[illegible]	[illegible]	[illegible]	[illegible]	[illegible]	[illegible]	[illegible]	[illegible]	[illegible]	[illegible]
1906.											
Ontario	[illegible]			[illegible]		[illegible]	[illegible]		[illegible]	[illegible]	
Quebec	[illegible]	[illegible]	[illegible]	[illegible]	[illegible]	[illegible]	[illegible]	[illegible]	[illegible]	[illegible]	
New Brunswick	[illegible]	[illegible]				[illegible]				[illegible]	
Nova Scotia	[illegible]		[illegible]			[illegible]					
Prince Edward Island	[illegible]					[illegible]			[illegible]		
Manitoba	[illegible]					[illegible]					
Alberta	[illegible]					[illegible]					
British Columbia	[illegible]					[illegible]					
Yukon Territory	[illegible]					[illegible]	[illegible]		[illegible]		
Sundries						[illegible]			[illegible]		
Totals	[illegible]	[illegible]	[illegible]	[illegible]	[illegible]	[illegible]	[illegible]	[illegible]	[illegible]	[illegible]	

Further column groups printed on the page (Remaining in Warehouse; Warehoused; Received from other Divisions; Totals; Army, Navy and Ships' Stores; Written off by Authority; Taken for Ex-warehousing; Remaining in Warehouse; Totals), subdivided into Tobacco (Lbs.), Cigarettes (No.), Canadian Tobacco (Lbs.), Combination Tobacco (Lbs.), Combination Cigarettes (No.): [illegible]

	1906.	1905.
Total duty collected, ex-manufactory and ex-warehouse, including Canada Twist and Raw Leaf	$ [illegible]	$ [illegible]
License Fees	[illegible]	[illegible]
Totals	$ [illegible]	$ [illegible]

INLAND REVENUE DEPARTMENT,
OTTAWA, August 29 1906.

W. J. GERALD,
Deputy Minister.

APPENDIX A—*Continued*—RAW LEAF TOBACCO, INCLUDING STEMS, SCRAPS AND CUTTINGS.

DR. No. 16.—WAREHOUSE RETURN for the Year ended June 30, 1906. CR.

Remaining in Warehouse from last year.	Imported.	Warehoused ex-Factory.	Received from other Divisions.	Totals.	Divisions.	Entered for Consumption. Quantity.	Entered for Consumption. Duty.	Removed to other Divisions.	Exported.	Written off.	Taken for Horticultural purposes, and destroyed.	Re-entered for Manufacture.	Remaining in Warehouse.	Totals.
Std. lbs.	Std. lbs.	Std. lbs.	Std. lbs.	Std. lbs.		Std. lbs.	$ cts.	Std. lbs.	Std. lbs.	Std. lbs.	Std. lbs.	Std. lbs.	Std. lbs.	Std. lbs.
3,045	878	5,424	13,473	22,820	Belleville, Ont.	14,248	1,424 80	2.872	2,552			305	2,843	22,820
33,916	09,112	10,399	1,287	155,414	Brantford, "	96,664	9,681 88	954	11,696		79	247	4574	155,414
			785	785	Cornwall, "						785			785
20,433	59,436¾	3,970	8,880	92,719¾	Guelph, "	61,938¾	6,351 76	1,917	4,529			2,288	22,047	92,719¾
1,488,743	1,819,668	279,451	9 995¼	3,597,857¼	Hamilton, "	1,664,238¼	166,873 35	14,308	274,950		101	4,866½	1,639,393½	3,597,857¼
54,143	78,541	10,859	5,912	149,455	Kingston, "	63,603	6,372 62	20,198	9,033			5,822	50,799	149,455
187,385	730,860½	113,287	13,237	1,044,769½	London, "	680,502	70,490 00	12,122	92,892			18,710	240,543½	1,044,769½
			7,148	7,148	Ottawa, "						7,148			7,148
1,516	9,775		1,442	12,733	Owen Sound, "	10,250	1,025 00	140					2,343	12,733
992		339	497	1,828	Perth, "	799½	79 95					½	1,028	1,828
1,056	1,389		1,879¼	4,324¼	Peterborough, "	1,484	148 40				1,760		1,080¼	4,324¼
2,685		597		3,282	Port Arthur, "	150	15 00	3,059				73		3,282
685	8,537			9,222	Prescott, "	6,463	646 30						2,759	9,222
17,109	20,386	1,632	4,640	43,767	St. Catharines, "	21 419	2,145 22	1,732	2,400		200	5,423	12,593	43,767
14,062	38,995½	3,033		56,090½	Stratford, "	35,490½	3,549 05	2,605	1,097		40		16,858	56,090½
125,367½	635,928	66,176	11,816¾	839,288¼	Toronto, "	468,799¼	52,190 41	8,036	64,981		533	14,707	282,232	839,288¼
20,779	35,079¾	2,320	675¼	58,854	Windsor, "	30,624	3,156 48	1,220	5,786				21,224	58,854
1,971,916½	3,549,286½	497,487	81,667½	6,100,357½	Totals	3,156,673¼	324,150 22	69,163	469,916		10,646	52,442	2,341,517¼	6,100,357½
4,123½	1,118		6,255½	11,497	Joliette, Que.	7,301½	1,643 85					945	3,250½	11,497
4,981,101	9,422,967¾	240,837½	42,843	14,687,749¼	Montreal, "	9,387,340¾	965,458 54	123,454¾	161,869¾		25,746	31,863	4,957,475	14,687,749¼
89,008	216,027½	7,729	31,133	343,897½	Quebec, "	255,909½	46,169 06	3,470	4,362			22,257½	57,898½	343,897½
15,622	21,011	68	4,571	41,272	St. Hyacinthe, "	24,629	2,799 22	4,526				618	11,499	41,272
166,539½	220,530	28,005	45,754¾	460,829¼	Sherbrooke, "	253,241¼	40,136 26	10,898	18,402			31,733	146,555	460,829¼
990	2,769½		1,814	5,573½	Three Rivers, "	4,861	755 13					½	712	5,573½
5,257,384	9,884,423¾	276,639½	132,371¼	15,550,818½	Totals	9,933,283	1,056,962 06	142,348¾	184,633¾		25,746	87,417	5,177,390	15,550,818½

47,612	27,913	6,884	2,389	84,798	St. John, N.B . .	33,478¾	4,392 12	11,720	3,862	6,060	150	3,622	25,905¼	84,798
3,061	9,520	340	1,155¼	14,076¼	Halifax, N.S.......	12,178¼	1,217 83	....	....	. . .	42	....	1,856	14,076¼
19,271	34,691	....	200	54,162	Pictou, "	33,938	3,842 40	....	....	.....	.....	....	20,224	54,162
22,332	44,211	340	1,355¼	68,238¼	......Totals........	46,116¼	5,060 23	....	....	......	42	....	22,080	68,238¼
45,386	161,479	....	....	206,865	Charlottettown, P.E.I	143,345	14,633 86	....	....	......	1,311	....	62,209	206,865
64,658	168,038	21,506	12,277¼	266,479¼	Winnipeg, Man.....	183,729½	18,414 51	5,052	16,830	......	213	611	60,043¾	266,479¼
4,719	20,435½	672	909¼	26,735¾	Calgary, Alta......	19,485¾	1,948 60	1,501	156	. ...	......	....	5,593	26,735¾
36,849	80,785½	11,658	2,480¾	131,773¼	Vancouver, B.C....	89,591¼	9,027 92	3,504	14,670	.....	191	177	23,640	131,773¼
9,912	31,644	3,598	628½	45,782½	Victoria, "	32,917½	3,306 15	790	3,508	....	.. ..	272	8,295	45,782½
46,761	112,429½	15,250	3,109¼	177,555¾	......Totals........	122,508¾	12,334 07	4,294	18,178	. ..	191	449	31,935	177,555¾
7,460,768½	13,968,216¼	818,784½	234,078¾	22,481,848	....Grand Totals...	13,638,620¼	1,437,895 67	234,078¾	693,575¾	6,060	38,299	144,541	7,726,673¼	22,481,848

W. J. GERALD,
Deputy Minister.

INLAND REVENUE DEPARTMENT,
OTTAWA, August 29, 1906.

APPENDIX A.—*Continued.*—RAW LEAF TOBACCO, INCLUDING STEMS, SCRAPS AND CUTTINGS.

No. 17.—Comparative Statement of Warehouse Returns for the Years ended June 30, 1905 and 1906.

Remaining in Warehouse from last year.	Imported.	Warehoused ex-Factory.	Received from other Divisions.	Totals.	Provinces.	Entered for Consumption.		Removed to other Divisions.	Exported.	Written off.	Taken for Horticultural purposes, and destroyed.	Re-entered for Manufacture.	Remaining in Warehouse.	Totals.
						Quantity.	Duty.							
Std. lbs.	Std. lbs.	Std. lbs.	Std. lbs.	Std. lbs.	1905.	Std. lbs.	$ cts.	Std. lbs.	Std. lbs.	S. lbs.	S. lbs.	Std. lbs.	Std. lbs.	Std. lbs.
1,231,386¼	3,952,365	506,870	122,715¼	5,813,336½	Ontario	3,253,156	335,564 67	76,812	441,415	782	12,569	56,686	1,971,916½	5 813 336½
5,615,898¼	8,322,651¾	352,704½	147,826	14,439,080½	Quebec	8,593,956¼	926,041 86	190,144¼	279,070¼	2,740	1,644½	[illegible]1¼	5,257,384	1[illegible]0½
52,791½	37,781	3,215	2,718¼	96,505¾	New Brunswick	43,603¾	5,492 39	....	3,620	.....	....	1,670	47,612	96,505¾
29,404	46,604	....	615	76,623	Nova Scotia	53,676	5,697 60	....	....	.....	615	....	22,332	76,623
71,458	135,723	....	....	207,181	P. E. Island	161,795	16,179 50	....	....	.....	.....	....	45,386	207,181
73,169¼	148,250¾	18,759	2,198¾	242,377¾	Manitoba	159,195¾	15,919 59	6,430	10,407	.....	279	1,408	64,658	242,377¾
8,536	9,163	544	....	18,243	N. W. Territories	11,732	1,173 20	1,001	791	.....	.....	....	4,719	18,243
62,545	97,191	15,653	2,266½	177,655½	British Columbia	110,261½	11,117 38	3,952	12,217	3,096	....	1,368	46,761	177,655½
7,145,188¼	12,749,729½	897,745½	278,339¾	21,071,003	Totals	12,387,376¼	1,317,186 19	278,339¼	747,520¼	6,618	15,107½	175,273¼	7,460,768½	21,071,003
					1906.									
1,971,916½	3,549,286½	497,487	81,667½	6,100,357½	Ontario	3,156,673¼	324,150 22	69,163	469,916	.....	10,646	52,442	2,341,517¼	6,100,357½
5,257,384	9,884,423¾	276,639½	132,371¼	15,550,818½	Quebec	9,933,283	1,056,962 06	142,348¾	184,633¾	.....	25,746	87,417	5,177,390	15,550,818½
47,612	27,913	6,884	2,389	84,798	New Brunswick	33,478¾	4,392 12	11,720	3,862	6,060	150	3,622	25,905¼	4,898
22,332	44,211	340	1,355¼	68,238¼	Nova Scotia	46,116¼	5,060 23	....	....	.....	42	....	22,080	68,238¼
45,386	161,479	....	....	206,865	P. E. Island	143,345	14,633 86	....	....	.....	1,311	....	62,209	206,865
64,658	168,038	21,506	12,277¼	266,479¼	Manitoba	183,729½	18,414 51	5,052	16,830	.....	213	611	60,043¾	266,479¼
4,719	20,435½	672	909¼	26,735¾	Alberta	19,485¾	1,948 60	1,501	156	.....	.....	....	5,593	26,735¾
46,761	112,429½	15,256	3,109¼	177,555¾	British Columbia	122,508¾	12,334 07	4,294	18,178	.....	191	449	31,935	177,555¾
7,460,768½	13,968,216¼	818,784½	234,078¾	22,481,848	Totals	13,638,620¼	1,437,895 67	234,078¾	693,575¼	6,060	38,299	144,541	7,726,673¼	22,481,848

W. J. GERALD,
Deputy Minister.

Inland Revenue Department,
Ottawa, August 29, 1906.

APPENDIX A—*Continued*—CANADA TWIST TOBACCO.

No. 18.—STATEMENT of Revenue collected from Canada Twist Tobacco for the Year ended June 30, 1906.

Divisions.	Licenses.		Canada Twist, at 5 cts. per pound.	Total Duty collected, including License Fees.
	No.	Fees.		
		$	Lbs.	$ cts.
Cornwall, Ont.	4	8	2,700	143 00
Ottawa "	10	20	2,970	168 50
Prescott "	1	2	160	10 00
Totals	15	30	5,830	321 50
Joliette, Que	8	13	9,872	506 60
Montreal "	36	72	20,638	1,103 90
Totals	44	85	30,510	1,610 50
Grand Totals	59	115	36,340	1,932 00

W. J. GERALD,
Deputy Minister.

INLAND REVENUE DEPARTMENT,
OTTAWA, August 29, 1906.

CANADA TWIST TOBACCO.

No. 19.—COMPARATIVE STATEMENT for Years ended June 30, 1905 and 1906.

Years.	Provinces.	Licenses.		Canada Twist, at 5 cents per pound.	Total Duty collected, including License Fees.
		No.	Fees.		
			$	Lbs.	$ cts.
1905	Ontario	7	14	1,140	71 00
	Quebec	29	57	31,727	1,643 35
	Totals	36	71	32,867	1,714 35
1906	Ontario	15	30	5,830	321 50
	Quebec	44	85	30,510	1,610 50
	Totals	59	115	36,340	1,932 00

W. J. GERALD,
Deputy Minister.

INLAND REVENUE DEPARTMENT,
OTTAWA, August 29, 1906.

APPENDIX A—*Continued*—CIGARS.

No. 20.—RETURN of Manufactures

Divisions.	Licenses.		Total Raw Leaf Tobacco and other Materials actually used.	Deficiencies paying duty.	Cigars at $7 per Thousand.		Cigars at
	No.	Fees.			Produced.	Paid duty	Produced.
		$ cts.	Lbs.	No.	No.	No.	No.
Belleville, Ont	1	75 00	8,555	....	....	....	396,050
Brantford "	6	450 00	87,613	....	1,500	1,500	4,846,125
Guelph "	9	675 00	61,303¾	....	....	....	3,703,900
Hamilton "	15	1,125 00	209,559¾	2,023	1,050	1,050	*38,600 10,191,545
Kingston "	2	150 00	60,777	....	....	....	3,187,020
London "	21	1,537 50	606,915	....	1,002	1,002	33,895,745
Owen Sound "	1	75 00	10,168	....	....	....	512,800
Perth "	1	75 00	999	....	....	....	61,100
Peterborough, Ont	1	75 00	1,492	....	....	....	100,700
Port Arthur "	1	75 00	254	....	....	....	14,350
Prescott "	1	75 00	5,756	....	....	....	313,600
St. Catharines "	12	862 50	25,114	....	....	....	1,504,100
Stratford "	3	225 00	34,197½	....	....	....	1,837,400
Toronto "	24	1,775 00	381,438¾	2,017	420	420	20,690,965
Windsor "	8	552 50	31,502	....	....	....	1,685,335
Totals	106	7,802 50	1,525,644¾	4,040	3,972	3,972	*38,600 82,940,735
Joliette, Que	5	320 00	59,589	....	....	....	109,100
Montreal "	34	2,347 50	1,151,298¼	22,836	1,170	1,170	60,843,200
Quebec "	6	420 00	152,239	....	....	....	7,940,635
St. Hyacinthe "	5	345 00	50,525	....	....	....	1,805,480
Sherbrooke "	5	350 00	164,858¼	....	....	....	9,147,060
Three Rivers "	2	140 00	12,037½	....	....	....	189,355
Totals	57	3,922 50	1,590,547	22,836	1,170	1,170	80,034,830
St. John, N.B	5	355 00	76,770¼	....	....	....	1,016,205
Halifax, N.S	3	225 00	11,930¼*	....	....	....	634,780
Pictou "	1	37 50	227	....	....	....	15,150
Totals	4	262 50	12,157¼	....	....	....	649,930
Winnipeg, Man	13	900 00	163,715½	....	14,997	14,997	8,789,560
Calgary, Alta	3	225 00	17,251¾	....	....	....	921,485
Vancouver, B.C	13	965 00	78,693½	....	2,844	2,844	4,330,350
Victoria "	11	815 00	29,660½	2,263	....	....	1,534,700
Totals	24	1,780 00	108,354	2,263	2,844	2,844	5,865,050
Grand Totals	212	15,247 50	3,494,440½	29,139	22,983	22,983	*38,600 180,217,795

* Repacked. † Destroyed by fire.

INLAND REVENUE DEPARTMENT,
OTTAWA, August 29, 1906.

for the year ended June 30, 1906.

$6 per Thousand.		Canadian Cigars at $3 per Thousand.			Combination Cigars at $3 per Thousand.			Total Duty collected ex-manufactory, including License Fees.
Paid duty.	Warehoused	Produced.	Paid duty.	Warehoused.	Produced.	Paid duty.	Warehoused.	
No.	No.	No.	No.	No.	No.	No.	No.	$ cts.
190,000	206,050							1,215.00
2,391,875	2,454,250							14,811.75
1,324,125	2,379,775							8,619.75
38,600 3,354,325	6,837,220							21,502.03
758,170	2,428,850							4,699.02
17,162,420	16,733,325							104,519.04
346,250	166,550							2,152.50
	61,100							75.00
86,200	14,500							592.20
300	14,050							76.80
45,000	268,600							345.00
1,247,250	256,850							8,346.00
635,600	1,201,800							4,038.60
16,263,455	4,427,510	133,350	133,350					99,770.82
903,335	782,000				46,700	25,425	21,275	6,048.79
38,600 44,708,305	38,232,430	133,350	133,350		46,700	25,425	21,275	276,812.30
94,100	15,000	643,150	248,650	394,500	2.754,550	†7,850 1,515,250	1,231,450	6,176.30
30,472,200	30,371,000				244,150	244,150		186,058.35
3,780,905	4,159,730				1,125,430	806,340	319,090	25,524.46
827,425	978,055				1,264,840	1,056,060	208,780	8,477.73
5,219,015	3,928,045	254,610	157,580	97,030				32,136.83
74,235	115,120				572,400	421,500	150,900	1,849.91
40,467,880	39,566,950	897,760	406,230	491,530	5,961,370	†7,850 4,043,300	1,910,220	260,223.58
308,380	707,825				3,519,000	258,550	3,265,450	2,965.93
375,610	259,170							2,478.66
15,150								128.40
390,760	259,170							2,607.06
3,726,705	5,062,855							23,365.21
491,210	430,275							3,172.26
4,074,750	255,600				54,900	54,900		25,598.11
1,206,650	328,050				48,825	48,825		8,214.93
5,281,400	583,650				103,725	103,725		33,813.04
38,600 95,374,640	84,843,155	1,031,110	539,580	491,530	9,630,795	†7,850 4,426,000	5,196,945	602,959.38

W. J. GERALD,
Deputy Minister.

APPENDIX A—*Continued*—CIGARS.

DR. No. 21.—COMPARATIVE STATEMENT of Manufactures

Provinces.	Licenses. No.	Licenses. Fees.	Total Raw Leaf Tobacco and other Materials actually used.	Deficiencies paying duty.	Cigars at $7 per thousand. Produced.	Cigars at $7 per thousand. Paid Duty	Cigars at $7 per thousand. Warehoused.	Cigars Produced.
1905.		$ cts.	Lbs.	No.	No.	No.	No.	No.
Ontario	107	7,892 50	1,515,606	13,030	9,840	6,840	3,000	83,146,520
Quebec	60	4,245 00	1,557,062½	18,582	10,590	10,590	.....	80,302,680
New Brunswick	4	290 00	65,024¼	....	....	....	.....	1,052,705
Nova Scotia	3	225 00	11,262	....	....	....	....	616,645
Manitoba	11	787 50	139,701¾	....	....	....	.....	7,468,725
North-west Territories	2	150 00	10,561	....	....	....	.....	572,675
British Columbia	26	1,920 00	98,277½	*6,275	....	....	.....	5,314,400
Totals	213	15,510 00	3,397,495	37,887	20,430	17,430	3,000	178,474,350
1906.								
Ontario	106	7,802 50	1,525,644¾	4,040	3,972	3,972	....	†38,600 82,940,735
Quebec	57	3,922 50	1,590,547	22,836	1,170	1,170	....	80,034,830
New Brunswick	5	355 00	76,770¼	....	....	....	.....	1,016,205
Nova Scotia	4	262 50	12,157¼	....	....	....	.....	649,930
Manitoba	13	900 00	163,715½	....	14,997	14,997	....	8,789,560
Alberta	3	225 00	17,251¾	....	....	....	.....	921,485
British Columbia	24	1,780 00	108,354	2,263	2,844	2,844	....	5,865,050
Totals	212	15,247 50	3,494,440½	29,139	22,983	22,983	....	180,217,795 †38,600

* 6,275 cigars from combination leaf at $3 per M. † Repacked. ‡ Destroyed by fire.

INLAND REVENUE DEPARTMENT,
OTTAWA, August 29, 1906.

for the years ended June 30, 1905 and 1906. CR.

At $6 per Thousand.		Canadian Cigars at $3 per Thousand.			Combination Cigars at $3 per Thousand.			Total Duty collected ex-Manufactory including License Fees
Paid Duty.	Warehoused	Produced.	Paid Duty	Warehoused.	Produced.	Paid Duty	Warehoused.	
No.	No.	No.	No.	No.	No.	No.	No.	$ cts.
45,981,595	37,164,925	....	....	....	481,550	166,650	314,900	284,408 08
33,606,590	46,696,090	2,460,390	2,069,190	391,200	3,624,250	2,597,395	1,026,855	220,069 91
284,100	768,605	....	....	....	2,862,900	6,000	2,856,900	2,012 60
320,270	296,375	....	....	....	....	....	....	2,146 62
3,049,850	4,418,875	....	....	....	....	....	....	19,086 60
215,450	357,225	....	....	....	....	....	....	1,442 70
4,553,575	760,825	....	....	....	120,500	120,500	....	29,621 80
88,011,430	90,462,920	2,460,390	2,069,190	391,200	7,089,200	2,890,545	4,198,655	558,788 31
38,600 44,708,305	38,232,430	133,350	133,350	....	46,700	25,425	21,275	276,812 30
40,467,880	39,566,950	897,760	406,230	491,530	5,961,370	‡7,850 4,043,300	1,910,220	260,223 58
308,380	707,825	....	....	....	3,519,000	253,550	3,265,450	2,965 93
390,760	259,170	....	....	....	....	....	....	2,607 06
3,726,705	5,062,855	....	....	....	....	....	....	23,365 21
491,210	430,275	....	....	....	....	....	....	3,172 26
5,281,400	583,650	....	....	....	103,725	103,725	....	33,813 04
95,374,640 38,600	84,843,155	1,031,110	539,580	491,530	9,630,795	4,426,000 ‡7,850	5,196,945	602,959 38

W. J. GERALD,
Deputy Minister.

APPENDIX A—*Continued*—CIGARS.

No. 22.—WAREHOUSE RETURN for the year ended June 30, 1906.

Dr. | Cr.

Remaining in Warehouse from last year: Foreign.	Canadian.	Combination.	Warehoused: Foreign.	Canadian.	Combination.	Received from other Divisions: Foreign.	Canadian.	Combination.	Totals: Foreign.	Canadian.	Combination.	Divisions.	Entered for Consumption: Foreign, at 86 p. M.	Canadian, at 83 p. M.	Combination, at 83 p. M.	Duty.	Removed to other Divisions: Foreign.	Canadian.	Combination.	Exported: Foreign.	Combination.	Written off: Foreign.	Combination.	Remaining in Warehouse: Foreign.	Canadian.	Combination.	Totals: Foreign.	Canadian.	Combination.
No.	No.	No.	No.	No.	No.	No.	No.	No.	No.	No.	No.		No.	No.	No.	$ cts.	No.	No.	No.	No.	No.	No.	No.	No.	No.	No.	No.	No.	No.
250,650			206,050						456,700			Belleville, Ont.	205,000			1,710 00	5,000							166,700			456,700		
710,835			2,454,250						3,165,085			Brantford "	2,428,450			14,570 70								735,635			3,165,085		
459,225			2,379,775						2,839,000			Guelph "	2,358,025			14,148 15								480,975			2,839,000		
3,663,275			6,837,220			4,105,000			14,605,495			Hamilton "	11,985,405			71,912 43	158,500			16,000				2,445,590			14,605,495		
717,225			2,428,850			5,000			3,151,075			Kingston "	2,167,350			12,944 10								983,725			3,151,075		
4,924,000			16,733,325						21,657,325			London "	13,784,550			82,707 30	2,900,000							4,972,775			21,657,325		
118,075						283,000			401,075			Ottawa "	282,425			1,694 85	20,000							99,250			401,075		
41,800			166,550						208,350			Owen Sound "	178,300			1,069 80								30,050			208,350		
132,255	7,000		61,100						193,355	7,000		Perth "	147,655	7,000		906 93								46,700			193,355	7,000	
42,550			14,500						57,050			Peterborough "	41,000			246 00								16,050			57,050		
23,100			14,050						37,150			Port Arthur "	18,175			109 05	18,975										37,150		
56,300			268,600						324,900			Prescott "	295,000			1,770 00								29,900			324,900		
132,425			256,850						389,275			St. Catharines "	285,175			1,711 05								104,100			389,275		
186,050			1,201,800						1,387,850			Stratford "	1,193,300			7,159 80								194,550			1,387,850		
1,814,520			4,427,510			158,500			6,400,530			Toronto "	5,057,465			30,344 79								1,343,065			6,400,530		
328,555		136,350	782,000		21,275				1,110,555		157,625	Windsor "	784,080		143,625	5,135 36								326,475		14,000	1,110,555		157,625
13,001,440	7,000	136,350	38,232,430		21,275	4,551,500			56,385,370	7,000	157,625	Totals	41,281,335	7,000	143,625	248,140 01	3,102,475			16,000				11,986,540		14,000	56,385,370	7,000	157,625
	220,000	150,350	15,000	394,500	1,231,450				15,000	614,500	1,381,800	Joliette, Que.		498,500	374,550	2,613 15	15,000	83,000	917,850				3,400		35,000	86,050	15,000	614,500	1,381,800
7,758,125		128,450	30,371,000			15,000		886,350	38,144,125		1,014,800	Montreal "	30,693,735		894,800	186,606 81	1,298,000			79,775		365,675		5,796,940		20,000	38,144,125		1,014,800
1,612,415		83,450	4,150,730		319,090	30,000	83,000	29,500	5,793,145	83,000	432,040	Quebec "	3,792,180	23,000	326,600	23,801 88								2,000,965	60,000	105,440	5,793,145	83,000	432,040
602,905			978,105		208,780	20,000			1,601,010		208,780	St. Hyacinthe "	1,335,585		208,780	8,639 85	243,000							22,425			1,601,010		208,780
1,325,985	14,000		3,928,045	97,720					5,254,030	111,720		Sherbrooke "	3,029,605	101,520		22,082 19								1,624,425	10,200		5,254,030	111,720	
85,730		53,600	115,120		150,900				200,850		204,500	Three Rivers "	124,650		172,000	1,263 90								76,200		32,500	200,850		204,500
11,376,210	234,000	413,850	39,566,950	491,520	1,910,220	65,000	83,000	917,850	51,008,160	809,220	3,241,920	Totals	38,485,755	621,020	2,076,730	245,007 78	1,556,000	83,000	917,850	79,775		365,675	3,400	9,520,955	105,200	243,910	51,008,160	809,220	3,241,920
549,745		678,750	707,825		3,265,450				1,257,570		3,944,200	St. John, N.B.	688,800		2,619,050	11,990 25				1,450	3,700			567,270		1,321,450	1,257,570		3,944,200
274,000			259,170			23,000			556,170			Halifax, N.S.	245,700			1,474 20				28,600				281,870			556,170		
1,032,200			5,062,855			18,975			6,114,030			Winnipeg, Man.	5,015,515			30,093 09								1,098,515			6,114,030		
105,150			430,275						535,425			Calgary, Alta.	443,000			2,658 00								92,425			535,425		
98,400			255,600						354,000			Vancouver, B.C.	300,300			1,801 80								53,700			354,000		
211,900			328,050						539,950			Victoria "	468,500			2,811 00				15,050				56,400			539,950		
310,300			583,650						893,950			Totals	768,800			4,612 80				15,050				110,100			893,950		
27,349,045	241,000	1,228,950	81,843,155	491,520	5,196,945	4,656,475	83,000	917,850	116,750,675	816,220	7,343,745	Grand Totals	87,928,975	628,020	4,839,405	543,976 13	4,656,475	83,000	917,850	140,875	3,700	365,675	3,400	23,666,675	105,200	1,579,360	116,750,675	816,220	7,343,745

INLAND REVENUE DEPARTMENT,
OTTAWA, August 29, 1906.

W. J. GERALD,
Deputy Minister.

APPENDIX A—*Continued*—CIGARS.

No. 23.—COMPARATIVE STATEMENT of Warehouse returns for the years ended June 30, 1905 and 1906.

Dr.

Provinces.	Remaining in Warehouse from last year. Foreign.			Warehoused. Foreign.	Canadian.	Combination.	Received from other Divisions. Foreign.	Canadian.	Combination.	Totals. Foreign.	Canadian.	Combination.
	Foreign.	Canadian.	Combination.									
	No.	No.	No.	No.	No.	No.	No.	No.	No.	No.	No.	No.
1905.												
Ontario	11,316,375		21,000	†37,167,925		314,900	4,997,000	10,000		53,480,290	10,000	335,900
Quebec	11,924,530	43,700	503,300	46,026,650	391,300	1,026,855	130,500		60,000	58,751,120	434,900	1,590,155
New Brunswick	424,325		840,935	708,695		2,856,900				1,192,880		3,697,835
Nova Scotia	258,585			296,375			45,000			509,960		
Manitoba	1,162,875			4,418,875						5,581,750		
N. W. Territories	84,125			357,225						411,350		
British Columbia	388,500			760,825			45,000			1,194,325		
Totals	25,528,295	43,700	1,365,235	90,485,920	391,300	4,198,655	5,217,500	10,000	60,000	121,211,715	444,900	5,623,890
1906.												
Ontario	13,601,440	7,000	136,350	38,232,430	491,530	21,275	4,551,500	83,000	917,850	56,385,370	7,000	157,625
Quebec	11,376,210	234,690	413,850	39,806,950		1,910,220	65,000			51,008,160	809,220	3,241,920
New Brunswick	549,745		678,750	707,825		3,265,450				1,257,570		3,944,200
Nova Scotia	274,000			208,170			23,000			556,170		
Manitoba	1,032,200			5,002,555			18,975			6,114,030		
Alberta	105,150			430,275						535,425		
British Columbia	310,300			583,650						893,950		
Totals	27,249,045	241,690	1,228,950	84,813,155	491,530	5,196,945	4,658,475	83,000	917,850	116,750,675	816,220	7,343,745

†3,000 of these cigars at $7 per M.

Cr.

Provinces.	Entered for Consumption. Foreign, at $6 per M.	Canadian, at $3 per M.	Combination at $3 per M.	Duty.	Removed to other Divisions. Foreign.	Canadian.	Combination.	Exported. Foreign.	Combination.	Written off. Foreign.	Combination.	Remaining in Warehouse. Foreign.	Canadian.	Combination.	Totals. Foreign.	Canadian.	Combination.
	No.	No.	No.	$ cts.	No.	No.	No.	No.	No.	No.	No.	No.	No.	No.	No.	No.	No.
1905.																	
Ontario	†37,096,540	3,000	198,550	223,189 83	2,779,300			3,000				13,601,440	7,000	136,350	53,480,290	10,000	335,900
Quebec	44,811,435	190,210	1,116,305	272,968 16	2,438,300	10,000	60,000	77,400		17,875		11,376,210	234,690	413,850	58,751,120	434,900	1,590,155
New Brunswick	643,186		3,009,085	12,886 37					10,000			549,745		678,750	1,192,830		3,697,835
Nova Scotia	274,460			1,646 76				51,500				274,000			509,960		
Manitoba	4,540,560			27,237 30								1,032,200			5,581,750		
N. W. Territories	306,200			1,837 20								105,150			411,350		
British Columbia	334,715			5,128 65				20,350		8,900		310,300			1,191,325		
Totals	88,566,145	193,210	4,324,940	544,954 33	5,217,500	10,000	60,000	152,250	10,000	26,775		27,249,045	241,690	1,228,950	131,211,715	444,900	5,623,890
1906.																	
Ontario	41,281,355	7,000	143,625	248,140 01	3,102,475		917,850	16,000				11,983,540		14,000	56,385,370	7,000	157,625
Quebec	39,185,755	621,020	2,076,730	245,007 78	1,556,000	83,000		79,775		365,675	3,400	9,329,955	105,200	243,940	51,008,160	809,220	3,241,920
New Brunswick	688,850		2,619,050	11,399 25				1,450	3,700			567,270		1,321,450	1,257,570		3,944,200
Nova Scotia	245,760			1,474 20				28,600				281,870			556,170		
Manitoba	5,015,515			30,093 09								1,098,515			6,114,030		
Alberta	443,000			2,658 60								92,425			535,425		
British Columbia	768,800			4,612 80				15,050				110,100			893,950		
Totals	87,928,975	628,020	4,839,405	543,976 13	4,658,475	83,000	917,850	140,875	3,700	365,675	3,400	23,656,675	105,200	1,579,390	116,750,675	816,220	7,343,745

	1905.	1906.
Total duty collected, ex-manufactory and ex-warehouse	$ 1,088,232 64	$ 1,131,688 01
Licence fees	15,510 00	15,247 50
Totals	$ 1,103,742 64	$1,146,935 51

INLAND REVENUE DEPARTMENT,
OTTAWA, August 29, 1906.

W. J. GERALD,
Deputy Minister

APPENDIX A—*Continued*—INSPECTION OF PETROLEUM.

No. 24.—RETURN of Canadian Petroleum and Naphtha inspected during the year ended June 30, 1906.

Division.	Licenses.		Petroleum.	Naphtha.	Total.
	No.	Fees.			
		$	Galls.	Galls.	Galls.
London....	2	2	15,740,771·31	2,893,383·55	18,634,154·86

W. J. GERALD,
Deputy Minister.

INLAND REVENUE DEPARTMENT,
OTTAWA, August 29, 1906.

No. 25.—COMPARATIVE STATEMENT of Petroleum and Naphtha inspected during the Years ended June 30, 1905 and 1906.

Provinces.	Licenses.		Petroleum.	Naphtha.	Totals.
	No.	Fees.			
1905.		$	Galls.	Galls.	Galls.
Ontario...	3	3	15,237,521·19	2,282,514·08	17,520,035·27
1906.					
Ontario...	2	2	15,740,771·31	2,893,383·55	18,634,154·86

W. J. GERALD,
Deputy Minister.

INLAND REVENUE DEPARTMENT,
OTTAWA, August 29, 1906.

APPENDIX A—*Continued*—MANUFACTURES IN BOND.

No. 26.—RETURN of Manufactures

Divisions.	Licenses.		Materials Used.			
	No.	Fees.	Spirits.	Beer, Wine, &c.	Nitric Acid.	Mercury.
		$ cts.	Galls.	Galls.	Lbs.	Lbs.
Brantford Ont.	1	50 00	5,196·45	37·50	....	....
Guelph "	1	50 00	....	....	....	....
Hamilton "	3	150 00	23,399·65	374·40	....	....
Kingston "	1	50 00	9,798·03	200·24	....	....
Ottawa "	1	50 00	358·92	6·70	....	....
Perth "	2	50 00	....	....	....	....
Prescott "	1	300 00	192,338·21	....	950,582	103,182
Toronto "	6	300 00	92,836·33	1,072·40	....	....
Windsor "	5	500 00	8,417·99	....	39,447	4,849½
Totals	21	1,500 00	332,345·58	1,691·24	990,029	108,031½
Montreal, Que.	7	350 00	33,495·72	390·30	....	....
Quebec "	2	50 00	4,928·60	170·00	....	....
St. Hyacinthe, Que.	1	100 00	20,720·99	388·43	....	....
Sherbrooke "	2	300 00	38,675·46	....	180,084	23,850
Totals	12	800 00	97,820·77	948·73	180,084	23,850
St. John, N.B.	2	100 00	9,243·46	116·00	....	....
Winnipeg, Man.	2	75 00	2,858·46	36·00	....	....
Vancouver, B.C.	1	50 00	8,231·18	118·70	....	....
Grand Totals	38	2,525 00	450,499·45	2,910·67	1,170,113	131,881½

INLAND REVENUE DEPARTMENT,
OTTAWA, August 29, 1906.

for the Year ended June 30, 1906.

Manufactured.		Paid Duty ex-Manufactory.		Warehoused.		Total Duty Collected ex-Manufactory, including License Fees.
Vinegar.	Crude Fulminate.	Vinegar.	Duty.	Vinegar.	Crude Fulminate.	
Galls.	Lbs.	Galls.	$ cts.	Galls.	Lbs.	$ cts.
33,471·13	....	33,471·13	1,338 84	....	....	1,388 84
....	....	....	....	....	....	50 00
152,371·90	....	44,238·05	1,769 50	108,133·85	....	1,919 50
70,683·75	....	16,233·67	649 34	54,450·08	....	699 34
1,233·26	....	1,233·26	237 88	....	....	287 88
....	....	....	....	....	....	50 00
....	125,278	....	....	....	125,278	300 00
566,734·20	....	286,809·96	11,472 36	279,924·24	....	11,772 36
....	5,621	....	....	....	5,621	500 00
824,494·24	130,899	381,986·07	15,467 92	442,508·17	130,899	16,967 92
185,436·35	....	123,222·96	4,928 95	62,213·39	....	5,278 95
16,488·56	....	16,488·56	659 55	....	....	709 55
106,243·88	....	60,459·96	2,418 42	45,783·92	....	2,518 42
....	26,574	....	....	....	26,574	300 00
308,168·79	26,574	200,171·48	8,006 92	107,997·31	26,574	8,806 92
56,419·79	....	42,986·44	1,719 46	13,433 35	....	1,819 46
16,917·62	....	16,917·62	676 71	....	....	751 71
53,145·03	....	18,516·75	740 67	34,628·28	....	790 67
1,259,145·47	157,473	660,578·36	26,611 68	598,567·11	157,473	29,136 68

W. J. GERALD,
Deputy Minister.

APPENDIX A—*Continued*—MANUFACTURES IN BOND.

No. 27.—COMPARATIVE STATEMENT of Manufactures

PROVINCES.	LICENSES.		MATERIALS USED.			
	No.	Fees.	Spirits.	Beer, Wine, &c.	Nitric Acid.	Mercury.
1905.		$	Galls.	Galls.	Lbs.	Lbs.
Ontario	17	1,600	221,332·70	1,452·13	524,222	57,936½
Quebec	13	900	133,044·87	974·69	236,938	31,275
New Brunswick	2	100	6,789·36	110·90	....	....
Manitoba	1	50	....	....	....	....
British Columbia	1	50	2,541·26	46·70	....	....
Totals	34	2,700	363,708 19	2,584·42	761,160	89,211½
1906.						
Ontario	21	1,500	332,345·58	1,691·24	990,029	108,031½
Quebec	12	800	97,820·77	948·73	180,084	23,850
New Brunswick	2	100	9,243·46	116.00	....	....
Manitoba	2	75	2,858·46	36·00	....	....
British Columbia	1	50	8,231·18	118·70	....	....
Totals	38	2,525	450,499·45	2,910·67	1,170,113	131,881½

INLAND REVENUE DEPARTMENT,
OTTAWA, August 29, 1906.

for the Years ended June 30, 1905 and 1906.

MANUFACTURED.		PAID DUTY EX-MANUFACTORY.		WAREHOUSED.		Total Duty collected, ex-Manufactory, including License Fees.
Vinegar.	Crude Fulminate.	Vinegar.	Duty.	Vinegar.	Crude Fulminate.	
Galls.	Lbs.	Galls.	$ cts.	Galls.	Lbs.	$ cts.
725,449·97	70,980	278,298·58	11,132 03	447,151·39	70,980	12,732 03
434,475·61	36,246	244,313·51	9,772 61	190,162·10	36,246	10,672 61
41,918·94	....	29,853·87	1,194 14	12,065·07	....	1,294 14
....	....	....	....	....	....	50 00
12,388·78	....	....	....	12,388·78	....	50 00
1,214,233·30	107,226	552,465·96	22,098 78	661,767·34	107,226	24,798 78
824,494·24	130,899	381,986·07	15,467·92	442,508·17	130,899	16,967 92
308,168·79	26,574	200,171·48	8,006 92	107,997·31	26,574	8,806 92
56,419 79	....	42,986·44	1,719 46	13,433·35	....	1,819 46
16,917·62	....	16,917·62	676 71	....	....	751 71
53,145·03	....	18,516·75	740 67	34,628·28	....	790 67
1,259,145·47	157,473	660,578·36	26,611 68	598,567·11	157,473	29,136 68

W. J. GERALD,
Deputy Minister.

APPENDIX A—*Continued*—MANUFACTURES IN BOND.

DR. No. 28.—WAREHOUSE RETURN for

Remaining in Warehouse from last year.	Warehoused.		Received from other Divisions.	Totals.		Divisions.
Vinegar.	Vinegar.	Crude Fulminate.	Vinegar.	Vinegar.	Crude Fulminate.	
Galls.	Galls.	Lbs.	Galls.	Galls.	Lbs.	
....	....	....	6,643 85	6,643 85	....	..Brantford, Ont.........
34,937 79	108,133 85	....	....	143,071 64	....	..Hamilton " ....
12,150 05	54,450 08	....	....	66,600 13	....	..Kingston " ....
544 06	....	....	....	544 06	....	..Ottawa " ....
....	....	125,278	....	....	125,278	..Prescott " ....
100,925 69	279,924 24	....	....	380,849 93	....	..Toronto " ....
....	....	5,621	....	....	5,621	..Windsor " ....
148,557 59	442,508 17	130,899	6,643 85	597,709 61	130,899	.......Totals........
78,365 79	62,213 39	....	....	140,579 18	....	..Montreal, Que.........
....	....	....	8,481 60	8,481 60	....	..Quebec " ....
29,831 43	45,783 92	....	8,509 78	84,125 13	....	..St. Hyacinthe, Que.....
....	....	26,574	....	....	26,574	..Sherbrooke, Que ....
108,197 22	107,997 31	26,574	16,991 38	233,185 91	26,574	........Totals........
7,524 60	13,433 35	....	....	20,957 95	....	..St. John, N.B.........
....	....	....	84,703 18	84,703 18	....	..Winnipeg, Man.........
....	34,628 28	....	....	34,628 28	....	..Vancouver, B.C.........
264,279 41	598,567 11	157,473	108,338 41	971,184 93	157,473	.......Grand Totals.....

INLAND REVENUE DEPARTMENT,
OTTAWA, August 29, 1906.

the Year ended June 30, 1906. CR.

Entered for Consumption.		Removed to other Divisions.	Free.	Exported.	Remaining in Warehouse.	Totals.	
Vinegar.	Duty.	Vinegar.	Vinegar.	Crude Fulminate.	Vinegar.	Vinegar.	Crude Fulminate.
Galls.	$ cts.	Galls.	Galls.	Lbs.	Galls.	Galls.	Lbs.
6,643 85	265 75	....	....	....	....	6,643 85	....
87,993 05	3,519 70	25,920 53	....	....	29,158 06	143,071 64	....
56,854 99	2,274 21	4,509 42	....	....	5,235 72	66,600 13	....
544 06	21 76	....	....	....	....	544 06	....
....	....	....	....	125,278	....	....	125,278
248,183 92	9,927 33	60,917 08	....	....	71,748 93	380,849 93	....
....	....	....	....	5,621	....	....	5,621
400,219 87	16,008 75	91,347 03	....	130,899	106,142 71	597,709 61	130,899
117,225 73	4,689 03	8,509 78	....	....	14,843 67	140,579 18	....
3,345 87	133 82	....	5,135 73	....	....	8,481 60	....
49,922 71	1,996 93	8,481 60	8,509 78	....	17,211 04	84,125 13	....
....	....	....	....	26,574	....	....	26,574
170,494 31	6,819 78	16,991 38	13,645 51	26,574	32,054 71	233,185 91	26,574
12,538 04	501 50	....	....	....	8,419 91	20,957 95	....
67,016 83	2,680 65	....	7,929 39	....	9,756 96	84,703 18	....
24,183 61	967 37	....	....	....	10,444 67	34,628 28	....
674,452 66	26,978 05	168,338 41	21,574 90	157,473	166,818 96	971,184 93	157,473

W. J. GERALD,
Deputy Minister.

APPENDIX A—*Continued*—MANUFACTURES IN BOND.

DR. No. 29.—COMPARATIVE STATEMENT of Warehouse Returns

Remaining in Warehouse from last year.	Warehoused.		Received from other Divisions.	Totals.		PROVINCES.
Vinegar.	Vinegar.	Crude Fulminate.	Vinegar.	Vinegar.	Crude Fulminate.	
Galls.	Galls.	Lbs.	Galls.	Galls.	Lbs.	1905.
132,544·59	447,151·39	70,980	....	579,695·98	70,980	..Ontario..............
120,318·41	190,162·10	36,246	9,917·88	320,398·39	36,246	..Quebec..............
5,245·63	12,065·07	....	....	17,310·70	....	..New Brunswick.......
2,975·00	....	....	60,366·01	63,341·01	....	..Manitoba...........
....	12,388·78	....	....	12,388·78	....	..British Columbia....
261,083·63	661,767·34	107,226	70,283·89	993,134·86	107,226	........Totals..........
						1906.
148,557·59	442,508·17	130,899	6,643·85	597,709·61	130,899	..Ontario............
108,197·22	107,997·31	26,574	16,991·38	233,185·91	26,574	..Quebec............
7,524·60	13,433·35	....	....	20,957·95	....	..New Brunswick.......
....	....	....	84,703·18	84,703·18	....	..Manitoba...........
....	34,628·28	....	....	34,628·28	....	..British Columbia.......
264,279·41	598,567·11	157,473	108,338·41	971,184·93	157,473	........Totals..........

INLAND REVENUE DEPARTMENT,
OTTAWA, August 29, 1906.

for the years ended June 30, 1905 and 1906. CR.

Entered for Consumption.		Removed to other Divisions.	Free.	Exported.	Remaining in Warehouse.	Totals.	
Vinegar.	Duty.	Vinegar.	Vinegar.	Crude Fulminate.	Vinegar.	Vinegar.	Crude Fulminate.
Galls.	$ cts.	Galls.	Galls.	Lbs.	Galls.	Galls.	Lbs.
378,041·35	15,121·60	53,097·04	....	70,980	148,557·59	579,695·98	70,980
195,014·32	7,800·56	17,186·85	....	36,246	108,197·22	320,398·39	36,246
9,786·10	391·43	....	....	....	7,524 60	17,310·70	....
63,341·01	2,533·62	....	....	....	....	63,341·01	....
12,388·78	495·54	....	....	....	....	12,388·78	....
658,571·56	26,342·75	70,283·89	....	107,226	264,279·41	993,134·86	107,226
400,219·87	16,008·75	91,347·03	....	130,899	106,142·71	597,709·61	130,899
170,494·31	6,819·78	16,991·38	13,645 51	26,574	32,054·71	233,185·91	26,574
12,538·04	501·50	....	....	....	8,419·91	20,957·95	....
67,016·83	2,680·65	....	7,929·39	....	9,756·96	84,703 18	....
24,183·61	967·37	....	....	....	10,444·67	34,628·28	....
674,452·66	26,978·05	108,338·41	21,574·90	157,473	166,818·96	971,184·93	157,473

	1905.	1906.
Total duty collected, ex-manufactory and ex-warehouse......	$ 48,441 53	$ 53,589 73
License Fees....	2,700 00	2,525 00
Totals....	$ 51,141 53	$ 56,114 73

W. J. GERALD,
Deputy Minister.

APPENDIX A—*Continued*—ACETIC ACID.

No. 30.—RETURN of Manufactures for the Year ended June 30, 1906.

Divisions.	Licenses.		Manufactured.	Paid Duty ex-Manufactory.		Total Duty collected ex-Manufactory, including License Fees.
	No.	Fees.	—	—	Duty.	
		$	Galls.	Galls.	$ cts.	$ cts.
Toronto, Ont.	1	50	....	....	....	50 00
Montreal, Que.	1	50	7,657 37	7,657 37	306 29	356 29
Totals	2	100	7,657 37	7,657 37	306 29	406 29

W. J. GERALD,
Deputy Minister.

INLAND REVENUE DEPARTMENT,
OTTAWA, August 29, 1906.

APPENDIX—A—*Continued*—ACETIC ACID.

No. 31.—*Comparative Statement* of Manufactures for the years ended June 30, 1905 and 1906.

Provinces.	Licenses.		Manufactured.	Paid Duty ex-Manufactory.		Warehoused.	Total Duty collected ex-Manufactory, including License Fees.
	No.	Fees.	—	—	Duty.	—	
1905.		$	Galls.	Galls.	$ cts.	Galls.	$ cts.
Ontario	1	50	152,387 72	69,339 82	2,773 59	83,047 90	2,823 59
Quebec	1	50	5,988 64	5,988 64	239 55	....	289 55
Totals	2	100	158,376 36	75,328 46	3,013 14	83,047 90	3,113 14
1906.							
Ontario	1	50	....	....	....	....	50 00
Quebec	1	50	7,657 37	7,657 37	306 29	....	356 29
Totals	2	100	7,657 37	7,657 37	306 29	....	406 29

W. J. GERALD,
Deputy Minister.

INLAND REVENUE DEPARTMENT,
OTTAWA, August 29, 1906.

APPENDIX A—*Continued*—ACETIC ACID.

No. 32.—Warehouse Return for the Year ended June 30, 1906.

Dr. Cr.

Remaining in Warehouse from last year.	Total.	Division.	Entered for Consumption.	Duty.	Total.
Galls.	Galls.		Galls.	$ cts.	Galls.
31,244·98	31,244·98	....Toronto, Ont...........	31,244·98	1,249 80	31,244·98

W. J. GERALD,
Deputy Minister.

Inland Revenue Department,
Ottawa, August 29, 1906.

APPENDIX A—*Continued*—ACETIC ACID.

DR. No. 33.—COMPARATIVE STATEMENT of Warehouse Returns for the years ended June 30, 1905 and 1906. CR.

Remaining in Warehouse from last year.	Warehoused.	Totals.	Provinces.	Entered for Consumption.	Duty.	Remaining in Warehouse.	Totals.
Galls.	Galls.	Galls.	1905.	Galls.	$ cts.	Galls.	Galls.
34,107·55	83,047·90	117,155·45	Ontario	85,910·47	3,436 42	31,244·98	117,155·45
28,601·58	....	28,601·58	Quebec	28,601·58	1,144 05	....	28,601·58
62,709·13	83,047·90	145,757·03	Totals	114,512·05	4,580 47	31,244·98	145,757·03
			1906.				
31,244·98	....	31,244·98	Ontario	31,244·98	1,249·80	....	31,244·98

	1905.	1906.
Total duty collected, ex-manufactory and ex-warehouse	$ 7,593 61	$ 1,556 09
License fees	100 00	100 00
	$ 7,693 61	$ 1,656 09

INLAND REVENUE DEPARTMENT,
OTTAWA, August 29, 1906.

W. J. GERALD,
Deputy Minister.

METHYLATED SPIRITS.

No. 34.—STATEMENT showing the quantity of Raw Materials on hand at beginning and end of year, and brought in and used during the year 1905-1906.

DR. (A) CR.

Names of Articles.	Stock on hand, July 1, 1905.	Brought in during the year.	Total to be Accounted for.	Used in manufacture of Methylated Spirits.	Sold.	Stock on hand, June 30, 1906.	Total Accounted for
	Pr'f galls.	Pr'f galls.	Pr'f. galls.	Pr'f galls.	Pr'f galls.	Pr'f galls.	Pr'f galls.
Alcohol..........	5,758·50	60,410·40	66,168·90	63,684·95	16·50	2,467·15	66,168·90
Wood Naphtha..	5,603·62	22,078·16	27,681·78	23,809·03	....	3,872·75	27,681·78

(B)

STATEMENT showing quantity of Raw Materials used, and Methylated Spirits produced therefrom.

Alcohol used, Statement (A) above.	Wood Naphtha used Statement (A) above.	Methylated Spirits used, Statement (C) below.	Total to be Accounted for.	Methylated Spirits produced.	Loss in Manufacture.		Total Accounted for.
Pr'f galls.	Pr'f galls.	Pr'f galls.	Pr'f galls.	Pr'f galls.	Pr'f galls.	p.c.	Pr'f galls.
63,684·95	23,809·03	....	87,493·98	84,856·59	2,637·39	3·21	87,493·98

(C)

STATEMENT showing the quantity of Methylated Spirits on hand at beginning and end of year, and brought in, sold and otherwise accounted for during the year.

Stock on hand July 1, 1905.	Manufactured as above, Statement (B)	Brought in during the year.	Total to be Accounted for.	Sold.	Used in Methylated Spirits Warehouse.	Re-used in Manufacture of Methylated Spirits.	Stock on hand June 30, 1906.	Total Accounted for.
Pr'f galls.	Pr'f galls.	Pr'f galls.	Pr'f galls.	Pr'f galls.	Pr'f galls.	Pr'f galls.	Pr'f galls.	Pr'f galls.
3,177·63	84,856 59	....	88,034 22	83,252 70	....	....	4,781·52	88,034·22

W. J. GERALD,
Deputy Minister.

INLAND REVENUE DEPARTMENT,
OTTAWA, August 29 1906.

DR. No. 35.—HYDRAULIC and other Rents, &c.,

Balances due July 1, 1905.	Rents accrued up to June 30, 1906.	Totals.	Number.	Location.	Original Lessees.	Present Occupants.
$ cts.	$ cts.	$ cts.				
100 00	200 00	300 00	1	Ottawa River	Perley & Pattee	J. R. Booth
50 00	100 00	150 00	2	"	Thomson & Perkins	"
150 00	300 00	450 00	3	"	Lyman Perkins	"
150 00	300 00	450 00	4	"	R. Blackburn *et al*	McKay Milling Co. Ltd
....	100 00	100 00	5	"	J. & J. Petrie	Ottawa Electric Co
....	100 00	100 00	6	"	A. H. Baldwin	"
....	300 00	300 00	7	"	Bank of Montreal	Ottawa Elec. Ry. Co.
....	400 00	400 00	8	"	Perley & Pattee	Ottawa Investment Co Ltd.
....	100 00	100 00	9	"	J. M. Currier	N. S. Blaisdell
....	600 00	600 00	10	"	Harris, Bronson & Co.	The Ottawa Power Co.
....	200 00	200 00	11	"	Levi Young	Ottawa Elec. Ry. Co.
....	104 00	104 00	12	"	J. R. Booth	"
10 00	10 00	20 00	13	"	Bronson & Weston	"
....	100 00	100 00	14	"	"	"
....	96 00	96 00	15	"	Perley & Pattee	J. R. Booth
80 00	8 00	88 00	16	"	L. M. Coutlée	Mary Conroy
570 84	....	570 84	17	"	John Rochester	"
....	25 00	25 00	18	"	Nérée Tétreau	Thos. Ahearn
200 00	....	200 00	19	"	Hon. J. Skead	....
96 00	....	96 00	20	"	"	....
....	1 00	1 00	21	"	G. A. Grier & Co.	Ottawa Elec. Ry. Co
380 00	....	380 00	22	"	John Rankin	....
75 00	150 00	225 00	23	"	J. R. Booth	....
70 00	5 00	75 00	24	"	Colin Dewar	....
....	50 00	50 00	25	"	Bronson & Weston	....
....	1 00	1 00	26	"	Alfred Desjardins	....
....	100 00	100 00	27	"	The Bronson Co.	....
....	10 00	10 00	28	"	Ottawa Electric Co.	....
....	1 00	1 00	1	St. Lawrence	Quebec Harb. Comiss'ners	....
175 00	25 00	200 00	2	"	Rich. & Ont. Nav. Co.	....
1 00	1 00	2 00	3	Quebec	Corporation of Quebec	....
....	1 00	1 00	4	"	Narcisse Blais	....
....	1 00	1 00	5	Rondeau Harbour	School Trustees	....
1 00	1 00	2 00	6	Collingwood	Great Northern Trans. Co	....
1 00	1 00	2 00	7	Ottawa	E. G. Laverdure	....
....	1 00	1 00	8	Walkerton, Ont	D. Robertson & J. Rowland	....
....	1 00	1 00	9	Three Rivers	Corp'n of Three Rivers	....
100 00	100 00	200 00	10	"	W. Ritchie	....
165 00	....	165 00	11	British Columbia	A. Peel	....
90 00	....	90 00	12	"	Jonathan Maury	....
25 00	25 00	50 00	13	"	Roderick Finlayson	....
25 00	25 00	50 00	14	"	Joseph Spratt	....
....	1 00	1 00	15	"	Bank of Brit. Columbia	....
....	1 00	1 00	16	"	W. Dodd	....
....	12 00	12 00	17	"	D. W. Gordon	....
5 00	....	5 00	18	"	S. Williams	....
15 00	5 00	20 00	19	"	Geo. A. Huff	....
1 00	1 00	2 00	20	"	Can. Pac. Ry. Co	....
....	50 00	50 00	21	"	John Reid	....

Lessees' Accounts, 1905–1906. CR.

Description of Property.	Number.	Date to which Account is made up.	Paid during the Fiscal Year.	Balances due on June 30, 1906.	Totals.
			$ cts.	$ cts.	$ cts.
Lots B and C, Chaudière st., service ground	1	June 30, 1906	200 00	100 00	300 00
Lot D	2	" 30, 1906	100 00	50 00	150 00
Lots E, F and G, South Head st	3	" 30, 1906	300 00	150 00	450 00
Lots H, I and J, grist mill, North Head st	4	" 30, 1906	300 00	150 00	450 00
Lot K, fanning mill, South Head st	5	Dec. 31, 1905	100 00		100 00
Lot L, service ground	6	" 31, 1905	100 00		100 00
Lots Q, R and T, service ground, North Middle st	7	" 31, 1905	300 00		300 00
Lots M, N, O and P, service ground (no water used)	8	" 31, 1905	400 00		400 00
Lot S, service ground	9	June 30, 1906	100 00		100 00
Lots U, V, W, X, Y and Z, service ground	10	" 30, 1906	600 00		600 00
Two strips of land	11	Jan. 1, 1907	200 00		200 00
Lumber yard at head of slides	12	Sept. 20, 1906	104 00		104 00
Bridge over slides	13	June 30, 1907	10 00	10 00	20 00
Strip of land, Amelia Island	14	Jan. 1, 1907	100 00		100 00
Reserve, head of Chaudière Island	15	" 1, 1907	96 00		96 00
Small Island, Deschênes Rapids	16	" 1, 1906		88 00	88 00
Portion of lot 39, Concession 'A,' Nepean	17	" 1, 1885		570 84	570 84
Excavated channel, slide and two dams, Little Chaudière	18	March 1, 1907	25 00		25 00
Water lot, opposite lot 30, Concession 'A,' Nepean	19	Dec. 1, 1891		200 00	200 00
Three small islands, Ottawa River	20	May 1, 1891		96 00	96 00
Covering over portion of Ottawa slides	21	Nov. 10, 1906	1 00		1 00
East portion of Hawley's Island	22	June 30, 1891		380 00	380 00
Piece of land, southwest end of Union Bridge	23	Nov. 12, 1906	150 00	75 00	225 00
Piece of land on Victoria Island	24	June 15, 1907		75 00	75 00
Piece of land, south side of Middle st., Victoria Island	25	Aug. 31, 1906	50 00		50 00
Piece of land, Longue Pointe Rouge Templeton, Ottawa County	26	Oct. 24, 1906	1 00		1 00
Southwest of lot No. 1, Amelia Island	27	" 9, 1905	100 00		100 00
Lot Pa, South Head st	28	Jan. 10, 1907	10 00		10 00
Small lot near Custom House, Quebec	1	Sept. 1, 1906	1 00		1 00
Roadway from pier at Coteau Landing	2	July 1, 1906		200 00	200 00
Old Provincial Govt. B'ldg. grounds, on Mountain Hill	3	June 25, 1907	1 00	1 00	2 00
Privilege to erect bridge on St. Charles River	4	Feb. 6, 1907	1 00		1 00
Use of old log house, formerly used as Custom House, Shrewsbury, Ont	5	Sept. 11, 1905	1 00		1 00
Use of breakwater for storing coal	6	Feb. 5, 1907	1 00	1 00	2 00
Southeast half of lot 8, Ottawa	7	Dec. 18, 1906		2 00	2 00
Right of way over strip of land	8	April 27, 1907	1 00		1 00
Lot of land on St. Christopher Island, St. Maurice River	9	Dec. 1, 1906	1 00		1 00
Outlet of River St. Maurice	10	June 30, 1906	100 00	100 00	200 00
Portion of Assay Office, New Westminster	11	July 1, 1889		165 00	165 00
" " "	12	" 1, 1889		90 00	90 00
Privilege to erect two bulkheads, Rock Bay, Victoria Harbour	13	" 1, 1907	25 00	25 00	50 00
Privilege to build a wharf opposite his own property, Victoria Harbour	14	" 1, 1907	25 00	25 00	50 00
Right of drainage through Govt. property, Nanaimo	15	Dec. 1, 1906	1 00		1 00
Old Government House, Yale	16	July 24, 1905		1 00	1 00
Beach lots, A, C, E and F, front of 7, 8, 9, Nanaimo Harbour	17	Aug 27, 1906	12 00		12 00
Frontage of lot 7, block M, Victoria	18	July 16, 1904		5 00	5 00
Permission to build a wharf on lot A, block 2, Sumas River, Alberni, B.C	19	Aug. 12, 1906		20 00	20 00
Portion of Custom House lot, New Westminster	20	April 14, 1907	2 00		2 00
Lot 1, block 13, corner Begbie and Columbia sts., New Westminster	21	May 12, 1907	50 00		50 00

DR. No. 35.—HYDRAULIC and other Rents, &c.,

Balance due July 1, 1906.	Rents accrued up to June 30, 1906.	Totals.	Number.	Location.	Original Lessees.	Present Occupants.
$ cts.	$ cts.	$ cts.				
70 00	....	70 00	22	Rivière du Lièvre....	Dom. Phosphate Co., Ltd.	....
1 00	....	1 00	23	Charlottetown.......	Rt. Rev. Bishop McIntyre	Rt. Rev. Bishop McDonald............
....	16 00	16 00	24	Antigonish, N.S.....	L. C. Archibald.........	....
....	1 00	1 00	25	Owen Sound..	G. T. Railway	....
....	5 00	5 00	26	County of Grey. Ont.	Jacob Duke Speers....	....
240 00	....	240 00	27	Windsor............	Archie McNee.........	....
....	1 00	1 00	28	Lévis, Que..........	Cyrille Robitaille	....
....	5 00	5 00	29	Bayfield, N.S. ...	Charles L. Gass.........	....
1 00	1 00	2 00	30	"	"	....
5 00	5 00	10 00	31	Village of Brook, Ont	William Pedwell........	....
2,852 84	3,647 00	6,499 84				

INLAND REVENUE DEPARTMENT,
OTTAWA, August 29, 1906.

Lessees' Accounts, 1905-1906—*Concluded.* CR.

Description of Property.	Number.	Date to which Account is made up.	Paid during the Fiscal Year.	Balances due on June 30, 1906.	Totals.
			$ cts	$ cts.	$ cts.
Permission to erect a landing at Little Rapids, Rivière du Lièvre	22	April 30, 1898	....	70 00	70 00
Leave to connect drain to main service of pub. building	23	May 16, 1902	....	1 00	1 00
Tract of land and water lot, McNair's Cove	24	Dec. 31, 1906	16 00	....	16 00
Lot of land, west of Sydenham River	25	" 31, 1906	1 00	....	1 00
Water lot	26	April 8, 1907	5 00	....	5 00
Lot on Ouelette st., Windsor, Ont.	27	" 30, 1900	....	240 00	240 00
Ground rent	28	" 4, 1907	1 00	....	1 00
Water lot	29	Dec. 7, 1906	5 00	....	5 00
"	30	June 8, 1907	1 00	1 00	2 00
"	31	Mar. 31, 1907	10 00	....	10 00
Totals	..	....	3,608 00	2,891 84	6,499 84

W. J. GERALD,
Deputy Minister.

APPENDIX

No. 35 (A).—HYDRAULIC and other Rents, &c.—

Balances due on July 1, 1905.	Totals.	Number.	Location.	Name of Proprietors.
$ cts.	$ cts.			LAND SALES—PRINCIPAL ACCOUNT.
12,092 83	12,092 83	1	Hamilton and Port Dover Road.	Choat & Kern ....
433 34	433 34	2	Bonner's property, Quebec.......	Timothy Sullivan, now M. Murphy..
333 34	333 34	3	....	John Bailey, now Alex. Powell.......
300 00	300 00	4	....	Abraham Thompson.................
147 80	147 80	5	....	John Boomer.......................
248 40	248 40	6	....	John Garbatz, now J. C. Nolan.......
154 80	154 80	7	....	N. H. Bowen.......................
600 00	600 00	8	....	Estate Robert Reid.................
333 33	333 33	9	....	John Chevalier.....................
533 33	533 33	10	....	Daniel Holden ....
333 33	333 33	11	....	George Creeley.....................
63 00	63 00	12	....	Thomas McAdam....................
15,573 50	15,573 50			
				LAND SALES—INTEREST ACCOUNT.
6,298 25	6,298 25	1	Hamilton and Port Dover Road..	Choat & Kern (matured).............
558 00	558 00	2	Bonner's property, Quebec.......	Timothy Sullivan, now M. Murphy....
120 00	120 00	3	....	John Bailey, now Alex. Powell.......
306 00	306 00	4	....	Abraham Thompson..............
155 22	155 22	5	....	John Boomer.......................
275 82	275 82	6	....	John Garbatz, now J. C. Nolan. ....
208 95	208 95	7	....	N. H. Bowen ....
828 00	828 00	8	....	Estate Robert Reid..................
190 00	190 00	9	....	John Chevalier ....
298 68	298 68	10	....	Daniel Holden.....................
35 91	35 91	11	....	George Creeley....................
100 00	100 00	12	....	Thomas McAdam...................
100 00	100 00	13	....	Joseph Brook, tenant............
9,474 83	9,474 83			

INLAND REVENUE DEPARTMENT,
OTTAWA, August 29, 1906.

SESSIONAL PAPER No. 12

A—*Concluded.*

LESSEES' Accounts, 1905-1906.—*Concluded.*

Description of Property.	Number.	Date to which the account is made up.	Balances due on June 30, 1906.	Totals.
			$ cts.	$ cts.
Hamilton and Port Dover and Caledonia Bridge	1		12,092 83	12,092 83
Lot No. 1, Wolfe Street	2		433 34	433 34
" 9 "	3		333 34	333 34
" 49 "	4		300 00	300 00
" 73 and 74, Tower Street	5		147 80	147 80
" 64, Wolfe Street, and 211 and 252 Ware Street	6		248 40	248 40
" 67 and 68, Monument Street	7		154 80	154 80
" 22 and 23, Wolfe Street	8		600 00	600 00
" 32, Wolfe Street	9		333 33	333 33
" 65 and 66, Wolfe Street	10		533 33	533 33
" 31, Wolfe Street	11		333 33	333 33
" 135, Church Street	12		63 00	63 00
			15,573 50	15,573 50
	1	June 30, 1874.	6,298 25	6,298 25
Lot No. 1, Wolfe Street	2	May 1, 1889	558 00	558 00
" 9 "	3	"	120 00	120 00
" 49 "	4	"	306 00	306 00
" 73 and 74, Tower Street	5	"	155 22	155 22
" 64 Wolfe Street, and 211 and 252 Ware Street	6	"	275 82	275 82
" 67 and 68, Monument Street	7	"	208 95	208 95
" 22 and 23, Wolfe Street	8	"	828 00	828 00
" 32, Wolfe Street	9	Nov. 1, 1863	190 00	190 00
" 65 and 66, Wolfe Street	10	"	298 68	298 68
" 31, Wolfe Street	11	"	35 91	35 91
" 135, Church Street	12	"	100 00	100 00
Monument Hotel	13	"	100 00	100 00
			9,474 83	9,474 83

W. J. GERALD,
Deputy Minister.

APPENDIX B.

No. 1.—Details of Excise Expenditures for the Year ended June 30, 1906.

To whom paid.	Service.	Deductions for Retirement.	Deductions for Superannuation.	Deductions for Guarantee.	Amounts paid.	Total amounts paid.
	Belleville.	$ cts.	$ cts.	$ cts.	$ cts.	$ cts.
Iler, B.	Salary as Collector for year	....	42 96	7 20	2,109 82	
Standish, J. G.	″ Special Class Exciseman for year	....	34 96	4 32	1,710 72	
Pole, C. W.	″ Deputy Collector for year	......	33 08	3 60	1,618 32	
McCoy, W.	″ Special Class Exciseman for year	.....	27 48	4 32	1,333 16	
McCuaig, A. F.	″ Deputy Collector for year	....	18 80	2 88	919 97	
McFee, A. C.	″ 1st Class Exciseman for year	....	37 56	2 88	1,034 52	
Brown, W. J.	″ ″ ″ ″	53 69	....	2 88	1,018 39	
Wilson, H. R.	″ Probationary 3rd Class Exciseman from Feb. 6 to June 30, 1906	10 03	... .	1 20	189 63	
	Salaries	63 72	194 84	29 28	9,934 53	
	Contingencies	....	....	....	736 71	
						10,671 24
	Brantford.					
O'Donohue, M.J.	Salary as Collector for year	.....	32 75	7 20	1,600 02	
Sloan, W. J	″ Deputy Collector for year	64 96	....	3 60	1,231 44	
Weyms, C.	″ 1st Class Exciseman for year	......	22 44	2 88	1,099 61	
Orr, H. N.	″ ″ ″ ″	....	38 73	2 88	1,064 64	
Brentnall, F. F.	″ ″ ″ Brought from Toronto Sept. 1, 1905, and transferred to Toronto from Feb. 1, 1906	21 85	....	1 20	414 45	
Newsome, I	″ Probationary 3rd Class Exciseman from Feb. 6, to June 30, 1906	10 03	....	1 20	189 63	
	Salaries	96 84	93 92	18 96	5,599 79	
	Contingencies	......	....	....	1,501 20	
						7,100 99
	Cornwall.					
Mulhern, M. M.	Salary as Collector for year	......	21 96	3 60	1,074 42	
	Contingencies	......	....	....	88 50	
						1,162 92
	Guelph.					
Powell, J. B	Salary as Collector for year	......	47 40	7 20	2,315 40	
Till, T. M.	″ Deputy Collector for year	.....	33 94	3 60	1,662 36	
Dawson, W.	″ Special Class Exciseman for year	......	34 96	4 32	1,710 72	
Woodward, G. W.	″ Special Class Exciseman for year	......	27 48	4 32	1,343 16	
Broadfoot, S.	″ Accountant for year	.....	25 80	4 32	1,259 88	
Bish, P	″ 1st Class Exciseman for year	......	22 44	2 88	1,099 61	
Spence, F. H.	″ ″ ″ ″	.....	22 44	2 88	1,099 61	
Bowman, A. W.	″ ″ ″ ″	...	22 44	2 88	1,099 61	
Egener, A.	″ ″ ″ ″	.....	22 44	2 88	1,099 61	
Brain, A. F.	″ ″ ″ from July 1, '05, to Jan. 31, '06, and removed to Windsor	......	22 96	1 68	633 01	
O'Brien, E. C.	″ 2nd Class Exciseman for year	.....	19 02	2 88	934 26	
Alteman, P. J.	″ 1st ″ ″ ″	.....	37 56	2 88	1,034 52	
Howie, A.	″ 3rd ″ ″ ″	.....	16 50	2 88	805 62	

APPENDIX B.—No. 1.—Details of Excise Expenditures, 1905–1906—*Continued.*

To whom paid.	Service.	Deductions for Retirement.	Deductions for Superannuation.	Deductions for Guarantee.	Amounts paid.	Total amounts paid.
	Guelph—Con.	$ cts.	$ cts.	$ cts.	$ cts.	$ cts.
Coutts, J. J.	Salary as 1st Class Exciseman for year.	53 69	....	2 88	1,018 39	
Hanlon, J. R.	" 3rd " " "	29 02	....	2 88	548 63	
Martin, N.	" Probationary 3rd Class Exciseman from Aug. 7, 1905, and confirmed as 3rd Class from Feb. 7, to June 30, '06	24 48	....	2 59	462 99	
	Salaries	107 19	355 38	53 95	18,127 38	
	Contingencies	.....	....	....	1,243 90	
						19,371 28
	Hamilton.					
Miller, W. F.	Salary as Collector for year	......	48 00	14 40	2,337 60	
Cameron, D. M.	" Special Class Exciseman for year	....	30 00	4 32	1,465 68	
Baby, W. A. D.	" " "	.....	34 96	4 32	1,710 72	
O'Brien, Jas	" Deputy Collector for year	80 58	....	7 20	1,524 72	
Crawford, W. P.	" Accountant for year	.....	....	4 32	1,450 68	
O'Brien, J. F.	" Special Class Exciseman for year	....	24 48	4 32	1,196 16	
Dumbrille, R. W.	" 1st Class Exciseman for year.	....	22 44	2 88	1,099 61	
Hobbs, G. N.	" " "	...	22 44	2 88	1,099 61	
Brennan, D. J.	" Special Class Exciseman from July 1, 1905, to Feby. 28, 1906, removed to St. Hyacinthe	....	14 80	1 92	724 89	
Hayhurst, T. H.	" 1st Class Exciseman for year.	53 69	....	2 88	1,018 39	
Boyd, J. F. S.	" 1st " "	......	37 56	2 88	1,034 52	
Logan, J.	" 2nd " "	....	19 02	2 88	934 26	
Amor, W.	" 2nd " "	..	19 02	2 88	934 26	
Bishop, J. B.	" 2nd " "	45 59	......	2 88	865 21	
Cheseldine, J. H.	" 1st " "	53 69	......	2 88	1,018 39	
Lawlor, J. J.	" 1st " "	53 69	....	2 88	1,018 39	
Blackman, C.	" Messenger for year	33 52	....	.....	636 48	
Elliott, W. J.	" Probationary 3rd Class Exciseman from March 29th to June 30, 1906	6 44	....	0 72	121 85	
Kirkpatrick, H. J.	" " "	6 44	....	0 72	121 85	
	Salaries	333 64	272 72	68 16	20,313 27	
	Contingencies	......	....	....	1,666 91	
						21,980 18
	Kingston.					
Dickson, C. T.	Salary as Collector for year	.....	....	7 20	1,772 75	
Grimason, T.	" Deputy Collector for year	......	25 96	3 60	1,270 44	
Hanley, A.	" Accountant for year	.....	19 96	2 88	977 16	
Lyons, E.	" 1st Class Exciseman for year.	.....	22 44	2 88	1,099 61	
O'Donnell, M. J.	" Messenger for year	....	16 50	2 88	805 62	
Fahey, E.	" 3rd Class Exciseman	....	15 60	2 88	761 52	
Hogan, J.	" 3rd "	32 21	....	2 88	609 91	
Montgomery, W. H.	" Probationary 3rd Class Exciseman from Feb. 6th, to June 30, 1906	10 03	....	1 20	189 63	
	Salaries	42 24	100 46	26 40	7,486 64	
	Contingencies	....	....	....	1,048 56	
						8,535 20
	London.					
Alexander, T.	Salary as Collector for year	...	19 75	7 20	2,343 05	
Spereman, J. J.	" Special Class Exciseman for year	.	31 96	4 32	1,563 72	
Davis, T. G.	" Deputy Collector for year	......	33 48	3 60	1,637 88	

APPENDIX B.—No. 1.—Details of Excise Expenditures, 1905–1906—*Continued.*

To whom paid.	Service.	Deductions for Retirement.	Deductions for Superannuation.	Deductions for Guarantee	Amounts paid.	Total amounts paid.
	London—Con.	$ cts.	$ cts.	$ cts.	$ cts.	$ cts.
Thrasher, W. A.	Salary as Deputy Collector for year	83 69	....	3 60	1,587 67	
Rose, J. A.	" " "	64 96	....	3 60	1,231 44	
Coles, F. H.	" Accountant for year	...	25 80	4 32	1,259 88	
Wilson, D.	" " "	....	22 96	2 88	1,124 16	
Stewart, J.	" 1st Class Exciseman for year	.....	22 44	2 88	1,099 61	
Lee, E.	" " "	.....	22 44	2 88	1,099 61	
Girard, I.	" " "	.....	22 44	2 88	1,099 61	
Boyle, P.	" " "	71 76	33 65	2 88	1,016 64	
Davis, J.	" " Exciseman from 1 July 1905, to March 1, 1906. Resigned	.....	14 00	1 92	509 08	
Foster, H.	" 1st Class Exciseman for year	......	37 56	2 88	1,034 52	
Webbe, C. E. A.	" 2nd " "	......	19 02	2 88	934 26	
Tracy, J. P.	" 2nd " "	......	19 02	2 88	934 26	
Talbot, J.	" 3rd " "	40 44	....	2 88	766 68	
Whitehead, J. P.	" Deputy Collector for year	32 48	....	2 88	614 64	
Fiddes, Jas.	" " "	26 63	....	2 88	503 57	
Fleming, C.	" 3rd Class Exciseman for year	27 48	....	2 40	520 09	
	Salaries	347 44	324 52	62 64	20,880 37	
	Contingencies	....	....	....	760 66	21,641 03
	Ottawa.					
Freeland, A.	Salary as Collector for year	85 98	....	7 20	1,626 78	
McGuire, T.	" Deputy Collector for year	64 96	....	3 60	1,231 44	
Slattery, R.	" 1st Class Exciseman for year	......	22 44	2 88	1,099 61	
Fox, T.	" 1st " "	......	22 44	2 88	1,099 61	
Hinchey, E. H.	" Accountant for year	...	19 96	4 32	975 72	
Bennett, Jas.	" Deputy Collector for year	45 00	....	2 88	852 12	
Laporte, G.	" " "	.....	16 96	2 88	830 16	
Casey, J.	" 3rd Class Exciseman for year	31 44	....	2 88	595 68	
	Salaries	227 38	81 80	29 52	8,311 12	
	Contingencies	......	....	....	259 17	8,570 29
	Owen Sound.					
Graham, W. J.	Salary as Collector for year	....	11 62	3 60	1,501 38	
Nichols, J. T.	" Deputy Collector from July 1, '05 to Feb. 1, '06 (died)	....	21 48	1 68	570 01	
Johnson, J. J.	" 1st Class Exciseman for year	.....	21 44	2 88	1,050 60	
Chisholm, W. N.	" Deputy Collector for year	53 69	....	3 60	1,044 96	
Blyth, A.	" 2nd Class Exciseman for year	7 88	....	2 88	1,018 39	
Cryderman, C. W.	" Deputy Collector from April 20 to June 30, '06	....	....	0 72	149 16	
	Salaries	61 57	54 54	15 36	5,334 50	
	Contingencies	.....	....	....	644 94	5,979 44
	Perth.					
McLenaghan, N.	Salary as Collector for year	78 42	....	7 20	1,484 34	
Mason, F.	" Special Class Exciseman for year	......	33 00	4 32	1,612 68	
Goodman, A. W.	" 1st Class Exciseman for year	.....	22 44	2 88	1,099 61	
Noonan, H. T.	" Deputy Collector for year	40 76	....	3 60	770 64	
Clarke, T.	" " "	40 04	....	2 88	757 08	
Rowan, W. E.	" " "	25 04	....	2 88	472 08	
Egan, W.	" " "	.....	....	2 88	397 08	
Baikie, D.	" " "	25 04	....	3 60	471 36	
George, J.	" " "	10 04	....	2 88	187 08	

APPENDIX B.—No. 1.—Details of Excise Expenditures, 1905-1906—*Continued.*

To whom paid.	Service.	Deductions for Retirement.	Deductions for Superannuation.	Deductions for Guarantee	Amounts paid.	Total amounts paid.
	Perth—Con.	$ cts.	$ cts.	$ cts.	$ cts.	$ cts.
Maurice, E.	Salary as Deputy Collector for year	19 96		2 88	377 16	
Murphy, J. L.	" " "	4 96		2 88	92 16	
	Salaries	244 26	55 44	38 88	7,721 27	
	Contingencies				731 42	
						8,452 69
	Peterborough.					
Rudkins, W.	Salary as Collector for year	64 50		3 60	1,221 90	
Rork, T	" Deputy Collector for year	48 00		3 60	908 40	
Howden, R.	" " "		16 04	2 88	781 08	
Bickle, J. W.	" " "		13 96	2 88	683 16	
	Salaries	112 50	30 00	12 96	3,594 54	
	Contingencies				286 98	
						3,881 52
	Port Arthur.					
Ironside, G. A.	Salary as Collector for year			3 60	1,096 38	
Sangster, F. H.	" Deputy Collector from July 1, '05, to April 5, '06 (resigned)	5 66		2 19	106 31	
Bridgman, M. W.	" 3rd Class Exciseman for year	28 42		2 88	537 48	
Aaron, J. D.	" Deputy Collector from June 21 to June 30, 1906	0 20		0 08	3 88	
	Salaries	34 28		8 75	1,744 05	
	Contingencies				270 27	
						2,014 32
	Prescott.					
Keilty, T.	Salary as Collector for year		38 84	7 20	1,896 31	
Gerald, W. H	" Special Class Exciseman for year		34 96	4 32	1,710 72	
Macdonald, A. D.	" " "		27 48	4 32	1,343 16	
Melville, T. R.	" Deputy Collector for year	71 05		3 60	1,348 61	
Keeler, G. S.	" 2nd Class Exciseman for year		19 02	2 88	934 26	
Wood, J. A	" Deputy Collector for year			2 88	897 12	
White, J. B	" " "	32 48		2 88	614 64	
Marshall, T. N.	" 3rd Class Exciseman for year	33 72		2 88	638 40	
McPherson, E. A.	{ " " " / Insurance }	31 44 / 44 64		2 88	551 04	
	Salaries	213 37	120 30	33 84	9,934 26	
	Contingencies				1,322 34	
						11,256 60
	Stratford.					
Rennie, Geo	Salary as Collector for year		34 38	7 20	1,678 38	
Tobin, T. S.	" Deputy Collector for year	59 09		3 60	1,119 79	
Hicks, W. H.	" " "		19 96	2 88	977 16	
Young, R. E.	" 1st Class Exciseman for year	53 69		2 88	1,018 39	
Jeffrey, A. J.	" Deputy Collector "	40 04		2 88	757 08	
Dalton, M. J	" " "	40 04		3 60	756 36	
	Salaries	192 86	54 34	23 04	6,307 16	
	Contingencies				357 83	
						6,664 99
	St. Catharines.					
Hesson, C. A.	Salary as Collector for year		27 00	7 20	1,315 80	
Harris, J. G	" Deputy Collector for year		34 96	2 88	962 16	
Milliken, E.	" 2nd Class Exciseman for year		19 02	2 88	934 26	

APPENDIX B.—No. 1.—Details of Excise Expenditures, 1905-1906—*Continued.*

To whom paid.	Service.	Deductions for — Retirement.	Deductions for — Superannuation.	Deductions for — Guarantee	Amounts paid.	Total amounts paid.
	St. Catharines—Con.	$ cts.	$ cts.	$ cts.	$ cts.	$ cts.
Schram, R. L. H.	Salary as 2nd Class Exciseman for year	.. .	31 92	2 88	878 88	
Simpson, W. A.	" 1st " "	51 17	....	2 88	970 92	
	Salaries	51 17	112 90	18 72	5,062 02	
	Contingencies	......	....	....	387 69	
						5,449 71
	Toronto.					
Frankland, H. R.	Salary as Collector for year	116 16	......	14 40	2,194 44	
Gerald, C.	" Special Class Exciseman for year	......	36 00	4 32	1,759 68	
Henderson, W.	" Deputy Collector for year	......	33 48	3 60	1,637 88	
Boomer, J. B.	" Accountant "	...	30 00	4 32	1,465 68	
McKenzie, J. H.	" Deputy Collector "	80 58	....	3 60	1,528 32	
Metcalf, W. F.	" Special Class Exciseman for year	....	27 48	4 32	1,343 16	
Boyd, S. I.	" Deputy Collector	.....	24 00	2 88	1,173 12	
Dick, J. W.	" Special Class Exciseman for year	......	28 04	4 32	1,367 04	
Evans, G. T.	" " "	...	27 48	4 32	1,343 16	
Jamieson, J. C.	" " "	......	27 48	4 32	1,343 16	
Flynn, D. J.	" " "	......	25 44	4 32	1,245 17	
Shanacy, M.	" Deputy Collector for year	......	22 04	2 88	1,075 08	
Elliott, T. H.	" " "	57 52	.....	2 88	1,047 84	
	" Insurance	41 76				
Dudley, W. H.	" 1st Class Exciseman for year	....	22 44	4 32	1,098 17	
Coleman, C.	" Deputy Collector "	.. ..	19 96	2 88	977 16	
Helliwell, H. N.	" 1st Class Exciseman "	......	22 44	2 88	1,099 61	
O'Leary, T. J.	" 1st " "	.....	22 44	2 88	1,099 61	
Graham, W. T.	" 1st " "	......	22 44	2 88	1,099 61	
Doyle, B. J.	" 1st " "	......	22 44	2 88	1,099 61	
Cooke, W. R.	" 1st " "	......	22 44	2 88	1,099 61	
Howard, W. W. S.	" 1st " "	....	22 44	2 88	1,099 61	
Hurst, L. B.	" 1st Class Exciseman from July, '05 to Mar. 29, '06 and promoted to Special Class Exciseman from Mar. 29 to June 30, '06	.... .	22 71	3 24	1,111 89	
Wardell, R. S. R.	" 1st Class Exciseman for year	....	39 29	2 88	1,082 76	
Barber, J. S.	" 2nd " "	......	19 02	2 88	934 26	
Murray, A. E.	" 2nd " "	......	19 02	2 88	934 26	
Dager, H. J.	" Deputy Collector "	45 00	....	2 88	852 12	
Brentnall, F. F.	" " from July 1 to Aug. 31, '05, transferred to Brantford and brought from Brantford, from Feb. 1 to June 30, '06	30 59	....	1 68	580 23	
Coulter, A.	" 1st Class Exciseman for year	......	37 56	2 88	1,034 52	
Ritchie, H.	" Deputy Collector "	43 71	....	2 88	828 36	
Jones, A.	" 1st Class Exciseman "	......	16 50	2 88	805 62	
Falconer, R. H.	" 1st " "	53 69	....	2 88	1,018 39	
Graham, A. L.	" 1st " "	53 69	....	2 88	1,018 39	
Burns, R. J.	" 1st " "	53 69	....	2 88	1,018 39	
Mahoney, H.	" 1st " "	53 69	....	2 88	1,018 39	
Gillies, A. L.	" 1st " "	51 17	....	2 88	970 92	
Walsh, W. H.	" 2nd " "	43 50	....	2 88	824 82	
Fielding, L. G.	" Stenographer "	21 48	....	....	408 48	
	Salaries	746 23	612 58	127 32	41,639 12	
	Contingencies	......	....	... ...	1,613 02	
						43,252 14

APPENDIX B.—No. 1.—Details of Excise Expenditures, 1905-1906—*Continued.*

To whom paid.	Service.	Deductions for Retirement.	Deductions for Superannuation.	Deductions for Guarantee.	Amounts paid.	Total amounts paid.
	Windsor.	$ cts.	$ cts.	$ cts.	$ cts.	$ cts.
McSween, J.	Salary as Collector for year	......	42 96	14 40	2,092 62	
Bouteiller, G. A.	" Special Class Exciseman for year	...	36 00	4 32	1,759 68	
Marion, H. R.	" Deputy Collector for year	80 58	......	7 20	1,524 72	
Dunlop, C.	" " "	......	25 96	3 60	1,270 44	
Brennan, J.	" Special Class Exciseman for year	....	27 48	4 32	1,343 16	
Belleperche, A. J. E	" Accountant for year	64 50	....	4 32	1,221 18	
Marcon, F. A	" 1st Class Exciseman for year	......	22 04	2 88	1,075 08	
Keogh, P. M.	" Deputy Collector "	......	19 96	3 60	976 44	
Thomas, R.	" 1st Class Exciseman "	......	22 44	2 88	1,099 61	
Bayard, G. A.	" 1st " "	.....	22 44	2 88	1,099 61	
Berry, H. L.	" 1st " "	53 69	....	2 88	1,018 39	
Jubenville, J. P	" 2nd " "	.....	18 68	2 88	913 44	
Falconer, J.	" 3rd " "	.....	16 50	2 88	805 62	
Cahill, J. W.	" 3rd " "	....	16 50	2 88	805 62	
Neil, Jas.	" 1st " "	53 69	....	2 88	1,018 39	
Chilver, F. W	" 1st " "	53 69	....	2 88	1,018 39	
McArthur, G. A.	" 1st " " from July 1, '05 to April 28, '06 and Special Class Exciseman from April 29 to June 30, '06	54 99	....	3 24	1,042 55	
Beneteau, S	" 1st Class Exciseman for year	51 17	....	2 88	970 91	
Adam, A. R.	" 3rd " "	32 21	....	2 88	609 91	
Love, G. G.	" 3rd " "	29 84	....	2 88	564 31	
Brain, A. F	" 1st " " from Feb. 1 to June 30, 1906—Brought from Guelph	..	16 40	1 20	452 15	
	Salaries	474 36	287 36	80 76	22,682 23	
	Contingencies	....	....	....	1,135 34	23,817 57
	Joliette.					
Labelle, L. V.	Salary as Collector for year	85 98	....	3 60	1,630 38	
Gow, J. E.	" Special Class Exciseman for year	....	28 44	4 32	1,392 17	
Moreau, A	" Deputy Collector from July 1, 1905, to Feb. 15, 1906—Resigned	24 97	....	2 25	472 73	
Ralston, T.	" Deputy Collector for year	37 44	....	3 60	708 96	
Gamache, J. N	" " "	37 44	....	1 80	710 75	
Olivier, H	" Probationary Exciseman for year	31 44	....	2 88	595 68	
Forest, M	" Deputy Collector for year	10 04	....	3 60	186 36	
Bourgeois, C.	" 3rd Class Exciseman from Feb. 6 to June 30, 1906	25 20	....	1 20	478 42	
Bernier, J. A.	" 1st Class Exciseman, from Aug. 1, 1905, to June 30, 1906—Brought from Montreal	49 32	....	2 64	935 50	
Daveluy, J. P.	" 3rd Class Exciseman, from Mar. 1 to June 30, 1906—Brought from Montreal	14 00	....	0 96	265 04	
	Salaries	315 83	28 44	26 85	7,375 99	
	Contingencies	......	....	....	1,310 82	8,686 81
	Montreal.					
Toupin, J. A.	Salary as Collector for year	...	42 96	14 40	2,092 62	
Cavon, W	" Deputy Collector for year	.....	33 48	7 20	1,634 28	

Appendix B.—No. 1.—Details of Excise Expenditures, 1905—1906—*Continued.*

To whom paid.	Service.	Deductions for			Amounts paid.	Total amounts paid.
		Retirement.	Superannuation.	Guarantee		
	Montreal—Con.	$ cts.	$ cts.	$ cts.	$ cts.	$ cts.
Forest, E. R	Salary as Accountant for year	....	28 04	7 20	1,364 76	
Fox, J. D	" " "	.....	29 84	4 32	1,455 84	
Lane, T. M	" " "	.....	25 04	2 88	1,222 08	
Walsh, D. J	" Special Class Exciseman for year	....	28 96	4 32	1,416 72	
Scullion, W. J	" 2nd Class Exciseman for year	......	22 44	2 88	1,099 61	
Normandin, G	" 1st " from July 1 to Sept. 1, 1905—Resigned and re-appointed to his former position from Dec. 19, 1905, to June 30, 1906	38 56	....	2 14	731 01	
Chagnon, C. P	" Deputy Collector for year	49 96	....	7 20	942 84	
Malo, T	" 2nd Class Exciseman for year	......	7 75	1 20	380 60	
Dumouchel, L	" " "	......	19 02	2 88	934 26	
Courtney, J. J	" " "	.....	19 02	2 88	934 26	
Verner, F	" " "	......	19 02	2 88	934 26	
Dixon, H. G. S	" " "	.....	19 02	2 88	934 26	
Andrews, A. A	" " "	....	33 41	2 88	919 87	
Codd, H. J. S	" " "	......	19 02	2 88	934 26	
Renaud, A. H	" 1st " "	......	37 56	2 88	1,034 52	
Desaulniers, J.E.A	" 1st " "	53 69	....	2 88	1,018 39	
Laurier, J. L	" 2nd " "	45 59	....	2 88	865 21	
Snowden, J. W	" 1st " " from July 1, 1905, to Mar. 31, 1906—Promoted to Special Class Exciseman from April 1 to June 30, 1906	54 99	....	3 24	1,042 55	
Millier, E	" 3rd Class Exciseman for year	.....	16 50	2 88	805 62	
Panneton, G. E	" 3rd " "	.....	16 50	2 88	805 62	
Costigan, J. J	" 3rd " "	......	16 20	2 88	790 92	
O'Flaherty, E. J	" 3rd " "	......	16 50	2 88	805 62	
Brabant, J.B.G.N	" 3rd " "	......	18 18	2 88	892 62	
Bélair, A. P	" 3rd " "	.....	16 50	2 88	805 62	
Ryan, W	" 3rd " "	41 21	....	2 88	780 91	
Mainville, C. P	" 3rd " "	......	16 50	2 88	805 62	
Daveluy, J. P	" 3rd " from July 1, 1905, to Mar. 1, 1906—Transferred to Joliette	27 21	....	1 92	515 87	
Comte, L. A. A. J	" 2nd Class Exciseman for year	......	31 92	2 88	878 88	
Kearney, D. J	" 1st " "	53 69	....	2 88	1,018 39	
Bousquet, J. O	" 1st " "	53 69	....	2 88	1,018 39	
Lambert, J. A	" 2nd " "	45 59	....	2 88	865 21	
Maranda, N. A	" 3rd " "	36 00	....	2 88	681 12	
David, T	" 2nd " "	45 59	....	2 88	865 21	
Harwood, J. O. A	" 2nd " "	45 59	....	2 88	865 21	
Bruyère, H. P	" Deputy Collector for year	32 48	....	3 60	613 92	
Patterson, C. E. A	" " "	34 96	....	3 60	661 44	
Marin, L. H	" 3rd Class Exciseman for year	34 44	....	2 88	652 68	
Gauvin, E	" 2nd " "	45 59	....	2 88	865 21	
Bernier, J. A	" 1st " from July 1 to Aug., 1905—Removed to Joliette	4 37	....	0 24	82 89	
St. Michel, F. X	" Deputy Collector for year	25 04	....	3 60	471 36	
Lamoureux, J. A	" 2nd Class Exciseman for year	43 50	....	2 88	824 82	
Crevier, L. H	" 3rd " "	30 72	....	2 88	581 40	
Longtin, H	" 2nd " "	43 50	....	2 88	824 82	
Thurber, G	" 3rd " "	29 55	....	2 88	558 68	
Milot, J. F	" 3rd " "	28 73	....	2 88	543 36	
Ledoux, A	" Stenographer	21 48	....	2 88	405 60	
O'Donnell, M. J	" Messenger	31 96	....	....	608 04	

APPENDIX B.—No. 1.—Details of Excise Expenditures, 1905-1906—*Continued.*

To whom paid.	Service.	Deductions for Retirement.	Deductions for Superannuation.	Deductions for Guarantee	Amounts paid.	Total amounts paid.
	Montreal—Con.	$ cts.	$ cts.	$ cts.	$ cts.	$ cts.
Graveline, D. P.	Salary as Probationary 3rd Class Exciseman from Feb. 6 to June 30, 1906	10 03		1 15	189 68	
	Salaries	1007 71	533 38	163 25	42,976 93	
	Contingencies				5,256 54	
						48,233 47
	Quebec.					
LaRue, Geo.	Salary as Collector for year		47 40	7 20	2,315 40	
Cahill, J. H.	" Deputy Collector for year			3 60	1,696 32	
Patry, J. H.	" " "	80 58		3 60	1,528 32	
Coleman, J. J.	" 1st Class Exciseman for year		22 44	2 88	1,099 61	
LaRue, A.	" Deputy Collector "		31 44	3 60	864 96	
Bourget, O.	" Unclassified Exciseman for year		16 96	2 88	830 16	
Lemoine, J.	" 3rd Class " "		16 50	2 88	805 62	
Lépine, L.	" 3rd " from 1st July, to 1st Oct., 1905 (Superannuated)		4 05	72	197 73	
LaRue, A. P.	" Deputy Collector for year	42 52		3 60	803 88	
Beaulieu, J. B.	" 3rd Class Exciseman "		28 14	2 88	771 48	
Pelletier, N. G.	" Deputy Collector "	25 04		3 60	471 36	
Timmons, R.	" 3rd Class Exciseman "	43 50		2 88	824 82	
McGuire, L. J.	" 2nd " "	43 50		2 88	824 82	
Michon, A. E.	" Deputy Collector "	8 30		1 50	156 80	
Courchesne, J. H.	" " from July 1 to Nov. 1, 1905 (Resigned)	1 65		60	31 07	
Courchesne, P.H.E	" from Dec. 13, 1905 to June 30, 1906	5 49		99	103 69	
Taylor, G. W.	" Special Class Exciseman for year, brought from St. Hyacinthe, March 1, 1906		11 00	1 50	537 50	
Rouleau, C. E.	" 3rd Class " "	9 21		1 06	174 22	
	Salaries	259 79	177 93	49 00	14,037 61	
	Contingencies				6,161 06	
						20,198 67
	Sherbrooke.					
Simpson, A. F.	Salary as Collector for year		35 57	7 20	1,737 18	
Quinn, J. D.	" Special Class Exciseman for year		27 48	4 32	1,343 16	
Chartier, E.	" Deputy Collector for year	64 96		3 60	1,231 44	
Bowen, F. C.	" 3rd Class Excisemen "	41 21		2 88	780 91	
de Grosbois, C. B.	" 3rd " "	36 72		2 88	695 40	
Rousseau, E. H.	" Deputy Collector "	34 96		3 60	661 44	
	Salaries	177 85	63 05	24 48	6,449 53	
	Contingencies				627 65	
						7,077 18
	St. Hyacinthe.					
Benoit, L. V.	Salary as Collector for year	84 00		7 20	1,588 80	
Taylor, G. W.	" Special Class Exciseman from July 1, 1905 to Mar. 1, 1906, Transferred to Quebec		22 00	2 82	1,075 18	
Murray, D.	" 1st Class Exciseman for year		22 44	2 88	1,099 61	
Fortier, J.J.O.	" Deputy Collector "		19 96	2 88	977 16	
Bernard, N. J. D.	" 1st Class Exciseman "	51 17		2 88	970 92	
Langelier, F.	" Deputy Collector "	45 82		1 95	868 89	

APPENDIX B.—No. 1.—Details of Excise Expenditures, 1905–1906—*Continued*

To whom paid.	Service.	Deductions for Retirement.	Deductions for Superannuation.	Deductions for Guarantee	Amounts paid.	Total amounts paid.
	St. Hyacinthe—Con.	$ cts.	$ cts.	$ cts.	$ cts.	$ cts.
Poirier, J. N.	Salary as Deputy Collector for year	....	28 04	2 88	769 08	
Deland, A. N.	" " "	40 04	....	3 60	756 36	
Dumaine, J. D.	" 2nd Class Exciseman from July 1 to Dec. 31, 1905, and promoted to 1st Class Exciseman from Jany. 1 to June 30, 1906	46 20	....	2 88	875 88	
Rouleau, J. C.	" " "	46 20	....	2 88	875 88	
Tétrault, J.	" Deputy Collector for year	7 44	....	3 60	138 96	
Portelance, P. A.	" " "	4 96	....	1 80	93 24	
Desmarais, H. F.	" " "	4 96	....	3 60	91 44	
Brennan, D. J.	" 1st Class Exciseman from Mch. 1, 1906 to June 30, 1906 and prom. to Special Class Exciseman from Mch. 29 to June 30, 1906, br'ght fr. Hamilton	....	7 91	1 32	387 00	
	Salaries	330 79	100 35	43 17	10,568 40	
	Contingencies	.....	....	....	2,917 14	
						13,485 54
	Three Rivers.					
Hébert, C. D.	Salary as Collector for year	....	27 00	3 60	1,319 40	
Duplessis, C. Z.	" Deputy Collector for year	....	19 78	3 60	969 17	
Auger, L. H.	" 3rd Class Exciseman "	31 44	....	2 88	595 68	
Morissette, J. W.	" Deputy Collector from July 1 to Sept. 1, 1905 (Resigned)	82	....	30	15 54	
Morissette, F. R.	" Deputy Collector from Nov. 4, 1905 to June 30, 1906	3 24	....	1 18	61 38	
	Salaries	35 50	46 78	11 56	2,961 17	
	Contingencies	.....	....	....	391 98	
						3,353 1
	St. John.					
Belyea, T. H.	Salary as Collector for year	...	34 38	7 20	1,678 38	
Clarke, J. A.	" Deputy Collector for year	....	25 96	3 60	1,270 44	
McCloskey, J. R.	" 1st Class Exciseman from July 1, 1905, to March 28, 1906, and promoted to Special Class Exciseman from March 29 to June 30, 1906	.....	22 71	3 24	1,111 89	
Fitzpatrick, W. J.	" 1st Class Exciseman for year	.....	22 44	2 88	1,099 61	
Geldart, O. A.	" 1st Class Exciseman from July 1, 1905, to March 28, 1906, and promoted to Special Class Exciseman from March 29 to June 30, 1906	.....	22 71	3 24	1,111 89	
Harrison, W. F.	" Deputy Collector from July 1 to Oct. 1, 1905.—Died	13 74	....	0 90	260 34	
Ferguson, J. C.	" 1st Class Exciseman for year	.....	21 48	2 88	1,050 60	
Dibblee, W.	" Deputy Collector "	.....	3 72	2 88	293 40	
Dwyer, D. T.	" " "	10 04	....	3 60	186 36	
McGowan, J.	" Probationary 3rd Class Exciseman from Feb. 6 to June 30, 1906	10 03	....	1 20	189 63	
	Salaries	33 81	153 40	31 62	8,252 54	
	Contingencies	.....	....	....	1,024 03	
						9,276 57

APPENDIX B.—No. 1.—Details of Excise Expenditures, 1905-1906—*Continued.*

To whom paid.	Service.	Deductions for — Retirement.	Superannuation.	Guarantee.	Amounts paid.	Total amounts paid.
	Halifax.	$ cts.	$ cts.	$ cts.	$ cts.	$ cts.
Grant, H. H.	Salary as Collector for year	.....	39 78	7 20	1,942 98	
King, R. M.	" Deputy Collector for year	.....	29 21	3 60	1,429 62	
James, T. C.	" Accountant "	..	22 44	4 32	1,098 17	
Carroll, D.	" 1st Class Exciseman "	.....	22 44	2 88	1,099 61	
Blethen, C. W.	" " " "	.....	22 44	2 88	1,099 61	
Hubley, H. H.	" " " "	.....	21 48	2 88	1,050 60	
Gorman, A. M.	" " " "	.	21 48	2 88	1,050 60	
Wainwright, F. G.	" 2nd Class " "	..	19 02	2 88	934 26	
Tompkins, P.	" 3rd " " "	.....	16 50	2 88	805 62	
Hagarty, P.	" 3rd " " "	.....	.....	2 88	807 12	
Munro, H. D.	" 3rd " " "	.....	16 20	2 88	796 92	
Waddell, S. J.	" Deputy Collector "	19 96	.....	3 60	376 44	
	Salaries	19 96	230 99	41 76	12,485 55	
	Contingencies	.....	.....	.....	422 55	
						12,908 10
	Pictou.					
Fraser, P.	Salary as Collector for year	.....	21 96	3 60	1,074 42	
Macdonald, A. J.	" Deputy Collector for year	37 44	.....	2 88	709 68	
Carroll, F. P.	" 3rd Class Exciseman for year.	34 44	.....	2 88	652 68	
	Salaries	71 88	21 96	9 36	2,436 78	
	Contingencies	....	.....	.....	432 86	
						2,869 64
	Charlottetown.					
Nash, S. C.	Salary as Collector for year	13 20	.....	3 60	1,333 20	
Moore, T.	" Deputy Collector for year	19 96	.....	2 88	977 16	
	Salaries	33 16	.....	6 48	2,310 36	
	Contingencies	..	.....	.....	77 29	
						2,387 65
	Winnipeg.					
Gosnell, T. S.	Salary as Collector for year	.....	48 00	7 20	2,344 80	
Code, A.	" Deputy Collector for year	.....	31 44	3 60	1,539 96	
Long, W. H.	" Accountant "	60 00	.....	4 32	1,135 68	
Hawkins, W. L.	" " "	.....	24 00	4 32	1,171 68	
Girdlestone, R. J. M.	" Deputy Collector "	.....	19 96	2 88	977 16	
Verner, T. H.	" 1st Class Exciseman "	.....	37 56	2 88	1,034 52	
LaRivière, A. C.	" 1st " " "	.....	37 56	2 88	1,034 52	
Sparling, J. W.	" Deputy Collector "	49 9	.....	2 88	947 16	
Conklin, W. M.	" 1st Class Exciseman "	53 69	.....	2 88	1,018 39	
Barnes, G.	" Deputy Collector "	30 00	.....	2 88	567 12	
Earl, R. W.	" 2nd Class Exciseman from July 1, 1905, to Feb. 5, 1906, and promoted 1st Class Exciseman from Feb. 6 to June 30, 1906	46 20	.....	2 88	875 88	
Hammond, T. W.	" 3rd Class Exciseman for year.	29 26	.....	2 88	553 32	
Morris, T. H.	" " " "	28 88	.....	2 88	545 99	
Ross, H. E.	" Deputy Collector for year	...	11 92	2 88	385 20	
Jameson, S. B.	" " "	.....	9 00	2 88	288 12	
McNiven, J. D.	" " "	17 48	.....	2 88	329 64	
	Salaries	315 47	219 44	54 00	14,749 14	
	Contingencies	....	.....	.....	3,209 13	
						17,958 27

APPENDIX B.—No. 1—Details of Excise Expenditures, 1905-1906—*Continued.*

To whom paid.	Service.	Deductions for: Retirement.	Deductions for: Superannuation.	Deductions for: Guarantee	Amounts paid.	Total amounts paid.
	Calgary.	$ cts.	$ cts.	$ cts.	$ cts.	$ cts.
Saucier, X........	Salary as Collector for year...........	......	28 04	3 60	1,368 36	
Fletcher, R. W...	" Deputy Collector for year...	40 30	....	3 00	763 30	
Osborne, F. A....	" " " from 1 July '05 to 1 June '06 (Resigned)	....	19 25	2 64	528 11	
Walker, J. H.....	" Deputy Collector for year....	15 00	....	2 88	282 12	
Kenny, J........	" " " " "	15 00	......	3 60	281 40	
Harbottle, H......	" Probationary 3rd Class Exciseman from Feb. 6 to May 31, 1906, Deputy Collector from June 1 to 30, 1906....	12 11	....	1 26	229 16	
	Salaries....	82 41	47 29	16 98	3,452 45	
	Contingencies		....	... .	2,494 88	5,947 33
	Vancouver.					
Miller, J. E.....	Salary as Collector for year..	......	36 00	7 20	1,756 80	
Allen, G. A.	" Special Class Ex. for year...	....	31 96	4 32	1,563 72	
Parkinson, E. B...	" Deputy Collector "	64 96	....	3 60	1,231 44	
McCraney, H. P..	" " " "	45 00	....	3 60	851 40	
Swannell, F. W. .	" " " "	60 00	....	3 60	1,136 40	
Power, J. F.......	" Accountant "	43 96	....	4 32	831 72	
Wolfenden, W....	" Deputy Collector "	34 96	....	3 60	661 44	
Thorburn, J......	" 3rd Class Exciseman "	36 00	....	2 88	681 12	
McCutcheon, H.M.	" Deputy Collector "	30 00	....	3 60	566 40	
Hodder, W. E....	" " " "	30 00	....	3 60	566 40	
Howell, T........	" " " "	25 04	....	3 60	471 36	
Marion, A. H.....	" 3rd Class Exciseman "	28 58	....	2 88	540 55	
Deeley, F..... ...	" " " "	27 73	....	2 88	524 45	
Stevens, D. B.....	" Deputy Collector from 1 July '05 to 1st May '06 (Services dispensed with)......	16 60	....	3 00	313 70	
Keay, W. S.	" Deputy Collector for year....	19 96	....	3 60	376 44	
Parsons, C. H.....	" " " "	10 04	... ...	3 60	186 36	
MacGregor, D. C..	" " " from 3 May to 30 June '06.......	1 60	....	58	30 06	
	Salaries	474 43	67 96	60 46	12,289 76	
	Contingencies....	.... .	....	.. . ...	4,323 01	16,612 77
	Victoria.					
Jones, R..........	Salary as Collector for year...	.....	35 57	7 20	1,737 18	
O'Sullivan, D.....	" Deputy Collector for year....	... .	45 52	3 60	1,250 88	
Henwood, G	" 1st Class Exciseman "	.. .	22 44	2 88	1,099 61	
Ridgman, A. H...	" " " "	......	37 56	2 88	1,034 52	
McAloney, J. A..	" Deputy Collector for year....	19 96	....	3 60	376 44	
	Salaries	19 96	141 09	20 16	5,498 63	
	Contingencies..................	......	....	....	882 75	6,381 38
	Yukon.					
MacDonald, J. F.	Salary as Collector for year.	49 96	....	7 20	....	942 84

Appendix B.—No. 1—Details of Excise Expenditures, 1905–1906—*Continued.*

To whom paid.	Service.	Deductions for Retirement.	Deductions for Superannuation.	Deductions for Guarantee	Amounts paid.	Total amounts paid
	Distrtct Inspectors.	$ cts.	$ cts.	$ cts.	$ cts.	$ cts.
	Ontario.					
Dingman, N. J....	Salary for year	......	48 00	9 00	2,343 00	
	Contingencies	......	....	....	718 80	3,061 80
Stratton, W. C....	Salary for year	....	33 28	9 00	2,457 68	
	Contingencies	......	....	....	319 42	2,777 10
Kenning, J. H....	Salary for year	......	....	9 00	2,491 00	
	Contingencies	......	....	....	342 21	2,833 21
	Quebec.					
Lawlor, H........	Salary for year	.....	50 00	9 00	2,441 00	
	Contingencies	......	....	....	371 15	2,812 15
Rinfret, C. I......	Salary for year	125 00	....	9 00	2,366 00	
	Contingencies	......	....	....	261 81	2,627 81
	New Brunswick.					
Burke, T..	Salary for year	......	50·00	9 00	2,441 00	
	Contingencies	......	....	....	641 20	3,082 20
	Manitoba.					
Barrett, J. K.....	Salary for year	..	50 00	9 00	2,441 00	
	Contingencies	......	....	....	1,493 65	3,934 65
	British Columbia.					
Gill, W....... ...	Salary for year	......	24 96	9 00	2,466 00	
	Contingencies	......	....	....	484 34	2,950 34
	Inspector of Bonded Factories.					
Stratton, W. C....	Salary for year	......	4 00	....	296 00	
	Contingencies	......	....	....	176 91	472 91
	Inspector of Breweries and Malt Houses.					
Barrett, J. K.. ..	Salary for year	......	6 00	....	294 00	
	Contingencies	......	....	....	865 80	1,159 80
	Inspector of Distilleries.					
Kenning, J. H. ..	Salary for year	......	......	....	300 00	
	Contingencies	......	....	....	467 17	767 17
	Inspector of Tobacco Factories.					
Lawlor, H........	Salary for year	......	6 00	....	....	294 00

APPENDIX B.—No. 1.—Details of Excise Expenditures, 1905-1906—*Continued.*

To whom paid.	Service.	Amounts paid.	Total amounts paid.
	General Excise.	$ cts.	$ cts.
American Bank Note Co.	To pay for stamps and labels supplied	39,000 00	
British American Bank Note Co	To pay for bottling labels	5,840 10	
The Pritchard & Andrews Co	Rubber stamps, pads, daters, repairs, &c	212 75	
Edwards, W. C. & Co	Lumber and cartage	89 24	
Negretti & Zambra	100 thermometers and freight on same	252 6[illegible]	
Butterworth & Co	12 tobacco ovens at $9.50	114 00	
Taylor, G. W	Travelling expenses	135 42	
Gerald, C	" "	136 25	
Gerald, W. H	" "	51 85	
Oertling, L	Repairing 16 hydrometers and 2 petroleometers	97 45	
Reid, Thomas	Law costs in *re* Rex *vs.* J. Cosgrove	82 00	
Eimer & Amend	3 doz. burettes and 3 doz. flasks, &c	67 50	
Dring & Fage	3 doz. receiver bottles for wine still	12 77	
Registrar of the Exchequer Court	2 writs of assistance in favour of D. Murray and R. Slattery	5 80	
Thorton & Trueman	Repairing locks and keys	10 95	
Lyman & Sons	Apparatus for officer H. L. Berry	6 36	
Graves Bros	General hardware supplied	4 61	
Whitehead, Mrs. J	Cleaning storerooms, for the year	156 50	
Michon, A	Cartage	1 00	
Grand Trunk Ry. Co	Freight	6 40	
Canadian Pacific Ry. Co.	"	23 78	
Canadian Express Co	Express charges	41 16	
Dominion Express Co	"	47 35	
Canada Atlantic Ry. Co.	Freight	5 25	
Potvin, N	Petty expenses	1 17	
	Total general contingencies		46,402 4[illegible]
	Law Costs.		
Robitaille & Roy	Law costs in *re* Rex *vs.* J. E. Lamothe	14 50	
"	" " A. S. Dombrowski	19 50	
"	" " N. Dion	10 00	
"	" " J. F. Demers	10 70	
"	" " P. Gervais	33 30	88 00
Gouin, Hon'ble Lomer	" " J. R. Beauchamp	10 00	
"	" " W. Bousquet	10 00	
"	" " M. Zadina	25 20	
"	" " Hyman Baisky	20 00	65 20
Davis, T. L	" " J. J. Cosgrove		75 00
McHarg, W. H	" " J. C. Young	20 00	
"	" " Lin Chrs	20 00	
"	" " Tamoki, J	20 00	60 00
Fagan, T. P	" " J. Brossard		15 80
Foran, T. P	" " "		10 00
	Total for law costs		314 00

APPENDIX B.—No. 1.—Details of Excise Expenditures, 1905-06—*Continued.*

To whom paid.	Place of Residence.	Service.	Amounts paid.	Total amounts paid.
		Commission to Customs Officers.	$ cts.	$ cts.
Ross, W. T	Picton, Ont	From July 1, 1904 to June 30, 1906	149 02	
Fraser, R	Trenton, Ont	" "	342 80	
Watson, G	Collingwood, Ont	" "	492 80	
Lownsborough W	Lindsay, Ont	"	208 95	
Daly, James A	Campbellford, Ont	"	292 80	
Britton, W. H	Gananoque, Ont	"	274 20	
Brodeur, S. A	Valleyfield, Que	"	492 80	
Kavanagh, A. J	Gaspé, Que	"	275 96	
Cauchon, Alp	Lac Mégantic, Que	" "	273 76	
Rathford, C. E	Amherst, N. S	"	271 58	
McPherson, Jos	North Sydney, N.S	"	292 80	
McDonald, J. F	New Glasgow, N. S	"	492 80	
Street, A. F	Fredericton, N.B	"	492 80	
Gilhuly, R. H	Selkirk, Man	"	285 20	
Pound, T. J	Morden, Man	"	392 80	
Mathers, T. J	Gretna, Man	"	254 37	
Binney, J. W	Moncton, N. B	"	492 80	
Park, W. A	New Castle, N. B	"	292 80	
Anderson, J. J	Sackville, N. B	"	267 22	
Kirk, James T	Sussex, N. B	"	249 95	
Gilpin, R. R	Grand Forks, B. C	"	342 80	
Busby, E. S	Dawson, Yukon	"	492 80	
Valleau, A. S	Deseronto, Ont	"	292 80	
Allison, John B	Napanee, Ont	" "	392 80	
Macpherson, M. J	Kincardine, Ont	"	20 89	
English, J. J	Maple Creek N.W.T.	"	48 97	
Cameron, A. McK	Meaford	" to December 20, 1905	244 72	
Ferguson, D	Chatham, N. B	" to April 30, 1905	205 33	
Marsh, R. J. F	Fort Francis, Man	" to June 30, 1905	38 82	
Walton, E. J. R	Medecine Hat N.W.T	"	26 43	
McKenzie, W	North Bay, Ont	"	246 40	
Gardner, W	Macleod, N. W. T	"	94 00	
Conway, T. D	Ladysmith, B. C	" "	18 40	
Boyd, A	Antigonish, N. S	" 1905 " 1906	107 43	
McKenzie, Geo	Moose Factory	January 1, 1906 "	83 35	
Watt, Geo	Chatham, N. B	May 1, 1905 "	287 47	
Ferguson, J. W	Saskatoon, Man	July 1, 1905 "	196 40	
White, H	Cranbrook, B. C	March 1, 1905 "	82 13	
Jackson, H. B	Rainy River, Man	December 8, 1904 " 1906	307 53	
Browne, George	Meaford, Ont	December 19, 1905 " 1906	99 49	
Busby, E. S	Dawson, Yukon	Guarantee 24 mos. up to June 30, 1906	7 20	
Conway, T. D	Ladysmith, B. C	" "	7 20	
English, J. J	Maple Creek, N.W.T	" "	7 20	
Gilhuly, H. R	Selkirk, Man	"	7 20	
Gilpin, R. R	Grand Forks, B. C	"	7 20	
Mathers, T. J	Gretna, Man	"	7 20	
Pond, J. T	Morden, Man	"	7 20	
Daly, James A	Campbellford, Ont	"	7 20	
Macpherson, M. J	Kincardine, Ont	"	7 20	
Watson, G	Collingwood, Ont	"	7 20	
Anderson, J. J	Sackville, N.B	"	7 20	
Binney, J. W	Moncton, N.B	"	7 20	
Kirk, L. J	Sussex, N.B	"	7 20	
McDonald, J. F	New Glasgow, N.B	" "	7 20	
McPherson, Jos	North Sydney, N.S	"	7 20	
Park, W. A	New Castle, N.B	"	7 20	
Ratchford, C. E	Amherst, N.S	"	7 20	
Street, A. F	Fredericton, N.B	"	7 20	
Allison, J. B	Napanee, Ont	"	7 20	
Britton, W. H	Gananoque, Ont	"	7 20	
Fraser, R	Trenton, Ont	"	7 20	
Ross, W. T	Picton, Ont	"	7 20	

APPENDIX B.—No 1.—Details of Excise Expenditures, 1905-1906—*Continued.*

To whom paid.	Place of Residence.	Service.	Amounts paid.	Total amounts paid.
		Commission to Custom Officers.	$ cts.	$ cts.
Valleau, A. S.	Deseronto, Ont	Guarantee 24 mos. up to June 30, 1906	7 20	
Brodeur, S. A	Valleyfield, Que	" "	7 20	
Cauchon, Alp	Lac Mégantic	" "	7 20	
Lownsborough, W.	Lindsay, Ont	" "	7 20	
Boyd, A	Antigonish, N.S	12 June 30, 1905	3 60	
Ferguson, J. W	Saskatoon, Man	" "	3 60	
Stanley, T. D.	St. Mary's, Ont	" "	3 60	
Tyson, A. M	Wiarton, Ont	" "	3 60	
Clarke, A. J	Campobello, N.B	"	3 60	
Nadeau, M.	Claire, N.B	"	3 60	
McKenzie, W	North Bay, Ont	"	3 60	
Campbell, G	Moyie City, B.C	"	3 60	
Douglass, H	Banff, Albt., N.W.T.	"	3 60	
Gardner, W	Macleod, N.W.T.	"	3 60	
Marsh, R. J. F.	Fort Francis	" "	3 60	
Stevenson, J. R.	Moose Jaw	" "	3 60	
White, H.	Cranbrook, B.C	March 1, 1905 to June 30, 1905	1 20	
Walton, E. J. R.	Medicine Hat, N.W.T	July 13, 1904 to June 30, 1906	7 08	
Jackson, H. B.	Rainy River	Jan. 1, 1905, to "	5 40	
Watt, G	Chatham, N.B	May 1, 1905, to "	4 20	
McKenzie, Geo	Moose Factory	Jan. 1, 1906, to "	1 80	
Brown, Geo	Meaford, Ont	Dec. 19, 1905, to "	1 92	
Beauchesne, P. C.	Paspébiac	July 1, 1905, to Jan. 31, 1906	2 10	
Ferguson, D	Chatham, N.B	Sept. 1, 1904, to June 30, 1905	3 00	
Cameron, A. McK.	Kincardine, Ont	July 1, 1904, to December, 1905	5 28	
Kavanagh, A. J	Gaspé, Que	June 1, 1904, to June 30, 1906	7 20	
Veniot, P. J	Bathurst, N.B	June 1, 1903, to June 30, 1905	7 20	
		Total to Customs Officers	10,493 95	10,493 95
		Commission on Tobacco Stamps.		
Grignon, A	St. Eustache	Allowance 5 per cent on sale of stamps	10 34	
Forest, J. O. F.	L'Epiphanie	" "	5 13	
Lapierre, J	St. Alexis	" "	19 30	
		Total	34 77	34 77
		Sundry Expenditures.		
Fréchette, A.		Technical translation		19 37
Miller, J. E		To pay for provisional allowance	523 25	
Gosnell, T. S		" "	324 74	
Saucier, X.		" "	175 00	
Jones, R		" "	75 00	
			1,097 99	1,097 99

APPENDIX B.—No. 1—Details of Excise Expenditures, 1905-1906—*Continued.*

To whom paid.	Service.	Amounts paid.	Total amounts paid.
	Duty-pay.	$ cts.	$ cts.
Boutellier, G. A.	From July 1, 1905, to June 30, 1906	200 00	
McArthur, G	" "	150 00	
Brennan, J	" "	100 00	
Thomas, R.	"	100 00	
Chilver, F. W	" "	100 00	
Falconer, J. E	" "	100 00	
Adams, A. R	" "	100 00	
Bayard, G. A.	" "	100 00	
Cahill, J. W	" "	100 00	
Marcon, F. E	" "	100 00	
Keogh, P. M.	" "	100 00	
Berry, H. L.	" "	150 00	
Gerald Chas.	"	200 00	
Jamieson, R. C.	" "	150 00	
Hurst, L. B	" "	100 00	
O'Leary, T. J	" "	100 00	
Doyle, B. J	" "	100 00	
Howard, W. W. S.	" "	100 00	
Graham, W. T	" "	100 00	
Jones, A.	" "	100 00	
Dawson, W	" "	100 00	
Howie, A.	" "	150 00	
Bish, P. (Estate of).	" "	100 00	
Woodward, G. W	" "	100 00	
Egener, A	" "	100 00	
Baby, W. A. D	" "	100 00	
Brennan, D. J	" "	150 00	
O'Brien, J. F.	"	116 66	
Bishop, James	" "	100 00	
Standish, J. G.	" "	100 00	
McFee, A. C.	" "	100 00	
Wilson, H. R	" "	100 00	
Gerald, W. H.	" "	150 00	
Macdonald, A. B.	" "	150 00	
Keeler, G. S.	" "	100 00	
McPherson, E. A.	" "	100 00	
Earl, Edgar	" "	100 00	
Mason, F	" "	100 00	
Goodman, A. W.	" "	100 00	
Gow, John C.	" "	150 00	
Bernier, J. A.	"	150 00	
Olivier, H	" "	100 00	
Ralston, T.	" "	100 00	
Walsh, D. J	" "	150 00	
Snowden, J. W	" "	100 00	
Taylor, G. W.	" "	150 00	
Bernard, A. J. D.	" "	100 00	
Allen, G. A.	" "	200 00	
McLachlan, H.	" "	100 00	
Cameron, D. M	" "	200 00	
Dick, J. W	" "	200 00	
Quinn, J. D	" "	150 00	
Coleman, J. J	" "	150 00	
Mulrooney, G.	" "	75 00	
Desaulniers, J. E. A.	" "	200 00	
Millier, E.	" "	150 00	
Scullion, W. J.	" "	100 00	
Traversy, F. X.	" "	100 00	
Murray, D.	" "	150 00	
Weyms, Chrs	" "	100 00	
Johnson, J. J	" "	100 00	
Young, R. E.	" "	200 00	

APPENDIX B.—No. 1.—Details of Excise Expenditures, 1905-1906—*Concluded.*

To whom paid.	Service.	Amounts paid.	Total amounts paid.
		$ cts.	$ cts.
McCoy, W.	From July 1, 1905, to February, 11, 1906	92 40	
Moreau, A.	" " 15, 1906	62 50	
Malo, T.	" October, 9, 1905	27 40	
Coulter, A.	From November 7, 1905, to June 30, 1906	65 07	
Martin, N.	" August 6, 1905, "	90 55	
Laurier, J. L.	" October 14, 1905, to November 1, 1905	4 89	
Davidson, J.	" November 2, 1905, to June 30, 1906	66 30	
Dumaine, J. D.	" July 3, to July 15, 1905, and from Sept. 12, to Sept. 27, 1905, and from February 20, 1906, to June 30, 1906	43 76	
Hayhurst, T. H.	" March 1, 1906, to June 30, 1906	33 32	
Brown, W. J.	" February 12, 1906, to June 30, 1906	57 60	
Daveluy, J. P.	" " "	37 50	
Brain, A. F.	" " 10, "	36 72	
	Total duty-pay		8,259 67
	Grand total		479,516 77
	ADD—Printing	4,013 94	
	Stationery	1,513 81	
	Lithographing and engraving, &c.	73 00	
			5,600 75
	Authorized disbursements (less superannuation, insurance, retirement and guarantee)		485,117 52
	ADD—Balances due to Collectors, July 1, 1905	49 08	
	" by " " 1906	343 98	
			393 06
			485,510 58
	LESS—Balances due by Collectors, July 1, 1905	343 98	
	" to " " 1906	603 79	
			947 77
	Actual disbursements agreeing with Statement No. 4, page 12		484,562 81

W. J. GERALD,

Deputy Minister.

INLAND REVENUE DEPARTMENT,

OTTAWA, August 29, 1906.

APPENDIX B—*Continued.*

No. 2.—Distribution of Seizures for the Year ended June 30, 1906.

Divisions.	To whom paid.	Service.	Amounts paid.	Totals.
			$ cts.	
Belleville	Brown, W. J	For his share of seizure, No. 11	50 00	
		" " "	3 00	
				53 00
London	Alexander, T	To pay informer penalty in seizure, No. 69	25 00	
		" " " 70	25 00	
				50 00
	Floody, E	For his share of seizure, No. 69	18 58	
		" " 70	18 57	
				37 15
Ottawa	Freeland, A	To pay informer penalty in seizure, No. 209	12 50	
		" " " 210	5 00	
		" " " 215	112 50	
		" " Genl. " 4927	12 50	
				142 50
		For his share of seizure, No. 208		5 55
	Slattery, R	" " " 208	5 55	
		" " " 209	10 02	
		" " " 210	03	
				15 60
	McGuire, T	" " " 209	10 03	
		" " " 210	02	
		" " " 211	4 25	
				14 30
Stratford	Rennie, G	To pay informer penalty in seizure, No. 104		25 00
	Floody, E	For his share of seizure, No. 104		15 65
Toronto	Frankland, H. R	To pay informer penalty in seizure, No. 410	25 00	
		" " " 411	12 50	
		" " " 412	25 00	
		" " 413	5 00	
		" " 414	25 00	
		" " 415	25 00	
		" " " 417	5 00	
				122 50
		For his share of seizure, No. 410	12 50	
		" " " 411	6 25	
		" " " 416	25 00	
		" " " 417	5 00	
				48 75
	Mahoney, H	" " " 410	12 50	
		" " " 414	25 00	
		" " " 415	19 40	
				56 90
	Henderson, W	" " " 411	6 25	
		" " " 412	15 00	
				21 25
	Floody, E	" " " 413		5 00
Joliette	Labelle, L. V	" " Genl. " 4948		10 00
Montreal	Toupin, J. A	To pay informer penalty in seizure, No. 1096	10 00	
		" " " 1098	12 50	
		" " " 1099	25 00	
		" " " 1100	12 50	
		" " " 1101	25 00	
		" " " 1102	50 00	
		" " " 1104	5 00	
		" " " 1105	5 00	
		" " " 1106	5 00	
		" " " 1107	50 00	
		" " " 1108	12 50	
		" " " 1109	12 50	

APPENDIX B—*Continued.*

No. 2—DISTRIBUTION of Seizures for the Year ended June 30, 1906—*Continued.*

Divisions.	To whom paid.	Service.	Amounts paid.	Totals.
			$ cts.	$ cts.
Montreal	Toupin, J. A	To pay informer penalty in seizure, No. 1110	12 50	
		" " " 1111	100 00	
		" " " 1113	5 00	
		" " " 1115	12·50	
				355 00
		For his share of seizure, No. 1099	4 14	
		" " 1104	3 70	
		" " 1105	2 82	
		" 1106	3 18	
		" 1113	2 65	
		" 1114	29 61	
				46 10
	Comte, L. A. A. J	" " 1090	0 60	
		" 1093	28 90	
		" 1101	11 75	
		" 1101	5 04	
		" 1102	27 57	
		" 1107	24 47	
		" 1108	7 55	
		" 1109	7 01	
		" 1111	87 55	
				200 44
	Brabant, J.B.G.N	" " 1090	0 60	
		" 1093	28 90	
		" 1096	7 28	
		" 1098	6 25	
		" 1099	4 15	
		" 1100	7 37	
		" 1101	11 75	
		" 1104	3 70	
		" 1105	2 83	
		" 1106	3 17	
		" 1107	24 48	
		" 1108	7 56	
		" " 1109	7 02	
		" " 1110	7 56	
		" " 1113	2 65	
		" 1114	29 62	
		" 1115	6 44	
				166 37
	Dixon, G. S	" " 1096	7 28	
		" 1100	7 37	
		" 1110	7 55	
				22 20
	Caven, W	" " 1098	6 25	
		" 1105	6 44	
				12 69
	Lawlor, H	" " 1099		4 14
	Kearney, D. J	" " 1102		27 57
Quebec	LaRue, G.	To pay informer penalty in seizure, No. 530.	25 00	
		" " " 531.	50 00	
		" " " 548.	25 00	
		" 551.	25 00	
		" " " 571.	50 00	
				175 00
	Bourget, O	For his share of seizure, No. 530	25 00	
		" " 531	18 75	
		" " 551	12 25	
		" 571	18 30	
				74 30

APPENDIX B—*Continued.*

No. 2.—Distribution of Seizures for the Year ended June 30, 1906—*Concluded.*

Divisions.	To whom paid.	Service.	Amounts paid.	Total amounts paid.
			$ cts.	$ cts.
Quebec	Trudel, E.	For his share of seizure, No. 531	18 75	
		" " 571	18 30	
				37 05
	Vallerand, F. O.	" " 530	25 00	
		" 548	25 00	
				50 00
	Corriveau, O	" " 551		12 25
St. Hyacinthe	Murray, D.	" Genl. No. 4989		55 00
St. John	Belyea, T. H.	To pay informer penalty in seizure, No. 124	50 00	
		" " " 125	25 00	
		" " " 126	50 00	
		" " " 127	25 00	
		" 128	25 00	
		" 129	25 00	
		" " 132. } " 133. }	25 00	
		" " " 134	25 00	
				250 00
	Bonness, J. D.	For his share of seizure, No. 121	50 00	
		" " 124	14 70	
				64 70
	Bonness, J. D. (Estate of)	" " 131	50 00	
		" 132 } " 133 }	25 00	
				75 00
	Kelly, J. T.	" " 125	25 00	
		" 126	50 00	
		" 127	25 00	
		" 128	10 05	
		" 129	10 05	
		" " 134	20 60	
				140 70
Vancouver	Miller, J. E.	To pay informer penalty in seizure, No. 33		50 00
	Thorburn, J.	For his share of seizure, No. 33		46 00
		Distribution of seizures		2,487 66

RECAPITULATION.

Ontario	$ 613 15
Quebec	1,248 11
New Brunswick	530 40
British Columbia	96 00
Total	$ 2,487 66

W. J. GERALD
Deputy Minister.

Inland Revenue Department,
Ottawa, August, 29, 1906.

APPENDIX B—*Continued.*

No. 3.—Details of Sundry Minor Expenditures for the Fiscal Year ended June 30, 1906.

To whom paid.	Service.	Deductions for Superannuation	Amounts paid.	Total amounts paid.
	Minor Expenditures.		$ cts.	$ cts.
Langley & Martin..... ...	Professional services in *re* Rex vs. G. H. Huff.......		....	9 29
	Adulteration of Food.	$ cts.		
Macfarlane, Thomas......	Salary as Chief Analyst, for the year.	60 00	2,940 00	
McGill, A	" 1st Assistant Analyst for the year	43 96	2,156 04	
Wright, S. E.............	" Clerk in laboratory "	....	699 97	
Davidson, F	" Clerk in laboratory from Sept. 1, 1905, to June 30, 1906.........	....	583 30	
Lemoine, A...............	" " "	....	583 30	
Valin, J. G..............	" " "	....	583 30	
Bélisle, E................	" " from Aug. 25, 1905, to June 30, 1906.........	....	548 15	
Ladouceur, Ls...........	" Messenger for the year...........	....	699 96	
Kidd, Thomas...........	" Food Inspector for the year......	....	500 00	
Costigan, J. J...........	" " "	7 00	343 00	
Ferguson, J. C...........	" " "	4 00	196 00	
Waugh, R. J.............	" "	....	350 00	
Conklin, W. M......	" "	....	200 00	
Fletcher, R. W........ ...	" "	....	200 00	
Parkinson, E. B..........	" " ..	....	200 00	
Rouleau, J. C............	" " "	....	200 00	
Moore, T................	" " "	....	200 00	
Roy, C. E	" Food Inspector from July 20, 1905, to June 30, 1906......	....	189 70	
Sanderson, A. E.........	" Food Inspector from July 26, 1905, to June 30, 1906......	... .	186 48	
Hogan, James...........	" Food Inspector for year..........	....	100 00	
McPhie, W. H............	" Food Inspector from Aug. 25, 1905, to June 30, 1906...............	....	72 28	
O'Sullivan, D.....	" Food Inspection from April 20, 1906, to June 30, 1906	....	19 71	
		114 96	....	11,751 19
	Contingencies.			
Macfarlane, T............	Travelling expenses............		226 95	
"	To pay for special assistance.........................		1,024 70	
"	" rent for laboratory............		366 67	
"	" sundries for laboratory.		1,640 46	
Kidd, Thomas...........	Travelling and purchases of samples............. ...		546 87	
Costigan, J. J...	" "		441 09	
Ferguson, J. C..........	" "		263 29	
Waugh, R. J.............	"		244 91	
Conklin, W. M	" "		480 01	
Fletcher, R. W...........	....		138 22	
Parkinson, E. B..........	"		213 78	
Rouleau, J. C............	"		425 25	
Moore, T.........	....		119 80	
Roy, C. E........... .. .	"		292 58	
Sanderson, A. E..........	"		229 22	
Hogan, James...........	" "		157 02	
McPhie, W. H...........	"		33 35	
				6,844 17

APPENDIX B—*Continued.*

No. 3.—Details of Sundry Minor Expenditures—*Concluded.*

To whom paid.	Service.	Amounts paid.	Total amounts paid.
	Contingencies.	$ cts.	$ cts.
Ellis, W. H.	Allowance under Act for retaining fees	200 00	
	" " rent	100 00	
	" " material used in analyses	100 00	
	Fees for analyses	775 00	
			1,175 00
Bowman, W	Allowance under Act for retaining fees	200 00	
	" " rent	100 00	
	" " material used in analyses	100 00	
	Fees for analyses	774 50	
			1,174 50
Valade, F. X.	Allowance under Act for retaining fees	200 00	
	" " rent	100 00	
	" " material used for analyses	100 00	
	Fees for analyses	155 00	
			555 00
Donald, J. T	Allowance under Act for retaining fees	200 00	
	" " rent	100 00	
	" " material used in analyses	100 00	
	Fees for analyses	952 60	
			1,352 60
Fagan, J. C.	Allowance under Act for retaining fees	200 00	
	" " rent	100 00	
	" " material used in analyses	100 00	
	Fees for analyses	534 67	
			934 67
Duberger, H. E.	Salary in connection with adulteration of drugs	600 00	
	Travelling expenses	639 03	
Fiset, M.	Expenses on chemical apparatus shipped to Ottawa	7 25	
The Pritchard & Andrews Co	Seals, stamps, repairs, &c	9 45	
Eimer & Amend	Chemical apparatus, &c	140 34	
Gooderham & Worts	46·02 gallons, alcohol for laboratory (including express charges)	65 19	
Lyman & Son Co	One scale, three thermometers and screw-cap jars	110 63	
Mills, N. M.	Professional services in *re* Rex *vs.* Ganong	5 00	
Latchford, F. R.	" " McGregor	10 00	
Chisholm, W.	" " D. J. Gillies	7 50	
Fairweather, F. L.	" " Asbell & Co.	5 00	
Langley & Martin	" " J. Moffatt	7 00	
Urquart & Urquart	" " Gadsby	10 00	
"	" " Eddy	15 00	
"	" " Star Grocery	15 20	
Howary, W. F.	" " Rubinowitz	15 00	
McGill, A.	Expenses in connection with the Montreal Grocers Association and pure food show	17 85	
The Chemists and Surgeons Supply Co.	Chemical apparatus	44 43	
Fréchette, L. A.	Technical translation	11 94	
			1,735 81
	Total adulteration of food expenditures		25,522 94
	Add for printing	1,401 59	
	" stationery	321 23	
	" lithographing	2 00	
			1,724 82
	Grand total, agreeing with statement No. 8, page 17		27,247 76

W. J. GERALD,
Deputy Minister.

Inland Revenue Department,
Ottawa, August 29, 1906.

APPENDIX B—*Continued.*

No. 4.—Details of Departmental Expenditures for the Year ended June 30, 1906.

Names.	Rank.	Period.	Deductions for Superannuations.	Deductions for Retirement.	Deductions for Insurance.	Amounts paid.	Totals.
			$ cts.	$ cts.	$ cts.	$ cts.	$ cts.
Brodeur, Hon. L. P.	Minister	From July 1 to Feb. 5	.....	.....	.....	4,187 48	
Templeman, Hon. W.	"	From Feb. 6 to June 30	.....	.....	.....	2,812 52	
Gerald, W. J.	Deputy Minister	For year	.....	.....	.....	4,000 00	
Himsworth, Wm.	Chief Clerk, Secretary	"	.....	.....	.....	2,700 00	
Campeau, F. R. E.	Chief Clerk, Chief Accountant	"	54 00	.....	.....	2,646 00	
Valin, J. E.	Chief Clerk, Assistant Accountant	"	38 00	.....	.....	1,862 00	
Shaw, James F.	Chief Clerk, Accountants Branch, Statistics	"	37 67	.....	.....	1,845 66	
Doyon, J. A.	Chief Clerk, Accountants Branch, Weights and Measures	"	37 33	.....	.....	1,829 32	
Carter, Wm.	Assistant Secretary	"	38 00	.....	.....	1,862 00	
Westman, T.	Accountant's Branch Clerk, Statistics	"	34 00	.....	.....	1,666 00	
Quain, R.	Accountant's Branch Clerk.	"	48 00	.....	61 92	1,490 08	
Fowler, G.	Clerk of Supplies, Secretary's Branch	"	.....	.....	.....	1,600 00	
Newby, F.	Secretary's Branch Clerk	"	30 00	.....	.....	1,470 00	
Dunne, J. P.	Accountant's Branch Clerk.	"	30 00	.....	.....	1,470 00	
Burns, John	Accountant's Branch Clerk, Weights and Measures	"	30 00	.....	.....	1,470 00	
Hudon, L. E.	Secretary's Branch Clerk	"	47 25	.....	.....	1,302 75	
Hughes, P. A.	Accountant's Branch Clerk.	"	45 50	.....	.....	1,254 50	
McCullough, A.	Secretary's Branch Clerk	"	26 00	.....	.....	1,274 00	
Halliday, W. A.	Accountant's Branch Clerk.	"	45 50	.....	.....	1,254 50	
Roy, L. G.	" "	"	44 19	.....	.....	1,218 31	
Garneau, Hector	Second Class Clerk	From July 1 to Sept. 30	.....	15 00	.....	285 00	
Wiallard, R. A.	" "	From July 1 to Feb. 28.	.....	41 68	.....	791 68	
Desaulniers, E. L.	" "	For year	.....	60 00	.....	1,140 00	
Nicholas, B. C.	" "	From March 24 to June 30	.....	16 29	.....	309 52	
Ostiguy, L. R.	Accountant's Branch Clerk, Statistics	For year	.....	53 33	.....	1,013 34	
Lawless, E. M.	Secretary's Branch Clerk	"	.....	45 00	.....	855 00	
Hagerty, B	" "	"	.....	45 00	.....	855 00	
Charbonneau, E.	" "	"	.....	45 00	.....	855 00	
Brodeur, P. E. S.	Accountant's Branch Clerk, Statistics	"	.....	43 75	.....	831 25	
Chateauvert, G. E.	Accountant's Branch Clerk, Statistics	"	.....	40 00	.....	760 00	
Gervais, J. H.	Accountant's Branch Clerk, Weights and Measures	"	.....	40 00	.....	760 00	
Doyle, E. F.	Secretary's Branch Clerk	"	.....	40 00	.....	760 00	
Watson, V. M.	Junior Second Class Clerk	"	.....	40 00	.....	760 00	
Goodhue, M. L. E. B.	Accountant's Branch Clerk, Weights and Measures	"	.....	40 00	.....	760 00	
Trumpour, G.	Junior Second Class Clerk	"	.....	40 00	.....	760 00	
Beard, M. H.	Third Class Clerk	From April 6 to June 30	.....	5 89	.....	112 15	
Furlong, C. J.	Accountant's Branch Clerk, Weights and Measures	From May 22 to June 30	.....	2 75	.....	52 35	

APPENDIX B—*Continued.*

No. 4.—DETAILS of all Departmental Expenditures for the Year ended June 30, 1906.

Names.	Rank.	Period.	Deductions for Superannuations.	Deductions for Retirement.	Deductions for Insurance.	Amounts paid.	Totals.
			$ cts.	$ cts.	$ cts.	$ cts.	$ cts.
Garneau, Hector....	Chief Private Secretary...	From July 1 to Sept. 30	......	......	.....	50 00	
Wiallard, R. A.....	Assistant Private Secretary	From July 1 to Feb. 5..	......	......	.....	239 26	
Desaulniers, E. L...	" " ..	From Oct. 1 to Feb. 5..	...	......	.....	69 61	
Nicholas, B. C.	Private Secretary..........	From Mar. 24 to June 30.......	.....	....	....	108 59	
Beard, M. H........	Assistant Private Secretary	From Mar. 26 to June 30........	......	......	.....	53 20	
Potvin, N..	Messenger....	For year....	24 50	... ..	......	675 50	
Yetts, R. P.........	"	"	21 35	.....	54 48	534 17	
			631 29	613 69	116 40	....	52,605 74

APPENDIX B—*Continued.*

No. 4.—DETAILS of Departmental Expenditures, 1905-1906—*Continued.*

Names.	Service.	Amounts paid.	Totals.
	Contingencies.	$ cts.	$ cts.
Robert, A.	Salary as messenger for the year	624 96	
Bourgeois, E.	" "	575 01	
Beard, M. H.	" extra clerk from March 26 to April 5, 1906, 11 days	15 00	
Templeman, Hon. W.	Travelling expenses	142 74	
Brodeur, Hon. L. P.	"	313 56	
Gerald, W. J.	"	92 45	
Himsworth, Wm.	"	57 52	
Shaw, J. F.	"	11 60	
Westman, T.	"	11 35	
Wiallard, R. A.	"	913 02	
Desaulniers, E. L.	"	106 19	
Kings' Printer	Printing	1,489 40	
"	Parliamentary publications	34 50	
"	Lithographing	127 10	
Controller of Stationery	Stationery	2,012 92	
Postmaster	Postage	41 86	
C. P. R. Telegraph Co.	Telegraphing	521 20	
G. N. W. Telegraph Co.	"	182 90	
The Bell Telephone Co.	Telephoning	54 35	
Graves Bros., Ottawa	Locks, &c.	5 40	
Sproule, W. H. & Co., Ottawa	Repairs to clocks, &c.	4 00	
Canadian Rubber Co., Montreal	Three sticks pure round rubber	2 54	
The Shareholder, Montreal	Subscription	2 00	
Jones Yarrell & Co., London, Eng.	"	20 68	
Saturday Night, Toronto	"	8 00	
Chronicle Printing Co., Quebec	"	3 00	
L'Avenir du Nord, St. Jérome	"	1 50	
Catholic Register, Toronto	"	1 00	
L'Echo de Quebec	"	3 00	
The Hanley Herald, Hanley	"	2 50	
Tobacco World Publishing Co.	"	1 00	
Le Canada Français, St. Jean	"	1 00	
Daily Telegram, St. John	"	5 00	
L'Action Libérale, Montreal	"	1 25	
Le Courrier de l'Ouest, Edmonton	"	2 20	
Scientific American, New York	"	7 00	
Bulletin des Recherches Historiques, Lévis	"	2 00	
Le Canada, Montreal	" 3 copies	9 25	
Le Temps, Ottawa	"	3 00	
Canadian Manufacturer, Toronto	"	1 00	
La Presse, Montreal	"	6 00	
Chatham Daily News, Chatham	"	4 00	
Le Courrier de Montmagny	"	1 38	
L'Union des Cantons de l'Est	"	1 00	
La Cultivateur, Montreal	"	1 00	
The Herald Publishing Co., Montreal	"	6 00	
La Patrie, Montreal	"	6 00	
The Mail and Empire, Toronto	"	4 00	
Witness Printing Co., Toronto	"	6 00	
Chronicle Publishing Co., Halifax	"	5 00	
Globe Printing Co., Toronto	"	8 00	
The Citizen, Ottawa	"	18 00	
Shareholded, Montreal	"	2 00	
Acadian Recorder, Halifax	"	5 00	
Journal Printing Co., Ottawa	"	6 00	
The News, Toronto	"	2 00	
Saturday Budget, Quebec	"	1 50	
The Star, Montreal	"	3 00	
L'Union, St. Hyacinthe	"	1 50	
Manitoba Free Press, Winnipeg	"	4 00	

APPENDIX B—*Continued.*

No. 4.—Details of Departmental Expenditure, 1905-1906—*Concluded.*

Names.	Service.	Amounts paid.	Totals.
	Contingencies.—Con.	$ cts.	$ cts.
Toronto World, Toronto	Subscription	3 00	
Le Bulletin, Montreal	"	1 00	
Canada Newspaper Co., Montreal	"	7 00	
The Colonist, Victoria	"	4 00	
Chronicle Printing Co., Quebec	"	3 00	
The News Advertizing Co., Vancouver	"	4 40	
Intelligencer, Belleville	"	3 88	
Toronto Daily Star, Toronto	"	1 00	
Daily Telegraph, St. John	"	4 59	
Acadiancis, St. John	"	3 00	
Gazette Printing Co., Montreal	"	12 00	
The Chronicle, "	"	4 00	
Canadian Mining Review, Montreal	"	4 00	
The New Freeman St. John	"	0 67	
The Canada Gazette, London, Eng	"	10 00	
Resources Publishing Co	"	1 00	
The Argus, Montreal	"	2 00	
The Farmer's Advocate, London	"	1 50	
La Tribune, St. Hyacinthe	"	1 00	
Canadian Express Co	Express charges	7 75	
Dominion " "	"	3 40	
Canadian Pacific Railway Co	Freight	1 34	
Ottawa Electric Railway Co	Street Car Tickets	35 00	
A. M. Storr	Cartage	120 35	
J. Mahoney	"	4 00	
M. Landreville	Cab hire	1 00	
J. Gardner	"	1 00	
Mrs S. Maveity	Washing towels	60 00	
H. Foisy	One tin pan	2 00	
Bryson Graham & Co.	Sundries	44 83	
J. B. Auger, Expressman	Christmas gratuity	1 00	
G. Taylor "	" "	1 00	
Telegraph Messengers, G. N. W.	" "	4 43	
" " C. P. R.	" "	3 51	
Dr. Robillard & Son	Soap, hair brushes, combs, whisks, fly paper, &c., &c.	26 95	
Mrs. A. Potvin	Sewing towels	1 50	
Graves Brothers	Tin pan	2 90	
Graham Brothers	Sundries	1 50	
L. N. Poulin	"	1 29	
N. Potvin	Petty expenses	2 95	
	Total departmental contingencies		7,904 67
	Authorized disbursements (less superannuation, retirement and insurance		60,510 41
	Add—Balance due June 30, 1906		16 66
			60,527 07
	Less—Balance due July, 1, 1905		16 66
	Actual disbursements agreeing with Statement No. 17, page 50		60,510 41

W. J. GERALD,
Deputy Minister.

Inland Revenue Department,
Ottawa, August 29, 1906.

APPENDIX B—*Continued.*

No. 5.—Details of Weights and Measures Expenditures, for the Year ended June 30, 1906.

To whom paid.	Service.	Deductions for Retirement.	Deductions for Superannuation.	Deductions for Guarantee	Amounts paid.	Total amounts paid.
		$ cts.	$ cts.	$ cts.	$ cts.	$ cts.
	Belleville.					
Johnson, W	Salary as Inspector for year		24 00	3 60	1,172 40	
Slattery, T	" Assistant Inspector for year		13 96	1 80	684 24	
Irwin, S	" " " from July 1, 1905, to June 1, 1906 (superannuated)		12 76	1 65	627 22	
Errett, R. W.	" Assistant Inspector for year			1 80	598 20	
Gallagher, T	" " " "			1 80	598 20	
Johnston, C. W.	" " " from Feb. 6 to June 30, 1906			0 75	240 32	
	Salaries		50 72	11 40	3,620 58	
	Contingencies				2,886 89	
						6,507 4
	Hamilton.					
Freed, A. T	Salary as Inspector for year			3 60	1,596 36	
McDonald, J.	" Assistant Inspector from July 1 to September 1, 1905 (died)		2 66	0 30	130 36	
Marentette, A	" Assistant Inspector for year		16 04	1 80	782 16	
Fitzgerald, E. W.	" " "			1 80	798 12	
Wheatley, A. E.	" " "			1 80	798 12	
Laidman, R. H.	" " "			1 80	748 20	
Jarvis, H	" " from July 1 to December 21, 1905 (died)			0 90	374 10	
Robins, S. W.	" Assistant Inspector for year			1 30	648 12	
	Salaries		18 70	13 80	5,875 54	
	Contingencies				1,071 71	
						6,947 25
	Ottawa.					
Macdonald, J. A.	Salary as Inspector for year			3 60	1,446 36	
Breen, J	" Assistant Inspector for year			1 80	698 16	
McFarlane, J.	" " "		13 96	1 80	684 24	
Winsor, J	" " "			1 80	698 16	
Findlay, R.	" "			1 80	632 28	
Scott, J	" "			1 80	498 12	
	Salaries		13 96	12 60	4,657 32	
	Contingencies				1,419 39	
						6,076 71
	Toronto.					
Kelly, D	Salary as Inspector for year			3 60	1,346 40	
Milligan, R. J.	" Assistant Inspector for year			1 80	798 12	
Wright, R. J.	" " "		16 04	1 80	782 16	
Smith, J. C.	" " "			1 80	698 16	
Murdoch, Jas	" "			1 80	698 16	
	Salaries		16 04	10 80	4,323 00	
	Contingencies				1,901 48	
						6,224 48
	Windsor.					
Hayward, W. J.	Salary as Inspector for year		30 00	3 60	1,466 40	
Coughlin, D	" Assistant Inspector for year			1 80	798 12	
Thomas, J. S.	" " "			1 80	798 12	
Hughes, R. A.	" " "			1 80	798 12	
Liddle, D.	" " from Feb. 6, to June 30, 1906			0 72	200 14	
	Salaries		30 00	9 72	4,060 90	
	Contingencies				2,196 89	
						6,257 79

APPENDIX B—*Continued.*

No. 5.—DETAILS of Weights and Measures Expenditures, for the Year ended June 30, 1906—*Continued.*

To whom paid.	Service.	Deductions for Retirement.	Deductions for Superannuation.	Deductions for Guarantee	Amounts paid.	Total amounts paid.
	Montreal.	$ cts.	$ cts.	$ cts.	$ cts.	$ cts.
Chalus, J. O.	Salary as Inspector for year		31 90	3 60	1,564 44	
Daoust, J. A.	" Assistant Inspector for year		16 04	1 80	782 16	
Hébert, J. A. P.	" " "			1 80	798 12	
Beaudet, E.	" " "			1 80	798 12	
Collins, D.	" " "			1 80	798 12	
Fournier, L. A.	" " from July 1 to August 1, 1905			0 15	58 18	
Beaulac, J. H.	" Assistant Inspector for year			1 80	698 16	
Hall, H. C.	" " from Feb. 6 to June 30, 1906			0 75	214 36	
	Salaries		48 00	13 50	5,711 66	
	Contingencies				2,943 44	
						8,655 10
	Quebec.					
Roy, C. E.	Salary as Inspector for year			3 60	1,146 36	
LeBel, J. A. W.	" Assistant Inspector from July 1, to Nov. 11, '05, and from Dec. 28, 05, to June 30, '06		38 52	1 80	918 65	
Kelly, M. J.	" Assistant Inspector for year	22 33	23 88	1 80	751 91	
Guay, A.	" " "			1 80	698 16	
Préfontaine, F. A.	" " "			1 80	690 75	
Knowles, C.	" "			1 80	748 20	
Petit, J. B.	" "		12 00	1 80	586 20	
Bourget, L. J.	" "			1 80	590 79	
Moreau, A.	" " "		2 00		98 00	
	Salaries	22 33	76 40	16 20	6,229 02	
	Contingencies				2,586 65	
						8,815 67
	St. Hyacinthe.					
Morin, J. P.	Salary as Inspector for year			3 60	896 40	
Tomlinson, W. M.	" Assistant Inspector for year			1 80	698 16	
Dessert, V.	" " "			1 80	698 16	
Thérien, J. F.	" " from Feb. 6, to June 30, '06			75	240 32	
	Salaries			7 95	2,533 04	
	Contingencies				1,389 90	
						3,922 94
	Three Rivers.					
Gravel, A. I.	Salary as Inspector for year			3 60	996 36	
Bolduc, E.	" Assistant Inspector for year			1 80	598 20	
	Salaries			5 40	1,594 56	
	Contingencies				713 09	
						2,307 65
	St. John.					
Barry, J.	Salary as Inspector for year			3 60	1,196 40	
Cowan, E.	" Assistant Inspector for year		15 00	1 80	733 20	
Bernier, J. A.	" " "			1 80	598 20	
Leblanc, F. X.	" " "			1 80	498 12	
	Salaries		15 00	9 00	3,025 92	
	Contingencies				558 94	
						3,584 86

APPENDIX B—*Continued.*

No. 5.—Details of Weights and Measures Expenditures, for the Year ended June 30, 1906.—*Continued.*

To whom paid.	Service	Deductions for Retirement.	Deductions for Superannuation.	Deductions for Guarantee	Amounts paid.	Total amounts paid.
	Cape Breton.	$ cts.	$ cts.	$ cts.	$ cts.	$ cts.
Laurence, G. C....	Salary as Inspector for year....	.....	.....	3 60	846 36	
	Contingencies....	.....	.....	.....	507 93	1,354 29
	Halifax.					
Frame, A.......	Salary as Inspector for year	.....	.....	3 60	1,046 40	
Waugh, R. J......	" Assistant Inspector for year..	.....	.....	1 80	648 12	
	Salaries....	.....	.....	5 40	1,694 52	
	Contingencies	.....	.....	.....	1,637 75	3,332 27
	Pictou.					
Dustan, W. M....	Salary as Inspector for year.,....	.....	19 96	3 60	976 44	
Chisholm, J. J....	" Assistant Inspector for year..	.....	.....	1 80	698 16	
	Salaries....	.....	19 96	5 40	1,674 60	
	Contingencies....	.....	.....	.....	279 14	1,953 74
	Charlottetown.					
Davy, E....... ...	Salary as Inspector for year	.....	.....	3 60	996 36	
Hughes, H.	" Assistant Inspector for year..	.....	.....	1 80	648 12	
	Salaries....	.....	.....	5 40	1,644 48	
	Contingencies....	.....	.....	.....	286 44	1,930 92
	Winnipeg.					
Magness, R......	Salary as Inspector for year	.....	.....	3 60	1,396 32	
McDonald, A. W.	" Assistant Inspector for year..	.....	.....	1 80	698 16	
Mager, J. G.....	" " " ..	.....	.....	1 80	98 16	
McKay, R.......	" " " ..	.....	.....	1 80	748 20	
Girdlestone, R. J. M	" " from July 1, '05 to Feb. 1, 06. Resigned....	.....	4 04	1 80	194 16	
Ross, H. E......	" Assistant Inspector for year..	.....	.....	1 05	58 26	
Gilby, W. F	" " " ..	.....	.....	1 80	498 12	
	Salaries....	.....	4 04	13 65	3,690 38	
	Contingencies....	.....	.....	.....	2,197 67	5,888 05
	Cape Breton.					
Saucier, X......	Salary as Inspector for year.	.....	.....	3 60	196 32	
Costello, J. W....	" Assistant Inspector for year.	.....	16 04	1 80	782 16	
	Salaries....	.....	16 04	5 40	978 48	
	Contingencies....	.....	.....	.....	461 15	1,439 63
	Nelson.					
Parker, Thos. ...	Salary as Inspector for year....	.....	.....	3 60	896 40	
	Contingencies....	.....	.....	.....	984 51	1,880 91

APPENDIX B—*Continued.*

No. 5.—DETAILS of Weights and Measures Expenditures, for the Year ended June 30, 1906—*Continued.*

To whom paid.	Service.	Deductions for Retirement.	Deductions for Superannuation.	Deductions for Guarantee	Amounts paid.	Total amounts paid.
	Vancouver.	$ cts.	$ cts.	$ cts.	$ cts.	$ cts.
Marshall, R	Salary as Inspector from July 25, '05 to June 30, '06	.....	....	3 36	838 57	
Findley, H.	" Assistant Inspector for year	....	....	1 80	898 20	
McAloney, J. A.	" " "	......	... .	1 80	348 12	
	Salaries	......	.....	6 96	2,084 89	
	Contingencies	......	....	......	725 92	
						2,810 81
	Victoria.					
Findley, H.	Contingencies	.....	....	......	....	148 61
	Yukon.					
MacDonald, J. F.	Salary as Inspector for year	.....	....	3 60	996 36	
	Contingencies	......	....	......	214 95	
						1,211 31
	Chief Inspector.					
Fyfe, Jas.	Salary as Chief Inspector for year		....	....	2,600 00	
	Contingencies	....	....	....	448 02	
						3,048 02

APPENDIX B—*Continued.*

No. 5.—DETAILS of Weights and Measures Expenditures, for the Year ended June 30, 1906—*Concluded.*

To whom paid.	Service.	Amounts paid.	Total amounts.
	General Contingencies.	$ cts.	$ cts
Burgess, T.	Salary as mechanical assistant for the year	900 00	
The Pritchard & Andrews Co	Copper brands steel crown stamps and General repairs, &c	192 20	
Lawson, Thomas & Sons	200 weights 50 lbs. each, brass corners, &c	311 60	
Graves Bros	General hardware supply	27 41	
Lunn, J. G. & Co	6 hand screw-press and 6 steel nose pieces for figures	240 00	
Avery, W. & T.	1 inspector outdoor balance	80 90	
American Bank Note Co	Printing stamps	32 35	
Carson, Hugh	12 leather cases	45 00	
Thornton & Trueman	Brass box covers, buttons, hooks, &c	50 40	
The Canadian Rubber Co	1, 12 gallon rubber bag, rubber tubing, &c	22 73	
Beauregard, Rainville & St. Julien	Law costs in *Rex vs.* Emery Fauteux	30 00	
Fyfe Scale Co	1 folding tri-pod and scale, &c	21 50	
The Dominion Plating Co	Nickleplating 5 scale kitts	12 50	
Bristow, M. G	Express charges	0 75	
Dominion Express Co	"	8 77	
Canadian Express Co	"	14 40	
Canadian Pacific Railway	Freight	3 67	
Potvin, N	Petty expenses	0 36	
	Total general contingencies		1,994 54
	PROVISIONAL ALLOWANCE.		
Magness, Robt	To pay for provisional allowance	299 94	
Saucier, X	" "	100 00	
	Total provisional allowance		399 94
	METRIC SYSTEM EXPENDITURES.		
McLennan, Prof. J. C.	Expenses in connection with lectures on the metric system	2,641 19	
Sauvalle, Marc	Treatise on metric system	250 00	
The Pritchard & Andrews Co	Brass checks, tokens, &c	105 00	
Edwards, W. C. & Co. Ltd.	Lumber and cartage	17 87	
Canadian Pacific Ry. Co.	Freight	25 30	
The Julian Sale Leather Goods Co	1 club bag for Prof. McLennan	12 00	
Carson, Hugh	2 leather straps	1 50	
The Canadian Express Co.	Express charges	47 00	
The Dominion Express Co.	"	39 00	
	Total for metric system		3,138 86
	Grand total		89,831 82
	ADD—Printing	760 67	
	Stationery	431 81	
			1,192 48
	Actual disbursements (less superannuation, insurance, retirement and guarantee)		91,024 30
	Add—Old balances due by inspectors July 1, 1906		193 26
			91,217 56
	LESS—Old balances due by Inspectors, July, 1, 1905		193 26
	Actual disbursements agreeing with statements Nos. (A.) and (B) pages 56 and 57		91,024 30

W. J. GERALD,
Deputy Minister.

INLAND REVENUE DEPARTMENT,
OTTAWA, August 29, 1906.

APPENDIX B—*Continued.*

No. 6.—DETAILS of Gas Inspection Expenditures, for the Year ended June 30, 1906.

To whom paid.	Service.	Deductions for Retirement.	Deductions for Superannuations.	Deductions for Guarantee	Amounts paid.	Total amounts paid.
	Barrie.	$ cts.	$ cts.	$ cts.	$ cts.	$ cts.
Shanacy, M.	Salary as Inspector for year		2 00	3 60		94 40
	Belleville.					
Johnson, W.	Salary as Inspector for year		7 04	3 60	339 36	
Stuart, W. E.	" Assistant Inspector for year			2 88	97 08	
	Salaries		7 04	6 48	436 44	
	Contingencies				100 00	
						536 44
	Berlin.					
Broadfoot, S.	Salary as Inspector for year			3 60	96 40	
	Contingencies				51 89	
						148 29
	Brockville.					
Johnston, C. W.	Contingencies					75 86
	Cobourg.					
Bickle, J. W.	Salary as Inspector for year		2 00	3 60	94 40	
	Contingencies				61 15	
						155 55
	Cornwall.					
Mulhern, M. M.	Salary as Inspector for year		2 00	3 60	94 40	
	Contingencies				37 45	
						131 85
	Guelph.					
Broadfoot, S.	Salary as Inspector for year		4 00	3 60	192 40	
	Contingencies				13 15	
						205 55
	Hamilton.					
McPhie, D.	Salary as Inspector for year		36 00	3 60	1,760 40	
McPhie, W. H.	" Assistant Inspector for year			1 80	648 12	
Dennis, W. A.	" " "			1 80	148 20	
Murphy F. E.	" " from Dec. 19 '05 to June 30, 06			0 96	320 00	
	Salaries		36 00	8 16	2,876 72	
	Contingencies				624 08	
						3,500 80
	Kingston.					
Gallagher, T.	Salary as Inspector for year			3 60	396 40	
	Contingencies				95 35	
						491 75
	Listowel.					
Male, T.	Salary as Inspector for year			3 60	96 40	
	Contingencies				92 99	
						189 39

APPENDIX B—*Continued.*

No. 6.—Details of Gas Inspection Expenditures, for the Year ended June 30, 1906 —*Continued.*

To whom paid.	Service.	Deductions for			Amounts paid.	Total amounts paid.
		Retirement.	Superannuation.	Guarantee		
	London.	$ cts.	$ cts.	$ cts.	$ cts.	$ cts.
Nash, A. F.	Salary as Inspector for year			3 60	1,196 40	
Folley, L. R.	" Assistant Inspector from Nov. 6, '05 to June 30, '06			1 17	390 49	
	Salaries			4 77	1,586 89	
	Contingencies				312 60	1,899 49
	Naranee.					
Johnston, W.	Contingencies					30 35
	Ottawa.					
Roche, H. G.	Salary as Inspector for year			3 60	1,146 36	
Bond, M. B.	" Assistant Inspector from June 19 to June 30, '06			0 09	19 91	
	Salaries			3 69	1,166 27	
	Contingencies				910 45	2,076 72
	Owen Sound.					
Graham, W. J.	Salary as Inspector for year		2 64	3 60	193 68	
	Contingencies				125 00	318 68
	Peterborough.					
Rork, T	Salary as Inspector for year			3 60	146 40	
	Contingencies				11 10	157 50
	Sarnia.					
Thrasher, W. A.	Contingencies					12 90
	Stratford.					
Rennie, G.	Salary as Inspector for year		4 00	3 60	192 40	
	Contingencies				15 00	207 40
	Toronto.					
Johnstone, J. K.	Salary as Inspector for year		34 04	3 60	1,662 36	
Pape, J	" Assistant Inspector for year			1 80	998 16	
White, J. A.	" " "			1 80	798 12	
Hunter, W. M.	" " "			1 80	698 16	
	Salaries		34 04	9 00	4,156 80	
	Contingencies				74 44	4,231 24
	Montreal.					
Aubin, A.	Salary as Inspector for year			3 60	1,596 36	
O'Flaherty, M. J.	" Assistant Inspector for year			1 80	898 20	
Aubin, Chs.	" " "			2 88	797 04	
	Salaries			8 28	3,291 60	
	Contingencies				462 45	3,754 05
	Quebec.					
LeVasseur, N.	Salary as Inspector for year		19 96	3 60	976 44	
Moreau, J. A.	" Assistant Inspector for year		10 00		490 00	
	Salaries		29 96	3 60	1,466 44	
	Contingencies				170 40	1,636 84

APPENDIX B—*Continued.*

No. 6.—DETAILS of Gas Inspection Expenditures, for the Year ended June 30, 1906—*Continued.*

To whom paid.	Service.	Deduction for Retirement.	Deduction for Superannuation.	Deduction for Guarantee	Amounts paid.	Total amounts paid.
	Sherbrooke.	$ cts.	$ cts.	$ cts.	$ cts.	$ cts.
Simpson, A. F.	Salary as Inspector for year	....	3 00	3 60	....	143 40
	St. Hyacinthe.					
Benoit, L. V.	Salary as Inspector for year	.....	....	1 80	....	98 20
	Fredericton.					
Fowler, J. D.	Salary as Inspector for year	.....	....	3 30	....	179 96
	St. John.					
Wilson, J. E.	Salary as Inspector for year	.....	....	3 60	1,096 40	
	Contingencies	.....	....	....	100 92	1,197 32
	Halifax.					
Miller, A.	Salary as Inspector from July 1, '05 to May 1, '06 (superannuated)	......	20 80	3 00	1,017 80	
Ritchie, A. J.	" Assistant Inspector from July 1, '05 to May 1, '06 and Inspector to June 30, '06	......	....	2 10	789 56	
Munro, H. D.	" Assistant Inspector for year	.....	1 96	1 80	96 24	
Cotter, W. F.	" " May 19 to June 30, '06.)	......	....	0 21	58 92	
	Salaries	.....	22 76	7 11	1,962 52	
	Contingencies	......	....	....	646 01	2,608 53
	Charlottetown.					
Bell, J. H.	Salary as Inspector for year	.....	....	3 60	....	446 40
	Winnipeg.					
Magness, R.	Salary as Inspector for year	...	....	3 60	296 40	
Mager, J. G.	" Assistant Inspector for year	......	....	2 88	697 08	
	Salaries	.....	....	6 48	993 48	
	Contingencies	. . .	....	....	269 88	1,263 36
	Nanaimo.					
McAloney, J. A.	Salary as Inspector for year	.....	....	3 60	....	96 40
	New Westminster.					
Wolfenden, W.	Salary as Inspector for year	5 00	....	3 60	....	91 40
	Vancouver.					
Miller, J. E.	Salary as Inspector for year	......	6 00	3 60	290 40	
	Contingencies	......	....	....	380 70	671 10
	Victoria.					
Jones, R.	Salary as Inspector for year	....	4 00	3 60	....	192 40
	Chief Inspector.					
Higman, O.	Salary as Chief Inspector for year	....	....	....	....	100 00

APPENDIX B—*Continued.*

No. 6.—Details of Gas Inspection Expenditures, for the Year ended June 30, 1906—*Concluded.*

To whom paid.	Service.	Amounts paid.	Total amounts.
	General Contingencies.	$ cts.	$ cts.
Sugg, W. & Co.	6 test meters and thermometers, &c.	433 76	
McGill, A	Travelling expenses in connection with the inspection of natural gas	146 25	
Fréchette, L. A.	Technical translation	30 40	
The Pritchard Andrews Co.	3 meter seals and general repairs, &c.	44 75	
Negretti & Zambra.	3 doz. India rubber cones	10 95	
The Canadian Rubber Co.	Rubber tubing, &c.	84 43	
Grand Trunk Railway	Freight	8 70	
Potvin, N.	Petty expenses	2 95	
	Total general contingencies	....	762 19
	Grand total	....	27,705 71
	Add—Printing	794 35	
	Stationery	274 89	1,069 24
	Authorized disbursement (less superannuation retirement and guarantee)	....	28,774 95
	Add—Balances due by Inspectors, June 30, 1906	....	218 88
			28,993 83
	Less—Balances due by Inspectors, July 1, 1905	....	218 88
	Actual disbursements, agreeing with statement No. 22, page 60	....	28,774 95

W. J. GERALD,
Deputy Minister.

Inland Revenue Department,
Ottawa, August 29, 1906.

APPENDIX B—*Continued.*

No. 7—DETAILS of Electric Light Inspection, Expenditures for the year ended June 30, 1906.

To whom paid.	Service.	Deduction for Guarantee.	Amounts paid.	Total Amounts paid.
	Belleville.	$ cts.	$ cts.	$ cts.
Johnston, C. W.	Salary as Inspector from Feby. 6 to June 30, '06	75	39 41	
	Contingencies		510 93	550 34
	Hamilton.			
McPhie, D.	Contingencies			83 08
	London.			
Nash, A. F.	Contingencies			251 45
	Ottawa.			
Roche, H. G.	Contingencies			129 00
	Owen Sound.			
Graham, W. J.	Contingencies			2 50
	Toronto.			
Johnstone, J. K.	Contingencies			487 87
	Montreal.			
Aubin, A.	Contingencies			55 85
	Quebec.			
Le Vasseur, N.	Contingencies			148 15
	Sherbrooke.			
Simpson, A. F.	Contingencies			70 70
	St. Hyacinthe.			
Provost, J. E.	Salary as Inspector for year	1 80	298 20	
	Contingencies		147 30	445 50
	Three Rivers.			
Dufresne, J. U.	Salary as Inspector for year		500 00	
	Contingencies		131 50	631 50
	St. John.			
Wilson, J. E.	Contingencies			220 15
	Halifax.			
Ritchie, A. J.	Contingencies			184 31
	Charlottetown.			
Bell, J. H.	Contingencies			81 19
	Winnipeg.			
Magness, R.	Contingencies			55 40
	Edmonton.			
Harbottle, N.	Salary as Inspector from Aug. 24, '05 to 30 June, '06	1 50	83 94	
	Contingencies		92 95	176 89

APPENDIX B—*Continued.*

No. 7.—DETAILS of Electric Light Inspection, Expenditures for the Year ended June 30, 1906—*Continued.*

To whom paid.	Service.	Deductions for Guarantee.	Amounts paid.	Total Amounts paid.
	Victoria.	$ cts.	$ cts.	$ cts.
Jones, R.	Contingencies			43 25
	Yukon.			
MacDonald, J. F.	Salary as Inspector for year	3 60		496 32
	Chief Electrical Engineer.			
Higman, O.	Salary as Chief Electrical Engineer for year		2,500 00	
Fontaine, A. A.	" " Ass't. " " from 1st July, '05 to 1st May, '06		666 60	
			3,166 60	
	Contingencies		830 06	3,996 66

APPENDIX B.—*Continued.*

No. 7.—DETAILS of General Electric Light Inspection, Expenditures for the Year ended June 30, 1906—*Concluded.*

To what paid.	Service.	Amount Paid.	Amount Paid.
		$ cts.	$ cts.
Ahearn & Soper	General electrical apparatus, repairs, &c	639 42	
British Insulated & Helsby Cables Co. Ltd	Cable wire, &c	135 54	
Wirt Electric Co	3 reostats	100 15	
Canadian Gen. Elec. Co	1 electrical drying oven and 1 heater	73 00	
Smith, S. & Sons	6 cronographs, 500 steel nuts, &c	111 53	
The Trumbull Electric Mfg Co	Electrical apparatus	71 50	
Shedrick, C. E	General repairs to wattmeters, &c	44 05	
Weston Electrical Instrument Co	500 receptacles, 1 multiplier, electrical apparatus and repairs	198 09	
Rutland Florence Marble Co	6 marble slabs	43 30	
Stewart Co.	25 meter brackets and board fixtures, &c	71 50	
Mills, A. R. & Sons	Marble and slate	5 75	
Blyth & Watt	1 galvanized tube and 12 pieces of tubing	8 20	
Machado & Roller	Repairing wattmeter	11 35	
The Robert Mitchell Co., Ltd	Adjustable brass levelling feet	18 00	
The Pritchard Andrews Co	Repairing 1 rubber stamp	0 20	
Duncan, H. J	Law costs in *re* Rex *vs.* W. Nichols	20 00	
The Ottawa Steel Casting Co	36 iron stands drilled, countersunked and tapped	10 80	
Workman & Co	Hardware supply	1 00	
The Eclipse Mfg. Co	Bolts, washers, and post holders, &c	3 80	
The Bell Telephone Co	32 feet wooden duet conduct	3 20	
American Vitrified Conduits Co	100 feet—2 duet conduits 2 feet=400 duet feet at 5¼c.	21 00	
The Dominion Express Co	Express charges	22 40	
The Canadian Express Co	"	18 88	
The Canadian Pac. Railway Co	Freight	13 73	
The Ottawa & New York Ry. Co	"	0 99	
The American Express Co.	Express charges	5 75	
Potvin, N	Petty expenses	0 62	
	Total electric light contingencies		1,653 75
	Grand total		9,763 86
	ADD—Printing	35 75	
	Stationery	46 96	82 71
	Actual disbursements, agreeing with statement No. 24 page 63		9,846 57

W. J. GERALD,
Deputy Minister.

INLAND REVENUE DEPARTMENT,
OTTAWA, August 29, 1906.

APPENDIX B—*Continued.*

No. 8.—List of Permanent Employees of the Inland Revenue Department employed on Salary, during the Year ended June 30, 1906.

Names.	Services.						
	Inside.	Excise.	Weights and Measures.	Gas.	Electric Light Inspection.	Preventive.	Food Inspection.
Adam, A. R.		1					
Adams, J. S.		1					
Alexander, Thos		1					
Allen, G. A		1					
Alteman, Peter J		1					
Amor, Wm		1					
Andrews, A. A.		1					
Armstrong, Walter		1					
Auger, L. H.		1					
Aubin, A.				1	1		
Aubin, Chs				1	1		
Baby, W. A. D		1					
Baikie, D.		1					
Barber, J. S		1					
Barnes, G.		1					
Barrett, J. K.		1					
Barry, James			1				
Bayard, Gilbert A.		1					
Beaulac, J. H.			1				
Beaulieu, J. B.		1					
Bélair, A. (Plessis dit)		1					
Bell, J. H.				1	1		
Belleperche, A. J. E.		1					
Belyea, T. H		1					
Béneteau, S.		1					
Bennett, James		1					
Benoit, L. V.		1		1			
Bernard, N. J. D.		1					
Bernier, J. A.			1				
Berry, H. L.		1					
Bickle, J. W		1		1			
Bish, Philip		1					
Bishop, J. B.		1					
Blackman, C.		1					
Blethen, C. W.		1					
Blyth, Alex.		1					
Bolduc, Ephrem			1				
Bonner, J. D.					1		
Boomer, J. B		1					
Boudet, E.			1				
Bourget, L. J.			1				
Bourget, O.		1					
Bourgeois, J. E	1						
Bousquet, J. O		1					
Bouteiller, G. A		1					
Bowman, Allan.		1					
Boyd, J. F. S.		1					
Boyd, S. I.		1					
Boyle, P.		1					
Bowen, F. C.		1					
Brabant, J. B. G. N		1					
Brain, A. F.		1					
Breen, John			1				
Brennan, D. J		1					
Brennan, John.		1					
Brentnall, F. F		1					
Bridgman, M. W		1					
Broadfoot, S.		1		1			
Brodeur, P. E. S.	1						

APPENDIX B—*Continued.*

No. 8.—List of Permanent Employees of the Inland Revenue Department, 1905–1906—*Continued.*

Names.	Services.						
	Inside.	Excise.	Weights and Measure.	Gas.	Electric Light Inspection.	Preventive.	Food Inspection.
Brown, W. J		1					
Browne, G. W		1					
Bruyère, H. P		1					
Burgess, Thomas H			1				
Burke, T		1					
Burns, John	1						
Burns, R. J		1					
Cahill, J. H		1					
Cahill, J. W		1					
Cameron, D. M		1					
Campeau, F. R. E	1						
Carroll, D		1					
Carroll, F. P		1					
Carter, William	1						
Casey, John		1					
Caven, A		1					
Caven, W		1					
Chagnon, C. P		1					
Chalus, J. O			1				
Charbonneau, E	1						
Chartier, Etienne		1					
Chateauvert, G. E	1						
Cheseldine, J. H		1					
Chilver, F. W		1					
Chisholm, J. J			1				
Chisholm, W. N		1					
Clark, James Alfred		1					
Clarke, Thomas		1					
Codd, Herbert J. S		1					
Code, Abraham		1					
Coleman, Charles		1					
Coleman, J. J		1					
Coles, F. H		1					
Collins, D			1				
Comte, L. A. A. J		1					
Conklin, W. M		1					1
Cook, W. R		1					
Costello, J. W			1				
Costigan, J. J		1					1
Coughlin, D			1				
Coulter, Alex		1					
Courtney, J. J		1					
Coutts, J. J		1					
Cowan, Edgar			1				
Crawford, W. P		1					
Crevier, J. H		1					
Dager, H. J		1					
Daignault, G		1					
Daoust, J. A			1				
Daveluy, J. P		1					
David, T		1					
Davis, T. G		1					
Davy, Edward			1				
Dawson, W		1					
Deland, A. N							
Dennis, W. A		1					
Deely, F				1			
Desaulniers, E. L	1	1					
Desaulniers, J. E. A		1					

APPENDIX B—*Continued.*

No. 8.—List of Permanent Employees of the Inland Revenue Department, 1905-1906—*Continued.*

Names.	Services.						
	Inside.	Excise.	Weights and Measures.	Gas.	Electric Light Inspection.	Preventive.	Food Inspection.
Desmarais, H. F.	.....	1	....	.....	.....	.....	.....
Dibblee, William	.....	1	....	.....	.....	.....	.....
Dick, J. W	.....	1	....	.....	.....	.....	.....
Dickson, C. T.	.....	1	....	.....	.....	.....	.....
Dingman, N. J	.....	1	....	.....	.....	.....	.....
Dixon, H. G. S.	.....	1	....	.....	.....	.....	.....
Doyle, B. J.	.....	1	....	.....	.....	.....	.....
Doyle, E. F.	1	.....	....	.....	.....	.....	.....
Doyon, J. A.	1	.....	....	.....	.....	.....	.....
Dudley, W. H.	.....	1	....	.....	.....	.....	.....
Dufresne, J. U.	.....	.....	....	.....	1	.....	.....
Dumaine, J. D. E.	.....	1	....	.....	.....	.....	.....
Dumbrille, R. W.	.....	1	....	.....	.....	.....	.....
Dumouchel, Léandre	.....	1	....	.....	.....	.....	.....
Dunlop, C.	.....	1	....	.....	.....	.....	.....
Dunne, J. P.	1	.....	....	.....	.....	.....	.....
Duplessis, C. Z	.....	1	....	.....	.....	.....	.....
Dustan, W. M.	.....	.....	1	.....	.....	.....	.....
Dwyre, D. T.	.....	1	....	.....	.....	.....	.....
Earl, R. W.	.....	1	....	.....	.....	.....	.....
Egan, Wm.	.....	1	....	.....	.....	.....	.....
Egener, A.	.....	1	....	.....	.....	.....	.....
Errett, R. W	.....	.....	1	.....	.....	.....	.....
Evans, G. T.	.....	1	....	.....	.....	.....	.....
Fahey, Ed.	.....	1	....	.....	.....	.....	.....
Falconer, James	.....	1	....	.....	.....	.....	.....
Falconer, R. H	.....	1	....	.....	.....	.....	.....
Ferguson, John C.	.....	1	....	.....	.....	.....	1
Fiddes, James	.....	1	....	.....	.....	.....	.....
Fielding, Laura G.	.....	1	....	.....	.....	.....	.....
Findlay, R.	.....	.....	1	.....	.....	.....	.....
Findley, Hugh	.....	.....	1	.....	.....	.....	.....
Fitzgerald, E. W.	.....	.....	1	.....	.....	.....	.....
Fitzpatrick, W. J	.....	1	....	.....	.....	.....	.....
Fleming, C.	.....	1	....	.....	.....	.....	.....
Fletcher, R. W.	.....	1	....	.....	.....	.....	1
Floody, E.	.....	.....	....	.....	.....	1	.....
Flynn, D. J	.....	1	....	.....	.....	.....	.....
Forest, E. R.	.....	1	....	.....	.....	.....	.....
Forest, M	.....	1	....	.....	.....	.....	.....
Fortier, J. J. O	.....	1	....	.....	.....	.....	.....
Foster, J. Henry	.....	1	....	.....	.....	.....	.....
Fowler, George	1	.....	....	.....	.....	.....	.....
Fox, J. D	.....	1	....	.....	.....	.....	.....
Fox, Thomas	.....	1	....	.....	.....	.....	.....
Frame, Archibald	.....	.....	1	.....	.....	.....	.....
Frankland, H. R.	.....	1	....	.....	.....	.....	.....
Fraser, P.	.....	1	....	.....	.....	.....	.....
Freed, A. T.	.....	.....	1	.....	.....	.....	.....
Freeland, Anthony	.....	1	....	.....	.....	.....	.....
Fyfe, James	.....	.....	1	.....	.....	.....	.....
Gamache, J. H.	.....	1	....	.....	.....	.....	.....
Gauvin, E.	.....	1	....	.....	.....	.....	.....
Geldart, O. A.	.....	1	....	.....	.....	.....	.....
George, John	.....	1	....	.....	.....	.....	.....
Gerald, C.	.....	1	....	.....	.....	.....	.....
Gerald, W. H.	.....	1	....	.....	.....	.....	.....
Gerald, W. J.	1	.....	....	.....	.....	.....	.....

APPENDIX B—*Continued.*

No. 8.—List of Permanent Employees of the Inland Revenue Department, 1905-1906—*Continued.*

Names.	Services.						
	Inside.	Excise.	Weights and Measures.	Gas.	Electric Light Inspection.	Preventive.	Food Inspection.
Gervais, J. H	1						
Gilby, W. F			1				
Gill, Wm		1					
Gillies, Archibald L		1					
Girard, Irénè		1					
Girdlestone, R. J. M.		1	1				
Goodhue, M. L. E. B.	1						
Goodman, A. W		1					
Gorman, Arthur M.		1					
Gosnell, T. S		1					
Gow, J. E		1					
Graham, A. L.		1					
Graham, W. J.		1		1			
Graham, W. T.		1					
Grant, H. H		1					
Gravel, A. I			1				
Grimason, Thomas.		1					
Grobois (de), Chas. B.		1					
Guay, Alphonse			1				
Hagan, James		1					
Hagarty, P		1					
Hagerty, B	1						
Halliday, W. A	1						
Hammond, T. W		1					
Hanley, A		1					
Hanlon, J. R.		1					
Harwood, J. O. A		1					
Harris, J. G		1					
Hawkins, W. L.		1					
Hayhurst, T. H		1					
Hayward, W. J.			1				
Hébert, C. D		1					
Hébert, J. A. P.			1				
Helliwell, H. N		1					
Henderson, W		1					
Henwood, George		1					
Hesson, C. A		1					
Hicks, W. H		1		1			
Higman, O				1	1		
Himsworth, Wm.	1						
Hinchey, E. H.		1					
Hobbs, G. N.		1					
Hodder, W. E		1					
Hogan, James		1					1
Howard, W. W. S.		1					
Howden, R		1					
Howell, Thomas		1					
Howie, A.		1					
Hubley, H. H		1					
Hudon, L. E.	1						
Hughes, Henry			1				
Hughes, P. A	1						
Hughes, R. A.			1				
Hunter, W. M				1	1		
Hurst, Levi B		1					
Iler, B.		1					
Ironside, G. A.		1					
James, T. C.		1					
Jameson, S. B.		1					

APPENDIX B—*Continued.*

No. 8.—List of Permanent Employees of the Inland Revenue Department, 1905-1906—*Continued.*

Names.	Services.						
	Inside.	Excise.	Weights and Measures.	Gas.	Electric Light Inspection.	Preventive.	Food Inspection.
Jamieson, R. C		1					
Jeffrey, A. J		1					
Johnson, C. W.				1			
Johnson, J. J.		1					
Johnson, Wm.			1	1	1		
Johnstone, J. K				1	1		
Jones, Andrew		1					
Jones, Richard		1		1	1		
Jubenville, J. P.		1					
Kearny, D. J		1					
Keay, W. S.		1					
Keeler, G. S		1					
Keilty, T		1					
Kelly, Daniel			1				
Kelly, J. F						1	
Kelly, M. J.			1				
Kenning, J. H.		1					
Kenny, John		1					
Keogh, P. M.		1					
Kidd, Thomas							1
King, R. M.		1					
Knowles, C			1				
Labelle, L. V		1					
Ladouceur, J							1
Laidman, Richard H.			1				
Lambert, J. A.		1					
Lamoureux, J. A.		1					
Lane, T. M		1					
Langelier, François		1					
Laporte, Geo		1					
LaRivière, A. C		1					
LaRue, A. P		1					
LaRue, George		1					
LaRue, J. B. Alexandre		1					
Laurence, G. C			1				
Laurier, J. L		1					
Lawless, E. M.	1						
Lawlor, H.		1					
Lawlor, John J		1					
LeBel, J. A. W.			1				
Leblanc, F. X			1				
Lee, Edward		1					
Ledoux, Alexina		1					
LeMoine, Jules		1					
LeVasseur, N.				1	1		
Logan, John		1					
Long, W. H. A		1					
Longtin, H		1					
Love, G. J.		1					
Lyons, E		1					
Macdonald, A. B		1					
Macdonald, J. A.			1				
Macdonald, J. F			1	1	1		
Macfarlane, Thos							1
Mackenzie, J. H.		1					
Mager, Joseph G			1				
Magness, Robt			1	1	1		
Mahoney, H		1					
Mainville, C. P		1					

APPENDIX B—*Continued,*

No. 8.—List of Permanent Employees of the Inland Revenue Department, 1905-1906—*Continued.*

Names.	Services.						
	Inside.	Excise.	Weights and Measures.	Gas.	Electric Light Inspection.	Preventive.	Food Inspection.
Male, Thomas				1			
Maranda, N. A		1					
Marcon, F. E		1					
Marentette, Alex			1				
Marin, L. H		1					
Marion, H. R		1					
Marrion, A. H		1					
Marshall, I. N		1					
Mason, F		1					
Maurice, E		1					
Metcalf, W. F		1					
Melville, T. R		1					
Miller, J. E		1		1	1		
Miller, W. F		1					
Millier, Elie		1					
Milligan, R. J			1				
Milliken, E		1					
Milot, J. F		1					
Moore, T		1					1
Morin, J. P			1				
Moreau, J. A			1	1			
Morris, T. H		1					
Mulhern, M. M		1		1			
Munro, H. D		1		1			
Murdoch, James			1				
Murphy, Jas. L		1					
Murray, A. E		1					
Murray, David		1					
McAloney, Joseph A		1	1	1			
McArthur, G. H		1					
McCloskey, J. R		1					
McCoy, Wm		1					
McCraney, H. P		1					
McCuaig, Aug. F		1					
McCullough, A	1						
McCutcheon, H		1					
McDonald, A. J		1					
McDonald, A. W			1				
McFarlane, J			1				
McFee, C		1					
McGill, A							1
McGuire, L. J		1					
McGuire, T		1					
McKay, R			1				
McLenaghan, N		1					
McNiven, J. D		1					
McPherson, E. A		1					
McPhie, Donald				1	1		
McPhie, W. H				1			
McSween, James		1					
Nash, A. F				1	1		
Neil, James		1					
Nash, S. C		1					
Newby, F	1						
Noonan, H. T		1					
Normandin, G		1					
O'Brien, E. C		1					
O'Brien, James		1					
O'Brien, J. F		1					

APPENDIX B—*Continued.*

No. 8.—List of Permanent Employees of the Inland Revenue Department, 1905–1906—*Continued.*

Names.	Services.						
	Inside.	Excise.	Weights and Measures.	Gas.	Electric Light Inspection.	Preventive.	Food Inspection.
O'Donnell, J.		1					
O'Donnell, M. J.		1					
O'Donohue, M. J.		1					
O'Flaherty, E. J.		1					
O'Flaherty, M. J.				1			
O'Leary, T. J.		1					
Orr, Henry N.		1					
O'Sullivan, D.		1					1
Panneton, G. E.		1					
Pape, James				1	1		
Parent, F.		1					
Parker, Thomas			1				
Parkinson, Edward B.		1					1
Parson, C. H.		1					
Patry, J. H.		1					
Patterson, C. E. A.		1					
Pelletier, N. G.		1					
Petit, J. B.			1				
Poirier, J. N.		1					
Pole, C. W.		1					
Popham, F. H.		1					
Portelance, P. A.		1					
Potvin, Napoléon	1						
Powell, J. B.		1					
Power, J. F.		1					
Préfontaine, F. H.			1				
Prosser, Elijah						1	
Provost, I. E.					1		
Quain, Redmond	1						
Quinn, J. D.		1					
Ralston, T.		1					
Renaud, A. H.		1					
Rennie, George		1		1			
Ridgman, A. H.		1					
Rinfret, C. I.		1					
Ritchie, A. J.				1	1		
Ritchie, R.		1					
Robins, S. W.			1				
Roche, H. G.				1	1		
Rork, T.		1		1			
Rose, John A.		1					
Rouleau, J. C., jr.		1					1
Rousseau, Elzéar H.		1					
Rowan, W. E.		1					
Roy, L. G.	1						
Rudkins, W.		1		1	1		
Ryan, Wm		1					
Saucier, X.		1					1
Schram, R. L. H.		1					
Scott, Jos.		1					
Scullion, W. J.		1					
Shanacy, M.		1		1			
Shaw, J. F.	1						
Simpson, A. F.		1		1	1		
Simpson, W. A.		1					
Slattery, R.		1					
Slattery, Thomas			1				
Sloan, W.		1					
Smith, J. C.			1				

APPENDIX B—*Continued.*

No. 8.—List of Permanent Employees of the Inland Revenue Department, 1905-1906—*Concluded.*

Names.	Services.						
	Inside.	Excise.	Weights and Measures.	Gas.	Electric Light Inspection.	Preventive.	Food Inspection.
Snowdon, J. W.		1					
Sparling, J. W.		1					
Spence, F. H.		1					
Spereman, J. J.		1					
Standish, J. G.		1					
Stewart, James		1					
Saint-Michel, F. X.		1					
Stratton, W. C.		1					
Stuart, W. E.				1			
Swannell, F. W.		1					
Talbot, John		1					
Taylor, G. W.		1					
Tétreault, J.		1					
Thomas, J. S.			1				
Thomas, Robert		1					
Thorburn, J.		1					
Thurber, J.		1					
Till, T. M.		1					
Timmons, R.		1					
Tobin, Thomas		1					
Tomlinson, W. M.			1				
Tompkins, P.		1					
Toupin, F. X. J. A.		1					
Tracy, J. P.		1					
Trasher, W. A.		1					
Trumpour, G.	1						
Valin, J. E.	1						
Verner, Francis		1					
Verner, Thomas H.		1					
Wainright, F. G.		1					
Walker, J. H.		1					
Walsh, Daniel J.		1					
Walsh, W. H.		1					
Wardell, R. S. R.		1					
Watson, V. M.	1						
Waugh, R. J.			1				1
Webbe, C. E. A.		1					
Westman, T.	1						
Weyms, C.		1					
Wheatley, Alfred E.			1				
White, J. B.		1					
Whitehead, J. P.		1					
Whyte, J. A.				1			
Wilson, David		1					
Wilson, J. E.				1	1		
Winsor, John A.			1				
Wolfenden, William		1		1			
Wood, James A.		1					
Woodward, G. W.		1					
Wright, Robert J.			1				
Wright, S. E.							1
Yetts, R. P.	1						
Young, R. E.		1					
Totals	32	343	66	41	24	3	16

APPENDIX B—*Continued.*

No. 9.—List of Permanent Employees of the Inland Revenue Department employed on salary during only a portion of the year ended June 30, 1906.

Names.	Period.	Services.						
		Inside.	Excise.	Weights and Measures.	Gas.	Electric Light Inspection.	Preventives.	Adulteration of Food.
Aaron, J. D	From June 21 to June 30, 1906		1					
Beard, Miss M. H	March 2 to June 30, 1906	1						
Belisle, E.	August 25, 1905 to June 30, 1906							1
Bond, M. B	July 19 to July 30, 1905				1	1		
Bonness, J. D	July 1, 1905 to April 30, 1906						1	
Bourgeois, C	February 6 to June 30, 1906		1					
Cotter, W. F	May 19 to June 30, 1906				1	1		
Courchesne, J. H	July 1 to October 31, 1905		1					
Courchesne, P. H. E	December 13, 1905 to June 30, 1906		1					
Cryderman, C. W.	April 20 to June 30, 1906		1					
Davis, Jas	July 1, 1905 to April 30, 1906		1					
Dessert, V	February 6 to June 30, 1906			1				
Elliott, W. J	March 29 to June 30, 1906		1					
Folley, L. R	November 6, 1905 to June 30, 1906				1	1		
Fontaine, A. A	July 1, 1905 to April 30, 1906					1		
Fournier, L. A	August 1 to July 31, 1905			1				
Fowler, J. D	July 1, 1905 to May 31, 1906				1			
Furlong, C. J	May 22 to June 30, 1906	1						
Garneau, H.	July 1 to September 30, 1905	1						
Graveline, D. P	February 6 to June 30, 1906			1				
Hall, H. C	February 6 to June 30, 1906		1					
Harbottle, N	August 24, 1905, to June 30, 1906		1			1		
Harrison, W. F	July 1 to September 30, 1905		1					
Irwin, S	July 1, 1905, to May 30, 1906			1				
Jarvis, H.	January 1 to June 30, 1906			1				
Johnston, C. W.	February 6 to June 30, 1906			1	1			
Kirkpatrick, A. J.	March 29 to June 30, 1906		1					
Lépine, L.	July 1 to September 30, 1905		1					
Liddle, D.	February 6 to June 30, 1906			1				
MacGregor, D. C.	May 3 to June 30, 1906		1					
Malo, T.	July 1 to November 30, 1905		1					
Marshall, R	July 25, 1905 to June 30, 1906			1				
Martin, N	July 25, 1905 to June 30, 1906		1					
Michon, A. E.	July 1, 1905 to April 30, 1906		1					
Miller, A	July 1, 1905 to April 30, 1906				1	1		
Montgomery, W. H.	February 6 to June 30, 1906		1					
Moreau, A	February 15 to June 30, 1906		1					
Morrisette, F	November 4, 1905 to June 30, 1906		1					
Morrisette, J. W	July 1 to August 31, 1905		1					
Murphy, F	December 19, 1905 to June 30, 1906				1	1		
McDonald, J	July 1 to August 31, 1905			1				
McGowan, J.	February 6 to June 30, 1906		1					
Newsome, I	February 6 to June 30, 1906		1					
Nichols, J. T	February 1 to June 30, 1906		1					
Osborne, F. A	July 1, 1905 to May 30, 1906		1					
Ross, H. E	February 1 to June 30, 1906			1				
Rouleau, C. E.	February 17 to June 30, 1906		1					
Roy, C. E	July 20, 1905 to June 30, 1906			1				
Sanderson, A. E.	July 15, 1905 to June 30, 1906							1
Sangster, F. H	July 1, 1905 to April 4, 1906		1					
Stevens, D. B.	July 1, 1905 to April 30, 1906		1					
Thérien, J. F	February 6 to June 30, 1906			1				
Wiallard, R. A	July 1, 1905 to February 28, 1906	1						
Wilson, H. R.	February 6 to June 30, 1906		1					
	Totals	4	28	12	7	7	1	2

APPENDIX B—*Concluded.*

No. 9.—List of Permanent Employees of the Inland Revenue Department employed on salary during the year ended June 30, 1906—*Concluded.*

RECAPITULATION.

Employed during the year	465
" a portion of the year	54
Total	519

SERVICES.

Employed in the Inside Service	36
" Excise	339
" Weights and Measures	68
" Gas	8
" Electric Light Inspection	4
" Preventive Service	4
" Food Inspection	8
" Excise, Weights and Measures aud Gas	1
" " and Gas	11
" " and Food Inspection	9
" Weights and Measures and Gas	2
" Gas and Electric Light Inspection	18
" Excise, Gas and Electric Light Inspection	4
" Weights and Measures, Gas and Electric Light Inspection	3
" " and Excise	1
" " and Food Inspection	1
" Excise and Electric Light Inspection	1
	519

W. J. GERALD,
Deputy Minister.

Inland Revenue Department,
Ottawa, August 29, 1906.

INDEX

REPORT, RETURNS AND STATISTICS

OF THE

INLAND REVENUES

OF THE

DOMINION OF CANADA

FOR THE FISCAL YEAR ENDED JUNE 30

1906

PART II

INSPECTION OF WEIGHTS AND MEASURES, GAS AND ELECTRIC LIGHT

PRINTED BY ORDER OF PARLIAMENT

OTTAWA
PRINTED BY S. E. DAWSON, PRINTER TO THE KING'S MOST
EXCELLENT MAJESTY
1906

[No. 13—1907.]

REPORT

OF THE

DEPUTY MINISTER OF INLAND REVENUE

ON THE

INSPECTION OF WEIGHTS AND MEASURES, GAS AND ELECTRIC LIGHT

To the Honourable
The Minister of Inland Revenue.

SIR,—I have the honour to submit herewith my annual report on the inspection of weights and measures, gas and electric light, with the usual statements in connection therewith, for the fiscal year ended June 30, 1906.

1. The total revenue collected during the year for the inspection of weights and measures, was $72,979.43, as against $65,088.33 collected during the year ended June 30, 1905.

2. The total expenditure was $91,518.87 as against $90,875.87 expended during the year ended June 30, 1905.

3. Appendix 'A' gives a summary statement of the receipts and expenditures of each inspection division.

4. In Appendices 'B,' 'C' and 'D' will be found a detailed statement of weights, measures and weighing machines presented for verification, verified and rejected during the year. The number of all descriptions may be summarily stated as follows :—

—	Presented.	Verified.	Rejected.	Percentage of Rejections.
Weights, Dominion	66,239	65,679	560	0·84
Measures of capacity, Dominion	107,049	106,945	104	0·09
Lineal measures	7,161	7,108	53	0·74
Balances, equal arms	13,332	13,168	164	1·23
" steelyards	4,038	3,983	55	1·36
" platform scales	42,013	41,192	821	1·95
Miscellaneous weights	683	679	4	0·58
" measures of capacity	2,295	2,288	7	0·30
" balances	8,006	7,970	36	0·44

Inspection of Gas.

5. The total revenue collected during the fiscal year ended June 30, 1906, for the inspection of gas and gas meters, was $41,439.25, as compared with $34,552.89 collected during the year ended June 30, 1905.

6. The total expenses were $29,063.26 as against $26,044.79 expended during the year ended June 30, 1905.

7. Appendix 'E' gives a summary statement of the receipts and expenditures of each gas inspection district.

8. A statement of the illuminating power and purity of gas inspected during the year will be found in Appendix 'F.'

9. The illuminating power, where inspection has been made, has been as follows:—

Places.	Number of tests made.	Number of times below Standard.	Places.	Number of tests made.	Number of times below Standard.
Barrie	12		Stratford	12	
Belleville	14		St. Catharines	12	
Berlin	12		St. Thomas	12	
Brockville	24		Toronto	104	
Chatham	12		Windsor	12	
Cobourg	12		Woodstock	12	
Cornwall	10		Montreal	104	
Deseronto	12		Quebec	12	
Galt	6		Sherbrooke	12	
Guelph	12		St. Hyacinthe	12	
Hamilton	104		Fredericton	34	2
Ingersoll	13	1	Moncton	9	
Kingston	24		St. John, N.B	42	
Listowel	12		Halifax	12	
London	105		Yarmouth	12	
Napanee	9		Charlottetown	16	
Ottawa	26		Winnipeg	22	
Owen Sound	11		Nanaimo	12	
Peterborough	24	1	New Westminster	12	
Port Hope	11		Vancouver	12	
Sarnia	12		Victoria	11	

The revenue derived from the inspection of electric light was as follows :—

Fees for inspection of meters, &c.	$29,974 75
Registration of companies	5,125 00
	$35,099 75
The expenses of inspection (annual)	8,117 76
	$26,981 99
Expended on standard instruments, &c.	1,736 46
Leaving a net revenue of	$25,245 53

Since the year 1896–97 the two services of gas and electric light inspection, which are conducted largely by the same staff of officers have reached that point at which they have ceased to be a burden upon the general taxpayer, as shown below :—

Years.	Gas and Electric Light.	
	Revenue.	Expenditure.
	$ cts.	$ cts.
*1899-1900	35,523 50	26,424 48
*1900–01	37,536 57	28,247 20
1901–02	45,663 05	33,328 48
1902–03	49,054 55	36,006 47
1903–04	50,218 75	33,426 15
1904–05	62,561 37	34,774 02
1905-06	76,539 00	38,917 48

*Exclusive of cost of standard instruments.

The kindred service of weights and measures inspection, it will be observed, earns slightly over 79 per cent of its actual cost, the expenditure as already stated having been $91,518.87 against a revenue of $72,979.43.

Sample sets of metric weights and measures are still being supplied to educational institutions throughout the country. Up to the present time nearly 650 of these sets have been sent out from the Department.

I have the honour to be, sir,

Your obedient servant,

W. J. GERALD,

Deputy Minister.

Inland Revenue Department,

Ottawa, August 29, 1906.

APPENDIX A.

STATEMENT of Weights and Measures Expenditures and Receipts for the Year ended June 30, 1906.

Inspection Divisions.	Inspectors and Assistants.	Expenditures. Salaries.	Special Assistance.	Seizures.	Rent.	Travelling Expenses.	Sundries.	Total.	Receipts.
		$ cts.	$ cts.	$ c.	$ cts.	$ cts.	$ cts.	$ cts.	$ cts.
Belleville...	Johnson, Wm.... Slattery, T....... Irwin, S......... Errett, R. W..... Gallagher, Thos. . Johnston, C. W. .	3,682 70	358 93	5 20	300 00	1,642 84	579 92	6,569 59	4,252 45
Hamilton..	Freed, A. T...... Marentette, A.... Fitzgerald, E. W. Robins, S. W.... Laidman, R. H... Wheatley, A. E.. Jarvis, H .... McDonald, J.....	5,908 04	....	....	......	995 31	76 40	6,979 75	7,917 18
Ottawa.....	Macdonald, J. A. Macfarlane, Jas.. Breen, John...... Winsor, J. A..... Findley, R....... Scott, J	4,683 88	....	....	125 00	1,046 63	247 76	6,103 27	4,574 98
Toronto.....	Kelly, D. .... Milligan, R. J. .. Wright, R. J..... Murdoch, Jas ... Smith, J. C......	4,349 84	....	....	......	1,744 15	157 33	6,251 32	7,748 55
Windsor....	Hayward, W. J. . Hughes, R. A.... Thomas, J. S..... Coughlin, D ..... Liddle, David....	4,100 62	299 06	....	.. ..	1,567 10	330 73	6,297 51	10,559 80
	Ontario......	22,725 08	657 99	5 20	425 00	6,996 03	1,392 14	32,201 44	35,052 96

APPENDIX A—*Continued.*

STATEMENT of Weights and Measures Expenditures and Receipts for the Year ended June 30, 1906—*Continued.*

Inspection Divisions.	Inspectors and Assistants.	Expenditures. Salaries.	Special Assistance.	Seizures.	Rent.	Travelling Expenses.	Sundries.	Total.	Receipts.
		$ cts.	$ cts.	$ c.	$ cts.	$ cts.	$ cts.	$ cts.	$ cts.
Montreal. . .	Chalus, J. O..... Daoust, J. O..... Hébert, J. A. P.. Collins, D........ Boudet, E..... Beaulac, J. H.... Hall, H. C.......	5,773 16	299 06	1 00	507 00	1,881 94	254 44	8,716 60	13,354 60
Quebec.	Roy, Chs. E..... Guay, Alph...... Petit, J. B....... Kelly, M.... ... Knowles, Chs.... LeBel, J. A. W.. Préfontaine, F. H. Bourget, L. J. ...	6,343 95	600 00	....	300 00	1,371 50	315 15	8,930 60	3,934 35
St. Hyacinthe. ...	Morin, J. P. ..... Dessert, V....... Tomlinson, Wm. . Thérien, J. F.....	2,540 99	299 05	....	......	994 67	96 18	3,930 89	3,077 91
Three Rivers	Gravel, A. I . .. Bolduc, E..	1,599 96	....	....	......	699 14	13 95	2,313 05	1,488 50
	Quebec	16,258 06	1,198 11	1 00	807 00	4,947 25	679 72	23,891 14	21,855 36
St. John, N.B	Barry, James..... Cowan, E..... .. LeBlanc, F. X.... Bernier, J. A....	3,049 92	....	....	......	492 70	66 24	3,608 86	2,427 26
Cape Breton	Laurence, G. C.....	849 96	....	...	37 50	395 12	75 31	1,357 89	746 90
Halifax.....	Frame, A........ Waugh, R. J..... Sargent, W. . .	1,699 92	799 92	.. .	300 00	391 98	145 85	3,337 67	983 20
Pictou......	Dustan, Wm...... Chisholm, J. J....	1,699 96	....	....	... ..	203 06	76 08	1,979 10	782 47
	Nova Scotia.....	4,249 84	799 92	....	337 50	990 16	297 24	6,674 66	2,512 57
Charlottetown, P.E.I	Davy, E... ..... Hughes, Henry...	1,649 88	....	....	......	223 20	63 24	1,936 32	628 55
Winnipeg, Man	Magness, R.. .. McKay, R. ..... Girdlestone,R.J.M McDonald, A. W. Ross, H. E....... Mager, J. G ..... Gilby, W. F......	3,708 07	....	....	....	2,063 48	134 19	5,905 74	7,288 68
Calgary, Albta	Saucier, X...... . Costello, J. W....	999 92	....	....	....	461 15	....	1,461 07	1,303 70

APENDIX A—*Concluded.*

STATEMENT of Weights and Measures Expenditures and Receipts for the Year ended June 30, 1906—*Concluded.*

Inspection Divisions.	Inspectors and Assistants.	Expenditures. Salaries.	Special Assistance.	Seizures.	Rent.	Travelling Expenses.	Sundries.	Total.	Receipts.
		$ cts.	$ cts.	$ c.	$ cts.	$ cts.	$ cts.	$ cts.	$ cts.
Nelson.....	Parker, Thos.......	900 00	....	....	165 00	551 90	267 61	1,884 51	702 15
Vancouver..	Marshall, R......; Findley, H.......; McAloney, J. A..	2,091 85	....	....	330 00	73 80	322 12	2,817 77	726 75
Victoria....	Findley, H. ...; McAloney, J. A..	....	....	....	15 00	126 36	7 20	148 61	62 30
	British Columbia	2,991 85	....	...	510 00	752 06	596 98	4,850 89	1,491 20
Dawson, Yukon...	Macdonald, J. F....	999 96	....	....	......	155 00	59 95	1,214 91	419 15

RECAPITULATION.

Divisions.	Expenditures. Salaries.	Special Assistance.	Seizures.	Rent.	Travelling Expenses.	Sundries.	Total.	Receipts.
	$ cts.	$ cts.	$ c.	$ cts.	$ cts.	$ cts.	$ cts.	$ cts.
Ontario..............	22,725 08	657 99	5 20	425 00	6,996 03	1,392 14	32,201 44	35,052 96
Quebec..............	16,258 06	1,198 11	1 00	807 00	4,947 25	679 72	23,891 14	21,855 36
New Brunswick..........	3,049 92	....	....	....	492 70	66 24	3,608 86	2,427 26
Nova Scotia..............	4,249 84	799 92	....	337 50	990 16	297 24	6,674 66	2,512 57
Prince Edward Island.....	1,649 88	....	....	....	223 20	63 24	1,936 32	628 55
Manitoba.................	3,708 07	....	....	....	2,063 48	134 19	5,905 74	7,288 68
Alberta..................	999 92	....	....	....	461 15	....	1,461 07	1,303 70
British Columbia.........	2,991 85	....	....	510 00	752 06	596 98	4,850 89	1,491 20
Yukon..................	999 96	....	....	....	155 00	59 95	1,214 91	419 15
Chief Inspector..........	2,600 00	....	....	....	199 07	248 95	3,048 02	....
General contingencies.....	....	....	....	....	....	1,994 54	1,994 54	....
Metric system...........	....	....	....	....	....	3,138 86	3,138 86	....
Printing................	....	....	....	....	....	760 67	760 67	....
Stationery..............	....	....	....	....	....	431 81	431 81	....
Provincial allowance.......	....	....	....	....	....	399 94	399 94	....
	59,232 58	2,656 02	6 20	2,079 50	17,280 10	10,264 47	91,518 87	72,979 43

INLAND REVENUE DEPARTMENT,

OTTAWA, August 29, 1906,

W. J. GERALD,

Deputy Minister.

APPENDIX

RETURN of Weights and Measures Inspected during the Fiscal Year ended June 30, each Division, for each Province,

Inspection Divisions.	Weights.									Measures of Capacity.					
	Dominion.			Troy.			Miscellaneous			Dominion.			Miscellaneous		
	Brought for Verification.	Verified.	Rejected.	Brought for Verification.	Verified.	Rejected.	Brought for Verification.	Verified.	Rejected.	Brought for Verification.	Verified.	Rejected.	Brought for Verification.	Verified.	Rejected.
Belleville	2,744	2,744	....	....	....	....	62	62	....	6,489	6,489	....	56	56	....
Hamilton	8,999	8,964	35	....	....	....	9	9	....	3,866	3,865	1	108	105	3
Ottawa	5,826	5,746	80	....	....	....	....	....	....	2,650	2,567	83	37	37	....
Toronto	5,616	5,610	6	19	19	....	20	20	....	15,993	15,993	....	428	428	....
Windsor	4,817	4,817	....	....	....	....	....	....	....	21,040	21,040	....	2	2	....
Ontario	28,002	27,881	121	19	19	....	91	91	....	50,038	49,954	84	631	628	3
Montreal	12,778	12,749	29	1,104	1,104	....	77	77	....	29,243	29,242	1	947	943	4
Quebec	8,252	7,865	387	....	....	....	389	385	4	6,221	6,215	6	76	76	....
St. Hyacinthe	3,330	3,326	4	....	....	....	....	....	....	4,457	4,451	6	109	109	....
Three Rivers	2,583	2,583	....	....	....	....	....	....	....	2,063	2,063		18	18	....
Quebec	26,943	26,523	420	1,104	1,104	....	466	462	4	41,984	41,971	13	1,150	1,146	4
St. John, N.B.	3,718	3,718	....	11	11	....	2	2	....	5,848	5,848	....	187	187	....
Cape Breton	574	555	19	....	....	....	....	....	....	405	398	7	41	41	....
Halifax	1,077	1,077	....	....	....	....	....	....	....	977	977	....	62	62	....
Pictou	598	598	....	....	....	....	1	1	....	474	474	....	49	49	....
Nova Scotia	2,249	2,230	19	....	....	....	1	1	....	1,856	1,849	7	152	152	....
Charlottetown, P.E.I.	824	824	....	....	....	....	5	5	....	324	324	....	23	23	....
Winnipeg, Man.	2,856	2,856	..	12	12	....	13	13	....	6,166	6,166	....	125	125	....
Calgary, Alberta	432	432	....	....	....	....	....	....	....	626	626	....	26	26	....
Nelson	213	213	....	....	....	....	....	....	....	133	133	....	1	1	....
Vancouver	848	848	....	....	....	....	....	....	....	63	63	....	....	....	....
Victoria	....	....	....	....	....	....	....	....	....	11	11	....	....	....	....
British Columbia	1,061	1,061	....	....	....	....	....	....	....	207	207	....	1	1	....
Dawson, Yukon	154	154	....	114	114	....	105	105	....	....	....	....	....	....	....

B.

1906, showing the Total Number brought for Verification, Verified and Rejected, for and for the whole Dominion.

Measures of Length.			Balances, &c.											
			Equal Armed.			Steelyards.			Platform Scales, Weigh Bridges, &c.			Miscellaneous.		
Brought for Verification.	Verified.	Rejected.	Brought for Verification.	Verified.	Rejected.	Brought for Verification.	Verified.	Rejected.	Brought for Verification.	Verified.	Rejected.	Brought for Verification.	Verified.	Rejected.
303	303	... .	503	503	....	82	82	...	2,473	2,473	......	451	451	....
181	181	....	2,576	2,496	80	1,169	1,151	18	5,526	5,246	280	1,723	1,703	20
485	485	....	828	790	38	17	16	1	3,770	3,647	123	297	297	....
1,090	1,090	....	1,174	1,174	....	304	304	....	3,037	2,953	84	1,750	1,750	....
349	349	...	909	903	6	273	272	1	6,454	6,398	56	700	699	1
2,408	2,408	....	5,990	5,866	124	1,845	1,825	20	21,260	20,717	543	4,921	4,900	21
2,213	2,213	....	2,932	2,927	5	1,359	1,344	15	7,562	7,476	86	1,207	1,195	12
791	747	44	1,159	1,144	15	204	197	7	1,878	1,826	52	159	159	....
394	394	....	563	561	2	202	200	2	2,073	2,016	57	98	98	....
85	85	...	410	395	15	37	36	1	1,104	1,096	8	32	32	....
3,483	3,439	44	5,064	5,027	37	1,802	1,777	25	12,617	12,414	203	1,496	1,484	12
63	63	....	718	717	1	59	59	....	1,269	1,267	2	358	358	....
107	98	9	103	103	....	7	7	...	330	326	4	90	90	....
67	67	....	246	245	1	42	42	....	596	582	14	178	175	3
74	74	...	123	123	....	14	14	....	312	312	......	79	79	....
248	239	9	472	471	1	63	63	....	1,238	1,220	18	347	344	3
20	20	....	160	160	....	25	25	....	443	443	......	58	58	....
584	584	....	624	624	....	138	128	10	3,699	3,655	44	498	498	....
333	333	....	79	78	1	16	16	....	494	489	5	143	143	....
22	22	....	47	47	....	28	28	....	363	361	2	79	79	....
....	....	....	168	168	....	48	48	....	512	508	4	76	76	...
......	......	....	......	....	....	......	......	...	19	19	....	10	10	....
22	22	....	215	215	....	76	76	....	894	888	6	165	165	....
......	......	....	10	10	...	14	14	....	99	99	......	20	20	....

APPENDIX

RETURN of Weights and Measures Inspected during the Fiscal Year ended June 30, each Division, for each Province,

RECAPITU

Inspection Divisions.	Weights.									Measures of Capacity.					
	Dominion.			Troy.			Miscellaneous			Dominion.			Miscellaneous		
	Brought for Verification.	Verified.	Rejected.	Brought for Verification.	Verified.	Rejected.	Brought for Verification.	Verified.	Rejected.	Brought for Verification.	Verified.	Rejected.	Brought for Verification.	Verified.	Rejected.
Ontario	28,002	27,881	121	19	19	....	91	91	....	50,038	49,954	84	631	628	
Quebec	26,943	26,523	420	1,104	1,104	....	466	462	4	41,984	41,971	13	1,150	1,146	3
New Brunswick	3,718	3,718	...	11	11	....	2	2	....	5 848	5,848	....	187	187	....
Nova Scotia	2,249	2,230	19	..	....	....	1	1	....	1,856	1,849	7	152	152	....
Prince Edward Island	824	824	....	...	....	....	5	5	....	324	324	....	23	23	....
Manitoba	2,856	2,856	....	12	12	....	13	13	....	6,166	6,166	....	125	125	....
Alberta	432	432	....	....	....	....	....	....	....	626	626	....	26	26	....
British Columbia	1,061	1,061	....	....	....	....	...	....	....	207	207	....	1	1	....
Yukon	154	154	...	114	114	...	105	105	...	....	....	....	....	....	....
Totals	66,239	65,679	560	1260	1260	....	683	679	4	107,049	106,945	104	2295	2288	7

INLAND REVENUE DEPARTMENT,

OTTAWA, August 29, 1906.

B—*Concluded.*

1906, showing the Total Number brought for Verification, Verified and Rejected, for and for the whole Dominion—*Concluded.*

LATION.

Measures of Length.			Balances, &c.											
			Equal Armed.			Steelyards.			Platform Scales, Weigh Bridges, &c.			Miscellaneous.		
Brought for Verification.	Verified.	Rejected.	Brought for Verification.	Verified.	Rejected.	Brought for Verification.	Verified.	Rejected.	Brought for Verification.	Verified.	Rejected.	Brought for Verification.	Verified.	Rejected.
2,408	2,408	....	5,990	5,866	124	1,845	1,825	20	21,260	20,717	543	4,921	4,900	21
3,483	3,439	44	5,064	5,027	37	1,802	1,777	25	12,617	12,414	203	1,496	1,484	12
63	63	....	718	717	1	59	59	....	1,269	1,267	2	358	358	....
248	239	9	472	471	1	63	63	....	1,238	1,220	18	347	344	3
20	20	....	160	160	....	25	25	....	443	443	......	58	58	....
584	584	...	624	624	....	138	128	10	3,699	3,655	44	498	498	....
333	333	....	79	78	1	16	16	....	494	489	5	143	143	....
22	22	....	215	215	....	76	76	....	894	888	6	165	165	....
....	.....	....	10	10	....	14	14	....	99	99	....	20	20	....
7,161	7,108	53	13,332	13,168	164	4,038	3,983	55	42,013	41,192	821	8,006	7,970	36

W. J. GERALD,

Deputy Minister.

APPENDIX

RETURN showing the number of Dominion Weights and Lineal Measures of each Fiscal Year ended

Inspection Divisions.	Dominion													
	Avoir													
	60 lbs.	50 lbs.	30 lbs.	20 lbs.	10 lbs.	7 lbs.	5 lbs.	4 lbs.	3 lbs.	2 lbs.	1 lb.	8 ozs.	4 ozs.	2 ozs.
Ontario.														
Belleville..	....	....	....	1	12	3	78	148	286	551	532	283	249	226
Hamilton	....	81	....	2	2	5	240	142	1,549	2,694	2,650	437	346	287
Ottawa	....	1	....	1	6	15	125	174	399	559	733	699	657	617
Toronto	....	....	....	1	31	6	154	247	532	1,348	1,234	474	406	400
Windsor	....	....	....	....	10	5	79	203	434	987	914	507	470	451
Total	....	82	....	5	61	34	676	914	3,200	6,139	6,063	2,400	2,128	1,981
Quebec.														
Montreal	313	191	6	7	52	28	721	680	899	2,481	2,357	1,455	1,230	1,053
Quebec	....	55	17	36	67	229	474	721	760	1,136	1,136	1,008	1,038	845
St. Hyacinthe	....	1	....	2	6	4	215	157	455	617	572	406	362	275
Three Rivers	....	....	....	....	4	4	204	134	357	441	412	344	308	214
Total	313	247	23	45	129	265	1,614	1,692	2,471	4,675	4,477	3,213	2,938	2,387
New Brunswick.														
St. John	....	....	....	3	15	21	154	250	316	797	752	435	340	285
Nova Scotia.														
Cape Breton	....	163	1	6	7	15	54	37	63	112	89	22	4	1
Halifax	....	4	1	....	2	11	33	57	125	307	252	94	75	52
Pictou	....	....	....	....	5	3	26	35	70	145	121	54	37	36
Total	....	167	2	6	14	29	113	129	258	564	462	170	116	89
Prince Edward Island														
Charlottetown	....	....	....	....	....	1	27	29	74	207	177	81	72	65
Manitoba.														
Winnipeg	....	3	1	3	8	35	22	159	261	708	559	239	174	201
Alberta.														
Calgary	....	....	....	....	1	....	16	11	38	90	75	34	33	32
British Columbia.														
Nelson	....	....	....	....	....	1	....	7	23	46	47	19	20	19
Vancouver	....	208	7	3	4	1	7	83	20	251	210	38	9	4
Victoria	....	....	....	....	....	....	....	....	....	....	....	....	....	....
Total	....	208	7	3	4	2	7	90	43	297	257	57	29	23
Dawson	....	....	....	....	....	....	10	13	21	52	40	12	2	1

C.

Denomination presented for Verification in each Inspection Division during the June 30, 1906—*Continued.*

Weights.									Lineal Measures.											
dupois.							Troy Weights.	Miscellaneous Weights.												Miscellaneous Measures.
1 oz.	8 drs.	4 drs.	2 drs.	1 dr.	½ dr.	Total Number.			6 feet.	5 feet.	1 yard.	½ yard.	2 feet.	1 foot.	½ foot.	100 feet chains.	66 feet chains.	Tape or riband.	Total Number.	
194	115	53	10	3	....	2,744	.....	62	...	..	303	..	..	..	..	..	..	..	303	.....
321	185	48	4	4	2	8,999	.....	9	....	....	181	..	..	..	..	..	..	..	181	......
694	615	517	9	5	....	5,826	.....	.....	....	....	485	..	..	..	..	..	..	..	485	......
404	221	94	27	37	..	5,616	19	20	....	....	1,090	..	..	..	..	..	..	..	1,090	.. ...
385	236	106	21	8	1	4,817	.....	.. ...	....	....	349	..	..	..	..	..	..	..	349	......
1,998	1,372	818	71	57	3	28,002	19	91	....	....	2,408	..	..	..	..	..	..	..	2,408	.. ...
706	322	126	61	84	6	12,778	1,104	77	....	....	2,213	..	..	..	..	..	..	..	2,213	.....
468	220	37	3	2	. .	8,252	.....	389	....	....	791	..	..	..	..	..	..	..	791	.....
186	58	10	3	1	....	3,330	.....	.....	....	....	394	..	..	..	..	..	..	..	394	......
127	30	3	1	....	....	2,583	....	.....	....	...	85	..	..	..	..	..	..	..	85	. .
1,487	630	176	68	87	6	26,943	1,104	466	...	....	3,483	..	..	..	..	..	..	..	3,483	......
231	81	33	5	....	....	3,718	11	2	....	...	63	..	..	..	..	..	..	..	63	.....
......	...	....	....	....	....	574	....	.....	....	....	107	..	..	..	..	..	..	..	107	......
39	17	6	2	...	....	1,077	.....	......	....	..	67	..	..	..	..	..	..	..	67	......
32	20	7	3	4	....	598	.....	1	....	....	74	..	..	..	..	..	..	..	74	......
71	37	13	5	4	....	2,249	.....	1	....	....	248	..	..	..	..	..	..	..	248	......
55	25	7	2	2	....	824	....	5	....	...	20	..	..	..	..	..	..	..	20	.....
191	111	90	53	37	1	2,856	12	13	....	...	584	..	..	..	..	..	..	..	584	.....
32	27	22	9	12	....	432	... ..	.....	....	....	333	..	..	..	..	..	..	..	333	....
16	9	5	1	....	....	213	.....	....	....	....	22	..	..	..	..	..	..	..	22	......
3	......	...	. ..	....	....	848	.. .	... .	....	....	......	..	..	..	..	..	..	..	......	.....
....	.....	....	....	. ..	....	....	.....	......	....	....	......	..	..	..	..	..	..	..	......	......
19	9	5	1	....	.. .	1,061	.....	...	....	....	22	..	..	..	..	..	..	..	22	
1	2	....	....	....	....	154	114	105	....	....	......	..	..	..	..	..	..	..	....	..

APPENDIX

RETURN showing the Number of Dominion Weights and Lineal Measures of each ended June

INSPECTION DIVISIONS.	DOMINION — Avoir													
	60 lbs.	50 lbs.	30 lbs.	20 lbs.	10 lbs.	7 lbs.	5 lbs.	4 lbs.	3 lbs.	2 lbs.	1 lb.	8 ozs.	4 ozs.	2 ozs.
Ontario.														
Belleville	....	....	....	1	12	3	78	148	286	551	532	283	249	226
Hamilton	....	81	....	2	2	5	239	140	1,547	2,691	2,646	431	342	283
Ottawa	...	1	....	1	6	14	114	168	377	548	711	694	655	617
Toronto	....	....	....	1	31	6	154	246	532	1,347	1,232	472	406	400
Windsor	....	....	...	....	10	5	79	203	434	987	914	507	470	451
Totals	....	82	...	5	61	33	664	905	3,176	6,124	6,035	2,387	2,122	1,977
Quebec.														
Montreal	313	191	6	7	52	28	719	680	895	2,477	2,352	1,449	1,226	1,050
Quebec	....	55	17	36	62	218	446	685	720	1,082	1,074	953	987	816
St. Hyacinthe	....	1	....	2	6	4	215	156	455	616	571	405	362	275
Three Rivers	....	....	....	....	4	4	204	134	357	441	412	344	308	214
Totals	313	247	23	45	124	254	1,584	1,655	2,427	4,616	4,409	3,151	2,883	2,355
New Brunswick.														
St. John	....	....	....	3	15	21	154	250	316	797	752	435	340	285
Nova Scotia.														
Cape Breton	....	163	....	6	7	12	50	33	62	109	86	22	4	1
Halifax	....	4	1	....	2	11	33	57	125	307	252	94	75	52
Pictou	....	....	....	....	5	3	26	35	70	145	121	54	37	36
Totals		167	1	6	14	26	109	125	257	561	459	170	116	89
P. E. I. Island.														
Charlottetown	....	....	....	....	....	1	27	29	74	207	177	81	72	65
Manitoba.														
Winnipeg	....	3	1	3	8	35	22	159	261	708	559	239	174	201
Calgary, Alberta	...	....	....	...	1	....	16	11	38	90	75	34	33	32
British Columbia.														
Nelson	....	....	....	....	....	1	....	7	23	46	47	19	20	19
Vancouver	....	208	7	3	4	1	7	83	20	251	210	38	9	4
Victoria	....	....	....	....	....	....	....	....	....	....	....	....	....	....
Totals	....	208	7	3	4	2	7	90	43	297	257	57	29	23
Dawson, Yukon	....	....	....	....	....	....	10	13	21	52	40	12	2	1

C—*Continued.*

Denomination, Verified in each Inspection Division during the Fiscal Year 30, 1906—*Continued.*

Weights.									Lineal Measures.											
dupois.							Troy Weights.	Miscellaneous Weights.												Miscellaneous Measures.
1 oz.	8 drs.	4 drs.	2 drs.	1 dr.	½ dr.	Total Number.			6 feet.	5 feet.	1 yard.	½ yard.	2 feet.	1 foot.	½ foot.	100 feet chain.	66 feet chain.	Tape or Riband.	Total Number.	
194	115	53	10	3	....	2,744	....	62	....	....	303	..	..	..	..	..	..	..	303	....
315	183	47	4	4	2	8,964	....	9	....	....	181	..	..	..	..	..	..	..	181	....
694	615	517	9	5	....	5,746	....	....	....	....	485	..	..	..	..	..	..	..	485	....
404	221	94	27	37	....	5,610	19	20	....	....	1,090	..	..	..	..	..	..	..	1,090	....
385	236	106	21	8	1	4,817	....	....	....	....	349	..	..	..	..	..	..	..	349	....
1,992	1,370	817	71	57	3	27,881	19	91	....	....	2,408	..	..	..	..	..	..	..	2,408	....
705	322	126	61	84	6	12,749	1,104	77	....	....	2,213	..	..	..	..	..	..	..	2,213	....
454	218	37	3	2	....	7,865	....	385	....	....	747	..	..	..	..	..	..	..	747	....
186	58	10	3	1	....	3,326	....	....	....	....	394	..	..	..	..	..	..	..	394	....
127	30	3	1	....	....	2,583	....	....	....	....	85	..	..	..	..	..	..	..	85	....
1,472	628	176	68	87	6	26,523	1,104	462	....	....	3,439	..	..	..	..	..	..	..	3,439	....
231	81	33	5	....	....	3,718	11	2	....	....	63	..	..	..	..	..	..	..	63	....
....	....	....	....	....	....	555	....	....	....	....	98	..	..	..	..	..	..	..	98	....
39	17	6	2	....	....	1,077		....	....	....	67	..	..	..	..	..	..	..	67	....
32	20	7	3	4	....	598	....	1	....	....	74	..	..	..	..	..	..	..	74	....
71	37	13	5	4	....	2,230	....	1	....	....	239	..	..	..	..	..	..	..	239	....
55	25	7	2	2	....	824	....	5	....	....	20	..	..	..	..	..	..	..	20	....
191	111	90	53	37	1	2,856	12	13	....	....	584	..	..	..	..	..	..	..	584	....
32	27	22	9	12	....	432	....	....	....	....	333	..	..	..	..	..	..	..	333	....
16	9	5	1	....	....	213	....	....	....	....	22	..	..	..	..	..	..	..	22	....
3	....	....	....	....	....	848	....	....	....	....	....	..	..	..	..	..	..	..	....	....
19	9	5	1	....	..	1,061	....	....	....	....	....	..	..	..	..	..	..	..	....	....
1	2	....	....	....	....	154	114	105	....	....	....	..	..	..	..	..	..	..	....	....

APPENDIX

RETURN showing the Number of Dominion Weights and Lineal Measures of each
June, 30,

Inspection Divisions.	Dominion													
	Avoir													
	60 lbs.	50 lbs.	30 lbs.	20 lbs.	10 lbs.	7 lbs.	5 lbs.	4 lbs.	3 lbs.	2 lbs.	1 lb.	8 ozs.	4 ozs.	2 ozs.
Ontario.														
Belleville	....	....	....	....	....	....	....	....	....	....	....	....	....	....
Hamilton	....	....	....	....	....	....	1	2	2	3	4	6	4	4
Ottawa	....	....	....	....	....	1	11	6	22	11	22	5	2	....
Toronto	....	....	....	....	....	....	....	1	....	1	2	2	....	....
Windsor	....	....	....	....	....	....	....	....	....	....	....	....	....	....
Totals	....	....	....	....	....	1	12	9	24	15	28	13	6	4
Quebec.														
Montreal	....	....	....	....	....	....	2	....	4	4	5	6	4	3
Quebec	....	....	....	....	5	11	28	36	40	54	62	55	51	29
St. Hyacinthe	....	....	....	....	....	....	....	1	....	1	1	1	....	....
Three Rivers	....	....	....	....	....	....	....	....	....	....	....	....	....	....
Totals	....	....	....	....	5	11	30	37	44	59	68	62	55	32
New Brunswick.														
St. John	....	....	....	....	....	....	....	....	....	....	....	....	....	....
Nova Scotia.														
Cape Breton	....	....	1	....	....	3	4	4	1	3	3	....	....	....
Halifax	....	....	....	....	....	....	....	....	....	....	....	....	....	....
Pictou	....	....	....	....	....	....	....	....	....	....	....	....	....	....
Prince Edward Island.														
Charlottetown	....	....	....	....	....	....	....	....	....	....	....	....	....	....
Manitoba.														
Winnipeg	....	....	....	....	....	....	....	....	....	....	....	....	....	....
Calgary, Alberta	....	....	....	....	....	....	....	....	....	....	....	....	....	....
British Columbia.														
Nelson	....	....	....	....	....	....	....	....	....	....	....	....	....	....
Vancouver	....	....	....	....	....	....	....	....	....	....	....	....	....	....
Victoria	....	....	....	....	....	....	....	....	....	....	....	....	....	....
Dawson, Yukon	....	....	....	....	....	....	....	....	....	....	....	....	....	....

INLAND REVENUE DEPARTMENT,

OTTAWA, August 29, 1906.

C—*Concluded.*

Denomination, Rejected in each Inspection Division during the Fiscal Year ended 1906—*Concluded.*

Weights.									Lineal Measures.											
dupois.																				
1 oz.	8 drs.	4 drs.	2 drs.	1 dr.	½ dr.	Total number.	Troy Weights.	Miscellaneous Weights.	6 feet.	5 feet.	1 yard.	½ yard.	2 feet.	1 foot.	½ foot.	100 feet chains.	66 feet chains.	Tape or riband.	Total number.	Miscellaneous Measures.
6	2	1	....	....	....	35	....	....	....	....	....	....	....	....	....	....	....	....	....	....
....	....	....	....	....	....	80	....	....	....	....	....	....	....	....	....	....	....	....	....	....
....	....	....	....	....	....	6	....	....	....	....	....	....	....	....	....	....	....	....	....	....
....	....	....	....	....	....	....	....	....	....	....	....	....	....	....	....	....	....	....	....	....
6	2	1	....	....	....	121	....	....	....	....	....	....	....	....	....	....	....	....	....	....
1	....	....	....	....	....	29	....	....	....	....	....	....	....	....	....	....	....	....	....	....
14	2	....	....	....	....	387	....	4	....	....	44	....	....	....	....	....	....	....	44	....
....	....	....	....	....	....	4	....	....	....	....	....	....	....	....	....	....	....	....	....	....
....	....	....	....	....	....	....	....	....	....	....	....	....	....	....	....	....	....	....	....	....
15	2	....	....	....	....	420	....	4	....	....	44	....	....	....	....	....	....	....	44	....
....	....	....	....	....	....	....	....	....	....	....	....	....	....	....	....	....	....	....	....	....
....	....	....	....	....	....	19	....	....	....	....	9	....	....	....	....	....	....	....	9	....
....	....	....	....	....	....	....	....	....	....	....	....	....	....	....	....	....	....	....	....	....
....	....	....	....	....	....	....	....	....	....	....	....	....	....	....	....	....	....	....	....	....
....	....	....	....	....	....	....	....	....	....	....	....	....	....	....	....	....	....	....	....	....
....	....	....	....	....	....	....	....	....	....	....	....	....	....	....	....	....	....	....	....	....
....	....	....	....	....	....	....	....	....	....	....	....	....	....	....	....	....	....	....	....	....
....	....	....	....	....	....	....	....	....	....	....	....	....	....	....	....	....	....	....	....	....
....	....	....	....	....	....	....	....	....	....	....	....	....	....	....	....	....	....	....	....	....
....	....	....	....	....	....	....	....	....	....	....	....	....	....	....	....	....	....	....	....	....
....	....	....	....	....	....	....	....	....	....	....	....	....	....	....	....	....	....	....	....	....

W. J. GERALD,
Deputy Minister.

APPEN

RETURN showing the Number of Dominion Measures of Capacity, Balances and Weighing during the Fiscal Year

Inspection Divisions.	Measures of Capacity.												
	Dominion.												
	Bushel.	½ Bushel.	Peck.	Gallon.	½ Gallon.	Quart.	Pint.	½ Pint.	Gill.	½ Gill.	Total Number.	Miscellaneous.	5 lbs. and under.
Ontario.													
Belleville	185	653	632	1,050	1,082	1,585	1,053	243	6	....	6,489	56	170
Hamilton	5	59	165	533	467	1,484	1,073	74	4	2	3,866	108	1,347
Ottawa	......	6	51	483	766	664	496	158	25	1	2,650	37	522
Toronto	220	212	575	1,986	2,655	3,357	5,668	1,297	23	....	15,993	428	509
Windsor	1,364	1,080	1,096	2,565	3,189	5,212	5,480	1,054	....	....	21,040	2	426
Totals	1,774	2,010	2,519	6,617	8,159	12,302	13,770	2,826	58	3	50,038	631	2,974
Quebec.													
Montreal	12	917	1,323	3,573	4,566	7,662	8,040	2,647	464	39	29,243	947	1,147
Quebec	13	258	302	986	1,439	1,397	1,231	510	85	....	6,221	76	203
St. Hyacinthe	22	150	256	708	1,098	1,126	701	317	79	....	4,457	109	122
Three Rivers	...	26	28	282	571	577	367	190	22	...	2,063	18	62
Totals	47	1,351	1,909	5,549	7,674	10,762	10,339	3,664	650	39	41,984	1150	1,534
New Brunswick.													
St. John	......	393	363	919	1,676	1,293	1,046	126	32	....	5,848	187	187
Nova Scotia.													
Cape Breton	2	.....	1	59	180	118	39	6	....	...	405	41	30
Halifax	4	3	31	209	302	256	103	56	8	....	977	62	66
Pictou	......	18	14	58	160	130	47	46	1	....	474	49	34
Totals	6	26	46	326	642	504	189	108	9	....	1,856	152	130
P. E. Island.													
Charlottetown	.....	.....	.....	13	55	139	97	20	...	....	324	23	50
Manitoba.													
Winnipeg	50	40	14	1,212	1,911	1,653	1,163	123	....	....	6,166	125	177
Calgary, Alberta	7	4	.. ..	148	219	154	84	10	....	....	626	26	39
British Columbia.													
Ne son	.....	......	1	29	43	41	18	1	....	...	133	1	26
Vancouver	.....	......	......	3	6	25	28	1	....	....	63	....	73
Victoria	.. .	......	......	. ..	2	3	4	2	....	....	11	....	.... .
Totals	.....	.....	1	32	51	69	50	4	....	...	207	1	99
Dawson, Yukon	....	. ..	.....	.....	... .	. ..	.....	......	....	. ..	....	...	3

DIX D.

Machines of each Denomination, Presented for Verification, in each Inspection Division, ended June 30, 1906.

BALANCES.

With equal arms.			Steel Yards with Divided Arms.				Weigh Bridges or Platform Scales.							
6 lbs. to 50 lbs.	51 lbs. to 100 lbs.	101 lbs. and upwards.	500 lbs. and under.	61 lbs. to 1,000 lbs.	1,001 lbs. to 2,000 lbs.	2,001 lbs. and upwards.	250 lbs. and under.	251 lbs. to 500 lbs.	501 lbs. to 2,000 lbs.	2,001 lbs. to 4,000 lbs.	4,001 lbs. to 6,000 lbs.	6,001 lbs. and upwards.	Total.	Miscellaneous.
333	....	....	74	3	2	3	833	197	960	155	73	255	3,058	451
1,229	....	....	1,153	14	1	1	3,212	92	1,622	213	78	309	9,271	1,723
304	2	....	16	1	....	....	825	153	2,593	48	50	101	4,615	297
665	....	....	278	17	6	3	1,088	136	1,027	321	82	383	4,515	1,750
483	....	....	271	1	1	....	920	106	4,599	301	68	460	7,636	700
3,014	2	....	1,792	36	10	7	6,878	684	10,801	1,038	351	1,508	29,095	4,921
1,769	10	6	1,317	20	....	22	3,109	1,166	2,545	225	167	350	11,853	1,207
895	5	56	169	35	....	....	717	612	436	19	13	81	3,241	159
441	....	....	201	....	1	....	717	456	651	35	81	133	2,838	98
348	....	....	37	....	....	....	364	359	333	13	19	16	1,551	32
3,453	15	62	1,724	55	1	22	4,907	2,593	3,965	292	280	580	19,483	1,496
530	1	....	56	1	2	....	552	260	337	29	19	72	2,046	358
71	....	2	7	....	....	....	173	43	63	2	6	43	440	90
178	1	1	41	1	....	....	317	72	121	12	9	65	884	178
88	....	1	13	....	1	....	137	52	65	11	12	35	449	79
337	1	4	61	1	1	....	627	167	249	25	27	143	1,773	347
109	1	....	24	....	....	1	132	41	225	18	14	13	628	58
444	3	....	133	4	....	1	1,052	55	820	287	782	703	4,461	498
40	....	....	11	2	3	....	137	12	203	18	25	99	589	143
21	....	....	20	4	4	....	139	10	156	11	3	44	438	79
95	....	....	35	8	5	....	234	25	201	28	5	19	728	76
....	....	....	....	....	....	....	7	....	6	1	....	5	19	10
116	....	....	55	12	9	....	380	35	363	40	8	68	1,185	165
....	7	....	1	3	10	....	40	6	46	2	1	4	123	20

APPENDIX

RETURN showing the Number of Dominion Measures of Capacity, Balances and Weighing ended June

Inspection Divisions.	Measures of Capacity.												
	Dominion.												
	Bushel.	½ bushel.	Peck.	Gallon.	½ gallon.	Quart.	Pint.	½ pint.	Gill.	½ Gill.	Total Number.	Miscellaneous.	5 lbs. and under.
Ontario.													
Belleville	185	653	632	1,050	1,082	1,585	1,053	243	6	....	6,489	56	170
Hamilton	5	59	165	533	466	1,484	1,073	74	4	2	3,865	105	1,335
Ottawa	....	5	45	453	746	658	477	157	25	1	2,567	37	499
Toronto	220	212	575	1,986	2,655	3,357	5,668	1,297	23	....	15,993	428	509
Windsor	1,364	1,080	1,096	2,565	3,189	5,212	5,480	1,054	....	....	21,040	2	423
Totals	1,774	2,009	2,513	6,587	8,138	12,296	13,751	2,825	58	3	49,954	628	2,936
Quebec.													
Montreal	12	917	1,322	3,573	4,566	7,662	8,040	2,647	464	39	29,242	943	1,145
Quebec	13	258	302	983	1,439	1,396	1,229	510	85	....	6,215	76	200
St. Hyacinthe	22	149	253	707	1,097	1,126	701	317	79	....	4,451	109	122
Three Rivers	.....	26	28	282	571	577	367	190	22	....	2,063	18	58
Totals	47	1,350	1,905	5,545	7,673	10,761	10,337	3,664	650	39	41,971	1146	1,525
New Brunswick.													
St. John	......	393	363	919	1,676	1,293	1,046	126	32	....	5,848	187	187
Nova Scotia.													
Cape Breton	2	.....	1	59	175	116	39	6	...	....	398	41	30
Halifax	4	8	31	209	302	256	103	56	8	....	977	62	66
Pictou	......	18	14	58	160	130	47	46	1	....	474	49	34
Totals	6	26	46	326	637	502	189	108	9	....	1,849	152	130
P. E. Island.													
Charlottetown	......	......	......	13	55	139	97	20	....	....	324	23	50
Manitoba.													
Winnipeg	50	40	14	1,212	1,911	1,653	1,163	123	....	....	6,166	125	177
Calgary, Alberta	7	4	..	148	219	154	84	10	....	....	626	26	39
British Columbia.													
Nelson	... .	......	1	29	43	41	18	1	....	....	133	....	26
Vancouver	......	......	......	3	6	25	28	1	....	....	63	1	73
Victoria	... .	..	.....	......	2	3	4	2	....	....	11	....	...
Totals	... ..	....	1	32	51	69	50	4	...	....	207	1	99
Dawson, Yukon	.....	.....	......	......	......	......	......	....	....	....	....	. .	3

D.—*Continued.*

Machines of each Denomination, Verified, in each Inspection, during the Fiscal Year 30, 1906.

BALANCES.

With Equal Arms.			Steel Yards with Divided Arms.				Weigh Bridges or Platform Scales.						Total.	Miscellaneous Balances.
6 lbs. to 50 lbs.	51 lbs. to 100 lbs.	101 lbs. and upwards.	500 lbs. and under.	501 lbs. to 1,000 lbs.	1,001 lbs. to 2,000 lbs.	2,001 lbs. and upwards.	250 lbs. and under.	251 lbs. to 500 lbs.	501 lbs. to 2,000 lbs.	2,001 lbs. to 4,000 lbs.	4,001 lbs. to 6,000 lbs.	6,001 lbs. and upwards.		
333	.....	.....	74	3	2	3	833	197	960	155	73	255	3,058	451
1,161	.....	.....	1,135	14	1	1	3,151	80	1,491	186	71	267	8,893	1,703
290	1	.....	15	1	.....	.....	787	144	2,545	40	43	88	4,453	297
665	.....	.....	278	17	6	3	1,078	132	1,002	313	77	351	4,431	1,750
480	..	..	270	1	1	.....	908	102	4,576	299	66	447	7,573	699
2,929	1	.....	1,772	36	10	7	6,757	655	10,574	993	330	1,408	28,408	4,900
1,766	10	6	1,302	20	.....	22	3,099	1,157	2,521	220	152	327	11,747	1,195
884	5	55	164	33	.....	.....	706	593	420	18	13	76	3,167	159
439	.....	.....	199	.....	1	.....	704	437	639	34	75	127	2,777	98
337	.....	.....	36	.....	.....	.....	361	358	330	13	18	16	1,527	32
3,426	15	61	1,701	53	1	22	4,870	2,545	3,910	285	258	546	19,218	1,484
529	1	.....	56	1	2	.....	552	260	335	29	19	72	2,043	358
71	.....	2	7	.....	.....	.....	170	42	63	2	6	43	436	90
177	1	1	41	1	.....	.....	317	69	116	12	8	60	869	175
88	.....	1	13	..	1	.....	137	52	65	11	12	35	449	79
336	1	4	61	1	1	....	624	163	244	25	26	138	1,754	344
109	1	.....	24	.....	.....	1	132	41	225	18	14	13	628	58
444	3	.....	123	4	.....	1	1,047	54	810	282	773	689	4,407	498
39	.....	.....	11	2	3	....	136	12	201	18	25	97	583	143
21	.....	.....	20	4	4	.....	139	10	155	11	3	43	436	79
95	.....	.....	35	8	5	.....	234	25	200	27	5	17	724	76
.....	.....	....	.....	..	....	.....	7	..	6	1	.....	5	19	10
116	.....	....	55	12	9	.....	380	35	361	39	8	65	1,179	165
....	7	.....	1	3	10	.....	40	6	46	2	1	4	123	20

APPENDIX

RETURN showing the Number of Dominion Measures of Capacity, Balances and during the Fiscal Year

Inspection Divisions.	Measure of Capacity.												
	Dominion.												
	Bushel.	½ Bushel.	Peck.	Gallon.	½ Gallon.	Quart.	Pint.	½ Pint.	Gill.	½ Gill.	Total Number.	Miscellaneous.	5 lbs. and under.
Ontario.													
Belleville	....	....	....	....	....	....	....	....	....	....	....	....	....
Hamilton	....	....	....	....	1	....	....	....	....	....	1	3	12
Ottawa	....	1	6	30	20	6	19	1	....	....	83	...	23
Toronto	....	....	....	....	....	....	....	....	....	....	....	....	....
Windsor	....	....	....	....	....	....	....	....	....	....	....	....	3
Totals	....	1	6	30	21	6	19	1	...	....	84	3	38
Quebec.													
Montreal	....	....	1	....	....	....	....	....	....	....	1	4	2
Quebec	....	....	....	3	....	1	2	....	....	....	6	....	3
St. Hyacinthe	....	1	3	1	1	....	....	.	....	....	6	....	....
Three Rivers	....	....	....	....	....	....	....	....	....	....	....	...	4
Totals	....	1	4	4	1	1	2	....	....	....	13	4	9
New Brunswick.													
St. John	....	....	....	....	....	....	....	....	....	....	....	....	....
Nova Scotia.													
Cape Breton	....	....	....	....	5	2	...	....	...	....	7	....	....
Halifax	....	....	....	....	....	....	....	....	...	....	....	....	....
Pictou	....	....	....	....	...	....	....	....	...	....	....	....	....
Totals	....	....	....	....	5	2	....	...	..	....	7	...	....
P. E. Island.													
Charlottetown	....	....	....	....	....	....	....	....	..	...	....	....	....
Manitoba.													
Winnipeg	....	....	....	....	....	....	...	....	....	....	....	....	....
N. W. Territories.													
Calgary, Alberta	....	....	..	....	....	....	....	....	....	....	....	....	....
British Columbia.													
Nelson	....	....	....	....	....	....	....	....	....	....	....	....	....
Vancouver	....	....	....	....	....	....	....	....	....	....	....	....	....
Victoria	....	....	....	....	....	....	....	....	....	....	....	....	....
Dawson, Yukon	....	....	....	....	....	....	....	....	....	....	....	....	....
Totals	....	....	....	....	....	....	....	....	....	....	....	....	....

INLAND REVENUE DEPARTMENT,
OTTAWA, August 29, 1906.

D—*Concluded.*

Weighing Machines of each Denomination, Rejected in each Inspection Division, ended June 30, 1906.

Balances.														
With Equal Arms.			Steel Yards with Divided Arms.				Weigh Bridges and Platform Scales.							
6 lbs. to 50 lbs.	51 lbs. to 100 lbs.	101 lbs. and upwards.	500 lbs. and under.	501 lbs. to 1,000 lbs.	1,001 lbs. to 2,000 lbs.	2,001 lbs. and upwards.	250 lbs. and under.	251 lbs. to 500 lbs.	501 lbs. to 2,000 lbs.	2,001 lbs. to 4,000 lbs.	4,001 lbs. to 6,000 lbs.	6,001 lbs. and upwards.	Total.	Miscellaneous.
....	....	....	....	....	....	....	....	....	....	....	....	....	....	....
68	....	....	18	....	....	....	61	12	131	27	7	42	378	20
14	1	....	1	....	....	....	38	9	48	8	7	13	162	....
....	....	....	....	....	....	....	10	4	25	8	5	32	84	....
3	....	....	1	....	....	....	12	4	23	2	2	13	63	1
85	1	....	20	....	....	....	121	29	227	45	21	100	687	21
3	....	....	15	....	....	....	10	9	24	5	15	23	106	12
11	....	1	5	2	....	....	11	19	16	1	....	5	74	....
2	....	....	2	....	....	....	13	19	12	1	6	6	61	....
11	....	....	1	....	....	....	3	1	3	....	1	....	24	....
27	....	1	23	2	....	....	37	48	55	7	22	34	265	12
1	....	....	....	2	....	....	....	....	....	....	....	....	3	....
....	....	....	....	....	....	....	3	1	....	....	....	....	4	....
1	....	....	....	....	....	....	....	3	5	....	1	5	15	3
....	....	....	....	....	....	....	....	....	....	....	....	....	....	....
1	....	....	....	....	....	....	3	4	5	....	1	5	19	3
....	....	....	....	....	....	....	....	....	....	....	....	....	....	....
....	....	....	10	....	....	....	5	1	10	5	9	14	54	....
1	....	....	....	....	....	....	1	....	2	....	....	2	6	....
....	....	....	....	....	....	....	....	....	1	....	....	1	2	....
....	....	....	....	....	....	....	....	....	1	1	....	2	4	....
....	....	....	....	....	....	....	....	....	....	....	....	....	....	....
....	....	....	....	....	....	....	....	....	....	....	....	....	....	....
....	....	....	....	....	....	....	....	....	2	1	....	3	6	....

W. J. GERALD,
Deputy Minister.

APPENDIX E.

STATEMENT of Gas Expenditures, and Receipts for the Year ended June 30, 1906.

Districts.	Inspectors.	Expenditures.						Receipts.
		Salaries.	Special Assistance.	Rent.	Travelling Expenses.	Sundries.	Totals.	
		$ cts.	$ cts.	$ cts.	$ cts.	$ cts.	$ cts.	$ cts.
Barrie	Shanacy, M.	100 00	....	......	......	......	100 00	176 50
Belleville	Johnson, Wm. Stuart, W.E.	449 96	....	100 00	......	......	549 96	285 00
Berlin	Broadfoot, S.	100 00	......	......	31 80	20 09	151 89	334 25
Brockville	Johnston, Chas. W.	....	58 31	......	......	17 55	75 86	345 50
Cobourg	Bickle, J. W.	100 00	......	......	32 15	29 00	161 15	178 00
Cornwall	Mulhern, M. M	100 00	......	......	......	37 45	137 45	47 75
Guelph	Broadfoot, S.	200 00	......	......	......	13 15	213 15	421 50
Hamilton	McPhie, D. McPhie, W. H. Murphy, F. C. Dennis, W. A.	2,920 88	.....	120 00	376 95	127 13	3,544 96	9,829 25
Kingston	Gallagher, T.	400 00	....	45 00	......	50 35	495 35	538 25
Listowel	Male, Thos.	100 00	......	78 00	......	14 99	192 99	47 50
London	Nash, A. F. Folley, L. R	1,591 66	24 00	....	213 45	75 15	1,904 26	3,043 00
Napanee	Johnson, Wm. (acting.)	....	......	......	28 85	1 50	30 35	42 00
Ottawa	Roche, H. G Bond, M. B.	1,169 96	540 00	300 00	......	70 45	2,080 41	971 25
Owen Sound	Graham, W. J.	199 92	......	125 00	......	...	324 92	118 25
Peterborough	Rork, Thos.	150 00	...	......	9 10	2 00	161 10	143 50
Sarnia	Thrasher, W. A.	....	......	......	6 90	6 00	12 90	441 00
Stratford	Rennie, Geo.	200 00	......	......	.....	15 00	215 00	191 00
Toronto	Johnstone, J. K. Pape, Jas. Whyte, J. A. Hunter, W. M.	4,199 84	......	......	12 60	61 84	4,274 28	10,599 75
	Ontario.	11,982 22	622 31	768 00	711 80	541 65	14,625 98	27,753 25
Montreal	Aubin, A. O'Flaherty, M. J Aubin, Chas.	3,299 88	....	240 00	53 25	169 20	3,762 33	8,605 50
Quebec	LeVasseur, N. Moreau, J. A.	1,500 00	......	150 00	......	20 40	1,670 40	384 50
Sherbrooke	Simpson, A. F.	150 00	......	......	.. ..	......	150 00	181 00
St. Hyacinthe	Benoit, L. V.	100 00	....	......	......	......	100 00	128 00
	Quebec.	5,049 88	......	390 00	53 25	189 60	5,682 73	9,299 00
Fredericton	Fowler. J. D.	183 26					183 26	153 00
St. John	Wilson, J. E.	1,100 00	.....	......	91 06	9 86	1,200 92	642 50
	New Brunswick	1,283 26	......	......	91 06	9 86	1,384 18	795 50
Halifax, N.S.	Miller, A. Ritchie, A. J Cotter, W. F. Munro, H. D	1,992 39	.....	300 00	253 41	92 60	2,638 40	378 00
Charlottetown, P.E.I	Bell, J. H	450 00	......	..	......	......	450 00	71 50
Winnipeg, Man.	Magness, R. Mager, J. G.	999 96	.. ..	.. .	200 55	69 33	1,269 84	1,437 50
Nanaimo	McAloney, J. A	100 00	.....	.. .	.....	... .	100 00	38 00
New Westminster	Wolfenden, Wm.	100 00	......	......	......	... .	100 00	61 75
Vancouver	Miller, J. E.	300 00	......	......	146 20	234 50	680 70	1,123 75
Victoria	Jones, R	200 00	....	......	......	......	200 00	481 00
	British Columbia.	700 00	......	.....	146 20	234 50	1,080 70	1,704 50

APPENDIX E—*Concluded.*

STATEMENT of Gas Expenditures and Receipts for the Year ended June 30, 1906.

RECAPITULATION.

Provinces.	Expenditures.						Receipts.
	Salaries.	Special Assistance.	Rent.	Travelling Expenses.	Sundries.	Totals.	
	$ cts.	$ cts.	$ cts.	$ cts.	$ cts.	$ cts.	$ cts.
Ontario	11,982 22	622 31	768 00	711 80	541 65	14,625 98	27,753 25
Quebec	5,049 88	....	390 00	53 25	189 60	5,682 73	9,299 00
New Brunswick	1,283 26	....	....	91 06	9 86	1,384 18	795 50
Nova Scotia	1,992 39	....	300 00	253 41	92 60	2,638 40	378 00
Prince Edward Island	450 00	....	....	....	....	450 00	71 50
Manitoba	999 96	....	....	200 55	69 33	1,269 84	1,437 50
British Columbia	700 00	....	....	146 20	234 50	1,080 70	1,704 50
Chief Inspector	100 00	....	....	....	....	100 00	....
General expenses	....	....	....	....	731 79	731 79	....
Printing	....	....	....	....	794 35	794 35	....
Stationery	....	....	....	....	274 89	274 89	....
Technical translation	....	....	....	....	30 40	30 40	....
	22,557 71	622 31	1,458 00	1,456 27	2,968 97	29,063 26	41,439 25

W. J. GERALD,

Deputy Minister.

INLAND REVENUE DEPARTMENT,

OTTAWA, August 29, 1906.

APPEN

RETURN of the Illuminating Power and Purity of Gas

Inspection Offices.	Illuminating Power.					Sulphur per 100		
	Highest.	Lowest.	Average.	No. of times below standard.	No. of Tests.	Highest	Lowest.	Average
	Candles.	Candles.	Candles.			Grains.	Grains.	Grains.
Barrie—								
July	....	....	18·50	0	1	....	....	....
August	....	....	19·80	0	1	....	....	....
September	....	....	19·50	0	1	....	....	....
October	....	....	19·00	0	1	....	....	....
November	....	....	16·02	0	1	....	....	....
December	....	....	16·30	0	1	....	....	....
January	....	....	18·50	0	1	....	....	....
Februury	....	....	19 30	0	1	....	....	....
March	....	....	16·30	0	1	....	....	....
April	....	....	18·02	0	1	....	....	....
May	....	....	17·00	0	1	....	....	....
June	....	....	19·30	0	1	....	....	....
				0	12			
Belleville—								
July	....	....	20·93	0	1	....	....	....
August	....	....	....	....	....	....	....	....
September	....	....	21·67	0	1	....	....	....
October	....	....	20·01	0	1	....	....	....
November	....	....	17·09	0	1	....	....	....
December	....	....	....	....	....	....	....	....
January	....	....	....	....	....	....	....	....
February	20·02	18·95	19·48	0	2	....	....	....
March	18·84	18·52	18·68	0	2	....	....	....
April	20·96	19·81	20·38	0	2	....	....	....
May	21·98	20·51	21·24	0	2	....	....	....
June	....	....	....	0	2	....	....	....
				0	14			
Deseronto—								
July	....	....	22·00	0	1	....	....	....
August	....	....	21·00	0	1	....	....	....
September	....	....	19·80	0	1	....	....	....
October	....	....	19·00	0	1	....	....	....
November	....	....	21·70	0	1	....	....	....
December	....	....	19·00	0	1	....	....	....
January	....	....	18·50	0	1	....	....	....
February	....	....	20·00	0	1	....	....	....
March	....	....	20 00	0	1	....	....	....
April	....	....	18·04	0	1	....	....	....
May	....	....	19·00	0	1	....	....	....
June	....	....	19·20	0	1	....	....	....
				0	12			

DIX F.

Inspected during the Year ended June 30, 1906.

Cubic Feet.		Ammonia per 100 Cubic Feet.					Sulphuretted Hydrogen.			Remarks.
No. of times in excess of allowance.	No. of Tests.	Highest.	Lowest.	Average.	No. of times in excess of allowance.	No. of Tests.	No. of times absent.	No. of times present.	No. of Tests.	
		Grains.	Grains.	Grains.						
...	...	...	...	...	...	...	1	0	1	
...	...	...	...	...	...	...	1	0	1	
...	...	...	...	...	...	...	1	0	1	
...	...	...	...	...	...	...	1	0	1	
...	...	...	...	...	...	...	1	0	1	
...	...	...	...	...	...	...	1	0	1	
...	...	...	...	...	...	...	1	0	1	
...	...	...	...	...	...	...	1	0	1	
...	...	...	...	...	...	...	1	0	1	
...	...	...	...	...	...	...	1	0	1	
...	...	...	...	...	...	...	1	0	1	
...	...	...	...	...	...	...	1	0	1	
							12	0	12	
...	...	...	...	...	...	...	1	0	1	
...	...	...	...	...	...	...	...	...	...	
...	...	...	...	...	...	...	0	1	1	
...	...	...	...	...	...	...	0	1	1	
...	...	...	...	...	...	...	1	0	1	
...	...	...	...	...	...	...	...	...	...	No tests made.
...	...	...	...	...	...	...	...	...	...	
...	...	...	...	...	...	...	2	0	2	
...	...	...	...	...	...	...	2	0	2	
...	...	...	...	...	...	...	2	0	2	
...	...	...	...	...	...	...	2	0	2	
...	...	...	...	...	...	...	2	0	2	
							12	2	14	
...	...	...	...	...	...	...	1	0	1	
...	...	...	...	...	...	...	1	0	1	
...	...	...	...	...	...	...	1	0	1	
...	...	...	...	...	...	...	1	0	1	
...	...	...	...	...	...	...	1	0	1	
...	...	...	...	...	...	...	0	1	1	
...	...	...	...	...	...	...	0	1	1	
...	...	...	...	...	...	...	1	0	1	
...	...	...	...	...	...	...	1	0	1	
...	...	...	...	...	...	...	1	0	1	
...	...	...	...	...	...	...	1	0	1	
...	...	...	...	...	...	...	1	0	1	
							10	2	12	

APPENDIX

RETURN of Illuminating Power and Purity of Gas

Inspection Offices.	Illuminating Power.					Sulphur per 100		
	Highest.	Lowest.	Average.	No. of times below standard.	No. of Tests.	Highest	Lowest.	Average
	Candles.	Candles.	Candles			Grains.	Grains.	Grains.
Berlin—								
July			17·93	0	1			
August			17·88	0	1			
September			17·59	0	1			
October			17·80	0	1			
November			18·47	0	1			
December			18·63	0	1			
January			18·99	0	1			
February			17·55	0	1			
March			19·35	0	1			
April			19·94	0	1			
May			18·91	0	1			
June			16·65	0	1			
				0	12			
Brockville—								
July	20·02	18·60	19.31	0	2			
August	22·65	20·00	21·32	0	2			
September	21·79	21·00	21·39	0	2			
October	22 37	19 00	20·68	0	2			
November	20·82	20·70	20·76	0	2			
December	20·90	20·68	20·79	0	2			
January	23·80	22·02	22·91	0	2			
February	20·05	20·02	20·03	0	2			
March	19·92	19·62	19·77	0	2			
April	21·65	20·60	21·12	0	2			
May	20·54	20·23	20·38	0	2			
June	19·76	19·16	19·46	0	2			
				0	24			
Cobourg—								
July			18·17	0	1			
August			18·07	0	1			
September			18·66	0	1			
October			16·97	0	1			
November			17·43	0	1			
December			16·95	0	1			
January			17·22	0	1			
February			17·03	0	1			
March			19·01	0	1			
April			16·72	0	1			
May			17·09	0	1			
June			17·22	0	1			
				0	12			

F—*Continued.*

Inspected during the Year ended June 30, 1906.

Cubic Feet.		Ammonia per 100 Cubic Feet.					Sulphuretted Hydrogen.			Remarks.
No. of times in excess of allowance.	No. of Tests.	Highest.	Lowest.	Average.	No. of times in excess of allowance.	No. of Tests.	No. of times absent.	No. of times present.	No. of Tests.	
		Grains.	Grains.	Grains.						
...	...	...	...	...	...	...	1	0	1	
...	...	...	...	...	...	...	1	0	1	
...	...	...	...	...	...	...	1	0	1	
...	...	...	...	...	...	...	1	0	1	
...	...	...	...	...	...	...	1	0	1	
...	...	...	...	...	...	...	1	0	1	
...	...	...	...	...	...	...	1	0	1	
...	...	...	...	...	...	...	1	0	1	
...	...	...	...	...	...	...	1	0	1	
...	...	...	...	...	...	...	1	0	1	
...	...	...	...	...	...	...	1	0	1	
...	...	...	...	...	...	...	1	0	1	
							12	0	12	
...	...	...	...	...	...	...	2	0	2	
...	...	...	...	...	...	...	2	0	2	
...	...	...	...	...	...	...	2	0	2	
...	...	...	...	...	...	...	2	0	2	
...	...	...	...	...	...	...	2	0	2	
...	...	...	...	...	...	...	2	0	2	
...	...	...	...	...	...	...	2	0	2	
...	...	...	...	...	...	...	2	0	2	
...	...	...	...	...	...	...	2	0	2	
...	...	...	...	...	...	...	2	0	2	
...	...	...	...	...	...	...	2	0	2	
...	...	...	...	...	...	...	2	0	2	
							24	0	24	
...	...	...	...	...	...	...	0	2	2	
...	...	...	...	...	...	...	2	0	2	
...	...	...	...	...	...	...	1	1	2	
...	...	...	...	...	...	...	0	2	2	
...	...	...	...	...	...	...	0	2	2	
...	...	...	...	...	...	...	0	2	2	
...	...	...	...	...	...	...	0	2	2	
...	...	...	...	...	...	...	1	1	2	
...	...	...	...	...	...	...	2	0	2	
...	...	...	...	...	...	...	2	0	2	
...	...	...	...	...	...	...	2	0	2	
...	...	...	...	...	...	...	2	0	2	
							12	12	24	

APPENDIX

RETURN of the Illuminating Power and Purity of Gas

Inspection Offices.	Illuminating Power.					Sulphur per 100		
	Highest.	Lowest.	Average.	No. of times below standard.	No. of Tests.	Highest	Lowest.	Average
	Candles.	Candles.	Candles.			Grains.	Grains.	Grains.
Port Hope—								
July			18·86	0	1			
August								
September			19·31	0	1			
October			19·83	0	1			
November			18·62	0	1			
December			18·92	0	1			
January			18·91	0	1			
February			18·27	0	1			
March			19·45	0	1			
April			18·90	0	1			
May			18·88	0	1			
June			18·55	0	1			
				0	11			
Cornwall—								
July			18·05	0	1			
August			18·10	0	1			
September			18·10	0	1			
October								
November								
December			18·00	0	1			
January			18·10	0	1			
February			18·05	0	1			
March			18·00	0	1			
April			18·05	0	1			
May			18·10	0	1			
June			18·10	0	1			
				0	10			
Guelph—								
July			18·59	0	1			
August			16·63	0	1			
September			16·89	0	1			
October			17·77	0	1			
November			17·27	0	1			
December			18·43	0	1			
January			21·11	0	1			
February			17·93	0	1			
March			20·21	0	1			
April			19·63	0	1			
May			19·36	0	1			
June			19·74	0	1			
				0	12			

F—*Continued.*

Inspected during the Year ended June 30, 1906.

Cubic Feet.		Ammonia per 100 Cubic Feet.					Sulphuretted Hydrogen.			Remarks.
No. of times in excess of allowance.	No. of Tests.	Highest.	Lowest.	Average.	Times in excess of allowance.	No. of Tests.	No. of times absent.	No. of times present.	No. of Tests.	
		Grains.	Grains.	Grains.						
......	......	......	......	......	......	......	2	0	2	
......	......	......	......	......	......	......	2	0	2	
......	......	......	......	......	......	......	2	0	2	
......	......	......	......	......	......	......	2	0	2	
......	......	......	......	......	......	......	2	0	2	
......	......	......	......	......	......	......	2	0	2	
......	......	......	......	......	......	......	2	0	2	
......	......	......	......	......	......	......	2	0	2	
......	......	......	......	......	......	......	2	0	2	
......	......	......	......	......	......	......	2	0	2	
......	......	......	......	......	......	......	2	0	2	
......	......	......	......	......	......	......	2	0	2	
							24	0	24	
......	......	......	......	......	......	......	1	0	1	
......	......	......	......	......	......	......	1	0	1	
......	......	......	......	......	......	......	1	0	1	
......	......	......	......	......	......	......	......	......	......	
......	......	......	......	......	......	......	1	0	1	
......	......	......	......	......	......	......	1	0	1	
......	......	......	......	......	......	......	1	0	1	
......	......	......	......	......	......	......	1	0	1	
......	......	......	......	......	......	......	1	0	1	
......	......	......	......	......	......	......	1	0	1	
......	......	......	......	......	......	......	1	0	1	
							10	0	10	
......	......	......	......	......	......	......	1	0	1	
......	......	......	......	......	......	......	1	0	1	
......	......	......	......	......	......	......	1	0	1	
......	......	......	......	......	......	......	1	0	1	
......	......	......	......	......	......	......	1	0	1	
......	......	......	......	......	......	......	1	0	1	
......	......	......	......	......	......	......	1	0	1	
......	......	......	......	......	......	......	1	0	1	
......	......	......	......	......	......	......	1	0	1	
......	......	......	......	......	......	......	1	0	1	
......	......	......	......	......	......	......	1	0	1	
......	......	......	......	......	......	......	1	0	1	
							12	0	12	

APPENDIX

RETURN of the Illuminating Power and Purity of Gas

Inspection Offices.	Illuminating Power.					Sulphur per 100		
	Highest.	Lowest.	Average.	No. of times below standard.	No. of Tests.	Highest	Lowest.	Average
	Candles.	Candles.	Candles.			Grains.	Grains.	Grains.
Hamilton—								
July	18·48	18·02	18·25	0	8	......	......	......
August	18·50	17·85	18·18	0	8	......	......	......
September	18·68	17·85	18·33	0	10	......	......	......
October	18·41	17·44	17·93	0	8	......	......	......
November	18·84	18·35	18·66	0	8	......	......	......
December	19·34	17·94	18·65	0	10	......	......	......
January	18·84	17·87	18·54	0	8	......	......	......
February	18·52	18·16	18·32	0	8	......	......	......
March	18·41	17·33	17·76	0	10	......	......	......
April	17·47	16·59	16·96	0	8	......	......	......
May	17·52	16·54	16·98	0	9	......	......	......
June	18·28	17·52	17·86	0	9	......	......	......
				0	104			
Brantford—								
July	......	......	......	......	......	......	......	......
August	......	......	......	......	......	......	......	......
September	......	......	......	......	......	......	......	......
October	......	......	......	......	......	......	......	......
November	......	......	......	......	......	......	......	......
December	......	......	......	......	......	......	......	......
January	......	......	......	......	......	......	......	......
February	......	......	......	......	......	......	......	......
March	......	......	......	......	......	......	......	......
April	......	......	......	......	......	......	......	......
May	......	......	......	......	......	......	......	......
June	......	......	......	......	......	......	......	......
				......	......			
Galt—								
July	......	......	18·02	0	1	......	......	......
August	......	......	19·35	0	1	......	......	......
September	......	......	18·02	0	1	......	......	......
October	......	......	19·34	0	1	......	......	......
November	......	......	20·01	0	1	......	......	......
December	......	......	19·50	0	1	......	......	......
January	......	......	......	......	......	......	......	......
February	......	......	......	......	......	......	......	......
March	......	......	......	......	......	......	......	......
April	......	......	......	......	......	......	......	......
May	......	......	......	......	......	......	......	......
June	......	......	......	......	......	......	......	......
				0	6			

F—*Continued.*

Inspected during the Year ended June 30, 1906.

Cubic Feet.		Ammonia per 100 Cubic Feet.					Sulphuretted Hydrogen.			Remarks.
No. of times in excess of allowance.	No. of Tests.	Highest. Grains.	Lowest. Grains.	Average. Grains.	No. of times in excess of allowance.	No. of Tests.	No. of times absent.	No. of times present.	No. of Tests.	
......	......	......	......	......	......	......	8	0	8	
......	......	......	......	......	......	......	8	0	8	
......	......	......	......	......	......	......	10	0	10	
......	......	......	......	......	......	......	8	0	8	
......	......	......	......	......	......	......	8	0	8	
......	......	......	......	......	......	......	10	0	10	
......	......	......	......	......	......	......	8	0	8	
......	......	......	......	......	......	......	8	0	8	
......	......	......	......	......	......	......	10	0	10	
......	......	......	......	......	......	......	8	0	8	
......	......	......	......	......	......	......	9	0	9	
......	......	......	......	......	......	......	9	0	9	
							104	0	104	
......	......	......	......	......	......	......	1	0	1	
......	......	......	......	......	......	......	1	0	1	
......	......	......	......	......	......	......	1	0	1	
......	......	......	......	......	......	......	1	0	1	
......	......	......	......	......	......	......	1	0	1	
......	......	......	......	......	......	......	1	0	1	
......	......	......	......	......	......	......	1	0	1	
......	......	......	......	......	......	......	1	0	1	
......	......	......	......	......	......	......	1	0	1	
......	......	......	......	......	......	......	1	0	1	
......	......	......	......	......	......	......	1	0	1	
......	......	......	......	......	......	......	1	0	1	
							12	0	12	
......	......	......	......	......	......	......	1	0	1	
......	......	......	......	......	......	......	1	0	1	
......	......	......	......	......	......	......	1	0	1	
......	......	......	......	......	......	......	1	0	1	
......	......	......	......	......	......	......	1	0	1	
......	......	......	......	......	......	......	1	0	1	
......	......	......	......	......	......	......	1	0	1	
......	......	......	......	......	......	......	1	0	1	
......	......	......	......	......	......	......	1	0	1	
......	......	......	......	......	......	......	1	0	1	
......	......	......	......	......	......	......	1	0	1	
......	......	......	......	......	......	......	1	0	1	
							12	0	12	

APPENDIX

RETURN of the Illuminating Power and Purity of Gas

Inspection Office.	Illuminating Power.					Sulphur per 100		
	Highest.	Lowest.	Average.	No. of times below standard.	No. of Tests.	Highest	Lowest.	Average
	Candles.	Candles.	Candles.			Grains.	Grains.	Grains.
Dominion Nat. Gas. Co.—								
July								
August								
September								
October								
November								
December								
January								
February								
March								
April								
May								
June								
Prov. Nat. Gas and Fuel—								
July								
August								
September								
October								
November								
December								
January								
February								
March								
April								
May								
June								
Mutual Nat. Gas Co—								
July								
August								
September								
October								
November								
December								
January								
February								
March								
April								
May								
June								

F—*Continued.*

Inspected during the Year ended June 30, 1906.

Cubic Feet.		Ammonia per 100 Cubic Feet.					Sulphuretted Hydrogen.			Remarks.
No. of times in excess of allowance.	No. of Tests.	Highest.	Lowest.	Average.	Times in excess of allowance.	No. of Tests.	No. of times absent.	No. of times present.	No. of Tests.	
		Grains.	Grains.	Grains.						
...	...	...	...	...	...	...	1	0	1	
...	...	...	...	...	...	...	1	0	1	
...	...	...	...	...	...	...	1	0	1	
...	...	...	...	...	...	...	1	0	1	
...	...	...	...	...	...	...	1	0	1	
...	...	...	...	...	...	...	1	0	1	
...	...	...	...	...	...	...	1	0	1	
...	...	...	...	...	...	...	1	0	1	
...	...	...	...	...	...	...	1	0	1	
...	...	...	...	...	...	...	1	0	1	
...	...	...	...	...	...	...	1	0	1	
...	...	...	...	...	...	...	1	0	1	
							12	0	12	
...	...	...	...	...	...	...	1	0	1	
...	...	...	...	...	...	...	1	0	1	
...	...	...	...	...	...	...	0	1	1	
...	...	...	...	...	...	...	0	1	1	
...	...	...	...	...	...	...	0	1	1	
...	...	...	...	...	...	...	0	1	1	
...	...	...	...	...	...	...	0	1	1	
...	...	...	...	...	...	...	0	1	1	
...	...	...	...	...	...	...	0	1	1	
...	...	...	...	...	...	...	0	1	1	
...	...	...	...	...	...	...	0	1	1	
...	...	...	...	...	...	...	0	1	1	
							2	10	12	
...	...	...	...	...	...	...	1	0	1	
...	...	...	...	...	...	...	1	0	1	
...	...	...	...	...	...	...	0	1	1	
...	...	...	...	...	...	...	0	1	1	
...	...	...	...	...	...	...	0	1	1	
...	...	...	...	...	...	...	0	1	1	
...	...	...	...	...	...	...	0	1	1	
...	...	...	...	...	...	...	0	1	1	
...	...	...	...	...	...	...	0	1	1	
...	...	...	...	...	...	...	0	1	1	
...	...	...	...	...	...	...	0	1	1	
...	...	...	...	...	...	...	0	1	1	
							2	10	12	

APPENDIX

RETURN of the Illuminating Power and Purity of Gas

Inspection Offices.	Illuminating Power.					Sulphur per 100		
	Highest.	Lowest.	Average.	No. of times below standard.	No. of Tests.	Highest	Lowest.	Average
	Candles.	Candles.	Candles.			Grains.	Grains.	Grains.
St. Catharines—								
July			16·15	0	1			
August			16·13	0	1			
September			16·83	0	1			
October			16·99	0	1			
November			16·68	0	1			
December			16·58	0	1			
January			16·71	0	1			
February			17·55	0	1			
March			16·69	0	1			
April			16·32	0	1			
May			16·10	0	1			
June			16·24	0	1			
				0	12			
Kingston—								
July	20·14	19·08	19·61	0	2			
August	19·00	18·71	18·65	0	2			
September	20·16	18·06	19·11	0	2			
October	20·52	19·50	20·01	0	2			
November	21·00	19·54	20·27	0	2			
December	19·10	18·90	19·00	0	2			
January	20·76	20·08	20·42	0	2			
February	19·93	18·50	19·21	0	2			
March	20·37	18·33	19·35	0	2			
April	20·08	19·12	19·60	0	2			
May	19·20	19·09	19·14	0	2			
June	18·14	18·06	18·10	0	2			
				0	24			
Listowel—								
July			20·88	0	1			
August			20·30	0	1			
September			18·00	0	1			
October			20·30	0	1			
November			20·44	0	1			
December			20·88	0	1			
January			17·26	0	1			
February			17·04	0	1			
March			16·05	0	1			
April			17·94	0	1			
May			20·01	0	1			
June			17·25	0	1			
				0	12			

SESSIONAL PAPER No. 13

F—*Continued.*

Inspected during the Year ended June 30, 1906.

Cubic Feet.		Ammonia per 100 Cubic Feet.					Sulphuretted Hydrogen.			Remarks.
No. of times in excess of allowance.	No. of Tests.	Highest	Lowest	Average	No. of times in excess of allowance.	No. of Tests.	No. of times absent.	No. of times present.	No. of Tests.	
		Grains.	Grains.	Grains.						
....	.....	....	....	....	....	.....	1	0	1	
....	.....	....	....	....	....	.....	1	0	1	
....	.....	....	....	....	....	.....	1	0	1	
....	.....	....	....	....	....	.....	1	0	1	
....	.....	....	....	....	....	.....	1	0	1	
....	.....	....	....	....	....	.....	1	0	1	
....	.....	....	....	....	....	.....	1	0	1	
....	.....	....	....	....	....	.....	1	0	1	
....	.....	....	....	....	....	.....	1	0	1	
....	.....	....	....	....	....	.....	1	0	1	
....	.....	....	....	....	....	.....	1	0	1	
....	.....	....	....	....	....	.....	1	0	1	
							12	0	12	
....	.....	....	....	....	....	.....	2	0	2	
....	.....	....	....	....	....	.....	2	0	2	
....	.....	....	....	....	....	.....	2	0	2	
....	.....	....	....	....	....	.....	2	0	2	
....	.....	....	....	....	....	.....	2	0	2	
....	.....	....	....	....	....	.....	2	0	2	
....	.....	....	....	....	....	.....	2	0	2	
....	.....	....	....	....	....	.....	2	c	2	
....	.....	....	....	....	....	.....	2	0	2	
....	.....	....	....	....	....	.....	2	0	2	
....	.....	....	....	....	....	.....	2	0	2	
....	.....	....	....	....	....	.....	2	0	2	
							24	0	24	
....	.....	....	....	....	....	.....	1	0	1	
....	.....	....	....	....	....	.....	1	0	1	
....	.....	....	....	....	....	.....	1	0	1	
....	.....	....	....	....	....	.....	1	0	1	
....	.....	....	....	....	....	.....	1	0	1	
....	.....	....	....	....	....	.....	1	0	1	
....	.....	....	....	....	....	.....	1	0	1	
....	.....	....	....	....	....	.....	1	0	1	
....	.....	....	....	....	....	.....	1	0	1	
....	.....	....	....	....	....	.....	1	0	1	
....	.....	....	....	....	....	.....	1	0	1	
....	.....	....	....	....	....	.....	1	0	1	
							12	0	12	

APPENDIX

RETURN of the Illuminating Power and Purity of Gas

Inspection Offices.	Illuminating Power.					Sulphur per 100		
	Highest.	Lowest.	Average.	No. of times below Standard.	No. of Tests.	Highest	Lowest.	Average
	Candles.	Candles.	Candles.			Grains.	Grains.	Grains.
London—								
July	18·01	17·17	17·53	0	9	...	...	...
August	20·29	18·00	18·82	0	8	...	...	...
September	19·32	16·40	17·06	0	10	...	...	...
October	20·91	16·78	19·11	0	8	...	...	...
November	20·50	17·55	19 12	0	8	...	...	...
December	23·86	18·36	20·16	0	8	...	...	...
January	22·32	16·48	19·52	0	10	...	...	...
February	21·13	18·75	20·02	0	8	...	...	...
March	22·95	19·03	20·45	0	10	...	...	...
April	23·13	18·84	20·39	0	8	...	...	...
May	22·10	18·20	20·20	0	8	...	...	...
June	20·91	16·50	19·30	0	10	...	...	...
				0	105			
Chatham—								
July	...	...	18·51	0	1	...	...	...
August	...	...	17·35	0	1	...	...	...
September	...	...	17·83	0	1	...	...	...
October	...	...	17·59	0	1	...	...	...
November	...	...	16·46	0	1	...	...	...
December	...	...	16·83	0	1	...	...	...
January	...	...	16·40	0	1	...	...	...
February	...	...	16·00	0	1	...	...	...
March	...	...	16·61	0	1	...	...	...
April	...	...	15·66	0	1	...	...	...
May	...	...	16·77	0	1	...	...	...
June	...	...	16·47	0	1	...	...	...
				0	12			
Ingersoll—								
July	...	...	16·11	0	1	...	...	...
August	...	...	21·51	0	1	...	...	...
September	...	...	9·85	1	1	...	...	...
October	...	...	16·08	0	1	...	...	...
November	...	...	18·47	0	1	...	...	...
December	...	...	17·64	0	1	...	...	...
January	...	...	16·28	0	1	...	...	...
February	...	...	16·29	0	1	...	...	...
March	...	...	18·67	0	1	...	...	...
April	...	...	17·39	0	1	...	...	...
May	...	...	17·09	0	1	...	...	...
June	15·44	13·34	14·39	0	2	...	...	...
				1	13			

F—*Continued.*

Inspected during the Year ended June 30, 1906.

Cubic Feet.		Ammonia per 100 Cubic Feet.					Sulphuretted Hydrogen.			Remarks.
No. of times in excess of allowance.	No. of Tests.	Highest.	Lowest.	Average.	No. of times in excess of allowance.	No. of Tests.	No. of times absent.	No. of times present.	No. of Tests.	
		Grains.	Grains.	Grains.						
...	...	...	...	...	...	...	9	0	9	
...	...	...	...	...	...	...	8	0	8	
...	...	...	...	...	...	...	10	0	10	
...	...	...	...	...	...	...	8	0	8	
...	...	...	...	...	...	...	8	0	8	
...	...	...	...	...	...	...	8	0	8	
...	...	...	...	...	...	...	10	0	10	
...	...	...	...	...	...	...	8	0	8	
...	...	...	...	...	...	...	10	0	10	
...	...	...	...	...	...	...	8	0	8	
...	...	...	...	...	...	...	8	0	8	
...	...	...	...	...	...	...	10	0	10	
							105	0	105	
...	...	...	...	...	...	...	1	0	1	
...	...	...	...	...	...	...	1	0	1	
...	...	...	...	...	...	...	1	0	1	
...	...	...	...	...	...	...	1	0	1	
...	...	...	...	...	...	...	1	0	1	
...	...	...	...	...	...	...	1	0	1	
...	...	...	...	...	...	...	1	0	1	
...	...	...	...	...	...	...	1	0	1	
...	...	...	...	...	...	...	1	0	1	
...	...	...	...	...	...	...	1	0	1	
...	...	...	...	...	...	...	1	0	1	
...	...	...	...	...	...	...	1	0	1	
							12	0	12	
...	...	...	...	...	...	...	1	0	1	
...	...	...	...	...	...	...	1	0	1	
...	...	...	...	...	...	...	1	0	1	
...	...	...	...	...	...	...	1	0	1	
...	...	...	...	...	...	...	1	0	1	
...	...	...	...	...	...	...	1	0	1	
...	...	...	...	...	...	...	1	0	1	
...	...	...	...	...	...	...	1	0	1	
...	...	...	...	...	...	...	1	0	1	
...	...	...	...	...	...	...	1	0	1	
...	...	...	...	...	...	...	1	0	1	
...	...	...	...	...	...	...	2	0	2	
							13	0	13	

APPENDIX

RETURN of the Illuminating Power and Purity of Gas

Inspection Offices.	Illuminating power.					Sulphur per 100		
	Highest.	Lowest.	Average.	No. of times below Standard.	No. of Tests.	Highest	Lowest.	Average
	Candles.	Candles.	Candles.			Grains.	Grains.	Grains.
St. Thomas—								
July	.....	.....	17·63	0	1	.....	.....	.....
August	.....	.....	18·04	0	1	.....	.....	.....
September	.....	.....	17·90	0	1	.....	.....	.....
October	.....	.....	18·65	0	1	.....	.....	.....
November	.....	.....	17·10	0	1	.....	.....	.....
December	.....	.....	20·33	0	1	.....	.....	.....
January	.....	.....	16·89	0	1	.....	.....	.....
February	.....	.....	17·54	0	1	.....	.....	.....
March	.....	.....	16·77	0	1	.....	.....	.....
April	.....	.....	16·12	0	1	.....	.....	.....
May	.....	.....	17·67	0	1	.....	.....	.....
June	.....	.....	17·37	0	1	.....	.....	.....
				0	12			
Windsor—								
July	.....	.....	18·32	0	1	.....	.....	.....
August	.....	.....	16·95	0	1	.....	.....	.....
September	.....	.....	17·31	0	1	.....	.....	.....
October	.....	.....	17·72	0	1	.....	.....	.....
November	.....	.....	18·28	0	1	.....	.....	.....
December	.....	.....	18·40	0	1	.....	.....	.....
January	.....	.....	17·46	0	1	.....	.....	.....
February	.....	.....	17·34	0	1	.....	.....	.....
March	.....	.....	17·87	0	1	.....	.....	.....
April	.....	.....	17·15	0	1	.....	.....	.....
May	.....	.....	19·06	0	1	.....	.....	.....
June	.....	.....	17·28	0	1	.....	.....	.....
				0	12			
Woodstock—								
July	.....	.....	16·58	0	1	.....	.....	.....
August	.....	.....	17·00	0	1	.....	.....	.....
September	.....	.....	18·08	0	1	.....	.....	.....
October	.....	.....	18·45	0	1	.....	.....	.....
November	.....	.....	17·55	0	1	.....	.....	.....
December	.....	.....	17·21	0	1	.....	.....	.....
January	.....	.....	17·05	0	1	.....	.....	.....
February	.....	.....	17·60	0	1	.....	.....	.....
March	.....	.....	16·10	0	1	.....	.....	.....
April	.....	.....	18·71	0	1	.....	.....	.....
May	.....	.....	19·04	0	1	.....	.....	.....
June	.....	.....	19·07	0	1	.....	.....	.....
				0	12			

SESSIONAL PAPER No. 13

F—*Continued.*

Inspected during the Year ended June 30, 1906.

Cubic Feet.		Ammonia per 100 Cubic Feet.					Sulphuretted Hydrogen.			Remarks.
No. of times in excess of allowance.	No. of Tests.	Highest.	Lowest.	Average.	No. of times in excess of allowance.	No. of tests.	No. of times absent.	No. of times present.	No. of Tests.	
		Grains.	Grains.	Grains.						
....	.....	....	....	....	....	.....	1	0	1	
....	.....	....	....	....	....	.....	1	0	1	
....	.....	....	....	....	....	.....	1	0	1	
....	.....	....	....	....	....	.....	1	0	1	
....	.....	....	....	....	....	.....	1	0	1	
....	.....	....	....	....	....	.....	1	0	1	
....	.....	....	....	....	....	.....	1	0	1	
....	.....	....	....	....	....	.....	1	0	1	
....	.....	....	....	....	....	.....	1	0	1	
....	.....	....	....	....	....	.....	1	0	1	
....	.....	....	....	....	....	.....	1	0	1	
....	.....	....	....	....	....	.....	1	0	1	
							12	0	12	
....	.....	....	....	....	....	.....	1	0	1	
....	.....	....	....	....	....	.....	1	0	1	
....	.....	....	....	....	....	.....	1	0	1	
....	.....	....	....	....	....	.....	1	0	1	
....	.....	....	....	....	....	.....	1	0	1	
....	.....	....	....	....	....	.....	1	0	1	
....	.....	....	....	....	....	.....	1	0	1	
....	.....	....	....	....	....	.....	1	0	1	
....	.....	....	....	....	....	.....	1	0	1	
....	.....	....	....	....	....	.....	1	0	1	
....	.....	....	....	....	....	.....	1	0	1	
....	.....	....	....	....	....	.....	1	0	1	
							12	0	12	
....	.....	....	....	....	....	.....	1	0	1	
....	.....	....	....	....	....	.....	1	0	1	
....	.....	....	....	....	....	.....	1	0	1	
....	.....	....	....	....	....	.....	1	0	1	
....	.....	....	....	....	....	.....	1	0	1	
....	.....	....	....	....	....	.....	1	0	1	
....	.....	....	....	....	....	.....	1	0	1	
....	.....	....	....	....	....	.....	1	0	1	
....	.....	....	....	....	....	.....	1	0	1	
....	.....	....	....	....	....	.....	1	0	1	
....	.....	....	....	....	....	.....	1	0	1	
....	.....	....	....	....	....	.....	1	0	1	
							12	0	12	

APPENDIX

RETURN of the Illuminating Power and Purity of Gas

Inspection Offices.	Illuminating Power.					Sulphur per 100		
	Highest.	Lowest.	Average.	No. of times below Standard.	No. of Tests.	Highest	Lowest.	Average
	Candles.	Candles,	Candles.			Grains.	Grains.	Grains.
Napanee—								
July	...	...	...	...	...	...	...	...
August	...	...	...	...	...	...	...	...
September	...	...	21·46	0	1	...	...	...
October	...	...	19·14	0	1	...	...	...
November	...	...	...	...	...	...	...	...
December	...	...	19·89	0	1	...	...	...
January	...	...	18·75	0	1	...	...	...
February	...	...	20·18	0	1	...	...	...
March	...	...	20·49	0	1	...	...	...
April	...	...	19·86	0	1	...	...	...
May	...	...	20.01	0	1	...	...	...
June	...	...	21·23	0	1	...	...	...
				0	9			
Ottawa—								
July	17·82	17·76	17·79	0	2	15·17	14·19	14·68
August	17·22	17·17	17·19	0	2	14·92	14·64	14·78
September	17·69	16·70	17·19	0	2	14·41	14·30	14·35
October	17·43	17·32	17·37	0	2	14·54	14·36	14·45
November	17·37	17·05	17·21	0	2	15·56	14·18	14·87
December	17.51	16·89	17·20	0	2	14·84	14·29	14·56
January	16·81	16·46	16·63	0	3	14·41	14·19	14·30
February	16·85	16·64	16·74	0	2	14·92	14·85	14·88
March	16·94	16·77	16·85	0	2	17·96	14·08	16·02
April	16·78	16·72	16·75	0	2	14·98	14·63	14·80
May	16·95	16·23	16·62	0	3	14·75	14·58	14·66
June	16·67	16·46	16·56	0	2	...	...	...
				0	26			
Owen Sound—								
July	...	...	16·40	0	1	...	...	...
August	...	...	16·10	0	1	...	...	...
September	...	...	16·00	0	1	...	...	...
October	...	...	...	...	...	...	...	...
November	...	...	17·02	0	1	...	...	...
December	...	...	18·80	0	1	...	...	...
January	...	...	16·50	0	1	...	...	...
February	...	...	16·25	0	1	...	...	...
March	...	...	16·20	0	1	...	...	...
April	...	...	16·78	0	1	...	...	...
May	...	...	16·09	0	1	...	...	...
June	...	...	16·20	0	1	...	...	...
				0	11			

F—*Continued.*

Inspected during the Year ended June 30, 1906.

Cubic Feet.		Ammonia per 100 Cubic Feet.					Sulphuretted Hydrogen.			Remarks.
No. of times in excess of allowance.	No. of Tests.	Highest.	Lowest.	Average.	No. of times in excess of allowance.	No. of Tests.	No. of times absent.	No. of times present.	No. of Tests.	
		Grains.	Grains.	Grains.						
...	...	...	...	...	...	...	...	...	...	
...	...	...	...	...	...	...	...	...	...	
...	...	...	...	...	...	...	1	0	1	
...	...	...	...	...	...	...	1	0	1	
...	...	...	...	...	...	...	...	...	...	
...	...	...	...	...	...	...	1	0	1	
...	...	...	...	...	...	...	1	0	1	
...	...	...	...	...	...	...	1	0	1	
...	...	...	...	...	...	...	1	0	1	
...	...	...	...	...	...	...	1	0	1	
...	...	...	...	...	...	...	1	0	1	
...	...	...	...	...	...	...	1	0	1	
							9	0	9	
0	2	2·19	1·68	1·93	0	2	2	0	2	
0	2	1·97	1·86	1·91	0	2	2	0	2	
0	2	2·36	1·53	1·96	0	2	2	0	2	
0	2	2·37	1·34	1·85	0	2	2	0	2	
0	2	2·05	1·70	1·87	0	2	2	0	2	
0	2	2·17	1·77	1·97	0	2	2	0	2	
0	2	2·13	1·94	2·03	0	2	3	0	3	
0	2	2·22	2·03	2·12	0	2	2	0	2	
0	2	2·34	1·95	2·14	0	2	2	0	2	
0	2	2·16	2·14	2·15	0	2	2	0	2	
0	2	2·10	1·99	2·04	0	2	3	0	3	
0	2	...	...	...	0	2	2	0	2	
0	24				0	24	26	0	26	
...	...	...	...	...	...	...	1	0	1	
...	...	...	...	...	...	...	1	0	1	
...	...	...	...	...	...	...	1	0	1	
...	...	...	...	...	...	...	...	...	...	
...	...	...	...	...	...	...	1	0	1	
...	...	...	...	...	...	...	1	0	1	
...	...	...	...	...	...	...	1	0	1	
...	...	...	...	...	...	...	1	0	1	
...	...	...	...	...	...	...	1	0	1	
...	...	...	...	...	...	...	1	0	1	
...	...	...	...	...	...	...	1	0	1	
...	...	...	...	...	...	...	1	0	1	
							11	0	11	

APPENDIX

RETURN of the Illuminating Power and Purity of Gas

Inspection Offices.	Illuminating Power.					Sulphur per 100		
	Highest.	Lowest.	Average.	No. of times below standard,	No. of Tests.	Highest	Lowest.	Average
	Candles.	Candles.	Candles.			Grains.	Grains.	Grains.
Peterborough—								
July	21·00	20·20	20.60	0	2	......	......	......
August	20·20	19·20	19·70	0	2	......	......	......
September	23·00	18·20	20·60	0	2	......	......	......
October	20·60	19·00	19·80	0	2	......	......	......
November	18·20	16·30	17·25	0	2	......	......	......
December	18·50	17·80	18·15	0	2	......	......	......
January	16·50	16·20	16·35	0	2	......	......	......
February	18 00	14·50	16·23	1	3	......	......	......
March	......	......	17·60	0	1	......	......	......
April	18·40	17·40	17·90	0	2	......	......	......
May	20·00	17·70	18·85	0	2	......	......	......
June	22·50	22·00	22·25	0	2	......	......	......
				1	24			
Sarnia—								
July	......	......	19·16	0	1	......	......	......
August	......	......	18·54	0	1	......	......	......
September	......	......	18·76	0	1	......	......	......
October	......	......	18·70	0	1	......	......	......
November	......	......	18·98	0	1	......	......	......
December	......	......	17·08	0	1	......	......	......
January	......	......	19·36	0	1	......	......	......
February	......	......	21·34	0	1	......	......	......
March	......	......	21·18	0	1	......	......	......
April	......	......	21·16	0	1	......	......	......
May	......	......	20·96	0	1	......	......	......
June	......	......	21·02	0	1	......	......	......
				0	12			
Stratford—								
July	......	......	17·05	0	1	......	......	......
August	......	......	17·06	0	1	......	......	......
September	......	......	17·35	0	1	......	......	......
October	......	......	16·74	0	1	......	......	......
November	......	......	17·46	0	1	......	......	......
December	......	......	17·68	0	1	......	......	......
January	......	......	17·53	0	1	......	......	......
February	......	......	17·30	0	1	......	......	......
March	......	......	16·59	0	1	......	......	......
April	......	......	16·89	0	1	......	......	......
May	......	......	16·77	0	1	......	......	......
June	......	......	17·46	0	1	......	......	......
				0	12			

F—*Continued.*

Inspected during the Year ended June 30, 1906.

Cubic Feet.		Ammonia per 100 Cubic Feet.					Sulphuretted Hydrogen.			Remarks.
No. of times in excess of allowance.	No. of Tests.	Highest.	Lowest.	Average.	No. of times in excess of allowance.	No. of Tests.	No. of times absent.	No. of times present.	No. of Tests.	
		Grains.	Grains.	Grains.						
....	......	....	....	....	....	.....	2	0	2	
....	......	....	....	....	....	.....	2	0	2	
....	......	....	....	....	....	.....	2	0	2	
....	......	....	....	....	....	.....	2	9	2	
....	......	....	....	....	....	.....	2	0	2	
....	......	....	....	....	....	.....	2	0	2	
....	......	....	....	....	....	.....	2	0	2	
....	......	....	....	....	....	.....	2	0	2	
....	......	....	....	....	....	.....	2	0	2	
....	......	....	....	....	....	.....	2	0	2	
....	......	....	....	....	....	.....	2	0	2	
....	......	....	....	....	....	.....	2	0	2	
							24	0	24	
....	......	....	....	....	....	.....	1	0	1	
....	......	....	....	....	....	.....	1	0	1	
....	......	....	....	....	....	.....	1	0	1	
....	......	....	....	....	....	.....	1	0	1	
....	......	....	....	....	....	.....	1	0	1	
....	......	....	....	....	....	.....	1	0	1	
....	......	....	....	....	....	.....	1	0	1	
....	......	....	....	....	....	.....	1	0	1	
....	......	....	....	....	....	.....	1	0	1	
....	......	....	....	....	....	.....	1	0	1	
....	......	....	....	....	....	.....	1	0	1	
....	......	....	....	....	....	.....	1	0	1	
							12	0	12	
....	......	....	....	....	....	.....	1	0	1	
....	......	....	....	....	....	.....	1	0	1	
....	......	....	....	....	....	.....	1	0	1	
....	......	....	....	....	....	.....	1	0	1	
....	......	....	....	....	....	.....	1	0	1	
....	......	....	....	....	....	.....	1	0	1	
....	......	....	....	....	....	.....	1	0	1	
....	......	....	....	....	....	.....	1	0	1	
....	......	....	....	....	....	.....	1	0	1	
....	......	....	....	....	....	.....	1	0	1	
....	......	....	....	....	....	.....	1	0	1	
....	......	....	....	....	....	.....	1	0	1	
							12	0	12	

APPENDIX

RETURN of the Illuminating Power and Purity of Gas

Inspection Offices.	Illuminating Power.					Sulphur per 100		
	Highest.	Lowest.	Average.	No. of times below standard.	No. of Tests.	Highest	Lowest	Average
	Candles.	Candles.	Candles.			Grains.	Grains.	Grains.
Toronto—								
July	19·29	18·21	18·62	0	8	16·99	15·66	16·32
August	19·52	18·81	19·11	0	9	17·01	15·34	16·17
September	19·57	18·67	18·97	0	9	14 18	11·47	12·83
October	19·38	18·40	18·79	0	8	15·67	14·05	14·86
November	19·80	18·17	18·92	0	9	11·47	11·25	11·36
December	18·88	17·98	18·44	0	9	11·61	11·32	11·46
January	19·20	18·06	18·51	0	9	12·24	9·79	10·51
February	18·89	17·69	18·42	0	8	13·86	12 66	13·26
March	19·52	18·55	18·95	0	9	12·24	9·87	10·55
April	19·73	18·65	19·01	0	8	11·42	8·71	10·06
May	19·26	18·51	19·01	0	9	11·29	9·95	10·62
June	19·20	18·10	18·75	0	9	12·62	11·39	12·00
				0	104			
Montreal—								
July	19·65	17·84	18·87	0	8	19·04	8·77	13·90
August	19·64	17·90	18·73	0	9	6·07	4·51	5·29
September	19·11	17·92	18·50	0	9	17·84	5·45	11·64
October	18·61	16·68	17·67	0	9	4·41	2·73	3·57
November	18·28	16·45	17·12	0	8	12·45	10·78	11·61
December	18·27	16·87	17·47	0	9	33·18	31·75	32·46
January	20·77	16·36	17·96	0	9	19·06	17·95	18·50
February	17·91	17·13	17·52	0	8	16·90	8·64	12·77
March	17·73	16·82	17·30	0	9	7·34	6·40	6·87
April	18·61	16·99	17·70	0	8	28·38	2·79	15 58
May	19·17	17·57	18·21	0	9	5·77	5·23	5·50
June	19·90	18·24	18·63	0	9	10·77	4·38	7·57
				0	104			
Quebec—								
July	....	....	18·88	0	1	22·98	16·73	19·85
August	....	....	18·31	0	1	19·71	19·04	19·37
September	....	....	17·91	0	1	20·33	16 77	18·55
October	....	....	18·34	0	1	20·59	18·53	19·56
November	....	....	18·56	0	1	19·74	17·36	18·55
December	....	....	18·89	0	1	22·36	19·68	21·02
January	....	....	18·36	0	1	20·13	16·50	18·31
February	....	....	18·07	0	1	22·02	19·64	20·83
March	....	....	18·54	0	1	19·77	19·62	19·69
April	....	....	18·44	0	1	20·08	15·07	17·57
May	....	....	18·47	0	1	19·48	19·05	19·20
June	....	....	18·63	0	1	20·18	16·36	18·27
				0	12			

F—*Continued.*

Inspected during the Year ended June 30, 1906.

Cubic Feet.		Ammonia per 100 Cubic Feet.					Sulphuretted Hydrogen.			Remarks.
No. of times in excess of allowance.	No. of Tests.	Highest.	Lowest.	Average.	No. of times in excess of allowance.	No. of Tests.	No. of times absent.	No. of times present.	No. of Tests.	
		Grains.	Grains.	Grains.						
0	2	0·89	0·52	0·70	0	2	8	0	8	
0	2	0·45	0·31	0·38	0	2	9	0	9	
0	2	0·26	0·20	0·23	0	2	9	0	9	
0	2	0·45	0·25	0·35	0	2	8	0	8	
0	2	0·28	0·24	0·20	0	2	9	0	9	
0	2	0·15	0·10	0·07	0	2	9	0	9	
0	2	0·15	0·10	0·12	0	2	9	0	9	
0	2	0·35	0·25	0·30	0	2	8	0	8	
0	2	0·15	0·10	0·12	0	2	9	0	9	
0	2	0·50	0·00	0·25	0	2	8	0	8	
0	2	0·46	0·25	0·35	0	2	9	0	9	
0	2	0·41	0·30	0·35	0	2	9	0	9	
0	24				0	24	104	0	104	
0	2	....	....	0·00	0	2	12	0	12	
0	2	....	....	0·00	0	2	12	0	12	
0	2	....	....	0·00	0	2	13	9	13	
0	2	....	....	0·00	0	2	13	0	13	
0	2	....	....	0·00	0	2	11	0	11	
0	2	....	....	0·00	0	2	13	0	13	
0	2	....	....	0·00	0	2	13	0	13	
0	2	....	....	0·00	0	2	12	0	12	
0	2	....	....	0·00	0	2	13	0	13	
0	2	....	....	0·00	0	2	12	0	12	
0	2	....	....	0·00	0	2	13	0	13	
0	2	....	....	0·00	0	2	13	0	13	
0	24				0	24	150	0	150	
0	2	....	....	0·00	0	2	1	0	1	
0	2	....	....	0·00	0	2	1	0	1	
0	2	....	....	0·00	0	2	1	0	1	
0	2	....	....	0·00	0	2	1	0	1	
0	2	....	....	0·00	0	2	1	0	1	
0	2	....	....	0·00	0	2	1	0	1	
0	2	....	....	0·00	0	2	1	0	1	
0	2	....	....	0·00	0	2	1	0	1	
0	2	....	....	0·00	0	2	1	0	1	
0	2	....	....	0·00	0	2	1	0	1	
0	2	....	....	0·00	0	2	1	0	1	
0	2	....	....	0·00	0	0	1	0	1	
0	24				0	24	12	0	12	

APPENDIX

RETURN of the Illuminating Power and Purity of Gas

Inspection Offices.	Illuminating Power.					Sulphur per 100		
	Highest.	Lowest.	Average.	No. of times below standard.	No. of Tests.	Highest	Lowest.	Average
	Candles.	Candles.	Candles.			Grains.	Grains.	Grains.
Sherbrooke—								
July	...	...	19·62	0	1	...	...	...
August	...	...	19·64	0	1	...	...	...
September	...	...	16·24	0	1	...	...	...
October	...	...	17·78	0	1	...	...	...
November	...	...	17·00	0	1	...	...	...
December	...	...	17·35	0	1	...	...	...
January	...	...	16·95	0	1	...	...	...
February	...	...	16·89	0	1	...	...	...
March	...	...	17·73	0	1	...	...	...
April	...	...	16·80	0	1	...	...	...
May	...	...	17·24	0	1	...	...	...
June	...	...	18·53	0	1	...	...	...
				0	12			
St. Hyacinthe—								
July	...	...	18·59	0	1	...	...	...
August	...	...	18·78	0	1	...	...	...
September	...	...	18·57	0	1	...	...	...
October	...	...	18·96	0	1	...	...	...
November	...	...	18·79	0	1	...	...	...
December	...	...	18·98	0	1	...	...	...
January	...	...	18·92	0	1	...	...	...
February	...	...	18·95	0	1	...	...	...
March	...	...	18·47	0	1	...	...	...
April	...	...	18·82	0	1	...	...	...
May	...	...	18·96	0	1	...	...	...
June	...	...	18·78	0	1	...	...	...
				0	12			
Fredericton—								
July	16·65	15·88	16·26	0	5	...	...	...
August	18·07	16·53	17·30	0	5	...	...	...
September	18·07	16·83	17·46	0	5	...	...	...
October	17·86	15·75	16·69	1	5	...	...	...
November	16·13	15·51	15·82	1	2	...	...	...
December	16·55	16·16	16·40	0	3	...	...	...
January	16·79	16·62	16·68	0	3	...	...	...
February	17·34	17·25	17·31	0	3	...	...	...
March	17·10	16·24	16·67	0	2	...	...	...
April	...	...	...	...	...	...	...	...
May	...	...	...	...	...	...	...	...
June	...	...	18·03	0	1	...	...	...
				2	34			

F—*Continued.*

Inspected during the Year ended June 30, 1906.

Cubic Feet.		Ammonia per 100 Cubic Feet.					Sulphuretted Hydrogen.			Remarks.
No. of times in excess of allowance.	No. of Tests.	Highest.	Lowest.	Average.	No. of times in excess of allowance.	No. of Tests.	No. of times absent.	No. of times present.	No. of Tests.	
		Grains.	Grains.	Grains.						
...	...	...	...	...	...	...	1	0	1	
...	...	...	...	...	...	...	1	0	1	
...	...	...	...	...	...	...	1	0	1	
...	...	...	...	...	...	...	1	0	1	
...	...	...	...	...	...	...	1	0	1	
...	...	...	...	...	...	...	1	0	1	
...	...	...	...	...	...	...	1	0	1	
...	...	...	...	...	...	...	1	0	1	
...	...	...	...	...	...	...	1	0	1	
...	...	...	...	...	...	...	1	0	1	
...	...	...	...	...	...	...	1	0	1	
...	...	...	...	...	...	...	1	0	1	
							12	0	12	
...	...	...	...	...	...	...	1	0	1	
...	...	...	...	...	...	...	1	0	1	
...	...	...	...	...	...	...	1	0	1	
...	...	...	...	...	...	...	1	0	1	
...	...	...	...	...	...	...	1	0	1	
...	...	...	...	...	...	...	1	0	1	
...	...	...	...	...	...	...	1	0	1	
...	...	...	...	...	...	...	1	0	1	
...	...	...	...	...	...	...	1	0	1	
...	...	...	...	...	...	...	1	0	1	
...	...	...	...	...	...	...	1	0	1	
...	...	...	...	...	...	...	1	0	1	
							12	0	12	
...	...	...	...	...	...	...	4	1	5	
...	...	...	...	...	...	...	5	0	5	
...	...	...	...	...	...	...	4	1	5	
...	...	...	...	...	...	...	4	1	5	
...	...	...	...	...	...	...	1	1	2	
...	...	...	...	...	...	...	3	0	3	
...	...	...	...	...	...	...	3	0	3	
...	...	...	...	...	...	...	2	1	3	
...	...	...	...	...	...	...	2	0	2	
...	...	...	...	...	...	...	...	...	...	
...	...	...	...	...	...	...	1	0	1	
							29	5	34	

APPENDIX

Return of the Illuminating Power and Purity of Gas

Inspection Offices.	Illuminating Power.					Sulphur per 100		
	Highest.	Lowest.	Average.	No. of times below Standard.	No. of Tests.	Highest	Lowest.	Average
	Candles.	Candles.	Candles.			Grains.	Grains.	Grains.
St. John—								
July	18·28	17·09	17·89	0	4			20·73
August	18·04	17·38	17·65	0	4			23·50
September	17·94	17·23	17·48	0	4			21·19
October	18·20	17·58	17·87	0	3			19·94
November	17·72	17·32	17·52	0	2			17·94
December	18·42	17·61	17·95	0	4			19·55
January	18·00	17·35	17·89	0	4			20·67
February	17·81	16·61	17·38	0	3			20·71
March	17·59	16·51	17·16	0	4			22·97
April	17·78	17·18	17·42	0	4			19·33
May	17·27	16·79	17·05	0	3			20·85
June	17·09	16·59	16·80	0	3			20·94
				0	42			
Moncton—								
July			20·36	0	1			
August			20·19	0	1			
September			19·69	0	1			
October			18·96	0	1			
November			18·86	0	1			
December			19·31	0	1			
January			18·28	0	1			
February								
March								
April								
May			18·89	0	1			
June			17·29	0	1			
				0	9			
Halifax—								
July			17·64	0	1			10·81
August			17·62	0	1			11·38
September			17·85	0	1			13·31
October			17·40	0	1			10·05
November			16·56	0	1			9·39
December			17·15	0	1			11·15
January			18·04	0	1			
February			18·08	0	1			13·76
March			17·71	0	1			17·63
April			17·73	0	1			16·86
May			17·88	0	1			17·11
June			17·06	0	1			25·93
				0	12			

F.—*Continued.*

Inspected during the Year ended June 30, 1906.

Cubic Feet.		Ammonia per 100 Cubic Feet.					Sulphuretted Hydrogen.			Remarks.
No. of times in excess of allowance.	No. of Tests.	Highest.	Lowest.	Average.	No. of times in excess of allowance.	No. of Tests.	No. of times absent.	No. of times present.	No. of Tests.	
		Grains.	Grains.	Grains.						
0	1	......	......	1·27	0	1	4	0	4	
0	1	......	......	1·52	0	1	4	0	4	
0	1	......	......	1·31	0	1	4	0	4	
0	1	......	......	1·10	0	1	3	0	3	
0	1	......	......	0·00	0	1	2	0	2	
0	1	......	......	0·00	0	1	4	0	4	
0	1	......	......	0·00	0	1	4	0	4	
0	1	......	......	0·00	0	1	3	0	3	
0	1	......	......	0·00	0	1	4	0	4	
0	1	......	......	0·00	0	1	4	0	4	
0	1	......	......	0·75	0	1	3	0	3	
0	1	......	......	0·00	0	1	3	0	3	
0	12				0	12	42	0	42	
......	......	......	......	......	......	......	1	0	1	
......	......	......	......	......	......	......	1	0	1	
......	......	......	......	......	......	......	1	0	1	
......	......	......	......	......	......	......	1	0	1	
......	......	......	......	......	......	......	1	0	1	
......	......	......	......	......	......	......	1	0	1	
......	......	......	......	......	......	......	1	0	1	
......	......	......	......	......	......	......	......	......	......	
......	......	......	......	......	......	......	......	......	......	
......	......	......	......	......	......	......	......	......	......	
......	......	......	......	......	......	......	1	0	1	
......	......	......	......	......	......	......	1	0	1	
							9	0	9	
0	1	......	......	0·00	0	1	1	0	1	
0	1	......	......	0·00	0	1	1	0	1	
0	1	......	......	0·00	0	1	1	0	1	
0	1	......	......	0·00	0	1	1	0	1	
0	1	......	......	0·00	0	1	1	0	1	
0	1	......	......	0·00	0	1	......	......	......	
......	......	......	......	......	......	......	1	0	1	
0	1	......	......	0·00	0	1	1	0	1	
0	1	......	......	0·00	0	1	1	0	1	
0	1	......	......	0·00	0	1	1	0	1	
0	1	......	......	0·00	0	1	1	0	1	
0	1	......	......	0·00	0	1	1	0	1	
0	11				0	11	11	0	11	

APPENDIX

RETURN of the Illuminating Power and Purity of Gas

Inspection Offices.	Illuminating Power.					Sulpher per 100		
	Highest.	Lowest.	Average.	No. of times below standard.	No. of tests.	Highest	Lowest	Average
	Candles.	Candles.	Candles.			Grains.	Grains.	Grains.
Yarmouth—								
July	......	......	16.85	0	1	......	......	......
August	......	......	17.49	0	1	......	......	......
September	......	......	19.40	0	1	......	......	......
October	......	......	17.91	0	1	......	......	......
November	......	......	16.77	0	1	......	......	......
December	......	......	18.76	0	1	......	......	......
January	......	......	18.37	0	1	......	......	......
February	......	......	16.48	0	1	......	......	......
March	......	......	16.53	0	1	......	......	......
April	......	......	19.23	0	1	......	......	......
May	......	......	18.38	0	1	......	......	......
June	......	......	17.93	0	1	......	......	......
				0	12			
Charlottetown—								
July	......	......	19.10	0	1	......	......	......
August	......	......	19.16	0	1	......	......	......
September	......	......	17.32	0	1	......	......	......
October	......	......	18.41	0	1	......	......	......
November	......	......	16.66	0	1	......	......	......
December	......	......	16.70	0	1	......	......	......
January	......	......	21.19	0	1	......	......	......
February	20.46	19.03	19.74	0	2	......	......	......
March	17.87	17.74	17.80	0	2	......	......	......
April	......	......	19.14	0	1	......	......	......
May	17.88	17.57	17.72	0	2	......	......	......
June	17.00	16.70	16.85	0	2	......	......	......
				0	16			
Winnipeg—								
July	......	......	18.09	0	1	......	......	......
August	......	......	16.06	0	1	......	......	......
September	18.58	17.35	17.96	0	2	......	......	......
October	18.09	17.18	17.64	0	2	......	......	......
November	17.83	16.63	17.23	0	2	......	......	......
December	17.70	16.68	17.19	0	2	......	......	......
January	18.54	16.82	17.68	0	2	......	......	......
February	19.66	16.00	17.83	0	2	......	......	......
March	17.83	17.48	17.65	0	2	......	......	......
April	17.07	17.00	17.04	0	2	......	......	......
May	18.58	17.07	18.14	0	2	......	......	......
June	18.90	16.76	17.83	0	2	......	......	......
				0	22			

F—*Continued.*

Inspected during the Year ended June 30th, 1906.

Cubic Feet.		Ammonia per 100 Cubic Feet.					Sulphuretted Hydrogen.			Remarks.
No. of times in excess of allowance.	No. of Tests.	Highest. Grains.	Lowest. Grains.	Average. Grains.	No. of times in excess of allowance.	No. of Tests.	No. of times absent.	No. of times present.	No. of Tests.	
							1	0	1	
							1	0	1	
							1	0	1	
							1	0	1	
							1	0	1	
							1	0	1	
							1	0	1	
							1	0	1	
							1	0	1	
							1	0	1	
							1	0	1	
							1	0	1	
							12	0	12	
							1	0	1	
							1	0	1	
							1	0	1	
							1	0	1	
							1	0	1	
							1	0	1	
							0	1	1	
							2	0	2	
							2	0	2	
							1	0	1	
							2	0	2	
							2	0	2	
							15	1	16	
							1	0	1	
							1	0	1	
							2	0	2	
							2	0	2	
							2	0	2	
							2	0	2	
							2	0	2	
							2	0	2	
							2	0	2	
							2	0	2	
							2	0	2	
							2	0	2	
							22	0	22	

APPENDIX

RETURN of the Illuminating Power and Purity of Gas

Inspection Offices.	Illuminating Power.					Sulphur per 100		
	Highest.	Lowest.	Average.	No. of times below Standard.	No. of Tests.	Highest	Lowest.	Average
	Candles.	Candles.	Candles.			Grains.	Grains.	Grains.
Nanaimo—								
July			18·92	0	1			
August			18·12	0	1			
September			18·35	0	1			
October			16·57	0	1			
November			18·45	0	1			
December			17·59	0	1			
January			16·19	0	1			
February			16·20	0	1			
March			16·18	0	1			
April			16·37	0	1			
May			17·91	0	1			
June			16·44	0	1			
				0	12			
New Westminster—								
July			19·09	0	1			
August			19·17	0	1			
September			19·21	0	1			
October			19·29	0	1			
November			18·82	0	1			
December			18·69	0	1			
January			18·91	0	1			
February			19·13	0	1			
March			18·72	0	1			
April			18·10	0	1			
May			18·38	0	1			
June			18·50	0	1			
				0	12			
Vancouver—								
July			17·45	0	1			
August			17·55	0	1			
September			17 60	0	1			
October			16·85	0	1			
November			17·10	0	1			
December			17·20	0	1			
January			16·90	0	1			
February			17·00	0	1			
March			17·35	0	1			
April			17·50	0	1			
May			17·40	0	1			
June			17·60	0	1			
				0	12			

F—*Continued.*

Inspected during the Year ended June 30, 1906.

Cubic Feet.		Ammonia per 100 Cubic Feet.					Sulphuretted Hydrogen.			Remarks.
No. of times in excess of allowance.	No. of Tests.	Highest.	Lowest.	Average.	No. of times in excess of allowance.	No. of Tests.	No. of times absent.	No. of times present.	No. of Tests.	
		Grains.	Grains.	Grains.						
......	......	......	......	......	......	......	1	0	1	
......	......	......	......	......	......	......	1	0	1	
......	......	......	......	......	......	......	1	0	1	
......	......	......	......	......	......	......	1	0	1	
......	......	......	......	......	......	......	1	0	1	
......	......	......	......	......	......	......	1	0	1	
......	......	......	......	......	......	......	1	0	1	
......	......	......	......	......	......	......	1	0	1	
......	......	......	......	......	......	......	1	0	1	
......	......	......	......	......	......	......	1	0	1	
......	......	......	......	......	......	......	1	0	1	
......	......	......	......	......	......	......	1	0	1	
							12	0	12	
......	......	......	......	......	......	......	1	0	1	
......	......	......	......	......	......	......	1	0	1	
......	......	......	......	......	......	......	1	0	1	
......	......	......	......	......	......	......	1	0	1	
......	......	......	......	......	......	......	1	0	1	
......	......	......	......	......	......	......	1	0	1	
......	......	......	......	......	......	......	1	0	1	
......	......	......	......	......	......	......	1	0	1	
......	......	......	......	......	......	......	1	0	1	
......	......	......	......	......	......	......	1	0	1	
......	......	......	......	......	......	......	1	0	1	
......	......	......	......	......	......	......	1	0	1	
							12	0	12	
......	......	......	......	......	......	......	1	0	1	
......	......	......	......	......	......	......	1	0	1	
......	......	......	......	......	......	......	1	0	1	
......	......	......	......	......	......	......	1	0	1	
......	......	......	......	......	......	......	1	0	1	
......	......	......	......	......	......	......	1	0	1	
......	......	......	......	......	......	......	1	0	1	
......	......	......	......	......	......	......	1	0	1	
......	......	......	......	......	......	......	1	0	1	
......	......	......	......	......	......	......	1	0	1	
......	......	......	......	......	......	......	1	0	1	
......	......	......	......	......	......	......	1	0	1	
							12	0	12	

APPENDIX

RETURN of the Illuminating Power and Purity of Gas

Inspection Offices.	Illuminating Power.					Sulphur per 100.		
	Highest.	Lowest.	Average.	No. of times below Standard.	No. of Tests.	Highest	Lowest.	Average.
	Candles.	Candles.	Candles.			Grains.	Grains.	Grains.
Victoria—								
July	....	....	18·24	0	1	....	....	....
August	....	....	18·02	0	1	....	....	....
September	....	....	....	....	....	....	....	....
October	....	....	16·07	0	1	....	....	....
November	....	....	17·13	0	1	....	....	....
December	....	....	16·63	0	1	....	....	....
January	....	....	17·53	0	1	....	....	....
February	....	....	17·32	0	1	....	....	....
March	....	....	17·49	0	1	....	....	....
April	....	....	17·38	0	1	....	....	....
May	....	....	17·68	0	1	....	....	....
June	....	....	16·69	0	1	....	....	....
				0	11			

INLAND REVENUE DEPARTMENT

OTTAWA, August 29, 1906.

F—*Concluded.*

Inspected during the Year ended June 30, 1906.

Cubic Feet.		Ammonia per 100 Cubic Feet.					Sulphuretted Hydrogen.			Remarks.
No. of times in excess of allowance.	No. of Tests.	Highest. Grains.	Lowest. Grains.	Average. Grains.	No. of times in excess of allowance.	No. of Tests.	No. of times absent.	No. of times present.	No. of Tests.	
....	......	....	....	....	....	......	1	0	1	
....	......	....	....	....	....	......	1	0	1	
....	......	....	....	....	....	......	....	....	......	
....	......	....	....	....	....	......	1	0	1	
....	......	....	....	....	....	......	1	0	1	
....	......	....	....	....	....	......	1	0	1	
....	......	....	....	....	....	......	1	0	1	
....	......	....	....	....	....	......	1	0	1	
....	......	....	....	....	....	......	1	0	1	
....	......	....	....	....	....	......	1	0	1	
....	......	....	....	....	....	......	1	0	1	
....	......	....	....	....	....	......	1	0	1	
							11	0	11	

W. J. GERALD,

Deputy Minister.

APPENDIX G.

STATEMENT of Gas Meters presented for Verification, Verified, Verified after first Rejection and Rejected during the Year ended June 30, 1906.

Inspection Offices.	Presented for Verification.	Kind.		Verified as coming within the Error tolerated by Law.			Verified after first Rejection.			Rejected.			Totals, Verified and Rejected.	
		Wet.	Dry.	Correct.	Fast.	Slow.	Correct.	Fast.	Slow.	Unsound.	Fast.	Slow.	Verified.	Rejected.
Barrie	147		147	6	47	81	1	1	5	3	1	2	141	6
Belleville	230		230	76	56	95				1	2		227	3
Berlin	258		258	96	159				1			2	256	2
Brockville	232		232	40	63	129							232	
Cobourg	105		105	4	30	69			1			1	104	1
Cornwall	13		13	11		2							13	
Guelph	342		342		90	247					3	2	337	5
Hamilton	6,759	1	6,758	1,292	1,038	4,388				2	36	3	6,718	41
Kingston	453		453	78	41	330					1	3	449	4
Listowel	11		11	6	2	3							11	
London	2,085		2,085	420	487	1,164				1	7	6	2,071	14
Napanee	3		3	1	1	1							3	
[illegible]	704		704	125	134	441				1	2	1	700	4
[illegible]	76		76	59	6	11							76	
Peterborough	63		63	30	3	28	1				1		62	1
Sarnia	354		354	180	60	113						1	353	1
Stratford	177		177	49	47	69				2	5	5	165	12
Toronto	10,532		10,532	2,095	3,514	4,900				4	16	3	10,509	23
Montreal	9,507		9,507	1,571	4,923	2,966				24	10	13	9,460	47
Quebec	234		234	77	79	78							234	
Sherbrooke	140		140	47	55	38							140	
St. Hyacinthe	92		92	32	28	32							92	
Fredericton	133		133	13	15	60				7		38	88	45
St. John	420		420	207	30	183							420	
Halifax	184		184	130	51	3							184	
[illegible]	38		38	3	10	13				9		3	26	12
Winnipeg	1,274		1,274	447	100	727							1,274	
[illegible]	2		2	2									2	
[illegible]	26		26	3	5	18							26	

Vancouver	1,033	....	1,033	289	314	430	....	....	....	....	....	....	1,033	....
Victoria	396	....	396	127	162	107	....	....	....	....	....	....	396	....
Totals	36,023	1	36,022	7,516	11,550	16,726	2	1	7	54	84	83	35,802	221

W. J. GERALD,
Deputy Minister.

INLAND REVENUE DEPARTMENT,
OTTAWA, August 29, 1906.

APPENDIX H.

STATEMENT of Electric Light Expenditures and Receipts for the Year ended June 30, 1906.

Districts.	Inspectors.	Expenditures.					Receipts.	
		Salaries.	Special Assistance.	Travelling Expenses.	Sundries.	Total.	Registration Fees.	Inspection Fees.
		$ cts.	$ cts.	$ cts.	$ cts.	$ cts.	$ cts.	$ cts.
Belleville	Johnson, Wm.	40 16	1 49	385 20	124 24	551 09	590 00	1,222 00
Hamilton	McPhie, D.			82 75	33	83 08	295 00	1,659 50
London	Nash, A. F.			249 85	1 60	251 45	590 00	1,922 50
Ottawa	Roche, H. G.			129 00		129 00	390 00	1,930 25
Toronto	Johnstone, J. K.			479 30	11 07	490 37	1,065 00	5,909 25
	Ontario	40 16	1 49	1,326 10	137 24	1,504 99	2,930 00	12,643 50
Montreal	Aubin, A.			26 05	29 80	55 85	165 00	6,262 00
Quebec	LeVasseur, N.			35 85	112 30	148 15	165 00	593 00
Sherbrooke	Simpson, A. F.			64 30	6 40	70 70	185 00	153 75
St. Hyacinthe	Provost, J. E.	300 00		143 60	3 70	447 30	205 00	478 00
Three Rivers	Dufresne, J. U.	500 00		130 40	1 10	631 50	65 00	191 75
	Quebec	800 00		400 20	153 30	1,353 50	785 00	7,678 50
St. John, N.B.	Wilson, J. E.			213 44	6 71	220 15	235 00	1,161 50
Halifax, N.S.	Ritchie, A. J.			180 74	3 57	184 31	395 00	1,044 00
Charlottetown, P. E. I.	Bell, J. H.			40 00	41 19	81 19	40 00	334 75
Winnipeg, Man	Magness, R.			42 30	13 10	55 40	385 00	3,456 00
Edmonton, Alberta	Harbottle, N.	85 44			92 95	178 39		216 75
Vancouver	Miller, J. E.						265 00	2,797 25
Victoria	Jones, R.			35 50	7 75	43 25	65 00	642 50
	British Columbia			35 50	7 75	43 25	330 00	3,439 75
Yukon	Macdonald, J. F.	499 92				499 92	25 00	
	Chief Elec. Eng'r.	3,166 60	24 44	455 00	350 62	3,996 66		
	General				1,653 75	1,653 75		
	Printing				35 75	35 75		
	Stationery				46 96	46 96		
	Grand Totals	4,592 12	25 93	2,693 28	2,542 89	9,854 22	5,125 00	29,974 75

W. J. GERALD,
Deputy Minister.

INLAND REVENUE DEPARTMENT,
OTTAWA, August 29, 1906.

APPENDIX I.

STATEMENT showing the number of Electric Light Meters Verified, Rejected, and Verified after first Rejection, in each Inspection District, for the Fiscal Year ended June 30, 1906.

Districts.	Number presented.	Verified as coming within the error tolerated by law.			Rejected.			Verified after first Rejected.		
		Correct.	Fast.	Slow.	Unsound.	Fast.	Slow.	Correct.	Fast.	Slow.
Belleville	1,008	534	289	185	....	....	....	....	....	....
Hamilton	1,252	300	356	595	....	....	1	....	....	....
London	1,772	1,310	221	233	....	7	1	....	....	....
Ottawa	2,424	580	207	1,633	1	2	1	....	....	....
Toronto	4,623	1,522	1,769	1,271	....	11	50	....	....	....
Montreal	5,219	4,161	1,021	23	4	5	5	....	....	....
Quebec	685	265	206	211	1	1	1	....	....	....
Sherbrooke	123	42	32	44	....	1	4	....	....	....
St. Hyacinthe	436	136	193	102	....	5	....	....	....	....
Three Rivers	138	64	34	40	....	....	....	....	....	....
St. John	788	391	174	219	....	2	2	....	....	....
Halifax	944	933	2	....	3	3	3	....	....	....
Charlottetown	330	161	96	73	....	....	....	....	....	....
Winnipeg	3,099	2,597	154	348	....	....	....	....	....	....
Edmonton	265	19	6	240	....	....	....	....	....	....
Vancouver	2,746	307	1,573	866	....	....	....	....	....	....
Victoria	807	408	207	192	....	....	....	....	....	....
Yukon	....	....	....	....	....	....	....	....	....	....
	26,659	13,730	6,540	6,275	9	37	68	....	....	....

W. J. GERALD,

Deputy Minister.

INLAND REVENUE DEPARTMENT,

OTTAWA, August 29, 1906.

APPENDIX J.

STATEMENT showing the Electric Light Companies registered under the Electric Light Inspection Act, during the Year ended June 30, 1906.

Districts.	From whom Collected.	Serial No.	By whom Collected.	Certificate for Fiscal Year.	Number of Lamps. Arc.	Incandescent.	Totals.	Registration Fees.	Totals.
								$ cts.	$ cts.
Belleville	The Marmora Electric Co., Ltd	1	C. I. R., Belleville	1905-1906	....	575	575	10 00	
	The Frankford Electric Light Co., Ltd	2	" "	"	....	290	290	5 00	
	[illegible] of [illegible]	3	" "	"	66	5,000	5,660	25 00	
	The Corporation of the Village of Madoc	4	" "	"	12	900	1,020	10 00	
	The Trenton Electric & Water Co., Ltd., Trenton & Belleville	5	" "	"	70	8,859	9,559	25 00	
	The [illegible] Electric Light and Power Co.	6	" "	"	5	1,100	1,150	10 00	
	Vankleek Hill Electric Light Co.	1	C. I. R., Cornwall	1905-1906	....	1,735	1,735	10 00	
	Thos. Ross & Sons, Hawksbury	2	" "	"	....	1,860	1,860	10 00	
	St. Lawrence Power Co., Ltd., Mille Roches	3	" "	"	230	620	2,920	25 00	
	Stormont Electric Light and Power Co., Cornwall	4	" "	"	14	1,600	1,740	10 00	
	The Corporation of the Town of Alexandria	5	" "	"	....	1,355	1,355	10 00	
	Jos. Bishop & Son, Crysler	6	" "	"	....	400	400	5 00	
	Corporation of the City of Kingston	1	C. I. R., Kingston	1905-1906	115	8,000	9,150	25 00	
	School of Mining and [illegible], Kingston	2	" "	"	8	22	102	5 00	
	Benjamin Manufacturing Co., Ltd., Yarker	3	" "	"	....	200	200	5 00	
	A. A. [illegible]y, Yarker	4	" "	"	....	140	140	5 00	
	The [illegible] Electric Light Co	1	C. I. R., Peterborough	1905-1906	....	575	575	10 00	
	The [illegible] Water & Electric Co., Ltd	2	" "	"	25	5,500	5,750	25 00	
	The Ontario Light, Heat and Power Co., Colborne	3	" "	"	20	796	996	10 00	
	Light, Heat and Power Co., Lindsay	4	" "	"	81	7,500	8,310	25 00	
	Havelock Electric Light and Power Co., Peterborough	5	" "	"	13	623	753	10 00	
	Lakefield Light and [illegible] Co.	6	" "	"	8	517	597	10 00	
	H. W. Fowlds & Co., Hastings	7	" "	"	12	500	620	10 00	
	[illegible] Power Co., Peterborough	8	" "	"	8	8,250	8,330	25 00	
	Water Works and Electric Light Commission, Cambellford	9	" "	"	37	2,433	2,803	25 00	
	Bowmanville Electric Light Co.	10	" "	"	18	1,900	2,080	25 00	
	The Port Hope Electric Light and Power Co., Ltd	11	" "	"	37	2,020	2,390	25 00	
	Peterboro Light and [illegible] Co.	12	" "	"	142	8,000	9,120	25 00	
	W. C. Harrison, Norwood	13	" "	"	13	425	555	10 00	
	J. G. [illegible], [illegible]k	14	" "	"	6	420	480	5 00	
	D. J. Galbraith, Newcastle	15	" "	"	....	400	400	5 00	

	The Board of Water, Light and Power Commission, Fenelon Falls	16	" "	"	10	1,604	1,704	10 00	
	Water and Light Commissioners, Prescott	1	C. I. R., Prescott	1905–1906	9	2,500	2,590	25 00	
	The Brockville Light and Power Department	2	" "	"	95	4,500	5,450	25 00	
	The Electric Light and Water Supply Co., Ltd	3	" "	"	25	1,500	1,750	10 00	
	Kemptville Milling and Light Co., Ltd	4	" "	"	......	1,000	1,000	10 00	
	Eager and Sanderson Co. Winchester	5	" "	"	......	900	900	10 00	
	The Municipality of the Village of Iroquois	6	" "	"	12	1,383	1,403	10 00	
	The Westport Electric Light and Milling Co., Ltd.	7	" "	"	......	575	575	10 00	
	Morrisburg Electric Light and Power Works	8	" "	"	......	2,800	2,800	25 00	
	Cardinal Electric Light Co., Ltd	9	" "	"	......	1,200	1,200	10 00	
	Merrickville Electric Light and Power Co	10	" "	"	......	455	455	5 00	
									590 00
Hamilton	James Munro, Embro	1	C. I. R., Brantford	1905–1906	......	432	432	5 00	
	The Brantford Street Railway Co	2	" "	"	5	210	260	5 00	
	The Brantford Electric & Operating Co., Ltd	3	" "	"	300	16,000	19,000	25 00	
	Corporation of the Town of Paris	4	" "	"	27	1,700	1,970	10 00	
	Simcoe Gas and Water Co	5	" "	"	30	......	300	5 00	
	Woodstock Water and Light System	6	" "	"	155	5,000	6,550	25 00	
	H. Webster, Norwich	7	" "	"	......	1,044	1,044	10 00	
	The Tilsonburg Electric Light Works	8	" "	"	5	1,550	1,600	10 00	
	The Ingersoll Electric Power & Light Co., Ltd	9	" "	"	57	2,653	3,223	25 00	
	Keileg & Fisher	10	" "	"	......	400	400	5 00	
	Port Rowan Electric Co	11	" "	"	9	150	240	5 00	
	The Hamilton Electric Light & Power Co	1	C. I. R., Hamilton	1905–1906	950	60,000	69,500	25 00	
	The Hamilton Cataract Power, Light & Traction Co	2	" "	"	......	260	260	5 00	
	The Electric Power and Manufacturing Co., Hamilton	3	" "	"	......	200	200	5 00	
	The Dundas Electric Co	4	" "	"	6	1,200	1,260	10 00	
	The Dunnville Electric Light Co., Ltd	1	C. I. R., St. Catharines	1905–1906	15	1,240	1,390	10 00	
	Corporation of the Town of Niagara Falls	2	" "	"	60	5,000	5,600	25 00	
	The Maple Leaf Rubber Co. Ltd., Port Dalhousie	3	" "	"	15	1,019	1,169	10 00	
	The Grimsby Electric Plant	4	" "	"	......	455	455	5 00	
	Hamilton Cataract, Power, Light & Traction Co., Ltd., Beamsville	5	" "	"	......	443	443	5 00	
	The Lincoln Electric Light & Power Co., Ltd., St. Catharines	6	" "	"	122	8,200	9,420	25 00	
	Merritton Electric Light Co	7	" "	"	24	1,500	1,740	10 00	
	Corporation of the Town of Thorold	8	" "	"	26	1,600	1,860	10 00	
	Corporation of the Town of Niagara	9	" "	"	......	700	700	10 00	
	Welland Electric Light Co	10	" "	"	20	600	800	10 00	
									295 00
London	The Petrolia Electric Light Heat and Power Co	1	C. I. R., London	1906–1906	6	2,400	2,460	25 00	
	The Power Equipment Co. of Ontario, London	2	" "	"	2	1,600	1,620	10 00	
	R. C. McLeay, Watford	3	" "	"	14	280	420	5 00	
	H. Cook & Sons, Lucan	4	" "	"	......	450	450	5 00	
	West Lorne Electric Light Co	5	" "	"	6	345	405	5 00	
	Hamilton & Prout, Forest	6	" "	"	12	360	480	5 00	
	Corporation of the Town of Strathroy	7	" "	"	18	3,060	3,240	25 00	
	The London Electric Co	8	" "	"	366	33,774	34,140	25 00	
	The Sarnia Gas and Electric Light Co	9	" "	"	89	4,000	4,890	25 00	

APPENDIX J—*Continued.*

STATEMENT showing the Electric Light Companies registered under the Electric Light Inspection Act, during the year ended June 30, 1906.

Districts.	From whom Collected.	Serial No.	By whom Collected.	Certificate for Fiscal Year.	Number of Lamps. Arc.	Incandescent.	Totals.	Registration Fees.	Totals.
								$ cts.	$ cts.
...m........	The City Light, Heat and Power Department, St. Thomas	10	C. I. R., London	1905-1906.	126	3,500	4,760	25 00	
	H. C. Baird & Son, Park Hill	11	" "	"	12	1,100	1,220	10 00	
	Alvinston Power Co., Ltd	12	" "	"	13	350	480	5 00	
	The Dutton Electric Co., London	13	" "	"	4	650	690	10 00	
	The Town of Aylmer Electric Department	14	" "	"	12	1,500	1,620	10 00	
	Corporation of the Town of St. Marys	1	C. I. R., Stratford	1905-1906.	35	3,500	850	25 00	
	The Seaforth Electric Light, Heat and Power Co	2	" "	"	35	2,000	2,350	25 00	
	Corporation of the Town of Goderich	3	" "	"	41	2,500	2,910	25 00	
	Brussels Electric Light Co	4	" "	"	9	350	440	5 00	
	Corporation of the Town of Mitchell	5	" "	"	6	1,200	1,260	10 00	
	John Patterson, Wroxeter	6	" "	"	....	360	360	5 00	
	Stratford Gas Co	7	" "	"	90	3,000	3,900	25 00	
	J. G. [illegible], [illegible]	8	" "	"	....	550	550	10 00	
	The Corporation of the Town of Wingham	9	" "	"	45	4,000	4,450	25 00	
	The Listowel Gas and Electric Light Co., Ltd	10	" "	"	25	....	250	5 00	
	J. A. Williams & Co., Zurich	11	" "	"	....	290	290	5 00	
	Thomas Welch, Hensall	12	" "	"	2	850	870	10 00	
	Clinton Electric Light Co	13	" "	"	14	1,500	1,640	10 00	
	Blyth Electric Light Co	14	" "	"	7	400	470	5 00	
	Corporation of the Town of Palmerston	15	" "	"	13	600	780	10 00	
	C. B. Snell, Exeter	16	" "	"	15	1,000	1,150	10 00	
	Hiram Walker & Sons, Ltd., Walkerville	1	C. I. R., Windsor	1905-1906.	15	3,500	3,650	25 00	
	The Sandwich, Windsor and Amherstburg Railway, Ltd., Windsor	2	" "	"	9	9,200	9,290	25 00	
	The Kingsville Electric Light Co	3	" "	"	....	1,300	1,300	10 00	
	The Corporation of the Town of Dresden	4	" "	"	2	950	970	10 00	
	The Corporation of the Village of Thamesville	5	" "	"	....	860	800	10 00	
	The Leamington Light and Heat Co., Ltd	6	" "	"	17	1,525	1,695	10 00	
	The Corporation of the Town of Bothwell	7	" "	"	15	330	480	5 00	
	D. W. Kett, Tilbury	8	" "	"	13	1,000	1,130	10 00	

	W. H. McMackon, Ridgeton	9	"	"	"	10	1,500	1,600	10 00	
	Chatham Gas Co.	10	"	"	"	20	8,000	8,200	25 00	
	Amherstburg Electric Light, Heat and Power Co	11	"	"	"	....	1,400	1,400	10 00	
	Chas. E. Naylor, Essex	12	"	"	"	6	1,000	1,060	10 00	
	Corporation of the Town of Blenheim	13	"	"	"	17	1,200	1,370	10 00	
	The Premier Electric Light and Power Co., Ltd., Wallaceburg	14	"	"	"	29	1,218	1,508	10 00	
	Walter Brush Grubb, Harrow	15	"	"	"	......	400	400	5 00	
	Wigle Bros., Windsor	16	"	"	"	....	400	400	5 00	
Ottawa	The Consumers' Electric Co., Ltd., Ottawa	1	C. I. R.,	Ottawa	1905-1906	174	28,136	29,876	25 00	590 00
	The Ottawa Electric Co., Ottawa and Hull	2	"	"	"	1,146	137,393	148,853	25 00	
	The Deschênes Electric Co., Ottawa	2	"	"	"	......	2,700	2,700	25 00	
	Robt MacLaren, Buckingham	4	"	"	"	30	2,500	2,800	25 00	
	The Capital Power Co., Ltd., Hull and Deschênes	5	"	"	"	.....	200	200	5 00	
	The Hull Electric Co., Hull and Aylmer	6	"	"	"	40	7,054	7,454	25 00	
	North Bay Light, Heat and Power Co	1	C. I. R.,	Perth	1905-1906	24	2,500	2,740	25 00	
	The Pembroke Electric Light Co., Ltd.	2	"	"	"	22	4,000	4,220	25 00	
	Mattawa Electric Light and Power Co., Ltd	3	"	"	"	13	1,070	1,200	10 00	
	The [illegible] Electric Light and Power Co	4	"	"	"	......	3,500	3,500	25 00	
	Carleton Place Electric Light Co	5	"	"	"	28	2,175	2,455	25 00	
	The Dowd Milling Co., Pakenham	6	"	"	"	..	425	425	5 00	
	Canadian Copper Co., Copper Cliff	7	"	"	"	9	1,128	1,218	10 00	
	Smith Falls Electric Power Co., Ltd.	8	"	"	"	102	4,400	5,420	25 00	
	The Canadian [illegible] and Water Power Co., Ltd., Perth	9	"	"	"	.....	3,000	3,000	25 00	
	The Renfrew Power Co., Ltd.	10	"	"	"	51	3,000	3,510	25 00	
	The Corporation of the Town of Almonte	11	"	"	"	17	1,920	2,090	10 00	
	The Sturgeon Falls Electric Light and Power Co., Ltd	12	"	"	"	......	2,300	2,300	25 00	
	Corporation of the Town of Perth	13	"	"	"	35	....	350	5 00	
	Corporation of the Town of Sudbury	14	"	"	"	......	1,975	1,975	10 00	
	Renfrew Electric Co., Ltd	15	"	"	"	......	1,500	1,500	10 00	
Toronto	The Berlin Light Commissioners	1	C. I. R.,	Guelph	1905-1906	112	4,000	5,120	25 00	390 00
	Corporation of the Town of Hespeler	2	"	"	"	....	1,000	1,000	10 00	
	Corporation of the Town of Mount Forest	3	"	"	"	15	1,200	1,350	10 00	
	George Leighton, Harriston	4	"	"	"	18	400	580	10 00	
	City of Guelph Light and Power Department	5	"	"	"	100	6,359	7,359	25 00	
	Galt Gas Light Co	6	"	"	"	58	5,000	5,580	25 00	
	Waterloo Electric Light and Power Co., Ltd	7	"	"	"	27	2,700	2,970	25 00	
	Fergus Electric Light and Milling Co	8	"	"	"	17	1,050	1,220	10 00	
	The Preston Heat and Light Commission	9	"	"	"	25	1,000	1,250	10 00	
	Jacob Morley, New Hamburg	10	"	"	"	20	1,000	1,200	10 00	
	Ratz Bros., Elmira	11	"	"	"	....	600	600	10 00	
	Ratz Bros., Elmira	12	"	" (1)	"	....	500	500	80 00	
	E. W. B. Snider, St. Jacobs	13	"	" (2)	"	......	240	240	85 00	
	Walkerton Electric Light and Power Co., Ltd	1	C. I. R.,	Owen Sound	1905-1906	16	1,725	1,885	10 00	
	H. Cargill & Sons, Cargill	2	"	"	"	......	500	500	5 00	
	Saugeen Electric Light and Power Co., Ltd., Walkerton	3	"	"	"	..	2,400	2,400	25 00	
	Canada Furniture Manufacturers Ltd., Wiarton	4	"	"	"	3	1,378	1,408	10 00	
	H. Grutzner, Hanover	5	"	"	"	19	1,595	1,785	10 00	

[1] For the years 1896 to 1905. [2] For the years 1896 to 1906.

APPENDIX J—*Continued.*

STATEMENT showing the Electric Light Companies registered under the Electric Light Inspection Act, during the Year ended June 30, 1906.

Districts.	From whom Collected.	Serial No.	By whom Collected.	Certificate for Fiscal Year.	Number of Lamps. Arc.	Number of Lamps. Incandescent.	Number of Lamps. Totals.	Registration Fees.	Totals
								$ cts.	$ cts.
to........	Corporation of the Town of Kincardine	6	C. I. R., Owen Sound	1905-1906	17	1,400	1,570	10 00	
	Paisley Electric Light Co	7	" "	"	.....	900	900	10 00	
	Crawford and McIntyre, Durham	8	" "	"	4	1,200	1,240	10 00	
	Thos. Andrews, Thornbury	9	" "	"	10	550	650	10 00	
	Fred. Deagle, Eugenia	10	" "	"	...	300	300	5 00	
	Walter Stewart & Son, Lucknow	11	" "	"	1	440	450	5 00	
	Teeswater Electric Light Co	12	" "	"	.....	300	300	5 00	
	Corporation of the Town of Owen Sound	13	" "	"	57	7,141	7,711	25 00	
	Minnis Bros., Markdale	14	" "	"	....	900	900	10 00	
	Corporation of the Town of Collingwood	15	" "	"	60	1,000	4,600	25 00	
	Corporation of the Village of Dundalk	16	" "	"	...	500	510	5 00	
	Chesley Electric Light Co	17	" "	"	23	1,050	1,280	10 00	
	W. Moore & Sons, Meaford	18	" "	"	22	1,300	1,520	10 00	
	N. Wenger & Bros., Ayton	19	" "	"	....	153	153	5 00	
	Brampton Electric Light Co	1	C. I. R., Toronto	1905-1906	28	1,700	1,980	10 00	
	The Hamilton Cataract, Power, Light and Traction Co. Ltd., Burlington	2	" "	"	.....	465	465	5 00	
	Corporation of the Town of Barrie	3	" "	"	51	5,500	16,010	25 00	
	The Togona Water and Light Co., Sault Ste. Marie	4	" "	"	224	11,199	3,439	25 00	
	I. J. Gould, Uxbridge	5	" "	"	12	1,200	1,320	10 00	
	Town of East Toronto	6	" "	"	30	325	625	10 00	
	Town of Gravenhurst	7	" "	"	...	1,900	1,900	10 00	
	John Phillips, Grand Valley	8	" "	"	....	1,200	1,200	10 0	
	Corporation of the Village of Beeton	9	" "	"	.....	630	630	10 00	
	Corporation of the Village of Acton	10	" "	"	.....	1,000	1,000	10 00	
	Corporation of the Town of Huntsville	11	" "	"	..	1,800	1,800	10 00	
	Toronto Electric Light Co. Ltd	12	" "	"	1,722	1 5000	167,220	25 00	
	Corporation of the Town of Bracebridge	13	" "	"	2	4,000	4,020	25 00	
	Jonas Byre, Stouffville	14	" "	"	...	488	488	5 00	

Toronto	The Penetanguishene and Midland Street Railway Light and Power Co. Ltd	15	"	"	"	16	1,400	1,560	10 00	
	The Municipality of Weston	16	"	"	"	18	690	870	10 00	
	The Oshawa Electric Light Co., Ltd	17	"	"	"	12	1,800	1,920	10 00	
	Georgetown Electric Light & Power Co.	18	"	"	"	14	1,500	1,640	10 00	
	Blind River Light, Heat & Power Co., Ltd.	19	"	"	"	....	750	750	10 00	
	Sunderland Electric Power Co., Ltd.	20	"	"	"	....	320	320	5 00	
	Corporation of the Town of Parry Sound	21	"	9	"	10	3,500	3,600	25 00	
	Corporation of the Town of Orillia	22	"	"	"	50	6,260	6,700	25 00	
	Corporation of the Town of Midland	23	"	"	"	23	4,000	4,230	25 00	
	Joseph K oxn Stayner	24	"	"	"	....	800	800	10 00	
	Alliston Electric Light Co	25	"	"	"	....	1,500	1,500	10 00	
	Corporation of the Town of Newmarket	26	"	"	"	....	2,700	2,700	25 00	
	C. W. Watson, Orangeville	27	"	"	"	30	1,400	1,700	10 00	
	The Aurora Electric Light Co.	28	"	"	"	2	450	470	5 00	
	W. H. Summerfeldt, Sutton West	29	"	"	"	....	400	400	5 00	
	Simon [illegible], [illegible]	30	"	"	"	....	500	500	5 00	
	Alex. Dobson, Beaverton	31	"	"	"	....	450	450	5 00	
	C. E. Copeland, Elmvale	32	"	"	"	....	475	475	5 00	
	The Knight Bros. Co., Burk's Falls	33	"	"	"	1	1,100	1,110	10 00	
	Cataract Electric Co	35	"	"	"	....	500	500	5 00	
	Corporation of the Town of Thessalon	34	"	"	"	13	700	830	10 00	
	Corporation of the Village of Markham	36	"	"	"	....	450	450	5 00	
	The Stark Telephone, Light & Railway System, Ltd., Toronto Junction	37	"	"	"	121	4,540	5,750	25 00	
	W. & A. McArthur Co., Ltd., Little Current	38	"	"	"	9	600	690	10 00	
	Milton Electric Light & Power Co.	39	"	"	"	20	550	750	10 00	
	Jas. Pickering, Shelbourne	40	"	"	"	22	800	1,020	10 00	
	Corporation of the Village of Port Perry	41	"	"	"	3	950	980	10 00	
	A. B. [illegible], Oakville	42	"	"	"	25	1,640	1,890	10 00	
	Corporation of the Town of Whitby	43	"	"	"	27	1,610	1,880	10 00	
	Corporation of the Village of Tottenham	44	"	"	"	....	600	600	10 00	
										1,065 00
Montreal	The Laurentian Water & Power Co., Ste. Agathe des Monts	1	C. I. R.,	Montreal	1905-1906	2	1,200	1,220	10 00	
	The Montreal Light, Heat & Power Co	2	"	"	"	3,069	328,219	358,909	25 00	
	La Compagnie d'Eclairage Electrique de Terrebonne	3	"	"	"	....	810	810	10 00	
	The [illegible] of the Village of Huntingdon	4	"	"	"	..	800	800	10 00	
	The Valleyfield Electric Co., Ltd	5	"	"	"	72	3,150	3 870	25 00	
	Gazette Printing Co., Montreal	6	"	"	"	..	700	700	10 00	
	Beauharnois Electric Light Co., Montreal	7	"	"	"	..	901	901	10 00	
	St. Jerome Power and Electric Co.	8	"	"	"	2	800	820	10 00	
	The Corporation of the Town of Lachine	9	"	"	"	58	2,000	2,580	25 00	
	The Lachute Electric Light Co	10	"	"	"	....	4,000	4,000	5 00	
	John T. Ayers, Lachute	11	"	"	"	....	950	950	10 00	
	Jean Roux, Ste. Thérèse	12	"	"	"	....	400	400	5 00	
	Central Electric Co., Montreal	13	"	"	"	15	1,500	[illegible]	10 00	
										165 00
Quebec	M. A. and Henri Grandbois, St Casimir	1	C. I. R.,	Quebec	1905-1906	....	250	250	5 00	
	La Compagnie d'Electricité de Roberval	2	"	"	"	1	1,665	1,675	10 00	
	The Quebec Jacques Cartier Electric Co	3	"	"	"	600	50,272	56,272	25 00	

APPENDIX J—*Continued.*

STATEMENT showing the Electric Light Companies registered under the Electric Light Inspection Act, during the Year ended June 30, 1906.

Districts.	From whom Collected.	Serial No.	By whom collected.	Certificate for Fiscal Year.	Number of Lamps. Arc.	Number of Lamps. Incandescent.	Number of Lamps. Totals.	Registration Fees.	Totals.
								$ cts.	$ cts.
Quebec	The Canadian Electric Light Co., Lévis	4	C. I. R., Quebec	1905-1906	26	15,626	15,886	25 00	
	Quebec Railway, Light and Power Co.	5	" "	"	216	59,000	61,160	25 00	
	La [illegible] Electrique de la Baie Ste. Paul	6	" "	"	....	500	500	5 0	
	Montmagny Light and Pulp Co.	7	" "	"	....	1,800	1,800	10 00	
	The Fraserville Co., Ltd	8	" "	"	11	3,000	3,110	25 00	
	J. Camille Pouliot, Bic	9	" "	"	....	200	200	5 00	
	La Cie des Eaux et de l'Electricité, Chicoutimi	10	" "	"	....	2,000	2,000	10 0	
	Chs. A. Julien, Pont Rouge	11	" "	"	....	300	300	5 00	
	Chs. A. Julien, St. Raymond	12	" "	"	....	500	500	5 0	
	La Compagnie Hydraulique et Electrique de Lorette	13	" "	"	....	687	687	10 0	165 00
Sherbrooke	The [illegible] of the Town of Magog	1	C. I. R., Sherbrooke	1905-1906	....	2,300	2,300	25 00	
	La [illegible] d'Eclairage Electrique du Village de Mégantic, Lake Megantic	2	" "	"	....	1,000	1,000	10 00	
	Parl[illegible] & [illegible], Dixville	3	" "	"	....	125	125	5 00	
	George [illegible], Sawyerville	4	" "	"	1	225	235	5 00	
	Ri[illegible] [illegible] Co.	5	" "	"	....	1,869	1,869	10 00	
	Brome Lake Electric Power Co., Waterloo	6	" "	"	....	1,600	1,600	10 00	
	Thos. Crockett, Danville	7	" "	"	....	800	800	10 00	
	Sherbrooke Power, Light & Heat Co	8	" "	"	99	15,500	[illegible]	25 00	
	Eastern Townships [illegible] Co., North Hatley	9	" "	"	....	1,200	1,200	10 0	
	[illegible] of the Town of Bromptonville	10	" "	"	....	410	460	5 00	
	La Compagnie [illegible] D'Israëli	11	" "	"	....	500	500	5 00	
	[illegible] of the Town of [illegible]	12	" "	"	50	2,580	3,080	25 0	
	[illegible] of the Village of Granby	13	" "	"	40	2,500	2,900	25 00	
	Stanstead Electric Light Co	14	" "	"	20	1,200	1,400	10 0	
	The [illegible] of the [illegible] of [illegible] Mills	15	" "	"	....	500	500	5 00	185 00
St. Hyacinthe	La Fonderie de Plessisville	1	C. I. R., St. Hyacinthe	1905-1906	....	2,800	2,800	25 00	
	La Compagnie de Gaz, Electricité & Pouvoir, St. Hyacinthe	2	" "	"	38	8,000	8,380	25 00	
	The Arthabaska Water & Power Co., Victoriaville	3	" "	"	....	4,000	4,000	25 0	

	La Compagnie Electrique de Sorel	4	" "	"	34	1,[illegible]5	2,[illegible]5	10 00	
	Farnham Electric Co	5	" "	"	......	1,400	[illegible]0	10 00	
	M. S. Connell & Sons, Stanbridge East	6	" "	"	......	[illegible]0	[illegible]0	5 00	
	Nelson Buzzell, Cowansville	7	" "	"	......	[illegible]0	[illegible]0	5 00	
	Deslandes & Chevrette, Actonvale	8	" "	"	......	[illegible]0	[illegible]0	5 00	
	The Corporation of the Town of Drummondville	9	" "	"	......	1,000	1,000	10 00	
	Corey & Campbell, Bedford	10	" "	"	2	[illegible]0	[illegible]0	10 00	
	St. Césaire Hydraulic Power, St. Johns	11	" "	"	15	6,000	6,150	25 00	
	The St. Johns Electric Light Co	12	" "	"	8	3,000	3,080	25 00	
	A. N. Dufresne, St. Césaire	13	" "	"	......	1,500	1,500	25 00	205 00
Three Rivers	La Corporation de la Ville de Joliette	1	C. I. R., [illegible]e	1905–1906	39	2,000	2,390	10 00	
	Felix Robert et Cie., St. Lin	2	" "	"	......	[illegible]2	[illegible]2	5 00	
	Forest & Forest, St. Roch, de l'Achigan	3	" "	"	......	[illegible]5	[illegible]5	5 00	
	L'Electrique de Grand Mère	1	C. I. R., Three Rivers	1905–1906	......	1,800	1,800	10 00	
	The Shawinigan Electric Light Co., Shawinigan Falls	2	" "	"	......	1,350	1,350	10 00	
	The North Shore Power Co., Three Rivers	3	" "	"	86	7,000	7,860	25 00	65 00
St. John	A. & R. Loggie, Loggieville	1	C. I. R., St John	1905–1906	......	[illegible]0	[illegible]0	5 00	
	The Bathurst Electric and Water Power Co	2	" "	"	......	1,000	1,000	10 00	
	[illegible]n of Campbellton	3	" "	"	30	1,[illegible]0	2,000	10 00	
	[illegible]e St. John Railway Co	4	" "	"	420	20,000	24,200	25 00	
	[illegible]n Electric Light and Power Co., St. John	5	" "	"	32	[illegible]0	[illegible]0	10 00	
	[illegible]. Stephen Electric Light Co., St. Stephen and Milltown	6	" "	"	51	1,876	2,386	25 00	
	The [illegible]k [illegible]c [illegible]ht [illegible] Ltd	7	" "	"	10	[illegible]0	1,000	10 00	
	C. M. Sherwood, Centreville	8	" "	"	5	[illegible]0	[illegible]0	5 00	
	The Sussex Manufacturing [illegible] Ltd	9	" "	"	3	[illegible]3	[illegible]3	10 00	
	The City of Moncton [illegible]er and Light Department	10	" "	"	92	7,700	8,620	25 00	
	The Sac[illegible]ille Electric Light [illegible] Telephone Co	11	" "	"	......	1,200	1,200	10 00	
	The [illegible]n of [illegible]w Castle	12	" "	"	21	2,700	2,910	25 00	
	The [illegible]n of the [illegible]n of Chatham	13	" "	"	7	3,000	3,070	25 00	
	Small & Fisher Co., Ltd., [illegible]	14	" "	"	......	[illegible]0	[illegible]0	5 00	
	The Kent Electric [illegible], Ltd., [illegible]ucto	15	" "	"	......	1,740	1,740	10 00	
	The Fredericton [illegible] Light [illegible]	16	" "	"	21	2,888	3,098	25 00	235 00
Halifax	Halifax Electric [illegible]y Co., Ltd	1	C. I. R., Halifax	1905–1906	368	36,[illegible]0	40,600	25 00	
	The [illegible]n of Annapolis Royal [illegible]c Ligh Works	2	" "	"	2	1,[illegible]0	1,[illegible]0	10 00	
	Dartmouth Gas, Electric Light, Heating and Power [illegible], Ltd	3	" "	"	......	1,800	1,800	10 00	
	[illegible] [illegible] Light Co., Wolfville	4	" "	"	......	1,600	1,[illegible]0	10 00	
	The [illegible]r Electric Light and Power [illegible], Ltd	5	" "	"	6	2,500	[illegible]0	25 00	
	The Kentville Electric Light and Power Co., Ltd	6	" "	"	1	1,350	1,360	10 00	
	Chambers' [illegible]c Light and [illegible]r Co., Ltd., [illegible]o	7	" "	"	2	8,500	8,520	25 00	
	Milton [illegible]ic Light, Power and Manufacturing Co., Ltd	8	" "	"	......	[illegible]0	[illegible]0	5 00	
	John Daley, Digby	9	" "	"	......	[illegible]0	[illegible]0	10 00	
	The [illegible]th Street Railway [illegible], Ltd	10	" "	"	......	[illegible]0	[illegible]0	5 00	
	Edison Electric Light and [illegible]r [illegible] of Springhill, Ltd	11	" "	"	2	[illegible]0	[illegible]0	10 00	
	The [illegible]n of Bridgewater	12	" "	"	......	1,[illegible]0	1,700	10 00	
	The Bridgetown Electric Light and Power Co., Ltd	13	" "	"	......	[illegible]0	[illegible]0	10 00	
	The Can[illegible] [illegible]ic Co., Amherst	14	" "	"	10	3,000	3,100	25 00	

APPENDIX J—*Continued.*

STATEMENT showing the Electric Light Companies registered under the Electric Light Inspection Act, during the Year ended June 30, 1906.

Districts.	From whom Collected.	Serial No.	By whom Collected.	Certificate for Fiscal Year.	Number of Lamps. Arc.	Number of Lamps. Incandescent.	Number of Lamps. Totals.	Registration Fees.	Totals.
								$ cts.	$ cts.
Halifax	The Town of Liverpool Electric Light Works	15	C. I. R., Halifax	1905-1906	24	1,500	1,740	10 00	
	Bear River Light, Heating and Power Co., Ltd	16	" "	"	.....	468	468	5 00	
	The Town of Parrsboro Electric Light Plant	17	" "	"	.....	1,000	1,000	10 0	
	The Lunenburg Gas Co., Ltd	18	" "	"	.....	1,985	1,985	10 00	
	Oxford Electric Co., Ltd	19	" "	"	.....	490	490	5 00	
	Mahone Bay Electric Light and Power Co	20	" "	"	.....	500	540	5 00	
	Logan & Co., Shubenacadie	21	" "	"	.....	300	300	5 00	
	The Antigonish Electric Co	1	C. I. R., Pictou	1905-1906	.....	1,100	1,100	10 00	
	Cape Breton Electric Co., Ltd., Sydney	2	" "	"	51	12,521	[illegible]	25 00	
	Sydney Mines Electric Co	3	" "	"	1	1,000	[illegible]	10 00	
	The Town of Glace Bay	4	" "	"	7	5,311	5,381	25 00	
	New Glasgow Electric Co., Ltd	5	" "	"	40	7,200	7,600	25 00	
	Inverness Railway and Coal Co	6	" "	"	6	315	375	5 00	
	Cape Breton Electric Co., North Sydney	7	" "	"	26	2,761	3,021	25 00	
	Corporation of the Town of Pictou	8	" "	"	34	3,000	3,340	25 00	
	Port Hood Development Co	9	" "	"	.....	500	500	5 00	395 0
Charlottetown	The Montague Electric Co	1	C. I. R., Charlottetown	1905-1906	.....	425	425	5 00	
	The Charlottetown Light and Power Co., Ltd	2	" "	"	85	800	850	25 00	
	The Summerside Electric Co., Ltd	3	" "	"	20	1,400	1,600	10 00	40 00
Winnipeg	Calgary Water Power Co., Ltd	1	C. I. R., Calgary	1905-1906	.....	3,000	3,000	25 00	
	City of Edmonton	2	" "	"	41	8,400	8,810	25 00	
	The Lethbridge Electric Co., Ltd	3	" "	"	2	1,800	1,820	10 00	
	Corporation of the Town of Wetaskiwin	4	" "	"	15	600	750	10 0	
	The Macleod Electric Light and Power Co., Ltd	5	" "	"	....	1,000	1,000	10 00	
	The Western General Electric Co., Ltd., Red Deer	6	" "	"	12	800	920	10 00	
	Board of Water and Light Commissioners, Fort William	1	C. I. R., Port Arthur	1905-1906	50	5,500	6,000	25 00	
	The Corporation of the Town of Port Arthur	2	" "	"	344	6,330	9,770	25 00	
	The Winnipeg Electric Street Railway Co	1	C. I. R., Winnipeg	1905-1906	147	[illegible]	60,634	25 00	
	Corporation of the Town of Neepawa	2	" "	"	13	2,245	2,375	25 00	

Winnipeg	[illegible]a Electric Light [illegible] Power Co	3	C. I. R., Winnipeg	1905-1906	4	600	640	10 00	
	Boissevain Electric Light [illegible]	4	" "	"		500	500	5 00	
	The Selkirk [illegible] [illegible] and [illegible] [illegible], Ltd	5	" "	"		1,400	1,400	10 00	
	[illegible] of the City of Regina	6	" "	"		4,000	4,350	25 00	
	[illegible] of the City of Prince Al[illegible]	7	" "	"	35	1,600	1,600	10 00	
	The Brandon Electric Light Co., Ltd	8	" "	"	40	1 [illegible]	10,400	25 00	
	[illegible] of the [illegible] of Kenora	9	" "	"	22	5,000	[illegible]	25 00	
	The [illegible] Electric Co., Ltd., Portage la Prairie	10	" "	"	13	[illegible]	[illegible]	25 00	
	The Morden [illegible] [illegible] Co	11	" "	"		1,000	1,000	10 00	
	The [illegible] Electric Light and Power Co., [illegible]	12	" "	"	3	1,000	1,030	10 00	
	The [illegible] of the City of [illegible] Jaw	13	" "	"	27	2,107	2,377	25 00	
	[illegible] [illegible], Estevan	14	" "	"		[illegible]	500	5 00	
	The Municipality of the [illegible] of Indian Head	15	" "	"	30	1,500	1,800	5 00	
	The Town of Dauphin	16	" "	"	14	1,[illegible]	1,890	5 00	
									385 00
Vancouver	The [illegible] Kootenay Power and Light Co., Ltd., Rossland	1	C. I. R., Vancouver	1905-1906	11	3,000	3, 10	25 00	
	The Sandon [illegible] Works [illegible] Light Co	2	" "	"	3	[illegible]	780	10 00	
	The [illegible] of the [illegible] of Grand Forks	3	" "	"	13	1,500	1,630	10 00	
	The [illegible] [illegible], [illegible] and Improvement Co	4	" "	"		[illegible]	[illegible]	5 00	
	The [illegible] Electric [illegible]	5	" "	"	6	1,400	1,460	10 00	
	[illegible] of the City of Kamloops	6	" "	"		4,000	4,000	25 00	
	The [illegible] of the City of Revelstoke	7	" "	"	5	1,900	1,[illegible]	10 00	
	The [illegible] Electric Lighting Co., Ltd	8	" "	"	2	[illegible]	870	10 00	
	The Canadian Smelting Works, Trail	9	" "	"	44	1,500	1,940	10 00	
	British Columbia [illegible] Railway Co., Ltd., Vancouver	10	" "	"	[illegible]	87,391	[illegible]	25 00	
	Crow's [illegible] Pass Electric Light Co., Ltd., Fernie	11	" "	"	1	[illegible]	[illegible]	25 00	
	Crow's [illegible] [illegible] Electric Light [illegible] Power Co., Ltd., Michell	12	" "	"		[illegible]	600	10 00	
	The Cranbrook [illegible] Light Co., Ltd	13	" "	"	3	1,800	1,830	10 00	
	Corporation of the City of [illegible]	14	" "	"	9	4,200	[illegible]	25 00	
	The [illegible] of the City of New Westminster	15	" "	"	13	7,500	[illegible]	25 00	
	[illegible] of the City of Verno[illegible]	16	" "	"		1,200	1,200	10 00	
	Kootenay Electric Co., Ltd., Kaslo	17	" "	"		[illegible]	840	10 00	
	The [illegible] Water Power [illegible] Light Co., Ltd	18	" "	"		20	20	5 00	
	Daly Reduction [illegible], Ltd., Hedley	19	" "	"		[illegible]	[illegible]	5 00	
									265 00
Victoria	The Nanaimo Electric Light, Power and Heating Co	1	O. I. R., Victoria	1905-1906	60	2,400	[illegible]	25 00	
	Cumberland Electric Lighting Co., Ltd	2	" "	"		1,600	1,600	10 00	
	Electric Railway Co., Ltd., Victoria	3	" "	"	66	[illegible]	7,[illegible]	25 00	
	Victoria Electric Co., Ltd	4	" "	"		260	260	5 00	
									65 00
Dawson	The Dawson Electric Light and Power Co	1	C. I. R., Dawson	1905-1906	3	4,500	4,530	25 00	25 00
	Grand total								5,125 00

INLAND REVENUE DEPARTMENT,

OTTAWA, August 29, 1906.

W. J. GERALD,

Deputy Minister.

Lightning Source UK Ltd.
Milton Keynes UK
UKHW040859250219
337881UK00008B/1057/P